PSYCHOLOGY

A EUROPEAN TEXT

PHILIP ZIMBARDO
Stanford University, USA

MARK McDERMOTT
University of East London, UK

JEROEN JANSZ
Leiden University, Holland

NICO METAAL
Leiden University, Holland

Harper
Collins

Adaptation (Psychology: A European Text) copyright
© 1995 by HarperCollins Publishers Ltd, UK.

Psychology and Life, 13th Edition,
Copyright © 1993 by Philip Zimbardo.

Adaptation published by arrangement with HarperCollins
Publishers, Inc, USA.

This edition first published in 1995 by
HarperCollins College Division
An imprint of HarperCollins Publishers Ltd, UK
77–85 Fulham Palace Road
Hammersmith
London W6 8JB

Jeroen Jansz, Mark McDermott and Nico Metaal assert the
moral right to be identified as the authors of the adapted
material.

British Library Cataloguing in Publication Data
A catalogue record for this book is available from the British
Library

ISBN 0-00-499002-1

Typeset by Dorchester Typesetting Group Ltd, Dorset
Printed and Bound by New Interlitho Italia, Italy
Cover design: The Senate

THE AUTHORS

Professor Philip Zimbardo is a Professor of Psychology at Stanford University, USA, where he has taught since 1968, after teaching at Yale University, New York University and Columbia University. He received his education at Brooklyn College (BA) and Yale University (MS and PhD). He is the author of more than 100 professional articles and chapters, and two dozen books. His introductory text, *Psychology and Life*, is the oldest, continuously selling psychology textbook in America. His trade books, *Shyness* and *The Shy Child*, have been bestsellers and translated into many languages. He recently designed, wrote and hosted the television series, *Discovering Psychology*. He continues his active research programme in the area of social psychology, focusing on aspects of situationally induced violence, the psychology of time perspective and some social-cognitive origins of madness.

Dr Mark McDermott, MSc PhD, has been a full-time lecturer, tutor and researcher in the Department of Psychology at the University of East London, UK, since 1989. He read his first degree in psychology at University College Cardiff (UCC) and also completed postgraduate teaching training there. He has published findings from his doctoral research on rebelliousness in adolescence as undertaken at UCC and the University of Illinois, USA, in a number of edited book chapters. His training thereafter as a clinical psychologist at Manchester University has led in recent years to teaching and research interests in health and social psychology, resulting in the publication of various co-authored journal articles. Currently, his ongoing empirical work focuses on forms of hostility as risk-factors for coronary artery disease and on social influence processes in occupational absenteeism.

Dr Jeroen Jansz, PhD, majored in theoretical psychology at Leiden University, Holland. He held several temporary teaching positions before undertaking doctoral research. After completion of his PhD thesis, he entered his current position as a lecturer in the history and theory of psychology in the Department of Experimental and Theoretical Psychology at Leiden University. Next to papers in Dutch and international journals, he has co-authored books about psychoanalysis and feminism (1983), the history of psychology (1986) and general psychology (1994). His current research is concerned with the interplay between identity and motivation, a theme that was covered in his book, *Person, Self, and Moral Demands* (1991).

Dr Nico Metaal, PhD, majored in social psychology at Leiden University, Holland. He has a long standing record of teaching the general introduction to psychology at this university. Currently, he is a lecturer in general psychology in the Department of Experimental and Theoretical Psychology at Leiden University. His past research has included the study of the quality of commercial courses in popular psychology. His recent research focuses on motives in ordinary explanation. This project resulted in a number of papers and in the monograph, *Persoonlijke autonomie* (1992). Recently, he co-authored the book, *Psychologie: de stand van zaken* (1994), which provides a general introduction to psychology. He is also an editor of the Dutch journal, *De Psycholoog*.

CHAPTER 10

MOTIVATION AND EMOTION   354

CHAPTER 12

PERSONALITY AND INDIVIDUAL DIFFERENCES 440

CHAPTER 14

ABNORMAL PSYCHOLOGY 538

PREFACE

This is the first four-colour, comprehensive, introductory psychology textbook that has been written specifically for European courses. In producing this new book, Philip Zimbardo's leading undergraduate text *Psychology and Life* was taken as a starting point. From there, the authors thoroughly revised the former American text by reducing some sections and adding in new material, changes being made to 40 per cent of the original text over all. This collaborative work has resulted in *Psychology: A European Text*. This new text focuses on the broad empirical basis of the subject and on the pluriform nature of psychology. It contains full coverage of core areas and methods, whilst also encompassing discussion of current issues of key importance for contemporary psychology.

Through a unique combination of the contributory efforts of the four authors from Britain, Holland and the United States of America, this textbook is international in content and orientation. The important work of psychologists in Europe is foregrounded and referenced alongside that of other internationally recognised psychologists. Present-day case studies and illustrative examples are included, the content of which are familiar and meaningful to a European readership. Statistics from European countries are incorporated where appropriate to examine similarities and differences between national populations in the incidence of various phenomena of interest to psychology.

The scope and substance of the book provides the reader with an intellectually engaging and critical introduction to psychology. Students are familiarised with important debates about key concerns: to name but a few as examples, these include gender issues, recovered memories, the universality of emotions, the status of subliminal perception, social constructionism, the current status of DSM and ICD classification and psychological aspects of AIDS.

The coverage of these and other central issues is supported by the retention of positive pedagogical features as present in the former American edition. These include the use of opening cases at the beginning of each chapter, 'close-up' boxes, interim summaries, recapping of main points and listing of key terms, and of major contributors at the end of each chapter.

Through its international and pluriform orientation, *Psychology: A European Text* provides information and evaluative skills which enable the reader to understand psychology's past and to participate in the debate about psychology's present and future. In so doing, this introductory text lays before the enquiring student the various ways in which psychology may enrichen understandings of the human condition.

ACKNOWLEDGEMENTS

We are indebted to colleagues whose help and support has sustained us through the process of writing this text. We would like to acknowledge the continuous encouragement and support given to us by **Martin Liu**, the Commisioning Editor at HarperCollins College Division, London and by the Divisional Managing Director **John Parsons.** Thanks are due also to the remainder of the HarperCollins team, in particular to **Sarah Mackey** and her colleagues for their ongoing endeavours with respect to *Psychology: A European Text*.

We would also like to acknowledge the contributions of our academic colleagues as made to the various stages in the production of this book. In particular, we would like to express our gratitude to the members of the Department of Psychology at the University of East London and the Department of Experimental and Theoretical Psychology at Leiden University for supporting our endeavours and helping to create the conditions in which our work could successfully take place.

We would also like to extend our thanks to colleagues who have commented upon portions of this text in draft form or who have helped indirectly through their conversations and other efforts with us, namely to: **Michael J. Apter**, Georgetown University, United States of America; **Carolien Baartman**, Leiden University, Holland; **Sacha Bem**, Leiden University, Holland; **Mary Boyle**, University of East London, England; **George Brown**, University of London, England; **Agneta H. Fischer**, University of Amsterdam, Holland; **Nico H. Frijda**, University of Amsterdam, Holland; **Ben Gammon**, University of East London, England; **Mark Griffiths**, University of Plymouth, England; **Lex van der Heijden**, Leiden University, Holland; **Denis Hilton**, Ecole Supérieure des Sciences Economiques et Commerciales, Cergy-Pontoise, France; **Gerard Kempen**, Leiden University, Holland; **Gerard Kerkhof**, Leiden University, Holland; **Antony Manstead**, University of Amsterdam, Holland; **Anastasia Marneth**, Rutgers Foundation, the Hague, Holland; **Harald Merckelbach**, University of Limburg, Holland; **John Pearce**, University of Wales College of Cardiff, Wales; **Melinda Rees**, University of London, England; **Els van Schie**, Leiden University, Holland; **Henderikus Stam**, University of Calgary, Canada; **Rien Verbaten**, Leiden University, Holland; **Marietta Vis**, Leiden University, Holland; **Willem Albert Wagenaar**, Leiden University, Holland; **David White**, University of Staffordshire, England; **Gezinus Wolters**, Leiden University, Holland; and **Vanda L. Zammuner**, University of Padova, Italy.

Our thanks are extended likewise to those colleagues who acted as reviewers of *Psychology and Life (13th edition)*, the forerunner of this volume, to: **Ian Boardman, Marina Brunton, Christine Bundy, Lilliemore Crowther, Jackie Fitzgerald**, University College of North Wales, Wales; **Nancy Kelly**, University of Huddersfield, England; **David Lloyd**, University College of North Wales, Wales, **Bjorn Lyxell**, Linkoping University, Sweden; **Gerry Mulhern**, Queens University, Belfast, Northern Ireland; **Karen Rowse** and **John Whitehurst**, University College of North Wales, Wales.

We would like to express our thanks to **Anne Stapleton, Susy Ajith, Vivian Ferris** (University of East London) and **Louise Radford** (HarperCollins, London) for their additional work on the reference list and to **Kevin Head, Ambi Ambihaipahan, Tony Britton, Claire Steed** and **John O'Leary** (University of East London) for their technical assistance.

Finally, we extend our thanks to our families and other friends not mentioned above by name who have tolerated our absences with equanimity during the course of our work.

Jeroen Jansz   Mark McDermott
Nico Metaal   Philip Zimbardo

Chapter 1

Probing the Mysteries of Mind and Behaviour

October 1992: at the end of her live performance of Bob Marley's song *War* on American television, Sinéad O'Connor tears up a photograph of the Pope and moments later says 'Fight the real enemy'. Aggressive telephone calls follow and a committee asks the public to destroy CDs and tapes of her music. When she appears on stage at Bob Dylan's fiftieth birthday celebration at New York's Madison Square Garden a few days later, her performance is disrupted by the American audience, one-half of which yells abuse and disapproval whilst the other shout support and encouragement. Sinéad grows fearful that she is going to be silenced by the crowd, that what she has to say in song and spoken word may go unheard, but continues as best she can nevertheless.

One wonders, though, why a successful singer would choose to engage in this ostensibly destructive act? Surely, Sinéad must have anticipated the pervasive reaction that followed? Why did she risk putting her popularity and career in jeopardy? Was it because she was at war with the faith within which she was brought up, or was it for other less obvious but more complex reasons? If the opinion of psychologists were to be sought, they might focus on her beliefs about religion, but in all likelihood they would take other factors into consideration in an effort to understand Sinéad's action and statement. However, before explanations can be given by anyone, by psychologists and others alike, it is necessary to take into account available background information. As soon as we collect biographical details about Sinéad and her career it becomes obvious that she has never avoided controversy.

Born in 1966, it was not long before Sinéad had to cope with many of life's hardships. She grew up in Dublin, Ireland, in a four-child family. Her parents divorced when she was eight. Sinéad had been subject to physical trauma and abuse by her mother until she moved to her father's home at the age of 13. After this relocation, however, she stopped going to school, truanting and shoplifting becoming frequent features of her existence. As a result, Sinéad was sent to a residential centre on the outskirts of Dublin for 'girls with behavioural problems'. She remained there for 18 months but was allowed to leave on condition that she attend a boarding school in Waterford, Ireland. After a year-and-a-half she left its confines, found herself a bed-sit in Dublin and, at 17, joined her first band. Tragically for Sinéad, not long after this in 1985, her mother was killed in a road accident. Though she was devastated by the loss, Sinéad's talent continued to flourish and was soon discovered. Contract in hand, she left Ireland some months later and in 1987 recorded *The Lion and the Cobra*, which appeared on a wave of publicity. This 21-year-old young woman with a bald, shaven head made an intriguing impression on many. Her voice was acknowledged widely as of an extraordinary quality, sounding on occasion turbulent and wild, whilst on others gentle and enchanting. In interviews she criticised the music business and the attitudes of many popstars. Although her image and music was 'alternative', she attracted a large audience. In 1990 her recording of *Nothing Compares 2 U* reached the top of the charts all over the world. However, it was also the year of a serious controversy. While touring the United States she broke with the American tradition of playing the American national anthem at the beginning of a big concert. American conservatives, headed by Frank Sinatra, publicly expressed their contempt for what they saw as O'Connor's anti-Americanism. The American press attacked her attitude and alleged arrogance. In interviews she disclosed that she found it hard to cope with the pervasive hostility shown towards her by the media. In the meantime she contributed to various benefit performances and worked on a new album.

So it was that in 1992, Sinéad came to play hostess to controversy once more, ripping up the Pope's image in an effort to extend the message of the song she was performing. But why elect to violate in front of millions of people a picture of one of the world's most influential religious leaders? This account of Sinéad opens up many questions for psychology. Were her action and words a response both to her personal experience of Catholicism as a young Irish woman and to the political unrest in Northern Ireland? Was she attempting to define her persona as a public figure or simply to increase her profile as a rock star? Perhaps, on the other hand, she was on the threshold of some kind of 'nervous breakdown'? Or do we have to look for quite different reasons behind the apparent ones?

As we will soon see, psychologists offer a variety of answers to questions like these. Some psychologists would argue, for example, that we need to go back to Sinéad's childhood if we want to understand her behaviour in 1992. In this vein, the destruction of the photograph could have been prompted by her distress about her mistreatment as a child, the Pope symbolising for her a universal parent against which she could express her anger and outrage. A crisis of confidence in herself may have been precipitated by an unwillingness within her family to recognise, express and resolve longstanding conflicts. Other psychologists, by contrast, would want to focus on Sinéad's own view of her future. Whichever of these approaches is preferred, psychology provides insight into what motivates actions like those of Sinéad's.

The major difference between a psychological interpretation of human action and one based on ordinary observation is that psychological knowledge is collected via systematic research and tested against professional standards. Through its theories and empirical work, psychology hopes to contribute to a better understanding of human functioning. It does so without claiming, however, that psychology has a monopoly on wisdom about the human condition. Human behaviour is variable and unpredictable to a large extent. As psychologists we cannot be certain, for example, whether or not Sinéad O'Connor will continue using her singer's voice to ensure her concerns are heard. Perhaps, though, she will persevere for 'silence' may be the 'real enemy' she feels compelled to overcome.

WE WANT TO welcome you to the subject of psychology. There are many routes that we can follow to understand 'the nature of human nature'. We will journey through the inner spaces of brain and mind and the outer dimensions of human behaviour. Between those extremes, we shall investigate things that you perhaps take for granted, such as how you perceive your world, communicate, learn, think, remember and even sleep. But we will also detour to try to understand how and why we dream, fall in love, feel shy, act aggressively, or become mentally ill.

The first goal of this book is to provide a comprehensive survey of psychological theories about the workings of the brain, mind and behaviour. The second goal is to show how the theories are scrutinised in psychological research. The third goal is concerned with the application of psychological knowledge in our everyday lives, and how psychology can be used wisely to enhance many aspects of the human condition. Many of the urgent issues of our time – global ecological destruction, drug addiction, urban crime, prejudice – can benefit from psychological perspectives. It should, however, be stressed that psychology does not claim to hold the key to the solution of these pressing problems. Next to the psychological aspects there are political, legal, economic and cultural dimensions to problems such as pollution, addiction, crime and prejudice. Therefore, a collaboration of psychologists with researchers from other disciplines is necessary. Psychologists have to keep in touch with policymakers who are formulating solutions to the pressing problems of our times.

◪ PSYCHOLOGY DEFINED

Academic psychology can be formally defined as the empirical study of the behavioural and mental functioning of individuals. Many psychologists seek answers to the fundamental question: what is the nature of human nature? Psychology answers this question by looking at processes that occur within individuals as well as those in the physical and social environment that may affect how people think, feel and act. But first let us examine each part of the definition of psychology: empirical, behaviour, mental and individual.

The *empirical* aspect of psychology requires that psychological conclusions are based on empirical evidence, i.e. reports of observations, technically called **data**, that are gathered through and by the senses of the observer. In this way, authority and personal beliefs should not determine whether a proposition about the human condition is accepted or refuted, but rather the methods used to make observations, collect data and formulate conclusions seek to do so in as unbiased a manner as possible. We will elaborate on the features of these methods later when we consider how psychologists conduct their research.

Behaviour is the means by which organisms adjust to their environment. Behaviour is action. The subject matter of psychology is largely the observable behaviour of humans and other species of animals. Smiling, crying, running, hitting, talking and touching are some obvious examples of behaviour that we can observe. Psychologists observe how an individual functions, what the individual does and how the individual goes about doing it within a given behavioural setting and social context.

Much human activity takes place as private, internal events-thinking, feeling, planning, reasoning, creating and dreaming. We therefore cannot understand human actions without also understanding **mental processes**, the workings of the human mind. Philosophy has produced much theoretical work on mental functioning. In psychology, the theoretical study of mental processes is connected to empirical investigation into the workings of *mind*.

The subject of psychological analysis is often the *individual* – a new-born infant, a student adjusting to her new life at university, a man in a mid-life crisis, or a young mother who succesfully combines her career with parenthood. However, the subject might also be

a chimpanzee learning to use symbols to communicate, a white rat navigating a maze, or a hungry pigeon learning to peck a button to release food. An individual might be studied in his or her natural habitat, or in the controlled conditions of a research laboratory. In recent years, researchers have even been studying computer simulations of animal behaviour and human mental processes.

◪ Ties to Other Disciplines

Psychology has numerous ties with so many different areas of knowledge. At one and the same time it is a social science, a behavioural science, a brain science and also a health science. As one of the social sciences, psychology draws from economics, political science, sociology and cultural anthropology. Because it systematically analyses activity in terms of its causes and consequences, psychology is a behavioural science. Psychologists share many interests with researchers in biological sciences, especially with those who study brain processes and the biochemical bases of behaviour. As a health science – with links to medicine, education, law and environmental studies – psychology seeks to improve the quality of our individual and collective well-being. Psychology also retains conspicuous ties to philosophy and areas in the humanities and arts such as literature, drama and religion.

It will soon become clear that psychological theory and research display a wide diversity of form and content. In this first chapter we will provide you with a number of strategies with which to bring some order to psychology's **pluriformity**, its numerous forms and guises. First, however, we will devote a few words to the historical and social context of modern psychology.

◪ PSYCHOLOGY AND INDIVIDUALISM

'Psychology has a long past, yet its real history is short', wrote one of the first German psychologists, Hermann Ebbinghaus (1908). The study of human nature stretches back thousands of years: philosophers have long asked important questions about how people perceive reality, the nature of consciousness and the origins of so-called 'madness'. This philosophical approach to psychological issues, however, was exclusively theoretical. In Ebbinghaus's day psychology emancipated itself from philosophy and became established as an empirical subject, employing scientific methods to observe and measure variation in behaviour.

The foundation of the first psychological laboratory by **Wilhelm Wundt** in Leipzig, Germany, 1879, is generally taken as the formal beginning of psychology as an independent empirical endeavour, using the methods of the natural sciences, such as physics and chemistry. Wundt was probably the first researcher to refer to himself as a 'psychologist'. At the end of the nineteenth century laboratories were founded in countries overseas and on the European continent: for example, the United States (1883), Russia (1886), Denmark (1886), Japan (1888), France (1889), Italy (1889), Canada (1890), Switzerland (1891), Belgium (1891), the United Kingdom (1891) and the Netherlands (1892).

Taking the foundation of Wundt's laboratory as the formal beginning of psychology is an attempt to reduce a complex interaction of numerous factors to one event at a specific time and place. The birth of modern psychology must actually be understood against the background of societal developments in nineteenth-century Europe. We will sketch briefly here the close links between psychology and Western societies. It will be argued that psychology is on the one hand a product of these Western individualistic cultures, while, on the other hand, it has made a significant contribution to Western individualism itself.

 Individualism

By the end of the nineteenth century the historical process of individualisation becomes visible in large segments of society. The ideology of individualism dominates the Western world from that moment on. **Individualism** can be characterised concisely by its assumption that the individual human being is the basic unit of society. Each individual is seen as a discrete entity possessing an inner core. The individual is further said to be free from the will of others and free to refrain from any involuntary relationships. Collectives are not denied, of course, but they are essentially seen as a summing-up of individuals.

Historians disagree as to the origins of individualism. For example, some trace individualism back to classical Greece, others link individualism quite strictly to private property, which first came into being in England around 1250. Most historians agree, however, on two major constituents of individualism: the Renaissance and Protestantism. It is generally acknowledged that the fifteenth-century Renaissance constituted a turning point in the conception of the individual. In the collectivist culture of the Middle Ages, each person was perceived as synonymous with his or her role in the group – the family, church, guild or city. In the Renaissance, *unique* artists appear on the

cultural stage, such as Michaelangelo and Leonardo da Vinci, and are honoured for their personal accomplishments and virtues. The emphasis on the *uniqueness* of people contributed to individualisation, but it should be noted that Renaissance individuality stops short of interest in the inner core of a person. An artist was perceived as unique because of his accomplishment, not for his personal psychological make-up. Renaissance individualism is further qualified by the fact that it was strangely restricted to the male cultural elite. The 'new' individuals were, generally speaking, outstanding artists of the male sex who belonged to the social aristocracy.

The Protestant rebellion against the Roman Catholic Church also pushed the individual human being to the centre of the stage. The Reformation of the fifteenth and sixteenth centuries stressed the individual's exclusive relation to 'God' in matters of faith. The believer could no longer lean on the priest or the Holy Church for the establishment of a relationship with the 'Almighty'. In their prayers, Protestants had themselves to account for their sins in private isolation. They could no longer rely on the priest who had the authority to give absolution after confession. Although Protestantism reached a wider audience than the cultural revolution of the Renaissance, its impact was largely confined to the northern and western parts of Europe and the east coast of the North-American continent. The other parts of Europe and America remained under the influence of Catholicism.

The Renaissance and Protestantism speeded up the process of individualisation, but it was not until the nineteenth century that individualism proliferated among all social strata in the Western world. The second industrial revolution (during the latter half of the nineteenth century) led to a drastic reorganisation of social life which had far-reaching consequences for individualisation. Mechanisation radicalised the system of being paid on a piece-meal basis. The individual accomplishment of the worker was now set against the standard of 'the one best way of doing the job'. The extent to which workers were able to reach this standard determined how much money each took home at the end of the day. Mechanised industries demanded skilled workers. In some countries this resulted in factory schools where labourers received a specialised education. Elsewhere, entrepreneurs supported the public demand for compulsory education. By the turn of the century most Western countries obliged their young citizens to spend a number of years in school. In class, grading systems were introduced to monitor the individual accomplishments of pupils.

Industrial production and schooling accelerated individualisation because of the emphasis on individual performance in these sectors. But the focus on the individual human being was also sustained at a more general level. Industrialisation generally led to rapid urbanisation. Former farmers and farm-hands had to leave the rural areas in order to build up a new life in the overpopulated towns. Many of them felt uprooted because they had to loosen ties with their families and local community. In this social climate people were thrown back upon themselves. They could no longer rely on their relatives and familiar members of the community. They had to decide themselves what they wanted from their lives and where to sell their labour in the market place.

At the ideological level, individualistic notions were forcefully supported by *Social Darwinism*. In this application of evolution theory to society, it was argued that the course of evolution should not be hindered by human interference. The natural drive of competition would in the end lead to the 'survival of the fittest' individuals. The burden of the people at the bottom of the social pyramid should therefore not be relieved. The Social Darwinists were against welfare programmes, free universal education, health services for the poor and similar projects. The uncompromising *laissez-faire* doctrine of Social Darwinism was immensely popular among the affluent in England and the United States of America. The theory legitimised the societal antagonisms of nineteenth-century individualism. It furthermore provided a 'scientific' explanation of the almost mythical story about the self-made man who had made it from 'rags to riches'.

The societal developments of the nineteenth century resulted in the domination of individualistic notions of person and society in the Western world. It should be noted at this point that individualism is largely a Western phenomenon. On a world scale, most cultures stress the importance of the group, or community, and attribute major importance to mutual responsibilities between members of the community. In other words, most cultures are dominated by *collectivism* (Hofstede, 1980; Triandis, 1990). It would, however, be a mistake to categorise cultures as either collectivistic or individualistic. Most cultures dominated by collectivism also have individualistic aspects. The people of China, for example, are achievement oriented but a different value is placed upon such striving – it is for the good of the collective, not of the individual. Even Western individualism, which maintains a strong position, has been (and is) contested by collectivist opposition. In Great Britain, for example, an economy based upon monetarism coexists with trade union movements and the benefits of a national health service. The history of the nineteenth-century is illustrative of this apparent paradox. Individualism was then gaining a large audience, but at the same time, the mass movements of socialism and nationalism subsumed individual interests under the interests of class or nation. The nineteenth-century mass movements were, however, not able to distract the historical process of individualisation from its course. The post-industrialist Western societies are today largely individualistic, although collectivist voices are always present to criticise individualism and its consequences.

◤ Psychology's Contribution

Psychology was institutionalised in the Western world by the end of the nineteenth century. The historical process of individualisation had implications on the development of psychology as a subject for emerging explanatory frameworks. Each person was conceived of as an autonomous individual and as a repository of personally unique thoughts. The notion began to take hold that such thoughts can be formed and expressed independently of the social and interpersonal context in which they were paradoxically yet necessarily formed (Jahoda, 1992). Arguably, such a starting point has had far-reaching consequences for the shape and form of contemporary psychology with its individualistic emphasis (Sampson, 1993). Throughout the same period, however, psychology started to make a specific contribution to Western individualism. Psychologists provided instruments to measure the differences between individuals. Psychologists were not the first to measure human differentiality. Physicians were already categorising people with respect to their physical condition; the practice of craniometry was widespread in Europe and North America. People who called themselves 'phrenologists' offered to measure a person's skull in order to determine the individual's various capacities. Bumps at specific locations on the head, for example, were taken as proof of a gift in mathematics; ones elsewhere as indications of outstanding capacity in other fields, or as centres for various psychological processes like affection or jealousy.

Nineteenth-century psychology quickly distanced itself from such measurements since the leading assumptions of phrenology soon became discredited. Psychology developed its own instruments and made a revolutionary contribution by measuring 'mental' differences more directly: the instrument of the psychological **test** was developed to measure mental capacities without any quantification of the body in terms of shape or location. Psychologists in France developed tests to determine in advance which pupils would be likely to do well in school and which pupils had to receive special education. In industry, psychologists proposed tests and other procedures to establish who was the most suitable man or woman for the job in question. On the eve of the First World

War, the psychological measurement of individual differences had become widespread in England, Germany and North America.

The First World War itself stimulated the development of psychology enormously. When the United States of America entered the war, American psychologists offered to test all recruits in order to determine their capacities and to decide who was capable of leadership and who was not. It resulted in the largest testing operation in the history of psychology. In Germany, psychologists were also involved in the selection of army personnel and in England psychologists were researching the fatigue that resulted from the monotonous labour in the munition factories. Many of the soldiers from both sides, who fought in the trenches of Flanders and Northern France, suffered from severe distress, called 'Shell Shock', something we might call 'post-traumatic stress reaction' today. Behind the front, soldiers affected in this way were treated, so laying the first foundation for psychotherapy.

Psychological tests contribute to individualisation in two ways: first, they assume the individual is the most important contributor to performance, irrespective of environmental influences; second, they quantify individual differences that cannot necessarily be observed without the aid of such an instrument. The rapid growth of psychological testing, as well as of other psychological interventions, is not without consequences. Since the 1950s onwards psychological terms, concepts and theories have been popularised on a large scale in the media. Psychological concepts like extraversion, intelligence, the unconscious and repression have become fully integrated in the vernacular. Without any hesitation people nowadays use such individualistic psychological vocabulary to describe their friends, colleagues, relatives and themselves.

The consequences of this popularisation of an individual-based psychology are debatable. It certainly is conceivable that the use of this psychological vocabulary changes the ways in which people think and feel about themselves and their fellow beings. Historians of Western culture are quite sure about this. They have observed the dissemination of a 'therapeutic attitude' in the past two decades. It has resulted in an essentialistic twist to individualism, which holds that each person has a unique core, or rather *essence* of feeling and intuition, that should be expressed if one wants to become a fully developed person. Thus, for better or worse, a psychological aspect has been inserted into the historical process of individualisation.

Later in this chapter we will present the dissemination of academic psychology and psychology's fields of practice. But first we will introduce a way in which we can organise psychology's theoretical pluriformity.

INTERIM SUMMARY

We defined psychology as the empirical study of the behavioural and mental functioning of individuals. Psychology has numerous ties with many different areas of knowledge because it is a social science, a behavioural science, a brain science and also a health science. From a historical perspective, psychology is on the one hand a product of Western individualistic societies while, on the other hand, psychology has made a significant contribution to Western individualism itself.

◤ CURRENT PSYCHOLOGICAL PERSPECTIVES

Psychology is characterised by a number of different theoretical perspectives about the behavioural and mental functioning of individuals. Rather than working from one theory generally accepted, psychologists have different viewpoints. Each perspective defines a different area important in the study of psychology which thus determines what to look for, where to look and (to an extent) what methods to employ. In some cases this theoretical pluriformity results in debates about contradictory claims. In other cases the perspectives have proven to be complementary.

This section outlines the perspectives that are conspicuous in contemporary psychology. We will first discuss the four foundational approaches, being behaviourism, psychoanalysis, cognitivism and biological psychology. Behaviourism and psychoanalysis were developed at the beginning of this century and although they lost a lot of their influence in favour of cognitivism, they still have an impact on contemporary psychology. After the foundational perspectives we will discuss humanist psychology, feminist psychology and social constructionism, which were originally developed as alternatives to mainstream psychology.

Psychology is concerned with real human beings made of flesh and blood. But what it is that makes a human animal into a human *person* is subject to debate. The theoretical perspectives differ with respect to the *image of the person* they implicitly or explicitly embrace. If human beings are assumed, for example, to be passive machines that function according to laws of nature, the image of the person is radically different from one wherein humans are assumed to be active, creative and responsible for their own doings and sayings. The image of the person is also related to questions about human freedom. Do people have free will or do they simply act out a script imposed by their heredity (biological determinism) or their environment (environmental determinism)?

Most theoretical perspectives use a *metaphor* to characterise human nature. Theorists in psychology are keen on metaphors because of the similarity between the processes to be explained and a system that is already understood. Using the computer as a metaphor for the human mind is a good example of this, one that incidentally replaced the earlier metaphor of mind as an elaborate form of telephone switchboard.

The theoretical perspectives further vary in their *temporal focus*, concentrating on either the past, present or future. Some psychologists look to past experiences to explain present behaviour, such as the influence of childhood sexual abuse or parental divorce on adult sexuality. Some psychologists focus on the present situation, observing how the behaviour of organisms is shaped by reward. Others study the importance of future events, investigating, for example, whether goal setting will influence the educational performance of underachieving students.

These psychological perspectives also vary in terms of how specific and precise they try to be and also in terms of how much they rely on empirical research findings. Although they are distinctive, at some points they overlap. Most psychologists nowadays borrow and blend concepts from more than one of these perspectives. Nevertheless, each represents a different approach to the central issues in psychology. In the chapters that follow, we will elaborate in some detail on the contributions of each approach, because taken together, they represent what modern psychology is all about.

◤ Behaviourism

In 1913, the young American animal psychologist **John B. Watson** published a provocative paper about psychology (Watson, 1913). He argued that psychology should only study overt behaviours that can be *objectively* recorded. By 'objective' is meant when an event can be observed simultaneously by more than one person. The behaviourist perspective is that psychologists should not be concerned with inner processes like motives or mental states, the experience of which may only be 'observed' by the person in whom they are occurring. From the behaviouristic perspective, inner processes are 'locked up' in a *black box*, the contents of which cannot be accessed by the scientific study of human behaviour. Due to its exclusive focus on overt behaviours, behaviourism is also known as stimulus-response (S → R) psychology. The specific behaviour that is being observed and

measured is termed the *response*. It has to be specific and measurable – blinking an eye, pulling a lever, or saying 'yes' following an identifiable stimulus (a light or a bell). A response is said to be triggered by an environmental condition known as a *stimulus* (the plural of stimulus is stimuli). Imagine, for example, that you are observing a baby: you might note that the baby exhibits a particular behaviour, crying, in response to the stimulus of a loud noise. For behaviourists, stimuli were forms of physical energy that cued responding.

Behaviourism in the past has used the analogy of a telephone switchboard as a metaphor to account for the ways in which external stimuli are linked to responses of the organism. The main objective of behavioural analysis is to understand how particular environmental stimuli control particular kinds of behaviour, or the *ABCs* of psychology (Blackman, 1980). First, behaviourists analyse the *A*ntecedent environmental conditions that precede the behaviour and 'set the stage' for responding or withholding a response. Next they look at the *B*ehavioural response, which is the main object of study – the action to be understood, predicted and modified. Finally, they look at the observable *C*onsequences that follow from the response – its impact on the environment and how these consequences may maintain the behaviour in question.

According to behaviourism, behaviour is wholly determined by conditions in the environment. People are neither innately 'good' nor 'evil' but simply reactive to their environment. That environment is of course composed of the actions of other people. Behaviour, then, can be changed by the proper arrangement of environmental conditions. Though heredity may place some limits on what environment can accomplish, behavioural psychologists assume that what people become is largely the result of *nurture* (experience) not inherited *nature*.

Behaviourists have typically done their research in the psychological laboratory. They insist on very precise definitions of the phenomena studied and rigorous standards of evidence, usually in quantifiable form. Often they study animal subjects such as rats and pigeons because, with animals, specification of all the conditions can be much more complete than with human subjects. They assume that the basic processes they investigate with their animal subjects are part of general principles that hold true for different species but that there are biological boundaries for each species which determine just how much behaviour can be affected by environmental contingencies.

Behaviourism originates in North America with Watson's work, but he himself was influenced by the Russian physiologist **Ivan Pavlov**. Pavlov discovered that the physiological response of salivation, thought to be produced only by eating food, could be elicited by the sight or sound of anything that was regularly paired with presentation of the food. Pavlov's primary interest was in the physiology of the learned relationship, known as **conditioning**.

Until Watson, the concept of an 'instinct' as an unobservable hereditary mechanism was used to explain personality and behaviour. Watson saw, however, that if all behaviour could be shown to be the result of learning, it would open up new possibilities for changing undesirable behaviour. He believed that mental events could not be studied scientifically, since he thought they could not be observed objectively. So he exiled all forms of mental processes from his form of behavioural analysis. He established a new direction in psychology – a search for causes in the environment rather than in a person – and was the first to insist that psychologists study only observable behaviour.

If Watson laid the groundwork for behaviourism, **Burrhus Frederic Skinner** was its major architect (Skinner, 1976). Skinner's plans and visions shaped behaviourism for many decades. He believed that the house of scientific psychology could accommodate only one tenant – observable behaviour. There was no room for boarders who made too much noise about consciousness, motivation, thoughtfulness or the brain. In Skinner's early blueprints, psychology could be described as scientific only if it restricted itself to the study of how behaviour *operates* on the environment and is changed by the consequences it has on that environment.

For much of this century, the behaviouristic model has dominated North American psychology and has been successfully exported to Western Europe. Its emphasis on the need for rigorous research and carefully defined concepts has influenced most areas of psychology. Although Skinner and his co-workers conducted their basic research with animal subjects, the principles of behaviourism have been widely and somewhat successfully applied to human problems. Behaviourist principles have proposed a more humane approach to educating children (through the use of rewards rather than punishment) and developing new therapies for modifying behaviour disorders. Skinner's behaviourism has been as practical as it is still provocative – provocative because critics maintain that the view of behaviourism was too narrow and for some decades retarded the development of psychology as a discipline that investigated the full range of human complexity. It did so, they say, by focusing attention, and the skills of many researchers, away from studying what makes human beings into human persons (such as inner subjective experiences, emotion, language, thought and consciousness in general). However, recent reassessments of Skinner's contribution are demonstrating that he also felt the study of these phenomena to be important (Richelle,

1993). The next theoretical perspective focuses on the intrapsychic forces that were marginalised within psychology by behaviourism.

◆ Psychoanalysis

According to **psychoanalysis**, behaviour is driven, or motivated, by powerful intrapsychic forces. In this view, human actions stem from inherited drives, and from attempts to resolve conflicts between personal needs and society's demands to act appropriately. Action is envisaged as the product of inner tension, but the main purpose of our actions is to reduce tension. According to psychoanalysis, the organism stops reacting when its needs are satisfied. The concept of **drive** is central in psychoanalytic theory. Drives are sources of energy and thus provide the power for behaviour. In psychoanalysis, human beings are steam engines, metaphorically speaking. The drives are assumed to be analogous to the coal that fuels the engine. Inner psychic tension is created by heating the water and if the tension gets too high and endangers the survival of the engine, safety valves are opened to bring relief. This perspective uses a *hydraulic model* of the build up and release of tension.

Psychoanalysis was originally developed by the Viennese physician **Sigmund Freud** in the late nineteenth and early twentieth centuries (Freud, 1923; 1949). Freud's ideas were not developed within the walls of a university, but grew out of his work with mentally disturbed patients. Freud believed that the principles he observed at work with his patients applied to both normal and abnormal behaviour. According to Freud's theory, each person is fully determined by a combination of heredity and early childhood experiences. He argued that infants are

Sigmund Freud developed the psychodynamic approach to behaviour.

driven by unlearned instincts for self-preservation and desires for physical pleasure. These primitive impulses are bottled up because they are opposed by taboos of parents and society. The child's personality develops according to the extent to which he or she resolves the conflict between the need to express and the need to inhibit such powerful impulses. Often this early conflict continues to influence behaviour and create emotional problems in ways that a person does not understand. Freud's model was the first to recognise that human nature is not always rational; that actions may be driven by motives that are not in conscious awareness. Freud is credited with making the **unconscious** worthy of serious inquiry.

In Freud's view, a person is pulled and pushed by a complex network of inner and outer forces. The nature of the human organism is portrayed negatively; violence is seen as a natural means of expressing primitive sexual and aggressive urges. This view implies that people need strong social controls if they are to be saved from their own passions for pleasure and destructiveness.

Freud's ideas have had a considerable influence on many areas of psychology. You will encounter different aspects of his contributions as you read about child development, dreaming, forgetting, unconscious motivation, personality, neurotic disorders and psychotherapy. His ideas will appear as frequent markers on our psychological journey. But you may be surprised to discover that his ideas were never the result of systematic research. Instead, they were the product of an exceptionally creative mind obsessed with unravelling the mysteries of human thoughts, feelings and actions. Freud closely observed his patients, others and most of all, himself. He may have been the world's greatest egoist, focusing the spotlight of intense analysis on his every action, from seemingly insignificant slips of the tongue to fragments of his dreams. Support for Freud's theories comes not so much from the psychological laboratory but in part from mythology, legend, drama and archaeology (Gay, 1988).

Many psychologists since Freud have taken psychoanalysis in new directions. North American and British neo-Freudian theorists have criticised Freud's deterministic image of the person: according to them, human beings are not at the mercy of their drives or of childhood experiences. They have broadened Freud's theory to include personal initiative and influences that occur over a lifetime, not just in infancy. Many neo-Freudians nowadays do research in collaboration with psychologists working from different theoretical perspectives (Eagle, 1984).

In France, psychoanalysis became part of the cultural movement that emerged after the student revolt of May 1968. The political uprising aimed at a radical reform of cultural norms and values. The students wanted to 'bring imagination to power', as they said at that time. When the May revolt fell short of its expectations, many activists turned to psychoanalysis for an answer. The key figure in French psychoanalysis is **Jacques Lacan**, who imported linguistic principles into Freudian theory. In his hybrid of linguistics and psychoanalysis, Lacan argues that the notion of Western personhood with its emphasis on the rational and the integrated self, or 'I', is an illusion. Human beings are torn between contradictory wishes and therefore in reality are decentred and essentially fragmentary. The symbolic system of Western languages, however, constructs the individual as a distinct, rational entity who is held responsible for his or her actions. In therapy, this symbolic accomplishment should be taken apart again by focusing on the words that are spoken in the session. In this context, Lacan advises young therapists to 'do crossword puzzles' as part of their training. Deconstructing the text and subtext of the rational 'I' is seen as the only way to cope with intrapsychic conflict (Lacan, 1974; 1979). Lacanian psychoanalysis is influential in cultural studies and in deconstructionist philosophy; however, its impact on academic psychology at present is limited in France as well as in other countries.

Despite the differences between Freud and his followers they share an emphasis on the energetic, or dynamic, side of human nature and on the emotional relations between individuals. Therefore, the multivarious psychoanalytic theories are often subsumed under the heading of *psychodynamic approaches*.

 **Cognitivism**

Cognitive psychologists focus on the rational and information processing aspects of human functioning. They are not concerned with intrapsychic dynamisms. Their subject matter is that which behaviourism has deliberately disregarded in scientific psychology: the contents of the black box. The so-called 'cognitive revolution' has emerged over the past three decades as a direct challenge to the limiting perspectives of behaviourism (**Ulric Neisser**, 1967). The centrepiece of the cognitive perspective is human thought and all the processes of knowing – attending, thinking, remembering, expecting, solving problems, fantasising and consciousness. From the cognitive perspective, people act because they think, and people think because they are human beings uniquely equipped to do so due to nature's design of our central nervous system, in particular of our brains. Cognitivists use the computer as a metaphor for human mental functioning. The software of language and thought runs on the hardware of the brain.

In the seventeenth century, the French philosopher **René Descartes** declared, 'I think, therefore I am'. This statement expresses a fundamental proposition about the nature of human existence: only through the awareness of individual thought processes can people have a sense of personal identity. In the Latin version of Descartes' proclamation, *'cogito ergo sum'*, 'cogito' means 'I think'. The word 'cognition' is derived from 'cogito'. Personal thoughts ascribe meaning to all experiences and shape perceptions and responses to the world.

According to cognitive psychologists, the processing or interpretation of information received about a stimulus is at least as important in determining behaviour as the stimulus input itself. These psychologists also assert that humans are not simply reactive creatures in this process but are also active creatures in choosing and creating individual stimulus environments. An individual responds to reality not as it is in the objective world of matter, but as it is represented within the subjective reality of the individual's inner world of thoughts and ideas.

In cognitive theories, behaviour is only partly determined by preceding stimulus events and past behavioural consequences, as behaviourists believe. Some of the most significant behaviour emerges from totally novel ways of thinking, not from predictable ways used in the past. The ability to imagine options and alternatives that are totally different from what is or was enables people to work toward new futures that transcend the realities of poverty or physical and emotional handicaps. In the cognitive approach, people start life as neither good nor evil, but with potential, in the form of mental templates, to be what they will. Cognitive psychologists are interested in the way people interpret the current stimulus environment. They want to know how people evaluate the various actions they might take and then decide what to do based on memories of what worked in the past and expectations of future consequences. They view thoughts as both results and causes of overt actions. Feeling regret when you have hurt someone is an example of thought as a result. But apologising for your actions after feeling regret is an example of thought as a cause.

Psychologist **Herbert Simon** was among the pioneers of cognitive psychology. He won a Nobel Prize in economics (1978) for his research on the way people make decisions under conditions of uncertainty, that is, without all the relevant information. He showed that economic models based on predictions from rational analyses of how people are supposed to behave do not work when the situation is unclear. Instead, people are far less rational in deciding than is often assumed. **George A. Kelly**, another pioneer of cognitivism, took the cognitive image of the person to its extremes by arguing that

ordinary human beings are like scientists (Kelly, 1955). Humans attribute personal meaning to the world by seeking explanations for what has happened and what will happen next. Therefore, they formulate hypotheses which are tested in reality. Sometimes the hypotheses need to be revised, at other times they are refuted and new hypotheses are needed. So, human beings are cognitive animals busy with gathering knowledge and testing it. They do so because the human mind thrives on curiosity and because such thinking fosters survival.

At present, **cognitivism** is the dominant theoretical perspective in psychology. But like any successful scientific endeavour, its programme is subject to criticism. Psychoanalysts were among the first to criticise cognitivism's sterile image of the person. Nowadays, many cognitivists themselves acknowledge that there is more to human life than the processing of information alone. Research into 'cold cognition' has to be supplemented with studies about 'hot motivation'. Keith Oatley (1992), for example, theorises about the relationship between rational planning, motivation and emotion. He argues that people are motivated to plan their future rationally, but due to environmental and personal conditions, people are not always able to fulfil their plans. Distressing emotions, like sadness or anger, occur when a plan goes badly. Happy emotions, like joy, appear when plans proceed smoothly. Cognitivism is further reproached for being too intellectualistic, because it almost exclusively focuses on the mental processes of individuals. Consequently, there is little attention paid to what people do and to the natural and social context wherein people function (Gardner, 1985).

Jerome Bruner, a leader of the first cognitive revolution, has recently argued in favour of a 'second cognitive revolution' (Bruner, 1990). He prefers a more interpretive approach to cognition concerned with 'meaning-making' instead of cognitivism's current emphasis on the processing of information. Then, he argues, a psychology could be developed around the concept of meaning and the processes by which meanings are created within a community. This is somewhat ironic, however, since pioneering cognitive psychologist **Frederic Bartlett** also stressed the necessity of moving toward a content and meaning based approach to understanding thought processes, away from a consideration of their structural components (Bartlett, 1932).

Whereas Bruner focuses on meaning as a particular human characteristic, other critics of cognitivism stress the beastlike nature of humankind. They defend a *naturalistic* shift that acknowledges that human beings are mammalian animals and thus are biologically driven organisms. They want to do away with the computer metaphor because of its emphasis on information processing. In psychology, the naturalistic stance has inspired the new field of connectionism which will be discussed in the next section.

 Biological Psychology

The **biological perspective** unites psychologists who search for the causes of behaviour in the functioning of genes, the brain, the nervous system and the endocrine system (controlling hormones). According to this biologically based framework, an organism's functioning is explained in terms of underlying physical structures and biochemical processes. All experiences and actions are understood as the result of the action of nerve impulses. The triggers for these actions are envisaged as coming from chemical and electrical activities taking place within and between nerve cells.

The four assumptions of this approach are that (a) psychological and social phenomena can be understood in terms of biochemical processes; (b) complex psychological phenomena can be understood by analysis, or reduction, into ever smaller, more specific biological units; (c) all behaviour – or behaviour potential – is determined by physical structures and largely by hereditary processes; and (d) experience can modify behaviour nevertheless by altering these underlying biological structures and processes. In the past this approach was known as physiological psychology, but now, with greater focus on unlocking the secrets of brain functioning and the need to integrate many ideas and methods from related areas, these researchers are more likely to refer to themselves as **neuroscientists**. They study processes ranging from the memory circuits in simple organisms such as snails to the way human brains react to surprising stimulus information.

In psychology, neuroscientists have contributed to the connectionist theorising that has developed in the last two decades (Bechtel & Abrahamsen, 1991). **Connectionism** crosses the borders between biological psychology and cognitivism. It criticises cognitive psychology because of its root metaphor. Computers are serial machines; they process information step by step. According to the connectionists, people process information in a radically different way. Human beings perceive many things at the same time. These impressions are processed next to each other, that is, in a parallel manner. *Parallel processing* functions in a network of nodes and relations between these nodes. Networks are modelled in the following way: nodes are represented by circles, the relations are represented by lines between the circles (see *Figure 1.1*).

The relation between nodes can be either active (technically called *excitation* and represented by an arrow), or passive (technically called *inhibition* and represented by a dot). The network model shows that activity in nodes 5 and 6 is produced by a complex interaction with nodes 1-3 and nodes 2-4. In more complex connectionist models, the relations are interactive. So node 5 may, for example, act back on node 2.

Connectionists use the neural network of the human brain as the metaphor for connectionist networks. This does not mean, however, that such a network is equivalent to the human brain. Our neurophysiological knowledge is not sufficient to base a connectionist psychology on the workings of the brain. In other words, 'the brain' is used metaphorically, like the steam engine, the telephone switchboard and the computer.

While many such neuroscientists work in fundamental research, others work in clinical settings. The former might study whether memory in elderly rats can be improved by grafting tissue from the brains of rat foetuses. Those working in clinical settings might study clients suffering memory loss following an accident or disease. Neuroscientists have won Nobel Prizes in physiology for explaining how the special cells in the eye's retina are designed to perceive

FIGURE 1.1	PARALLEL PROCESSING

A very simple network of six nodes which illustrates that activity in nodes 5 and 6 is produced by interaction with nodes 1 to 3 and nodes 2 to 4.

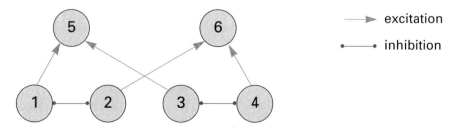

different features of the environment (**David Hubel** and **Torsten Wiesel**, 1981) and how the human brain of patients with epilepsy functions when its two halves are disconnected by surgery (**Roger Sperry**, 1981). We will say more in later chapters about their discoveries.

INTERIM SUMMARY

Behaviourism, psychoanalysis, cognitivism and biological psychology were presented as the four foundational approaches in psychology. Behaviourism is dedicated to the study of observable behaviour. Psychoanalysis studies how unconscious inner forces purportedly produce urges and wishes which drive our behaviour. Cognitivism researches the ways in which people mentally process information. Biological psychology seeks to explain human functioning in terms of underlying physical structures and biochemical processes. Each perspective defines a different area of study; their theoretical claims on occasions result in contradictions. Sometimes, the approaches have proven to be complimentary.

 ALTERNATIVE PERSPECTIVES

The foundational perspectives of behaviourism, psychoanalysis, cognitivism and biological psychology have all been subjected to criticism. From the 1960s onwards, some of these critics have been able to emancipate themselves from a marginal position to find a place within the landscape of psychology. In this section, we will first discuss humanistic psychology which has had a major impact on psychological practice and on the popular image of the discipline. We will further discuss the alternative approaches of feminist psychology and of social constructionism which have recently challenged some of the assumptions of mainstream academic psychology.

 Humanistic Psychology

Humanistic psychology emerged in the 1950s as an alternative to the determinism of psychoanalysis and behaviourism. In the humanistic view, people are neither driven by the powerful drives postulated by the Freudians nor manipulated by, and victims of, their environments, as proposed by the behaviourists. Instead, people are viewed as *active* creatures who are essentially 'good' and capable of choice. According to

the humanistic approach, the main task for human beings is to strive for growth and development of their potential. This image of men and women is not translated into a metaphor because humanists think metaphors result in a reduction of the manifold characteristics of humankind. Therefore, a human being is to be understood as a *person*.

The humanistic psychologist studies behaviour, but not by reducing it to components, elements and variables in laboratory experiments. Instead, the humanist looks for patterns in the life histories of people. In sharp contrast to the behaviourists, humanistic psychologists focus on the *subjective* world experienced by the individual, rather than the objective world as seen by external observers and researchers. In this respect, humanists are influenced by philosophical phenomenology which focuses on the individual actor's personal view of events. Early humanists, such as Rollo May, owe much to European existential thought with its emphasis on the constructive aspects of consciousness and subjectivity. Humanistic psychology is also tributary to **Gestalt psychology**. This approach was developed in Germany from the 1920s onwards. It criticised the reduction of human functioning to its elements by arguing that the whole is always more than the sum of its component parts. In humanism, the whole person is assumed to have an added value with respect to the elements that make up a human being. As a matter of consequence, humanistic psychology practises a **holistic** approach to the person that integrates the mind, body and behaviour of the individual with social and cultural forces.

Two important contributors to this perspective were **Carl Rogers** (1951) and **Abraham Maslow** (1970). Rogers emphasised the notion of the individual's natural tendency toward psychological growth and health and the importance of a positive self-concept in this process. Maslow developed a humanistic psychology of motivation: he postulated the need for *self-actualisation* and studied the characteristics of people he judged to be self-actualised.

The humanistic approach expands the realm of psychology beyond the confines of science to include valuable lessons from the study of literature, history and the arts. In this manner, psychology becomes a more complete discipline that balances the rigorous methods of science with the imaginative and interpretative approaches of the humanities (Korn, 1985). Many critics of this view see humanism as unscientific, 'feel-good, pop psychology'. Some humanists respond by advocating a more rigorous approach to the concepts, definitions and principles central to the humanistic approach (Rychlak, 1979). Others argue that their view is the yeast that will help psychology rise above its stifling focus on negative forces and on the animal-like aspects of humanity.

Feminism and Psychology

Simone de Beauvoir (1949) was among the first to criticise psychological theories for their male bias. In the 1960s her criticism was widely shared by European and North American feminists. Psychology is reproached for being a male stronghold throughout its history. Many prominent psychologists are men, and where women succeeded in coming through, their work was often marginalised (Russo & Denmark, 1987). Psychology's male bias is further shown in the fact that women and their contributions were infrequently studied. In 1968, this criticism was expressed by the American feminist **Naomi Weisstein** who argued in a seminal paper that psychology had nothing to say about what women are really like, what women need and what women want because psychology did not know (Weisstein, 1968). Furthermore, feminists have pointed to the sexist nature of psychological theories. Freud was the first in psychology to picture woman as the 'weaker' or 'different' sex, and he had many followers in psychoanalysis as well as in psychology in general.

Feminist criticism led to systematic research into gender differences. Many studies showed that the psychological differences between men and women were actually smaller than gender stereotypes led us to believe. By the end of the 1970s the focus within **feminist psychology** had shifted from criticism to the development of feminist theories. Research indicates that the social position of women results in a specific psychological perspective on many issues. In several studies it was found, for example, that most women have an *interdependent* and *collectivist* conception of themselves as a person, stressing their relations with others, whereas most men function from an independent, individualistic sense of self. Feminist theorising about stereotypes, communication, emotion, motherhood and fatherhood, psychopathology and sexual preferences has resulted in much empirical research and debate (Wilkinson, 1986).

Recently, feminist psychology has developed into *gender studies*. It is argued that the difference between male and female is a major focus around which cultures organise their view of reality. As such, cultures provide their subjects with the 'lenses of gender' through which their world is looked at (**Sandra Bem**, 1993). Ordinary language is a strong example of this: learning the English pronouns (he, she, him, her) requires wearing the lenses of gender; German and French cannot be spoken correctly without awareness of the gendered nature of language. In general, researchers in gender studies are interested in the ways in which the biological distinction between male and female (i.e. the **sex** of a person) is given meaning at a psychological and social level (i.e. the **gender** of a person). They stress that

the equating of male with masculine and female with feminine is a social construct and not necessarily a fact of nature. In fact, men and women have more similarities than differences.

Radical feminists take the gender issue one step further. They use *deconstructionism* (a branch of modern philosophy) and Lacanian psychoanalysis to reason that the notion of masculinity and femininity should be taken apart ('deconstructed') in order to show how the oppression of women is woven into our language and other symbolic systems of our culture (Burman, 1990).

 ## Social Constructionism

Like feminist psychology, social constructionism started as a critical endeavour. It criticised psychology for its almost exclusive focus on the abstract, apparently self-sufficient individual. Social constructionists unmask this individualistic image of the person as ideological because they consider it as nothing but importing the values of Western individualism into psychology. As such, **social constructionism** is critical of both Western psychology and of society. Social constructionists counter psychology's focus on the individual human being by stressing that human persons are always a product of their cultural and personal histories and of their immediate social contexts. This so-called 'primacy of the social' has far-reaching consequences because it directs analysis away from the study of individual minds and behaviour to the study of the relations *between* people that produce the 'inner worlds' of subjective experience. Psychological notions like 'mind', 'emotion', 'self' and 'memory' are not natural givens, the constructionists say, but are produced in the conversations and other discursive practices within which people are permanently engaged (Harré & Gillett, 1994; Shotter, 1993).

Some social constructionists adopt a radical *relativism* with respect to psychological knowledge. They argue that the psychological 'reality', which is generally taken for granted, is actually produced through language and other symbolic exchanges. They argue against the existence of a reality that can be unravelled by psychological research, resisting those who claim to have revealed fundamental 'truths' about the human condition. According to these constructionists, psychological knowledge is always dependent on the specific cultural and historical context and therefore cannot be generalised to any other ones. Most social constructionists, however, argue that our knowledge is inherently dependent on communities of shared meaning and therefore will always be governed by *normative rules* – principles of conduct that are 'typical' or 'usual' for a given group of people (**Kenneth Gergen**, 1985). It should be clear by now that Bruner's interpretive cognitive psychology, discussed above, is woven out of the same fabric as social constructionism.

◤ COMPARING PERSPECTIVES: FOCUS ON SINEAD O'CONNOR

Each of the perspectives discussed rests on a different set of assumptions and leads to different ways of accounting for behaviour. As an illustration, let us briefly return to the example we presented at the beginning of this chapter and compare how psychologists of different persuasions *might* seek to explain and comment upon Sinéad O'Connor's action.

Behaviourist

A behavioural analyst would look for an explanation in Sinéad's past and present overt reactions to public evaluation. How she has behaved on stage to signals of approval and disaproval would be studied in detail. The researcher might discover that her own home audiences always rewarded her with supportive cheers when she performed ostensibly outrageous acts live on stage. Such a perspective might also examine opportunities wherein she had observed similar behaviour enacted by others and seen it applauded as a consequence. Perhaps she had previously watched other rock musicians mutilate national emblems of authority during their stage shows and witnessed the encouraging approval of their audiences.

Psychoanalytic

In a psychoanalytic interpretation the focus would be on Sinéad's past. This approach would ask whether her political attack on the authority of a religious leader was motivated by personal reasons. The key to the puzzle might be found in her father's likely denial and repression of what had happened to his children when young. In this vein, it could be argued that Sinéad's tearing of the photograph symbolised a breaking of parental silence. At the same time, it could have signified a profound grief and anger as directed toward her mother and father, who like the Pope, she expected to care about her and nurture her unconditionally. Her tempestuous emotions could be interpreted as gaining impetus from the way in which they resonated with and revitalised her childhood anguish and mourning about being abused and implicitly rejected.

Cognitivist

A cognitive perspective would study how Sinéad processed information about the way in which the Catholic faith had shaped her education and thought. This perspective might propose, for example, that her thinking was the product of filtering in information about how the Church manages to impose constraints upon the activities and roles of young Irish women. Other forms of incoming information about the functions served elsewhere by the Pope by contrast become less salient for Sinéad.

Biological

Researchers in biological psychology would be interested mainly in the biochemical processes that took place within Sinéad's internal environment, her brain and body, before she tore the image in two. They might hypothesise, for instance, that continued hostility shown towards her by her parents had incited biochemical events over time that cumulatively gave rise to an uncontainable and dramatic state of rage and destructiveness. Alternatively, biologically oriented psychologists might look to complications created by health problems, medications and other physical factors in order to explain this sudden action.

Humanistic

Humanistic psychologists might explore the idea that Sinéad's own goals tended to be at odds with her public image, that her personal objectives of making music and expressing herself authentically were being compromised by the religious imperatives associated with her Irish heritage. Thereby, realising that she was experiencing difficulty actualising herself as both a secular and spiritual individual, she could see no other way forward than to renounce publically her ties with the Catholic Church by desecrating the image of its most revered representative.

Feminist

Feminist psychology researchers might wish to focus on the consequences of being a young Irish woman in showbusiness. Her attacks on the institutions and leaders of a patriarchal society could be understood as the actions of an oppressed woman who has learned to assert herself and fight back. Media assaults upon her could be seen as defensive male manoeuvres.

From this standpoint, her assault upon the Papacy could be interpreted as breaking with the traditional female gender-role of passivity and subordination by taking a stand against this paternal archetype.

Social constructionist

A social constructionist interpretation of her actions might try to debunk the image of the autonomous, rebellious young woman that had been created by media coverage of her. Broadly speaking, this perspective would argue that her controversial actions were shaped within a localised social context of friends and colleagues. Of interest would be to what extent the positions Sinéad discursively defended and enacted were fashioned through conversations with others and were intended as a catalyst for further debate.

In applying these diverse theoretical perspectives to Sinéad O'Connor, for reasons of clarity, we have presented them as somewhat separate and mutually exclusive. In actual practice, however, most psychologists borrow and utilise theories from a number of different perspectives when they are asked to interpret or explain a person's biography of behaviour. Thus, the preceding explanations of Sinéad's actions are by no means definitive. Indeed, before attempting to explain such a complex behavioural act (or, for that matter, the reactions of others to it, such as those of the audience and media), psychologists of all persuasions would want to know much more about the person and about the context in which the behaviour took place. Nevertheless, the very questions psychologists would ask and the information they would seek would be influenced in large part by their guiding theoretical perspective.

◤ WHAT PSYCHOLOGISTS DO

What is your image of a typical psychologist? What kind of work do psychologists do and where do they do it? Based on what you have seen on television or read in the newspapers, you may envision a therapist who works in his or her private office treating the mental health difficulties of troubled patients. But the kinds of tasks that psychologists engage in are much broader than therapy or helping people in distress. The roles they play and the settings in which they work are remarkably varied. In this section we will briefly describe what psychologists do in fields of practice, at universities or in research laboratories. The percentage

of psychologists in the population is greatest in Western industrialised nations and one-third of all psychologists work in the United States (See *Table 1.1,* next page).

But this picture will probably change. About a decade ago it became evident that a revival or new interest in psychology took place in many countries – notably in the eastern part of Europe and China (Rosenzweig, 1982; Sexton & Hogan, 1992).

A major distinction to be made is between *basic areas* in psychology and the psychological *fields of practice* (Van Strien, 1987). The basic areas are concerned with the development of theories. The principal aim of psychologists working in the basic areas is the accumulation of *knowledge*. Psychologists in the fields of practice are largely concerned with *helping* people in the broadest sense of the term. The fields of practice are generally known as *applied psychology*, which is really a misnomer because it suggests that psychology was first developed at universities and then applied to problems outside the laboratory. The history of psychology shows that this was hardly ever the case. Most advances in psychology were either caused by the fact that psychologists tried to solve practical problems or by the interaction between theoretical and practical work (Rose, 1990).

◤ Basic Areas

Psychological research is carried out in all branches of psychology, but most researchers work in one of the basic areas of psychology, where they pursue the accumulation of knowledge on a specific subject matter. A researcher in the basic area of developmental psychology, for example, wants to know which factors stimulate intellectual growth in the child; a researcher in cognitive psychology wants to understand how people learn a list of words by rote. These examples show that the rudimentary areas are called 'basic' for different reasons. Therefore, there is no generally accepted classification of basic areas in psychology. Nevertheless, we think it is fruitful to distinguish the following six: *developmental psychology* studies human development across the entire life span; *personality psychology* is concerned with differences between individuals; *social psychology* studies the way that behaviour and thought are affected by social contexts; *biological psychology* studies the biological bases of behaviour, feelings and mental processes; *cognitive psychology* is concerned with the workings of processes such as perception, language and memory; and *theoretical psychology*, which does not study human beings *per se*, but psychological theories about them.

The relationship between the basic areas and the theoretical perspectives we discussed above is

TABLE 1.1 PREVALENCE OF PSYCHOLOGISTS AROUND THE WORLD

Country	Psychologists per million of population
The Netherlands	884
Belgium	606
Israel	568
Finland	540
Switzerland	531 a
Spain	528
United States of America	521
Norway	514
Federal Republic of Germany	490 b
Brazil	433
Uruguay	387
Italy	348
Australia	342 a
Argentina	323
France	322
Canada	313
New Zealand	247
Great Britain	244
Czechoslovakia	226
Venezuela	202
Yugoslavia	192
Cuba	186
Austria	178
Poland	159
Ireland	157
German Democratic Republic	151
Colombia	143 c
Dominican Republic	134
Hungary	113
South Africa	83
Greece	60
Hong Kong	36
Japan	36
Romania	32
Armenia	29
Union Soviet Socialist Republics	18
Turkey	14
The Philippines	9
India	7
Korea	7
Pakistan	6
Zimbabwe	6

a – For these countries, the density was estimated using the mean of the range given for the number of psychologists.

b – Although there were 490 psychologists/million in the FRG, only 261/million were active psychologists.

c – The number of students of psychology in Columbia is double that of the number of psychologists currently active.

Source: Sexton, V.S. & Hogan, J.D. (eds) (1992) *International Psychology: Views from around the world*, Lincoln, University of Nebraska Press.

complex: biological psychologists are, for example, generally working from the biological perspective, although some embrace cognitivism. Social psychologists on the other hand can be working from entirely different perspectives, although they study the same subject matter. Some use behaviourism, others employ social constructionism. In other words, theoretical perspectives cross the borders of the basic areas, although some basic areas are mainly working from one theoretical perspective. We will delve a little deeper into the six basic areas.

- *Developmental psychology*. How does human development change over the course of an individual's lifetime? This is the question studied by specialists in developmental psychology. The developmental psychologist focuses on how human functioning changes over time, identifying the factors that shape behaviour from birth through childhood, adolescence, adulthood and old age.

- *Personality psychology*. What makes each of us unique? What are the distinctive characteristics that create individual differences in the way people respond to the same stimulus situation? The answers to such questions are the province of personality psychologists who use psychological tests and inventories, amongst other methods, to assess unique traits and individual differences. These psychologists also advance theories about the origins of personality and the factors that influence the development of personality.

- *Social psychology*. Conformity, compliance, persuasion, aggression and altruism are just some of the topics social psychologists try to understand. In order to understand how individuals are influenced by other people the social psychologist studies how behaviour and thought are affected by the social context in which interpersonal influences are experienced. They emphasise the potency of situational and interpersonal factors in influencing behaviour.

- *Biological psychology*. Researchers in this specialisation study the biological mediation of behaviour, feelings and mental processes. They seek to discover how biological systems affect learning, memory, emotion, sexual arousal and other basic processes vital to human and animal functioning. In our discussion of the biological theoretical perspective, we noted that many biological psychologists refer to themselves as neuroscientists. Psychopharmacology is another branch of biological psychology. It investigates the effects of drugs on behaviour. Psycho-pharmacologists may work for pharmaceutical companies, testing the behavioural effects of various drugs, but they also conduct basic research to understand the brain mechanisms that cause the special effects of certain drugs.

- **Cognitive psychology.** The research of cognitive psychologists focuses on consciousness and on mental processes, such as remembering and forgetting, thinking and communicating, judgement and decision making, reasoning and problem solving. Such cognitive psychologists who study the vicissitudes of the mind share the interests of scholars of philosophy, linguistics, anthropology and artificial intelligence many of whom want to understand how information is represented and processed. Taken together, these interrelated interests have formed the core of the rapidly expanding area of cognitive science.

- **Theoretical psychology.** In this last, and by far the smallest basic area, a *meta perspective* is adopted ('meta' meaning *'about'*): theoretical psychology is about the construction of psychology itself and is assumed to have four general goals (Koch, 1951; Stam, 1991). First, it focuses upon the study of the history of psychology and its theories. Further, it is concerned with the philosophical foundations of psychological theories. Its third aim is to make a contribution to the development of new theories in specific areas of psychology, by providing conceptual analyses and critiques (Hyland, 1981). Its fourth aim is an ambitious one. As you will notice in reading this book, much of psychology looks like a patchwork: its variety is hard to describe and summarise. Through taking a meta perspective, theoretical psychology ultimately seeks a certain unification of this diversity. It is worth noting, however, that unlike the other five areas, theoretical psychology is not content based. Rather, its foundations and substance are conceptual. In this way it is dissimilar to the remaining basic areas but in no sense is it diminished because of this.

◤ The Psychological Fields of Practice

Psychologists have been quite successful in convincing the general public that they have something to contribute to the solution of practical problems. The study of psychology has caused a wide variety of practical, or applied, psychologies. Some are closely connected to a basic area of which an example is the development of tests, mainly carried out by personality psychologists.

At present, most fields of practice follow rather separate paths. They have their own educational programmes and their own professional standards that require post-graduate psychologists to take extra training. Despite the breadth of practical psychology,

most applied psychologists work in one of three main fields of practice: private life, school or work. Next to these, psychologists work in applied domains of a lesser magnitude. For example, environmental psychologists contribute to the design of housing projects, offices and shopping centres that meet the needs of the community. Forensic psychologists apply psychological knowledge to human problems in the field of law enforcement. They may work with the courts to determine the mental competency of defendants, or help lawyers with problems such as the (un)reliability of eyewitness testimony. Sports psychologists analyse the performance of athletes and use motivational principles and behavioural techniques to teach them how to achieve peak-performance levels.

Private life

The majority of psychologists working in this domain concentrate on the diagnosis and treatment of emotional and behavioural problems with which individuals have to cope. *Clinical psychologists* tackle not only mental distress in all its forms but also juvenile offending, drug addiction, criminal behaviour, learning disabilities and marital and family conflict. The role of clinical psychologists is easily confused with those of allied professions. Thus, it is necessary to make some basic distinctions. *Psychiatrists* are medical specialists. They primarily treat people with mental health problems and work in private practices, clinics or hospitals. They also engage in research to better understand the nature and treatment of mental ill-health. Of the many professionals concerned with helping those suffering from mental problems, only psychiatrists can prescribe medication or treatments involving physical-biological methods, such as the use of electric shock therapy for extreme and intractible forms of depression. Clinical psychologists also treat people who show behavioural disorders, and do so in private practices or in clinics and hospitals. They have a broader background in psychology than do psychiatrists. Clinical psychologists conduct all psychological testing and psychometric evaluation for mental hospitals, clinics, schools, courts and other services. *Psychoanalysts* are therapists, either psychiatrists or clinical psychologists, with additional specialised training in the principles of Freudian psychoanalysis.

Counselling psychologists are similar to clinical psychologists, but they often work on problems of a less severe nature and the treatment they provide is usually shorter in duration. They tend to work in community rather than hospital settings. *Health psychologists* are also concerned with the well-being of individuals. Their work, however, focuses less on the treatment of illness and more on prevention of ill-health and on the promotion of good health. Health psychologists collaborate with medical researchers to understand how different lifestyles affect physical health and how to manage or prevent stress.

School

Educational psychologists study to improve all aspects of the learning process. These psychologists help design school curricula and teacher-training programmes. They have responsibility for carrying out psychometric assessments of children with specific learning difficulties and for making recommendations regarding remedial education for these young people. They also advise teachers on how best to help pupils with particular learning needs and how to manage behaviour in the classroom. Most educational psychologists are also trained in developmental psychology. It helps them to cope with general developmental issues related to school performance. Educational psychologists who work with disabled children are often hybrids of educational and clinical psychology, as far as their own education is concerned.

Work

Psychologists in this field specialise in the relationship between people and their jobs. *Occupational psychologists* work to solve problems related to employee selection, morale, productivity, job enrichment, management effectiveness and job stresses. A subcategory of occupational psychology – human factors psychology (or ergonomics) – studies the interaction between worker, machines and working environment. Human factors psychologists study how to make equipment, such as computers, 'user friendly', as well as how to design airplane cockpits, space shuttles and automobile display panels for their optimal effectiveness by a human operator.

Some occupational psychologists refer to themselves as *organisational psychologists*, because their work in post-industrial societies is mainly concerned with organisational issues related to work. For example, they study communication patterns in commercial companies, or work flow between different sections of an organisation.

Thus far, we have discussed psychology's theoretical pluriformity – in its numerous forms and guises – and presented the various areas in which psychologists work. The next section is concerned with the ways in which psychologists accumulate knowledge about the behavioural and mental functioning of individuals. It will provide you with an understanding of *how* psychologists come to know *what* they do about human and animal behaviour.

INTERIM SUMMARY

The pluriformity of psychology is conspicuous at a theoretical level, and also with respect to what psychologists do. The distinction between basic areas and fields of practice brings some order into the manifold nature of the discipline. The basic areas of developmental psychology, personality psychology, social psychology, biological psychology, cognitive psychology and theoretical psychology principally pursue the accumulation of knowledge. The fields of practice also strive after this, but are largely concerned with advising and helping people in their 'private' life, at school, or at work.

WHAT IS PSYCHOLOGICAL RESEARCH?

Before we examine in detail what researchers have found in each of the major areas of psychology, we need to examine the ways by which psychologists know what they do about behaviour and mental processes. In the first section, 'What is scientific research?' we will briefly discuss the principles of scientific method. The second section, 'Doing scientific research', provides a bird's-eye view of the methods used in psychological research. Both sections will also help you to think more critically about empirical research and what it does and does not show us. Like it or not, you are a daily consumer of mass media reports on research findings, some valuable, some worthless, some confusing and some misleading.

The goal of the psychologist conducting research is to accumulate knowledge in order to arrive at an *understanding* of mental and behavioural processes. In this respect, research psychologists do not differ that much from ordinary human beings. When a middle-aged man, for example, starts crying in a crowded pub, the onlookers will ask themselves why and make inferences about the reason why he is crying. In seeking an explanation, people will employ the implicit and explicit psychological knowledge they have about behaviour in pubs, about reasons for crying and about crying men. They use their knowledge out of curiosity, but this knowledge also contributes to smooth social interaction. In this example, ordinary psychological knowledge tells us that it is very exceptional to cry in public, especially for men. So, onlookers may infer that the grieving man is seriously distressed and is thus in need of support. The example presents us with the question about the difference between ordinary psychological knowledge as used by lay persons and the knowledge that is provided by psychological research as conducted by professional psychologists.

History has shown that ordinary psychological knowledge should be met with a sound amount of distrust. For example, not too long ago, it was generally assumed among Westerners that the people of colonised Africa and Asia were mentally inferior to their Caucasian rulers. To give another example, at the beginning of this century many were convinced of the idea that academic work would seriously hurt the mind and body of young women. History shows many more examples of exclusion and oppression based on 'ordinary' psychological knowledge (Jahoda, 1992). Research by psychologists and by workers in the neighbouring disciplines has contributed to the debunking of stereotypes about Africans, Asians and women. In contrast with everyday psychological knowledge which is accumulated without much critical scrutiny, psychological research is essentially critical. It should shatter everyday illusions, half-truths and lies and replace them with sound knowledge about what is the case, given the current state of psychological knowledge.

There is, however, no absolute guarantee that psychological research always provides us with unbiased knowledge. Psychologists are also prone to distortions in their judgement as after all, they are human beings too. But, psychological researchers utilise a powerful instrument that helps to minimise biases in their knowledge. This instrument is **scientific method**. It is made up of a set of principles that governs the ways in which knowledge is gathered. After first presenting the general principles of scientific method, we will consider why some philosophers and contemporary psychologists are critical of the method and its foundations.

◤ Quantitative Methods

The roots of scientific method as it is currently employed are to be found in European philosophy of the 1920s. In those days, a new philosophy of science was developed by a group of philosophers and scientists who called themselves 'The Vienna Circle'. Their philosophy, which came to be known as **logical positivism**, holds that science should concern itself only with 'positive' knowledge, based on empirical evidence: reports of observations that are gathered through and by the senses of the observer. The logical positivists felt that criteria were needed to distinguish once and for all 'sensible knowledge' from common sense and metaphysical nonsense. The principle of **verifiability** is an example of a criterion to guide scientific research: statements are meaningful only if their truth may be verified in empirical research. This enables the scientist to label theological propositions as meaningless scientifically (whatever their personal value to believers) because their truth cannot be verified. Logical positivism linked verifiability and other criteria to prescriptive rules that were meant to govern scientific research.

Logical positivism exerted a powerful influence on academic psychology. It resulted in the so-called **empirical-analytical methodology** of conducting research (De Groot, 1969). This scientific method argues that if psychologists want to obtain true knowledge about the human condition they have to rely on *objective*, empirical evidence. Evidence is considered to be 'objective' only if it can be observed simultaneously by more than one person. Objectivity also requires *impartiality* of the researchers. Personal commitments, interests, values and preferences must be put aside. The empirical-analytical methodology is further characterised by quantification. The empirical evidence is translated into numbers because this allows researchers to determine the relationships between the data with mathematical precision. The help of statistics is summoned to test new evidence and to compare such evidence against what is already known. Statistical analysis is used to estimate whether what is found is really the result of varying conditions under study, or the operation of chance occurrences.

Objective, impartial empirical research is meant to result in general laws of human functioning. Their purpose is to provide a systematic explanation of the behavioural and mental activity of individuals. The ultimate aim for many researchers employing empirical-analytical methodology is to *predict* (and '*control*') behaviour. It is argued that psychological laws allow psychologists to predict behaviour across time and place. This is exactly the target at which behaviourism aims. Behavioural analysts took great pains to discover the law-like principles that govern human behaviour. They assert that one cannot be sure an explanation is correct unless it is used to predict what will happen.

The empirical-analytical method has dominated psychological research since the development of logical positivism in philosophy. The methodology and its philosophical roots, however, were subjected to criticism from the beginning. In philosophy, **Karl Popper** argued in the 1930s that impartiality is difficult to attain because researchers cannot do away with theoretical preconceptions; their observations are always theory-laden and therefore, importantly, science should aim at falsification of what is generally accepted, instead of verifying existing truth-claims (Popper, 1934). Falsification amounts to a deliberate attempt by researchers to try to refute what they think they have discovered empirically. So, if their observations lead them, for example, to conclude that swans are white, they should look for a non-white swan.

In general, scientific method demands a critical

and sceptical attitude toward any conclusion until it has been duplicated repeatedly by independent investigators. This need for *replication* requires a critical open-mindedness from the researcher. Good researchers are critical of the work done by their colleagues as well as of their own contribution. A good researcher is eager to be contradicted. The resulting debate contributes to a deepening of insight into the topic under study.

◆ Qualitative Methods

In psychology, humanist psychologists took the lead in criticising logical positivism (Gabriel, 1990). Feminists and social constructionists joined the critical choir more recently. They all employ a hermeneutic methodology in opposition to the empirical-analytical one. **Hermeneutics** is philosophical reflection on the practice of interpretation. In psychology, hermeneutics has resulted in a methodology that stresses empirical phenomena are always dependent parts of larger contexts in which they are given meaning and *interpreted* (Terwee, 1990). It is argued that conclusions from psychological research are context-bound and historically, culturally and linguistically contingent. The so-called psychological 'laws' that are meant to transcend specific contexts are always embedded in the local situations where they were discovered. It is therefore difficult, if not impossible, to generalise these specific regularities found in particular research contexts to humankind in general.

In the 1960s, hermeneutic principles were translated into a methodology that focused on understanding rather than prediction. In opposition to the quantification of logical positivism it was called **qualitative methodology**. In empirical research this is concerned with natural language, which is studied as it is spoken or written down in ordinary life. For example, people are interviewed, or their personal letters or diaries are studied. These data are analysed in an interpretive fashion, that is, without translating the words or sentences into numbers. It allows the researcher to keep his or her focus on the context of what was said or written. The interpretive approach of qualitative methodology is very time-consuming, therefore the research is generally limited to the study of a small number of people. Sometimes, *case studies* are employed in which the life of one person is studied intensively.

Qualitative researchers are critical of the impartiality required by logical positivism because it results in an unequal subject-to-object relationship between the researcher and the persons studied. The participants are said to be reduced to 'objects' whose functioning is expressed as a set of numbers. Qualitative methodology, by contrast, aims at the establishment of a subject-to-subject relationship between researcher and participants. This equal relationship honours the indispensable contribution participants pay to the scientific enterprise and recognises that such an enterprise involves the coming together and negotiating of two equally important sets of subjective experience.

In the 1970s qualitative methodology was appropriated by feminism in an attempt to develop a feminist methodology. Some feminists, especially those outside psychology, strongly objected to quantifying results because they felt such practices reduced people to dehumanising numbers. Most feminist psychologists, however, employ a variety of qualitative and quantitative methods, although there is a widespread conviction that many of the issues with which feminist psychology is concerned are better served by the subject-to-subject approach of qualitative research than by empirical-analytical objectivism (Peplau & Conrad, 1989).

◆ The Inter-subjective Standards of Scientific Method

The debate about the methodological principles of logical positivism and the development of a qualitative methodology has had consequences for the methodological stances psychological researchers take. Some psychologists refute altogether the search for knowledge that transcends local contexts. They strongly oppose impartiality, objectivism and quantification. Instead, they focus in their case studies on understanding the functioning of one individual in his or her specific context. Most contemporary psychological researchers, however, feel guided by the general principles of scientific method, although perhaps in a watered-down version. Empirical-analytical methodology is generally followed in its emphasis on *empirical* evidence obtained through controlled observation and careful measurement. When data clash with the opinion of experts, data win. Empirical researchers nowadays accept the **inter-subjective** nature of the psychological enterprise, which means they conduct their research in a way that is agreed as acceptable by their colleagues in the scientific community. They come to a consensus view about particular psychological knowledge through peer review and commentary upon their contributions. The abstract standard of objectivity is thus traded for standards which are established in the community of researchers. These standards, however, are continually being explored, renegotiated and redefined so as to encompass the pluriform nature of psychology's subject matter. Being secretive about results is not encouraged because all data and methods must eventually be open for public **verifiability**; that is, other researchers must have the opportunity to inspect, criticise, replicate or refute the data produced and the methods used.

Psychological research is generally dedicated to the discovery of *regular patterns* in human functioning, but most psychologists are reluctant to assume that these regularities have a law-like nature. If a lawful pattern is presented by a researcher, though, it is expressed in probabilistic terms. Such a 'law' indicates the probability (or 'likelihood') of the occurrence of a certain behaviour or mental activity under specific circumstances.

Most contemporary investigators seek to be impartial. They try to exclude personal preferences and commitments from their research, although they are generally aware of the fact that it is difficult to ban totally the influence of personal experience. Research in the psychology of perception has shown convincingly that all human observations are biased by personal factors (see Chapter 6). The procedures of scientific method help to indicate the sources of **bias** in order to minimise them.

◪ Becoming a Wiser Research Consumer

We have emphasised an appreciation of scientific method, with its concomitant critical attitudes and values. Even if you do not intend to engage in empirical research professionally, understanding the principles of scientific method is useful. It may help to improve your critical thinking skills by teaching you how to ask necessary questions and evaluate the answers about psychological phenomena.

Because psychology is so much a part of our everyday lives and is often misrepresented in the media, psychologists are extremely concerned about communicating accurate information to the public about what is thought to be known and about how one can go about evaluating its worth. Most psychology in the public domain does not come from the books, articles and reports of accredited psychologists. Rather, this information comes from newspaper and magazine articles, television and radio shows and books on self-help. Furthermore, a lot of 'pop' psychology is employed by 'pseudosciences', like astrology and some contributions to the 'New Age' movement. The pseudoscience industry sells its diverse products to the legions of 'true believers' who come prepared to accept the unexplained, the

unevaluated and the undemonstrated. It is not surprising that many cult leaders find willing recruits to their never-ending array of quasi-religious movements. Common to many such cults are attacks on the rational and empirical foundation of our knowledge about the world. Since such 'authorities' can mislead us, it becomes vital to cultivate the open-minded scepticism that is central to scientific method.

Contemporary society, which is often over-loaded with information, is filled with claims about 'truth' and with biased conclusions that serve special interests. When you read, for example, that a toothpaste is '37 per cent more effective', do you run out and buy some, or do you ask, 'Compared with what?' Compared with not brushing at all or with brushing with sugar, maybe? When you learn from an advertisement that four out of five doctors recommend Brand X aspirin, do you want to know if the sample size for this research was only five doctors? While these instances may seem extreme, we are asked to believe many such claims, not only by advertisers but by journalists as well.

Recently, a famous North American report about sexual behaviour was found to be based on faulty sampling procedures for gathering data. According to the conclusions of the Hite Report (contained in the popular book, *Woman and Love*, by Shere Hite, 1987), 98 per cent of married North American women reported they were dissatisfied with some aspect of their marriages and three-quarters of these married women had engaged in extramarital affairs as a result. These and other sensational findings were based on the answers from a reasonably large group of 4,500 American women, aged 14 to 85. However, when the same questions were posed to another group of women by ABC News and *The Washington Post*, the results were quite different. Only seven per cent reported having affairs and the majority, 93 per cent, were emotionally satisfied with their relationships (*The Washington Post*, 27 October 1987).

Which report about the mental, emotional and social state of North American women in modern times provides us with a more accurate picture? The answer lies in how the data were gathered. The Hite Report mailed the questionnaire to women in church and political groups. But the 4,500 women who returned the form represented only a 4.5 per cent return of the 100,000 questionnaires sent out. Their answers can hardly be taken as representative of American women's attitudes and marital relationships. Unfortunately married women or those with more active fantasy lives may have been more likely to take the time to answer. The study conducted to check the claims of the Hite Report used a procedure with only 1,505 participants. To assure that all groups were proportionally represented, subjects were selected according to US Census figures on age, education, race and sex. The Hite Report is a case of science-coated journalism. Precise percentages are given to convey the aura of science, but the methods employed to collect them are so flawed that the data on which they are based are worthless. Thereby, the figures likewise are so.

Studying psychology will help you make wiser decisions based on evidence gathered either by you or by others. Some of these decisions are the everyday ones about which products to buy or services to use. Others are more substantial. They may affect your entire life. It is therefore necessary to retain a critical open-mindedness when examining truth-claims from advertisers and journalists, as well as those made by psychologists and other scientists.

INTERIM SUMMARY

Empirical research in psychology is a highly systematised enterprise guided by a set of principles known as scientific method. It stresses inter-subjective standards and verifiability of the procedures and results of empirical study. Most psychological researchers employ quantitative methods. Their procedures originate in the philosophy of logical positivism. This emphasises objectivity, impartiality of the researcher and quantification of what is observed. A growing number of psychologists, however, carry out research by employing qualitative methods. This approach is inspired by the philosophy of hermeneutics. The focus of qualitative methodology is upon exploring subjective interpretations. It is wary of objectification and quantification because it wishes to make conspicuous the indispensable contribution participants make to the products of the empirical process.

◤ THE WHY, WHAT, WHO, WHERE AND HOW OF DOING RESEARCH

Doing psychological research is a goal-directed and methodical enterprise. Researchers first ask well-defined questions about a theoretical issue or a practical problem. Then they try to find answers to these questions according to rules that are prescribed by the scientific community. In the preceding section we have seen that most psychological researchers conform to a methodology that is empirical and stresses inter-subjective standards and verifiability. These general principles can be translated into a standard procedure for conducting psychological research which is summarised here in five questions. Each question describes a step in the research process. The five questions are: *Why* do we want to do this particular research? *What* is our research question? *Who* are the subjects we want to study? *Where* do we do the study? *How* are we going to collect and analyse the information needed to answer our research question?

◤ Why: Motivation and Relevance of the Research

Psychological research is always done for a certain purpose. Before embarking on the empirical investigation itself, researchers thoroughly study the topic. They may come across a contradiction, a problem, or a bottleneck that prompts the study to be designed in a particular way. The research project is carried out to answer the question that has been formulated. It may also attempt to solve the problem or bottleneck.

Empirical investigations can pursue either theoretical goals or practical ones. In some studies, one tries to serve both aims. A psychologist who designs an investigation to test a theory about gender differences in emotional expression conducts theoretical or 'basic' research. The researcher who investigates a malfunctioning company does practical or 'applied' research. Although there are many differences between applied and basic (also referred to as 'pure') research, both kinds of research employ a design that is based on what is known already about the issues studied. The researchers from our example would both begin their report with an account of the thoughts and preliminary investigations that motivated them to design their empirical study the way they did. In other words, they would first answer the question of *why* they wanted to do this particular research.

◤ What: the Research Question

The reader of this text who constantly asks themself questions about the information provided is being a better student than one who only thinks that everything he or she reads is quite interesting and understandable. Asking questions is the best way to acquire new knowledge. However, learning is not only a matter of just asking questions, but of asking the 'right' questions. The six-year-old child who asks his parent why his toy car, when given a firm push, always comes to a stop instead of rolling on forever, is asking the right question. The same holds true for researchers. After answering the question *why* they are doing this particular research, investigators have to formulate the question their research is supposed to answer. *What* is it that they want to look for? This **research question** is their guideline and the key for succesful research. If they have no question, they do not know what to look for. If they ask a poorly formulated question, their investigation is likely to be worthless.

A good research question contains many presuppositions. The investigator who starts research in a failing commercial company with the question 'What is going wrong?' does not yet know what to look for or where. The only presupposition is that something is wrong and that is not much of a guideline. The question 'Is something wrong with the lines of communication between the diverse departments?' is much more specific. Probably the investigator has done some preliminary investigation that has suggested that the departments do function well as separate units, but not in conjunction with each other. The question 'Does the fact that the heads of the departments all view themselves as the potential successor of the retiring head of the company, lead to a deliberate withholding of vital information?' contains a lot more presuppositions. The investigator not only has the idea that something is amiss with the communication between departments but also what is causing this. This last question, when phrased as a statement, is called a hypothesis.

A **hypothesis** is a provisional statement of a possible relationship between two or more events. Often hypotheses are hunches about what ideas or events go together, based not only on theories, but also on a psychologist's observations, introspection, creative intuition, or analysis of a pattern of available evidence. The psychologist who is investigating the malfunctioning company comes to a hypothesis by looking around, talking with people, using his or her imagination in combination with a knowledge of occupational psychology. If the hunch is right and the following research is well designed and executed, he or she has achieved the research objective. If the hunch proves to be wrong, then a perfectly designed and executed investigation will not show otherwise. Thus, at the beginning of any investigation, creative thinking and ingenuity on the part of the researcher are necessary.

After formulating a hypothesis researchers have the task of translating concepts into ones that have a commonly accepted meaning for everyone using them. The company-researcher has, for instance, to specify what is meant by 'vital information'. Otherwise the hypothesis is not testable. The strategy for standardising the meaning of concepts is called **operationalisation**. When Peter tells us he likes his tea very sweet, we try to operationalise 'very sweet' by asking him to specify what 'very sweet' means in terms of number of lumps of sugar. If Mary says that she is very intelligent, a psychologist would probably ask her how high is her IQ-score on an intelligence test. Thus, intelligence is operationally defined in terms of the questions used to make up an intelligence test. An operational definition avoids the ambiguity of everyday descriptive terms, for example, 'depressed', 'stressed' or 'rewarding'. Such a definition allows both research participants and researchers to understand clearly how a given concept is being used. Take the case of a group of researchers who tried to discover whether their subjects had sex frequently by stating the question: 'Are you sexually active?' When one of the men who answered 'no' on this question was interviewed later, he told them he had sexual intercourse a few times a week, but he was not 'active' in bed at all. 'I just lie there', he said. This misunderstanding was due to the fact that 'sexually active' is a poor operationalisation of the frequency of having sexual intercourse.

When researchers know why they want to do their research and what their research questions, hypotheses and operationalisations are, they can look for the means by which they are going to find their 'answers'. They need willing participants and a place to carry out the investigation. This is the *who* and *where* of the research. They also need a method, such as observation, a questionnaire or an experiment. This is the *how* of the research. We will move on to consider the who and where.

◤ Who and Where: the Subjects and their Settings

To answer their research questions psychologists study empirical phenomena. Most of the time these are human persons, but there are also psychologists who study animals or human products, like paintings, diaries, or even the contents of waste bins. These empirical phenomena are sometimes referred to as research objects, but when human persons are studied we more appropriately refer to them as subjects or participants. Of course *who* is studied is very much determined by the research question.

When the research question, for instance, concerns the amount of time Scandinavian students spend reading a newspaper, we do not have to observe or interrogate all of them. In this case, all Scandinavian students form the **population** of the research, but the psychologist collects information only from a carefully selected group of the population. This group, called a **sample**, is believed to have attributes that are representative of the entire population. Well-known examples of the use of samples are the determination of television viewing figures and political opinion polls. The conclusions about national opinions are often based on a sample of about 1,500 subjects, though this may vary from country to country.

The researcher, but also the wiser research consumer, has to be aware of errors in sampling. We already mentioned that the conclusions of the Hite Report (Hite, 1987) were based on a sample that was not representative. Another example of unrepresentative sampling occurs when psychological research in the laboratory is done with psychology students, because they are easily available. Despite the fact that a group of psychology students is not a representative sample of all adults, the results are often presented as if they are so.

Another decision researchers have to take is *where* to study their subjects. Do they go to them or do they invite participants to come to a psychological laboratory? There are many cases in which the research question logically determines the research setting. If you want to study the effect of erotic pictures on pupil size, heartbeat, skin resistance and the blood pressure of women as compared with men, you need an equipped laboratory. If your research question concerns the behaviour of drivers on a motorway in foggy weather, you have to make observations in the *naturalistic setting*, in this case on a motorway. The question of setting is relatively easily settled when researchers intend to study what people say. A questionnaire or an interview can be given almost anywhere, so long as the subject is not severely distracted by the environment. However, when the research question concerns what people do and the researcher has a choice, the setting is often a big issue. Is it better to observe children's play in the laboratory or at the playground? Is it better to study group decision-making with an artificial arrangement in the laboratory or in a naturalistic setting, like a board-meeting in a company? Where they have such a choice psychologists often choose the laboratory. It is cheaper, quicker, easier and it gives the opportunity to *control* the relevant variables.

The question arises, however, as to whether results from a laboratory study can be generalised to 'real life'. This issue is known as the problem of the **ecological validity** of laboratory research. Some psychologists believe that behaviour is relatively independent of the situation in which that behaviour takes place. In such a case laboratory findings are transferable to the natural, ecological setting. Other psychologists maintain the opinion that people's actions are, most of the time, locally situated. When the situation and their companions change, their behaviour changes also. The effect of alcohol on behaviour, for instance, is different when people are drinking with strangers as compared with friends or family members. It also makes a difference whether they drink at home, in a pub or in a laboratory. In this case results of laboratory research do not say anything about real life; they do not have ecological validity. Concerns about ways to increase **validity** are pressing and perennial ones in psychology.

◤ How: Methods of Collecting and Analysing Data

The next step in the research process psychologists have to decide is *how* to get the relevant information from their research objects or subjects. For this purpose there are many *methods of data collection* available. Hereafter we will review some of the major methods used to collect data of psychological relevance. Once collected, data must be analysed. Researchers present their results in an orderly fashion. Methods of data analysis are needed to translate the unorganised, overwhelming and confounding array of observations into neatly organised tables, graphs, or other forms of summary. We will go on to conclude this part of the chapter by describing some *methods of data analysis*.

◤ METHODS OF COLLECTING DATA

Psychologists following the principles of empirical-analytical methodology, either in a strict or a watered-down sense, use some procedure for assigning numbers to, or *quantifying*, different levels, sizes, intensities or amounts of the empirical evidence they collect to answer a research question, or to verify or falsify a hypothesis. They can, for example, measure the speed at which a subject reacts to a red light, or scale a subject along a continuum that orders their emotional stability in some systematic way, or code the explanations subjects give for the behaviour of others into categories that can be quantified. These numerical values are called research **data**.

Researchers have to choose the method that provides the data crucial for answering their research question. For instance, if the researcher of a malfunctioning commercial company has decided to study the correspondence between departments, human products are being analysed, for which analysis an instrument of *content analysis* has to be developed. If it is the behaviour of the people involved at the place of work which is of interest, some method of *observation* of their behaviour is applied. If verbal information is required, a *questionnaire* or an *interview* is used. If the researcher wants to watch the heads of the departments communicate with each other in a more controlled setting in which, for example, the flow of information can be manipulated and varied, an *experiment* is set up.

Analysing People's Products

Whether investigators use paintings, utensils or garbage as research objects, they need an instrument to analyse them. That holds also for the products psychologists are especially interested in: verbal material such as documents, newspaper articles, diaries, letters, or speeches. **Content analysis** is a research technique for making replicable and valid inferences from natural language (Krippendorff, 1980). With content analysis researchers try to capture the meaning of the utterances in the text in a systematic way. The standard procedure is to divide the text, or the transcribed talk, into elements (words, sentences, expressions) that are relevant in the light of the research hypothesis. The prevalence of the elements is counted in order to test the hypothesis. One may, for instance, use content analysis to classify the way political spokespersons glorify their own party and degrade the others, or one may develop an instrument that identifies and categorises explanations people give for their own behaviour. One may look for the number of aggressive themes in children's stories. A conspicious example of content analysis in psychology is the analysis of the stories produced on the TAT (Thematic Apperception Test, see Chapter 10).

Discourse analysis is also concerned with natural language but does not focus on quantifying in order to test a hypothesis. Rather it is concerned with what language is being used for and what function it serves; it offers a detailed description of all the twists and turns in language, of all the rhetorical devices and vocabularies used. Discourse analysis is an example of a qualitative methodology in which quantification is considered unnecessary. The strict separation between data collection and data analysis, which is standard in the empirical-analytic methodology, is not followed. Discourse analysts do not want to reduce the richness of language; they want to stay as close to the studied texts as possible. Further, they do not avoid engagement with their subjects, because it is a prerequisite to adopt their perspective in order to understand and represent them (Potter & Wetherell, 1987; Burman & Parker, 1993).

Observing People's Behaviour

The most direct way to get information about people's behaviour is simply to watch them. In everyday life, walking on the street, sitting in a restaurant, or waiting in a queue, we do it all the time. We 'see' a couple quarrelling, a woman flirting, or a man boasting. When a psychologist observes people's behaviour in the same unsystematic manner, it is called *free observation*. Often a psychologist starts an inquiry that way, not yet knowing what to look for, just noticing what looks worthwhile or remarkable. Free observation is often used when the research is still in an exploratory phase; the researcher does not yet have a clear research question. These initial observations are meant to provide clues to be used in formulating a specific research question, or hypothesis, which will be tested later.

When the psychologist takes on the role of a member of the group that is being studied and participates, to some extent at least, in its functioning, this method of observation is called *participant observation*. In a now classic example, Whyte (1943) moved into one of the slums of Boston to study the structure, culture and functioning of 'the Norton Street gang' and 'the Italian Community Club'. More recently Campbell (1984) spent two years with a number of female gangs in New York. Participant observation has been most highly developed in anthropological research, where participating often is the only way to study a community with a culture that differs completely from those in the West.

By standing behind a one-way mirror, a researcher can watch a child at play and record his or her observations without influencing or interfering with the child's behaviour.

Both free observation and participant observation are examples of unstructured observation, where the investigators have no predetermined set of categories at their disposal. The data consist of their notes made during the observation or, more often, afterwards at home or in the office. Unstructured observation has the advantage of the open mind that registers everything worthwhile. However, the question is, what is worthwhile? No two researchers using unstructured observation will produce the same data. The investigator needs a more direct, controlled, structured or systematic method of observation. With *systematic observation* behaviour is observed according to rules that are developed in advance. The researchers have made categories with which to classify behaviour; they work according to a **research design**. For instance, when researchers want to study interaction within groups and they have developed a research question which stresses the difference between (a) remarks that give social support to the other members of the group and (b) remarks that concern the task at hand, they simply have to tally remarks in the category *social-emotional* and the category *task-oriented* (Bales, 1970). Part of their design also is the use of trained observers who have been instructed to classify the same behaviour in the same category.

 Asking People Questions

In daily life, sometimes we are interested in the kind of behaviours that are very difficult or impossible to observe, such as sexual activities or family life. Sometimes we are not interested at all in what people do, but rather in what they think and feel. Thus, if we want to know more about people than meets the eye, observing behaviour is not enough. We also ask people questions about their behaviour and their thoughts and feelings and listen to their answers. If we want a general impression, we formulate a general question and let them talk freely. If we want specific information, our question will be more precise and we will interrupt if the subject dodges the question. Psychologists who try to find answers to their research questions simply by posing questions act in a similar way. They rely on the information of spoken or written **self-reports**.

If the self-report consists of the reflection of a face-to-face dialogue between a researcher and a subject, the instrument is called an *interview*. In an interview the researcher has a conversation with the participant. It is interactive. An interviewer may vary the questioning to follow up on something the respondent said. Competent interviewers are also sensitive to the process of the social interaction as well as to the information revealed. They are trained to establish 'rapport', a positive social relationship with the respondent that encourages trust and the sharing of personal information. A *questionnaire* is a written set of questions, ranging in content from questions of fact ('Are you a registered student?') to questions about past or present behaviour ('How much do you drink?'). It may also include questions about attitudes and feelings ('How satisfied are you with your present job?'). The researcher need not be present when subjects write down their answers. When questionnaires are used to gather information efficiently from a large number of people, it is called a **survey**.

Like observations, both interviews and questionnaires may vary in the extent to which they are structured. When the interviewer does not work with a predetermined set of questions and the respondent is free to talk, the interview is like a conversation. This form of self-report is the least structured, comparable with free observation. More structure is present when the respondents give answers to questions that are constructed in advance by the researcher. If the respondents are allowed to answer these questions freely in their own words, these are called *open-ended questions*. Questionnaires that pose specific questions on which the subject can only answer by marking one of a few fixed alternatives, such as *'agree'*, *'undecided'* or *'do not agree'*, are the most structured. The amount of structure should be determined by the research question and the hypothesis of the researcher. If the research question is about political preferences, it suffices to let respondents put a mark against the party they intend to support. However, if the research concerns the reasons why people vote for a particular party, something more sophisticated is needed. Unfortunately, the research question is not the only thing that determines the choice of research instrument. Time and money are also important factors. A researcher who allows respondents to answer in their own words, because of interest in the precise reasons behind their political preferences, has to make tape-recordings of the interviews. After making written or typed transcripts of these, the texts must be analysed. Thus, an instrument with which to carry out the content analysis must be constructed. Categories must be made to classify the provided reasons. It is less time consuming to make up these categories in advance and to present them in the questionnaire as fixed alternatives. Of course, the danger of this more efficient approach is that the answers of the respondents are forced into the categories of the researcher. It may well be that they would have answered differently given the opportunity to do so. Consequently, the choice of the kind of self-report researchers consider suitable for their goals, and the amount of structure they want to impose, is often a matter of balancing competing considerations.

The most well-known type of self-report is the **test**. Most tests are highly structured. Respondents have to solve specific problems for which they get points, or they have to answer specific questions by marking one of a few fixed alternatives. The total score on the structured test gives information about the subjects' characteristics or capacities by way of one or a few numerical scores. Intelligence tests, for example, provide an IQ (Intelligence Quotient). Personality tests often place the respondent on a scale of a few major personality traits, such as extraversion and emotional stability. A test is a kind of questionnaire, sometimes an interview. One of the reasons a test has its own methodological status is that a test is **standardised**, which means that the distribution of the test scores across the population for which the test is designed, is known. Otherwise, your score would not tell you very much. What would an IQ of 115 express if you did not know that the mean of the population of an intelligence test is 100 and that about 68 per cent of adults score between 85 and 115?

There are also less structured tests, for instance, *projective tests*. In these tests subjects are confronted with an ambiguous stimulus, like an inkblot or a multi-interpretable picture and asked what the inkblot looks like (an object or an event) or what is happening in the picture. Their answers are considered to be 'projections' of their own inner states. Thus a frightened person will project fear into the inkblots, seeing, for instance, all kinds of horrifying monsters. Often the answers on a projective test will undergo a meticulous form of content analysis by the research or clinical psychologist.

From the standpoint of the researcher who embraces the empirical-analytical approach in a strict sense, asking people questions can generate invalid data. The interview situation allows personal biases and prejudices to affect how the interviewer asks questions and thereby how the respondent answers them. Respondents who are aware of the interviewer's purpose may fabricate information about themselves, perhaps in order to get a job or to get themselves declared unfit for military service. Even if respondents do their utmost to present themselves as they think they really are, the issue arises as to whether this manifested self-image provides a flattering portrait instead of the 'real' picture. These researchers prefer a method that gives more opportunity to control the immense amount of factors that simultaneously influence or determine individual behaviour: namely, the experimental method.

The Controlled Conditions of the Psychological Experiment

In psychological research we want to discover relations among variables. A **variable** is something that can occur with different values. For example, the amount of caffeine people consume daily is a variable, and so is their alertness. There is a *relationship* between these two variables, but what is the exact relationship? Asking people how much coffee they drink and how alert they are does not bring us very far toward specifying this relationship. Not only do we not know how much caffeine is consumed with 'five cups' or what is meant by 'very alert', but we especially have no information about other variables that may influence alertness. These might be what and how much people eat, whether they are physically active or not, how much sleep they get and whether they drink alcohol or use medicines. Such variables can be controlled by asking a group of people to participate in an **experiment** in which they all eat the same food, get the same physical exercise, have the same amount of sleep and so on. The only variable that should be varied in such an experiment is the amount of consumed caffeine. Of course, the experimenters also have to come up with a good operationalisation of alertness. They may, for instance, develop an instrument in which reaction time and speed of completing a task is measured. The design of the experiment should be such that the resulting differences in the alertness test, if there are any, are attributable to the amount of caffeine only. This is the case when the experimenter succeeds in controlling *all* relevant other variables that might have an influence on the outcome being measured.

The ability to exercise precise control over variables distinguishes the experimental method from other methods of empirical research. In a *controlled experiment* specific behaviour is measured under systematically varied conditions. An experimenter manipulates a stimulus or variable and measures its effects on one or more behavioural outcomes. The stimulus or stimulus condition that is systematically manipulated or varied by the experimenter – in our example the amount of caffeine – is known as the **independent variable**. That aspect of a subject's behaviour or experience that is observed or measured as a predicted change resulting from the manipulation of the independent variable – in our example alertness – is known as the **dependent variable**. Its variations depend upon variations in the independent variable, when the experiment 'works' as expected.

Apart from the independent variable, all other relevant variables, extraneous conditions and personal biases are controlled or eliminated so that all alternative explanations (other than the one proposed by the experimental hypothesis) can be ruled out.

This is a difficult task. In our caffeine example, for instance, the researchers have to face the fact that individual differences in alertness exist regardless of coffee-drinking. Thus, they have to make sure that their participants are *randomly assigned*, by chance procedures, to the different experimental conditions (in this case different amounts of caffeine). **Randomisation** is a critical feature of experimentation. This is so because it makes it more probable that there are no important differences between members of the experimental group (that receives the independent variable) and the control group (that does not) prior to the introduction of the independent variable. They also have to use *standardised procedures* to make sure that subjects receiving different amounts of caffeine are treated in exactly the same way.

Take, for example, a situation where two research assistants could help the experimenters by administering the alertness test. One of them is young, cheerful and attractive, while the other is middle-aged, solemn and homely. In this case the researchers should wonder whether involving both assistants is a wise decision. It would be better to control the variable (here, the research assistant) in order to make sure that differences in the dependent variable (alertness) are not attributable to it. Furthermore, all instructions, room temperature, tasks, the way the researcher is dressed, time allotted, how the responses are recorded and many more details of the experimental situation need to be similar for all subjects to ensure that their experience is the same. The only difference in their experiences should be that introduced by the independent variable (in our example, the amount of caffeine).

The possibility of controlling variables and making exact measurements with accurate instruments is greatest in a room where the conditions to do so are optimal. For this reason most experiments take place in a laboratory. However, the experimental method is not a matter of location, but of logic. It can also be used outside the laboratory. For example, it is possible to investigate the effect of a psychotherapeutic technique by dividing patients with comparable symptoms into two groups. One, the **experimental group**, receives treatment, the other, the **control group**, does not. Of course in this *field experiment* the investigator also has to make sure that the two groups are comparable on variables like age, physical health and medication.

When a difference between the experimental and control group has been found, the investigator has to be sure that it is not attributable to the effects of another variable. Perhaps the experimental group, by pure coincidence, included far more people who, for example, have an enduring relationship. The effect, then, could be attributed to social support instead of to the psychotherapeutic technique. In such a case, it

is best to replicate the study with two groups that are also *matched* for 'having a supportive partner'. If the effect still holds, the evidence for the effectiveness of the psychotherapeutic technique is stronger, but it always remains possible that *the* vital variable has been overlooked. It could be asserted, for instance, that it is not this particular method that is responsible for the 'cure', but the attention which the experimental group receive for their problems while the control group does not. Thus, a third experiment would have to be set up, in which next to the experimental group and the control group, a third group is created, that is treated with another therapeutic technique but where there is the same amount of attention shown to the participants as in the experimental treatment group. If the effect is still demonstrated, people now may be convinced that this particular treatment works, until a fourth variable . . . This may look endless and frustrating to you, but remember what is said about the scientific enterprise: a good researcher is always eager to be contradicted and an assertion about behaviour is only 'true' as long as it is not falsified by other research.

One of the limits and disadvantages of the experimental method is the **ecological validity** of laboratory research as mentioned earlier – the extent to which experimental contexts and findings have generality with regard to 'normal' life conditions – is not always evident. When behaviour is studied in an artificial environment, the situational factors may be controlled so comprehensively that the environment may distort the behaviour from the way it would occur in a naturalistic setting. Another 'problematic' factor is the unavoidable fact that experimental subjects are only human: they know they are in an experiment and are being tested, measured and observed. They may react to this awareness by trying to please the researcher, by attempting to 'work out' the research purpose, or by changing their behaviour from what it would be if they were unaware of being monitored. Critics within psychology claim that much of the richness and complexity of natural behaviour patterns are lost in controlled experiments, sacrificed to the simplicity of dealing with only one or a few variables and responses at a time. Still another point of argument concerns the ethics of experimental research. At the end of this chapter we will consider some of the ethical issues raised by carrying out research.

◤ Physiological Measures

Some researchers, especially biological psychologists, do not focus on psychological measurements, but rather on physiological ones. How, for instance, does

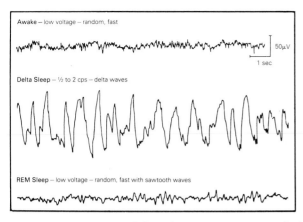

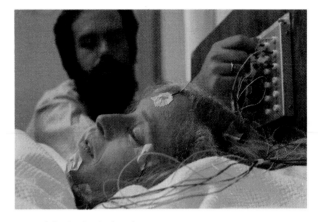

By connecting subjects to EEG machines, scientists can study the activity of the brain during sleep.

a researcher know what the brain is doing when someone is asleep or solving a problem? Instruments are available which demonstrate these internal reactions in a measurable form. For example, by amplifying the brain's electrical signals and recording them on a computerised graph, or by monitoring the blood flow in the brain, it is possible to get a picture of an individual's state of mental activity. The electroencephalogram (EEG) permits researchers to record patterns of brainwave activity. Researchers then study how these patterns vary as consciousness is altered when a subject goes from a state of wakefulness to sleeping and dreaming. Researchers interested in discovering how information is processed in specialised cells in the brain can do so by carefully implanting minute electrodes into single brain cells and recording their pattern of activity. One disadvantage of such technology is that it is physically invasive. Because the equipment is attached to the research subjects, they are prevented from moving about freely and acting as they might ordinarily. It thereby also invades the subjects awareness and therefore may modify usual reactions.

 METHODS OF ANALYSING DATA

Psychologists use **statistics** to make sense of the data they collect. They also use statistics to provide the quantitative foundation for the conclusions they draw. *Descriptive statistics* are used to describe and summarise numerically sets of data collected from research subjects, and to describe relationships among two or more variables. Descriptive statistics indicate what scores are most typical, or central, and also how variable, or dispersed, the rest of the scores are from the central one. *Inferential statistics* are used to determine what conclusions can be drawn about a given population from the sample data collected. A difference, or relationship, between two sets of data is said to be *statistically significant* if the probability that the difference obtained being due to chance is less than five per cent of the time. That effect, less than five times out of 100, is the agreed standard in psychology for determining whether a result is statistically significant. If so, a researcher can conclude that, because the effect was unlikely to be due to chance or random factors, the results obtained are more likely to have occurred as the consequence of the manipulation of the independent variable.

Knowledge of the basics of statistics is essential not only for planning and conducting empirical research, but also for understanding the presentation and interpretation of psychological research. For this reason, most European universities give their psychology students a course in statistics, parallel to the introductory units at the start of the statistics curriculum. That is why we restrict ourselves here to the elaboration of a few basic statistical principles and indices.

Measures of **central tendency** give a single, representative summary score that can be used as an index of the most typical score obtained by a group. The measures of central tendency are the mode, the median and the mean. The *mode* is the score that occurs most often. The *median* is the middlemost score: half the scores are above and half below this value. The *mean* is the most cited measure of central tendency: it is the average score (of a distribution of scores) which takes account of the size of each individual score. The mean is computed by adding the scores and dividing this value by the total number of scores.

Measures of *variability* indicate how close together or spread apart are the scores in a distribution. Two measures of variability are the *range,* the highest and lowest scores; and the **standard deviation**, the average distance each score is from the mean of all scores.

Psychologists often want to determine to what extent two variables, traits or attributes are related. Is intelligence associated with creativity? Are optimistic people healthier than those with a pessimistic outlook? What is the link between social isolation and mental health? To determine the relationship between two variables, psychologists use two sets of scores to compute a statistical measure known as the **correlation coefficient** (r). Its numerical value can vary between +1.0 and −1.0, where +1.0 is a perfect positive correlation, −1.0 is a perfect negative correlation and 0.0 means there is no correlation at all. A *positive* correlation coefficient means that as the magnitude of one set of scores increases, that of a second set also increases. For example, there exists a positive correlation between drinking alcohol and making errors on a perceptual motor-skills task, like driving a car. The more one drinks, the more mistakes are made. The reverse is true for *negative* correlations; the second set of scores descends when the first ascends. For example, when units of alcohol consumed increase, reaction time decreases. Correlation coefficients that are closer to zero show that there is a weak relationship or no relationship between scores on two measures. As the correlation coefficient gets larger, closer to the ±1.0 maximum, predictions about one set of scores based upon information about the other set of scores (for the other characteristic) become increasingly more accurate. For example, if there exists a high correlation between school achievement and scores on an intelligence test (IQ), knowing someone's IQ makes it possible to forecast (more or less) someone's school performance.

A sizeable correlation only indicates that two sets of data co-vary in a systematic way; the correlation does not necessarily mean that one of them *causes* the other. Take, for example, a group of researchers exploring the relationship between worker productivity and stress. They might measure how much stress people are experiencing in their lives and how well they are performing at work. Felt stress might be operationally defined as scores on a stress questionnaire. Job productivity might be defined as the number of units of a given product that a worker produces each day. The researchers could then measure these two variables for many different workers and compute the correlation coefficient between them. Suppose they detect a strongly negative score: as felt stress goes up, productivity goes down, and vice versa. Suppose furthermore that, based on this sizeable negative correlation, the researchers advise the management board that the way to increase productivity would be to lower stress. Such a conclusion does not necessarily follow. Of course, a negative stress and work productivity correlation might mean that stress at home causes people to do poorly at work, but it might also mean that poor job productivity makes people experience more stress. It might even mean that people of a certain personality type are more likely to experience stress and also to perform poorly on the job.

If we formulate the matter in more technical terms, a correlation between two variables, X and Y, could reflect any one of several cause and effect possibilities, or even none at all. It could mean that X causes Y, or that Y causes X. It could also mean that both X and Y are the effect of an underlying cause, Z. The correlation might even exist only by coincidence. An example of the last possibility is that the migration of birds might occur every year around the time of your birthday. But it is a coincidence that your birthday falls at a time when birds migrate. As obvious as this seems, people often fail to recognise the possibility that coincidence rather than causation or correlation is operating.

Because correlations are relationships between sets of measurements usually taken of many people, predictions based on them are group predictions. Correlations are rarely accurate predictions for individuals. For example, the high positive correlation repeatedly found between heavy smoking and incidence of lung cancer indicates that there will be more cancer among heavy smokers than among non-smokers. It does *not* tell us whether any particular heavy smoker will get cancer or whether a given non-smoker will remain free of lung cancer.

INTERIM SUMMARY

Psychological research is empirical and stresses inter-subjective standards and verifiability. These general principles of scientific method were translated into procedures for conducting psychological research. These were summarised in terms of five questions, each of which described a step in the research process. The five questions were: WHY do we want to do this particular research? WHAT is our research question? WHO are the subjects we want to study? WHERE do we study them? HOW are we going to collect and analyse the information needed to answer our research question?

✕ ETHICAL ISSUES IN HUMAN AND ANIMAL RESEARCH

Respect for the basic rights of humans and animals who participate in psychological research is a fundamental obligation of all researchers. To guarantee that these rights are honoured, special committees oversee research proposals, imposing strict guidelines issued by the national governing bodies. Psychology departments in universities, hospitals and research institutes each have ethics committees that approve and reject proposals for human and animal research. In a sense, these institutional review boards try to adjust the balance of power between experimenters and research participants. Professional organisations like the *British Psychological Society* (BPS), the *American Psychological Association* (APA), and the *Netherlands Institute of Psychologists* (NIP) have established detailed guidelines for ethical standards for researchers. In Europe a 'task force on ethics', consisting of delegates from all European professional organisations of psychologists, is engaged in integrating the different rules. What are some of those guidelines and ethical concerns?

 ## Informed Consent

Typically all research with human subjects begins by giving a full description of the procedures, potential risks and expected benefits that participants will experience. Before beginning the research, subjects are given this information and asked to consider and sign statements indicating that they give their **informed consent** to participate. The subjects are assured in advance that they may leave an experiment at any time they wish, without penalty and should be given the names and telephone numbers of officials to contact if they have any grievances. In addition, the privacy of subjects is protected; all records of their behaviour are kept strictly confidential or any public sharing of them must be approved by the subjects in advance. Finally, participants have the right to withdraw their data if they feel it has been misused or their rights abused in any way.

 ## Risk/Gain Assessment

Most psychological investigations carry little risk to the subjects, especially where participants are merely asked to perform routine tasks. However, some studies that examine more personal aspects of human nature – such as emotional reactions, self-images, conformity, stress, or aggression – can be upsetting or psychologically disturbing. Therefore, whenever a researcher conducts such a study it is important that he or she includes, as a basic feature of the research process, procedures designed to protect the subjects' physical and psychological well-being (Diener & Crandall, 1978). Risks must be minimised, subjects

must be informed of the risks and suitable precautions must be taken to deal with strong reactions by the subjects. Where any risk is involved, its potential costs are carefully weighed by each institution's ethics committee in terms of that institution's necessity for achieving anticipated benefits for the subject matter of psychology, for society and indeed for the participants of the study. Similar precautions are to be exercised in animal research, where the humane and considerate treatment of all animal subjects is clearly recognised as essential.

 ## Intentional Deception

For some kinds of research it is not possible to tell the subjects the whole story in advance without biasing the results. If you were studying the effects of deception on subjects in an experiment, for example, you could not tell them what you were studying because then they would not be able to react naturally to being deceived. However, many critics argue that deception is never justified in research because it violates the basic right of informed consent (Korn, 1987). Others assert that the immorality of any deception does harm to the subjects, the profession of psychology and society (Baumrind, 1985). On the other hand, one could argue that participating in a deception experiment may reveal previously unthought of aspects of one's personality.

Perhaps the most controversial study in psychology was one in which subjects were made to think they should follow the orders of an authority figure who instructed them to deliver painful shocks to another subject. In fact, they were not actually hurting the victim, although they did not know this. In this study of blind obedience to authority, the subjects were quite torn between honouring their research commitment by doing as they were told and quitting the experiment (Milgram, 1974). The researcher reported that over 80 per cent of the subjects reported afterwards when asked that they were 'very glad' or 'glad' to have been in the study; only one per cent said they were 'sorry' or 'very sorry', and the rest were neither glad nor sorry to have participated (Milgram, 1977).

Yet, if even one subject feels harmed by participating in a deception experiment, doesn't that make it unethical? Alternatives to deception research are put into practice wherever possible and safeguards are instituted to reduce the potential risks. In risky experiments, the ethics committee may impose constraints, insist on monitoring the procedure of the study with a view to halting the experiment if unwarranted distress occurs, or they simply deny approval (Steininger *et al*, 1984).

◤ Debriefing

Participation in psychological research should always be a mutual exchange of information between researcher and subject. The researcher may learn something new about a behavioural phenomenon from the participant's reactions, while the subject should be informed of the purpose, hypothesis, anticipated results and expected benefits of the study. At the end of an experiment, each subject must be given a careful debriefing in which the researcher provides as much information about the study as possible and makes sure that no one leaves feeling confused, upset or embarrassed. If it was necessary to mislead the subjects during any stage of the research, the experimenter carefully explains the reasons for this deception.

◤ Issues in Animal Research

Should animals be used in psychological and medical research? Before we consider the pro and con sides of this issue, let us first outline some reasons why psychologists sometimes focus upon animal subjects in their research. First, it is easier to distinguish between heredity and environmental factors that influence performance and brain functioning in animals bred and reared under controlled conditions than it ever could be in humans. Second, since many species breed more rapidly than humans, studies of developmental processes that occur over many generations are possible. Third, in some species, basic processes such as sensation, learning, memory and even social status are comparable to those in humans. Since in animals they occur in less complex forms that can be more readily investigated, animal models of these processes shed light on human functioning, despite obvious dissimilarities in terms of linguistic abilities and consciousness. Fourth, other psychologists study animal behaviour not for what it may reveal about humans, but to better understand general laws of behaviour demonstrable across species or simply to learn about a given animal species. Much of the psychological knowledge that we will study in this book has come from research that investigated the behavioural and physiological functioning of animals.

In recent years, concern over the care and treatment of animals used in psychological and biomedical research has led to strict guidelines that researchers must follow in order to receive research funds and conduct their research. Most countries require that every effort is made to minimise pain and discomfort and to seek alternative procedures that are not stressful.

Seldom, however, are these precautions and procedures acknowledged by animal rights activists. The dominant goal of most of these groups is 'to stop the exploitation of animals for any purpose, and in particular, to abolish animal experimentation altogether' (McCabe, 1990). While some of the activists push for restrictive legislation to inhibit and prohibit much animal research, others take more direct action. The so-called Animal Liberation Fronts in the United States, Britain, the Netherlands and elsewhere have taken credit for 'liberating' research animals from laboratories and for breaking into laboratories and damaging the facilities. Such acts have interfered with and, in many cases, halted basic biomedical research. The debate over animal testing goes beyond issues of ethics in research. It centres on society's recognition of the contribution that carefully conducted research with animals, and with humans, makes daily to the health and well-being of humans and animals alike. The benefits of animal research include the discovery and testing of drugs that treat anxiety, mental illnesses and Parkinson's disease; new knowledge about drug addiction; rehabilitation of neuromuscular disorders; and currently work on the desperately sought cure for AIDS (Miller, 1985).

Animal activists claim that not a single medical advance has depended on animal experimentation. Oxford professor of physiology, Colin Blakemore

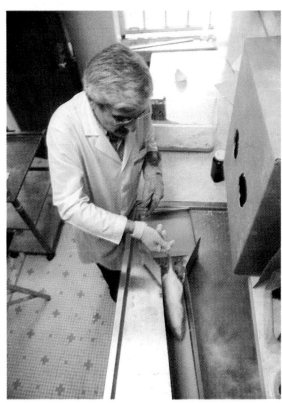

Rats are often used for experiments because the experimental variables are easy to control for them and we know their genetic history.

(1990), rebuts their assertion. He says, 'I cannot think of a single advance that has not depended on animals at some stage' (*Science*, 8/31/90, p.981). A different perspective on the debate comes from a catalogue of benefits that animal research has made to animals. On a worldwide basis, immunisations for various animal diseases, such as rabies, distemper and anthrax, are preventing suffering and untimely deaths in billions of domestic animals. Psychological researchers have shown how to alleviate the stresses of confinement experienced by zoo animals. Their studies of animal learning and social organisation have led to the improved design of shelters and animal facilities that promote good health (Nicoll *et al, 1988*).

A balanced consideration of the information and arguments both 'for' and 'against' should guide decisions on this issue.

◤ CONCLUSION

In this opening chapter we have presented the pluriformity of contemporary Western psychology. Psychologists may work from different theoretical perspectives, although the field is currently dominated by cognitivism. There are many ongoing discussions about fundamental issues in psychology. Such debates are at the core of what researchers try to accomplish: the accumulation of knowledge in a critical way. Open-minded scepticism is a primary prerequisite for this.

This book is devoted to psychological knowledge that has been derived from empirical research in all its forms and contexts. In the following chapters, the focus is on the most important recent developments in psychology. About a century ago psychology began in Europe, with its most fervent development in Germany. By the 1930s the power base of psychology shifted to the United States, where it has remained for more than half a century. This shift was partly caused by the fact that many European intellectuals had to flee from their countries during the rise of the Third Reich. Thus, numerous influential contributions to psychology have been made by European émigres who as exiles continued their work in the USA. The dominance of North American psychology, however, has never been all-encompassing. Innovations have continued to emerge from Europe (Sexton & Hogan, 1992). Recently, psychologists from Asia, for example, have raised fundamental questions about the nature of psychology as a typically Western enterprise. Nowadays, the international orientation of psychology is growing, although most of its key figures are still from the United States. As Rosenzweig documented a decade ago, this picture may change in the future. Indeed, the growth of psychology in many countries is more rapid than in the USA. As a consequence, North American psychology will become an increasingly smaller part of the international psychological community (Rosenzweig, 1982). Now that psychologists from all over the world contribute to the understanding of the mental and behavioural functioning of individuals in a variety of contexts, psychology's ties with Western individualism may loosen. Through its numerous forms and guises psychology is ready to be developed into a truly international enterprise.

This book reflects the changes in modern psychology. Much of the research presented here was carried out by North American psychologists, but a substantial amount of the studies cited stem from Europe and other countries outside the USA. Through this international orientation, we will try to provide you with the information and evaluative skills to participate in the debate about psychology's present and future. We also hope to show how psychology may enrich our understandings of the human condition and can be of relevance to people's lives.

According to Genesis in the Bible, humans 'have dominion over the fishes of the sea and over the birds of the air and over every living thing that moves upon the earth'. This attitude of separateness from, and superiority over, nature differs dramatically from the attitudes of people without a Judeo-Christian heritage. Contrast the following creation story, told by a Sanpoil chief from the Pacific Northwest, with Genesis. Consider the different human–animal relationship each implies.

Sweat Lodge was a chief long, long ago; but he wasn't called Sweat Lodge then. He was just called chief. He decided to create all the animals and all the birds. So he created them and named them all . . . Then he told each one of them: 'In times to come, when people have been created, they will send their children out, during the day or during the night, and you will talk with them and tell them what they will be able to do when they grow up' (James, 1953).

Native Americans have traditionally followed an elaborate code of respectful behaviour toward animals – each animal is believed to have its own spirit, power and sensitivity – and they have demonstrated a commitment to accommodate and adapt to the environment, taking from it only what they need for survival and looking upon natural resources as precious gifts. In the Native American tradition, anyone who violates this code risks bad luck, illness, or even death (Nelson, 1989).

Although North America was inhabited for about 25,000 years

before the Europeans arrived, there is little evidence that the indigenous people disturbed the land or eliminated any species of animal (*The Harper Atlas of World History*, 1986). Yet, in the comparatively short span of only 500 years, European settlers and their descendants have defoliated immense tracts of forest, degraded agricultural lands, polluted the air and ocean and driven untold numbers of animal and plant species to extinction (Brown, 1989). While we no longer shoot into herds of buffalo from moving trains for sport, Alaska's Fish and Game Department shoots wolves from aircraft, even as conservationists are trying to restore the species to the land (Williams, 1989).

A fundamental belief common to all industrialised nations is that the environment, including outer space, is controllable through technology and that it is human destiny to control it. This orientation toward domination over the environment, rather than accommodation to it, has led people to exploit its limited resources. In *The Control Revolution* (1986), social scientist James Beniger defines control as

'purposive influence toward a predetermined goal'. In extolling the virtues of interlinking systems of technical, economic, and information control that have reshaped society in the last century, Beniger points to the control that seems to matter most: control over people. He argues that the great transformation of traditional into modern society was based on the appearance of technical and social systems better able to control or influence human behaviour.

This control orientation has led people to exploit one another. Europeans took from Native Americans their land, their freedom and their way of life. In exchange, they gave them the gun, alcohol, reservations, smallpox and the assembly line. Although when two cultures meet it is not inevitable that one will completely dominate the other, it is inevitable that both will change. Poet Robert Bly reminds us of an ancient reality in which shamans 'entered into the realm of the spirits, . . . wrestled with them, outwitted them, and saved people who had become ill through the mischievous activity of those spirits' (1990). To ears attuned to bleepers and cellular telephones, such notions may sound strange. However, some psychologists have begun to listen to the voices of other cultures (Bornstein & Quinna, 1988). These voices sensitise us to the realisation that control as a goal of life may result in costs and limitations as well as gains. When interventions designed to modify behaviour for the noble ends of accumulating knowledge or therapy are perceived as manipulation by those who are to be changed, then the means must be questioned. Recognising this alternate perspective on the complexity of control broadens and enriches our quest to understand the nature of human nature – and helps to create a psychology of all people.

recapping main points

Psychology: Definition

At the beginning of our journey into psychology, we defined the discipline as the empirical study of the behavioural and mental functioning of individuals. We briefly sketched the close links of modern Western psychology with the historical process of individualisation.

Psychological Perspectives

Psychology itself is a pluriform enterprise. We discussed seven theoretical perspectives that are conspicuous in contemporary psychology. Behaviourism, psychoanalysis, cognitivism and biological psychology were presented as the four foundational approaches. Humanistic psychology, feminist psychology and social constructionism were discussed next. These perspectives originated as critical approaches, but in due course have made specific theoretical contributions to psychology. Each perspective in contemporary psychology has defined a different area of study, which sometimes results in contradictory claims. In other cases, the perspectives have proven to be complimentary. This theoretical diversity has its counterpart in the work psychologists do. It ranges from providing therapeutic support to carrying out research on the psychobiological mechanisms in human vision.

Psychological Research

Empirical research is a highly systematised enterprise which is guided by a set of principles called scientific method. It stresses inter-subjective standards and verifiability of the procedures and results of the study. Though most psychologists try to put the principles of scientific method into practice, there is ongoing debate about its assumptions and practical consequences.

The procedures for conducting psychological research can be summarised in terms of five questions: WHY do we want to do this particular research? WHAT is our research question? WHO are the subjects we want to study? WHERE do we study them? HOW are we going to collect and analyse the information needed to answer our research qustion?

Ethical Issues in Human and Animal Research

Research as well as practical interventions may result in ethical problems. Professional organisations of psychologists all over the world have developed ethical codes that stress the actions of psychologists must always be guided by the interests of their clients or participants in research.

key Terms

behaviourism
bias
biological psychology
central tendency
cognitivism
conditioning
connectionism
content analysis
control group
correlation coefficient
data
debriefing
dependent variable
discourse analysis
drive
ecological validity
empirical investigation
empirical-analytical methodology
experimental group
feminist psychology
gender
Gestalt psychology
hermeneutics
holistic
humanistic psychology
hypothesis
independent variable
individualism
informed consent
inter-subjectivity

logical positivism
mental processes
neuroscience
observational methods
operationalisation
pluriformity
population
psychoanalysis
psychological experiment
qualitative methods
quantitative methods
randomisation
reliability
research design
sample
scientific method
sex
self-reports
significance
social constructionism
standard deviation
standardisation
statistics
survey
test
unconscious
validity
variable
verifiability

major Contributors

Bartlett, Frederic (1886–1969)
Bem, Sandra
Bruner, Jerome
de Beauvoir, Simone (1908–86)
Descartes, René (1596–1650)
Freud, Sigmund (1856–1939)
Gergen, Kenneth
Hubel, David
Kelly, George A. (1905–66)
Lacan, Jacques (1901–81)
Maslow, Abraham (1908–70)

Neisser, Ulric
Pavlov, Ivan (1849–1936)
Popper, Karl (1902–94)
Rogers, Carl (1902–87)
Simon, Herbert
Skinner, Burrhus Frederic (1904–90)
Sperry, Roger (1913–94)
Watson, John B. (1878–1958)
Weisstein, Naomi
Wiesel, Torsten
Wundt, Wilhelm (1832–1920)

Chapter 2

Biopsychology and Neuroscience

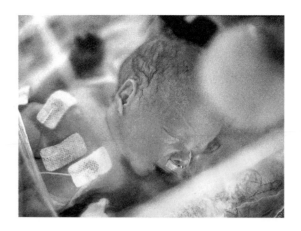

$\blacksquare$ ive-and-a-half weeks before her twins were due, Christine felt the first sharp pains of labour. Her husband drove her to the hospital where, for 16 hours, the two of them followed the breathing instructions given to them during their natural childbirth class. A foetal monitor then showed that the heartbeat of one of the babies was weakening. Doctors quickly performed a caesarean section. Within minutes, Nicola, at 1.8 kilos, and Alex, at 1.75 kilos, had entered the world.

Immediately after birth, Nicola and Alex joined half a dozen other babies in the Neonatal Intensive Care Unit. For two-and-a-half weeks, electronic devices monitored their vital signs. Experienced nurses tended to their physical needs and held them frequently. Christine spent a good part of each day with her babies, holding and rocking them and feeding them her breast milk from bottles, awaiting the day when she could actually breast-feed them. The twins looked fragile and unfinished. With no layers of baby fat, every little rib in their bodies showed.

Had Nicola and Alex been born 20 years earlier their first few weeks of life would have been quite different. Until the late 1970s, prematurely-born infants were touched as little as possible. Parents and medical personnel feared that any unnecessary contact with the outside world might harm the babies. Fortunately for Nicola and Alex, we now know better.

Research with infant rats and humans has led researchers to conclude that brain functioning can be altered by touch and that, for newborns, touch is essential for normal growth and development.

Biologist **Saul Schanberg** found that when rat pups were removed from their mothers, the levels of an enzyme important for growth in the pups decreased dramatically (Schanberg *et al*, 1990). The longer they were deprived of maternal contact, the less responsive the pups became. The effects of maternal deprivation could be reversed in only two ways: by returning them to the mother, who immediately started licking them, or by having a researcher vigorously stroke them with a small paintbrush. Schanberg (1990) concluded that, 'The need for a mother's touch is really brain-based. It isn't just nice to have it. It's a requirement for the normal development and growth of the baby'.

Psychologist **Tiffany Field**, who had collaborated with Schanberg (Field & Schanberg, 1990), conducted similar stimulation studies of prematurely-born human infants. Her research team randomly selected 20 premature babies to receive periodic massages throughout the day, while 20 others received normal hospital treatment in the intensive care unit – treatment which did not include massages. According to Field, 'The premature babies who were massaged for 45 minutes a day for ten days before they were discharged gained 47 per cent more weight than the babies who did not get massaged. They were more active. They were more alert'. Eight months later, the massaged babies had maintained their weight advantage and were also more advanced in motor, cognitive and emotional development (Field, 1990). This research is being extended and replicated in larger samples of premature babies in order to establish the power of human touch on biological and psychological health.

Many infants are born prematurely each year. Those who are touched and cuddled often leave the hospital several days sooner than is usual for babies who are not, substantially reducing care costs per child. Unfortunately, not all hospitals apply what researchers have learned about the positive effect of early touch on development. If they did, the lives of thousands of children would be improved and large amounts of health care money each year could be saved – both very practical benefits of this basic research.

When Nicola and Alex left the hospital, they were still rather small, but were developing so well that the doctors felt confident they would be alright. At home the babies shared a cot in the living room, where relatives and friends who remarked on their tiny size were encouraged to pick up the babies gently and cuddle them. Christine and her husband were acutely aware that providing such physical stimulation is apparently critical for optimal development of the brain and, in turn, the mental and physical processes the brain controls.

WHEN FULLY MATURED, the brain weighs only 1.36 kilos, less than Nicola or Alex did at birth. But, despite its small weight, and the fact that it is made up of the same basic chemical molecules found throughout the universe, the brain is the most complex structure in the known universe. This little biocomputer contains more cells than there are stars in our entire galaxy – over 100 billion nerve cells – designed to communicate and store information. What is even more difficult to comprehend is that within this biochemical structure is the basis for communicating all the information that it is ever possible for the brightest of us to know or the most sensitive of us to experience. Because of our brains each of us is a self-contained miracle, able to do many things more easily and more automatically than even the most powerful computers.

The human brain, which has developed over millions of evolutionary years, is the subject of study for a new breed of researchers in the rapidly emerging field of neuroscience, a multidisciplinary attempt to understand the functioning of the nervous system. Psychologists in neuroscience are also identified as researchers in biopsychology, a rapidly growing area that studies the relationships among biology, behaviour and environment. These psychologists believe that everything the brain does is ultimately caused by physical, chemical or biological events taking place in specific regions of the brain. The first task of biopsychologists is to reduce behavioural phenomena to the smallest units in the biochemical mechanisms that underlie the actions of all living creatures. Once they have an elemental understanding of the biological substrate, they move on to the more difficult task of synthesising the complex repertoire of human actions. The ultimate question for biopsychologists is how the human mind emerges from this mass of tangled organic tissue.

Many questions arise as we charge the brain with the task of understanding itself. How does the biological machinery of the brain and its connections to the rest of the nervous system – the spinal column and the nerves of the body – become the basis for intelligent life? How can a series of on-off electrical impulses within the brain's nerve cells, and the flow of chemical transmitter substances between these cells, be the basis for our every thought, dream, feeling, motive and action? How can an organ that does not generate enough energy to light an ordinary light bulb be the most powerful creative and destructive force on earth? Then there is the grand illusion fostered by the brain: each human mind comes to believe that it is more powerful than the combined, emerging properties of all the brain's structure and functions. The conscious aspect of mind – the sense of self that looks out at the world and in at its own thoughts and mortality – seems to exist independently of its biology, which it perceives as inferior. But when brain cells are destroyed by disease, drugs and accidents, we are suddenly reminded of the biological basis of the human mind. In such cases, we are forced to recognise the physical matter from which sensation and language, learning and memory, passion and pain, human reason and madness spring forth.

The goal of this chapter is to demonstrate the way psychology as a discipline investigates the relationship of biological systems to the outside world. First, we will explore how evolution and heredity determine our biology and behaviour. We will then examine how laboratory and clinical research provide a view into the workings of the brain, the nervous system and the endocrine system. We will consider some intriguing relationships among these biological functions and some aspects of the human experience of consciousness. Finally, we will study how touch and other stimulation can actually modify the brain, which will explain why we perceive the brain as responsive and dynamic. In this way, understanding biological considerations will enable you to appreciate more fully the complex interplay among brain, mind, behaviour and environment that creates the unique experience of being human.

■ EVOLUTION, HEREDITY AND BEHAVIOUR

Before we can even begin to appreciate the brain's involvement in our behaviour and thought processes, we need to ask two questions: how did this marvellous piece of biology come to be and why are the brains of all species, although similar, so different? The answers to these questions will provide us with a powerful perspective from which we can appreciate the significance in everyday life of the brain and nervous system. The first question will lead us to consider evolution, the theory that, over time, organisms originate and adapt to their unique environments through the interaction of biological and environmental variables (outlined in Chapter 1). The second question will lead us to consider heredity, the biological transmission of traits from parent to offspring.

■ Evolution

About 50 years before Wilhelm Wundt established psychology's first experimental laboratory, **Charles Darwin**, newly out of college with a degree in theology, set sail on a five-year cruise that would change his life and the history of science forever. In 1831 the H.M.S. Beagle, an ocean-research vessel, set sail from England to survey the coast of South America. During the trip, Darwin collected everything that crossed his path: marine animals, birds, insects, plants, fossils, seashells and rocks. His extensive notes became the foundation for his books on topics ranging from geology to emotion to zoology. The book for which he is most remembered is *On the Origin of Species*, published in 1859. In this work, Darwin set forth science's grandest theory: the evolution of life on planet earth.

While he was at sea, Darwin only briefly entertained some of the ideas that lead to evolution. What made him develop these ideas into a theory? For years after his return to England, he marvelled at the differences among his specimens and re-read and revised his notes countless times. Darwin argued theory and data for long hours with other naturalists. He even

began to dabble in selective breeding, a procedure for purposely mating plants or animals to produce offspring that possess specific and highly desirable traits.

It was Darwin's research into selective breeding that eventually gave rise to some of his most important ideas on evolution. He began to think that some analogous mechanism in nature might be responsible for the ways different species either adapted to their environment or became extinct. After all, if humans could select for specific traits in breeding animals and plants, why couldn't nature, in all its grandeur and power, do the same? Thinking along these lines eventually led Darwin to the conclusion that, in a species' struggle for existence, some characteristics are favoured and preserved by nature while others are not favoured and are destroyed. The result of this process, he wrote, 'would be the formation of a new species' (Darwin, 1859).

Natural selection

Darwin called his theory – that some members of a species tend to produce more offspring than others – the theory of **natural selection**. Organisms well adapted to their environment, whatever it happens to be, will produce more offspring than those less well adapted. Over time, those organisms possessing traits more favourable for survival will become more numerous than those not possessing those traits. In evolutionary terms, an individual's success is measured only by the number of offspring he or she produces. Let us look at a specific example.

One of the many places that Darwin visited on his voyage was the Galapagos Islands, a volcanic archipelago off the west coast of South America. These islands are a haven for diverse forms of wildlife, including 13 species of finches, now known as 'Darwin's Finches'. How did so many different

Charles Darwin (1809–82)

species of finches come to inhabit the islands? They couldn't have migrated from the mainland, for those species do not exist there. The answer to the question is found in natural selection. Apparently, long ago, a small flock of finches found their way to one of the islands; they mated among themselves and eventually their numbers multiplied. Food resources and habitats vary considerably from island to island. Some of the islands are lush with berries and seeds, others are covered with cacti and others have plenty of insects. Over time, some finches migrated to different islands in the archipelago. What happened next is the process of natural selection. Birds that migrated to islands rich in berries and seeds survived and reproduced only if they had thick beaks. On those islands, birds with thinner, more pointed beaks, unsuitable for crushing or breaking open seeds, died. Birds that migrated to insect-rich islands survived and reproduced only if they had thinner, more pointed beaks. There, birds with thick beaks, not selected for eating insects, died. The environment of each island determined which finches would live and reproduce and which would perish, leaving no offspring. The diversity of habitats on these islands permitted the different species of Darwin's Finches to evolve from the original ancestral group.

Recent research has shown that natural selection can have dramatic effects, even in the short term. In a series of studies by **Peter Grant** (1986), involving one species of Darwin's Finches, records were kept of rainfall, food supply and the population size of these finches on one of the Galapagos Islands. In 1976, the population numbered well over 1,000 birds. The following year brought a murderous drought that wiped out most of the food supply. The smallest seeds were the first to be depleted, leaving only larger and tougher seeds. That year the finch population decreased by more than 80 per cent. However, smaller finches with smaller beaks died at a higher frequency than larger finches with thicker beaks. Consequently, and as Darwin would have predicted, the larger birds became more numerous in the following years. Why? Because only they, with their larger bodies and thicker beaks, were fit enough to respond to the environmental change caused by the drought. Interestingly, in 1983, rain was plentiful and seeds, especially the smaller ones, became abundant. As a result, smaller birds outlived larger birds, probably because their beaks were better suited for pecking the smaller seeds. As Grant's study shows, while evolutionary effects occur over a very long time-frame, natural selection can have noticeable effects even over short periods.

Variation and competition

Although the environment is the driving force behind natural selection, it is not the only cause. Two other

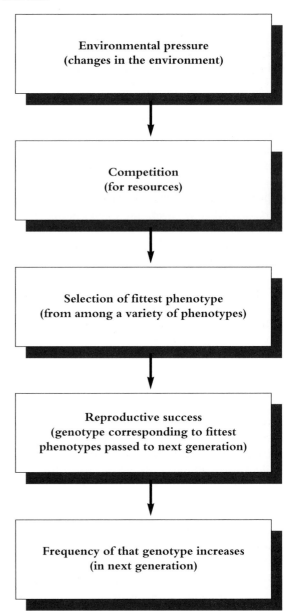

FIGURE 2.1 HOW NATURAL SELECTION WORKS

Environmental changes create competition for resources among species members. Only those individuals possessing characteristics instrumental in coping with these changes will survive and reproduce. The next generation will have a greater number of individuals possessing these genetically based taits.

Environmental pressure
(changes in the environment)

Competition
(for resources)

Selection of fittest phenotype
(from among a variety of phenotypes)

Reproductive success
(genotype corresponding to fittest phenotypes passed to next generation)

Frequency of that genotype increases
(in next generation)

factors, variation and competition, also play key roles.

Variation refers to differences in biological and psychological traits among individuals within a given population. Some people are big and strong; others are intelligent; and still others are big, strong and intelligent. Each finch species studied by Grant differed from the others in its **phenotype** (i.e. the many features by which an individual is recognised). These phenotypes included physical traits (beak size) and behavioural traits (ability to crack different kinds of seeds). The differences among the finches went deeper than outward appearances and seed-cracking abilities. Each finch also possessed a different **genotype**, or genetic structure inherited from its parents. Genotypes determine the extent to which the environment can influence an organism's development and behaviour. Any organism's phenotype is determined by one and only one process: the interaction of the organism's genotype with the environment. Ultimately, natural selection operates at the level of the genotype; if the phenotype is not well adapted to an environment, then neither is the particular genotype that gave rise to it.

During times of drought and scarcity of small seeds, larger birds outsurvived and outreproduced smaller birds. Had there been no phenotypic variation among the finches, that is no differences among the finches in terms of their physical traits and abilities, none or all would have survived. But because there was phenotypic variation, and because that variation was genetically based, the larger finches had a selective advantage and they survived and reproduced. When environmental conditions reversed and small seeds became more plentiful, birds with the smaller phenotype had a selective advantage. Then the smaller phenotypes were better suited to the environment and the larger birds, carrying the corresponding genotype, were selected against.

Because members of the same species occupy the same ecological niche, strong competition for food,

territory and mates occurs. This means that for every seed consumed by one finch, there is that much less food for other finches. A small piece of real estate protected by one bird is that much less territory that can be occupied by another. In times of food scarcity, competition gets even tougher, and only those with the fittest phenotype will survive and pass along the corresponding genotype to the next generation. *Figure 2.1* (previous page) is a simplified model of natural selection, including how variation and competition are involved in the selection of the fittest phenotypes.

■ Human Evolution

What sort of role, if any, has natural selection played in human evolution? We sometimes forget that first and foremost we are biological creatures. Occasionally, we are reminded of this fact, when we become ill or have to visit the dentist to have a tooth filled. For the most part, however, the comforts of modern culture dispose us to take our biology for granted. As in Darwin's times, some people still argue that natural selection applies to animals, but not to us. We seldom appreciate that our lifestyle, with all of its conveniences and luxuries, is the result of the natural selection of certain genotypes passed along to us from our ancient ancestors.

Through the combined efforts of hundreds of

FIGURE 2.2	APPROXIMATE TIME LINE FOR THE MAJOR EVENTS IN HUMAN EVOLUTION

Bipedalism freed the hands for grasping and tool use. Encephalisation provided the capacity for higher cognitive processes such as abstract thinking and reasoning. These two adaptations probably led to the other major advances in our evolution.

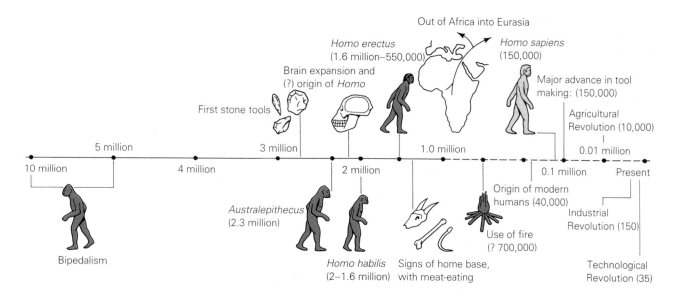

naturalists, biologists, anthropologists and geneticists, we now know that in the evolution of our species, natural selection favoured two adaptations – bipedalism and encephalisation. Together, they made possible the rise of human civilisation. Bipedalism refers to the ability to walk upright and encephalisation refers to increases in brain size. These two adaptations are responsible for most, if not all, of the other major advances in human evolution, including cultural development (see *Figure 2.2*, previous page). As our ancestors evolved the ability to walk upright, they were able to explore new environments and exploit new resources. As brain size increased, our ancestors became more intelligent and developed capacities for complex thinking, reasoning, memory and planning. (However, the evolution of a bigger brain did not guarantee that humans would become more intelligent – what was important was the kind of tissue that developed and expanded within the brain.) Because the opposable thumb evolved, humans fashioned and used tools. They developed simple strategies for hunting big game and they used fire for heating and cooking. The genotype coding for intelligent and mobile phenotypes slowly squeezed other, less well-adapted genotypes from the human gene pool, affording only intelligent bipeds the opportunity to reproduce.

After bipedalism and encephalisation, perhaps the other most important evolutionary milestone for our species was the advent of language (see Diamond, 1990). The capacity for language, of course, stemmed directly from encephalisation. If bipedalism and encephalisation are the cornerstones upon which modern civilisation is built, then language is the tool by which cultures are fashioned and refashioned. Think of the tremendous adaptive advantages that language conferred upon early humans. Simple instructions for making tools, finding a good hunting or fishing spot and avoiding danger would save time, effort and lives. Conversation, even humour, would strengthen further the social bonds among members of a naturally gregarious species. Most importantly, the advent of language, particularly the written word, would provide for the transmission of accumulated wisdom from one generation to future generations. Language is the basis for cultural evolution, which is the tendency of cultures to respond adaptively to environmental change through learning. Cultural evolution gave rise to major advances in toolmaking, to improved agricultural practices and to the development and refinement of industry and technology. In short, cultural evolution is critical to the development and maintenance of the kinds of lifestyles enjoyed by our species today.

In contrast to biological evolution, cultural evolution allows our species to make very rapid adjustments to changes in environmental conditions. Instead of taking thousands, even millions, of years for an adaptation to evolve, adaptations may appear within a single generation. As the basic unit of biological evolution is the gene, the basic unit of cultural evolution is the written or spoken word. But cultural evolution does have a genetic basis; without genotype coding for the capacities to learn and to think abstractly, cultural evolution would not occur. Culture – including art, literature, music, scientific knowledge and philanthropic activities – is possible only because of the human genotype. The influence of genes on our behavioural and cognitive abilities explains why psychologists are so keenly interested in genetics.

The marvellous piece of biology we call the brain exists because it was favoured by natural selection in our ancient ancestors' quest for survival. Our brains differ from those of other species for much the same reason (Harvey & Krebs, 1990). The earliest humans lived and survived in an environment different from those of other species so their brains evolved differently to meet the needs of their unique environment.

Genes and Behaviour

You have learned that, in the struggle for existence, environment determines a genotype's ability to live. Now let us briefly consider how the genes themselves are related to behaviour. You differ from your parents in part because you grew up and continue to live in a different environment from that in which they grew up. However, you differ from them also because you possess a combination of genes different from theirs. Your mother and father have endowed you with a part of what their parents, grandparents and all past generations of their family lines have given them, resulting in a unique biological blueprint and timetable for your development. The study of heredity, the inheritance of physical and psychological traits from ancestors, is called genetics.

Basic genetics

In the nucleus of each of our cells is genetic material called *DNA* (deoxyribonucleic acid). DNA contains the instructions for the production of proteins. These proteins regulate the body's physiological processes and the expression of phenotypic traits: body build, physical strength, intelligence and many behaviour patterns. DNA is organised into tiny units called genes that are found on rodlike structures, known as *chromosomes*.

At the very instant you were conceived, you

inherited from your parents 46 chromosomes, 23 from your mother and 23 from your father. Each of these chromosomes contains thousands of genes. The union of a sperm and egg will result in only one of many billion possible gene combinations. Although you have a full 50 per cent of your genes in common with your brothers or sisters, your set of genes is unique unless you have an identical twin. The difference in your genes is one reason why you are distinguishable, physically and behaviourally, from your brothers and sisters. (The other reason is that you do not live in exactly the same environment as they do.)

The sex chromosomes are those that contain genes coding for development of male or female physical characteristics. You inherited an X chromosome from your mother and either an X or a XY chromosome from your father. An XX combination codes for development of female characteristics; an XY combination codes for development of male characteristics. Consider for a moment the psychological implication of this one factor of your biology. How your parents reared you; how your relatives, friends, teachers and others treat you; whether you can bear children; the kinds of athletic, social and occupational opportunities afforded you; and even your self-perception stem, by and large, from this one very critical genetic factor. Is your psychology, how you get along in the world, rooted in your biology? Whether we answer this question in terms of your behaviour, cognition, social perception, or physical appearance, the answer is an unequivocal yes.

Remember, though, that genes do not code for destinies; they code for *potential*. Although only women can bear children, largely they do so by choice. Just because you are tall does not mean you will play volleyball or basketball. Also keep in mind that it is not only genetic factors that determine who you are. Physical size, for example, is determined jointly by genetic factors and nutritional environment. Physical strength can be developed in both males and females through special exercise programmes. Intellectual growth is determined by both genetic

potential and educational experiences. Neither genes nor the environment alone determines who you are or what kind of person you ultimately become. Genes only control the range of effects that the environment can have in shaping your phenotype. Thus, nature and nurture are inextricably linked. It is their interaction, the continual meeting of biological and psychosocial determinants, that accounts for human behaviour and experience in all its richness and diversity.

Genetics and psychology

The task for psychologists is to determine which environments help people develop their full potential. Consider, for example, people with Down's Syndrome. Down's Syndrome is caused by an extra chromosome in the 21st pair (resulting in three chromosomes instead of two in the pair). It is characterised by impaired psychomotor and physical maturation as well as by arrested intellectual development and associated learning difficulties. (The majority of Down's Syndrome babies are born to mothers and fathers over the age of 40.) Without intervention from psychologists and other skilled professionals, people with this disorder depend almost wholly on others to fulfil their basic needs. However, special educational programmes can help people with Down's Syndrome to care for themselves, find and hold manageable jobs, and establish a degree of personal independence.

The behaviour of people with Down's Syndrome can be modified through training. This fact underscores an important relationship that is emerging between psychology and genetics. Researchers in both fields have united forces in an interdisciplinary effort to accomplish two goals: to understand how genes influence behaviour and to determine how environmental variables (training programmes, diet and social interactions) can be used to modify behaviour that has a strong genetic basis. Human behaviour genetics is a relatively new field uniting both geneticists and psychologists interested in determining the genetic basis of behavioural traits and functioning, such as intelligence, mental disorders and altruism (Fuller, 1982; Plomin & Rende, 1991). Much of the research conducted by behaviour geneticists involves selective breeding, similar to the research once practised by Darwin. (Recall that selective breeding is the artificial selection of specific phenotypic traits.) They also investigate the inheritance of certain behavioural traits, such as intelligence, among individuals who vary in their degree of genetic similarity. Psychologists working in the field of developmental disabilities are primarily responsible for designing programmes to improve the

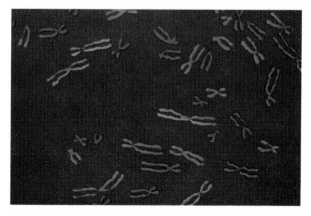

Human chromosomes

quality of life for individuals born with genetically-based disorders.

Genetic research over the past two decades has brought us to a threshold of understanding which was once thought unobtainable. We are on the verge of being able to map all of the human genes and use that knowledge to improve our quality of life by gigantic leaps (Delisi, 1988). Genetic mapping is the attempt to decipher the DNA code for each of our estimated 100,000 genes. Once these codes are broken – once we know which genes give rise to which traits – scientists will be able to conduct more accurate diagnostic tests for genetically-based disorders. In the past 20 years, the genes involved in juvenile diabetes, some forms of cancer, arthritis, blindness and manic-depressive disorder have been identified. Identifying defective genetic coding is the first step in developing effective intervention and treatment programmes. For example, since 1970, regular diagnostic tests for Tay-Sachs disease (which involves massive neurological damage and usually ends in death before the age of four) have been routinely performed on persons believed to be at risk for this disorder. Since the tests have been conducted, the incidence of Tay-Sachs has plummeted by over 90 per cent (*Consumer Reports*,

1990). The test warns people of the possibility that their children may be born with the disorder, allowing them to make an enlightened decision about whether to have children. With increased knowledge of how genes contribute to the development of physical and psychological traits, it may soon be possible to provide gene therapy for people with certain medical and psychological disorders (Anderson, 1984). Already researchers have found ways to produce human insulin and vaccines from genes to use in the treatment of diseases; use of genetic materials to treat some immune system disorders appears likely in the next few years. Other research has demonstrated that gene therapy is highly effective in treating cancerous tumours in mice. Based on this success, similar research with humans is expected to begin soon (Culliton, 1990). If these advances are not amazing enough, research is currently under way that may soon provide for the actual replacement or repair of defective genes. As we learn more and more about genes and their relationship to behaviour and psychological disorders, psychologists will likely be called on even further to provide guidance about the way that knowledge might be put to its most effective use (Wingerson, 1990).

INTERIM SUMMARY

Species originate and change over time because of natural selection, which is the tendency of organisms to reproduce differently due to the interaction of phenotypic traits with the environment. Because members of a species vary in their biological and behavioural characteristics and because that variation is genetically based, changes in environmental conditions may favour organisms possessing special characteristics. In terms of the evolution of our species, natural selection has favoured two adaptations: bipedalism and encephalisation. These adaptations are responsible for subsequent evolutionary advances, including language and culture.

The basic unit of evolution is the gene – a small unit of DNA found along chromosomes. Genes alone do not determine the specific nature of a phenotype. Rather, genes set the range of effects that environmental factors can have in influencing expression of phenotypic traits. Because behaviour is determined by both genetic and environmental variables, psychologists and geneticists have united to accomplish two goals: to understand better how genetic variables influence behaviour and to use that knowledge to improve the quality of life. Advances in genetic mapping promise to provide researchers with surer diagnoses of genetically-based disorders, which will lead to more effective clinical treatments.

BRAIN AND BEHAVIOUR

Long before Darwin made preparations for his trip aboard the Beagle, scientists, philosophers and others debated the role that the brain and nervous system play in everyday life. One of the most important figures in the history of brain studies was the French philosopher **René Descartes** (1596–1650). He was important because he proposed what at that time was a very new and very radical idea: the human body is an 'animal machine' that can be understood scientifically – by discovering natural laws through empirical observation. He raised purely physiological questions, questions about body mechanics and motion that led him to speculate about the forces that control human action. Basically, Descartes argued that human action is a mechanical reflex to environmental stimulation. He explained that physical energy excites a sense organ. When stimulated, the sense organ transmits this excitation to the brain in the form of 'animal spirits'. The brain then transmits the animal spirits to the appropriate set of muscles, setting in motion a reflex. Today, the idea of reflexive behaviour is something that most of us, especially psychologists, take for granted. In the seventeenth century, the idea had serious implications that could have angered religious leaders. At the time, the prevailing religious dogma taught that humans were special, endowed by a higher agency with the power of free will. Descartes'

René Descartes (1596–1650)

idea of reflexive behaviour, however, implied that humans were not different from animals.

But Descartes did believe that humans and animals were different. He believed that, unlike animals, humans have souls that guide their actions, enabling them to make rational choices between right and wrong. Because animals do not possess souls, he argued, they cannot be aware of their actions; their behaviour is wholly mechanistic and they are driven completely by primitive needs.

Although Descartes' idea of a soul kept him in good graces with the church, the value of this notion as a hypothetical construct is debatable at a time now when our actions are understood by contemporary neuroscience to be mediated by the workings of the brain. But we should not dismiss Descartes' other ideas as being unworthy of our consideration. In fact, it was those other ideas – that the human body can be subject to scientific study, that behaviour can be thought of as a response to environmental stimulation, and that the brain is somehow involved in that response – that eventually led subsequent researchers to examine more closely the relationships between the brain and behaviour.

So, Descartes was way ahead of his time: discoveries relating the brain and nervous system did not come for another 140 years. In 1811, researchers discovered that there are two basic types of nerves: sensory and motor. Almost 40 years later, in 1838, **Johannes Müller** formulated his doctrine of specific nerve energies, which states that one's sensory experience (of seeing and hearing, for example) is determined not by the stimulus input but by the specific part of the nervous system activated by that input. In 1861, **Paul Broca** discovered that damage to the left side of the brain impairs language abilities, the first suggestion of a connection between brain structure and brain function. Descartes' notion of the reflex did not have valid scientific support until 1906 when **Charles Sherrington** discovered that reflexes are composed of direct connections between sensory and motor nerve fibres at the level of the spinal cord. Sherrington also developed the idea that the nervous system involves both excitatory (increasing neural activity) and inhibitory (decreasing neural activity) processes. It was also not until this century that scientists knew anything at all about the basic unit of the nervous system, the neuron. In 1933, Santiago Ramon y Cajal theorised that the nervous system is comprised of neurons; 20 years later, with the aid of the electron microscope, other scientists supported his ideas. Since then, our understanding of the brain and nervous system has mushroomed. In 1948, Canadian psychologist **Donald Hebb** proposed that the brain is not merely a mass of tissue but a highly integrated series of structures, or 'cell assemblies', that perform specific functions.

Today, neuroscience is one of the most rapidly growing areas of science. Time between important discoveries is now measured by weeks, sometimes even days. What is permitting such rapid advances in neuroscience? Broadly speaking, the answer to that question is cultural evolution. Knowledge and wisdom acquired over hundreds of years of research, in combination with advances in technology, has given today's neuroscientists both the intellectual resources and the technological wizardry necessary for eavesdropping on the brain.

■ Eavesdropping on the Brain

Neuroscientists have four ways of plumbing the depths of the brain to uncover its secrets: studying patients suffering from brain damage, chemically or electrically producing lesions at specific brain sites, electrically stimulating and recording brain activity, and using computer-driven scanning devices to 'photograph' the brain. Each of these techniques serves a dual function: first, to produce new knowledge about the structure, organisation, and biochemical basis of normal brain functions; second, to diagnose brain disease and dysfunctions and then clinically evaluate therapeutic effects of specific treatments.

Brain damage

In September 1848, Phineas Gage, a 25-year-old railway worker in Vermont, was tamping (a process of packing down firmly with a special 'tamping iron') a charge of black powder into a hole drilled deep into a rock in preparation for blasting. The powder exploded unexpectedly, blowing the tamping iron,

'My mother didn't answer the door when I came to pick her up for Christmas dinner. She had passed out on the floor next to an empty bottle. It was typical. Thirty years earlier, the same thing had happened with my grandmother. Back then my mother said, 'If I ever get to be like grandma, I want you to tell me.' Sometimes I wonder: should I tell my son the same thing?'

This 42-year-old university lecturer is not an alcoholic. But his mother was not an alcoholic at 42 either. Over the years, her drinking increased; then she was involved in a car crash after which she was arrested for driving while intoxicated. The Christmas incident was one of several binges that the family wanted to overlook.

Individual differences in the frequency and total amount of alcohol drunk as well as reactions to heavy drinking are determined by many factors. What does it mean to have a predisposition for alcoholism and what factors, genetic, biological, sociocultural and environmental, influence how that tendency expresses itself?

Many different fields of research in brain and behavioural sciences contribute aetiologic information about alcoholism – i.e. information about the causes of alcoholism. Knowledge about the relative contributions of biological and environmental factors to alcohol dependence comes from studies of human families and from research on animals.

Psychologists compare the concordance rates of alcoholism in monozygotic twins (those who are genetically identical) and dizygotic twins (those who, like siblings, share only half their genes). When both members of a pair of twins have the same diagnosis – alcoholic or nonalcoholic – they are concordant for alcoholism. If one twin is alcoholic and the other is not, they are discordant for alcoholism. All major studies of alcoholism in twins have found that monozygotic (MZ) twins are more similar in both being alcoholic or both being nonalcoholic than dizygotic (DZ) twins (*Alcohol & Health*, 1990). It is important to note, however, that the MZ twins' concordance rates, although higher than those for DZ twins, show a wide range from a low of 26 per cent in one study (Hrubec & Omenn, 1981) to a very high 74 per cent in an earlier study (Kaij, 1960). This variability in concordance rates (using reliable measures) suggests that environmental factors can strongly influence whether a person with a genetic predisposition will become an alcoholic.

A second line of research compares children reared by alcoholic adoptive parents and those raised by alcoholic biological parents. While children reared by alcoholic adoptive parents are at no greater risk of becoming alcoholics than anyone else, the children of alcoholic biological parents are more likely than others to abuse alcohol – even when they are reared apart from their parents since infancy and placed in stable homes (Cloninger, 1987). Such findings tend to implicate the effects of genetic predispositions. However, environment does play an important role when a child is reared in a 'provocational' environment. The risk of alcoholism increases significantly among adopted sons living with fathers who drink heavily and are in unskilled occupations. When the adopted son comes from a biologically alcoholic parent and is reared in a similarly provocative milieu, the chances of severe alcohol abuse more than double.

Curiously, the genetic patterning of alcoholism for women is different from that for men. This difference is related to two different types of alcoholism. Type 1 involves the inability to stop binges once begun but the ability to abstain for long periods. Type 2 involves those who have persistent alcohol-seeking behaviours and an inability to abstain. Although both types of alcoholism are common in men, women predominantly develop Type 1 alcoholism, and men who are being treated in hospitals for severe alcoholism are largely Type 2. These subgroups of alcoholics differ in their neurophysiological and neurochemical reactions to various types of stimulation from their environment. New theorising links such reactions both to genetic predispositions and possibly to some personality variables.

Biopsychologists are trying to find biological markers to help them identify individuals likely to develop problems with alcohol. Markers are any measurable indicators that reliably predict the behaviour or reaction under investigation; they may be **precursors** or **correlates** of the event but not necessarily the causes of the event. As the search for markers continues, researchers are also learning how environmental factors can modify the extent to which genetic similarity determines drinking habits. In an Australian study of almost 2,000 pairs of female twins, married twins were much less similar to one another in their alcohol consumption patterns than were unmarried twins (Heath *et al*,

1989). This finding suggests that something about the experience of marriage decreased the degree to which genetic factors influenced drinking. It might also be hypothesised that unmarried twins were more likely to have lower levels of social support than married twins and we know that social isolation is causally related to many forms of pathological behaviour, among them alcoholism.

Will the lecturer continue his family's legacy of alcohol problems?

Today's science cannot answer that question with certainty, but many researchers are working to discover the extent to which genetic and environmental factors contribute to this widespread, self-destructive behaviour. Once we can identify people who are genetically and psychosocially predisposed to alcoholism, we will be able to learn much more about how the interplay of biology and environment contribute to a dependence on alcohol.

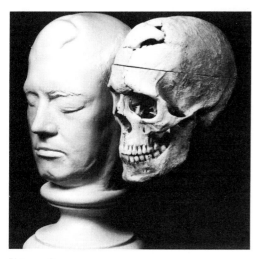

Phineas Gage

over a metre long and weighing six kilograms, right through Gage's head. Still conscious, Gage was taken by wagon to his hotel, where he was able to walk upstairs. The doctor who attended him noted that the hole in Gage's skull was eight centimetres wide, with shreds of brain all around it. He dressed the wound. Two days later, Gage became delirious and remained near death for the next two weeks, but he eventually revived. Incredibly, Gage lived for another 12 years.

Gage's physical impairment was remarkably slight: he lost vision in his left eye, and the left side of his face was partially paralysed, but his posture, movement and speech were all unimpaired. Yet, psychologically, he was a changed man, as his doctor's account makes clear:

'His physical health is good, and I am inclined to say that he has recovered. He has no pain in (his) head, but says it has a queer feeling which he is not able to describe. . . . His contractors, who regarded him as the most efficient and

capable foreman in their employ previous to his injury, considered the change in his mind so marked that they could not give him his place again. He is fitful, irreverent, indulging at times in the grossest profanity (which was not previously his custom). . . . Previous to his injury . . . he possessed a well-balanced mind, and was looked upon by those who knew him as a shrewd, smart businessman, very energetic and persistent in executing all his plans of operation. In this regard his mind was radically changed, so decidedly that his friends and acquaintances said he was "no longer Gage"' (Bigelow, 1850).

At about the same time that Gage was convalescing from his injury, **Paul Broca**, a French neurosurgeon, was studying the brain's role in language. His first laboratory research in this area involved a *post mortem* of a man whose name was derived from the only word he had been able to speak, 'Tan'. Broca found that the left front portion of Tan's brain had been severely damaged. This finding led Broca to study the brains of other persons who suffered from language impairments. In each case, Broca's work revealed similar damage to the same area of the brain. He concluded that language ability depended on the functioning of structures in a specific region of the brain.

Lesions

As the remarkable story of Gage and word of Broca's carefully conducted laboratory research spread, more and more researchers began to wonder about the role the brain plays in helping people to manage their day-to-day affairs. But some of these researchers did not stop at studying the effects of accidental brain damage on behaviour; they began, with considerable deliberation and skill, to lesion (destroy sections of) the brains of otherwise intact animals (typically rats and other small creatures) and to then measure systematically the outcomes.

The problem with studying accidentally damaged brains, of course, is that researchers have no control over the location, extent of the damage, or its other related complications (infection, blood loss, traumas). If science was going to produce a well-founded understanding of the brain and its relationship to behavioural and cognitive functioning, Broca's colleagues needed a better method. Instead of waiting for patients with brain damage to show up in hospital labs, researchers asked, 'Why not deliberately produce carefully placed lesions in the brains of experimental research subjects?' Although we can now appreciate the ethical implications of this question, early neuroscientists believed this was a productive strategy.

Lesions are carefully inflicted injuries to specific brain areas. Researchers create three types of lesions: they either surgically remove specific brain areas, cut the neural connections to those areas, or, destroy those areas through application of intense levels of heat, cold or electricity or through laser surgery. Our conception of the brain has been radically changed since researchers have repeatedly compared and co-ordinated the results of lesioning experiments on animals with the growing body of clinical findings on the effects of brain damage on human behaviour. Knowledge of brain functions gained from laboratory studies has also been supplemented by observation of the effects of lesions used for medical therapy. For example, a type of lesion used widely with epileptic patients involves severing the nerve fibres connecting the two hemispheres, or sides, of the brain. In addition to easing the suffering of patients, these types of studies have also revealed to us important information about the brain's role in everyday conscious experience, a topic we will take up at the end of this chapter.

Electrical stimulation and recording

Before the Canadian neurosurgeon **Wilder Penfield** operated on the brain of a patient suffering from epileptic seizures, he made a map of the cortex so that he could localise the origin of the seizures and leave unharmed other areas vital to the patient's functioning. His map-making tool was an electrode, a thin wire through which small amounts of precisely regulated electrical current could pass. As Penfield touched one cortical surface after another with this surgical wand, the conscious patient (under local anaesthetic only, since there are no pain receptors in the brain itself) reacted in various ways. When stimulating some sites, Penfield observed motor reactions of hand clenching and arm raising; when touching others, he witnessed 'experiential responses' as the patient vividly recalled past events or had sudden feelings (such as fear, loneliness, or elation) with a *déjà vu* familiarity about them. As if he had pushed an electronic memory button, Penfield touched memories stored silently for years in the deep recesses of his patient's brain (Penfield & Baldwin, 1952). Penfield's explorations of the surface of the brain, together with many subsequent studies, have permitted researchers to draw precise maps of the brain's surface.

In the mid-1950s, **Walter Hess** pioneered the use of electrical stimulation to probe structures deeper in the brain. For example, Hess put electrodes far into specific parts of the brain of a freely moving cat. By pressing a button, he could then send a small electrical current to the brain at the point of the electrode. Hess carefully recorded the behavioural consequences of stimulating each of 4,500 brain sites in nearly 500 cats. Electrical stimulation of certain regions of the brain led the otherwise gentle cats to bristle with rage and hurl themselves upon a nearby object – which, in the early days, was sometimes the startled experimenter! Sleep, sexual arousal, anxiety or terror could be provoked by the flick of the switch – and turned off just as abruptly.

Other neuroresearchers discovered another application of the new electrode technology. Instead of electrically stimulating the brain, they simply used electrodes to record the electrical activity of the brain as it occurred in response to environmental stimulation.

The brain's electrical output can be monitored in two ways. First, by inserting ultrasensitive micro-electrodes into the brain, researchers can record the electrical activity of a single brain cell. Usually invertebrates, such as the sea slug Aplysia, are used in this kind of research because they have relatively few neurons and these neurons are large enough to be easily identified, enabling researchers to record the electrical activity within each nerve cell. Such recordings will eventually illuminate the fundamental mechanisms used to process information in human brains as well. Second, by placing a number of electrodes on the surface of the head, researchers can record larger, integrated patterns of electrical activity. These electrodes transmit signals regarding the brain's electrical activity to a machine called an electroencephalograph. In turn, the machine produces an electroencephalogram (EEG), or an amplified tracing of the activity. An EEG is used to study the brain during states of arousal and has been particularly useful in helping researchers study processes involved in sleeping and dreaming. In one recent experiment, changing aspects of human thought were detected by

124 EEG sensors applied to the scalps of each subject. In the split second before they were to respond behaviourally, the subjects' brains showed activity in brain areas that would be activated during execution of the task, suggesting mental rehearsal prior to acting (Givens, 1989a; Barinaga, 1990).

By developing a large set of brain electrical-activity data from healthy people and from people with various brain and psychiatric disorders, ranging in age from six to 90 years old, researchers are now able to diagnose brain dysfunctions reliably. Using just a single 60-minute EEG sample, researchers and clinicians can perform computer-assisted diagnosis and classification of different disorders with accuracy, a process known as *neurometrics* (John *et al*, 1988).

Brain scans

The most exciting technological innovations for studying the brain are machines originally developed to help neurosurgeons detect brain abnormalities, such as tumours or damage caused by strokes or diseases. These machines, or brain scanners, produce images of different regions of the living brain. Research using brain scans does not require surgery or other intrusive procedures that may damage brain tissue. Three brain-scanning devices are currently used.

Perhaps the most widely used scanner is the computerised tomography scanner, better known as the CT scanner. The CT scanner projects X-rays through the head at various angles. A computer then

CT scans allow neuroscientists and neurosurgeons to produce computer-enhanced images of the brain to help them understand brain structures and their relationship to behaviour.

calculates the amount of radiation passing through the brain from the various angles and integrates that information into an image that can be seen on a monitor. By looking at the image, researchers can locate abnormalities in brain tissue, which permits them to link brain structure to the psychological symptoms exhibited by the individual.

An even more powerful scanner is the positron

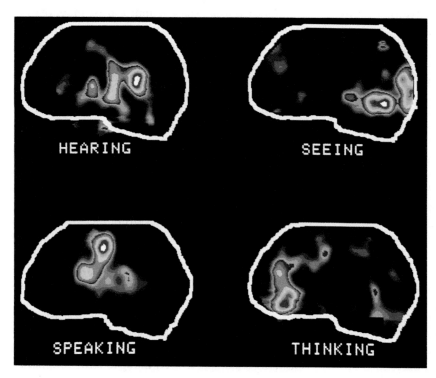

These PET scans show that different tasks stimulate neural activity in distinct regions of the brain.

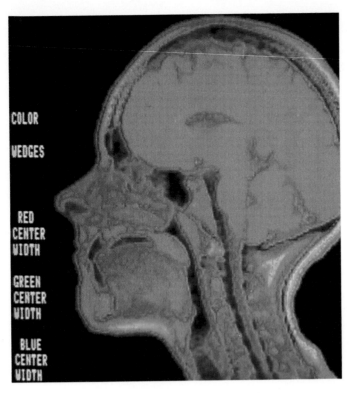

Magnetic resonance imaging (MRI) produces this colour-enhanced profile of a normal brain. MRI uses a combination of radio waves and a strong magnetic field to view soft tissue. This technique provides a truer image than other imaging techniques.

emission tomography scanner, or **PET scanner**. In PET research, subjects are given different kinds of radioactive (but safe) substances that eventually travel to the brain, where they are taken up by active brain cells. Recording instruments outside the skull can detect radioactivity emitted by the cells that are active during different cognitive or behavioural activities. This information is then fed into a computer that constructs a dynamic portrait of the brain and projects it onto a monitor, showing where different types of neural activity are actually occurring.

Another new technology allowing brain researchers and neurosurgeons to explore the living brain is magnetic resonance imaging, or **MRI**. MRI uses magnetic fields and radio waves to generate pulses of energy within the brain. By tuning the pulse to different frequencies, some atoms line up with the magnetic field. When the magnetic pulse is turned off, the atoms vibrate (resonate) as they return to their original positions. These vibrations are picked up by special radio receivers that channel information about the vibrations into a computer. In turn, the computer generates maps of the location of different atoms in areas of the brain. These maps enable researchers to see which cells are functioning normally and which are not. In addition, researchers can use the maps to study the different kinds of activity taking place in specific areas of the brain or the spinal cord in response to various types of physical and psychological stimulation.

Brain imaging is a very promising tool for achieving a better understanding of normal brain structure, physiology, chemistry and functional organisation. By directly imaging the brain's structure and the biochemical processes underlying psychological disorders, we can learn how to evaluate and better design the medications used to treat those disorders (Andreason, 1988). Three hundred years have passed since Descartes sat in his candle-lit study and theorised how the brain functions; over 100 years have passed since Broca discovered in his crude *post mortem* of Tan that brain regions seem to be linked to specific functions. In the time since these developments, cultural evolution has provided neuroscientists with the kinds of technology necessary to reveal some of the brain's most important secrets. The remainder of the chapter describes some of these secrets and discusses how they are related to our behaviour, our thinking and, in short, our psychology.

Brain Structures and their Functions

The development of the brain in any species follows strict genetic coding for the foundation, or hardwiring, of certain basic neural circuits. The way the brain forms and separates into divisions is similar in many species; but the higher the species is on the evolutionary scale, the larger and more complex the brain becomes and the more sophisticated the functions it can perform become. In the human brain, the genetic instructions lead to a remarkably precise, efficient communication and computational system unmatched by any other species.

Environmental stimulation is necessary to fine-tune the brain. Without this stimulation, many brain structures will not develop properly. Enriched early experience has been shown to develop superior adult learners and physically change the human brain (Rosenzweig, 1984b).

The human brain is a triarchic structure: it is composed of three interconnected layers, each corresponding to different epochs in our evolutionary history (MacLean, 1990). In the deepest recesses of the brain, in a region called the **central core**, are structures involved primarily with autonomic processes such as heart rate, breathing, swallowing and digestion. Enveloping the central core is the **limbic system**, which is involved with emotional and sexual behaviours as well as with eating, drinking and aggression. Wrapped around these two 'primitive'

FIGURE 2.3 — THE CENTRAL CORE, LIMBIC SYSTEM AND CEREBRAL CORTEX

From an evolutionay perspective, the central core is the oldest part of the brain; the limbic system evolved next; and the cerebral cortex is the most recent achievement in brain evolution.

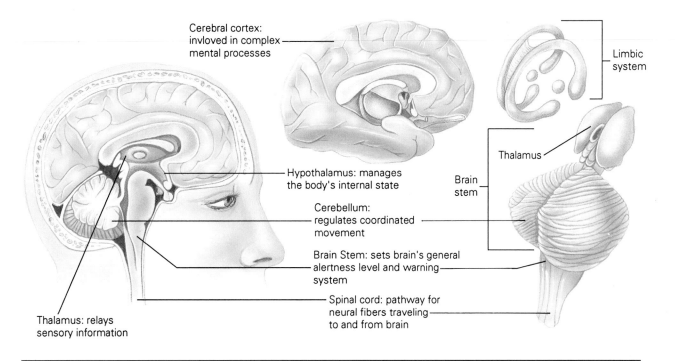

brains is the pinnacle of human evolution: the **cerebral cortex**. For each of us, the universe of the human mind exists in this region, just beneath the scalp. Without the cerebral cortex we would be no different from the lowliest of animal species. With it, we can design new ways to challenge the limits imposed by heredity on our human nature. The cerebral cortex integrates sensory information, coordinates our movements, and facilitates abstract thinking and reasoning (see *Figure 2.3*).

Before we move on to consider these regions in more detail it must be noted, however, that the three systems of the brain do not always necessarily function in harmony. Although the cortex provides us with advanced ways of coping with the world, our evolutionary past may bother us as when, for example, the activity of the limbic system is involved in the regulation and mediation of emotions. The cortex may allow us to refrain from, say, immoral acts because we know they will harm others; nevertheless, impulsions from the central core and limbic system often interfere with our culturally-valued standards and our desires to function with maximum efficiency and accuracy. Consider, for example, air-traffic controllers who must optimally perform the complex task of safely landing an aircraft: they need all their available powers of decision making and composure just at the point when they are also feeling most

aroused and stressed; heart rate peaks during these moments of the job, whether the shift is during the day or night (Dixon, 1994). In such instances, where cortical functioning is compromised by the activity of the limbic and core regions, the brain's triarchic structure in one way can be construed as a biological anachronism humankind could well do without. On other occasions, however (for instance, when resisting an aggressor or fleeing from physical danger), the sub-cortical components of this three-part structure can be viewed more positively since they promote adaptive functioning – namely, 'fight' or 'flight' from threat.

The structures of the brain perform specific activities that can be divided into five general categories: (a) internal regulation, (b) reproduction, (c) sensation, (d) motion and (e) adaptation to changing environmental conditions. The first two are the brain's way of controlling bodily processes that keep us alive, well, and prepared to reproduce and nourish offspring. The third activity enables the brain to make contact with the outside world by processing sensory information from receptors located throughout the body. The brain also monitors internal sensations that provide information about balance, gravity, movements of limbs and orientation. Some neuroscientists believe that the fourth activity, motion, is the major role of the brain. The brain must get the muscles to move so that an organism can

FIGURE 2.4   THE STRUCTURES OF THE CENTRAL CORE

The structures of the central core are primarily involved with basic life processes: breathing, pulse, arousal, movement, balance and rudimentary processing of sensory information.

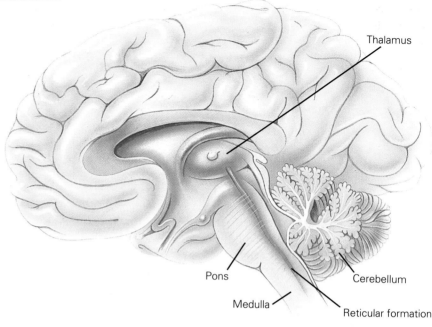

effect changes in its environment to produce desired consequences. As 'a mechanism for governing motor activity', the brain's 'primary function is essentially the transforming of sensory patterns into patterns of motor coordination' (Sperry, 1952). The final function – adapting to the environment – involves the brain's remarkable ability to modify itself as it learns, store what it has experienced and direct new actions based on feedback from the consequences of its previous actions. Let us look more closely at the three major brain regions that regulate these numerous activities beginning with the central core.

The central core

The central core is found in all vertebrate species. It contains five structures that collectively regulate the internal state of the body (see *Figure 2.4*). The **medulla**, located at the very top of the spinal cord, is the centre for breathing, waking, sleeping and the beating of the heart. Because these processes are essential for life, damage to the medulla can be fatal. Nerve fibres ascending from the body and descending from the brain cross over at the medulla, which means that the left side of the body is linked to the right side of the brain and the right side of the body is connected to the left side of the brain. Directly above the medulla is the **pons**, which is involved in

dreaming and in waking from sleep. The **reticular formation** is a dense network of nerve cells situated between the medulla and pons. It serves as the brain's sentinel. It arouses the cerebral cortex to attend to new stimulation and keeps the brain alert even during sleep. Massive damage to this area often results in a coma. The reticular formation has long tracts of fibres that run to the **thalamus**, a relay station that channels incoming sensory information to the appropriate area of the cerebral cortex, where that information is then processed. For example, the thalamus relays information from the eyes to the visual cortex, a portion of the cortex located at the very rear of the head. The **cerebellum**, attached to the brain stem at the base of the skull, coordinates bodily movements, controls posture and maintains equilibrium. Damage to the cerebellum interrupts the flow of otherwise smooth movement, causing it to appear uncoordinated and jerky.

The limbic system

The central core is found in all vertebrates, but only mammals are equipped with the more recently evolved limbic system. The limbic system mediates motivated behaviours, emotional states and memory processes. It also regulates body temperature, blood pressure and blood-sugar level and performs other

FIGURE 2.5   THE LIMBIC SYSTEM

The structures of the limbic system, which are present only in mammals, are involved with motivated behaviour, emotional states and memory processes.

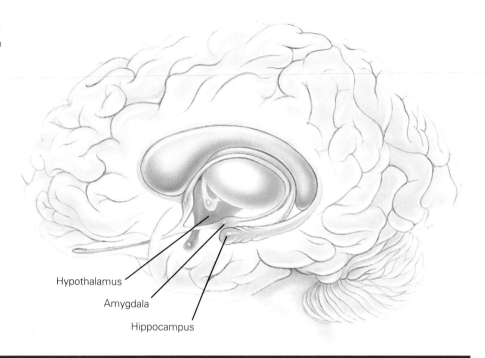

Hypothalamus

Amygdala

Hippocampus

housekeeping activities. The limbic system comprises three structures: the hippocampus, amygdala and hypothalamus (see *Figure 2.5*).

The **hippocampus**, the largest of the limbic system structures, plays an important role in memory, especially in long-term storage of information (Galluscio, 1990). Damage to the hippocampus does not impair the learning of new information, but it does impair the ability to remember it. Thus, if you were in an accident and sustained damage to your hippocampus, you would still be able to learn new tasks, but you would not be able to remember having done so! In other words, your life would always be in the present: everything you learn today, you would have to relearn tomorrow. Evidence for the hippocampus' role in memory is derived mostly from clinical evidence, notably from studies of a patient, 'H.M.', perhaps psychology's most famous subject.

When he was 27, H.M. underwent surgery in an attempt to reduce the frequency and severity of his epileptic seizures. During the operation, parts of his hippocampus were accidentally removed. As a result, H.M. could only recall the very distant past; his ability to put new information into long-term memory was gone. Long after his surgery, he continued to believe he was living in 1953, which was the year the operation was performed. However, and for some unknown reason, comparable damage to the hippocampus in other animals, such as rhesus monkeys, does not result in the same degree of memory impairment (Salmon *et al*, 1987).

The **amygdala** is known best for its role in aggression, although it is also involved in feeding, drinking and sexual behaviours. Studies with several animal species, including humans, have shown that lesioning the amygdala has a calming effect on those prone to frequent uncontrollable outbursts of aggression. In some cases, animals who have undergone amygdalectomies (surgical removal of the amygdala) show bizarre sexual behaviour, attempting to copulate with just about any available partner. In one early experiment, a cat was observed trying to copulate with a dog, a chicken and a monkey (Schreiner & Kling, 1963).

The **hypothalamus** is one of the smallest structures in the brain, yet it plays a vital role in many of our most important daily actions. It is actually composed of several nuclei, small bundles of neurons that regulate physiological processes involved in motivated behaviour (including eating, drinking, temperature regulation and sexual arousal). The hypothalamus also regulates the activities of the endocrine system, which secretes hormones. The hypothalamus basically maintains the body's internal equilibrium. When the body's energy reserves are low, the hypothalamus is involved in stimulating the organism to find food and to eat. When body temperature drops, the hypothalamus causes blood-vessel constriction, or minute involuntary movements we commonly refer to as the 'shivers'. This bodily thermostatic function is a form of **homeostasis** – maintaining an internal balance or equilibrium.

FIGURE 2.6 THE CEREBRAL CORTEX

Each of the two hemispheres of the cerebral cortex has four lobes. Different sensory and motor functions have been associated with specific parts of each lobe.

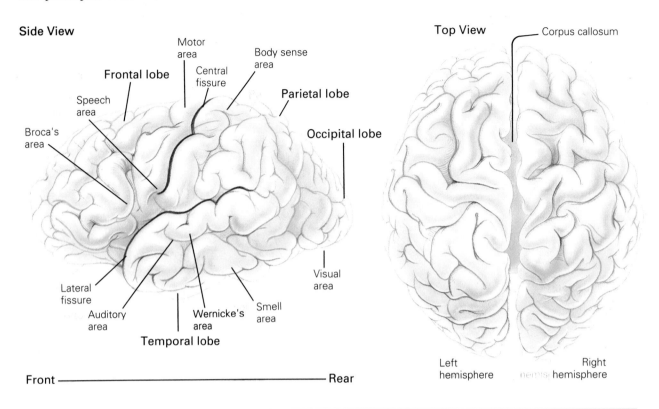

The cerebral cortex

When someone says that you 'really have brains', he or she is referring to your cerebral cortex. In humans, the cerebral cortex dwarfs the rest of the brain, occupying two-thirds of its total mass. Its role is to regulate the brain's higher cognitive and emotional functions. The cerebral cortex is divided into two almost symmetrical halves, the **cerebral hemispheres**, each mediating different cognitive and emotional functions. The *left cerebral hemisphere* is involved with spontaneous use of language (both written and spoken), integration of complex movement, memory for words and numbers, and anxiety and positive emotions. The *right cerebral hemisphere* regulates memory for music and geometric patterns, facial recognition and feelings of negative emotions. The two hemispheres are connected by a thick mass of nerve fibres, collectively referred to as the **corpus callosum**. This pathway sends messages back and forth between the hemispheres.

Neuroscientists have mapped each hemisphere using two important landmarks as their guides. One deep groove, called the **central fissure**, divides each hemisphere vertically and a second similar groove, called the **lateral fissure**, divides each hemisphere horizontally (see *Figure 2.6*). These vertical and horizontal divisions create four areas, or brain lobes, in each hemisphere. Each of these lobes serves specific functions. The **frontal lobe**, which is involved with motor control and cognitive activities, such as planning, making decisions, setting goals and relating the present to the future through purposeful behaviour, is located above the lateral fissure and in front of the central fissure. Accidents that damage the frontal lobes can have devastating effects on human action and personality, as in the case of Phineas Gage. The **parietal lobe** is involved with controlling incoming sensory information and is located directly behind the central fissure, toward the top of the head. The **occipital lobe**, the final destination for visual information, is located at the back of the head. The **temporal lobe**, where auditory information is processed, is found below the lateral fissure, on the sides of each cerebral hemisphere.

It would be misleading to say that one specific lobe alone controls any one specific function by itself. The structures of the brain perform their duties in harmony, working smoothly as an integrated unit, similar to a symphony orchestra. Whether you are washing the dishes, solving a calculus problem, or chatting to a

FIGURE 2.7 THE MOTOR CORTEX

Different parts of the body are more or less sensitive to environmental stimulation and brain control. Sensitivity in a particular region of the body is related to the amount of space in the cerebral cortex devoted to that region. In this figure, the body is drawn so that size of body parts is relative to the cortical space devoted to them. The larger the body part in the drawing, the greater its sensitivity to environmental stimulation and the greater the brain's control over its movement.

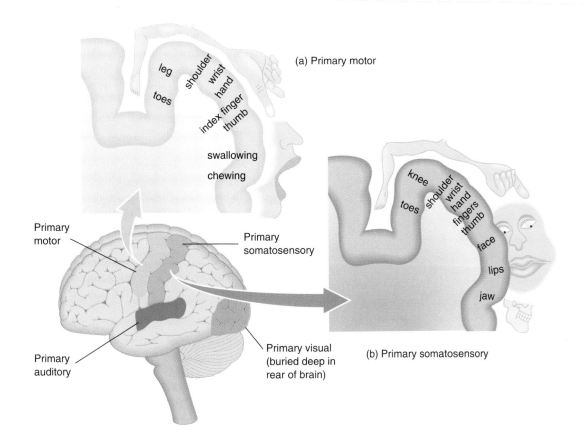

friend, your brain works as a unified whole, each lobe interacting and cooperating with the others. Nevertheless, neuroscientists can identify areas of the four lobes of the cortex that are *necessary* for specific functions, such as vision, hearing, language and memory.

The actions of the body's voluntary muscles, of which there are more than 600, are controlled by the **motor cortex**, located just in front of the central fissure in the frontal lobes. Muscles in the lower part of the body, for example the toes, are controlled by neurons in the top part of the motor cortex. Muscles in the upper part of the body, such as the throat, are controlled by neurons in the lower part of the motor cortex. As you can see in *Figure 2.6*, the upper parts of the body receive far more detailed motor instructions than the lower parts. In fact, the two largest areas of the motor cortex are devoted to the fingers – especially the thumb – and to the muscles involved in speech, reflecting the importance in human activity of manipulating objects, using tools,

eating and talking. Remember that commands from one side of the brain are directed to muscles on the opposite side of the body. So, the motor cortex in the right hemisphere of your brain controls the muscles in your left foot.

The **somatosensory cortex** is located just behind the central fissure in the left and right parietal lobes. This part of the cortex processes information about temperature, touch, body position and pain. As with the motor cortex, the upper part of the sensory cortex relates to the lower parts of the body and the lower part to the upper parts of the body. Most of the area of the sensory cortex is devoted to the lips, tongue, thumb and index fingers, the parts of the body that provide the most important sensory input (see *Figure 2.7*).

Auditory information is processed in the **auditory cortex**, which is in the two temporal lobes. The auditory cortex in each hemisphere receives information from both ears. One area of the auditory

FIGURE 2.8	HOW A WRITTEN WORD IS SPOKEN

Nerve impulses, laden with information about the written word, are sent by the retinas to the visual cortex via the thalamus. The visual cortex then sends the nerve impulses to an area in the rear of the temporal lobe, the angular gyrus, where visual coding for the word (the arrangements of letters and their shapes, etc.) is compared to its acoustical coding (the way it sounds). Once the proper acoustical code is located, it is relayed to an area of the auditory cortex known as Wernicke's area. Here it is encoded and interpreted. Nerve impulses are then sent to Broca's area which sends the message to the motor cortex. The motor cortex puts the word in your mouth by stimulating the lips, tongue and larynx to act in synchrony.

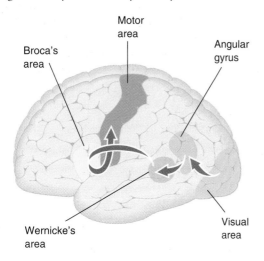

Speaking a written word

cortex is involved in the production of language and a different area is involved with language comprehension. Visual input is processed at the back of the brain in the **visual cortex**, located in the occipital lobes. Here the greatest area is devoted to input from the central part of the retina at the back of the eye, the area that transmits the most detailed visual information.

Not all of the cerebral cortex is devoted to processing sensory information and commanding the muscles to action. In fact, the majority of it is involved in integrating information. Processes, such as planning and decision making, are believed to occur in all the areas of the cortex not labelled in *Figure 2.6*, or the **association cortex**. Animals located on higher rungs of the evolutionary ladder have more of their cortex devoted to association areas than do lower animals. This difference in the relative size of association areas reflects a physiological, structural difference among animals, but it also reflects a behavioural difference. For example, humans, at the top of the evolutionary ladder, show greater flexibility in behaviour because

their genotypes code for proportionately more of their cortex to be devoted to association areas.

How do these different areas of the brain work in unison? Consider, as an example, the biology of speaking a written word (see *Figure 2.8*). Imagine that your psychology lecturer hands you a piece of paper with the word 'chocolate' written on it, and he or she asks you to say the word aloud. Saying the word 'chocolate' is probably a very easy thing for you to imagine yourself doing, if only because you have probably said the word many times before. But the biological processes involved in the action are subtle and complex. Neuroscience can break down your verbal behaviour into numerous steps. First, the visual stimulus (the written word 'chocolate') is detected by the nerve cells in the retinas of your eyes, which send nerve impulses to the visual cortex (via the thalamus). The visual cortex then sends nerve impulses to an area in the rear of the temporal lobe (called the *angular gyrus*) where visual coding for the word is compared to its acoustical coding. Once the proper acoustical code is located, it is relayed to an area of the auditory cortex known as *Wernicke's area*, where it is decoded and interpreted. Nerve impulses are then sent to *Broca's area*, which, in turn, sends a message to the motor cortex, stimulating the lips, tongue and larynx to produce the word 'chocolate'.

That is a lot of mental effort for just one word. Now imagine what you require of your brain every time you read aloud a book or even a road sign. The truly amazing thing is that your brain responds effortlessly and intelligently, translating thousands of scribbles and marks on paper into a biological code, informing other brain areas about what is going on and finally, putting words in your mouth (Montgomery, 1990).

INTERIM SUMMARY

Descartes' speculation that the human body is governed by natural laws and that the brain is somehow involved in regulating behaviour laid the foundation for modern neuroscience. Neuroscience is a multidisciplinary approach used in understanding the relation between brain and behaviour. Modern neuroscientists use four methods of research in this area: studying patients suffering from brain damage, chemically or electrically producing lesions at specific brain sites, electrically stimulating and recording brain activity, and employing computer-driven scanning devices to photograph the brain. Precise use of these methods has permitted neuroscientists to make important discoveries about the way brain structures process information, generate thoughts and co-ordinate complex behaviour patterns.

The brain is divided into three integrated layers:

the central core, the limbic system and the cerebral cortex. The central core is the oldest part of the human brain and is chiefly responsible for life-sustaining functions: breathing, digestion and heart rate. Encircling the central core are the structures of the limbic system, which are involved in storage of long-term information, aggression, eating and drinking, and sexual behaviour. The most recently evolved area of the brain is the cerebral cortex, which surrounds the central core and limbic system and accounts for most of the brain's mass. The cerebral cortex is divided into two roughly symmetrical halves called hemispheres. Different areas of the cortex either process different kinds of environmental stimulation or initiate movement. But the brain functions as an integrated whole; no one brain region operates independently of the others. On occasions, however, such functioning may not be harmonious and complementary, given the environmental tasks at hand.

■ THE ENDOCRINE AND NERVOUS SYSTEMS

Think of someone you know, perhaps your closest friend. For whatever reason, this person has come to play a significant role in your life. He or she can make you smile and laugh, keep you company when you're feeling lonely, cause you to question your motives for taking a certain course of action, and make you angry sometimes and joyful at other times. The relationship you have with this person can be traced to your experiences together, but the ways your friend makes you feel, think, or act is more than the mere sum of your interactions with each other. How you react to your friend is largely influenced by the way your brain processes information about his or her actions and by the way your brain tells your body and mind to respond. In more technical terms, your response to environmental stimulation is mediated by an electrochemical communications system, whose

FIGURE 2.9	ENDOCRINE GLANDS IN FEMALES AND MALES

The pituitary gland is shown on the far right; it is the master gland that regulates the glands shown to the left. The pituitary gland is under the control of the hypothalamus, an important structure in the limbic system.

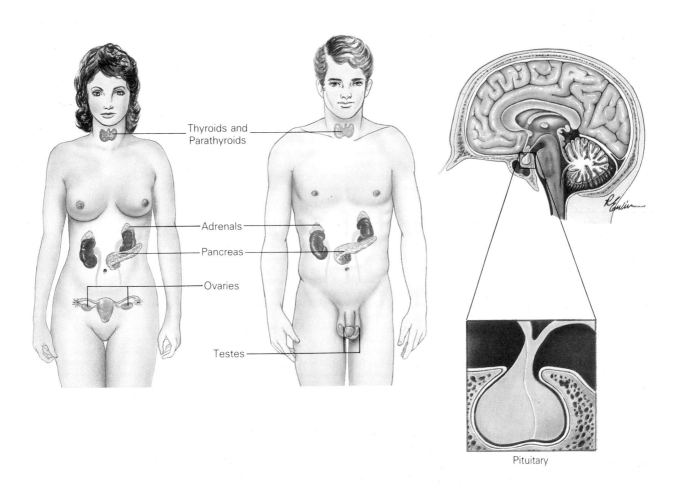

Pituitary

job it is to relay sensory information to the brain and, in turn, relay behavioural information from your brain to various parts of your body.

We actually have two distinct and highly complex communication systems. One system, the **endocrine system**, is a network of glands that manufacture and secrete chemical messengers called hormones into the bloodstream (see *Figure 2.9*, previous page). The other system, the **nervous system**, is a massive network of nerve cells that rapidly relays messages to and from the brain using different kinds of chemical messengers called **neurotransmitters**.

■ Glandular Control of Behaviour and Internal Processes

Hormones are important in everyday functioning, although they are more vitally important at some stages of life and in some situations than others. Hormones are involved in a wide array of bodily functions and behaviours. They influence your body growth; initiate, maintain and stop development of

primary and secondary sexual characteristics; moderate levels of arousal and awareness; serve as the basis for mood changes; and regulate metabolism, the rate at which the body uses its energy stores. The endocrine system promotes the survival of an organism by helping fight infections and disease. It advances the survival of the species through regulation of sexual arousal, production of reproductive cells and production of milk in nursing mothers.

Endocrine glands respond to the levels of chemicals in the bloodstream or are stimulated by other hormones or by nerve impulses from the brain. Hormones are then secreted into the blood and travel to distant target cells with specific receptors; hormones exert their influence on the body's programme of chemical regulation only at the places that are genetically predetermined to respond to them. In influencing diverse, but specific, target organs or tissue, hormones can regulate such an enormous range of biochemical processes that they have been called 'the messengers of life' (Crapo, 1985). This multiple-action communication system allows for control of slow, continuous processes such as maintenance of blood-sugar levels and calcium levels, metabolism of carbohydrates, and general body growth. But what

TABLE 2.1	MAJOR ENDOCRINE GLANDS AND THE FUNCTIONS OF THE HORMONES THEY PRODUCE
These glands:	**Produce hormones that regulate:**
Hypothalamus	Release of pituitary hormones
Anterior pituitary	Testes and ovaries Breast milk production Metabolism Reactions to stress
Posterior pituitary	Water conservation Breast milk excretion Uterus contraction
Thyroid	Metabolism Growth and development
Parathyroid	Calcium levels
Gut	Digestion
Pancreas	Glucose metabolism
Adrenals	Fight or flight responses Metabolism Sexual desire in women
Ovaries	Development of female sexual traits Ova production
Testes	Development of male sexual traits Sperm production Sexual desire in men

happens during sudden crises? For example, what happens to your body when you see a child run out in front of your car? The endocrine system releases the hormone **adrenaline** (epinephrine) into the bloodstream, which energises your body so that you can respond quickly to avert disaster. A similar process happens when you are frightened. Suddenly, you become tremendously alert, your muscles tense, readying you to spring into action: to fight or to flee.

Hormones are produced in several different regions of the body. These hormone 'factories' make a variety of hormones, each of which regulates different bodily processes, as outlined in *Table 2.1* (previous page). Let us examine the most significant of these hormones.

In charge of the endocrine system is the **hypothalamus**, a bundle of small nuclei that reside at the base of the brain. The hypothalamus is an important relay station among other parts of the brain, the endocrine system, and the central nervous system. Specialised cells in the hypothalamus receive messages from other brain cells commanding it to release a number of different hormones to the pituitary gland, where they either stimulate or inhibit the release of other hormones.

The **pituitary gland** is often regarded as the most important gland, because it secretes about ten different kinds of hormones that influence the secretions of all the other endocrine glands as well as a hormone that influences growth. The absence of this growth hormone results in dwarfism; its excess results in gigantic growth. In males, pituitary secretions activate the testes to secrete testosterone, which stimulates production of sperm. The pituitary gland is also involved in the development of male secondary sexual characteristics, such as facial hair, voice changes and physical maturation. Testosterone may even increase aggression and sexual desire. In females, a pituitary hormone stimulates production of oestrogen, which is essential to the hormonal chain reaction that triggers the release of ova from a female's ovaries, making her fertile. Certain birth-control pills work by blocking the mechanism in the pituitary gland that controls this hormone flow, thus preventing the ova from being fertilised.

Neuronal Control of Behaviour and Internal Processes

The body's other communication system, the nervous system, is more extensive and acts more quickly than the endocrine system. The nervous system is composed of billions of highly specialised nerve cells, or neurons, that are organised either into densely packed clusters called nuclei or into pathways (some of which are very extensive) called nerve fibres. The major task of the nuclei is to process information; the chief job of nerve fibres is to relay information to and from these nuclei. We have already discussed these nuclei in detail, they make up the brain. To a lesser degree, nuclei are found outside the brain, mainly along the spinal cord where they receive and relay sensory and motor information to and from the brain.

The brain and the nerve fibres that are found throughout the body constitute the nervous system. The nervous system is subdivided into two major

FIGURE 2.10	PHYSICAL ORGANISATIONS OF THE HUMAN NERVOUS SYSTEM

The sensory and motor nerve fibres that constitute the peripheral nervous system are linked to the brain by the spinal cord.

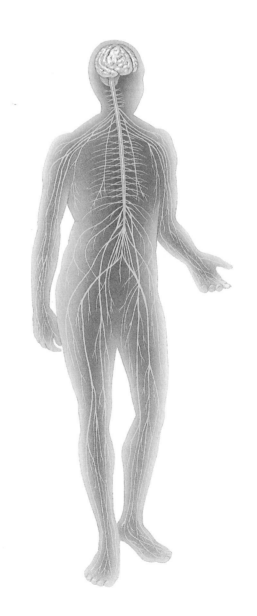

FIGURE 2.11   HIERARCHICAL ORGANISATION OF THE HUMAN NERVOUS SYSTEM

The central nervous system is composed of the brain and the spinal cord; the peripheral nervous system is divided according to function; the somatic nervous system controls voluntary actions; and the autonomic nervous system regulates internal processes. The autonomic nervous system is subdivided into two systems: the sympathetic nervous system governs behaviour in emergency situations, and the parasympathetic nervous system regulates behaviour and internal processes in routine circumstances.

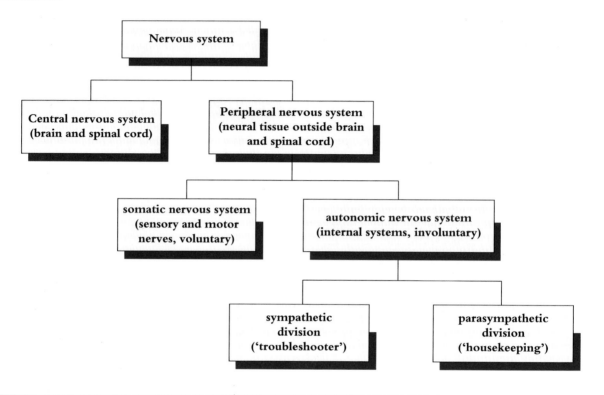

divisions: the **central nervous system (CNS)** and the **peripheral nervous system (PNS)**. The CNS is composed of all the neurons in the brain and spinal cord; the PNS is made up of all the neurons forming the nerve fibres that connect the CNS to the body. *Figures 2.10* (previous page) and *2.12* (next page) show the relationship of the CNS to the PNS.

The job of the CNS is to integrate and coordinate all bodily functions, process all incoming neural messages, and send out commands to different parts of the body, depending upon the environmental situation. The CNS sends and receives neural messages through the spinal cord, a mainline of neurons that connects the brain to the PNS. The mainline itself is housed in a hollow portion of the spinal cord called the **spinal column**. Spinal nerves branch out from the spinal cord between each pair of vertebrae in the spinal column, eventually connecting with sensory receptors, muscles and glands throughout the body. The spinal cord also coordinates the activity of the left and right sides of the body and is responsible for simple reflexes that do not involve the brain. For example, an organism whose spinal

cord has been severed from its brain can still withdraw its limb from a painful stimulus. Though normally the brain is notified of such action, the organism can complete the action without dir-ections from above. Damage to the nerves of the spinal cord can result in paralysis of the legs or trunk, as seen in paraplegic individuals. The extent of paralysis depends on how high up on the spinal cord the damage occurred.

Despite its commanding position, the CNS is isolated from any direct contact with the outside world. It is the role of the PNS to provide the CNS with information from sensory receptors, such as those found in the eyes and ears, and to relay commands from the brain to the body's organs and muscles. The PNS is actually composed of two subdivisions of nerve fibres (see *Figure 2.11*). The **somatic nervous system** regulates the actions of the body's skeletal muscles. For example, right now I am typing these words on a microcomputer. Movement of my fingers over the keyboard is managed by my somatic nervous system. As I think about what it is that I want to say, my brain sends commands to my fingers to press certain keys. Simultaneously, the

FIGURE 2.12 THE AUTONOMIC NERVOUS SYSTEM

The parasympathetic nervous system, which regulates day-to-day internal processes and behaviour, is shown on the left. The sympathetic nervous system, which regulates internal processes and behaviour in stressful situations, is shown on the right. Note that on their way to and from the spinal cord, the nerve fibres of the sympathetic nervous system innervate, or make connections with ganglia, specialised clusters of neuron chains.

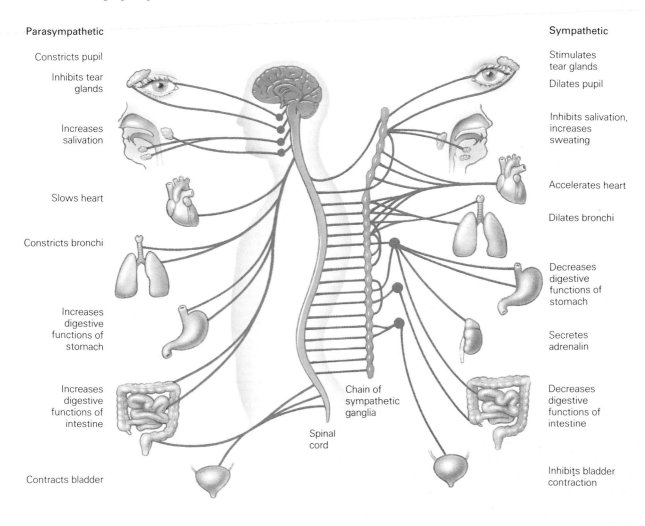

fingers send feedback about their position and movement to the brain. When I strike the wrong key the somatic nervous system informs the brain, which then issues the necessary correction and, in a fraction of a second, I delete the mistake and hit the right key.

The other subdivision of the PNS is the **autonomic nervous system** (ANS), which sustains basic life processes. This system is on the job 24 hours a day, regulating bodily processes that we usually do not consciously control, such as respiration, digestion and arousal. It must work even when the individual is asleep and it also sustains life processes during anaesthesia and prolonged coma states. The autonomic nervous system deals with survival matters of two kinds: those involving threats to the organism and those involving bodily maintenance. To accomplish these tasks, the autonomic nervous system is further subdivided into the sympathetic and **parasympathetic nervous system** (see *Figure 2.11*). These divisions essentially work together 'in opposition' to accomplish their tasks. The sympathetic division governs responses to emergency situations, when large amounts of energy must be mobilised and behaviour initiated with split-second timing. The parasympathetic division monitors the routine operation of the body's internal functions. The sympathetic division can be regarded as a troubleshooter; in an emergency or stressful situation, it arouses the brain structures for 'fight or flight'. Digestion stops, blood flows away from internal organs to the muscles, oxygen transfer increases, heart rate increases and the endocrine system is stimulated to facilitate motor responses. After the danger is over, the parasympathetic division takes charge to decelerate these processes, and the individual begins to calm down. Digestion resumes, heartbeat slows, and breathing is relaxed. Basically, the parasympathetic division carries out the body's non-emergency housekeeping chores, such as elimination of bodily wastes, protection of the visual system (through tears and pupil constriction) and long-term conservation of body energy. The separate duties of the sympathetic and parasympathetic nervous systems are illustrated in *Figure 2.12* (previous page).

INTERIM SUMMARY

Both the endocrine system and the nervous system function as communications systems. The endocrine system is a slow-acting system of glands that produce and secrete chemical substances called hormones into the blood stream. Hormones are involved in body growth, development of primary and secondary sexual characteristics, metabolism, digestion and arousal. The endocrine system is controlled by the hypothalamus, which receives messages from higher-order brain centres regarding when and how to stimulate the pituitary gland. The pituitary gland then secretes the appropriate hormone, which in turn stimulates one or more of the other endocrine glands into operation. Two of the more important hormones are oestrogen, which triggers the release of ova, and testosterone, which stimulates production of sperm.

The nervous system is composed of billions of neurons and is divided into two major subdivisions: the CNS, which is composed of the brain and spinal cord, and the PNS, which is composed of all the neurons connecting the CNS to the body. The PNS is further divided into two subdivisions: the somatic nervous system, which regulates the body's skeletal muscles, and the autonomic nervous system, which governs basic life-support processes. The sympathetic division of the autonomic nervous system springs into action during times of stress and emergency and the parasympathetic division operates under more routine circumstances.

◼ THE NERVOUS SYSTEM IN ACTION

To interact with the world, we depend more on the nervous system than we do on the endocrine system. Although both systems are critical to our ability to live the way we do, the nervous system allows us to sense and to respond to the outside world. For that reason, one of the major goals of early physiologists was to understand better how the nervous system operates. In large measure, modern neuroscientists have accomplished this goal, although they continue to work on finding smaller pieces of the puzzle. Our objective in this section is to analyse and understand how all the information available to our senses is ultimately communicated throughout our body and brain by nerve impulses. We begin by discussing the properties of the basic unit of the nervous system, the neuron.

◼ The Neuron

A neuron is a cell specialised to receive, process, and/or transmit information to other cells within the body. Neurons vary in shape, size, chemical composition and function – over 200 different types have been identified in mammalian brains – but all neurons have the same basic structure (see *Figure 2.13*, next page).

At birth, or shortly afterward, your brain will have all the neurons it is ever going to have. Unlike the brains of fish, amphibians and birds, in which new neurons appear even in adults, the human brain has a fixed number of neurons. This stable set of neurons may be essential for the continuity of learning and memory over a long lifetime (Rakic, 1985). However, human neurons die in astonishing numbers, somewhere in the neighbourhood of 10,000 each and every day of your life! Fortunately, because we start out with so many neurons, we will lose less than two per cent of our original supply in 70 years. The deteriorated brain functioning that sometimes occurs in old age is usually not a result of the decrease in the number of neurons but an effect of destructive changes within the neurons themselves or in the chemical substances that carry signals between neurons.

Understanding how individual neurons function is important because it has the potential for opening up new directions in the use of therapeutic drugs and genetic engineering to control nerve transmission. With such new directions usually comes the betterment of human lives.

Neurons typically take in information at one end and send out messages from the other. The part of the cell that receives incoming signals is a set of branched fibres called **dendrites**, which extend outward from the cell body. The basic job of the dendrites is to receive stimulation from other neurons or sense receptors. The **cell body**, or soma, contains the nucleus of the cell and the **cytoplasm** that sustains its life. The soma integrates information about the stimulation received from the dendrites (or in some cases received directly from another neuron) and passes

FIGURE 2.13 — TWO DIFFERENT KINDS OF NEURONS

Note the differences in shape and dendritic branching.

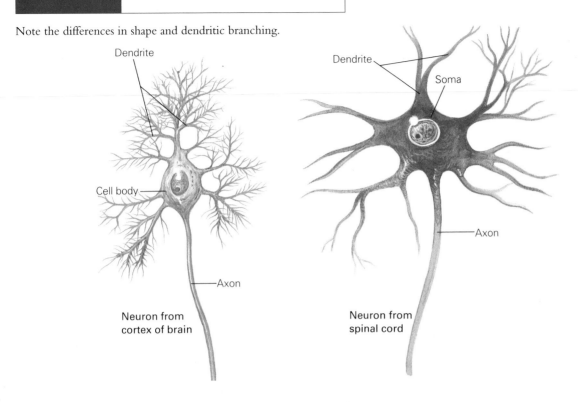

Neuron from cortex of brain

Neuron from spinal cord

FIGURE 2.14 — THE MAJOR STRUCTURES OF THE NEURON

The neuron receives nerve impulses through its dendrites. It then sends the nerve impulses through its axon to the terminal buttons where neurotransmitters are released to stimulate other neurons.

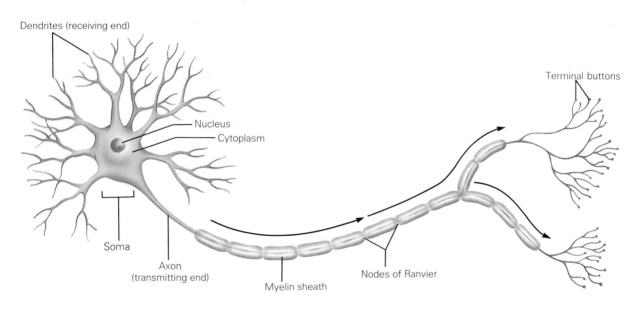

it on to a single, extended fibre, the **axon**. In turn, the axon conducts this information along its length, which, in the spinal cord, can be a couple of metres long and in the brain, less than a millimetre. At the other end of axons are swollen, bulb-like structures called **terminal buttons** through which the neuron is able to stimulate nearby glands, muscles or other neurons. Neurons transmit information in only one direction: from the dendrites through the soma to the axon to the terminal buttons. This is known as the *law of forward conduction* (see *Figure 2.14*, previous page).

In general, there are three major classes of neurons. **Sensory neurons**, also called afferent neurons, carry messages from sense-receptor cells toward the central nervous system. **Receptor cells** are highly specialised cells that are sensitive to light, sound and body position. **Motor neurons**, also called efferent neurons, carry messages away from the central nervous system toward the muscles and glands. Sensory neurons rarely communicate directly with motor neurons, however. Most of the billions of neurons in the brain are **interneurons**, which relay messages from sensory neurons to other interneurons or to motor neurons. For every motor neuron in the body there are as many as 5,000 interneurons in the great intermediate network that forms the computational system of the brain (Nauta & Feirtag, 1979).

As an example of how these three kinds of neurons work together, consider the pain-withdrawal reflex (see *Figure 2.15*). When pain receptors near the skin's surface are stimulated by a sharp object, they send messages via sensory neurons to an interneuron in the spinal cord. The interneuron responds by stimulating motor neurons, which, in turn, excite muscles in the appropriate area of the body to pull away from the pain-producing object. It is only after this sequence of neuronal events has taken place and the body has been moved away from the stimulating object, that the brain is informed of the situation. In cases such as this, where survival depends on swift

FIGURE 2.15	THE PAIN-WITHDRAWAL REFLEX

The pain-withdrawal reflex shown here involves only three neurons: a sensory neuron, a motor neuron, and an interneuron.

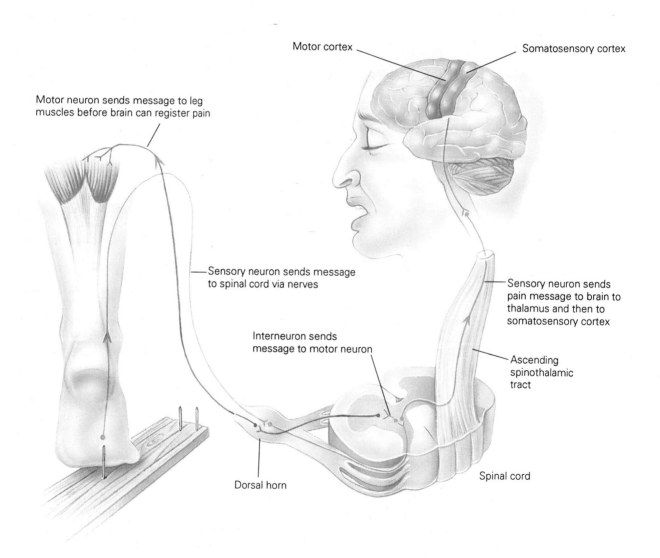

action, our sensation and subsequent perception of pain often occurs after we have physically responded to the danger. Of course, then the information from the incident is stored in the brain's memory system so that the next time we avoid the potentially dangerous object altogether before it can begin to hurt us.

Interspersed among the brain's vast web of neurons are about ten times as many **glial cells** (glia). The word glia is derived from the Greek word for glue, which gives a hint of one of the major duties performed by these cells: they bind neurons to each other (although not so close that they actually touch). In vertebrates, glial cells also have several other important functions. Their first function is garbage removal. When neurons are damaged and die, glial cells in the area multiply and clean up the cellular junk left behind; they can also take up excess chemical substances in the gaps between neurons. Their second function is insulation. Glial cells form an insulating cover, called a *myelin sheath*, around some types of axons. This fatty insulation greatly increases the speed of nerve signal conduction. The third function of glial cells is to prevent poisonous substances in the blood from reaching the delicate cells of the brain. Specialised glial cells, called *astrocytes*, make up a blood-brain barrier, forming a continuous envelope of fatty material around the blood vessels in the brain. Substances that are not soluble in fat do not dissolve through this barrier and since many poisons and other harmful substances are not fat soluble, they cannot penetrate the barrier to reach the brain.

■ Graded and Action Potentials

How is the violent discharge of an electric eel when disturbed by an intruder similar to the gentle lullaby of a mother putting her baby to sleep? Both are the outcomes of the same kind of electrochemical signals used by the nervous system to process and transmit information. Both electrical messages involve changes in the electrical activity of a single neuron. These changes are caused by the flow of electrically-charged particles, called **ions**, through the neuron's membrane, a thin 'skin' separating the cell's internal and external environments.

Think of a nerve fibre as macaroni parcels, filled with salt water and proteins, floating in a salty soup. The soup and the fluid in the macaroni both contain ions – atoms of sodium (NA), chloride (CL), calcium (CA) and potassium (K) – that have either positive or negative charges. The membrane, or the surface of the macaroni, plays a critical role in keeping the ingredients of the two fluids apart or letting them mix a little. In other words, the membrane determines the polarity of the macaroni's (or cell's) fluid, or its electrical state in relation to the soup (or outside fluid). When a cell is inactive, or in a polarised state, there are about ten times as many potassium ions inside as there are sodium outside. (Think of the ions being kept 'poles apart'.) Even in a polarised state, the fluid inside a neuron has a slightly negative voltage relative to the fluid outside. In a polarised or resting state, the neuron is simply prepared to respond; whether it actually does or not depends upon the activity of its neighbouring neurons. It is similar to a battery ready to be used.

The membrane is not a perfect barrier; it is semipermeable. It 'leaks' a little, allowing some sodium ions to slip in while some potassium ions slip out. To correct for this, nature has provided transport mechanisms within the membrane that pump out sodium and pump in potassium. The nervous system uses a great deal of energy to maintain this polarised state of readiness for every neuron in the body (Kalat, 1984).

When a neuron is stimulated, it becomes less negatively charged, or depolarised, and starts producing its own electrical signals. In a depolarised state, ions flow in and out of the neuron through the membrane. All neural messages in all organisms are initiated by this process of ion flow; it is the basis of all sensation, experience, thought and action. The neuron's universal language consists of two basic types of electrical signal: **graded potentials** and **action potentials**.

The graded potential

A graded potential is produced by the external physical stimulation of the dendrite or soma and varies in size according to the magnitude of the stimulus. The more intense the stimulation, the larger the graded potential. For example, in sensory receptors, such as the retina of the eye, light is converted or transduced into a graded potential (often called a receptor potential). The size of this potential will depend upon how intense or bright the light is. Graded potentials are only useful as short-term, local signals within the neuron, usually between the dendrite and axon, because they weaken over long distances. Graded potentials can only have a significant influence on overall nervous system activity when they are of sufficient strength to cause the cell membrane to depolarise suddenly to a certain critical level or threshold (see *Figure 2.16*, next page).

The action potential

When one neuron stimulates another to the point that its threshold is met or exceeded, a dramatic event

FIGURE 2.16	GRADED ACTION POTENTIALS

A graded action potential is caused when one neuron stimulates the dendrite or soma of another neuron. The graded potential increases with the intensity of the stimulation. Because they weaken over distance, graded potentials serve only as localised signals within the neuron, usually between the dendrite and the axon. However, if the graded potential is of sufficient intensity when it reaches the axon, the cell membrane will depolarise and give rise to an action potential. The action potential is propagated along the axon in an all-or-nothing fashion; once its threshold is met, it will travel at a constant speed down the axon regardless of the intensity of the originating stimulus. Its final destination is the terminal button where it stimulates release of chemical messengers called neurotransmitters.

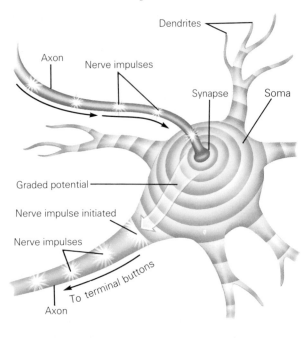

takes place: the nerve impulse or action potential is generated along the axon. The action potential is caused by the chemical and electrical changes that occur within the neuron when its state is changed from being polarised (slightly negative) to being depolarised (slightly positive). In other words, when a neuron is depolarised, the fluid inside becomes more positively charged relative to that outside the neuron (see *Figure 2.17*).

Unlike the graded potential, whose intensity is directly proportional to the intensity of the stimulus, the action potential is unaffected by properties of the stimulus. The action potential is said to obey the all-or-none law: the speed with which the action potential travels along the axon is unaffected by increases in the size or intensity of stimulation beyond the threshold level. Once the threshold level is reached by the incoming, graded potential, a uniform

and complete action potential is generated. If the threshold is not reached, no action potential happens. In this way, propagation of an action potential along the axon is analogous to flushing a toilet: no matter how hard you press the lever beyond some minimal level, the speed of the water into the toilet bowl and down the drain is the same.

A second important characteristic of the action potential is that its speed or size will not decline with the length of the axon: the action potential just keeps moving along at the same speed until it reaches its final destination, the terminal buttons. In this sense, the action potential is said to be **self-propagating**; once started, it needs no outside stimulation to keep itself moving. It is similar to a lit fuse on a firework.

A third characteristic of the action potential is actually a feature of the neuron in which the action potential is occurring. Just after an action potential is finished and the neuron is attempting to return to its polarised state, further stimulation, no matter how intense, cannot cause another action potential to be generated (see *Figure 2.17*). This period of total unresponsiveness lasts only 0.5 to 2 milliseconds and is called the *absolute refractory period*. Have you ever tried to flush the toilet while it is filling back up with water? There must be a critical level of water for the toilet to flush again. Similarly, in order for a neuron to be able to generate another action potential, it must 'reset' itself and await stimulation beyond its threshold. However, when the neuron is in the

FIGURE 2.17	TIMETABLE FOR ELECTRICAL CHANGES IN THE NEURON DURING AN ACTION POTENTIAL

Sodium ions entering the neuron cause its electrical potential to change from slightly negative during its polarised or resting state to slightly positive during depolarisation. Once the neuron is depolarised, it enters a brief refractory period during which further stimulation will not produce another action potential. Another action potential can occur only after the ionic balance between the inside and the outside of the cell is restored.

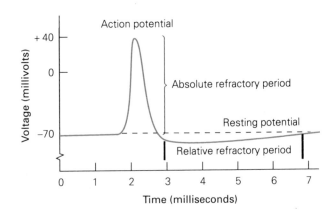

process of returning to its polarised state, very strong stimulation will cause it to fire again. This *relative refractory period* lasts for a few milliseconds before the threshold returns to normal.

How can this uniform, all-or-none, action potential transmit information about differences in intensity of stimulation? A more intense stimulus does two things to make its presence known to the nervous system. First, it triggers more frequent action potentials in each neuron (faster rate). Second, it also triggers action potentials in more neurons (greater quantity). Somewhere in the brain this information about rate and quantity is combined and encoded, resulting in an appropriate reaction to an ever-varying outer world.

Different neurons conduct action potentials along their axons at different speeds; the fastest have signals that move at the rate of 200 metres per second, the slowest plod along at 10 centimetres per second (Bullock *et al*, 1977). The axons of the faster neurons are covered with a myelin sheath, making this part of the neuron resemble long beads on a string. The tiny breaks between the beads are called *nodes of Ranvier* (see *Figure 2.14*). In neurons having myelinated axons, the action potential literally skips along from one node to the next. Damage to the myelin sheath throws off the delicate timing of the action potential and causes serious problems. Multiple sclerosis (MS) is a devastating disorder caused by deterioration of the myelin sheath. It is characterised by double vision, tremors and eventually paralysis. In MS, specialised cells from the body's immune system actually attack myelinated neurons, exposing the axon and disrupting normal synaptic transmission (Joyce, 1953 Fall).

The key to understanding how the action potential is generated along the axon is understanding the properties of the neuron's cell membrane. All electrical signalling in the nervous system involves the flow of ions through ion channels in the cell membrane (Catterall, 1984; Hille, 1984). Ion channels are excitable portions of the cell membrane that produce and change electrical signals. They do so by opening or closing pores, tiny tunnels in the membrane, which selectively permit certain ions to flow in and out. Three positively charged ions (sodium, potassium and calcium) and one negatively charged ion (chloride), appear to be the ones moving through these channels. The signal-processing property of neurons is determined by how many ion channels are packed into a given area in each part of the cell and the type of ion involved.

The high density of sodium channels in the part of the axon nearest the soma reduces the threshold for generating the action potential and typically starts the impulse on its way. The way is slow if the axon is not myelinated, because there are relatively few sodium channels operating; but it becomes speedy with myelinated axons because of their great density of sodium channels. The most sodium channels are found at the nodes of Ranvier where the electrical signals literally jump from node to node. Why? Because the great concentration of sodium channels at these nodes requires fewer ions to move into the cell while moving the action potential down the axon. Thus the action potential can buzz along with little time lost in ion exchange or cost in metabolic energy.

While sodium is rushing into the neuron, potassium is rushing out through its own channels. As a result, the inside of the neuron becomes positive relative to the outside, meaning the neuron has become fully depolarised. How does the neuron return to its original resting state of polarisation? The microscopic transport mechanisms embedded in the cell membrane work to re-establish ionic equilibrium by pumping sodium out of the cell, and potassium and chloride back into the cell. (These are the same transport mechanisms or pumps that also help the neuron maintain its resting state.)

▣ Synaptic Transmission

There is more to the action potential than its leapfrogging journey down the axon. When this train of impulses finally arrives at the station, there is no direct connection to the next destination – no two neurons ever touch. So, somehow, there must be an indirect connection with the next impulse train. Action potentials set off the activity at a **synapse**, a junction of two or more neurons. Once the action potential reaches the terminus station, it sets in motion a series of truly remarkable events called **synaptic transmission**, which is the relaying of information from one neuron to another across the synaptic gap (see *Figure 2.18*, next page). Four basic steps are involved in synaptic transmission. First, upon arriving at the terminal station the action potential causes small round packets called *synaptic vesicles* to move toward and affix themselves to the interior membrane of the terminal button. The action potential also opens calcium ion channels that admit positive ions into the terminal button. Inside each vesicle are **neurotransmitters**, biochemical substances whose function is to stimulate other neurons. Second, synaptic vesicles rupture, spilling the neurotransmitters into the synaptic cleft, the tiny space separating the *presynaptic membrane* (the terminal button of the sending neuron) from the *postsynaptic membrane* (the surface of a dendrite or soma of a receiving neuron). Researchers believe that the influx of positive ions through the calcium channels causes the rupture of the synaptic vesicles and the release of whatever neurotransmitters they contain (Zucker & Lando,

FIGURE 2.18 SYNAPTIC TRANSMISSION

The action potential in the presynaptic neuron causes neurotransmitters to be released into the synaptic gap. Once across the gap, they stimulate receptor molecules embedded in the membrane of the postsynaptic neuron.

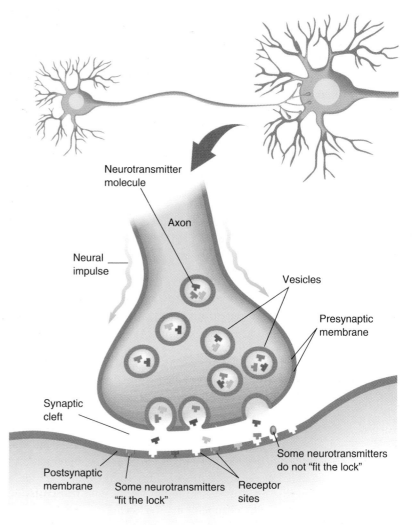

1986). Third, neurotransmitters are dispersed rapidly across the synaptic cleft to the *postsynaptic membrane*. And fourth, the neurotransmitters attach themselves to receptor molecules embedded in the postsynaptic membrane.

The neurotransmitters will bind themselves to the receptor molecules under only two conditions. First, no other neurotransmitters or other chemical substances must be attached to the receptor molecule. Second, the shape of the neurotransmitter must match the shape of the receptor molecule, as precisely as a key fits into a keyhole. If neither condition is met, the neurotransmitter will not attach itself to the receptor molecule, and therefore it will not be able to stimulate the postsynaptic membrane. If the neurotransmitter does become attached to the receptor molecule, then it may initiate a graded potential, and the message it contains is passed on to the next synaptic gap and so on. Once the neurotransmitter has completed its job, it detaches itself from the receptor molecule and drifts back into the synaptic gap. There it is either decomposed through enzymatic action or reabsorbed into the presynaptic terminal button for reuse with the next graded potential.

So far we have a system for generating action, but what about inaction? How is some of our behaviour inhibited, prevented from being activated? Synapses come in two types. In excitatory synapses, the binding of the neurotransmitter to receptor molecules causes the postsynaptic neuron to generate action potentials or generate them at a higher rate. In inhibitory synapses, the binding of the neurotransmitter to receptor molecules causes the postsynaptic neuron not to generate action potentials or to generate them at lower rates. Interestingly, it is not the neurotransmitter that determines whether the postsynaptic neuron will be excited or inhibited. Instead, it is the nature of the receptor molecule that determines what the effect will be. The same neurotransmitter may be excitatory at one synapse but inhibitory at another, depending on whether the receptor excites or inhibits nerve signals.

A single neuron may have synapses with thousands of other neurons. Whether that postsynaptic neuron will generate action potentials and at what rate it will generate them is determined by the sum of all the excitatory and inhibitory effects acting on it. If the majority of its synapses are excitatory, then it will generate action potentials when stimulated. If the majority of its synapses are inhibitory, then it will not generate action potentials.

You may be wondering why we have taken you so deep into the caverns of the nervous system. After all, this is a psychology course, and psychology is supposed to be about behaviour, thinking and emotion. Synapses, though, are the biological medium in which all of these activities occur. If you change the normal activity of the synapse, then you change how people behave, how they think and how they feel. Understanding the functioning of the synapse has led to tremendous advances in our understanding of learning and memory, emotion, psychological disorders, drug addiction and, in general, of biochemical processes involved in mental health. There is good reason to believe that the synapse is the space where evolution has etched one of its most significant contributions to humanity (Rose, 1973).

■ Neurotransmitters and their Functions

More than 60 different chemical substances are known or suspected to function as neurotransmitters in the brain. To qualify as a neurotransmitter, a substance must meet a set of technical criteria. It must be manufactured in the presynaptic terminal button and must be released when an action potential reaches that terminal. Its presence in the synaptic cleft must produce a biological response in the postsynaptic membrane and, if its release is prevented, no

subsequent responses can occur. Six substances that qualify as neurotransmitters have been studied intensely, largely because they have been found to play such an important role in the daily functioning of the brain. These six are acetylcholine, GABA, dopamine, noradrenalin (norepinephrine), serotonin and endorphins.

Acetylcholine is found in both the central and peripheral nervous systems. In the brain, it appears to be involved with memory processes. Memory loss among patients suffering from Alzheimer's disease, a degenerative disease that is increasingly common among older persons, is believed to be caused by the deterioration of neurons that secrete acetylcholine. Acetylcholine is also excitatory at junctions between nerves and muscles, where it causes muscles to contract. A number of toxins affect the synaptic actions of acetylcholine. For example, botulinum toxin, which is often found in food that has been preserved incorrectly, poisons an individual by preventing release of acetylcholine in the respiratory system. This poisoning, known as botulism, can cause death by suffocation. Curare, a poison Amazon Indians use on the tips of their blowgun darts, produces a similar effect, paralysing lung muscles.

GABA (gamma-amino butyric acid) is affected by a variety of depressants, chemical compounds that reduce central nervous system activity. For example, barbiturates are believed to bind to receptor molecules sensitive to GABA, causing sedation. This effect implies that low levels of GABA may be responsible for anxiety (Paul *et al*, 1986).

The catecholamines are a class of chemical substances that include two important neurotransmitters, *dopamine* and *noradrenaline* (norepinephrine). Both have been shown to play prominent roles in psychological disorders, such as schizophrenia and mood disturbances. Noradrenaline appears to be involved in some forms of depression. Drugs that increase brain levels of this neurotransmitter also elevate mood and relieve depression. Higher than normal levels of dopamine have been found in persons with schizophrenia. As you might expect, one way to treat people with this disorder is to give them a drug that decreases brain levels of dopamine. In the early days of drug therapy, an interesting but unfortunate problem arose: high doses of the drug used to treat schizophrenia produced Parkinson's disease-like symptoms, involving disruption of motor functioning and tardive dyskinesia: involuntary, stereotyped and rhythmic movements of the upper body and face. Parkinson's disease is caused by the deterioration of neurons that manufacture most of the brain's dopamine. This important finding led to research that improved drug therapy for schizophrenics and to research that focused on drugs that could be used in the treatment of Parkinson's disease.

The last 30 years have witnessed an explosion of worldwide drug use and abuse. Drug addiction, which we will read about in the next chapter, is a growing social and economic problem: tremendous personal losses are incurred by abusers, addicts and their families. Because of the criminal activity associated with the need to support expensive drug habits, addiction is putting a severe strain on the legal and punitive systems as well as on our health care system. An interest in reducing drug addiction has led to increased research aimed at understanding its biological components, at discovering the specific brain systems responsible for the variety of pleasurable effects and negative withdrawal effects experienced by drug users. Much of the research to date has been conducted on those drugs that are being abused most widely, for example, cocaine.

Over the past ten years, cocaine addiction has evolved in the United States of America from a very rare problem to one of its greatest national health concerns. One report estimates that one in two adults between the ages of 25 and 30 – as many as 25 million Americans – have tried cocaine. Five to ten million people there use cocaine on a monthly basis, with as many as three million cocaine abusers estimated to be in need of treatment, six times the number of heroin addicts (Gawin, 1991; Ray & Ksir, 1987). In Great Britain, accounts were given during the 1980s of relatively frequent cocaine use among high-earning workers in stressful occupations, such a pattern of use being concentrated in London and the south-east of England. By the spring of 1990, however, cocaine in an alternative, smokeable form –

'crack' – had reportedly reached the status of a 'standard commodity' on the covert drug markets of Britain's major cities, with recent surveys estimating cocaine over-use rates at 2–3 per cent of young adults (Institute for the Study of Dependence, 1992). As yet in the UK, neither cocaine nor crack has found a place in wider youth culture.

Whilst cocaine has been around for a fairly long time, crack cocaine is a comparatively new variation of the drug. Crack is an incredibly powerful and dangerous central nervous system stimulant. It is made by mixing cocaine with water and baking soda. When the mixture dries, it forms a rock or crystal that may be smoked. Many people prefer crack to regular cocaine because it is cheaper and more easily available, and because smoking cocaine provides a much more rapid and powerful high than snorting cocaine. This is because the surface area of the lungs is larger than that of the mucus

membranes of the nose, and so it permits more of the drug to enter the central nervous system. Intravenous injection of cocaine produces even more powerful effects, but is not as popular because many people are afraid of needles, infections and AIDS transmission.

Cocaine is one of the most powerful reinforcers known in humans and animals. Experimental animals will press a lever thousands of times for a single dose of cocaine, and they will work incessantly to obtain continuous, rapid intravenous administration of the drug for several weeks, until they die (Johanson & Fischman, 1989). In humans, cocaine produces feelings of profound euphoria, well-being and alertness. It magnifies the intensity of almost all known pleasures except for those associated with eating, which, in fact, are diminished. Cocaine and crack users find the effects of the drug so rewarding that they use it more and more and eventually may become physiologically addicted to it. Chronic drug addiction is maintained in part by the psychological symptoms of drug withdrawal, unpleasant mood states and cravings for drug euphoria. The earlier distinction between psychological and physiological addiction and dependence has been replaced by the World Health Organization with the term 'neuroadaptation' to indicate the more typical combination of both consequences of chronic drug use.

About ten to 15 per cent of initial cocaine users become abusers. We do not yet know why some users progress to addiction and others stop experimenting with cocaine. However, once addiction develops, the typical pattern is high-dose, long-duration binging, with repeated use of cocaine every 10 to 30 minutes for 4 to 24 hours until the supply runs out. Binges, which average from one to seven a week, are followed by several days of abstinence. Addicts report that, during binges, everything in life, except the cocaine euphoria, loses its significance – including one's own survival.

Abstaining from cocaine results in a three-phase pattern: an initial crash of mood and energy, intense craving, depression and anxiety; a withdrawal phase a few days later when all normal pleasurable experiences are diminished; and an extinction phase when craving is gradually reduced as the learned associations of cues conditioned to taking cocaine are weakened. Between 30 and 90 per cent of cocaine abusers who remain in drug treatment programmes cease cocaine use. Those programmes usually combine psychotherapy with pharmacological interventions designed to break the binging cycles and to prevent relapse.

How can cocaine have such powerful control over otherwise rational individuals? The answer is found in the way the drug interacts with the central nervous system. Cocaine (and amphetamines) produces pleasure or reward by increasing the activity of certain brain neurotransmitters. Specifically, after being released at the synapse, cocaine inhibits the re-uptake of dopamine and the neurotransmitters noradrenalin and serotonin. This means that nerve-

signal activity continues, causing continual, heightened activity among the neurons meeting at these synapses (Ritz *et al*, 1987). The brain experiences or interprets this increased activity as pleasurable and any actions that led to it are reinforced. Ultimately, then, the lure of cocaine resides in the action at the synapse. Long-term cocaine abuse generates neurophysiological changes in brain systems that regulate the psychological processes associated with feelings of pleasure. Cocaine works on the human mind by changing the pattern of synaptic transmission in the brain. Research is showing that virtually all drugs exert their psychological and physiological effects by altering the activity of synapses, either by blocking or enhancing the release of certain neurotransmitters or by affecting how they bind to specific postsynaptic drug receptors in the brain. This knowledge has come from 'basic animal research, thus underscoring the value of basic research directed at unravelling the neurophysiological mysteries of human experiences of pleasure and pain' (Gawin, 1991).

Another important neurotransmitter is *serotonin*. All serotonin-producing neurons are located in the brain stem, which is involved with arousal and many autonomic processes. Hallucinogenic drugs such as LSD (lysergic acid diethylamide) appear to have profound effects on these serotonin neurons by influencing one kind of postsynaptic receptor molecule to which they attach (Jacobs, 1987). By exerting their influence on these receptors, hallucinogens produce vivid and bizarre sensory experiences, some of which last for hours.

The *endorphins* are a very interesting group of chemical substances that are usually classified as neuromodulators instead of neurotransmitters. A neuromodulator is any substance that modifies or modulates the activities of the postsynaptic neuron. Endorphins were discovered fairly recently during

experiments on morphine conducted by Candace Pert and Solomon Snyder (1973). Pert and Snyder found that morphine (which is derived from the opium poppy) binds to specific receptor sites in the brain. Quite logically, they reasoned that morphine exerts its pain-relieving and euphoric effects at these sites.

But why should morphine have its own receptor sites in our brains? In fact, the brain produces its own morphine-like substances. Researchers have discovered a number of chemical brain substances that have binding sites on receptors in the limbic system and that produce effects similar to those of morphine (Hughes *et al*, 1975). Endorphins, for example, are naturally occurring, morphine-like chemicals produced in the brain that play an important role in the control of emotional behaviours (anxiety, fear, tension, pleasure) and pain. Endorphins have been called 'nature's link between pleasure and pain', and their study is helping us understand more about the nature of drug addiction.

An interesting research paradigm has been developed for the study of the painkilling effects of chemicals suspected to be one of the endorphins. Naloxone is a drug that has only one known effect; it blocks morphine and endorphins from binding to receptors (Hopson, 1988). Any procedure that reduces pain by stimulating release of endorphins becomes ineffective when naloxone is administered. So researchers concluded that endorphins are involved in pain mediation, because when naloxone was administered, along with the medical treatment designed to reduce pain, no pain medication effects were observed. By using this 'negative method', researchers have implicated release of endorphins as being at least partially responsible for the pain-reducing effects of acupuncture (Watkins & Mayer, 1982) and even for placebos (Fields & Levine, 1984).

◼ Neural Networks

You now know how the nervous system relays information between cells, but it must do much more to generate organised and complex reactions of thought, feeling and action. The other major task of the nervous system is to process a wealth of information in an integrated fashion; this means that it must be able to handle large amounts of information coming and going simultaneously between a large number of structures. At the most basic level of processing there is the combination of graded potentials in the cell body and the modification of synaptic transmission to inhibit or increase nerve cell activity. Higher levels of information processing require neural networks, circuits or systems of neurons that are functioning together to perform tasks that individual cells cannot carry out alone. We have already looked at one of the simplest neural networks, the pain-withdrawal reflex (review *Figure 2.15*).

Neural networks follow a basic principle of nature: all life processes are organised hierarchically. In other words, simpler units, structures and processes are organised into levels of ever greater complexity, with higher ones exercising some control over lower ones. At each level of complexity there are limits and constraints that can be overcome only by a more complex system (Jacob, 1977). Just as new capabilities become available at each level from molecule to cell to organ to organism, new potential for information processing becomes available with increasingly complex neural networks.

Because neural networks in humans can be so complex, scientists often study the neural networks of simple organisms such as invertebrates. This research helps them understand the biological basis of more complex behaviour. A favourite subject of study has been the large sea slug, Aplysia, because its relatively few neurons are large enough to be identified so that they can be traced and so that 'wiring diagrams' can be worked out for given types of behaviour. For example, Aplysia's heart rate is controlled by a simple neural network involving only a few cells: some excite it to pump and others inhibit it. These cells are command cells, individual cells at a critical position to control other cells and, thus, to trigger entire behavioural sequences.

A more complex neural network is found in Aplysia's gill-withdrawal reflex, a defensive response that protects organs vital to its survival. Tactile stimuli applied to the siphon of Aplysia at first elicit gill withdrawal. With repeated stimulation, however, the gill-withdrawal response habituates: it becomes weaker and weaker until it is not made at all. Yet if a strong stimulus is now applied to another part of the body, the gill-withdrawal reflex returns. This effect is called dishabituation.

When **Eric Kandel** and his associates searched for the biochemical basis of this gill-withdrawal reflex, they found that, because of the action of a particular neural network during habituation, a smaller amount of neurotransmitter than usual was being released (Kandel, 1979). This finding is important because it identifies a specific biochemical mechanism that explains a simple learned behaviour, habituation of the gill-withdrawal reflex (see *Figure 2.19*, next page).

Eric Kandel with Aplysia

FIGURE 2.19 | NEURAL NETWORK FOR THE GILL-WITHDRAWAL REFLEX IN APLYSIA

The top left drawing shows the sea slug in its normal state. The top right drawing shows it with the gill withdrawn. The schematic diagram represents the neural network controlling the reflex. The sensory neurons involved are indicated by a single line, but each of the motor and interneurons is shown.

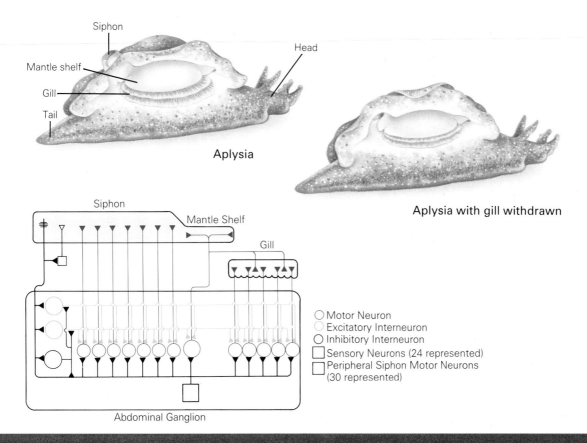

Aplysia

Aplysia with gill withdrawn

○ Motor Neuron
○ Excitatory Interneuron
○ Inhibitory Interneuron
▢ Sensory Neurons (24 represented)
▢ Peripheral Siphon Motor Neurons
(30 represented)

Abdominal Ganglion

INTERIM SUMMARY

The neuron is the basic unit of the nervous system. Its function is to receive, process and relay information to other cells, glands or muscles. Neurons relay information in only one direction: from the dendrites through the cell body to the axon to the terminal buttons. Sensory neurons receive messages from specialised receptor cells and send them toward the central nervous system. Motor neurons channel messages from the brain away from the central nervous system to muscles and glands. Interneurons relay information from sensory neurons to other interneurons or to motor neurons. Glial cells help bind neurons together; they also perform basic housekeeping duties for the cell and the synapse.

Within a neuron, information is passed from the dendrites to the soma in the form of graded potentials, which are proportional in size to the intensity of the stimulus causing them. Once the graded potential exceeds a specific threshold, an action potential, which obeys the all-or-none law, is sent along the axon to the terminal buttons. Action potentials are actually caused by the opening of special ion cells that allow sodium ions to enter the cell and potassium ions to leave. The arrival of the

action potential at the terminal buttons causes neurotransmitters to be released into the synaptic cleft. Once across the cleft, they can become lodged in the receptor molecules found in the postsynaptic membrane. The effects of these neurotransmitters – whether they excite or inhibit the postsynaptic membrane – depend upon the nature of the receptor molecule. Of the more than 60 known neurotransmitter substances, six have been particularly well researched. Each of these neurotransmitters is involved with specific functions of the brain and with behaviour. Drugs affect behaviour and cognition by influencing synaptic transmission.

Neural networks are involved in higher-level processing of information. Because they possess large but relatively few neurons, invertebrates such as Aplysia are ideal subjects for the study of simple neural networks. In his research with Aplysia, Kandel discovered all the components of a neural network that serves as the basis for a form of simple learning involving habituation of the gill-withdrawal reflex. Such findings are apt to lead to future research involving more complex neural networks and correspondingly more complex behaviour.

■ THE NERVOUS SYSTEM AND CONSCIOUS EXPERIENCE

Understanding what neuroscience has to say about the operation of the nervous system is important because the nervous system is the basis for all of our conscious experience. Anything that changes how the nervous system operates also changes normal consciousness – sensing, perceiving, thinking and behaving are all affected – usually for the worse. In the next chapter, we will focus our attention on the realm of consciousness, but first we want to inquire about some links between the biology of the brain and the nervous system and the human experience of consciousness.

We now know that the part of the brain responsible for consciousness is the cerebral cortex. Interestingly enough, each hemisphere of the cortex appears to be involved in regulating different aspects of conscious experience. How does this occur?

■ Cerebral Dominance

If you were a neuroscientist investigating the functions of the cerebral hemispheres, what might you conclude from these three clues?

1. Patients suffering strokes that paralyse the right side of their bodies often develop speech disturbances.
2. Patients suffering strokes that damage the left hemisphere often develop problems in using and understanding language. (Recall Paul Broca's early findings.)
3. The left hemisphere is usually slightly larger than the right one (Galaburda *et al*, 1978).

Though the two hemispheres appear to be physically similar, both clinical and experimental evidence clearly indicates dissimilarity in their functions. In fact, each hemisphere tends to dominate the control of different functions. Cerebral dominance is the term for the command of one cerebral hemisphere over bodily movements and speech. For the vast majority of right-handed people, language-related functions are dominated by the left hemisphere (a smaller majority of left-handers are also left-hemisphere dominant for language). This dominance explains why the left hemisphere is usually larger and why damage to it may cause language disorders. It also explains why people suffering paralysis on the right side due to a stroke may have speech problems. Right-side paralysis indicates that the damage was to the left side of the brain (the effects are contralateral, i.e. to the opposite side of the body).

Neuroscientists have found that only about five per cent of right-handers and 15 per cent of left-handers have speech controlled by the right hemisphere, while another 15 per cent of left-handers have language functions occurring in both sides of the brain. Persons with right-brain dominance in language functions are at higher risk of developing disorders interfering with language-related functions such as reading. Interestingly, males are more likely than females to be left-handed and also to have more speech-related learning disorders.

Much of our knowledge about cerebral dominance derives from observing people who have suffered brain damage on one side or whose cerebral hemispheres could not communicate with each other (see *Figure 2.20*). Patients with right-hemisphere damage are more likely to have perceptual and attentional problems, possibly including serious difficulties in spatial orientation. For example, they may feel lost in a previously familiar place or be unable to fit geometric shapes together. Patients with right-hemisphere damage in the right parietal lobe may show a syndrome in which they totally ignore the left side of their bodies and left visual fields, eating only what is on the right side of a plate of food, for example.

FIGURE 2.20	THE EFFECTS OF DAMAGE TO ONE SIDE OF THE BRAIN

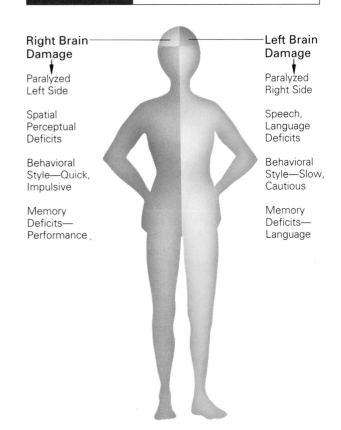

Right Brain Damage
- Paralyzed Left Side
- Spatial Perceptual Deficits
- Behavioral Style—Quick, Impulsive
- Memory Deficits—Performance

Left Brain Damage
- Paralyzed Right Side
- Speech, Language Deficits
- Behavioral Style—Slow, Cautious
- Memory Deficits—Language

FIGURE 2.21 SPECIALISATION OF THE CEREBRAL HEMISPHERES

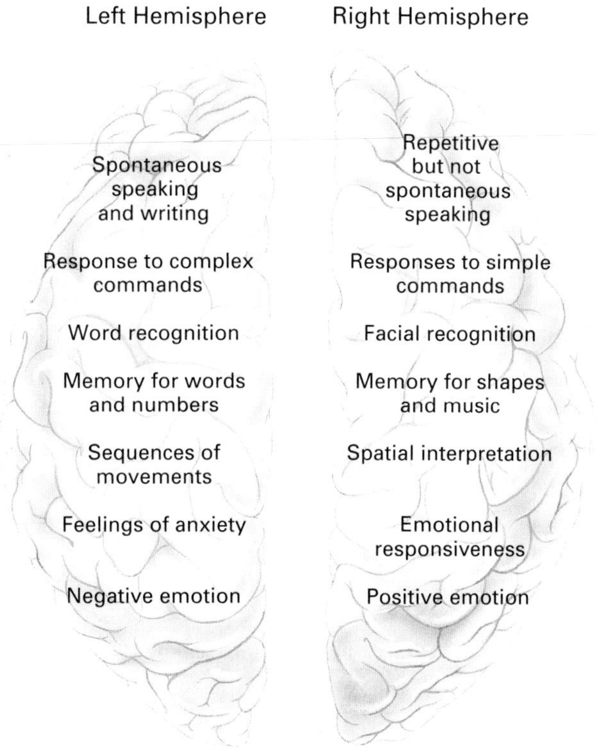

Left Hemisphere   Right Hemisphere

Spontaneous speaking and writing

Repetitive but not spontaneous speaking

Response to complex commands

Responses to simple commands

Word recognition

Facial recognition

Memory for words and numbers

Memory for shapes and music

Sequences of movements

Spatial interpretation

Feelings of anxiety

Emotional responsiveness

Negative emotion

Positive emotion

FIGURE 2.22 THE CORPUS CALLOSUM

The corpus callosum is a massive network of nerve fibres that channels information between the two hemispheres. Severing the corpus callosum impairs the communication process.

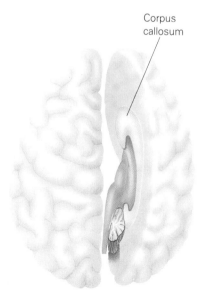

Corpus callosum

In general, studies of healthy individuals have shown that the left side of the brain is more involved in controlling verbal activities, and the right side is more important in directing visual-spatial activities. However, the two hemispheres often make different contributions to the same function. For example, both hemispheres contribute to language and memory functions, to perceptual-cognitive functions, and to emotional functions (see *Figure 2.21*). As evidence for this generalisation, consider a study in which subjects were given tasks requiring a series of split-second decisions and actions while brain-wave recordings were taken of the electrical activity of both hemispheres. Brain-wave activity rapidly bustled back and forth between the two hemispheres, depending on the kind of judgement and response being made at the moment. The researchers referred to this shifting pattern of brain-wave activity as 'shadows of thought' (Gevins *et al*, 1983).

Canadian psychologist **Doreen Kimura** has found that there are gender differences in the size of each hemisphere and in how the left hemisphere is organised to control language abilities. In females, the left hemisphere appears to be somewhat larger; in men, it is the right hemisphere that is slightly larger. This corresponds roughly to gender differences in language (controlled by the left hemisphere) and spatial abilities (controlled by the right hemisphere): women

FIGURE 2.23 THE NEURAL PATHWAYS FOR VISUAL INFORMATION

The neural pathways for visual information coming from inside portions of each eye cross from one side of the brain to the other at the corpus callosum. The pathways carrying information from the outside portions of each eye do not cross over. The ultimate destination of all visual information is the visual cortex. Severing the corpus callosum prevents information selectively displayed in the right visual field from entering the left hemisphere where it would be integrated with language formation.

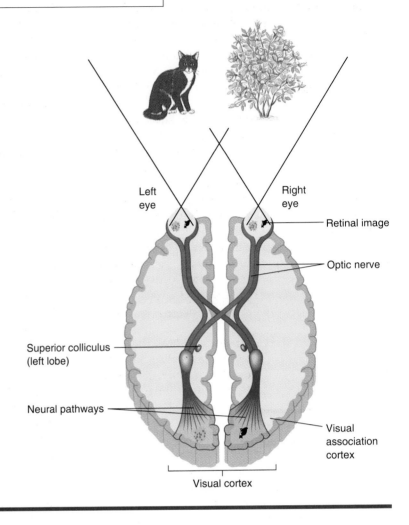

tend to outperform men on verbal tasks and men tend to do better on spatial tasks. Kimura's work with brain-damaged persons shows that women are more prone to suffer speech impairments when the front portion of the left hemisphere is damaged. For men, similar problems arise when the rear portion of the left hemisphere is damaged. Nevertheless, the magnitude and origins of these anatomical differences is still being argued over, with the biological debate firmly located within wider socio-political power struggles ongoing between the sexes (Fausto-Sterling, 1993). Further, why the left hemisphere is organised differently for men and women is not exactly clear, although Kimura believes that hormonal influences during brain development may have a role (Holloway, 1990).

Early neuroscientists concluded that left hemisphere language functions would be found only in humans. We now know that this is not the case. For example, the development of a canary's songs is controlled by the left side of its brain. Also, rats handled frequently when young were found to have stored early experiences in the right hemisphere of

their brains. As adults, these rats were less aggressive than those rats not given early handling. This effect was eliminated in animals that had the right hemispheres of their brains removed. Such research has led investigators to conclude that 'no animal species, no matter how humble, lacks cerebral dominance' (Geschwind, cited in Marks, 1981).

◼ Two Brains or One?

That we have two cerebral hemispheres, each of which appears to have different functions, raises an intriguing question: would each half of the brain be able to act as a separate conscious mind if it were separated from the other in some way? The chance to investigate this possibility has been provided by a treatment for severe epilepsy in which surgeons sever the **corpus callosum**, that bundle of about 200 million nerve fibres that transfers information back and forth between the two hemispheres (see *Figure 2.22*, page 79). The goal of this surgery is to prevent the violent electrical rhythms that accompany epileptic seizures from crossing between the hemispheres (Wilson *et al*, 1977). The operation is usually successful and a patient's subsequent behaviour in most circumstances appears normal. Patients who undergo this type of surgery are often referred to as 'split-brain patients'.

What gave researchers the idea that the two hemispheres may be able to function independently? When sensory input from the eyes, for example, is registered by the receptors, part of it is directed across to the opposite side of the brain (right eye to left hemisphere; left eye to right hemisphere). However, the information is shared by both hemispheres through the corpus callosum (see *Figure 2.23*, previous page). So when they can coordinate input from both eyes, split-brain patients can function without problems. But when given special tasks that present separate information to each eye or each hand, the effects of the split-brain surgery are quite dramatically abnormal.

The first split-brain operations on human patients were performed by neurosurgeon William Van Wagener in the early 1940s (Van Wagener & Herren, 1940). Over a decade later, researchers cut the corpus callosum in animals and then trained the animals in visual discrimination tasks with one eye covered. When the eye patch was switched to the other eye, the animals took as long to learn the tasks as they had the first time. The one side of the brain had not learned anything from the experience given to the other side (Myers & Sperry, 1958).

To test the capabilities of the separated hemispheres of epileptic patients, **Roger Sperry** (1968) and **Michael Gazzaniga** (1970) devised situations that could allow visual information to be presented separately to each hemisphere (see *Figure 2.24*).

The researchers found that the left hemisphere was superior to the right hemisphere in problems involving language or requiring logic and sequential or analytic processing of concepts. The left hemisphere could 'talk back' to the researchers while the right hemisphere could not. Communication with the right hemisphere was achieved by confronting it with manual tasks involving identification, matching, or assembly of objects, tasks that did not require the use of words. The right hemisphere turned out to be better than the left at solving problems involving spatial relationships and at pattern recognition. However, it could only add up to ten and was at about the level of a two-year-old in the use and comprehension of word combinations.

The two hemispheres also seemed to have different 'styles' for processing the same information. For example, on matching tasks, the left hemisphere matched objects analytically and verbally, by similarity in function. The right hemisphere matched things that looked alike or fitted together to form a whole pattern. Thus, when pictures of a hat, a knife and a fork were presented only to the left hemisphere, a split-brain subject asked to match the correct one with a picture of cake on a plate would report, 'You eat cake with a fork and knife'. When the test stimuli were presented to the right hemisphere, the same patient might match the hat with the cake since the items were similar in shape (Levy & Trevarthen, 1976).

FIGURE 2.24	COORDINATION BETWEEN EYE AND HAND

Coordination between eye and hand is normal if a split-brain patient uses the left hand to find and match an object that appears in the left visual field because both are registered in the right hemisphere. However, when asked to use the right hand to match an object seen in the left visual field, the patient cannot do so because sensory messages from the right hand are going to the left cerebral hemisphere, and there is no longer a connection between the two hemispheres. Here the cup is misperceived as matching the pear.

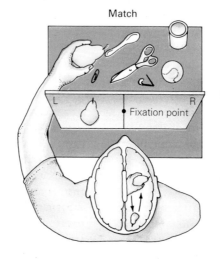

Match

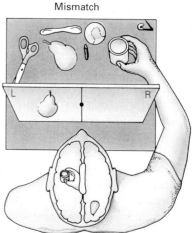

Mismatch

The brain is designed to function as a whole with a vast, precise communication network integrating both hemispheres. When the hemispheres are disconnected, the result is two separate brains and a duality of consciousness. Each hemisphere can respond independently and simultaneously when stimuli are presented separately to each side. When stimuli are presented to only one side, responses are either emotional or analytic, depending on which hemisphere gets the task of interpreting the message. Lacking language competence, however, the disconnected human right hemisphere has limited and vastly inferior visual-spatial skills as compared to the cognitive skills of the left hemisphere. The right hemisphere has failed to develop not only language facility but also a range of mental processes necessary for comprehension and understanding of both external and internal events.

Consider the following demonstration of a split-brain subject using his left-half brain to account for the activity of his left hand, which was being guided by his right-half brain.

A snow scene was presented to the right hemisphere while a picture of a chicken claw was simultaneously presented to the left hemisphere. The subject selected, from an array of objects, those that 'went with' each of the two scenes. With his right hand, the patient pointed to a chicken head; with his left hand he pointed to a shovel. The patient reported that the shovel was needed to clean out the chicken shed (rather than to shovel snow). Since the left brain was not privy to what the right brain 'saw' because of the severed corpus callosum, it needed to explain why the left hand was pointing at a shovel when the only picture the left hemisphere was aware of seeing was a chicken claw. The left brain's cognitive system provided a theory to make sense of the behaviour of different parts of its body. It appears that the dominant left hemisphere interprets the meaning of overt behaviours, emotional responses, and the experiences of the right hemisphere (Gazzaniga, 1985).

We must be cautious, however, about generalising such findings from split-brain patients into a basic view of the way that normal brains function. Does the brain function holistically as a uniform central command system, or is it organised according to specialised functions for each hemisphere? A number of investigators propose that the human mind is neither a single entity nor even a dual entity but rather a confederation of multiple *mind modules*. These 'miniminds' are each specialised to process almost automatically a specific kind of information, such as spelling or arithmetic. The input from these many separate modules is then synthesised and coordinated for action by central, executive processors (Fodor, 1983; Hinton & Anderson, 1981; Ornstein, 1986a). Some researchers and practitioners have gone beyond

theory to develop techniques designed to enhance right hemisphere functioning in the hope of boosting creativity (Buzan, 1976; Edwards, 1979).

Other neuroscientists and psychologists are sceptical about the importance and validity of hemispheric specialisation. Despite the striking fact that the human brain is not completely symmetrical, these investigators still suspect that any asymmetries are explainable in terms of specialised processes located in each hemisphere (Efron, 1990). Ideally, the debate between these two views of the brain will generate a fuller understanding of how our brain works so effectively. It should also provide insights into why the human brain sometimes fails to function rationally or wisely.

INTERIM SUMMARY

The cerebral cortex is the basis of consciousness. If it did not exist or if it were different in the slightest of ways, our conscious experience of the world would be changed. The cerebral cortex is divided into two halves or hemispheres by the corpus callosum. Although the hemispheres are physically symmetrical, their functions are not. Language, memory for words and numbers, word recognition, feelings of anxiety and negative emotions are regulated by the left hemisphere. The right hemisphere controls spatial interpretation, facial recognition, memory for shapes and music and positive emotions. The two hemispheres can be physically disconnected by surgically severing the corpus callosum. As long as stimuli are presented to the visual or auditory fields of both hemispheres, the brain will continue to work as an integrated whole. But when stimuli are selectively presented to the visual or auditory field of only one hemisphere, the other one is neither aware of that stimulation nor of the kind of cognitive activities that are taking place in the other hemisphere. (However, the left hemisphere often constructs explanations and theories to account for reactions generated by stimulating the right hemisphere.) Severing the corpus callosum, then, creates two brains, each capable of independent functions.

◼ OUR RESPONSIVE BRAIN

In this chapter, we have peeked at a small portion of the marvellous 1.36-kilogram universe that is our brain. It is one thing to recognise that the brain controls behaviour and our mental processes, but quite another to understand how it carries out all those functions that we take for granted when it functions normally and what happens when it does not. Neuroscientists are engaged in this fascinating quest to understand the interplay between brain, hormones, behaviour, experience and environment.

We began our study of the biology of behaviour with the example of how touch can have a biological effect in transforming the growth of premature infants (for more on the effects of touch, see Brown, 1984, and Gunzenhauser, 1990). This positive effect of physical stimulation on bodily growth is mediated by changes in brain functioning. The massaged babies gained more weight than the unstimulated control infants (despite similar nutritional and calorie intake), they became more physically active and their sleep patterns changed. These stimulated babies showed significantly higher catecholamine levels, releasing more of several neurotransmitters. The key to weight gain in both premature human infants and rat pups deprived of a mother's touch is stimulating the activity of a special brain enzyme (ODC) which synthesises growth proteins that are essential for normal development. Whilst maternal deprivation restricts production of the growth hormone, massaging the infants maintains the brain's release of the hormone (Field & Schanberg, 1990). So here is a clear case where the brain's functioning is modified in profound ways by external stimulation. Also, it has been found that therapeutic touch profoundly improves the mental and physical health of the elderly (Fanslow, 1984).

Much new research, across a wide range of species, is demonstrating that the brain is a dynamic system capable of changing itself – both its functions and its physical structure – in response to various kinds of stimulation and environmental challenges (Fernald, 1984; Sapolsky, 1990). We are thus led to a new perspective about the nature of the brain. In addition to the well-known behaving brain which controls behaviour, there is the responsive brain which is changed by the behaviour it generates and by environmental stimulation. This capacity for its own internal modification makes the complex human brain the most dynamic, responsive system on the planet (Rosenzweig, 1984b).

recapping main points

⊃ Evolution, Heredity and Behaviour

Species originate and change over time because of natural selection. In the evolution of humans, bipedalism and encephalisation were responsible for subsequent advances including language and culture. The basic unit of evolution is the gene. Genes determine the range of effects that environmental factors can have in influencing expression of phenotypic traits.

⊃ Brain and Behaviour

Neuroscientists use four methods to research the relation between brain and behaviour: studying brain damaged patients, producing lesions at specific brain sites, electrically stimulating and recording brain activity, and scanning the brain with computerised devices. The brain consists of three integrated layers: central core, limbic system and cerebral cortex. The central core is responsible for breathing, digestion and heart rate. The limbic system is involved in long-term memory, aggression, eating, drinking and sexual behaviour. The cerebral cortex consists of two hemispheres. Different areas of the cortex process different kinds of stimulation, form associations, or initiate movement.

⊃ The Endocrine and Nervous Systems

The endocrine system produces and secretes hormones into the bloodstream. Hormones help regulate growth, primary and secondary sexual characteristics, metabolism, digestion and arousal. The hypothalamus controls the endocrine system by stimulating the pituitary gland. The pituitary gland then secretes the appropriate hormone to stimulate one or more of the other endocrine glands.

The brain and the spinal cord make up the central nervous system (CNS). The peripheral nervous system (PNS) is composed of all neurons connecting the CNS to the body. The PNS consists of the somatic nervous system, which regulates the body's skeletal muscles and the autonomic nervous system (ANS), which regulates life-support processes. The sympathetic division of the ANS is active during stress. Its parasympathetic division operates under routine circumstances.

⊃ The Nervous System in Action

The neuron, the basic unit of the nervous system, receives, processes and relays information to other cells, glands and muscles. Neurons relay information in a fixed direction from the dendrites through the cell body to the axon and then on to the terminal buttons. Sensory neurons receive messages from specialised receptor cells and send them toward the CNS. Motor neurons channel messages away from the CNS to muscles and glands. Interneurons relay information from sensory neurons to other interneurons or motor neurons.

Information passes from dendrites to the soma in the form of graded potentials. Once the graded potential exceeds a specific threshold, an action potential is sent along the axon to the terminal buttons. Action potentials are caused when the opening of ion cells allows an exchange of positive and negative ions across the cell membrane. Neurotransmitters are released into the synaptic gap. Once across the gap, they lodge in the receptor molecules of the postsynaptic membrane. Whether these neurotransmitters excite or inhibit the membrane depends on the nature of the receptor molecule.

⊃ The Nervous System and Conscious Experience

The cerebral cortex is the basis of consciousness. Language, word and number memory, anxiety and negative emotions are regulated by the left hemisphere. The right hemisphere controls spatial interpretation, facial recognition, memory for shapes and music and positive emotions. If the hemispheres are surgically severed, each functions independently of the other and is not aware of stimulation or cognitive activities that affect the other half.

The behaving brain initiates and controls behaviour. The responsive brain's functions and structure are changed by stimulation from the environment and from its own behaviour.

⊃ Our Responsive Brain

Research has shown that the brain's functioning is modified in profound ways by external stimulation. New research is showing that the brain is a dynamic system, responsive to environmental stimulation and capable of self-modification.

key Terms

action potential
all-or-none law
amygdala
association cortex
auditory cortex
autonomic nervous system (ANS)
axon
bipedalism
central core
central nervous system (CNS)
cerebellum
cerebral cortex
cerebral dominance
cerebral hemispheres
corpus callosum
CT scanner
dendrite
developmental disability
electrode
electroencephalogram (EEG)
encephalisation
endocrine system
endorphin
evolution
gene
genetics
genotype
glial cells (glia)
graded potential
heredity
hippocampus
homeostasis
hormone
human behaviour genetics
hypothalamus
interneuron
ion channel

law of forward conduction
lesion
limbic system
medulla
motor cortex
motor neuron
MRI
natural selection
nervous system
neural network
neuromodulator
neuron
neurotransmitter
oestrogen
parasympathetic division
peripheral nervous system (PNS)
PET scanner
phenotype
pituitary gland
pons
reaction potential
receptor cell
refractory period
reticular formation
sensory neuron
sex chromosome
soma
somatic nervous system
somatosensory cortex
sympathetic division
synapse
synaptic transmission
terminal button
testosterone
thalamus
visual cortex

major Contributions

Broca, Paul (1824–80)
Darwin, Charles (1809–82)
Descartes, Rene (1596–1650)
Field, Tiffany
Gazzaniga, Michael
Grant, Peter
Hebb, Donald
Hess, Walter

Kandel, Eric
Kimura, Doreen
Müller, Johannes
Penfield, Wilder (1891–1976)
Schanberg, Saul
Sherrington, Charles (1861–1952)
Sperry, Roger (1913–94)

Chapter 3

Mind, Consciousness and Altered States

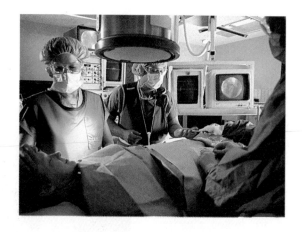

'One hundred, 99, 98, 97 . . .' Karen counted as the anaesthetic flowed from the needle to her vein. Geometric patterns oscillated wildly before her. '92, 91, 9 . . .' Darkness descended. Sensation and awareness shut down. Karen's surgery began.

Karen had not worried about this operation – it was only minor surgery to remove a cyst in her mouth. Minutes into the operation, however, the surgeon exclaimed, 'This may not be a cyst at all. It may be cancer!' Fortunately, the biopsy proved him wrong. In the recovery room he told Karen, who was still groggy and slightly nauseated, that everything was fine; the operation was a complete success.

That night, Karen felt anxious and had trouble falling asleep. She started crying for no apparent reason. Finally, when she did fall asleep, she dreamed about a puppy she could not have because of her allergy to dogs. She woke feeling sad and was depressed all day. At first, Karen attributed her bad mood to her dream. But when all attempts to restore her usual good spirits failed and her depression worsened, Karen sought professional help.

A therapist hypnotised Karen and then asked her to lift her hand if something was disturbing her. Karen's hand rose, and the therapist suggested that she report what was disturbing her. Karen exclaimed, 'The cyst may be cancerous!'

After receiving assurances that the cyst was benign, Karen's depression lifted. Consciously, Karen had not understood the source of her anxiety. But even in an unconscious, anaesthetised state, some part of her mind had comprehended the surgeon's words. The terrible meaning of that information became psychologically traumatic to Karen.

Karen's case is not unusual. Accumulating evidence indicates that many patients who are fully anaesthetised and have no conscious recall of their operation may still hear what is going on during their surgery. Our hearing sensitivity appears to remain on alert even under adequate anaesthesia. The reasons for this auditory alertness may be deeply rooted in our evolutionary history – animals in the open had to respond swiftly to possible danger sounds even when asleep. Whatever the reason, highly specialised cells in the auditory nerve make signals passing along it exceptionally clear and hard to block out with anaesthetics. Because of this sensitivity, even casual remarks in the operating room can be dangerous.

The possibility that patients might experience auditory awareness during general anaesthesia has led to research and stimulated considerable controversy among psychologists and physicians. Recent studies have supported the notion that at least some information that is processed under general anaesthesia is retained afterwards (Ghoneim & Block, 1992; Jelicic et al, 1992). Negative messages have been shown to induce anxiety following surgery, as in Karen's case (Blacher, 1987; Eich et al, 1985; Levinson, 1967). On the positive side, encouraging messages during surgery have been linked to shorter hospital stays and decreased needs for post-operative pain-killing medication (McLintock et al, 1990).

KAREN'S CASE INTRODUCES us to the complexities of human consciousness. Her ordinary state of conscious awareness was influenced by memories that she was not able to acknowledge, such as her frustrated desire for a puppy and her fear of cancer. Even when her body was immobilised by a general anaesthetic, her brain was still subconsciously processing environmental stimuli.

What is ordinary *consciousness*? Can unconscious mental events really influence our thoughts, emotions, and behaviour, as they seemed to do for Karen? Our search for answers to these questions inevitably leads to another inquiry, notably one about the nature of mind. Consciousness and mind are linked closely because conscious and unconscious information processing, awareness and attention are all functions of the human mind. These mental processes are mediated by the brain and are a prerequisite for all that we think, feel and do.

At the end of the previous chapter, we began to examine brain mechanisms involved in some alterations of consciousness. In this chapter, we continue our exploration of the mind by first reflecting briefly on the relationship between brain and mind. Next, we will analyse the nature of consciousness – its functions, levels and different structures. Then we will shift to the regular mental changes we all experience during day-dreaming, sleeping and night-dreaming. Finally, we will look at how people sometimes try to alter their state of consciousness.

⬤ SOUL, MIND AND BRAIN

Throughout human history, people have tried to account for human behaviour. Our early ancestors traced the causes of human actions to their *anima*, or inner life force, and the operation of outer spiritual forces – divine and demonic – that they believed existed in nature. In these *animistic explanations* of behaviour, the same kinds of spiritual force guided all creatures of nature. An individual's spirit, or soul, was assumed to be separate from the body, doing all those things that make people human: seeing, talking, remembering and feeling. When evil spirits entered a person's body, they could cause disease or bizarre behaviour. Puncturing the person's skull was thought to allow these evil spirits to escape. When the spirit left, whether it had been good or evil, the person could do nothing, and the body died.

Across the centuries philosophers, such as those from ancient Greece, have debated over the relationship between brain and mind – the sources of all actions and thoughts. A sketch of some major positions in this debate will be a useful starting point for learning about human consciousness.

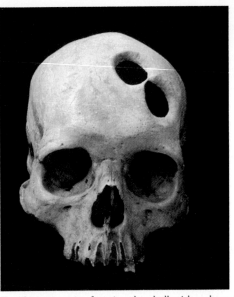

Trephination – perforating the skull with a sharp instrument – was long thought to be a means of treating mental disorders. The process was originally believed to drive out the evil spirits causing the disturbance.

⬤ The Mind–Body Problem

The problem of the relationship between the mind and the brain has long perplexed philosophers and defied easy solutions. On one side of the debate are those who hold that the mind does not exist in solid form: they believe that the term is merely a popular hypothetical construct used to describe what the brain does. It is only the *brain*, they say, that thinks about the brain's activities, just as a computer's diagnostic programs check on its own circuits and functioning. On the other side are those who believe that *mind* encompasses much more than brain activities. They believe that mind and consciousness are central to what it means to be human.

Plato was one of the first Greek philosophers to try to distinguish between notions of mind and body. In his view, the mind and its mental processes were absolutely distinct from the physical aspects of body and brain. Plato gave the mind a special position. He believed it went beyond the directly sensed physical world to consider abstractions and 'ideal realities', and he speculated that the mind survived the death of the body. Plato's view became known as dualism. **Dualism** proposes that the mind is fundamentally different from and independent of the brain: the mind and brain are dual aspects of human nature.

In the mid-1600s, the French philosopher and mathematician **René Descartes** advanced the radical new theory that the body was an 'animal machine'. Its workings could be studied scientifically by *reducing* all sensations and actions to their underlying physical components. In this *mechanistic approach*, animal behaviours and some basic human behaviours are reflex reactions to physical energies exciting the senses. It follows from Descartes' theory that, as a machine, the body can not be subject to moral principles, so, other human behaviours – reasoning, decision making, and thinking about oneself, for example – are based on the operation of the soul, or human mind. Descartes' dualistic view enabled him to resolve the dilemmas he faced as a devoutly religious Catholic (who believed in the spiritual soul), a rational thinker (who believed in the ephemeral mind) and a scientific observer (who believed in the mechanistic view of perception and reflex actions).

In opposition to dualism is **monism**, which was defended by Descartes' contemporary, **Thomas Hobbes**. Monists hold that the sum total of reality can be reduced to matter: a human being is nothing but a body. In this sense, mental phenomena are nothing but the products of the brain. Monists contend that mind and its mental states are reducible, in principle, to brain states; that is, all thought and action have a physical, material base.

Psychology's Conception of the Mind

Throughout psychology's short history, there has been an ongoing, vigorous tug-of-war between dualists and monists. As psychology gradually diverged from philosophy in the early 1800s it became 'the science of the mind'. In Germany, Wundt used the laboratory method of controlled introspection to discover the contents of the conscious mind, and the American philosopher **William James** observed his own 'stream of consciousness'. In fact, James asserted on the very first page of his *Principles of Psychology* (1890) that 'Psychology is the description and explanation of "consciousness" as such'.

Watson's objective behaviourism dismissed these psychologists' introspection and stream of consciousness studies as unscientific, substituting their methods with research on directly observable behaviour and observations of learned habits of responding. During the decades that behaviourism dominated American and European psychology, psychology lost not only its mind but also its brain, as behaviourists focused solely on external actions and behaviour.

Around 1960, humanist psychologists publicly expressed their unease with behaviourism's reduction of human beings to mechanistic automata. According to the humanists, psychology could not do without an account of consciousness. In fact, humanist psychologists made the study of individual consciousness the foundation of their approach. Their central concept of self-actualisation underlined each person's capacity to raise his or her awareness and state of being.

The cognitive psychologists of the 1960s also opposed behaviourist reductionism. During the so-called 'cognitive revolution', psychology parted company from its self-conceptualisation as the science of behaviour and was re-conceptualised as 'the science of the mind' (Gardner, 1985). Cognitive psychologists studying thought examined the workings of the mind, its mental products and conscious awareness. Does this mean that modern cognitive psychologists have rediscovered Cartesian dualism? It does not and remains not the case. By and large, cognitive psychologists seem not to concern themselves about the nature of mind. If they do, they tend to defend **functionalism** as a position that supercedes the classical dichotomy between dualism and monism.

The basic thesis of functionalism is best explained in computer terminology. When a small personal computer and a large mainframe computer perform the same computation, they are functionally identical, although they have little in common from a physical standpoint. Similarly, if different programs, like word-processing or a computer game, are run on the same personal computer, their basic physical properties of computation are the same, but the functional interpretation of word-processing and a game are different. In other words, the functional characteristics are of primary importance; the physical basis of the operations is of secondary importance. An emphasis on a *functional role* likewise can be defended with respect to human mental processes. Functionalism maintains that mental processes, including consciousness, can be defined according to their functional role in a network of causal relations which involves stimulus inputs, other mental states and the organism's actions (Flanagan, 1991). Thus, the mental state of joy may be induced by a beautiful gift; at the same time it may produce a conscious awareness of happiness and it may finally result in the act of embracing the one who gave the gift.

Nevertheless, functionalists hold that the functional role of mind can only be executed because of a physical embeddedness – just as software would be nothing without hardware. However, functionalists are reluctant to perform a one-to-one reduction of the functional level of operation to the physical level of, for example, firing neurons. Cognitive psychology thus concerns itself with the properties and roles of mental states at the functional level.

The emergence of brain sciences has led biologically oriented psychologists to champion a modern version of the monist position. They believe that the brain alone sits at the head of the table of life and that mind and brain are one. Implicitly they endorse ideas such as those expressed by Armstrong, who has previously defended a union of mind and brain within psychology: 'The mind is nothing but the brain . . . We can give a complete account of man in purely physio-chemical terms' within a 'purely electrochemical account of the workings of the brain' (Armstrong, 1968). Some would go so far as to assert that consciousness can also be purged from our explanatory psychological frameworks. The **eliminative materialists** want to eliminate mentalistic terminology from the scientific account of human functioning. They criticise functionalism for importing such ordinary verbiage and explanations into psychology. Functionalists have uncritically followed commonsense notions in assuming that people have a consciousness and that they know, believe, hope, desire and so on. According to the eliminative materialists, researchers should stop following psychology's mentalism and start doing neuroscience instead. In neuroscience, they argue we can do away with 'mind' and 'consciousness' because human functioning allegedly can be explained entirely in neuro-chemical terms (Churchland, 1986).

The eliminatist view and the monist conceptions of consciousness are challenged by the research of **Roger Sperry** and **Michael Gazzaniga** in which surgical disconnections of the cerebral hemispheres created a duality of conscious experience in patients (see Chapter 2). Out of this research came a new perspective, called the **emergent-interaction theory** of mind–brain relationships. This theory asserts that: (a) brain activities give rise to mental states, but these mental states are different from, more than, and not reducible to, brain states; (b) the mind and conscious experience are dynamic, *emergent* properties of brain activity (as water is an emergent property of hydrogen and oxygen molecules); (c) the phenomenon of 'inner experience' is a high-order emergent property of the brain's hierarchical organisation of control and regulation; (d) brain and mind *interact*, so that while the brain acts on the mind, the mind acts on the brain to govern, rule and direct neural and chemical events; and (e) the conscious mind exerts top-level causal influence over the brain in directing and controlling behaviour.

This new form of dualism is compatible with the perspectives of most psychologists, and it fuses science and our common experience:

> 'The mind has been restored to the brain of experimental science . . . The subjective is no longer outside the mainstream of objective science, nor something that will eventually be reducible in principle to neurophysiology . . . Scientific theory has become squared finally with the impression of common experience: we do in fact use the mind to initiate and control our physical actions' (Sperry, 1987).

The fact that we shall treat mind and consciousness as central psychological concepts does not imply that controversies about their nature and about their subsequent relations to the brain are closed. It should be noted that although we, as sensate beings, cannot perceive moment-by-moment the totality of the processes that give rise to the human mind, we are aware recurrently of its products, such as language, and of our own state of consciousness. Both give us a subjective sense of awareness – a cognisance of there being natural phenomena external or internal to ourselves (Searle, 1992). However, even this alleged fact of ordinary experience may be an illusion: in this vein, the philosopher **Daniel Dennett** (1991) has argued that our human consciousness is not the source, but rather the product of the tales humans tell about themselves.

THE NATURE OF CONSCIOUSNESS

Think of *consciousness* as the front page of the mind and *attention* as the headlining story. Awareness is the knowledge that the story is in the newspaper of your mind. Ordinary waking consciousness includes the immediate mental experiences comprising your perceptions, thoughts, feelings and desires at a given moment – all the mental activity on which you are focusing your attention. You are conscious of focusing attention not just on what you are doing but on the fact that you are doing it and, at times, on the realisation that others are observing, evaluating and reacting to what you are doing. A *sense of self* comes out of this experience of watching ourselves from this privileged 'insider' position. Taken together, these various mental activities form the *contents* of consciousness.

However, there is more to consciousness than its contents. We also use the term consciousness to refer to a general state of mind rather than to its specific contents. In sum, **consciousness** can mean simply that you are aware of the general condition of your mind, or are aware of particular mental contents, or are self-aware.

Functions of Consciousness

Why does consciousness exist, what purpose does it serve? The general functions of consciousness are to aid our survival and enable us to construct both personal realities and culturally shared realities.

Aiding survival

From a biological perspective, consciousness probably evolved because it helped individuals to make sense of environmental information and to use that information in planning the most appropriate and effective actions. Usually we are faced with a sensory-information overload, because of the massive amount of information that strikes our sensory receptors in an unstructured way. Consciousness helps us adapt to our environment by making sense of this 'profusion of confusion' in three ways.

First, it reduces the flow of stimulus input by *restricting* what we notice and to what we pay attention. All that is evaluated as 'irrelevant' becomes background noise to be ignored while we focus conscious awareness on 'relevant' input. Second, consciousness helps us select and store personally meaningful stimuli from the flow of all relevant environmental input. This *selective storage* function of consciousness allows us to form and retain a mental representation, a short-term or working memory, of the stimulus after it is no longer physically present (Baddeley, 1986; Atkinson & Shiffrin, 1968; see Chapter 8). The third function of consciousness is to make us stop, think, consider alternatives based on past knowledge and imagine various consequences. This *planning* or executive control function enables us to suppress strong desires when they conflict with our values, ethics or practical concerns. For all these reasons, consciousness gives us far more potential than other species have for flexible, appropriate responses to the changing demands in our lives (Ornstein, 1986b; Rozin, 1976).

Personal and cultural constructions of reality

No two people interpret every situation in exactly the same way. Cognitive psychologists have shown that your *personal construction of reality* is your unique interpretation of a current situation based on a broader scheme or model that includes your general knowledge, memories of past experiences, current needs, values, beliefs and future goals (Fiske & Taylor, 1991; Neisser, 1976). Each person attends more to certain features of the stimulus environment than to others precisely because her or his personal construction of reality has been formed from a selection of unique inputs. When your personal construction of reality remains relatively stable, your sense of self is given unity and continuity over time and across situations.

Individual differences in personal constructions of reality are even greater when people have grown up in different cultures or lived in different environments within a culture. The opposite is also true: because the people of a given culture share many of the same experiences, they often have similar constructions of reality. *Cultural constructions of reality* are ways of thinking about the world that are shared by most members of a particular group of people (Bruner, 1990; Shweder, 1991). When a member of a culture develops a personal construction of reality that fits in with the cultural construction, it is affirmed by the culture and, at the same time, it affirms the cultural construction. This mutual affirmation of conscious constructions of reality is known as **consensual validation** (Natsoulas, 1978; Rozin & Fallon, 1987).

Levels of Consciousness

Psychologists identify three different levels of consciousness (see *Figure 3.1,* next page). They correspond roughly to: (a) a basic level of awareness of the world; (b) a second level of reflection on what we are aware of; and (c) a top level of awareness of ourselves as conscious, reflective individuals (Hilgard, 1980; Natsoulas, 1981; Tulving, 1985).

At the basic level, consciousness is being aware that we are perceiving and reacting to available perceptual information. At the second level, consciousness relies on symbolic knowledge to free us from the constraints of real objects and present events – it gives us imagination. We can contemplate and manipulate objects in their absence, visualise new forms and uses for the familiar, plan utopias and invent new products. The top level of consciousness is *self-awareness*, awareness that personally experienced events have an autobiographical character. Self-awareness gives us our sense of personal history and identity (Freeman, 1993). At this level of consciousness, if we have personally experienced an orderly, predictable world, we come to expect it, and this expectation equips us to choose the best present actions and plans for the future (Lachman & Naus, 1984).

Clearly, consciousness is crucial to the control of our behaviour. But is behaviour controlled only by mental processes of which we are consciously aware? Were you aware of your heartbeat just now? Probably not; its control is part of non-conscious processes. Were you thinking about your last holiday or the author of *Ulysses*? Again, probably not; control of those kinds of thoughts are part of pre-conscious memories. Were you aware of background noises, such as a clock ticking or traffic or a nearby street? You could not be and still pay full attention to the meaning of the material in this chapter, because awareness of non-relevant stimuli is part of non-conscious awareness. Finally, are you aware of how

FIGURE 3.1	THE ICEBERG METAPHOR FOR LEVELS OF CONSCIOUSNESS

If conscious experience were represented as an iceberg, conscious processes would be located above the surface, while the unconscious would be submerged. Subconscious and preconscious processes would both be beneath the surface, but are accessible through special attention and recall. Non-conscious processes influence bodily functions, but never become accessible to consciousness.

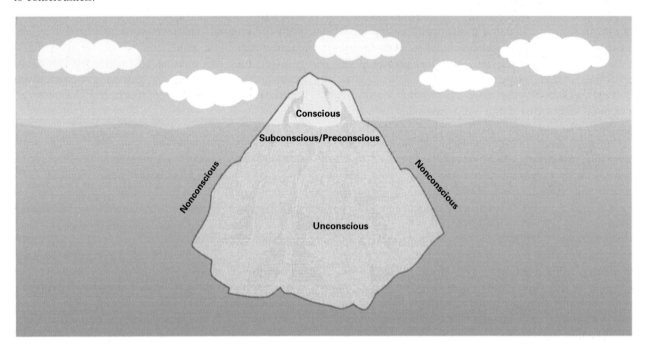

some of your early life experiences, sexual desires and feelings of aggression affect what you say and do now? According to psychodynamic analysis, awareness of these strong, disruptive emotions is blocked by powerful forces that are part of the unconscious.

Non-conscious processes

Non-conscious processes involve information not represented in either consciousness or memory but that still influences fundamental bodily or mental activities. An example of non-conscious processes at work is the regulation of blood pressure, in which physiological information is detected and changes are acted on continually without our awareness. Another is the basic perception of figure and ground, as you can see in *Figure 3.2*. We instantly separate the figure from its background, but we are unaware of the organising processes that give rise to this perceptual response. We only become aware of the fact that such processes must be going on behind the scenes when we look at an ambiguous drawing, such as the right-hand image and have to search for a recognisable ground behind the figure (see also Chapter 6).

Preconscious memories

Memories accessible to consciousness only after something calls our attention to them are known as *preconscious memories*. They include all kinds of knowledge you accumulated earlier, from language concepts to the procedures for skilled performances (such as riding a bicycle). Preconscious memories function silently in the background of our mind until needed or stimulated, or until we are trying to teach others what we know how to do automatically, such as tying shoelaces.

Subconscious awareness

Subconscious awareness involves processing information not currently in consciousness but retrievable from memory by special recall or attention-getting procedures. Much research indicates that we are influenced by stimuli not perceived consciously (Kihlstrom, 1987). In the case that opened this chapter, Karen's depression was the result of a subconscious process; once it was brought into her consciousness by hypnotic therapy, she could recognise it and deal with it appropriately.

FIGURE 3.2 FIGURE GROUND STIMULI

The Unconscious

In common speech, we use the term unconscious to refer to someone who has fainted, fallen into a coma or undergone general anaesthesia. In psychology, however, the term has a special meaning. In **Sigmund Freud's** psychoanalytic theory, the **unconscious** refers to mental processes that are kept out of conscious awareness by the mechanism of repression, because they refer to traumatic memories and taboo desires. Freud believed that when the content of original, unacceptable ideas or motives are repressed – put out of consciousness – the strong feelings associated with the thoughts still remain and show up in various forms. One of Freud's contributions was discovering how much adult activity is influenced by unconscious processes that originate in early life.

Measuring Mind and Consciousness

If consciousness is a subjective process that only *you* can experience, how can it ever be studied empirically? A number of general approaches and specific methods have been developed to assess what is not directly observable. In this section, we will briefly review some of the most important traditional methods and a few of the newest techniques of studying mind and consciousness. The methods differ in the extent to which they require conscious awareness on the part of the experimental subjects. Reaction times, for example, can be used to measure responses to stimuli of which subjects may not be entirely conscious. Likewise participants do not need to be conscious of their cortical state for brainwave patterns to be monitored. Introspection, on the other hand, demands the focal attention of the subject on conscious processing.

Measuring reaction time

Reaction time is one of the most basic measurements that psychologists use to assess what goes on in the mind. Reaction time is the elapsed time between the presentation of some stimulus or signal and a subject's response to it. Underlying differences in mental processes are inferred from differences in reaction times, with slower reaction times taken to indicate more complex mental processing.

For example, it has been found that *simple reaction time*, the single response to a single stimulus, is shorter than *discrimination reaction time*, in which different stimuli are presented and the subject is required to respond only to one as designated. *Choice reaction time*, in which a different response must be made for each of several different stimuli, is the longest. Adopting the principle that complex mental processes take longer, researchers today are using reaction time in a number of research designs from which to infer the occurrence of various mental processes.

Introspection and think-aloud protocols

Introspection was developed by **Wilhelm Wundt** in the late 1800s. It involved training people to analyse the contents of their own consciousness into component parts, such as sensations, images and feelings. Although it yielded catalogues of the elements of consciousness, the introspective approach provided no clues about the actual sequences of mental processes in life situations. When the introspections of two people differed in the same situation, there was no empirical way to resolve the discrepancy between them. Moreover, many mental processes are not even available for conscious inspection, because often people are simply not aware of the process of thinking – only of its product.

Introspection can be used to supplement other methods, but it can never be satisfactory as a technique for studying consciousness or its features. However, researchers have found a way to use introspection as an exploratory procedure to help map out more precise research. During the process of working on a task, experimental subjects describe what they are doing and why. Researchers use their reports, called **think-aloud protocols**, to infer the mental strategies that subjects employ to represent knowledge and to accomplish an experimental task (Ericsson & Simon, 1984; Newell & Simon, 1972).

An example of a think-aloud protocol is found in an investigation of the way people plan everyday shopping trips.

Subjects were presented with a map of the city identifying several stores and businesses. They were assigned several items to purchase and required to plan a day's shopping trip, thinking aloud while they planned. From the protocols, the researchers discovered that planning is not a logical, organised, hierarchical process. Instead, it is an opportunistic process: a person follows many trains of thought simultaneously, jumping back and forth while discovering information that is relevant to one line of thought or another (Hayes-Roth & Hayes-Roth, 1979; Oatley, 1992).

Experience sampling

In the **experience sampling method**, subjects wearing electronic pagers are asked to write down or describe to a portable tape recorder what they are feeling and thinking whenever the pager signals. A radio transmitter activates the pager at various random times each day for a week or more (Emmons, 1986; Hurlburt, 1979). Whenever the pager signals, subjects may also be asked to respond to questions, such as 'How well were you concentrating?' In this way, researchers can keep a running record of people's

thoughts, awareness and attention foci as they go about their everyday lives (Csikszentmihalyi, 1990).

Reading the mind in brain waves

Sensory stimuli elicit electrical waves in the brain that can be measured at the scalp. A brainwave evoked by stimulus events is called an evoked potential, or an **event-related potential** (ERP), to distinguish it from the spontaneous electrical activity that is going on all the time in the living brain. It appears that an ERP first reflects properties of the stimulus, such as its intensity, but then begins to reflect cognitive processes, such as the person's evaluation of the stimulus. For example, the evoked potential is larger for the last word in the sentence 'He took a sip from the computer' because it is more unusual and unexpected than the word 'glass' might be (Donchin, 1975; Woods et al, 1980). One component of ERPs is a brain response that is measured to determine attention and detection of low probability events – surprises. It is also measured as an index of the mental workload involved in certain tasks – such as those performed by air-traffic controllers. This brain response is called the *P-300 component* because it is a positive waveform that peaks 300 milliseconds after a stimulus event (Donchin, 1985).

Brainwaves can help us read the mind in other ways. Electroencephalograms (EEGs), described in Chapter 2, are used to probe the relationship between the functioning of the two cerebral hemispheres in mental tasks. For example, it has been found that tasks with attentional demands are reflected in EEG alpha waves with middle frequencies (8 to 15 Hz), while cognitive and emotional tasks are reflected in higher frequency beta waves (16 to 24 Hz). Moreover, alpha-wave activity is sensitive to the type of attentional task. It is greater for tasks, such as mental arithmetic, that require a focus on internal processes than it is for tasks that require monitoring of environmental stimuli (Ray & Cole, 1985).

There are several other applications of measurement of the electrical activity of the brain to index mental processes. One research programme uses recordings from many electrodes placed on the scalp to measure the rapidly changing patterns of brain electrical activity that occur prior to a subject's overt response to a cue. The human brain seems to 'program' different regions or subsystems in anticipation of the need to process certain types of information and take certain kinds of action. Analyses of the brainwave patterns of these *preparatory sets* enable researchers to predict whether a response will be accurate or inaccurate. Performance is likely to be inaccurate when these preparatory sets are incomplete

FIGURE 3.3	EEG BRAIN MAPS USED FOR DIAGNOSES

The figure shows brain mapping by multiple EEG scalp recordings that are averaged over a large sample of normally functioning people and then compared to the EEG recordings from the same brain sites of those with various mental problems and brain dysfunctions. The columns show different brainwave frequencies, and the four rows show the EEG data for each of these frequencies in samples of normal adults and those with alcoholism, schizophrenia and a cognitive impairment. Deviations from the dark colour pattern of the normal group are indicated by lighter reds and blues. Diagnosis of individuals can be made by comparing their EEG patterns with those from a variety of samples that differ in brain/mind dysfunctions.

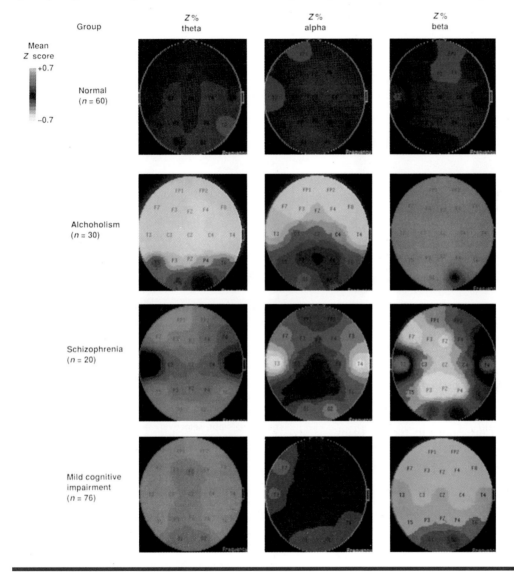

or incorrect – when the mind is not properly prepared to direct the correct response (Gevins *et al*, 1987).

E. R. John and his associates have developed a practical way to read the mind through EEG patterns (1988). By comparing the brain electrical activity of healthy people, ages six to 90, with those of individuals suffering from disorders of brain functioning, mental illness and cognitive impairments, it is possible to make accurate diagnoses of the nature and severity of many types of brain dysfunctions. *Figure 3.3* shows a series of 'brain maps' of the average

EEGs of normal subjects and the EEGs of comparison subjects with alcoholism, schizophrenia and a mild cognitive impairment. The power of each of three different bands of EEG waves are converted to a colour code so that normal is the dark colour and deviations from normal are toward blue or, in the opposite direction, toward red. The extent and brain location of each type of dysfunction can be read from such comparative maps. Thus, any new, undiagnosed patient's EEG pattern can be computed relative to these group norms. Then, a diagnosis can be made.

In the past decade, technological breakthroughs

FIGURE 3.4	BRAIN IMAGES OF REGIONAL CEREBRAL BLOOD FLOW

Cerebral blood-flow patterns differ in episodic and semantic retrieval. The brain image on the left shows recently acquired semantic knowledge (news about elections). The brain image on the right shows a recently experienced personal episode (thinking about an outing of a few days before).

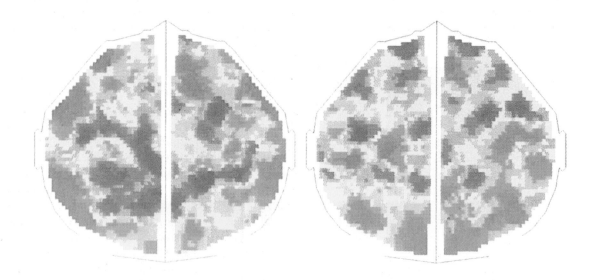

have made it possible to map brain structure and function in normal human beings while they perform mental tasks. These *brain imaging techniques* include those discussed in Chapter 2: CAT and PET scans and magnetic resonance imaging (MRI). Researcher **Michael Posner** (1990) is using PET to study basic cognitive-processing during reading and imaging. He uses cognitive theory to guide his hypotheses and then traces the predicted operations to specific brain structures and processes that can be imaged, or visualised, as a subject works on particular cognitive tasks.

Another psychologist, **Endel Tulving** (1989), is using a different technique for imaging brain functions, the pattern of cerebral blood flow in different regions of the brain. A radioactive tracer is injected into the bloodstream of an alert person and special sensors detect its flow through the brain. Each tiny area is assigned a colour code according to the rate of blood activity there, and it is portrayed in a computer-generated visual mosaic. *Figure 3.4* illustrates two brain images of regional cerebral blood flow as a subject performs two tasks: thinking about events in his episodic memory and then in his semantic memory. While some brain regions are active during the first task, they become less so and others take over during the second memory task. These results are brain-based evidence for Tulving's cognitive model about the different types of memory, which will be discussed in Chapter 8.

INTERIM SUMMARY

In this section we examined the functions, levels and structures of consciousness. We also looked at approaches to research on consciousness. Consciousness aids our survival in several ways. By restricting input, selectively storing currently relevant information, and using past and current knowledge to plan future actions, it allows us to make intentional, flexible responses. It also enables individuals to construct versions of 'reality' and communities to create culturally shared representations of their social worlds. There are at least three different levels of consciousness: (a) a basic level of world awareness; (b) a level of reflection about what we are aware of; and (c) a top level of self-consciousness. Structures of consciousness can influence our behaviour, thoughts and feelings. These structures include non-conscious processes that automatically regulate bodily functions and perceptual decisions, preconscious memories, subconscious awareness (retrievable only with special procedures) and the unconscious, as hypothesised by Freud. Research designed to observe these private events of consciousness employs a variety of techniques: reaction time is one of the most common techniques. It assumes that greater cognitive complexity is reflected in longer reaction times. Introspection has been revived in a more useful format: think-aloud protocols. These protocols require subjects to verbalise their thoughts as they work on a cognitive task. Experience sampling is another technique to focus attention on what one is thinking, feeling and doing.

In the search to understand mental functioning, researchers have gone directly to the brain to map its structure and activity during mental tasks. New techniques of brain imaging, such as PET scans and cerebral-flow mapping, are allowing psychologists to peer literally into the alert brain as it learns, thinks and remembers.

EVERYDAY CHANGES IN CONSCIOUSNESS

Watch children stand on their heads or spin around in order to make themselves dizzy and then ask them why they do it. 'So everything looks funny.' 'It feels weird.' 'To see things tumble around in my head.' Answers such as these support the belief that 'human beings are born with a drive to experience modes of awareness other than the normal waking one; from very young ages, children experiment with techniques to change consciousness' (Weil, 1977).

As they grow older, some people continue these mind experiments by taking drugs that alter ordinary awareness, including legal drugs such as alcohol, tobacco and caffeine. We all change our consciousness every time we day-dream or slip from wakefulness into sleep and have night dreams. In this section we will look at everyday changes in consciousness that are unavoidable, occur naturally and play important functions in our lives.

Day-dreaming

Day-dreaming is a mild form of consciousness alteration that involves a shift of attention away from the immediate situation or task to thoughts that are elicited in a semi-automatic way, either spontaneously or intentionally. Day-dreams include fantasies and thoughts focused on current concerns. Day-dreaming occurs when people are alone, relaxed, engaged in a boring or routine task, or just about to fall asleep. People are least likely to day-dream just after awakening or when eating (Singer, 1966; 1975).

Do you day-dream? In one sample of 240 respondents with some university education, ages 18 to 50, 96 per cent reported day-dreaming daily. Young adults, ages 18 to 29, reported the most day-dreaming; there was a significant decline with age

(Singer & McCraven, 1961). Psychologists generally believe that day-dreaming serves valuable functions and that it is often healthy for children and adults alike (Klinger, 1987). Current research using the experience-sampling method suggests that most day-dreams dwell on practical and current concerns, everyday tasks, future goals (trivial or significant) and interpersonal relationships. Day-dreaming reminds us to plan for things to come, helps us solve problems and gives us creative time-outs from routine mental activities.

What triggers day-dreams? Usually the trigger is a cue from the environment or our own thoughts in the form of words or pictures. However, we may also deliberately initiate day-dreams to relieve the tedium of a boring lecture or job, or to prepare ourselves for a particular task. One study revealed that more than 80 per cent of lifeguards and truck drivers day-dream at times to ease their boredom at work (Klinger, 1987). Sports psychologists often have athletes deliberately day-dream as part of visualisation training, and soldiers going into battle may prepare themselves by day-dreaming of the hated enemy (Keen, 1986).

Surprisingly, sexual and violent day-dreams account for only a small per centage of all day-dreams: explicitly sexual day-dreams average only about five per cent of the total, while violent fantasies are even less frequent. The most common fantasy is having sex with someone other than the actual partner. Others include having sex in a more romantic setting and forcing a partner to have sex or being forced into sex (Pelletier & Herold, 1983). Men tend to have more reality-based sexual day-dreams whereas women tend more toward purely imaginative situations.

Research on day-dreaming by **Jerome Singer** reveals that day-dreamers differ from one another in three ways. They vary in how many vivid, enjoyable day-dreams they have regularly, how many of their day-dreams are ridden with guilt or fear, and how easily they are distracted or can maintain their attention (Singer & Antrobus, 1966).

Sleeping and Dreaming

Sleep can be described as a recurring state that is characterised by a reduced awareness of and interaction with the external environment, a reduced muscular activity with a partial or complete cessation of voluntary behaviour and self-consciousness (Anch *et al*, 1988). We spend about one-third of our life in this altered state of consciousness. The rhythm of waking and sleeping are part of the rhythm of nature, yet they are expressed at the micro level of the activity of single brain cells and neural networks.

Circadian rhythms

All creatures are influenced by nature's rhythms; humans are attuned to a time cycle known as **circadian rhythms**, patterns that repeat approximately every 24 hours. An individual's circadian rhythm corresponds to daily changes in the physiological activities of his or her nervous system. Arousal levels, metabolism, heart rate, body temperature and hormonal activity ebb and flow according to the ticking of the individual's internal clock. For the most part, these human activities reach their peak during the day – usually during the afternoon – and hit their low point at night while we sleep. There are, however, interesting differences between individuals in the tuning of their internal clocks: the 'early birds' function best in the morning and the 'night owls' among us are most happy and productive during the (late) evening (Kerkhof, 1985).

What happens to the circadian rhythm when people are deprived of all social clues and of all information about time? To find out how the 'real' internal clock works, Aschoff and Wever built an underground bunker laboratory equipped with all the home comforts of everyday domestic life. The only things of which their subjects were deprived were clocks and a means by which they could make contact with the outside world. Spending several weeks in the bunker, each participant came under the control of his or her own natural circadian rhythm. It turned out that the 'real' biological clock operates on a cycle with a mean of 24.7 hours (Wever, 1979). Thus, our circadian rhythm results from external cues that force our intrinsic biological clock into a strict daily rhythm of 24 hours.

Circadian rhythms are very sensitive to environmental change. Anything that throws off our natural biological clocks affects how we feel and act. Perhaps the most dramatic example of how changes in daily routine affect circadian rhythms is air travel. When people fly across many time zones, they may experience *jet lag*, a condition whose symptoms include fatigue, irresistible sleepiness and subsequent unusual sleep–wake schedules. Jet lag occurs because the internal circadian rhythm is out of phase with the normal temporal environment. For example, your body says it is six in the evening when local time is noon. Jet lag fatigue is a special problem for flight crews and is often responsible for pilot errors that cause aeroplane accidents (Coleman, 1986).

What variables influence jet lag? The direction of travel and the number of time zones passed through are the most important variables. Travelling east-bound creates greater jet lag than does west-bound flight since our biological clocks can be extended more readily than shortened as required on east-bound trips (it is easier to stay awake longer than it is to fall asleep sooner).

The problems night-shift workers in factories and hospitals face are similar to the ones induced by air travel across time zones. For most people it is very difficult to adjust to the night-work cycle because shifts are rotated regularly. Furthermore, night-workers generally have to shift to the ordinary cycle on weekends if they want to participate in social activities. The health problems night-workers face and their high rates of accidents may be explained by the fact that they have not the opportunity to adjust to inverted time-schedules (Anch *et al*, 1988; Coleman, 1986).

Rapid eye movements

About a third of our circadian rhythm is devoted to that period of quiescence called sleep. Most of what we know about sleep concerns the electrical activities of the brain. The methodological breakthrough for the study of sleep came in 1937 with the development of a technology that records brainwave activity of the sleeper in the form of an **electroencephalogram** (EEG). With the EEG, researchers discovered that brainwaves change in form at the onset of sleep and show further systematic, predictable changes during the entire sleep period (Loomis *et al*, 1937).

The next significant discovery in sleep research was that bursts of **rapid eye movement** (REM) occur at periodic intervals during sleep (Aserinsky & Kleitman, 1953). During this period, according to the

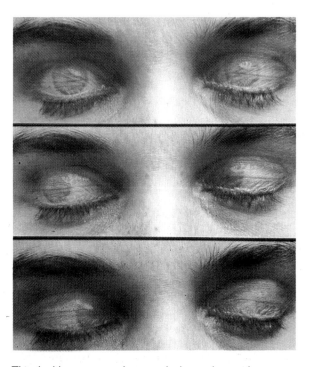

This double exposure photograph shows the rapid eye movements associated with dreaming.

EEG, the brain is relatively active, and the muscles are in such a relaxed state that it seems they are almost paralysed. When subjects in sleep laboratories are awakened during REM sleep, they often report dreams. So, initially it seemed that rapid eye movements are reliable behavioural signs that a sleeper's mental activity is centred around dreaming. **William Dement** and his colleagues were the first to use this new objective pathway to study this previously hidden side of human activity (Dement, 1976; Dement & Kleitman, 1957).

The time when a sleeper is not showing REM is known as **non-REM sleep (NREM)**. We now know that dreaming is not restricted to REM sleep. The mind is active in NREM sleep as well. NREM dream reports are mostly filled with brief descriptions of ordinary daily activities, similar to waking thoughts. A certain proportion, however, consists of true dreams with perceptual images and temporal progression, that originally were considered characteristic of REM dreams only. Dream reports from REM sleep are usually longer, the dreams are sometimes more bizarre and more vivid, and they involve more physical activity and emotion (Hobson, 1989). However, the difference between the two forms of sleep is gradual. Actually, most dreams, in REM sleep as well as NREM sleep, are remarkably representative of everyday life. We often think our dreams are bizarre, because of the selectivity of our memories. Unusual events are remembered better than ordinary tales (Farthing, 1992).

The sleep cycle

When you are preparing to go to bed, EEG recordings show that your brainwaves are moving along at a rate of about 14 cycles per second (cps). Once you are comfortably in bed, you relax and your brainwaves slow down to a rate of about 8 to 12 cps. When you fall asleep, you first enter NREM sleep, which will be reflected in even further changes in the EEG. In fact, over the course of the night, your sleep cycle will move through several stages, each of which shows a distinct EEG pattern.

NREM sleep is divided in four stages. In stage 1, the EEG records brainwaves of about 3 to 7 cps. Through a short stay in stage 2, a very deep state of relaxed sleep (stages 3 and 4, also known as *deep sleep*) is then reached. Your breathing and heart rate decrease, and your brainwaves slow to about 1 to 2 cps. These 'slow' waves are known as delta waves, so deep sleep is also referred to as *delta sleep*. Then REM sleep sets in. The electrical activity of your brain increases and your EEG trace looks very similar to those recorded during stages 1 and 2. Your muscle tone declines, and your eyes move rapidly back and

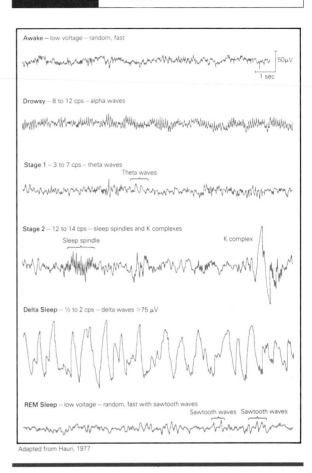

| FIGURE 3.5 | EEG PATTERNS REFLECTING THE STAGES OF A REGULAR NIGHT'S SLEEP |

Adapted from Hauri, 1977

forth. In *Figure 3.5* the EEG patterns associated with the different stages are shown. Because the EEG pattern during REM sleep resembles that of an awake person, REM sleep was originally termed *paradoxical sleep*.

Humans and most animals have regular sleep–wake cycles, orderly stages of sleep and a standard ratio of REM to NREM sleep. The sleep–wake cycle has been found to correspond with activity in specific areas of the brain, such as certain brainstem neurons and cells in the thalamus, the principal gateway to the cerebral cortex (Steriade & McCauley, 1990). Sleep–wake cycles are affected also by the release of chemicals that influence sleeping and waking (Maugh, 1982). For instance, sleep is promoted when large amounts of the hormone melatonin are released from the pineal gland (Binkley, 1979), and serotonin seems to be involved with changes in arousal levels.

Sleep patterns

For a young adult living on a conventional sleep–wake cycle without sleep complaints, the pattern of sleep follows a standard schedule. Cycling through the first four stages of NREM sleep requires about 90 minutes. Next, REM sleep lasts for about ten minutes. Over the course of a night's sleep, you pass through this 100-minute cycle four to six times. With each cycle, the amount of time you spend in deep sleep (stages 3 and 4) decreases, and the amount of time you spend in REM sleep increases. During the last cycle, you may spend as much time as an hour in REM sleep (see *Figure 3.6*). Thus, NREM sleep accounts for 75 to 80 per cent of total sleep time, while REM sleep makes up 20 to 25 per cent of sleep time (Carskadon & Dement, 1989).

The length of nocturnal sleep depends on many factors. The two most general factors are a genetic sleep need which is programmed into each species and, most importantly for humans, volitional determinants. People actively control sleep length in a number of ways, such as by staying up late and using alarm clocks. Sleep duration is also controlled by circadian rhythms, so that time asleep may depend on one's personal peak times for REM.

What accounts for variations in amount of sleep? Individuals who sleep longer than average are found to be more nervous and worrisome, artistic, creative and non-conforming. Short sleepers tend to be more energetic and extraverted (Hartmann, 1973). Strenuous physical activity during the day increases the amount of time spent in the slow-wave sleep of stage 4, but it does not affect REM time (Horn, 1988). Mental problems seem to have a great effect on extending REM sleep. In a study of individuals depressed about divorce that was undertaken in the sleep laboratory of **Rosalind Cartwright**, it was found their sleep was often disrupted with REM periods starting too early or lasting too long (Cartwright, 1984).

Of further interest is the dramatic change in

patterns of sleep that occurs over an individual's lifetime (shown in *Figure 3.7*). We start out in this world sleeping for about 16 hours a day, with nearly half of that time spent in REM sleep. By the time we are old, we sleep very little and spend only about 15 per cent of the time in REM sleep. Young adults typically sleep seven to eight hours, with about 20 per cent REM.

The function of sleep

Because humans and other mammals exhibit regular sleep–wake cycles, orderly stages of sleep, and a standard ratio of REM to NREM sleep, there would appear to be both an evolutionary basis and a biological need for sleep. Why do we sleep as we do and what functions do sleeping and dreaming serve?

The two most general functions for sleep may be *conservation* and *restoration*. Sleep may have evolved because it enabled animals to conserve energy at times when there was no need to forage for food, search for mates or work (Allison & Cicchetti, 1976; Cartwright, 1982; Webb, 1974). On the other hand, sleep also enables the body to engage in housekeeping functions and to restore itself in any of several ways. During sleep, neurotransmitters may be synthesised to compensate for the quantities used in daily activities and postsynaptic receptors may be returned to their optimal level of sensitivity (Stern & Morgane, 1974).

If sleep serves an important function, you should expect that sleep deprivation causes serious damage. However, until now such consequences have not been found. Sleep deprivation does affect our behaviour, notably higher functions like attention, speech and memory, but these disturbances are not permanent. In 1965, the 17-year-old Randy Gardner stayed awake

FIGURE 3.6	STAGES OF SLEEP

A typical pattern of the stages of sleep during a single night includes deeper sleep in the early cycles but more time in REM in the later cycles.

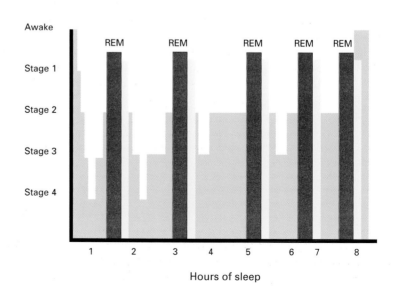

FIGURE 3.7 PATTERNS OF HUMAN SLEEP OVER A LIFETIME

The graph shows changes with age in total amounts of daily REM and NREM sleep and percentage of REM sleep. Note that the amount of REM sleep decreases considerably over the years, while NREM diminishes less sharply.

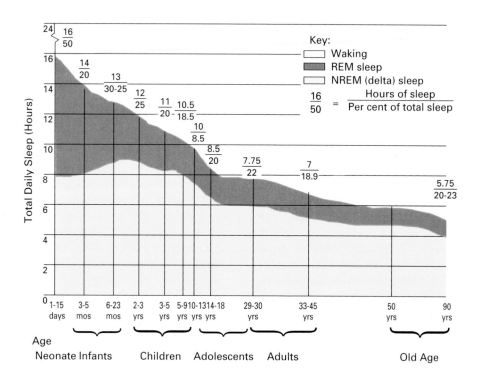

for 11 days. He completed his waking period with a comprehensible story on a press conference. After sleeping 14 hours and 40 minutes, he was tested by psychologists, who could not find anything unusual (Dement, 1972). You may have experienced yourself that, after skipping one night of sleep, it suffices to sleep two eight-hour nights in order to recover completely. Hence, sleep may serve conservation and restoration, but physiological processes of vital importance that are only active during sleep, have not yet been found (Farthing, 1992).

If you were to be deprived of REM sleep for a night, you would find that you would have more REM sleep than usual the next night. This so-called *REM rebound* suggests that REM sleep serves an important function. A number of interesting, but not yet fully demonstrated, benefits have been attributed to REM sleep. For example, it appears that, during infancy, REM sleep is responsible for establishing the pathways between our nerves and muscles that enable us to move our eyes. REM sleep may also establish functional structures in the brain, such as those involving the learning of motor skills. REM sleep can also play a role in the maintenance of mood and emotion, and it may be required for storing memories and fitting recent experiences into networks of

previous beliefs or memories (Cartwright, 1978; Dement, 1976; Nielsen *et al*, 1989).

A radical version of the restorative function of sleep is found in the theory that holds that sleep and dreams help the brain to flush out the day's accumulation of unwanted and useless information. In other words, we need to sleep because only then does our neural system get its nightly spring-cleaning. In this view, dreams serve to reduce daytime fantasy and obsession, thereby minimising otherwise bizarre connections amongst our many memories. REM sleep is said to result in a 'reverse learning mechanism' – people dream in order to forget (Crick & Mitchison, 1983; 1986).

Sleep disorders

For millions of people, a shortage of sleep represents a persistent, serious problem that can lead to personal distress, disrupt intimate relationships and interfere with their occupational lives. Of those whose time-tables include night-shifts, more than half drop off to sleep at least once a week whilst at work. In fact, some of the world's most serious accidents –

Three Mile Island, Chernobyl, Bhopal and the Exxon Valdez Disaster – have occurred during the late evening hours. It has been speculated that these accidents occurred because key personnel failed to function optimally as a result of insufficient sleep. A persistent shortage of sleep, however, is not always caused by shifts in our circadian rhythm. There are several forms of *sleep disorders,* some of which are biological and some more psychological in origin.

When people are dissatisfied with their amount or quality of sleep, they are suffering from **insomnia**. This chronic failure to get adequate sleep is characterised by an inability to fall asleep quickly, frequent arousals during sleep and/or early morning awakening (Bootzin & Nicasio, 1978). Insomnia is a complex disorder caused by a variety of psychological, environmental and biological factors (Borkovec, 1982). However, when insomniacs are studied in sleep laboratories, the objective quantity and quality of their actual sleep varies considerably, from disturbed sleep to normal sleep. Research has revealed that many insomniacs who complain of lack of sleep actually show completely normal patterns of sleep – a condition described as *subjective insomnia.* Equally curious is the finding that some· people who show detectable sleep disturbances report no complaints of insomnia (Trinder, 1988). The discrepancies may result from differences in the way people recall and interpret a state of light sleep.

Two unusual sleep disorders that can wreak havoc on the lives of those afflicted are narcolepsy and sleep apnea. **Narcolepsy** is a sleep disorder characterised by a periodic compulsion to sleep during the daytime. It is often combined with cataplexy, a total loss of muscle control brought on by emotional excitement (such as laughing, anger, fear, surprise or hunger) that causes the afflicted to fall down suddenly. When they fall asleep, narcoleptics enter REM sleep almost immediately. This rush to REM causes them to experience – and be aware of – vivid hallucinations or images of their dreams that break into daytime consciousness. Because narcolepsy runs in families, scientists assume the disease has a genetic basis. Approximately five people in a thousand suffer from narcolepsy (Farthing, 1992; Guilleminault *et al*, 1989; Joyce, 1990 winter).

Sleep apnea is an upper-respiratory sleep disorder in which the person stops breathing while asleep. When this happens, the blood's oxygen level drops and emergency hormones are secreted, causing the sleeper to awaken, to begin breathing again and then to fall back to sleep. While most of us have a few such apnea episodes a night, someone with sleep apnea disorder can have hundreds of such cycles every night. Apnea during sleep is frequent in premature infants who sometimes need physical stimulation to start breathing again. Sometimes apnea episodes frighten the sleeper, but often they are so brief that the sleeper fails to attribute accumulating sleepiness to them (Guilleminault, 1989).

Excessive *daytime sleepiness* is an inevitable consequence of most central nervous system sleep disorders, circadian rhythm disruptions due to jet lag or shift-work, and drug use. It is also experienced by many people who simply do not get an adequate amount of nocturnal sleep or good quality sleep due to their lifestyles. About four to five per cent of the general population surveyed reports excessive daytime sleepiness (Roth *et al*, 1989). This sleepiness causes diminished alertness, delayed reaction times and impaired performance of motor and cognitive tasks. Nearly half the patients with excessive sleepiness report motoring accidents and more than half have had job accidents, some serious.

One may wonder at this point if it is an exaggeration to call sleepiness a disorder. Can boring lectures, overheated rooms or monotonous tasks be the cause of this sleepiness? The researchers contradict this supposition by arguing that such conditions only unmask the presence of physiological sleepiness – they do not cause it (Roth *et al*, 1989). Although the cause of daytime sleepiness is not simply insufficient sleep – tension, worry, depression and agitation are often responsible – learning how to get longer, more restful sleep can reduce its undesirable symptoms.

Dreams

Of all our dreams, we are especially fascinated by the bizarre ones. During every ordinary night of our life, we experience vivid, colourful, completely nonsensical hallucinations characterised by complex mini-plots that transform time, sequence and place. Dreamers may float or fly or feel as immobile as sacks of potatoes while some kind of danger swiftly approaches. They may talk, hear sounds and experience sexual excitement, but they can not smell, taste or feel pain. Overall, these bizarre dreams are best characterised as 'theatre of the absurd' – chaotic dramas that appear illogical when analysed in the rational mindset of our waking hours.

Freud called dreams 'transient psychoses' and models of 'everynight madness'. He also called them 'the royal road to the Unconscious'. In the past few decades, a new path to understanding the inter-action of the brain's biology and the mind's psychology has been worn. Once only the province of prophets, psychics and psychoanalysts, dreams have become a vital area of study for many researchers. Dream research got its impetus from sleep laboratory findings that correlated rapid eye movements, unique

EEG patterns and the sleeper's report of having dreamed.

As we already mentioned, dreams are not restricted to REM sleep. Dreaming (of a different quality) also takes place during NREM periods. Dreaming associated with NREM states is less likely to contain dramatic story content. It is full of specific thoughts but has little sensory imagery. Subjects recall a much higher percentage of REM dreams than NREM dreams, as shown in ten different studies that used a variety of definitions of dreaming (Freeman, 1972). NREM dreaming is enhanced in those with sleep disorders and in normal sleepers during the very late morning hours (Kondo *et al*, 1989).

Freudian dream analysis

Sigmund Freud made the analysis of dreams the cornerstone of psychoanalysis with his classic book, *The Interpretation of Dreams* (1900). 'When the work of interpretation has been completed, we perceive that a dream is the fulfilment of a wish,' he wrote. Freud saw dreams as symbolic expressions of powerful, unconscious, repressed wishes. These wishes appear only in disguised form because they harbour forbidden desires, such as sexual yearning for the parent of the opposite sex. The two dynamic forces operating in dreams are, thus, the wish and the censor, a defence against the wish. The censor transforms the hidden meaning, or **latent content**, of the dream into **manifest content**, which appears to the dreamer after a distortion process that Freud referred to as *dream work*. The manifest content is the acceptable version of the story; the latent content represents the socially or personally unacceptable version but also the true, 'uncut' one.

In the Freudian perspective, the two main functions of dreams are to guard sleep and to serve as an arena in which wish fulfilment can take place. Dreams act as the guardians of sleep by draining off psychic tensions created during the day, allowing the dreamer to work through repressed and unconscious desires. For the therapist who uses dream analysis to understand and treat a patient's problems, dreams reveal the patient's unrecognised wishes, the fears attached to those wishes, and the characteristic defences the patient employs to handle the resulting psychic conflict between such desires and apprehensions.

In Freudian dream analysis, the images that occur are regarded as symbols and metaphors and are always subject to interpretation within the context of the person's dream. Nevertheless, Freud did propose some universal symbols, many of a sexual nature, that purportedly have the same meanings from dream to dream.

A cognitive account of dreaming

Many dream analysts followed Freud in his emphasis upon the hidden meaning of the dream world. Cognitive psychologist **David Foulkes** (1990), however, has taken issue with the Freudian interpretation of dreaming. Foulkes argues that, during the night, the brain shows random cortical activity which activates bits of knowledge from memory. The mind copes with this chaotic array of memory units by doing that which it is designed to do best: it tries to make sense of all input it receives, to impose order on chaos and to synthesize separate bursts of electrical stimulation into a coherent story by creating a dream. Therefore, in this account, the story and contents of dreams do not reveal any repressed or threatening material, but rather consist of a creative reshuffling of what was encountered during the day.

The bizarre nature of some dreams is explained by observing that the narrative reorganisation combines elements from different episodes and from what was encountered before. For example, a dream in which one gets anxious during an imaginary dinner with the Queen, may actually be composed of a recollection of the Queen's appearance on television and by the memory of a previous formal invitation to a dinner by one's boss and partner. Notice the connection here between Foulkes' interpretation of dreams and the view of **Michael Gazzaniga,** presented in the previous chapter, that in split-brain patients the left hemisphere of the brain tries to make sense of the activities controlled by the silent right hemisphere.

Activation-synthesis theory of dreaming

The Freudian view is facing its severest challenge from a new biologically based theory that partly accords with Foulkes' theory. It states that all dreams begin with random electrical discharges from deep within the brain. The signals emerge from a primitive part of the brain, the *brain stem,* and then stimulate higher areas of the brain's cortex. These electrical discharges are automatically activated about every 90 minutes and stay activated for 30 minutes or so – a time period equivalent to REM sleep periods. They are sent to the forebrain and associated areas of the cortex, where they trigger memories and connections with the dreamer's past experiences. There are no logical connections, no intrinsic meaning and no coherent patterns to these random bursts of electrical signals.

The proponents of this controversial theory, **J. Allen Hobson** and **Robert McCarley** (1977), argue that REM sleep furnishes the brain with an internal source of activation, when external stimulation is tuned down, in order to promote the growth and development of the brain. This view does not say the content of dreams is meaningless, only that their source is random stimulation and not unconscious wishes. Hobson (1988) claims that the meaning is added as a kind of brainstorm afterthought.

The activation-synthesis approach helps explain many of the mysteries of sleep we posed earlier. The 'stuff' of dreams may be a brain chemical, *acetylcholine*, which is turned on by one set of neurons in the brain stem during REM. Those neurons are 'on' only when the others, which trigger the release of *serotonin* and *noradrenaline*, are 'off'. Those brain chemicals are necessary to store memories. We forget some 95 per cent of our dreams because they are only stored temporarily in our short-term memory. They cannot be transferred to more permanent memory because serotonin and noradrenalin (norepinephrine) are shut off during the dream. Our dreams are vivid but devoid of smells and tastes because only visual neurons are stimulated by the electrical discharges during REM. We dream with such rich, vivid images because the brain uses symbols and metaphors to store higher-order knowledge; the dream is simply utilising this warehouse of material to find some pre-existing meaning in the madness of chaotic brain discharges. Our eyes move, but our other muscles do not, during REM sleep because of the action of a particular group of cells in the brain stem.

Unique to the dream state, then, are the dual processes of *distributed activation* across the cortex – which ordinarily executes perceptual, cognitive and motor responses in the waking state – and *massive inhibition* of sensory and proprioceptive inputs. The results of these processes are thoughts and dreams without physical action or speech. New views assume that there is a common set of processing modules in the brain that produces both dreaming and waking perceptions (Steriade & McCarley, 1990). By better understanding the mechanisms of dreaming, we can enhance our knowledge of waking aspects of imagery and conscious thought processes (Antrobus, 1991).

INTERIM SUMMARY

In this section, we saw that everyday changes in consciousness include day-dreaming, sleeping and dreaming. Day-dreaming is a common, mild consciousness alteration that works by shifting attention away from a current situation to practical personal concerns or future goals.

Many changes in consciousness correspond to the body's circadian rhythm. Daily stresses, physical exertion and travelling across time zones are examples of the kinds of activities that can disrupt circadian rhythms. For all of us, sleep represents an important change in consciousness. Sleep is characterised by a reliable series of changes in the brain's electrical activities. These changes can be described in terms of stages, which we cycle through several times during a night's sleep. REM sleep is significant because of the corresponding heightened electrical activity that occurs in the brain and because the dreams that fascinate us the most – the bizarre stories – occur primarily in this stage. The standard sleep cycle follows predictable patterns of alternating between REM and NREM sleep throughout the night. Sleep disorders result in complaints of poor quality of sleep or lack of adequate sleep. Among the major types of sleep disorders are insomnia, narcolepsy, sleep apnea and excessive daytime sleepiness.

Dreams are the most common variations of consciousness. Vivid dreaming occurs during REM sleep, which is brought on by nerve cell signals in the brain stem. In Freudian interpretation, dreams are manifestations of unconscious wishes. Cognitive theory and activation-synthesis theory argue that dreams are biologically based, caused by the random activation of nerve discharges, which the mind then tries to make sense of and synthesise into a coherent story.

EXTENDED STATES OF CONSCIOUSNESS

In every society, people have been dissatisfied with purely ordinary transformations of their waking consciousness. They have developed practices that take them beyond familiar forms of consciousness to experiences of extended states of consciousness. Psychological researchers and therapists have also developed procedures for deliberately altering states of consciousness, such as training people to control their dreams or using hypnosis to modify ordinary mental and emotional processes.

Lucid Dreaming

Is it possible to be aware that one is dreaming? Proponents of the theory of **lucid dreaming** argue that being consciously aware that one is dreaming is a learnable skill that enables dreamers to control the direction of their dreams (Garfield, 1975; LaBerge, 1986). The Dutch physician Van Eeden coined the term 'lucid dream' and described some of the dreams in which he had been able to control the dream action (Van Eeden, 1913). In laboratory sleep research, dreamers wear specially designed goggles that detect their rapid eye movements when they are having a dream. When the goggles detect REM sleep, they begin to flash a red light in the subject's eyes. The subjects had learned previously that the red light was a cue for becoming consciously aware that they were dreaming. This procedure is being used both in laboratory studies and with volunteers at home. Once aware of dreaming, yet still not awake, sleepers move into a state of lucid dreaming in which they are able to take control of their dreams, directing them according to their personal goals. The ability to have lucid dreams reportedly increases with one's intention to do so (LaBerge & Rheingold, 1990).

The idea of consciously controlling one's dreams is very controversial. Therapists who use dream analysis as part of their understanding of a patient's problems oppose such procedures because they feel that they distort the natural process of dreaming. On the other side, researchers such as **Stephen LaBerge** argue that gaining control over events previously thought to be uncontrollable is healthy because it enhances self-confidence.

⬤ Hypnosis

Most people find hypnosis fascinating. As portrayed in popular films, the hypnotist need only speak a few words in order to cause major changes in the behaviour of the hypnotic subject. What is hypnosis, what are its important features and what are some of its valid psychological uses?

Hypnosis is a term derived from *Hypnos*, the name of the Greek god of sleep. Sleep plays no part in hypnosis, except in a subject's appearance of being in a deeply relaxed, sleep-like state, in some cases. If a subject were in fact asleep, he or she would not respond to hypnosis. There are many different theories about what hypnosis is and how it works. A broad definition of hypnosis is an alternate state of awareness induced by a variety of techniques and characterised by the special ability some people have to respond to suggestion with changes in perception, memory, motivation and sense of self-control (Orne, 1980). In the hypnotic state, the subject experiences heightened responsiveness to the hypnotist's suggestions. Not only does a hypnotised subject follow suggestions but often feels that his or her behaviour is performed without intention or any conscious effort.

Hypnotisability

Most dramatic stage performances of hypnosis give the impression that the power of hypnosis lies with the hypnotist. However, the real star is the person who is hypnotised. The hypnotist is only a coach or experienced travel guide who shows the way. In fact, some individuals can even practice self-hypnosis, or *autohypnosis*.

The single most important factor in hypnosis is a participant's ability to become hypnotised. **Hypnotisability** represents the degree to which an individual is responsive to standardised suggestions to experience hypnotic reactions. It is a unique cognitive ability, a special aspect of the human imagination. There are wide individual differences in this susceptibility, varying from a complete lack of responsiveness to any suggestion to total responsiveness to virtually every suggestion. A highly hypnotisable person may respond to suggestions to change motor reactions, experience hallucinations, have amnesia for important memories and become insensitive to powerful pain stimuli.

Figure 3.8 shows the percentage of adolescent subjects at various levels of hypnotisability the first time they were given a hypnotic induction test. This objective measure of hypnotisability is the most important single predictor of a person's responsiveness to a variety of hypnotic phenomena. For example, high scorers are more likely than low scorers to experience pain relief as a result of hypnosis (*hypnotic analgesia*) and to respond to hypnotic suggestions to have perceptual distortions of various kinds.

Hypnotisability is a relatively stable attribute. An adult's scores remain about the same when measured various times over a ten-year period (Morgan *et al*, 1974). In fact, when 50 men and women were retested 25 years after their first hypnotisability assessment (as college students), the results indicated a remarkably high correlation coefficient of 0.71

FIGURE 3.8	LEVEL OF HYPNOSIS AT FIRST INDUCTION

The graph shows the results for 533 subjects hypnotised for the first time. Hypnotisability was measured on the Stanford Hypnotic Susceptibility Scale which consists of 12 items.

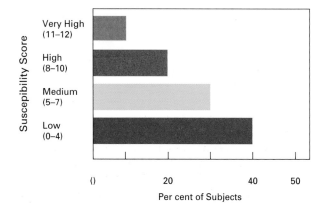

(Piccione *et al*, 1989). Hypnotisability develops early in life along with the sense of being able to become completely absorbed in an experience. Children tend to be more suggestible than adults; hypnotic responsiveness peaks just before adolescence and declines thereafter.

Hypnotisability is not the result of gullibility or conformity, and it is not a conscious attempt at role playing or a reaction to the social demands of the situation (Fromm & Shor, 1979). A hypnotisable person is one who is capable of deep involvement in the imaginative feeling areas of experience, such as in reading novels or listening to music. A hypnotisable person can be hypnotised by anyone he or she is willing to respond to, while someone unhypnotisable will not respond to the tactics of the most skilled hypnotist (Lynn *et al*, 1990).

Induction of hypnosis

Hypnosis begins with hypnotic induction, a preliminary set of activities that prepare a participant for the alternate state of awareness that accompanies hypnosis. Induction activities involve suggestions to imagine certain experiences or to visualise events and reactions. When practiced repeatedly, the hypnotic induction procedure functions as a learned signal. Induction minimises distractions and encourages the subject to concentrate only on suggested stimuli and to believe that he or she is about to enter a special state of consciousness.

The typical induction procedure uses suggestions for deep relaxation, but some people can become hypnotised with an active, alert induction – even suggesting that the subject imagine jogging or riding a bicycle. A child in the dentist's chair can be hypnotised while his or her attention is directed to vivid stories or to imagining the exciting adventures of a favourite TV character. Meanwhile, the dentist drills and fills cavities, using no anaesthesia, but the child feels no pain (Banyai & E. Hilgard, 1976). Responsiveness to hypnotic suggestion can be slightly enhanced with intensive practice as well as with sensory deprivation or drugs, such as LSD or mescaline (Diamond, 1974; Sanders & Reyhen, 1969; Sjoberg & Hollister, 1965). These procedures do not transform unsusceptible subjects into highly responsive ones, however.

The fruits of hypnosis

It is necessary to maintain rational scepticism about the claims made about hypnosis, especially when they are based on individual case reports or research lacking proper control conditions (Barber, 1969). Researchers disagree about the psychological mechanisms involved in hypnosis (Fromm & Shor, 1979). Some argue that hypnosis is nothing more than heightened motivation (Barber, 1976) and others believe it is only social role playing, a kind of placebo response of trying to please the hypnotist (Sarbin & Coe, 1972). However, research has shown that the specific effects hypnosis produces in deeply hypnotised subjects is distinguishable from both the expectancy effects of placebo responding and general suggestibility effects (Evans, 1989).

A reliable body of empirical evidence suggests that hypnosis can exert a powerful influence on many psychological and bodily functions (Bowers, 1976; Burrows & Dennerstein, 1980; E. Hilgard, 1968; 1973). One of the most valuable uses of hypnosis has been in therapy with patients who develop multiple personalities. (This use is discussed in Chapter 14.)

In general, hypnotherapy has been more successful with involuntary disorders, such as chronic pain, asthma and migraine headaches, than with voluntary disorders, such as smoking, overeating and alcoholism (Farthing, 1992). Pain control is accomplished through a variety of hypnotic suggestions: distraction from the pain stimulus, imagining the part of the body in pain as non-organic (made of wood or plastic) or as separate from the rest of the body, taking one's mind on a vacation from the body and distorting time in various ways. Hypnosis has proven especially valuable to surgery patients who cannot tolerate anaesthesia, to extreme burn patients, to mothers in natural childbirth and to cancer patients learning to endure the pain associated with the disease and its treatment (Hilgard & Hilgard, 1983). Self-hypnosis is the best approach to controlling pain because patients can then exert control over their pain whenever it arises. In a study of 86 women with cancer, those using self-hypnosis for pain control reported having only half the pain as others (Spiegel *et al*, 1989).

Meditation

Many religions and traditional psychologies of Asian cultures work to direct consciousness away from immediate worldly concerns, external stimulation and action. They seek to achieve an inner focus on the mental and 'spiritual' self. **Meditation** is a form of consciousness change designed to enhance self-knowledge and well-being by reducing self-awareness. During meditation, a person focuses on and regulates breathing, assumes certain bodily positions (yogic positions), minimises external

Meditation through yoga.

stimulation and either generates specific mental images or frees the mind of all thought.

One consequence of meditation is mental and bodily relaxation. Meditation reduces anxiety, especially in those who function in stress-filled environments (Benson, 1975; Shapiro, 1985). However, meditative practices can function as more than valuable time-outs from tension. When practiced regularly, some forms of meditation serve the functions of heightening consciousness, achieving enlightenment by enabling the individual to see familiar things in new ways, and freeing perception and thought from the restrictions of automatic, well-learned patterns. Moreover, meditation is said to lead to mindful awareness in one's daily life. Mindfulness of the routine activity of breathing especially creates a sense of peace. One of the foremost Buddhist teachers of meditation, Nhat Hanh (1991), recommends awareness of breathing and simple appreciation of our surroundings and minute daily acts as a path to psychological equilibrium.

Meditative practices were given a boost in Western countries when *The Beatles* followed a guru to India and proclaimed the virtues of meditation. Although many music fans rushed to follow in the footsteps of the 'fab four', the practice of using meditation to achieve peace of mind, a sense of connectedness with the world and spiritual awakening requires neither group participation nor a group leader. Any individual who is sufficiently motivated to try modifying the standard operating procedures of his or her consciousness can effectively practice meditation. There is some controversy over the measurable effects of meditation. Advocates claim wide-ranging positive influences while opponents report no reliable experimental evidence that regular meditation leads to a heightened state of consciousness (Holmes, 1984).

Hallucinations

Under unusual circumstances, a distortion in consciousness occurs during which the individual sees or hears things that are not really present. **Hallucinations** are vivid perceptions that occur in the absence of objective stimulation; they are a mental construction of an individual's altered reality. However, a critical feature of hallucinations is their apparent reality for the person who is hallucinating; he or she really sees the object or hears the voice 'out there' (Slade & Bentall, 1988). They differ from *illusions*, which are misinterpretations of the sensory stimulus shared by most people in the same perceptual situation. Illusions are inherent to the way human information processing is effectuated. We will elaborate on the subject of illusions in Chapter 6.

Hallucinations can occur during high fever, epilepsy and migraine headaches. They also occur in cases of severe mental disorders when patients respond to private mental events as if they were external sensory stimuli. Some psychologists wonder why we do not hallucinate all the time. They believe that the ability to hallucinate is always present in each of us, but normally inhibited by interaction with sensory input, by our constant reality checks, and by feedback from the environment. When sensory input and feedback are lacking and there is no way to test our ideas against outer reality, hallucinations are more likely.

The complex functioning of the brain requires some constant level of external stimulation, but when it is lacking the brain manufactures its own. Some subjects, when kept in a special environment that minimises all sensory stimulation, show a tendency to hallucinate. Sensory isolation 'destructures the environment' and may force subjects to try to restore meaning and stable orientation to a situation. Hallucinations may be a way of reconstructing a reality in accordance with one's personality, past experiences and the demands of the present experimental setting (Zubeck *et al*, 1961; Suedfeld, 1980).

Psi Phenomena

The past decades have been host to a controversy among psychologists about a particular kind of extended state of consciousness, notably the phenomena known as psi. **Psi phenomena** are processes of information and energy transfer that cannot be explained in terms of the physical mechanisms thus far discovered and acknowledged by the natural sciences. Psi phenomena are the subject matter of **parapsychology** (Broughton, 1991; Edge et al, 1986). Telepathy and clairvoyance are examples of psi phenomena. The alleged effects of human consciousness upon the activity of electrical and mechanical devices (such as random number generators) also provides us with other intriguing examples of possible psi phenomena (Jahn, 1994; 1992). The debate among (para)psychological researchers has focused recently on the so-called **ganzfeld procedure** (Bem & Honorton, 1994). The following shows what happens in a ganzfeld experiment:

In one room the 'receiver' is placed in mild perceptual isolation from the outside world: the light has been dimmed and a constant low-level noise is played to the participant – known as the 'receiver' – through headphones. This environment of reduced auditory and visual sensation is called the ganzfeld (total field). In another room, the 'sender', who also is in acoustic isolation, is presented with a visual stimulus (for example, a slide). The sender must concentrate on this stimulus, or 'target'. At the same time, the receiver in the other room is invited to verbalise everything that comes to his or her mind. After the session, the receiver is shown four pictures, one of which is the target. The receiver is asked to rate the degree to which each of the pictures matches what was experienced during the ganzfeld procedure.

In 1985 the parapsychologist **Charles Honorton** published a review of a large number of ganzfeld experiments which showed that receivers were able to select the visual target 38 per cent of the time. However, critics of parapsychology were not persuaded by this result. Among them, **Ray Hyman** (1985) publicly expressed his doubts. He and others pointed to flaws in the procedures – for example, to the risk of sensory leakage so that the receiver may obtain information. They also pointed to the problem of randomly selecting the target stimulus. This is crucial, because sender and receiver may both be familar with particular kinds of images. The debate between Honorton and Hyman produced an interesting result: they agreed on a set of guidelines which future ganzfeld experiments should follow.

A sequel to the earlier ganzfeld debate has been provided by Bem & Honorton (1994). Attracting much attention inside and outside psychology, they claimed – on the basis of ganzfeld experiments which conformed to guidelines – that this kind of psi was still confirmable. In response, Hyman (1994) acknowledged that whilst recent studies are methodologically superior to previous parapsychological experiments, patterns in the results

compel the research community to require further replication of such data. This request no doubt will result in a continuation of the debate about the existence of psi phenomena.

⬤ Mind-altering Drugs

Since ancient times, people have taken drugs that altered their perception of reality. There is archaeological evidence for the uninterrupted use of sophora seed (mescal bean) for over 10,000 years in the southwestern United States and Mexico, from the ninth millennium BC to the nineteenth century AD. Ancient Americans smoked sophora to bring about ecstatic hallucinatory visions. Sophora was later replaced by the more benign peyote cactus, which is still used in the sacred rituals of many native American tribes.

Today, drugs are associated less with sacred communal rituals than with recreational pleasure. Individuals throughout the world take various drugs to relax, cope with stress, avoid facing the unpleasantness of current realities, feel comfortable in social situations or to experience an alternate state of consciousness. Using drugs to alter consciousness has been popularised by numerous authors (Casteneda, Kerouac, Burroughs, Baldwin, Leary) but notably by the publication of *The Doors of Perception* by Aldous Huxley (1954). Huxley took mescaline as an experiment on his own consciousness. He wanted to test the validity of poet William Blake's assertion in *The Marriage of Heaven and Hell* (1793): 'If the doors of perception were cleansed everything would appear to man as it is, infinite. For man has closed himself up, till he sees all thro' narrow chinks of his concern'.

In the United States, Europe and beyond, post-World War II youth culture began to appropriate experimentation with psychotropic drugs as part of its social repertoire. For example, during the 1970s nearly 55 per cent of American final-year pupils at school (in annual surveys of over 16,000 young people) reported using one or more illegal drugs during the last 12 months of their school career. Although this figure has declined steadily since 1982 (to about 38 per cent in 1987), the number of adolescents addicted to drugs has reached epidemic proportions (Johnston et al, 1989). It is interesting to note that males are more likely to use drugs and to know more users than females (Brunswick, 1980). Recreational drug use has become a serious social problem. With addiction to illegal drugs come crime and crime-related problems that plague all levels of society.

Dependence and addiction

Psychoactive drugs are chemicals that affect mental processes and behaviour by temporarily changing conscious awareness. Once in the brain, they may attach themselves to synaptic receptors, blocking or stimulating certain reactions. By doing so, they profoundly alter the brain's communication system, affecting perception, memory, mood and behaviour. However, continued use of a given drug lessens its effect on the nervous system. A reduced effectiveness with repeated use is called **tolerance**. As tolerance develops, greater dosages are required to achieve the same effect. Hand-in-hand with tolerance is **physiological dependence**, a process in which the body becomes adjusted to and dependent on the substance, in part because neurotransmitters are depleted by the frequent presence of the drug. The tragic outcome of tolerance and dependence is **addiction**. A person who is addicted requires the drug in his or her body and suffers painful withdrawal symptoms (shakes, sweats, nausea and, in the case of alcohol withdrawal, even death) if the drug is not present.

When an individual finds the use of a drug so desirable or pleasurable that a craving develops, with or without addiction, it is known as **psychological dependence**. Psychological dependence can occur with any drug – including caffeine and nicotine. We noted in Chapter 2 that a new term, *neuroadaptation*, is being used for both kinds of dependence – physiological and psychological – because it is often difficult to separate their interrelated effects. The result of drug dependence is that a person's lifestyle comes to revolve around drug use so wholly that his or her capacity to function is limited or impaired. In addition, the expense involved in maintaining a drug habit of daily – and increasing – amounts can often drive an addict to robbery, assault, prostitution or drug pushing. One of the gravest dangers currently facing addicts is the threat of contracting HIV through sharing hypodermic needles – intravenous drug users can unknowingly inject themselves with drops of bodily fluid from others who have this deadly immune deficiency disease.

Teenagers who use drugs to relieve emotional distress and to cope with daily stressors suffer long-term negative consequences. An eight-year study of teenage drug use starting in 1976, involving 1,634 school pupils in their early teenage years from Los Angeles, collected complete annual data on 739 subjects. While fewer than ten per cent of those studied were regular or chronic drug users, fewer than ten per cent reported not using any drugs. The results can be grouped into four major findings:

- Daily drug use had a negative impact on personal and social adjustment, disrupting relationships, reducing educational potential, increasing non-violent crime and encouraging disorganised thinking.
- Hard drugs, such as stimulants and narcotics, increased suicidal and self-destructive thoughts whilst reducing social support, thereby promoting loneliness.
- Drug effects varied with the type of drug and mixed use of drugs, so that cocaine increased confrontations and weakened close relationships, but the combination of hard drugs and cigarettes was most damaging to psychological and physical health.
- Nevertheless, teenagers who used alcohol moderately and no other drugs 'showed increased social integration and increased self-esteem'. However, these students may have been better adjusted to begin with than their peers (Newcomb & Bentler, 1988). Alternatively, it is equally plausible that time spent drinking alcohol in social settings, such as in pubs or at parties, provided opportunities to widen social networks.

Varieties of psychoactive drugs

A summary of common psychoactive drugs is listed in *Table 3.1* (next page). We noted in the previous chapter how drugs have differing effects on the central nervous system – stimulating, depressing or altering neurotransmission. Here we will summarise some of the major psychological experiences created by these drugs and the conditions under which they are taken.

The most dramatic changes in consciousness are produced by drugs known as hallucinogens, or

Alcohol is one of the most commonly used of psychoactive drugs.

TABLE 3.1 PSYCHOACTIVE DRUGS: USES, DURATION AND DEPENDENCIES

	Medical Uses	Duration of Effect (hours)	Dependence	
			Psychological	Physiological
Opiates (Narcotics)				
Morphine	Painkiller, cough suppressant	3-6	High	High
Heroin	Under investigation	3-6	High	High
Codeine	Painkiller, cough suppressant	3-6	Moderate	Moderate
Hallucinogens				
LSD	None	8-12	None	Unknown
PCP (Phencyclidine)	Veterinary anaesthetic	Varies	Unknown	High
Mescaline (Peyote)	None	8-12	None	Unknown
Psilocybin	None	4-6	Unknown	Unknown
Cannabis (Marijuana)	Nausea associated with chemotherapy	2-4	Unknown	Moderate
Depressants				
Barbiturates (e.g. Seconal)	Sedative, sleeping pill, anaesthetic, anticonvulsant	1-16	Moderate-High	Moderate-High
Benzodiazepines (e.g. Valium)	Antianxiety, sedative, sleeping pill, anticonvulsant	4-8	Low-Moderate	Low-Moderate
Alcohol	Antiseptic	1-5	Moderate	Moderate
Stimulants				
Amphetamines	Hyperkinesis, narcolepsy, weight control	2-4	High	High
Cocaine	Local anaesthetic	1-2	High	High
Nicotine	Nicotine gum for cessation of smoking habit	Varies	Low-High	Low-High
Caffeine	Weight control, stimulant in acute respiratory failure, analgesic	4-6	Unknown	Unknown

psychedelics; these drugs alter both perceptions of the external environment and inner awareness. As the name implies, these drugs often create hallucinations and a loss of the boundary between self and all that is non-self. Hallucinogenic drugs, such as LSD, act in the brain at specific receptor sites for the chemical neurotransmitter serotonin (Jacobs, 1987). The four most commonly known hallucinogens are *mescaline* (from cactus plants), *psilocybin* (from a mushroom), and *LSD* and *PCP* (angel dust), which are synthesised in chemical laboratories. Of these, young people are most likely to abuse PCP. PCP produces a strange

dissociative reaction in which the user becomes insensitive to pain, becomes confused and feels apart from his or her surroundings.

One of the most widespread hallucinogens is *cannabis*, which is a plant with psychoactive effects. Its active ingredient is THC, found in both hashish (the solidified resin of the plant) and marijuana (the dried leaves and flowers of the plant). The experience derived from inhaling THC depends on its dose – small doses create mild, pleasurable highs, and high doses result in long hallucinogenic reactions. The positive reports from regular users include changes at a sensory and perceptual level – notably, euphoria, well-being, distortions of space and time and, occasionally, out-of-body experiences. However, depending on the social context and other factors, the effects may be negative – fear, anxiety and confusion. Because motor co-ordination is impaired with marijuana use, those who work or drive under its influence suffer more industrial and automobile accidents (Gieringer, 1988). Cannabinoids, the active chemicals in marijuana, work by binding to specific receptors in the brain that are designed to be activated only by that drug.

Opiates, such as heroin, suppress physical sensation and response to stimulation. The initial effect of an intravenous injection of heroin is a rush of pleasure – feelings of euphoria supplant all worries and awareness of bodily needs. There are no resulting major changes in consciousness, but serious addiction is likely once a person begins to inject heroin.

The *depressants* include barbiturates – most notably alcohol. These drugs tend to depress (slow down) the mental and physical activity of the body by inhibiting or decreasing the transmission of nerve impulses in the central nervous system. High dosages of barbiturates induce sleep but reduce the time spent in REM sleep. After the withdrawal of barbiturates which were given over prolonged periods, extended REM periods are punctuated by frightening nightmares. Overdoses of barbiturates lead to loss of all sensations and coma. More deaths are caused by overdoses of barbiturates, taken either accidentally or with suicidal intent, than any other poison (Kolb, 1973). One of the most subtly addictive depressants is valium, which is prescribed as a tranquilliser to reduce temporary anxiety. Valium often becomes a permanent habit that is very difficult to give up.

Alcohol was apparently one of the first psychoactive substances used extensively by our ancestors. Under its influence, some people become silly, boisterous, friendly and talkative; others become abusive and violent; still others become quietly depressed. At small dosages, alcohol can induce relaxation and slightly improve an adult's speed of reaction. However, the body can break down alcohol at the rate of only approximately one ounce per hour, and greater amounts consumed in a short time period overtax the central nervous system. Driving fatalities and accidents occur six times more often to individuals with 0.10 per cent alcohol in their bloodstream than to those with half that amount. Another way alcohol intoxication contributes to accidents is by dilating the pupils, thereby causing night vision problems that drunk drivers are not aware of having. When the level of alcohol in the blood reaches 0.15 per cent, there are gross negative effects on thinking, memory and judgement along with emotional instability and motor inco-ordination.

In our drug-using culture, the line between use and abuse is easy to cross for many who become addicted.

Alcohol-related automobile accidents are the leading cause of death among people between the ages of 15 and 25. When the amount and frequency of drinking alcohol interferes with job performance, impairs social and family relationships, and creates serious health problems, the diagnosis of *alcoholism* is appropriate. Physical dependence, tolerance and addiction all develop with prolonged heavy drinking. For some individuals, the problem of alcoholism is associated with an inability to abstain from drinking. For others, alcoholism manifests itself as an inability to stop drinking once the person takes a few drinks (Cloninger, 1987).

Stimulants, such as amphetamines and cocaine, have three major effects that users seek. These are increased self-confidence, greater energy and hyperalertness, and mood alterations that approach euphoria. Heavy users experience frightening hallucinations and develop beliefs that others are out to harm them. These beliefs are known as paranoid delusions. A special danger with cocaine use is the contrast between euphoric highs and very depressive lows. This leads users to increase uncontrollably the frequency of drug use and the dosage. One survey of 1,212 cocaine users who went to the hospital for a variety of reasons found that about 20 per cent had severe seizures and impaired psychological functioning (Petit, 1987).

A new, particularly destructive street drug is 'crack', a highly purified form of cocaine. It produces a swift high that wears off quickly. Because it is sold in small, cheap quantities that are readily available to the young and the poor, 'crack' is destroying social communities. Despite the well-publicised deaths of prominent American athletes from 'crack' overdoses, there is little evidence that its use is declining at present.

Two stimulants that we rarely think of as psychoactive drugs are caffeine and nicotine. As you may know from experience, within ten minutes, two cups of strong coffee or tea administer enough caffeine to have a profound effect on heart, blood and circulatory functions. They can also disturb your sleep. Like all addictive drugs, nicotine mimics natural chemicals released by the brain. These chemicals stimulate receptors that make us feel good whenever we have done something right – a phenomenon that aids our survival. Unfortunately, nicotine teases those same brain receptors into responding as if it were good for us to be smoking. By short-circuiting our brains, nicotine shortens our lives as well. The total negative impact of nicotine on health is greater than that of all other psychoactive drugs combined, including heroin, cocaine and alcohol.

The pioneering work of Doll and Peto (1976) clearly demonstrated the relationship between cigarette use and cancer: they found that people who smoke 15 to 24 cigarettes a day have ten times the lung cancer rate of non-smokers; further, those consuming more than 25 per day had 22 times the rate of cancer. The British National Health Service attributes 58,000 deaths (one per cent of the total population) annually to cigarettes. While smoking is the leading cause of preventable sickness and mortality, it is both legal and actively promoted – millions are spent annually on its advertising and distribution. Although anti-smoking campaigns have been somewhat effective in reducing the overall level of smoking, a third of people in the United Kingdom aged 16 or over smoke cigarettes (Foster *et al,* 1990). The smoking habit often starts early, with some 15-year-olds smoking at least one cigarette a day (MORI, 1990).

⬤ POSTSCRIPT: WHY CONSCIOUSNESS?

It is reasonable to reflect briefly on the ordinary, fundamental nature as well as the extraordinary capacities of human consciousness. Why do we have a conscious mind and why do we sometimes try to alter it?

The evolution of the human brain permitted survival of those of our forebears who could cope with a hostile environment, even when their sensory and physical abilities were not adequate. They compensated for their relative lack of highly specialised sense receptors, strength, speed, protective coloration or safe habitat by developing a unique set of mental skills. Humans became capable of *symbolic*

representation of the outer world and of their own actions – enabling them to remember, plan, predict and anticipate (Craik, 1943). Instead of merely reacting to stimuli in the physical present or to biological needs, *Homo sapiens'* complex brain was able to model its world; to imagine how present realities could be transformed into alternative scenarios.

This symbolic representation was a tremendous new survival tool. The capacity to deal with objective reality in the here-and-now was expanded by the capacity to bring back lessons from the past (memory) and to imagine future options (foresight). A brain that can deal with both objective and subjective realities needs a mechanism to keep track of the focus of attention. It must know whether the source of the stimulation being processed consists of external objects and events or internal thoughts and concepts. That part of the brain is the *conscious mind.*

The prominence of *Homo sapiens* among all other creatures may be attributed to the development of a human intelligence and consciousness that was forged in the crucible of competition with the most hostile force in its evolutionary environment – other humans. The origin of the human mind may have evolved as a consequence of the extreme *sociability* of our ancestors, perhaps originally as a group defence against predators and to create more efficient exploitation of resources. However, close group living then created new demands for co-operative as well as competitive abilities with other humans. Natural selection favoured those who could think, plan and imagine alternative realities that could promote both bonding with kin and victory over adversaries. Those who developed language and tools won the grand prize of survival of the fittest mind – and fortunately, passed it on to us (Lewin, 1987).

So why did we ever become dissatisfied with our everyday working minds and seek to alter our consciousness? Ordinarily, our primary focus is on meeting the immediate demands of tasks and situations facing us. This focus forces our attention to serve as an ever-shifting searchlight illuminating relevant dimensions of our current experience. However, we are aware of these reality-based constraints on our consciousness. We realise they limit the range and depth of our experience and do not allow us to fulfil our vast intellectual potential. Perhaps, at times, we all long to reach beyond the confines of ordinary reality (Targ & Harary, 1984). The human need to expand consciousness is the mental equivalent of learning to walk erect when it is easier to crawl, and of seeking the uncertainty of freedom instead of settling for the security of the status quo. Extending our consciousness broadens the universal experience of what it means to be a thoughtful human being.

recapping main points

Soul, Mind and Brain

A continuing debate in psychology and philosophy has centred on the relationship between mind and body, between the physical brain and the ephemeral mind. Dualism considers them separate; monism postulates they are one. Contemporary solutions to the mind–body problem include functionalism, emergent-interaction theory and eliminative materialism. Functionalists focus on the functional role of mental processes without reducing them to brain states. The emergent-interaction approach offers a reconciliation of the two positions by proposing that: brain activities give rise to mental states; these states are emergent properties of the brain's hierarchical organisation; that brain and mind interact; and that the mind can exert causal influences over the brain in the control of behaviour. Eliminative materialists wish to do away with concepts like mind and consciousness because they maintain that neuroscience will verify that mental phenomena are nothing but brain states.

The Nature of Consciousness

Consciousness is an awareness of the mind's functioning and its contents. Consciousness aids our survival and enables us to construct both personal and culturally shared realities. Three levels of consciousness are identifiable as: (a) a basic awareness of the world; (b) reflection upon that of which we are aware; and (c) self-awareness. The structure of consciousness involves non-conscious processes, preconscious memories, subconscious awareness, conscious awareness and the unconscious. Many different research techniques are employed to study different aspects of consciousness. These include reaction time measures, think-aloud protocols, experience sampling and techniques for registering what is going on in the brain.

Everyday Changes in Consciousness

Ordinary alterations of consciousness include day-dreaming, sleep and dreams. Day-dreaming is a common experience when attention is shifted from the immediate situation to other thoughts that are elicited semi-automatically. Both genetic and volitional factors determine the length of sleep for humans. We have regular sleep–wake cycles, orderly stages of sleep and a standard ratio of REM to NREM sleep. The mind is active in REM sleep as well as in NREM sleep. About one-quarter of sleep is REM. Sleep disorders are more common than usually recognised, especially among over-active people. Insomnia, narcolepsy and sleep apnea can be modified with psychological and medical therapy.

Freud proposed that the content of dreams is unconscious material stimulated by the day's events. Both the cognitive theory and the activation-synthesis theory of dreaming challenge Freud's psychodynamic approach with an account that is based on biological processes.

Extended States of Consciousness

Lucid dreaming is an awareness that one is dreaming coupled with an attempt to control the course of the dream. Hypnosis is an alternate state of consciousness characterised by the ability of hypnotisable people to respond to suggestions from the hypnotiser with changes in perception, motivation, memory and self-control. Pain control is one of the major benefits of hypnosis.

Meditation changes conscious functioning by ritual practices which focus attention away from external concerns to inner experience that may enhance self-knowledge. Hallucinations are vivid perceptions occurring in the absence of objective stimulation. The processes of information and energy transfer that are known collectively as psi phenomena are a specific kind of altered state of consciousness. The debate about the confirmation and existence of psi phenomena continues.

Psychoactive drugs affect mental processes by temporarily changing consciousness as they modify CNS activity. Among the psychoactive drugs that alter consciousness are hallucinogens, stimulants, opiates and depressants, including alcohol, caffeine and nicotine.

key Terms

addiction
circadian rhythms
consciousness
consensual validation
day-dreaming
dualism
electroencephalogram
eliminative materialism
emergent-interaction theory
event-related potential
experience sampling method
functionalism
ganzfeld procedure
hallucinations
hypnosis
hypnotisability
insomnia
latent content
lucid dreaming

manifest content
meditation
monism
narcolepsy
non-REM sleep (NREM)
non-conscious processes
parapsychology
physiological dependence
psi phenomena
psychoactive drugs
psychological dependence
rapid eye movement (REM)
sleep apnea
think-aloud protocols
tolerance
unconscious

major Contributors

Cartwright, Rosalind
Dement, William
Dennett, Daniel
Descartes, René (1596–1650)
Foulkes, David
Freud, Sigmund (1856–1939)
Gazzaniga, Michael
Hobbes, Thomas (1588–1679)
Hobson, J. Allen
Honorton, Charles (1946–92)

Hyman, Ray
James, William (1842–1910)
John, E.R.
LaBerge, Stephen
McCarley, Robert
Posner, Michael
Singer, Jerome
Sperry, Roger (1913–94)
Tulving, Endel
Wundt, Wilhelm (1832–1920)

Chapter 4

Child and Life-Span Development

1984. The tiny figures in blankets are not quite three weeks old. Then, Nicola wakes up. She lies there, quite content, listening to her mother in the kitchen. Ten minutes later, Alex awakens. Almost immediately, she begins to howl. The babies' mother runs in, picks up Alex and reaches for a clean nappy.

Nicola and Alex are genetically identical, the products of a fertilised ovum that split some time in the first two weeks of pre-natal life. However, because of their positions on the placenta, Nicola was always first to get the nutrients. Thus, at birth she weighed 1.75 kilos; Alex weighed a little less. Although no one can tell the girls apart when they are dressed identically, there are some important differences between the babies.

1985. Much to her mother's dismay, Alex starts climbing on chairs as soon as she learns to crawl. Nicola follows suit in a couple of days. Alex takes her first step on her first birthday. Nicola watches. In less than a week, she is walking too. After her morning baby food, Alex sits on her daddy's knee and opens her mouth wide for bites of his scrambled eggs. She never seems to be able to get enough. When anyone offers eggs to Nicola, she turns away and grimaces. She sticks to baby food.

1986. When Alex and Nicola are 19 months old, their mother goes away for four days. This is the first time she has ever left her daughters for more than a day. The girls accompany their father to the hospital where their mother and a new-born baby, Michael, are waiting. Nicola greets her mum with a big smile and a hug, as though nothing has happened. Alex looks away, fidgets and shows little emotion.

1987. Both girls are wild about clothes. They both like to admire themselves before a full-length mirror. Alex claims pink and green are her favourite colours and is very possessive about them. Nicola likes purple, but allows Alex to wear 'her colour' if she wants.

Nicola likes sleeping alone, while Alex often gets anxious if she feels she has lost track of her sister. Sometimes Alex wakes up in the night, crying 'I dream't I lost Nici and I couldn't find her anywhere'. Together or apart, they sleep in

identical, sometimes mirror-image, positions.

When they work at their little table, Alex scribbles intently on sheets of paper, 'writing' letters and stories that she later dictates to her mother. Nicola is more interested in three-dimensional art projects: she models clay and makes collages out of objects she finds. Nicola still sucks her thumb and likes to stay close to her mum.

1990. Although Alex sometimes eats up to three times as much as Nicola, their weight never differs by more than one-fifth of a kilo (Nicola is heavier). Nicola loves fruits and vegetables. Alex prefers eggs and meat. Nicola takes violin lessons and practices every day. Alex would like to take lessons, too, but she does not want to practice. While Nicola practices, Alex reads. She can read anything, even the instructions for the family's new computer. When Nicola picks up a book, she looks first at the pictures and then reads each word carefully.

On holiday, Alex likes to sleep with her aunt and grandma. Nicola prefers to stay with her mother. When Nicola is nearby, Alex is theatrical and outgoing, but when she is on her own she seems more withdrawn. Nicola seems less dependent on social approval. Alex reacts immediately and intensely to everything that happens, her emotions seemingly just beneath her skin. Nicola is more likely to watch and wait passively, not revealing what she is feeling.

At the end of each day, the girls brush their teeth (which grew at the same time but on opposite sides of their mouths). After listening to a bed-time story, Alex and Nicola climb into their beds and curl up in those same mirror-image positions.

Although Alex and Nicola developed from the same egg and sperm, the previous excerpts from their baby book illustrate how very different they already were three weeks after birth and what unique characteristics and behaviours each was exhibiting six years later. How is it possible that two people with identical origins could develop so differently?

■ APPROACHES TO DEVELOPMENT

THIS CHAPTER PRESENTS an overview of *developmental psychology*, the branch of psychology that is concerned with the changes in physical and psychological functioning that occur during the processes and stages of growth, from conception across the entire life span. The task of developmental psychologists is to find out how human beings change over time. Therefore, individuals are studied at various ages. Psychologists make a distinction between **chronological age** – the number of months or years since birth – and **developmental age** – the chronological age at which most children show a particular level of physical or mental development. For example, a three-year-old child who has verbal skills typical of most five-year-olds is said to have a developmental age of five for verbal skills.

Before going into a dicussion of development in the different phases of life (infancy, childhood, adolescence, adulthood and old age) we will discuss a number of topics that are foundational in the study of development. We will first explore the role of genetic factors and then focus on the interaction of nature and nurture. Finally, we will see how development is conceptualised and how it is studied empirically.

Genetic Influences on Behaviour

Your body build, behaviour and development were all determined, to some extent, at the moment the genetic material in sperm and egg cells of your parents united. Your genetic inheritance imposes certain constraints, but it also makes possible for you certain behaviours that are not possible for members of other species.

As we have seen in Chapter 2 you inherited 23 chromosomes from your mother and 23 from your father. Each of these chromosomes contains thousands of genes. **Genes** are segments along the chromosome strands that contain the 'blueprints' or instructions for the development of our physical characteristics and even some of our psychological attributes. Genes determine not only what characteristics we will develop but also when. These instructions are carried out through the synthesis of proteins, which results in a protein-making code. If any of the codes are incorrect, then the genes will synthesise the wrong kind of protein. The result of incorrect codes might be a genetic disease that impairs normal functioning or even premature death.

A baby born with the normal complement of 46 chromosomes has as many as 100,000 genes in each of its many body cells. A full set of genes – all of the genes inherited from both parents – is an organism's *genotype*. The set of characteristics an organism actually develops – observable features, such as body build and eye colour – is called its *phenotype*. Most of the genetic components deal with characteristics that are specific to each species, the rest with individual differences within that species. It is not always possible to tell the genotype from the phenotype, but, as we noted in Chapter 2, the field of research known as *behaviour genetics* attempts to identify the genetic bases of psychological attributes, such as intelligence and personality (Plomin & Rende, 1991).

Research in behaviour genetics has determined that most human characteristics in which heredity plays a role are **polygenic**, or dependent on a combination of genes. Genes that are always expressed when they are present in an individual, regardless of their combination with another gene, are called *dominant genes*. Genes that are expressed only when paired with a similar gene are called *recessive genes*. For example, an individual who has a gene for brown eyes, a dominant gene, will always have brown eyes, whether that gene pairs with a blue-eye gene or a brown-eye gene. However, an individual who has a gene for blue eyes, a recessive gene, will only have blue eyes if that gene pairs with another blue-eyed gene. All-or-nothing characteristics, such as eye colour, are controlled by either a single gene or by a pair of genes, depending on whether the characteristic is dominant or recessive. Characteristics that vary in degree, such as height, are thought to be controlled by several genes.

When the environmental requirements are specific and predictable, genes rigidly programme behaviour. The result is *stereotyped*, unlearned behavioural patterns. Animals that are higher on the *phylogenetic*, or animal development, scale face more varied environmental challenges. Through experience and learning, they have replaced the stereotyped behaviour patterns seen in lower animals with more complex and flexible patterns.

There are many events that occur after the organisational work of genes and before any given behavioural ability emerges. Environmental influences – from biological to physical and social – help determine the outcome of each of these intermediate events. For example, the very first event in the long process of development is that neighbouring genes regulate whether a particular gene will be turned 'on or off'. During the first months of pregnancy, environmental factors such as malnutrition, radiation or drugs can prevent the normal formation of organs and body structures. In the early 1960s, several hundred women took a tranquiliser called *thalidomide* (also known under the trade name *Softenon*) in early pregnancy to prevent morning sickness and insomnia. The unanticipated side effect was that the drug 'turned off' normal foetal growth of limbs. These mothers gave birth to babies whose arms and legs had not developed fully.

Understanding the gene-environment-behaviour pathway has led to a remarkably simple treatment for one kind of mental deficiency, *phenylketonuria*, or PKU. A PKU infant lacks the genetic material to produce an enzyme that metabolises the amino acid *phenylalanine*. Because of this deficiency, phenylalanine accumulates in the infant's nervous system and interferes with normal growth and brain development. Changing the infant's diet to eliminate or greatly reduce food substances containing phenylalanine (such as lettuce) counteracts the genetic predisposition and intellectual development moves into the normal range (Koch *et al*, 1963).

◧ Nature and Nurture in Development

To what extent is human behaviour determined by heredity (nature) and to what extent is it a product of learned experiences (nurture)? The **nature–nurture controversy** is a long-standing debate among philosophers, psychologists and educators concerning the relative importance of heredity and learning. To appreciate one of the classic elements in this controversy, we must go back in time to a curious event that took place in 1800.

In those days, philosophers strongly disagreed about the origins of human skills and knowledge. On one side of the debate were those who believed that the human infant is born without knowledge or skills: experience, in the form of human learning, etches messages on a blank tablet – or *tabula rasa* – of the infant's unformed mind. This view, proposed by the British philosopher **John Locke**, is known as *empiricism*, which credits human development to experience. What directs human development is the stimulation people receive as they are nurtured.

Among the scholars opposing empiricism was the French philosopher **Jean Jacques Rousseau**. He held the *nativist* view that nature, or what we bring into the world from our evolutionary legacy, is the mould that shapes development. He argued that at birth people are 'noble savages', likely to be spoiled or corrupted by contact with society (Cranston, 1991).

The nature–nurture debate was intensified by the discovery of a wild boy who had apparently been raised by animals in the forests around the region of Aveyron, France. This 12-year-old, uncivilised child, who became known as the *Wild Boy of Aveyron*, was thought to hold the answers to these profound questions about human nature. A young doctor, Jean Marie Itard, accepted the challenge of trying to civilise and educate the Wild Boy, whom he named Victor. At first, Itard's intensive training programme seemed to be working; Victor became affectionate and well-mannered and learned to follow instructions. After five years, however, progress stopped and the teacher reluctantly called an end to the experiment (Itard, reprinted, 1962).

Victor, the Wild Boy of Aveyron.

To this day, the controversy persists about what this curious case study actually revealed. Did nature or nurture fail? Perhaps Victor had been abandoned as an infant because he was developmentally disabled. If that were the case, any training would have only limited success. If not, would modern training procedures have helped the boy develop more fully than Itard's methods? Among contemporary scholars it is generally believed that the case shows clearly the devastating effects of social isolation or, conversely, the vital role of early social contact on communication and mental growth (Lane, 1976; 1986).

Today, thanks to the work of many researchers and scholars, we know that the extreme positions of Locke's empiricism and Rousseau's nativism do injustice to the richness of human functioning. Locke's blank slate view of the new-born infant is challenged by the observation that babies, even within the first few hours of life, will turn their heads toward anything that strokes their cheeks – a nipple or a finger – and begin to suck it. Sucking is the only behaviour that is common among all mammals (Blass & Teicher, 1980). Sucking is an exceedingly complex, but already highly developed, behaviour pattern. Babies know how to suck from the start, which seems to support nativism. This is, however, only partly the case, because the appropriate stimulus, in this case stroking, is needed for sucking to appear. Once it is there, sucking can be changed by its consequences. The sweeter the fluid, the more continuously and also

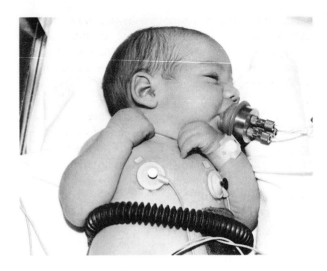

Infant with Lipsitt sucking device.

the more forcefully an infant will suck (Blass, 1990; Lipsitt et al, 1976).

Almost any complex action is shaped both by an individual's biological inheritance and by personal experience, including learning. Heredity and environment have a continuing mutual influence on each other: each makes possible certain further advances in the other, but each also limits the other's contributions.

Heredity sets a reaction range of potential; experience determines where in that range any individual will be. For example, your heredity

FIGURE 4.1	REACTION RANGES FOR HEIGHT AS A FUNCTION OF ENVIRONMENT

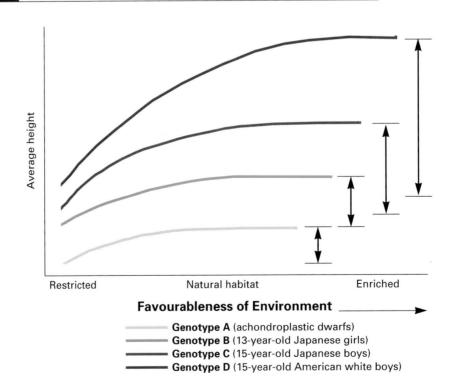

Average height

Restricted   Natural habitat   Enriched

Favourableness of Environment ⟶

Genotype A (achondroplastic dwarfs)
Genotype B (13-year-old Japanese girls)
Genotype C (15-year-old Japanese boys)
Genotype D (15-year-old American white boys)

determines how tall you can grow; how tall you actually become depends partly on nutrition, an environmental factor. *Figure 4.1* (previous page) illustrates the interaction of height and favourableness of environment for groups of children with different genotypes for height.

Although the nature–nurture controversy continues, most investigators today are more interested in how heredity and environment interact to contribute to development than in the relative importance of each (Plomin & McClearn, 1993). In the following discussion of physical growth, constitutional factors in development, sensory development and social interaction, it will be evident that genetic and environmental factors interact in almost every instance.

In later chapters we will focus on the nature–nurture interaction with respect to, for example, perception, intelligence and mental disturbances.

Physical growth

The blueprint provided by the genes directs the physical development of a human being in a predictable sequence, so that physical growth seems to 'unfold from within'. **Maturation** refers to this unfolding process. It is the process of growth typical of all members of a species who are reared in the species' usual habitat. Maturation describes the

FIGURE 4.2	THE DEVELOPMENT OF THE HUMAN BRAIN

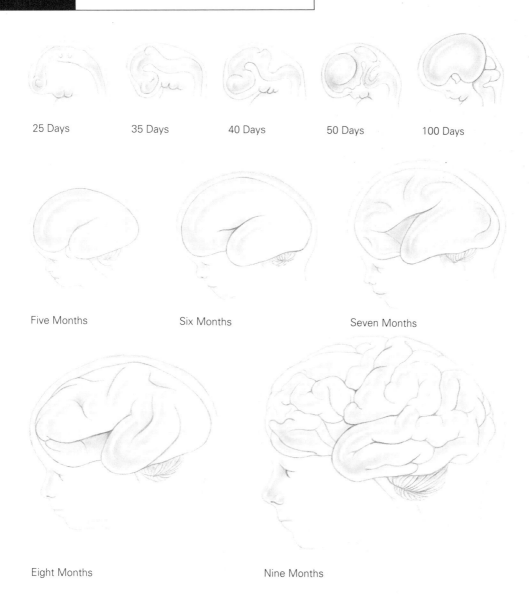

25 Days   35 Days   40 Days   50 Days   100 Days

Five Months   Six Months   Seven Months

Eight Months   Nine Months

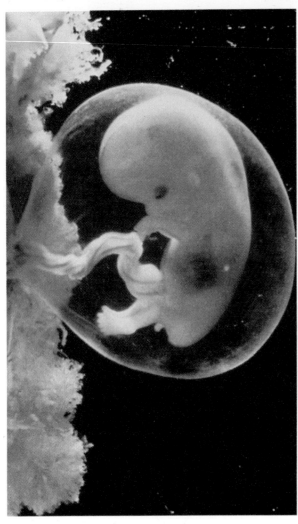

As the brain grows in the developing foetus, it generates 250,000 new neurons per minute.

FIGURE 4.3	GROWTH CURVES FROM BIRTH TO EARLY ADULTHOOD

Neural growth occurs very rapidly in the first year of life. It is much faster than overall physical growth. By contrast, genital maturation does not occur until adolescence.

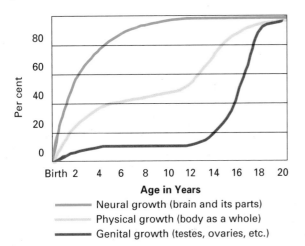

Neural growth (brain and its parts)
Physical growth (body as a whole)
Genital growth (testes, ovaries, etc.)

systematic changes occurring over time in bodily functioning and behaviour, that are influenced: by (a) genetic factors that instigate the maturational changes that make an individual ready for new experiences and learning; (b) chemical factors in the pre-natal and post-natal environments (nutritive or toxic influences); and (c) sensory factors that are constant for all members of the species, such as the force of gravity or basic social contacts (Gottleib, 1983; Hebb, 1966). In other words, maturational sequences of growth are determined by the interaction of inherited biological boundaries and environmental inputs that are normal for a given species. The influence of maturation is most apparent in early development, but it continues throughout life. Maturation in the nervous system, for example, changes the amount and type of sleep we need at different stages of life (see Chapter 3).

The earliest behaviour of any kind is the heartbeat. It begins in the pre-natal period, before birth, when the embryo is about three weeks old and half a centimetre long. Responses to stimulation have been observed as early as the sixth week, when the embryo is not yet three centimetres long. Spontaneous movements are observed by the eighth week (Carmichael, 1970; Humphrey, 1970). After the eighth week the developing embryo is called a foetus. The mother feels foetal movements in about the sixteenth week after conception, although these movements may be heard with a stethoscope a week or two earlier. In the sixteenth week, the foetus is about 18 centimetres long (the average length at birth is 50 centimetres). An infant's body weight doubles in the first six months and triples by the first birthday; by the age of two, a child's torso is about half of its adult length.

As the brain grows in utero, it generates new neurons at the rate of 250,000 per minute, reaching a full complement of over 100 billion neurons by birth (Cowan, 1979). In humans and many other mammals, this cell proliferation and migration of neurons to their correct locations takes place pre-natally, while the development of the branching processes of axons and dendrites largely occurs after birth (Kolb, 1989). The sequence of brain development, from 25 days to nine months, is shown in *Figure 4.2* (previous page).

The neural tissue of the brain (the total mass of brain cells) grows at an astonishing rate, increasing by 50 per cent in the first two years and 80 per cent above birth size in the next two and levelling off by about 11 years of age.

The growth of the sex organs and the secondary sex characteristics follows a very different maturational timetable. Genital tissue shows little change until puberty in the teenage years, and then develops rapidly to adult proportions. *Figure 4.3* shows the systematic, though different, patterns of growth for neural and genital tissues, compared with overall body growth.

FIGURE 4.4   MATURATIONAL TIMETABLE FOR LOCOMOTION

The development of walking requires no special teaching. It follows a fixed time-ordered sequence that is typical of all physically capable members of our species. In cultures where there is more stimulation, children begin to walk sooner (Shirley, 1931).

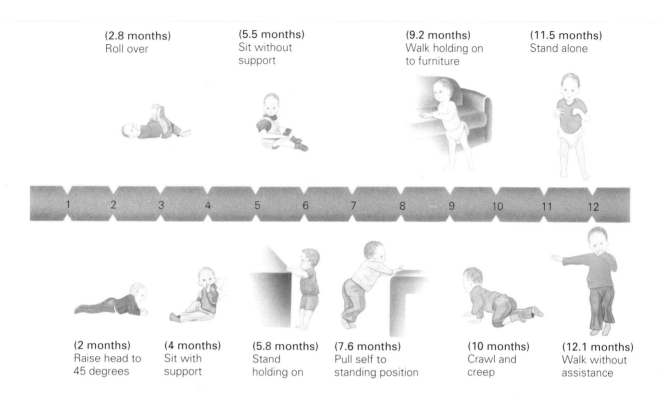

Maturation is also responsible for making possible the appearance of certain behaviours at roughly the same time for all normal members of a species, as we noted with twins Nicola and Alex, although there are some cultural variations. For example, in the sequence for locomotion, as shown in *Figure 4.4*, a child learns to walk without special training.

Development of walking follows a fixed, time-ordered sequence that is typical of all physically capable members of our species. The maturation of locomotion thus follows inner promptings but they need a bit of refinement, which comes through experience. If this environmental stimulation is not obtained, or postponed, the maturational table changes, as illustrated by the native American practice of carrying babies in tightly bound back cradles. This practice retards walking, but once released, the child goes through the same sequence.

For example, most children sit without support by seven months of age, pull themselves up to a standing position a month or two later and walk soon after their first birthday. Once the underlying physical structures are sufficiently developed, proficiency in these behaviours requires only a minimally adequate environment and a little practice. They seem to follow an inner, genetically determined timetable that is characteristic for the species. Consequently, it is almost impossible to speed up the development of these behaviours.

Constitutional factors

By birth, or soon afterward, genetic and early environmental influences result in the development of basic physical and psychological characteristics, such as body build, predispositions to certain physical and mental illnesses and personality style (or temperament; see Chapter 12). These **constitutional factors** are basic physiological and psychological tendencies resulting from the interaction of genetically determined characteristics, or endowment, with early life experiences and environmental influences. Constitutional factors remain fairly consistent throughout a person's lifetime. Research on constitutional factors has shown, for example, that some babies are more sensitive to stimulation than others, some have a high energy level and some are placid and not easily upset. Basic reaction tendencies such as these may affect the way children interact with their environment and, thus, what they will experience and how they will develop (Miyake *et al*, 1985).

Jerome Kagan's research on temperament has shown that about ten to 15 per cent of infants are 'born shy' or 'born bold' (Kagan & Snidman, 1991; Kagan *et al*, 1986). They differ in sensitivity to physical and social stimulation: the unresponsive baby is more easily frightened and less socially receptive. People are less likely to interact and be playful with the unreactive baby, accentuating the child's early disposition.

Sensory development

In the past century, it was a widely held belief among psychologists that the human infant was a totally helpless and confused organism, who after the tranquility of life in the womb, was assailed on all sides by perceptual stimulation. However, psychological research in the past two decades has pointed to the radically different conclusion that babies come into the world with the ability to carry out all sorts of amazing mental and perceptual tasks. A few minutes after birth, a new-born's eyes are alert, turning in the direction of a voice and searching inquisitively for the source of certain sounds that it prefers or stretching out an exploratory hand.

Babies are also born with prejudices. For example, as early as 12 hours after birth they show distinct signs of pleasure at the taste of sugar water or vanilla and they smile when they smell banana essence. Infants prefer salted to unsalted cereal, even when they had virtually no prior experience with salted foods (Bernstein, 1990; Harris *et al*, 1990). But they recoil from the taste of lemon or shrimp or from the smell of rotten eggs.

Their hearing functions even before birth, so they are prepared to respond to certain sounds when they are born. They prefer female voices, are attentive to clicking sounds, fall asleep to the beating of a heart, and recognise their mothers' speech a few weeks after birth. Some of these auditory preferences may be due to the embryo's familiarity with such sounds, having experienced them in the uterine environment.

Vision is less well developed than the other senses at birth. This is because the new-born has not yet developed a sufficient number of photoreceptor cells and neuronal connections in order to produce good vision. However, these immature systems develop very rapidly and, as they do, the baby's visual capacities

become evident (Banks & Bennett, 1988). Early on, infants can perceive large objects that display a great deal of contrast. A one-month-old child can detect contours of a head at close distances; at seven weeks the baby can scan the interior features of the care-giver's face and as the mother or father talks the baby can scan her or his eyes. As early as two months of age, the baby begins to see a world of colour, differentiating patterns of white, red, orange and blue. At three months, the baby can perceive depth and is well on the way to enjoying the visual abilities of adults.

From the moment of birth on, infants start to build up their knowledge of the world by processing sensory information. They also seem to extract relations between related sensory events. Through interaction of inherited tendencies and learned experiences, babies, in time, develop the ability to process vast amounts of sensory information.

Interacting socially

Babies are designed to be sociable. They prefer human voices to other sounds and human faces to most other patterns (Fantz, 1963). Babies not only respond to, but also interact with, their care-givers. High-speed film studies of this interaction reveal a remarkable degree of synchronicity – the gazing, vocalising, touching and smiling of mothers and infants are closely co-ordinated (Martin, 1981; Murray & Trevarthen, 1986). Babies respond and learn, but they also send out messages to those who comfort them and attend to their needs. Not only are the behaviours of mothers and infants linked in a socially dynamic fashion, but their feelings are also matched (Fogel, 1992). A three-month-old infant may laugh when its mother laughs and frown or cry in response to her negative mood (Tronick *et al*, 1980).

Developmental psychologists studying what babies can do are becoming ever more impressed with how precocious (smart for their age) babies are. They seem to arrive equipped to accomplish three basic tasks of survival: sustenance (feeding), maintenance of contact with people (for protection and care) and defence against harmful stimuli (withdrawing from pain or threat). These tasks require perceptual skills, some ability to understand experiences with people and objects and basic thinking skills that combine information from different senses (von Hofsten & Lindhagen, 1979).

Some investigators have concluded that children are born with the ability to distinguish among experiences and to put this information into separate categories. This ability to categorise the flow of conscious experience is essential for building a knowledge base (Masters, 1981).

Continuity, Stages and Critical Periods

An important issue in developmental psychology is the extent to which development is characterised by continuity or discontinuity. Some psychologists take the position that development is essentially *continuous*; they believe it occurs through the accumulation of quantitative changes. According to this view, we become more skilful in thinking, talking or using our muscles in much the same way that we become taller – through the cumulative action of the same continuing processes. In contrast, other psychologists see development as a succession of reorganisations – behaviour is qualitatively different in different age-specific life periods. In this view, particular aspects of development are *discontinuous*, although development, as a whole, is a continuous process. Thus, new-borns are seen not as less dependent on the mother than they were before birth (a quantitative change) but as dependent in different ways.

Psychologists who believe development is discontinuous look for and theorise about **developmental stages**, qualitatively different levels of development. They believe that different behaviours` appear at different ages or life periods, because different underlying processes are operating during those periods. The term *stage* is reserved for an interval of time in which there are some observed qualitative differences in physical, mental or behavioural functioning. Children may go through the stages at different rates but not in different orders.

The concept of stages implies a step-wise progression toward an expected *end state*, which generally is adult functioning (Cairns & Valsiner, 1984). The end state is used as the criterion to determine whether the child progresses in development. Progress is measured by the extent in which the transfer from one stage to the next has approximated the end state. The stage theories that are discussed in this chapter each describe the step-wise progression toward specific end states. Freud's theory of psychosexual development describes progression toward adult functioning in which earlier sexual conflicts are resolved. Piaget's theory of cognitive development shows the step-wise approximation of rational and abstract adult thinking. Kohlberg's account of moral reasoning is concerned with the question as to whether people have reached the goal of using the principle of justice in their moral reasoning. Finally, Erikson's theory of social development describes the step-wise progression towards adulthood in which social conflicts are dealt with in a balanced way.

Although the stage concept is at the core of many developmental theories, there is also a lot of debate about the adequacy of the concept. Some theorists argue that stages cannot be conceptualised in a general sense but have to be specified to particular developmental tasks. For example, rather than giving a step-wise account of general cognitive development, stage theories should focus on the developmental steps in reading ability, perceptual skills and speech-production (Van Geert & Mos, 1990).

The widespread stage concept is fundamentally criticised by the *dynamic systems approach* to development. In this approach, it is argued that mutual interaction between children and their environment usually have unpredictable outcomes. Dependent upon what happens between participants in the interaction, development can proceed smoothly as a continuous process, but it can also result in sudden jumps or temporal regressions. A central concept of the dynamic systems approach is *non-linearity*, which boils down to the fact that small causes can have big effects (Van Geert, 1994). If, for example, a three-year-old who is known as a 'friendly buddy' suddenly aggressively bites a peer in the day-care centre, his biting results in a restructuring of the child-environment interaction which may result in fundamental changes in the developmental trajectory.

Related to the concept of developmental stages is the concept of critical periods. A **critical period** is a sensitive time during development when an organism is optimally ready to acquire a particular behaviour if certain stimuli and experiences occur. If those stimuli and experiences do not occur, the organism does not develop the behaviour at that time and it will have a difficult time doing so later. Experimental evidence supports the idea that critical periods for certain functions occur in animals and humans. For example, salamander tadpoles usually start swimming immediately upon birth. If they are prevented from swimming during their first eight days (by being kept in an anaesthetising solution), they swim normally as soon as they are released. However, if they are kept in the solution four or five days longer, they are never able to swim – the critical period has passed (Carmichael, 1926).

The case of a tragically abused girl, Genie, 'the wild child of California', illustrates both the critical-period effect on language development and the human ability to overcome early intellectual deficits (Pines, 1981).

In 1970, a mistreated girl of 13 was found in California. She had been isolated in a small dark room by her father and had not heard human speech since infancy. She was a pitiful, malnourished, unsocialised creature of only 25 kilos, unable to stand erect or to speak. She had been kept naked and harnessed in nearly total isolation, forced to sleep in a straightjacket in a caged cot and forbidden to make any noise or to have anyone speak to her. Her mother, nearly blind and unable to take care of her daughter, was terrified of her violent, disturbed husband. Eventually, she ran away with the child.

When first tested, Genie scored at the level of normal one-year-olds. But with guidance and intensive training, Genie made rapid progress in many areas of functioning. Her performance on many tests that did not require verbal abilities increased consistently over the years; her IQ score nearly doubled from 38 in 1971 to 74 in 1977 (which is still well below the average of 100). Although she learned many hundreds of words and could communicate effectively, Genie seemed to have passed the critical period for language acquisition. She never asked questions and because she could not understand grammatical principles that put order and meaning in language, her speech was similar to a garbled telegram. Genie's right-brain activities had not been impaired by her years of deprivation, but the development of her left hemisphere had been seriously limited by her failure to use language for all those years. Despite training and practice, normal language development would now be unlikely (Curtiss, 1977; Rymer, 1993).

◨ Developmental Research

In studies of development it is common practice to observe, compare and test babies, children, adolescents and adults at different ages. With respect to the very young ones, however, investigators have to tackle the complicated issue of how to extract information about internal processes from subjects who are too young to say what they perceive, think and feel. Modern developmental researchers have solved this problem by noting what infants can do and then inferring the meaning that certain patterns of behaviour have for those infants. Infants move their eyes to look at things, reach out to touch objects and suck liquids. Researchers use these simple behaviours to index their abilities, capacities and psychological states.

In order to do this, researchers use the paradigm of habituation. Experimenters record whether an infant looks at one stimulus more than another as an indication that the infant can perceive the difference between them. Too much of the same stimulus quickly loses its appeal to babies who soon stop responding to it. This decrease in response to any repeatedly presented event is known as **habituation**. It is a basic response process found in most species and is especially evident in new-borns. **Dishabituation** occurs when, after the baby has habituated to a

familiar stimulus, another stimulus is presented to which the infant responds. This new attentional focus reveals that the baby perceives it to be different from the previous stimulus. Researchers use the babies' looking time and reaching as measures of attention, preference or perceptual ability. For example, a baby sees one object added to a second and then the screen is dropped to block the objects from view. When the screen is quickly raised, revealing three objects, the baby stares longer at them than the first two objects. This is taken to mean that the baby has developed a basic sense of numbers or addition, long before any formal arithmetic training (Baillargeon, 1986).

In addition to recording these simple responses and others, such as smiling, crying and sticking the tongue out, devices can record electrical responses from specific brain regions, degree of dilation of the pupil of the eye, or heart rate. Each of these responses tells the researcher something about babies' responses to different events.

In developmental research across childhood and the life span, different investigative designs are used. We will discuss four of them: normative investigations; longitudinal investigations; cross-sectional designs; and sequential designs.

Normative investigations seek to describe a characteristic of a specific age or developmental stage. By systematically testing individuals of different ages, researchers can determine developmental landmarks, such as those listed in *Table 4.1*. The data provide *norms* – standard patterns of development or achievement, based on observation of many children during the first eight months after their births. Thus, a child's performance can be compared in terms of its position relative to the standard for the typical individual at the same age. Extreme deviations on some behaviours are predictive of abnormal development. For instance, children who are slow in learning to talk might be given special assistance in order to catch up.

Developmental psychologists use time-based research designs to understand possible mechanisms of change and causal influences on behaviour. Most characteristic of their approach is the **longitudinal design**, in which the same individuals are repeatedly observed and tested over time, often for many years. An advantage of longitudinal research is that, because the subjects have lived through the same socio-economic period, age-related changes cannot be confused with variations in differing societal circumstances. However, there are several disadvantages. The results can be generalised only to a very limited group: those born at the same time period of the data collection. Also, with longitudinal designs, it is difficult to keep track of the subjects over extended time periods in a society that is so highly mobile.

Most research on development uses a **cross-**

TABLE 4.1 NORMS FOR INFANT MENTAL AND MOTOR DEVELOPMENT (based on the Bayley Scales)

ONE MONTH

Responds to sound

Becomes quiet when picked up

Follows a moving person with eyes

Retains a large easily grasped object placed in hand

Vocalises occasionally

TWO MONTHS

Smiles socially

Engages in anticipatory excitement (to feeding, being held)

Recognises mother

Inspects surroundings

Blinks to object or shadow (flinches)

Lifts head and holds it erect and steady

THREE MONTHS

Vocalises to the smiles and talk of an adult

Searches for sound

Makes anticipatory adjustments to lifting

Sits with support, head steady

FOUR MONTHS

Head follows dangling ring, vanishing spoon and ball moved across table

Inspects own hands and fingers

Shows awareness of strange situations

Picks up cube with palm grasp

Sits with slight support

FIVE MONTHS

Discriminates strange from familiar persons

Makes distinctive vocalisations (e.g. pleasure, eagerness, satisfaction)

Makes effort to sit independently

Turns from back to side

Has partial use of thumb in grasp

SIX MONTHS

Reaches persistently, picks up cube deftly

Lifts cup and bangs it

Smiles at mirror image and likes frolicking

Reaches unilaterally for small object

SEVEN MONTHS

Makes playful responses to mirror

Retains two of three cubes offered

Shows clear thumb opposition in grasp

Scoops up pellet from table

EIGHT MONTHS

Vocalises four different syllables (such as da-da, me, no)

Listens selectively to familiar words

Rings bell purposively

Attempts to obtain three presented cubes

Shows early stepping movements (pre-walking progression)

This table shows the average age at which each behaviour is performed up to eight months. Individual differences in rate of development are considerable, but most infants follow this sequence.

sectional design, in which groups of subjects, of different chronological ages, are observed and compared at one and the same time. A researcher can then draw conclusions about behavioural differences that may be related to those age differences. In experiments using a cross-sectional design, those in the experimental group receive a particular treatment or stimulus condition, while those in the control group – subjects of the same age distribution – are not exposed to the independent variable. Using a cross-

sectional design, researchers can investigate an entire age range at one time. The disadvantage of cross-sectional design comes from comparing individuals who differ by year of their birth as well as by their chronological age differences. Age-related changes are confounded by differences in the social or political conditions experienced by different birth cohorts (those born in the same year). Thus, a study comparing samples of ten and 18-year-olds now might differ from that of ten and 18-year-olds who grew up in the 1970s in ways related to their different eras as well as to their developmental stages. Therefore, cross-sectional designs cannot really distinguish between age effects and those of one's environment.

The best features of cross-sectional and longitudinal approaches are combined in **sequential design**. In this method, subjects span a certain, small age range. The subjects are grouped according to the years of their births and the groups are observed repeatedly over several years. For example, a sequential design study might start in 1992 with four

birth cohorts of children ages five (1987), four (1988), three (1989) and two (1990), tested each year for three years. By choosing cohorts whose ages will overlap during the course of the study, a researcher avoids the problems of both the cross-sectional and the longitudinal approaches: age and time-of-birth effects and lack of generalisability.

INTERIM SUMMARY

Developmental psychologists study the processes and changes that accompany different ages and stages of human development, from conception throughout the entire life-span. A major concern to psychologists is the understanding of the contribution of genetics to the human condition. Physical growth and the development of many abilities follow a genetically based timetable of maturation, but early experience also plays a role in maturation. Environmental inputs can modify, to some extent, genetically inherited predispositions. The sensory systems that are most well-developed around the time of birth are hearing, smell and touch. Vision, however, develops more slowly.

The debate regarding the relative contribution of nature and nurture to human development dates back to the antagonistic philosophical doctrines of empiricism and nativism. Current wisdom suggests that nature and nurture always interact to determine complex behavioural patterns. Infants are born with many abilities and active minds pre-wired to survive by demanding nourishment, defending against harm and making social contact with adult care-givers. Researchers have studied the behaviour of infants through normative investigations that establish standards of behaviour typical for each age period; research using longitudinal, cross-sectional and sequential designs; and studies of overt behaviours (such as sucking, looking and touching) that index the baby's preferences, feelings and mental functioning.

While some developmental psychologists argue that development is continuous over time, others take the discontinuity view that specific functions are qualitatively different at varying age periods. The latter also outline a series of stages that all children must go through in a fixed sequence to achieve optimal performance; there are critical periods when the organism is most ready to profit from appropriate stimulation and will suffer handicaps if severely deprived during these times.

INFANCY AND CHILDHOOD

In this section, our focus is on psychological development that takes place during the early years of infancy and childhood (see *Table 4.2*). It is in this period that the transformations are rapid and varied. Our plan is to understand how an apparently 'know-nothing' new-born becomes such a competent, mentally sophisticated organism in such a relatively brief period.

For most of us, psychologists and other people, it is common to talk about infancy and childhood as periods that are distinct from later stages (like adolescence and adulthood). In developmental psychology, this is reflected in the fact that 'the child' is a distinct entity of study, as are 'the adolescent' and 'the adult'. However, before immersing ourselves in the study of childhood, it should be noted that today's notion of 'the child' is a rather recent historical construction (Ariès, 1962; Ariès & Duby, 1985).

TABLE 4.2	STAGES IN EARLY LIFE-SPAN DEVELOPMENT	
Stage	**Age Period**	**Some Major Characteristics**
Prenatal Stage	Conception to birth	Physical development
Infancy	Birth at full term to about 18 months	Locomotion; rudimentary language; social attachment
Early Childhood	About 18 months to about six years	Well-established language; gender typing; group play; ends with 'readiness' for schooling
Late Childhood	About six years to about 13 years	Many cognitive processes become adult except in speed of operation;

Before the first half of the eighteenth century, children older than six years of age were considered small adults and were expected to perform as adults whenever their competencies allowed it. Parents and employers had virtually unlimited power over children; many children were abused, abandoned, sold as slaves and mutilated (McCoy, 1988; Pappas, 1983). In those times of high infant and child mortality, adults considered young children to be more interchangeable and replaceable than perhaps is the case today: children's individual identities were not acknowledged. All that mattered was their ability to contribute to the welfare of the family. During the 1800s, people began to perceive that many conditions associated with industrialisation, urbanisation and immigration were threatening to children. These concerns led to child labour laws, compulsory education and juvenile court systems.

In Europe and the United States, it was not until the beginning of the twentieth century that children became valued as potential persons. Child-oriented family life, in which children have a protected social and emotional status, had become widespread and external sources of influence on child care, such as developmental psychology and the juvenile judicial system, had evolved. But the child's status as a 'person in his own right' did not receive societal acknowledgement until this century. The emerging status of the child as an individual afforded children legal rights, including protection from abuse and neglect. Today children are recognised as competent persons worthy of considerable freedom (Horowitz, 1984).

■ Psychosexual Development

Our examination of early psychological development begins with one of the oldest 'stage' theories. In the theory of **psychosexual stages** as developed by **Sigmund Freud** at the beginning of this century, sexuality is assumed to provide the energy for psychological growth. During infancy and early childhood, sexuality is totally concerned with bodily stimulation; it takes years before the complex patterns of adult sexuality emerge. Psychosexual development proceeds in an invariant sequence of stages, according to Freud (1905). Each psychosexual stage is organised around a so-called *erogenous zone*, which is a part of the body that provides pleasure when stimulated. In the *oral stage*, which comes first in development, the mouth is the erogenous zone. Touching the lips, sucking, biting and eating are the primary sources of pleasure for the baby. In the second stage, the experience of gratification shifts to the anus. In this *anal stage*, toddlers seek pleasure by retaining and subsequently expelling

their excrement. Somewhere between the ages of three and five, children enter the *phallic stage*: now, pleasure is derived from the genitals. The use of the term phallic (as derived from *phallus*, meaning the male sexual organ) illustrates that male sexuality is presented as the norm in Freud's theory. This stage is the scene for the unfolding of the **Oedipus complex,** in which both boys and girls are said to develop an unconscious sexual desire for the parent of the opposite sex. However, this lust is coupled with repressed hatred for the same-sex parent. According to Freud, the resolution of the Oedipus complex is accomplished when the child has learned to trade his hatred for his identification with the same-sex parent.

The phallic stage is succeeded by the *latent stage*. Between the ages of five and 11 years, children are assumed to be in a period of relative calm with respect to sexuality. Upon reaching puberty, they enter the last phase, the *genital stage*. The sexual diversity of earlier stages must now be streamlined into an orientation of sexual energy toward an appropriate member of the opposite sex.

One of the fundamental assumptions of psychoanalysis is that developments over the life span are determined during early childhood (see Chapter 1). Psychosexual development is no exception to this rule: in psychoanalytic theory, disturbances in ordinary adult functioning tend to be explained by arrested psychosexual development. When persons have not been able to progress from one stage to the other, they suffer from *fixation*: they remain attached to the pleasures of an earlier stage – for example, as an adult, seeking oral rather than genital stimulation.

Within psychology, Freud's theory of psychosexual development is controversial. On the one hand, there are psychologists who express objections to Freud's alleged one-sided emphasis on sexuality as the dynamic factor in development; on the other, there are many theorists who acknowledge Freud's influence upon their thinking, even though the empirical evidence supporting his stage theory is weak (Fisher & Greenberg, 1985). An important example of a radical reformulation of psychoanalytic developmental theory is Erikson's work, which is discussed later in this chapter. We will shift our attention now from sexuality to cognition.

■ Cognitive Development

Theories of **cognitive development,** which are concerned with the processes and products of the mind as they emerge and change over time, originate from the pioneering work of the Swiss biologist and psychologist **Jean Piaget**. For nearly 50 years, he observed the progression of children's intellectual capacities, thereby laying the foundations of a psychology of cognitive development. This domain of study addresses questions such as how and when do children begin to reason, think, plan strategies and solve problems? Cognitive development is also concerned with the *child's theory of mind* (Wellman, 1990), observing at what age their everyday understanding of mental states and reasoning emerges. For example, it is investigated at what point children know that it is possible to believe in ideas that are unverifiable and that people, but not objects, have desires and dreams.

Piaget's interest in cognitive development grew out of his interest in philosophical questions about the accumulation of knowledge and his training in biological methods of observation which helped him investigate human cognition as a form of biological adaptation. Piaget saw the human mind as an active biological system that seeks, selects, interprets and reorganises environmental information to fit with or adjust to its own existing mental structures. According to Piaget children are innately motivated to be effective in dealing with their physical environment. They enjoy, and get excited about, *mastering* their physical environment. However, children also want to understand their social as well as their own internal world of ideas, desires and feelings (Buck, 1988).

Piaget began his quest to understand the nature of the child's mind by carefully observing the behaviour of his own three children. He would pose problems to them, observe their responses, slightly alter the situations and once again observe their responses. How does a child transform specific, concrete information gathered through sensory experience into general, abstract concepts that are not limited to any immediate stimulus situation? Piaget studied the ways children perceive certain situations and the ways they come to know about physical reality. His interest was not in the amount of information children possessed, but in the ways their thinking and inner representations of outer reality changed at different stages in their development.

There are three key components of Piaget's approach to cognitive development: schemes; assimilation and accommodation; and the four stages of cognitive growth.

Schemas

A three-month-old infant thinks and knows about the world in very practical, hands-on, mouth-on motor-action responses to sensory stimulation. This infant cognition involves sensorimotor intelligence, rather than symbolic representation consisting of **schemas**.

The latter are mental structures or programmes that guide sensorimotor sequences, such as sucking, looking, grasping and pushing. Schemas are enduring abilities and dispositions to carry out specific kinds of action sequences that aid the child's adaptation to its environment, with little or no thought as we know it. With practice, elementary schemas are combined, integrated and differentiated into ever more complex, diverse action patterns, as when a child pushes away undesired objects to seize a desired one behind her. At first, these sensorimotor sequences are dependent on the physical presence of objects that can be sucked, watched or grasped, for example. But thereafter, mental structures increasingly incorporate symbolic representations of outer reality. As they do, the child performs more complex mental operations (Gallagher & Reid, 1981; Piaget, 1977).

Assimilation and accommodation

According to Piaget, there are two basic processes at work in cognitive growth – assimilation and accommodation. In assimilation, the new is changed to fit the known; in accommodation, the known is changed to fit the new.

Assimilation modifies new environmental information to fit into what is already known. External sensory data reaching the child are changed in line with existing internal, cognitive-structural units of its sensorimotor schemes. **Accommodation** restructures or modifies the child's existing schemas so that new information can fit in better. Consider the transitions a baby must make from sucking at its mother's breast, to sucking the nipple of a bottle, to sipping through a straw and then to drinking from a cup. The initial sucking response is a reflex action present at birth, but it must be modified somewhat so that the child's mouth fits the shape and size of the mother's nipple.

In adapting to a bottle, an infant still uses many parts of the sequence unchanged (assimilation), but he must grasp and draw on the rubber nipple somewhat differently than before and learn to hold the bottle at an appropriate angle (accommodation). Piaget saw cognitive development as the result of constant interweaving of assimilation and accommodation in an upward spiralling process. Assimilation keeps and adds to what exists, thereby connecting the present with the past. Accommodation results from new problems posed by the environment. These discrepancies between the child's old ideas and new experiences are an important motivator of changes in cognitive development. Through these two processes, children's behaviour and knowledge becomes less dependent on concrete external reality, coming to rely more on abstract thought.

Stages of cognitive development

There are four qualitatively different Piagetian stages of cognitive growth: the **sensorimotor stage** (infancy), the **pre-operational stage** (early childhood), the **concrete operational stage** (middle childhood) and the **formal operational stage** (adolescence). Distinct styles of cognition emerge at each stage in this progression from sensory-based reaction to reflective, logical thought. All children are assumed to progress through these stages in the same sequence, although one child may take longer to pass through a given stage than another.

Sensorimotor stage (roughly from birth to age two). So many new cognitive achievements appear during the first two years of a child's life that Piaget subdivided this first stage of sensorimotor cognitive development into six sub-stages. We will summarise only the two main trends in this period: changes in how the infant interacts with its environment and the infant's understanding of object permanence.

During the first year, the sensorimotor sequences are improved, combined, co-ordinated and integrated (sucking and grasping, looking and manipulating, for example). They become more varied as the infant tests different aspects of the environment, discovers that her actions have an effect on external outer events and begins to perform what appear to be intentional, directed behaviours toward clear goals. But in the sensorimotor period, the child is tied to her immediate environment and motor-action schemes because she lacks the cognitive ability to represent objects symbolically.

The most important cognitive acquisition of the infancy period is the ability to form mental representations of absent objects, those with which the child is not in direct sensorimotor contact. By the end of the second year, the child has developed this ability. **Object permanence** refers to a child's perceptions that objects exist and behave independently of their actions or awareness. In the first months of life, Nicola and Alex would follow objects with their eyes, but when the objects disappeared from view, the girls turned away as if the objects had also disappeared from their minds. Around three months of age, however, they showed surprise if their mother left their bedroom through one door and returned soon after through another. The results indicate that object permanence develops gradually during this first stage of cognitive development and is solidly formed before age two (Flavell, 1985).

Pre-operational stage (roughly from two to seven years of age). The big cognitive advance in this next developmental stage is the consolidation of representational thought, the ability to represent objects mentally that are not physically present. Except for this development, Piaget characterises the pre-operational stage according to what the child cannot do, such as solving problems by using logical operations. Three of the most interesting features of the child's mind in this period are egocentrism (self-centred focus), the inability to distinguish mental from physical worlds and centration (focus on only central features of objects).

Egocentrism is evident during their conversations with other children: they often look as if they are talking to themselves, rather than interacting. Egocentrism refers to children's inability to take the perspective of another person or to imagine a scene from any perspective other than their own. Piaget showed children a three-dimensional, three-mountain scene and asked them to describe what a teddy bear standing on the far side would see;

 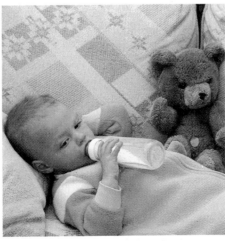 

Although an infant will begin to suck a bottle just the way he or she sucked a breast (assimilation), the infant will soon discover that some changes are necessary (accommodation). The child will make an even greater accommodation in the transitions from bottle to straw to cup.

his subjects could not describe this scene from that other perspective accurately until about age seven (Piaget & Inhelder, 1967). In later research, however, when looking at scenes more familiar to them, children of three and four were able to turn movable images to show someone else's view, though they still did poorly with a stationary scene such as the one Piaget used (Borke, 1975).

The child is unable to distinguish her or his mental world from the physical world. We can see this in their tendency to physicalise mental phenomena, such as when they say that dreams are pictures on the walls that everyone can see. We can also see this in their *animistic thinking* – attributing life and mental processes to physical, inanimate objects and events. Thus, clouds cover the sun 'on purpose' because 'we ought to go to sleep' (Piaget, 1929).

Children at the pre-operational stage typically ignore the less noticeable features of objects because they are captivated by more perceptually striking features. A child's central focus on a single perceptual factor is called *centration*. Piaget's classic *conservation task* provides an example of centration. When an equal amount of lemonade is poured into two identical glasses, children of ages five, six and seven all report that the glasses contain the same amount; but when the lemonade from one glass is poured into a tall, thin glass, they have differing opinions. The five-year-olds know that the lemonade in the tall glass is the same lemonade (qualitative identity), but they believe that somehow it has become more. The six-year-olds are uncertain about the nature of the changed quantity, but also say the tall glass has more. The seven-year-olds know there is no difference between the amounts. The younger children still rely on appearance, centring on a single perceptual salient dimension – the height of the liquid in the glass; the older ones rely on a rule, two dimensions – height and width.

Concrete operational stage (roughly from seven to 11 years of age). At this stage, the child is capable of mental operations but still cannot reason abstractly. For example, if a child sees that Mark is taller than Antony and, later, that Antony is taller than Simon, the child can reason that Mark is the tallest of the three. But if the information about their relative heights is presented to the child verbally and he is not permitted to observe directly their height, he cannot make the correct conclusion. At this stage, children begin to break through their centration, decentring from one physically obvious characteristic, becoming capable of taking others into account.

The seven-year-olds in the lemonade study had mastered the concept of what Piaget called **conservation**: physical properties do not change when nothing is added to them or taken away from them, even though their appearance changes. Successful completion of the lemonade conservation task illustrates an understanding of conservation of area, number and shape.

Although these children learn to use logic and inference in solving concrete problems, the symbols they use in reasoning are still symbols for concrete objects and events and not abstractions. The limitations of their thinking are shown in the game of '20 Questions', the goal of which is to determine the identity of an object by asking the fewest possible questions of the person who thinks up the object. Children at the concrete operational stage usually stick to very specific questions, such as 'Is it a bird?' or 'Is it a cat?' They usually do not ask abstract questions, such as 'Does it fly?' or 'Does it hunt?'

Formal operational stage (approximately from age 11 on). In this final stage of cognitive growth, thinking becomes abstract. Adolescents can see how their particular reality is only one of several imaginable realities and they begin to ponder deep questions of meaning, values and existence. Most young adolescents have acquired all the mental structures needed to go from being naive thinkers to informed thinkers. The approach of adolescents and adults to the '20 Questions' game demonstrates their ability to use abstractions and to adopt an information-processing strategy that is not merely random guesswork. They impose their own structures on the task, starting with broad categories and then formulating and testing hypotheses in the light of their knowledge of categories and relationships. Their questioning moves from general categories ('Is it an animal?') to subcategories ('Does it fly?') and then to specific guesses ('Is it a bird?') (Bruner *et al*, 1966).

Recent perspectives on cognitive development

Within contemporary developmental psychology, Piaget's theory of the dynamic interplay of assimilation and accommodation is presented as an account of the way in which a child's mind develops. Piaget's stage approach to cognitive development is a model many developmental psychologists rely on to understand how other mental and behavioural processes may develop. For instance, there is some evidence that the left cerebral hemisphere shows EEG activity in growth spurts around the ages that correspond with some of Piaget's stages (Thatcher *et al*, 1987).

However, contemporary researchers have devised new conceptions of the child's cognitive abilities. Their research has shown that children are much more intellectually sophisticated at each stage than perhaps Piaget realised (Wellman & Gelman, 1992). Investigators are also challenging his theory of the sensorimotor foundations of thought (J. Mandler, 1992) and looking more to information-processing models of cognitive development (Siegler, 1983).

We will present a brief overview of conclusions relating to perceptual and conceptual development that have emerged from recent studies. An important theoretical problem with Piaget's work is that he did not distinguish between *performance* (doing) and *competence* (knowing), therefore assuming that failure to perform verbally or behaviourally was evidence of a lack of underlying cognitive competence. On some of his tasks, the young child may not have understood his verbal instructions or was perhaps without sufficient motivation to carry out the complex routine required. Recent research shows that the difference in conceptual understanding between pre-operational and concrete operational children may actually be a discrepancy in immediate or short-term *memory* rather than a variation in task comprehension (Case, 1985). Children at the pre-operational stage are unable to perform tasks that overload their more limited memory system, even when they understand the basic concepts involved in the task.

New research designs that employ habituation–dishabituation, are demonstrating that infants know much more than they can tell us and that young children may think in ways that are not reflected in Piagetian tasks. When the situation and task are changed, it appears that children in the pre-operational period can do what they are not supposed to: break through their egocentrism, differentiate physical and mental worlds and decentre their perceptions. In one study, one-month-old infants were habituated to sucking on dummys with either bumpy or smooth surfaces, but they were not allowed to see them. When the dummys were removed and the infants were shown both kinds of dummys, they looked longer at the type of dummy they had felt

tactually in their mouths (Meltzoff & Borton, 1979; Gibson & Walker, 1984). This is taken as evidence for very early sensory co-ordination and visual recognition of objects felt but never seen.

Infants as young as three months see objects as solid and as having boundaries; they can discriminate these objects from their backgrounds as is shown in the following experiment.

A stick was moved repeatedly back and forth behind a block of wood until habituation occurred. Then the subjects were shown two displays of sticks moving as before but missing the block. One display consisted of a solid stick; the other display consisted of two sticks, one above and one below where the solid block used to be (see Figure 4.5). Which display did the babies prefer? They preferred the broken rod to the more familiar, habituated, whole stick. Thus they can determine object boundaries by perceiving relative motion (Kellman & Spelke, 1983; Spelke et al, 1989).

In a series of studies, **Renée Baillargeon** (1985; 1986) was able to show that infants as young as three months old have already developed a kind of *object permanence*. They apparently understand the basic principle that solid objects cannot pass through other solid objects; when they think they perceive such an event, they show surprise. This is illustrated in the following experiment.

The infants sat in front of a large display box. Directly before them was a small screen; to the left of the screen was a long ramp. The infants watched the following event: the screen was raised (so the infants could see there was nothing

---

FIGURE 4.5 TASK STIMULI USED TO DEMONSTRATE THAT INFANTS PERCEIVE OBJECTS AND BOUNDARIES

Three-month-old infants can develop concepts of objects and object boundaries as shown by their preferences in a habituation paradigm. They habituate to the top display of a rod moving behind a block. Then they are tested with each of the two lower displays: the moving rod without the block in front and two pieces of moving rods that appear as parts of the rod seen above and below the block before. The infants continue to habituate to the whole rod, instead preferring to look at the 'novel' broken rod. They show no preference for either kind of stationary rod after seeing a stationary rod behind the block.

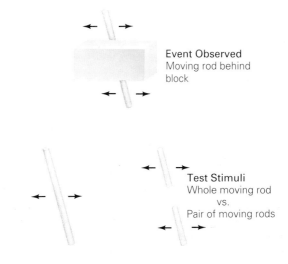

Event Observed
Moving rod behind block

Test Stimuli
Whole moving rod
vs.
Pair of moving rods

behind it) and then lowered; a toy car was pushed on to the ramp; the car rolled down the ramp and across the display box, disappearing as it shot behind the screen, reappearing at the end of the screen, and finally exiting the display box to the right (see Figure 4.6).

After the infants habituated to this event, they saw two test events. These events were identical to the habituation event except that, in both test events, a box was placed behind the screen so that, when the screen was raised, it revealed the box. The only difference between the test events was the location of the box behind the screen. In the possible event the box was placed at the back of the display box, behind the tracks of the car, so the car could roll freely through the display. In the impossible event the box was placed on top of the tracks so that it blocked the car's path; but, during the event, the car still appeared to roll freely through it. The infants showed more surprise and looked longer at this impossible event (Baillargeon, 1986).

Further evidence of conceptual functioning during the sensorimotor stage is seen when nine-month-old children imitate actions they saw performed a day earlier. After having seen an experimenter perform an unusual action on a novel object – pressing a recessed button that made a beeping sound come from a box – the subjects were able to reproduce the action 24 hours later. The subjects recalled a pattern of events that they had not practiced (Meltzoff, 1988).

Evidence that pre-operational children are not totally *egocentric* is apparent when they can take the perspective of others if the task is simplified. When shown a card with a horse on one side and an elephant on the other, they can say that the experimenter sitting across from them sees the elephant while they are seeing the horse (Masangkay *et al*, 1974). Children can also adapt their communication to different types of listeners. When a four-year-old tells a two-year-old about a toy, she uses shorter, simpler utterances than she does when telling a peer or adult about that toy (Shatz & Gelman, 1973).

Children in the pre-operational stage can differentiate between mental and physical worlds if the right questions are asked of them. When shown a photograph of two boys, one thinking about a biscuit and one holding a biscuit, children can tell which boy can actually eat the biscuit (Wellman & Estes, 1986). A related study showed that these pre-operational children can decentre their perceptions by sometimes focusing on less perceptually salient physical features of stimuli. Children at this young age preferred to describe people according to their mental states, rather than their physical actions; when shown drawings that illustrated both, they would be less likely to say, 'He's wiping up his spilled milk' than 'He's feeling sad about his spilled milk' (Lillard & Flavell, 1990).

■ Acquiring Language

The development of language is linked inextricably with cognitive development. On the one hand, children need their cognitive abilities to learn the

FIGURE 4.6	A SCHEMATIC REPRESENTATION OF HABITUATION AND TEST EVENTS

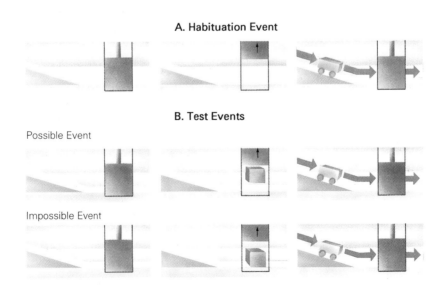

rules of language. On the other hand, ideas, reasons, arguments and other fruits of cognitive development are generally expressed in language. In this section, the nature–nurture interaction will again be a major character on the developmental stage. First, we will describe some of the language-learning abilities children are born with. However, as we shall see, this innate language readiness is only part of the story, since social factors in conversational language also play major roles in language acquisition. Here we will discuss some major topics in the development of language production and comprehension. The phenomenon of language will be treated more comprehensively in Chapter 9.

Innate precursors to language learning

Linguists agree that the ability to learn language is biologically based but that there is no universal language. This means that the predisposition to learn language must be remarkably flexible as well as strong (Meier, 1991).

There are five factors that many developmental linguists point to as especially important in language mastery by children: their high level of social interest, their speech perception and speech production abilities, their language acquisition device and finally, the time they spent listening to their mothers' sounds while still in utero. Let us see how each of these factors contributes to making children language experts so quickly.

Social interest. Infants are social beings. To new-borns, humans are very interesting and emotionally important stimuli. For example, studies show that infants prefer stimuli that have many rounded contours and edges and that move and emit sounds – in other words, objects that look and act similar to people. Without this interest in social interaction and in communicating with others, there would be no motivation for children to learn language.

Speech perception abilities. Except for children born with hearing deficits, all infants can hear many of the sound contrasts that languages use to distinguish between different meanings. In English, 'bit' and 'pit' have different meanings. We know that they are different words because we can hear the difference between /b/ and /p/, which are different *phonemes*, or minimal, meaningful sound units. There are about 45 distinct phonemes in English. Researchers using the habituation paradigm to study perception of speech sounds in infants from one to four months of age have shown that new-borns can distinguish all of them. Moreover, recent studies have shown that infants can hear sound differences that their parents

cannot. No language uses all of the speech sound contrasts that can be made. A well-known example is the lack of differentiation between the English /r/ and /l/ in Japanese. Native speakers of Japanese often have a very hard time hearing the difference between these sounds when they study English. English speakers are also plagued with this problem when they learn new languages: there are a number of sound contrasts that are used in other languages that adult English speakers have a very hard time hearing. Several such contrasts are used in Hindi.

In one of the studies, the researchers measured the ability of infants learning English and Hindi as well as adults who spoke English and Hindi to hear the differences between the Hindi phonemes. They found that all of the infants, regardless of which language they were learning, could hear the differences until the age of eight months. However, after eight months and of the adults, only the Hindi-speaking subjects could hear the Hindi contrasts. Thus, infants start out with sensitivities to sounds that they lose if these contrasts are not used in their language (Werker & Lalonde, 1988). The researchers argue that these developmental changes are best understood as a form of perceptual reorganisation rather than a complete loss of earlier abilities (Werker & Pegg, 1992).

Speech production abilities. In addition to their abilities to perceive speech sounds, infants have a biological predisposition to make certain sounds that will later be used in language. The basic apparatus for speech production (the vocal tract) is innate. Moreover, well before they begin to use true words, infants babble, making speechlike sounds (such as 'mamama' or 'bububu') and the age of onset of babbling seems to be biologically determined. Indeed, some linguists have argued that babblings are the direct precursors of speech sounds. Specifically, they suggest that a baby babbles all sounds in all languages and the repertoire is eventually narrowed down only to those sounds found in the language he or she learns (Mowrer, 1960). This view is not entirely accurate because a baby does not babble certain speech sounds (consonant clusters such as 'str' in 'strong' and 'xth' in 'sixth'). In addition, some sounds ('r' and 'l', for example) are present in babbling but not in a child's first words. Babbling allows children learning spoken languages to practice making sounds with the vocal apparatus, grouping the sounds into sequences and adding intonation to those sequences (Clark & Clark, 1977).

The language acquisition device. The linguist **Noam Chomsky** (1965, 1975) has argued that, in addition to these innate abilities, there is a biologically based **language acquisition device** (LAD) that plays a major role in children's language learning. Chomsky holds that children are born with biologically pre-determined mental structures that facilitate the comprehension and production of speech. Chomsky assumes that the LAD is mainly concerned with grammatical patterns and relationships. *Grammar* is a language's set of rules about combining word and word units in order to make understandable sentences. Different languages use considerably different rules about grammatical combinations.

In his days, Chomsky took issue with Skinner and other behaviourists who explained language acquisition in terms of children's actual language experience. Chomsky's principal argument against the behaviourist language theory is the so-called *poverty of stimulus argument* (Chomsky, 1980). It states that there is not enough information in the samples of speech children hear to account for the rich and complex language children develop. He further noted that virtually all children (except those with extreme impairments or those who experienced early social deprivation) learn language very quickly and he also argued that parents hardly ever provide feedback on grammatical rules – if they do correct or comment on their children's grammatics, this feedback is not sufficient to teach children grammatical rules. Children's talk, however, shows that they very quickly learn to apply implicitly the very complex set of grammatical rules.

Care-givers tend to correct children's utterances on the basis of their *truth value* rather than on their accurate grammatical quality. When a child says, 'One, two, I have two foots!', the care-giver may respond enthusiastically, 'That's right! You really know how to count now'. The care-giver is unlikely to frown and say, 'No, silly, you have two FEET, not two foots!' However, when children utter a grammatically correct but factually incorrect sentence, they are likely to be corrected. Neither learned imitation nor care-giver correction, then, can explain grammatical development very well. Moreover, many aspects of language emerge and evolve at particular periods – critical language acquisition periods – that correspond more closely with physical and cognitive maturation than with particular learning experiences (Lenneberg, 1969).

Pre-natal listening experience. One final factor that favours early language acquisition is pre-natal listening experience. Until recently, researchers have assumed that experience with language begins at birth. A compelling series of studies, however, challenges this assumption, suggesting that babies listen to sounds while they are still in utero. Researchers used rate of sucking as a dependent measure of preferences for sounds heard in the womb.

In the first study, mothers-to-be read aloud from a story-book, twice a day during the last two months of pregnancy.

A day or two after birth, their babies were tested for story preferences. The infants were given a non-nutritive nipple to suck. If the infant sped up their rate of sucking, a tape of one story was played; if she slowed down her rate of sucking, another story was played. One story was the same as the story the infant had heard pre-natally, while the other was a new story. In order to control for effects of particular rates of sucking, half of the infants heard the 'familiar' story when they sped up and half heard it when they slowed down. The researchers found that infants adjusted their rate of sucking in order to hear the story their mothers had read aloud during pregnancy. This means that they preferred listening to stories they had heard in utero, showing that they must have been listening (DeCasper & Spence, 1986). The studies also showed that new-borns prefer their mother's voices over those of strangers (DeCasper & Fifer, 1980).

There still is much unclear about pre-natal listening – for example, at what point is the foetus mature enough to perceive speech? It is clear, however, that these studies strongly suggest that babies are prepared to perceive speech at birth.

Communication skills

Without language you cannot communicate abstract ideas, but by using non-verbal gestures you can indicate you are hungry or tired; pre-linguistic infants use non-verbal means to communicate. They cry when distressed and coo and smile when pleased. At first, infant communication relies greatly on parents as interpreters, but over time, children take on more of the communication burden. The development of *pointing* is illustrative of the interaction between child and care-giver. Initially, this gesture is nothing more than an unsuccesful attempt to grasp something: the child's hands, stretched toward the desired object remain posed in the air. When a care-giver comes to the child's aid and realises that his or her movements indicate something, the situation changes fundamentally. The attempt to grasp something is interpreted as pointing, which is a gesture for others. In other words, the child's unsuccessful attempt engenders a reaction not from the object he or she seeks but from another person and, so, a new aspect of meaning is communicated (Bruner, 1986; Vygotsky, 1978).

Care-givers work to keep their infants' interest and to introduce them to language. When adults speak to infants and young children they use a special form that differs from adult speech: an exaggerated, high-pitched intonation known as **motherese**, also known as the *Baby Talk Register*. This way of speaking appears to serve a number of functions, among them to get and hold the infant's attention, communicate affect and mark turn-taking in parent–infant dialogues. Motherese intonations offer flexibility and instruction, containing affective messages without words. Care-givers use rising intonation to engage babies' attention, falling intonation to comfort them, and short staccato bursts as prohibitions. Cross-cultural research has shown that parents in many different cultures use these patterns and that babies understand them, even if they are not in their native tongue (Fernald *et al*, 1989).

Care-givers work to introduce their infants to language by engaging them in proto-dialogues. At first, these dialogues are very one-sided; care-givers will talk and pause at certain points to let infants respond. Care-givers will accept as valid responses anything the babies do, even burping or sneezing. As babies get older, care-givers become more demanding conversational partners, requiring at first that babies verbalise, later that they use actual words and later still that they use words relevant to the topic at hand. This pattern of gradually increasing demands on the child and decreasing parental support is called *scaffolding*. With this experience, young children become less reliant on their parents as interpreters of communication. The infants learn to use gestures (pointing) and non-verbal vocalisations (whining) to communicate their desires and interests. Eventually, children use their first words for making assertions and requests; they seem to use their very first words to communicate messages to others (Greenfield & Smith, 1976).

This is illustrated by the fact that children who know the word 'lemonade' will not utter the word (or an equivalent pattern of sounds) when they are alone. They will, however, pronounce 'lemonade' when others are present in order to ask for a drink. Therefore, utterances are communicative: children's words invite their care-givers to take their turn in the social interaction (Rogoff, 1990).

Learning words

Young children are excellent word learners. By the age of six, the average child is estimated to understand 14,000 words (Templin, 1957). Assuming that most of these words are learned between the ages of 18 months and six years, this works out to about nine new words a day, or almost one word per waking hour (Carey, 1978). The cumulative growth of a child's vocabulary is shown in *Figure 4.7*.

Initially, during the *one-word stage*, children use only one word at a time. These first single words are

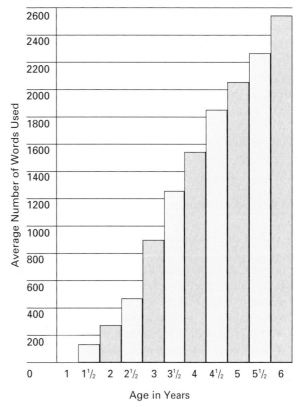

FIGURE 4.7 CHILDREN'S GROWTH IN VOCABULARY

The number of words a child can use increases rapidly between the ages of $1^1/_2$ and 6. This study shows children's average vocabularies at intervals of six months. *Source:* B. A. Moskowitz, 'The Acquisition of Language', Scientific American, Inc. All rights reserved. Reprinted by permission.

usually concrete nouns or verbs. Children use them to name objects that move, make a noise or can be manipulated – such as, 'mama', 'ball' and 'dog'. During the one-word stage, children sometimes over-extend words, using them incorrectly to cover a wide range of objects. For example, they may use the word 'dog' to refer to all animals or the word 'moon' to refer to all round objects, including clocks and coins.

At around 18 months, children's word learning often takes off at an amazing rate. At this age, children might point to every object in a room and ask, 'What's that?' Researchers have called this phase *the naming explosion* because children begin to acquire new words, especially names for objects, at a rapidly increasing rate.

Learning the names for objects is only the first stage of language learning. Before they fully grasp the reference from words to objects in the outside world, they sometimes use a kind of fantasy word in referring to the world outside language. Children can be highly consistent in using these personalised words. For example, the child who referred to ice cream as

'ABCDE'. It took his parents some time before they understood this peculiar referential expression. If the parents wanted something that they did not want their child to know they spelled out the word, as in 'Would you like some I-C-E-C-R-E-A-M?' Full spelling was too complicated for the child, so he spelled the letters he knew (Reich, 1986).

As children grow older, they begin to express more abstract meanings, going beyond talking about their physical world to begin talking about their psychological world as well. For example, around the age of two, children begin to use words such as 'dream', 'forget', 'pretend', 'believe', 'guess' and 'hope', as they talk about internal states (Shatz et al, 1983). Finally, after cognitive advances that occur later in childhood, they understand and use abstract words such as 'truth', 'justice' and 'idea'.

Acquiring grammar

As adult users of language, we know how to combine words into meaningful larger units. Combining words greatly increases the number of meanings and the level of complexity of those meanings. For example, 'Christine put the package in Philip's box' and 'Philip put the box in Christine's package' use the same words but have very different meanings.

During the one-word stage, the child actively develops hypotheses about the way to combine words into sentences. After the naming explosion, which occurs between 18 months and two years, children begin to use their one-word utterances in sequence to convey more complex meanings. By combining words into two-word utterances, children can communicate more meaning than simple identification. For adults to understand two-word utterances, they must know the context in which the words are spoken. 'Susan ball', for example, could mean, 'Susan wants the ball' or 'Susan throws the ball'. At this two-word stage, children across widely differing language communities tend to break down the world into similar linguistic categories with two-word utterances. For instance, ten children speaking different languages (English, Samoan, Finnish, Hebrew and Swedish) were found to talk mostly about three categories: movers, movable objects and locations (Braine, 1976).

After two words, sequence size continues to increase. From the two-word stage on into early multi-word sentences, children's speech is telegraphic: filled with short, simple sequences or sentences, using many content words (mostly nouns and verbs) but lacking tense endings and plurals. Telegraphic speech also lacks function words, such as 'the', 'and' and 'of' – for example, 'Bill hit ball window break' is a telegraphic message.

In addition to learning how to fill out the full grammatical form of sentences, children must learn how to put words together. For example, by the age of two, English-speaking children have learned that word order is important and that the three critical elements are actor–action–object, usually arranged in that order – for instance, 'The lamb followed Mary'. However, young children may misinterpret 'Mary was followed by her little lamb to school' which has a different word order and function words. Children must also learn how to rearrange the elements of a statement to form questions and negatives. To make a sentence negative, young children may simply put 'no' in front of it: 'No the sun is shining'. Later, they learn where to insert the negative: 'The sun is not shining'.

An additional grammatical skill that children need to acquire is using morphemes, which are the smallest units of meaning in a language (see Chapter 9). Suffixes such as -'s, -ed and -ing are morphemes and they mark certain kinds of meaning, such as possession (Maria's), past tense (danced) and continuing action (still laughing). It is apparent that they try out hypotheses about the way grammatical morphemes should be used. Sometimes, of course, their hypotheses are wrong.

One very common error is **over-regularisation**, in which a rule is applied too widely, resulting in incorrect linguistic forms. For example, once children learn the past-tense rule (adding -ed to the verb), they add -ed to all verbs, forming words such as doed and breaked. Over-regularisation is an especially interesting error to psycholinguists, as children who have learned the general rule for the past tense, will immediately extend it to all verbs, even to words that are exceptions to the rule – words that they previously used correctly. To researchers, such mistakes are evidence that language learning depends on acquiring general rules of grammar, rather than just imitating what adults say (Slobin, 1979). So, for developmental psychologists, the common errors of childhood offer exciting glimpses into the complex mental processes that underlie all human speech.

Social and Emotional Development

A child competent solely in language and cognitive skills would still be lacking appropriate social and emotional capabilities. Children's basic survival also depends on forming meaningful, effective relationships with other people. They need to learn and internalise their society's sets of rules which order much of the individual's behaviour and the interpersonal transactions of its members. This life-long process of shaping behaviour patterns, values, standards and motives in order to become a competent member of society is called **socialisation**. Many people are involved in the socialising practices, starting with the parents in the case of infants, followed by the influence of peers and of institutions such as school and college. In this section we will discuss firstly Vygotsky's pioneering work on development, who argues that all aspects of development, including the growth of language and cognitive abilities, are basically social in nature. Secondly, we will focus on the work of Erikson who presented an influential theory about the stages involved in social development throughout the life-course. Finally, we will briefly consider some important aspects of social development, notably attachment and the development of emotions and gender.

Individual development as a social product

The Russian psychologist **Lev Vygotsky** produced theoretical work on development in the revolutionary 1920s. Educated in literature and cultural history, he started teaching psychology shortly after the Russian October Revolution. His first book was on the psychology of art in which he coupled his love for literary research with his interest in psychology (Van der Veer & Valsiner, 1991).

In the following years he devoted himself to the theory and practice of psychology. In his theoretical work, echoing the Marxist theory of his time, he assumed that individual development is the outcome of an interaction between the biological development of the species and the historical progression of human culture. In this way, as soon as individual human beings are born they are, thus, both biologically and culturally equipped with that which was accumulated by earlier generations. In the same vein, Vygotsky argued that the individual's dimension of consciousness is a derivative of the social dimension of consciousness: from the moment of birth on, the infant is addressed as if he or she already possesses a consciousness, being referred to by name and addressed by the linguistic form of 'you' long before the child can use his or her name or the first person singular as a means of self-reference (Shotter, 1989).

Vygotsky goes on to argue that the so-called higher mental processes like cognition, memory and perception are to a large extent shaped by the culture a child lives in. This part of the theory was tested by Luria and his team in rural Russia. There, in a community of illiterate peasants, they tried to verify whether the concepts of thinking used by the peasants were different from the concepts used by educated people from Moscow. Although Luria and Vygotsky interpreted the results of these field experiments as support for the Vygotskean assumptions, later analyses showed that there were some missing links in the empirical evidence (Luria, 1976; Van der Veer & Valsiner, 1991).

Most of Vygotsky's work, however, was devoted to the study of development in mother–child interaction (Wertsch, 1985). In theoretical and empirical work, Vygotsky showed that thinking develops from the child's actions on its social and natural environment. This contrasts with the insights of his contemporary Piaget, who focused on the unfolding of cognitive capacites from their biological roots. The Vygotskean and Piagetian perspectives most clearly collide with respect to the relation between language and thought. Piaget was mainly concerned with the development of thinking capacities as a prerequisite for the acquisition of language; Vygotsky concentrated on the roots of thought in communicative interaction – for example, in play or 'conversation' – where mother and child jointly produce an understanding of the situation which is expressed in some form of language. Thus, communicative skills interact with cognitive structures and contribute to the development of mind (Vygotsky, 1987).

The particular psychological process involved in the social construction of mind through interaction is called **internalisation**. It is the process in which the child gains voluntary control over communicative forms, including language, that were originally external to him or her (Wertsch & Stone, 1985). This is illustrated in the following experiment.

A mother and her child of pre-school age are engaged in the solution of a jigsaw puzzle: pieces have to be put together to form a truck. Solving the puzzle evidently requires an exchange between mother and child. The researchers distinguish four levels in the interaction, which roughly correspond to different age levels. At the first level, the child's definition of the situation is so different from the adult's that communication is difficult, if not impossible. The mother's directives are not understood, communication is totally external to the child. By the second level a child begins to participate: he starts to pick up pieces for example, showing a partial understanding of the task. However, the mother still is the one who directs the actions toward the goal. At the third level, the child shows effective responses – for example, by copying his mother's actions. At the fourth level, the child takes the initiative and will generally direct his mother to a marginal position. Now, he is capable of solving the puzzle task himself and is eager to do so. The communicative forms that originally were provided by his mother, are now under his voluntary control; they have shifted from external to internal (Wertsch, 1979; Wertsch et al, 1980).

Social interaction as a prerequisite for cognitive development is also exemplified by Vygotsky's *Zone of Proximal Development*. He defined this specific kind of framework as the difference between a child's attained developmental level as determined by independent problem-solving and the higher level of potential development, estimated via problem solving under adult guidance or in collaboration with more capable peers (Vygotsky, 1978). The concept of the zone of proximal development has consequences for the design of methods of instruction: teachers should structure the tasks in school so that the teacher–child transaction invites the child to reach just above his or her actual capacities.

For a long time, Vygotsky's work was little known in Western Europe and the United States. In the past two decades, however, many developmental psychologists have followed the lead given earlier by **Jerome Bruner**, and used the theory about the social origins of children's minds in their own work (Wertsch & Tulviste, 1992).

Psychosocial stages of development

The most comprehensive theory of social development was presented by **Erik Erikson**. As a middle-aged immigrant to America from Germany, he became aware of conflicts he faced because of his new status, his thoughts being refined by his work with native Americans and returning World War II veterans. His awareness caused him to reflect on many such conflicts all individuals face in the life-long process of development. His reflection ultimately resulted in a new way of thinking about human development in terms of a sequence of conflicts and challenges that emerge at many stages in the life course, from infancy to old age. His background in psychoanalysis manifested itself in his insistence that the resolution of conflicts in the early phases of life are of consequences for later social development. However, he parted from the Freudian emphasis upon sexuality: rather than positioning stages that are *psychosexual* in nature, Erikson located *psychosocial* stages at the core of his theory. **Psychosocial stages** are successive orientations toward oneself and others that influence personality growth across the entire life span. Each stage requires a new level of social interaction; success or failure in achieving this can change the course of subsequent development in a positive or negative direction.

Erikson (1963) identified eight psychosocial stages in the life cycle. The four stages that cover infancy and childhood are discussed here (see *Table 4.3*). The other stages, which cover life from puberty onward, are discussed below in the section on adolescence and adulthood.

Each of the four stages that follow is characterised by a particular *crisis* or conflict. Although the conflict continues in different forms and is never resolved once and for all, it needs to be sufficiently resolved at a given stage if an individual is to cope successfully with the conflicts of later stages.

- *Trust vs Mistrust:* in the first stage an infant needs to develop a basic sense of trust in the environment through interaction with care-givers. Trust is a natural accompaniment to a strong attachment relationship with a parent who provides food, warmth and the comfort of physical closeness. But a child whose basic needs are not

TABLE 4.3 ERIKSON'S FIRST FOUR PSYCHOSOCIAL STAGES

Approximate Age	Crisis	Adequate Resolution	Inadequate Resolution
0–1½	Trust vs mistrust	Basic sense of safety	Insecurity, anxiety
1½–3	Autonomy vs self-doubt	Perception of self as agent capable of controlling own body and making things happen	Feelings of inadequacy to control events
3–6	Initiative vs guilt	Confidence in oneself as initiator, creator	Feelings of lack of self-worth
6–puberty	Competence vs inferiority	Adequacy in basic social and intellectual skills	Lack of self-confidence, feelings of failure

met, who experiences inconsistent handling, lack of physical closeness and warmth and the frequent absence of a caring adult, may develop a pervasive sense of mistrust, insecurity and anxiety. This child will not be prepared for the second stage which requires the individual to be adventurous.

- **Autonomy vs Self-doubt:** according to Erikson, with the development of walking and the beginnings of language, there is an expansion of a child's exploration and manipulation of objects (and sometimes people). With these activities should come a comfortable sense of *autonomy* and of being a capable and worthy person. Excessive restriction or criticism at this second stage of development may lead instead to self-doubts, while demands beyond the child's ability, as in too-early or too-severe toilet training, can discourage the individual's efforts to persevere in mastering new tasks. They also can lead to stormy scenes of confrontation, disrupting the close, supportive parent–child relationship that is needed to encourage the child to accept risks and meet new challenges. The two-year-old who insists that a particular ritual be followed or demands the right to do something without help is acting out of a need to affirm his or her autonomy and adequacy.

- **Initiative vs Guilt:** toward the end of the pre-school period, a child who has developed a basic sense of trust, first in the immediate environment and then in her or himself, has become a person who can now initiate both intellectual and motor activities. The ways that care-givers respond to the child's self-initiated activities either encourage the sense of freedom and self-confidence needed for the next stage or produce guilt and feelings of being an inept intruder in an adult world.

- **Competence vs Inferiority:** during the first of the school years, the child who has successfully resolved the crises of the earlier stages is ready to go beyond random exploring and testing to the systematic development of competencies. School and sports offer arenas for learning intellectual and motor skills, interaction with peers offers a space for developing social skills, opportunities develop through special lessons, organised group activities and perseverance of individual interests. Successful efforts in these pursuits lead to feelings of competence.

Erikson's first four psychosocial stages provide an organised perspective on social development in infancy and childhood. Now we will slightly shift our focus of attention. We will concentrate on three important aspects of social development in the first phases of life by discussing attachment, the development of emotions, and gender.

Attachment

Erikson's trust–mistrust stage already pointed to the importance of a high-quality bond between children and care-givers. In fact, social development begins with the establishment of a close emotional relationship between a child and regular care-giver. This intense, enduring, social-emotional relationship is called an **attachment**. Attachment behaviours appear to occur instinctively in many species. Among rats, for example, the mother's licking of the new-born or eating of the placenta activates hormones that prime her to provide care and protection for her young (Pedersen *et al*, 1982). In other species, the infant automatically forms an attachment to the first moving object it sees or hears (Johnson & Gottlieb, 1981). When this attachment occurs rapidly and during a critical period of development and it has a lasting effect on later social behaviour, the process is called **imprinting**. The response in newly hatched ducklings to their mother's movements is a classic example of imprinting. Because the mother is usually the first moving object the duckling sees, the infant normally imprints on an appropriate adult member of its species. However, young geese raised by a human will imprint on the human instead of on one of their own kind, as demonstrated by ethologist **Konrad Lorenz** (1937).

Human infants and human care-givers may have similar instinctive attachment behaviours. In the 1970s, it was reported that human mothers were more

Konrad Lorenz, the researcher who pioneered in the study of imprinting, graphically demonstrates what can happen when young animals become imprinted on someone other than their mother.

likely to 'bond' with their babies if they were allowed to see and hold the babies immediately after delivery (Klaus & Kennell, 1976). Researchers proposed that child-birth activated bonding hormones in the mothers. Although later research has shown that physical contact immediately after delivery is neither critical for, nor enough to, stimulate human attachment. Hormones alone cannot account for attachment and human babies also cannot rely on their own locomotor capacities to achieve closeness to and get attention from a care-giver. Human babies do, however, seem to have built-in behaviours that signal to others to respond to them (Campos *et al*, 1983). Smiling, crying and vocalising are examples of these proximity-promoting signals. Successful attachment, of course, depends on an infant's ability to emit these signals and also on an adult's tendency to respond to the signals. According to the pioneer of attachment research, **John Bowlby** (1973), infants will form attachments to individuals who consistently and appropriately respond to their signals. The desired result is secure attachment which provides a psychological home base which enables the child to explore the environment, take risks and accept intimacy in personal relationships.

The empirical study of attachment

Many theorists both inside and outside psychology have argued that babies become attached to their parents because the parents provide them with food. This is called the *cupboard theory* of attachment. However, it may be that the cupboard explanation is only part of the story. There are many times when infants seem to be very interested in developing social relationships and participating in playful interactions with people who have never given them food.

Harry Harlow (1965) did not believe that the cupboard theory completely explained the motivation for and importance of attachment. He set out to test the cupboard theory of attachment against his own hypothesis that infants might also attach to those who provide **contact comfort**. Harlow separated macaque monkeys from their mothers at birth and placed them in cages where they had access to two artificial 'mothers': one consisted of an exposed wire structure and the other was covered with soft towelling cloth.

Harlow found that the baby monkeys nestled close to the soft cloth mother and spent little time on the wire one. They did this even when only the wire mother gave milk! The baby monkeys also used the cloth mother as a source of *comfort when frightened and as a base when exploring new stimuli. When a fear stimulus (for example, a toy bear beating a drum) was introduced, the baby monkeys would run to the cloth mother. When novel and intriguing stimuli were introduced, the baby monkeys would gradually venture out to explore and then return to the towelling cloth mother before exploring further. When new stimuli were presented in the cloth mother's absence, the monkeys would often freeze in a crouched position or run from object to object screaming and crying. The infant monkeys became more attached to and actually preferred the mother that provided contact comfort than to the one that provided food (Harlow & Zimmerman, 1958).*

Further studies by Harlow and his colleagues found that the monkeys' formation of a strong attachment to the mother substitute was not sufficient for healthy social development. At first, the experimenters thought the young monkeys with soft cloth mothers were developing normally, but a very different picture emerged when the female monkeys who had been raised in this way became mothers. If these monkeys had been deprived of interaction with other monkeys in their early lives, they had trouble forming normal relationships in adulthood. After the birth of her baby, the first of these unmothered mothers ignored her infant and sat relatively motionless at one side of the living cage. If a human observer approached and threatened either the baby or the mother, there was no counter-threat. As the infant matured and became mobile, it made continual,

One of Harlow's monkeys and its artificial terry-cloth mother. Harlow found that the contact comfort mothers provide is essential for normal social development.

desperate attempts to accomplish maternal contact. These attempts were consistently repulsed by the mother. She would brush the baby away or restrain it by pushing the baby's face to the woven-wire floor (Harlow, 1965).

Human babies are subjected to different kinds of research procedures. One of the most widely used methods for assessing attachment is the *Strange Situation Test* developed by **Mary Ainsworth** and her colleagues (Ainsworth *et al*, 1978). In the standard version of this test the following procedure is followed. First, the child is brought into an unfamiliar room filled with toys. With mother present, the child is encouraged to explore the room and to play. After several minutes, a stranger comes in, talks to the mother and approaches the child. Next, the mother exits the room. After this brief separation, the mother returns, there is a reunion with her child, and the stranger leaves. The researchers record the child's behaviours at separation and reunion.

The researchers have found that children's responses fall into three or, perhaps, four general categories. *Securely attached* children show some distress when the parent leaves the room; seek proximity, comfort and contact upon reunion and then gradually return to play. *Insecurely attached-avoidant* children seem aloof and may actively avoid and ignore the parent upon her return. *Insecurely attached-ambivalent* children become quite upset and anxious when the parent leaves; at reunion they cannot be comforted and they show anger and resistance to the parent but, at the same time, express a desire for contact. More recently, another classification has been added to describe children who act dazed and confused upon reunion. After the parent's return, these *insecurely attached-disorganised* children may stop moving completely or show contradictory behaviour patterns, such as gazing away while in contact with the parent (Main *et al*, 1985).

Observations of human infants in ordinary settings have also demonstrated the critical value of contact comfort. A lack of close, loving relationships in infancy has been shown in many studies to affect physical growth and even survival. Studies of hospitalised infants found that, despite adequate nutrition, the children often developed respiratory infections and fevers of unknown origin, failed to gain weight and even showed signs of physiological deterioration (Bowlby, 1969; Sherrod *et al*, 1978; Spitz & Wolf, 1946).

A tragedy has occurred in recent times in institutions in Romania where as many as 40,000 homeless infants and children have been kept under the worst possible conditions. Many of these children are called 'non-recoverables'; a more accurate translation is 'lost forever'. Dictator Nicolae Ceaucescu (overthrown in 1990) started a campaign to increase Romania's population, at any cost. The country's extremely poor economic conditions caused such hardships that many mothers abandoned the babies they had conceived in response to Ceaucescu's campaign. Many of these children who were left in state institutions 'appear to suffer chiefly from isolation and neglect . . . Babies may have been born normal but arrive at the orphanage totally unresponsive, the result of never having been shown affection or being touched'. Relief workers have found 'children tied to their beds, starving and filthy. Often, the children have never been touched or held. No one has talked to them. They rock back and forth, staring blankly' (Sachs, 1990). It is doubtful whether any form of intervention can fully overcome this early trauma of having no attachment to a caring adult.

The controversy surrounding Bowlby's theory and empirical research on attachment is whether these behaviour patterns seen in infants at 12 and 18 months of age are stable over time. In other words, do insecurely attached infants become insecurely attached pre-schoolers and perhaps even insecurely attached adults? A common result of studies on abused children, who as a rule are insecurely attached, is that they are hostile and aggressive toward their peers. In one study of ten abused toddlers, ages one to three years, researchers found that the children did not respond appropriately when a peer was in distress. When another child is upset and crying, toddlers will normally respond by showing concern, empathy or sadness. By contrast, the abused children were more likely to respond with fear, anger or physical attacks (Main & George, 1985).

Research on attachment has shown that social development requires affectionate relationships with other members of the species. In the earlier studies, the focus was attachment to the biological mother. Subsequent research has, however, shown that the early proximity of the child to the biological mother is not necessary for attachment and healthy social development (Rutter, 1979). Positive bonds can be formed with any care-giver who is *comforting*, *interacts* actively, and is *responsive* to a baby's signals (Ainsworth, 1973).

During the past decade, many researchers have devoted their attention to attachment relations in institutional forms of care, such as day-care centres. In the relationship between professional care-givers and children, the quality of attachment is as crucial as the mother–child bond. If professional care-givers interact actively with the children and are comforting and responsive, a high-quality attachment is usually formed (Goossens & Van IJzendoorn, 1990). In general, studies using measures of attachment to evaluate social and emotional development find no important differences between maternal and non-maternal care (Scarr & Eisenberg, 1993).

Emotional development

Thus far we have discussed emotion in a very rudimentary sense. Research on attachment has shown that children require family bonds that enable the expression of emotion. Now we briefly turn to the specific issue of emotional development. Our discussion will show that human beings are not fully equipped with a fine-tuned emotional repertoire at birth. Like every other human attribute, this aspect of the person needs to be developed. The process of emotional development is directly linked to that of social development but also includes cognitive aspects.

The study of emotional development is a rather recent topic of research (Harris, 1989). Emotions are difficult to study in children, especially in the very young, because at these ages we have to rely totally on facial and other bodily expressions to provide us with information. It is not until the development of self-reflexive cognitions and their linguistic expression that complex emotions like shame and guilt can be studied in detail.

Bridges (1932) observed that children display a dichotomous emotional life at birth: they express pleasure when their needs are satisfied, and distress is acted out when they feel frustrated. After about three months babies tend to show signs of joy when they are cherished by familiar people, usually their caregivers. The expression of this emotion by smiling is one way in which children have a significant impact on their social environment. The aphorism, 'smile and the world smiles back', seems to be applicable to the earliest forms of interaction (Fridlund, 1990). In about the same period sadness becomes evident – for example, when positive stimulation is withdrawn or when the care-giver leaves the room suddenly. Disgust also appears at about the age of three months, disgust being shown when, for example, a taste or smell is disliked (Lewis, 1993).

Anger and fear emerge in the second half of the first year (Lewis, 1991; Stenberg et al 1983). The former is expressed, for example, when the child's movement is frustrated, whilst fear generally arises in response to unfamiliar circumstances. The more complex emotions like embarrassment and envy appear later on the scene. These emotions presuppose the development of self-awareness, because they imply an acknowledgement of individuality. This cognitive capacity has been shown to arise at about 18 months (Lewis, 1991). The class of emotions that emerges latest in development is concerned with the evaluation of the child's behaviour against a code or standard. This class includes, for example, pride, shame and guilt. These emotions are expressed and understood from about the age of two-and-a-half (Lewis, 1993).

The links with more specific kinds of cognitive operations are stressed by researchers who argue that children first have to understand that people generally act from goals, desires and beliefs before they are capable of comprehending that people will be sad if they do not get what they want, or happy if they do. Soon, this understanding is translated into the realisation that there is nothing inherently delightful or distressing about a given outcome; one person may be pleased to be given milk, whereas another may be unhappy because she wanted juice instead (Harris, 1993).

The social embeddedness of emotional development is emphasised by the fact that children are well aware of the type of situation that elicits a particular emotion and that they know the actions and expressions that accompany particular emotions (Harris et al, 1987). It has been found that six-year-olds who appeared capable of indicating situations that would result in either pride, shame or guilt were in fact describing ones in which their *parents* would experience these emotions. They were able to apply the emotional concept to a specific situation, but would not necessarily be able to experience the emotion themselves (Smiley & Huttenlocher, 1989). From a Vygotskean point of view, it has been argued that children learn to understand emotions like embarrassment and guilt through the internalisation of their parents' actions. When parents feel embarrassed in a particular circumstance, because, for example, their child has knocked over a pile of cans in a supermarket, they will communicate this feeling of embarrassment through action, thus displaying what it means to act out 'embarrassment' (Semin & Papadopoulou, 1990). In other words, the interaction between parent and offspring provides an emotional education for the child.

The development of gender

Undeniably males and females are anatomically different. However, the apparent dissimilarities in their behaviour are largely influenced by their varying roles and socially constructed identities as designated within a given society. Some of these behavioural contrasts are linked to biological ones, but many stem from differences in *socialisation processes*. Throughout the course of their development, boys and girls learn about the frequently divergent expectations that their culture and society place on them. In order to study these processes and expectations more closely, it is useful to begin by looking at what is generally understood by the terms sex and gender.

Sex refers to the biologically based characteristics

Young children tend to be segregationists and seek out peers of the same sex.

that distinguish males and females. These characteristics include distinctive reproductive attributes and dissimiliarities in terms of hormones and anatomy. These biologically based differences may result in differential behaviour for boys and girls. For example, boys tend to be more physically active and aggressive than girls and to engage in rough play after infancy (Maccoby, 1980). In contrast to biological sex, **gender** is a social and psychological phenomenon referring to learned, sex-related behaviours and attitudes. Cultures vary in how strongly gender is linked to daily activities and in the amount of tolerance of what is perceived as gendered and cross-gendered behaviour. **Gender identity** incorporates an individual's sense of 'maleness' and 'femaleness'; it includes awareness and acceptance of one's sex. Some individuals, such as transsexuals, experience conflict between their biological sex and their gender identity. A sense of gender identity that is acceptable to oneself and others is assumed to be important to a child's psychological well-being.

Psychological theories have given different accounts of the development of gender differences and gender identity. First, we will discuss the perspective that stresses the social construction of gender. Next we will sketch Chodorow's psychodynamic theory and then finish with a presentation of Bem's cognitive theory.

The social construction of gender roles. **Gender roles** are patterns of behaviour that are traditionally regarded as socially appropriate for males and females within a particular societal context. They provide the guiding definitions for 'masculinity' and 'femininity'. Much of what we consider masculine or feminine is shaped by our culture (Hare-Mustin & Maracek, 1988; 1990; Williams, 1983). Children learn the gender roles of their cultures in many ways; they often imitate the behaviour of people around them or

of people in films, TV programmes or books. Adults may reward them for gender-congruent behaviour and punish them for actions that are gender-incongruent. In many cultures, boys and girls receive strong negative responses from their parents when they engage in cross-gender behaviour (Langlois & Downs, 1980). Finally, children also develop and are reinforced for beliefs about rules which limit gender roles ('Girls can't play football').

Gender-role socialisation begins at birth. In one study, parents described their new-born daughters, using words such as 'little', 'delicate', 'beautiful' and 'weak'. By contrast, parents described their new-born sons as 'firm', 'alert', 'strong' and 'co-ordinated'. The babies actually showed no differences in height, weight or health (Rubin *et al*, 1974). The differences in the responses of these parents seems to be based on *gender-role stereotypes*.

Eleanor Maccoby (1988) has found evidence that play styles and toy preferences are not highly correlated with parental preferences or roles. Maccoby believes that many of the differences in gender behaviour among children are the results of peer relationships. Because of gender-role socialisation, boys and girls grow up in different psychological environments that shape their views of the world and their ways of dealing with problems. Children between the ages of two and six seem to have more extreme and inflexible perceptions of gender than do adults (Stern & Karraker, 1989). The children's extreme reactions may be linked to the fact that they are at the age when they are rather uncertain about their own gender and, thus, tend to accentuate gender stereotypic behaviour in an effort to consolidate their emerging sense of self. Consequently young children tend to be segregationists: they seek out peers of the same sex even when adults are not monitoring their behaviour or in spite of adult encouragement for mixed-group play.

The reproduction of mothering. The theory of feminist psychologist **Nancy Chodorow** (1978) blends insights from psychoanalysis with more recent work concerning the social construction of gender. Chodorow argues that the traditional nuclear family of the Western middle-class creates a socio-emotional context that inevitably dichotomises gender. In most middle-class families, fathers spend much time working in locations that lie beyond the walls of the family home, whereas mothers spend their days taking care of the children. From the moment of birth onwards, mothers see themselves consciously and unconsciously reflected in their little girls because they are of the same sex. The result is a close emotional bond between mother and daughter. Likewise, girls will consciously or unconsciously acknowledge that they are woven out of the same fabric as is their mother. Therefore, they develop a relational identity in which the need for intimacy and the expression of feelings are crucial features. Thus, from the earliest years, girls are socialised to become mothers themselves.

Boys, on the other hand, are generally treated as 'others' and will therefore draw back from their mothers, separating themselves off from this primary relational context. Furthermore, they have to identify with an absent father – that is, with an ideal rather than with a real person made of flesh and blood. This results in a male identity which is characterised by autonomy and an independent ego, and also in the repression of emotions – men fearing loss of control and absorption into others during these potentially vulnerable states. Chodorow's account has precipitated studies which indeed show that women are generally more oriented towards social relationships whilst men place more value on their independence and personal accomplishments (Chodorow, 1989; Gilligan, 1982; Hyde, 1991).

Through the lenses of gender. Cognitive theorists have argued that at about two-and-a-half years of age, a conceptual awareness of gender differences begins to emerge. During the pre-operational stage, children quickly learn to value what is modelled to them by same-sex peers and adults, consequently seeking out that which is designated as sex-appropriate activity. They develop *gender constancy* – that is the understanding that a person's sex remains the same despite changes in appearance. Gender constancy parallels the principle of conservation and is, for example, tested by asking children whether a doll's sex could be changed if the children wanted to. Most four-year-olds answer in the affirmative, whereas most six-year-olds say it is not possible (Kohlberg, 1966).

In *gender schema theory,* it is argued that children develop their gender identity with reference to schemas that are culturally embedded (Bem, 1981b). Due to the fact that Western culture is gender-polarising in its discourse and social institutions (Burman, 1994), children assimilate these values without even being aware of this process. In the terminology of **Sandra Bem**, children learn to perceive the world and themselves 'through the lenses of gender' (Bem, 1993). When they mature

INTERIM SUMMARY

Freud assumed that sexuality motivated development. In his account, infancy and childhood are divided into psychosexual stages. The oral, anal and phallic stage are followed by a latency stage after which the genital stage describes the fulfilment of psychosexual development.

Piaget formulated a stage theory concerning the way the child's conceptual abilities emerge and expand. His key ideas centre on the development of schemes, assimilation (which fits new input into existing mental structures), accommodation (which changes current aspects of thinking to fit new input) and the four-stage theory of discontinuous cognitive development. The earliest sensorimotor stage is one in which infants are assumed to know and think in very limited ways and to be perceptual-behaving creatures rather than conceptual ones. In the pre-operational stage, the ability to represent absent events becomes well organised. During the concrete operational stage, earlier mental deficiencies wane. The child can perform a range of mental operations involving concrete, but not symbolic, thoughts. The final stage of formal operations involves acquiring all the mental structures necessary to reason logically and abstractly.

Many features of Piaget's theories are being challenged by current investigators. There is now evidence that perceptual and conceptual functioning occur at much earlier ages and that the sensorimotor stage may not be a necessary first stage of cognitive development.

Children are master language-learners. Some researchers believe that we have an in-born language-acquisition device. Culture and parental interaction are essential parts of the language acquisition process. There are fixed stages of word-learning that proceed from a pre-verbal babbling stage, to a one-word stage, a two-word stage and finally towards the limitless utterances of short sentences in the telegraphic stage. Language development and cognitive development are intertwined.

Developmental psychologists who work from a social perspective, like Vygotsky, hold that individual development is essentially produced in a social context. Through interaction with care-givers, children learn to internalise what is relevant to them. Erikson proposed a stage theory for social development in which each stage is characterised by a particular social crisis that has to be resolved before the next stage is entered.

Socialisation begins with an infant's attachment to a care-giver. Failure to make this attachment may lead to numerous physical and psychological problems. Research on emotional development has shown that joy, sadness and disgust are evident very soon after birth. More complex emotions like anger and fear develop later because they are linked to the child's actions within and upon the environment. Pride, shame and guilt emerge still later because they presuppose cultural knowledge on the part of the child. Gender is a psychological phenomenon referring to learned, sex-related behaviour and attitudes. Gender-role socialisation begins at birth. A variety of socialising agents reinforce gender stereotypes.

cognitively they come to understand that gender is a primary organisational principle in society and they also learn to apply this information to themselves. Contemporary Western societies are full of examples of gender polarisation: from the pink and blue clothes and baby rooms in the first years of life to the conceptions of what is psychologically appropriate for boys and girls. For example, feelings of vulnerability and affection for same-sex peers are generally considered inappropriate for boys. Gender schema theory thus situates the motivation for a match between sex and behaviour in the gender polarisation of the culture rather than in that of the child's mind (Bem, 1993).

ADOLESCENCE AND ADULTHOOD

In the preceding section it was clear that the theorists who influenced the study of individual development, such as Sigmund Freud and Jean Piaget, focused mainly on early life periods. They assumed that the burden of development is carried on only through adolescence; after that the person and the psyche were set for life and would experience relatively few important changes. Erikson happens to be the exception to this rule: for him, development is a life-long process.

The long-held notions in developmental psychology about the insignificance of adult mid-life and the irreversible decline of biological and psychological functioning in the elderly are also challenged by recent empirical studies. Emerging from this research is the basic premise of *life-span developmental psychology*: that personality, mental functioning and other vital aspects of human nature

continue to develop and change throughout the entire life cycle.

Life-span development explores the continuities, stabilities and changes in physical and psychological processes that characterise human functioning from conception through to the final phases of life (Honzik, 1984). Though childhood years are formative, we have a remarkable capacity for change across the entire life-span (Brim & Kagan, 1980). The long-term effects of early infant and childhood experiences are highly variable and continue to be influenced by later experiences (Henderson, 1980; Simmel, 1980).

Adult Ages and Stages

Development in adolescence and adulthood has also been subjected to stage-like divisions, with researchers of development across the life-span having proposed different and diverse stages (Levinson 1978; 1986; Vaillant, 1977). The most influential theory of stages across the life-span is that of Erikson. In the preceding section we discussed the first four of his psychosocial stages concerned with infancy and childhood. Now we will turn to the next four stages which describe the characteristic conflicts that are said to emerge from adolescence onwards.

- *Identity vs Role confusion:* Erikson believed that the essential crisis of adolescence is discovering one's true identity amid the confusion created by playing many different roles for the different audiences in an expanding social world. Resolving this crisis helps the individual to develop a sense of a coherent self; failing to do so adequately may

TABLE 4.4	ERIKSON'S LATER PSYCHOSOCIAL STAGES (ADOLESCENCE TO LATER ADULT)		
Approximate Age	**Crisis**	**Adequate Resolution**	**Inadequate Resolution**
Adolescent	Identity vs role confusion	Comfortable sense of self as a person	Sense of self as fragmented; shifting, unclear sense of self
Early adult	Intimacy vs isolation	Capacity for closeness and commitment to another	Feeling of aloneness, separation; denial of need for closeness
Middle adult	Generativity vs stagnation	Focus of concern beyond oneself to family, society, future generations	Self-indulgent concerns; lack of future orientation
Later adult	Ego-integrity vs despair	Sense of wholeness, basic satisfaction with life	Feelings of futility, disappointment

result in a self-image that lacks a central stable core. Erikson coined the term **identity crisis** to describe the unfavourable outcome of this stage. According to him, adolescents who have not been able to develop a basic sense of trust during infancy, are at risk to suffer from an identity crisis.

- *Intimacy vs Isolation:* the essential crisis for the young adult is to resolve the conflict between intimacy and isolation – to develop the capacity to make full emotional, moral and sexual commitments to other people. This requires the individual to compromise some personal preferences, accept some responsibilities and yield some degree of privacy and independence. Failure to resolve this crisis adequately leads to isolation and the inability to connect to others in psychologically meaningful ways. Much research (see Chapter 11) supports the conclusion that anything that isolates us from sources of *social support* – from a reliable network of friends and family – puts us at risk for a host of physical ills, mental problems and even social pathologies.

- *Generativity vs Stagnation:* according to Erikson, the next major opportunity for growth occurs during adult mid-life and is known as *generativity.*

People in their 30s and 40s move beyond a focus on self and partner to broaden commitments to family, work, society and future generations. Those who have not resolved earlier life-stage crises of identity and intimacy, however, may experience a mid-life crisis. These people are still self-preoccupied, question past decisions and goals, want to sacrifice commitments for one last fling and pursue freedom at the expense of security.

- *Ego–integrity vs Despair:* awareness of one's mortality and changes in body, behaviour and social roles sets the stage for Erikson's final stage of late adulthood. Resolving the crises at each of the earlier stages prepares the older adult to resolve the crisis of late adulthood – to look back without regrets and to enjoy a sense of a meaningful, integrated life. When previous crises are left unresolved, aspirations remain unfulfilled and the individual experiences futility, despair and self-depreciation. The overall result is that a person may fail to solve the crisis at this final developmental stage as well. Some elderly people, confronted by this ultimate sense of failure, choose to end their lives, rather than continue to experience such emotional pain.

Erikson's psychosocial stages provide an organising principle for social development across the life-span. We now turn to the specific characteristics of adolesence and adulthood.

Adolescence

For successive cohorts of adolescents, each of the stages of life are played out against a background of ever-changing values and social, economic and political patterns. In many European nations and in

Many cultures have initiation rites that signal a child's passage into adulthood. Shown above left is a bar mitzvah, a Jewish ceremony marking a boy's 13th birthday. The photo on the bottom left records the puberty rites of the White Mountain Apaches of Arizona. On the right is a photo of the initiation ceremony of a young Lamaist monk.

the United States, the conformity and conservatism of the post-World War II 1950s manifested itself in terms of patriotic fever, unthinking obedience to authority, traditional values and a baby boom. Coupled with sexual freedom bolstered by the development of birth control technology, this sowed the seeds of the adolescent revolution of the 1960s and early 1970s. Although we all experience the developmental stage of adolescence in our lives, the particular shapes and forms of this stage differ widely from generation to generation as prevailing social conditions change from one decade to the next.

Adolescence is commonly defined as the stage of life that begins at the onset of **puberty**, when sexual maturity, or the ability to reproduce, is attained. However, where adolescence ends and adulthood begins is not so clear. Although the physical changes that take place at this stage seem to be universal, the social and psychological dimensions of the adolescent experience are highly dependent on the cultural context.

Transition and intiation rites

Most non-industrial societies do not identify an actual adolescent stage as we know it. Instead, many such societies have rites of passage or **initiation rites**. These rituals usually take place around puberty and serve as a public acknowledgment of the transition from childhood to adulthood. They vary widely from extremely painful ordeals to instruction in sexual and cultural practices or periods of seclusion involving survival ordeals. In many cultures, separate rites are carried out for males and females, reflecting gender polarisation.

A common psychodynamic interpretation of initiation rites is that male children must confront and come to terms with power relations before entering adult status. They are to identify themselves with powerful males, like their fathers, rather than harbour any impulses of violence toward them. This process is known as and involves 'identification with the aggressor'. Young men are also required to give up being dependent on their mothers, so that they are neither ambivalent about their male status nor likely to violate incest taboos (DeVos & Hippler, 1969).

In many traditional societies, the period of adolescence as a transition between childhood and adulthood lasts for only the few hours or the few months of the rite of passage. Once individuals have passed through that period, there is no ambiguity about their status – they are adults and the ties to their childhood have been severed. In white Western European secular society, there are few transition rituals to help children clearly mark their new

adolescent status; therefore, adolescence can extend for more than a decade, through the teens to the mid-20s.

Tasks of adolescence

Of all the issues that are important in adolescence, we will focus on two developmental tasks that commonly confront adolescents in Western society: (a) coming to terms with adult sexuality; and (b) redefining social roles, including achieving personal autonomy. Each of these issues is a component of the central task of establishing an integrated identity. Consistent with Erikson's (1968) description of the social context of identity, each of these issues can be looked at as a different way in which young people define themselves in relation to others.

Physical maturity and sexuality. Puberty is generally signified by *menarche* (the onset of menstruation) in girls and this generally occurs between 11 and 15 years of age. For boys, puberty is signified by the production of live sperm, accompanied by the ability to ejaculate, first occuring on average, at about 14 years. There are, however, considerable variations in this timing.

Part of achieving a personal identity involves coming to terms with one's physical self. The term **body image** refers to the way one subjectively views one's appearance. This image is dependent not only on measurable features, such as height and weight, but also on other people's assessments and on cultural standards of attractiveness. During adolescence, dramatic physical changes and heightened emphasis on peer acceptance (especially peers of the opposite sex) can lead to an increased, if not excessive, concern with one's body image (Hatfield & Sprecher, 1986). In one study, approximately 44 per cent of adolescent girls and 23 per cent of boys claimed that they 'frequently felt ugly and unattractive' (Offer *et al*, 1981a). Even more striking, in another study, physical appearance was the biggest source of concern for a group of 240 secondary school students (Eme *et al*, 1979).

The self-concepts of girls are closely tied to perceptions of their physical attractiveness, while boys seem to be more concerned with their physical prowess, athletic ability and effectiveness (Lerner *et al*, 1976). These differences probably mirror a Western cultural preoccupation with female beauty and male strength, and as some adolescents may not embody the cultural stereotypes of attractiveness, it is not surprising that this preoccupation can become a major source of concern. Uncertainty about one's body image sometimes results in rigid dieting and serious eating disorders, such as anorexia and bulimia (see Chapter 10).

A new awareness of sexual feelings and impulses accompanies physical maturity. In early adolescence, masturbation is the most common expression of sexual impulses. About 50 per cent of boys and 37 per cent of girls report masturbating by the age of 13; 80 per cent of boys and 69 per cent of girls report masturbating by the age of 18 or 19 (Hass, 1979; Sorensen, 1973). Homosexual experiences are also common in adolescence. Between 14 and 17 per cent of teenage boys report some homosexual experiences, although the actual rate may be considerably higher. The rate is about half as high for adolescent girls (Hass, 1979; Sorensen, 1973). The proportion of adolescents engaging in sexual intercourse has risen substantially in the last 20 years. It is estimated that at least half of all young people have engaged in intercourse before age 18 and about 75 per cent have done so by the age of 20 (Chilman, 1983; London *et al*, 1989).

Empirical investigations indicate that the initial sexual experiences of boys and girls differ substantially. The vast majority of girls become sexually involved with individuals with whom they are in love. In contrast, for most adolescent males, personal relationships appear to be less important than the sexual act itself – the young male reports no emotional involvement with his first sexual partner (Miller & Simon, 1980).

Social relationships. Erikson asserted that the essential crisis of adolesence is discovering one's true identity amid the confusion of playing many different roles. Family ties are stretched as the adolescent spends more time outside the home. In Western societies, this change typically means that the adolescent experiences less structure and adult guidance, is exposed to new and perhaps conflicting values and develops a strong need for peer support and acceptance. Adolescents report spending more than four times as much time talking to peers as adults and also a preference for talking to their peers (Csikszentmihalyi *et al*, 1977). Peers become an increasingly important source of social contact and emotional support; but it appears that, as needs for close friendships and peer acceptance become greater, there is also an increase in the anxiety that may become associated with being rejected. Conformity to peer values and behaviours rises to a peak around ages 12 and 13. Concerns with peer acceptance and popularity are particularly strong for girls who appear to be more focused upon social relations than their male counterparts; but girls are less likely to conform to group pressures to engage in anti-social behaviours than are boys (Berndt, 1979).

The dual forces of parents and peers at times constitute opposing influences on adolescents and this conflict can fuel the dynamic processes of separating

from parents and of identifying increasingly with like-minded, same-age people. In general, however, parents and peers may be seen as serving complementary functions and fulfilling different needs in the lives of adolescents (Davis, 1985).

If the adolescent is not able to establish new relationships, loneliness becomes significant. Between 15 and 25 per cent report feeling very lonely (Offer *et al*, 1981a). Shyness reaches its highest level in early teenage years as desire for social acceptance markedly increases (Zimbardo, 1990).

The myth of adolescent 'sturm und drang'

The traditional 'sturm und drang' or 'storm and stress' view of adolescence holds that it is a uniquely tumultuous period of life, characterised by extreme mood swings and unpredictable, difficult behaviour. This view can be traced back to Romantic writers of the late eighteenth and early nineteenth centuries. Indeed, it was Goethe who made famous the 'sturm und drang' phrase. More recently, this conception of adolescence was strongly propounded by **G. Stanley Hall**, the first psychologist of the modern era to write at length about adolescent development (1904). Following Hall, the major proponents of this view have been psychoanalytic theorists (for example, Blos, 1967; A. Freud, 1946; 1958). Some of them have argued that not only is extreme turmoil a normal part of adolescence, but that failure to exhibit such angst is a sign of arrested development. **Anna Freud** writes that 'to be normal during the adolescent period is by itself abnormal' (1958).

TABLE 4.5	THE PSYCHOLOGICAL SELF OF THE NORMAL ADOLESCENT

Item	Percentage of Adolescents Endorsing Each Item
I feel relaxed under normal circumstances.	91
I enjoy life.	90
Usually I control myself.	90
I feel strong and healthy.	86
Most of the time I am happy.	85
Even when I am sad I can enjoy a good joke.	83

It was not until large studies were undertaken of representative adolescents however, that the turmoil theory finally began to be widely questioned within psychology. The results of such studies have been consistent: most adolescents (four out of every five) do not experience the inner turmoil and unpredictable behaviour ascribed to them (Offer *et al*, 1981a; Oldham, 1978b). Offer and his colleagues asked over 20,000 adolescents about their personal experiences. The researchers concluded that the majority of adolescents 'function well, enjoy good relationships with their families and friends and accept the values of the larger society' (1981; see *Table 4.5*).

Other studies have found that while adolescents may differ greatly from their fathers and mothers in terms of preferences for music, fashion and other issues of personal taste, their fundamental values tend to remain similar to those of their parents (Conger, 1991).

There also appears to be much more consistency in personality development from early adolescence to adulthood than the traditional turmoil theory would predict. Successful adjustment in adolescence tends to predict appropiate adaptation in adulthood and although adolescence is experienced by some young people as a stressful time, those few adolescents who experience serious trauma during this period are likely to continue doing so as they move into adulthood (Bachman *et al*, 1979; Offer & Offer, 1975; Vaillant, 1977). A recent study clearly points to the strong pathway between adolescent conduct problems and subsequent adult criminality:

> *A large-scale longitudinal study of adolescents (ages ten to 13) attending school in a Swedish town compared their conduct status (from teachers' reports) and biological functioning with the likelihood of their having criminal records or other adjustment problems as young adults (ages 18 to 26). Among the boys, those who showed early aggressiveness, restlessness (hyperactivity) and low levels of adrenaline were significantly more likely to develop into adults who would commit registered criminal offences. In addition, a more severe pattern of early maladjustment is correlated with other indices of adult adjustment problems as well, such as alcohol abuse and being under psychiatric care (Magnusson, 1987; Magnusson & Bergman, 1990).*

◧ Adulthood

In adulthood people are generally exploring options for commitment and social acceptance, while, at the same time, seeking greater change and risks. When they reflect on their own development they may re-examine earlier choices in light of new knowledge.

The tasks of adulthood

We owe to Freud a classical statement about adulthood. He said that, despite the many variations in adult life-styles, adult development is driven by two basic needs: 'lieben und arbeiten' (or 'love and work'). Abraham Maslow (1968) described these needs as *love* and *belonging* which, when satisfied, develop into the needs for success and esteem. Other theorists describe these basic needs as affiliation or social acceptance needs and achievement or competence needs. Recall that, for Erikson, the comparable needs are intimacy and generativity.

Erikson perceived young adults as consolidating clear and comfortable senses of their identity in preparation for embracing the risks and potentials of intimacy. However, the sequence from identity to intimacy that Erikson described may not accurately reflect present-day realities. The trend in recent years has been for young adults to live together before marrying. As a result, they tend to marry later in life than people did in the past. These societal developments suggest that many individuals today must struggle with identity issues, such as vocational choice, at the same time that they are dealing with intimacy issues.

In addition, marriage and intimate partnerships today often occur more than once. In fact, married adults are now divorcing at a rate four times greater than adults did 50 years ago. The current prevalence of divorce and separation leads many adults to re-examine their conceptions of and capacity for intimacy at later points in the life cycle. A major factor in the rising divorce rate is that spouses have higher expectations for each other and of what constitutes an ideal marriage and family structure (Cleek & Pearson, 1985). However, some studies have indicated that communication between modern spouses is substantially better than it was in earlier times (Caplow, 1982).

Those who have not successfully resolved the crises of identity and intimacy may still be trying to do so in their later adulthood, perhaps with an increasing sense of insecurity and failure. A crisis that may develop at this middle stage of life is the struggle between the desire for security, with its comforting stability and predictability, and the desire for freedom, with its exciting potential for adventure and new experiences. In many traditional marriages, women give up much more of their personal freedom and autonomy than men in the hope of achieving security, which is often illusory and short-lived.

TABLE 4.6 DIFFERENCES BETWEEN BEST AND WORST-OUTCOME SUBJECTS ON FACTORS RELATED TO PSYCHOSOCIAL MATURITY

	Best Outcomes (30 men)	Worst Outcomes (30 men)
Childhood environment poor	17%	47%
Pessimism, self-doubt, passivity and fear of sex at 50	3%	50%
Personality integration rated in bottom fifth percentile during college	0	33%
Subjects whose career choice reflected identification with father	60%	27%
Dominated by mother in adult life	0	40%
Failure to marry by 30	3%	37%
Bleak friendship patterns at 50	0	57%
Current job has little supervisory responsibility	20%	93%
Children's outcome described as good or excellent	66%	23%

Systematic studies documenting the details of individual development in adulthood are comparatively recent and are still mapping previously unmarked territory. **George Vaillant** (1977) studied the personality development of 95 highly intelligent American men through interviews and observations over a 30-year period following their graduations from university in the mid-1930s. Many of the men showed great changes over time and their later behaviour was often quite different from their conduct in early adulthood. The interviews covered the topics of physical health, social relationships and career achievement. At the end of the 30-year period, the 30 subjects with the best outcomes and the 30 with the worst outcomes were identified and compared in a number of ways, including in terms of their maturity as defined by Erikson's psychosocial stages. *Table 4.6* compares the scores of the two groups on several items that indicate degree of psychosocial maturity.

By middle life, the best-outcome men were carrying out generativity tasks, assuming responsibility for others and contributing in some way to the world. Their maturity even seemed to be associated with the adjustment of their children – the more mature fathers were more able to give children the help they needed in adjusting to the world. In a supplementary study of 57 members of the sample, the ongoing importance of the capacity for intimacy was confirmed. The purpose of the study was to predict psychosocial adjustment in middle age from measures of social motivation 17 years earlier. The best predictor of mental, physical and social adjustment was *intimacy motivation*, 'a recurrent preference or readiness for experiences of close, warm and communicative interpersonal exchange' (Vaillant, 1977). The two areas of adjustment that were most highly correlated with intimacy motivation were enjoyment of job and marital satisfaction (McAdams & Vaillant, 1982).

In general, less is known about the adult personality development of women. In light of changing sex roles over the last few decades, a central issue for adult women has become the integration of occupational and family aspirations. Women seem to be more realistic than men when they express uncertainty about vocational choice. They are well aware that it takes effort to combine a job with parenthood. Men, on the other hand, seem not to be bothered much about the responsibilities of parenthood. It was also found that women who have families and work outside the home tend to be more satisfied with their lives than either single working women or married home-makers (Crosby, 1982; Sheehy, 1976).

Many developmental theorists have proposed that the quality of adult relationships and social functioning can be traced to the quality of parent–child relationships, especially in the early years of life (Ainsworth, 1989; Freud, 1949; Hartup, 1989; Hazen & Shaver, 1987). To evaluate empirically the effects of early life experiences on subsequent adult development, it is necessary to carry out longitudinal prospective research in which data about early relationships is collected when the subjects are children. However, much research has been of a retrospective nature, assessing the childhood rearing patterns and parent–child relationships of adult subjects. Such research may provide biased or mis-remembered accounts. A large-scale American study has carefully examined the childhood antecedents of social accomplishment of mid-life adults by using a prospective longitudinal design. The social accomplishment that the researcher measured was a subject's capacity to maintain a marriage, a family and outside friendships.

The study began in 1951 with interviews of 379 mothers about the child-rearing practices they used with their five-year-olds who attended nursery school. Additional data about the social and personal adjustment of each child (202 boys and 177 girls from both working-class and middle-class backgrounds) were collected from the nursery teachers. Until the children turned 18, researchers also made measures of sources of family stress, including divorce, death, hospitalisation and moving. When these subjects turned 41, those who could be contacted completed questionnaires and interviews. The final sample consisted of 76 married or previously married white subjects – 33 men and 43 women – primarily from middle-class backgrounds. Measures of social adjustment were taken in the form of reports about various aspects of each subject's life history, including marriage, divorce and the quality of personal relationships. Other measures taken included physical health, life satisfaction, feelings of stress and well-being.

The key finding in this study was that the mothers' reports of feelings of warmth felt and expressed for their five-year-old child were significantly associated with the child's conventional social accomplishment more than three decades later. Adults with warm, affectionate mothers or fathers were able to sustain long and relatively happy marriages, raise children and be involved with friends at mid-life. Contrary to expectations, parental harmony did not relate to social accomplishment in the adults, nor did having a difficult childhood. Socially accomplished adults were

emotionally stable, active, reliable and self-disciplined. Compared to the subjects who tested low on this measure of conventional social adjustment, the socially accomplished subjects had higher levels of psychological well-being, had less strain and showed a greater sense of generativity. In addition, those whose marriages and family lives were working best were also more committed to and involved with their life work (Franz et al, 1991).

Adult thinking

Adults' thinking differs from adolescents' in several distinctive ways. In the process of meeting the tasks of adulthood, adults change their style of thinking to become more highly focused and channelled in specific directions. They must more often take into account the differing perspectives of people from a wider range of ages and backgrounds than they did as adolescents. They must discover how to negotiate disputes and resolve conflicts through compromise, bargaining and generating alternative goals or paths.

Recall that, according to Piaget, the final stage of cognitive development is that of formal operational thought, achieved in adolescence through maturation and educational experience. Formal thinking enables one to reason logically and to use abstract thought to solve general problems. But most of the everyday, practical problems of adults occur in ambiguous, unstructured social and work relationships. Dealing with these unknowns and partial truths with formal thought is too limiting and rigid. What adult life requires is a more dynamic, less abstract and less absolute way of thinking that can deal with inconsistencies, contradictions and ambiguities. This pragmatic, world-wise cognitive style that adults use is referred to as **post-formal thought** (Basseches, 1984; Labouvie-Vief, 1985).

K. Warner Schaie (1978) studied adult thinking and suggested that the cognitive style of adults occurs in stages. *Table 4.7* outlines the five stages of cognitive

TABLE 4.7	SCHAIE'S STAGES OF COGNITIVE DEVELOPMENT		
Childhood and Adolescence	**Early Adulthood**	**Middle Adulthood**	**Late Adulthood**
Acquisition (Piaget's four stages)	Achieving (goal-directed learning)	Responsible (concern for others) Executive (concern for social systems)	Reintegrative (wisdom)

development across the life course. Through adolescence, the person acquires information and techniques for solving problems that are generic and not typically relevant to personal-life situations. In early adulthood this 'liberal arts' knowledge gives way at the achieving stage to a focus on information used for more narrowly defined, self-relevant purposes, such as achieving specific goals. With middle adulthood comes the responsible stage, a broadening of this 'entrepreneurial' style of personal goal-seeking to a focus on responsibilities to others, especially to family and community. For some people in this mid-adult period, the feeling of responsibility extends to a deeper, more complex concern for social welfare and for harmony between social, political and occupational groups. Schaie identifies this deeper level as the executive stage, where the person thinks in terms of obligations and commitments to larger systems. Finally, during late adulthood, the individual re-focuses cognitive style inward to make sense of his or her own life and, simultaneously, outward to deal with broad issues, such as the meaning of life and death and concerns about the survival of the planet. At this re-integrative stage, the individual develops a thinking style that is best characterised as evidence of wisdom.

Moral development

One of the hallmarks of adult thinking is the development of higher levels of moral reasoning.

Morality is a system of beliefs, values and underlying judgements relating to the rightness or wrongness of human acts. Developing an understanding and internalisation of morality is an important part of socialisation. Society wants children to become adults who accept its moral value system and whose behaviour is guided by moral principles. However, there is an important difference between moral reasoning and actually practising the principles of moral behaviour.

Moral reasoning. Piaget (1960) sought to tie the development of moral judgement to a child's general cognitive development, as discussed earlier in this chapter. As the child progresses through the stages of cognitive growth, he or she assigns differing relative weights to the consequences of an act and to the actor's intentions. For example, to the pre-operational child, someone who breaks ten cups accidentally is 'naughtier' than someone who breaks one cup intentionally. As the child gets older, the actor's intentions weigh more heavily in the judgement of morality. The best-known psychological approach to moral development was created by **Lawrence Kohlberg** (1964; 1973; 1981). Kohlberg, who based his theory on Piaget's earlier work, focused on the stages of development of moral reasoning. Each stage is characterised by a different basis for making moral judgements. *Table 4.8* summarises the seven stages proposed by Kohlberg.

The lowest level of moral reasoning is based on self-interest, while higher levels centre on social good,

| TABLE 4.8 | KOHLBERG'S STAGES OF MORAL REASONING |

Levels and Stages	Reasons for Moral Behaviour
PRE-CONVENTIONAL MORALITY	
Stage 1 Pleasure/pain orientation	**To avoid pain or not to get caught**
Stage 2 Cost-benefit orientation; reciprocity – an eye for an eye	**To get rewards**
CONVENTIONAL MORALITY	
Stage 3 Good child orientation	**To gain acceptance and avoid disapproval**
Stage 4 Law and order orientation	**To follow rules, avoid censure by authorities**
PRINCIPLED MORALITY	
Stage 5 Social contract orientation	**To promote the society's welfare**
Stage 6 Ethical principle orientation	**To achieve justice and avoid self-condemnation**
Stage 7 Cosmic orientation	**To be true to universal principles and feel oneself part of a cosmic direction that transcends social norms**

regardless of personal gain. The stages are acquired in order and each can be seen to be more cognitively sophisticated than the preceding one. Acquisition of these stages generally parallels the development of stages of cognitive ability proposed by Piaget. Stages 1 to 3 are traversed by most people over the course of cognitive development; almost all children reach stage 3 by the age of 13. In contrast, not all people attain stages 4 to 7. Sometimes adults who have attained a higher stage drop back a stage or two under certain circumstances. The higher stages are not associated with any particular age or type of cognitive achievement. Empirical research on moral reasoning is generally done with adult subjects. To measure the kinds of moral reasoning that people use at these different stages, Kohlberg used a series of moral dilemmas that pit different moral principles against one another.

In one dilemma, a man named Heinz is trying to help his wife obtain a certain drug needed to treat her cancer. An unscrupulous pharmacist will only sell it to Heinz for ten times more than the cost price. This is much more money than Heinz has and more than he can raise. Heinz becomes desperate, breaks into the pharmacist's shop and steals the drug for his wife. Should Heinz have done that? Why?

The scoring is based on the reasons the person gives for the decision and not on the decision that is made. For example, a subject who says that the man should steal the drug because of his obligation to his dying wife or that he should not steal the drug because of his obligation to uphold the law of society (despite his personal feelings about saving his wife's life) is expressing concern about meeting established obligations and is scored at stage 4.

There are four principles governing Kohlberg's moral stage model: (a) an individual can be at one and only one of these stages at a given time; (b) everyone goes through the stages in a fixed order; (c) each stage is more comprehensive and complex than the preceding; and (d) the same stages occur in every culture. These principles apply more clearly to the first three stages of moral reasoning than they do to the last four.

Kohlberg's stages of moral reasoning have generated considerable controversy. The content of the stages themselves appears to be somewhat more subjective and it is harder to understand each successive stage as more comprehensive and sophisticated than the preceding. For example, 'avoiding self-condemnation', the basis for moral judgements at stage 6, does not seem obviously more sophisticated than 'promoting society's welfare', the basis for judgements at stage 5. In addition, the

universality of the stages is questionable. The higher stages are not found in all cultures and appear to be associated with education and verbal ability in Western culture and therefore are inappropriate measures for cultures that do not emphasise a high degree of abstraction and education (Gibbs, 1977; Simpson 1974). Thus, these features should not necessarily be prerequisites for moral achievement (Rest & Thoma, 1985).

Additionally, many researchers have questioned Kohlberg's decision to study moral reasoning instead of moral action; these critics believe that what people say (intentions) and what they do (behaviour) when faced with moral choices often differ (Kurtines & Greif, 1974). Also controversial is the early claim Kohlberg made that women lag behind men in moral development, typically stopping at a less advanced level than men do. We will now examine these last two criticisms more closely below.

Gender differences in moral judgement. There has been considerable controversy over the question of gender differences in moral reasoning. In early experiments, Kohlberg (1969) and others using his measurement paradigm (Alker & Poppen, 1973) found that most men reach stage 4, a law-and-order orientation, while most women remain at stage 3, where moral reasoning involves living up to the expectations of others. This conclusion is challenged by some researchers. **Carol Gilligan** (1982) has proposed that Kohlberg's finding that women's morality is less fully developed than men can be explained by the fact that his coding scheme is biased in favour of men. His original work was developed from observations of boys only. Gilligan believes that women develop differently, not less morally. She proposes that women's moral development is based on a standard of caring for others and progresses to a stage of self-realisation, whereas men base their reasoning on a standard of justice. In addition, men may refer more to fairness (Lyons, 1983). Other researchers dispute whether gender differences in moral reasoning really exist at all (Baumrind, 1986; Greeno & Maccoby, 1986). These variations may also be attributable to the artificial distinction made between the ethic of care and the ethic of justice, which is common in most empirical studies of the subject (Nunner-Winkler, 1984). One review of the empirical literature shows that gender differences in moral reasoning are rarely found and when they are found, they are explained by the male subjects in a particular study having a higher than average education level than the female subjects (Walker, 1984). These possibly different orientations may not necessarily correspond to women and men scoring differently on Kohlberg's scale or other moral reasoning scales (Gibbs *et al*, 1984; Lyons, 1983). The jury is still out on this complex issue.

Moral action. Of course, the alleged gender differences in moral judgement may have absolutely nothing to do with moral behaviour. The majority of studies of gender differences in pro-social or moral behaviours have found no consistent differences between the sexes (Eisenberg & Mussen, 1989; Radke-Yarrow *et al*, 1983). In addition, very different patterns of moral reasoning and understanding may lead to the same moral behaviours. Furthermore, one's level of moral understanding may have little to do with one's display of moral action (Blasi, 1980).

Kohlberg's theory of moral development does not address human motivation to act morally as he was interested in the cognitive aspect of moral reasoning and not in the moral behaviour itself. However, if we want to understand moral development more completely, we must consider what it is that motivates people to behave honestly, co-operatively or altruistically. Several groups of psychologists recently have begun to investigate the emotional and social roots of morality. **Martin Hoffman** (1987), among others, argues that emotions within the child, especially empathy, may provide the motivation for moral behaviour. Observational studies reveal that children experience empathy at very young ages and some researchers believe that empathy may actually be an innate response (such as sucking or crying).

Empathy is the condition of identifying oneself mentally with someone else's emotion. Feeling another person's distress may trigger a sympathetic response. First, children feel distress with and then sorrow for another individual. Children then may want to reduce these unpleasant feelings and they discover that acting positively towards the distressed person helps accomplish this. Young children are capable of positive social behaviours designed to help or comfort others in apparent distress. Many psychologists now believe these types of behaviour signal the start of moral development. Empathy may represent part of the foundation for future moral behaviour (Zahn-Waxler & Radke-Yarrow, 1982).

INTERIM SUMMARY

Life-span theorists have proposed stage models to describe the development of adult personality, cognition and moral reasoning. The most influential theory about adult development is Erikson's, in which four stages are proposed from adolescence to life's end. In Western societies, adolescence is a loosely defined period between childhood and adulthood marked by the onset of puberty. In some societies, relatively dramatic initiation rites more clearly define the transition between childhood and adulthood, but individuals in these cultural settings may not actually go through an 'adolescent' stage. Despite reports of the turmoil experienced during these teenage years, evidence from self-reports of adolescents reveals that this period for the majority is not a time of 'storm and stress'; most adolescents report being relatively satisfied with their lives. However, an over-concern about appearance and social rejection is common, as are shyness, feelings of loneliness and eating disorders. The adolescent is faced with resolving two main issues: forming a coherent sexuality; and establishing personal autonomy and adaptive social and sexual relationships with parents and peers.

A major change during adulthood is the emergence of post-formal thinking which is pragmatic, problem-oriented, socially sensitive and sufficiently flexible to cope with the ambiguities of adult life. Moral reasoning follows a clear stage model of development at the lower levels, but it does not do so for the hypothesised higher levels. Controversy exists about the nature of gender differences in moral reasoning. Some investigators have found differences in the moral levels of men and women: it is argued that females are more responsive to social relationships and obligations (which gives them lower scores on corresponding measurement scales) than males who are focused largely on the issue of justice as the moral touchstone of their reasoning. Psychologists have studied moral reasoning but have overlooked moral behaviour. Conditions have been examined under which children and adults behave in moral or immoral ways, but disregarding the cognitive components that underlie their moral reasoning.

OLD AGE

One of the fastest-growing specialised fields in psychology is **behavioural gerontology**, the study of all the psychological aspects of aging and of the elderly. The expansion of this area is undoubtedly stimulated by the changing composition of populations. At the beginning of this century in most European countries and the United States less than five per cent of the population was over 65. Today that figure is about ten per cent, and when the baby-boom generation reaches old age around the year 2020, nearly a quarter of the population in Western countries will be in this oldest group. By that time the age-class over 65 will be larger than the one under 20 years of age – a dramatic reversal of all previous demographics (Pifer & Bronte, 1986). With such drastic changes occurring in the age distribution of our society, it is more essential than ever for us to understand the nature of aging as well as the particular abilities and needs of the elderly.

Research Approaches to Aging

Traditionally research about aging has focused on age changes – the way people change as they grow older. Usually, however, empirical data demonstrate age differences – the way people of different ages differ from one another. Why is this so? Cross-sectional research designs are more commonly used than longitudinal research. Age differences uncovered in cross-sectional studies sometimes reflect age-changes, but sometimes they do not. They may instead represent *cohort effects* – that is, differences between people born at different times in history, rather than differences in what the same people at different chronological ages can do.

Consider an imaginary study on computer literacy as an example of the way research can be misleading. You sit people of varying ages in front of word-processors. Then you ask the subjects to perform basic word-processing tasks. You discover that the older the subjects are, the less well they perform the task. It would be inaccurate to assume that as people age, they lose their abilities to use computers. Many older generations did not have access to such technology until they were well into their adult years, if ever. This is an example of the cohort effect. The critical difference is not the age of the person but the experience of the different cohorts. The study informs us only of differences or similarities between younger people and older people.

Perspectives on Aging

Aging can mean different things depending on which perspective is taken. From a physiological viewpoint, biological aging typically means decline: energy reserves are reduced, cells decay and muscle tone diminishes. However, from a psychological standpoint aging is not synonymous with decline. Many aspects of the human condition improve with age. The life-long accumulation of experience, for example, may culminate in wisdom during old age. One recent theoretical approach to studying change and stability views development – at any age – in terms of the joint occurrence of gains and losses (Baltes, 1987). For example, as a child gains the ability to talk, to some extent she loses the ability to get what she wants by simply crying. In old age, a person may lose energy reserves but gain an ability to control emotional experiences and thereby conserve energy. Viewed in this way, we can expect two kinds of changes, gains and losses, as we grow older.

A successful aging strategy might consist of making the most of gains while minimising the impact of the losses that accompany normal aging. This strategy for successful aging, proposed by psychologists **Margaret**

Baltes and **Paul Baltes**, is called **selective optimisation with compensation** (Baltes, M., 1986; Baltes, P., 1987). *Selective* here indicates that people scale down the number and extent of their goals for themselves. *Optimisation* refers to people exercising or training themselves in areas that are of highest priority to them. *Compensation* means that people use alternative ways to deal with losses (for example, choosing age-friendly environments). While this general strategy of adapting to losses and taking advantage of gains may be universal, each individual's adaptations will likely take on quite different forms.

Fortunately, many older people have discovered particular strategies that help them age successfully. However, there are those who experience trouble or personal difficulty in aging, which may be caused by cultural myths of aging and stereotypes of the elderly. **Agism** is the term for prejudice against older people. Agism leads to discrimination against the elderly that limits their opportunities, isolates them and fosters negative representations of them. Our society values growth, strength and physical appearance and worships youthfulness; the enemy is the aging process marked by signs of decline and weakness (Butler & Lewis, 1982). Even undergraduate psychology texts have been found guilty of agism. A survey of 139 texts written over the past 40 years reveals that many of the texts failed to cover the period of late adulthood or presented stereotypical views of the elderly (Whitbourne & Hulicka, 1990). But a more dramatic instance of agism is shown in the personal experiences of a reporter who deliberately 'turned old' for a while.

Pat Moore disguised herself as an 85-year-old woman and wandered the streets of over 100 American cities to discover what it means to be old in America. Clouded contact lenses and earplugs diminished her vision and hearing; bindings on her legs made walking difficult; and taped fingers had the dexterity of arthritic ones. This 'little old lady' struggled to survive in a world designed for the young, strong and agile. She could not open jars, hold pens, read labels or climb up the stairs on the bus. The world of speed, noise and shadows frightened her. When she needed assistance, few people offered it. She was often ridiculed for being old and vulnerable and was even violently attacked by a gang of adolescents (Moore in Discovering Psychology, *1990, Programme 18).*

The Changes of Age

Old age does increase susceptibility to illness. Even so, it is crucial to distinguish changes associated with normal aging – changes most people can expect as they grow old – from those associated with disease or illness. Making this distinction is not as simple as it sounds. At one time, it was a commonly held myth that anyone would become senile if he or she lived long enough. Now, most severe cognitive deficits are attributed to specific age-related diseases – some of which are avoidable or treatable – rather than to natural consequences of the aging process. The boundaries between what we consider normal age changes and what we consider the effects of disease and illness are changing with our expanding medical and psychological knowledge. Indeed, we now know that most cognitive abilities do not show major or significant decline under ordinary circumstances of ageing. In this final section of our study of development, normal aging is examined.

Physiological Changes

Some of the most obvious changes that occur with age concern people's physical appearances and abilities. As we grow older, we can expect our skin to wrinkle, our hair to thin and become grey and our height to decrease about five centimeters. Our hearts and lungs operate less efficiently with age and, therefore, we can expect decreased physical stamina. We can also expect some of our senses to dull. These changes occur gradually, beginning as soon as early adulthood. Below are some common age-related sensory and physical changes, their effects and some ways people effectively deal with them.

Vision. The vast majority of people over 65 experience some loss of visual ability. With age, the lenses of people's eyes become more rigid, making close sight and night vision more difficult. The lens becomes yellow and this is thought to be responsible for diminished colour vision experienced by some older people. Colours of lower wavelengths – violets, blues and greens – are particularly hard for some elderly people to discriminate. Without corrective lenses, half of the elderly would be considered legally blind.

Hearing. Hearing loss is common among those of 60 years and older. The average older person will have difficulty hearing high frequency sounds (this impairment is greater for men than for women). Understanding speech, particularly that spoken by high-pitched voices, becomes harder. Deficits in hearing can be quite gradual and hard for an individual to notice until they are extreme. Perhaps even when the person becomes aware of it, he or she may wish to deny it because it is perceived as an undesirable sign of old age.

Hearing loss that remains undetected or denied,

however, can have far-reaching implications (Maher & Ross, 1984; Manschreck, 1989). An elderly person may think that those around him are whispering so that he will not be able to hear them converse. If this is how someone makes sense of his inability to understand other people's speech, it is easy to see how *mild paranoia* can develop. It is not uncommon for nursing home residents to exhibit mild paranoid symptoms.

In a controlled laboratory study, healthy college student subjects were hypnotised to have temporary partial hearing loss with amnesia for the hypnotic suggestion. When others in the room could not be clearly understood, each of the experimental subjects began to respond with suspicion, hostility and eventually with paranoid-like thinking. Their reactions were undone with debriefing (Zimbardo *et al*, 1981). Thus, it may well be that the prevalence of paranoid thinking among the institutionalised elderly is not so much a function of changes in mental functioning due to aging as it is a function of undetected hearing loss.

Sexual functioning. One myth about aging is that old people cannot or should not be sexual. While some age-related changes affect sexual functioning, belief in a myth such as this can be a greater obstacle to having a satisfying sex life in old age than actual physical limitations. Although sex loses its reproductive functions in old age, it does not lose its capacity to provide pleasure. Indeed, sex is one of life's 'healthy pleasures' which should be practiced with regularity whenever possible to enhance successful aging, since it is arousing, provides aerobic exercise, stimulates fantasy and is a form of social interaction (Ornstein & Sobel, 1989). There is no age, for women or for men, at which orgasm ceases. The most noticeable change older women experience after menopause (the cessation of menstruation and ovulation) is less natural lubrication and less fatty tissue surrounding the vagina and clitoris. In general, there is less known about how men's sexual functioning changes with age. Older men seem to place less emphasis on ejaculation as the primary means of achieving sexual pleasure. Consequently, older men can maintain their erections longer, which can lead to greater sexual satisfaction for both partners. Sexuality is one clear domain where experience can compensate for physical changes.

Cognitive changes

One of the great fears about aging is that it is accompanied by the loss of cognitive abilities: thinking productively and creatively, remembering, planning and making good decisions. Is this fear justified?

Intelligence. There is little evidence to support the notion that general cognitive abilities decline among the healthy elderly. Only about five per cent of us will become senile and experience major losses in cognitive functioning. The majority of us will experience more difficulty in forming new associations and we can expect to acquire new information more slowly by the time we are in our 70s or 80s, but we will probably not undergo dramatic changes in the way we think. There is even evidence that some aspects of intellectual functioning are superior in older people. For instance, psychologists are now exploring age-related gains in *wisdom* – expertise in the fundamental pragmatics of life (Baltes, 1990).

When age-related decline in cognitive functioning occurs, it is usually limited to only some abilities. When intelligence is separated into the components that make up our verbal abilities (*crystallised intelligence*) and those that are part of our ability to learn quickly and thoroughly (*fluid intelligence*), only fluid intelligence shows slight decline with age (Botwinick, 1977).

Individuals vary greatly in their later-life intellectual performance. Elderly people who pursue high levels of environmental stimulation, tend to maintain high levels of cognitive abilities. Diversity in cognitive functioning among older individuals leads psychologists to reject claims that cognitive decline in old age is caused by systematic physiological decay of the central nervous system. Instead, it appears that *disuse*, rather than decay, may be responsible for isolated deficits in intellectual performance (Schaie, 1989). It is even possible to learn how to reuse cognitive abilities after not using them with, for instance, cognitive training techniques for inductive reasoning and spatial orientation (Schaie & Willis, 1986).

Memory. A common complaint among older people is the feeling that their ability to remember things is not as good as it used to be; this is also borne out in the results of memory tests for adults over 60 years of age (Hultsch *et al*, 1990). While trying to evaluate these complaints, psychologists have learned that not all memory systems show deficits with age. As yet, they have also been unable to come up with a complete explanation for the mechanisms that underlie memory impairment in old age (Light, 1991). Memory difficulties appear primarily in that part of the memory system known as short-term or *working memory*, where new memories are processed and stored for less than a minute (Poon, 1985). Aging does not seem to diminish long-term memory for an event that occurred long ago, for instance, remembering the faces and names of classmates from school (Bahrick *et al*, 1975).

There are many different theories about the effects of age on memory. Some theories focus on differences between old and young people in their efforts to organise and encode the information that is to be remembered later; others point to the elderly's reduced attentional capacity; and still others suggest that the elderly's belief that their memory is poor may impair performance.

Other theories look to differences in the brain. There are two general ways in which age-related, neurobiological changes might result in impaired memory. The first is cell loss or decay in the brain itself. The second is deficiencies in the biochemicals, or *neurotransmitters,* that flow through the brain (see Chapter 2). If the brain mechanisms responsible for memory are intact in older people, but these mechanisms are not optimally fuelled by neuroendocrine systems, then memory impairment might be lessened by increasing neurotransmitter levels. For example, it was found that long-term memory was enhanced among elderly subjects who were given drinks containing glucose (which helps the brain to utilise neuroendocrines). This suggests that neuroendocrine systems may be responsible for memory loss and that pharmacological treatment may improve memory in the elderly (Manning *et al*, 1990).

Both cognitive theories and neurobiological theories of memory changes related to ageing are being vigorously investigated at this time. The hope is to improve not only our general understanding of the nature of human memory and the ageing process, but to develop strategies and procedures for preventing memory impairment.

Social changes

One unfortunate consequence of living is that you can expect to outlive some of your friends and family

As people age, they become more selective in choosing their companions, maintaining only the most rewarding social contacts.

members; older people will be particularly aware of this. Some older people find it difficult getting out and socialising with friends and family because their mobility is restricted by light or serious disabilities. Given these considerations, it is not surprising that people become less socially active in old age. This finding is well-established, supported by both cross-sectional and longitudinal studies. Yet, rates of social contact in later life decrease more substantially than can be explained solely by the deaths of friends and loved ones and reduced mobility.

One early explanation assumed that the elderly voluntarily withdraw from society in symbolic preparation for inevitable death (Cumming & Henry, 1961). This *disengagement view of aging* has been largely discredited for a number of reasons. The first reason is that it fails to acknowledge that older people do remain vitally involved with some people, particularly family members and long-time friends. Interestingly, having one intimate relationship (with either a friend or family member) has been found to be more important in promoting older people's health, well-being and longevity than having dozens of casual friends. Having a pet seems to have similar benefits (Siegel, 1990). The second reason the disengagement view has been criticised is that older people are not emotionless or emotionally withdrawn as the disengagement view implies (Levenson *et al*, 1991; Malatesta & Kalnok, 1984). There is even some evidence that, in old age, emotions become more central determinants of people's social preferences (Frederickson & Carstensen, 1990). It has also been suggested that, as people age, they become more selective in choosing their social partners, maintaining only their most rewarding relationships. Selective social interaction may also be a practical means by which people can regulate their emotional experiences and conserve their physical energy (Carstensen, 1987; 1991).

Psychological disorders

The incidence rates for most functional mental disorders appear to be lowest after age 65, with the exception of perhaps depression and the dementias, such as *Alzheimer's disease* (Kay & Bergmann, 1982; see Chapter 8). The normal course of aging does not usually or necessarily entail worsened mental health.

Depression has long been assumed to be the most common psychological disorder among the elderly, with risk of onset increasing steadily as people age. Recent epidemiological studies, however, have called this assumption into question. Some studies suggest that initial onset of major depression is less prevalent among those 65 and older than in younger groups

(Robins *et al*, 1984). Regardless, depression presents a major problem for many older people: it is the number one reason for psychiatric hospitalisation in old age. Depression often accompanies the dependence and helplessness caused by many illnesses. However, older people seem less susceptible to depression as a result of physical disability than are middle-aged people. Perhaps this is so because older adults come to expect some degree of dependence in old age.

At Life's End

For all of us, death is inevitable and yet, while medical advances cannot prevent death, they have changed our manner of dying. Chronic illnesses now constitute the major causes of death. So, for most people, dying will now be a lengthy process. Preparing for our deaths and responding to the deaths of others are parts of life that psychologists want to understand so that they may help people cope with them.

Dying a good death

According to some theorists, notably **Elisabeth Kubler-Ross**, all dying patients go through the same series of emotional stages (Kubler-Ross, 1969, 1975). The first is *denial*. This initial stage may actually help the person to maintain hope by avoiding overwhelming grief. The second stage is *anger*. This anger arises from the loss of personal control over present and future life-plans. The third stage is *bargaining*. At this stage, a dying person might, for example, make an agreement with God in exchange for a little more time. The fourth stage is *depression*. This depression may arise from an anticipated or actual turn for the worse. The final stage is *acceptance*. With enough time and emotional support from caring family, friends or institutional care-givers, people can work through their anguish and calmly accept their impending death. Kubler-Ross believes that, if people accept their own death, it is easier for them to die in peace and dignity.

Other researchers studying the reactions of dying people have observed more fluidity and complexity than is suggested by this fixed-stage model. Denial, anger and depression may reappear at different times during the dying process, depending on the context of the death and if an illness such as cancer or AIDS is involved (Kastenbaum, 1986). These emotional reactions vary according to the perceived stigma of one's illness, the social support during treatment and whether there is progressive, steady decline or periodic improvement. Still others suggest that people's responses to their own terminal illnesses remain fairly constant and do not proceed through stages at all.

Another way to characterise the dying process is in terms of the physical and socio-emotional needs of dying people (Schulz, 1978). The single most important need may be the alleviation of physical pain using, most commonly, drug therapy. Dying people (as well as their families and friends) also have a number of social and emotional needs that have to be acknowledged. The need to maintain a sense of dignity and self-worth can be met, in part, by allowing dying people control over the course of their treatments or control over the end of their own lives. Needs for social closeness and emotional support can be satisfied by involving family members in the treatment process and by allowing dying people ample private time with their loved ones.

The loss of a spouse after decades of marriage can be particularly traumatic.

Bereavement

The impact of death does not end when a person dies. Family and friends cope with their own feelings of grief and bereavement for months and years after the death of someone close to them. **Margaret Stroebe** and **Wolfgang Stroebe** (1983; 1987) have documented in their research that the loss of a spouse after decades of marriage can be particularly traumatic; it can substantially increase illness and mortality rates. Compared to the general population, widows and widowers have two times as many diseases as do those of the same age who are single or married (Stroebe *et al*, 1982). Because women typically live longer and marry men older than themselves, losing a spouse is much more common for women than for men. Yet there is some evidence that the stress of losing a spouse is harder on men than on women. Research also indicates that intense grief can alter the immune system response to illness. It led to the hypothesis that changes in the immune system following bereavement are related to the increased mortality of bereaved widowers (Schliefer *et al*, 1983). Although susceptibility to illness tends to increase during bereavement, the actual number of widows

and widowers who 'die of a broken heart' is fairly small. Most recover from their grief and return to their normal and sometimes stronger selves.

Some investigators have identified distinct *stages of mourning* (Kalish, 1985). The first *shock stage* is followed by the *longing phase* involving desire to be with the deceased. The third major reaction is the *depression stage* with despair at the loss, sometimes combined with anger and confusion. Finally, the last stage of mourning is the *recovery phase* when the death is put into a meaningful perspective.

With anticipated deaths (as opposed to sudden, accidental deaths), people have time to prepare for the inevitable endings of their important relationships with others and work through anticipatory grief. Preparing for such endings might entail sharing innermost feelings and spending intimate time together. There is some evidence that, after a partner died, these last interactions represent what a survivor remembers about his or her relationship with the deceased (Fredrickson, 1990). A memory of the deceased individual lives on in all those who were somehow touched by his or her presence. In this sense, the human life cycle can to be said to extend beyond the demise of our corporeal selves.

recapping main points

Approaches to Development

Developmental psychologists study the processes and changes that accompany different ages and stages of human development. The debate over the relative contribution of nature and nurture to human development dates back to the antagonistic philosophical doctrines of empiricism and nativism. Current wisdom suggests that nature and nurture always interact to determine any complex behavioural pattern. While some psychologists argue that development is continuous over time, others propose stages that stress discontinuity, specific functions being qualitatively different at different age periods.

Infancy and Childhood

In Freud's theory sexuality motivates development. Piaget formulated a stage theory about the growth of the child's cognitive capacities. His key concepts are schemes, assimilation and accommodation. The four stages of cognitive development are the sensorimotor, the pre-operational, the concrete operational and the stage of formal operations. Children are master language-learners. Culture and parental interaction are essential parts of the language-acquisition process, alongside innate factors.

Vygotsky and Erikson focus on the social context of development. Erikson proposed a theory of psychosocial stages to elaborate and explicate life-span development. The need for attachment and the emergence of emotion and gender are specific aspects of social development.

Adolescence and Adulthood

Developmental psychologists now recognise that development occurs throughout a person's entire lifetime. Adolescence is a loosely defined period between childhood and adulthood, marked by the onset of puberty. Research reveals that most adolescents are satisfied with their lives but that they are over-concerned about their appearance and with being accepted socially. Adult thought involves the emergence of post-formal thinking. Moral reasoning in adults conforms to a clear stage model of development at the lower levels but not at hypothesised higher levels. There is considerable debate over possible gender differences in moral reasoning.

Old Age

Successful aging can be characterised by people optimising their functioning in select domains that are of high priority to them and compensating for losses by using substitute behaviours. Age-related declines in cognitive functioning are typically evident in only some abilities; individuals vary greatly in intellectual performance as they grow old. Declines in performance can often be reversed with educational training. This suggests that isolated cognitive deficits are caused by disuse rather than by decay of the central nervous system. People become gradually less socially active as they grow older. It appears that as people age they selectively maintain only those relationships that matter most to them. Emotional closeness within these select relationships may even increase with age. Most people will die in old age from chronic illnesses of long duration. Kubler-Ross suggests that the process of dying involves five emotional stages: denial, anger, bargaining, depression and acceptance. While these stages should not be considered fixed or universal, they offer insight into people's psychological responses to their own mortality and impending demise.

key Terms

accommodation
adolescence
agism
assimilation
attachment
behavioural gerontology
body image
chronological age
cognitive development
concrete operational stage
conservation
constitutional factors
contact comfort
critical period
cross-sectional design
developmental age
developmental stages
dishabituation
egocentrism
empathy
formal operational stage
gender
gender identity
gender roles
genes
habituation

identity crisis
imprinting
internalisation
language acquisition device (LAD)
longitudinal design
maturation
morality
motherese
nature–nurture controversy
normative investigations
object permanence
Oedipus complex
over-regularisation
polygenic
post-formal thought
pre-operational stage
psychosexual stages
psychosocial stages
puberty
schemas
selective optimisation with compensation
sensorimotor stage
sequential design
sex
socialisation

major Contributors

Ainsworth, Mary
Baillargeon, Renée
Baltes, Margaret
Baltes, Paul
Bem, Sandra
Bowlby, John (1907–90)
Bruner, Jerome
Chodorow, Nancy
Chomsky, Noam
Erikson, Erik (1902–94)
Freud, Anna (1895–1982)
Freud, Sigmund (1856–1939)
Gilligan, Carol
Hall, G. Stanley (1844–1924)
Harlow, Harry (1905–81)

Hoffman, Martin
Kagan, Jerome
Kohlberg, Lawrence (1927–87)
Kubler-Ross, Elisabeth
Locke, John (1632–1704)
Lorenz, Konrad
Maccoby, Eleanor
Piaget, Jean (1896–1980)
Rousseau, Jean Jacques (1712–78)
Schaie, K. Warner
Stroebe, Margaret
Stroebe, Wolfgang
Vaillant, George
Vygotsky, Lev (1896–1934)

Chapter 5

Sensation

The Senses: Fundamental Features   **167**
The Senses: an Overview
Is Perceiving Believing?

Psychophysics   **169**
Signal Detection: Absolute Thresholds
Subliminal Perception
Signal Detection Theory
Difference Thresholds

Interim Summary   **174**

Vision   **174**
The Physics of Light
The Sense Organ: the Eye
The Receptors in the Retina
Visual Pathways to the Brain
The Visual Cortex
Colour Vision
Seeing Form, Depth and Movement

Interim Summary   **187**

Audition   **187**
The Physics of Sound
Detection and Transduction
Psychological Dimensions of Sound

Theories of Pitch Perception
Sound Localisation
Close-up: Noise Pollution Fills the Air

Interim Summary   **194**

The Other Senses   **194**
Smell
Taste
Position and Movement
Touch
Pain

Recapping Main Points   **200**

Key Terms   **201**

Major Contributors   **201**

Five months before her second birthday, Helen Keller was struck by a mysterious illness that deprived her of both sight and hearing. Helen's other senses became highly developed – a phenomenon experienced by many people who suffer long-term sensory deprivation – and her sensory experiences were eloquently documented: 'I cannot recall what happened during the first months after my illness. I only know that I sat in my mother's lap or clung to her dress as she went about her household duties. My hands felt every object and observed every motion, and in this way I learned to know many things . . . Sometimes I stood between two persons who were conversing and touched their lips. I could not understand, and was vexed' (Keller, 1902).

In her seventh year, Helen Keller became the pupil of Annie Sullivan, a young woman whose vision was partially impaired. In letters to a matron at the Perkins School in Boston, USA, where Annie had been educated, she wrote of the pleasure Helen derived from her remaining senses: 'On entering a greenhouse her countenance becomes radiant, and she will tell the names of the flowers with which she is familiar, by the sense of smell alone . . . She enjoys in anticipation the scent of a rose or a violet; and if she is promised a bouquet of these flowers, a peculiarly happy expression lights her face' (Sullivan, 1908).

Helen herself wrote about the way her sense of smell gave her advance warning of storms. 'I notice first a throb of expectancy, a slight quiver, a concentration in my nostrils. As the storm draws near my nostrils dilate, the better to receive the flood of earth odours which seem to multiply and extend, until I feel the splash of rain against my cheek. As the tempest departs, receding farther and farther, the odours fade, become fainter and fainter, and die away beyond the bar of space' (Keller, in Ackerman, 1990).

Annie Sullivan reported that Helen's 'whole body is so finely organised that she seems to use it as a medium for bringing herself into closer relations with her fellow creatures'. Annie was puzzled at first by Helen's 'inexplicable mental faculty' to pick up emotions and physical sensations. She soon realised, though, that Helen had developed an exquisite sensitivity to the muscular variations of those around her. 'One day, while she was out walking with her mother . . . a boy threw a torpedo, which startled Mrs Keller. Helen felt the change in her mother's movements instantly, and asked, "What are we afraid of?"' (Sullivan, 1908). During a hearing test, Helen astonished a roomful of people when 'she would turn her head, smile, and act as though she had heard what was said'. However, when Annie let go of Helen's hand and moved to the opposite side of the room, Helen remained motionless for the rest of the test (Sullivan, 1908).

Although she could neither see nor hear, Helen Keller extracted a great deal of sensory information from the world. She did not perceive colour, light and sound through the ordinary channels. Instead, she 'heard' symphonies by placing her hands on a radio to feel the vibrations, and she 'saw' where a person had been by picking up the scent of his or her clothes. Her ability to compensate for her sensory disabilities hints at the intricate co-ordination within human sensory systems and the interaction of sensory and brain processes. It also makes us aware of the extent to which our senses work in unison to weave experience of the world around us into the fabric of our very being.

IN SPITE OF the loss of two senses, Helen Keller adapted wonderfully well to her environment. The way she achieved this was remarkable, but of course the fact that she adapted with every conceivable means to a changing environment is not. All organisms have to adapt to what happens in the outside world, and thus, each one needs equipment to receive, process and respond to external stimuli. In other words, organisms need sensory systems to detect and process incoming information to the brain – known as **afferent pathways** – and motor systems to process outgoing information from the brain to the muscles and glands – referred to as **efferent pathways**. In this and the next chapter we focus on afferent processes. How do the sensory systems work and how does our brain, locked in the dark, silent chamber of the skull, process afferent stimuli? How do we see, hear, smell, taste and feel pain? In short, how do we perceive?

Perceiving is a process that can be divided into several steps. It starts with detecting 'something' in the external world. Since the world is composed of different kinds of physical energy, the first step consists of making contact with these stimuli. This job is done by several stimulus detector units which each are susceptible to a different kind of energy. These collecting devices are the *sense organs* and their function is detection. Once a stimulus has been detected, the nervous system takes over. Because the nervous system is composed of neurons, and neurons only operate via electrochemical energy (see Chapter 2), a conversion must take place. The transformation of physical energy into neural energy is called **transduction** and is effectuated by the *receptors*, which are situated inside the sense organs. For example, the eye is the sense organ that detects electromagnetic energy and the so-called 'rods' and 'cones' in the retina are the receptors that perform the transduction of this form of energy into nerve impulses.

Following transduction, nerve fibres transport the stimulus energy to specific brain centres, where the signals are 'translated' into elementary or **primary sensations**. Primary sensations of vision, for example, consist of 'seeing' particular forms, colours and movements. This whole process, from detection through transduction to primary sensations is called *sensation*. However, primary sensations are far from the end result of the process of perceiving. Using sight again as an example, our 'seeing' involves much more than visual sensations of movement for particular

forms with certain colours. We see children at play, people in love and sheep grazing. In other words, what we see is always given meaning. The process of assigning meaning to sensory signals is called *perception*. Hence, sensation is the process by which a stimulated sensory receptor gives rise to neural impulses that result in an elementary sensory experience; perception, on the other hand, is the elaboration, interpretation and assignment of meaning to a sensory experience.

The boundaries between sensation and perception are not distinctly drawn. Nevertheless, psychologists often distinguish the two processes – a convention we will follow in our presentation of this subject. This chapter deals with *sensory processes* which fundamentally involve initial stimulus detection, as followed by transduction, then conduction of neural energy to the brain (where further processing takes place), resulting finally in the experience of a primary sensation. The bringing in and organising of information from the environment are often referred to as 'world-driven' or 'data-driven' processes. They are themselves identifiable as so-called **bottom-up processes** because they start down at the level of sensory information and work their way 'upward' to the brain. The chapter following this one, however, will deal with perceptual processes. Perception is often associated with the opposite of bottom-up processing, that is to say with **top-down processing**.

Although you experience your perception of the sheep instantaneously and effortlessly, it is in fact the result of a complicated process.

The latter refers to the processing of information as it is influenced by pre-existing, subjectively held concepts, thoughts or ideas about the material being processed – that is to say, perception is conceptually impelled and subject-driven. In top-down processing, higher mental processes control the way incoming stimulation is managed and even what qualifies as relevant.

THE SENSES: FUNDAMENTAL FEATURES

If asked how many senses we have, most people refer to the five senses as enumerated by Aristotle: vision (sight), audition (hearing), taste, smell and touch. But what of sensations such as pain, warmth and coldness, and of balancing and moving? In addition, there are receptors in the digestive tract that are involved in sensations such as hunger and thirst; receptors in the brain monitor the chemical makeup and temperature of the bloodstream. However, we will not continue with an exhaustive list. Instead, we will briefly introduce the most well-known senses by way of a classification that takes its impetus from the physical energy to which the receptors respond. Four kinds of receptors can be distinguished, each of which are designed to receive a different form of energy, namely: photoreceptors, mechanoreceptors, chemoreceptors and thermoreceptors. After the following overview of these, we will briefly compare the process of sensation as described by empirical researchers with the commonsense notion that what we see is simply a copy of the outside world.

 ## The Senses: an Overview

Our **photoreceptors** – the rods and cones – are situated in the retina at the back of the eye. They respond to fractions of electromagnetic energy which we call light. Only when the eye is struck by this particular part of the electromagnetic spectrum, do the photoreceptors transduce the physical energy into neural impulses. Through several intermediate stations, the signals of the rods and cones are transported by nerve fibres to the primary visual cortex, a part of the occipital cortex at the back of the brain. It is called 'primary' because only the first step in visual processing takes place here. We will discuss the process of detection, transduction and processing of light extensively in the section on vision.

There are several types of **mechanoreceptors** that respond to different forms of mechanical energy.

The mechanical energy for hearing consists of the vibration of molecules through a medium, usually air. Like the receptors of the eye, the mechanoreceptors of the ear respond only to a part of the available vibrational energy. Inside the ear the airborne soundwave is transformed into movements of fluid that cause the receptors – tiny hairs in the so-called basilar membrane – to bend. Subsequently, neural impulses are sent to the auditory cortex. This process will receive detailed attention in the section on audition.

Also located in the inner ear are mechanoreceptors that respond to gravity and acceleration. Hair cells in the semicircular canals of the inner ear respond to the movement of fluid, which is caused by movements of the head. The resulting sense is one of balance and equilibrium. Nerve endings in tendons, muscles and joints detect whether our body is moving or stationary and inform us of the position and movement of our body parts. This sense is called kinesthesis. Other mechanoreceptors are located in the skin. Tiny hairs and free nerve endings respond to pressure and send their signals to the brain where they are 'translated' into the sensations of touch and pain.

A third class of receptors is called **chemoreceptors**. Chemical energy is the physical stimulus for smell and taste. The process of smelling starts when molecules that float in the air attach themselves briefly to haircells that are located in a relatively small area in the upper part of the nose. Taste arises when the taste buds on the tongue are stimulated by the molecules of substances.

As a final group we must mention here **thermoreceptors**. Thermal energy or temperature is sensed in the skin by nerve endings. There are 'cold' nerve fibres which respond to cooling of the skin with an increase in firing; and there are 'warm' nerve fibres which become more active when the temperature increases. *Table 5.1* (next page) summarises the forms of energy humans are capable of detecting by the use of the corresponding sense organs, receptors and sensations.

 ## Is Perceiving Believing?

The world is filled with all kinds of energy. Although we only detect a fraction of it, we have many senses that enable us to enjoy this abundance. An initial glimpse at the way in which the sensory systems operate, however, makes one wonder how this diversity is accommodated. There is no elaborate pipework lined on the inside with miniscule mirrors that can convey electromagnetic energy to the brain; nor are there sound corridors along which vibrational

TABLE 5.1 THE SENSES: FUNDAMENTAL FEATURES

Stimulus	Sense	Sense Organ	Receptor	Primary Sensation
ELECTROMAGNETIC ENERGY	Vision	Eye	Rods and cones of retina	Colours, patterns, textures
MECHANICAL ENERGY				
Sound waves	Audition	Ear	Hair cells of the basilar membrane	Sounds
Gravity, acceleration	Equilibrium	Inner ear	Hair cells of semi-circular canals and vestibule	Spatial movement, gravitational pull
Movement of joints	Kinesthetis	Tendons, muscles and joints	Nerve endings	Body movement
Pressure on skin	Skin sensations	Skin	Nerve endings, tiny hairs	Touch, pain
CHEMICAL ENERGY				
Volatile substances	Smell	Nose	Hair cells of olfactory epithelium	Odours (musky, flowery, burnt, minty)
Soluble substances	Taste	Tongue	Taste buds of tongue	Flavours (sweet, sour, salty, bitter)
THERMAL ENERGY	Skin sensations	Skin	Various types in skin and tissues	Warmth, cold

energy can be transported in its original form. Rather, the nervous system is composed of neurons; it only recognises one kind of 'messenger' – action potentials – and one kind of 'clerk' – graded potentials – which bring the messages together and sort them into some form of order (as detailed in Chapter 2). Thus, during the process of transduction, diverse forms of physical energy are turned into a somewhat dreary uniformity. How then do we apprehend the intensity and quality of our various sensory experiences?

The main way stimulus intensity is coded is in terms of the rate of neural impulses. For example, a slight touch on the skin will generate a series of electrical impulses in nerve fibres at that point. As the pressure is increased, the impulses do likewise in their frequency of firing. Thus, for all sensory modalities, the perceived magnitude of stimulus intensity is a function of the rate of neural firing. A second way that intensity is coded is by the regularity in the temporal patterning of these nerve impulses. At weak intensities, the firing is spaced and irregular, but as the intensity increases, the patterning becomes not only more closely spaced but also more constant.

The constantly variable patterning of action potentials makes a diversity of changes in intensity understandable. But how do we manage to experience different sensory *qualities*? How can the highly stereotyped events of action potentials give rise to completely different sensations such as seeing, hearing and smelling? It appears the experience of these individual qualities depend on the particular patterning of neural activity associated with each type of sensation and on the area of the brain where the impulses are processed. The visual cortex 'translates' action potentials into visual sensations, the auditory cortex into auditory sensations, and so on. Strange experiences would be generated if, for example, the optic nerves could be connected with the auditory cortex. We would experience inconceivable sensations such as 'hearing light'.

This short introduction into the mechanisms of sensation already shows that, strictly speaking, everyday language about sensation is misleading. We often say we see with our eyes, hear with our ears and smell with our nose. We also speak of a red light, a bitter taste and a loud sound. However, our eyes are only collecting devices that work rather passively. The actual 'seeing' is done by the brain. Furthermore, there is no such thing 'out there' as red; there is electromagnetic energy with a particular wavelength that our brain 'translates' into a visual sensation which we call 'red'. One of the first to argue this view was **Isaac Newton** in 1671:

'For the rays (of light), to speak properly, are not coloured. In them there is nothing else than a certain power and disposition to stir up a sensation of this or that colour. For as sound, in a bell or musical string or other sounding body, is nothing but a trembling motion, and in the air nothing but that motion propagated from the object . . . so colours in the object are nothing but a disposition to reflect this or that sort of ray more copiously than the rest.'

It is no wonder, however, that more than four centuries later, people are still duped by the process of sensation. In our own everyday experience, we are not conscious of a process occurring. The accessability of the world through our senses is instantaneous. We see a red rose without knowing how we accomplish this act. Nobody knows how he or she has constructed an internal visual representation of an object in the external world. The self-evidential act of seeing leaves most people believing that what they apprehend with their own eyes is what truly exists in the physical structure of the external world: *seeing apparently is believing*. In this respect the eye often is compared with a camera, that 'objectively' registers what 'really' is out there.

The notion that our internal visual representations are duplicates of reality itself goes back to the Greek philosophers. They assumed that copies of the outside world (*eidola*) are projected on to the retina of our eyes. We now know that the Greeks, and along with them so-called common sense, were incorrect. Seeing – and for that matter all the other sensory processes – has nothing to do with duplication. Human perception only accommodates a fraction of the external world and the way it handles this small part can be better designated as 'calculation' and as a 'search for meaning' than as simple 'reproduction'. We will elaborate on this notion in the ensuing sections.

PSYCHOPHYSICS

Psychophysics represents the oldest field of empirical psychology (Levine & Shefner, 1981). Its central task is the study of lawful correlations between physical stimuli and the experienced sensations the stimuli evoke. Nowadays psychophysicists answer questions such as: how loud must a fire alarm at a factory be in order for workers to hear it over the din

of the machinery; how bright must a traffic light be so as to be visible with the sun behind it; and how loud should a motorcycle be before its driver is accused of noise pollution? Practical questions such as these often arise when people are making decisions about safety regulations, product design and legal issues.

The most significant figure in the history of psychophysics was the German physicist and philosopher, **Gustav Fechner**. He coined the term 'psychophysics' – 'psyche' refers to mind and 'physike' to naturally occurring phenomena. Fechner not only laid the foundations of the philosophical basis of psychophysics, but also developed ways to measure the relations between sensations and physical stimuli. His procedures for relating the intensity of a physical stimulus – measured in physical units – to the magnitude of the sensory experience – measured in psychological units – are still in use today (Fechner, 1860).

One of psychophysics' central concerns is the study of the sensitivity of the sensory systems. A number of questions are pertinent here. The first one concerns the basic task for any sensory system, the detection of the presence of a stimulus in the environment: what magnitude of stimulus is necessary for an individual to be aware of its presence? This minimal amount of energy, be it electromagnetic, mechanical, chemical or thermal, is called the *absolute threshold*. With respect to the latter, a subsidiary question arises as to whether it is possible to perceive things without being aware of it – a phenomenon called *subliminal perception*. In the following section then, to answer these questions, we will examine *signal detection theory* and in so doing consider by how much two stimuli must differ in order to be discriminated as not the same. Within such a theoretical framework, the threshold for the perception of a difference is known as the *difference threshold*.

Signal Detection: Absolute Thresholds

The minimum amount of physical energy needed to produce a sensory experience is called the **absolute threshold**. Researchers measure absolute thresholds psychophysically by asking vigilant observers to perform detection tasks, such as trying to see a dim light in a dark room. During a series of trials, the stimulus is presented at varying intensities and on each trial the observers indicate whether or not they were aware of it. If you have ever had the sensitivity of your hearing evaluated, you have participated in an absolute threshold test.

FIGURE 5.1   CALCULATION OF ABSOLUTE THRESHOLDS

Because a stimulus does not become suddenly detectable at a certain point, absolute threshold is defined as the intensity at which the stimulus is detected half of the time over many trials.

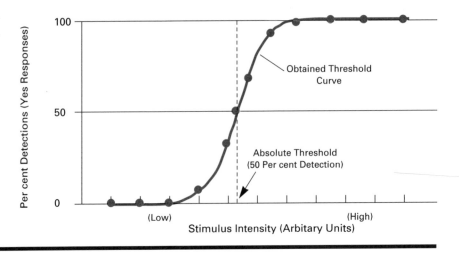

The results of an absolute threshold study can be summarised in a **psychometric function**: a graph that shows the percentage of detections (plotted on the vertical axis, or Y-axis) of each stimulus intensity (plotted on the horizontal axis, or X-axis). A typical psychometric function is shown in *Figure 5.1*. For very dim lights, which are clearly below threshold, detection is at 0 per cent; for bright lights, which are clearly above threshold, detection is at 100 per cent. In between, there is a region of transition from no detection to occasional detection to detection all of the time. The existence of this region demonstrates that there is not a true absolute threshold, no single value below which there is always a 'no' and above which there is always a 'yes'.

Since a stimulus does not suddenly become clearly detectable at a specific point, a person's absolute threshold is arbitrarily indicated as the stimulus level at which a sensory signal is detected half of the time. Thresholds for different sense modalities can be measured in the same way, simply by changing the physical energy. *Table 5.2* shows absolute threshold levels for several familiar natural stimuli.

✸ Subliminal Perception

In the mid-1950s an unsuspecting cinema audience in New Jersey, USA, was confronted with verbal messages that were superimposed on the regular film. The slogans, such as 'eat popcorn' and 'drink Coke', appeared so briefly that they could not be consciously detected. According to the researcher, sales of the recommended products increased drastically. Claims about the effect of such 'hidden persuaders' are still made today. For example, in almost every esoteric bookshop, you can buy so-called subliminal self-help tapes. The tapes contain music, but also, superimposed on the music, encouraging phrases, such as 'You'll be very successful today'. These messages cannot be heard consciously. There are cassettes for different kinds of problems. One tape guarantees a better sex life, another a quick cure for low self-esteem, a third promises safe and effective weight loss. The turnover of these tapes in the United States of America is rated at several tens of millions of dollars a year.

The phenomenon of perceiving something without awareness is known as **subliminal perception**. The popcorn study has stirred much concern among the public. What if cult leaders, politicians or advertisers were to use tapes with

TABLE 5.2   APPROXIMATE THRESHOLDS OF FAMILIAR EVENTS

Sense Modality	Detection Threshold
Light	A candle flame seen at 30 miles (48 km) on a dark clear night
Sound	The tick of a watch under quiet conditions at 6 metres
Taste	One teaspoon of sugar in 9 litres of water
Smell	One drop of perfume diffused into the entire volume of a 3-room apartment
Touch	The wing of a bee falling on your cheek from a distance of 1 centimetre

subliminal messages? Since the intensity of their communications must be below our absolute threshold, we cannot detect whether they contain propaganda – so we could easily become the targets of such 'brainwashing' techniques. On the other hand, since detection of the subliminal stimuli should be 0 per cent, messages have to be sent well below our absolute threshold (see *Figure 5.1*). Are our senses capable of detecting such low intensities, and if so, are our brains capable of giving meaning to these vague stimuli without us being consciously aware of them?

Although there are psychologists who believe in the effectiveness of subliminal perception, most psychologists conducting experimental research, however, have been very reluctant to acknowledge these claims. The absence of a theoretical framework and the many methodological flaws in this line of enquiry has bred much scepticism (Holender, 1986). One of the main problems is that it is very difficult to offer incontrovertible support for the occurrence of subliminal perception. In cognitive terms, the dilemma of subliminal perception can be reformulated as follows: is it possible for there to be a dissociation between the availability of the information to the processing system and its availability to conscious awareness? The answer to this question depends in large part upon our definition of '(un)conscious'. If in a subliminal perception experiment an effect is found, whilst a subject may report that 'I did not perceive anything', most researchers would conclude that processing did take place but without conscious awareness. Can they be sure, however, that the subject's report is correct? Some researchers maintain that subjective reports should not be trusted and must be replaced by more objective measures.

There is some evidence that the subliminal presentation of single words or physical features like faces, does have an effect and can be perceived subliminally (Merikle, 1992). In one experiment subjects were shown a number of portraits. For half of them, each photograph was immediately preceded by an unpleasant picture (for example, a disgusting face) that was presented subliminally. The other participants saw pleasant subliminal stimuli, such as a smiling baby. Those who were shown the unpleasant subliminal stimuli expressed more negative attitudes toward the persons on the portraits than did the other subjects (Krosnick *et al*, 1992).

Evidence for an effect of subliminally presented material that goes beyond the analysis of the meaning of a single word, however, has not been forthcoming (Greenwald, 1992). Research, for example, has demonstrated that self-help tapes have no effect (Greenwald *et al*, 1991; Russell *et al*, 1991). Also the claims in the 1950s concerning the buying of products under the influence of subliminal messages have never been substantiated (Loftus & Klinger, 1992).

Information processing under subliminal conditions appears to be very limited. **Daniel Holender**, for instance, criticises most of the research into unconscious information processing, stating that under neatly controlled laboratory research conditions the evidence for the effectivenesss of subliminal perception appears to be rather meagre (Holender, 1986; Greenwald, 1992).

 Signal Detection Theory

Fechner originally assumed that each person had a more or less fixed threshold for each sense. Psychophysicists soon found, however, that people's apparent sensitivity can fluctuate. Indeed, our sensitivity depends upon our desires, expectations and habits. When we want something to happen very much, our sensitivity for that particular stimulus is far greater than if we are unconcerned about its occurrence or non-occurrence. Our expectations may also influence our readiness to detect a sensory event: radar operators are more likely to detect the weak blip on a sonar scope if they are on a ship during wartime than if they are on a yacht during peacetime. People also develop habitual ways of responding: some people are inclined to say 'yes' and some 'no'; under conditions of uncertainty this means that some will over-report the presence of a stimulus event while others will consistently under-report it.

The **theory of signal detection** (TSD), however, is an alternative to the classical approach to psychophysics (Green & Swets, 1966). According to TSD, sensation is a graded or continuous experience, wherein we not only have to deal with a stimulus from the outside world, but also with the inside 'noise' produced by our sensory systems. Like electronic snow on a television screen, there is always some fluctuating background neural activity in the sensory systems. A stimulus simply adds to this activation. Thus, if you are confronted with a weak stimulus on a threshold test, you have to decide whether there is a genuine stimulus or just background noise. Because you cannot always tell for sure, you make a guess. According to TSD you make this guess by setting for yourself a criterion. If the perceived stimulus intensity exceeds your decision criterion you say 'yes', if not you say 'no'. Thus, where the classical approach to psychophysics holds the sensory system responsible for setting the threshold, in TSD the threshold is also determined by processes which involve decision-making.

In a typical signal detection experiment, subjects are told that after a warning light appears, a tone may or may not be presented. The basic design is given in

FIGURE 5.2 THE THEORY OF SIGNAL DETECTION

Matrix A shows the possible outcomes when a subject is asked if a target stimulus occurred on a given trial. Matrices B and C show the typical responses of a *yea sayer* and a *nay sayer*.

A. Response Given

Stimulus Signal	Yes	No
On	Hit	Miss
Off	False alarm	Correct rejection

B. 'Yea Sayer' Responses

	Yes	No
On	92%	8%
Off	46%	54%

C. 'Nay Sayer' Responses

	Yes	No
On	40%	60%
Off	4%	96%

Figure 5.2. A weak stimulus is presented in half the trials. No stimulus is presented in the other half; these are so-called 'catch trials'. In each trial, subjects respond by saying 'yes' if they think the signal was present and 'no' if they think it was not. As shown in matrix A of the Figure, each response is scored as a hit, a miss, a false alarm, or a correct rejection, depending on whether a signal was, in fact, presented and whether the observer responded yes or no.

As shown in matrix B, an observer who is a 'yea sayer' (inclined to say yes) will give a high number of hits, which is good, but will also have a high number of false alarms, which is bad. A 'nay sayer' will be appreciated for a high number of correct rejections, but at the same time condemned for a higher number of misses, as is shown in matrix C.

Combining the percentages of hits and false alarms creates a mathematical relationship that differentiates sensory thresholds from decision criteria. This procedure makes it possible to find out whether two observers have the same sensitivity despite large differences in their decision criteria. The decision criterion reflects the observer's strategy for responding in a particular situation. By providing a way of separating sensory process from decision criteria, the theory of signal detection allows an experimenter to identify and separate the roles of the sensory stimulus and the individual's decision criterion in producing the final response.

The TSD approach now dominates modern psychophysics. In addition, it provides a model of decision-making that can be used in other contexts as well. Many everyday decisions are taken on the basis of probabilities and of costs and benefits. For example, before going for a walk on a cloudy day, we assess whether or not to take an umbrella. Driving down the motorway with an almost empty fuel tank, we deliberate over whether to refuel immediately or at the next station. When we are not feeling well, we assess the need to call a busy doctor out, weighing up whether or not our symptoms indicate something serious or minor. Such decisions involve different rewards for every 'hit' and 'correct rejection' and penalties for every 'miss' and 'false alarm'. Decisions are likely to be biased by the schedule of anticipated gains and losses. If saying 'yes' ('I will call the doctor out') when a stimulus is really present (you have a virus) will result in a substantive gain (that you will be cured), and if saying 'no' ('I won't call the doctor out') when it *is* present will probably result in a significant loss (that you will become very ill), then a 'yes' bias will prevail. Drawing up what is called a payoff matrix, as shown in *Figure 5.2*, may help you to arrive at and make the best decision.

TSD can also be used during the course of making a medical diagnosis (Swets, 1992). Suppose a doctor thinks it is necessary to intervene in the course of an illness, but he or she is not sure about the cause, severity or very existence of the suspected disease; in such a case, the physical and psychological consequences for the patient of the planned intervention will affect the doctor's decision criterion as to whether or not the treatment should in fact be carried out. In the case of a possible bacterial infection, the doctor will not require much evidence for the decision to be taken to prescribe antibiotics. For both the patient and the doctor there is little to lose in the instance of a 'false alarm' and much to gain in that of a 'hit'. On other occasions much more evidence is required: for example, if during a dangerous surgical operation a malignant cancerous growth is not actually found to be present, the decision that has already been taken to operate could turn out to be a costly one. Of course the payoff matrix of the doctor is not always the same as that for the patient. Thus, the decision-maker must consider the available evidence, the relative costs of each type of error and the relative gains from each type of correct decision. More conservative decisions result when there is a high cost for a false alarm and a low cost for a miss.

FIGURE 5.3 | JUST NOTICEABLE DIFFERENCES AND WEBER'S LAW

The longer the standard bar, the greater the amount you must add (ΔL) to see a just noticeable difference. The difference threshold is the added length detected on half the trials. In plotting these increments against standard bars of increasing length, the proportion stays the same – the amount added is always one-tenth of the standard length. The relationship is linear, producing a straight line on the graph. We can predict that the ΔL for a bar length of 5 will be 0.5.

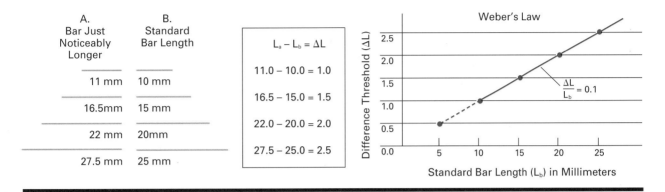

 Difference Thresholds

Suppose you are a programmer inventing a new video game. You have decided to use bars to represent the enemy spaceships that have been captured; each time a ship is downed, the striker's bar gets a little longer. You want the players to be able to tell which of the two bars is longer so they will know who is winning, but you also want the additions to the bar length to be small enough so that as many spaceships as possible can be represented. To do this, you need to determine the **difference threshold**, the smallest physical difference between two stimuli that can still be recognised as a difference.

You would determine a difference threshold in much the same way that you would determine an absolute threshold, except that you would use a pair of stimuli on each trial and ask your subjects whether the two stimuli were the same or different. For the video game problem, you would show your subjects two bars on each trial, one of some standard length and one just a bit longer. After many such trials, you would plot a psychometric function by graphing the per cent of *different* responses on the vertical axis as a function of the actual differences in length which you would plot on the horizontal axis. The difference threshold is the length difference at which the curve crosses the 50-per cent value. This difference threshold value is known as the **just noticeable difference**, or JND.

Suppose you perform your experiment with a standard bar length of ten millimetres, and you find the difference threshold to be about one millimetre. Can you go ahead and design your video-game display now? Unfortunately, you are not ready yet,

because the difference threshold is not the same for long and short bars. With a standard bar of 20 millimetres, for instance, you would have had to add about two millimeters to get a JND; with a bar of 40 millimetres the JND would be four millimetres. *Figure 5.3* shows some examples of JNDs with bars of several lengths: the JNDs increase steadily as the length of the standard bar increases.

Fortunately, there is something that does remain the same for both long and short bars. It is the ratio of the size of the increase that produces a JND to the length of the standard bar; both 1:10 and 2:20 equals 0.1. In 1834, **Ernst Weber** discovered this relationship and found that it held for a wide range of stimulus dimensions. The only difference he found between stimulus dimensions was the particular value of the ratio. He summarised all his findings in a single equation now called **Weber's law**: *the JND between stimuli is a constant fraction of the intensity of the standard stimulus.* Thus, the bigger or more intense the

TABLE 5.3 | WEBER'S CONSTANT VALUES FOR SELECTED STIMULUS DIMENSIONS

Stimulus Dimension	Weber's Constant
Sound frequency	.003
Light intensity	.01
Odour concentration	.07
Pressure intensity	.14
Sound intensity	.15
Taste concentration	.20

standard stimulus, the larger the increment needed in order to get a just noticeable difference, and vice versa. A few drops of water added to a test tube are more likely to be noticed than the same amount added to a jug. This is a very general property of all sensory systems. The formula for Weber's law is $\Delta I/I = k$, where I is the intensity of the standard; ΔI, or *Delta I*, is the size of the increase that produces a JND; and k is the constant ratio for the particular stimulus dimension, or Weber's constant. Weber's law provides a good approximation, but not a perfect fit to experimental data, of how the size of JND increases with intensity. We see in *Table 5.3* (previous page) that Weber's constant has different values for different sensory dimensions – there is greater sensitivity as the value becomes smaller. So this table tells us that we can differentiate two sound frequencies more precisely than light intensities, which, in turn, are detectable with a smaller JND than odour or taste modalities are.

INTERIM SUMMARY

Sensation is the first stage in the process of perception. It involves the detection of physical energy, the transduction of that energy into neural codes and the processing of these signals into primary sensations. Different kinds of receptors respond to various forms of physical energy. Accordingly, four groups of receptors can be distinguished: photoreceptors, mechanoreceptors, chemoreceptors and thermoreceptors. Because our perception of the world is instantaneous and effortless, it is often thought by non-psychologists that the act of perceiving involves the mere copying or mirroring of the outside world. In actual fact a great deal of 'working over' and 'calculating' *vis-à-vis* that input occurs in between the initial detection of physical energy and the experience of a primary sensation.

Psychophysicists look at the measurable relationships between psychological responses and physical stimuli. One of their central concerns is the study of the sensitivity of sensory systems. Within that realm of endeavour, these psychologists try to determine absolute thresholds as well as difference thresholds. Since people's sensitivity fluctuates, such thresholds are not fixed. Signal detection theory offers a way of separating out the influence of sensory from decisional processes in the detection of physical stimuli. There is some evidence that simple stimuli can be perceived without us being aware of it. Nevertheless, fears surrounding the uncontrollable effects of subliminal perception seem unfounded.

We turn now to examine the special features of each of our different sensory modalities.

 ## VISION

For humans, vision is the most complex and highly developed sense. The entire visual cortex consists of a network of connected areas or *modules* that takes up as much as 60 per cent of the brain. Vision is also the most well studied of all sense modalities, and therefore we will cover vision here in greater detail than the other senses. Our coverage of the process of seeing follows the path that the energy takes: physical energy – electromagnetic radiation – is collected by a sense organ – the eye – wherein receptors – the rods and cones – transduce the physical energy into neural impulses. Nerve fibres transport the signals to the brain where processing in the visual cortex gives rise to a visual sensation. After elaborating upon this process, we will consider the subject of colour vision and that of the perception of form, depth and movement.

 ### The Physics of Light

The physical stimulus for vision, or seeing, is electromagnetic radiation. All electromagnetic energy comes in tiny, indivisible particles called *quantums*. The quantums of that part of the electromagnetic spectrum we call light are known as *photons*. Quantums often act as if they travel in an oscillating wave, with the wavelength defined as the physical distance between the peaks of the waves. Electromagnetic energy can have wavelengths over a broad range, varying between trillionths of a centimetre and 30 kilometres. This energy contains, among others, gamma rays, X-rays, radar, TV waves and radio waves. As is shown in *Figure 5.4*, light constitutes just a tiny portion of the total electromagnetic spectrum, namely the range of wavelengths from 380 to about 760 nanometres. A nanometre (nm) is one billionth of a metre.

Roughly speaking, different wavelengths within the range of the spectrum used for vision give way to different sensations of colour. Starting with the short end of the 'visible' spectrum, humans perceive the colour of light changing from violet through blue, green, yellow and orange to red. We will elaborate on the way seeing colour takes place, in the section about colour vision below.

 ### The Sense Organ: the Eye

The eye is a collecting device. Its function is to focus the part of the electromagnetic energy we

FIGURE 5.4 THE VISIBLE SPECTRUM

The range of the electromagnetic spectrum is portrayed at the bottom. Human eyes are sensitive only to the visible spectrum. Differing light wavelengths in the visible spectrum create perception of various colours.

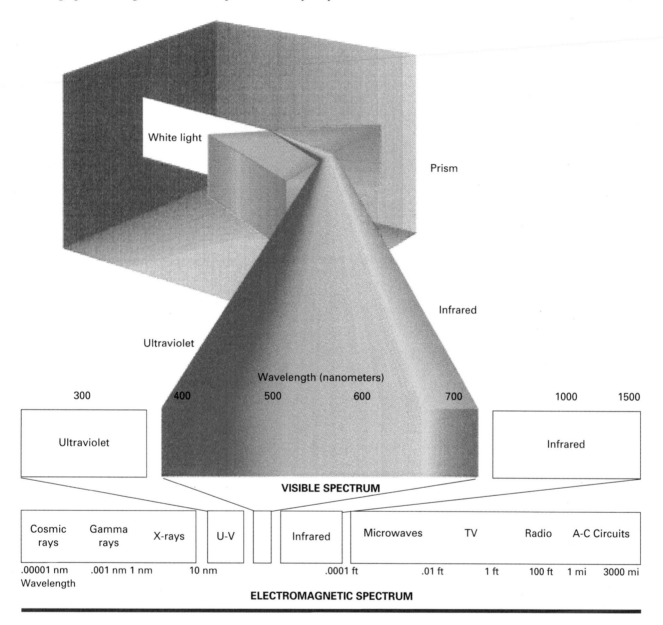

call light on to the back of the eyeball, where photoreceptors transduce the physical energy into neural energy. To achieve this, the eye must bend or refract the light waves. This process starts at the front of the eye in a dome-like window, about 13 mm in diameter, called the *cornea*, and proceeds when light waves travel through a small chamber filled with a watery fluid called *aqueous humor*. The next device, as you can see in *Figure 5.5* (next page), is the *iris*. The iris is the coloured membrane that attracts our attention when we look into someone's eyes. The colour of your eyes, which actually is the colour of your irises, is genetically determined.

The light waves proceed through a hole in the iris, called the *pupil*. The function of the iris seems to be to control the amount of light entering the eye by contracting – in response to bright light – and dilating – in dim light – the pupil. Pupil size does not only vary in response to light variations, however. Psychological factors can also affect pupil dilation – positive emotional reactions dilate the pupil and negative ones constrict it. When, for example, you look at pictures of people you find very attractive, your pupils may expand by about 30 per cent. Pupil size also reflects mental effort, decreasing when concentration is intense. Any of these changes in

FIGURE 5.5 STRUCTURE OF THE HUMAN EYE

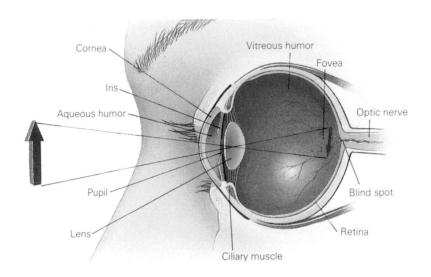

pupil size are involuntary and occur without your awareness (Hess, 1972).

Directly behind the pupillary aperture is located a bean-shaped crystalline lens. The lens changes its shape, thinning to focus on distant objects and thickening to focus on near ones. The ciliary muscles, from which the lens is suspended, can change the thickness of the lens and, hence, its optical properties in a process called **accommodation**.

Many people suffer from accommodation problems. For example, people who are nearsighted – who have myopia – cannot focus upon distant objects properly, while those who are farsighted cannot focus on nearby ones. The lens starts off as clear, transparent and convex. As people age, however, the lens becomes more amber tinted, opaque and flattened, and it loses its elasticity. The effect of some of these changes is that the lens cannot become thick enough for close vision. When people pass the 45-year mark, the blur point – the closest point at which they can focus clearly – gets progressively farther away. When this happens, people who have never needed glasses before begin to need them for reading and other close work. People who already wear glasses may need bifocals – glasses that provide a nearer focus on the bottom half and a far one on the upper half.

The lens of the eye focuses light on a thin sheet that lines the rear wall of the eyeball, the *retina,* reversing and inverting the light pattern as it does so. Before striking the retina, the waves traverse the large chamber of the eye, filled with a jellylike substance called *vitreous humor.* The retina contains the photoreceptors that are responsible for transduction.

 The Receptors in the Retina

After detection of light, which also includes refraction, *transduction* must take place. This occurs in the **retina**, where integration of the input also begins. Under the microscope, we see the retina's highly organised, layered structure. The retina has five types of neurons (each with its own layer): (a) the rods and cones, (b) the bipolar neurons, (c) the ganglion cells, (d) the horizontal cells and (e) the amacrine cells. The first three types of neurons are arranged in a hierarchical pattern that achieves divergent processing of incoming light, thus maximising its detection. The last two types of neurons in the retina are inhibitory cells that restrict the spread of the visual signal within the retina.

Rods and cones

The basic conversion from light energy to neural energy is performed in the retina by *photoreceptors*: the rods and cones. Intriguingly, these receptor cells are positioned in the rearmost layer of the retina. Light rays must travel through a maze of preceding neurons to reach the two types of photoreceptors. Subsequently, after transduction, the (now neural) impulses are relayed forward to the other neurons of the retina (see *Figure 5.6*).

Nature has provided two different kind of receptor cells, one for seeing in dim light and the other for seeing in bright light. The 120 million thin **rods** 'see in the dark' and give rise to sensations of black and white. The six million **cones** are active in daylight (or in electric

FIGURE 5.6 — RETINAL PATHWAYS

This is a stylised and greatly simplified diagram showing the pathways that connect three of the layers of nerve cells in the retina. Incoming light passes through all these layers to reach the receptors at the back of the eyeball which are pointed away from the source of light. Note that the bipolar cells gather impulses from more than one receptor cell and send the results to several ganglion cells. Nerve impulses (blue arrows) from the ganglion cells leave the eye via the optic nerve and travel to the next relay point.

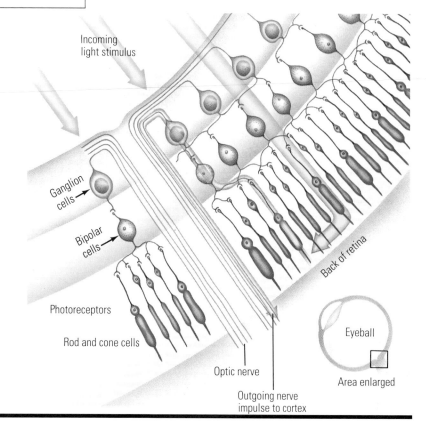

light) and give rise to the visual sensations of colour. In the very centre of the retina is a small region called the **fovea** that contains nothing but densely packed cones – it is rod free. The fovea is the area of sharpest vision – both colour and spatial detail will be most accurate when light strikes the fovea.

Bipolar and ganglion cells

The retina's bipolar and ganglion cells gather the responses of many nearby rods and cones. The **bipolar cells** combine impulses from many receptors. Next, the **ganglion cells** integrate the impulses from many bipolar cells into a single rate of firing. The axons of the ganglion cells make up the **optic nerve**, which carries this visual information out of the eye and toward the brain. Considering that each optic nerve fibre contains 'only' one million axons, which has to transport the signals of millions and millions of rods and cones, a lot of neural processing already takes place in the retina itself.

The ganglion cells provide a starting point for a distinction that continues to exist in the subsequent

FIGURE 5.7 — FIND YOUR BLIND SPOT

To find your blind spot, hold this book at arm's length, close your right eye and fixate on the bank figure with your left eye as you bring the book slowly closer. When the dollar sign is in your blind spot, it will disappear, but you will experience no gaping hole in your visual field. Instead, your visual system fills in this area with the background whiteness of the surrounding area so you 'see' the whiteness, which isn't there.

To convince yourself that higher brain processes 'fill in' the missing part of the visual field with appropriate information, close your right eye again and focus on the cross as you bring the book closer to you. This time, the gap in the line will disappear and be filled in with a line that completes the broken one. At least in your blind spot, what you see with your own eye may be a false view of reality.

processing of visual information in the pathways to the brain, as well as in the visual cortex itself. Two types of ganglion cells are distinguishable: parvo and magno cells. The majority of the ganglion cells consists of **parvo cells**. These are small cells – 'parvo' is the latin term for 'small' – with relatively short branches that are especially located in the fovea region and that are 'colour sensitive'. **Magno cells** are 'colour blind'; they are bigger – 'magno' being the Latin term for 'large' – and have longer branches and subsequently more connections with other cells. Virtually no magno cells have been found in the fovea region and their number increases as we move outward into the peripheral retina. Parvo cells have a lower conduction rate than magno cells.

As the optic nerve exits the eye, it leaves a small area of the retina without receptor cells. This area is the blind spot. You do not normally experience blindness there because what one eye 'misses' the other eye registers, and the brain 'fills in' the information that is most likely missing. To find your own blind spot, look at *Figure 5.7* (previous page) and follow the instructions.

 Visual Pathways to the Brain

The bundled axons of the ganglion cells forming the *optic nerve* start the process of carrying the information from the retina to the brain. The two – one from each eye – optic nerves come together at the base of the hypothalamus in the optic chiasma, which resembles the Greek letter χ (chi). In humans, the axons in the optic nerve are divided into two bundles at the optic chiasma; a bundle from the inner-half of each eye crosses over to the other side to continue its journey toward the back of the brain, as shown in *Figure 5.8*.

Beyond the optic chiasma the pathway is no longer called the optic nerve, but rather the **optic tract**. The optic tract consists of two distinct anatomical routes. The primary visual pathway goes first to the **lateral geniculate nucleus** of the thalamus. The cells in this nucleus also can be divided in parvo-like cells and magno-like cells, which successively receive their input from the parvo ganglion cells and the magno ganglion cells. The cells in the lateral geniculate nucleus do not only receive signals from the retina, but also from higher visual centres in the cortex. These signals may be considered a form of feedback based on previous information. Thus, the lateral geniculate nucleus is the first station where the processing of information is being influenced both in a 'bottom-up' and a 'top-down' fashion (Coren *et al*, 1994). This demonstrates

thereby the artificiality of the distinction between sensation and perception. In a large fan of fibres the signals are finally sent to the primary visual cortex.

The secondary (smaller) pathway from the optic chiasma goes to the **superior colliculus**, a cluster of nerve cell bodies in the brain stem. This visual centre is, in an evolutionary sense, much older than the cortex. It contains mainly cells of the magno-type. In addition to being activated by visual stimuli, this area also responds to auditory and tactile stimuli. It suggests that the superior colliculus serves as a site for integration between sensory modalities (Meredith & Stein, 1985). From the superior colliculus, the signals go through the thalamus – but *not* the lateral geniculate nucleus – to the visual cortex.

FIGURE 5.8	PATHWAYS IN THE HUMAN VISUAL SYSTEM

The diagram shows the way light from the visual field projects on to the two retinas and shows the routes by which neural messages from the retina are sent to the two visual centres of each hemisphere. Of course, the projections of the animals on to the retina and hemispheres must not be taken literally; the eye is not a camera and visual representations are not copies of the outside world.

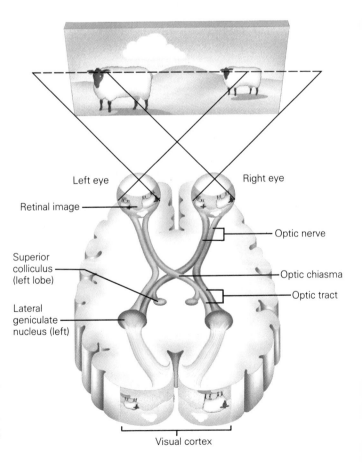

FIGURE 5.9   PATHWAYS IN THE VISUAL CORTEX

Sensory information enters the brain at the primary visual cortex. The results of a gross analysis performed there are sent to the secondary visual cortex and then on to the temporal lobe (the parvo cellular pathway) and the parietal lobe (the magno cellular pathway).

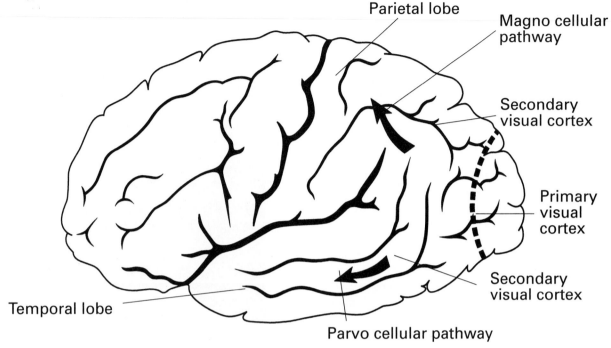

The Visual Cortex

At the back of the brain is a special area where most signals coming from the photoreceptors enter the cortex. It is the part of the occipital cortex known as the **primary visual cortex,** or striate cortex. This area can be regarded as a centre for detection of the complete range of stimulus properties, such as colour, movement and orientation. The primary visual cortex distributes its information over a large number of higher order visual areas in the **secondary visual cortex,** which, as you can see in *Figure 5.9*, is located in the front of the primary visual cortex. These areas consist of relatively isolated networks of neurons, called **modules,** that appear to be specialised in the analysis of limited aspects of the visual field. For example, one module might be relatively specialised for colour, another for orientation or movement, yet another for distance or texture, and so on.

From the secondary visual areas the information seems to travel in one of two distinctly different pathways that find their origin in the parvo and magno ganglion cells respectively. Thus, there are not only two different types of ganglion cells and corresponding visual pathways to the brain, but also two distinct information-processing systems within it. These intra-cortical pathways project to different areas in the visual cortex (Van der Heijden, 1992).

From the secondary visual cortex, the **parvo cellular pathway** leads to the temporal lobes. It is suggested that this area, comprising of many modules, processes identity information – that is to say, it is concerned with analysing the '*what*' of our world. It appears that the identification of that which is in the perceptual field is independent from the position or the movement of the object concerned. You can identify a chair or your mother irrespective of where they are located and whether or not they are moving around. People with lesions in specific parts of the right temporal lobe cannot identify objects or individuals. Some of these people are suffering from visual agnosia, a deficit that received popular attention through the book *The Man Who Mistook His Wife for a Hat* (Sachs, 1985). These patients apprehend all parts of the visual field, but what they see does not mean anything to them. Thus, the temporal lobes appear to be involved in the fine-grained, relatively time-consuming perception of patterns and colours. This is in line with the structure of the parvo cells – small cells with relatively short branches and a low conduction rate.

The **magno cellular pathway** leads from the secondary visual cortex to the parietal lobes. The suggestion is that this pathway is concerned with the spatial relationships among stimuli, analysing the '*where*' of objects. In line with the structure of the magno cells, the parietal lobes seem to be involved in quick but relatively gross perception of location and movement, and also with gross pattern perception.

The current view among neuroscientists is that within the brain, the various attributes of the visual world are analysed separately in different modules. Evidence for the modular organisation of the visual cortex came from patients who lost parts of their brain capacity as a result of various types of strokes. Some suffered surprisingly selective visual losses, such as the loss of colour discrimination, but not of form perception or the loss of motion perception (Livingstone & Hubel, 1988). These clinical studies are now supported by anatomical, physiological and psychological experiments. For example, in one region of the temporal lobe of monkeys, cells have been found that respond selectively to faces. Responses on the presentation of cartoon caricatures were weaker than those to realistic monkey-like faces (Bruce *et al*, 1981; Perrett & Mistlin, 1887).

Taken together, the visual cortex is nowadays considered a hierarchically organised system of modules, wherein the modules decompose the complex visual input. They function as building blocks in the information-processing system. By performing the analysis of different visual attributes in parallel, rather than in series, much more processing can be accomplished in a short period of time. Furthermore, the brain seems to function in such a way that identity and location are independently represented by separate cortical systems.

By now you will probably be convinced that the process of vision has nothing to do with 'copying' the outside world and that terms such as 'computation' and 'calculation' are more appropriate to describe what happens in between the initial detection of light and the ensuing experience of a visual sensation. We will encounter again the structure and functioning of the visual cortex, especially on the level of the neurons itself, when we examine the seeing of form, depth and movement.

 **Colour Vision**

In the seventeenth century Newton discovered that when white light shines through a prism it separates into a rainbow of colours: the visible spectrum. Each colour you see is the result of experiencing light rays of a particular wavelength – for example, violet-blue at the low frequency end of the visual spectrum and red-orange at the high frequency end. Sunlight combines all of these wavelengths in equal amounts, thereby giving rise to the sensation of whiteness.

Isaac Newton showed that white light passing through a prism yields a rainbow of all colours of the spectrum.

Colour, as noted before, is a psychological property of sensory experience, created when the brain processes the information coded in the light source. Despite the complexity of the processes involved, colour vision is one of the best understood aspects of our visual experience.

Hue, brightness and saturation

All experiences of colour can be described in terms of three basic dimensions of our perception of light: hue, brightness and saturation. **Hue** is the dimension that captures the essential colour of a light in terms of the wavelength entering the eye. In pure lights that contain only one wavelength (such as a laser beam) the psychological experience of hue corresponds directly to the physical dimension of the light's wavelength. **Brightness** is the dimension of colour experience that captures the intensity of light. White has the most brightness; black has the least. **Saturation** is the psychological dimension that captures the purity and vividness of colour sensations. Undiluted colours have the most saturation; muted, muddy and pastel colours have intermediate amounts of saturation; and greys have zero saturation. When colours are analysed along these three dimensions, humans are capable of visually discriminating among thousands of different colours. If brightness and saturation are held constant, most people can discriminate at least 200 different hues (Coren *et al*, 1994).

Our perception of colour of any one object depends on our comparisons with the colours of other objects in the scene as well as on the remembered colours of certain objects and the names we have for different colours. Although there is a high degree of agreement across different cultures in naming colours, interesting differences exist. For example, the Japanese only recently introduced a word into their language for blue; previously, the word 'aoi' stood for the range of colours from green and blue to violet.

The colour circle

Let us return to Newton's rainbow of colours. To answer the question of how all colours combine to form white light, we need to refer to the colour circle in *Figure 5.10*. It shows the hues arranged in a circle, according to their perceived similarity, with those that are most similar in adjacent positions. Their order mirrors the order of hues in the spectrum. Four hues are unique – red, yellow, green and blue –

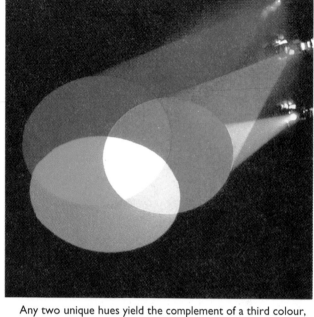

Any two unique hues yield the complement of a third colour, but the combination of the three wavelengths produces white light.

because they are not combinations of other hues as are all the rest. These unique, pure hues are equally spaced. Colours that are directly opposite are **complementary colours**; when they stimulate the

FIGURE 5.10	THE COLOUR CIRCLE

Colours are arranged by their similarity. Complementary colours are placed directly opposite each other. Mixing complementary colours yields a neutral grey or white light at the centre. The numbers next to each hue are the wavelength values for spectral colours, those colours within our region of visual sensitivity. Nonspectral hues are obtained by mixing short and long spectral wavelengths.

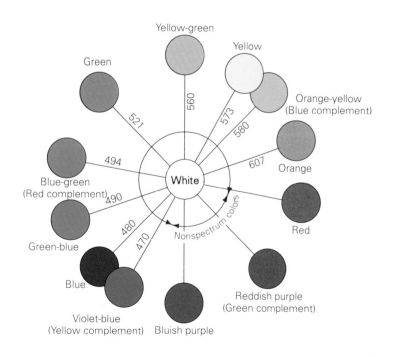

FIGURE 5.11 COLOUR AFTERIMAGES

Stare at the dot in the centre of the picture for at least 30 seconds. Then fixate on the centre of a sheet of white paper or a blank wall.

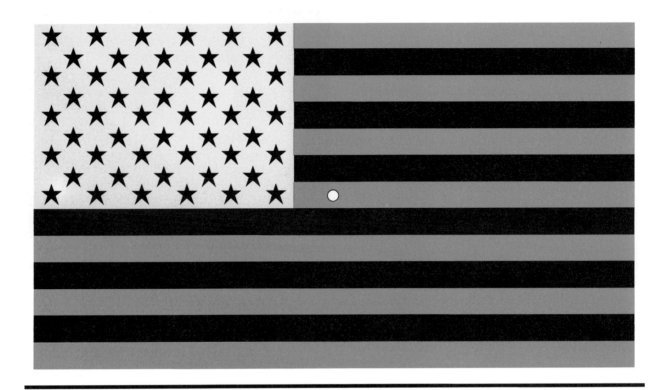

same part of the retina simultaneously, their added effects yield white light (at the centre of the colour circle). This phenomenon is called additive colour mixture. Yellow and blue lights, for example, produce an additive colour mixture. However, yellow and blue paints produce green. When paint or crayon pigments are mixed, some wavelengths of light are absorbed or subtracted from the light. This phenomenon is called subtractive colour mixture. The remaining reflected wavelength the eye detects gives the painted object the colour we perceive.

Through the phenomenon of additive colour mixture, combining any two of the hues red, green and blue will form a complement; green and red will form yellow, for example. However, mixing all the unique hues yields white light, as shown in the photograph on the previous page.

Another interesting aspect of complementary colours is what happens after you stare at a brightly coloured object for a while and then turn away to look at a blank surface. As in *Figure 5.11*, you will see its complementary colour as a visual after-image.

Not everyone sees colours in the same way; some people are born with a colour deficiency. Colour-blindness is the partial or total inability to distinguish colours. The negative after-image effect of

viewing the green, yellow and black flag will not work if you are colour-blind. Colour-blindness is usually a sex-linked hereditary defect associated with a gene on the X chromosome. Males more readily develop this recessive trait than females, because they have a single X chromosome; females would need to have it on both X chromosomes to become colour-blind. Estimates of colour-blindness among Caucasian males are about 10 per cent, but less than 0.5 per cent for females.

There are different forms of colour-blindness. People with colour weakness can not distinguish pale colours, such as pink or tan. Most typical colour-blindness involves trouble distinguishing red from green, especially at weak saturations. Those who confuse yellows and blues are rare – about one or two people per thousand. Rarest of all are those who see no colour at all and see only variations in brightness. Only about 500 cases of this total colour blindness have ever been reported.

To see whether you have a major colour deficiency, look at *Figure 5.12* (next page) and note what you see. If you see the numbers '2' and '6' in the pattern of dots, your colour vision is probably normal. If you see something else, you are probably at least partially colour blind.

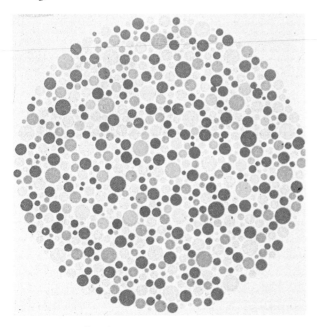

FIGURE 5.12	THE ISHIHARA COLOUR BLINDNESS TEST

A person who cannot discriminate between red and green colours will not be able to identify the number hidden in the figure.

Theories of colour vision

What theories have psychologists proposed to account for how we see colour? We will consider the two most prominent models: trichromatic theory and opponent-process theory.

The first scientific theory of colour vision was proposed by **Thomas Young** around 1800. He suggested that only three types of receptors in the normal human eye would be necessary to produce all primary colour sensations: red, green and blue. All other colours, he believed, were combinations of these three primaries. Young's theory was later refined and extended by **Hermann von Helmholtz** and came to be known as the Young–Helmholtz **trichromatic theory**.

Trichromatic theory provided a plausible explanation for the production of people's colour sensations and for colour blindness (according to the theory, colour-blind people had only one or two kinds of receptors); but other facts and observations were not as well explained by the theory. For example, why do colour-blind people always fail to distinguish pairs of colours: red and green or blue and yellow?

Answers to these questions became the cornerstones for a second theory of colour vision proposed by **Ewald Hering** in the late 1800s. According to his **opponent-process theory**, all colour experiences arise from three underlying systems, each of which includes two opponent elements: red versus green, blue versus yellow, or black (no colour) versus white (all colours). Hering theorised that colours produced complementary after-images because one element of the system became fatigued (from over-stimulation) and, thus, increased the relative contribution of its opponent element. In Hering's theory, types of colour blindness came in pairs because the colour system was actually built from pairs of opposites, not from single primary colours.

After years of dispute about which theory was correct, scientists eventually recognised that the theories were not really in conflict; they simply described two different stages of processing that corresponded to successive physiological structures in the visual system (Hurvich & Jameson, 1957). We know now that there are, indeed, three types of cones – each of which is most sensitive to light at a particular wave-length – and they work very much as predicted by the original Young–Helmholtz trichromatic theory. The responses of these cone types correspond to the three primary colours in the Young–Helmholtz theory. People with red–green colour-blindness, for instance, have one malfunctioning cone system; that is to say, they are insensitive to the long wavelengths others perceive as red.

The retinal ganglion cells then combine the outputs of these three cone types in different ways, in accordance with Hering's opponent-process theory (R. De Valois & Jacobs, 1968). According to the modern version of opponent-process theory, as supported by Hurvich & Jameson (1974), the two members of each colour pair work in opposition (are opponents) by means of neural inhibition. Some cells are excited by light that produces sensations of red, and some are inhibited by light that produces sensations of green. Other cells in the system do the opposite: they are excited by light that looks green and are inhibited by light that looks red. Together, these two types of ganglion cells form the physiological basis of the red–green opponent-process system. Other ganglion cells make up the blue–yellow opponent system. The black–white system contributes to our perception of colour saturation and brightness.

Molecular basis of colour vision

Recent discoveries from genetics and neurobiology laboratories support psychological theories about the way colour vision functions. We perceive different colours by analysing the inputs from cones that are sensitive to wavelengths that give rise to sensations of either red, green or blue. Each cone contains pigments that detect one of these kinds. The colours we see depend on how strongly light entering the eye excites each of these three types of cone cells. Using

FIGURE 5.13 BRIGHTNESS CONTRAST

These four (objectively) identical grey squares are set on different backgrounds. As you can see, the lighter the background, the darker the grey squares appear.

the powerful tools of molecular genetics, researchers have isolated and identified the genes that direct the development of the three colour vision proteins (Nathans *et al*, 1986).

Other vision researchers have developed a technique for analysing the electrical activity of a single cone cell from the retinas of macaque monkeys and humans (which are quite similar). Single cone cells were 'sucked up' into a special hollow glass tube that was less than 1/25th the diameter of a human hair. Light of various wavelengths was shone on the

tube and the strength of electrical signals emitted from the cone cell was amplified and measured. Using this technique, the researchers found that some cells were tuned to respond maximally to light wavelengths of 435 nanometers (blue cells), others to 535 nm (green cells) and others to 570 nm (red cells). Now researchers are trying to identify the biochemical activities of these cells that are triggered by light and start the process of transduction of external energy into neural energy that underlies our visual sensation (Baylor, 1987).

A

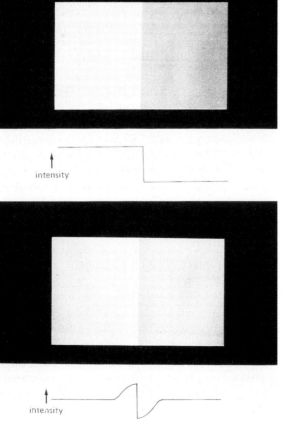

intensity

B

Seeing Form, Depth and Movement

Seeing form, depth and movement is clearly of survival value. It is a prerequisite for moving toward desirable objects and away from undesirable ones. Thus, besides colour vision, the visual system also

FIGURE 5.14 THE ILLUSION OF CONTOUR

The power of edges to define a visual field is seen in the two rectangular surfaces. Rectangle A and rectangle B seem similar – they both have dark right halves and light left halves. To prove that the right half of rectangle A is darker than the left half, place a pencil along the centre of the rectangle. Note the brightness difference on either side of the pencil. To prove that your perception of the world can be distorted, place the pencil along the centre of rectangle B. Visual magic! The difference between the left and right halves has vanished. A light meter moved across rectangle A records the sharp change in light intensity at the mid-point of the rectangle; but the bottom rectangle is shown to have the same light intensity throughout, except at the mid-point between the two halves where there is a gradual shift toward brighter on the left side and darker on the right. The mid-point border creates a false impression of contrast that misleads your visual system into seeing a difference where there is none.

must detect the form or shape of objects, their depth or distance away and their movement in space. In this final section on the visual system, we will first consider the information we use to perceive the shape and form of objects in space and then examine the way the visual system enables us to transform that stimulus input into the 'right' neural codes for accurate identification of its properties.

Contrast effects

Any typical visual field consists of many shapes, colours and textures that impinge on the retina. How do we see what is important? First, we must separate figures from their background so that we can make subsequent detailed analysis of their properties. This figure-ground segregation occurs largely automatically at the earliest stages of processing. Nevertheless, a visual scene filled with figures is quite complex. The key to perceiving different objects in space is finding contrasts in brightness to form boundaries and distinct edges that give objects shape, size and orientation in space. The visual system accentuates the edges between objects to make them stand out clearly by searching for contrasts.

A patch of grey appears lighter against a dark background than it does against a light background, as shown in *Figure 5.13* (previous page). This brightness-contrast effect makes the response to a constant stimulus greater as the intensity difference between it and its background increases. In the retina, adjacent areas are accentuated by this brightness-contrast effect, causing perceived boundaries between surfaces to be sharpened. *Figure 5.14* (previous page) demonstrates the power of edges to define a visual field.

Receptive fields and feature-detectors

While discussing the general principles of visual information-processing, we indicated that the visual system is characterised by specialisation. In the hierarchically organised visual system, each module appears to analyse only some limited aspects of the visual field. This specialisation already exists on the level of the single cell. The firing rate of single ganglion cells – the frequency with which they discharge impulses – is dependent on the specific properties of the stimulus as well as on the specific zone of the retina that is stimulated. For example, one particular ganglion cell may only respond if a straight line in the upper-left region in the visual field stimulates a zone of the lower-right side of the retina. For any particular ganglion cell, the region of retinal

stimulation to which the cell responds is known as the **receptive field** of that cell (Coren *et al*, 1994).

Receptive fields of retinal ganglion cells are of two types: (a) those in which stimulation in the centre of the receptive field produces excitation while stimulation in the surrounding part produces inhibition; and (b) those with the opposite organisation. Ganglion cells respond to differences in stimulation – that is, they are most excited by *stimulus contrast*. Those with 'on' centres – an excitatory centre – fire most strongly in response to a bright spot surrounded by a dark border while those with 'off' centres – an inhibitory centre – fire most vigorously in response to a dark spot surrounded by a light border. Uniform illumination causes the centre and surround to inhibit each other's activity – the cell is not as excited by uniform illumination as it is by a spot or bar of light.

When a receptor cell is stimulated by light it transmits information in two directions: upward to the brain and sideways to neighbouring receptor cells. Impulses are sent out to adjacent cells to inhibit the transmission of those receptor cells. This sideways suppression is called **lateral inhibition** and is the basis for the brightness contrast effect we have previously noted. Lateral inhibition exaggerates the difference between stimuli, generating messages to the brain that there is more contrast than 'actually' exists.

The geography of the visual field is not only retained on the level of retinal processing, but also in the visual cortex. **David Hubel** and **Thorsten Wiesel** pioneered the study of the receptive fields of cells in the visual cortex and, in 1981, won a Nobel prize for their work. They recorded the firing rates from single cells in the visual cortex of cats in response to moving spots and bars across the visual field. When Hubel and Wiesel mapped out the receptive fields of these cortical cells, they found both excitatory and inhibitory regions; but they found that the receptive fields of the cortical cells were almost always elongated rather than round. Accordingly, these cortical cells were strongly excited (or inhibited) by bars of light or by edges configured in particular orientations (Hubel & Wiesel, 1962; 1979). Because these cortical cells were simply and directly related to specific receptive fields, Hubel and Wiesel called them simple cells. Their output, in turn, is processed by other, more complex types of cortical cells (see *Figure 5.15*, next page).

When the electrical activity of single cells in the visual cortex was recorded in response to stimulation of different types, it turned out that, within their receptive fields, these cortical cells responded only to patterns of specific shapes and angles of orientation. Some cells responded to lines, some to edges, some to particular positions or orientations of a stimulus, some to particular shapes and some to movement in a

FIGURE 5.15   RECEPTIVE FIELDS OF GANGLION AND CORTICAL CELLS

The receptive field of a cell is the region of retinal stimulation to which the cell responds. The receptive fields of the ganglion cells in the retina are circular (A, B); those of the simplest cells in the visual cortex are elongated in a particular orientation (C, D, E, F). In both cases, the cell responding to the receptive field is excited by light in the regions marked with plus signs and inhibited by light in the regions marked with minus signs.

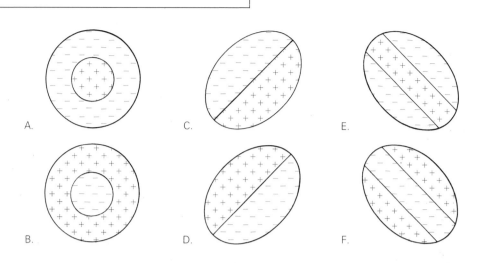

particular direction. Thus, it appears that the brain is designed to extract certain simple features from the complex stimuli that bombard the visual system, such as lines, edges, angles and corners. For example, simple cortical cells in the visual cortex might respond to a triangle in such a way that some of the cells would detect horizontal lines and others would detect straight lines at 60°. More complex cortical cells might detect 60° corners. The information from the different cells would then be combined to trigger the sensation of a triangle somewhere at a higher level of brain processing. Hubel and Wiesel called these cortical cells **feature-detection** cells because they responded most strongly by discharging impulses when specific stimulus features were present in their receptive fields.

The feature-detection model postulates that feature detectors are arranged hierarchically – the simple input from lower centres is combined and expanded at each successive stage along the visual pathway. While there is some evidence to support this view, the theory does not explain the whole story. Rather than merely responding to simple bars that have the same contrast, most cortical cells are even more sensitive to successive, contrasting bands of dark and light. Some have argued that our nervous system constructs visual scenes by decoding visual images in patterns of light and dark. In doing so, it acts like a computer that only deals with zero's and one's (De Valois & De Valois, 1980).

Sets of cortical cells may be organised into

FIGURE 5.16   HIGH AND LOW SPATIAL FREQUENCIES

Detection of only low spatial frequencies would give us the blurry view in A. Detection of only the high spatial frequencies would give us the outline view in B. Normal detection of all frequencies gives us the full view in C.

A.   B.   C.

channels that are tuned to respond to different spatial frequencies. Some channels, specific to low frequencies, pick up blobs of light, others detect high frequencies and others are specific for frequencies in between. Together, they provide all the information needed to represent a visual scene by combining the range of spatial frequencies that define its dark–light pattern. Any two-dimensional pattern – from a national flag to a photograph of Groucho Marx – can be analysed mathematically and broken down into computer codes as the sum of its many spatial frequencies. *Figure 5.16* of Groucho Marx reveals what you would see of him with only low spatial frequencies – the overall shape in the blurry picture, A. The high spatial frequencies are responsible for the sharp edges and fine detail in the outline picture, B. What we ordinarily see is the combination of all spatial frequencies, as in picture C.

Do we really know that what these nerve cells in the visual system are responding to affects what the brain perceives and how we behave? In the last few years the answer to this question has been an affirmative. Stimulating distinct circuits of receptive fields of neurons in the visual cortex not only excites the neurons but also causes certain perceptions to occur (Newsome & Pare, 1988). In another recent study, a causal connection between neuronal activity of cells in the visual cortex and perceptually judged direction of movement was demonstrated (Salzman *et al*, 1990).

We started this chapter by referring to the adaptational nature of our sensory system. In this section about vision, it by now has become clear that we can move adequately, and grasp and manipulate objects thanks to specialised cells in the central nervous system that play a key role in spatial attention. The models as presented increase our basic understanding of how we are able to act accurately on the basis of what we perceive. Such insight also has practical utility for clinical interventions with patients suffering from problems of visual-movement impairments (Wise & Desimone, 1988).

 AUDITION

Similar to vision, audition, or hearing, provides us with spatial information over extended distances. However, hearing may be even more important than vision in orienting us toward distant events. We often hear stimuli before we see them, particularly if they take place behind us or on the other side of opaque objects such as walls. Although vision is better equipped for identifying an object than hearing is, we often see the object only because we have used our ears to turn our eyes in the right direction.

Besides orienting us, hearing plays a crucial role in our understanding of spoken language; it is the

INTERIM SUMMARY

The visual system is the most thoroughly studied of the sensory pathways. The process of seeing starts when the eye focuses the small part of the electromagnetic energy we call light on to the back of the eyeball, where photoreceptors – the rods and cones – transduce the physical energy into neural impulses. Ganglion cells in the retina integrate the input from receptors and bipolar cells; their axons form the optic nerves which meet at the optic chiasma. From there, the optic tract consists of two distinct anatomical routes: the primary visual pathway goes to the lateral geniculate nucleus of the thalamus; while the secondary – smaller – pathway goes to the superior colliculus.

Within the brain, the various attributes of the visual world are analysed separately in different modules. After a first, basic analysis of incoming visual information in the primary visual cortex, modules in the secondary visual cortex perform a more specialised analysis. From there the information travels along one of two distinctly different pathways: the parvo cellular one, leading to the temporal lobes, is concerned with analysing the *what* (i.e. the identity of stimulus objects);

the magno cellular pathway, leading to the parietal lobes, deals with analysing the *where* (i.e. the spatial location of stimuli).

Colour is a psychological property of sensory experience created when the brain processes the information encoded within the light source. Colour sensations differ in hue, saturation and brightness. The colour circle arranges colours in such a way that complementary colours are placed opposite each other. Current colour vision theory combines the Young–Helmholtz trichromatic theory (receptor processing) and the opponent-process theory (ganglion cell processing).

Researchers disagree about whether spatial information is detected by feature-detectors or analysed as spatial frequency patterns. Detection of spatial frequencies is studied by analysis of patterns of light–dark cycles known as sine-wave gratings. New research demonstrates that by stimulating the receptive fields of visual neurons, perceptual judgements can be produced: the brain starts perceiving what the neuron is 'seeing'.

principal sensory modality for human communication. People who lack the capacity to hear are excluded from much normal human interaction and, as a result, may suffer psychological problems associated with feelings of frustration, rejection and isolation. If the onset of a hearing impairment is gradual, often the individual who is experiencing the impairment does not recognise what is occurring in this respect. Depression and paranoid disorders may accompany such undetected loss of hearing (Post, 1980; Zimbardo *et al*, 1981). The importance of hearing and the tragedy of its loss is captured in this eloquent description:

> *The world will still make sense to someone who is blind or armless or minus a nose. But if you lose your sense of hearing, a crucial thread dissolves and you lose track of life's logic. You become cut off from the daily commerce of the world, as if you were a root buried beneath the soil (Ackerman, 1990).*

Similar to our coverage of the process of vision, in this section about audition we will discuss first the general principles of the physics of sound as well as those of detection and transduction. We will then elaborate on three subjects: the psychological dimensions of sound, theories of pitch perception and sound localisation.

The Physics of Sound

If you clap your hands together, whistle, or tap your pen on the table, you will cause objects to vibrate. This vibration is transmitted to the surrounding medium – usually air – as the vibrating objects push the molecules of the medium back and forth. The resulting slight changes in pressure spread outward from the vibrating objects in the form of waves, as shown in *Figure 5.17*, travelling – in air – at a rate of 340 metres per second. When this form of mechanical pressure is detected, transduced and processed by our hearing system, we experience sound. Sound cannot be created in a true vacuum (such as outer space) because there are no molecules in a vacuum for vibrating objects to move.

Air pressure changes – changes in the density of air molecules in space – are often called *sine waves*. Strictly speaking, there is no sound in the outside world, so there are no sound waves either. Sound is a psychological property of sensory experience. Nevertheless, for reasons of simplicity of language use, we will also use 'sound waves' to refer to the mechanical pressure that forms the raw material for the process of hearing.

A sine wave has two basic physical properties

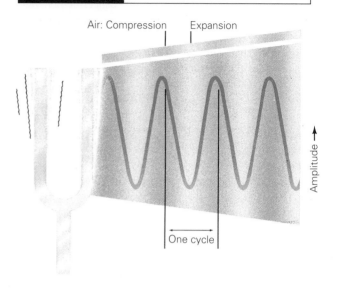

that determine how it sounds to us: frequency and amplitude. *Frequency* measures the number of cycles the wave completes in a given amount of time. A cycle, as indicated in *Figure 5.17*, is the left-to-right distance from the peak in one wave to the peak in the next wave. Frequency of waves is usually expressed in cycles per second (cps) or **Hertz** (Hz). When the ear of a healthy young person is struck by waves between 20 and 20,000 Hz, the mechanoreceptors (hair cells of the basilar membrane inside the ear) convert the physical energy into neural impulses. By comparison, the lowest tone of a piano is about 50 Hz, the highest 4,000 Hz. *Amplitude* measures the physical property of strength of the sound wave, as shown in its peak-to-valley height. Amplitude is defined in units of sound pressure or energy.

The sounds we hear that are produced by a single sine wave, such as those made by tuning forks, are called 'pure tones'. A pure tone has only one frequency and one amplitude. Most sound waves in our daily world are not pure as they are produced by complex sound waves containing a combination of frequencies and amplitudes. We hear differing qualities of sounds (clarinet versus piano, for example) because most waves contain differing combinations of frequencies and amplitudes.

Detection and Transduction

The ear can be divided into three major parts: the external, middle and inner ear (see *Figure 5.18*). The visible part of the ear, which belongs to the external

FIGURE 5.18 STRUCTURE OF THE HUMAN EAR

Sound waves are channelled by the external ear, or pinna, through the external canal, causing the tympanic membrane to vibrate. This vibration activates the tiny bones of the inner ear – the hammer, anvil and stirrup. Their mechanical vibrations are passed along from the oval window to the cochlea where they set in motion the fluid in its canal. Tiny hair cells lining the coiled basilar membrane within the cochlea bend as the fluid moves, stimulating nerve endings attached to them. The mechanical energy is then transformed into neural energy and sent to the brain via the auditory nerve.

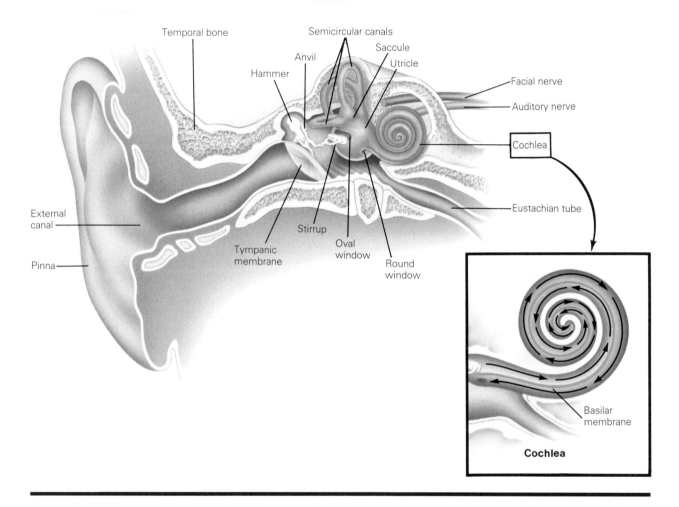

ear, is called the *pinna*. Like all sense organs, the ear is a collecting device. Its function is to collect and intensify vibrational energy. Thus, the process of hearing starts when vibrating air molecules hit the external ear. Some sound waves enter the ear directly and some enter after having been reflected off the pinna. The wave travels along the auditory canal until it encounters a thin membrane called the eardrum, or tympanic membrane. The eardrum is set into motion by pressure variations of the sound wave and thereby transmits the wave from the outer ear into the middle ear.

The middle ear is a chamber that contains the three smallest bones in the human body: the hammer, the anvil and the stirrup. These bones form a mechanical chain of events that transmits and amplifies the vibrations from the eardrum to a

membrane, called the *oval window,* that constitutes the entrance of the inner ear.

If the bones in the middle ear are not functioning properly, the resulting hearing impairment is called 'conduction deafness'. This problem concerning the conduction of the air vibrations to the cochlea can sometimes be corrected in microsurgery by insertion of an artificial anvil or stirrup.

The **cochlea**, located in the inner ear, is a fluid-filled, coiled tube that has a membrane known as the **basilar membrane** running down its middle and along its length. When the stirrup vibrates against the oval window at the base of the cochlea, the fluid in the cochlea is set into wave motion. This fluid wave travels down the length of the coiled tube, around the end, and back to the base on the other side of the basilar membrane, where it is absorbed by the round window. As the fluid moves, it causes the basilar membrane to move in a wave-like motion.

The wave-like motion of the basilar membrane bends the tiny hair cells connected to the membrane. As the hair cells bend, they stimulate nerve endings, transforming the mechanical vibrations of the basilar membrane into neural activity. The nerve impulses leave the cochlea in a bundle of fibres called the **auditory nerve**. These fibres meet in the cochlear nucleus of the brain stem. Similar to the crossing over of nerves in the visual system, stimulation from one ear goes to both sides of the brain. Auditory signals pass through a series of other nuclei on their way to the **auditory cortex** in the temporal lobes of the cerebral hemispheres. The higher order processing of these signals begins in the auditory cortex. We will have to say more about the auditory visual cortex when we discuss two theories of pitch perception.

Hearing impairment that is caused by a defect in the neural mechanisms that create nerve impulses in the ear or relay them to the auditory cortex, is called 'nerve deafness'. Obviously, damage to the auditory cortex can also create nerve deafness. Currently, there are no known ways to modify nerve deafness.

Psychological Dimensions of Sound

Three important psychological dimensions of sound – sound as we experience it – are pitch, loudness and quality (or timbre). While practising singing or playing a musical instrument, with the production of each tone of the musical scale, you are varying the **pitch**. The most important physical determinant of our experience of pitch is the frequency of the sound wave: high frequencies produce high pitch and low frequencies produce low pitch. The full range of human sensitivity to pure tones for young adults extends from frequencies as low as 20 Hz to frequencies as high as 20,000 Hz. Frequencies below 20 Hz may be experienced through touch as vibrations rather than as sound. With age a progressive loss in sensitivity occurs, especially for high frequencies.

The psychophysical relationship between pitch and frequency is not a linear one: at the low end of the frequency scale, increasing the frequency by just a few Hz raises the pitch quite noticeably; but at the high end of frequency, we require a much bigger increase in order to hear the difference in pitch. For example, the two lowest notes on a piano differ by only 1.6 Hz, whereas the two highest ones differ by 235 Hz – a difference that is more than 140 times greater than the difference between the two lowest notes.

The experienced loudness of a sound is greatly affected by the intensity of the physical stimulus. If everything else is held constant, the greater the amplitude of the sound waves the greater the experienced loudness. The human auditory system is sensitive to an enormous range of physical intensities. At the low end of the scale, we can hear the tick of a wristwatch at six metres. This seems an appropriate absolute threshold, because with any further sensitivity we would literally hear the blood flowing in our ears. At the other extreme, a jet airliner taking off 90 metres away is so loud that it can be painful. In terms of physical units of sound pressure, the jet produces a sound wave with more than a billion times the energy of the ticking watch.

FIGURE 5.19	LOUDNESS OF FAMILIAR SOUNDS

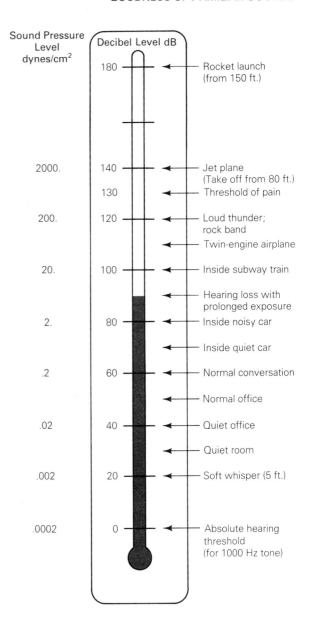

LOUDNESS OF FAMILIAR SOUNDS

Because the range of hearing is so great, physical intensities of sound are usually expressed in ratios rather than absolute amounts; loudness is measured in units called **decibels** (db). *Figure 5.19* shows the loudness of some representative natural sounds in decibel units. It also shows the corresponding sound pressures for comparison. Notice that sounds louder than about 90 db can produce hearing loss, depending on how long one is exposed to them.

Only a few sound sources produce pure tones. Everyday sounds consist of enormously complex waveforms. The **timbre** of a sound reflects the specific quality of such complex sound waves. For example, you can differentiate between a piano and a violin because the waveforms they produce, even when playing the same note, are different. A complex sound can be analysed as a sum of many different pure tones, each with a different amplitude and frequency. *Figure 5.20* shows the complex waveforms that correspond to several familiar sounds. The graph in the figure shows the sound spectrum for middle C on a piano – the range of all the frequencies actually present in that note and their amplitudes.

In a complex tone such as middle C, the lowest frequency (about 256 Hz) is responsible for the pitch we hear; it is called the 'fundamental'. The higher frequencies are called 'harmonics' (or overtones) and are simple multiples of the fundamental. The complete sound we hear is produced by the total effect of the fundamental and the harmonics shown in the spectrum. If pure tones at these frequencies and intensities were added together, the result would sound the same to us as middle C on a piano. Amazingly, the human ear actually analyses complex waves by breaking them down into these component waves.

The sounds that we call noise do not have the clear, simple structures of fundamental frequencies and harmonics. Noise contains many frequencies that are not systematically related to each other. For instance, the static noise you hear between radio stations contains energy at all audible frequencies; you perceive it as having no pitch because it has no fundamental frequency.

 Theories of Pitch Perception

To explain how the auditory system converts sound waves into sensations of pitch, two distinct theories have been proposed: place theory and frequency theory.

Place theory was initially proposed by **Hermann von Helmholtz** in the 1800s and was later modified, elaborated and tested by **Georg von Békésy**, who

FIGURE 5.20	WAVEFORMS OF FAMILIAR SOUNDS

Below the complex waveforms of five familiar sounds is the sound spectrum for middle C on the piano. The basic wavelength is produced by the fundamental, in this case at 256 cycles, but the strings are also vibrating at several higher frequencies that produce the jaggedness of the wave pattern. These additional frequencies are identified in the sound spectrum.

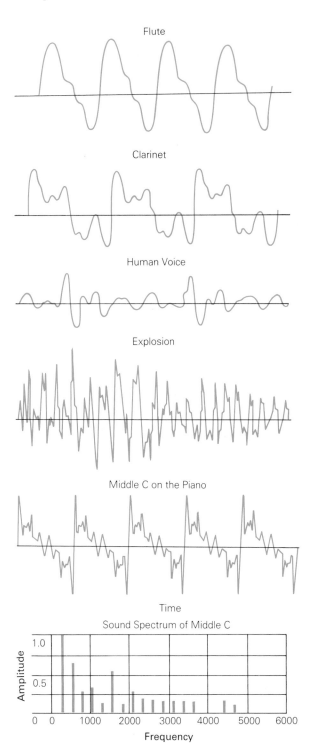

won a Nobel prize for this work in 1961. Place theory proposes that pitch perception depends on which part of the receptor is stimulated. It is based on the fact that the basilar membrane moves when sound waves are conducted through the inner ear. Different frequencies produce most movement at particular locations along the basilar membrane. For high-frequency tones, the wave motion is greatest at the base of the cochlea, where the oval and round windows are located. For low-frequency tones, the greatest wave motion of the basilar membrane is at the opposite end. So, place theory states that perception of pitch depends upon the specific place on the basilar membrane where the greatest stimulation occurs.

The second theory, **frequency theory**, explains pitch by the timing of neural responses. Its main hypothesis is that neurons fire only at a certain phase in each cycle of the sine wave – perhaps at the peaks. Their firing rate is determined by a tone's frequency. This rate of firing is the code for pitch. One problem with this theory is that individual neurons cannot fire rapidly enough to represent high pitch sounds, because none of them can fire more than 2,000 times per second. This limitation makes it impossible for one neuron to distinguish sounds above 2,000 Hz. This limitation is overcome by the **volley principle** which explains what might happen when the peaks in a sound wave come too rapidly for any single neuron to fire in response to each peak. As shown in *Figure 5.21*, several neurons in a combined action, or volley, could fire at the frequency that matched the stimulus tone (Wever, 1949).

FIGURE 5.21	THE VOLLEY PRINCIPLE

The total collective activity of the auditory (black) nerve cells has a pattern that corresponds to the input sound wave (red) even though each individual fibre may not be firing fast enough to follow the sound wave pattern.

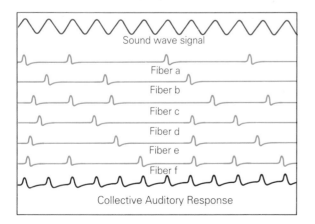

As with the trichromatic and opponent-process theories of colour vision, the place and frequency theories of pitch perception were long thought to be in direct conflict. Recently, it has become clear that both are correct, each accounting for only a portion of the audible frequency range. Frequency theory accounts well for coding frequencies below about 5,000 Hz; at higher frequencies neurons cannot fire quickly and precisely enough to code a signal adequately, even in volley. Place theory accounts well for perception of pitch at frequencies above 1,000 Hz. Below 1,000 HZ, the entire basilar membrane vibrates so broadly that it cannot provide to the neural receptors a signal that is distinctive enough to be used as a means of distinguishing pitch. Between 1,000 and 5,000 Hz both mechanisms can operate. As in the case of the competing colour theories, the two pitch theories have proven to be compatible. A complex sensory task is divided between two systems that, together, offer greater sensory precision than either system alone could provide.

Sound Localisation

Porpoises and bats do not use vision to locate objects in dark waters or dark caves. Instead, they use echolocation – they emit high-pitch sounds that bounce off objects, giving them feedback about the objects' distances, locations, sizes, textures and movements. Although we humans lack this special ability, we do use sounds to determine the location of objects in space, especially when seeing them is difficult. We do so through two mechanisms: relative timing of sounds to each ear and relative pitch of sound from each ear.

The first mechanism involves neurons that compare the relative times when incoming sound reaches each ear. A sound on your right side, for example, reaches the right ear before the left. Neurons are arranged in rows, so that every other row is stimulated by one of the two ears. Another set of neurons compares the times when these rows are stimulated and computes the relative arrival times of sounds to each ear. This mechanism is quite sensitive, detecting differences in arrival times as small as 1/10th millionth of a second, under ideal conditions.

The second mechanism relies on the principle that, as sound travels around your head, it changes ever so slightly in pitch. Another set of detector neurons compares the relative pitch of sounds from each ear, providing a second source of information about the location of a target sound. A simple demonstration of how these mechanisms are put into practice occurs when a sound is directly in front of or

During the 1980s, in the USA, some communities in California banned the use of leaf blowers, because these motorised substitutes for a garden rake had the potential to blast bystanders with sounds as loud as 91 decibels – about the same loudness as Niagara Falls (Carlton, 1990). In San Francisco, problems with noise pollution in general have become so serious that the police force has a special noise abatement unit. These officers are equipped with devices to measure the decibel level of the offending sounds. If it is more than five decibels over the background noise, they issue warnings. A second violation leads to formal notification within police records. If the source of the noise is a night club, its operating permit may even be revoked (Krieger, 1990).

Prolonged exposure to intense sounds not only provokes stress, but it can also produce permanent hearing loss. Impairment depends both on the duration and intensity of a sound. A sudden explosion at 200 dbs can cause massive damage in a fraction of a second, but routine, continued exposure to sounds more than and even less than 100 dbs can also cause significant hearing impairment. Many people report stimulation deafness for up to several hours after listening to a rock concert in an enclosed area. Rock musicians may suffer more permanent hearing loss because they are exposed to intense sound levels so frequently.

Rock musicians are not the

only ones adversely affected by the noise levels in modern society. While the majority of 70-year-olds living near the Sudanese–Ethiopian border could hear a whisper from 90 metres away (Krieger, 1990), about one in four Americans over 65 needs a hearing aid to detect whispers across the room (Clayman, 1989).

Sustained exposure to loud noises damages the sensitive hair cells that convert the motion of the basilar membrane into neural impulses. Once damaged, these cells do not regenerate and they cannot be surgically repaired. Short exposure to very loud sounds – a pneumatic drill nearby, a jet engine at 100 feet, or a rock concert from the front row – can cause damage in less than half an hour. Short blasts of loud but less intense sounds, such as those caused by a

power mower (about 85 db), may be safe but earplugs are advised. In the USA, the federal government regulates the maximum noise exposure allowed in the workplace. While the limit for 90 db noise is eight hours a day, workers cannot legally be exposed to 110 dbs for longer than half an hour daily.

Loud noise primarily affects sensitivity to high frequencies (at or above 4,000 HZ). With age, almost everyone in our noisy society loses some ability to hear at these frequencies. The data from East Africa suggest that this loss may not be a physiological consequence of aging but could be the cumulative effect of a lifetime's exposure to environmental noise. If so, those who want to preserve their hearing might consider cleaning up their gardens the old fashioned way – with a rake.

behind you. In order to overcome the problem of equidistance from your ears, in all likelihood you will move the position of your head – and thereby of your ears – so that their sound localisation function can be performed in the way for which they were designed.

INTERIM SUMMARY

The process of hearing starts when the ear detects vibrations of molecules in the air. These waves vary in frequency, amplitude and complexity, and correspondingly, our sensations of sound vary in pitch, loudness and timbre (quality). In the cochlea, sound waves are transformed into fluid waves that move the basilar membrane. When the tiny hairs on the basilar membrane bend in response to this movement, they stimulate neural impulses that are sent along to the auditory cortex.

Place theory accounts best for the coding of high frequencies; together, frequency theory and the volley principle account best for the coding of low frequencies. While conductance deafness may be corrected, nerve deafness, which involves defects in neural transmission of sound codes, cannot. Localising sounds in space involves the interplay of two neuronal mechanisms: one computes the relative timing of sounds coming to each ear; the other estimates the relative pitch of sounds from each ear. Prolonged exposure to sources of noise pollution diminishes hearing ability and can lead to permanent hearing impairment.

 ## THE OTHER SENSES

In humans, seeing and hearing are considered the two most important senses. As Helen Keller demonstrated, this does not mean that people whose world is restricted to smells, tastes, touches and feelings of warmth and cold or of pain cannot have a rich and varied perceptual life. Moreover, many animals rely almost exclusively on the so-called 'minor senses'. In this last section, we will first briefly discuss the two chemically based senses: smell and taste. We will then close our discussion of sense modalities with a brief analysis of the essential features of some mechanical senses: these concern the detection of position and movement by the vestibular and kinesthetic senses, and the skin sensations of touch and pain.

 ## Smell

The sense of smell involves a sequence of biochemical activities that trigger the firing of action potentials. The first stage of this sequence consists of the interaction of odours with receptor proteins on the membrane of tiny hairs in the nose (*olfactory cilia*). Only eight molecules of a substance are required to initiate one of these nerve impulses, but at least 40 nerve endings must be stimulated before the organism can smell the substance. Once initiated, these nerve impulses convey odour information to the **olfactory bulb**, located just above the receptors and just below the frontal lobes of the cortex. Odour stimuli may start the process of smell by stimulating an influx of chemical substances into ion channels in olfactory neurons, which, as you may recall from Chapter 2, triggers an action potential (Restrepo *et al*, 1990).

The brain centre that is specialised to process information about smell is the *rhinencephalon*, one of the oldest parts of the brain. Several facts have led researchers to conclude that smell is our most primitive sense. First, the human rhinencephalon looks very similar to that of other organisms – for example, the lizard – suggesting that the sense evolved long before major differences among organisms began to evolve. Second, while sensory signals from all other sense modalities pass through the relay station of the thalamus before going on to their destination in the sensory cortex, smell signals do not. Instead, they go directly to the brain's smell centre.

Smell presumably evolved as a system for detecting and locating food (Moncrieff, 1951). It is also used for detecting potential sources of danger. Because smell is a distance sense – organisms do not have to come into direct contact with other organisms in order to smell them – it is particularly useful for alerting organisms to danger. In addition, smell can be a powerful form of active communication. Members of some species communicate with each other by secreting and detecting chemical signals called **pheromones**. Pheromones are chemical substances used as communication within a given species to signal sexual receptivity, danger, territorial boundaries and food sources. Worker ants and bees use pheromone signals to let others in their colony or hive know where they have found a food source (Marler & Hamilton, 1966).

The significance of the sense of smell varies greatly across species. Dogs, rats, insects and many other creatures for whom smell is central to survival have a far keener sense of smell than we do; thus, relatively more of their brain area is devoted to smell. Humans primarily seem to use the sense of smell in conjunction with taste to seek and sample food, but there is some evidence that humans may also secrete and sense sexual pheromones. Particularly suggestive is the fact that, over time, menstrual cycles of close friends in women's dormitories have been shown to fall into a pattern of synchrony. This phenomenon is known as the McClintock effect (McClintock, 1971). Humans give off scents that carry signals to other humans that affect their physiological responses. It has been reported that about a fourth of the people with smell disorders find that their sex drive disappears (Henkin, in Ackerman, 1990).

 ## Taste

Although food and wine gourmets are capable of making remarkably subtle and complex taste distinctions, many of their sensations are really smells and not tastes. Taste and smell work together closely when food is actually being eaten. In fact, when you have a cold, food seems tasteless because your nasal passages are blocked and you cannot smell the food. This principle is easily demonstrated by holding your nose and then trying to tell the difference between foods of similar texture but different tastes, such as pieces of apple and raw potato.

There are only four primary, taste qualities: sweet, sour, bitter and saline (salty). These qualities define your *taste space* (analogous to colour space) in which the primary tastes are positioned at the corners of a prism (as shown in *Figure 5.22*) and various taste combinations lie within its boundaries.

The taste receptor cells are gathered in clusters called the **taste buds**. From the tops of these cells come small tendrils, or papillae, similar to shoots of a plant, that have the taste receptor sites embedded in them. They are distributed in the mouth cavity, particularly on the upper side of the tongue, as shown in *Figure 5.23* (next page). Sensitivity to sweetness is greatest at the tip of the tongue; to sourness on the edges; and to bitterness at the back. Sensitivity to saltiness is spread over the whole surface. Taste is also mediated by three of the cranial nerves, which activate different parts of the tongue, mouth and throat.

The tendrils and their taste receptors can be damaged by many things we put in our mouths, such as alcohol, cigarette smoke and acids. Fortunately, our taste receptors get replaced every few days – even more frequently than smell receptors. Indeed, the taste system is the most resistant to damage of all our sensory systems; it is extremely rare for anyone to suffer a total, permanent taste loss (Bartoshuk, 1990).

Single-cell recordings of taste receptors show that individual receptors respond somewhat to all the taste stimuli. Tastes seem to be coded in terms of relative activity in the different types of receptors. For instance, all receptors fire to both salt solutions and sweet solutions, but some fire more to one, and some

FIGURE 5.22	TASTE SPACE

Shown are the four primary tastes and the names of substances in which each taste predominates. Although different parts of the tongue and mouth are more sensitive to one taste or another, individual taste receptors seem to respond to all tastes in varying proportions.

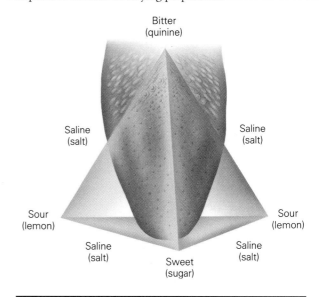

fire more to the other (Pfaffman, 1959).

Taste sensitivity is exaggerated in infants and decreases with age. Many elderly people who complain that food has lost its taste really mean that they have lost much of their sensory ability to detect differences in the taste and smell qualities of food.

 ## Position and Movement

In our presentation of the fundamental features of the senses (see *Table 5.1*) we introduced two senses that inform us about the position and movement of the body. The sense of equilibrium, also called the vestibular sense, as well as kinesthesis both rely on mechanical energy.

To move around purposefully in our environment we need constant information about where our limbs and other body parts are in relation to each other and to objects in the environment. Without this knowledge, even our simplest actions would be hopelessly unco-ordinated. The **vestibular sense** tells us how our body – especially our head – is oriented in the world with respect to gravity. It also deals with acceleration; it tells us when we are moving or, more precisely, when the direction or rate of our motion is changing.

The receptors for this information are tiny hairs in

FIGURE 5.23 RECEPTORS FOR TASTE

Part A shows the distribution of the papillae on the upper side of the tongue. Part B shows a single papilla enlarged so that the individual taste buds are visible. Part C shows one of the taste buds enlarged.

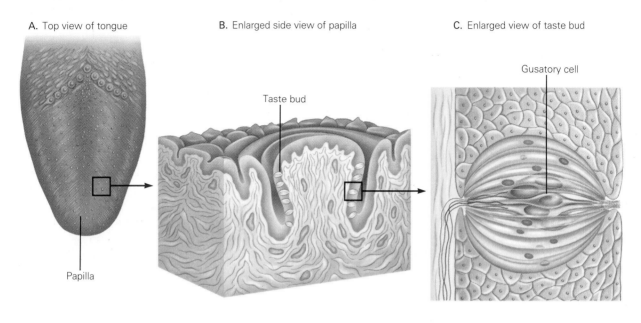

A. Top view of tongue

Papilla

B. Enlarged side view of papilla

Taste bud

C. Enlarged view of taste bud

Gusatory cell

fluid-filled sacs and canals in the inner ear; the hairs bend when the fluid moves and presses on them, which is what happens when we turn our heads quickly. The *saccule* and *utricle* shown in *Figure 5.18* tell us about acceleration or deceleration. The three canals, called the *semicircular canals*, are at right angles to each other and, thus, can tell us about motion in any direction. They inform us how our heads are moving when we turn, nod or tilt them. The vestibular sense also helps us keep ourselves upright. People who lose their vestibular sense because of accidents or disease are initially quite disoriented and prone to falling and dizziness. However, most of these people eventually compensate by relying more heavily on visual information. Motion sickness can occur when the signals from the visual system conflict with those from the vestibular system. Feeling nauseous when reading in a moving car is common because the visual signal is of a stationary object, while the vestibular signal is of movement. Drivers rarely get motion sickness because they are seeing and also feeling motion.

Whether we are standing erect, riding bicycles, drawing pictures, removing splinters with tweezers or making love, our brains need to have accurate information about the current positions and movement of our body parts relative to each other. The **kinaesthetic sense** (also called kinaesthesis) provides constant sensory feedback about what the body is doing during motor activities. Without it, we would be unable to co-ordinate most of the voluntary movements we make so effortlessly.

We have two potential sources of kinaesthetic information: receptors in the joints and receptors in the muscles and tendons. Receptors that lie in the joints respond to pressures that accompany different positions of the limbs and to pressure changes that accompany movements of the joints. Receptors in the muscles and tendons that hold bones together respond to changes in tension that accompany muscle shortening and lengthening and tendons. They are involved in motor control and co-ordination but tell us little about body position.

 Touch

The skin is a remarkably versatile organ. In addition to protecting us against surface injury, holding in body fluids and helping regulate body temperature, it contains nerve endings that produce sensations of pressure when stimulated by mechanical energy, and warmth and cold when stimulated by thermal energy. Here we will confine ourselves to pressure.

The skin's sensitivity to pressure varies tremendously over the body. For example, we are ten times more accurate in sensing the position of stimulation on our fingertips than the position of stimulation on our backs. The variation in sensitivity of different body regions is shown by the greater density of nerve endings in these regions and also in the greater amount of sensory cortex devoted to them. In Chapter 2, we learned that our sensitivity is greatest where we need it most – on our faces, tongues and hands. Precise sensory feedback from these parts of the body permits effective eating, speaking and grasping.

One aspect of the skin senses plays a central role in human relationships, emotions, and sexuality: *touch*. Through touch we communicate to others our desire to give or receive comfort, support, love and passion. Our language reflects the importance of touch – it is filled with touch metaphors: it is good to 'be in touch with your feelings', to show a 'touch of class' and to have 'that personal touch'; but it is bad to be 'touchy' and terrible to be 'untouchable'. Touch is the primary stimulus for sexual arousal in humans. However, where you get touched or touch someone else makes a difference; those areas of the skin surface that are especially sensitive to stimulation and give rise to erotic or sexual sensations are called 'erogenous zones'. Other touch-sensitive erotic areas vary in their arousal potential for different individuals depending on learned associations and the concentration of sensory receptors in the areas.

In Chapter 2, we already mentioned the positive effects of touch (in the form of massage) for premature babies – massaged babies not only grew faster than untouched premature babies, but their mental development was also enhanced by touch. Comparable research with rats shows that vigorous stimulation releases growth hormones and activates the growth enzyme ODC (onithine decarboxylase) in the brain and other vital organs. Deprivation of touch stimulation has been shown to stunt the growth of rat babies and human children.

In one study, rat pups that were handled daily in their early lives showed a life-long enhancement of many aspects of their health. The stimulated pups, as compared to unstimulated control animals, were more resistant to stress and in the process of aging sustained more brain cells and better memory processes (Meany et al, 1988).

The practical message is clear: touch those you care about often and encourage others to touch you – it not only feels good, but it is healthy for you and for them (Lynch, 1979; Montague, 1986).

Pain

Pain is the universal complaint of the human condition – from the pain associated with birth to the periodic pain of teething, injury, sickness, menstruation and headache, and to chronic pain such as arthritis, lower back pain and pain with unknown origins. About one-third of North Americans have been estimated to suffer from persistent or recurring pain (Wallis, 1984). Depression and even suicide can result from the seemingly endless nagging of chronic pain.

Pain is the body's response to stimulation from noxious stimuli – those that are intense enough to cause tissue damage or threaten to do so. The pain response is complex, involving a remarkable interplay between chemical reactions at the site of the pain stimulus, nerve impulses to and from the spinal cord and brain, and a number of psychological and cultural factors. Simply put, pain is a hurt we feel. 'It is always more than a distressing sensation. It is useful to think of pain as a person's emotional experience of a distressing sensation; thus, morale and mood can be as important as the intensity of the feeling itself in determining the degree of pain' (Brody, 1986).

Acute pain is studied experimentally in laboratories with paid volunteers who experience varying degrees of a precisely regulated stimulus, such as heat applied briefly to a small area of the skin. This procedure can test a subject's *tolerance* for pain as well as measure the sensory and subjective responses to it – without causing any damage to the skin tissue. In some cases, a human subject's nerve impulses are monitored by passing a slender recording sensor through the skin into the nerve fibre itself. This enables the researcher to listen to signals being sent by cells in the peripheral nervous system to the brain. Chronic pain is typically studied in hospital research clinics as part of the treatment programme to find new ways to alleviate it.

Almost all animals are born with some type of pain defence system that triggers automatic withdrawal reflexes to certain stimulus events. When the stimulus intensity reaches threshold, organisms respond by escaping – if they can. In addition, they quickly learn to identify painful stimulus situations, avoiding them whenever possible.

You might think that it would be nice never to experience pain. Actually, such a condition would be deadly. People born with congenital insensitivity to pain feel no hurt, but their bodies often become scarred and their limbs often become deformed from injuries that they could have avoided had their brains been able to warn them of danger. In fact, because of their failure to notice and respond to tissue-damaging stimuli, they tend to die young (Manfredi *et al*, 1981). Pain serves as an essential defence signal – it warns us of potential harm.

People can suffer from two kinds of pain: nociceptive and neuropathic. **Nociceptive pain** is the negative feeling induced by a noxious external stimulus; for example, the feeling you have when you touch a hot stove with your hand. Specialised nerve endings in the skin send the pain message up your arm, through the spinal cord, and into your brain which issues the 'pull away' command. By pulling away, you can make this type of pain stop. **Neuropathic pain** is caused by the abnormal functioning or over-activity of nerves. It comes from injury or disease of nerves caused by accidents or cancer, for example. Drugs and other therapies that calm the nerves can relieve much of this type of pain.

Pain mechanisms

It has been difficult to learn how the pain system works, because of the complexity of the interconnections and pathways involved in the perception of pain and also because of the fact that

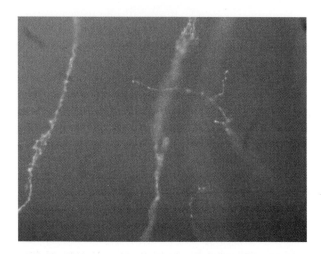

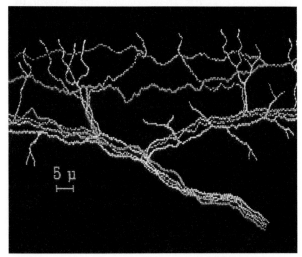

Shown is a microscopic nerve fibre that was filled with fluorescent dye so that it could be photographed. Also shown is a computerised simulation of nerve fibres. Each colour responds to different pain-producing stimuli.

much pain involves psychological factors as well as purely stimulus factors. Scientists have only recently been able to identify the specific sets of nerves that respond to pain-producing stimuli. They have learned that some nerves respond only to temperature, others to chemicals, some to mechanical stimuli, and still others to combinations of pain-producing stimuli. These nerves set off action potentials that eventually get to the brain. This network of pain fibres is a fine meshwork that covers your entire body; there are about 6,000 of these nerve fibres in one-square millimetre of the cornea of your eye.

Although researchers have no clue yet about how the brain interprets the neural signals it receives as pain, they have been able to map the actual procedure involved in signalling the brain. Powerful chemicals are stored in or near free nerve endings. When an injury occurs, the chemicals at the site of injury are released, and the nerves transmit impulses to the spinal cord. Peripheral nerve fibres send pain signals to the central nervous system by two pathways: a fast-conducting set of nerve fibres that are covered with a myelin sheeting; and slower, smaller nerve fibres without any myelin coating. From the spinal cord, the impulses are relayed to the thalamus and then to the cerebral cortex, where the location and intensity of the pain are identified, the significance of the injury is evaluated and action plans are formulated (McKean, 1986).

New research has used both PET scans and magnetic-resonance imaging (MRI) to discover where in the brain pain is represented. In experimental studies with healthy, awake volunteers subjected to nociceptive heat pain, the researchers found that pain information is not distributed over large areas of the cortex. Instead, signals of pain intensity are processed by specific sites in the parietal and frontal cortical areas. Emotional reactions to pain are processed in a different region – by the limbic system (Talbot *et al*, 1991).

One of the strategies adopted by the brain is to send white blood cells to the area of injury to fight infection. The brain also releases endorphins – the brain's own morphine. Endorphins produce analgesia (pain reduction) by reducing sensitivity to pain stimuli. They appear to be responsible for the pain relief achieved by acupuncture and direct electrical stimulation of the brain stem (Hosobuchi *et al*, 1979). People who suffer from chronic pain that is not relieved by standard medical treatments have abnormally low concentrations of endorphins in their cerebrospinal fluid (Akil, 1978).

One theory about the way pain may be modulated is the **gate–control theory**, developed by **Ronald Melzack** (1973, 1980), which assumes that the nervous system is able to process only a limited amount of sensory information at any one time. If too much information is being sent through, certain cells in the spinal cord act as neurological gates, interrupting and blocking some pain signals and letting others get through to the brain. Small fibres in the spine open these gates when signals from injured tissues are received, while the large fibres of the spine close the gates, shutting down the pain response. Treatment for chronic pain sometimes involves electrical stimulation designed to activate the gate-closing function of the large neural fibres. Other sensory influences that close the pain gates may include massaging of the hurt area, the emotional arousal accompanying competition, and distracting mental activities.

The psychology of pain

Our emotional reactions, context factors and our interpretation of the situation can be as important as the actual physical stimuli in determining how much pain we experience. In fact, the sensation of pain may not be directly related to the intensity of the noxious stimulus at all or even to its presence or absence.

The importance of central processes in the experience of pain is shown in two extreme cases – one where there is pain but there is no physical stimulus for it; and another where there is no pain but there is an intensely painful stimulus. For example, up to ten per cent of people who have limbs amputated report extreme or chronic pain in the limb that is no longer there – the 'phantom limb phenomenon'. The perceived reality of a phantom limb may show that the unique experiences of one's body are invested with emotional tone and cognitive meaning (Melzack, 1989). In contrast, some individuals taking part in religious rituals are able to block out pain while participating in activities involving intense stimulation, such as walking on a bed of hot coals or having their bodies pierced with needles.

Much research points to the conclusion that the pain one feels is affected by the meaning one attaches to the experience, culturally learned habits, social support and attention, and learned gender roles (Weisenberg, 1977). Because pain is in part a psychological response, it can be modified by treatments that make use of mental processes, such as hypnosis, deep relaxation and thought-distraction procedures. The Lamaze method of preparation for childbirth reduces the woman's intense labour pains

The sensation of pain may not be directly related to the intensity of the stimulus. Individuals taking part in religious rituals, such as walking on a bed of coals, are able to block out pain.

by combining several of these methods. Lamaze breathing exercises aid relaxation and focus attention away from the pain area. The use of distracting, pleasant images, massage that creates a gentle counter-stimulation, and the social support of a coaching spouse or friend all work to give a prospective mother a greater sense of control over this painful situation.

One of the most potent of all treatments for pain is placebo therapy (Fish, 1973). Pain can be relieved by drugs expected to be painkillers that are, in fact, inert substances with no medicinal value. Believing that a particular treatment will lead to pain reduction is sufficient to bring about major psychological and physiological relief in many people. It appears that belief, as well as perception of pain, can trigger the release of painkilling endorphins in the brain. It has been suggested that the one-third of the population who are positive placebo responders may have higher concentrations of endorphins than other people do (Levine, 1978).

The way you perceive your pain, what you communicate about it to others, and even the way you respond to pain-relieving treatments may reveal more about your psychological state – about the kind of inferences you are making – than about the intensity of the pain stimulus. What you perceive may be different from, and even independent of, what you sense – as we will see in our study of the psychology of perception in Chapter 6.

recapping main points

The Senses: Fundamental Features

Sensation is the first stage in the process of perception. It involves the detection of physical energy, its transduction into neural codes and the processing of these signals into primary sensations. Because in everyday life our perception of the world is instantaneous and effortless, non-psychologists often think that perceiving is merely a matter of copying or mirroring the outside world. In actuality much 'working over' of this input and 'calculating' is involved between the initial detection of physical energy and seeing something.

Psychophysics

Psychophysics investigates the relation between psychological responses and physical stimuli. To study sensation, researchers measure absolute thresholds and difference thresholds. Signal detection theory offers a way of separating out the influence of sensory versus decisional processes in the detection of physical stimuli. There is some evidence that simple stimuli can be perceived without us being aware of this. However, fears about the uncontrollable effects of subliminal perception seem unfounded.

Vision

Photoreceptors in the retina – rods and cones – convert electromagnetic energy into neural impulses. Via ganglion cells in the retina, the signals are transported by the optic nerves to the optic chiasma. From there, the primary visual pathway leads to the lateral geniculate nucleus of the thalamus. The secondary (smaller) pathway is connected to the superior colliculus. Within the brain, a first basic step in the analysis of incoming visual information is performed in the primary visual cortex. Modules in the secondary visual cortex perform a more specialised form of analysis. From there, the parvo cellular pathway leading to the temporal lobes is concerned with analysing the 'what' of physical stimuli; the magno cellular pathway on the other hand, leads to the occipital lobes and deals with analysing the 'where' – the spatial location of stimuli.

The wavelength of light is that property which is the stimulus for colour. Colour sensations differ in hue, saturation and brightness. Contrasts in brightness form boundaries and distinct edges that give objects size, shape and spatial orientation. Colour vision theory combines the trichromatic theory of three colour receptors with the opponent-process theory of colour systems as composed of opponent elements. Detection of stimulus features occurs through the action of feature detection cells in the retina and higher visual centres and through the analysis of spatial frequencies of light-dark cycles.

Audition

The process of hearing starts when the ear detects vibrations of molecules in the air. These waves vary in frequency, amplitude and complexity. Correspondingly, our sensations of sound vary in pitch, loudness and timbre (quality). In the cochlea, sound waves are transformed into fluid waves that in turn move the basilar membrane. Hairs on the basilar membrane stimulate neural impulses that are sent to the auditory cortex. Place theory explains the coding of high frequencies and frequency theory explains the coding of low frequencies. Exposure to intense sounds may cause temporary hearing impairment.

The Other Senses

Smell and taste respond to the chemical properties of substances, working together when we seek and sample food. The sense of smell is achieved via odour-sensitive cells deep within the nasal passages. Taste receptors are taste buds embedded in papillae, mostly within the tongue. The vestibular sense gives information about the direction and rate of body motion. The kinaesthetic sense gives information about the position of body parts and helps co-ordinate motion. The skin senses provide us with touch sensations. Pain is the body's response to potentially harmful stimuli. The physiological response to pain involves both chemical reactions at the site of the pain stimulus and nerve impulses moving between the brain and spinal cord. Pain is in part a psychological response that can be modified by treatments that emphasise mental processes and thought distraction.

key Terms

absolute threshold
accommodation
afferent pathways
auditory cortex
auditory nerve
basilar membrane
bipolar cells
bottom-up processing
brightness
chemoreceptors
cochlea
complementary colours
cones
decibel (db)
difference threshold
efferent pathways
feature-detection
fovea
frequency theory
ganglion cells
gate-control theory
Hertz (Hz)
hue
just noticeable difference (JND)
kinaesthesis
lateral geniculate nucleus
lateral inhibition
magno cells
magno cellular pathway
mechanoreceptors
modules
neuropathic pain
nociceptive pain

olfactory bulb
opponent-process theory
optic nerve
optic tract
pain
parvo cells
parvo cellular pathway
pheromones
photoreceptors
pitch
place theory
primary sensations
primary visual cortex
psychometric function
psychophysics
receptive field
retina
rods
saturation
secondary visual cortex
subliminal perception
superior colliculus
taste buds
theory of signal detection (TSD)
thermoreceptors
timbre
top-down processing
transduction
trichromatic theory
vestibular sense
volley principle
Weber's law

major Contributors

Fechner, Gustav (1801–87)
Hering, Ewald (1834–1918)
Holender, Daniel
Hubel, David
Melzack, Ronald
Newton, Isaac (1642–1727)

von Békésy, Georg (1899–1972)
von Helmholtz, Hermann (1821–94)
Weber, Ernst (1795–1878)
Wiesel, Thorsten
Young, Thomas (1773–1829)

Chapter 6

Perception

One night in late 1965, a United Airlines Boeing 727 began a steady descent to Chicago's O'Hare Airport from an altitude of 22,000 feet. Nineteen miles off the shore of Lake Michigan, the plane plunged into the lake.

One month later, also at night, an American Airlines Boeing 727, preparing to land at Kentucky's Boone County Airport, followed the thread of the Ohio River toward the runway which began at the river's steep south bank. The plane never touched down. It crashed into the bank, 12 feet below the runway.

One night in early 1966, an Al Nippon Airlines Boeing 727 headed toward Tokyo Bay. The pilot could see the lights of Tokyo and Yokohama clearly. He requested and received permission to approach using visual cues rather than relying exclusively on the plane's instruments. The pilot had not even let down the wheels or extended the flaps when, six-and-a-half miles from the runway, the plane dove into Tokyo Bay at a speed of 240 knots.

Preliminary analyses of these and other similar cases showed that all the accidents occurred at night, under clear weather conditions, with the planes flying over a dark area of water or land. In every case, irregular patterns of light (as opposed to grids of neatly intersecting lines of street lights) in the distance had been visible to the pilots.

In a way, the new Boeing 727 design was partly responsible for the accidents because it was so well engineered. In earlier, less stable models, feedback from vibrations and sounds and kinaesthetic sensations would have warned the pilots that they were descending too rapidly. However, it was more than an improved design that had caused the accidents.

Using a flight simulator, engineering psychologist **Conrad Kraft** found that an error in the pilot's visual perception was responsible for each of the accidents. Pilots making a visually guided approach over a dark terrain relied on the relatively constant visual angle between their planes and the distant light patterns in determining their altitudes. If they were approaching flat terrain, their altitude estimates were generally correct, but if the terrain sloped upwards, with the farthest lights higher than the closer ones, even the most experienced pilots descended to dangerously low altitudes. With no visual information from the 'dark hole' below them, the pilots overestimated their distance from the ground and inappropriately adjusted their descent angles.

Why did the pilots not also use their altimeters? When landing an airplane, a pilot must monitor several functions simultaneously – speed, engine power, altitude, direction – while responding to air-traffic controller directions and watching for other aircraft. With all of these responsibilities, especially when visibility is good, pilots may fail to check their altimeters.

After Conrad Kraft solved the mystery of the accidents, commercial airlines around the world informed pilots of the conditions under which they might misjudge altitude on approach to landing. Psychologists, such as Conrad Kraft, study perception in order to learn how the human sensory systems help (and sometimes trick) us in gathering information about the environments in which we live and work.

THE TERM PERCEPTION, in its broad usage, stands for the overall process of apprehending objects and events in the external environment. In the previous chapter we divided this process into sensation and perception, thereby using perception in a more narrow sense. *Sensation*, the subject of the previous chapter, is what gets the overall process started. Sensation involves detection and transduction of physical energy, and transportation of neural signals to the brain, where processing or 'calculating' finally result in primary sensations. The processes of bringing in and organising information from the environment are often called world-driven, data-driven or **bottom-up processes**.

Perception, in its narrow terminological usage, is the process of assigning meaning to sensory signals. Those who study perception are interested in how we form a conscious representation of the outside world. Perception is often associated with the opposite of bottom-up processes – that is to say, with subject-driven, conceptually-driven or **top-down processes**. In top-down processing, higher mental processes control the way incoming stimulation is managed and even what qualifies as relevant. Thus, our knowledge, beliefs, values, expectations, motivations and emotions influence the selection, organisation and interpretation of sensory data.

As we noted in the chapter on sensation, the division between sensation and perception is misleading in so far as it suggests that the two processes can be separated. Actually, visual information processing consists of the interaction between and integration of bottom-up and top-down processes. Nevertheless, for the sake of clarity of exposition, we will follow the convention of discussing sensation and perception separately. This chapter deals with perceptual processes, the systems associated with the higher level activity of the central nervous system.

Most of the time, perceiving occurs so effortlessly, continuously and automatically that we take it for granted. We only have access to the results of this complex process. For example, look around the room you are in first by moving your head slowly and then by moving it quickly. Did any objects move? In your experience they did not, but according to the sensory information from your retina, all the objects in the room were whirling around. How does your brain 'know' that they were not moving? After shutting this book, hold it at arm's length, rotating it completely. Move it toward your face and then set it down on your lap and open it again. Did any images in the book change shape or size? How does it transpire that the book – or your hand for that matter – did not seem to undergo size and shape transformations corresponding to the changing images they projected on to the retina as they moved?

In this chapter, we will unmask the perceptual apparatus to discover how it manages to drive our perceptions so well. Our discussion will be mainly about vision because it has been more intensively studied than any of the other modalities and also because it is possible on the printed page to provide visual demonstrations of some of the effects we will be explicating. In so doing, we will learn about some of the ways in which we make sense of the host of messages that are sent from sense receptors to the brain and back again to response systems for action. We will also learn how the mind interprets external reality and goes beyond the physics of sensation to design its own imaginative and personalised versions (or 'percepts') of reality.

◆ THE TASK OF PERCEPTION

We might say that the role of perception is to make sense of sensation. 'Making sense' means creating a personal understanding of the experienced physical world. It involves many different mental processes, including: synthesising elements into combinations; judging sizes, shapes, distances, intensities and pitches; estimating the unknown or uncertain from known features; remembering past experiences via given perceptual stimuli; comparing different stimuli currently being experienced; and associating the perceived qualities of stimuli with appropriate ways of responding to them. Every act of perception becomes, then, a series of very complex computational problems to be solved by the perceiving person.

The task of perception is to extract the continuously changing, often chaotic, sensory input of external energy sources and organise it into stable, orderly percepts of meaningful objects that are relevant to a perceiver. A **percept** is what is perceived – the phenomenological or experienced outcome of the process of perception. It is not a physical object nor its image in a receptor but rather a representation of it – the psychological product of perceptual activity.

Psychologists who study perception come to this field from many directions (Banks & Krajicek, 1991). Some are interested in it from a neuroscience perspective, using a molecular level of analysis. They track sensory stimuli through the sensory receptors, pathways in the brain and the visual cortex. Others want to understand perception at a broader level by discovering the principles governing certain perceptual phenomena, such as the way we perceive motion and depth. Researchers from the field of *artificial intelligence* (AI) are bringing new conceptual tools to the study of perception as they distinguish between the biological hardware of perception and the rules that specify how each perceptual process works. A third basic approach to perception comes from the descendants of what is known as the *Gestalt tradition*, which constitutes modern perceptual psychology. These researchers study the laws of perceptual organisation and the units of perception.

Other psychologists are interested in the relationships between perception and other processes that influence it (such as memory, cognition and motivation) or that are influenced by it (such as learning and social interaction). For example, researchers have discovered relationships between vision problems in childhood and adolescence and subsequent learning problems and juvenile delinquency (Dowis, 1984; Harris, 1989; Snow, 1983).

Finally, because perception is the way we make contact with our social and physical worlds, many psychologists apply perceptual knowledge and theory to the development of improved technology. During the development of flight simulators, robots and space-vehicle workstations, psychologists collaborate with engineers to help them apply perceptual theory in the creation of their designs. So, too, improvements in telephone reception, television viewing and prosthetic devices that aid hearing and sight-impaired people have come from knowledge of the psychology of audition and vision.

◆ PERCEPTION: FUNDAMENTAL FEATURES

Those who study perception are interested in how we create a conscious representation of the outside world and in the accuracy of that representation. Perception involves *synthesis* (integration and combination) of simple sensory features, such as colours, edges and lines, into the percept of an object. If synthesis results in a representation of an object, you will wonder whether you have seen the object before. The question 'Does this representation look familiar to me?' concerns the **recognition** of an object. **Identification** assigns meaning to percepts. We compare the percept to a memory representation, attach a label to it and decide what it is. Circular objects 'become' either footballs, coins, clocks or oranges. Moving objects may be identified as cars, cats or persons, and a specimen of the last category may be identified as your aunt, your neighbour or a stranger. Our recognition of an object as something we have seen before, and our labelling or categorising of that object, enables us to retrieve information about its likely behaviour and thereby to activate the behaviour

we should perform in order to deal with it effectively. These perceptual processes merge with cognitive processes, which include our theories, memories, values, beliefs and attitudes concerning the object. Thus, the boundaries between perception and cognition are as permeable as they are between sensation and perception (Coren *et al*, 1994).

Consider the case of Dr Richard, whose brain damage left his sensation intact but altered his perceptual processes.

Dr Richard was a psychologist with considerable training and experience in introspection. However, tragically, he suffered brain damage that affected his visual perception. Since the damage did not affect his capacity for speech production, he was able to describe his subsequent unusual visual experiences quite clearly. In general terms, the brain damage seemed to have affected his ability to put sensory data together properly. For example, he reported that if several persons were in his visual field he sometimes was not able to see one person as a whole. He saw the different parts of one person as separate parts not belonging together in a single form. If the person moved, however, so that all parts went in the same direction, Dr Richard would then see them as one complete person. Without some common factor – such as motion – to help 'glue' things together, he tended to see a confusion of separate objects, all of which were simultaneously present in his field of view but which he did not experience as going together.

Sometimes perceiving a common element would result in absurd configurations. He would frequently see objects of the same colour, such as a banana, a lemon and a canary, going together even if they were separated in space. At other times, however, Dr Richard had difficulty combining the sound and sight of the same event. When someone was singing, he might see a mouth move and hear a song, but it was as if the sound had been dubbed with the wrong tape in a foreign film. Dr Richard's experiences of his environment during such episodes were disjointed, fragmented and bizarre – quite unlike what he had been used to before his problems began (Marcel, 1983).

There was nothing wrong with Dr Richard's eyes or with his ability to analyse the properties of stimulus objects – he saw the parts and qualities of objects accurately. Rather, his problem lay in perceptual synthesis: putting the bits and pieces of sensory information together properly to form a unified, coherent perception of the event in the visual scene. His case makes salient the distinction between sensory and perceptual processes. It also serves to remind us that

FIGURE 6.1 | INTERPRETING RETINAL IMAGES

both sensory analysis and perceptual synthesis must be going on all of the time even though we are unaware of the way they function or even that they are there.

A. Physical Object (Distal Stimulus)

Interpreting Retinal Images

Imagine you are the person in section A of *Figure 6.1*. You are sitting in a chair. Section B of *Figure 6.1* portrays the visual field of your left eye as you sit in the room. Reflected light from the visual field forms a *retinal image*, consisting of a distribution of light of various intensities and wavelengths on your retina. How does this retinal image compare with the environment that produced it?

One very important difference is that the retinal image is two-dimensional whereas the environment is three-dimensional. Compare the shapes of the physical objects out there in the world with the shapes of their corresponding retinal images. The shapes in *Figure 6.1* that you 'know' are really rectangular are not necessarily rectangular in your retinal image. As you can see in section C of *Figure 6.1*, only the window, viewed straight on, actually produces a rectangle in your retinal image. The other shapes are distorted into trapezoids, or partially blocked by other objects. In fact, when you consider all the differences between the environmental objects and the images of them on your retina, it is surprising that you can perceive the scene as well as you do.

The differences between a physical object in the world and its retinal image are so profound and important that psychologists distinguish carefully between them as two different stimuli for perception. The physical object in the world is called the **distal**

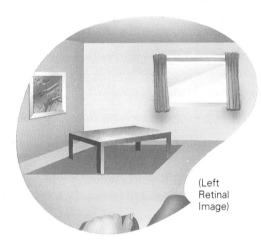

(Left Retinal Image)

B. Optical Image (Proximal Stimulus)

FIGURE 6.2 | DISTAL AND PROXIMAL STIMULUS

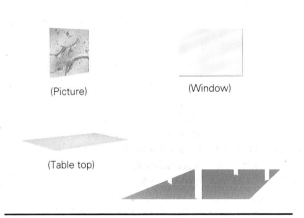

(Picture)   (Window)

(Table top)

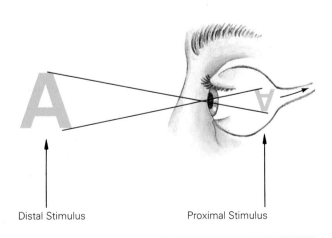

Distal Stimulus   Proximal Stimulus

stimulus (distant from the observer) and the optical image on the retina is called the **proximal stimulus** (proximate or near to the observer), as shown in *Figure 6.2*.

The major problem of visual perception can be

thought of as the process of getting from the flat patches of light that make up the retinal image (the proximal stimulus) to the world of objects around us (the distal stimulus).

The distinction between proximal and distal

FIGURE 6.3 BOTTOM-UP AND TOP-DOWN PROCESSES

The diagram outlines the processes that give rise to the transformation of incoming information at the stages of sensation, perception and identification/recognition. Bottom-up processing occurs when the perceptual representation is derived from the information available in the sensory input. Top-down processing occurs when the perceptual representation is affected by an individual's prior knowledge, motivations, expectations and other aspects of higher mental functioning.

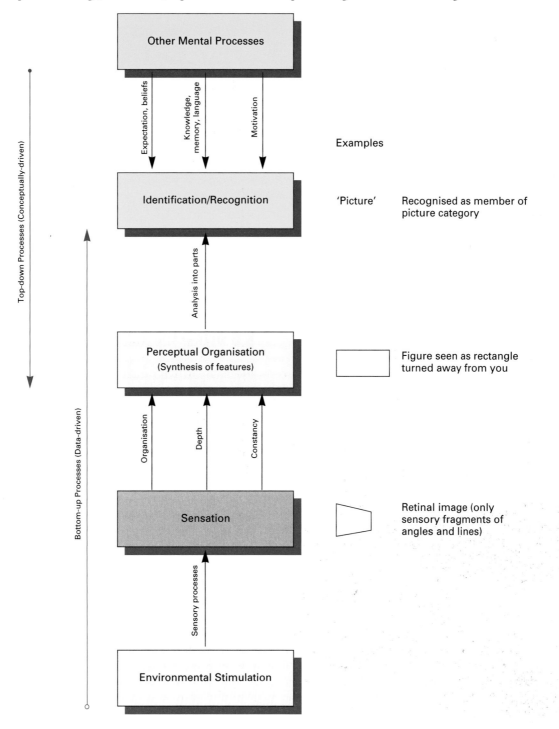

stimuli applies to all kinds of perception, not just to vision. Auditory images – the patterns of sound waves that enter your ears – differ from the physical objects that produce them. Also tactile images – the patterns of pressure and temperature that you feel on your skin as you actively explore objects with your hands – are not the same as the physical objects that cause them. In each case, perception involves processes that somehow use information in the proximal stimulus to tell you about properties of the distal stimulus.

There is much more to perceiving a scene, however, than just determining the physical properties of the distal stimulus. You see objects as familiar and meaningful: a window, a picture, a table and a rug. Besides accurately perceiving the shapes and colours of the objects, you interpret them in terms of your past experience with similar objects. This process of recognition and identification is also part of what you do automatically and almost constantly as you go about perceiving your environment.

Let us examine one of the objects in the scene from *Figure 6.1*: the picture hanging on the wall. *Figure 6.3* (previous page) is a flow chart, in which seeing the picture is divided into several stages. The *bottom-up processes* are depicted as upward pointing arrows between the boxes. They represent the sensory stage, in which the sensory data of the retinal image – the two-dimensional trapezoid – are sent upward for extraction and analysis of relevant information. Bottom-up processes are those that are anchored in empirical reality and deal with bits of information and the transformation of concrete, physical features of stimuli into physiological codes and ultimately into abstract representations. The *top-down processes* are depicted as arrows pointing down. They represent the perceptual stage in which the trapezoid is seen as a rectangle turned away from you in three-dimensional space and in which you recognise this rectangular object

as a picture. The perceptual stage involves a perceiver's past experience, knowledge, expectations, memory, motivations, cultural background and language in the interpretation of the object of perception. As we noted before, the two types of processes usually interact as we perceive our environment.

◆ Reality, Ambiguity and Distortions

A primary goal of perception is to get a functional 'fix' on the world – to recognise predators, prey, possible danger and pleasure, and to behave appropriately. Survival depends on the way we perceive objects and events in our environment, but the environment is not always easy to 'read'. Take a look at the photograph of black and white splotches in *Figure 6.4*. What is it? Try to extract the stimulus figure from the background. Try to see a Dalmatian taking a walk. The dog is hard to find because it blends with the background.

Experience teaches you sometimes not to trust your sensations entirely and to supplement what your senses tell you with your knowledge. For example, when you return to your neighbourhood, after driving a car for hours on a motorway, it is hard to imagine that hitting a fence at a speed of 16 kilometres per hour (10 mph) will be a real crash. You know it will, but it does not 'feel' that way.

◆ Visual Illusions

Psychologists who study perception are fascinated by perceptual ambiguities and the illusions they generate. People's perceptions are called **illusions** when they experience a stimulus pattern in a manner that is demonstrably incorrect (see also Chapter 3). Typically, illusions become more common when the stimulus situation is ambiguous, or when information our perceptual system needs is missing, or when elements are combined in unusual ways and familiar patterns are not apparent. Since the first scientific analysis of illusions was published by J. J. Oppel in 1854, literally thousands of articles have been written about illusions in nature as well as in art. Oppel's modest contribution to the study of illusions was a simple array of lines that appeared longer when divided into segments than when only the end lines were present:

versus

| |

| FIGURE 6.4 | AMBIGUOUS PICTURE |

Oppel called his work the study of *geometrical optical illusions*. Illusions point out the discrepancy between percept and reality. They can demonstrate the abstract conceptual distinctions between sensation and perception and can help us understand some fundamental properties of perception (Coren & Girgus, 1978).

First examine an illusion that works at the sensation level: the *Hermann grid* in *Figure 6.5*. As you stare at the centre of the grid, dark, fuzzy spots appear at the intersections of the white bars. However, if you focus closely on one intersection, the spot vanishes. As you shift focus, you transform the spots into little dancing dots. This phenomenon is caused by the way receptor cells interact with each other. The firing of certain ganglion cells in the retina prevents or inhibits the firing of adjacent cells. Because of this *lateral inhibition* – a concept already discussed in the last chapter – you see dark spots instead of white areas at white intersections just outside your focus. Apparently your knowledge cannot overcome the illusion, because it operates at a more basic, sensory level.

To study illusions that reveal the operations of perception, psychologists rely on ambiguous figures – stimulus patterns that can be seen in two or more distinct ways. **Ambiguity** is an important concept in understanding perception because it shows that a single image at the sensory level can result in multiple interpretations at the perceptual level.

Sometimes ambiguity arises early in the process of

FIGURE 6.5	THE HERMANN GRID

This Hermann Grid has two ganglion cell receptive fields projected on it. It is an example of an illusion at the sensory stage.

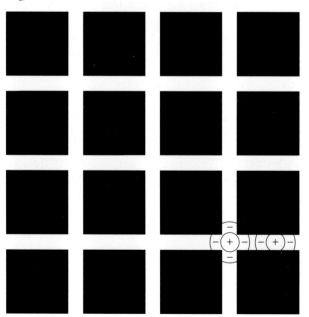

FIGURE 6.6	A – PERCEPTUAL ILLUSIONS B – RECOGNITION ILLUSIONS

A.

Vase or Faces?

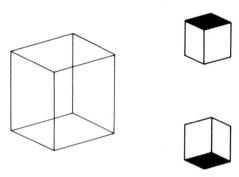

The Necker Cube: Above or Below?

B.

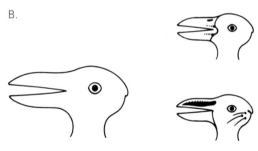

Duck or Rabbit?

perception when an object can be interpreted as two or more different objects in the environment. Ambiguity can also arise in a later stage when the object being perceived can be interpreted as belonging to different categories.

Figure 6.6 shows three examples of ambiguous figures. Each figure is accompanied by two unambiguous but conflicting interpretations. Notice that once you have seen both of them, your perception flips back and forth between them as you look at the ambiguous figure. This perceptual instability of ambiguous figures is one of their most important characteristics.

The vase/faces can be seen as either a central

white object on a black background or as two black objects with a white area between them. The Necker cube can be seen as a three-dimensional hollow cube either below you and angled to your left or above you and angled toward your right. With both vase and cube, the ambiguous alternatives are different physical arrangements of objects in three-dimensional space, both resulting from the same stimulus image. Because it cannot recognise both alternatives at the same time, your perceptual system has jumped to a decision

about how to synthesise the elements into a whole on the basis of attending to certain local features.

The duck/rabbit figure is an example of ambiguity in recognition. It is perceived as one physical shape, but ambiguity arises in determining the kind of object it represents and in how best to categorise it given the mixed set of information available. Transforming ambiguity and uncertainty about the environment into a clear interpretation is a fundamental property of normal human perception.

FIGURE 6.7 SIX ILLUSIONS TO TEASE YOUR BRAIN

A. Use a ruler to answer each question.

Which is larger: the brim or the top hat?

Top Hat Illusion

Is the diagonal line broken?

Poggendorf Illusion

Which central circle is bigger?

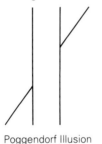

Ebbinghaus Illusion

Which horizontal line is longer?

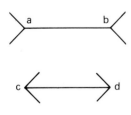

Müller–Lyer Illusion

Are the vertical lines parallel?

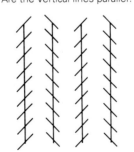

Zöllner Illusion

B. Which of the boxes are the same size as the standard box? Which are definitely smaller or larger? Measure them to discover a powerful illusory effect.

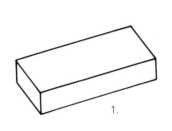

1.

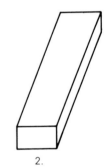

2.

Standard

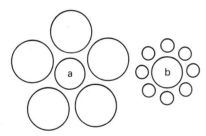

3.

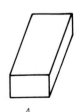

4.

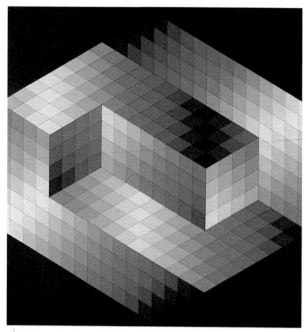

Paintings by Victor Vasarely (above), M. C. Escher (top right) and Salvador Dali.

Perceptual illusions make us aware of two considerations: the active role the brain plays in constructing a view of the world and the effects of context on the way we perceive stimuli. Psychologists have discovered many illusions (such as those in *Figure 6.7*) not only in vision (Robinson, 1972) but also in other sensory modalities (Bregman, 1981; Shepard & Jordan, 1984). These illusions demonstrate that the central nervous system does not simply record events. Instead, the system involves complex processes for detecting, integrating and interpreting information about the world in terms of what we already know and expect; thus, what we 'see' goes beyond present physical stimulus properties. The fact that these processes usually occur effortlessly and are helpful in decoding the world around us does not mean that they are simple or error-free.

Ambiguity in art

Several prominent modern artists fascinated with the visual experiences created by ambiguity have used perceptual illusions as a central artistic device in their work. Consider the three examples of art shown on this page. *Gestalt Bleue* by Victor Vasarely produces depth reversals like those in the Necker cube. The corners of the surfaces can be seen either as coming out toward you or going away from you. In *Sky and Water* by M. C. Escher you can see birds and fish only

through the process of figure-ground reversal, as in the vase/faces picture. Notice that after you look at the unambiguous birds at the top, you tend to see birds rather than fish in the ambiguous centre section; but after you look at the unambiguous fish at the bottom, you tend to see fish rather than birds in the centre section. This tendency demonstrates the influence of context on your perception, a topic we will discuss later in more detail.

The final example is *Slave Market with the Disappearing Bust of Voltaire* by Salvador Dali. This work reveals a more complex ambiguity in which a whole section of the picture must be radically reorganised and reinterpreted to allow perception of the 'hidden' bust of the French philosopher Voltaire. Although it might be difficult at first to 'find' the picture-in-the-picture, once you have seen Voltaire you will see him every time you look.

Illusions in reality

Illusions are not just peculiar arrangements of lines, colours and shapes used by artists and psychologists to plague unsuspecting people. They are also an inescapable aspect of our 'seeing the world'. Even though we may recognise an illusion, it can continue to occur and fool us again and again. You know the sun does not sink into the sea, but you cannot help seeing it that way. When a full moon is overhead, it seems to follow you wherever you go even though you know the moon is not in pursuit. When you are sitting on a ship while dreamily staring out of the window to a part of the quayside, you may for a moment experience the departure of the ship as a movement of the quay. You know this cannot be true, so the illusion will be corrected very quickly. The same illusion may occur when your train is standing next to another at the railway station. Because trains are supposed to move and quays are not, more time is needed to decide that your own train is moving and not the other one.

People can control illusions to achieve desired effects. Architects and interior designers use principles of perception to make spaces seem larger or smaller than they really are. A small apartment becomes more spacious when it is painted with light colours and sparsely furnished. Set and lighting directors of films and theatrical productions purposely create illusions on film and on stage.

The everyday use of illusion can be seen in our choices of cosmetics and clothing (Dackman, 1986). Light-coloured clothing and horizontal stripes can make our bodies seem larger while dark-coloured clothing and vertical stripes can make our bodies seem slimmer. Illusions also appear in more tragic contexts, as we noted in our opening case about pilot error. These kind of examples again demonstrate that perceiving has nothing to do with duplicating. Seeing constitutes working, calculating and correcting errors if what we apprehend does not correspond with what we know. Sometimes it can involve making errors if what appears comprehensible actually is not.

◆ Nurture and Nature

In Chapter 4 we introduced the debate between empiricists and nativists. These two views about the origins of human skills and knowledge have also played an important role in theories of perception. **Empiricists** argue that people are born as if a virgin soil – a *tabula rasa* – and that all their knowledge results from learning experiences. According to this *nurture* view, new-born babies only 'see' a confusing,

chaotic array of stimuli. They have to learn, for example, that the world is not whirling around when they move their head, and that people who are walking away from them do not shrink into little puppets. **Nativists** hold that people make sense of the world by innate mechanisms. According to this *nature* view, new-born babies are perfectly able to organise the incoming stimuli, for example, by ordering sensations in terms of cause and effect.

Advocates of both the environment and heredity positions assume that some perceptual attributes, such as colour and brightness, are built into the sensory system. Their disagreement is over the mechanisms for perceiving relational qualities, such as the size and location of objects in space (Hochberg, 1988). We will begin with the dominant approach perception has followed for about a hundred years, as represented by the experiential theory of Hermann von Helmholtz. We will contrast this with two other views – the view of the Gestalt approach and James Gibson – that propose innate bases for perception.

Helmholtz's classical theory

Hermann von Helmholtz (1866; 1962) argued for the importance of experience in perception. His theory emphasised the role of mental processes in interpreting the often ambiguous stimulus arrays that excite the nervous system. An observer makes sense of the proximal stimulus by using prior knowledge of the environment. On the basis of this experience, the observer makes hypotheses, or inferences, about what he or she is seeing.

Looking, for example, for the first time at the picture of the vase and the faces, an observer's hypothesis might well be: 'Is this a vase?' If this hunch seems believable, he or she will confirm it: 'Yes, this is a vase!' From then on, seeing the picture again, there is no need to 'really' look anymore. The observer just recognises the vase until someone suggests that it could be something else: 'These are (also) two faces'. If this second perceptual hypothesis is confirmed as well, and the two hypotheses are equally acceptable, the observer is perfectly able to switch between the two.

Perception is thus an inductive process, moving from specific images to inferences (reasonable hunches) about the general class of objects or events that the images might represent. Since this process takes place out of our conscious awareness, Helmholtz termed it **unconscious inference**. Ordinarily, these inferential processes work well. However, as we have demonstrated, sometimes perceptual illusions can result when unusual circumstances in the stimulus array or viewing position allow multiple interpretations of the same stimulus or favour an old, familiar interpretation when a new one is required.

The Gestalt approach

Founded in Germany in the second decade of this century, **Gestalt psychology** maintained that psychological phenomena could be understood only when viewed as organised, structured *Gestalts* and not when broken down into primitive perceptual elements. The term 'Gestalt' roughly means 'whole' or 'configuration'. Gestalt psychology challenged atomistic views of psychology as proposed, for example, by the behaviourists, by arguing that the whole is more than the sum of its parts. For example, a particular melody is perceived as having attributes such as beautiful, slow and sad, that do not apply to the seperate notes. Gestalt psychologists argued further that we organise our perceptions the way we do, not because we have learned to do so, but because it is inherent to our perceptual system. Our organisation of perception is build into the structure and physiology of the brain. Although Gestalt psychology has ceased to exist as a separate school of psychology, some of its basic ideas and questions are still being actively studied by researchers in perception and other areas of psychology.

Gibson's ecological optics

The modern nativists argue for innately determined principles that order incoming sensory information. One proponent of this view, **James Gibson** (1966; 1979), searched for the aspects of the proximal stimulus that provide information about the distal stimulus. According to Gibson, we directly pick up information about the invariant properties of the environment. There is no need to take raw sensations into account or to look for higher level systems of perceptual inference – perception is direct. Not only do we have information about the retinal colour, size and shape of each object, we also have information about the relative positions, sizes and shapes of these objects and even about our own position with respect to these objects. While the retinal size and shape of each object changes, depending on the object's distance and on the viewing angle, these changes are not random. Such changes are systematic and certain properties of objects remain invariant under all such changes of viewing angles and viewing distances. Our visual system is tuned to detect such invariances because we have evolved in the environment in which these invariances were important for our survival (Palmer, 1981).

Much of the earlier laboratory research on perception involved having subjects sit in one place while viewing simple, unmoving stimuli under highly restricted and artificial conditions. Gibson and others argued that perceptual systems evolved in organisms who were on the move – seeking food, water, mates and shelter – in a complex and changing environment (Gibson, 1979; Pittenger, 1988; Shaw & Turvey, 1981; Shepard, 1984). Instead of trying to understand perception as a result of an organisms' structure, Gibson proposed that it could be better understood through an analysis of the immediately surrounding environment (or its *ecology*). As one writer put it, Gibson's approach was, 'Ask not what's inside your head, but what your head's inside of' (Mace, 1977).

In effect, Gibson's theory of ecological optics is concerned with the perceived stimuli rather than with the mechanisms by which we perceive stimulus objects. This approach was a radical departure from all previous theories. Gibson's ideas emphasised perceiving as active exploration of the environment. When an observer is moving in the world, the pattern of stimulation on the retina is constantly changing over time as well as space. Gibson stressed the richness of this optical flow in perceptual events. The theory of ecological optics tried to specify the information about the environment that was available to the eyes of a moving observer. It had little to say about optical illusions because, according to Gibson, such illusions only occur when the viewing conditions are constrained and unnatural and the stimuli are artificially constructed in the laboratory. In the real world, subjects would have a lot more information available to them about the nature of ambiguous stimuli.

Gibson's ecological perception shares with the Gestalt viewpoint the belief that perception is determined directly by the stimulus configuration presented to the viewer, and both reject any view of perception as being mediated by constructions built up from sensory elements.

Current positions explaining perception incorporate the best of these approaches. Following the insights provided by Gibson, many researchers are well aware of the need to study the ecological constraints on perception and the dynamic nature of the sensory information available to the brain (Shaw & Turvey, 1981; Cutting, 1981; Pittenger, 1988). Yet, most of the researchers do not believe that perception is direct and immediate, as Gibson and some Gestalt psychologists claimed. They compare the process of perception to conceptual problem-solving (Beck, 1982; Kanitza, 1979; Pomerantz & Kubovy, 1986; Rock, 1983; 1986; Shepp & Ballisteros, 1989). New approaches emphasise both the role of past experience (as Helmholtz did) and the role of simplicity and economy (as Gestalt psychologists did) in perceptual organisation.

INTERIM SUMMARY

The term perception is often used to refer to the overall process of apprehending objects and events in the external environment; that process can be divided into two parts. Sensation is what gets the overall process started. It starts with the detection of physical energy and ends with the experience of primary sensations. Perception essentially organises and combines sensations into meaningful units. Perceptual processes allow us to construct, recognise and identify physical objects (distal stimuli) from the information available to us in the form of neural activity in the receptive field (proximal stimuli).

When the sensory data are incomplete or ambiguous, illusions may occur. Some illusions can be explained by simple sensory mechanisms; others occur because the same image can be interpreted as two or more different objects in the environment, thus requiring explanation at the perceptual organisation or at the identification stage.

Helmholtz argued for the importance of experience in perception. He took the empiricist position that we learn to make sense of proximal stimuli by using our prior experience of the world. Gestalt psychologists believed that we organise stimulus information as whole units and not as sensory elements because our brain is designed to function in this integrated, co-ordinated fashion. Gibson, a nativist, believed that information available to us in the proximal stimulus unambiguously and directly determines the distal stimulus because we are 'tuned' to detect certain invariances in our environment.

SELECTIVE ATTENTION

In everyday life millions of stimuli impinge on our sense organs. Since we cannot react to every one of them, and certainly not to all of them at the same time, somewhere somehow in the process a selection has to be made – a choice about what deserves further processing and what does not. The ways in which we select and make choices among all of the incoming information are often grouped together under the general label **selective attention**.

Before reading any further, experience how attention works by following the instructions in *Figure 6.8* (adapted from Rock & Gutman, 1981).

While performing the experiment, you probably experienced that paying attention is very simple. We asked you to attend to the red shapes and you just did so without much effort. You may have also apprehended that paying attention is rewarding because you remembered the red shapes in the figure much better than the other shapes. But paying attention to something does not necessarily mean that nothing at all is remembered of the unattended shapes. Presumably you did remember some basic features, such as their colour, and whether they were drawn continuously or contained gaps. It is as though our visual system extracted some of the simple features of the unattended objects but never quite managed to put them together to form whole percepts.

In everyday life people do not take much notice of the act of attending. We do it automatically, and if we are aware of enacting it – if we take a deliberate decision to attend to something – we only perceive the result of this process. As was said before, nobody has access to the processing of information that goes on 'inside our heads', and selective attention is no exception to this rule. However, many researchers in numerous laboratories are trying to access this process. By performing experiments, they are attempting to unravel an experience that we usually take for granted. In particular, they are endeavouring to work out how bottom-up and top-down processes in our perceptual systems make it possible for us to be capable of attending to that precise information which is of relevance to ordinary functioning.

In this section we will explore this avenue of experimentation and related theories of attention. It will become apparent that ideas about how attention works have changed over time, generally as a result of new insights. However, progress in research has not yet resulted in general agreement. To begin with, though, we will discuss some classic experiments concerning what is called the *cocktail party phenomenon*. Then we will introduce the current view of selective attention which considers it to be a consequence of limited information-processing capacity. The opposite of this *limited capacity and early selection* view will be presented thereafter, namely that of *unlimited capacity and late selection*. By then it will be evident that the *concept of attention* has many different meanings. Necessarily at such a point, then, we will consider these in more detail. The section will end with a discussion of the latest developments concerning the *unlimited capacity and early selection* viewpoint.

The Cocktail Party Phenomenon

Imagine you are at a party listening to one of your fellow guests. If what he or she has to say is sufficiently interesting, you will be perfectly able to ignore the conversations going on around you. If you are bored, however, but too polite to walk away, you will find it also perfectly easy to shift your attention back and forth between the surrounding conversations, rapidly enough to understand some parts of each of them. However, you will find it impossible to follow several conversations simultaneously or even listen to two of them at once. You must selectively attend to only one spoken message at a time if you are to understand fully and remember anything.

In the early 1950s **Colin Cherry** studied this **cocktail party phenomenon** experimentally. At first, Cherry (1953) presented two messages with different meanings simultaneously on one audio tape, spoken by the same person. It proved very difficult to follow just one of the messages. Obviously, meaning is not the right cue for the selection process, otherwise it would be possible to follow one of the communications. Cherry went on looking for the signals that people do use for shifting attention from one source to another. The answer was provided by his experiments using the so-called **dichotic listening** task. His subjects, wearing headphones, again listened to two tape-recorded messages played simultaneously, but this time a different message was delivered into each ear. They

FIGURE 6.8	AN EXAMPLE OF OVERLAPPING FIGURES

Cover all but the left column of the figure with a piece of paper. Look at the pictures of overlapping coloured shapes in the left column. Try to attend to the red shapes only and rate them according to how appealing they seem to you. Next, cover the left column of the figure and uncover the right side. Now test your memory for the red (attended) figures and the blue and green (unattended) figures. Put a check mark next to each figure you definitely recall seeing on the left. How well do you remember the attended versus the unattended shapes?

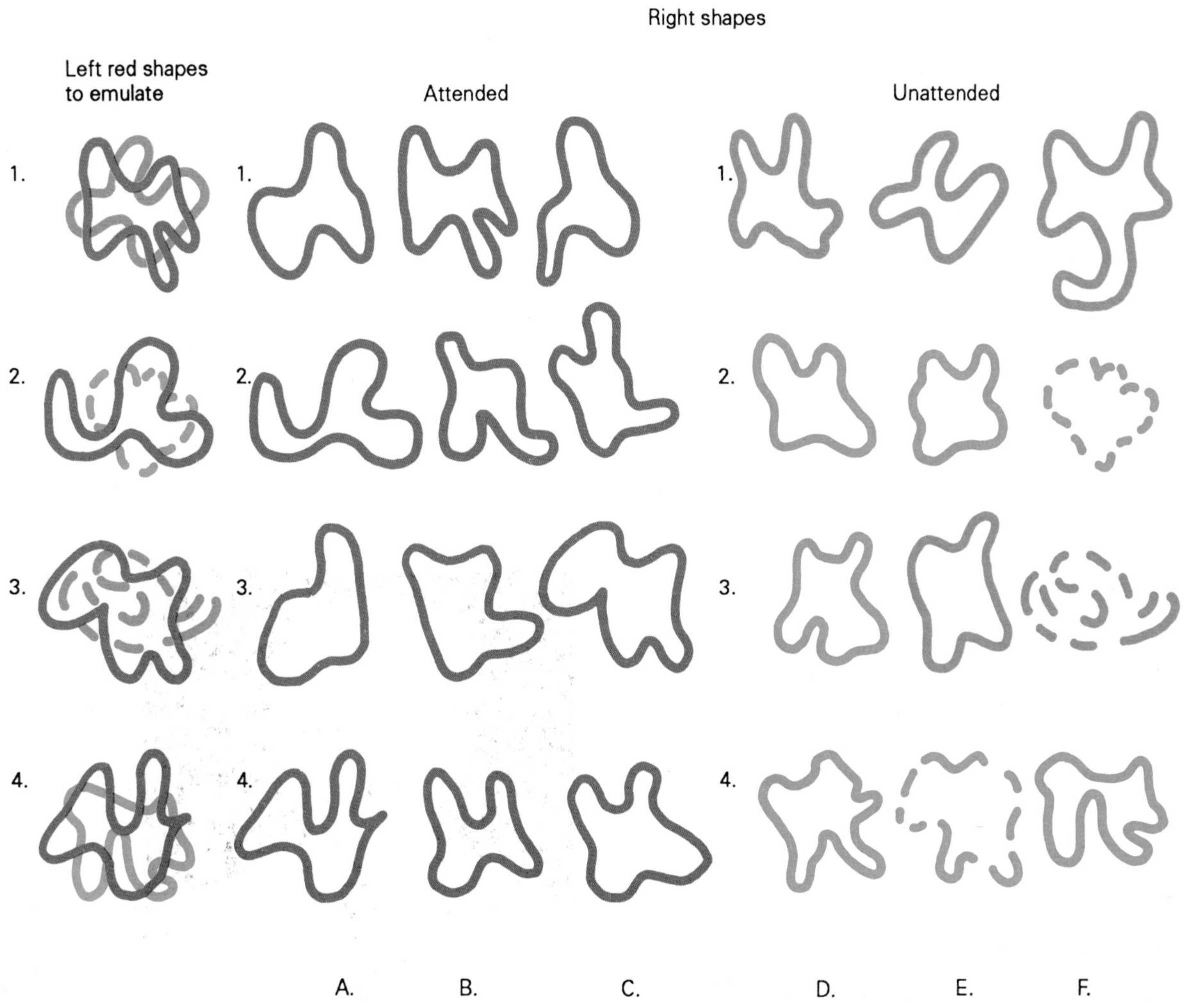

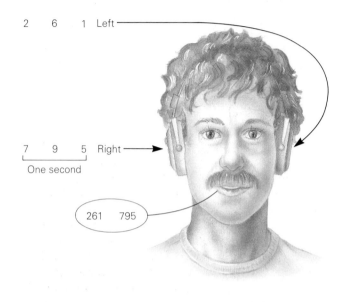

FIGURE 6.9   DICHOTIC LISTENING TASK

A subject hears different digits presented simultaneously to each ear: 2 (left), 7 (right), 6 (left), 9 (right), 1 (left) and 5 (right). He reports hearing the correct sets – 261 and 795. However, when instructed to attend only to the right ear input, the subject reports hearing only 795.

were instructed to repeat back only one of the two messages to the experimenter, whilst ignoring the other – a technique called *shadowing* (see *Figure 6.9*). Now, the subjects had no problem in following the attended message while ignoring the other one, even when the two messages were delivered by the same voice. Thus, it is apparent that people are able to attend to one message by using direction or location as cues for selective attention.

In general, participants in dichotic listening experiments remember very little of the ignored message. They do not even notice major alterations, such as changing the language from English to German or playing the tape backward. However, subjects do notice some things, especially marked physical changes. For example, substantially raising the pitch by changing the speaker's voice from male to female, changing the intensity of the sound, and inserting something completely different (like a pure tone in the middle of the speech) are noticed and remembered.

◆ Limited Capacity and Early Selection

In the light of results such as those of the dichotic listening experiments, **Donald Broadbent** conceived

of attention as a selective filter that deals with the overwhelming flow of incoming sensory information by blocking out some sensory input and passing on the input that is selected for further processing. Thus, hopping from one conversation to another seems to be controlled by a kind of mental switch – an internal mechanism that keeps all the incoming communication lines closed, except one.

Broadbent's filter theory

Let us consider Broadbent's *filter theory of attention* in a little more detail. According to Broadbent (1958), stimuli from the outside world enter the information-processing system in a parallel fashion. This means that processing starts with the absorption of *all* stimuli presented at any given time, and that those stimuli are processed at the same time next to each other. The information is temporarily stored in a *sensory buffer* (see also Chapter 8). Because this store has to contain lots of information, its capacity must be large. Further on in the system, however, the capacity to deal with information is limited. There, information is processed in serial, that is step by step. So, somewhere in between these two systems there appears to be a bottleneck and that is the point at which Broadbent located his *filter*. It is the task of the filter to regulate the information-traffic between the two systems. Note that Broadbent's filter is a special mechanism in that it is uniquely devoted to the selection of information. Apparently we need something specific to do the selection task. Information that is not selected by the filter remains very briefly in the sensory buffer and then decays rapidly. Only information that passes through the filter is processed further in the sense that it comes in actuality to be 'perceived'. So recognition and identification, or in general 'assigning meaning', is only reserved for information that passes the attention filter.

Donald Broadbent

216   CHAPTER 6 ····· PERCEPTION

The filter theory of attention is based on the assumption that the brain cannot deal with the enormous amount of stimulation the outside world bombards us with. Because of this **limited capacity** of processing, there has to be a selection mechanism. Selection is based on rough physical characteristics of the stimuli, such as the direction from which the sound comes. The filter cannot select in terms of content, because meaning is determined by the 'deeper' processing that takes place after the information is filtered. Thus, according to Broadbent, selection occurs very early in the process; that is to say, a selection mechanism is operating at a stage prior to that concerned with categorising the information. In other words, this pre-categorical or **early selection** is meaning-independent.

Treisman's attenuation theory

Broadbent's theory was first challenged when it was discovered that some subjects were perceiving things they would have been unable to if attention had been totally blocking all irrelevant material. While waiting in a cafeteria queue, your attention is focused on the conversation you are engaged in and you are seemingly oblivious to a nearby vocal exchange – until you overhear your name mentioned. Suddenly, you are aware that you must have been monitoring the conversation to detect that special signal amidst the background noise. (Because nowadays cocktail parties hardly exist anymore, this effect is sometimes called *the lunch-line effect* (Farthing, 1992)). In dichotic listening tasks, subjects sometimes not only notice their own names in a message they were instructed to ignore, but also other personally relevant information (Cherry, 1953). When a story being shadowed in one ear was switched to the unattended ear and replaced by a new story, some subjects continued to report words from the original story which was then entering the supposedly ignored ear. The subjects did so even though they had been accurately following the instruction about which ear to shadow (Treisman, 1960).

Apparently, an unattended message can be processed far more thoroughly than was allowed for in Broadbent's theory. Accordingly, alternative theories were proposed. **Anne Treisman** (1986; 1988), for example, proposed an *attenuation theory*. In the attenuation theory, there is also an early selective filter with about the same properties as Broadbent's filter, except that it does not completely block out the unwanted messages but merely attenuates them. Thus, the 'ignored' information also receives some higher-level, meaningful analysis, but the analysis is only partial, is not guaranteed and frequently does not

Anne Treisman

reach consciousness. Whether you become aware of it depends on a second selection – a 'late' selection concerning the analysis of meaning. Highly important or relevant information (for example, your name) has a low threshold and therefore a high probability of being noticed. The attended channel still receives far more processing than the unattended channel because processing of the unattended message is attenuated or reduced – but nevertheless more processing is conceived as taking place than in Broadbent's theory. By comparison with Broadbent's framework, Treisman's early filter is viewed as 'leaky', and so a second, 'late' filter enters the picture. But like Broadbent, Treisman still assumes that a special mechanism is needed to guard us against stimulation overflow. Her model is still based upon a *limited capacity therefore selection* theory (Bundesen, 1990).

◆ Unlimited Capacity and Late Selection

Nowadays, like Broadbent and Treisman, most theorists in information-processing psychology maintain that the human brain has only a limited capacity for processing information – that is to say, for its categorisation or identification. This *limited capacity therefore selection* view, however, also has its opponents. Two main issues are raised: one concerns the complex, if not impossible task the filter faces; the other concerns the point that not remembering the unattended message does not necessarily indicate that it is not processed.

Broadbent's filter has to evaluate the significance of stimuli. This task is highly relevant for survival, so selection must take place very carefully. But how is it possible to select prudently if there is only a limited capacity for processing – for really understanding what the incoming information is all about? How can we choose when the selection made by the filter is pre-categorical, which implies the impossibility of weighting all incoming information? Saying that *we* do not choose but the filter does, is proposing an 'explanation' that forces us to answer the question who or what is this little-creature-inside-our-head – this *homunculus* – that takes these incredibly complex decisions for us? In other words, proposing an early filter as an explanation for selective attention does not explain anything if the supposed capacities of such a mechanism makes the filter as complicated as our whole information-processing system itself.

A second critical issue concerns the assumption that not remembering a message means that it is not processed at all. What evidence do we have that unattended information is not processed completely? In the previous chapter we noted that people only have access to the outcomes of their own perceptual processing. You see a red rose without knowing how you accomplished that feat. If there is an outcome – such as an internal representation of a red rose – we infer that there also must have been processing of information. But if we are not aware of an outcome, does that necessarily mean that there has been no processing either? Furthermore, from the discussion on subliminal perception, also in Chapter 5, we learned that even objects we do not 'see' are sometimes processed by our perceptual system. Thus, all we can conclude from the demonstration (and its supporting research) described in *Figure 6.8*, is that people are not consciously aware of the shapes of the unattended figures, but also that we do not know whether our visual system did not in fact put these shapes together correctly and completely without our awareness.

Deutsch and Deutsch's response selection theory

Issues like those mentioned above, inspired **Anthony** and **Diana Deutsch** to propose an information-processing theory that constitutes a radical departure from that of Broadbent. In their *response selection theory of attention* the assumption that we need a filter because our capacity is limited is rejected. According to the Deutschs, all sensory inputs may be processed completely without attention (Deutsch & Deutsch, 1963; Driver & Tipper, 1989). Each message will subject to the same treatment: it will be categorised and recognised, and its importance will be weighted. If it is sufficiently important, we will 'perceive' the message; if not, we will be unaware of it. Attention has not so much to do with 'perceiving' but with 'thinking'. Thus, according to Deutsch and Deutsch a

selection mechanism operates at a stage where the information already has meaning. Selective attention regarding meaningful material has to do with the weighting inputs in terms of importance, and is called post-categorical or **late selection**.

A demonstration of non-conscious awareness of unattended information is provided in *Figure 6.10*. Try to read the red letters in each column. Disregard the overlapping green letters. Did you notice that one of the columns is harder to read? Which one? Now look carefully at the green letters. In the first column, there is no relationship between the green letters and the red letters. However, in the second list, beginning with the second red letter, each red letter is the same as the green letter above it. A number of experiments show that subjects take longer to read the second list (Tipper & Driver, 1988; Driver & Tipper, 1989).

According to the authors of such experiments,

FIGURE 6.10	A TEST OF YOUR ATTENTIONAL MECHANISMS

First read aloud the red letters in column one as quickly as possible, disregarding the green. Next, quickly read the red letters in column two, also disregarding the green. Which took longer?

Column One   Column Two

subjects take longer to read the second column because they actually process the green letters unconsciously and have to inhibit or prevent themselves from responding to them. When, after having inhibited a particular letter, subjects are asked to respond to it; but they are slowed down because they have to unblock or disinhibit the letter and make it available as a response.

If *limited capacity therefore selection* is wrong, why should we make a selection at all? Why not replace it by *unlimited capacity therefore no selection*? The answer is that according to the late selection view, we are limited not on the afferent processing or input side but rather on the efferent processing or output side. Selective attention is necessary, not because we are limited in the amount of information we can process but because we are limited in the number of responses we can make at a given time. We cannot respond to numerous stimuli simultaneously; survival depends on being able to respond correctly and swiftly only to those that are most important. Thus, what makes selection necessary is not limited capacity but rather our inability to manage and respond to **unlimited capacity** or 'too much capacity'. That is why the theory of Deutsch and Deutsch is called a response selection theory of attention, and its credo could well be summarised as *selection for action*.

Before describing further developments in this discussion about selection being early or late, and capacity being limited or unlimited, we first have to deal with a conceptual problem. So far, the concept of attention and the contexts in which the term has been used implies that it can have a number of different meanings. It is necessary to pause for a moment and draw some distinctions between several forms of attention.

◆ The Concept of Attention

Until now, the concept of attention has been used in ways that imply different meanings. At a party, your attention directed towards one individual is the consequence of a deliberate decision to look at and listen to this person, and to think carefully about what he or she is saying. In this instance, you are in control of paying attention and processing is mainly top-down (or *subject-driven)*. However, if your name is used in one of the other conversations going on around you, you cannot help noticing it. In this case attention is mainly bottom-up (or *world-driven)*. If both acts are called *attention*, are we talking about the same phenomenon or does the concept of attention have such a broad meaning that we need to differentiate between several forms of attention? The

latter seems to be the case. Despite the fact that everybody intuitively knows what attention is, the concept is still highly ambiguous and elusive. At least three different forms of 'attention' can be distinguished (Van der Heijden, 1992). Let us take selective attention in vision as an example.

You are reading this chapter. Your gaze is attracted to black curved lines and to black straight lines with different angles on a white background. If you turn the page, however, your attention may well shift to something colourful. It turns out that this book also contains pictures, which, in this example, distract you momentarily from your reading. When you try to go back to the letters, suddenly your attention may be attracted by a movement in the upper-left corner of your visual field. After you locate this moving object and identify it as a harmless insect, you direct your attention back again to the book. This first 'attentional' factor deals with the *where* – the position or spatial location of the stimulus – and with some gross physical features of the stimulus, such as colour and form. It concerns 'seeing'. The early selection mechanisms we have discussed up until now, such as Broadbent's filter, deal with this form of attention. When psychologists carrying out research into perception talk about attention, they are referring in large part to this *early* or *pre-categorical selection*. From now on then, when we write of 'attention', we are likewise referring to this more narrow usage of the term.

While you are reading this chapter, your attention is also directed at grasping the meaning of words, sentences and paragraphs. You compare what you read with what you already know; you anticipate on the basis of your expectations. Focusing attention in this case is trying to concentrate your thinking on the text. It is the same form of 'attention' you need in order to understand what a fellow guest at a party is saying. This second 'attentional' factor concerns a way of directing our thoughts, often called an *expectation,* and has to do with the *what* – the identity of the stimulus. This selection mechanism seems to operate at a stage where the information already has meaning. We encountered the notion of 'expectation' previously when discussing selective attention as a late selection mechanism that is meaning-dependent. The weighting of importance of input at this later stage of processing being *late* or *post-categorical selection.* Whereas attention (in its narrow usage) concerns 'seeing' or, in general, 'perceiving', expectations can be aligned with 'knowing'.

If you want to study this chapter seriously, your attention will be directed at making the necessary preparations. You need a comfortable chair and a table on which the book is to be placed in front of you. You need pen and paper on one side and a lamp or overhead light. A quiet surrounding is preferable, where there are no other things to attend to for the next few hours, and so on. In general terms, this 'attentional' factor concerns advance preparation with regard to you defining the limits of whether and how you may react in designated circumstances. This 'attentional' factor is often called *intention*. Although research into intention is presently uncommon, it definitely is an important form of attention.

Distinguishing between three 'attentional' factors is a contrivance in the sense that in reality it is impossible to divide them one from the other. Information-processing is always a combination of bottom-up and top-down processing – of attention, expectation and intention working together. But these three 'attentional' factors can be conceptually distinguished and such a tripartite distinction may help us to clarify some of the problems mentioned earlier.

Unlimited Capacity and Early Selection

Current researchers in visual attention, notably **Alan Allport**, **Odmar Neumann** and **Lex van der Heijden**, reject that a choice has to be made between limited capacity and early selection on the one hand and unlimited capacity and late selection on the other. They argue that as far as visual attention (in the narrow usage of the term) is concerned, unlimited capacity is combined with early selection (Neumann *et al*, 1986). Here we will present their argument concerning the capacity dilemma and thereafter will discuss the problem of where selection takes place.

Central capacity: limited or unlimited?

Of course nobody would claim that our visual system will process every stimulus that meets our eyes. In the previous chapter we stated that the sense organ and the receptors – the eye, and the rods and cones – reduce the amount of incoming stimuli. The eye itself, then, can be regarded as a 'filter' that protects the visual system from an overload. We also noted that only two million retinal ganglion cells are available to process the signals of millions and millions of rods and cones, and that they have to transport the signals again to millions and millions of cells in the visual cortex. Hence, very early in the process, a kind of bottleneck is built into the visual system. Furthermore, lateral inhibition can also be interpreted in terms of reducing the capacity for storage and transmission. But it is exactly the presence of these *peripheral* 'structural' limitations which makes it

unnecessary to postulate an extra *central* mechanism especially devoted to the task of protecting us from the possibility of overload (Allport, 1987; 1989; Van der Heijden, 1990; 1992).

This line of reasoning is supported by current knowledge of the neurophysiology of visual information processing. Also in the previous chapter, we referred to the view among neuroscientists that within the brain, the various attributes of the visual world are analysed separately in different modules. This modular organisation makes it possible to process many forms of information at a time. So if the brain in visual perception not only operates serially but also in parallel, and the visual system itself has several built-in selection mechanisms, again we do not need to propose that some mysterious filtering homunculus protects us against perceptual overload (Marcel, 1983; Neumann, 1987, 1990). Thus, within the constraints of the visual system itself, its capacity for processing information seems to have no limitations imposed upon it.

Selection: late or early?

There is no question that selection of responses, or late selection, does occur. We cannot do everything at once, so we must choose what is most important and we do so by using 'expectation' and 'intention'. In the laboratory this selection of action is artificially induced by the instruction that is given by the experimenter. In the experiment in *Figure 6.8*, you will have experienced how a simple instruction can model your expectations and intentions and thereby lead your perceptions. If you followed the instructions, you attended to the red shapes and as a result, if action should be required, you could efficiently react to them but not to the unattended ones. This form of selection thus has to solve the problem of identifying which action from the total repertoire of possible ones should be given temporal priority.

If processing is unlimited and expectation and intention are the basis of late selection, is there still need for attention as a distinct phenomenon? Is there more to selection in an early phase than, say, the processing that takes place in the eye? According to researchers – including Allport, Neumann and Van der Heijden – there definitely exists early selection in the form of attention. This selective attention is needed because a selected action can generally be directed to only one of among a number of simultaneously available objects at a time. Attention has to solve the problem of which object to act upon at a given moment. But of what exactly does this early selection consist?

Experiments on visual attention have shown that

early selection is based on physical features such as colour, form, brightness and size but not on meaning (for example, the meaning of words). If a paragraph contains ten words in italics, you will have no problem pointing to them very quickly. It is as if you do not have to 'think' about it; you just 'see' them in an instant. However, you do have to 'think' when you are asked to point to ten adjectives in a text. Thus, in visual selection early selection does take place, and it is concerned with 'seeing' (or 'apprehending') and not with 'knowing' (or 'comprehending'); it is pre-categorical and not post-categorical. Furthermore, it transpires that visual selection always has something to do with position in visual space. Even if people select according to colour or form, location is a very important intermediary. Thus, selective attention concerns the *where* of a stimulus (Van der Heijden, 1992).

Van der Heijden relates the evidence from psychological experiments for an early selection mechanism concerning the where of a stimulus to the neurophysiological insights about a separation of processing channels in the brain, as discussed in the previous chapter. The relatively slow *parvo cellular pathway* is involved in the *what*, the identification of a stimulus. The relatively fast *magno cellular pathway* is involved in determining the *where*, the location and direction of a stimulus. Only in humans and some apes is the parvo system a few times larger than the magno channel. Thus, it appears that the parvo system is a latter-day evolutionary device designed for 'higher' processes such as recognition and identification; and furthermore – it takes its time. The magno system on the other hand is much more 'primitive'. It is a fast-working pathway that enables us to react inmediately to a stimulus, even before we have had the time to recognise or identify it. Equipped with only a magno system, we would spend the day snapping at every moving object that was smaller than ourselves and jumping away from big objects snapping at us, without even knowing what it is we are fleeing from or attacking. So the magno system seems perfectly equipped to underake the task of *selection-for-action* and consequently selective attention should be studied as one of the results of the workings of this system.

More research needed

We have devoted some space to the development of experimentation and to theorising about selective attention, not only because it is an important subject, but also to show how empirical psychological research progresses steadily, step by step. Within this context, we used the *unlimited capacity and early selection* view as an example, without spuriously claiming that there exists general agreement among researchers in this field. The worn-out phrase 'more research is needed' in order to settle ongoing disputes can be applied to most areas of psychology and selective attention is no exception. As we noted before in this section, however, most researchers still adhere to the *limited capacity and early selection* view. The important advantage of the preceding view is that there is no further need to postulate a separate mechanism – an homunculus somewhere inside our heads – in order to explain our natural ability to be selective in perception. According to this view, selective attention is built into our perceptual system and it serves not just seeing – by regulating potential overload – but in particular it is directed at action. And that is what life is also all about.

INTERIM SUMMARY

The ways in which we select and make choices among all of the incoming information are often grouped together under the general label of selective attention. The cocktail party phenomenon demonstrates that most people do not find it difficult to attend to one message whilst ignoring others. Broadbent's theory of attention explains this ability by postulating a filter that is situated at an early point in the processing of information. The filter is necessary because the brain has a capacity that is too limited to deal with the enormous amount of stimulation with which the outside world bombards us.

However, the fact that we hear our name when it is used in an ongoing background conversation to which we are not attending, shows that some processing of the messages we choose to ignore does take place. According to Treisman's attenuation theory, this happens because the filter is 'leaky'. She states that processing of the unattended message does take place but in an attenuated or reduced form. Deutsch and Deutsch wonder how such an early filter manages to make such skilful decisions. They deny the existence of such an homunculus and state that a selection mechanism only operates at a stage wherein the information already has meaning. This late selection goes hand in hand with a potentially unlimited capacity on the part of the visual system. We do have limitations, however, but they concern our behavioural repertoire. Thus, we do not select for perception but for action.

One of the problems in the debate pertains to the meaning of the concept *attention*. Three 'attentional' factors can be distinguished: attention in a narrow sense; expectation; and intention. The first one deals with the early selection of the '*where*' of a stimulus. The other ones are concerned with the late selection of the '*what*' of a stimulus. Allport, Neumann and Van der Heijden hold that attention has to do with 'seeing' (or 'apprehending') and expectation and intention with 'knowing' (or 'comprehending'). They postulate an early selection mechanism within the visual system, notably in the magno cellular pathway. It solves the problem of which stimulus to act upon at a given moment in time. They also state that other than the constraints laid down by the visual system itself, its capacity for processing information has no limitations imposed upon it. Thus, the old dichotomy between the 'limited capacity and early selection' view on the one hand and the 'unlimited capacity and late selection' one on the other can be replaced by an 'unlimited capacity and early selection' approach. But this does not mean that the familiar phrase 'more research is needed . . .' is not applicable to the subject of selective attention. Ongoing disputes therein – as elsewhere within psychology – are in need of resolution.

◆ ORGANISATIONAL PROCESSES IN PERCEPTION

In this section, we will explore what is known about several kinds of processes that transform sensory information into perception of real-world objects. In *form perception* we will discuss the way our visual system transforms incoming stimulation into perceptual objects. Then we will elaborate on the subject of the *perception of space, time and motion*, followed by a discussion of *depth perception*. Under the heading *perceptual constancies*, we will complete this section by answering the question of how we manage to perceive a relatively constant world out of continually changing retinal images.

◆ Form Perception

Imagine how confusing the world would be if we were unable to put together and organise the information available from the output of our millions of retinal receptors. Processes of *perceptual organisation* put sensory information together to afford us the perception of coherence. For example, your percept of the two-dimensional geometric design in section A of *Figure 6.11* is probably three diagonal rows of figures, the first being composed of squares, the second of arrowheads and the third of diamonds. Nothing seems remarkable about this until you analyse all the organisational processing that you must be performing to see the design in this way. Many of the organisational processes we will be discussing in

this section were first described by Gestalt theorists who argued that what we perceive depends on laws of organisation, or simple rules by which we perceive shapes and forms.

Region segregation

Consider your initial sensory response to section A of *Figure 6.11*. Because your retina is composed of many separate receptors, your eye responds to this stimulus pattern with a mosaic of millions of independent neural responses coding the amount of light falling on tiny areas of your retina. This mosaic pattern is represented in section B of *Figure 6.11*. The first task of perceptual organisation is to determine which of these tiny areas belong with which others. In other words, the

FIGURE 6.11	PERCEPT OF A TWO-DIMENSIONAL GEOMETRIC DESIGN

What is your percept of the geometrical design in A? B represents the mosaic pattern that stimulus A makes on your retina.

A.

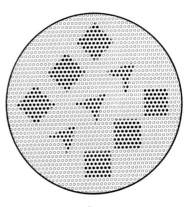

B.

outputs of the separate receptors must be combined into larger regions that are uniform in their properties.

The primary information for this *region segregation* process comes from colour and texture. An abrupt change in colour (hue, saturation or brightness) is interpreted as the presence of a boundary between two regions. Abrupt changes in texture can also mark boundaries between visibly different regions.

Many researchers now believe that the cells in the visual cortex, discovered by Hubel and Wiesel (see Chapter 5), are involved in these region-segregating processes (Marr, 1982). Some cells have elongated receptive fields that are ideally suited for detecting boundaries between regions that differ in colour. Others have receptive fields that seem to detect little bars or lines such as those that occur in grassy fields, wood grains and woven fabrics. These cortical line-detector cells may be responsible for our ability to discriminate between regions that have different textures (Beck, 1972; 1982; Julesz, 1981).

Figure and ground

As a result of region segregation, the stimulus in *Figure 6.11* has now been divided into ten regions: nine small dark ones and a single large light one. Another organisational process divides the regions into figures and background. A **figure** is seen as an object-like region in the forefront, and **ground** is seen as the backdrop against which the figures stand out. In section A of *Figure 6.11*, you probably see the dark regions as figures and the light region as ground. However, figure and ground can also be reversed, like the vase/faces drawing and the Escher art, which results in the image of a large white sheet of paper that has nine holes cut in it through which you can see a black background.

The tendency to perceive a figure as being in *front* of a ground is very strong. In fact, you can even get this effect in a stimulus when the perceived figure does not actually exist! In the first image of *Figure 6.12*, you probably perceive a fir tree set against a ground containing several red circles on a white surface. But actually there is no fir tree shape; the figure consists only of three solid red figures and a base of black lines. You see the illusory white triangle in front because the wedge-cuts in the red circles seem to be the corners of a solid white triangle. To see an illusory six-pointed star, look at the other image in *Figure 6.12*. Here, the non-existent 'top' triangle appears to blot out parts of red circles and a black-lined triangle.

Contours and closure

If you perceive the white area in both pictures of *Figure 6.12* as two different regions, an illusory white triangle and a white ground, you have created illusory **subjective contours**. These contours do not actually exist in the distal stimulus but only in your subjective experience.

Your perception of the white triangles in *Figure 6.12* also demonstrates another powerful organising process: **closure**. Closure makes you see incomplete figures as complete and supplies the missing edges beyond gaps and barriers. Humans have an innate tendency to perceive stimuli as complete and balanced, even when there are pieces missing.

Perceptual grouping

In section A of *Figure 6.13* (next page) a six-by-six array of circles is presented – that is, it is ambiguous in

FIGURE 6.12	SUBJECTIVE CONTOURS THAT FIT THE ANGLES OF YOUR MIND

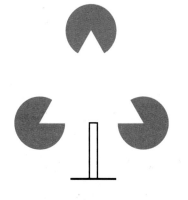
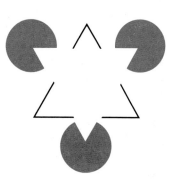

FIGURE 6.13 GROUPING PHENOMENA

We perceive each array from B through G as being organised in a particular way, according to different Gestalt principles of grouping.

A.

B.

C.

D.

E.

F.

G.

the array, he was able to formulate a set of laws of grouping. One of these laws is the **law of proximity**: all else being equal, the nearest (most proximal) elements are grouped together.

In section D, the colour of the dots instead of their spacing has been varied. Although there is equal spacing between the dots, your visual system automatically organises this stimulus into rows because of their similar colour. Most people will see the dots in section E as being organised into columns because of similar size, and the dots in section F as being organised into rows because of similar shape and orientation. These grouping effects can be summarised by the **law of similarity**: all else being equal, the most similar elements are grouped together.

When elements in the visual field are moving, similarity of motion also produces a powerful grouping. We already alluded to this phenomenon in describing Dr Richard's observation that an object in his visual field became organised properly when it moved as a whole. This principle is called the **law of common fate**: all else being equal, elements moving in the same direction and at the same rate are grouped together. If the dots in every other column of section G were moving upward, as indicated by the blurring, you would group the image into columns because of their similarity in motion. The same effect is demonstrated at a ballet when several dancers move in a pattern different from the others.

The Gestalt grouping laws operate only when two or more elements are simultaneously present in a visual field. According to the Gestaltists, the whole stimulus pattern somehow determines the organisation of its own parts: the sum is more than just a collection of its parts. Perceiving the whole - the Gestalt – is itself more basic and takes place at the same time or earlier than the perception of its elements.

Once a given region has been segregated and selected as a figure against a ground, the boundaries must be further organised into specific shapes. You might think that this task would require nothing more than perceiving all the edges of a figure, but the Gestaltists showed that visual organisation is far more complex. If a whole shape were merely the sum of its edges, then all shapes having the same number of edges would be equally easy to perceive. In reality, organisational processes in shape perception are also sensitive to something the Gestaltists called **figural goodness** or the **law of symmetry**, a concept that includes perceived simplicity, symmetry and regularity. *Figure 6.14* shows several figures that exhibit a range of figural goodness even though each has the same number of sides. Figure A is the 'best' figure (or most standard looking) and figure E is the 'worst' (or least standard looking).

Experiments have shown that 'good' figures are more easily and accurately perceived, remembered

its grouping, for you can see it equally well as either rows or columns of dots. However, when the spacing is changed slightly so that the horizontal distances between adjacent dots are less than the vertical distances, as shown in B, you see the array unambiguously as organised into horizontal rows; when the spacing is changed so that the vertical distances are less as shown in C, you see the array as organised into vertical columns. This problem of grouping was first studied extensively by Gestalt psychologist **Max Wertheimer** (1923). Wertheimer presented subjects with arrays of simple geometric figures. By varying a single factor and observing how it affected the way people perceived the structure of

FIGURE 6.14	FIGURAL GOODNESS – 1

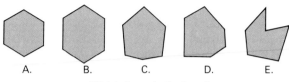

Which figure is the best?

FIGURE 6.15	FIGURAL GOODNESS – 2

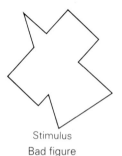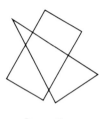

Stimulus
Bad figure

Perception
Good figures

and described than 'bad' ones (Garner, 1974). Such results suggest that shapes of 'good' figures can be coded more rapidly and economically by the visual system than those of 'bad' figures. In fact, the visual system sometimes tends to see a single 'bad' figure as being composed of two overlapping 'good' ones, as shown in *Figure 6.15*.

We have mentioned the law of proximity, the law of similarity, the law of common fate and the law of symmetry (or figural goodness). Gestalt psychologists believed that all of these laws are just particular examples of a general principle, the **law of Prägnanz**, that states that the simplest organisation requiring the least cognitive effort will always emerge. Perhaps the most general Gestalt principle is this: we perceive the simplest organisation that fits the stimulus pattern – the *minimum principle of perception*.

✦ The Perception of Space, Time and Motion

Higher levels of organisation are achieved when the shapes of figures are perceived relative to reference frames established by the spatial and temporal context.

The perceptual effects of reference frames are demonstrated in *Figure 6.16*: the left-hand image in section A is seen as a diamond, whereas the right-hand image is seen as a square. When these images are parts of diagonal rows, as shown in section B, the shapes reverse. Most people do not see the left-hand image as a collection of diamonds, but as a tilted column of squares. In the same way the right-hand figure is seen as a tilted column of diamonds and not as a group of squares. The shapes of the images look different when they are in diagonal rows because the orientation of each image is seen in relation to the **reference frame** established by the whole row (Palmer, 1984; 1989).

There are other ways to establish a contextual reference frame that has the same effect. These same images appear inside of rectangular frames tilted 45 degrees in section C of *Figure 6.16*. If you cover the frames, the left image resembles a diamond and the right one a square. When you uncover the frames, the left one changes into a square and the right one into a diamond.

Spatial and temporal integration

Reference frames are just one example of the visual system's tendency to organise individual parts in

FIGURE 6.16	REFERENCE FRAMES

Diamond

Square

A.

Tilted Squares

Tilted Diamonds

B.

Tilted Squares

Tilted Diamond

C.

relation to larger *spatial* contexts. In fact, even the whole visual field at any moment is seldom perceived as ending at the edges of our vision. Instead, we perceive it as a restricted glimpse of a large visual world extending in all directions to unseen areas of the environment.

People also must be able to integrate their perceptions from these restricted glimpses of the world in *time*. A momentary fixation on a figure is somehow properly integrated with what has been seen in the previous fixation, which was properly integrated with the one before that, and so on. If this phenomenon were not true, we would not perceive the same objects in successive views; we would see a hotchpotch of unrelated and overlapping shapes.

The process of putting together visual information from one fixation to the next in both space and time is absolutely critical for useful perception. The world around us is so much larger than a single field of view that we could never know about the spatial layout of the surroundings without organisational processes that integrate the visual information from many eye fixations into a single continuing episode of related images (Hochberg, 1968; Parks, 1965).

Complex objects often require several eye fixations before a complete spatial interpretation can be built up, even when the objects are small enough to fit into a single field of view. One interesting consequence of the way we put together the information from different fixations is that we are able to perceive 'impossible' objects, such as the ones in *Figure 6.17*. For example, in image A, each fixation of corners and sides provides an interpretation that is consistent with an object that seems to be a three-dimensional triangle; but, as shown in image B, when you try to integrate them into a coherent whole, the pieces just do not fit together properly. Image C has two arms that somehow turn into three prongs right before your vigilant gaze, and the perpetual staircase in image D forever ascends or descends.

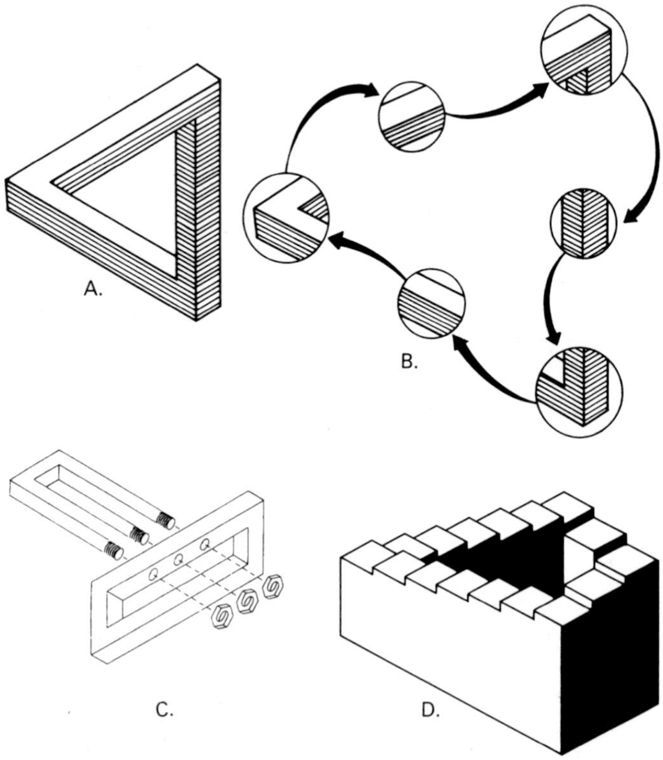

Motion perception

Being able to perceive motion is critical for survival. Although the basis for motion perception can be found in 'motion-detector' cells in our brains, as described in the last chapter, the whole process is a far more complicated affair, requiring that higher levels of perceptual organisation in the brain integrate and interpret the responses of different retinal cells over time.

Similar to orientation, motion is not perceived absolutely but relative to a reference frame. If you sit in a darkened room and fixate on a stationary spot of light inside a lighted rectangle that is moving very slowly back and forth, you will perceive instead a moving dot going back and forth within a stationary rectangle. This illusion, called **induced motion**, occurs even when your eyes are quite still and fixated on the dot. Your motion-detector cells are not firing at all in response to the stationary dot, but presumably are firing in response to the moving lines of the rectangle creating the perception of motion. To see the dot as moving requires some higher level of perceptual organisation in which the dot and its supposed motion are perceived within the reference frame provided by the rectangle.

There seems to be a strong tendency for the visual system to take a larger, surrounding figure as the reference frame for a smaller figure inside it. You have probably experienced induced motion many times without knowing it. The moon (which is nearly stationary) frequently looks as if it is moving through a cloud. The surrounding cloud induces perceived movement in the moon just as the rectangle does in the dot (Rock, 1983; 1986).

Sometimes, when you are moving, you might experience the illusion that components of the visual field are moving, while you are stationary. The illusions of the moving quay and the moving train next to you, which we referred to in our discussion of illusions in reality, are actually examples of this

FIGURE 6.17 IMPOSSIBLE FIGURES

A.

B.

C.

D.

The moon appears to move through the clouds when, actually, it is the clouds that are moving rapidly.

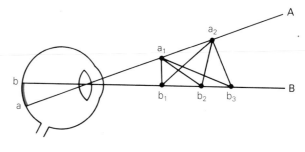

FIGURE 6.18 | DEPTH AMBIGUITY

phenomenon. Another movement illusion that demonstrates the existence of some higher-level organising processes for motion perception is called **apparent motion**. The simplest form of apparent motion, the **phi phenomenon**, occurs when two stationary spots of light in different positions in the visual field are turned on and off alternately at a rate of about four to five times per second. This effect occurs on outdoor advertising signs and in disco light displays. Even at this relatively slow rate of alternation, it appears that a single light is moving back and forth between the two spots. There are multiple ways to conceive of the path that leads from the location of the first dot to the location of the second dot. Yet, human observers normally see only the simplest path – a straight line (Shepard, 1984).

All the organisational processes we have discussed so far explain how humans can see a unified world in the successive, partial and unorganised patterns of stimulation that affect our sensory organs. Unlike Dr Richard, we are able to synthesise the many bits of sensory information we receive to make sense of them. There is no question that our brain performs this synthesis very well, but perception psychologists are still trying to figure out how the brain manages to accomplish this task.

Depth Perception

Until now, we have considered only two-dimensional patterns on flat surfaces. Everyday perceiving, however, involves objects in three-dimensional space. Perceiving all three spatial dimensions is absolutely vital to approach what we want and avoid what is dangerous. This perception requires accurate information about *depth* (the distance from you to an object) as well as about its *direction* from you. Your ears can help in determining direction, but they are not much help in determining depth.

Seeing how far away an object is, is done by a visual system that can only rely on retinal images that have two spatial dimensions – vertical and horizontal. To illustrate the problem of having a 2-D retina doing a 3-D job, consider the situation shown in *Figure 6.18*. When a spot of light stimulates the retina at point a, how do you know whether it came from position a1 or a2? In fact, it could have come from anywhere along line A. Similarly, all points on line B project on to the single retinal point b. To make matters worse, a straight line connecting any point on line A to any point on line B (a_1 to b_2 or a_2 to b_1, for example) would produce the same image on the retina. The net result is that the image on your retina is ambiguous in depth: it could have been produced by objects at any one of several, different distances. For this reason, the same retinal image can be given many different perceptual interpretations.

The ambiguity of the Necker cube in *Figure 6.6* results from this ambiguity in depth. The fact that you can be fooled under certain circumstances, shows that depth perception requires an interpretation of sensory input and that this interpretation can be wrong. Your interpretation relies on many different *depth cues* about distance, among them binocular cues, motion cues and pictorial cues.

Binocular cues

Having two eyes instead of one enables us to get information about depth. The two sources of binocular depth information are binocular disparity and convergence.

Because the eyes are about five to eight millimetres apart, they receive slightly different views of the world. To convince yourself of this, try the following experiment. First, close your left eye and use the right one to line up your two index fingers with some small object in the distance, holding one finger at arm's length and the other about 30 centimetres in front of your face. Now, keeping your fingers stationary, close your right eye and open the left one while continuing to fixate on the distant object. The second eye does not see your fingers lined up with the distant object any more because it gets a slightly different view.

This displacement between the horizontal positions of corresponding images in our two eyes is called **binocular disparity**. It provides depth information because the amount of disparity, or difference, depends on the relative distance of objects from the perceiver. For instance, when you switched eyes, the closer finger was displaced farther to the side than was the distant finger.

When you look at the world with both eyes open, most objects that you see stimulate different positions on your two retinas. The object you directly focus on projects on to the two foveae. Any other objects that happen to be at that same distance from you will also project on to corresponding retinal positions in the two eyes, but all other objects will actually produce images at different places on the two retinas because of binocular disparity. If the disparity between corresponding images in the two retinas is small enough, the visual system is able to fuse them into a perception of a single object in depth. However, if the images are too far apart, as when you cross your eyes, you actually see the double images. Thus, the visual system interprets horizontal displacement between the two retinal images as depth in the three-dimensional world.

Other binocular information about depth comes from **convergence**. The two eyes turn inward to some extent whenever they are fixated on an object (see *Figure 6.19*). When the object is very close (for example, ten centimetres) in front of your face, the eyes must turn toward each other quite a bit for the same image to fall on both foveae. You can actually see the eyes converge if you watch someone focus first on a distant object and then on one nearby.

Convergence information sent back to the brain from the eye muscles is useful for depth perception only up to about three metres, however. At greater distances the angular differences are too small to detect because the eyes are nearly parallel when you fixate on a distant object.

Motion cues

To see how motion produces depth information, try the following demonstration. Close one eye, line up your two index fingers with some distant object as you

FIGURE 6.19   CONVERGENCE CUES TO DEPTH

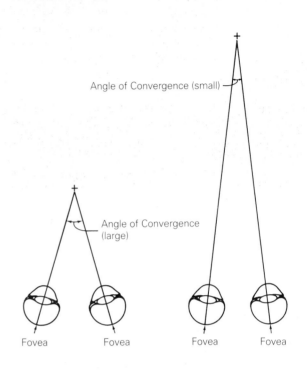

Angle of Convergence (small)

Angle of Convergence (large)

Fovea   Fovea   Fovea   Fovea

did before, and then move your head to the side while fixating on the distant object and keeping your fingers still. As you move your head, you see both your fingers move, but the close finger seems to move farther and faster than the more distant one. The fixated object does not move at all. This source of information about depth is called **relative motion parallax**.

Motion parallax provides information about depth because, as you move, the relative distances of objects in the real world determine the amount and direction of their relative motion in your retinal image of the scene. When you are moving in a stationary environment, the speed and direction of motion of points in your retinal image depends on their distance in depth relative to the fixated point (which does not move).

Pictorial cues

People who are used to seeing with only one eye are not deprived of seeing depth. There are sources of information about depth available from even just one eye and no motion of the head. These sources are called *pictorial cues* because they include the kinds of depth information found in pictures. Artists make skilled use of pictorial cues.

Interposition, or *occlusion*, arises when an opaque object blocks the light coming toward your eye from an object behind it so that only the front object is fully present in your retinal image. Interposition gives you depth information indicating that the occluded object is farther away than the occluding one. Opaque surfaces block light, creating shadows, and produce more depth information about three-dimensional shape and about the position of the light source.

Three additional sources of pictorial information are all related to the way light projects from a three-dimensional world on to a two-dimensional surface (such as the retina): relative size, linear perspective and texture gradients.

Relative size involves a basic rule of light projection: objects of the same size at different distances project images of different sizes on the retina. The closest one projects the largest image and the farthest one the smallest image. This rule is called the *size/distance relation*. Thus, relative size is a cue for depth perception.

Linear perspective is a depth cue that also depends on the size/distance relation. When parallel lines recede into the distance, they converge toward a point on the horizon in your retinal image. This very important fact was discovered around 1400 by Italian Renaissance artists who were then able to paint depth compellingly for the first time. Prior to the discovery of linear perspective, artists had incorporated in their paintings information from interposition, shadows and relative size, but they had been unable to depict

realistic scenes that showed objects at various distances. Application of Euclidean theorems of geometry to create illusionistic effects (as first devised by Brunelleschi) had a great impact on the history of Western art (Kemp, 1990).

The third kind of pictorial depth cue comes from Gibson's **texture gradients**. Images of uniform texture are smaller at greater than closer distances because they are projected on to smaller areas of the retina. The wheat field in *Figure 6.20* is an example of the way texture is used as a depth cue. The gradients result from the size/distance relation but are applied to textures of surfaces rather than to edges. Although the texture of a surface, such as a rug or tile floor, is actually uniform, the size/distance relation requires that its texture elements that are far away appear smaller than those that are closer.

By now, it should be clear that there are many sources of depth information. Under normal viewing conditions, however, information from these sources comes together in a single, coherent three-dimensional interpretation of the environment. We experience depth, not the different cues to depth that existed in the proximal stimulus. In other words, we do not perceive double images, differential motion, interposition, shadows, relative size or convergence of parallel lines, even though all these factors are constantly present in the patterns of light that enter the eyes. Rather, the visual system uses these sources of information automatically, without our conscious awareness, to make the complex computations that

FIGURE 6.20	EXAMPLES OF TEXTURE AS A DEPTH CUE

The wheat field is a natural example of the way texture is used as a depth cue. Notice the way wheat slants. The geometric design uses the same principles.

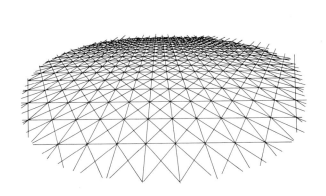

| FIGURE 6.21 | THE PONZO ILLUSION |

The converging lines add a dimension of depth, and, therefore, the distance cue makes the top line appear larger than the bottom line, even though they are actually the same length.

give us a perception of depth in the three-dimensional environment, which is what we consciously experience.

It may even be true that depth perception processes are at work when we do not consciously experience depth. This idea underlies the usual explanation of the **Ponzo illusion** (see *Figure 6.21*). The upper line looks longer because you unconsciously interpret the converging sides according to linear perspective as parallel lines receding into the distance, similar to railroad tracks. Thus, you unconsciously process the upper line as though it were farther away, so you see it as longer. The illusion is created by the converging lines that add a dimension of depth and by the distance cue.

◆ Perceptual Constancies

The goal of perception is to obtain information about the world around us, not about images on our sensory organs. We have already shown a number of ways in which the human visual system meets this goal by going beyond the information it is given directly. Another very important way it meets the goal is by perceiving an unchanging world despite the constant changes that occur in viewing conditions, creating different patterns of stimulation on the retina.

If you move your head closer to this book, the book stimulates a much larger part of your retina then when it would at a normal reading distance. Nevertheless you see the book's size as constant. If you set the book upright and try tilting your head clockwise, the image of the book rotates counter-clockwise on your retina, but you still perceive the book to be upright: its perceived orientation is constant. In general, then, you see the world as invariant, constant and stable, despite changes in the stimulation of your sensory receptors. Psychologists refer to this general phenomenon as **perceptual constancy**. Roughly speaking, it looks like you perceive the properties of the distal stimuli, which are generally constant, rather than the properties of proximal stimuli, which change every time you move your eyes or head. For survival it is critical that we perceive constant and stable properties of continuing objects in the world despite the enormous variations

The two little men may not look it, but they are exactly the same size. Most people see the little man on the right as smaller because they unconsciously use distance to judge the size of something familiar.

in the properties of the light patterns that stimulate our eyes. The task of perception is to discover invariant properties of our environment despite the variations in our retinal impressions of them.

Under extreme conditions, perceptual constancy may break down. For example, when you look at people from the top of the Eiffel Tower, they resemble ants. However, under normal circumstances, constancy holds over almost all visible properties. In this section we will discuss only three such properties in which constancy has been intensively studied: size, shape and orientation.

Size and shape constancy

The perception of an object's actual size is, in part, based on the size of its retinal image. However, the demonstration of the constancies of size and orientation while handling this book showed that the size of the retinal image depends on both the actual size of the book and its distance from the eye. Because of this relation between size and distance (the same one we discussed in the section on depth perception), the perceptual system must determine an object's actual size by combining information from the size of its retinal image with other information about its distance. We already noted that information about distance is available from a variety of depth cues. The visual system combines that information with retinal information about image size to yield a perception of an object size that usually corresponds to the actual size of the distal stimulus. **Size constancy** refers to this ability to perceive the true size of an object despite variations in the size of its retinal image.

The theory that size constancy is achieved by comparing retinal size to distance was first proposed by Helmholtz (Cutting, 1987). As we said before, he called the perceptual process that makes the comparison **unconscious inference**. It is a process of inference because the visual system must figure out, or infer, the size of an object by combining several different kinds of information. It is unconscious because the observer is not aware of knowing the size/distance relation or of using it to perceive objective size. Unconscious inferences about the true sizes of objects seem to be made rapidly, automatically and without conscious effort of any sort.

If the size of an object is perceived by taking distance cues into account, then we should be fooled about size whenever we are fooled about distance. One such illusion occurs in the Ames room shown in *Figure 6.22*. You perceive the room to be rectangular, with the two back corners at equal distance. Thus, you perceive the actual size of Philip Zimbardo as being consistent with the size of the images on your

A.

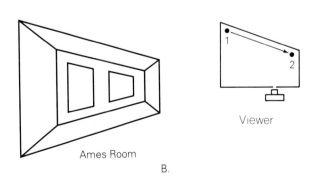

Ames Room

Viewer

B.

FIGURE 6.22   THE AMES ROOM

retina in both cases. In fact, however, he is not at the same distance. The Ames room appears to be a rectangular room, but it is actually made from non-rectangular surfaces at odd angles in depth and height

FIGURE 6.23 | SHAPE CONSTANCY

As a coin is rotated, its image becomes an ellipse that grows narrower and narrower until it becomes a thin rectangle, an ellipse again, and then a circle. At each orientation, however, it is still perceived as a circular coin.

as you can see in the drawings that accompany the photos. Any person on the right, even a smaller person like Philip Zimbardo's daughter, will make a larger retinal image because he or she is twice as close to the observer.

Another way that the perceptual system can infer objective size is by using prior knowledge about the characteristic size of similarly shaped objects. For instance, once you recognise the shape of a house, a tree or a dog, you have a pretty good idea of how big each is, even without knowing its distance from you. Most of the time your perception is correct, but, as movie directors are well aware, miniature scenery constructed to scale can give you a perception of normally sized, real objects.

Shape constancy is closely related to size constancy. The actual shape of an object is perceived correctly even when it is slanted away from the perceiver, making the shape of the retinal image substantially different from that of the object itself. For instance, a circle tipped away from you projects an elliptical image on to the retina; a rectangle tipped away projects a trapezoidal image (see *Figure 6.23*). Yet the shapes usually are perceived as a circle and a rectangle slanted away in space. When there is good depth information available from binocular disparity, motion parallax or even pictorial cues, the visual system can determine an object's true shape simply by taking the distance from its different parts into account.

Orientation constancy

When you tilted your head to the side in viewing your book, the world did not seem to tilt; only your own head did. **Orientation constancy** is our ability to recognise the true orientation of the figure in the real world, even though its orientation in the retinal image is changed. This form of constancy, too, results from a process of unconscious inference. Information about the orientation of an object in the environment is inferred from the orientation of its retinal image. In addition, head tilt is taken into account, largely through the vestibular system in the inner ear

(discussed in Chapter 5). By using the output of the vestibular system with retinal orientation, the visual system is usually able to create a perception of the orientation of an object in the environment.

In familiar environments, prior knowledge provides additional information about objective orientation. While we are good at recognising simple and familiar objects, complex and unfamiliar figures are not as recognisable, especially when they are seen in unusual orientations (see as an example *Figure 6.24*)

When a figure is complex and consists of subparts, each part must be rotated mentally. It may not be possible to rotate so many parts at the same time (Rock, 1986). So, while one part is undergoing rotation, another part may still be perceived as unrotated. Look at the two upside-down pictures of former British Prime Minister Margaret Thatcher on the next page before reading further. You can probably tell that one of them has been altered slightly around the eyes and mouth, but the two pictures look pretty similar. Now turn the book upside down and look again. The same pictures look extraordinarily different now. Your failure to see that obvious difference before turning the book upside down may

FIGURE 6.24 | AFRICA ROTATED 90°

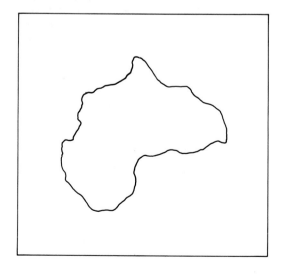

Which photograph was taken after Margaret Thatcher resigned? Turn the book around for a different orientation.

be due to your inability to rotate all of the parts of the face at the same time. It is also a function of years of perceptual training to see the world right-side up and to perceive faces in their correct visual orientation. You could try this Thatcher test with young children to determine whether they detect the 'ghoul' more quickly than adults do.

◆ RECOGNITION AND IDENTIFICATION

The perceptual processes described so far provide reasonably accurate knowledge about physical properties of the distal stimulus – the position, size, shape, texture and colour of three-dimensional objects in a three-dimensional world. With just this knowledge and some basic motor skills, you would be able to walk around without bumping into objects, manipulate objects that are small and light enough to move and make accurate models of the objects that you perceive. However, you would not know whether you had seen them before and what these objects were. Your experience would resemble a visit to an alien planet where all the objects were new to you; you would not know what to eat, what to put on your head, what to run away from or what to approach.

To get information about the objects you perceive, you need to be able to recognise them as something you have seen before and to identify them as members of the meaningful categories that you know about from experience. Recognition and identification attach meaning to percepts.

INTERIM SUMMARY

The processes that put sensory information together to give us the perception of a coherent scene over the visual field are called the processes of perceptual organisation. At the sensory stage, abrupt changes in colour and texture result in region segregation – deciding which parts of the visual field belong together. A further distinction that emerges is that between the figure (object-like regions) and ground (background against which the figures stand out). Sometimes, we even perceive figures that are physically not there – such as illusory contours. Illusory contours demonstrate another important principle in perceptual organisation – the principle of closure. We tend to perceive whole figures, complete disconnected borders and fill in occluded parts. Several disjointed figures or parts may be perceived as a group if they are close to each other (the law of proximity), similar to each other (the law of similarity), move together (the law of common fate) or if they form a 'good' figure (the law of symmetry). An underlying principle for the grouping laws has been suggested by Gestalt psychologists; the simplicity or Prägnanz principle states that the simplest configuration requiring least cognitive effort will emerge.

The spatial and temporal context in which the figures occur establishes a reference frame and the figures are perceived relative to this. The role of the reference frame is particularly evident in motion perception. We assume larger objects are stationary, and we perceive the motion of smaller objects relative to the larger ones. Apparent motion occurs when two stationary spots of light are turned on and off in different positions in the visual field at given rates. Both the reference frame effects and the existence of apparent motion demonstrate the contribution of higher level perceptual processes in motion perception.

The most striking difference between the retinal image and the percept is that the retinal image is two-dimensional whereas the percept is three-dimensional. Depth perception requires interpretation of sensory input and this interpretation relies on a number of depth cues, such as binocular cues, motion parallax and pictorial cues. These factors affect the retinal image of the object, yet we correctly perceive the unchanging distal object; this paradox is the phenomenon of perceptual constancy. We have constancy for size, shape and orientation of objects, as well as for other aspects of perception, such as brightness. Our ability to recognise a figure in unusual orientations is limited by our familiarity with the figure and especially by the figure's complexity. Simple figures are easily recognised in unfamiliar orientations; complex figures are harder to recognise. When a figure consists of multiple parts, the human perceptual system is not able to rotate all of the parts at the same time.

FIGURE 6.25	DROODLES

Do you see a woman scrubbing the floor (A) and a giraffe's neck (B)? Each of these figures can be seen as representing something familiar to us, although this perceptual recognition usually does not occur until some identifying information is provided.

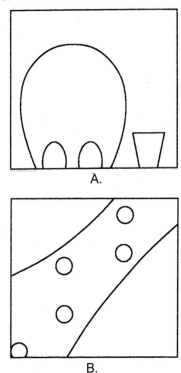

A.

B.

◆ Top-down Processing

Recognising and identifying objects implies matching what you see against your stored knowledge; it is primarily *top-down processing*. As we have seen several times before, top-down processes (also called conceptually-driven) originate in the brain and influence the selection, organisation or interpretation of sensory data. Abstract thoughts, prior knowledge, beliefs, values and other aspects of an individual's higher mental processes control the way incoming stimulation is managed and even what qualifies as relevant (review *Figure 6.3*).

The importance of top-down processes can be illustrated by drawings known as *Droodles* (Price, 1953; 1980). Without the labels, these drawings are meaningless, but once identified, their meaning is obvious (see *Figure 6.25*). Our inclination to organise our percepts is used in the so-called **projective tests**. When confronted with meaningless or multi-interpretable pictures, people 'see' meaningful and

explicit objects or events. The most well-known projective tests are the *Rorschach test* – using inkblots – and the *Thematic Apperception Test* (TAT) – using pictures of events. Because of the ambiguity of the pictures, people organise and give meaning to them. This making-sense is influenced by current motives and conflicts, thereby giving psychologists insight into the (hidden) motives of their clients (see Chapter 12).

Recognition and identification give our experiences continuity over time and across situations. This part of the process of perceiving involves memory, conceptual analysis, expectation, motivation, personality characteristics and social experience. *Conception* is added to perception, and meaning to *facts*.

What makes us decide that a grey, oddly shaped, medium-sized, furry moving thing is actually a cat? Presumably, we have a memory representation of a cat, and the identification process consists of matching

FIGURE 6.26	RECOGNITION BY COMPONENTS

Suggested components of 3-dimensional objects and examples of how they may combine. In the top half of the figure, each 3-D object is constructed of cylinders of different sizes. In the bottom half of the figure, several different building blocks are combined to form familiar objects.

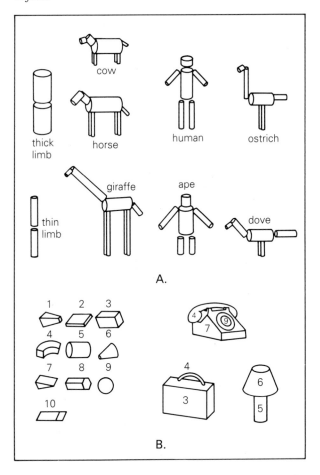

such a memory representation to the newly constructed percept and deciding that they are the same. Because computer scientists are attempting to teach computerised robots to recognise objects, they are especially interested in how these matches between memory representation and percept are accomplished. One possibility is that the memory representations of various objects consist of components and information about the way these components are attached to each other. Several different theories exist about the nature of such components (Biederman, 1985; 1987; Cooper, 1989; Marr & Nishihara, 1978). See, for example, *Figure 6.26*.

After the percept is constructed from primitive features (such as colours or edges) it also gets divided up into components (such as cylinders, cubes and pyramids) of various sizes. Then the components of the memory representation of the object get matched against the components of the percept. If a close match is found, the object is recognised and identified.

◆ Contexts and Expectations

If you meet people you know in places where you do not expect to see them, such as in the wrong city or the wrong social group, it takes much longer to recognise them and sometimes you are not even able to identify them. This demonstrates the importance of the *context*; you did not *expect* them to be there. The spatial and temporal context provides an important source of information for classifying objects because once you have identified the context, you have expectations about what objects you are and are not likely to see nearby (Biederman, 1989).

Perceptual identification depends on your expectations as well as on the physical properties of the objects you see – object identification is a constructive, interpretive process. Depending on what you already know, where you are, what else you see around you, and your expectations from context, the identification you make will vary. Read the following words:

THE CAT

Taken together, they say THE CAT. Now look again at the middle letter of each word. Physically, these two letters are exactly the same, yet you perceived the first as an H and the second as an A. Clearly, your perception was affected by what you know about words in English. The context provided by T–E makes an H highly likely and an A unlikely, whereas the reverse is true of the context of C–T (Selfridge, 1955).

To account for contextual effects, it has been suggested that interpretation of perceptual data depends on complex information structures in memory. Instead of storing information in memory in isolated bits, we organise our knowledge of the world into integrated packages. We already referred to these clusters of information as **schema**. The concept of schema reflects the way perception of reality is actively constructed through the interplay of external stimulus information and the personal experiences and knowledge that we bring into every perceptual setting. In Chapters 8 and 9 – about remembering, and thought and language – we will have a more detailed look at the working of schemata.

Perceptual set

Another aspect of the influence of context and expectation on perception (and response) is set. Set is a temporary readiness to perceive or react to a stimulus in a particular way. A **motor set** is a readiness to make a quick, prepared response. A 100-metre runner trains by perfecting a motor set to come out of the blocks as fast as possible at the sound of the starting gun. A **mental set** is a readiness to deal with a situation, such as a problem-solving task or a game, in a way determined by learned rules, instructions, expectations or habitual tendencies. A mental set can actually prevent you from solving a problem when the old rules do not seem to fit the new situation (see Chapter 9). However, set can facilitate responding by inhibiting irrelevant or wrong responses. Game-show contestants who compete to answer first typically reveal the operation of this set. A **perceptual set** is a readiness to detect a particular

FIGURE 6.27	A. YOUNG BEAUTY

stimulus in a given context. For example, a new parent is perceptually set to hear the cries of his or her child. Often, a perceptual set leads you to see an ambiguous stimulus in a way you were expecting.

Read quickly through the series of words in row 1. Then do the same with row 2.

1. FOX; OWL; SNAKE; TURKEY; SWAN; D?CK
2. BOB; RAY; DAVE; BILL; HENRY; D?CK

Probably, the meaning of the words before D?CK have influenced you in filling in the missing letter in the same ambiguous stimulus D?CK.

Labels form another context that can create a perceptual set for an ambiguous figure. Look carefully at the picture of the woman in Figure 6.27A (previous page); have a friend examine Figure 6.27B on this page. Next, together look at Figure 6.27C on the next page – what do each of you see? Did the prior exposure to the unambiguous pictures with their labels have any effect on either perception of the ambiguous image? People can easily develop different views of the same target after prior conditions have created different sets. Similarly, sets can influence social attitudes or bias how we interpret some part of the world.

◆ Personal and Social Factors

People from the same culture share basic, accepted social categories that determine standards for, for example, beauty, danger, appropriateness or unacceptability. Our culturally defined attitudes can function as anchors or standards by which new inputs are often evaluated without conscious awareness of their influence (Deregowski, 1980). People from other cultures, who do not share our cultural truisms, may 'see' objects or events differently. Because, as we said before, in everyday life 'seeing is believing' these differences lie at the basis of misunderstanding, miscommunication and mistrust between people from different cultures.

There are not only differences in perception between cultures, but also between individuals within a culture. For example, in reconciling contradictory perceptual data, some people rely more heavily on internal vestibular information and others more heavily on visual information from the external environment. This last group of people is known as more **field dependent** than the first one. Many attempts have been made to link these individual differences in the way we organise our perception of the physical world to the way we organise our perception of the social world – how we see people – and our own internal world – how we see ourselves.

Of course it is very tempting to postulate a *cognitive style* that encompasses our total style of information-processing (Witkin & Goodenough, 1977).

A well-known test for field dependence in perception requires subjects to judge when lines are vertical (aligned with gravity) in situations in which there is conflicting visual information. In one version of the test – the rod-and-frame test – subjects are shown a tilted rod inside a tilted frame with no other visual information. They are asked to adjust the tilt of the rod so that it is upright with respect to gravity. Some people are able to do this quite accurately despite the tilt of the frame. These people are field independent *because they seem to rely almost exclusively on internal bodily information provided by their vestibular and kinaesthetic systems to define the vertical and are able to ignore contradictory information from the visually tilted frame. These people have been classified by personality tests as being self-reliant, inner-directed and individualistic (Klein, 1970). Other people, however, adjust the rod so that it is strongly tilted toward the orientation of the frame. These people are* field dependent *because they seem to depend more upon the external field information provided by the frame and less on internal information. They have been characterised by the same tests as being socially dependent, eager to make a good impression and conforming (Ruble & Nakamura, 1972).*

The correspondence between people's social preferences and their behaviour on the rod-and-frame test suggests that we each have our own unique cognitive style that determines how we seek, acquire and evaluate information about our environment, both physical and social (G. Klein, 1970). Another attempt to link perception and personality in terms of cognitive style concerns the distinction between levelling and sharpening. *Levellers* tend to smooth over

FIGURE 6.27	B. OLD HAG

FIGURE 6.27   C. NOW WHAT DO YOU SEE?

perception'. However, there is yet to emerge a comprehensive theory that integrates the complex network of processes involved in perception, cognition and personality.

 Conclusion

Top-down processing highlights the important fact that perceptual experience in response to a stimulus event is a response of the whole person. In addition to the information provided when sensory receptors are stimulated, our final perception depends on who we are, whom we are with, and what we expect, want and value. We often see what we want to see.

The interaction of top-down and bottom-up processes points to the fact that perception is an act of *constructing* reality to fit one's assumptions about how reality probably is or should be. If perceiving were completely data-driven, we would all be bound to the same mundane, concrete reality of the here and now. We could register experience but not profit from it on later occasions, nor would we see the world differently under different personal circumstances. If processing in perception were completely hypothesis-driven, however, we would each be lost in our fantasy worlds of what we expect and hope to perceive. A proper balance between the two extremes achieves the basic goal of perception: to experience what is out there in a way that maximally serves our needs as biological and social beings as we move about and adapt to our physical and social environment.

what seems irregular, novel or unusual and omit details in order to give a more homogenous and less incongruous interpretation of the stimulus event. Levellers are also more likely to miss subtle differences – their perceptions are dominated by similarities apparently because their perceptual processing is too greatly influenced by memory of what has gone before. By contrast, when given a task with a sequence of gradually changing stimuli, *sharpeners* see the elements of each stimulus display as independent of what went before, accentuating and over-emphasising current details. They tend to perceive the elements of a situation more accurately than do levellers, but they may miss the 'forest' by focusing too closely on the 'trees'.

Many interesting findings have emerged from attempts to understand the process of perception, particularly by 'putting the *person* back into

recapping main points

The Task of Perception

The task of perception is to extract the continuously changing, often chaotic, sensory input from external energy sources and organise it into stable, orderly percepts of meaningful objects that are relevant to a perceiver. Another way to formulate it is by saying that perception has to do with making sense of sensation.

Fundamental Features of Perception

At the sensory level of processing, physical energy is detected and transformed into neural energy and sensory experience. At the perceptual level, brain processes organise sensations into coherent images and give us the perception of objects and patterns. These percepts of objects are then compared against memory representations so as to be recognised as familiar and identified as meaningful objects or not. Thus, perception is a constructive process of going beyond sensory stimulation to discover what objects exist in the world around us. When the same sensory information is organised into different percepts, or when the same percepts can be interpreted or identified differently, we may experience illusions. Knowledge about perceptual illusions can give us clues about normal organising processes.

Selective Attention

Attention refers to our ability to select part of the sensory input and disregard the rest. There are several competing theories about attention. The *limited capacity and early selection* view postulates a filter that is situated in an early phase of the processing of information. The filter is needed because the brain has a limited capacity. The *unlimited capacity and late selection* view states that the capacity for processing information is unlimited. We do have limitations, however, but they concern our capacity to respond. Thus, selection is not selection-for-perception but selection-for-action.

One of the problems in the debate pertains to the meaning of the concept *attention*. The first view deals with a narrow usage of the term, concerning the '*where*' of objects. The second view has to do with attention as expectation and intention, and it concerns the '*what*' of stimulus events. Recently a third view – *unlimited capacity and early selection* – is emerging. It holds that within the constraints of the visual system itself, the capacity for processing information seems to have no limitations. We do need to make early selections because of the problem of deciding which object to act upon at a given moment in time. This selection mechanism, however, does not consist of a special filter, but is part of the functioning of the magno cellular pathway.

Organisational Processes in Perception

Organisational processes segregate our percepts into regions and organise them into figures that stand out against the ground. We tend to see incomplete figures as wholes; group items by similarity; and see 'good' figures more readily.

We tend to organise and interpret parts in relation to the spatial and temporal context in which we experience them. We also tend to see a reference frame as stationary and the parts within it as moving, regardless of the actual sensory stimulus. In converting the two-dimensional information on the retina to a perception of three-dimensional space, the visual system gauges object size and distance: distance is interpreted on the basis of known size and size is interpreted on the basis of various distance cues. We tend to perceive objects as retaining the same size, shape and orientation. Prior knowledge normally reinforces these and other constancies in perception.

Recognition and Identification

The processes of recognition and identification give meaning through ones that draw on memory, expectation, motivation and personality characteristics. Expectations, schemas and perceptual sets may guide recognition of incomplete or ambiguous data in one direction rather than in another, equally possible one. Personality characteristics, motives and social influences contribute to the meanings of perceptual data and may lead us to create our own world. Perception, thus, depends not only on the nature of the sensory stimulus, but also on who we are, what we know and expect.

key Terms

ambiguity
apparent motion
binocular disparity
bottom-up processing
closure
cocktail party phenomenon
convergence
dichotic listening
distal stimulus
early selection
empiricism
field dependence
figural goodness
figure-ground
Gestalt psychology
identification
illusions
induced motion
interposition
late selection
law of common fate
law of Prägnanz
law of proximity
law of similarity
law of symmetry
limited capacity

linear perspective
mental set
motor set
nativism
orientation constancy
percept
perceptual constancy
perceptual set
phi phenomenon
Ponzo illusion
projective tests
proximal stimulus
recognition
reference frame
relative motion parallax
schema
selective attention
set
shape constancy
size constancy
subjective contours
texture gradients
top-down processing
unconscious inference
unlimited capacity

major Contributors

Allport, Alan
Broadbent, Donald (1926–93)
Cherry, Colin
Deutsch, Anthony
Deutsch, Diana
Gibson, James (1904–79)

Kraft, Conrad
Neumann, Odmar
Treisman, Anne
van der Heijden, Lex
von Helmholtz, Hermann (1821–94)
Wertheimer, Max (1880–1943)

Chapter 7

Learning and Behaviour Analysis

During a routine check-up, the doctor finds that your blood pressure is dangerously high. She explains that untreated hypertension can lead to heart failure, stroke, kidney damage, retinal damage and even seizures. You are not overweight or diabetic and you reassure the doctor that you do not smoke or drink. Yes, life is a little stressful, especially since college, work and family concerns all make demands on you at the same time, but you cannot do much about that right now. The doctor tells you that she is putting you on an anti-hypertensive drug. You express concern about side effects – you know someone who lost his libido when he took the same drug. The doctor says not to worry – side effects should give you little trouble after the first few weeks. To your relief, after a short time, your blood pressure returns to normal.

Unbeknown to you, a few weeks after you started taking the drug, your doctor replaced the real medication with a placebo – in this case, a drug that has no actual physiological effect. Today, use of the placebo is one of the most promising developments in modern medicine. Researchers **Robert Ader** and **Anthony Suchman** have found that hypertensive patients who were taken off medication while continuing to be treated with placebos maintained healthy blood pressures longer than patients who did not get placebos (Suchman & Ader, 1989).

How can an inert pill cure hypertension? After repeated exposures to the real drug, the physical ritual involved in taking the drug became associated with the physiological changes involved in lowering blood pressure. Patients did not have to learn consciously that a medication reduced the force of the heartbeat, increased salts and water excreted in urine, or dilated blood vessels. Instead, through repeated association of these effects with the act of taking the medicine, subjects' bodies became conditioned to respond appropriately, even after the active ingredients were withdrawn. The medicine-taking ritual alone initiated the body's conditioned responses. However, it did so only after the medicine had been taken with the belief that it was effective medicine and the entire procedure of medicine-taking (pharmacotherapy) became part of this placebo effect. Although side effects as well as positive changes could become conditioned to a placebo, the side effects would be likely to diminish in time as other, stronger stimuli elicited incompatible responses.

In an earlier experiment, Ader and colleague Nathan Cohen demonstrated that some functioning of the immune system could be controlled by psychological factors (Ader & Cohen, 1981). They taught one group of rats to associate sweet-tasting saccharin with weakened immunity by giving them a drug that depressed the immune system after giving them saccharin. A control group received only the saccharin. Later, when both groups of rats were given only saccharin, the animals that had originally received saccharin and the drug still produced significantly fewer anti-bodies to foreign cells than those that had been given only saccharin. The learned association alone was sufficient to elicit suppression of the immune system, making them vulnerable to a range of diseases. The learning effect was so powerful that, later in the study, some of the rats died after drinking only the saccharin solution.

Until recently, it was assumed that immunological reactions – rapid production of antibodies to counterattack substances that invade and damage the organism – were automatic, biological processes that occurred without any involvement of the central nervous system. It is now clear that the vital immune system is under both psychological and biological control. In other words, our brains and bodies learn messages from the environment that can enhance or diminish our health. Usually this learning occurs unconsciously, but, by understanding how it works, psychological researchers can develop strategies for teaching us how to learn the right messages about resisting disease and to block the wrong ones about vulnerability to disease. Pharmaceutical companies will not be happy about these results. Periodic substitution of placebos for potent drugs could enable patients to maintain therapeutic effects with only minimal levels of medication and much reduced side effects. It is possible that, soon, modern medicine will be applying basic principles of learning theory to help us teach our bodies how to stay healthy.

THE STUDY OF LEARNING

PSYCHOLOGISTS HAVE LONG been interested in conditioning, or the ways in which events, stimuli and behaviour become associated with one another. Although the study of conditioning is historically rooted in the study of animal behaviour, research over the last half century shows that the principles of conditioning can also be applied to humans, with some important points of departure between ourselves and other species in this respect also having been noted (Lowe *et al*, 1978; Lowe & Horne, 1985).

Psychologists have explored two basic types of conditioning: **classical conditioning** and **operant conditioning**. In classical conditioning, one stimulus becomes associated with a second in such a way that the latter takes on some of the properties of the first and can thereafter elicit responses similar to those produced by the initial stimulus but notably can do so in its absence – indeed when it is no longer being paired with the original stimulus. Thus, a stimulus previously unassociated with another, comes to likewise be able to predict reliably the occurrence of a particular response. To return to our opening example, ingestion of the drug (initial or 'first' stimulus) – and later the placebo ('second' stimulus) – became *associated* with the absence of physiological symptoms (i.e. the 'response') related to high blood pressure. The placebo was a stimulus that came to influence bodily changes that previously had been produced only by the drug. In operant conditioning, behaviour becomes associated with its *consequences*. For people addicted to smoking, inhaling cigarette smoke is associated with a pleasurable sensation and the reactions of the nervous system are associated with the nicotine. It is difficult to break this habit because of these conditioned associations as well as the physiological dependence on the drug's direct effect – when a smoker has gone without a cigarette for a long period, smoking will relieve negative withdrawal symptoms. The behavioural act of smoking gets conditioned to both the learned pleasurable sensations and the reduction of the negative symptoms associated with withdrawal. Cigarette smoking thus becomes a learned psychological and physiological addiction.

In this chapter, we will examine the ways researchers have studied these two kinds of conditioning and the conclusions their empirical investigations have drawn about how we learn important information that helps us to survive and prosper. We will also examine a growing body of evidence that shows the complexity of what we assume to be simple kinds of learning. Finally, we will note how the procedures used to study the learning process have become powerful tools also used to investigate the effects of many different variables on behaviour and mental processes.

Before we begin our study of learning in earnest, let us consider the significance of learning from an evolutionary perspective. Learning is as much a product of our genetic endowment as any other phenotype. Similar to physical phenotypes, learning is influenced by experience: that is, nature does not bequeath us a fixed tendency to learn only certain things. Instead, we inherit a capacity for learning. Whether that capacity is realised – and to what extent – depends on the individual and on environmental opportunities. While most of us have similar capacities for learning, we learn different things and in different degrees because of our unique individual life experiences. Sociobiologist David Barash expressed the matter eloquently when he wrote, 'It may well be true that we are born able to lead a thousand different lives, but it is no less true that we die having lived just one' (1982).

There can be little doubt that our capacity for learning is what separates us from our fellow creatures. The capacity for learning varies among animal species according to their genetic blueprint and with the availability of environmental affordances that enable it to occur (Timberlake, 1993; Mayr, 1974). Some creatures, however, such as reptiles and amphibians, benefit less than others from interactions with the environment. For them life is more of a series of stimulus-response patterns than of behavioural changes occurring as a function of experience. Their survival depends on living in a relatively constant habitat in which their responses to specific environmental events get them what is needed or away from what must be avoided. For creatures higher on the evolutionary ladder, such as monkeys and humans, genes play much less of a role in determining specific behaviour–environment interactions and allow for greater plasticity, or variability, in learning. These animate creatures are more equipped to learn according to the ways in which their behaviour produces changes in their environment.

Since the turn of the century, as Le Ny (1985) has pointed out, both psychologists working in Europe and the United States have been fascinated by learning. In all likelihood this is because it reflects the democratic and capitalistic ideology that people can shape their lives largely by their actions and endeavours. Since learning theory is posited upon the assumption that people's behaviour can change via experience, essentially they are conceived therein as not being ultimately limited by factors such as biology, family history or social conditions. Rather, people are viewed as being autonomous entities, able to a great degree to aspire to better lives, regardless of their origins. It is perhaps no coincidence, then, that the principles of, for example, operant conditioning – of behaviour being functionally related to its consequences – were elaborated from within the context provided by contemporary capitalist societies, these highly individualist cultures stressing personal rather than social responsibility for behaviour and that the 'delivery' of rewards (particularly of a financial kind) must always be made contingent upon prior 'work' in the form of actions and performance (Kim et al, 1994). Ironically, however, reappraisal of such theorising reveals it to be also highly 'social' in its account of the human condition in that it stresses the importance at core of contextual and environmental influences upon behaviour (Blackman, 1991; Richelle, 1993). Psychologists all over the world have realised that learning is linked to the development of both adaptive and maladaptive behaviours. The same person who learned how to use the rules of logic could equally learn to be superstitious, develop phobias and adopt the irrational beliefs which form the basis of some mental disorders. So, at the heart of much that is human nature – for better or for worse – is the psychology of learning.

What is Learning?

The process of **learning** can be said to have occurred when a relatively permanent change in behaviour or behaviour potential has been produced by experience. Let us look more closely at the three critical parts of this definition.

A change in behaviour or behaviour potential

It is obvious that learning has taken place when you are able to demonstrate the results, such as driving a car or earning a high score on a test. Learning is not observed directly but is inferred from changes in observable behaviour. Learning is apparent from improvements in your **performance**. Cohen (1984) calls this **procedural learning** which can be understood in terms of Ryle's (1949) concept of 'knowing how', referring to the tacit ability to perform skilled actions. Often, however, your performance does not show everything that you have learned. The test questions may be unfair, or you may do poorly because test anxiety interferes. When your motivation is either very weak or very strong, performance may not be a good indicator of learning. Sometimes, too, you have acquired general attitudes such as an appreciation of modern art or an understanding of Eastern philosophy, that may not be apparent in your measurable actions. Cohen (1984) calls this **declarative learning** which can be aligned with Ryle's (1949) concept of 'knowing that', referring to factual knowledge as represented within consciousness. In such instances, you have learned a potential for behaviour change because you have learned attitudes and values that can influence what you do – for example, the kind of books you read or the way you spend your leisure time. Learning involves change in behaviour potential because we may know and learn much that does not show up in specific performances. This is an example of the declarative-procedural learning distinction – the difference between what has been learned as knowledge and what is expressed in overt behaviour in terms of performance. It is sometimes also summarily referred to as the **learning-performance distinction**.

From a behavioural perspective, overt performance is the primary index of learning. From a cognitive standpoint, however, learning has been conceptualised in terms of information-processing and as the general betterment of cognitive capacities (Bower & Hilgard, 1981). Thus, as learning theorists we may also wish to discover, for example, what infants or animals know in declarative terms when they cannot tell us, what mental patients know when they will not tell us and what shy people know when they are too anxious to tell us. As researchers, psychologists have devised special testing procedures to make external, observable and measurable the silent cognitive knowledge and covert learning that lie hidden within an organism. Indeed, it is the creative task of most psychological researchers to find ways of measuring and quantifying external indices of internal changes within the organisms they study.

Whilst learning is not observed directly but is inferred from changes in observable behaviour, we should be careful, however, not to infer learning from all changes in behaviour or behaviour potential. Sometimes behaviour changes occur for reasons other than learning. Some changes are due to physical maturation or the development of the brain as the organism ages. Other changes occur because of disease, illness, brain damage or the effects of drugs. Similarly, you must have noticed that your performance in many areas is lowered by fatigue, boredom and anxiety, while it is boosted by encouraging reactions of team-mates, an inspirational pep talk and especially attractive incentives. These biological and motivational variables affect performance of what has been learned but not learning itself.

A relatively permanent change

To qualify as learned, a change in behaviour or behaviour potential must be relatively permanent. Once you learn to swim, you will probably always be able to do so. Some changes in behaviour, however, are transitory and not learned. For example, your pupils dilate or contract as the brightness of light changes. This change in behaviour is a reflex that is dependent on the effects a given stimulus has on your nervous system. On the other hand, much of your learning, especially knowledge of ideas, is eventually forgotten or changed by what you learn later; learned changes may not necessarily last forever.

A process based on experience

Learning can take place only through experience. Experience includes taking in information (and

evaluating and transforming it) and making responses that affect the environment. Psychologists are especially interested in discovering what aspects of behaviour can be changed through experience and how such changes come about. Some lasting changes in behaviour require a combination of experience and maturational readiness. For example, consider the timetable that determines when an infant is ready to crawl, stand, walk, run and be toilet trained. No amount of training or practice will produce those behaviours before the child has matured sufficiently.

Under most circumstances, learning can be said to have taken place when the three conditions we have outlined exist. However, sometimes it is not obvious to the person or observers that these conditions are present. For example, changes in physiological responses, such as those in the immune system, can only be monitored with technical equipment. Learning of a broad rather than specific nature – such as adopting a value system of respect for authority or love of one's country – is very difficult to measure. Finally, what constitutes experience varies from person to person. We say that prejudice is learned by experience, but that experience may consist of accepting biased views held by other people and not of personal negative contact with the targets of that prejudice. Similarly, a phobic fear of snakes, for example, may be learned but not based on actual experience with snakes. These exceptions or extensions of the definition of learning highlight the need for researchers to be precise when determining the conditions associated with different types of learning.

■ Behaviourism and Behaviour Analysis

Much of modern psychology's view of learning finds its roots in the work of **John Watson** (1878–1958). As you might recall from Chapter 1, Watson founded the school of psychology known as behaviourism. For nearly 50 years, American psychology was dominated by the behaviourist tradition expressed in Watson's 1913 article *Psychology as the Behaviourist Sees It*. Watson was influential in advancing the assumptions and methods of behaviour theory into many areas of psychological research – most notably, the field of learning. His early work on the way rats learn to solve mazes used a method that other researchers readily adopted; later, he adapted Ivan Pavlov's theory of conditional response as the unit of learned habit (which we will soon study). In perhaps his most influential work, *Psychology from the Standpoint of a Behaviourist*, Watson (1919) argued that

John Watson

introspection – verbal reports of sensations, images and feelings – was not an acceptable means of studying behaviour because it was too subjective. After all, psychology is a science and the hallmark of science is objective methodology. What, then, should be the subject matter of psychology? Watson's answer was observable behaviour. In Watson's words, 'States of consciousness, like the so-called phenomena of spiritualism, are not objectively verifiable and for that reason can never become data for science' (Watson, 1919). In Watson's view, then, behaviour – not mental states – was the only acceptable subject matter for psychology.

Watson's ideas had direct influence on a young man who went on to become one of the most famous psychologists of his time. **Burrhus Frederic Skinner** (1904–90) began his graduate study in psychology at Harvard after reading Watson's 1924 book *Behaviourism*. During his career, Skinner pioneered a new brand of behaviourism known as radical behaviourism. Skinner's complaint against internal states and mental events dealt not so much with their legitimacy as data as with their legitimacy as causes of behaviour (Skinner, 1990). In Skinner's view, mental events, such as thinking and imaging, do not cause behaviour. Rather, they are examples of behaviour that are caused by environmental stimuli. Suppose that we deprive a pigeon of food for 24 hours, place it in an apparatus where it can obtain food by pecking a small disc and find that it soon does. Skinner would say that the bird's behaviour is explained by food deprivation, an event that was manipulated environmentally. He would also say that it adds nothing to our account to say that the bird pecked the disc because it was hungry or that it did so because it wanted to get the food. The animal's behaviour can be explained by an environmental event –

deprivation. The subjective feeling of hunger, which cannot be directly observed or measured, is not a cause of the behaviour but the result of deprivation. So, too, the behaviour of pecking the disc with its consequence of getting food is a result of the initial deprivation followed by the consequences on the environment of the animal's actions.

Behaviourism serves as the philosophical cornerstone of behaviour analysis, the area of psychology that focuses on discovering environmental determinants of learning and behaviour. In general, behaviour analysts argue that human nature can be fully understood only by using extensions of the methods and principles of natural science – especially physics. The task is to discover the regularities in human action that are universal, occurring to all types of people and other animal species under comparable situations. Although experience changes people's actions, the actual changes follow orderly principles. Identifying these principles will achieve the primary goal of behaviour analysis: to explain behaviour in terms of its controlling variables. It is the relationship between behaviour and environmental events and not the relationship between behaviour and mental events that concerns the behaviourists. The causes of behaviour are found solely in the environment.

Behaviour analysts approach their work with two basic assumptions: (a) learning is largely due to the processes involved in classical and operant conditioning and (b) the behaviour of humans and other animal species can be explained by the same

INTERIM SUMMARY

Learning may be defined as a relatively permanent change in behaviour or behaviour potential based on experience. Our capacity for learning depends upon both our genetic heritage and the nature of our environment. The study of learning has been dominated by the behaviouristic approach as represented in the work of Watson, Pavlov and, more recently, Skinner. Behaviourism serves as the philosophical bedrock of behaviour analysis, the area of psychology that focuses on discovering the environmental determinants of learning and behaviour. Behaviour analysts operate under two general assumptions: first, learning can be explained according to the processes involved in classical and operant conditioning; second, the behaviour of all organisms can be described by the same general laws of learning. Behaviour analysis has recently come under attack from psychologists who have shown that learning is determined both by biological and cognitive factors in addition to environmental ones.

general laws of learning. First, the two types of conditioning are sufficient to explain most or all of human and animal behaviour. Second, in the language of classical and operant conditioning, learning occurs under two conditions: (a) when two environmental stimuli coincide so that the presence of one reliably predicts the presence of the other and (b) when behaviour produces a change in the organism's environment.

Although the behaviouristic position has yielded many valuable explanations of human nature, we will see that it has been challenged by other psychologists who insist on keeping a thinking brain and a rational mind in control of the behaving body.

CLASSICAL CONDITIONING: LEARNING PREDICTABLE SIGNALS

In the story that began our chapter, we saw how the body can become conditioned to respond to a novel stimulus based on an association of the latter with a pre-existing stimulus event. The beneficial effects of a drug became associated with the act of taking a particular pill, even when that pill contained no medically active ingredients. This type of conditioning is known as **classical conditioning**, a form of basic learning in which one stimulus or event comes to predict the occurrence of another stimulus or event. What is learned is a new association between an originally neutral stimulus and an existing response by pairing the neutral stimulus (which did not previously elicit the target response) with a stimulus that was already able to produce the response by itself. Following associative conditioning then, the formerly neutral stimulus elicits a response that is similar – if not identical – to the original response. Thus, classical conditioning is about stimulus *substitution*: one stimulus takes on the properties of another via association, so can be substituted for it and elicit the same response. Such simple pairings of stimulus events are experienced in our everyday environments and have

significant implications for us both of a social and therapeutic kind (Thomas & O'Callaghan, 1981).

Pavlov's Surprising Discovery

The Russian physiologist **Ivan Pavlov** (1849–1936) is credited with discovering the basic principles of classical conditioning. Pavlov did not set out to study classical conditioning or any other psychological phenomenon. He happened upon classical conditioning while conducting research on digestion, research for which he won a Nobel Prize in 1904.

Pavlov had devised a technique to study digestive processes in dogs by implanting tubes in their glands and digestive organs to divert bodily secretions to containers outside their bodies so that the secretions could be measured and analysed. To produce these secretions, Pavlov's assistants put meat powder into the dogs' mouths. After repeating this procedure a number of times, Pavlov observed an unexpected behaviour in his dogs – they salivated before the powder was put in their mouths! They would start salivating at the mere sight of the food and later, at the sight of the assistant who brought the food or even at the sound of the assistant's footsteps. Indeed, any stimulus that regularly preceded the presentation of food came to elicit salivation. Quite by accident, Pavlov had discovered that the environmental control of behaviour can be changed as a result of two stimuli becoming associated with each other.

To Pavlov, this finding did not make sense, at least from a purely physiological point of view. After all, why should stimuli unrelated to a given stimulus (eating) come to elicit the same kind of behaviour (salivation) that the stimulus (eating) does? Salivating to footstep sounds had no apparent survival value, for example. Pavlov believed that other principles had to be at work. It has been said that 'chance favours the prepared mind', and Pavlov was ready to realise the significance of these 'psychic secretions', as he called them. He ignored the advice of the great physiologist

To study classical conditioning, Pavlov placed his dogs in a restraining apparatus. The dogs were then presented with a neutral stimulus, such as a tone. Through its association with food, the neutral stimulus became a conditional stimulus, eliciting salivation.

of the time, Charles Sherrington, that he should abandon his 'foolish' investigation. Pavlov, at that point a distinguished, middle-aged physiologist, became consumed by his unusual finding. He abandoned his work on digestion and in so doing changed the course of psychology forever (Pavlov, 1928).

The behaviour Pavlov studied was the reflex. A **reflex** is an unlearned response, such as salivation, pupil contraction, knee jerks or eye blinking, that is naturally elicited by specific stimuli that have biological relevance for the organism. Simply put, a reflex is an elicited behaviour that promotes biological adaptation to a changing environment. For example, salivation, the reflex Pavlov studied, helps digestion. After conditioning, organisms make reflexive responses to new stimuli having no such original biological relevance for them.

Pavlov knew that, in order to discover what was causing his dogs to salivate, he would have to manipulate various aspects of his experimental setting and observe what effects, if any, would follow. His strategy was elegant and simple. He first placed a dog in a restraining harness. At regular intervals, a tone was sounded and the dog was given a small amount of food. As you might imagine, the dog's first reaction to the tone was only an orienting response – the dog pricked its ears and moved its head to locate the source of the sound. However, with repeated pairings of the tone and the food, the orienting response stopped and salivation began. What Pavlov observed in his earlier research was no accident, the phenomenon could be replicated under controlled conditions. A neutral stimulus – such as the tone – when paired with another, more relevant stimulus – such as food – will eventually elicit a response similar to the original reflex – such as salivation.

The main features of Pavlov's classical conditioning procedure are illustrated in *Figure 7.1*. Any stimulus, such as food, that naturally elicits a reflexive behaviour is called an **unconditional stimulus** (UCS) because learning is not a necessary condition for the stimulus to control the behaviour. The behaviour elicited by the unconditional stimulus is called the **unconditional response** (UCR). During conditioning trials, a neutral stimulus, such as a tone, is repeatedly paired with the unconditional stimulus so that it predictably follows the neutral stimulus. After several trials, the tone is presented alone. Now it elicits the same response as the UCS does – in this case, salivation. The tone stimulus has acquired some of the properties to influence behaviour that were originally limited to the unconditional stimulus. The neutral stimulus paired with the unconditional stimulus is now called the **conditional stimulus** (CS) because its effectiveness in eliciting behaviour is conditional upon its

FIGURE 7.1	BASIC FEATURES OF CLASSICAL CONDITIONING

Before conditioning, the unconditional stimulus (UCS) naturally elicits the unconditional response (UCR). A neutral stimulus, such as a tone, has no eliciting effect. During conditioning, the neutral stimulus is paired with the UCS. Through its association with the UCS, the neutral stimulus becomes a conditional stimulus (CS) and elicits a conditional response (CR) that is similar to the UCR.

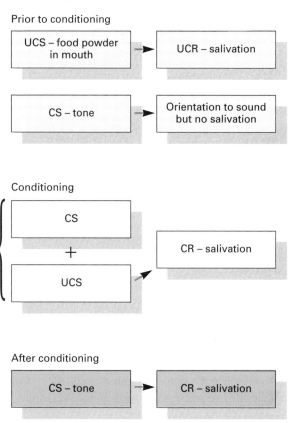

association with the UCS. The reflexive behaviour elicited by the CS is called the **conditional response** (CR). In other words, nature provides the UCS–UCR connections, but the learning produced by classical conditioning creates the CS–CR connection.

Pavlov's careful laboratory experiments showed how otherwise neutral stimuli could come to exert control over reflexive behaviour. He used many stimuli, such as metronome ticking, lights and tones, to demonstrate that virtually any of them could become substitutes for biologically significant unconditional stimuli. Pavlov's work was important because it demonstrated a new behavioural phenomenon. However, Pavlov was not content to stop his research there. For the remainder of his life, he continued to search for the variables that influence classically conditioned behaviour. His research uncovered a number of important processes involved in classical conditioning, most of which are still being studied by modern psychologists. Classical conditioning is also called *Pavlovian conditioning* because of Pavlov's discovery of the phenomenon of conditioning and his dedication to tracking down the variables that influence it. It is to these phenomena that we now turn.

◼ Basic Processes

What conditions are optimal for classical conditioning? This general question has been asked in many different ways and answered in literally thousands of different studies. The answers provide clues to the fundamental processes underlying learning. In this section, we will review what is known about these processes.

Acquisition

In general, the CS and UCS must be paired several times before the CS reliably elicits a CR. **Acquisition** refers to the process at the beginning of a classical conditioning experiment by which the CR is first elicited and gradually increases in frequency over repeated trials. The far left panel in *Figure 7.2* shows the acquisition phase of a hypothetical experiment. At first, very few CRs are elicited by the CS. With continued CS–UCS pairings, however, the CR is elicited with increasing frequency and a conditioned response is acquired by the organism.

In studying conditioning, an experimenter may vary several aspects of Pavlov's procedure, such as the number of trials an organism receives, the time interval between successive trials, the time interval

between the CS and UCS and the intensity or quality of either or both stimuli. Variations in these and other aspects of the situation are the independent variables. The four major dependent variables that index the effectiveness of the conditioning are: (a) the amplitude (or the strength) of the CR; (b) the latency (or time delay) between when the CS is presented and the CR is made; (c) the rate at which (or how often) the CR is elicited; (d) and the persistence of the CR (or how long the CR continues to be elicited by the CS) in the absence of the UCS. This last measure is very important in conditioning; it is also known as **resistance to extinction**.

In conditioning, as in telling a good joke, timing is critical. The CS and UCS must be presented close enough in time to be perceived by the organism as being related. Four temporal patterns between the two stimuli have been studied, as shown in *Figure 7.3*. The most widely used type of conditioning is called forward conditioning, in which the CS comes on prior to and stays on until the UCS is presented, overlapping it. In trace conditioning, the CS is turned off just before the UCS is presented. Trace refers to the memory that the organism must have of the CS which is no longer present when the UCS appears. In simultaneous conditioning, both the CS and UCS are presented at the same time. Finally, in the case of backward conditioning, the CS is presented after the UCS.

Conditioning is usually better with a short interval between the CS and UCS. The range of time intervals between the CS and UCS that will produce the best conditioning depends upon the response being conditioned. For motor and skeletal responses, such as eye blinks, a short interval of a second or less is best. For visceral responses, such as heart rate and salivation, however, longer intervals of five to 15 seconds work best. Conditioned fear usually requires longer intervals of many seconds or even minutes to develop.

FIGURE 7.2	ACQUISITION, EXTINCTION AND SPONTANEOUS RECOVERY IN CLASSICAL CONDITIONING

During acquisition (CS + UCS), the strength of the CR increases rapidly. During extinction, when the UCS no longer follows the CS, the strength of the CR drops to zero. The CR may reappear after a brief rest period, even when the UCS is still not presented. The reappearance of the CS is called 'spontaneous recovery'.

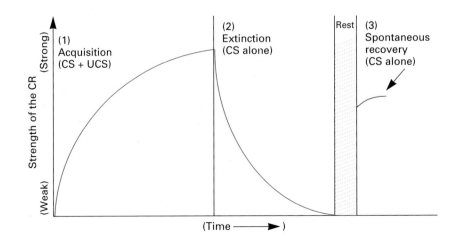

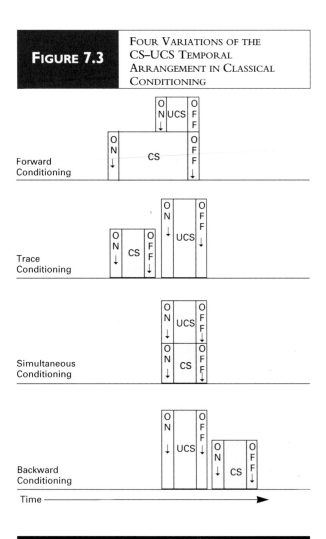

FIGURE 7.3 FOUR VARIATIONS OF THE CS–UCS TEMPORAL ARRANGEMENT IN CLASSICAL CONDITIONING

Forward Conditioning

Trace Conditioning

Simultaneous Conditioning

Backward Conditioning

Time ⟶

Conditioning is generally poor with a simultaneous procedure and very poor with a backward procedure. Evidence of backward conditioning may appear after a few pairings but disappear with extended training as the animal learns that the CS is followed by a period free of the UCS. In both cases, conditioning is weak because the CS does not actually signal the onset of the UCS.

Conditioning occurs most rapidly when the CS stands out against the many other stimuli that are also present. Thus, a stimulus will be more readily noticed the more intense it is and the more it contrasts with other stimuli. Either a strong, novel stimulus in an unfamiliar situation or a strong, familiar stimulus in a novel context leads to good conditioning (Kalat, 1974; Lubow *et al*, 1976). According to the Rescorla and Wagner (1972) model of associative learning, the feature of the CS that most facilitates conditioning is its informativeness – its reliability in predicting the onset of the UCS. Thus, the key to developing a strong conditioned response is to increase the signal-to-noise ratio of the CS by making it a stronger signal than all other competing events – background stimuli or irrelevant noise.

Extinction and spontaneous recovery

Once a conditional response is acquired, does it last forever? When the UCS no longer follows the CS, the CR becomes weaker over time and eventually stops occurring. When the CR no longer occurs in the presence of the CS (and absence of UCS), **extinction** is said to have occurred (see *Figure 7.2*, second panel from left). Conditional responses, then, are not necessarily a permanent aspect of the organism's behavioural repertoire. However, the CR will reappear in a weak form when the CS is presented alone again (see *Figure 7.2*, far right panel). Pavlov referred to this sudden reappearance of the CR after a rest period, or time-out, without further exposure to the UCS as **spontaneous recovery**.

With further postextinction training (further pairings of CS and US), the CR gets rapidly stronger. This more rapid relearning is an instance of **savings**: less time is required to reacquire the response than to acquire it originally, so some of the original conditioning must be retained by the organism even after experimental extinction appears to have eliminated the CR. In other words, extinction has only weakened its performance, not wiped out the original learning.

Stimulus generalisation

Once a CR has been conditioned to a particular CS, similar stimuli may also elicit the response. For example, if conditioning was to a high frequency tone, a lower tone may also elicit the response. A child bitten by a big dog is likely to respond with fear even to smaller dogs. This automatic extension of responding to stimuli that have never been paired with the original UCS is called **stimulus generalisation**. The more similar the new stimulus is to the original CS, the stronger the response will be. When response strength is measured for each of a series of increasingly dissimilar stimuli along a given dimension, a generalisation gradient, or slope, is found.

Because important stimuli rarely occur in exactly the same form every time in nature, stimulus generalisation builds in a similarity safety factor by extending the range of learning beyond the original specific experience. With this feature, new but comparable events can be recognised as having the same meaning or behavioural significance despite apparent differences. For example, a predator can make a different sound or be seen from a different angle and still be recognised and responded to quickly.

Stimulus discrimination

Though stimuli similar to the original CS may elicit a similar response, it is possible for an organism to respond only to one particular CS and not to respond to other stimuli, regardless of how similar they are. **Stimulus discrimination** is the process by which an organism learns to respond differently to stimuli that are distinct from the CS on some dimension (for example, differences in hue or in pitch). An organism's discrimination among similar stimuli (tones of 1,000, 1,200, and 1,500 cps, for example) is sharpened with discrimination training in which only one of them (1,200 cps, for example) predicts the UCS and in which the others are repeatedly presented without it. Early in conditioning, stimuli similar to the CS will elicit a similar response, though not quite as strong. As discrimination training proceeds, the responses to the other, dissimilar stimuli weaken: the organism gradually learns which event-signal predicts the onset of the UCS and which signals do not.

For optimum adaptation, the initial perceptual tendency to generalise and respond to all somewhat similar stimuli needs to give way to discrimination among them, with responses only to those that are, in fact, followed by the UCS. Ideally, then, conditioning is a process in which discrimination ultimately wins over generalisation; but it is a balancing act between these two counteracting tendencies of being over-responsive and over-selective.

■ Significance of Classical Conditioning

Pavlov's work helps us understand significant everyday behaviour. Many of the emotions we experience and many of our attitudes can be explained by classical conditioning. Let us take a closer look at how classical conditioning can help us understand emotion and attitude development.

Fear conditioning

Pavlov's conditioning with meat powder is an example of **appetitive conditioning** – conditioning in which UCS is of positive value to an organism – related to its appetites. However, classical conditioning may also involve an aversive, painful UCS. Aversive conditioning occurs when the CS predicts the presentation of an aversive UCS, such as electrical shock. An organism's natural response to such stimuli is reflexive behaviour that reduces the intensity of the

UCS or removes it entirely. Through its association with the UCS, the CS also comes to elicit these kinds of responses when it is presented later independently of the UCS. In eyelid conditioning, a puff of air to the eye (UCS) forces an eyeblink or lid closure (UCR). When a tone (CS) is paired with the airpuff, it soon elicits the eyeblink (CR).

This simple procedure for classically conditioning the eyelid closure response has been used in the study of the neurobiological circuits of the brain systems involved in each of the components of the overall response – response to the airpuff, to the tone and to the stored memory trace of the CS–UCS connection as conditioning develops (Thompson, 1986). It is also being used to compare the effects of age differences in learning and memory of humans, rabbits and other mammals (Woodruf-Pak & Thompson, 1988).

An important discovery from aversive conditioning studies has been that the organism learns not only a specific conditional muscle response but a generalised fear reaction as well. The subject learns a specific response to a stimulus and re-evaluates the previously neutral stimulus as affectively negative. Withdrawal from the negative stimulus is accompanied by reactions of the autonomic nervous system – changes in heart rate, respiration and electrical resistance of the skin (the galvanic skin response, or GSR). These changes become part of an overall conditional fear response.

Interestingly, when strong fear is involved, conditioning may take place after only one pairing of a neutral stimulus with the UCS. Traumatic events in our lives that may occur only once can condition us to respond with strong physical, emotional and cognitive reactions that are highly resistant to extinction. Conditional fear is often easy to acquire

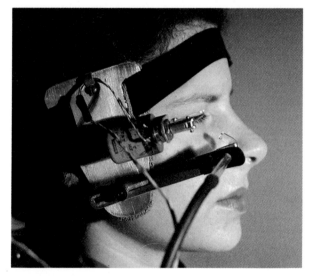

In eyelid conditioning, a puff of air to the eye (UCS) forces an eyeblink or lid closure (UCR). When a tone (CS) is paired with the airpuff, it soon elicits the eyeblink (CR).

and difficult to extinguish. For example, a man who was in a bad car accident during a rain storm, every time now it begins to rain while he is driving, becomes panic-stricken, sometimes to the extent that he has to pull over and wait for the storm to pass. Occasionally, he crawls into the back and lies on the car floor, face down, until the rain subsides.

A classic study of conditional fear in a human being was conducted by psychologists **John Watson** and **Rosalie Rayner** with an infant named Albert.

Watson and Rayner (1920) trained Albert to fear a white rat he had initially liked by pairing its appearance with an aversive UCS – a loud gong struck just behind him. The unconditional startle response and the emotional distress to the noxious noise was the basis of Albert's learning to react with fear to the appearance of the white rat. His fear was developed in just seven conditioning trials. The emotional conditioning was then extended to behavioural conditioning when Albert learned to escape from the feared stimulus. The infant's learned fear then generalised to other furry objects, such as a rabbit, a dog and even a Father Christmas mask! In the early days of psychology, careful attention to possible harmful effects of experiments on subjects was sometimes lacking. In fact, Albert's mother, a wet nurse at the hospital where the study was conducted, took him away before the researchers could remove the experimentally conditioned fear. So we do not know whatever happened to Little Albert (Harris, 1979).

We know now that conditioned fear is highly resistant to extinction. Even if the overt components of muscle reaction eventually disappear, the reactions of the autonomic nervous system continue. This leaves an individual vulnerable to arousal by the old signals, sometimes without awareness of why the reaction is occurring. Conditional fear reactions may persist for years, even when the original frightening UCS is never again experienced, as shown in the following study.

During World War II, the signal used to call sailors to battle stations aboard US Navy ships was a gong sounding at the rate of 100 rings a minute. To personnel on board, the sound was associated with danger; thus, it became a CS for strong emotional arousal. Fifteen years after the war, a study was conducted on the emotional reactions of hospitalised Navy and Army veterans to a series of 20 different auditory stimuli. Although none of the sounds were current signals for danger, the sound of the old 'call to battle stations' still produced strong emotional arousal in the Navy veterans who had previously experienced that association. Their response to the former danger signal, as determined by galvanic-skin-response measures, was significantly greater than that of the Army veterans (Edwards & Acker, 1962). Such learning, then, may in part explain the prevalence and persistence decades later of somatic and anxiety-related disorders amongst ex-combatants and prisoners of World War II as documented by numerous studies (Rahe, 1988; Venn & Guest, 1991; Sutker et al, 1993).

All of us retain learned readiness to respond with fear, joy, or other emotions to old signals (often from our childhood) that are not appropriate or valid in our current situation. When we are unaware of their origins, these once reasonable fear reactions may be interpreted as anxiety and we get more upset because we seem to be reacting irrationally without adequate cause or reason (Dollard & Miller, 1950). Aversive conditioning has been used as part of therapeutic programmes to stop undesirable behaviour, as we shall see in Chapter 15.

Conditioned social behaviour

Many of our attitudes have been formed by conditioning processes that take place without our awareness (Staats & Staats, 1958). Attitudes are often defined as an individual's learned tendencies to respond behaviourally, emotionally and cognitively to particular target stimuli, such as people, ideas or objects, with a positive or negative evaluation (Fishbein & Ajzen, 1975). Stimuli may acquire their power to elicit attitudinal responses by being paired with UCSs that elicit emotional or affective responses. Words, symbols and pictures that naturally elicit strong positive responses will become conditional arousers of similarly positive reactions. This principle has been applied by advertisers and promoters who want us to like their products enough that we will purchase them.

In one research study, researchers demonstrated that pairing food words with meaningless trigrams such as 'jik' or 'zad', led to attitudes toward the trigrams that were more positive among college students who were food deprived than among those who had eaten (Staats et al, 1972). In another study, trigrams were paired with items that were of negative interest to students. The students then evaluated these trigrams as unpleasant (Staats et al, 1973). A large body of research shows that social behaviour – aggression, altruism, persuasion, co-operation and competition – can be studied as a response system formed through classical conditioning (Lott & Lott, 1985; Weiss et al, 1971).

The ability of neutral stimuli to acquire through

Advertisers understand how to use pictures associated with strong UCSs that elicit strong positive responses.

classical conditioning was due to the mere pairing of the CS and the UCS. In his view, to classically condition a response the CS and the UCS must occur close together in time, that is, be **temporally contiguous**. Pavlov's theory dominated classical conditioning until the mid 1960s when **Robert Rescorla** (1966) conducted a very telling experiment using dogs as subjects. Rescorla placed dogs in one side of a shuttlebox (see *Figure 7.4*). Occasionally they would be given unsignalled electric shocks through the grid floor. Rescorla had trained his animals to jump the barrier that divided the box in half. If they did not jump, they received a shock; if they did jump, the shock was postponed. Rescorla used the frequency with which dogs jumped the barrier as a measure of fear conditioning. The more often they jumped the greater the amount of fear conditioning.

When the dogs were jumping across the barrier regularly, Rescorla randomly divided his subjects into two groups and subjected them to another training procedure. Each group was exposed to a different CS–UCS relation where the CS was a tone and the UCS was a shock. To the random group, the UCS was delivered randomly and independently of the CS. Thus, the UCS was as likely to be delivered in the absence of the CS as it was in its presence, which means that the CS had no predictive value. For the Contingency Group, however, the UCS always followed the CS. Thus, for this group, the sounding of the tone was a reliable predictor of the delivery of the shock.

Once this training was complete, the dogs were

conditioning the power to elicit strong responses automatically makes us all vulnerable to our emotions and attitudes. Although there are some limitations to this process – to be discussed later – the tremendous implications of the ease with which conditioning takes place should not escape you. A very powerful conclusion has emerged from the many years of psychological research on conditioning: virtually any stimulus you can perceive can be associated with almost any response so that you learn to value, desire, or fear the stimulus. (For notable exceptions, see the last section of this chapter on biological constraints.) We learn to use information about impending events to help us make preparatory responses; we prepare for the future on the basis of our conditioning history. Even our immune system, as you will recall from our opening story in this chapter, is influenced by classical conditioning and conditioning can kill, as shown in the Close-up on the next page.

FIGURE 7.4	A SHUTTLEBOX

Rescorla used the frequency with which dogs jumped over the barrier as a measure of fear conditioning.

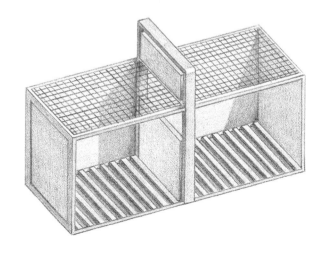

■ The Role of Contingency and Informativeness

So far, we have described classical conditioning, but we have not yet explained it. Pavlov believed that

A man's body lay in an inner-city alley, a half-empty syringe dangling from his arm. Cause of death? The coroner called it an overdose, but the man had ordinarily shot up far greater doses than the one that had supposedly killed him. This sort of incident had happened before, and it baffled investigators. How could a regular user with high drug tolerance die of an overdose when he did not even get a full hit?

Psychologist **Shepard Siegel** thought something else might be happening. Studies of rats had convinced him that tolerance – decreased responsiveness to a drug after repeated use – involved more than just physiological changes in the brain. He thought learning – an association of the drug with the physical setting and rituals normally associated with its use – also contributed to tolerance.

Some time ago, Pavlov (1927) and later his colleague Bykov (1957) pointed out that tolerance to opiates can develop when an individual anticipates the pharmacological action of a drug. Perhaps with advance notice – provided by the conditional stimulus associated with the ritual of injection – the body somehow learns to protect itself by preventing the drug from having its usual effect. In settings ordinarily associated with drug use, the body physiologically prepares itself for the drug's expected effects. Over time, larger doses are needed to achieve the desired effect.

In one study, Siegel classically conditioned rats to expect heroin injections (UCS) in one setting (CS) and dextrose (sweet sugar) solution injections in a different setting (CS) (Siegel *et al*, 1982). In the first phase of training, all rats developed heroin tolerance. On the test day, all subjects received a larger-than-usual dose of heroin – nearly twice the previous amount. Half of them received it in the setting where heroin was expected; the other half received it in the setting where dextrose solutions had been given during conditioning. More than twice as many rats died in the dextrose-solution setting when heroin was not expected as when it was expected in the usual heroin setting – 82 per cent versus 31 per cent! Those receiving heroin in the usual setting had valid expectations and were more prepared for this potentially dangerous situation, perhaps by initiating a physiological response that countered the drug's typical effects.

In order to find out if a similar process might operate in humans, Siegel and a colleague interviewed heroin addicts who had come close

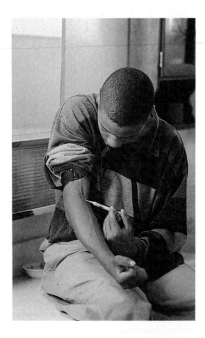

to death from supposed overdoses. In seven out of ten cases, the addicts had been shooting up in a new and unfamiliar setting (Siegel, 1984). Although this natural experiment provides no conclusive data, it suggests that a dose for which an addict has developed tolerance in one setting may become an overdose in an unfamiliar setting. Conditioned cues may be powerful elicitors of a learned tolerance response. Without this protective reaction, the drug's effects could be more potent than usual, increasing the addict's susceptibility to overdose and death.

FIGURE 7.5	THE ROLE OF CONTINGENCY IN CLASSICAL CONDITIONING

Rescorla showed that dogs trained under the contingent CS–UCS relation showed more jumping (and thus conditioned fear) than did dogs trained under the contiguous but noncontingent CS–UCS relation. The arrows indicate the onset and offset of the CS tone.

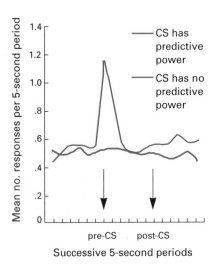

put back into the shuttlebox but this time with a twist. Now, the tone used in the second training procedure occasionally sounded, signalling shock. What would the dogs do? According to Rescorla, if Pavlov was correct, both groups of dogs should show about the same amount of conditioned fear in the presence of the tone – dogs in both groups should jump with about the same frequency because the temporal contiguity between the CS and UCS was the same for both groups. However, if classical conditioning is dependent upon a contingent CS–UCS relation in addition to contiguity, then dogs in the Contingency Group should jump more frequently than the other group.

Rescorla's results, shown in *Figure 7.5*, indicate that Pavlov's explanation of classical conditioning is inadequate. Dogs exposed to the contingent (predictable) CS–UCS relation jumped more frequently in the presence of the tone than did dogs exposed only to the contiguous (associated) CS–UCS relation. Thus, in addition to contiguity, it appears that the CS must reliably predict the occurrence of the UCS in order for classical conditioning to occur. This finding makes considerable sense (Rescorla, 1988). After all, in natural situations, where learning enables organisms to adapt to changes in their environment, stimuli come in clusters and not in neat, simple units as they do in traditional laboratory experiments. To survive, the animal must be able to detect which of all the available stimuli signal rewards and which signal danger.

Although Rescorla's work demonstrated that contingency plays a crucial role in classical conditioning, other researchers wondered if there was more to the story. One such researcher was **Leon Kamin**, who conducted an experiment equally as ingenious as that of Rescorla's (see *Figure 7.6*).

Kamin's study involved two groups of rats. The experimental group was first trained to press a lever in the presence of a tone (CS) to avoid shock (UCS). Next, a second CS – a light – was added; now the UCS was preceded by two CSs: the tone (CS) and the light (CS). The control group was exposed only to this sequence of tone-light-shock; it never experienced the tone alone as a predictor of shock delivery. Kamin then tested both groups of rats for fear conditioning to the light alone or to the tone alone. If contingency is sufficient to explain classical conditioning, then both groups of rats should have responded in equal amounts to the light and the tone.

Interestingly, that is not what Kamin found. The experimental rats responded to the tone but not the light, whereas control rats responded equally to both the tone and the light. Kamin explained his results in terms of the informativeness of the conditional

FIGURE 7.6	KAMIN'S PROCEDURE FOR PRODUCING THE BLOCKING EFFECT

Rats in the experimental group were trained to respond to a tone (CS_1). Next they were trained to both a tone (CS_1) and a light (CS_2). Rats in the control group were trained only to the compound light and tone (CS). When tested for conditioning to light alone and to tone alone, only the control rats responded to both stimuli. According to Kamin, experimental rats did not respond to the light because it contained no new information predicting the occurrence of the UCS. The tone's effect blocked the light's effect.

Experimental group		Control group
	Training Phase 1.	
CS_1		
UCS → CR		$\emptyset$
	Phase 2.	
CS_1		CS_1
CS_2		CS_2
UCS → CR		UCS → CR
	Testing	
CS_1 → CR		CS_1 → CR
CS_2 → No CR		CS_2 → CR

CS_1 = tone CS_2 = light

stimuli. For experimental rats, the previous conditioning to the tone in the first phase of the experiment, *blocked* any subsequent conditioning that could occur to the light. In other words, the previous experience with the tone overshadowed the significance of the light as a predictor of the UCS. From the rat's point of view, the light may as well not have existed; it provided no additional information beyond that already given by the tone. The ability of the first CS to reduce the informativeness of the second CS because of previous experience with the UCS is called **blocking**. For control rats, both the light and the tone were equally informative – the rats had no previous experience with either CS so that one would reduce the informativeness of the other.

Classical conditioning, then, is much more complex than Pavlov originally theorised. Simply pairing a neutral stimulus with a UCS will not result in classical conditioning. For a neutral stimulus to become a CS, it must satisfy two other criteria beside contiguity. First, according to Rescorla, it must reliably predict the occurrence of the CS (there must be a contingent relationship between the CS and the UCS). Second, the CS must also be informative. If two CSs are equally predictive, as was the case for Kamin's experimental rats, then the CS that is more informative will become the more potent CS. Kamin's study showed that once an organism learns about the UCS on the basis of one dependable signal, it does not bother to learn about other stimuli that are also consistently present, presumably because their information is redundant. The power of any particular neutral stimulus to become a CS thus depends on the presence of other stimuli that could also serve as potential signals.

It must be noted, however, that competing theories have emerged which have challenged the basis of the Rescorla's work as fully articulated within the later Rescorla and Wagner (1972) model. One factor that appears to be important for successful conditioning is whether or not subjects are familiar with the CS prior to conditioning. When a CS is novel then conditioning is rapid, but if it has been presented for a number of trials alone then conditioning initially is rather slow. According to several theorists, this slow conditioning is a consequence of subjects failing to attend to the CS. There is some debate, however, concerning the factors that govern the amount of attention a stimulus will receive. According to Wagner, any CS that is unexpected, such as one that is novel or occurs in a new context will receive attention and be learned about rapidly. In contrast, Pearce and Hall (1980) maintain that animals will attend to a stimulus if they are uncertain what it signals, but if the stimulus is followed reliably by some event then they will tend to

ignore it. Thus, this theory predicts that animals will ignore, and hence learn slowly not only about a stimulus that is followed by nothing, but also a stimulus that is followed repeatedly by the same UCS. Evidence in support of this latter prediction can be found in Hall and Pearce (1979).

More latterly, **John Pearce** (1987) has raised further objections to the Rescorla-Wagner model, arguing that it takes an essentially *elemental* approach to associative learning in which the separate components of the stimulus pairing are conceived as being individually predictive of the CR. Instead, he proposes a theory of conditioning in which the pairing and presentation of two stimuli is said to result internally in a *configural* representation of the pattern of this stimulation as a whole which then becomes associated as a unity with the CR.

Consider a discrimination in which food follows one stimulus, a tone (T), but not a simultaneous **compound** of a tone and a light (TL). According to Pearce's (1994) **configural theory**, this training will result in animals learning that the TL compound signals the absence of food, whereas the Rescorla-Wagner model predicts they will learn that it is the light (L) which signals the absence of food. The difference between these *configural* and *elemental* viewpoints can be readily observed by considering an experiment by Pearce and Wilson (1991), who first trained animals with the above discrimination prior to trials in which L was paired with food. According to an elemental viewpoint this should erase entirely the effects of the original training, and result in L exciting a CR. To test this prediction, Pearce and Wilson (1991) then exposed animals to the original discrimination where they found that responding during TL was rather weak. This finding should not occur, according to Rescorla and Wagner, because the light now serves as a signal for the presence, not the absence of food. In contrast, this finding can be readily explained by Pearce's (1994) configural theory: because the animals have learnt that the tone-light compound signals the absence of food in the first stage of the experiment, the training with the light by itself does not abolish this learning, and so they still show a weak CR during the compound (TL) in the final stage of the experiment. In more general terms, this result highlights that elemental theories predict much greater effects of **retroactive interference** (wherein associations are overwritten and unlearned as a result of later conditioning) than is often the case. Configural theories are less prone to this failing.

Notably, these developments reflect contemporaneous moves within learning theory since the 1960's away from accounts of conditioning in terms of overt behaviours and towards more cognitive models of associative learning (Mackintosh, 1994).

INTERIM SUMMARY

One widely used procedure for investigating learning, especially how organisms learn about the relationships between stimulus events in their environment, is classical conditioning. In this procedure, developed by Pavlov, a biologically significant stimulus, called an unconditional stimulus (UCS), elicits a reflex, called an unconditional response (UCR). A neutral stimulus that is then paired repeatedly with the UCS becomes a conditional stimulus (CS), which elicits a similar response, called the conditional response (CR). However, if the UCS no longer follows the CS, extinction, or disappearance, of the CR occurs. After a rest period, though, spontaneous recovery may occur – the CR returns when the CS is presented alone again. Stimuli similar to the CS also elicit the CR; this phenomenon is called stimulus generalisation. If these stimuli are not followed by the UCS, stimulus discrimination occurs – the organism stops responding to the irrelevant stimuli and responds only to the original CS. According to the results of Rescorla's and Kamin's research, for classical conditioning to occur, two criteria must be met. First, Rescorla's research showed there must be a contingent relation between the CS and UCS – the CS must reliably predict the occurrence of the UCS. Second, the CS also must be informative. If two CSs are equally predictive, as in Kamin's experiment, then the more informative CS will become the better predictor of the presentation of the UCS and responding will be directed toward only that CS. Despite these results, theoretical rivals have persisted, notably in the form of the Pearce–Hall model of associative learning and more latterly in terms of Pearce's configural theory. Classical conditioning is a powerful means by which we learn to respond emotionally to a host of desirable or fearful stimuli; it is also a way in which certain attitudes are formed.

■ OPERANT CONDITIONING: LEARNING ABOUT CONSEQUENCES

At about the same time that Pavlov in Russia was using classical conditioning to induce dogs to salivate to the sound of a bell, **Edward L. Thorndike** (1898) in America was watching cats trying to escape from puzzle boxes (see *Figure 7.7*). He reported his observations and inferences about the kind of learning he believed was taking place in his subjects:

When put into the box, the cat shows evident signs of discomfort and develops an impulse to escape from confinement. It tries to squeeze through any opening; it claws and bites at the bars or wire; it thrusts its paws out through any opening and claws at everything it reaches . . . It does not pay very much attention to the food outside (the reward for the hungry cat) but seems simply to strive instinctively to escape from confinement. The vigour with which it struggles is extraordinary. For eight or ten minutes it will claw and bite and squeeze incessantly . . . Whether the impulse to struggle be due to an instinctive reaction to confinement or to an association, it is likely to succeed in letting the cat out of the box. The cat that is clawing all over the box in its impulsive struggle will probably claw the string or loop or button so as to open the door. And gradually all the other unsuccessful impulses will be stamped out and the particular impulse leading to the successful act will be stamped in by the resulting pleasure, until, after many trials, the cat will, when put in the box, immediately claw the button or loop in a definite way (Thorndike, 1898).

What did Thorndike's cats learn that was different from what Pavlov's dogs had learned? According to Thorndike's procedure, learning was an association not between two stimuli but between stimuli in the situation and a response that a subject learned to

FIGURE 7.7	A THORNDIKE PUZZLE BOX

To get out of the puzzle box and obtain food, Thorndike's cat had to manipulate a mechanism that would release a weight that would then pull the door open.

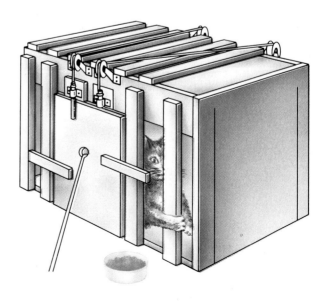

make: a stimulus-response (S-R) connection. Thorndike believed that responses repeatedly followed by reward brought satisfaction and were strengthened, or stamped in, while nonrewarded responses were weakened, or stamped out. Thorndike's conditioning procedure allowed an animal to respond freely, but only one of its responses would have a satisfying consequence.

◻ The Law of Effect

According to Thorndike's 'connectionist' theory, the learning of reinforced S-R connections occurs gradually and automatically in a mechanistic way as the animal experiences the consequences of its actions through blind trial-and-error. Gradually, the behaviours that have satisfying consequences increase in frequency; they eventually become the dominant response when the animal is placed in the puzzle box. Thorndike referred to this relationship between behaviour and its consequences as the **law of effect**.

The law of effect has an important conceptual parallel to natural selection in evolution (Skinner, 1981). For both, the environment acts as the agent of selection. In natural selection, the environment determines which genes become more frequent in future populations. Similarly, the law of effect describes how environmental changes produced by behaviour increase the frequency of that behaviour in the future. Behaviours leading to satisfying or rewarding consequences are selected; they are likely to occur more frequently in the future than behaviours leading to unsatisfying or punishing consequences.

Thorndike believed that the law of effect is also applicable to human learning. His ideas had a major impact on the educational psychology of his time, even though he believed that learning involved trial-and-error without conscious thought. By the 1950s, over a thousand research reports a year on factors influencing animal learning were being published. These researchers generally assumed that elementary processes of learning were conserved across species, which meant that, from the lowest to the highest level animal species, these processes are comparable in their basic features. Complex forms of learning represent combinations and elaborations of these simpler processes. The study of animal learning was easier and allowed greater control over relevant variables than did the study of human learning. In most cases, the ultimate hope was that this basic research with simpler animals would shed more light on the mysteries of human learning – on how we have earned the many habits that formed our behavioural repertoires.

◻ Experimental Analysis of Behaviour

Burrhus Frederic Skinner embraced Thorndike's view that environmental consequences influence the responses that precede them, but he rejected all assumptions about satisfaction and about S-R habits being learned and any interpretation that resorted to inferences about an organism's intentions, purposes, or goals. What an animal wants was not important.

A natural datum in a science of behaviour is the probability that a given bit of behaviour will occur at a given time. An experimental analysis deals with that probability in terms of frequency or rate of responding . . . The task of an experimental analysis is to discover all the variables of which probability of response is a function (Skinner, 1966).

The **experimental analysis of behaviour** means discovering, by systematic variation of stimulus

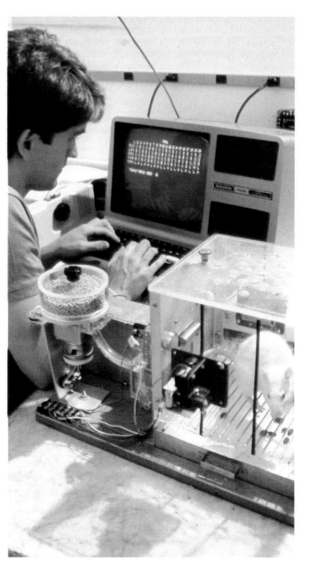

An operant conditioning laboratory

conditions, all the ways that various kinds of environmental conditions affect the probability that a given response will occur. Skinner's analysis is experimental rather than theoretical – theorists are guided by derivations and predictions about behaviour from their theories, but empiricists, such as Skinner, advocate the bottom-up approach, starting with the collection and evaluation of data within the context of an experiment. Skinner refused to make inferences about what happens inside an organism. No intervening variables are assumed; in his analysis inner conditions such as hunger are defined operationally, in terms of the procedures an experimenter can carry out – for example, deprivation of food for 24 hours. While approaching food and eating it can be observed and recorded, desire for food or pleasure at receiving it cannot.

To analyse behaviour experimentally, Skinner developed operant conditioning procedures in which he manipulated the consequences of an organism's behaviour in order to see what effect they had on subsequent behaviour. An **operant** is any behaviour that is emitted by an organism and can be characterised in terms of the observable effects it has on the environment. Literally, operant means affecting the environment, or operating on it (Skinner, 1938).

Operants are not elicited by specific stimuli as classically conditioned behaviours are. Pigeons peck, rats search for food, babies cry and coo, some people gesture while talking and others stutter or say 'like' and 'you know' frequently. The probability of these behaviours occurring in the future can be increased or decreased by manipulating the effects they have on the environment. Operant conditioning, then, modifies the probability of different types of operant behaviour as a function of the environmental consequences they produce.

Behaviour analysts manipulate contingencies of reinforcement to study behaviour. Usually, this manipulation occurs within the highly controlled environment of a special apparatus invented by Skinner: the *operant chamber* (Baron *et al*, 1991). *Figure 7.8* shows how the operant chamber works.

In many operant experiments, a cumulative recorder is used to record the animal's responding and delivery of reinforcers. Each response 'steps' a pen vertically across paper that is being rotated outward by a small moving drum. The greater the animal's response rate, the steeper the line drawn by the pen. Delivery of reinforcers is denoted by tiny hash marks drawn downward from this line.

FIGURE 7.8   OPERANT CHAMBER AND CUMULATIVE RECORDER

In the operant chamber typical of those used with rats, presses on the lever are followed by delivery of a food pellet. Each response moves the pen one step vertically along a sheet of moving paper. The steeper the response record, the greater the rate of responding.

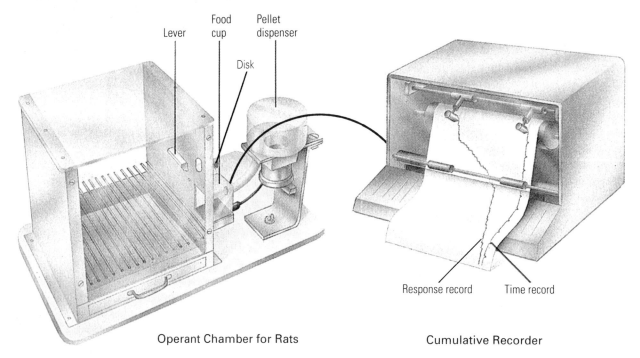

Operant Chamber for Rats   Cumulative Recorder

Reinforcement Contingencies

A **reinforcement contingency** is a consistent relationship between a response and the changes in the environment that it produces. For example, a pigeon's pecking (the response) is generally followed by the presentation of grain (the corresponding change in the environment). This consistent relationship, or reinforcement contingency, will usually be accompanied by an increase in the rate of pecking. For delivery of grain to increase only the probability of pecking, it must be contingent only on the pecking response – it must occur regularly after that response but not after other responses, such as turning or scratching.

Based on Skinner's work, contemporary behaviour analysts seek to understand behaviour wholly in terms of reinforcement contingencies. The primary goal of behaviour analysis is to understand complex behaviour in terms of the reinforcement contingencies that engender and maintain it. Behaviour analysts have been successful in applying their understanding of reinforcement contingencies to a wide variety of everyday situations. Notably this accomplishment has occurred via the application of behavioural analysis largely in two settings: in education (Blackman, 1974), wherein benefits have been noted particularly for children with substantive learning difficulties (Tennant et al, 1981; Lambert, 1990); and in clinical and therapeutic contexts, for example in relation to the modification of chronic pain (Fordyce, 1976; Flor et al, 1987) and in the behavioural analysis of risk behaviour for HIV infection (Bayés, 1990). Notwithstanding behaviour analyst's achievements in these two fields of practice, the utility of the approach extends elsewhere into every corner of our everyday occupational and interpersonal lives. Let us take a closer look then, at how reinforcement contingencies operate.

Consequences of behaving

Significant events that can strengthen an organism's responses if they are contingently related are called **reinforcers**. Reinforcers are always defined empirically – in terms of their effects on changing the probability of a response. Reinforcers in operant conditioning differ from unconditional stimuli in classical conditioning only because of the variations between the procedures used in each form of conditioning and not because of any special properties of the stimuli themselves. A **positive reinforcer** is any stimulus that – when made contingent upon a behaviour – increases the probability of that behaviour over time. The delivery of a positive reinforcer contingent upon a response is called *positive reinforcement*. A food pellet positively reinforces a rat to press a lever. Getting a laugh positively reinforces a human to tell a joke. Your attention positively reinforces your professor to lecture.

Because behaviour that produces desirable consequences is reinforced and repeated, we can use this principle to find out what is desirable for organisms that cannot tell us, such as newborn babies. Newborn infants younger than three days of age have been shown to learn a response (sucking on a non-nutritive nipple in certain ways) that gives them the opportunity to hear their mothers' voices instead of hearing the voice of another female. The evidence shows that new-borns can discriminate between speakers and prefer their own mothers' voices and that operant conditioning can be used to assess such perceptual and motivational capacities (DeCasper & Fifer, 1980).

A **negative reinforcer** is any stimulus that – when removed, reduced or prevented – increases the probability of a given response over time. The removal, reduction or prevention of a negative reinforcer following a response is called *negative reinforcement*. Using an umbrella to prevent getting wet during a downpour is a common example of a behaviour that is maintained by negative reinforcement. The negative reinforcer, rain, is avoided by using an umbrella. An car door buzzer also serves a negative reinforcing function: its annoying sound is terminated when the driver closes the door securely.

To clearly distinguish between positive and negative reinforcement, try to remember the following: both positive and negative reinforcement increase the probability of the response that precedes them. Positive reinforcement increases response probability by the presentation of a positive stimulus following a response; negative reinforcement does the same in reverse through the removal, reduction or prevention of a negative stimulus following a response. In the umbrella example, staying dry is a positive stimulus that positively reinforces you to use an umbrella; the rain is a negative stimulus that negatively reinforces you to use an umbrella.

Positive and negative reinforcement explain how new behaviours are acquired and old ones maintained. Suppose, however, that you wanted to eliminate an existing operant? How would you do it? One way would be to use **operant extinction**, a procedure in which delivery of a positive reinforcer is withheld. If the behaviour does not produce any consequences, it returns to the level it was before operant conditioning – in other words, it is extinguished. For example, smiling and nodding are behaviours that may reinforce your professor to look at you often. Withholding of those reinforcers will decrease the probability of the lecturer looking at you as often. Have you ever had the experience of dropping a few coins into a vending machine and getting nothing in return? If you kicked the machine and your drink or chocolate bar then came out, kicking would be reinforced. However, if your kicking produced no drink or chocolate bar and only a sore foot, kicking would quickly be extinguished.

An unwanted response is extinguished only if all reinforcers can really be withheld. Complete withholding is difficult outside the laboratory where many aspects of a person's environment are not under the control of readily identifiable reinforcers. Extinction is, thus, more likely to occur when withholding of reinforcers is combined with positive reinforcement to increase the probability of the desired response. Clowning in class to get attention is most likely to stop if the student finds that it does not work any more (extinction) and discovers that other, more socially approved behaviours do elicit attention (positive reinforcement).

Punishment

Another technique for decreasing the probability of a response is **punishment**. A punisher is any stimulus that – when it is made contingent upon a response – decreases the probability of that response over time. Punishment is the delivery of a punisher following a response. Touching a hot stove, for example, produces pain that punishes the preceding response so that you are less likely next time to touch the stove. Responses that are punished immediately tend to decrease in frequency. However, responses that produce delayed aversive consequences are only suppressed (Estes, 1944). When a formerly punished response no longer produces aversive consequences, it tends to increase in frequency to prepunishment levels.

Although punishment and negative reinforcement are closely related operations, they differ in important ways. A good way to differentiate them is to think of each in terms of its effects on behaviour. Punishment, by definition, always reduces the probability of a response occurring again; negative reinforcement, by definition, always increases the probability of a response recurring. For example, some people get severe headaches after drinking caffeinated beverages. The headache is the stimulus that punishes and reduces the behaviour of drinking coffee. However, once the headache is present, people often will take aspirin or another pain reliever to eliminate the headache. The aspirin's analgesic effect is the stimulus that negatively reinforces the behaviour of ingesting aspirin.

A word of caution is in order regarding the use and abuse of punishment in family and institutional settings. To eliminate undesired behaviours, it is always preferable to reinforce the alternative, desired behaviour than it is to punish the undesired behaviour. When reinforcement is not possible or does not stop the unwanted action swiftly enough and punishment is the only alternative, psychological research shows that punishment should meet a number of conditions. It should be swift and brief; be administered right after the response occurs; be limited in intensity; be specific to responses and never to the person's character; be limited to the situation where the response occurs; give no mixed messages to the person being punished; and consist of penalties in the form of withdrawal of access to reinforcers and not of the administration of physical pain (Walters & Grusec, 1977).

Serious long-term problems arise with the use of punishment to control human behaviour because the conditions just mentioned are rarely met by angry parents and emotional teachers. In some cultures, children are punished often and hard. In the United States and Britain, for example, surveys reveal that corporal punishment is still meted out in some private schools, mostly to elementary school boys 'by teachers or administrators wielding wooden paddles to whack students across their buttocks' (Schmidt, 1987). In more enlightened societies wherein the 'carrot' is preferred to the 'stick', as in Holland for example, such physically coercive forms of behavioural control are forbidden by law. Although some parents and school officials argue that corporal punishment enables discipline and order at home and in school to be maintained, its continuing presence signals that they do not fully appreciate how to motivate and influence children in positive ways by the intermittent use of various forms of reward. Desired behaviour can be strengthened and accentuated by giving praise and attention immediately after the behaviour has been emitted; unwanted behaviour, on the other hand, can be gradually extinguished and eliminated by consistently ignoring it or by minimising *all* forms of response and attention following its occurrence (Herbert, 1989). Punishment is often counter-productive, suppressing the punished response only in the presence of authority and causing physical harm, emotional scars, stigmatisation (when given in public) and hatred for the institution in which it is experienced. Worst of all, the physically punished child learns that physical aggression is an acceptable means of controlling the behaviour of others (Bongiovani, 1977; Hyman, reported in Schmidt, 1977).

Behaviour analysts assume that any behaviour that persists does so because that behaviour results in reinforcement. Any behaviour, they argue – even irrational or bizarre behaviour – can be understood by discovering what is the reinforcement or payoff. Sometimes, behaviours may be maintained by reinforcers different from those involved in the original conditioning. For example, symptoms of mental or physical disorders are sometimes maintained because the person gets attention and sympathy and is excused from normal responsibilities. These **secondary gains** reinforce irrational and sometimes self-destructive behaviour. Excessively shy behaviour, for example, can be maintained through reinforcement even though the person would prefer not to be shy.

Three-term contingency

Organisms learn not only to behave but also how to behave in certain situations. Through their associations with reinforcement or punishment, certain stimuli that precede a particular response, or **discriminative stimuli**, later come to set the occasion for that behaviour. Discriminative stimuli do not signal other stimuli as CSs in classical conditioning do. Through experience with different stimuli and behavioural consequences, organisms learn that in the presence of some stimuli but not others their behaviour is likely to have a particular effect on the environment. For example, in the presence of a green street light, the act of crossing an intersection in a motor vehicle is reinforced. When the light is red, however, such behaviour may be punished – it may result in a police caution or an accident. An awareness of the discriminatively learned nature of traffic light colours becomes apparent if visiting Naples for the first time: many tourists new to the city are often nearly run down by drivers who simply do not stop or even slow up when the traffic lights are at red – unless a police officer is standing on a nearby corner, effectively serving the invaluable function as a discriminative stimulus for Neopolitan motorists!

Skinner referred to the sequence of discriminative stimulus-behaviour-consequence as the **three-term contingency** and believed that it could explain most human action (Skinner, 1953). *Table 7.1* describes how the three-term contingency might explain several different kinds of human behaviour.

Skinner's belief that human behaviour can be explained by the three-term contingency was based on work with laboratory rats and pigeons. Under laboratory conditions, manipulating the consequences of behaviour in the presence of discriminative stimuli

TABLE 7.1	THE THREE-TERM CONTINGENCY: RELATIONSHIPS AMONG DISCRIMINATIVE STIMULI, BEHAVIOUR AND CONSEQUENCES		
	Discriminative Stimulus (S^D)	**Emitted Response (R)**	**Stimulus Consequence (S)**
1. **Positive Reinforcement:** a response in the presence of an effective signal (S^D) produces the desired consequence. This response increases.	Soft-drinks machine	Put coin in slot	Get drink
2. **Negative Reinforcement (escape):** an unpleasant situation is escaped from by an operant response. This escape response increases.	Heat	Fan oneself	Escape from heat
3. **Negative Reinforcement (avoidance):** a stimulus signals to the organism that an unpleasant event will occur soon. An appropriate response avoids its occurrence. This avoidance response increases.	Sound of car door buzzer	Close door securely	Avoid aversive noise
4. **Extinction Training:** an operant response is not followed by a reinforcer. It decreases in rate.	None or S^Δ	Clowning behaviour	No one notices and response becomes frequent
5. **Punishment:** a response is followed by an aversive stimulus. The response is eliminated or suppressed.	Attractive matchbox	Play with matches	Get burned or get caught and spanked

can exert powerful control over that behaviour (Mazur, 1990). For example, a pigeon might be given grain after pecking a disc in the presence of a green light but not a red light. The green light is a discriminative stimulus that sets the occasion for pecking; the red is a discriminative stimulus that sets the occasion for not pecking. The green light is a positive discriminative stimulus or S^D (pronounced 'ess dee'). The red light is a negative discriminative stimulus or $S\Delta$ (pronounced 'ess Delta').

Organisms learn quickly to discriminate between these two conditions, responding regularly in the presence of S^Ds and not responding in the presence of $S\Delta$s. By manipulating the components of the three-term contingency, we can exert powerful stimulus control over our own behaviour as well as that of others.

Organisms also learn to generalise responses to other stimuli that resemble the S^D. Once a response has been reinforced in the presence of one discriminative stimulus, a similar stimulus can become a discriminative stimulus for that same response. For example, pigeons trained to peck a disc in the presence of a green light, will also peck the disc in the presence of lights that are lighter or darker shades of green than the original discriminative stimulus. This kind of **generalisation** is at the heart of some of life's most embarrassing moments. Have you ever had the experience when walking down the street of thinking you see someone you know? After waving or calling to the person, you realise that he or she is a complete stranger.

▪ Properties of Reinforcers

Whether through discrimination or generalisation, the three-term contingency describes the conditions under which behaviour is controlled by particular stimuli. Such control is acquired through the repeated association of behaviour producing reinforcing or punishing consequences in the presence of those stimuli.

Reinforcers have a number of interesting and complex properties. They can start out as weak and become strong, can be learned through experience rather than biologically determined and can be activities rather than objects. In some situations, even powerful reinforcers may not be enough to change a dominant behaviour pattern (in this case, we would say that the consequences were not actually reinforcers).

Reinforcers and punishers are the power brokers of operant conditioning – they change or maintain behaviour. Contingent reinforcement strengthens responding; contingent punishment suppresses responding. When stimuli are presented non-contingently, their presence has little effect on behaviour – for example, when a parent praises your bad work as well as your good efforts or a teacher is overly critical regardless of the quality of your performance. Such non-contingent consequences reveal more to us about the attributes of the loving parent or hostile teacher than about your performance.

Humans, unlike most other species, can learn even when behavioural consequences are not apparently immediate but delayed. You typically get feedback on examination performance days after you study for and take the test, but if the feedback is positive, the response of studying for the next test is likely to be strengthened. Although your test score is the reinforcer of interest in testing situations, taking a test does have other consequences. For example, you do not need to wait to get your test back to know that you answered some of the questions right. The fact that you can respond to a test question quickly and without a great deal of deliberation serves to reinforce your studying and test-taking behaviour. If you have another test before you get the results of the previous test, you are likely to approach studying for it in the same way you did the first one.

Conditioned reinforcers

In operant conditioning, otherwise neutral stimuli paired with primary reinforcers, such as food and water, can become **conditioned reinforcers** for operant responses. When they do, they can come to serve as ends in themselves. In fact, a great deal of human behaviour is influenced less by biologically significant primary reinforcers than by a wide variety of conditioned reinforcers. Money, grades, praise, smiles of approval, gold stars and various kinds of status symbols are among the many potent conditioned reinforcers that influence much of our learning and behaviour. When a conditioned reinforcer controls a wide range of responses, it is said to be a generalised conditioned reinforcer. Money, for example, controls so much human behaviour because it can be traded for many significant events in our lives. It is a reinforcer that can maintain a high level of responding even when a person hoards it and never exchanges it for property and pleasures of the mind or flesh.

Virtually any stimulus can become a conditioned reinforcer by being paired with a primary reinforcer. In one experiment, simple tokens were used as conditioned reinforcers with animal learners.

In an early study, chimps were trained to learn how to solve problems with edible raisins as primary reinforcers. Then

Inedible tokens can be used as conditioned reinforcers with animals. In one study, chimps deposited tokens in a 'chimp-o-mat' in exchange for raisins.

tokens were delivered along with the raisins. When only the tokens were presented, the chimps continued working for their 'money' because they could later deposit their hard-earned tokens in a 'chimp-o-mat' designed to exchange tokens for the raisins (Cowles, 1937).

Teachers and experimenters often find secondary conditioned reinforcers more effective and easier to use than primary reinforcers because: (a) few primary reinforcers are available in the classroom, whereas almost any stimulus event that is under control of a teacher can be used as a conditioned reinforcer; (b) they can be dispensed rapidly; (c) they are portable; and (d) their reinforcing effect may be more immediate since it depends only on the perception of receiving them and not on biological processing as in the case of primary reinforcers (food).

In some institutions, token economies have been set up based on these principles. Desired behaviours (grooming or taking medication, for example) are explicitly defined and token payoffs are given by the staff when they are performed. These tokens can later be exchanged by the patients for a wide array of rewards and privileges (Ayllon & Azrin, 1965; Holden, 1978). These systems of reinforcement are especially effective in modifying patients' behaviours regarding self-care, upkeep of their environment and, most importantly, frequency of their positive social interactions.

Preferred activities as positive reinforcers

Positive reinforcers in the laboratory are usually substances such as food or water. However, outside the laboratory there are many more behaviour reinforcers in operation. We know that nursery-school children enjoy running and shouting much more than sitting still and listening to someone talk. What would happen if the opportunity to run and shout were made contingent on a period of sitting still first? Would there be an increase in the sitting-still behaviour? The answer is yes. In a classic study, when pleas, punishment and some screaming proved unsuccessful, a teacher reprogrammed her classroom contingencies. The procedure the teacher used may seem unusual, but it worked.

Short periods during which the children sat quietly in their chairs facing the blackboard were occasionally followed by the sound of a bell and the instruction, 'Run and scream'. The students immediately jumped out of their chairs and ran around the room screaming and having a good time. After a few minutes, another signal alerted them to stop and return to their chairs. Later in the study, the children were given the opportunity to earn tokens for engaging in low-probability behaviours, such as practising arithmetic. The children could use the tokens to buy the opportunity to participate in high-probability activities, such as playing with toys. With this kind of procedure, control was virtually perfect after a few days (Homme *et al*, 1963).

The principle that a more preferred activity can be used to reinforce a less preferred one is called the **Premack principle**, after its discoverer **David Premack** (1965). He found that water-deprived rats learned to increase their running in an exercise wheel when running was followed by an opportunity to drink. Other rats that were not thirsty but exercise-deprived would learn to increase their drinking when that response was followed by a chance to run. According to the Premack principle, a reinforcer may be any event or activity that is valued by the organism. The Premack principle is often used by parents and teachers to get children to engage in low-probability activities. For a socially outgoing child, playing with friends can reinforce the less pleasant task of finishing homework first. For a shy child, reading a new book can be used to reinforce the less preferred activity of playing with other children. Whatever activity is valued can be used as a reinforcer and thus increase the probability of engaging in an activity that is not currently valued. Over time, there is the possibility that the less-favoured activities will come to be valued as exposure to them leads to discovery of their intrinsic worth.

The Premack principle is enormously useful for self-management. If you wish you could get your studying done early in the evening before you get tired but you are easily distracted, try promising yourself a half-hour break to engage in an activity you really want to do – but only after you have studied for a given period of time or have read a given number of pages. A Premack moral is that pleasure before study makes study a pain; pleasure after study makes study a gain.

▢ Shaping and Chaining

Similar to classical conditioning, operant conditioning does not usually occur in one trial. Reinforcing behaviour only once or even twice in the presence of a discriminative stimulus is usually not sufficient to produce learning. In the laboratory, behaviour analysts train new behaviours with a method called **shaping by successive approximations**, which means reinforcing any responses that successively approximate and ultimately match the desired response.

Suppose that you wish to train an animal – a rat – to press a lever in an operant chamber. The rat has learned to use its paws in many ways, but it probably has never pressed a lever before. First, you deprive the rat of food for a day. (Without deprivation, food is not likely to serve as a reinforcer.) Next, you teach it to eat food from the food hopper in an operant chamber. When the rat is properly motivated and has learned where the food is located, you can begin the actual shaping process. You start by making delivery of food contingent upon specific aspects of the rat's behaviour, such as orienting itself toward the lever. Next, food is delivered only as the rat moves closer and closer to the lever. Soon, the requirement for reinforcement is actually to touch the lever. Finally, the rat must depress the lever for food to be delivered. Now the rat is ready to be left on its own; it has learned that it can produce food by pressing the lever.

Shaping is a procedure for changing behaviour in small steps that successively approximate the desired terminal stage performance. When shaping begins, any element of the target response is reinforced. When this element occurs regularly, only responses more like the final goal response are reinforced. By carefully combining differential reinforcement for the currently correct response (rather than any of the former responses) with gradual raising of the criteria for desired performance, an experimenter can shape the desired, higher-level action. Shaping is not effective on nonhuman animals alone; it has important practical applications for human behaviour as well. Consider the following example involving a young schizophrenic child.

The patient was a three-year-old boy who was diagnosed as having childhood schizophrenia. He lacked normal social and verbal behaviour and was given to ungovernable tantrums and self-destructive actions. After a cataract operation, he refused to wear the glasses that were essential for the development of normal vision. So, first, he was given a bit of candy or fruit at the clicking sound of a toy noisemaker; through its association with food, the sound became a conditioned reinforcer. Then, training began with empty eyeglass frames. At first, the noisemaker was sounded after the child picked up the glasses. Soon, though, it sounded only when the child held the glasses and, later, only when he carried them. Slowly and through successive approximations, the boy was rewarded for bringing the frames closer to his eyes. After a few weeks, he was putting the empty frames on his head at odd angles and, finally, he was wearing them in the proper manner. With further training, the child learned to wear his glasses up to 12 hours a day (Wolf et al, 1964).

In everyday life, you can rarely get by with a single response to a situation. Usually, you must perform long sequences of actions to complete a behavioural episode. You write essays that consist of many strings of responses, your teacher delivers a lecture that involves many different responses and any sports skill you have acquired is composed of a host of components. To teach a sequence of actions, you could use a technique called **chaining**, a procedure in which each response in a sequence is followed by a conditioned reinforcer and the final response is followed by a primary reinforcer. In chaining, the last response of the sequence is reinforced (with the primary reinforcer) first. This final response then becomes a conditioned reinforcer for the response that occurs just before it. Each link in the behaviour chain serves as a discriminative stimulus for the next response in line and as a conditioned reinforcer for the response that immediately precedes it. Consider, for example, the chain of behaviours involved in eating. How would you go about teaching a child to eat with the proper utensils? Three separate actions are involved in this operant chain: putting food onto the spoon, raising the spoon to the mouth and inserting the spoon into the mouth. First, by reinforcing the last behaviour in the chain, you would actually put food into the child's mouth. Next, you would reward lifting the spoon (you would have already placed food onto the spoon for the child). Putting food into the mouth reinforces the action of lifting the spoon and serves as a discriminative stimulus for chewing. Only after the child has learned to lift the spoon and insert it into his or her mouth, is the child actually trained to put food on to the spoon.

▪ Schedules of Reinforcement

In the laboratory, shaping and chaining are used by behaviour analysts to train new behaviours in their subjects. By systematically manipulating the consequences of an organism's behaviour in the presence of discriminative stimuli, new patterns of responding, some of them quite complex, can be created and studied. The basic principles of operant behaviour that we have discussed so far – reinforcement, punishment and extinction – were each discovered and subsequently studied with variations of this simple approach. The most commonly used variation is to expose subjects to different **schedules of reinforcement**, in which reinforcement (or punishment) is dependent on either the number of responses emitted or a single response made after a given time interval has elapsed. So, instead of getting one unit of reward for one unit of response every time, different patterns of responding are required to get that same unit of reward. Sometimes many responses are necessary to get it or one response will obtain the prize but only after a given time period since the last reward. Different reinforcement schedules have different effects on behaviour. Let us take a closer look at how these schedules operate and how they influence behaviour.

Sometimes when you raise your hand in class, the teacher calls on you and sometimes not. In baseball, the best batters hit .30 for an entire season, which means that their attempts at hitting succeed only three times out of ten, but on any given day they might get four hits in four. Some slot-machine players continue to put coins in the one-armed bandits even though the reinforcers are delivered only rarely. Obviously, behaviour is not always followed by reinforcement or by punishment. The relationship between behaviour and reinforcement may vary according to a variety of patterns or schedules, four of which we discuss below.

There is a legendary story about the way the first schedule of reinforcement was accidentally discovered by young B. F. Skinner. It seems that one weekend he was secluded in his laboratory with not enough of a food-reward supply for his hard-working rats. He economised by giving the rats pellets after every two responses rather than after each one. From the rats' points of view, half the time they responded they got reinforcers and half the time they did not. Under this condition of **partial** (or **intermittent**) **reinforcement**, the rats still acquired the operant response, although more slowly than usual. What do you predict happened when these animals underwent extinction training and their responses were now followed by no pellets at all? How did the extinction curve of these partially reinforced subjects look compared to those who were reinforced on a one-to-one schedule? The animals trained under partial reinforcement continued to respond longer and more vigorously than did the rats who had gotten payoffs after every response. Half as many experiences of the response-reinforcer contingency had produced a more durable response. The partial reinforcement effect is now a widely established principle: responses acquired under schedules of partial reinforcement are more resistant to extinction than those acquired with continuous reinforcement (Bitterman, 1975). To keep a learned response going for a long time in the absence of rewards, researchers deliver reinforcement during training occasionally but not continuously.

The discovery of the effectiveness of partial reinforcement led to extensive study of the effects of different reinforcement schedules on human and animal behaviour (see *Figure 7.9*). Reinforcers can be delivered according to either a ratio schedule, after a certain number of responses, or an interval schedule, after the first response following a specified interval of time. In each case, there can be either a constant, or fixed, pattern of reinforcement or an irregular, or variable, pattern of reinforcement, making four major types of schedules in all. Even when the amount and kind of reinforcement are the same and deprivation is constant, performance will vary enormously according to the schedule on which reinforcers are given (Ferster *et al*, 1975).

| FIGURE 7.9 | REINFORCEMENT SCHEDULES |

These different patterns of behaviour are produced by four simple schedules of reinforcement. The hash marks indicate when reinforcement is delivered.

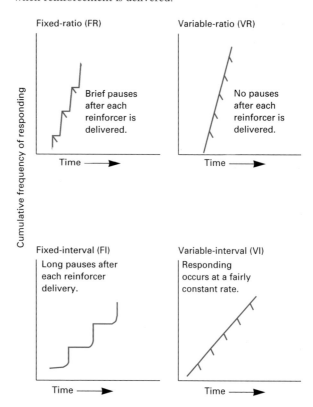

Fixed-ratio (FR) schedules

In fixed-ratio schedules, the reinforcer comes after the organism has emitted a fixed number of responses. When reinforcement follows one response, the schedule is called an FR-1 schedule. When the first 24 responses are unreinforced and reinforcement follows only every twenty-fifth response the schedule is an FR-25 schedule. The FR-1 schedule, or continuous reinforcement schedule, is the most efficient for rapidly shaping an animal to acquire a new response. FR schedules generate high rates of responding because there is a direct correlation between responding and reinforcement – the more responses the more often reinforcement is delivered. When workers get paid once after making or selling a given total number of units, FR schedules are in operation. The higher the ratio, the more rapid the responding but also the longer the pause after each reinforcement. Stretching the ratio too thin by requiring a great many responses for reinforcement without first shaping the organism to emit that many responses may lead to extinction.

Variable-ratio (VR) schedules

In a variable-ratio schedule, the number of responses required for reinforcement varies from one reinforcer delivery to the next. A VR-10 schedule means that, on average, reinforcement follows every tenth response; but it might come after only one response or after 20 responses. Variable-ratio schedules generate the highest rate of responding and the greatest resistance to extinction, especially when the VR value is large. A pigeon on a VR-110 schedule will respond with up to 12,000 pecks per hour and will continue responding for hours even with no reinforcement. Keep in mind, though, that the pigeon's behaviour was shaped – at first, it was exposed to low VR values (for example, VR-5) and, then, to increasingly larger values. Gambling would seem to be under the control of VR schedules. The response of dropping coins in slot machines is maintained at a high, steady level by the payoff that is delivered only after an unknown, variable number of coins has been deposited. VR schedules leave us guessing when the reward will come – we gamble that it will be after the next response and not much later.

Fixed-interval (FI) schedules

On a fixed-interval schedule, a reinforcer is delivered for the first response made after a fixed period of time has elapsed. On an FI-10 schedule, the subject, after receiving any one reinforcer, will have to wait at least ten seconds before another response is reinforced. Other responses in between, before the time interval has elapsed, have no programmed consequences – they do not count towards reinforcement. Response patterns under FI schedules show a scalloped pattern. Immediately after each reinforced response, the animal makes few if any responses – it takes a time out without making meaningful responses. As time passes, the animal responds more and more until, eventually, it is payoff time.

Variable-interval (VI) schedules

With variable-interval schedules, the first response, after a variable period of time has elapsed from the last reinforcement, is reinforced. On a VI-20 schedule, reinforcers are delivered, on average, once every 20 seconds. Thus, a response after ten seconds is sometimes followed by a reinforcer, but sometimes 30 seconds must pass before a response is reinforced. Responses during the intervening interval have no effect on reinforcement. No wonder this schedule generates a low but very stable response rate. Extinction under VI schedules is gradual and much slower than under fixed-interval schedules. Although there is a steady decline in responding without reinforcement, subjects trained under a long VI schedule continue to respond for long periods. In one case, a pigeon pecked 18,000 times during the first four hours after reinforcement stopped and required 168 hours before its responding extinguished completely (Ferster & Skinner, 1957). Such persistence of performance during extinction is one of the most powerful effects of partial reinforcement schedules.

◼ Biofeedback: Boosting Weak Response Signals

Imagine that your task is to help someone learn how to scores goals from the penalty spot. Your task sounds relatively straightforward; however, there is a catch: you are blindfolded. How will you give your pupil the feedback needed to correct misses or reinforce hits? Now, remove the blindfold. Is there any difference in the procedure or the outcome? You can now verbalise what is needed to help the penalty taker put the ball past the goalkeeper.

How can we extend this soccer metaphor to learning to control heart rate, blood pressure and brainwaves? It is possible to learn to control

After five years flat on her back in the hospital, Sue Strong used biofeedback to learn to increase her blood pressure to the point where she could sit up. She was also helped by a monkey who had been operantly shaped to comb her hair, feed her, turn book pages and make other responses Sue could not do on her own because of paralysis.

involuntary behaviours that are otherwise controlled by the autonomic nervous system. **Biofeedback training** is a procedure for providing clear external signals of ordinarily weak or internal responses to make an individual aware of those responses. When you are blindfolded, you cannot easily increase the soccer player's penalty kick percentage. However, when you can see that the player's leg does not fully follow through after the shot, you can make some necessary suggestions. Similarly, in biofeedback training, the subject can 'see' his or her own bodily reactions which are monitored and amplified by special equipment that transforms them into lights and sound cues of varying intensity. The subject's task is then to control the level of these external cues; for example, a subject might have to keep lit a light on a meter or maintain a tone at a given intensity. Achieving control of the level of the cues is the reinforcer. In biofeedback, as in football, the reinforcer is rarely a tangible substance but more often the personal pride or sense of accomplishment that accompanies meeting the criterion reaction.

Biofeedback, as pioneered by psychologist **Neal Miller** (1978), has helped many people gain control over a variety of nonconscious biological processes. When combined with other behavioural techniques, biofeedback is useful in the treatment of many conditions, such as headaches, neuromuscular disorders, hypertension, hypotension, Raynaud's disease and faecal incontinence (Olton *et al*, 1980). Biofeedback has made some dramatic changes in severely handicapped patients, as in the case of Sue Strong. A physical condition made it impossible for her to sit up without fainting; when she would try, her blood pressure would suddenly plummet. Biofeedback enabled Sue to monitor her blood pressure and learn how to increase it gradually to the point where she no longer fainted. Thanks to biofeedback, patients who had been immobilised on their backs for years now can sit up and function more effectively (Miller, 1985).

Learned Helplessness

We have noted that contingency between responding and reinforcement increases desirable responding, while response-contingent punishment suppresses undesirable responding. What happens when the individual gets punished arbitrarily regardless of the response? Imagine that, after years of raising your hand in class to get the teacher's attention, you take a class in which the teacher makes fun of you for raising your hand, suggesting that you must think you are in elementary school. In addition, the teacher never calls on you, no matter how you signal that you want to ask or answer a question. What do you do? One simple answer is that you give up – you stop trying to get the teacher's attention. Because environmental consequences do not seem to be related in any contingent or meaningful way to what you do, you stop trying to control them. This passive resignation that follows prolonged, non-contingent, inescapable punishment is termed **learned helplessness**.

Learned helplessness was discovered by **Martin Seligman** and **Steven Maier** (1967) in a study on dogs who received painful, unavoidable shocks. Some of them could escape these shocks by learning to press a switch that stopped the shock (negative reinforcement). However, others continued to get shocked no matter what response they made (non-contingent punishment). In the next phase, each dog was put into a shuttlebox (similar to the one used by Rescorla). The dogs could escape the shocks on the grid floor by jumping over the small hurdle between the two compartments of the box. Just before a shock was given, a tone sounded (the conditional stimulus). Some of the dogs – those who had learned to escape before by pressing the switch – soon learned that tone reliably predicted shock and escaped to the safe side of the box as soon as the tone signal came on. The dogs who had been exposed previously to non-contingent punishment, however, did not escape the painful shocks, even when it was possible and easy to do so. Instead, they crouched, barked, or shook with fear; they seemed to have given up.

The passively resigned dogs' impaired performance included three components: motivational deficits –

INTERIM SUMMARY

Drawing from his research on cats in puzzle boxes, Thorndike formulated his law of effect: behaviour that produces 'satisfying' outcomes tends to be repeated. Skinner incorporated the law of effect into his study of operant conditioning. Emitted behaviours are called operants because they operate on or change the environment. Skinner's analytic approach centres on manipulating contingencies of reinforcement and observing the effects on behaviour. A positive reinforcer is any stimulus that, when made contingent upon a behaviour, increases the probability of that behaviour over time. A negative reinforcer is any stimulus that, when removed, reduced, or prevented following a response, increases the probability of that response over time. Two ways to reduce or eliminate behaviour are extinction, or the withholding of a positive or negative reinforcer and punishment, or the delivery of an aversive stimulus contingent upon responding. Based on his work, Skinner argued that behaviour could be explained in terms of the three-term contingency: manipulating the consequences for behaving in the presence of discriminative stimuli results in powerful control over behaviour.

Primary reinforcers are biologically important stimuli that function as reinforcers even though an organism may have had no previous experience with them. Conditioned reinforcers are learned; for humans, they include money, praise and status symbols. New complex responses may be learned by shaping or chaining procedures. A desired response may be shaped through successive reinforcement of closer approximations of the desired response. A chain of responses may be taught by making completion of each link a conditioned reinforcer for the response that comes before it and a discriminative stimulus for the next one in the chain. Partial or intermittent reinforcement leads to greater resistance to extinction than continuous reinforcement. Behaviour is affected by schedules of reinforcement that may be fixed or that vary in the number of responses or in the temporal patterning of reinforcers. On ratio schedules, reinforcers are delivered after a certain number of responses that may be constant (fixed) or irregular (variable). On interval schedules, reinforcers are delivered after a specified interval of time that may also be fixed or variable.

Biofeedback is a procedure for changing behaviour. It amplifies usually weak or non-observable responses so they can be reinforced. Biofeedback has been used successfully to help people control pulse rate, blood pressure and migraine headaches.

When punishment is non-contingent on behaviour but occurs regardless of what the organism does, a state of learned helplessness may emerge. The learned helplessness syndrome includes the triad of deficits in motivation, emotion and cognition; it is also implicated in states of human depression.

they were slow to initiate known actions; emotional deficits – they appeared rigid, listless, frightened and distressed; and cognitive deficits – they demonstrated poor learning in new situations where simple new responding would be reinforced. Even when these sad dogs were repeatedly dragged over the hurdle to the safe side of the box, they did not learn to jump over on their own (Maier & Seligman, 1976).

There are some obvious parallels between learned helplessness in animals and depression in humans (Seligman, 1975). However, in the case of humans, we must consider cognitive factors – the ways in which they interpret situations of non-contingency. Do humans attribute failure to personal factors or to situational features? How important is it for them to have a sense of control over their outcomes (Abramson *et al*, 1978)? We will answer these questions in Chapter 14 when we investigate clinical depression.

LEARNING, BIOLOGY AND COGNITION

The bulk of research on animal learning has focused on arbitrarily chosen responses to conveniently available stimuli in artificial laboratory environments. The laboratory approach was adopted purposely by researchers who believed that the laws of learning they uncovered would be powerful general principles of behaviour for all organisms and all types of learning. Critics have argued that traditional behaviour theory did not do justice to the conception of humans as controllers of their own lives; personal autonomy, inner directedness, or reason-based actions had no rightful place in this view of learning (Schwartz & Lacy, 1982). In addition, central to the approach of operant conditioners was the assumption that the specific responses, discriminative stimuli and reinforcers used in their studies were all arbitrarily chosen merely to demonstrate the power of the general principles of learning. They had no intrinsic value to the organism but were determined operationally according to what worked in the laboratory control of behaviour.

Curiously, the contemporary view that a single, general account of the associationist principles of learning is common to humans and all animals was first proposed centuries ago by English philosopher David Hume in 1771. Hume reasoned that 'any theory by which we explain the operations of the understanding, or the origin and connexion of the passions in man, will acquire additional authority, if we find that the same theory is requisite to explain the same phenomena in all other animals' (Hume, 1951).

The appealing simplicity of such a view has come under attack in the last three decades as psychologists have discovered certain constraints, or limitations, on the generality of the findings regarding conditioning. Some constraints are imposed by the biological makeup of the organism and the environmental habitats to which particular species must normally adapt (Leger, 1992). Other constraints are imposed by the fact that animal learners cannot think, reason, interpret and attribute meaning and causality to stimulus events and to behaviour. The operation of these cognitive processes serves to make conditioning less mechanical and more flexible than originally believed – making possible more complex kinds of learning than those envisaged in the simpler views of conditioning.

Biological Constraints on Learning

Organisms that survive the particular challenges their ancestors faced pass on their genotypes to future generations. In order to fit a given ecological niche, each species must develop certain behavioural repertoires that aid survival. For instance, birds living on steep cliffs must make nests in such a way that their eggs will not roll out; the offspring of those that make the wrong kind of nests die and fail to pass on their genes. Some animals develop particular sense modalities (eagles have superior vision and bats have excellent hearing) and others develop special response capabilities, such as speed or strength, suggesting that different species may have different capabilities for learning in a given situation – notably the habitat in which their species usually functions. Some relationships between CSs and UCSs, or behaviour and its consequences, may be more difficult for some organisms to learn than others, depending on their relevance to survival. In this vein, Seligman (1970) articulated the concept of **preparedness**: he recognised that people and animals are biologically *prepared* to learn behaviours that are allied to their survival needs, whilst are *unprepared* to learn ones that are not relevant in this respect and appear *contraprepared* to respond or learn associations which run contrary to any naturally occurring behavioural predisposition or tendency.

Biological constraints on learning are any limitations on learning imposed by a species' genetic endowment. These constraints can apply to the animal's sensory, behavioural and cognitive capacities. Biological constraints challenge assumptions of the traditional behaviour-analytic approach; they suggest that the principles of conditioning cannot be universally applied to all species across all situations and that not all reinforcement contingencies work equally well to produce learning in any given species. If they must take into account the natural environments of different species and their genetic makeup, the laws of learning are neither universal nor even very general. Two areas of research were forerunners to Seligman's (1971) preparedness concept and show clearly that behaviour-environment relations can be biased by an organism's genotype: namely, species-specific behaviour and taste-aversion learning.

Species-specific behaviour

You have seen animals performing tricks on television, in the circus, or at zoos or fairs. Some animals play soccer or table tennis and others drive tiny racing cars. For years, **Keller Breland** and **Marion Breland** had used operant conditioning techniques to train thousands of animals from many different species to perform a remarkable array of such behaviours. The Brelands had believed that general principles derived from laboratory research using virtually any type of response or reward could be directly applied to the control of animal behaviour outside the laboratory.

At some point after their training, however, some of their animals began to 'misbehave'. For example, a raccoon was trained, after great difficulty, to pick up a coin, put it into a toy bank and collect an edible reinforcer. The raccoon, however, would not immediately deposit the coin. Later, when there were two coins to be deposited, conditioning broke down completely – the raccoon would not give up the coins at all. Instead, it would rub the coins together, dip them into the bank and then pull them back out. (Such behaviour seems strange until you consider that raccoons often engage in rubbing and washing behaviours as they remove the outer shells of a favourite food, crayfish.) Similarly, when pigs were given the task of putting their hard-earned tokens into a large piggy bank, they instead would drop the coins onto the floor, root (poke at) them with their snouts and toss them into the air. (Pigs root and shake their food as a natural part of their inherited food-getting repertoire.)

This experience convinced the Brelands that, even when animals have learned to make operant responses perfectly, the newly 'learned behaviour drifts toward instinctual behaviour' over time. They termed this tendency **instinctual drift** (Breland & Breland, 1951; 1961). The behaviour of their animals is not explainable by the three-term contingency; but it is understandable, if we consider the species-specific tendencies imposed by an inherited genotype – raccoons naturally rub objects together before eating them and pigs naturally root their food as they eat it.

These tendencies override the temporary changes in behaviour brought about by operant conditioning. In fact, the inherited behavioural pattern is incompatible with the operant conditioning task. The tokens might have elicited the natural response of the animal to food in the way a CS does a CR. The animals' misbehaviours were a manifestation of the embedding of classical conditioning (involving natural, biologically significant relationships) in an operant conditioning procedure designed to teach new contingencies present in the response-token-food sequence. The intrusion of competing contingencies occurs when an animal responds to the token (CS) as if it were food (UCS) and not simply a conditioned reinforcer for the preceding operant response.

Taste-aversion learning

Perhaps we can all recount occasions whereupon we have become nauseous after eating a particular meal. Although no one else may have become ill from the same meal as prepared for all eating it, the unpalatable taste of the food for you has thereby become associated with feelings of sickness, irrespective of whether or not a stomach virus or some other cause may have in fact been the determinant of your condition. For some days, weeks or months afterwards, the very smell of the specific food or offending sauce with which it was adorned would be sufficient to trigger the reaction of nausea. Such a bias is not strange however since humans and many animals readily form associations between feelings of illness and a small class of likely causes: namely, food. Did we learn this bias or is it a part of our genetic endowment? We must look to experimental psychology for a plausible answer to this question.

Taste-aversion learning, or the tendency to associate a substance's taste with illness caused by eating that substance, represents a genetic bias in learning. Indeed, studies of taste aversion seem to violate usual principles of conditioning but make sense when viewed as part of a species' adaptiveness to its natural environment. Suppose that a rat eats poisoned bait and many hours later becomes ill but survives. After only this one pairing and despite the long interval (up to 12 hours) between tasting the food (CS) and experiencing poisoned-based illness (UCS), the rat learns to avoid other foods with that specific flavour. There is no principle in classical conditioning that can adequately explain such one-trial learning and why such a long CS-UCS interval is effective in eliciting a CR.

Interestingly enough, other stimuli present at the same time are not avoided later – only those associated with taste. This was demonstrated in a study by the psychologist, **John Garcia**, who was the first to articulate the principles of **taste-aversion learning**, or the 'Sauce Bernaise phenomenon', as it was called initially following his own experience of a particular meal's distressing gastrointestinal effects. Only thereafter however did he realise their significance for learning theory.

Garcia and his colleague, **Robert Koelling** (1966), designed an ingenious study to demonstrate that some CS–UCS combinations can and some cannot be classically conditioned in particular species of animals. In this study, rats were shown to learn an association between the flavour of a liquid and later illness but not between flavour and simultaneous pain. They also demonstrated the capacity to associate the cues of sound and light with shock-produced pain but not with illness.

In phase 1, thirsty rats were first familiarised with the experimental situation in which licking a tube produced three CSs: saccharine-flavoured water, noise and bright light. In phase 2, when the rats licked the tube, half of them received only the tasty water and half received only the noise, light and plain water. Each of these two groups was again divided: half of each group was also given electric shocks that produced pain, and half was given X-ray radiation that produced nausea and illness.

The amount of water drunk by the rats in phase 1 was compared with their drinking in phase 2 when pain and illness were involved (see Figure 7.10). Big reductions in drinking occurred when flavour was associated with illness (taste aversion) and when noise and light were associated with pain. However, there was little change in behaviour under the other two conditions when flavour predicted pain or when the 'bright-noisy water' predicted illness. This experimental design generated the conclusion that rats show taste aversion by avoiding a sweet-tasting (usually preferred) saccharine water when it predicts illness. The pattern of results suggests that rats have an inborn bias to associate particular stimuli with particular consequences (Garcia & Koelling, 1966).

Even without conditioning, most animals show bait shyness, an unlearned reluctance to sample new foods or even familiar food in a strange environment. Of all the stimuli available to them, animals seem to use the sensory cues – of taste, smell, or appearance – that are most adaptive in their natural environments for responding to potential edible or dangerous foods. Evolution has provided organisms with a survival mechanism for avoiding foods that are toxic and thus illness-producing, and perhaps all unfamiliar foods are responded to as potentially toxic until proven otherwise.

FIGURE 7.10   INBORN BIAS

Results from Garcia and Koelling's study (1966) showed that rats possess an inborn bias to associate certain cues with certain outcomes. Rats avoided saccharine-flavoured water when it predicted illness but not when it predicted shock. Similarly, rats avoided the 'bright-noisy water' – when it predicted shock but not when it predicted illness.

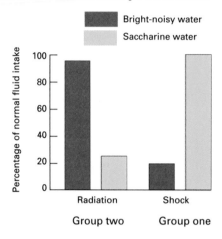

Several recent programmes of research illustrate the practical application of the principles discovered about conditioned food aversions. For example, to stop foxes from killing chickens (and poultry farmers from shooting foxes), the work of John Garcia and colleagues suggests putting noxious chicken burgers covered in feathers on the outskirts of fenced-in areas of free-range poultry farms. The foxes who eat these chicken burgers get sick, vomit and develop an instant distaste for chicken meat. Their subsequent disgust at the mere sight of chickens makes them back away from them instead of chasing them around the farm. This type of taste-aversion learning depends on the powerful feedback from the animal's nervous system, which occurs without awareness and does not even depend on memory to be effective. In another experiment, animals taste a special food, are put to sleep under deep anaesthesia and are given a drug that produces nausea. When awake and exposed to the food they had tasted just before the anaesthesia, the animals recoil and avoid it (Garcia, 1990).

Cancer patients often develop aversions to normal foods in their diets to such an extent that they become anorexic and malnourished. Their aversions are, in part, a serious consequence of their chemotherapy treatments, which produce nausea and which often follow meals. Researchers are working to prevent the development of aversions to nutritive foods – necessary in the diets of children with cancer – by arranging for meals not to be given just before the chemotherapy and by presenting the children with a 'scapegoat' aversion. They are given sweets or ice cream of unusual flavours to eat before the treatments so that the taste aversion becomes conditioned only to those special flavours. Extension of this practical solution to cancer may be a lifesaver for some cancer patients (Bernstein, 1988).

Some instances of conditioning, then, depend not only on the relationship between stimuli and behaviour, as was long thought, but also on the way an organism is genetically predisposed toward stimuli in its environment (Barker *et al*, 1978). What any organism can and cannot readily learn in a given setting is as much a product of its evolutionary history as it is a product of reinforcement contingencies.

Cognitive Influences on Learning

Despite Skinner's insistence on building a psychology of learning based solely on observable behavioural events, cognitive processes are significant in many kinds of learning (Hill, 1990). Cognition is any mental activity involved in the representation and processing of knowledge. Cognitive activities include thinking, remembering, perceiving and using language. Although the next two chapters are devoted to cognitive psychology, here we will discuss briefly how cognitive processes influence learning.

Observational learning

If important stimuli carry information for us, then we must be able to pay attention to them and decode their meaning. Observational responses can be made through any sense modality and are reinforced by the information obtained. When are you most likely to make observational rather than action responses? Unless you enjoy risk taking, chances are that you look before you leap into new ventures and uncertain situations. Recognising the right cues enables you to behave appropriately and avoid embarrassment.

Much social learning occurs in situations where learning would not be predicted by traditional conditioning theory, because a learner has made no active response and has received no tangible reinforcer. The individual has simply watched another person exhibiting behaviour that was reinforced or punished and later behaved in exactly the same way or refrained from doing so. **Observational learning** is the type of learning that occurs when someone uses observations of another person's actions and their consequences to guide his or her future actions. Observational learning results in the formation of certain expectations. In essence, after observing a model, you may think to yourself, 'If I do exactly what she does, I will get the same reinforcer or avoid the same punisher'. For example, the three-year-old boy who imitates his mother baking cakes does so because he expects that he will 'have fun just like Mummy'.

A classic demonstration of observational learning occurred in the laboratory of **Albert Bandura**. After watching adult models punching, hitting and kicking a large plastic BoBo doll, the children in the experiment later showed a greater frequency of the same behaviours than did children in control conditions who had not observed the aggressive models (Bandura *et al*, 1963). Subsequent studies showed that children imitated such behaviours just from watching filmed sequences of models, even when the models were cartoon characters.

There is little question now that we learn much – both prosocial (helping) and antisocial (hurting) behaviours – through observation of models, but what variables are important in determining which models will be most likely to influence us? Although this is a complex issue to resolve, the following general conclusions appear warranted (Baldwin & Baldwin, 1973 Bandura, 1977a). A model's observed behaviour will be most influential when: (a) it is seen as having reinforcing consequences; (b) the model is perceived positively, liked and respected; (c) there are perceived similarities between features and traits of the model and the observer; (d) the observer is rewarded for paying attention to the model's behaviour; (e) the model's behaviour is visible and salient – it stands out as a clear figure against the background of competing models; and (f) it is within the observer's range of competence to imitate the behaviour.

The capacity to learn from watching as well as from doing is extremely useful. It enables us to acquire large, integrated patterns of behaviour without going through the tedious trial-and-error process of gradually eliminating wrong responses and acquiring the right ones. Observational learning also enables us to profit from the mistakes and successes of others. How to recognise snakes or mushrooms that are poisonous or how to protect our eyes during a solar eclipse are examples of dangerous lessons better learned through observation than experience.

As you might expect, given Bandura's findings and the great amount of time most of us spend watching television, much psychological research has been directed at assessing the behavioural impact that TV's modelled behaviour has on viewers (Huston, 1985). Because of the high level of violence in American society and elsewhere, there is concern over the possible influence of televised violence. Does exposure to acts of violence – murder, rape, assault, robbery, terrorism and suicide – increase the probability that viewers will imitate them? The

conclusion from psychological research is yes – it does for some people (Milavsky *et al*, 1982; National Institutes of Mental Health Report, 1982). In controlled laboratory studies, the two major effects of filmed violence were a reduction in emotional arousal and distress at viewing violence, or psychic numbing and an increase in the likelihood of engaging in aggressive behaviour (Murray & Kippax, 1979).

Because much behaviour is under the control of thoughts and internalised images, a cognitive analysis of behaviour has been very influential in guiding new forms of therapy. Cognitive behaviour-modification involves the use of cognitive principles to modify behaviour patterns that are undesirable for clients. Bandura's work (1986) has been influential in redirecting approaches that were originally limited to behaviour change principles to a broader conception that integrates cognitive and behaviour change. Getting patients to restructure their thinking about distressing situations, relationships with other people, memories of past experiences and personal goals is proving effective in helping them overcome certain types of mental disorders. In Chapter 15 we will describe this therapy in detail.

Rule learning

Smoking is dangerous to your health; do not smoke. To reduce the risk of AIDS, practice safe sex. These are just two of many recommendations that attempt to influence our behaviour. Watching models may help us to learn some information faster or better, but verbal instructions can serve as rules that guide our actions in a wider variety of situations, especially those we have never personally observed. Rules are guidelines for behaviour in certain situations that are verbally encoded as instructions, suggestions, commands, hints, proverbs and morality tales. Rules are essentially discriminative stimuli. **Rule learning** involves recognising the contexts in which rules are relevant and perceiving the consequences for obeying or violating them. Through rules, a society passes along its accumulated wisdom and prejudices to future generations. Rules help its members behave appropriately as they attempt to acquire reinforcers and avoid punishers. The most powerful rules, however, are those that are internalised – self-instructions regarding what one can and cannot do. Attempts to change the negative behaviour patterns of ineffective, shy, aggressive or neurotic people often involve teaching them to modify patterns of limiting rules they impose on themselves (Martin & Pear, 1983). Behaviourists argue that rule-controlled behaviour is under reinforcement contingencies that support formulating the rules and following the rules, so it is not a challenge to their viewpoint (Zettle, 1990).

Cognitive maps

The importance of cognitive processes in learning was demonstrated by psychologist **Edward C. Tolman** (1886–1959). He accepted the behaviourists' idea that psychologists must study observable behaviour, but he created many situations in which mechanical, one-to-one associations between specific stimuli and responses could not explain the behaviour that he observed. Tolman (1948) claimed that learning probably involved two components: a **cognitive map**, or inner representation of the learning situation as a whole, and an **expectancy** about the consequences of one's actions.

To show that animals are capable of learning more than just a fixed response stamped in by reinforcement, Tolman and his students performed a series of studies on place learning. They demonstrated that, in a maze, when an original goal-path is blocked, an animal will take the shortest detour around the barrier, even though that particular response was never previously reinforced (Tolman & Honzig, 1930). *Figure 7.11* shows the arrangement of one such maze. Rats behaved as if they were responding to an internal cognitive map, rather than blindly exploring different parts of the maze through trial-and-error. More recent experiments on cognitive maps in rats, chimpanzees and humans have confirmed Tolman's

FIGURE 7.11	USE OF COGNITIVE MAPS IN MAZE LEARNING

Subjects preferred the direct path (path 1) when it was open. With a block at A, they preferred path 2. When a block was placed at B, the rats usually chose path 3. Their behaviour seemed to indicate that they had a cognitive map of the best way to get the food.

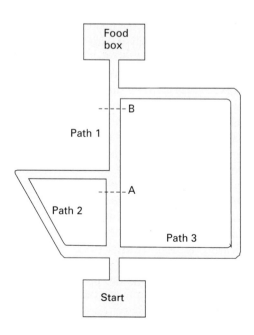

earlier findings (Menzel, 1978; Moar, 1980; Olton, 1979). Organisms learn the general layout of their environment by exploration, even if they are not reinforced for learning particular paths. In fact, when foraging animals have found food in one spot, they tend to seek it elsewhere and not return to the original site for a while.

Tolman's results showed that learning is neither blind nor simple. Conditioning involves more than forming an association between sets of stimuli or between responses and reinforcers. It includes the learning of expectancies, predictions and information evaluation – cognitive factors – as well as learning about other facets of the total behavioural context (Balsam & Tomie, 1985).

Insight learning

Based on his experiments with cats, Thorndike believed that all learning depended on trial-and-error. His conclusion supported educational practices of the time, which emphasised rote practice and were not concerned with what learners might be perceiving and understanding. A young German psychologist in the Gestalt tradition, **Wolfgang Köhler**, challenged Thorndike's view of learning. He pointed out that, although the cats could only have escaped by the means they used, many puzzles in real life have meaningful internal relationships providing clues to the appropriate responses. Sometimes these puzzles require putting known facts together in new ways; sometimes they enable one to formulate hypotheses to test new theories that make sense of partial knowledge.

During World War I, Köhler was on Tenerife off the coast of Africa. Köhler imported chimpanzees to use as subjects for his research on problem solving. He put them in enclosed areas where tasty morsels were in sight but out of reach – suspended high up or placed a few feet outside the enclosure. Typically, his subjects would first try unsuccessfully to reach the food directly and then stop and survey the situation. After a period of time and often suddenly, they would try an approach based on a novel way of using the objects at hand: they would drag a box under the fruit and climb onto it to reach the prize (later, when the fruit was hung higher, they reached it by piling boxes on top of each other) and they would rake in the food placed outside the enclosure with a stick, or they would use the short, accessible stick to rake in a longer stick that could do the job (Köhler, 1925).

Köhler concluded that, whether an organism will solve a problem by trial-and-error or by **insight** – a sudden understanding of the relationships among elements in the situation for the solution to a

A pigeon is initially baffled but then uses a box to get a banana that is out of reach.

particular goal – depends on: (a) whether there are relationships in the problem that can be discovered and (b) whether they are within the cognitive capacity of the organism. Even if the latch in Thorndike's puzzle boxes had not been out of sight, the cats might not have had the ability to understand its mechanism by looking at it.

Conditioning in the laboratory provides little opportunity for subjects to make much use of the full range of their higher cognitive processes, but, even there, the subject is clearly an active processor of information, scanning the environment for significant events, storing experience in memory, integrating and organising this stored information in useful ways and drawing on appropriate parts of that information to decide on the best response to the current situation. According to the cognitive view, changes in behaviour are manifestations of cognitive processes that also change the way some organisms think about their environment and understand themselves.

In the past two decades, despite Skinner's (1987; 1990) persuasive objections to psychology as a cognitive science of mind, there has been a significant shift among psychologists from a behavioural viewpoint toward cognitive approaches to learning. At the same time, there has been an increased recognition of the significance of evolutionary and neurological processes in learning (Garcia & Garcia y Robertson, 1985; McGaugh *et al*, 1985; Thompson, 1986).

▣ Connectionist Learning Models

Another area of learning theory that has made a surge of progress in the past few years is the development of *connectionist learning models*, hypothesised systems that try to rigorously describe the processes, structures and features that are involved in learning. These models can be used to gain understanding and make predictions about what and how humans and animals will learn in different situations. The concern with the 'what' and 'how' of learning is one of the

characteristics that sets these models apart from the learning paradigms of the behaviourists, which primarily are concerned with just describing when learning occurs. Because these learning models actually hypothesise the way learning can take place, researchers have taken to writing computer programs in an attempt to model the proposed elements of various learning processes. This comparatively new approach allows great flexibility in both the testing and modifying of hypothetical models. While the ideas involved in some contemporary approaches to the psychology of learning are not new, the appropriation of computer technology and of the main elements of programming principles into the modelling of cognitive processes has spurred the study of so-called connectionist learning theories in recent years.

As the term implies, *connectionist models* deal with the learning of connections between the component features of either external or internal events, the latter including components of thought such as concepts and sensations. A term first used by Thorndike (1898) to describe his associationistic theory of conditioning, **connectionism** refers to the notion that mental and behavioural learning can be explained with reference to the links made during these processes between simpler mental or behavioural elements. At an overtly behavioural level of analysis, this elemental approach can refer for example to the connection formed between a stimulus and a response, as favoured by Thorndike (1911). At a more cognitive level of analysis however, such a framework can also make reference to the connections that are purportedly formed between internal *mental representations* of actions and outcomes in associative learning experiments (Wasserman *et al*, 1993). It is at this cognitive level of analysis that connectionism since the 1980s has had most impact, concerning itself with explaining the processes involved in such phenomena as language acquisition (Elman, 1990), memory (McClelland & Rumelhart, 1985) and of pattern recognition (Marr, 1982). Lastly and importantly, a connectionist framework is predicated upon the assumption of a neurobiological substrate to learning wherein links are said to occur between *neural units* which display activation corresponding with the occurrence of mental representations of, for example, UCS and CS events, as in classical conditioning. Such units constitute a network of **nodes**, with any association between nodes being possible. From a connectionist standpoint, what occurs during learning is that the strength of the connections between nodes changes. This is a somewhat different definition of learning to the one given at the beginning of the chapter – *any permanent change in behaviour as a function of experience*. However, they are not incompatible, the latter being representable in connectionist terms.

Thus, connectionist models consist of a collection of interlinked elements or *units* which represent different features or combinations of features of events involved in the learning process. Each connection has a certain strength associated with it, corresponding to the strength of the relationship between the items it connects. If the connection strength between a unit that corresponds to the concept 'chocolate' and a unit that corresponds to the sensation 'delicious' is positive, then chocolate and delicious are positively associated with each other – in other words, 'chocolate implies delicious'. On the other hand, if the connection strength between a unit that corresponds to 'pork' and the 'delicious' unit is negative, then there is a negative association between these two notions and so 'pork' implies 'not delicious'. The greater the connection strengths, positive or negative, the more strongly the relation between the two concepts is implied. If the connection strength between a 'water' unit and the 'delicious' unit is zero, then there is no particular association or implication between water and what it tastes like.

A connectionist model can have many such conceptual units with connections of various strengths between them, capturing the associations and implications between the collection of concepts and sensations represented. The connectionist learning model also specifies how those connection strengths are acquired. The simplest type of learning rule we might think of to change connection strengths between conceptual units in our model is purely associational, just as we saw in classical conditioning. So, whenever two units are 'activated' simultaneously, we will positively strengthen the connection between them. For instance, whenever we have chocolate that is delicious, we strengthen the positive connection between these two concepts. Soon, we will have learned that chocolate is, in fact, always delicious. Such connectionist learning is often called **Hebbian learning** after **Donald Hebb**, who proposed it in a general form (Hebb, 1949). If we apply this type of learning model to classical conditioning, we can model how an animal might build up associations between conditional stimuli (an auditory tone) and unconditional stimuli (an electric shock) and its

unconditional response (fear).

While connectionist learning is a useful beginning for modelling some forms of conditioning, it errs by the implied build up of associations between any conceptual units that happen to be 'activated' close together in time. For example, imagine that a tone and a shock are presented together. A learning model using a Hebbian learning rule will come to associate these two sensations with each other, as expected. Now, imagine that a tone and a light are paired with the shock. Hebbian learning will continue to take place, this time also strengthening the association between the light and the shock, since they occur near in time to each other. Thus, the model will predict that a tone implies the shock and a light also implies the shock. As we saw in the blocking experiments, however, animals do not learn this second association; they pick up only the first one. Thus, a connectionist model of animal learning fails in this case and we are left asking 'what is the mechanism of learning in this instance'? A connectionist approach answers such a question by positing one of a number of possible learning rules (or *algorithms*) to explain this blocking situation.

Our proposed learning rule is derived from the notion of informativeness of the CS, which we saw was thought to be important for classical conditioning to occur. We will change the interpretation of the interaction of units in the model slightly. Instead of merely associating pairs of concepts or sensations, we will use the connections between units to predict some concept or sensation given the presence of others. The connection between the tone unit and the shock unit represents the prediction about whether a tone will be followed by a shock: if there is a strong positive connection between the two, then a tone will predict a shock, but if there is a zero-strength connection between them, then hearing a tone neither implies a shock nor guarantees that there will not be one. The learning rule we will posit states that the connection between two present concepts or sensations is strengthened whenever the prediction about the second one is wrong (see *Figure 7.12*, next page).

For example, imagine that the network begins with zero-strength connections between a tone unit and a shock unit, and between a light unit and the same shock unit. If we present the network with a tone, the connection from the tone unit to the shock unit is zero; the network will not predict that a shock is about to happen. When we turn on the tone unit to correspond to a shock sensation, the network is mistaken in its prediction and the new learning rule causes the strength between the tone unit and the shock unit to be increased. After we do this tone–shock pairing a few times, the strength of the connection between the two corresponding units will

FIGURE 7.12   CONNECTIONISM

In a connectionist network, a subject can expect food in response to a light stimulus or a bell stimulus but not both. The network includes the AND unit in the centre which comes on when both the light and the bell are perceived, turning off the food expectation unit (hence the strong negative connection from it to the top unit). An extended version of error-correcting learning (the generalised Delta rule) is necessary to learn the proper connections in such a network.

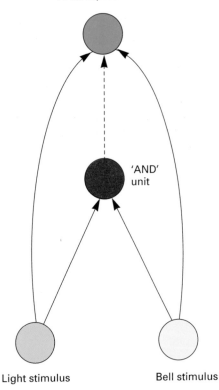

Food expectation

'AND' unit

Light stimulus   Bell stimulus

with the difference, or delta, between predictions and reality (Widrow & Hoff, 1960; Rumelhart & McClelland, 1986). The delta rule can model a variety of learning situations but is still quite limited. For instance, imagine that you want to train an animal to respond to expect food either when a light comes on or when a bell is rung but not when both the light and bell occur together. You cannot merely have a connectionist network using the delta rule that learns a positive connection from a light unit to a food unit and from a bell unit to the same food unit, because then food will be predicted for either stimulus *and* for both. In fact, you need a more powerful learning rule that is able to create *new units* to help solve difficult learning situations. For instance, if you had a learning rule that could create a new unit that was only activated when both the bell and light were 'on' and that had a strong negative connection to the food unit, this network would predict no food when both the bell and the light were witnessed.

Until fairly recently, there was no known learning rule that could solve such a problem of conceptual restructuring. Now, however, the **generalised delta rule** (Rumelhart & McClelland, 1986), among others, allows this more flexible type of learning and has spurred recent interest in connectionist learning models (Kruschke, 1992). These models are providing us with novel understandings of ways in which people and animals learn about their worlds. They extend our appreciation of the wide-ranging nature of research about learning and no doubt will suggest new directions in the future for further work.

Applied Behaviour Analysis

The final point to be made in this chapter is that behaviour-analysis is used routinely by many different psychologists to investigate a broad range of topics or to advance prosocial activity of various kinds. Of note here in applied settings has been a reworking of Skinner's three-term contingency in terms of an 'Antecedent-Behaviour-Consequence' (ABC) functional analytic framework as proponed by behavioural analyst **Derek Blackman**. A persistent opponent of 'cookbook behaviourism', he and others stress the importance of always analysing *behaviour* in terms of the environmental *antecedents* which precipitate it and in relation to the *consequences* which maintain its occurrence (Blackman, 1980; Owens & Ashcroft, 1982). Only then can behaviour be properly understood in terms of how it is functionally related to environmental events. Thereafter, a meaningful intervention (involving the modification of the antecedents and consequences) can be planned and

be sufficient enough so that the next time we present a tone, the model will predict a shock. When the shock occurs, however, it will not be a surprise, and no further learning will take place. If we then turn on the tone and light units together, the tone–shock connection will still predict a shock, and when we produce the shock, no learning will take place, and there will be no change in the connection strength between the light and the shock units. In this case, the light sensation is not informative and so its association is not learned. In this way, we have achieved blocking with our new learning rule, and we have added another degree of realism to our learning model (Rescorla & Wagner, 1972).

Because this new rule only causes a change in the connection strengths (i.e. causes learning) when the network makes a mistake in its prediction about the world, it is known as **error-minimising learning**. It is often referred to as the *delta rule* because it deals put into effect. Employing an ABC analysis thereby ensures that resultant behaviour modification programmes are tailored to the specific needs of the individual concerned whilst the temptation to pluck inappropriate techniques from behavioural 'cookbooks' is avoided.

The experimental analysis of behaviour provides a framework within which to:

- Study the learning capacities of a species by defining the variables and conditions that favour or disfavour learning and using the results to infer the capabilities of a particular type of organism.
- Study the memory capacities of a species by assessing performance on recognition tasks and other behavioural tests.
- Determine the sensory and perceptual capacities of a species through discrimination learning tasks and habituation-dishabituation paradigms.
- Encourage animals, infants and people without language to tell us what they know and experience

when such knowledge is otherwise 'behaviourally silent'.
- Uncovers the relationships between brain structure, brain function and behaviour.

Our understanding of how humans and animals learn has come a long way from the early studies of Pavlov, Thorndike and Skinner. The basic principles of conditioning and learning are being extended in many new and fruitful directions. Interest in mapping the biological boundaries of learning and in the cognitive dimension of human learning have grown steadily in recent decades. The new evolutionary perspective adds another dimension. We are also witnessing a wider, practical utilisation of learning theory in education, psychotherapy, programmes for stress reduction and health management. In addition, there are many applications of learning theory to situations that occur in everyday life. It has been used in numerous settings, including homes, sports arenas, businesses, supermarkets, industry and transit systems (Krasner, 1985).

recapping main points

The Study of Learning

The capacity for learning depends on genetic heritage and environmental influences. The study of learning has been dominated by behaviourism. Behaviourists believe that learning can be explained by the processes involved in classical and operant conditioning. They also believe that the same principles of learning apply to all organisms. Recently, challengers to the behaviourist view have shown that learning is determined by a combination of biological, cognitive and environmental factors.

Classical Conditioning

Classical conditioning, 'discovered' by Pavlov, is widely used for investigating relationships between stimulus events. In classical conditioning, an unconditional stimulus (UCS) stimulates an unconditional response (UCR). A neutral stimulus paired with the UCS becomes a conditional stimulus (CS) which elicits a similar response, called the conditional response (CR). Extinction occurs when the UCS no longer follows the CS. Stimulus generalisation is the phenomenon whereby stimuli similar to the CS elicit the CR. For classical conditioning to occur, there must be a contingent relationship between the CS and UCS. The CS must be informative as well as predictive.

Operant Conditioning

Thorndike's law of effect states that satisfying outcomes tend to be repeated. Skinner's behaviour analytic approach centres on manipulating contingencies of reinforcement and observing the effects on behaviour. There are two kinds of reinforcers: negative and positive. Withholding a reinforcer and punishment are the two ways of eliminating a behaviour. According to Skinner, behaviour can be explained by the three-term contingency of discriminative stimulus-behaviour-consequence.

Primary reinforcers are stimuli that function as reinforcers even when an organism has not had previous experience of them. Conditioned reinforcers are learned. Complex responses may be learned through chaining or shaping. Partial or intermittent reinforcement leads to greater resistance to extinction than does continuous reinforcement. Behaviour is affected by schedules of reinforcement that may be varied or fixed and delivered in intervals or in ratios.

Biofeedback is a procedure for changing behaviour by amplifying weak or nonobservable responses so they can be reinforced. Learned helplessness occurs when there is a non-contingent relationship between behaviour and environmental consequences.

Learning, Biology and Cognition

Several lines of research evidence suggest that learning is constrained by genetic heritage and cognitive abilities. The species-specific repertoires of different organisms, adaptive in their natural environments, make some CS–UCS and response-reinforcement connections easier to learn than others. They may even prevent conditioning from occurring in laboratory settings. Cognitive influences on learning are shown in observational learning, rule learning and insight learning. People (and some animals) can learn through observation. Rule learning is another type of cognitive learning. The most powerful rules are those internalised as one's own rules. Current research on conditioning and learning reveals that organisms can do much more than learn specific responses and associations among concrete events. They can also learn abstract, symbolic associations, general response patterns, rules and an understanding of the meanings of relationships connecting stimuli to responses. Behaviour-analytic procedures have many applications outside of the laboratory in everyday life. Researchers currently use these procedures and paradigms in studies of memory, sensation, perception, language and brain structure and function.

key Terms

acquisition
appetitive conditioning
biofeedback training
biological constraints on learning
blocking
chaining
classical conditioning (Pavlovian)
cognitive map
compound stimulus
conditional response (CR)
conditional stimulus (CS)
conditioned reinforcers
configural theory
connectionism
declarative learning
discriminative stimuli
error minimising learning
expectancy
experimental analysis of behaviour
extinction
generalisation
generalised delta rule
Hebbian learning
insight
instinctual drift
law of effect
learned helplessness
learning
learning-performance distinction
negative reinforcer

nodes
observational learning
operant
operant conditioning
operant extinction
partial (or 'intermittent') reinforcement
performance
positive reinforcer
Premack principle
preparedness
procedural learning
punishment
reflex
reinforcement contingency
reinforcers
resistance to extinction
retroactive interference
rule learning
savings
secondary gain
schedules of reinforcement
shaping by successive approximations
spontaneous recovery
stimulus discrimination
stimulus generalisation
taste-aversion learning
temporal contiguity
three-term contingency
unconditional response (UCR)
unconditional stimulus (UCS)

major Contributors

Ader, Robert
Bandura, Albert
Blackman, Derek
Breland, Keller
Breland, Marion
Garcia, John
Hebb, Donald Olding (1904–85)
Kamin, Leon
Koelling, Robert
Köhler, Wolfgang (1887–1967)
Maier, Steven
Miller, Neal

Pavlov, Ivan Petrovitch (1849–1936)
Pearce, John
Premack, David
Rayner, Rosalie
Rescorla, Robert
Seligman, Martin
Siegel, Shepard
Skinner, Burrhus Frederic (1904–90)
Suchman, Anthony
Thorndike, Edward Lee (1874–1949)
Tolman, Edward Chace (1886–1959)
Watson, John Broadus (1878–1958)

Chapter 8

Remembering and Forgetting

On 25 April 1988 a Jerusalem court sentenced John Demjanjuk – accused of being 'Ivan the Terrible' – to death for crimes against humanity, including the slaughter of 850,000 Jews in the Treblinka gas chambers. From the very beginning Demjanjuk denied that he was Ivan the Terrible and claimed that he had never worked in a Nazi death camp. Hence the legal case, to a large extent, was dependent upon proving that Demjanjuk was indeed Ivan: the man who at Treblinka between August 1942 and August 1943 was one of the operators of the diesel engine which produced the lethal fumes used in the gas chambers and who was feared for his cruelty by the victims.

The identification of Ivan was problematic. The only people who survived the confrontation with Ivan at Treblinka were those (about 50) who managed to escape from the death camp in the summer of 1943. The survivors of this group, who 35 years later were still able to testify, had to compare the face and physique of John Demjanjuk in 1988 with that of their memory of Ivan in 1943.

Can people make such an identification in a reliable way? For many of us this goes without saying. The notion that copies of our significant experiences are hidden somewhere in the vast storehouse of our memory and that you only have to find the right repository to reveal them, is widespread. Commonsense ideas about memory tell us that his face should be indelibly printed in memory, especially when it concerns such a horrifying and threatening person as Ivan, with whom many of the survivors had daily contact for about a year. Psychological research into memory,

however, has revealed that recalling a face seldom proceeds as simply as if looking for a picture-in-the-head. Remembering a face is a very complex process: people construct an image, combining parts from the original memory of the target face with, for example, pieces of a photograph they may have seen a few years later of someone who reminded them of the person to be recalled. Then they may add their imaginings of the face years later during a conversation, and so on. All this is woven together into a coherent picture, but errors easily infiltrate this process.

The Dutch psychologist **Willem A. Wagenaar** was asked to give expert testimony during the trial of Demjanjuk. In his book, Wagenaar (1988) tells the story of how Demjanjuk came to be identified as, and accused of being, the mass murderer. He applies knowledge from psychological research to the identification procedures and practices as utilised to gather evidence. Wagenaar elucidates pitfalls in these methods and proposes rules that should be followed which are based on empirical research. One of the rules, for example, specifies that witnesses should be asked to identify the subject only once, because in subsequent attempts it would be possible to rely on the image remembered from previous identifications. Another procedural rule indicates that identification of a suspect through pictures requires that the photograph of the suspect should be presented amidst others of innocent look-alikes, that are matched with the description of the suspect on a number of dimensions. Wagenaar criticises the interrogators of the witnesses for the prosecution in the Demjanjuk trial for not following many of these advisable rules, regarding such oversights as largely unnecessary.

When empirical research reveals that our psyches function differently from our commonsense ideas, and when the implications of such findings are applied to others, reactions can often be pronounced. In this case witnesses felt they were treated as if they were 'liars' or 'incompetent' – as if they could ever forget *that* face. But the question of forgetting is not the issue here. Rather, of importance is whether it is probable that a slight fading or reconstruction of memory over 35 years is possible, just enough to create confusion with another person who looks remarkably similar. The problem is also how to

deal with the fragmented and fragile memories of the persons involved in such a way that their accounts are as reliable as possible. The final acquittal of Demjanjuk in 1993 by the Supreme Court of Israel was premised upon a consideration that the concentration camp witnesses could have been inexact in their recognition of an alleged former tormentor – a verdict made poignant and ironic given the relatively unsophisticated practices that had been used to test the credibility of their recollections. Wagenaar's analysis illustrates, then, that psychological knowledge about the workings of human memory can be applied in legal procedures for prosocial effect by maximising the reliability of witnesses' all-important accounts.

IN THIS CHAPTER we will see how psychologists think about, and do research into, the ways in which we encode, store, process and retrieve information – in short, how we remember and forget. What good would all your learning be were it not for a brain that could store its lessons and a mental system that could call them upon demand – for example, during a multiple-choice examination? It is estimated that the average human mind can store 100 trillion bits of information, yet sometimes we cannot recall where we have put the car keys, or we forget a promise to call home. We all would like to be able to improve our memories – for trivial information, names, faces, musical tunes and funny jokes – and so some psychologists are engaged in developing techniques for memory enhancement.

For psychologists, the study of memory is very important because memory underlies so much of our behaviour and our humanity. Try to think of any activity that does not require the use of memory in some form or another. For example, try to imagine what it would be like if you suddenly had no memory of your past – no memory of people you have known or of events that have happened to you. Without such 'time anchors', how would you maintain a sense of who you are, a sense of your personal identity? Memory raises a variety of issues for psychologists in many different areas, and empirical research on the processes and structures of human memory is almost as old as psychology itself. Nowadays, most memory research is done from a *cognitive* perspective. Until recently,

the empirical studies were almost exclusively done in the psychological laboratory and such experiments have provided us with detailed accounts of how information is encoded in and retrieved from memory, to be described later in this chapter. We will discuss the memory systems that are postulated, and outline the mental processes that transform the sensory stimuli and the thoughts and feelings we experience into remembered bits of information.

After our discussion of laboratory-based research about human memory, we will shift our attention to researchers inside and outside cognitive psychology who grew dissatisfied with the exclusive focus on laboratory research in the study of memory. Their research on *everyday memory* deliberately takes place outside the psychological laboratory in more or less natural settings. We shall also look at the biological reality of memory, outlining some insights coming from neurobiologists who are charting the brain's hardware and the chemistry of memory.

◆ WHAT IS MEMORY?

Memory is the mental capacity to store and, later, recall or recognise events that were previously experienced. For most cognitive psychologists, memory is an active mental system that receives, encodes, modifies and retrieves information.

Memory also refers to what is retained – the total body of remembered experience as well as a specific event that is recalled. We use the term remembering to mean either retaining or recalling experiences.

Memory differs from a photograph or documentary film in that memories are rarely exact copies of earlier experiences, as photographs and film frames are. What you remember is influenced by many factors – some operating at the time of the original event, others operating when you are storing the information for later use and still others operating when you are recalling the original information. Your memories can also be affected by your physical health, attention, emotions and prejudices. The net effect of the many influences on your memory is that you remember a collage of the events you experience, second-hand descriptions of events, your expectations, your fantasies and even your sense of what is socially desirable. So, your most vivid memories may actually be distortions of what really happened. Perhaps you even 'remember' being somewhere you never were but only heard about.

 Encoding, Storage and Retrieval

The ability to recall an experience at some later time requires the operation of three mental processes: encoding, storage and retrieval. Encoding is the translation of incoming stimulus energy into a unique neural code that your brain can process. Storage is the retention over time of encoded material. Retrieval is the recovery at a later time of the stored information.

Encoding requires that you first select some stimulus event from among the huge array of inputs nearly always available to you. Then you must identify the distinctive features of that experienced event. Both bottom-up and top-down processing are involved here; you react to the sensory features of the stimulus and bring to bear all you know about similar stimuli and the beliefs and attitudes you have formed about them (see Chapter 6 for a discussion of bottom-up and top-down processing).

Is the event a sound, a visual image or a smell? If it is a sound, is it loud, soft or harsh? Does it fit with other sounds into some pattern that forms a name, a melody or a cry for help? Is it a sound you have heard before? During encoding, you try to tag an experience with a variety of labels. Some of these labels are specific and unique ('It's Adam Z'). Others put the event into a general category or class ('He's a rock musician'). This encoding process is usually so automatic and rapid that you are not aware that you are doing it.

A further encoding process relates the new input to other information you already possess or to goals or purposes for which it might later prove relevant. This process is called *elaboration*. Retention is better when you can link new information with what you already know. Some researchers believe that you remember relationships between single memories by forming networks of ideas that link together the information you know.

Storage is the process which retains encoded information over some period of time. Encoded information tends to be lost when it cannot be linked to already stored information, or if it is not periodically practised or used. The more often some bit of information is rehearsed, the more likely it is to be retained.

Retrieval is the payoff for all your earlier effort. When it works, it enables you to gain access – sometimes in a split second – to information you stored earlier. Can you remember what comes before storage: decoding or encoding? The answer is simple to retrieve now, but will you still be able to retrieve encoding as swiftly and with as much confidence when you are tested on this chapter's contents weeks from now? You might assume that you either know something or you do not and that any method of testing what you know will give the same results. Not so. The two most common testing methods – recall and recognition – give quite different results.

Recall means reproducing the information to which you were previously exposed. **Recognition** means realising that a certain stimulus event is one you have seen or heard before. When trying to identify a criminal, the police would be using the recall method if they asked the victim, or witness, to describe, from memory, some of the perpetrator's distinguishing features: 'Did you notice anything unusual about the attacker?' They would be using the recognition method if they showed the victim photographs, one at a time, from a file of criminal suspects, or if they asked the victim to identify the perpetrator in a police line-up.

Both recall and recognition require a search using given cues. However, recall questions usually give fewer and less specific cues than recognition questions. There is another important difference between recognition and recall. For recognition, you need simply to match a remembered stimulus against a present perception; both the stimulus and perception are in your consciousness. For recall, however, you must reconstruct from memory something that is not in the present environment and then describe it well enough so that an observer can be sure, from your words or drawings, that it really is 'in' your mind.

It is hardly surprising, therefore, that you can usually recognise far more than you can recall, that most students find multiple-choice questions (recognition) easier than essay questions (recall) and that recognition tests usually lead to better test performance. It is important to note, however, that as the incorrect alternatives become more similar to the correct answer, recognition becomes more difficult and recall can actually be easier.

We saw in Chapter 6 that perceptual processes can alter sensory information and that past memories can sometimes distort perception. In this chapter, we will see that there is a continuing interplay between what we perceive and what we remember. This interaction among encoding, storage and retrieval is complex and disturbances that occur during any one of these processes will affect what we remember.

◆ Metaphors of Memory

The memory system is difficult to understand, because we can neither see nor touch it. In ordinary life, we are only aware of its functioning or dysfunctioning. Therefore, people have developed an almost endless variety of metaphors for human memory (Roediger, 1980). Most metaphors can be categorised into two types: the *storehouse* metaphors and the *traces* metaphors. The former pictures memories as traces, for example, in soft wax, snow or an expanse of sand. The latter is concerned with putting memories in storage. This storehouse metaphor is common in contemporary ordinary language: we are inclined to say that 'we keep things in memory'; we are sure we 'have put it somewhere' although we cannot 'find it' anymore.

This metaphorical language of storage, however, is quite misleading because it suggests that people possess a memory-system at some unspecified location within the brain in which they store pieces of information. Cognitive psychologists argue that this is not correct: memory is not a substance but rather is a *process*. This distinction explains why 'remembering' is a more apposite term to use than 'memory'. Thus, in contemporary cognitive psychology, the computer program is more generally employed as an appropriate metaphor for the workings of human memory: what we encode, store and retrieve is the software that runs on the hardware of the human brain.

◆ Two Pioneers of Memory Research: Ebbinghaus and Bartlett

The first significant study that provided a quantitative measure of memory was published in 1885 by the German psychologist **Hermann Ebbinghaus**. He was the pioneering force in the experimental investigation of human verbal memory. Ebbinghaus concentrated on the activity of memorising; he had a basic conception of memory as a kind of *work* (Danziger, 1990). How he studied the activity of remembering is as interesting as what his research found. Ebbinghaus used different series of nonsense syllables – meaningless three-letter units consisting of a vowel between two consonants, such as CEG or DAX. He used nonsense syllables, rather than meaningful three-letter words, because he hoped to obtain a 'pure' measure of memory – one uncontaminated by previous learning or associations that the person might bring to the experimental memory task.

Not only was Ebbinghaus the researcher, he was also his own subject, which was common practice in those days. He performed all the research tasks himself and then measured his own performance. The task he assigned himself was serial learning, or memorisation, of a set of items. Ebbinghaus chose to use rote learning, memorisation by mechanical repetition, to perform the task.

Ebbinghaus started the study by examining a list of the nonsense syllables. He read through the items one at a time until he finished the list. Then he read through the list again in the same order and again until he could recite all the items in the correct order – the criterion performance. Then he distracted himself from rehearsing the list by forcing himself to learn many other lists. Next, instead of trying to recall all the items on the original list, Ebbinghaus measured his memory by seeing how many trials it took him to relearn the original list. If he took fewer trials to relearn it than he had to learn it, he had saved information from his original study.

For example, if Ebbinghaus took 12 trials to learn a list and 9 trials to relearn it several days later, his savings score for that elapsed time would be 25 per cent (12 trials – 9 trials = 3 trials; 3 trials:12 trials = 25 per cent). Using this savings method, Ebbinghaus recorded the degree of memory lost after different time intervals. The curve he obtained is shown in Figure 8.1. *As you can see, he found a rapid initial loss of memory, followed by a gradually declining rate of loss. Ebbinghaus's curve is typical of results from experiments on rote memory of meaningless material.*

Following Ebbinghaus' lead, for many decades psychologists studied verbal learning by observing subjects learning series of nonsense syllables. This research was based on the assumption that there was only one kind of remembering. By studying memory in as 'pure' a form as possible, uncontaminated by meaning, researchers hoped to find basic principles that could then be used to understand more complex examples of remembering.

FIGURE 8.1	EBBINGHAUS'S FORGETTING CURVE

The curve shows how many nonsense syllables individuals using the savings method can remember when tested over a 30-day period. The curve decreases rapidly and then reaches a plateau.

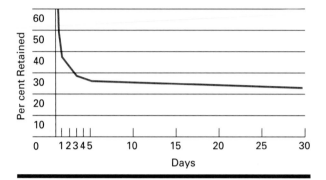

Although Ebbinghaus' general experimental approach to studying memory proved valuable, it also may have done a disservice to psychology by relegating meaning to the status of a confounding variable rather than treating it as the most significant aspect of memory.

The second pioneer of modern memory research, **Frederic Bartlett**, was among the first to stress the importance of *meaning* in the study of memory. He was very critical of the memory research of his day because it was totally dominated by experiments that used meaningless material, like nonsense syllables. Bartlett took the view that human learning at core was spurred on by an 'effort after meaning'. Memory researchers therefore should study the encoding and retrieval of salient material. In his own research, Bartlett (1932) found that people who perform a memory task do not simply repeat what they have learned but actively reconstruct what they remember. So-called **schema** – structures of prior knowledge – are responsible for this unintentional reconstruction of past events. We will discuss Bartlett's views on reconstruction and schema below in the section on remembering as a constructive process.

Bartlett's prominence as a psychologist could not prevent the study of retrieving meaningful material from being neglected until the recent past. In 1978, however, **Ulric Neisser** revived Bartlett's objections and since then there has been a growing interest in studying meaningful material in natural contexts of remembering.

 Types of Memory

Two main varieties of memory can be designated – procedural and declarative – each distinguished by the kind of information it holds. Memory is concerned with **procedural knowledge** – ways to do things, such as brushing your teeth or riding a bicycle; but it also pertains to **declarative knowledge** – facts about events in the world, about how they are related and about what they mean. Researchers have concluded that procedural (skill) knowledge and declarative (fact) knowledge must somehow be stored differently.

Procedural memory

Procedural memory is the way we remember how things get done. It is used to acquire, retain and employ perceptual, cognitive and motor skills (Anderson, 1982; Tulving, 1983). Skill memories are memories of actions, such as bicycle riding or climbing a staircase. They are acquired by practice and observation of models and they are difficult to learn but even harder to forget (Bandura, 1986). Skill memories are consciously recalled only during early phases of performance. Experts perform their skilled tasks without conscious recall of the appropriate skill memories. In fact, experts are often unable to think consciously through their tasks without hindering their performance – try to explain how to tie a shoelace or how to swim. It is easier to perform the task than describe how to do it.

Declarative memory

Unlike procedural memory, declarative memory – the way we recall explicit information – involves some degree of conscious effort. There is another important difference between the two types of memory. Procedural memory is thought to be a capacity of subcortical areas in the evolutionarily old brain; the declarative memory system evolved more recently, built upon the primitive base. This difference may account for the fact that both human and animal babies develop skill memories earlier than fact memories. Young monkeys were tested at different ages on both a skill-acquisition task and a simple memory-association task. At three months of age, they were as proficient as adults on the skill task but could not do the other task until they were six months old, and did not develop adult proficiency at it until they were almost two years old (Mishkin, 1982).

There are two different types of declarative memory, as first proposed by Canadian psychologist **Endel Tulving** (1972):

- *Semantic memory:* this is the generic, categorical memory that stores the basic meanings of words and concepts without reference to their time and place in experience. It more closely resembles an encyclopedia than an autobiography. The meaning-based relationships in your semantic memory are organised around abstract and conceptual information. Among other information, your semantic memory includes generic facts (true for others, regardless of personal experience) about grammar, musical composition and scientific principles. For example, the formula $E=(MC)^2$ is stored in semantic memory.

- *Episodic Memory:* this second variety of declarative memory storage involves remembering events that have been personally experienced. Episodic memory stores autobiographical information – an individual's own perceptual experiences – along with some temporal coding (or time tags) to identify when the event occurred and some content coding for where it took place. For example, memories of a happiest birthday or of a first love affair are stored in episodic memory and so are memories of daily life and the atrocities in the Nazi camps.

Successful recall of much of the factual information you have learned in school can also involve episodic memory because many events, formulas and concepts are stored, in part, according to a variety of personally relevant context features. For example, in trying to answer a particular test question, you remember which course the material came from; whether you heard the information during a lecture, read it in the class textbook or discussed it in a study group and whether you recorded it in your notes.

Implicit and explicit memory

Semantic and episodic memories are what we usually think of when we talk about memory – the conscious recollection of knowledge and our past experiences. However, what we have learned from past experiences can sometimes be expressed *non-consciously*. In recent years, the study of non-conscious memory has received much attention. **Implicit memory** is the learning that emerges from experiences you are unaware of that improve your performance on a task (Roediger, 1990).

Implicit memory is a non-conscious form of memory because you need not explicitly remember the original learning event that is influencing your current performance, as, at the time, you did not attend to the fact that you were learning something. Attention is crucial in this respect. The amount of attention people pay to the stimuli that are presented has large consequences for retrieval in explicit

remembering. With respect to implicit memory, however, attention has hardly any effect on the performance (Jelicic *et al*, 1992). One example of a task involving implicit memory that has been studied in detail is word-fragment completion. In this task, people are presented with word fragments, such as 'ssssn', and asked to fill in the blanks with the letters that will make it a word. What researchers have found is that people are much more likely to solve this fragment correctly if they have recently seen the word assassin in a list, whether they remember having seen the word or not. This kind of improvement on a task is known as a **priming effect** (Schacter, 1987).

Interestingly, *amnesiacs* – that is, people who suffer from memory-loss as a consequence of brain damage – display normal implicit memory. In other words, amnesiacs benefit from learning experiences as much as normal subjects when their memory is tested with an implicit task, such as word-fragment completion (Graf *et al*, 1984). Implicit memory has even been demonstrated in otherwise normal patients suffering from anaesthesia-induced anterograde amnesia (for recent events), which clearly demonstrates the distinction between explicit, or conscious, memory and implicit, or non-conscious, memory (Kihlstrom *et al*, 1990). Although amnesiacs are not able to consciously recall their past experiences, they are nevertheless affected by them and show they have learned from them. What is it they have learned? Psychologists disagree about what produces implicit memory. Some believe that it reflects the residual activation of the memory system and is only a temporary benefit to performance on tasks that require memory. Others believe it may reflect a separate memory system that encodes perceptual events and helps a person perceive more quickly and accurately after the events (Tulving & Schacter, 1990).

 An Information-processing View

Most contemporary psychologists who study memory view the mind as an information-processing system. They find it helpful to talk about mental processes in terms of the language of computer programming and functioning because it enables the complex process of remembering to be broken down into simpler subprocesses or stages.

Using the analogy between the brain and a computer, psychologists suggest that units of information are stored in our brains as memories in much the same way that bits of information are stored in a computer's databank. However, the human mind operates in more complex and subtle ways than any computer. A digital computer processes one bit of information at a time, using transistors that respond to only two signals: 1 (on) and 0 (off). A brain, however, uses graded and changing signals as well as processing many different kinds of information at the same time. Digesting one piece of information at a time, as a digital computer does, is called *serial processing*. Digesting different types of information at the same time, as a human does, is known as *parallel processing*.

Humans and computers also differ in the stability of their memories. A computer does not spontaneously add to or modify its stored memories. The trillions of synapses in the brain that vary in their excitability–inhibitory strengths permit processing far more complex than that provided by any computer developed so far (Sinclair, 1983). On the other hand, the brain's memory units are not as stable and unchanging as those of computer memory. The very act of recalling information changes a memory in some way.

Clearly there are significant differences between a computer and the human brain. Nonetheless, borrowing from computer science has helped researchers formulate hypotheses about remembering and forgetting that can be tested experimentally amongst human participants. We will first discuss an influential model of memory that uses computer-architecture as a metaphor to conceptualise memory as three systems. Then we will present two alternatives for this model: firstly, the levels of processing perspective which focuses on the depth at which information is processed in memory, thereby also employing the language of the computer analogy; and secondly, connectionist models of memory which use neural networks as a metaphor, thus in a way effectively distancing themselves from a computer-based model (see Chapter 1).

Psychologists suggest that units of information are stored in our brains as memories in much the same way that bits of information are stored in a computer's databank.

◆ The Multi-store Model: Three Memory Systems

The most influential model for human memory was proposed by **Richard Atkinson** and **Richard Shiffrin** (1968). In their **Multi-Store Model (MSM)**, they put forward three memory systems: sensory memory, short-term memory and long-term memory. Sensory memory preserves fleeting impressions of sensory stimuli – sights, sounds, smells and textures – for only a second or two. Short-term memory includes recollections of what we have recently perceived; such limited information lasts only up to 20 seconds unless it receives special attention. Long-term memory preserves information for retrieval at any later time – up to an entire lifetime. Information in long-term memory constitutes our knowledge about the world.

Imagine as you are passing a cinema, you notice the odour of popcorn and hear loud sounds from inside (fleeting sensory memories). When you get home you decide to check the time of the next film, so you look up the cinema's number and then dial the digits. Your short-term memory holds these digits for the brief period between when you look up the number and when you dial it; if the line is busy, you will have to work at remembering the number or have to look it up again. Once the cinema's message machine gives you the film times, you rehearse them. Then you can rely on your long-term memory to get you to the film on time.

The three memory systems are also thought of as stages in the sequence of processing information. They differ, not only in how much information they can hold and how long they can hold it, but also in the way they process it. Memories that get into long-term storage have passed through the sensory and short-term stages first. In each stage, the information is processed in ways that make it eligible for the next stage. Sense impressions become ideas or images; these, in turn, are organised into patterns that fit into existing networks in long-term memory.

The three systems or stages of remembering are conceptual models of the way psychologists believe we process incoming information, retain it and then later use it. Psychologists do not know whether these stages involve physically separate brain areas. The stages seem to be functionally distinct sub-systems within the overall system of remembering and recalling information. By finding out how information is processed in each sub-system, psychologists hope to understand why some conditions help us remember experiences, even trivial ones, while other conditions make us forget even important experiences. *Figure 8.2* (next page) shows the hypothesised flow of information into and among these sub-systems.

FIGURE 8.2 A MODEL OF THE HUMAN MEMORY SYSTEM

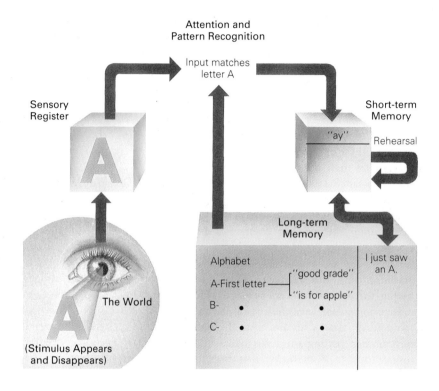

INTERIM SUMMARY

Memory is the mental capacity to store and, later, recall or recognise events that were previously experienced. For most psychologists, memory is an active mental system that encodes, stores and retrieves information. Metaphors of memory help us to conceive and understand memory and its functions. Through history, two types of metaphors have been employed: that of the storehouse and that of the trace. In contemporary psychology on human memory, the computer program is also used metaphorically.

The empirical study of memory began with Ebbinghaus whose legacy to us was his methodology based on the use of nonsense syllables. Bartlett was the second pioneer. He stressed the importance of meaning in memory research.

It is common to distinguish different types of memory. Procedural memory is the way we remember how things

get done. Declarative memory is concerned with the recall of information. The latter is subdivided into semantic and episodic memory. We can also distinguish types of memory with respect to the ways in which information is processed: implicit memory is distinguishable from explicit memory because people do not always explicitly remember the original learning event.

Many contemporary psychologists who study memory view the mind as an information-processing system. The most influential model based on this view, the Multi-Store Model (MSM), postulates three memory systems – sensory memory, short-term memory and long-term memory – each being thought of as stages in the sequence of processing information.

 SENSORY MEMORY

A **sensory memory** – also called a **sensory register** – is an impression formed from input of any of the

senses. Sensory memory represents a primitive kind of memory that occurs after sensation but before a stimulus is assigned to some category during the process of pattern recognition. Psychologists believe that sensory memory, which is the first stage of most information-processing models of human memory, is a register for each sense and holds appropriate incoming stimulus information for a brief interval. It holds this information in a form that faithfully reproduces the original stimulus. That form is called pre-categorical, because it takes place prior to the process of categorisation (Crowder & Morton, 1969).

Psychologists know more about visual and auditory memories than those of other senses (although the senses of taste and smell are obviously of great importance for survival among free-ranging animal species). A visual memory, or **icon**, lasts about one-half second. An auditory memory, or **echo**, lasts several seconds (Neisser, 1967). You can easily demonstrate the difference between the sensory registers for yourself. When you turn off a radio, the sounds of the music literally echo in your head for a while after the sound is gone, but if you pull down a window shade, the scene outside is gone almost at once.

What would happen if icons and echoes did not occur? Without them, we could see and hear stimuli only at the moment they were physically present, which would not be long enough for recognition to occur. These sensory registers are essential to hold input until it is recognised and passed on for further processing.

Encoding for Sensory Memory

To enter the sensory register, the physical stimuli that impinge on your sensory receptors must be encoded into the biochemical processes that give rise to sensations and perceptions. Even at the first stage, selectivity is occurring. Stimuli of vital importance to organisms take priority over others that are not as important – for example, soldiers who are focusing on detecting enemy gunners may be unaware of the pain from their wounds. Through **sensory gating**, which is directed by processes in the brain, information in one sensory channel is boosted while information in another is suppressed or disregarded.

Storage: How Much and How Long?

Though fleeting, your sensory storage capacity is large – more than all your senses can process at one time. Early researchers underestimated the amount of stimuli that could actually be stored during this brief interval. **George Sperling** suspected that the number of items actually produced on a recall task might

not be an accurate indication of the number that actually had entered the sensory memory. In 1960, he devised an ingenious method – the **partial-report procedure** – to test his hypothesis.

Sperling flashed the same arrays of three sets of three consonants for the same amount of time (one-twentieth of a second) but now asked his subjects to report only one row rather than the whole pattern. A signal of a high, medium or low tone was sounded immediately after the presentation to indicate which row from the entire set the subjects were to report. He found that, regardless of which row he asked for, the subjects' recall was nearly perfect. Sperling took this to indicate that all the items must have gotten into the sensory memory. When, next, three rows of four items were flashed to other subjects, the subjects were 76 per cent accurate in their reports – indicating again that there were nine items (9 divided by 12 = 75 per cent) available in sensory memory for immediate recall (Sperling, 1960; 1963).

Would it be better if sensory memories lasted longer so we would have more time to process them? Not really. New information is constantly coming in and it must also be processed. Sensory memories last just long enough to give a sense of continuity but not long enough to interfere with new sensory impressions. There is another way that sensory registers are cleared: new inputs that are similar can erase iconic and echoic representations.

In one study, two rows of letters were flashed briefly, and 100 milliseconds later, a circle was flashed where one of the letters had been. Normally, all the letters would have been seen 100 milliseconds after presentation, but, instead of seeing all the letters with a circle around one of them, the subjects saw the two rows with the circle in place of one of the letters (Averbach & Coriell, 1961).

What happened in the study was that a stimulus following another of a similar kind erased or masked the preceding one; this phenomenon is known as **backward masking** (see *Figure 8.3*, next page). Backward masking is simply an interference with the ongoing perceiving process. It is an unusual experience in that what comes later prevents what came earlier from being recognised and remembered.

At the first stage of information processing there is a race against the clock to complete pattern recognition and other coding before the sensory memory fades away. Most sensory inputs lose that race and fail to make it out of the sensory register into either short-term or long-term memory.

FIGURE 8.3	SEQUENCE OF EVENTS IN BACKWARD MASKING

In backward masking, a stimulus that appears in the same position as one just perceived (here the letter Q) masks or blocks it from being perceived. It is an anomaly that a later event blocks out an earlier one.

Display On: A X Q P N B L M
                 V T C H R E V K

Display Off:

Mask On: ◯

What a Person Sees: A X ◯ P N B L M
(Q is Masked)   V T C H R E V K

 Transfer to Short-term Memory

Though sensory gating has kept some stimulus input from being translated into sensations and perceptions, you still receive far more sensory information than you can remember or than you can use if you do remember. Actually, only a tiny fraction of what you sense stays with you permanently, as you may have discovered when you tried to remember everything you saw and heard on an exciting trip. How do sensory memories move into short-term memory?

The only way to move sensory memories into short-term memory is to attend to them. Of the vast range of sense impressions you experience and retain briefly in your sensory memory, only those to which you attend become eligible for more lasting memory. **Selective attention** – being aware of only part of the available sensory input – is a familiar experience for you. At a party you can participate intelligently in only one conversation at a time; you manage to tune out the others going on around you. Similarly, parents can detect their baby's cry over the noise of a houseful of guests who may not register the crying at all. Through selective attention we can choose which inputs to focus upon. Only those inputs that somehow command attention become candidates for further processing and storage in short-term memory.

As we saw in earlier chapters, the global process of taking in sensory input actually involves three stages: transforming stimulus energy into sensory data (sensation), organising data from individual receptors into groupings (perception), and classifying new information in long-term memory through top–down processes. This third perceptual stage includes pattern recognition and incorporates influences from expectations or personal needs.

What kinds of information have the best chance of receiving attention and getting into short-term memory? In general, familiar information will make it into this stage of processing most easily. For example, a pseudo-word such as 'eetpnvma' will not be processed as well as a real word such as 'pavement', even though both contain the same letters. Similarly, it is hard for people growing up in Western cultures to remember music with the tonal scales of Southeast Asian traditional music. However, the principle of familiarity does not always hold. When something is repeated so often that it becomes boring we become habituated to it and tune out the stimulus.

The representation of information in some encoded form in storage is called a **memory code**. When there is no memory code already in long-term memory that matches or relates to a new stimulus, encoding for short-term memory is harder, takes longer and is less likely to occur. Thus, it is easier to remember new information if you can relate it to something you already know or associate it with something bizarrely memorable.

INTERIM SUMMARY

The Multi-Store Model assumes that sensory memory is the first stage of information-processing. In sensory memory, each sense briefly retains incoming stimuli. Information is encoded as physical stimuli impinge on sensory receptors. Sensory gating is a process by which our sensory apparatus responds more strongly to important stimuli and less strongly to personally irrelevant ones. Sensory memory does not store the icons and echoes for long, but nevertheless it has a large capacity.

Only a small fraction of the information stored in sensory memory can be transferred to short-term memory. You can selectively attend to only a few inputs so as to accommodate them in a short-term store.

 SHORT-TERM MEMORY (STM)

A stimulus that has been recognised is likely to be transferred to **short-term memory** (STM). STM occurs between the fleeting events of sensory memory and the more permanent storage of long-term memory. A number of interesting characteristics distinguish this memory-processing phase.

Short-term memory has a very limited capacity. Much less information is stored in this stage than in either of the other two stages. It also has a short retention duration: what is stored is lost after about 18–20 seconds unless it is held in consciousness. But short-term memory is the only memory stage in which conscious processing of material takes place, and material held in it survives as long as it is held in conscious attention – far beyond the 20-second limit when material is held without attention. This is why short-term memory is sometimes equated with *consciousness*: it is part of our psychological present. Short-term memory sets a context for new events and links separate episodes together into a continuing story. It enables us to maintain and continually update our representation of a changing situation and to keep track of the topics during a conversation. In short, it is the workbench of the mind.

The active processing of information, which is assumed to be characteristic of STM, inspired **Alan Baddeley** to theorise on a **working memory**, which is concerned with working over, thinking about and organising material from either sensory or long-term memory (both of them non-conscious). In short, much of the mental work people do is carried out in this system (Baddeley, 1986). Short-term memory and working memory overlap. The major distinction between the two is that STM is a unitary store, whereas working memory consists of a number of different components each encoding a limited amount of specific information (for example, speech-based information or visio-spatial information).

Working memory is assumed to function in *parallel* with sensory and long-term memory (Baddeley, 1992). For example, suppose a waiter carrying a tray of used dishes passes your table while you are deeply engaged in conversation. A minute or so later, you hear an enormous crash. You know that you have not just heard a falling tree or a car accident; you may immediately interpret the sound as the crashing of dishes from that waiter's tray. In this example, working memory is using auditory and visio-spatial information from a recent event and from LTM about the sounds of different types of events to help you interpret a new current perception (Baddeley & Hitch, 1974).

 ## Encoding in STM

Information enters short-term memory as organised images and patterns that are usually recognised as familiar and meaningful. Verbal patterns entering short-term memory usually seem to be held there in acoustic form – according to the way they sound – even when they come through an individual's eyes rather than ears. We know this from research in which subjects were asked to recall lists of letters immediately after seeing them. Errors of recall tended to be confusions of letters that sounded similar, rather than letters that looked similar. For example, the letter 'D' was confused with the similar-sounding 'T' rather than with the more

similar-looking 'O' (Conrad, 1964). Our use of an acoustic code in short-term memory may be tied to our preference for verbal rehearsal of information.

You may be wondering how hearing-impaired people can manage if short-term memory uses acoustic encoding. Apparently, the hearing-impaired use two alternatives to the acoustic coding most hearing people use. They rely on visual encoding (identifying letters, words and sign-language symbols) and, to a lesser extent, on semantic encoding (identifying the categories or classes to which visually observed events belong). The basis for this deduction comes from the nature of the errors they make in controlled experimental trials: confusing items that are similar in appearance or in meaning instead of similar in sound (Frumkin & Anisfeld, 1977). Even though hearing persons generally rely on acoustic encoding in short-term memory, there is evidence that they, too, sometimes rely on visual and semantic encoding (Conrad, 1972).

 ## Storage in STM

The limited, brief storage capacity for short-term memory is called **immediate memory span**. When the items to be remembered are unrelated, the capacity of short-term memory seems to be between five and nine bits of information – about seven (plus or minus two) familiar items: letters, words, numbers or almost any kind of meaningful item. Cognitive psychologist **George Miller** referred to this phenomenon as the *magical number seven* (Miller, 1956). When you try to force more than about seven items into short-term memory, earlier items are lost to accommodate more recent ones, as the following exercise illustrates:

Read the following list of random numbers once, cover them, and write down as many as you can in the order they appear.

8 1 7 3 6 4 9 4 2 8 5

How many did you get correct?

Now read the following list of random letters and perform the same memory test.

J M R S O F L P T Z B

How many did you get correct?

If your short-term memory is similar to that of most others, you probably recalled about seven numbers and seven letters. Some people will recall five units, some as many as nine – that is, seven, plus or minus two.

Processing in STM

There are two important ways to increase the limited capacity of short-term storage so that more of the information there can be transferred into long-term memory. These two methods are chunking and rehearsal, and both are effective in such transferring because they keep the information in the focus of attention.

Chunking

A **chunk** is a meaningful unit of information. A chunk can be a single letter or number, a group of letters or other items, or even a group of words or an entire sentence. For example, the sequence 1–9–8–4 consists of four digits that could constitute four chunks – about half of what your short-term memory can hold. However, if you see the digits as a year or the title of George Orwell's book, *1984*, they constitute only one chunk, leaving you much more capacity for other chunks of information. Chunking is the process of recoding single items by grouping them on the basis of similarity or some other organising principle or by combining them into larger patterns based on information stored in long-term memory.

See how many chunks you find in this sequence of 20 numbers:

19181945187119391914

FIGURE 8.4	SHORT-TERM RECALL WITHOUT REHEARSAL

When the interval between stimulus presentation and recall was filled with a brief distracting task, recall became poorer as the interval grew longer.

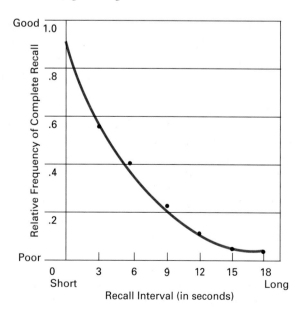

You can answer '20' if you see the sequence as a list of unrelated digits, or '5' if you break down the sequence into the dates of major wars in European history. If you do the latter, it is easy for you to recall all the digits in proper sequence after one quick glance. It would be impossible for you to remember them all from a short exposure if you saw them as 20 unrelated items. Your memory span can always be greatly increased if you can discover how to organise the available body of information into a smaller number of chunks.

You can also structure incoming information according to its personal meaning to you (linking it to the ages of friends and relatives, for example). Even if you cannot link new stimuli to rules, meanings or codes in your long-term memory, you can still use chunking. You can simply group the items in a rhythmical pattern or temporal group (181379256460 could become 181, pause, 379, pause, 256, pause, 460).

Rehearsal

Everybody is familiar with the necessity of repeating the digits of a telephone number to keep them in mind. This memorisation technique is called **maintenance rehearsal**. The fate of unrehearsed information was demonstrated in a clever experiment.

Subjects heard three consonants, such as F, C and V. They had to recall those consonants when given a signal after a variable interval of time, ranging from 3 to 18 seconds. To prevent rehearsal, a distractor task was put between the stimulus input and the recall signal – the subjects were given a three-digit number and told to count backward from it by threes until the recall signal was presented. Many different consonant sets were given and several short delays were used over a series of trials with a number of subjects.

As shown in Figure 8.4, recall got increasingly poorer as the time required to retain the information got longer. After even 3 seconds, there was considerable memory loss, and, by 18 seconds, loss was nearly total. In the absence of an opportunity to rehearse the information, short-term recall was impaired with the passage of time (Peterson & Peterson, 1959).

Recall suffered from not being able to rehearse the new information. It also suffered from interference from the competing information of the distractor task. (Interference as a cause of forgetting will be discussed later in this chapter.)

Rehearsal keeps information in short-term

memory (or working memory) and prevents competing inputs from pushing it out; but maintenance rehearsal is not an efficient way to transfer information to long-term memory. To make sure that information is transferred, you need to engage in **elaborative rehearsal**, a process in which the information is not just repeated but actively analysed and related to already-stored knowledge. This process happens when you note that the telephone number 358–9211 can also be thought of as 3+5 = 8 and 9+2 = 11. This elaboration depends upon your having addition rules and summations stored in and transferred from long-term memory. If you do, then you can find patterns and meanings in otherwise unrelated and meaningless items. Similarly, once you have learned the rules of syntax – how words can be arranged to form acceptable sentences – you can group the words in English sentences into chunks. We will have more to say about elaborative rehearsal later when we discuss encoding for long-term memory.

The limited capacity of short-term memory is one of the fundamental and stable features of the human memory system. However, there are memory experts who can remember long strings of numbers after a single presentation or multiply large numbers in their heads in a few seconds. Apparently, part of their secret is learning to shift information back and forth between short-term and long-term memory. To see how this skill might be developed, cognitive psychologist William Chase worked with a student identified as S.F.

At the beginning, S.F. could repeat only the standard seven numbers in proper sequence, but after two-and-a-half years of practice (an hour a day, two to five days a week), he could recall up to 80 digits or reproduce perfectly a matrix of 50 numbers – and do so more quickly than lifelong memory experts.

S.F. was neither coached nor given special training. He merely put in hundreds of hours of practice listening to random digits being read one per second and then recalling them in order. When he reported them correctly, another digit was added on the next trial; if he was incorrect, one digit was dropped on the next trial. After each trial, S.F. gave a verbal report (a protocol) of his thought process.

S.F.'s protocols provided the key to his mental wizardry. Because he was a long-distance runner, S.F. noticed that many of the random numbers could be grouped into running times for different distances. For instance, he would recode the sequence 3, 4, 9, 2, 5, 6, 1, 4, 9, 3, 5 as 3:49.2, near record mile; 56:14, ten-mile time; 9:35, slow two miles. Later, S.F. also used ages, years of special

events, and special numerical patterns to chunk the random digits. In this way, he was able to use his long-term memory to convert long strings of random input into manageable and meaningful chunks. S.F.'s memory for letters was still only seven, plus or minus two, because he had not developed any chunking strategies to recall alphabet strings (Chase & Ericsson, 1981; Ericsson & Chase, 1982).

INTERIM SUMMARY

Short-term memory is the link between the rapidly changing sensory memory and our permanent store of long-term knowledge. Short-term memory has, however, a very limited capacity, and its information is lost after about 20 seconds unless it is actively rehearsed. Short-term memory is also known as working memory because it is the stage at which conscious processing of material takes place. Information enters short-term memory as organised patterns from sensory memory. The immediate memory span is the limited capacity of short-term memory; it consists of about seven chunks, plus or minus two.

The capacity of short-term memory can be increased by chunking and rehearsing information. In some cases, maintenance rehearsal will work; in most cases, however, elaborative rehearsal is necessary to transfer information to long-term memory.

 LONG-TERM MEMORY (LTM)

An elderly woman from San Francisco vividly recalls the 1906 earthquake and subsequent fire. She remembers exactly how she felt as she and the other children scrambled to fetch water from the bay to drench big, burlap bags. Her father took the bags she soaked and draped them over the roof, hoping to save their home from the hungry flames. For this 96-year-old woman, the San Francisco earthquake of 1989 had little impact. Nothing could ever rekindle the terror and excitement she had felt as a young girl watching her city being levelled to the ground.

Somehow, despite all the experiences and thoughts she has had in the years since the earthquake, this lady has maintained her memories of 1906. This is the miracle of long-term memory, our third memory system. **Long-term memory** (LTM) is the 'storehouse' of all the experiences, events, information, emotions, skills, words, categories, rules and judgements that have been transferred into it from sensory and short-term memories. LTM constitutes each person's total knowledge of the world and of the self. This memory system enables you to do much more than just retain a record of past events or thoughts. Material in long-term memory helps you deal with and store new information through *top–down processing*. It also makes it possible for you to solve new problems, reason, keep future appointments and apply a variety of rules to the manipulation of abstract symbols – to think about situations you have never experienced, or to create.

Given the amount of information in long-term memory, it is a marvel that it is so accessible. You can often get the exact information you want in a split second: who discovered classical conditioning? Name a play by Shakespeare. Your responses to these challenges probably came effortlessly because of several special features of long-term memory: (a) words and concepts have been stored in it or encoded by their meanings, which have given them links to many other stored items; (b) the knowledge in your long-term memory is stored in a well-organised, orderly fashion; and (c) many alternative cues are stored to help you retrieve exactly what you want from all that is there.

 ## Encoding for LTM

We have seen that short-term memory is similar to an office in-tray. Items are stored in your short-term memory sequentially in a temporal order according to their arrival. Long-term memory, by contrast, more closely resembles a set of file cabinets or a library. Items are stored according to their meanings and all items are catalogued and cross-referenced. There are consequently many indices to help you retrieve most items from your brain.

Meaningful organisation

The role that meaningful organisation plays in long-term storage was demonstrated in a pioneering study about chess by psychologist **Adriaan de Groot** (1965).

In the experiment, subjects were shown positions that were derived from actual chess games. After five seconds, the position was erased from the chess board and subjects were then asked to reconstruct it. Grandmasters and Masters of chess did not have any difficulty with putting the pieces

back togther again into the form of the previous constellation. Ordinary subjects, by contrast, had serious difficulties with this task. However, if the chess experts and the ordinary subjects were asked to reproduce a random configuration of pieces, there was no difference in performance between the two groups. De Groot's explanation focuses on the experts being able to encode the real positions in memory by reference to meaningful patterns with which they were already very familiar, something that was impossible to achieve with sets of randomly placed pieces.

Meaningful organisation in long-term storage is also evident when you remember the gist or sense of an idea rather than the actual sentence you heard. For example, if you hear the sentence, 'Sarah picked up the book', and later hear, 'The book was picked up by Sarah', you might think that the second sentence was the same as the one you heard earlier, because the meaning was the same even though the form was different (Bransford & Franks, 1971). Moreover, if you do not understand the meaning of a piece of text, you will be unable to organise it into a memorable unit of information. Even descriptions of common events cannot be properly understood and remembered without sufficient organisational cues. Read the following passage and then write down as much as you can recall. Then, read the passage's title, which was 'misplaced' on the next page (Bransford & Johnson, 1972; 1973).

The procedure is actually quite simple. First you arrange items into different groups. It is important not to overdo things. That is, it is better to do too few things at once than too many. In the short run, this may not seem important, but complications can easily arise. A mistake can be expensive as well. At first, the whole procedure will seem complicated. Soon, however, it will become just another facet of life. It is difficult to foresee any end to the necessity for this task in the immediate future, but then, one never can tell. After the procedure is completed, arrange the materials into different groups again. Then you can put them into their appropriate places. Eventually they will be used once more and the whole cycle will have to be repeated; however, that is part of life.

There are several things you can do to organise the material and give it meaning. Material can usually be meaningfully organised in more than one way. As we have seen, chunking and elaborative rehearsal are helpful in preparing material for long-term storage because they organise the material and make it more meaningful. When you are not limited to the 20 seconds of short-term memory, but can study material in front of you, it is possible to use a number of strategies of meaningful organisation. These techniques of memory enhancement will be discussed later in the section on mnemonics.

Encoding specificity

Your method of organising material in the encoding stage directly affects not only how the material is stored but, equally importantly, what cues will work when you want to retrieve it. The close relationship among encoding, storage and retrieval is called the **encoding specificity principle** (Tulving & Thomson, 1973). The better the match between your organisation for encoding and the cues you are likely to be given later, the better your recall will be. If you expect essay questions on a test, during encoding you should look for, and try to remember, general information about abstract relationships, implications and conceptual analysis, because that is probably what you will be asked to retrieve. If you expect multiple-choice questions, you should pay more attention to specific, concrete, right-or-wrong factual details, comparisons and distinctions.

The encoding specificity principle also means that when you are learning new material, you will be encoding details about the circumstances around you at the time you are encoding – the principle of **context dependence**. Your learning can provide additional retrieval cues if you are in similar circumstances when you try to retrieve the material you have studied. The power of such context dependence was demonstrated by the finding that divers who learned material underwater remembered it better when tested underwater, even when the material had nothing to do with water or diving (Baddeley, 1982). Context dependence is one reason that studying in a noisy environment may not help your retrieval when you will be tested in a quiet room.

 Storage in LTM

The system of LTM is filled with the names of sensations, world facts, your opinions and values, and dates and places important to you. It is your personal museum. How are all these different kinds of information represented in this LTM storage?

The title of the passage on page 294 is 'Procedure for Washing Clothes'.

Information representation

We know that information in LTM is stored in organised patterns, with networks of meaningfully related concepts and multiple connections for many – perhaps all – chunks of knowledge. The functional differences among our three types of memory – procedural, semantic and episodic – indicates that there is probably a difference in the ways or places these chunks are stored. Also, one memory ability can be lost and another retained, which means that they must be structurally different as well as functionally different. We know that in LTM there must also be representations of past sensory experiences (sights, sounds and smells, for example), emotional experiences, experiences of movement (as in skill learning) and even episodes of interpersonal experiences. These representations are not only stored, but stored with interconnections (Forgas, 1982). Because of the enormous complexities involved, we know little about the way all forms of the experiences we remember are actually represented in long-term memory. Psychologists have put forth three hypotheses about the ways that people represent ideas and experiences in long-term memory. These three are propositional storage, dual-code memory and eidetic imagery.

Propositional storage. Researchers who study the comprehension and memory of verbal material have hypothesised that memory code is verbal – that people store representations of ideas in some type of linguistic code. The smallest unit of meaning that people store is called a *proposition*. A proposition is an idea that expresses a relationship between concepts, objects or events; to express that relationship, the proposition is comprised of a subject and a predicate. 'People drink water' and 'Grandparents spoil children' are examples of propositions. As you can see, propositions are not facts – they are merely assertions that can be judged to be true or false.

An abstract proposition can be represented in numerous linguistic forms. For example, the meaning conveyed by the sentence 'They drank water' is also conveyed by the sentences 'They imbibed H_2O' and 'They swallowed the liquid that comes out of a tap'. All of the sentences are different, but they all mean the same thing because they are all based on the same abstract proposition (see Chapter 9).

According to some theorists, networks of propositions form the structural building blocks of LTM. These semantic (meaning) networks enable us to locate stored information, alter it or add to it (Anderson, 1976). It is not always easy, however, to retrieve information stored in LTM. It takes longer to understand the meaning of sentences containing more propositions, even when the number of words in the sentences is the same (Kintsch, 1974). Researchers have also shown that when subjects are asked to remember a set of interrelated sentences, the more propositions there are related to a given concept, the longer it takes to recall any one of those propositions (Anderson & Bower, 1973). These two facts provide evidence for the importance of propositions in our thought processes.

Dual-code memory. Other investigators believe that people use visual codes in addition to verbal ones for storing memories. This hypothesis is known as the *dual-code model of memory* (Begg & Paivio, 1969; Paivio, 1983). According to this view, sensory information and concrete sentences are more likely to be stored as images, while abstract sentences are coded verbally. Verbal codes cannot act as indices or reference pegs for visual codes. One version of this dual-code theory asserts that images reside in a visual buffer – a spatial medium – where they can be worked on and transformed in various ways (for example, rotated or scanned) by other cognitive processes (Kosslyn, 1983).

Researchers continue to debate what memory codes are used to represent information. Some psychologists have proposed that memory uses different types of codes to represent different types of information (Day, 1986) – for example, propositional networks are used to encode test information (Anderson & Bower, 1973), and mental images are used for maps (B. Tversky, 1981) and mentally rotating complex figures (Cooper & Shepard, 1973). It seems that the answer to the debate is that both propositions and images represent information, but at different times and for different processing demands.

Eidetic imagery. Actual images may be stored in memory. We know this because of the phenomenon of photographic memory, known technically as **eidetic imagery**. Research subjects who claim to have eidetic imagery report seeing a whole stimulus picture in front of their closed eyes as if they were experiencing it directly rather than scanning memory for traces of it. Instead of asking subjects to describe pictures they have been shown, researchers now use a more demanding test for eidetic imagery. Researchers show subjects two pictures in succession, each meaningless by itself, but together forming a meaningful composite. The subjects must hold the two images in visual memory in enough detail so the images will fuse to form a single picture that is not predictable from either part alone. As the test progresses, the pictures become more complex. When tested with this method, only a small number of people qualify as true 'eidetikers' (Gummerman *et al*, 1972; Leask *et al*, 1969) – only about five per cent of those studied (Gray & Gummerman, 1975). The debate about eidetic imagery is far from over. It seems that the only certainty is the rarity of this phenomenon.

INTERIM SUMMARY

Long-term memory is the permanent store of one's experiences, knowledge and skills. Information transferred from STM is encoded into LTM by its meaning and associations with other pieces of information already there. Encoding is facilitated by organisation strategies. The way one encodes a bit of information also affects its retrieval. The encoding specificity principle states that when retrieval cues match the organisation of encoding, recall will be enhanced.

There are several theories concerning how information is represented in LTM. One theory holds that ideas are stored as propositions that express the relation between concepts. The dual-code theory proposes that there are two forms of storage – a verbal code and a visual code. Abstract information might be stored as propositions, but visual and spatial information would be stored as mental images.

◆ CHALLENGES TO THE MULTI-STORE MODEL

Most of the information in this chapter about memory is based on the multi-store model of memory. It assumes a serial processing of information from temporary sensory memory to short-term memory and, finally, to long-term memory (Atkinson & Shiffrin, 1968). *Figure 8.5* presents an elaborate version of the multi-store model, with a summary of its main features.

Although the multi-store model dominates memory research, it has also been challenged. One alternative theory is that there may be a single system of memory with variations in levels of processing: deeper processing involves more analysis, interpretation, comparison and elaboration, and so it results in better and lengthier memory. This view is called the **levels-of-processing theory** (Craik & Lockhart, 1972; Lockhart & Craik, 1990). The second alternative approach is **connectionism**. This criticises the MSM for its exclusive emphasis on serial processing and for its employment of the computer as a root metaphor (McClelland *et al*, 1986).

◆ The Levels-of-Processing Theory

According to the levels-of-processing theory, the word 'memory' can be processed at three levels:

FIGURE 8.5   THE MAIN FEATURES OF THE MULTI-STORE MODEL

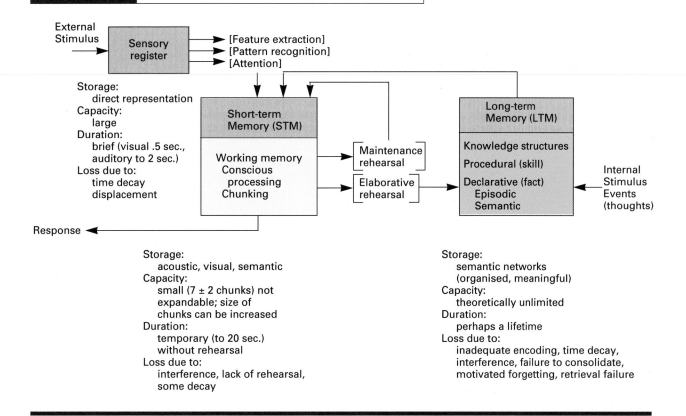

- *Physical:* in terms of its appearance and the size and shape of the letters.
- *Acoustic:* involving the sound combinations that distinguish it from similar-sounding words (such as 'memo').
- *Semantic:* according to its meaning.

Levels-of-processing theorists claim that these processes differ in depth. It takes little mental work to process input at a physical level, more at an acoustic level, and still more at a semantic level. Moreover, within any of these three levels of processing, there can also be more variations in depth. For example, it should now require deeper processing for you to complete the sentence 'Memory means . . .' than it did before you started this chapter, because the word is now linked to many more concepts and associations.

One way that level of processing is shown to influence memory comes from research on subjects working on tasks that require either low-level processing or deep processing. Those subjects who simply read sentences and rated their pleasantness recalled more total words from the sentences (deep processing) than did subjects who read the same sentences but focused on counting the number of 'e' letters in them (shallow processing) (Jenkins, 1979).

This levels-of-processing view is important because of the emphasis it places on the varying depths at which information can be processed. However, it has not yet replaced the Multi-Store Model. A major problem with the levels-of-processing theory is that it is often difficult to determine in advance whether a task will require deep or shallow processing. Moreover, the MSM is bolstered by evidence from studies of amnesia, brain responses and serial position effects. Let us briefly review this evidence.

The first evidence is that amnesiacs retain long-term memory for events prior to the brain injury and short-term memory for events currently taking place, but have no ability to transfer new information from short-term to long-term memory. Others with amnesia have shown more impairment of long-term than short-term memory, suggesting that there are two memory systems (Milner, 1966; Squire *et al*, 1993; Wingfield & Byrnes, 1981).

A second source of support for the MSM (that there is a separate short-term memory system) comes from a physiological study of brain responses during a test of recall. A unique brain wave form (a particular evoked potential) was found to be related to recall in a standard task that measured memory for very recent events within the short-term memory period. The researchers interpreted this result as evidence for a memory storage system that holds incoming information for a short time (Chapman *et al*, 1978).

FIGURE 8.6 THE SERIAL POSITION EFFECT

The graph shows the effects of a distracting task performed between the presentation of the list and the request for recall. The items on the beginning of the list are recalled best regardless of the delay-distraction. The items at the end are recalled well without delay-distraction but gradually worse as the delay-distraction is lengthened. The poorer recall at the middle of the list is due to the serial position effect (After Glanzer & Cunitz, 1966).

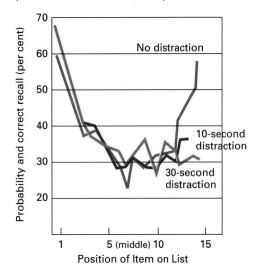

even when different types of material are presented and when different modes of presentation are used (Roediger & Crowder, 1976). When learning the alphabet, children make most errors on the middle letters (I to M). Most spelling errors also occur in the middle of words. College students fail more examination items on material from the middle of a lecture than on material from the start or end of the lecture (Holen & Oaster, 1976; Jensen, 1962).

 Connectionist Models of Memory

The connectionist or *parallel distributed processing* models of memory were developed recently. The structure and functioning of connectionist models is based upon knowledge about the structure and functioning of the brain. In these models the brain itself is utilised as the metaphor for memory (see Chapter 1) (Bechtel & Abrahamsen, 1991). Memories are stored in several interconnected units in the network, rather than in a simple location. As a result, network memories show a characterstic called *graceful degradation*. Unlike a computer memory that functions either perfectly or not at all (as in the case of input error or of minor damage to the system), the functioning of network memories gradually declines when the input becomes more irregular or when the connections within the network are progressively impaired. The strength of the connections among these units increases as a function of learning. If, for example, a particular person is encountered often, the units that are activated on these occasions become more strongly associated. In addition, information about this person will activate other units, connections between these becoming strengthened but also associated with those units that already represent the individual concerned. Subsequent meetings with this person will be characterised by easier access to and activation of the network of units associated with the person and by more fluid spreading of unit activations as associated with information about him or her. For instance, if the individual happens to be a bus-driver, not only do units associated with 'bus-driver' become activated, but so do those associated with 'busses', 'driving' and 'rush-hour'.

We will also see in the section on neurobiology that different biochemical processes seem to operate in temporary storage as opposed to permanent storage.

The third type of evidence supporting the MSM comes from studies of the **serial position effect** in episodic memory. When a subject is free to recall, in any order, unrelated items presented for memorisation, he or she recalls best those at the beginning and end of the list, as shown in *Figure 8.6*. Presumably, the subject would have processed all items at the same level in this case. The greater recall of items at the beginning and end of the list can be explained, however, by the existence of two memory systems. At recall time, the items at the beginning of the list would have been transferred to long-term storage and those at the end would still be in short-term memory. Those in the middle would have neither advantage, and their recall would be further hampered by interference from items before and after. This interpretation of the results is bolstered when subjects are given a distracting task after exposure to the list but before the testing: subjects recall the items in the last part of the list as poorly as those in the middle of the list, whereas they remember early items as well as ever (Glanzer & Cunitz, 1966; Postman & Phillips, 1965).

Having a poorer memory for the middle position of any series is a general phenomenon that occurs

The structure of parallel processing in networks is responsible for the fact that memories within them are *content addressable*. This means that retrieval does not require the specification of a location or performance of a serial search in one or more memory stores. Rather, it results from the direct activation of all units that are (partly) associated with the memory to be accessed. Connectionist networks are used to explain why people possess both episodic and semantic memories. For example, we retain information about a number of specific chairs with which we are familiar (episodic) and also we have knowledge of the general concept of 'chair' (semantic) (Eysenck, 1994). As soon as we are confronted with the stimulus word 'chair', many units will be activated in a parallel fashion: both the units referring to particular chairs and the units that are associated with knowledge about chairs in general (McClelland & Rumelhart, 1986).

INTERIM SUMMARY

The Multi-Store Model of memory is challenged by the levels-of-processing theory which proposes that there is a single memory system but that the level to which inputs are processed varies: material may be analysed at the physical, acoustic or semantic level. The durability and retrievability of information from memory increases with the depth to which that information was originally processed. Connectionist models of memories challenge the serial processing in the MSM and stress the network-like representation of memories.

REMEMBERING

Some researchers believe that information is never lost from memory. They argue that all information encoded in long-term memory is stored there permanently. Retrieval failures, however, occur when the appropriate retrieval location or pathway for a given memory is forgotten (Linton, 1975). A great deal of research has focused on the retrieval process and on the cues that are most effective for locating specific memories among the massive number present in the memory system.

The stimuli available to us as we search for a memory are known as **retrieval cues.** These cues may be provided externally, such as questions on a quiz ('What research procedure do you associate with Ebbinghaus?') or generated internally ('Where have I met him before?'). In the same way that the correct identification code will get us the library book we want, a suitable retrieval cue will unlock the particular stored memory we are seeking. We have already mentioned the importance of encoding specificity for retrieval. As we have seen, cues can be provided both by the content of a stimulus and by the context during encoding.

Since information is organised in LTM storage, it is not surprising that cues based on organisation can also help you retrieve what you know, whether the organisation is imposed by the experimenter or generated by the subject (Mandler, 1972). In one study, subjects were given a list of words to memorise for free recall. The words were arranged by categories; a label preceded each category of words. The category labels were not mentioned in instructions – subjects were simply told to memorise the words. During the recall test, half the subjects were given the category labels as retrieval cues, while the other subjects were asked only to recall as many items as they could. Recall was much better for the subjects given the category labels as retrieval cues. In the second recall test, both groups were given the category retrieval cues, and they remembered equally well. The information had evidently been available in the long-term memory store of all the subjects, but was just not as accessible without the retrieval cues to help locate the items (Tulving & Pearlstone, 1966).

Even with good cues, not all stored content is equally accessible, as you know only too well. In the case of familiar, well-learned information, more aspects of it have been stored and more connections between it and the many different parts of the memory network have been established, so a number of cues can give you access to it. On the other hand, when trying to find the one key that will unlock a less familiar memory, you may have to use special search strategies.

Distinctivenss

We all know from ordinary interaction that unusual events are easier to remember than common occurrences. When some event, person or object is distinct, it stands out and is generally given more attention. Distinctiveness also functions as an aid to retrieval on memory tasks in the laboratory. If people are asked, for example, to remember '167', they have more difficulty in doing so when '167' is presented in a list of 100 other numbers than when '167' is presented among a list of words. The retrieval cue 'number' would be distinct among words but not among digits (Von Restorff, 1933).

So-called *flashbulb memories* are another example of the functionality of distinctiveness. People often have a clear recollection of what they were doing when an extremely important event took place. In the recent past researchers have concentrated on the explosion of the *Challenger* space shuttle in 1986. Psychologists asked people a few days after the explosion what they were doing when they saw or heard of the explosion.

People often have a clear recollection of what they were doing when an extremely important event took place, such as the *Challenger* disaster.

They also asked people to indicate how confident they were of their responses. A second group was tested eight months later. In general, people seemed to have vivid, flashbulb memories of the event and their activities which coincided with the explosion. The confidence in their own recollections turned out to be related to their emotional reaction to the event and to the extent to which they discussed the disaster with relatives and friends (Bohannon, 1988). There is considerable debate, however, about whether flashbulb memories are represented in a specific system, or simply as part of long-term memory (McCloskey *et al*, 1988).

◆ Odour Recognition

What is the smell that brings back a flood of childhood memories for you? Is it the smell of baking bread or Eau de Cologne? Unlike visual and auditory memories, odour memories uniquely recreate significant past episodes in your life. In his novel, *A la recherche du temps perdu*, Marcel Proust describes how the aroma and flavour of a morsel of food triggered long-forgotten memories of his childhood: 'When from a long-distant past nothing subsists, . . . the smell and taste of things . . . bear unfaltering, in the tiny and almost impalpable drop of their essence, the vast structure of recollection'.

While we can have vivid, long-lasting recognition of odours, our recall of them is at best limited. You can recall the size, colour and shape of a banana, but

FIGURE 8.7	THE SPECIAL STRENGTH OF ODOUR MEMORY

The relative permanence of the ability to recognise a given odour is apparent when one compares it to recognition memory for pictures. The recognition of episodic odours (those associated with significant experiences) remains close to initial strength as time passes. By comparison, one's ability to recognise pictures shown in a laboratory experiment, while as strong as odour recognition initially, decreases rapidly. Laboratory odours are not recognised well after a minimal time interval but show little long-term loss.

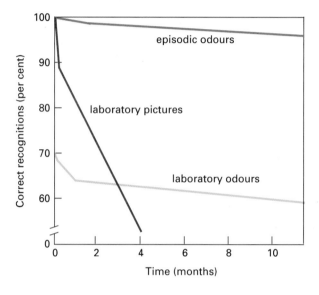

you cannot conjure up its odour sensation. There is no controllable recall of odour perceptions because the primary function of the sense of smell is to respond immediately to odours when they are experienced – not to permit later recall for the purpose of cognitive analysis (Engen, 1987). *Figure 8.7* compares the special strength of odour memories – both natural episodic odours and laboratory-presented odours – with visual memory for pictures.

◆ Remembering as a Constructive Process

We have been talking as if we simply store and remember varying amounts of the information we receive. Sometimes what we remember is either more than or different from what we actually experienced. Laboratory studies about the way people process and remember meaningful material have forced psychologists to begin to conceptualise remembering as a continuation of the active, constructive process of perception. According to this view, as we organise material to make it meaningful, we frequently add details to make it more complete or change it to make it fit better with other, already existing information in our personal memory store. As first noted by psychologist **Jerome Bruner**, when we construct memories, we 'go beyond the information given' (1973). In some cases, going beyond the information given is so radical that people retrieve 'information' that was not there when encoding took place. A clear example of this is provided by the recollections of eminent psychologist Jean Piaget. He believed for a long time, that as a young child he was the victim of an attempted kidnapping. He reported that he had retained vivid and detailed memories of the alleged occurrence. Later, it transpired that the event had been completely fabricated by his nanny (Loftus, 1993).

Adding new information to what we take in is a constructive process that happens when the given information seems incomplete and we fill in the rest to make a 'coherent picture'. Changing information to make it conform to knowledge already in memory is a distortion process. When a new idea or experience is incompatible with your values, beliefs or strongly felt emotions, you may alter it unintentionally to be more consistent with your worldview or self-concept.

Construction can occur at the encoding stage (when the material is first processed), at the retrieval stage, and perhaps even in between, during storage, as apparent inconsistencies and contradictions are managed. In other words, a person brings more to every situation than his or her memory recording device. What is perceived and remembered is a function of the individual's past history, current values and future expectations, as well as the nature of the stimulus being committed to memory.

Although the study of constructive processes in memory has only recently become popular in memory research, it was actually begun over 50 years ago by **Frederic Bartlett.** In one of his studies he focused on the kinds of constructions that take place when people try to remember material that is unfamiliar to them (Bartlett, 1932). He observed the way British undergraduates transmitted and remembered simple stories whose themes and wording were taken from another culture. His most famous story was *The War of the Ghosts*, an American Indian tale.

Bartlett used two procedures to study the way his subjects transformed this story into a coherent narrative that made sense to them. In serial reproduction, one person would read the story and tell it from memory to a second person, who communicated it to a third, and so on. In repeated reproduction, the same person would retell the story from memory over a number of repeated sessions (in some cases years apart). In both cases, memory was very inaccurate; the recalled story that emerged was often quite different from the original story that was read.

Bartlett found that constructive processes were intervening between input and output. The original story was evidently unclear to the subjects because of their lack of cultural understanding. The subjects unknowingly changed details to fit their own preconceptions so that the story would make sense to them. The distortions involved three kinds of constructive processes:

- *Levelling:* simplifying the story.
- *Sharpening:* highlighting and overemphasising certain details.
- *Assimilation:* changing the details to better fit the subject's own background or knowledge.

Bartlett introduced the concept of **schema** to account for the constructions taking place. A schema is a general conceptual framework or cluster of knowledge and preconceptions regarding certain objects, people and situations. Schemata are 'knowledge packages' that guide our further knowledge, memories, and provide expectations for the future. In Bartlett's experiment, schemata facilitated transformations of details so that these were more consistent with the student's view of the world.

The importance of schemata in helping us organise and make sense of details – and remember them – has been shown in many studies, a few of which are described here. In general, story titles give us schemata that help us make sense of elements in the plot and enable us to remember relevant sections of the story. When the elements do not fit with the title, reconstructive memory has trouble, as seen in the following study.

While some subjects read a story titled Watching a Peace March from the Fortieth Floor, *other subjects read the exact same story but retitled* A Space Trip to an Inhabited Planet. *Most of the story was ambiguous enough to fit under either title, but one sentence fit only the space trip title: 'The landing was gentle, and luckily the atmosphere was such that no special suits had to be worn'.*

More than half of those who were given the space trip title remembered this sentence, but only a few remembered it from the 'peace march' story. The titles seemed to have activated different schemata. For one schema, the critical sentence fit was interpreted as relevant and was remembered; for the other, it had no meaning and was lost or not retrievable (Bransford & Johnson, 1972).

The construction of memories is also influenced by the person's emotional state, or *mood*. **Gordon Bower** (1981) and his students have experimentally uncovered two effects of moods on memory: mood-congruent processing and mood-dependent retrieval. *Mood-congruent processing* occurs when people are selectively sensitised to encode information that agrees with their current mood state. Material that is congruent with one's prevailing mood is more likely to be attended to, noticed and processed more deeply in memory with greater elaborative associations. This type of processing causes people to improve learning of information that is congruent with their mood (Gilligan & Bower, 1984).

Mood-dependent retrieval refers to the recall of a prior emotional event, wherein such recollection specifically occurs when the same mood felt at the time of the original event is again experienced. People remember more events that were originally sad when they are feeling sad. Happy people are more likely to retrieve happy events from their past. A similar constructional process occurs when clinically depressed patients are asked to recall events from their personal biographies: their negative mood guides their recollecting so as to retrieve more negative memories from the past (Blaney, 1986). In part, this tendency is due to the *encoding specificity principle*. When you are happy, your mood serves as a retrieval cue for happy information and it biases recall towards positive events.

The constructive nature of remembering confronts us with a serious problem. If memories are the outcomes of a constructive process which is directed by our strivances toward establishing meaningful, coherent and self-enhancing narratives, our memories may well be seriously distorted, especially concerning events that happened a long time ago. Can we rely, then, on our own autobiography? Are the narratives we have told our friends (and ourselves) about what we did and who we are trustworthy? Can we believe other persons when they confront us with the details of an incident they witnessed? Since people are usually quite unaware of their constructions, these questions become all the more pressing. Not only are people oblivious of their self-deceit, but they also show remarkable confidence about their false memories (Spiro, 1977). Even the very vivid memories people sometimes report of emotionally charged events – for example, the flashbulb memories we discussed earlier – are often highly inaccurate. Indeed, Weaver (1993) argues that the undue confidence with which these memories are held is a defining feature of flashbulb memories. So should we be troubled by these revelations about memory processes?

In later sections on 'motivated forgetting' and 'eye-witness testimony' we will see that sometimes we should indeed be highly concerned. Memorising, especially if it focuses upon events that happened in the distant past, is a far from perfect process. Under some conditions people adapt, embellish or distort their recollections. Like Piaget, they can even experience compelling illusory recollections. But at the same time memories also can be wonderfully detailed and accurate. Despite its faults, constructive memory is an enormously positive feature of creative minds at work. More often than not, it helps us to make sense of our uncertain world by providing the right context in which to understand, interpret, recollect and act on minimal or fragmentary evidence. Without it, our memories would be little more than simple transcription services that would be unable to assign any special significance to our many experiences.

The continuing research of cognitive psychologists is refining our understanding of the ways memories are changed by subsequent information – how they are lost, suppressed or merged. Researchers are also testing variables to explore the limits of the conclusion that 'misleading mentions may make memories mucky' (see Bekerian & Bowers, 1983; McClosky & Egeth, 1983; Jacoby *et al*, 1989; Johnson *et al*, 1993). As we already noted with respect to the case of Demjanjuk, objections from the public are often particularly pronounced when scientific research contradicts commonsense notions, especially when psychologists assert that people are not as infallible as commonsense holds. Instead of worrying about the fact that remembering is not like replaying a video of the past, we should use the results of psychological research to be more aware of the dynamics and possible pitfalls of remembering.

Gordon Bower

INTERIM SUMMARY

We have emphasised that remembering is a constructive process. When the information we were originally given is incomplete or not fully understandable, we frequently add to it; we make inferences and assumptions that allow us to retain a more complete and organised memory. Schemata are knowledge structures that summarise our knowledge within a limited domain. They help us recall information by providing a framework for us to use when evaluating experiences. The construction of memories is also influenced by the mood people are in: mood congruent processing and mood dependent retrieval specify the effects moods have on memory.

 ## FORGETTING

We all remember an enormous amount of material over long periods of time. College students can accurately recall details about the births of younger siblings even when those events occurred 16 years earlier (Sheingold & Tenney, 1982). Conductor Arturo Toscanini, even at an advanced age, supposedly knew 'by heart every note of every instrument of about 250 symphonic works and the words and music of about 100 operas' (Marek, 1975).

Knowledge in semantic memory is retrieved even better than knowledge in episodic memory, regardless of the time lapsed since the actual experience of the knowledge. In semantic memory, you will retain generalisations longer than details. For long-term retention, as for efficient encoding and retrieval, meaningful organisation seems to be the key.

However, even well-learned material may be irretrievable over time. We forget much of what we have learned. Why? In this section, we will explore the following four perspectives on forgetting (each one offers an explanation for what has happened to stored information when we cannot remember it):

- *Decay:* stored information is lost over time, similar to the colours of a picture bleached by the sun.
- *Interference:* stored information is blocked by similar inputs, as when multiple exposures of a negative interfere with the clarity of the original image.
- *Retrieval failure:* stored information cannot be located, as when someone cannot find their car in a huge car park.
- *Motivated forgetting:* stored information is hidden from consciousness for some personal reason, as when you forget the name of someone you do not like.

 ## Memory Traces Decay

Some early psychologists theorised that we forget because we suffer gradual storage loss; the **memory traces** decay over time, just as batteries lose their charge. However, to prove that decay is to blame for forgetting, research would have had to show that: (a) no mental activity that could change or interfere with the memories occurs between original learning and recall and (b) decayed memories are, in fact, gone from the brain and not merely inaccessible for some reason. Although it seems plausible that decay is partly responsible for the inability to remember material learned long ago, all we can say with certainty is that decay is an important factor in sensory memory loss and in short-term memory loss when all maintenance rehearsal is prevented.

In fact, some memories do not seem to become weaker over time. Remember that learned motor skills are retained for many years even with no practice. Once you learn to swim, you never forget how. In addition, trivia and irrelevant information, such as song titles and commercial jingles, seem to persist in memory, as do memories of odours from childhood.

 ## Interference

We never learn anything in a vacuum; we have other experiences before and after we learn new material. Both our learning and our retention of new material are affected by these interferences from other experiences, as demonstrated by the serial-position effect when end list input interferes with middle list recall. **Proactive interference** (*pro* means forward acting) refers to the phenomenon that occurs when the vocabulary list you learned yesterday interferes with your learning of today's list. **Retroactive interference** (*retro* means backward acting) describes what happens when studying today's list interferes with your memory for yesterday's list.

There are three general principles governing interference. First, the greater the similarity between two sets of material the greater the interference between them – two vocabulary lists in the same foreign language would interfere with each other more than a vocabulary list and a set of chemical formulas. Second, meaningless material is more vulnerable to interference than meaningful material.

Third, the more difficult the distracting task between learning and recall, the more it will interfere with memory of material learned earlier.

Ebbinghaus, after learning dozens of lists of nonsense syllables, found himself forgetting about 65 per cent of the new ones he was learning. 50 years later, students at an American university who studied Ebbinghaus' lists had the same experience – after many trials with many lists, what the students had learned earlier interfered proactively with their recall of current lists (Underwood, 1948; 1949).

The most obvious prediction that emerges from interference theory is that information undisturbed by new material will be recalled best. A classic study by Jenkins and Dallenbach (1924) provided support for this hypothesis. Subjects who went to sleep immediately after learning new material recalled it better the next morning than those who spent the same amount of time after learning performing their usual activities. Another finding from interference research is that short-term memory seems most vulnerable to interference. Evidence from the studies of the serial-position effect suggests that once material is firmly encoded in long-term memory, it is less subject to interference from later presented material.

 ## Retrieval Failure

An apparent memory loss often turns out to be only a failure of retrieval. A question worded a little differently will guide us to the information, or a question requiring only recognition will reveal knowledge that we could not access and reproduce by recall. The American students who were having trouble recalling Ebbinghaus' lists often remembered better when retrieval cues were given. But even the best retrieval cues will not help if a person did not store the material properly, just as a book not listed in the card catalogue will not be retrievable even if it is on a shelf somewhere in the library. In any case, it seems clear that much of our failure to remember reflects poor encoding or inadequate retrieval cues rather than loss of memory. Failure to call up a memory is never positive proof that the memory is not there.

Why do we forget the names of many of our primary-school classmates or even university teachers whom we meet in town away from the university? One reason is that the social context in which we met those people originally is changed and with that change we have lost the *social-context retrieval cues* we used to form memories for those acquaintances (Reiser *et al*, 1985). Memories of people are formed

around the social contexts in which they were encountered, and only later with more interaction, do we add secondary retrieval cues based on the personality traits and personal attributes of those people (Bond & Brockett, 1987).

 ## Motivated Forgetting

Another important reason to forget is that we merely do not wish to remember. Sometimes, we are motivated to forget some ideas we do not want to recognise as part of us, appointments we do not want to keep, names of people whom we do not like, and past events that threaten our basic sense of self or security. **Sigmund Freud** (1923) was the first to emphasise that memory and forgetting are dynamic processes. When memories are unacceptable or painful, we repress them in order to protect ourselves. **Repression** is an active but unconscious process by which threatening and conflict-laden (sexual or aggressive) impulses are pushed out of consciousness.

When *motivated forgetting* exceeds ordinary forgetfulness, and this inability to remember is not due to an organic cause, it is called *psychogenic amnesia*. The essential feature of **amnesia** is an inability to recall important personal information. Amnesia mostly occurs after a traumatic incident. Pynoos and Nader (1989), for example, studied memory distortions of children who, while playing in the schoolyard, were shot at by a disturbed man. Interviews showed that the children who had been most at risk tended to reduce the perceived danger. For example, they were inclined to overestimate the distance between themselves and the offender. On the other hand, the less endangered children erroneously remembered that the man had approached them directly, thereby increasing the perceived danger. Some children later completely forgot that they had been hit and thereby wounded.

There is considerable doubt whether Freud's 'repression' is an apposite concept with which to explain motivated forgetting (Holmes, 1990). It is beyond doubt, however, that traumatic events may precipitate the taking of mental 'escape routes', like exaggerating some and weakening other details or even forgetting parts of the traumatic incident altogether. But can traumatic experiences also lead to a blockade of the remembrance of an entire event or even a whole series of events? Does *total* amnesia as a consequence of psychological trauma exist and if it does, can it be undone? These questions have become important issues because of the many legal cases, especially in America, wherein adults accuse their parents of having abused them in their childhood.

For years they may have completely repressed the painful memories, but suddenly recollections of these menacing events come to the fore as **recovered memories** – take, for example, the case of Eileen Franklin.

In 1969, Eileen's eight-year-old friend Susan Nason vanished from her neighbourhood. For 20 years, no one knew what had happened to her. Then, in 1989, with the help of psychotherapy, Eileen claimed that she had recalled a long-repressed, horrifying memory about what had happened to Susan. On an autumn day two decades earlier, Eileen had witnessed her father sexually assault her friend and then bludgeon her to death with a rock (Marcus, 1990). He had threatened to kill Eileen if she ever told anyone. In a courtroom Eileen not only testified about the murder she had witnessed, but she also testified that, when she was a child, her father had beaten and sexually molested her. She said that the memory of the murder was triggered by a profound moment of eye contact with her daughter who reminded her of Susie. Suddenly, gazing into the eyes of her little girl, she remembered the look in Susie's eyes during her father's brutal assault. Eileen's father was found guilty and sentenced to life imprisonment.

Alongside the many legal cases about recovered memories concerning childhood abuse, several popular books on this subject have been published – sales are enormous and so is the attention from the media. The goal of all this consideration is a sincere desire to help people. Arguably, total amnesia is plausible and possible. Indeed, according to Lindsay and Read (1994), there is general agreement among memory researchers that some adults who were abused as children would not remember the abusive events. Recovery of these memories is also possible. With the help of appropriate cues such memories may be recollected. However, as we noted at the end of our discussion of remembering as a constructive process, there is also strong evidence about the existence of *illusory memories*. The already cited memory distortion of Piaget is but one example of many well-known anecdotes describing errors in autobiographical memory. These anecdotes can be supported by experiments demonstrating that people's expectations and beliefs can distort their recollections of specific autobiographical events (Lindsay and Read, 1994). Moreover, some people in particular conditions are susceptible to suggestions, especially from authority figures. Subjects may have the genuine belief that they are remembering something they witnessed, when in fact they have constructed memories on the basis of misleading suggestions (Ross *et al*, 1994; Loftus, 1993).

Of course, the suggestion alone that some people under some conditions may create false memories is appalling for the people involved, as we have already noted in our opening case about Demjanjuk. The notion of illusory memories is at odds with the intense feelings of suffering and also contradicts commonsense ideas about how memory works. Notably, some clinical psychologists and psychiatrists who supervise the process of recollection find it a difficult concept to accept and take on board. Nevertheless, there is considerable evidence that the same memory recovery techniques that help clients to recollect traumatic childhood events, can also lead to the creation of illusory memories and false beliefs (Loftus, 1993). We must take into account that people who go into therapy because of transient problems of daily living are susceptible. The client's readiness to designate external causes for their difficulties, in combination with the therapist's eagerness to uncover the existence of traumas, may eventually result in a reconstruction of the past that is erroneous. Ironically, then, the attention this topic receives in the mass media may unintentionally run the risk of reinforcing the creation of illusory memories of childhood sexual abuse.

In his book about Ivan the Terrible, Wagenaar (1988) proposed rules that should be followed if we are to rely on people's memory for the identification of a suspect. The same holds for recovered memories. Both proponents and critics of memory recovery therapies should share, for example, an interest in developing methods that are as non-suggestive and open-minded as possible in order to minimise the risk of creating illusory memories of childhood sexual abuse (Lindsay and Reed, 1994). This delicate matter is not helped by a polarisation between experimental psychologists on the one side and clinical psychologists and their traumatised clients on the other. Co-operation is urgently needed.

◆ Mnemonics: How to Prevent Forgetting

We are all eager to improve our memories in order to prevent ourselves from forgetting things we want to remember. There are special procedures and strategies that help us to encode material and to retrieve more easily. These strategies are known as **mnemonics** (from the Greek word meaning *to remember*). Mnemonics are short, verbal devices that encode a series of ideas by associating them with familiar and previously encoded information. The mnemonic procedures date back to the earliest cultures known to humankind. Before printing came into practice, it was absolutely necessary to learn a lot of information by heart. Orators and minstrels, for example, had to learn their speeches, tales and songs by heart (Yates, 1966). Mnemonics, however, have not lost their value in the contemporary culture of information exchange. They are especially useful for rote memorisation and when a lot of complex material, like this textbook, has to be memorised. In this section we will discuss the following mnemonic strategies: organisational schemes, visual imagery, the method of loci and the PQ4R method.

The simplest mnemonic devices use *organisational schemes* that put the items into a pattern that is easy to remember. For example, a mnemonic to remember the colours of the spectrum in their proper sequence becomes a person's name: 'Roy G. Biv' (red, orange, yellow, green, blue, indigo, violet). Sometimes an *acronym* in which each letter stands for a name can function as a mnemonic device. For example, 'WASPLEG' is an acronym for the so-called seven deadly sins: wrath, avarice, sloth, pride, lust, envy and gluttony. Also, 'VITARI' may help you to remember the capitals of the Baltic States: Vilnius, Tallinn and Riga.

Visual imagery as a mnemonic is a little more complex than simple organisation. It is an effective form of encoding because the material to be remembered later is encoded at both the verbal and the visual level. In retrieval, visual imagery gives you codes for both verbal and visual memories simultaneously (Paivio, 1986). You remember words by associating them with visual images – the more vivid and distinctive the images the better. For example, if you want to remember the names 'Ben' and 'Justin' you might conjure up an image of a man hurrying past the Houses of Parliament clock tower in London, thereby evoking a connection with 'Big Ben' and the phrase 'Just-in-time'. Delayed recall is enhanced when you encode the separate bits of information into a creative, unusual story line (Bower, 1972).

A mnemonic strategy that has been employed from classical Greece to the present day is *the method of loci*. The singular of loci is *locus*, and it means 'place'. The method of loci is a means of remembering the order of a list of names or objects by associating them with some sequence of places with which you are familiar. To remember a list of people you are meeting, you might mentally put each one sequentially in a separate room in your house; to remember their names, you mentally walk through your house and find the name associated with each location.

The mnemonics discussed thus far are well suited for systematic encoding of simple material like lists of names, persons and objects. When the memory task is more demanding, however, we need a more complex mnemonic procedure. The *PQ4R method*, which stands for 'Preview, Question, Reading, Reflect, Recite and Review', is an example of a complex mnemonic strategy that improves reading and retrieval of course material (Anderson, 1990). A chapter in this book is most effectively studied if you do so in the following step-wise fashion:

1 *Preview:* you start with a cursory survey of the entire chapter whereby you identify the hierarchy structure of the information that is implicit within the organisation of headings and subsequent sections.

2 *Question:* try to ask as many questions as is practically possible. Ask yourself, for example, why a particular section appears at that point; or question the illustrations in the book. With such questions in mind, you read with purpose.

3 *Reading:* read each section carefully and try to find answers to your questions. The answers generally lead to new questions and so a deeper level of text processing begins to occur.

4 *Reflect:* when you read and look for answers, try to actively think about what you are reading. A fruitful procedure to guide your critical thinking is trying to relate new material to things you already know.

5 *Recite:* after you have read a substantial block of text, for example a whole section, try to recite what you have learned. If you run into problems with this, go back to the text and try to fill in the gaps in your memory. You can recite alone or talk the section over with a friend.

6 *Review:* after you have read the chapter, try to recall its main points and the problems you faced working through the text. Try to ensure that you have answers now to all the questions that you posed earlier.

The PQ4R method is effective, but like most mnemonically-based strategies it has one disadvantage: it is rather time consuming to read a chapter in this way. You can be almost certain, however, that you will later benefit from this time investment.

INTERIM SUMMARY

Some early psychologists attributed forgetting to the gradual decay of memory traces over time. But research has never demonstrated any evidence of people forgetting in the absence of intervening mental activity. More widely held views attribute forgetting to interference. Proactive interference is the negative impact on memory of earlier learning; retroactive interference is the negative impact of later learning. Not all forgetting reflects the loss of information from memory; forgetting can sometimes be a failure of retrieval. Items that once could not be recalled may eventually be remembered in the presence of more effective retrieval cues.

In some cases, forgetting is prompted by personal motives, though there is much debate about the actual existence of recovered memories.

In ordinary circumstances, memory profits from mnemonic strategies. The key to success in employing mnemonics is spending time on using them.

 ## EVERYDAY MEMORY

This chapter on remembering and forgetting has largely been concerned with memory as studied in the psychological laboratory. In this section we will discuss an approach to the study of memory which argues that psychologists should go out of the laboratory and study memory phenomena as they occur in 'natural' contexts. This approach, which has become known as *everyday memory research* (Conway, 1991) is a recent development. At the end of the 1970s, **Ulric Neisser** (1978) argued that the study of memory neglected the fact that memory, like other cognitions, takes place in everyday environments and interacts with these settings. Memory research lacked *ecological validity*, he said, meaning that its results had little relevance outside of the laboratory (see Chapter 1). Neisser explained this lack of relevance by pointing out that the large majority of memory researchers studied the encoding, storage and retrieval of essentially *meaningless* material. Neisser argued in favour of an 'ecological approach to memory', which he linked to Bartlett's early work.

Since Neisser's provocative remarks, the field of everyday memory emancipated itself from the classical laboratory-based approaches. Everyday memory researchers study the ways in which people encode, store and retrieve information that has salience for them in their daily lives (Conway, 1991; Klatzky, 1991). Everyday memory research tries to shed light, for example, on how people remember such things as faces, music, appointments or what they were taught at school. The following study by Ceci and Bronfenbrenner (1991) illustrates how memory-related behaviour is contextually influenced.

The researchers had children bake cupcakes. One group did the baking in the laboratory, the other group used the ovens in their homes. A child who had his or her cakes in the oven had to remember to check a wall-clock at regular intervals to prevent the cakes from burning. Careful observation of their clock-checking behaviour showed that the children in the laboratory checked the clock approximately 30 per cent more often than did their counterparts in their own homes. According to the researchers, this difference originated from the children at home using the early minutes of the period to callibrate their psychological clocks to the wall-clock. In the unfamiliar context of the laboratory, the children had more difficulty callibrating their psychological clocks, so they made greater use of the wall-clock to remember and monitor the baking time.

A second example of everyday memory research is derived from the common experience in ordinary life of using memory to learn a second language. One such study showed how people retained the Spanish they had learned previously in school. The researchers were able to construct 50-year forgetting functions which showed that people forget a significant amount of their Spanish in the first five years after learning it. Then, however, the rate of forgetting drops to zero, even in the absence of any rehearsal or despite not being used at all (Bahrick, 1984).

A lot of research about the practical aspects of memory in ordinary life is focused upon two specific topics: autobiographical memory and eyewitness testimony. Both are discussed below. Our consideration of everyday memory will conclude with a brief account of the *discursive approach* to memory.

 ## Autobiographical Memory

This field of study concerns itself with the capacity of people to recollect their earlier lives (Baddeley, 1992). As such it is closely related to the concept of *self*: certain events are much more important with respect to who and what persons consider themselves to be than are others.

Willem A. Wagenaar conducted a systematic study of his own memory wherein he recorded 2,400 events over a period of six years and tried to recall them afterwards (Wagenaar, 1986; 1992). All events were recorded in terms of four defining features: (a) *what* the event was; (b) *who* was involved; (c) *where* and (d) *when* it happened. Each event was scaled for saliency, emotional involvement and pleasantness. Recall was cued by different combinations of these recorded features. For instance, supplied with the *what* cue, the task then was to reproduce the correct information concerning *who*, *where* and *when*: if he drew a card from the file which said 'visiting The Last Supper', he had to recall that he went to see da Vinci's painting with persons 'R' and 'L' (*who*), in Milan (*where*) and on a certain day (*when*). A systematic evaluation of the recollections showed that 20 per cent of events were very difficult to retrieve, but there were also indications that none of the events were completely forgotten. Pleasant events were generally recalled more often than unpleasant ones. However, unpleasant events of which Wagenaar was the instigator were far better remembered than unpleasant events which he had only witnessed. The involvement of self thus seems to partly determine the extent to which events are recalled.

Other studies of **autobiographical memory** have been concerned with, for example, the dating of events that took place in bygone years (Linton, 1986; Rubin & Baddeley, 1989) and with the patterns evident in the autobiographical recollections of elderly people (Rubin *et al*, 1986).

◆ Eyewitness Testimony

The opening case study about Demjanjuk has already provided some insight into the complex nature of memories in the non-laboratory based setting of the courtroom. In countries where juries are an integral part of the administration of justice, it can be observed that members of the jury tend to give much weight to the testimony of witnesses who were 'at the scene' and report on what they saw 'with their own eyes'. But if memory is reconstructed to fit our pre-existing schemata, how far should the memory of such witnesses be trusted? The ease with which we can be misled into 'remembering' false information has been amply demonstrated in the laboratory research of **Elizabeth Loftus** (1979; 1984) and her colleagues. During the research, bright college students with good memories were misled into

Chernobyl trial, Russia: the way in which a witness is questioned about an event can affect his or her recall.

'recalling' that, 'at the scene,' a 'give way' sign was a 'stop' sign, that a nonexistent barn supposedly existed and that a green 'go-light' was shining red.

The basic research design used in these studies typically involved two groups of students, both of which viewed the same stimulus materials on film or as slides. Members of the experimental group later received information designed to 'contaminate' their memories – indirect suggestions that certain events happened or certain actions occurred. For example, they might have heard another 'witness' report something about a man's moustache when, in fact, the man had no facial hair. Although many subjects resisted being misled, a significant proportion integrated the new information into their memory representations and confidently reported the nonexistent moustache, barn and stop sign as part of what they actually saw 'with their own eyes'.

The way in which a witness is questioned about an event can affect his or her recall. Sometimes words used in questioning suggest a particular interpretation. These words then function as misleading retrieval cues.

In one study, people were shown a film of an automobile accident and were asked to estimate the speeds of the cars involved. However, some people were asked, 'How fast were the cars going when they smashed into each other?', while others were asked, 'How fast were the cars going when they contacted each other?' When the word 'smashed' was used within the question, the eyewitnesses reported that the cars had been going at over 40 miles (circa 65 kilometres) per hour. Those same cars were reported to be travelling at 30 miles (circa 50 kilometres) per hour by eyewitnesses who had been asked the question containing the word 'contacted'.

About a week later, all the eyewitnesses were asked, 'Did you see any broken glass?' In actual fact, no broken glass had appeared in the film. However, of the eye-witnesses who had been asked the 'smashed' question the week before, about a third reported that there had been broken glass. Only 14 per cent of the 'contacted' questioned eyewitnesses said they had seen broken glass. Clearly, the type of verb used in the original question altered people's memories of what they had witnessed. Moreover, these witnesses had filled in the gaps with plausible details so as to fit the general context suggested by the particular verb used (Loftus, 1979).

This line of research has conspicuous practical value and also contributes to basic knowledge. The process by which a person perceives an event, encodes that information and recalls it at a later time is at the core of psychological interest in learning and memory. Thus, the issues that are involved in this research are of central importance to both psychologists and professionals working in the legal system. The limitations of memory processes and the perceptual and cognitive biases that may be involved have profound implications for the use of eyewitness testimony in courtroom trials.

◆ The Discursive Approach to Memory

Psychologists who study memory tend to focus on the ways in which cognitive systems process information. As we have seen, most research on cognitive processing is done under laboratory conditions, although a growing number of researchers study memory-related processing outside the laboratory. The discursive approach to memory differs fundamentally from the cognitive one.

Here, the object of study is *discourse* about past events as it naturally occurs. The focus is on talk about the past and on the functions of this form of collective remembering. Researchers who embrace the discursive approach argue that people use knowledge of the past in current interaction to generate shared meanings and facilitate communication (Edwards *et al*, 1992). Thus, remembering is seen as the social construction of shared knowledge about the past, rather than as an individual mental process. One of the discursive studies, for example, showed that a small group of people that tried to remember the film *E.T.* constructed together a joint version of the film. In discussing their memories of the movie, the participants shared the burden of recall and were constantly comparing recollections and inserting out-of-sequence reminiscences. In other words, the participants constructed a shared understanding of the film through their conversation (Edwards & Middleton, 1986). In another study, families were recorded and observed as they talked about their holiday snapshots. Again, this practice of collective remembering produced a shared understanding of each family's past (Edwards & Middleton, 1988).

The discursive approach to memory is still in its early days. Its main concern is with how people use knowledge of the past in the present, rather than with how such knowledge was acquired, retained and retrieved – the usual concerns of both laboratory-based and everyday memory-based research in the

cognitive tradition (Conway, 1992).

Both everyday memory and **discursive remembering** have attracted a lot of attention recently amongst psychologists. Some researchers from the laboratory tradition are critical of these new approaches (Banaji & Crowder, 1989), whilst others express an intellectual openness and curiosity about what the future of this kind of memory research will bring (Roediger & Wheeler, 1992).

INTERIM SUMMARY

Psychologists who study everyday memory tend to do so in natural contexts. They study how prior, personally meaningful knowledge is processed in memory. In autobiographical memory the focus is on the capacity of people to recollect their earlier lives. The study of eyewitness testimony is linked to the constructive aspects of memory as discussed earlier. Research on testimonies shows that eyewitnesses are susceptible to biases when trying to recall past events, especially details about those events. Such recall also depends in large part upon the retrieval cues that are given by legal professionals to witnesses within the form and content of their questions.

Discursive remembering is the most recent development in everyday memory research. The discursive approach does not study the mental processes of remembering and forgetting, but is concerned with the ways in which people talk about their past so as to construct a shared present.

THE NEUROBIOLOGY OF MEMORY

If you want to understand how your personal computer handles information, you have to examine the software. For your understanding of the way a computer program works, it is not necessary to know anything about the machinery of the computer, namely, the hardware. The same can be said about the study of memory. In describing the way memory operates, one can separate reflection about its formal operations (the software) from reflections about the mechanisms (the hardware) used to implement those operations. Questions concerning the software of the memory process (for example, how information is encoded, stored, processed and retrieved) are studied by psychologists. In so doing, theoretical models are created of an information-processing system that forms, associates and encodes learned experiences. Psychologists test their theories with behavioural data from a variety of experiments in the laboratory or in natural settings.

Questions concerning the hardware (for example how experience modifies various components of the nervous system) are studied by neurobiologists. Two of the many tactics that emerge from this more molecular level of analysis are studying the anatomy of memory – where the brain forms and stores memories – and analysing the changes in synapses and neurons that are assumed to constitute memory. Let us examine some of the evidence being uncovered by neuroscientists.

 The Anatomy of Memory

In addition to encoding genetic information in the DNA of every cell nucleus, nature encodes experiential information in the neurons of the brain. The general term for this coding of acquired information in the brain is the engram or memory trace. The sum of a person's store of engrams is the biological substrate of human memory and the foundation upon which each human being's uniqueness rests.

Where in the vast galaxy of the brain are these memory traces to be found? Are they localised in particular brain regions or are they distributed throughout many different areas? The search for the engram was begun many years ago by physiological psychologist **Karl Lashley** (1929; 1950). He trained rats to learn mazes, removed portions of their cerebral cortexes, and then retested their memories for the mazes. He found that memory impairment from brain lesioning was proportional to the amount of tissue that was removed. The impairment grew worse as more of the cortex was damaged. However, memory was not affected by the area in the brain from where the tissue was removed. Lashley gave up in disappointment, prematurely concluding that the elusive engram did not exist in any localised regions of the brain but was widely distributed throughout the entire brain.

We now know that Lashley was partly correct – and partly incorrect. Maze learning, which involves spatial, visual and olfactory signals, is complex and memory for complex sets of information is distributed across many neural systems. However, memory for each specific type of sensory information and memory for discrete types of knowledge are separately processed and localised in limited regions of the brain. Modern neuroscientists are now able to trace the neural circuitry that is necessary and sufficient for a particular type of learning – and for its remembrance.

There are four major brain structures involved in memory:

- *The cerebellum:* essential for procedural memory, memories acquired by repetition and classically conditioned responses.
- *The striatum:* a complex of structures in the forebrain; the likely basis for habit formation and for stimulus-response connections.
- *The cerebral cortex:* for sensory memories and associations between sensations.
- *The amygdala and hypothalamus:* largely responsible for declarative memory of facts, dates and names, and also for memories of emotional significance.

Other parts of the brain, such as the thalamus, the basal forebrain and the prefrontal cortex, are involved also as way stations for the formation of particular types of memory (see *Figure 8.8*).

Neuropsychologist **Richard Thompson** (1987) has been investigating the anatomy of memory for the past 20 years and claims to have found the engram – at least one of them. He uses Pavlovian eyelid conditioning in rabbits as a model for an organism's adaptive behavioural responding to known brain circuits. Thompson conditions rabbits to blink when they hear a tone that signals that an air puff will shoot at their eyes. He has discovered that a lesion of only one cubic millimetre of cell tissue in the cerebellum of a rabbit causes permanent loss of the conditioned eyeblink. (The cerebellum is found to play an essential role in both the learning and memory of specific conditioned responses to aversive events.) The memory deficit is highly specific to that learned association – the animal can still hear the tone, respond to the air puff and learn the conditioned response in the other eye, but it cannot relearn the response in the first eye.

The entire circuitry for learning and storing this simple conditioned response has been traced to specific nuclei in and around the cerebellum. In more complex conditioning, as when the subject learns to remember that there is a delay between the tone and the air puff, circuits in the hippocampus also become involved (McCormick & Thompson, 1984).

The hippocampus and amygdala, both parts of the limbic system, are currently believed to be involved in encoding the kind of information that is dealt with in declarative memory. The cerebral cortex is probably the storage centre of long-term memory (McGaugh *et al*, 1985). Studies of human patients with amnesia have identified the important role of the hippocampus in encoding new fact memories. Comparable memory deficits are found in monkeys with lesions in the hippocampus and amygdala (Mishkin *et al*, 1984).

Some researchers are studying memory in cortical networks by stimulating or blocking smell memory. The olfactory system is unique among the senses because it has fairly direct connections to the hippocampus, amygdala and the thalamus. This fact

FIGURE 8.8	BRAIN STRUCTURES INVOLVED IN MEMORY

This simplified diagram shows some of the main structures of the brain that are involved in the formation, storage and retrieval of memories.

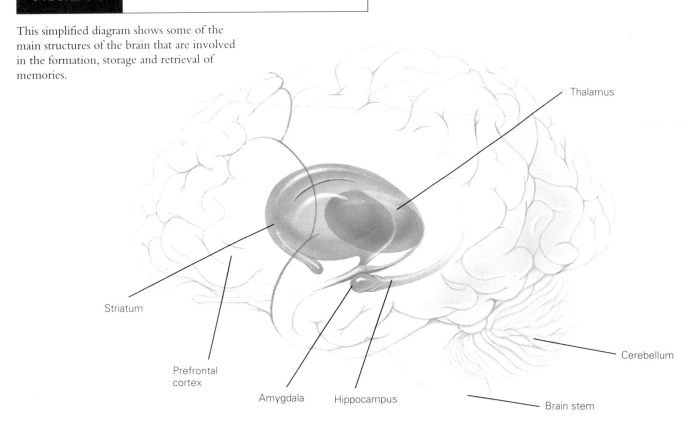

may account for the power of certain odours to evoke strong childhood memories in humans. Remarkable parallels occur between the smell memory of rats and humans. Lesions that separate the olfactory system and the hippocampus in rats produce forgetting for learned odours similar to the amnesia experienced by humans who have suffered damage to their temporal lobe and hippocampus (Lynch, 1986).

Other research supports theories that the brain organises memory functions around two different systems for information storage. The distinction we encountered earlier between procedural (skill) and declarative (fact) knowledge is supported by a variety of experiments with patients who experienced temporarily impaired memories as a result of electroconvulsive shock therapy and with brain-lesioned monkeys (Squire, 1986; Thompson, 1986; Mishkin & Appenszeller, 1987).

Skill learning and stimulus-response habits appear to be more primitive than fact, or cognitive, learning in the evolution of learning systems. Skill learning may involve a collection of special purpose abilities that are stored in structures evolutionarily even more primitive than the limbic system (which includes the amygdala and hippocampus). These structures are not affected by brain damage to higher level brain centres. In an extensive series of well-controlled experiments with

monkeys, **Mortimer Mishkin** and his associates have convincingly demonstrated that different neural systems underlie memories for information and memories for simple habits (Mishkin & Petri, 1984). While fact learning seems to be centred in the hippocampus and amygdala, skill learning may be located in the striatum (a group of cell bodies in the forebrain).

The hippocampus is also implicated in another vital aspect of memory we have not yet mentioned – the way stored information and new information are connected. Memory is not fixed at the time of learning but is gradually transformed into a durable long-term memory code by the dynamic process known as *consolidation* (Hebb, 1949; McGaugh & Herz, 1972). This stabilising or consolidating of memories can proceed for as long as several years in humans and for weeks in lower animals. It is the mechanism for the transition from short-term to long-term memory and is currently hypothesised to occur in the hippocampus.

◆ Alzheimer's Disease

Further evidence of the hippocampus' importance to memory comes from the tragic disorder known as

Alzheimer's disease. This disease strikes more than 10 per cent of people over the age of 65 and almost half of those over 85. The disease is marked by a gradual, but ultimately severe, decline in intellectual ability and memory. The symptoms of Alzheimer's are alarming: once independent and competent individuals begin to lose the ability to take care of themselves. It often starts with an atrophy in the hippocampus that causes anterograde amnesia. For example, while looking for a match after the gas is turned on, a coffee pot may come to mind which in turn may serve as a reminder to buy a new jar of a favourite brand, perhaps even right away. So the search for the match becomes a search for some money with which the purchase can be made but this new line of thought may also bring other objects to mind or in view, and so on. Patients forget what they are doing midway through an activity because they are no longer able to suppress information that is irrelevant for completing the task at hand. Later on, other parts of the brain (for example, the pre-frontal and temporal associative areas) are involved. Patients are no longer able to hold on to plans and a general cognitive deterioration sets in. Patients slowly forget how to enact skills they have performed most of their lives, including how to make a hot drink, wash themselves and find their way about their own home. In late stages of the disease, patients may even fail to remember and recognise who family members are. They may even forget the fact of having had their own children and in the end lose their own identity. This profound loss of past memories in addition to the disruption of new learning sets Alzheimer's disease apart from other amnesia syndromes.

Alzheimer's disease is clearly linked to degeneration of the hippocampus and related areas of the mid-brain. Autopsies have shown that up to three-quarters of the neurons in these areas may be lost in Alzheimer's patients and the remaining neurons damaged. Massive tangles of fibres appear in the cell bodies, and there is a decline in production of the neurotransmitters necessary for neurons to communicate with one another. Such degeneration of the hippocampus is not a necessary part of growing older since recent research shows that some cases of Alzheimer's have a genetic cause. However, the disorder points out the importance of the hippocampal system in the encoding and storage of new memories. Moreover, it suggests that these structures may also play a role in the act of retrieval, because of Alzheimer's devastating effects on old memories.

◆ Cellular Mechanisms of Memory

Neuroscientists now generally accept that human memory involves changes in the physiology and/or structure of synaptic membranes (Lynch, 1986) – neural impulses that signal specific experiences modify subgroups of the many billions of synapses in the cortex (see *Figure 8.9*). In this view of the biology of memory, the chemistry of memory must be able to modify irreversibly the structure of a small group of synaptic contacts on a single cell – without affecting neighbouring units.

Researchers have reached this conclusion by using high frequency stimulation of inputs to the hippocampus. This stimulation increased memory strength for new learning for 32 months. This technique, called *long-term potentiation*, was found to cause changes in the shapes of synapses, to lead to the formation of new synaptic contacts on nerve cells, and to increase the number of receptors for the neurotransmitter glutamate used by the hippocampus (McGaugh *et al*, 1985).

This long-lasting potentiation effect alters cortical synapses through several chemical processes triggered by neural impulses (or the experimental high-frequency stimulation). One such chemical process appears to involve the sudden increase in calcium within neurons. Calcium activates a special kind of enzyme called calpain, which causes the breakdown of parts of the cell membrane by influencing a protein, spectrin, that changes the shape of the dendritic spines. This forms new receptors on the membrane which make it more sensitive to subsequent signals from connecting neurons. Calpain's effects are permanent and irreversible, thus making it ideal for producing long-lasting changes in cellular chemistry and anatomy.

In addition, inputs to neurons also increase levels of neurotransmitters, the chemical messengers by which neurons communicate with one another. New evidence shows that neurons maintain a number of neurotransmitters, each independently regulated (Black *et al*, 1987). Learning modifies the levels of these neurotransmitters.

◆ Integrating the Biology and the Psychology of Memory

Understanding the human mind is the central goal of much psychological research. The learning and memory of experiences fills our minds with ideas that give meaning to our existence and purpose to our actions. There can be no mind without memory and no sense of human consciousness without mind. The psychological study of memory in the laboratory and in real life has provided new insights into the multiplicity of systems and operations involved in processing information into memory codes.

| **FIGURE 8.9** | HOW MEMORIES ARE FORMED |

A nerve spine in the hippocampus changes shape after receiving the type of stimulation that occurs during a learning experience. Below left, the first of several bursts of electricity causes a chemical neurotransmitter to be released from a neighbouring neuron onto the receptors of the nerve spine shown here. Calcium enters the cell. The calcium activates calpain (orange), an otherwise dormant enzyme, which begins to degrade fodrin, the structural material of the spine. With additional bursts of electricity, the fodrin continues to break down, and more receptors appear, below right. More receptors result in a greater influx of calcium, and therefore more calpain activation and even greater fodrin degradation. With significant loss of structural material, the spine changes shape. A new spine may also begin to extend through the membrane. These permanent changes result in new connections between neurons in the brain, a plausible explanation for memory.

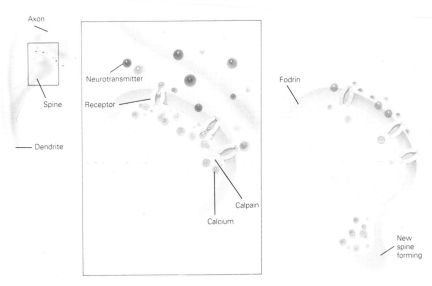

Theoretical speculations on the part of cognitive psychologists about the dual coding of short-term and long-term memory and distinctions among procedural, semantic and episodic memory have now been confirmed by the research of neurobiologists and neuropsychologists. These investigators study the brain as the biological substrate of the mind and memory as 'the essential brain substrate for all higher mental processes' (Thompson, 1984). Despite differences in the way each of these disciplines approach the study of memory, there is a new level of co-operation and integration between them. The ultimate goal of cognitive psychologists, neurobiologists and neuropsychologists is to be able to provide formal descriptions of cognition, underlying brain systems, and the neurons and cellular events within these systems (Squire, 1986). A memory may be vulnerable to distortion and loss over time, and we could all improve the ways we commit information to memory; but, to psychologists, memory is the 'Queen of the Cognitive Sciences' and, to poets, the very crux of being human.

recapping main points

What is Memory?

Psychologists study how remembering is a way of processing information. Many view it as a three-stage process in which information that arrives through our senses is encoded, stored and later retrieved. Three separate memory systems have been proposed: sensory, short-term and long-term.

Sensory Memory

In encoding for sensory memory, stimulus energy is changed to a neural code. Sensory memory has a large capacity but a very short duration. Attention and pattern recognition help sensory information to get into short-term memory.

Short-term Memory

Short-term memory (STM) has a limited capacity (seven plus or minus two items) and lasts only briefly without rehearsal. STM, as part of our psychological present, is also called working memory. Material may be transferred to it from either sensory or long-term memory. Information can be consciously processed only in STM.

Verbal information entering STM from sensory memory is usually encoded acoustically. STM's capacity can be increased by chunking unrelated items into meaningful groupings. Maintenance rehearsal extends the duration of material in STM indefinitely. Elaborative rehearsal prepares it for long-term storage.

Long-term Memory

Long-term memory (LTM) constitutes our total knowledge of the world and of the self. It is nearly unlimited in capacity. Meaningful organisation is the key to encoding for LTM: the more familiar the material and the better the organisation, the better the retention.

The more specifically material is encoded in terms of expected retrieval cues, the more efficient later retrieval will be, if the same cues are available at the time of retrieval. Similarity of context in which learning and retrieval takes place also aids retrieval.

Three kinds of memory content are procedural, semantic and episodic memory. Procedural memory is memory for skills – how things get done. Semantic memory is memory for the basic meaning of words and concepts. Episodic memory is concerned with memory of events that have been personally experienced.

There is debate and disagreement about whether there are actually three different memory systems (sensory, short-term and long-term) or whether there is only one memory within which we simply process memories at different levels, using varying depths of processing. Others have proposed that memory functions like a neural network.

Remembering

Remembering is not simply recording but a constructive and selective process. We remember what we want to and what we are prepared to remember based on our cultural and personal history. Schemata play a major role in constructive memory processes. Schemata are cognitive clusters built up from earlier experience that provide expectations and a context for interpreting new information and, thus, influence what is remembered.

Information or misinformation provided during retrieval can bias our recall without our realising it, making eyewitness testimony unreliable when contaminated by after-the-fact input.

Forgetting

Explanations for forgetting include decay, interference, retrieval failures and motivated forgetting. Each one is shown to play a role in some specific instances of forgetting. Mnemonic techniques can help prevent forgetting.

Everyday Memory

Memory is also studied in contexts where remembering and forgetting occur naturally – for example, when people recall the events from their lives (autobiographical memory) or when witnesses testify in court about what they have seen.

The Neurobiology of Memory

Study of the neurobiology of memory occurs in three areas: identification of brain structures involved in the formation and storage of memories; analysis of the synaptic and neuronal changes assumed to underlie memory; and discovery of the physiological systems that regulate or modify memory storage.

Different brain structures (including the hippocampus, the amygdala, the cerebellum and the cerebral cortex) have been shown to be involved in different types of memory, in the formation of new memories and the storage of old memories. It appears that memory may involve lasting changes in the membranes of neurons at some synapses and in the levels of certain neurotransmitters. Hormones such as adrenalin (epinephrine) may play a role in regulating memory.

Cognitive psychologists and neurobiologists are working together to unlock the secrets of memory, an achievement which will stand as one of the major accomplishments of modern science.

key Terms

Alzheimer's disease
amnesia
autobiographical memory
backward masking
chunk
connectionism
context dependence
declarative learning
discursive remembering
dual-code memory
echo
eidetic imagery
elaborative rehearsal
encoding
encoding specificity principle
episodic memory
icon
immediate memory span
implicit memory
levels-of-processing theory
long-term memory (LTM)
maintenance rehearsal
memory code
memory trace
mnemonics

motivated forgetting
Multi-Store Model
partial-report procedure
priming effect
proactive interference
procedural learning
propositional storage
psychogenic amnesia
recall
recognition
recovered memories
repression
retrieval
retrieval cues
retroactive interference
schema
selective attention
semantic memory
sensory gating
sensory memory
sensory register
serial position effect
short-term memory (STM)
storage
working memory

major Contributors

Atkinson, Richard
Baddeley, Alan
Bartlett, Frederic (1886-1969)
Bower, Gordon
Bruner, Jerome
Chase, William
de Groot, Adriaan
Ebbinghaus, Hermann (1850-1909)
Freud, Sigmund (1856-1939)
Lashley, Karl (1890-1958)

Loftus, Elizabeth
Miller, George
Miskin, Mortimer
Neisser, Ulric
Shiffrin, Richard
Sperling, George
Thompson, Richard
Tulving, Endel
Wagenaar, Willem A.

Chapter 9

Thought and Language

At the age of 16, Edith Eva Eger's world turned upside down. She and her family were suddenly arrested and interned in Auschwitz, a Nazi concentration camp in Poland. Shortly after they arrived at Auschwitz, her mother was sent to the gas chamber. Before she was taken away, she urged Edith and her sister to live their lives fully: 'Remember,' she said, 'what you put inside your brain, no one can take away' (Eger, 1990).

In the horror-filled existence of concentration camp life, Edith found that the basic logic of the world was reversed. The notions of good behaviour she had learned whilst growing up 'were replaced by a kind of animal quiver, which instantly smelled out danger and acted to deflect it'. Matters of life and death were decided as casually as flipping a coin – you could be sent to the 'showers of death' for having a loosely tied shoelace.

After years of being brutalised, the camp inmates longed for freedom, yet paradoxically, also dreaded it. When their liberators arrived, some prisoners 'rushed forward but most retreated and even returned to their barracks'.

Edith was a fortunate survivor. She later married, emigrated to the United States and became a clinical psychologist. Recently, at the age of 61, Dr Eger's need to understand the twisted reality of the camps caused her to return to Auschwitz. 'I came to mourn the dead and celebrate the living. I also needed to formally put an end to the denial that I had been a victim and to assign guilt to the oppressor' (Eger, 1990). For many years, she had denied the horrible truths of her camp experiences, but, eventually, denial was unacceptable to her. By reliving the events of her incarceration and forcing herself to think about the meaning of that horror, Dr Eger believes she has become better able to help others understand events that seem inexplicable in the context of their everyday lives. Edith took her mother's last

words to heart. No one can take away what she has 'put inside her brain'. By becoming a psychotherapist, Dr Eger chose a career in which she helps others cope with personal realities that defy rational explanation.

The fundamental human desire to comprehend the nature of one's existence that motivated Dr Eger was eloquently described by another survivor of Auschwitz, Italian writer Primo Levi. He reports, 'It might be surprising that in the camps one of the most frequent states of mind was curiosity. And yet, besides being frightened, humiliated and desperate, we were curious: hungry for bread and also to understand. The world around us was upside down and somebody must have turned it upside down . . . to twist that which was straight, to befoul that which was clean' (Levi, 1985).

Even in the hell of a concentration camp, the human mind still insists on enquiring into how such malevolence could occur. We appear to be driven by a basic need to understand the nature of our existence and to try to apprehend the causes of our thoughts, feelings and actions. In earlier chapters, we considered consciousness, learning and memory. We are now in a position to understand how humans think and reason and how our thoughts are communicated through language.

THE ACTIVITY OF thinking and translating our thoughts into language are generally taken for granted because we are engaged in these activities continually during most of our waking hours. However, when we witness a child's joy at solving a puzzle or when we are absorbed in an interesting conversation we may reflect upon the extraordinary nature of our human intellectual and communicative capacities.

In this chapter psychological approaches to human thought and language are discussed. Firstly, we will present some major issues in the psychology of thinking. The second part of the chapter is devoted to the psychological study of language. The serial nature of this presentation is somewhat misleading in suggesting that thought and language are separate matters. In fact, thought and language are hard to disentangle: people most probably use linguistic structures to think and they definitely employ spoken or written language to express their thoughts. Furthermore, it is very difficult to conceive how we would be able to discuss the psychology of thinking without using language.

It should also be noted that thought's connections extend beyond language. The study of thinking is part of research into *cognition* – that is, the study of all higher mental processes (see Chapter 1). Therefore, thinking is linked directly to the cognitive processes of perception, attention, remembering and forgetting, which were discussed in the preceding chapters.

In our dicussion of human thought we will focus on *intentional thinking* – that is, the process of thinking in a directed sense. Intentional thinking is the mental activity that is concerned with reasoning about something, solving a problem or deciding what to do. Our discussion of language embodies a presentation of the basic processes in language comprehension and production, but it is also concerned with language as a communicative tool. At the end of the chapter we will concern ourselves with the relation between language and thought.

THOUGHT: MENTAL STRUCTURES FOR THINKING

In the last chapter we showed that the act of remembering usually involves top-down processing of stored information. The sensory input is matched against our mental structures or internal representations. This matching enables us to identify the input as new or familiar, dangerous or desired and useful or irrelevant – which guides our actions. This process of basic pattern recognition helps new input get past the sensory register into short-term memory. Once there, further organising processes help us store it more permanently in long-

term memory. Pattern recognition and the later organisational processing, in turn, are the first stages of our higher mental processes – the beginnings of thinking. They go beyond the information contained in the sensory input by using stored knowledge as a context for interpretation (Bruner, 1973).

Human thought processes are at the upper end of the information-processing sequence, building on the more fundamental components of lower-order cognitions, such as pattern recognition, perceptual analysis and memory. What happens when we reach that ultimate stage of information-processing called *thinking*? Thinking is a complex mental process of forming a new representation by transforming available information. That transformation involves the interaction of many mental attributes, such as inferring, abstracting, reasoning, imagining, judging, problem-solving and, at times, creativity. From the perspective of cognitive psychology, thinking has three general features (Mayer, 1981):

- It is assumed to occur in the *mind,* although it may be inferred from observable behaviour.
- It is a process that manipulates *knowledge* in a person's cognitive system.
- It is *intentional*, which means that it is directed toward finding solutions to problems facing the individual.

Thinking relies on a variety of mental structures. These structures include concepts, schemes, scripts, propositions and pictures. Let us examine how we utilise them to form thoughts.

Concepts and Concept Formation

A basic process in thinking is to categorise individual experiences. Categorising, which amounts to giving the same label to members of a category and to take the same action towards them, is regarded as one of the most basic abilities of thinking organisms (Mervis & Rosch, 1981). The categories we form, which are mental representations of kinds of related items that are grouped in some way, are called **concepts**. Concepts are the building blocks of thinking. They enable us to organise knowledge in systematic ways. Concepts may represent objects, activities, or living organisms. Concepts may also represent properties (such as red or large), abstractions (such as truth or love) and relations (such as smarter than), which tells us about a difference between two organisms but does not tell us about either of the individuals being compared (Smith & Medin, 1981). Because they can never be observed directly, concepts, as mental structures, must be discovered through research.

A concept is a mental event that represents a category or class of objects. The concept of flower encompasses many different flowers.

Psychological theories serve the function to postulate concepts and the relations between them.

A basic task of thinking is concept learning or **concept formation** – identifying the stimuli properties that are common to a class of objects or ideas. We live in a world filled with untold numbers of individual events from which we are continually extracting information about how to combine them into an ever smaller, simpler set that we can manage mentally. The mind lives by the principle of **cognitive economy**, minimising the amount of time and effort required to process information. We learn not only features that form concepts, such as the colours of traffic lights, but also conceptual rules by which these features are related. For example, consider traffic light rules: If red, stop; if yellow, slow down and prepare to stop; if green, go.

Critical features versus prototypes

What is the unit of information that is stored in memory when we form a concept? Psychologists have not yet agreed on the unit. Currently, two competing theories attempt to account for the form in which information is stored.

- The **critical feature** approach suggests that we store definitions or lists of critical features that are necessary and sufficient conditions for a concept to be included in a category. A concept is a member of the category if, and only if, it has every feature on the list.
- The **prototype** approach suggests that categories are structured around an ideal or most representative

instance which is called a prototype (Rosch, 1973). A concept is classified as a member of a category if it is more similar to the prototype of that category than it is to the prototype of any other category. Prototype theories assume that a prototype of averaged features is stored along with some allowable variations of its features. A stimulus might not fit precisely within the limits of a stored category, but would still be classified as belonging to it if its variation from the prototype was within an acceptable range. For example, although the following fonts are very different, we still recognise them as belonging to the same category of the letter Z.

It appears that we use both methods of storing concepts – critical features and prototypes – but we use each for different kinds of concepts. Concepts in science are often based on definitions of critical features. For example, *mammals* are defined as vertebrates that nurse their young. The boundaries between mammals and non-mammals are well defined and a list of critical features seems to work to distinguish among them. How is the concept *bird* defined? The dictionary defines a bird as 'a warm-blooded vertebrate with feathers and wings'. However, bird is a fuzzy·concept because it has no well-defined boundaries between some members of its class (Zadeh, 1965). Some aspects of the definition do not fit every type of bird. If you were asked to build a cage for a bird, you would probably construct a cage that would be far too small for an ostrich or a penguin, both of which are birds. Your concept of bird seems to include something about *typicality* – the most typical member of the class – which goes beyond the list of critical features that qualifies creatures for birdhood.

A wide variety of studies have shown that people respond more quickly to typical members of a category than to its more unusual ones. Reaction time to determine whether a robin is a bird is quicker than reaction time to determine whether an ostrich is a bird, because robins resemble the prototype of a bird more than ostriches do (Kintsch, 1981; Rosch *et al*, 1976). One reason reaction time is faster for prototypes is that a prototype is formed on the basis of frequently experienced features. These features and their relations are stored in memory and the more often they are perceived the stronger their overall memory strength is. Thus, the prototype can be rapidly accessed and recalled.

Hierarchies and basic levels

Concepts are often organised in hierarchies, from general to specific, as seen in *Figure 9.1*. The broad category of animal has several sub-categories, such as bird and fish, which in turn are subdivided into their types, such as canary, ostrich, shark and salmon. The animal category is itself a sub-category of the still larger category of living beings. These concepts and categories are arranged in a hierarchy of levels,

with the most general and abstract at the top and the most specific and concrete at the bottom. They are also linked to many other concepts: some birds are edible, some are endangered, some are national symbols.

There seems to be a level in such hierarchies at which people best categorise and think about objects. That level – the *basic level* – can be retrieved from memory most quickly and used most efficiently. For example, the chair at your desk belongs to three obvious levels in a conceptual hierarchy: furniture, chair and desk chair. The lower level category, desk chair, would provide more detail than you generally need, whereas the higher level category, furniture, would not be precise enough. When spontaneously identifying it, you would be more likely to call it a chair than a piece of furniture or a desk chair. If you were shown a picture of it, your reaction time would be faster if you were asked to verify that it was a chair than if you were asked to verify that it was a piece of furniture (Rosch, 1978). Research indicates that our dependence on basic levels of concepts is another fundamental aspect of thought.

Schemas and Scripts

The concept of **schema** was introduced in the previous chapter as a general conceptual framework of

FIGURE 9.1	HIERARCHICALLY ORGANISED STRUCTURE OF CONCEPTS

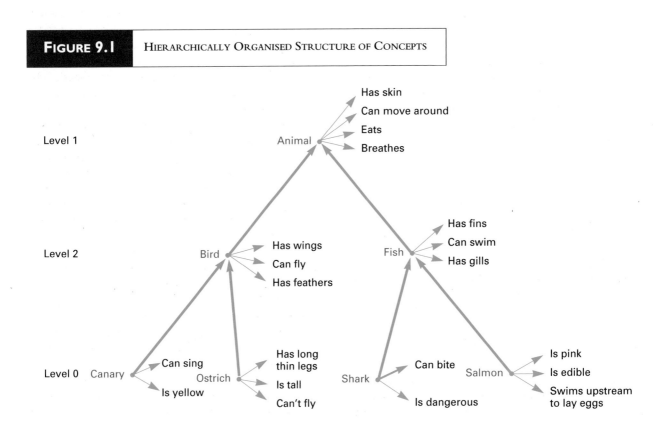

320   CHAPTER 9 ····· THOUGHT AND LANGUAGE

knowledge regarding objects, people or situations. Schemas influence what we perceive and remember by facilitating top-down processing of information. We now turn to the functioning of schemas as structures for thinking.

Schemas include expectations about what attributes and effects are typical for particular concepts or categories. New information, which is often incomplete or ambiguous, makes more sense when we can relate it to existing knowledge in our stored schemas. So we may say that, in addition to the functions of encoding new information (interpreting and organising it) and influencing memory for old information, schemas also enable us to make inferences about missing information. What can you infer about the statement, 'Ernie was upset to discover, upon opening the basket, that he had forgotten the salt'? With no further information, you can infer a great deal about this event that is not explicit in the description given. Salt implies that the basket is a picnic basket. The fact that Ernie is upset that the salt is missing suggests that the food in the basket is food that is usually salted, such as hard-boiled eggs and vegetables. You automatically know what other foods might be included and, equally important, what definitely is not: everything in the world that is larger than a picnic basket and everything that would be inappropriate to take on a picnic – from a boa constrictor to your favourite chair. The body of information you now have has been organised around a 'picnic' schema. By relating the statement about Ernie to your pre-established picnic schema, you understand the statement better.

Schemas also guide our thinking and understanding of new information. Comprehension seems to occur then through integrating consistent new input with what we already know and/or through overcoming the discrepancy between new input and stored schemas by changing a knowledge structure or by changing or ignoring the new input. This integrative process can be illustrated in the following way:

What do the following sentences mean to you?

The notes were sour because the seam was split.
The haystack was important because the cloth ripped.

Taken alone, these sentences make little sense. What notes are being referred to and how does a split seam cause sour notes? Why should ripped cloth make a haystack important?

Now, how does your thinking change with the addition of two words: *bagpipes* and *parachute*?

The sentences suddenly become understandable, because the information included is integrated into knowledge that already existed: into appropriate schemas. The notes were sour because the seam in the bag of the bagpipe was split. If you were falling from a plane in a torn parachute, the haystack could save your life. Thinking, similar to perceiving and remembering, is a *constructive process* in which we draw on our existing mental structures to make as much sense as possible out of new information.

The schematic organisation of thinking is concerned with a variety of topics. There are schemas about objects and environmental events but also about persons, roles and ourselves. *Person schemas* contain information about particular people as well as people in general and their traits, goals and ideas about what causes them to behave as they do. *Role schemas* include expected behaviours that are appropriate for a person in a particular social setting, such as a doctor, a waiter or a parent. *Self schemas* are the conceptions we have of ourselves that guide the way we process all self-relevant information, such as shyness, generosity and femininity (Fiske & Taylor, 1991).

An event schema or **script** is a cluster of knowledge about sequences of inter-related, specific events and actions expected to occur in a certain way in particular settings. A script is to procedural knowledge (*how*) what a schema is to declarative knowledge (*what*). We have, for example, scripts for going to a restaurant or using the library and scripts that govern the relations between women and men. Scripts generally vary across cultures, which is the case with sexual scripts, but also, for example, with scripts that govern gift-giving and gift-receiving.

Similar to a script in a play, a mental script outlines the 'proper' sequence in which actions and reactions are expected to happen in given settings. When all people in a given setting follow similar scripts, they all feel comfortable because they have comprehended the 'meaning' of that situation in the same way and have the same expectations for each other (Abelson, 1981; Schank & Abelson, 1977). When all people do not follow similar scripts, however, they are made uncomfortable by the script 'violation' and may have difficulty understanding the scene. Imagine, for example, what would happen if someone enters a restaurant, sits down, is given the menu and then says, 'Why do you bring me this list? I am here for eating, not for reading'.

We have trouble comprehending situations that do not fit scripted patterns. One way to reduce the discrepancy between new stimuli and existing structures of thinking is to enlarge and change our mental structures in appropriate ways to make a broader understanding possible. This process of *accommodation* begins in infancy and continues as long as we increase our knowledge and competence in any field. Being open to new possibilities that challenge old actualities is the way the mind matures. Mental flexibility means adjusting schemas and scripts to fit new ideas and experiences. By contrast, mental rigidity means forcing the new into old moulds and merely making exceptions for events that do not fit the rule, without ever changing the basic rule for using the schema or the script.

Propositions and Pictures

Thus far, we have presented the mental structures that are employed in thinking. We have shown that our internal psychological world is an organised one: thinking is assumed to be embedded in mental structures that are neatly designed. In this section we will address the question of what these mental structures are made of. We will concern ourselves with the question of whether people think in words or whether they (sometimes) think in pictures and spatial relationships.

Most cognitive psychologists assume that people think in words and sentences: people employ an internal mental language in thought. This means that facts, inferences and other aspects of thought are primarily represented in an internal language-like propositional structure that is largely unconscious and that is translated into natural language when we talk. Due to its abstract and formal nature, this language of thought (sometimes called *mentalese)* is fundamentally different from natural languages, although they share their propositional nature (Fodor, 1975; Pylyshyn, 1984).

A resolute minority in cognitive psychology, however, has argued in favour of a pictorial representation, next to the propositional one. The pictorialists hold that thinking partly proceeds in images (Kosslyn, 1983; Paivio, 1986). Among the arguments that are cited in favour of the pictorial thesis is the fact that mnemonics generally use some kind of visual imagery (see Chapter 8). Many contemporary cognitive scientists believe that visual thought differs from verbal thought, although there is no agreement on the relative importance of one representation or the other.

History is full of examples of famous discoveries made on the basis of mental imagery. For example, Albert Einstein claimed to have thought entirely in terms of visual images, translating his findings into mathematical symbols and words only after the work of visually based discovery was finished. Michael Faraday, who discovered many properties of magnetism, knew little about mathematics, but he was able to work by placing the supposed properties of magnetic fields in a visual image of relationships (Shepard, 1978).

Evidence of the psychological reality of mental images is provided in the following study that shows

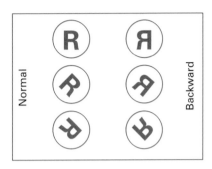

| FIGURE 9.2 | ROTATED R USED TO ASSESS MENTAL IMAGERY |

Subjects presented with these figures in random order were asked to say, as quickly as possible, whether each figure was a normal R or a mirror image. The more the figure was rotated from upright, the longer the reaction time was.

the behavioural consequences of images. Each subject was shown examples of the letter R and its mirror image that had been rotated various amounts, from 0 to 180 degrees (see *Figure 9.2*). As the letter appeared, the subject had to identify it as either the normal R or its mirror image. The reaction time taken to make that decision was longer the more the figure had been rotated. This finding indicated that a subject was imagining the figure in his or her 'mind's eye' and rotating the image into an upright position, before deciding whether the figure was an R or a mirror image. Such results support the idea that thinking processes using visual imagery are similar to the processes involved in visually perceiving real-world objects (Shepard & Cooper, 1982).

Not only are the processes (of using visual imagery and visually perceiving real-world objects) similar, so are the way people scan their mental images of objects and scan the actual perceived objects.

In one study, subjects first memorised pictures of complex objects, such as a motorboat (see Figure 9.3). Then they were asked to recall their visual images of the boat and focus on one spot – for example, the motor. When asked if the picture contained another object – a windshield or an anchor, for example (both were present) – they took longer to 'see' the anchor than the windshield, which was only half as far away as the anchor from the motor. The researcher regarded the reaction-time difference as evidence of the visual scanning times required to examine the objects at different physical distances in their mental images (Kosslyn, 1980).

Visual thought adds complexity and richness to our thinking, as do forms of thought that involve the other senses: sound, taste, smell and touch. Visual thinking can be very useful in solving problems in

FIGURE 9.3	VISUAL SCANNING OF MENTAL IMAGES

Subjects studied a picture of a boat and then were asked to look at the motor in their own image of the boat. While doing so, they were asked whether the boat had a windshield or an anchor. The faster response to the windshield, which was closer than the anchor, was taken as evidence that they were scanning their visual images.

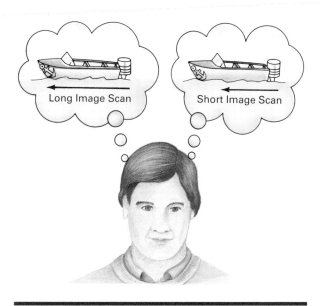

which relationships can be grasped more clearly in diagram form than in words. Visual thought, for example, is useful in spatial or geographical relationships. A cognitive representation of physical space is called a mental map, or *cognitive map*. Learning theorist **Edward Tolman** was the first to hypothesise that people form mental maps of their environment as they learn their way through life's mazes, and these internal maps guide their future actions toward desired goals (see Chapter 7). Cognitive maps help people get where they want to go. They also enable them to give directions to someone else. By using cognitive maps, people can move through their homes with their eyes closed or go to familiar destinations even when their usual routes are blocked (Hart & Moore, 1973; Thorndyke & Hayes-Roth, 1979).

The ways in which cognitive maps may work are illustrated by the following questions:

Which is farther north: New York or Florence?
Which is farther west: Avignon or Amsterdam?

To find the answers to these questions, you must use a mental representation of the spatial environment as you have personally experienced it, remember it from a map you have seen, or reconstruct it from separate bits of information that you possess. Although everybody seems to develop cognitive maps to navigate through the complex environments in which they live, these maps can sometimes be misleading. Did you know that Florence is farther north than New York? And did you know that Amsterdam and Avignon have the same eastern longitudinal position? Most people think, however, that New York is farther north, because they probably associate Florence with a southern climate. In the same vein, people generally think that Amsterdam is farther west. Similarly, on the cognitive maps of Parisians, the River Seine curves only gently through Paris instead of curving more sharply as it actually does. Thus, some Parisians misjudge places that are on the right bank of the Seine as being on the left bank (Milgram & Jodelet, 1976).

INTERIM SUMMARY

Thinking is a higher-order mental process that goes beyond the information given by sensory processing. Thinking transforms available information into new abstract representations. Human thought relies on many types of mental structures. One of the most basic abilities of thinking organisms is categorising individual experiences. Concepts, the building blocks of thinking, are mental representations that group related items in particular ways. We form concepts by identifying those properties that are common to a class of objects or ideas. This process is part of the mind's attempt to ensure cognitive economy – to minimise processing time and effort whenever possible. Conceptual rules specify how we think the features of concepts are related. We store their critical features as definitions of some types of concepts, such as well-defined scientific concepts. For concepts with ill-defined boundaries, we seem to store the prototypical or the most average instance of the concept. We respond to prototypes more quickly and recall them with more confidence than non-prototypical instances. Concepts are often arranged in hierarchies, from general to specific, and there is an optimal level of describing a complex concept, the basic level, to which we respond most effectively.

Other mental structures that guide thinking are the knowledge packages of schemas and scripts. They help to encode and store information in memory and also to form expectations about appropriate attributes and effects of concepts. Scripts are event schemas, organised knowledge about expected sequences of action in given settings. In addition to these verbal thinking structures, we rely on visual imagery which adds further richness to thinking. Mental maps are cognitive representations of physical space. They are useful in learning our way around our environment.

◤ REASONING AND PROBLEM-SOLVING

Our thoughts range between two extremes: the autistic and the realistic. **Autistic thinking** is a personal, idiosyncratic process involving fantasy, day-dreaming, unconscious reactions and ideas that are not testable by external reality criteria. This type of individualised thought is part of most creative acts. However, when it generates delusions and hallucinations, it can be evidence that the individual has lost touch with reality and is suffering from some type of mental illness. Autistic thinking is always top-down processing. **Realistic thinking**, by contrast, requires that ideas fit into the reality of situational demands, time constraints, operational rules and personal resources. Thinking realistically involves frequent checks on reality and tests that measure the appropriateness and correctness of one's ideas against some acceptable standard.

Reasoning is a process of realistic, goal-directed thinking in which conclusions are drawn from a set of facts. In reasoning, information from the environment and stored information are used in accordance with a set of rules (either formal or informal) for transforming information. There are two types of reasoning: deductive and inductive.

 ## Deductive Reasoning

Deductive reasoning is drawing a conclusion that follows logically according to established rules from two or more statements or premises. More than 2,000 years ago, Aristotle introduced the form of deductive reasoning known as the **syllogism**, which has three components: a major premise, a minor premise and a conclusion. He also developed rules for syllogistic reasoning – if these rules are adhered to, the conclusion will be drawn validly from the premises. Consider the following example:

Major premise: All people are thinking creatures
Minor premise: Descartes was a person
Valid conclusion: Therefore, Descartes was a thinking creature

Invalid conclusion: Therefore, all thinking creatures are Descartes.

If the conclusion is not derived by the rules of logic it is invalid, as shown in the second conclusion of the example. You immediately knew the second conclusion was invalid – evidence that deductive reasoning is a fundamental part of reasoning ability (Rips, 1983).

Validity and truth need to be distinguished in syllogistic thinking. If one of the premises is false, then the conclusion must also be false even though it can be drawn validly from them. If the conclusion is not logically derived from the premises, it is invalid even if it is true. Consider the following examples that mix truth and validity.

Major premise: Some psychologists study cognitions
Minor premise: Some cognitions are about women
True but invalid conclusion: Some psychologists are women
Major premise: All lecturers have cognitions
Minor premise: All cognitions are intelligent
False but valid conclusion: All lecturers have intelligent cognitions

Cognitive psychologists study the errors people make in logic and syllogistic reasoning in order to understand their mental representations of premises and conclusions (Johnson-Laird & Byrne, 1989). Some errors occur because the individual's personal beliefs about the premises and conclusions get in the way of logic. People tend to judge as valid those conclusions with which they agree and as invalid those with which they do not (Janis & Frick, 1943). The **belief-bias effect** occurs when a person's prior knowledge, attitudes or values distort the reasoning process by influencing the person to accept as valid those arguments that are invalid but believed to be true, or as invalid those arguments that are believed to be false (Evans *et al*, 1983).

Psychological research into deductive reasoning has been influenced strongly by **Peter Wason's** studies. He developed a reasoning task that is generally known as the *Wason selection task*. In its rudimentary version, the experimental task is as follows (Wason, 1966). There are four cards lying on a table, as shown below:

| E | F | 4 | 7 |

Each card has a letter on one side and a number on the other. The participants are invited to test the following hypothesis:

If a card has a vowel on one side, it has an even number on the other side.

In their testing, the participants were to select only those cards that would need to be turned over in order to see whether or not the rule is correct.

The experiment showed that most participants tested the hypothesis by following syllogistic 'if-then' reasoning in a positive sense: they turned over the 'E' card to see whether the hypothesis was confirmed. Very few participants, however, executed a complete test by also turning the '7' card. This is necessary to verify whether the '7' card has a vowel on its flip side. Most participants flipped both the 'E' and the '4' card. The latter does not prove anything, because even if there is a consonant on the other side, the hypothesis is not falsified. The poor performance of almost everyone on the Wason task is generally explained by pointing to the fact that people tend to seek *confirmation* and not falsification in reasoning.

A second explanation for the problems people have with this kind of deductive reasoning points to the abstract nature of the task. In a later study, Wason and Shapiro (1971) used the following cards:

MANCHESTER	LEEDS	CAR	TRAIN

In this particular case, the hypothesis to be tested was:

Every time I go to Manchester I travel by car.

Again the task was to turn only those cards that needed to be checked to confirm or falsify the hypothesis. The use of this concrete and meaningful material turned out to make the Wason task easier: 62 per cent of the participants said correctly that the 'Manchester' and 'train' cards needed to be turned.

 ## Inductive Reasoning

Inductive reasoning is a form of reasoning that uses available evidence to generate a conclusion about the likelihood of something. The process of inductive reasoning involves constructing a hypothesis based on limited evidence and then testing it against other evidence. The hypothesis is not drawn inescapably from the logical structure of the argument as it is in deductive reasoning. Rather, inductive reasoning requires leaps from data to decisions. These leaps are accomplished by integrating past experience, perceptual sensitivity, weighted value of the importance of each element of evidence and a dash of creativity. Psychologists generally rely on inductive reasoning in their research (see Chapter 1).

After solving a difficult mystery, Sherlock Holmes frequently exclaims to his sidekick, 'It's a matter of deduction, my dear Dr Watson'. In fact, Holmes' solutions involve shrewd *induction* – he pieces together shreds of data into a compelling web of evidence that eventually supports his hypothesis about the agent of and motive for the crime.

 ## Problem-solving

What goes on four legs in the morning, on two legs at noon and on three legs in the twilight? According to Greek mythology, this was the riddle posed by the Sphinx, an evil creature who threatened to hold the people of Thebes in tyranny until Oedipus could solve the riddle. To break the code, Oedipus had to recognise elements of the riddle as metaphors. Morning, noon and twilight represented different periods in a human life. A baby crawls and so has four legs; an adult walks on two legs; and an older person walks on two legs but uses a cane, making a total of three legs. Oedipus's solution to the riddle was *Man*.

While our daily problems may not seem as monumental as the one faced by young Oedipus, problem-solving activity is a basic part of our everyday existence. We continually come up against problems that require solutions: how to manage work and tasks within a limited time frame, how to break off an intimate relationship, how to avoid sexually transmitted diseases, to name a few. For psychologists, **problem-solving** is thinking that is directed toward solving specific problems and that moves from an initial state to a goal state by means of a set of mental operations. Researchers **Herbert Simon** and **Alan Newell** were the pioneers in the systematic study of problem-solving. In the 1950s they developed computer programs to simulate human problem-solving, thereby providing new ways of studying mental processes (Newell *et al* 1958).

Many problems are discrepancies between what you know and what you need to know. When you solve a problem, you reduce that discrepancy by finding a way to get the missing information. To get into the spirit of problem solving yourself, try the problems in *Figure 9.4* (the answers are on page 329).

Cognitive psychologists have disentangled a problem to three parts (Newell & Simon, 1972):

- An *initial state*: the incomplete information you start with that perhaps corresponds to some unsatisfactory set of conditions in the world.
- A *goal state:* the set of information or state of the world you hope to achieve.
- A set of *operations*: the steps you must take to move from an initial state to a goal state.

Together, these three parts define the problem space. You can think of solving a problem as walking through your town (the problem space) from your

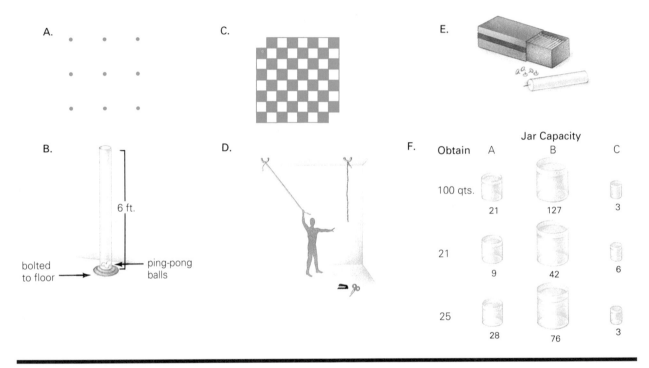

FIGURE 9.4 A. CAN YOU SOLVE IT?

A. Can you connect all the dots in the pattern by drawing four straight, connected lines without lifting your pen from the paper?

B. A prankster has put three ping-pong balls into a six-foot long pipe that is standing vertically in the corner of the physics lab, fastened to the floor. How would you get the ping-pong balls out?

C. The chessboard shown has had two corner pieces cut out, leaving 62 squares. You have 31 dominoes, each of which covers exactly two chessboard squares. Can you use them to cover the whole chessboard?

D. You are in the situation depicted and given the task of tying two strings together. If you hold one, the other is out of reach. Can you do it?

E. You are given the objects shown (two candles, tacks, string, matches in a matchbox). The task is to mount a lighted candle on the door. Can you do it?

F. You are given three 'water-jar' problems. Using only the three containers (water supply is unlimited), can you obtain the exact amount specified in each case?

home (the initial state) to the bookshop (the goal state), making a series of turns (the allowable operations).

Intelligent problem-solving

For those not involved in academic psychology, problem-solving and intelligence often are conceived as two sides of the same coin. People are designated as being intelligent when they show the ability to solve problems in a swift and inventive manner. Although psychologists in the past have provided many different definitions of intelligence (see Chapter 12), cognitive psychologists generally underpin a common-sense view of intelligence. They hold that intelligence is concerned with reasoning and problem-solving and they direct their attention to the cognitive processes that are used in intelligent behaviour.

One proponent of the cognitive processes view, **Earl Hunt** (1983), believes that the interesting individual differences in people's intelligence are to be found in the way different individuals go about solving a problem. He identifies three ways cognitive processes may differ in individuals: (a) choice about the way to represent internally (mentally) a problem; (b) strategies for manipulating mental representations; and (c) the abilities necessary to execute whatever basic information-processing steps a strategy requires.

Hunt encourages cognitive scientists to do something they have largely avoided: study individual differences instead of only the averaged reactions of many people to the same experimental stimuli. Using Hunt's model, special tasks can be designed to allow cognitive psychologists to observe individual differences in the way people represent problems (using images or verbalisation, for example), the way they encode material and the way information is transferred in their working memories. This approach encourages psychologists to see the flexibility and adaptiveness of human thinking (Hunt, 1984).

Robert Sternberg (1986a) also stresses the importance of cognitive processes in problem-solving. For intellectual tasks that involve general information, vocabulary, arithmetic, insight or analytic reasoning, Sternberg recommends componential analysis of the processes used to solve them. He identifies three types of *components* that are central to his model of information processing: (a) knowledge acquisition components, for learning new facts; (b) performance components, for problem-solving strategies and techniques; and (c) metacognitive components, for selecting a strategy and monitoring progress toward success.

However, these components tell only part of the story. In addition to this *componential intelligence* (which is reflected in school grades, for example), Sternberg identifies two other important types of intelligence: experiential and contextual (Sternberg, 1985). *Experiential intelligence* is reflected in creative accomplishments. It involves the ability to picture the external world using alternate types of internal (mental) representations and the ability to combine very different experiences in unique and original ways. It is easy to see how artists, such as Pablo Picasso, Harold Pinter and Peter Greenaway, captivate audiences by representing common-place things in unusual ways. Others, such as Albert Einstein and Sigmund Freud, have used their experiential intelligence to develop provocative scientific theories. *Contextual intelligence* is reflected in the practical management of day-to-day affairs. It involves your ability to adapt to new and different contexts, make the most of your available resources and effectively shape your environment to suit your needs. Contextual intelligence is what people sometimes call 'street wise' or 'business sense'.

Another important cognitive theory of intelligence has been proposed by **Howard Gardner** (1983). He identifies intelligence in terms of numerous abilities, each of which is equally important. The value attached to any of these abilities is culturally determined, according to what is needed by, useful to and prized by a given society. Gardner goes beyond cognition, reasoning and problem-solving in their ordinary sense by proposing seven intelligences that are each concerned with information-processing and problem-solving at different levels of functioning. The seven intelligences are:

- Linguistic ability.
- Logical-mathematical ability.
- Spatial ability (navigating in space, forming, transforming and using mental images).
- Musical ability (perceiving and creating pitch patterns).

Howard Gardner

- Bodily-kinesthetic ability (skills of motor movement, co-ordination).
- Interpersonal ability (understanding others).
- Intrapersonal ability (understanding oneself, developing a sense of identity).

Gardner argues that Western society promotes the first two intelligences (linguistic and logical-mathematical), while other societies value others. For example, sailors from the Caroline Island of Micronesia, must be able to navigate long distances without maps, using only their spatial intelligence and bodily-kinesthetic intelligence. Such abilities count more in that society than the ability to write a dissertation. In Bali, where artistic performance is part of everyday life, musical intelligence and talents involved in co-ordinating intricate dance steps are highly valued. Interpersonal intelligence is more central to collectivist societies where collective action and communal life are emphasised than it is in individualistic societies (Triandis, 1990).

Well-defined and ill-defined problems

There is an important distinction between well-defined and ill-defined problems (Simon, 1973). A *well-defined problem* is similar to an algebra problem in which the initial state, the goal state and the operations are all clearly specified. The task is simply to discover how to use allowable known operations to get the answer. By contrast, an *ill-defined problem* is similar to designing a home, writing a novel or finding a cure for AIDS; the initial state, the goal state and/or the operations may be unclear and vaguely specified. In such cases, the problem-solver's major task is first to define exactly what the problem is – to make explicit a beginning, an ideal solution and the possible means to achieve it. Once that is done, the

Designing a building is an example of an ill-defined problem, the architects must determine the function, location and capacity of the building and then draw the plans.

task becomes a well-defined problem that can be solved by finding a sequence of operations that will, in fact, achieve an acceptable solution.

Expertise

The way people solve problems is also dependent on their expertise. In general, 'experts' possess more relevant knowledge than novices and they also have better strategies for working towards a solution. **Adriaan de Groot** (1965) initiated research into the differences between experts and novices by studying the game of chess. When de Groot posed various chess problems to masters of chess, to experienced players and to novices and asked them to select the next move, he found that masters were more likely to elect for continuations that held greater promise of winning the game. Novices and players with only little experience, on the other hand, did not select preliminary moves so often that would lead to a winning position.

A central element in the explanation given by de Groot and others is that experts structure the chess positions in terms of conceptually broad strategies from which the moves to be made thereafter follow on with apparent ease and fluidity (de Groot, 1965; Chase & Simon, 1973). Experts are assumed also to represent mentally the chess game in more numerous and larger chunks, an inference drawn from the observation that experts comprehend chess positions in a shorter time and are also more successful at remembering the details of the various positions than less experienced players (see Chapter 8). Later

research has pointed to another difference between experts and novices: chess experts look further ahead in their mental calculations about the game (Holding, 1985).

Artificial intelligence

Many researchers who have studied human problem-solving have stressed the analogy between the human mind and computers by pointing to the fact that both are *information-processing systems* (Turing, 1950). Cognitive psychologists and others who work in the area of **artificial intelligence**, or AI, translate the theoretical analogy into computer programs. AI theories therefore in effect take the form of computer programs, the software that is tested by the outcomes generated when a program is run on the computer. AI research is concerned with the way symbols are manipulated and combined according to the instructions expressed in the language of computer programs. However, AI is not the study of computers as much as the study of intelligence in thought and action. Computers are only the tools that AI researchers use to study human thinking, in particular problem-solving.

Much work in artificial intelligence is concerned with the development of *expert systems*. These are problem-solving programs that have an enormous amount of relevant knowledge stored in their memories. An expert system is built around automatised procedures with respect to the ways in which a goal state is to be reached from an initial state (Newell & Simon, 1972). Most expert systems deal with well-defined problems in a very specific domain where it is possible for a human expert to translate his or her know-how into computer language.

AI programs have their limitations in dealing with problem-solving. A major difficulty is that AI cannot cope efficiently with ill-defined problems. There we still need the unpredictable and creative human mind. AI further lacks *metacognition* – that is, an understanding of what one is thinking about and thoughts about thinking itself (see below). AI programs follow the orderly steps that are built into them, being at present unable to jump to creative solutions no one has ever thought of before.

Mental sets: enhancers and inhibitors

The strings and the candle problems in *Figure 9.4* show a phenomenon called **functional fixedness** (Duncker, 1945; Maier, 1931). Functional fixedness is a mental block that adversely affects problem-solving

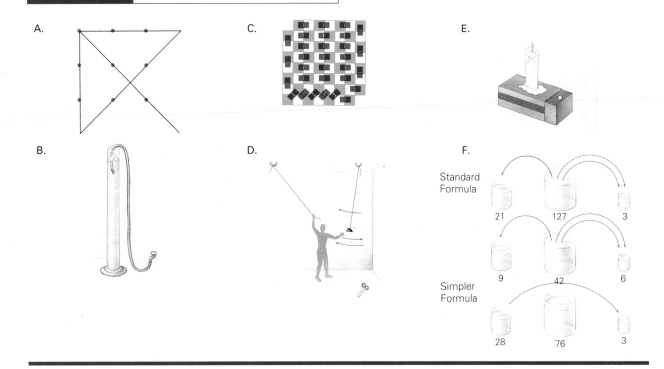

FIGURE 9.4 | B. SOLUTIONS TO THE PROBLEMS

A.

B.

C.

D.

E.

F.

Standard Formula

21   127   3

9   42   6

Simpler Formula

28   76   3

and creativity by inhibiting the perception of a new function for an object that was previously associated with some other purpose. You put your conceptual 'blinders' on and use only your familiar schemas, which shows again the power of schemas to guide or misguide perceptions of reality.

Another kind of mental rigidity may have hampered your solution of the water-jar problem. If you had discovered in the first two problems the conceptual rule that B–A–2(C) = answer, you probably tried the same formula for the third problem and found it did not work. Actually, simply filling jar A and pouring off enough to fill jar C would have left you with the right amount. If you were using the other formula, you probably did not notice this simpler possibility – your previous success with the other rule would have given you a mental set. A **mental set** is a pre-existing state of mind, habit or attitude that can enhance the quality and speed of perceiving and problem-solving under some conditions, but inhibit or distort the quality of our mental activities at times when old ways of thinking and acting are non-productive in new situations. Having a mental set, or readiness, to respond to new problems by using the same procedure, rules or formula that worked in the past is known as the **Einstellung effect** (Luchins, 1942). The term was coined by Gestalt psychologists who studied problem-solving in terms of the way a task and its elements are perceived. Much problem-solving involves 'breaking set' – temporarily giving up reliance on past learning

and mental habits for fullest participation in the stimulus array of the present moment in order to view options from a new perspective.

The Best Search Strategy: Algorithms or Heuristics?

After the problem space is known, the problem is well defined but not yet solved. Solving the problem requires using the operations to get from the initial state to the goal state. Using the problem-as-a-maze analogy, you must still decide on a strategy for selecting the right path.

One search strategy is an **algorithm**, a methodical, step-by-step procedure for solving problems that guarantees that eventually, with sufficient time and patience, a solution will be found. For example, there are 120 possible combinations of the letters 'otrhs'; you could try each one to find the only combination that is also a word: 'short'. For an eight-letter group such as 'teralbay', there are 40,320 possible combinations ($8 \times 7 \times 6 \times 5 \times 4 \times 3 \times 2 \times 1$). A search of all the combinations would eventually reveal the solution, but the search would be long and tedious. Luckily, there is an alternative approach that we can use to solve a great many problems every day. In problem-solving, just as in making judgements, we can use a **heuristic**, which is an informal rule of thumb that provides shortcuts, reducing complex problem-solving to more simple judgemental operations. Heuristics are general strategies that have often worked in similar situations in the past and may work also in the present case. For example, a heuristic that can help you solve the word jumble of 'teralbay' is: 'Look for short words that could be made from some of the letters and then see if the other letters fit around them'. Using such a strategy, you might generate 'ably' (tearably?), 'able' (raytable?) and 'tray' (latraybe?). By using this particular search strategy, you would probably not need to try more than a few of the possibilities before you came up with the solution: 'betrayal' (Glass *et al*, 1979).

Using a heuristic does not guarantee that a solution will be found; using an algorithm, tedious though it might be, does. Heuristics do work often enough; as we use them, we gradually learn which ones to depend on in which situations. One way experience helps us become better problem-solvers is by teaching us when and how to use heuristics appropriately. When there are few possible combinations of elements, use an algorithm to reduce them to the solution; when there are a great many, go for the heuristic. This last statement is itself one kind of heuristic that can guide rational problem-solving strategies.

◤ Metacognitive Knowledge

Once it is clear how to get from initial to end state, we are close to the nub of problem-solving. Reaching the end state, however, also presupposes that we have an overview of the process of thinking. This overview is called **metacognitive knowledge**. It comprises an awareness of what one already knows – the level of comprehension of current information about the task, situation and options – and one's assessment of personal resources for dealing with the immediate problem. Metacognitive processes enable people to analyse what they need to know, predict the outcome of different strategies (and check the results later) and evaluate their progress. In general, experts employ more metacognitive knowledge than novices in solving problems. You use your metacognitive knowledge when you organise your studying differently for a multiple-choice examination than for an essay examination or when you take the early train because you know that you are usually late for appointments.

When you are dealing with a task, your metacognitive knowledge search leads you to: (a) evaluate your own skills; (b) search your stored knowledge for various possible strategies and evaluate them; (c) decide how much knowledge you have and how much you still need; and (d) assess how much attention to pay to incoming information. These four variables – person, task knowledge, strategy and sensitivity – may act separately to influence your decisions, but more often they interact (Brown & DeLoache, 1978).

John Flavell (1981) is a pioneering theorist and researcher in metacognition. He believes that a better understanding of the way metacognitive knowledge develops and is used or misused will help greatly in teaching children and adults to gather information and evaluate the strategies they are using. Young children seem to lack metacognition: children who have been taught to remember a list of names by reciting them aloud generally fail to apply this simple technique if asked to memorise items on a shopping list. Their failure to recognise and employ a 'master plan' precludes the possibility of remembering the items on the list (Flavell & Wellman, 1979). Metacognitive knowledge is also used in perception: it enables us to enact mental operations that lie beyond the confines of our literal perceptions. Metacognition is employed, for example, when we recognise perspective and manipulate it and when we distinguish between reality and illusion (Flavell *et al,* 1983).

The implications of research on metacognitive processes are profound. To become proficient, we need to go beyond learning specific knowledge and skills. We must train ourselves to monitor our progress (or lack of it) to detect confusion in ourselves or in information sources and to recognise when we need additional information. When we take charge of our own search for knowledge, we may become experts and metacognition may help us to become our own teachers (Scardamalia & Bereiter, 1985).

INTERIM SUMMARY

The extremes of human reasoning are autistic and realistic. The first is idiosyncratic, without reference to external validity checks; the second is governed by reality constraints. In between the two lies the territory where most reasoning takes place. Deductive reasoning involves drawing conclusions from premises on the basis of rules of logic. Validity and truth of conclusions are not the same; sometimes our beliefs bias reasoning so that we falsely believe as valid those statements we favour and as invalid those that are contrary to our beliefs. Inductive reasoning involves inferring a conclusion from evidence on the basis of its likelihood or probability. Hypothesis formation and testing in psychology are typically based on inductive reasoning.

When solving problems, we must define the initial state, the goal state and the operations that can get us from the first to the second – a difficult task in ill-defined problems. Expert systems that are built by researchers in the area of artificial intelligence may help us to solve specific problems. Functional fixedness and other mental sets can hamper creative problem-solving and require attempts at breaking set. Algorithms ensure an eventual solution if there is one, but are impractical in many cases. Heuristics are mental shortcuts that often help us reach a solution quickly. We also rely on metacognitive knowledge that provides a background mental picture of the task at hand and also of the skills and background we use to solve it.

 ## JUDGING AND DECIDING

We can never be completely confident in our predictions about how people will behave or how events will unfold. Despite this uncertainty, we are constantly called upon to make personal, economic and political decisions that have enormous impacts on our lives. Are there accepted guidelines or models for making good decisions? When scientists, physicians, lawyers, politicians, stockbrokers and parents make their decisions, what procedures do they follow in order to get the best possible outcomes? In this section, we will see that decision-making is always subjective and often error-prone. In addition, we will see that human reason is fallible, at times leading us to make obvious mistakes.

Psychologists often distinguish between judgement and decision-making. **Judgement** is the process by which we form opinions, reach conclusions and make critical evaluations of events and people on the basis of available information. Judgements are also the product or the conclusion of that mental process. We often make judgements spontaneously, without prompting. **Decision-making**, on the other hand, is the process of choosing between alternatives, selecting and rejecting available options. Judgement and decision-making are interrelated processes. For example, you might meet someone at a party, and after a chat and a dance together, judge the person to be intelligent and interesting. You might then decide to spend the rest of the party with that person.

 ## Making Sense of the World

Our everyday world is a complicated place and we often have to rely on relevant knowledge we have accumulated previously to guide our behaviour.

Unlike Dr Eger, whose experience in the chaos of a concentration camp had no parallels in her experience, most of the situations in which we find ourselves share basic properties with previous situations we have encountered. Our judgements are based on **inference**, the reasoning process of drawing a conclusion on the basis of a sample of evidence or on the basis of prior beliefs and theories.

We employ a variety of inferential strategies to simplify the inferences we make. Ordinarily, these strategies serve us well. In some circumstances, however, we misapply these strategies to new data. In particular, when faced with new information that is inconsistent with previous knowledge, we are often too ready to try to fit it into an established theory rather than considering the possibility that the theory itself requires revision. Some psychologists believe that people are *cognitive misers*, always trying to minimise mental effort whenever sustained attention, comprehension or analysis is required (Taylor, 1980). People habitually use mental shortcuts to make up their minds quickly, easily and with maximum confidence (Kahneman *et al*, 1982). They are often too ready to be led astray by their theories about what ought to be and their values, ignoring data about what really is (Nisbett & Ross, 1980).

It is important to be aware that people can sometimes be misled by the very same cognitive processes that work remarkably effectively with respect to other judgements and decisions. However, just because these processes can sometimes lead us to apparently irrational conclusions, they are not themselves irrational – it might, for example, make more sense to use a mental shortcut, like a heuristic, than to employ a more ideal approach that always yields the correct answer but does so at the price of a great deal of mental effort.

 ## Perseverance of False Beliefs

We often continue to persevere in beliefs, theories and ways of doing things because we *assimilate* data or new experiences in a *biased* fashion (Ross & Lepper, 1980). Data consistent with our beliefs are given little attention before they are filed away mentally as evidence supporting our views because they are expected. Any ambiguity in the data is resolved, often without full awareness, in terms of our existing beliefs. Our attention is drawn, quite naturally, to aspects of the data that are incongruent and may challenge our theories, and we devote our efforts to reinterpreting and explaining this information within the context of our schemata or scripts. This process is known as **biased assimilation**.

Our tendency to cling on to initial schemes and scripts can lead to *over-confidence* in the truth of our beliefs because it causes us to underestimate the probability that these beliefs could be wrong. The workings of over-confidence were shown in a study in which American students living in dormitories were asked to predict the behaviour of their room-mates. They were asked to predict, for instance, whether their room-mates would keep or hand in a five-dollar bill found on the floor of a local campus café and how their room-mates would respond to a hypothetical choice between two magazine subscriptions. When compared to the actual responses of their room-mates, subjects' predictions were over-confident; subjects believed their predictions would be correct significantly more of the time than they actually were (Dunning *et al*, 1990).

Over-confidence can also lead people to overestimate their abilities. When asked about their driving skills and safety, for example, people typically judged themselves to be better drivers than 85 per cent of all the people they know. Thus, subjects believe that they are safer on the roads than the majority of drivers, which is not a plausible claim to make statistically speaking (Svenson, 1981). Over-confidence leads to what Weinstein (1980) has called **unrealistic optimism**. Researchers are currently debating vigorously about whether this kind of optimism does more harm than good (Klein & Kunda, 1993; Taylor & Brown, 1988). On the one hand, unrealistic optimism may help you to accomplish feats you might not otherwise have tried to aspire towards. On the other hand, unrealistic optimism in relation, for example, to underestimating the danger of contracting a sexually transmitted disease, may prevent you from taking action to avoid such undesirable outcomes (Van der Pligt, 1991). In the explanation given for this kind of over-confidence, motivational factors interact with cognitive ones. Unrealistic optimism can be understood as a manifestation of a motive for self-enhancement or as a pervasive tendency to see oneself as superior to others (Hoorens, 1993).

Cognitive Biases

Every now and then people seem to lose their capacity for rational thinking, deciding and problem-solving. Psychology offers a variety of explanations for these apparent lapses into irrationality. Some have pointed to the distinction between human reason and animal-like passions. When driven by desires that demand immediate gratification, people cease to be rational. Freudian psychoanalysis argues that sexual

and aggressive drives that are hidden in the unconscious exercise a powerful motivational influence on perception and thought. Rationality is pitted against emotionality and a focus on satisfying one's immediate desires. Society's task, often accomplished with the help of religion and education, is to suppress these 'primitive' urges by replacing them with more lofty principles and rules of conduct.

Modern cognitive psychology offers a different view of irrationality by arguing that erroneous judgements are the result of the misapplication or over-extension of normal, rational processes. In other words, the failures of human reason and the achievements of human thought are cut from the same rich fabric of cognitive processes. Let us consider this notion of ordinary irrationality in more detail.

The mental strategies or shortcuts we use can result in a **cognitive bias**, or a systematic error in the inferences we draw from evidence, the judgements we base on our inferences and the decisions we make using these judgements. At times, these biases are not errors but differences in emphasis or perspective that we bring to a situation we are trying to understand. The fact that the processes we use yield biased conclusions does not necessarily mean the processes are incorrect in themselves, but rather that we do not adequately discriminate between appropriate and inappropriate conditions for their use.

Personal experience teaches many useful lessons and obviously aids in making sense of the world. Under many circumstances, however, conclusions based solely on personal intuition have been shown to be inferior to those based on statistical evidence compiled objectively from many such similar cases – the base rate of average responding (Dawes *et al*, 1989; Dawes, 1979; Meehl, 1954). Nevertheless, we often maintain confidence in the validity of our intuitions in these situations and as a result, sometimes ignore or discard better objective evidence that is less susceptible to subjective error.

Researchers have identified a number of different biases in judgement. For example, we tend to perceive random events as non-random, correlated events as causally related and people as causal agents instead of situational variables. We have noted that heuristics are mental shortcuts useful in solving a problem by means of a direct procedure that reduces the range of possible solutions. Sometimes, using a mental shortcut causes you to overlook important information that would suggest a different conclusion.

Anchoring bias

Try this interesting experiment with a group of friends or family members. First, divide your subjects arbitrarily into two groups. Then, once they are separated from each other, give members of the first group five seconds to estimate the following mathematical product:

$$1 \times 2 \times 3 \times 4 \times 5 \times 6 \times 7 \times 8$$

Then, give members of the second group the same amount of time to estimate the answer to the same equation but in reverse order:

$$8 \times 7 \times 6 \times 5 \times 4 \times 3 \times 2 \times 1$$

After you have collected everyone's estimates, compute the median estimate for each group – that is, the number above and below which half of the estimates fall.

If your results are similar to those found by **Amos Tversky** and **Daniel Kahneman** (1973), two pioneering researchers in the area of judgement and decision-making, you will find that members of the first group give lower estimates than do members of the second group. In their original experiment, these researchers reported a median estimate of a low 512 for members of the first group and a high 2,250 for members of the second group (neither of which, incidentally, bore any resemblance to the correct answer of 40,320). The researchers explained these findings in terms of an **anchoring bias**, the insufficient adjustment – up or down – from an original starting value when judging the probable value of some event or outcome. Because members of the first group began to evaluate the product with low digits, their estimates were anchored to low numbers. In contrast, members of the second group began with the higher digits and were, therefore, anchored to relatively high numbers.

Surprisingly, the effects of anchoring also do not disappear with outrageously extreme anchors. In another experiment, subjects were asked whether the number of *Beatles* records that had made the

Amos Tversky and Daniel Kahneman

American Top Ten fell above or below 100,025; whether the average price of a textbook was more or less than $7,128.53. After the subjects responded, the researchers asked them to estimate the precise number of Top-Ten *Beatles* hits and the average price of a textbook. What these researchers found was that, instead of disregarding the unreasonably high anchor values, subjects were affected as much as when more plausible anchors were provided in the opening round of questions (Quattrone *et al*, 1984). The influence of anchoring grows with the discrepancy between the anchor and the 'pre-anchor estimate' (the average estimate subjects make without explicit anchors) until the effect reaches a plateau.

These results pose intriguing questions for future research. In particular, they raise the possibility that current or initial positions can have a large effect on later ones, inducing a 'status quo bias' (Samuelson & Zeckhauser, 1988) in which the current course of action is more likely to be continued than changed.

Availability heuristic

Are there more words in the English language that begin with the letter 'k' or more words that have 'k' as their third letter? If you are like the participants in the study by Tversky and Kahneman (1973), then you probably judged that 'k' is found more often at the beginning of words. In fact, the letter 'k' appears about twice as often in the third position.

How do the number of deaths from tornadoes annually in the United States compare with those from asthma and how do accidental deaths compare with deaths from disease? When asked to estimate the frequency of deaths from all causes, subjects overestimated those that were rare but dramatic and sensational and underestimated those that were more frequent but occurred in private, ordinary circumstances (Slovic, 1984). Asthma causes about 20 times more deaths than tornadoes, and diseases kill 16 times as many people as do accidents. Nonetheless, the subjects judged accidents and disease to be equally lethal and tornadoes to be three times more deadly than asthma.

When we use the **availability heuristic**, we estimate the likelihood of an outcome based on how easily similar or identical outcomes can be brought to mind or imagined. This heuristic causes us to judge as more frequent or probable those events that are more readily imagined or retrieved from memory. It is easier, for example, to recall words beginning with the letter 'k' than it is to think of words with 'k' in the third position; so, words beginning with a 'k' seem more numerous. The ease with which we can recall or imagine some event is usually a good cue for making frequency and probability judgements. However, rare events that are dramatised and sensationalised are more memorable and so we tend to believe mistakenly that they are also more frequent (Tversky & Kahneman, 1973; 1980).

Representativeness heuristic

Another judgemental heuristic that simplifies the complex task of social judgement under conditions of uncertainty is the **representativeness heuristic**. It is based on the presumption that belonging to a particular category implies having the characteristics considered typical of members of that category. When estimating the likelihood that a specific instance is a member of a given category, we look to see whether the instance has the features found in a typical category member. This process should remind you of *prototype theory*, which was discussed earlier in this chapter.

Consider the following question: we have a friend in London who is a lecturer. He is an excellent gardener, reads poetry, is shy and is slight of build. Would you judge that he probably teaches (a) Japanese studies or (b) psychology?

If you decided that our friend taught Japanese studies, you were matching the description of him with your *stereotypes* of people in the two fields. You probably did not take into consideration the fact that a much larger number of lecturers teach psychology and thus, the greater statistical probability that the friend is a psychologist. Neither did you consider the probability that, as psychologist, we would be likely to have more friends in our own area of study (Nisbett & Ross, 1980).

Relying on representativeness and neglecting the relevant *base-rate information* can lead people to be particularly confident even when making particularly unlikely predictions. For example, subjects presented with a description of a person that fits the stereotype of an engineer were equally confident that the person was an engineer whether they were told the description was drawn at random from a list containing 70 per cent engineers or from a list containing only 30 per cent engineers (Kahneman & Tversky, 1973).

Consider the following scenario: (a) a massive flood somewhere in North America in the next year in which more than 1,000 people drown; (b) an earthquake in California some time in the next year causing a flood in which more than 1,000 people drown. Although scenario (a) includes the possibility of scenario (b) and therefore must be more likely, subjects in a study by Tversky and Kahneman (1983) rated (b) as more likely, because the added detail made the scenario seem more probable. Reliance on

representativeness, then, can lead to judgements that violate basic rules of probability.

Availability and representativeness are just two of many heuristics that we use in making judgements about the world every day. The biased judgements resulting from these and other rules of thumb can distort our views of reality, but in many cases they are the best we can do, given the constraints and uncertainties of the situation.

◤ The Psychology of Decision-making

Classic economic theory, which is based on a 'rational actor' model, starts with the assumption that people act to maximise gain, minimise loss and allocate their resources efficiently. It provides a normative model of the way reasonable people ought to behave in an ideal world. It assumes that people do the best they can with available information and that most people have the same set of information and act as if they understand and can apply the laws of probability properly. However, a descriptive analysis of actual human choice and decision-making by cognitive psychologists shows that the assumptions of economic theory often do not hold (Simon, 1955; Tversky & Kahneman, 1986). People do not always understand and correctly apply the laws of probability and they are often required to make decisions under *conditions of uncertainty* in which the relevant probabilities are not known anyway.

Once we understand the way people actually behave, it comes as less of a surprise that people often do not follow normative rules. Two criticisms of the rational choice model come from (a) demonstrations that alternative descriptions of the same decision problem can result in different choices and (b) analyses of risk preferences.

Decision frames

In decision-making, preferences between options should be consistent, regardless of the way the decision is presented to them. This invariance principle is an essential aspect of normative models of choice. However, decisions are influenced by the way in which a decision problem is presented or framed, even when the alternatives are formally equivalent or technically the same. Consider, for example, the choice between surgery and radiation for treatment of lung cancer. Statistical information about the results of each treatment for previous patients can be presented either in terms of survival rates or mortality rates.

First, read the survival frame for the problem and choose your preferred treatment; then, read the mortality frame and see if you feel like changing your preference.

Survival frame
Surgery: Of 100 people having surgery, 90 live through the post-operative period, 68 are alive at the end of the first year and 34 are alive at the end of five years.
Radiation therapy: Of 100 people having radiation therapy, all live through the treatment, 77 are alive at the end of one year and 22 are alive at the end of five years.

What do you choose: *surgery* or *radiation*?

Mortality frame
Surgery: Of 100 people having surgery, ten die during surgery or the post-operative period, 32 die by the end of one year and 66 die by the end of five years.
Radiation therapy: Of 100 people having radiation therapy, none die during treatment, 23 die by the end of one year and 78 die by the end of five years.

What do you choose: *surgery* or *radiation*?

Note that the data are objectively the same in both frames. When people were actually asked to take the decision, however, results indicated that the decision frame had a marked effect on choice of treatment. Radiation therapy was chosen by only 18 per cent of the participants in the study given the survival frame, but by 44 per cent of those given the mortality frame. This framing effect held equally for a group of clinic patients, statistically sophisticated business students and experienced physicians (McNeil *et al*, 1982).

Other factors in decision-making

When we are faced with complicated judgements and decisions, we rely on heuristics to help us simplify the problem. However, when these strategies distort our perception of the information leading to the best course of action, we sometimes make faulty decisions. We may also make faulty decisions even when people do not fall prey to cognitive biases. For example, we can be influenced by non-rational psychological factors, such as 'wishful thinking'. If we want something very much we may underestimate the likelihood of negative outcomes and overestimate the likelihood of positive ones.

Groups can make the same kind of mistake, even at the highest levels of political decision-making. The disastrous Bay of Pigs invasion of Cuba in 1960 was approved by President Kennedy after Cabinet meetings in which contrary information was minimised or suppressed by those advisors to the president who were eager to undertake the invasion. **Irving Janis** (1982b) has coined the term **group think** for the tendency of a decision-making group to erect 'mind guards' that filter out undesirable input so that a consensus may be reached, especially if it is in line with the leader's viewpoint.

New views of *negotiation* recast it as a judgemental process in which expert negotiators sometimes use heuristics that are inappropriate for the given situation, have difficulties interpreting the ambiguous feedback available and frequently fail to give adequate consideration to the other side's perspective. The success of negotiators may be improved by training them to understand the effect that decisional heuristics have on the choices they make and to recognise that similar processes operate to determine the strategy taken by the other side (Neale & Bazerman, 1991; Raiffa, 1982).

Analysis of decision-making has traditionally split the topic into a *probability component* and a *value* (or *utility*) *component*. In short, when we make a decision, we consider the likelihood of various possible outcomes and how much we value each one. Most of the research on decision-making has focused mainly on people's probability estimates and related concepts. This work assumes that errors in decision-making arise mainly from inaccurate estimates of probability, not value. Recently, however, psychologists have turned their attention to the value component and have raised some fascinating questions.

One area of particular interest is our ability to predict how much we will like something at a later time or after repeated exposure. Tastes change and we might not like something as much after being exposed to it every day. Anticipation of such changes should be taken into account when making decisions. For instance, you should be less willing to buy an entire box of some food item you sampled in the grocery store if you think you would quickly become tired of it. Recent evidence suggests that people are not always accurate predictors of changes in their tastes (Kahneman & Snell, 1990) and that their theories of how tastes change lead them to decisions they later regret. For instance, you might decide to buy a house near a highway because you believe you will adapt to the noise, when, in fact, such adaptation is unlikely (Weinstein, 1982).

We can avoid many common pitfalls in decision-making by becoming better information processors. Awareness of the biasing effects of beliefs and theories, over-sensitivity to vivid cases, failure to take into account base-rate information, misuse of heuristics and decision frames and personal attitudes toward risk can help improve decision-making.

Fifty years ago, geneticist Russ Hoelzel would not have applied for a permit to do biopsy darting on orcas (killer whales). No agency regulated whale research. However, in the 1980s, Hoelzel's proposal to collect tissue samples sparked an ongoing international controversy. Conservationists pitted themselves in a struggle over the values of science and the rights of animals in the wild.

Decision-making is hard enough when all the facts are on the table, but in this and other ecological issues, decisions are negotiated on the basis of probabilities about uncertain future events. Since Hoelzel first applied for his research permit in 1985, organisations ranging from Greenpeace to the National Marine Fisheries Service have adopted official positions on the subject. To formulate these positions, they negotiated among themselves, calling upon fragments of data, assumptions, beliefs and values that seemed relevant to their decisions.

The information available to these organisations is summarised below. After weighing the pros and cons of each argument, decide whether you would grant the permit to Hoelzel?

Background: Hoelzel applied for permission to collect tissue samples from 45 orcas in the Puget Sound region. He planned to follow the animals and, when a target orca was within range, he would shoot it with a specially designed arrow. The arrow's sterilised tip was hollow to one inch and would be kept from penetrating further by a rubber stopper. 'After the arrow impacts the whale, it bounces out with the biopsy sample in its core and it is then reeled in using fishing

line attached to the end of the arrow' (Osborne, 1987).

Arguments for: this technique has been used with several species of whales and dolphins. Although short-term startle and avoidance effects have been observed, no long-term effects are known. Orcas in the Puget Sound region are part of an ongoing longitudinal study in which every animal's identity and reproductive history is known. With data from biopsies, the precise genetic relationships among these orcas could be determined. In addition, levels of environmental contaminants in the animals could be measured. Biologist John Calambokidis maintains that 'knowing the contaminant levels of these individuals is a unique opportunity for correlating reproduction with contaminants' (Calambokidis, 1986).

Arguments against: Paul Spong is a physiological psychologist whose experiments with captive orcas transformed him from a 'tank researcher' to an ardent advocate of whale rights. He contends that Hoelzel's

proposal 'is insulting and insensitive to the orcas' (Spong, 1988). Spong believes that their patterns of swimming and eating could be severely disrupted by the darting programme and fears they might leave the area – a long-term effect that might be irreversible. Residents of the islands around which the whales forage (for salmon and marine mammals) share Spong's concerns. They argue that data from tissue samples should not make any difference in the formulation of environmentally sound policies. Spong agrees: 'Do we really need more proof before taking action against the industrial wastes that are poisoning Puget Sound?' (Spong, 1988).

Based on this limited information, would you support or oppose Hoelzel's plan? Reflect on your decision-making process. Did you make any judgements about the motives of the people supporting either point of view? What are the rational aspects of your decision and the emotional, or value-laden, influences that could have biased it?

INTERIM SUMMARY

Decision-making is always subjective and prone to error. Awareness of mental traps is the first step in avoiding them. Inferential strategies normally serve us well, but occasionally we misapply these strategies to new data; we may not consider that new data inconsistent but prior knowledge could indicate a need to revise a particular theory. We continue to hold certain beliefs and theories or to persist in certain ways of doing things because we assimilate data or new experiences in a biased way.

Cognitive biases are now assumed to generate most apparently irrational decisions. Anchoring bias occurs when there is insufficient adjustment up or down from an original starting value. The availability heuristic leads us to estimate an outcome according to how easily similar or identical outcomes can be imagined. The representative heuristic is based on the presumption that belonging to a category implies having the characteristics considered typical of all members of that category. The psychology of decision-making shows that people often do not follow normative behavioural rules. Decisions are influenced by the way a problem is framed, even when alternatives are technically the same. People also have attitudes toward risk that influence decision-making. Finally, an optimistic bias can influence decisions.

THE PSYCHOLOGY OF LANGUAGE

Language is the most subtle tool of communication that people have at their disposal. Words and sentences are employed to communicate an endless variety of messages. Politicians, for example, express their ideas in language, actors use language to communicate the roles they play and judges use language when formally pronouncing sentence upon the accused. However, language is also necessary to communicate about less elevated matters in daily life. We use words and phrases to express our feelings, to ask for such mundane things as the table salt and to reflect on what perhaps we will do next summer. Language is so pervasive that we tend to forget how complex this communicative tool is. Under certain conditions, the complexity of language forces itself upon us − for example, when we try to learn a language that is structured differently from our native tongue, or when we try to explain the difference between the language of bees and humans.

We will turn here to a detailed discussion of the psychology of language. Firstly, we will describe the phenomenon of language and we will introduce terminology as used in the analysis of linguistic structures. These introductory remarks are followed by a section on language comprehension. After that, the production of language in the form of speech is discussed. The last part of the chapter is devoted to a social perspective on language: within this, a discussion of the communicative functions of speech and writing is followed by some remarks about the relations between language, thought and culture.

Characteristics and Functions

The complexity of language can be expounded upon by discussing its characteristics and functions. The first of four characteristics of language is apparent in the opening sentence of this section: language is the most *subtle tool of communication* people can use. Strictly speaking, language is one communicative instrument among others: for example, people can communicate a message by not showing up at an appointment, but no other tool can surpass the communicative nuances of a language. The second characteristic is language's *structured nature*: a linguistic message must conform to rather strict rules in order to be intelligible (for example, with respect to the order of words). At the same time, however, language is characterised by its *accessibility*. This third property underlines the creative nature of speaking and writing: competent language users are capable of creating an endless variety of new sentences from their linguistic knowledgebase and they are also able to understand novel sentences generated by others. The fourth characteristic is the *interpersonal nature* of language: what people say is generally intended as a message to be received by other people. Furthermore, a context constituted of interpersonal communication is a necessary condition for language acquisition to occur (as we have seen in Chapter 4).

As a precision instrument, language serves four functions:

- *Communication:* this is a function that is served evidently by this communicative tool.
- *Referentiality:* our meaningful expressions are assumed to refer to real or imaginary objects, persons and events outside language. It allows us to talk about objects, persons and ideas that are not present in order to put them on the agenda of communication. Reference can be rather simple, as in the case of the reference to a 'tree'. It can also be very complex when we refer, for example, to abstract entities like 'communism' or 'justice'.

- **Intentionality:** language is a goal-directed form of action. When we write or talk we always serve goals, for example, clarifying a complex issue in a lecture.
- **Reflection:** as members of the human species, we use language to reflect upon our own pronouncements, as is demonstrated by what you are reading now and by your ongoing evaluation of the text.

◪ Psycholinguistics

Language is studied by linguists as well as psychologists. Linguists tend to focus on linguistic competence – that is, the abstract knowledge people are assumed to possess about language. Psychologists who study language are known as *psycholinguists*. They are mainly interested in linguistic performance and therefore study how language is actually used. Most psycholinguists work from a cognitive perspective and they hold that studying the mental processes involved in comprehending and producing language is necessary in order to understand linguistic performance. Other psychologists may focus on the communicative function of language, or study the ways in which language is acquired, as we have seen in Chapter 4. In Chapter 2 we have already discussed some insights from *neurolinguistics* about the interplay between language and the brain – for example, when we discussed the functioning of *Wernicke's* and *Broca's areas* in word perception and speech production. Alongside this, neurolinguists have examined the extent to which difficulties in language use can be explained from what is known about deficits in functioning that are produced when brain damage has occurred.

The study of language can be divided into four broad areas:

- **Phonology** deals with the elements and systems of sound in a language.
- **Syntax** is concerned with the rules that specify which sequence of words is well formed and acceptable.
- **Semantics** deals with the meaning of words and sentences.
- **Pragmatics** deals with language in terms of its use and with the social rules with respect to language use.

The largest part of this chapter is devoted to syntax and semantics, but we will also discuss the pragmatic aspect of language when we consider the communicative function of language.

◪ Language Units

Human language is organised hierarchically. The sounds of speech make up the basic level. The most complex level is discourse, where sentences are combined to communicate meaning in a story-like fashion. In this section we will discuss the structure of language bottom-up: from sounds via words and sentences to discourse.

Sounds

Every language consists of meaningless sounds, or phones, that are combined to form meaningful elements. The category of **phonemes** connects the perception of sounds to words, because phonemes are defined as the smallest unit of speech that distinguishes one utterance from another. For example, the /p/ of English 'pin' and the /f/ of English 'fin' are different phonemes. Languages differ in the phonemes that can be distinguished as perceptual units and as produced by its speakers. The number of phonemes that are actually used is relatively small in all languages. For example, the English language uses about 45 phonemes.

Words

At the next level of the hierarchy are **morphemes**. These are the smallest units that contribute either to the meaning or to the structure of a sentence, or both. Words can consist of a single morpheme, like in 'lock', or of a combination of morphemes. When the morpheme '-er', for example, is added to 'lock' (a verb), the result – 'locker' – is composed of two morphemes, the addition resulting in a noun with a new meaning. The complete set of morphemes in a language is generally very large: most languages have tens of thousands of them.

Sentences

Words are combined to form phrases and the combination of phrases results in sentences. This hierarchical structure is shown in *Figure 9.5*.

The sentence 'the woman pays the bill' is a composition of a noun phrase and a verb phrase. Although the composition of a sentence is hierarchically organised and governed by rules, there is no limit to the number of grammatically acceptable sentences in a language. The creativity of language is

FIGURE 9.5 THE HIERARCHICAL ORGANISATION OF THE SENTENCE 'THE WOMAN PAYS THE BILL' INTO PHRASES

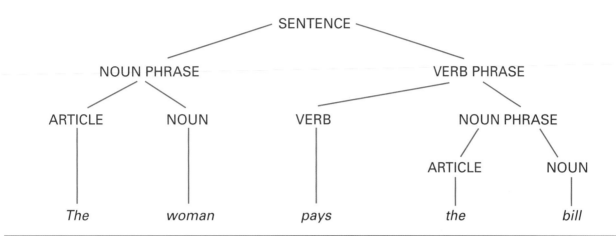

paramount at this level in the hierarchy. The endless variety of correct sentences can be illustrated easily in the following way: take an ordinary sentence from a conversation or from a journal or a textbook, and then look for the identical sentence from another source. You will be looking for quite a while (Carroll, 1994).

Given the infinite number of possible sentences, the question arises as to how people are able to produce and understand them all. It is not very conceivable, neither would it be useful, for language users to encode in long-term memory all of the sentences they read or hear. Psycholinguists nowadays usually assume that a limited set of rules for creating sentences is stored, rather than all the possible individual sentences themselves.

Discourse

People rarely speak in isolated words or sentences. In ordinary conversation, sentences are combined to form discourse – that is, an organised and coherent sequence of sentences. The structure of discourse cannot be defined in strict rules, as the following illustrations show. A fairy-tale is an example of discourse with a clear beginning ('Once upon a time . . .') and a clear end ('. . . and they lived happily ever after.'). But a polite conversation between strangers, which also is an example of discourse, does not have these clear markers at the beginning and the end. Some episodes of discourse are confined to specific social contexts: sermons and lectures are instances of this.

INTERIM SUMMARY

Language is the most subtle tool of communication. It is a highly structured phenomenon, but at the same time, language is open and creative because its basic elements can be combined endlessly. Language is also characterised by its interpersonal nature. Language serves four functions: the first one is communication; the second one is referentiality, which deals with the fact that language refers to a real or imaginary world outside language; the third function, intentionality, expresses the goal-directedness of language; and the last function is reflection, which is concerned with the fact that humans employ language to talk about language.

The study of language can be divided into four areas: phonology deals with sounds; syntax is concerned with the rules that specify the combination and order of words; semantics deals with meaning; while pragmatics studies language-in-use. Language as a phenomenon is hierarchically structured: the units of sound, phonemes, are combined to form the smallest units of structure and meaning, morphemes. Words are composed of morphemes and are combined to form phrases, which are the building blocks of sentences. Discourse is the coherent combination of sentences.

UNDERSTANDING LANGUAGE

The sounds that are spoken are meant to communicate messages, like the written letters of the alphabet. Therefore, sound patterns and letters have to be recognised and connected to the meaningful words that are stored in long-term memory (LTM). Comprehension starts at the basic level of discriminating sounds and letter patterns that are meaningful. However, understanding a language is not a simple bottom-up process where sound and letters are translated into meaning. This section will document the necessity of top-down interpretation as well as bottom-up processing in understanding speech and written text.

Understanding Words and Sentences

Perceiving and interpreting speech

In order to gain an understanding of what is said, sounds have to be analysed as the transporting units of meaning. The first task that is accomplished by the listener is segmentation. Speech reaches us as a continuous stream of sounds. In listening, or rather interpreting what is said, we have to cut this stream of sound into meaningful units. Correct segmentation has consequences for the meaning of a sentence, as the following example shows:

(1) a light house keeper

This phrase was used by Bolinger and Gerstman (1957) to illustrate that a brief pause changes the meaning. If a pause is inserted between 't' and 'h', the stress would be shared between 'light' and 'house' – the meaning becoming 'a housekeeper who does light housekeeping'. Without the pause, the stress is heard on 'light' – thereby the meaning being 'a keeper of lighthouses'. This example illustrates the general phenomenon that segmenting by means of pauses and stresses has consequences for what is understood. The importance of segmentation is evident when we listen to a conversation in a foreign language: more often than not the exchanges sound like a continuous stream, without many pauses.

When sounds are recognised as phonemes, decoding speech proceeds to a higher level. **William Marslen-Wilson** and **Lorraine Tyler** have developed the so-called **cohort model** of speech perception. It describes what happens in a step-wise fashion and stresses the interaction between the recognition of sounds and the context within the sentence of those particular sounds (Marslen-Wilson & Tyler, 1980). At the onset of the auditory presentation of a word, the 'word-initial cohort' is activated – that is, all words which are consistent with the sound that has been heard. For example, if one hears 'al' it may lead to the activation of 'allegation', 'allege' and some other words

FIGURE 9.6	THE WORD-INITIAL COHORT

The word-initial cohort is gradually reduced while hearing a word

allegation allege allegedly alimony alimentary	alimony alimentary	alimony
/al/	/alim/	/alimo/

(see *Figure 9.6*). This word-initial cohort is gradually thinned out as the speaker progresses, because some words are inconsistent with subsequent sounds: if the second sound combines with the first to produce 'alim', all words beginning with 'alle' are eliminated. Processing subsequent auditory signals continues until the so-called *uniqueness point* is reached. There, only one word in the word-initial cohort is consistent with the available evidence. In our example, the uniqueness point is reached at 'alimo' for the word 'alimony'. The example shows that the word can already be recognised before all auditory information is perceived.

Other researchers have concentrated their studies on the importance of the context in speech perception. Lieberman (1963), for example, taped words from spoken sentences and presented them on their own – that is, stripped of the original context in which they were originally voiced. These single words could only be recognised on about 50 per cent of the occasions; written words presented on their own, on the other hand, were accurately recognised in 100 per cent of the cases. Research on the so-called *phonemic restoration effect* has also underlined the importance of semantic context for the comprehension of a sound pattern. In one of their studies, Warren and Warren (1970) presented the following sentences to listeners. The asterisks indicate the place where a part of the word was masked by a sound (i.e. a cough) so that the subject could not hear it.

(2) It was found that the *eel was on the axle
(3) It was found that the *eel was on the shoe
(4) It was found that the *eel was on the orange
(5) It was found that the *eel was on the table

The experimental subjects heard the same speech sound 'eel', but their reports showed that what they heard was strongly affected by the sentence context. The listeners to (2) heard 'wheel' while the others heard 'heel', 'peel' and 'meal' respectively. In other words, speech perception was also determined by the semantic context.

The cohort model of speech perception is not without its problems. It has serious difficulty in explaining the recognition of mispronounced words. Imagine, for example, that someone who is obviously drunk approaches us with the request, 'Scuze m'zzzirr, can-yoo zzzpare a zzzji-igaredd?' According to the cohort model, we would not be able to recognise the word 'cigarette', because 'cigarette' would not be part of the word-initial cohort based on 'zzzji'. A second problem is the recognition of words in improbable contexts. If you say, for example, 'The baker bakes a tablecloth', the 'tablecloth' would not be recognised according to the cohort model, because during the search process a contextual analysis would eliminate 'tablecloth' as nonsensical (Dijkstra & Kempen, 1993).

Perceiving and interpreting written language

In understanding writing, the reader has to decode perceptual stimuli and differentiate them from that which is the case in speech perception. In the earliest stages of visual language processing in reading, the features of letters and the letters themselves are decoded. During reading, the eyes move very quickly, scanning in short bursts back and forth across the text. These *saccadic eye movements* usually occur at a rate of about four or five per second. One saccade takes between 30 and 40 milliseconds in duration. In between these movements the eyes are relatively still for periods of about 150 to 350 ms. These periods are called *fixations*, during which the part of the visual world at which the eye is directed, is projected on the high acuity, foveal region of the retina (Van der Heijden, 1992). During saccades the eyes move too quickly to pick up information from the printed pages. The saccadic eye movements proceed in either forward or backward directions. They each traverse an average of ten letters. Jumping backward is an indication of misperceiving or misunderstanding the text: the reader goes back in order to see what went wrong earlier.

Several models have been proposed for letter recognition. Most models consider features to be crucial. In experiments where isolated letters were presented very briefly (50 milliseconds) and participants were asked to report what they saw, perceivers tended to confuse letters with similar features, such as 'E' and 'F' or 'R' and 'P' (Rumelhart, 1970; see also Chapter 5 on feature detectors). The analysis of features in order to recognise letters (and words) is an example of bottom-up processing: the visual input activates or inhibits simple features at a basic level which in its turn can activate or inhibit more complex feature detectors at the next level. The disadvantage of a bottom-up model of feature perception is that it cannot explain context effects. This was shown in studies of the *word-superiority effect*, which holds that letters are better recognised when they are part of an existing word than when they are presented as part of a non-word ('owrd') or individually (Reicher, 1969).

There are many differences between the comprehension of speech and written text at the feature and letter level. Particular visual phenomena, like saccades, have no auditory counterpart. However, next to these differences are many similarities between the processing of speech and of written text. At the higher levels of understanding words, sentences and discourse, there is much similarity between written and oral language.

The internal lexicon

We have seen that perceptual units like speech-sounds and features of letters are combined to form the meaningful units of phonemes, morphemes, letters and words. At the morpheme and word level, meaning is established by drawing elements from our **internal,** or **mental, lexicon**. This is the representation of meaningful units, like words, in long-term memory. In producing and comprehending language we constantly draw from our lexicon. For example, we search for the meaning of the sound pattern 'frog'. When the word has been found, the properties associated with it become available. These properties include the meaning of the word ('small jumping animal living both in water and on land'), its spelling and pronunciation and its relationship to other words and meanings. These properties correspond to what is found in an ordinary dictionary, but the interal lexicon is assumed to contain also information that is not strictly linguistic. For many people, the activation of 'frog' will also result in the associated knowledge that a frog is a major character in *The Muppet Show*!

The lexicon stores an enormous amount of words. For an adult, it has been estimated at more than 50,000 words. Human speech proceeds at a velocity of about three words per second, which means that speakers as well as listeners have to choose among the database of lexical elements within one-third of a second (Dijkstra & Kempen, 1993). It is clear that this selection task can only be completed successfully if *lexical access* – that is, the process by which words and meanings are activated – can be realised very quickly. From our discussion of the cohort model (above), we have already seen that the choice among alternatives is most probably carried out in an interactive combination of bottom-up and top-down processing.

Rapid lexical access also presupposes that the

FIGURE 9.7	THE STRUCTURE OF THE INTERNAL LEXICON

The structure of the internal lexicon as assumed by the spreading activation model.

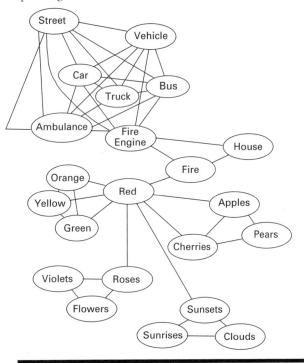

closely related concepts are more likely to be activated than distant concepts.

Parsing a sentence

One of the basic processes in comprehending a sentence is *parsing*. It involves working out the grammatical structure of a sentence by assigning elements of its surface structure to linguistic categories. The tree-like diagram of *Figure 9.5* might be the result of parsing a sentence. A lot of experimental research on parsing has employed so-called **garden path sentences**. The following sentence is an example of this:

(6) The steel ships are transporting is expensive.

This is called a garden path sentence because the meaning of the sentence seems to 'lead the reader up the garden path'. It would not be unusual for someone who read sentence (6) aloud to insert a pause between 'transporting' and 'is expensive', because at that point the original parsing no longer makes sense.

internal lexicon is organised efficiently. The organisation of the lexicon bears a close resemblance to the general organisation of knowledge in the cognitive system which was discussed earlier in this chapter in the section about mental structures for thinking. The theoretical proposals for the structure of the lexicon are as varied as they are with respect to the organisation of concepts. Some theorists have advocated a hierarchical network model, and others have argued in favour of storage by means of the semantic features of words. One important example is the *spreading activation model* of Collins and Loftus (1975). It is a revision of classical hierarchical network models. It holds that words are represented in the internal lexicon within a network of relationships, but the network itself is not hierarchically organised (Collins & Loftus, 1975). As *Figure 9.7* shows, the network is a web of inter-connecting nodes. In this example, words reside at the nodes, but morphemes may also be represented there. The distance between nodes expresses structural characteristics like shared category membership and functional relations (for example, the degree of association between words or meaningful elements). The way in which semantic information is retrieved occurs by a process of *spreading activation*. Wherever a person sees or hears a word, activation begins at a single node and then spreads in parallel form throughout the network. The distance between nodes influences activation, because

Syntactic analysis and semantic interpretation of sentences

An analysis at the syntactic level is a clear prerequisite for understanding. The sentence has to be parsed and syntactic properties have to be drawn from the internal lexicon. For example, it must be established to which category a word belongs and in which syntactic context the word fits. Next to these syntactic analyses, a semantic interpretation is needed. Take, for example, the following sentence:

(7) My boyfriend saw the Pyrenees flying to Brussels.

Syntactic analyses of what is said here will not provide the proper understanding of the sentence. To understand the meaning of (7) we need semantic knowledge of a general nature – for example, that the Pyrenees are a mountain range and not a type of aircraft. In some extreme cases, we can do without syntactic structures in communication as is for example shown in:

(8) storm tree walk hurt

It is most probable that we are able to determine immediately what is meant here, without relying on syntactic information.

Sentences have syntactic and semantic aspects, but the issue as to what extent both contribute to understanding a grouping of words has not been solved. Do syntax and semantics interact on equal terms or does one aspect dominate the other? Some defend the view that syntax and semantics interact during the comprehension process. In one study, subjects were presented ambiguous sentences in which the first clause biased the listener toward one of the possible interpretations (Marslen-Wilson & Tyler, 1980). For example, the subjects heard (9) and (10):

(9) If you walk too near the runway, landing planes . . .
(10) If you've been trained as a pilot, landing planes . . .

The semantic context suggests different interpretations of 'landing planes' in (9) and (10). After the subjects heard the sentences, a word was presented visually that was or was not appropriate: 'are' is appropriate for sentence (9) and 'is' is appropriate for (10). Reaction times of the subjects showed that appropriate words were named more quickly than inappropriate ones. This suggests that the semantic context was used immediately to assign one or another structural meaning. Other studies have, however, shown that the syntactic aspects of parsing exert a powerful influence on comprehension that cannot be undone by semantic interpretation. It seems safe to conclude that syntactic analysis and semantic interpretation are partially autonomous in their interaction (Dijkstra & Kempen, 1993).

Understanding Discourse

We have seen that the comprehension of words and sentences is an interactive process. Often we need, for example, to examine the structure of a sentence in order to understand the meaning of a word. In this section we will move one step up in the hierarchy by presenting a model for the comprehension of discourse. In many cases, understanding the discursive context of a sentence is necessary if one is to understand the sentence itself.

Cognitive psychologists and linguists generally assume that an integrated understanding of discourse is the result of relating current elements in the passage with elements that have come before (Carroll, 1994). The role of *propositions* is crucial in this respect. A proposition is a unit of meaning that consists of a predicate plus one or more arguments – for example, 'is-a (dog, animal)' and 'can (dog, bark)'. Basically, arguments are what the proposition is about ('dog, animal, bark') and the predicates are what is asserted about the arguments ('is-a', 'can'). Simple sentences consist of one proposition, but most sentences are combinations of a number of propositions. For example (from Carroll, 1994):

(11) George got into a quarrel with Harry, hit him and then left the bar.
(12) Initiated (George, Harry, quarrel)
(13) Hit (George, Harry)
(14) Left (George, bar)

In their model of discourse comprehension, **William Kintsch** and **Teun van Dijk** (Kintsch & van Dijk, 1978; 1983) have focused on the propositional nature of (written) text. Following the cognitive modelling of memory, they assume that text and other semantic information is stored propositionally in memory. The limited capacity of short-term memory (or working memory; see Chapter 8) precludes readers from processing all the propositions in a sentence or paragraph at once. Instead, readers work their way through the text in cycles of propositions. As soon as the first phrase is read, its basic proposition is determined. This propositional determination is repeated for every new phrase or sentence. In every new case, it is determined whether the current proposition can be linked to propositions that occurred just before the current one and, if so, are stored in memory. The links, for example, may be established on the basis of a common argument, like in sentences (13) and (14) above. If attaching a new proposition to those within the most recent sentence turns out to be impossible, the search is directed towards propositions that appeared earlier, or new ones are generated that link the actual representation of the text with earlier propositions.

Research on the propositional nature of discourse comprehension has implications for the readability of a text. Traditionally, readability was determined on the basis of superficial characteristics of the text, like the frequency of the words used and the length of the sentence. The Kintsch and Van Dijk model suggests that readability is rather determined by the processing operations that are needed for comprehension – for example, how easy the propositions are determined and how much time it takes to retrieve earlier propositions from memory. Indeed, empirical research has shown that the time required to read a text for the purposes of later recall is influenced by the number of propositions. Every new proposition adds about one and a half seconds to the reading time (Graesser *et al*, 1980; Kintsch & Keenan, 1973).

In more recent theories of discourse comprehension, it is argued that readers go beyond the information given in the propositions because they want to establish cohesion: readers try to match what they read to familiar knowledge. This matching process can exert a powerful influence over the understanding of a text. The following example was used in a study about the effects of cohesion establishment (Barton & Sanford, 1993). Subjects were asked to read the text and to answer the question.

There was a tourist flight travelling from Vienna to Barcelona. On the last leg of the journey, it developed engine trouble. Over the Pyrenees, the pilot started to lose control. The plane eventually crashed right on the border. Wreckage was equally strewn in France and Spain. The authorities were trying to decide where to bury the survivors.

What is the solution to the problem?

To experience the impact earlier knowledge can have on the understanding of a new text, you should try to answer the question yourself. Most probably, you are not different from the experimental subjects in failing to notice that survivors do not have to be buried. This misreading of written discourse can be explained theoretically by pointing to the influence of schematic knowledge on comprehension. Reading about an air crash and burial probably activates words like 'victims' before 'survivors' is read.

INTERIM SUMMARY

The comprehension of spoken and written language presupposes both bottom-up and top-down processing. To be able to understand speech, segmentation of the sequence of sounds is necessary. According to the cohort model, phonemes are compared with units from the internal lexicon in a bottom-up procedure. Top-down activity is underlined by the phonemic restoration effect.

Access to the internal lexicon is crucial for understanding. This database is the representation of words and their (associated) meaning in memory. Several models have been suggested for the structure of this lexicon. Parsing a sentence is a necessary step in the process of understanding sentences. Research about the ways in which parsing takes place has shown that both syntactic analysis and semantic interpretation are necessary in the comprehension of sentences.

Understanding discourse is the most complex level of language comprehension. Psycholinguists generally assume that the propositions in discourse are the building blocks of which understanding is formed.

◤ PRODUCING LANGUAGE

The fact that language is a communicative instrument presupposes that language users are both capable of understanding what others have said (or written) and capable of expressing their own thoughts in some linguistic form. Empirical research on language shows, however, an interesting discrepancy: most of psycholinguistic research is concerned with the comprehension of language, the production of language is studied less often. A major reason for this unequal distribution of attention is that the production of language is difficult to examine empirically. Psycholinguistics and cognitive psychology still struggle with the issue as to how thoughts are translated into the production of speech. The comprehension of speech – that is, the progression from language to thought – is easier to study, because it is possible, for example, to determine the success of comprehension by asking participants to recall a passage they listened to earlier.

In this section we will briefly describe some important aspects of producing spoken language. However, we will not discuss the production of written language. In our presentation we will draw upon the work of **Willem Levelt** (1989) who distinguished three stages of speech production: conceptualising, formulating and articulating. We will present the stages sequentially for reasons of clarity. Whether speech production actually *is* a sequential process is the subject of debate. Therefore, we will also present theories and research that stress parallel processing. However, before we look at speech production, we will discuss *slips of the tongue* because the analysis of these errors in speech production has provided psycholinguists with much of their knowledge about speech production.

◤ Slips of the Tongue

Spontaneous conversation in natural language shows errors in speech production on a regular basis. We sometimes say 'you can bake my bike' if we intend to lend our bicycle. The famous Oxford clergyman, the Reverend William Spooner, had the involuntary habit of exchanging initial sounds as in sentence (15):

(15) You have hissed my mystery lecture. (. . . *missed my history. . .*)

As a tribute to the reverend, these sound-exchanges are nowadays known as **spoonerisms**. Collections of speech errors show that these slips of the tongue are hardly random. These extreme cases of language production seem to occur in regular patterns. Therefore, the analysis of spontaneous slips is a way of gaining insight into the way in which language is produced (Fromkin, 1971). As a general rule, errors in an utterance tend to occur at one linguistic level only. In some cases, a single phoneme is added or exchanged; in other cases whole words or phrases may be substituted. For example, when someone mistakenly substitutes one word for another, the sentence can be correct nevertheless at the syntactic and phonological levels, as in sentence (16):

(16) My fear of crying bothers me. (. . . *fear of flying* . . .)

Another regular pattern is that slips of the tongue are generally consistent with the phonological rules of the language. English speakers may slip and say 'corcodile', which is a conceivable sequence of sounds, but 'crcoodile' will never be heard as a linguistic slip because this phonetic sequence is impossible to pronounce in English.

Psychologists from different theoretical perspectives have given different explanations for the occurence of speech errors. Freud has given a classical account of 'Freudian slips' in arguing that errors in speech production always have their basis in repressed, unconscious motives. In his work on speech errors he gave the following example:

One day he asked one of his patients how her uncle was doing; the patient answered by saying that she did not know, because she only saw her uncle 'in flagranti' (meaning, 'in the course of committing an illicit sexual act'); she immediately corrected herself and shamefully said that she meant 'en passant'. According to Freud, this and similar slips occur when the mechanism of repression weakens for a moment (Freud, 1900).

Errors like the above are rare, but some researchers have been successful in the induction of 'Freudian slips' in the laboratory. Motley (1987) found that spoonerisms that were sexually related, such as 'bare shoulders' for 'share boulders' and 'fast passion' for 'past fashion', were more common when the cognitive set of an experimental subject was predominantly sexual. This cognitive perspective was induced in a male group of subjects, for example, by the provocative attire of a female organiser. In that case, more sexually related slips were produced than when the organiser of the group was male.

Most psycholinguists and cognitive psychologists are not convinced by the Freudian explanation of slips of the tongue. Rather, they focus on the mechanisms of speech production than on unconscious drives. Their research on speech errors has provided valuable insights for linguistic theory – for example, that many of the units which are exchanged or substituted in slips of the tongue are precisely those as postulated by linguistic theories. According to some researchers, this means that the patterns of sound, the phonemes, and

the morphemes constitute the basic planning units in the production of speech (Fromkin, 1971). We will now turn to a description of the steps in speech production.

 Conceptualising

This first step is concerned with the thoughts the speaker wants to express. The speaker will conceptualise what he or she wants to say and probably also what is intended by the verbal expression. In other words, *planning* is a crucial aspect of language production (Zammuner, 1991). In our earlier section on mental representation, we discussed the issue as to how thoughts are represented in the cognitive apparatus before they are translated into linguistic form. If we accept for the moment that there is some kind of 'language of thought', then we could argue that conceptualising takes place in this representational system (Fodor, 1975). There is not much agreement, however, as to the ways in which the language of thought is translated into ordinary linguistic forms.

Conceptualising is the first step in the production process, but speakers do not always conceptualise first before they proceed with the next step. It is a common experience to hear ourselves speak without having thought before hand; every speaker needs pauses to reflect back on what he or she intended to say and on what will be said next (Garrett, 1984).

Formulating

The second step, *formulating*, is concerned with translating conceptual structures into a linguistic form. There is much debate among psycholinguists about the ways in which linguistic plans are put into practice. Most researchers, however, generally agree that speech production proceeds through a series of stages (Dijkstra & Kempen, 1993; Fromkin, 1971; Garrett, 1988). Disagreement has arisen about the first stage in the sequential production of speech. Fromkin (1971), for example, assumes that the syntactic structure of what is intended to be said is laid out first. After that, content words are fitted into this structure. Other models, by contrast, are lexically driven, which means that the first stage is concerned with the selection of the appropriate words from the mental lexicon (Dijkstra & Kempen, 1993; Kempen & Hoenkamp, 1987). We will sketch some important aspects of the last model.

What we want to express is first encoded at a grammatical level and then at the phonetic one. At the grammatical level, words are selected from the internal lexicon on the basis of the ideas to be expressed. These words generally trigger a syntactic structure, but syntax is also determined by the meaning to be expressed. Then, phonological encoding takes place. According to Levelt (1989), syllables play a crucial role at this level. The hundreds of thousands of words in ordinary language are composed of some thousand syllables. Because this sample of syllables is rather small, they are used on a regular basis and this permanent practice probably

allows speakers to prepare for the actual production of speech in a routine, automatic fashion.

Articulating

The third step is *articulation*. At this point the grammatically and phonologically encoded material is translated into actual speech sounds. The brain is

---

FIGURE 9.8   COLOUR PATTERNS USED IN LEVELT'S STUDY

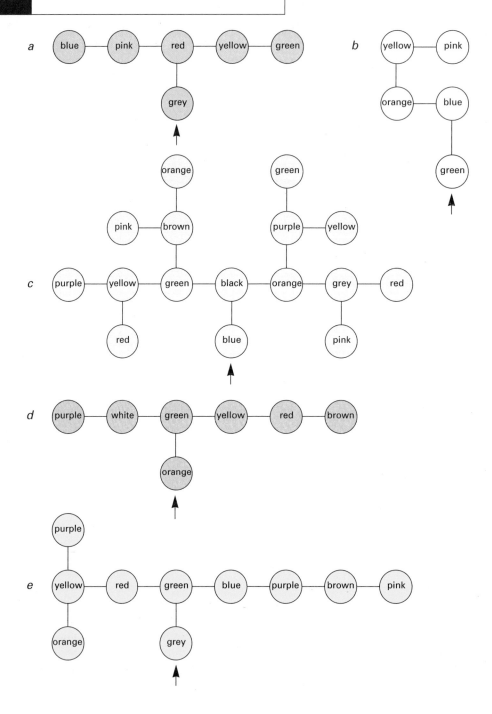

required to send signals to the muscles in the speech system so that they can execute the appropriate movements in order to produce the required sounds. What is actually articulated is also dependent on the sounds that came before and the sound that will follow. This phenomenon is known as **co-articulation**, which holds that the shape of the vocal system for any sound often accommodates to the shape needed for surrounding sounds. An example of co-articulation for upcoming sounds is the rounding of the lips in the production of the 'b' in 'boo', which anticipates the rounding needed for the sound 'oo', as opposed to their formation in, for example, 'bed' (Carroll, 1994).

Our sequential presentation of the processes of formulating and articulating suggests that they appear in strict alternation. However, **Gerard Kempen** and his colleagues have argued that the processes generally overlap (Kempen & Hoenkamp, 1987). They have coined the term **incremental processing** for the notion that people seem to plan one portion of their utterances as they articulate another portion ('increment' means increase or added amount). This kind of parallel processing is possible because people generally have very little conscious awareness of the work involved in articulation. Incremental processing can be illustrated in the following way. A sentence is a series of units. In translating a conceptual structure into the unit of a sentence, we have to plan unit X before we can articulate unit X. In this sense, speech production is serial. But, at the same time that we are articulating unit X, we are planning unit X + 1; in this sense processing is parallel (Carroll, 1994). In short, incremental processing allows us to implement new linguistic plans while we are articulating older ones.

When we are articulating a word, phrase or sentence, we check whether what we actually say is what we intended to say. People spontaneously interrupt themselves to correct their speech. This kind of correction typically takes the following form: the speaker interrupts himself after he has detected an error; then he utters some kind of editing expression, like 'uh', 'rather' or 'I mean'; the last step in correcting is concerned with repairing the mistake. Levelt (1983), in studying self-repairs, showed the participants in the study a pattern like the one in *Figure 9.8* (previous page), and they were then asked to descibe the pattern in such a way that someone else who had not seen it would be able the draw the pattern on the basis of the verbal description.

It was found that self-repairs were performed quickly: 18 per cent of the corrections were within a word, as in sentence (17); another 51 per cent occurred immediately after the error, as in (18). The remaining corrections were delayed by one or more words.

(17) We can go straight on to the ye . . . to the orange node.
(18) Straight on to green . . . to red.

Levelt's studies have shown that speakers routinely monitor their speech and quickly repair what went wrong in order to maximise listeners' comprehension.

INTERIM SUMMARY

Language production has been given less attention by psycholinguists than language comprehension. The production of speech has often been studied by analysing slips of the tongue, because these naturally occurring speech errors provide insight into the mechanisms of speech production. Speech production is an activity that proceeds step by step, although the stages generally overlap. We first conceptualise what we want to say and then formulate a plan in linguistic terms. The formulation is connected with articulation, during which we also check as to whether it is what we wanted to say. Research on incremental processing has shown that speakers implement new plans while they are articulating older ones.

◤ LANGUAGE AND COMMUNICATION

Much of the language we produce serves communicative purposes: we say something to someone in order to get a message across and in most cases the person we talk to will react with his or her own contribution to the conversational interaction. Many psychologists have argued that the communicative context of language production and comprehension is crucial for a complete understanding of human language. In this section we will therefore focus on the *pragmatic aspects* of language.

◤ Speech Acts

When people communicate with each other, they give voice to sentences like 'I promise you to . . .', 'I bet . . .' and 'I congratulate . . . These verbal utterances are different from others, because they primarily express a kind of action. The philosopher **John Austin** called these linguistic expressions **speech acts** and made them the cornerstone of his theory about the pragmatic function of language. The central assumption of Austin's speech act theory is that all utterances state things and do things – in other words, they have a *meaning* and a *force* (Austin, 1962; Searle, 1969). The difference between the two is illustrated in the following example of an indirect speech act:

(19) Can you shut the window?

The meaning of the sentence is an inquiry about an ability, but almost everyone who is addressed by this sentence will understand its implicit force: sentence (19) is a request to perform the closing of the window. In some cases, however, both meaning and force of the utterance are implicated in the verb used:

(20) I order you to shut the window.

Whether speech acts like (19) and (20) result in the desired action does not primarily depend on the truth or falsity of their meaning. Rather, it is crucial that certain conditions are met for speech acts to be accomplished. These conditions are called **felicity conditions**. In this closing-a-window case, felicity conditions would include, for example, whether or not the person addressed has the ability or willingness to shut the window. If the speech act does not meet the felicity conditions, it is generally considered awkward or inappropriate. This would be the case if request (19) were to be addressed to someone sitting in a room where none of the windows were open.

Psychologists who have used speech act theory in their research have focused on the pragmatics of human language. They are primarily interested in language as a tool to get things done rather than in language as an abstract system or in the mental representation of language. Recently, British social psychologists have followed Austin's inspiration by developing an approach called *discourse analysis* (Potter & Wetherell, 1987), which will be discussed later in the chapter on social psychology.

Conversational Principles

The communicative interaction between participants in a conversation is complex in nature. In ordinary conversation, there are no explicit rules that prescribe how conversational interaction must take place. Research on conversations has shown, however, that almost all conversational interactions follow implicit rules and conventions (Sacks *et al*, 1974; Heritage, 1985). One of the most important rules is that participants in a conversation *take turns,* which results in a rhythm of one participant talking at a time and

the other one listening and reinforcing what is said by 'hmm-ing' or nodding. The smooth transition from one speaker to the other is accomplished by a number of cues. In some cases it is done by directing a question to the person who listens. In most cases, however, more fine-tuned signals are employed. Among the signals that indicate that the speaker will soon conclude his or her turn are, for example, a drop in pitch and loudness, a drawl on the final syllable or the insertion of an expression like 'you know'. In one study a direct relationship was found between the number of cues and the listener's attempts to take a turn: the more turn-taking cues, the more attempts were made (Duncan, 1972). Turn-taking signals implicitly help participants to speak one at a time. However, utterances sometimes overlap, which occurs most commonly at the point of turn changes.

Another important reason why most conversations proceed smoothly is because participants generally interact on the basis of shared conventions. Grice (1975) identified conventions, or *maxims* as he called them, that govern conversational interaction. We will discuss the most important ones. The first one is that speakers strive to be as *informative* as is required, but not more informative than is needed in that particular conversation. The second one is that speakers must try to be *truthful* – in other words, they should not say things that they believe to be false. The third convention is that speakers should make their contribution *relevant* to the aims of the ongoing conversation. The fourth and last convention is that speakers should be *clear* in what they are saying. They must try to avoid obscurity and disorder in the language they use. In actual practice, speakers fall short of these four conventions from time to time. They are either purposively or accidentally uninformative, deceitful, irrelevant and unclear in what they say. These transgressions, however, do not undermine Grice's central point, which is that the conventions provide a basis for interpreting what others mean because we generally assume, unless we have information to the contrary, that speakers conform to these ground rules for successful conversations. The following fragment is an example of what happens when a convention is violated (Clark & Clark, 1977):

Steven: Jonathan is meeting a woman for dinner tonight.
Susan: *Does his wife know?*
Steven: Of course she does. The woman he is meeting is his wife.

In this conversation, the initial misunderstanding between the participants is caused by Steven's violation of Grice's first convention: he is not providing enough information and, thus, Susan is misled.

Gender Differences in Language and Conversation

Researchers who focus on the communicative functions of language have shown particular interest in the extent to which the individual's language is determined by social categories such as educational level, gender or societal position. Empirical research on gender differences has shown that the common stereotype of female 'chatterboxes' and 'gossips' who supposedly talk far more than men is not correct. Most studies by contrast have shown that men talk more than do women: their stretches of talk are longer and they take more time to explain their views (Hyde, 1991). Lakoff (1975) has argued that women are socialised to speak in different ways than men: women's language is, for example, generally characterised by polite constructions, such as indirect requests ('Can you open the door?'). Women also tend to favour modal constructions which express doubt ('can', 'could', 'shall') and use more *tag questions* than men. A tag question is a short phrase at the end of a declarative sentence that turns it into a question – for example, 'This is a great film, *isn't it?*' In one study it was found that women used about twice as many tag questions as men (McMillan *et al*, 1977).

The analysis of conversational interactions in mixed-gender groups has documented that men are more prone to interrupt women than vice versa. It was also found that the display of interest in what the speaker was saying by minimal responses (like nodding and 'hmm-ing') was far more frequent amongst female contributions to the conversation than in the male ones (McMillan *et al*, 1977; Zimmerman & West, 1975).

Feminist psychologists and linguists argue that gender differences in language and conversational style reflect and support the societal position of men and women (Davis, 1988; Hyde, 1991). In Western patriarchal societies, men predominantly occupy positions of power and their language underlines their societal status. Thus, many women are subjected to male authority and their polite, somewhat uncertain language both corroborates their own relative lack of power and supports the male power position. It should also be noted, however, that modal constructions and tag questions serve an important communicative function in encouraging communication, rather than closing it with a declarative statement. In this sense, female language reflects greater interpersonal sensitivity because it leaves room for other views to be expressed in the conversation. The linguist **Deborah Tannen** (1990) has argued recently that gender differences in language are also determined by different ways of thinking. Men tend to think hierarchically, in terms of 'one-up' and 'one-down': in conversations, they are far more afraid to lose their 'one-up' status than are women. Consequently, they tend to argue in a peremptory tone and try to determine the conversational process by interrupting a lot.

INTERIM SUMMARY

The pragmatic aspects of language are concerned with the communicative function of language. Speech act theory seeks to describe how people do things with words: people use language, for example, to request, apologise and threaten. Human conversation is characterised by turn-taking. Participants in a conversation generally share the conventions of being informative, truthful, relevant and clear in what they are contributing.

Research has pointed to gender differences in language and conversational style. Women generally use more modal forms of language than men and they interrupt less often, thus leaving room for other contributions.

LANGUAGE, CULTURE AND THOUGHT

Language serves many functions as a communicative instrument. It is an indispensable tool if, for example, we want to note something, make a claim or ask a question. The communicative properties of language, however, extend beyond the here and now. Without language, we would not know culture as it is in its many present forms. One could argue that language is the memory and repository of a culture because without language we could utilise only a small part of the knowledge accumulated by earlier generations. It is concluded here, therefore, that language and culture are linked inextricably.

The consequence of the link between language and culture is that organisms without a culture do not have a language in the human sense of the word. But does this also mean that they are not capable of acquiring a human-like language? Over the past decades, Gardner and Gardner have been rather successful in teaching a chimpanzee a human language by immersing the chimpanzee into our human, culturally embedded ways of communicating. They were able to teach the chimpanzee a large amount of American Sign Language, a non-vocal human language that is also used by deaf people. The chimpanzee was capable of acquiring many signs and of using them appropriately (Gardner & Gardner,

1969; Gardner *et al*, 1992). Despite this, and other successes in teaching primates a human sign language, two big differences remain: chimpanzees do not develop syntactic knowledge; and humans generally acquire a language without apparent difficulty, whereas chimpanzees have to devote years of practice to the development of this communicative system.

There are many different cultures and different languages across the globe. The consequences of this differentiation are readily apparent: people from different cultures and people who speak different languages have to face difficulties in communicating with one another. Common experience shows us that it is no easy task to translate one language/culture into another language/culture. On most occasions, it takes some effort to communicate when you are from different linguistic and cultural backgrounds. In the last section of this chapter we will take this issue one step further by asking whether or not these communicative problems are determined by different ways of thinking. In other words: does language determine thought?

The question of the relationship between language and thought has resulted in a long-standing debate in psychology and psycholinguistics. In the past and present, most theorists and researchers have assumed that thought determines language rather than the other way around. Language is designed to express propositional thought; the structure of language should therefore reflect the structure of thought. We will focus here on the opposite claim by discussing the hypothesis of **linguistic relativity** which holds that language shapes thought and, therefore, also holds that when languages are different, thinking is likewise different.

Linguistic Relativity

The hypothesis that language shapes thought was most strongly advocated by **Benjamin Whorf**. Thus, the hypothesis of linguistic relativity is known generally as **Whorf's hypothesis**. Whorf's thinking about the relation between language and cognition was influenced by the anthropologist Sapir who in his studies of native American linguistics suggested that languages are diverse in the way that they structure reality. Whorf radicalised Sapir's suppositions by arguing that a language determines cognitive processes – in other words, learning a language changes the way a person thinks. Consequently, Whorf claimed that speakers of different languages think in different ways (Whorf, 1956).

Researchers that have followed Whorf and studied the relation between language and thought commonly distinguish between a strong and a weak version of the Whorf hypothesis (Schwanenflugel *et al*, 1991). The *strong version* states that language determines cognition – that is, the presence of linguistic categories creates the cognitive categories that are employed in thinking. The *weak version* of the hypothesis assumes that the presence of linguistic categories influences the ease with which various cognitive operations are performed – that is, certain thought processes may be more accessible or more easily performed by members of one linguistic community in comparison with another (Carroll, 1994). We will discuss some examples of empirical research about linguistic relativity. However, it should be noted that when studies provide support for Whorf's thinking, it is always in relation to the weak version of his hypothesis. There is no empirical evidence to support the strong version.

Lexical differentiation

Whorf himself discussed many examples of lexical differentiation in languages: some languages have only one word for a particular thing or phenomenon, other languages have a more differentiated vocabulary. He observed, for example, that in Hopi (a native American language) there are only two words for everything that flies. The first word refers to bird, the other word includes everything else, from insects to airplanes. This categorical differentiation is rather broad from the standpoint of an English speaker. The second example is concerned with snow: Inuit, the language of the Inuit (Eskimo) people, contains multiple terms with which to describe snow, the vast majority of which are not available in English. According to Whorf, the vocabulary enables the Inuit to differentiate in their thought, perception and talk about the various kinds and states of snow that are evident to them in their everyday lives.

Whorf's ideas about lexical differentiation were criticised by those who argued that it is unclear what counts as a word in a language and between languages. Languages differ in their morphological constructions; in some languages it is more common to create new words by means of the addition of suffixes than it is in other languages. A count that is based exclusively on root words will produce a smaller number than a count that includes suffixed versions of root words (for example: 'powder-snow', 'wet-snow', 'thick-snow'). According to recent studies, then, the claim that the Inuit show greater discriminativeness with respect to different types of snow has yet to be settled and accepted by all (Pullum, 1991).

At a lexical level, it is clear that languages differ

The Inuit (Eskimo) people within their language have multiple terms with which to describe snow.

with respect to the words they have for colour. For example, whilst English has many colour terms, other languages have only two: black and white. The Whorf hypothesis raises the question as to whether speakers of such different languages perceive colours in a different way. In an early study, support was found for the Whorf hypothesis (Lenneberg & Roberts, 1956). The researchers found that Zuni-speakers in New Mexico made more mistakes in recognising yellows and oranges than did English-speakers. This problem could be explained by the fact that Zuni has only a single word to describe yellows and oranges.

Research by Heider (1972), however, showed contradictory results. She studied the Dani of New Guinea whose language has only black and white as colour terms. The study showed that Dani people are able to perceive colour variation in the same way as English speakers wherein there are 11 colour terms within the language. This result is clearly at odds with Whorf's hypothesis. In more recent research, however, Whorf's hypothesis is again supported (Kay & Kempton, 1984). The researchers compared the performance of English-speakers with that of people who spoke a native Mexican language that does not have the blue and green colour terms. English-speakers were more successful at discriminating the blues and greens than the native Mexicans were. Thus, the availability of colour terms seems to have some influence on the ease with which people can label the colours they perceive. It is still an open

question though, as to whether their perception of the colours is different.

A final example of linguistic relativity is the use of personal pronouns. In a recent overview, Mühlhäusler and Harré (1990) have documented that the different ways in which personal pronouns are used has consequences for people's identity. We will confine ourselves here to one example.

The use of 'I' as a self-referential category, which is a central characteristic of languages like English, German, French and Dutch, does not exist in Inuit. If a group of Eskimos is asked who will prepare dinner tonight, the potential cook will not answer by saying 'I will', but will reply with 'The being here mine'. In cases where English speakers would say 'I hear him', Inuit speakers use the expression 'His making of a sound with reference to me'. For Inuit speakers, cooking and hearing are not activities that originate within the autonomous individual, but are social processes of which the individual is an intrinsic part. The absence of a self-referential linguistic category like 'I' is related to the fact that autonomous individuality among Eskimos is not as important as it is in Western Europe and North America (Mühlhäusler & Harré, 1991).

The empirical evidence for the Whorf hypothesis is not conclusive. Some studies support Whorf's theory, other studies have not substantiated his thinking. However, Whorf and his followers have sensitised us to the importance of linguistic categories for the way in which we cope with our environments. In many instances, it is helpful to have a specific vocabulary to draw distinctions that we could not have made previously. Imagine, for example, what happens when studying a textbook like this: as readers progress, their psychological vocabulary grows and, thus, provides a finely honed tool with which to analyse psychological issues. Or, as another example, imagine what happens when people listen to music: a ordinary listener will probably differentiate implicitly between 'happy music' and 'sad music'; but someone who has studied the theory of music, in all likelihood, will be able to provide a much more richly descriptive account of what was heard and will probably have noted more points of detail in what was being played.

recapping main points

Mental Structures for Thinking

Thinking is a higher-order mental process that uses concepts as its building blocks. We form concepts by identifying those properties that are common to a class of objects or ideas. The organisation of concepts is either by their critical features or prototypically. Concepts are often hierachically organised. Schema and scripts guide thinking because they help to encode and store information in memory and also to form expectations. In addition to these language-like thinking structures, we rely on visual imagery in thought.

Reasoning and Problem-solving

Deductive reasoning involves drawing conclusions from premises on the basis of rules of logic. Inductive reasoning involves inferring a conclusion from evidence on the basis of its likelihood or probability. When solving problems, we must define the operations that can get us from the initial state to the goal state. Artificial intelligence programs have proven to be helpful in problem-solving. Mental sets can hamper problem-solving and require attempts at breaking set. Algorithms ensure an eventual solution if there is one, but generally are impractical. Heuristics are mental shortcuts that often help us reach a solution quickly. We also rely on metacognitive knowledge in problem-solving.

Judging and Deciding

Decision-making is always subjective and prone to error. Cognitive biases are now assumed to generate most apparently irrational decisions. Examples are the anchoring bias, the availability heuristic and the representativeness heuristic. The psychology of decision-making shows that decisions are influenced by the way a problem is framed and that people tend to rely on unrealistic optimism.

The Psychology of Language

Language is the most subtle tool of communication. It is a highly structured phenomenon, but at the same time, language is open and creative. Language is hierarchically structured: the elements of sound, phonemes, are combined to form the smallest unit of meaning, morphemes. Words are composed of morphemes and are combined to form phrases which are the building blocks of sentences. Discourse is the combination of meaningful sentences.

The comprehension of language presupposes both bottom-up and top-down processing. According to the cohort model, phonemes are compared with units from the internal lexicon in a bottom-up procedure. Top-down activity is underlined by the phonemic restoration effect. Access to the internal lexicon is crucial for understanding and so is parsing the sentence. Psycholinguists generally assume that propositions are the building blocks from which understanding of discourse is formed.

The production of speech is generally studied by analysing slips of the tongue, because these naturally occurring speech errors provide insight into the mechanisms of speech production. Speech production is an activity that proceeds step by step, but research on incremental processing has shown that speakers implement new plans while they are articulating older ones.

Speech act theory seeks to describe how people do things with words: people use language, for example, to request, apologise and threaten. Human conversation is characterised by turn-taking. Many studies have pointed to gender differences in language and conversational style. Women generally use more modal language forms than men and they interrupt less often.

Most contemporary psycholinguists and cognitive psychologists assume that language expresses propositional thought. Some, however, have argued that it is the other way around: language shapes thought. This theory of linguistic relativity has been tested in a number of cultures. Some empirical studies have found differences in perception that were related to the vocabulary used in the culture. Other studies have contradicted the linguistic relativity hypothesis.

key Terms

algorithm
anchoring bias
artificial intelligence
autistic thinking
availability heuristic
belief-bias effect
biased assimilation
co-articulation
cognitive economy
cognitive bias
cohort model
concept formation
concepts
critical feature
decision-making
deductive reasoning
Einstellung effect
felicity conditions
functional fixedness
garden path sentences
group think
heuristic
incremental processing
inductive reasoning
inference
intentionality
internal (or mental) lexicon

judgement
linguistic relativity
mental set
metacognitive knowledge
morphemes
parsing
phonemes
pragmatics
problem-solving
prototype
psycholinguistics
realistic thinking
reasoning
referentiality
reflection
representativeness heuristic
schema
script
semantics
speech acts
spoonerism
spreading activation model
syllogism
syntax
unrealistic optimism
Whorf's hypothesis

major Contributors

Austin, John (1911–60)
de Groot, Adriaan
Flavell, John
Gardner, Howard
Hunt, Earl
Janis, Irving (1918–90)
Kahneman, Daniel
Kempen, Gerard
Kintsch, William
Levelt, Willem
Marslen-Wilson, William

Newell, Allan (1927–92)
Simon, Herbert
Sternberg, Robert
Tannen, Deborah
Tolman, Edward (1886–1959)
Tversky, Amos
Tyler, Lorraine
van Dijk, Teun
Wason, Peter
Whorf, Benjamin (1897–1941)

Chapter 10

Motivation and Emotion

On the 16th of May 1993, Rebecca Stephens reached the top of Mount Everest at 29,028ft/8,848m. She was the first British woman to scale the highest mountain in the world. Through this accomplishment she joined the elite company of mountaineers who succeeded before her. Ever since the calculation of its height in 1852, Mount Everest has attracted climbers who have aimed to reach its summit. There were many attempts, but few were successful. In 1924, George Leigh Mallory and Andrew Irvine came close, but it is not certain they ever reached the top because their lives were lost on the peaks of this inhospitable mountain. Their tragic and mysterious disappearance gave Mount Everest an aura of enchantment that it has not yet lost. Everest became a 'Third Pole', a frontier of human accomplishment to replace those already conquered. Many attempts followed, but the first men that actually stood on the 'roof of the world' were New Zealander Edmund Hillary and the sherpa Tenzing Norgay on 29 May 1953.

What did Rebecca Stephens and her predecessors experience? To climb a mountain higher than approximately 26,000ft/8,000m is to ask the human body to do something it should not. At such altitudes, lungs gasp for oxygen, the blood thickens, and a stroke becomes a real risk. The kidneys slowly cease to function. This produces the possibility of a cerebral oedema – a swelling of the brain that impairs judgement and can be potentially lethal. Besides this, there is the wind and the cold. These exhausting conditions raise the question of how people endure this terrible ordeal. Andrew Peacock, an expert on medical effects of high altitude, maintains that mountaineers like Rebecca Stephens have special physical characteristics. As a member of Stephens's expedition, Peacock discovered that he lacked these special features: 'At 26,000ft I was far gone, but Rebecca was able to continue' (*The Independent on Sunday*, 23 May 1993). Peacock's experience confirmed his belief that people who reach the summit react more slowly to the effects of lack of oxygen.

From a psychological point of view, however, we are inclined to ask *why* people feel the need to scale Mount Everest. As psychologists we are not satisfied with Mallory's legendary answer 'because it is there'.

THE ONGOING SAGA involving Mount Everest raises some of the fundamental questions about human motives which we will tackle in this chapter. What impels people to act as they do? How are passive creatures energised into action? What makes us persist to attain a goal despite the high effort, pain and financial costs involved? Why do we procrastinate too long before starting to work on some tasks, or give in and quit too soon on others?

In daily life, we often use the term 'motivation' to represent very complex psychosocial concepts: 'I didn't do well on that test because I didn't like the teacher; he just never got me motivated enough'. We hear sports commentators proclaim, 'They won because they wanted to win more than their over-confident, undermotivated opponents'. As we follow detective stories, we try to figure out the hidden motive for the crime, which will provide a clue to the culprit's identity. Millions of faithful soap opera fans peer day after day into a seething cauldron of complex motives – greed, power and lust – bathed in the fiery and impassioned emotions of love, hate, jealousy and envy. These examples show that motivation is dynamic: it is concerned with energising behaviour in order to attain a goal. They also show that *motivation* is also inextricably tied to *emotion*.

Contemporary motivational psychologists look for the dynamic sources of our goal-directed behaviour. To explain the diversity of human behaviour many different *needs* are postulated, ranging from fundamental physiological needs (such as hunger) to social needs (such as love). Needs do not operate in a simple way. For some Australian aboriginals a plate covered with crawling termites may make their mouth water, while our appetite vanishes with the thought of eating live insects. The biological need of hunger also combines with cognitive and social needs. For instance, needs for personal control and social acceptance can affect eating behaviour in such a way that they produce an eating disorder. This miscellany of motives and the nature of motivation are the subjects of the first part of this chapter. We will explore theories, research and applications. In the second part of the chapter, we will look in depth at three forms of motivation, each important in a different way and each varying in the extent to which biological, cognitive and social factors operate; these three are hunger, sex and achievement. In the last part of this chapter the subject of emotion will be examined.

✖ THE PSYCHOLOGY OF MOTIVATION

Motivation is the general term for all the processes involved in starting, directing and maintaining physical and psychological activities. It is a broad concept that embraces the host of internal mechanisms involved in (a) *preferences* for one activity over another; (b) *vigour* or strength of responses; and (c) *persistence* of organised patterns of action toward relevant goals. The highly motivated person seeks out certain activities over others; practises behaviours and perfects skills required to attain the objective; and focuses energy on reaching the goal despite frustrations.

The word *motivation* comes from the Latin *movere* which means *to move*. *Action* is the fundamental property of living systems. All organisms approach some stimuli and avoid others as dictated by their appetites and aversions. Evolution favours organisms that can move toward and obtain that which they need for survival and move away from or oppose that which threatens them. Some appetites escalate into manias and addictions, dominating all other motivational systems. Some aversions become pathological fears and freeze our behavioural options. Between the extremes of frenzied action and immobility lie the motivational currents that shape the flow of our daily lives.

The multiplicity of human motivation generates a problem for classification. Until now there has been no taxonomy of motives that is accepted by a majority of psychologists. In this chapter, however, we will identify three main motivational systems: biological, cognitive and social. The **biological motivation** system consists of drives, associated with physiological needs that developed during the evolution of the human species. This system is mainly supposed to operate according to the principle of drive reduction. Examples are hunger and thirst. The other two systems concern more general needs in the sense that they are not directed at a specific goal (as are drives). Rather, they have the more general 'goal' of adapting the individual to the environment. These **cognitive motivation** and **social motivation** needs are more open to learning. However, cognitive and social needs are also biologically mediated, involving evolutionarily 'new' brain structures, which concern two inborn energy sources undifferentiated at birth, which direct the organism to explore the environment and relate to care-givers (Buck, 1988). In time and in interaction with others, the cognitive system develops into a system of *meaning-making* that enables the individual to deal effectively with the environment. In the same way, the social system develops into a system of *belongingness*. Cognitive and social motives therefore develop during the individual's life, within the shared context provided by other's behaviours, meanings and motives. Before considering these three motivational systems in more detail, we must first examine the functions served by various motivational concepts.

Functions of Motivational Concepts

Psychologists have used the concept of motivation for five basic purposes:

- **To account for behavioural variability.** Why might you do well on a task one day and poorly on the same task another day? Why does one child do much better at a competitive task than another child with roughly the same ability and knowledge? We use motivational explanations when the variations in people's performance in a constant situation cannot be traced to differences in ability, skill, practice, reinforcement history, or chance. If behaviour never varied, there would be no need for motivational concepts – or, for that matter, psychology.

- **To relate biology to biological processes.** The concept of motivation reminds us that we are biological organisms with complex internal mechanisms automatically regulating our bodily functioning, permitting us to survive. Deprivation states trigger these mechanisms which then motivate us through the sensations of hunger, thirst or cold to take action to restore the body's balance.

- **To infer private states from public acts.** There are two ways to respond to someone's behaviour. We can take it at face value, or we can see it as a significant symptom of an underlying emotional or motivational state. Put differently, we can respond to the surface or to the latent meaning of behaviour. Sigmund Freud's belief that hidden motives instigate much of our behaviour has had a profound effect on psychologists' study of motivation. Researchers in cognitive and social psychology are investigating the inferences that people make about inner and outer determinants of behaviour. How do we account for our own actions and the actions of others?

- **To assign responsibility for actions.** The concept of personal responsibility is fundamental to law, religion and ethics. Personal responsibility presupposes inner motivation and the ability to control one's actions. People are judged less responsible for their actions when (a) they did not intend negative consequences to occur; (b) external forces were powerful enough to provoke the behaviours; or (c) the actions were influenced by drugs, alcohol, intense emotion, or other internal influences. The concept of personal responsibility dissolves without the concept of consciously directed motivation.

- **To explain perseverance despite adversity.** Finally, motivational constructs also help us to understand why organisms can continue to perform consistently despite marked variations in stimulus conditions. Motivation gets you to work or class on time even when you are exhausted. The intense desire of Rebecca Stephens to prove to herself and others that she could perform the daring act of scaling a mountain was the result of strong motivational forces. Motivation helps you persist in playing the game to the best of your ability even when you are losing and realise that you cannot possibly win.

In the 1984 Olympic Games women's marathon, the world watched, stunned, as the last runner staggered into the stadium long after the winner had crossed the finish line. Somehow, she was propelled forward by her wobbly legs toward the finish line. Her face contorted in pain, her body bent and twisted, she doggedly pushed onward, refusing offers of help, until she had completed her mission to finish the race.

'I just hate to give up,' she later told reporters. During interviews she expressed her regret that the heat had not overcome her outside the stadium so she would have been spared the shame of her awkward, tension-filled laps in the stadium (Los Angeles Times, 1984).

While completing the Olympic Marathon, Gabriella Anderson-Schiess staggered to the marathon finish, nearly fell and was assisted from the track by medics, but only after she successfully completed her goal of finishing the Olympic Marathon.

INTERIM SUMMARY

Psychologists use motivation as a dynamic concept to describe the processes involved in starting, directing and maintaining activities. Psychology employs the concept of motivation for five purposes: (i) to account for behavioural variability; (ii) to relate behaviour to biology; (iii) to infer private states from public acts; (iv) to assign responsibility for actions; and (v) to explain perseverance despite adversity.

 ## THEORIES OF MOTIVATION

Psychologists have sought to explain the origins of animal and human behaviour via a host of different theories. We have categorised these theories in three main motivational systems: biological, cognitive and social.

 ## Biological Motivation

Under the heading biological motivation three theories are discussed: instinct, drive and arousal theory.

Instinct theories

For centuries, philosophers made a distinction between humans who were guided in their actions by reason and free will and nonhumans whose actions were determined by 'brute appetites'. **Charles Darwin's** theory of evolution challenged this dichotomy, paving the way for a theory in which instincts stimulated not only animal behaviour, but human behaviour as well. The theory of evolution had a lasting effect on the study of the psychology of motivation: it inspired psychologists to look at the adaptation or adjustment of all creatures to their environment as a motivational factor.

According to **instinct theories**, organisms are born with certain preprogrammed tendencies that are essential for the survival of their species. Animals engage in regular cycles of activity that enable their species to survive. Salmon swim thousands of miles back to the exact stream where they were spawned, leaping up waterfalls until they come to the breeding spot, where the surviving males and females engage in ritualised courtship and mating. Fertilised eggs are deposited, the parents die, and, in time, their young swim downstream to live in the ocean until a few years later, when it is time for them to return to complete their part in this continuing drama. Similarly remarkable activities can be reported for most species of animals. Bees communicate the location of food to other bees, army ants go on highly synchronised hunting expeditions, birds build nests and spiders spin complex webs – exactly as their parents and ancestors did.

The relation between an instinct and the succeeding behaviour was considered linear. That is to say, a certain behaviour is almost directly caused by an instinct, without for example intervening psychological factors. This principle of **monocausality** makes it necessary to explain the complexity of human behaviour by postulating a huge number of different instincts. **William James**, for instance, stated in 1890 that humans rely on more instincts than lower animals do to guide their behaviour. In addition to the biological instincts they share with animals, a host of human social instincts, such as sympathy, modesty, sociability and love, come into play. For James, both human and animal instincts were purposive. They served important purposes in the organism's adaptation to its environment. This view of the vital role of human instincts was extended by psychologist **William McDougall**. McDougall (1908) made a list of basic instincts, defining instincts as inherited dispositions that had three components: a general energising aspect, an action aspect, and goal directedness.

By the 1920s however, lists of over 10,000 human instincts were being compiled by psychologists (Bernard, 1924). The notion of instincts as explanations for human behaviour was beginning to stagger under the burden of the monocausality principle. Critics pointed out that postulating an instinct for every action does not explain anything at all, and that instincts do not provide a useful explanation of behaviour because they overemphasise fixed inborn mechanisms, and fail to recognise that much behaviour is clearly modifiable by learning. Meanwhile anthropologists, such as Ruth Benedict (1959) and Margaret Mead (1939), had observed enormous behavioural variation between cultures. This finding contradicted the motivational theories that considered only the universals of inborn instincts. Gradually instincts disappeared from the psychological stage to be replaced by the concept of drives.

Drive theories

Like instincts, drives are conceived of as biological needs. **Primary drives** are said to be internal

Humans and animals often participate in activities to increase stimulation.

biological disturbances that result from natural tissue needs, such as those for food, water, avoidance of pain and temperature regulation (Buck, 1988). Unlike instincts however, drives do not lead to behaviour in a straightforward way. **Sigmund Freud** (1915), for example, thought that human behaviour is determined by two main drives: a drive for life (Eros) and a death drive (Thanatos). He believed that drives exist to satisfy bodily needs and that they create a psychic energy[1]. This tension guides us toward activities or objects that will reduce the tension. However, drives neither have conscious purpose nor predetermined direction. A drive is only the fuel of action: it consists of *non-specific energy*. Other mechanisms, such as the way a child learns to cope with society's demands, guide action in appropriate directions.

The behaviourist **Clark Hull** (1943, 1952) believed motivation is necessary for learning to occur and that learning is essential for successful adaptation to the environment. In the same vein as Freud, Hull emphasised the role of tension in motivation; he believed that tension reduction is reinforcing. In his view, a new-born child possesses only a few primary drives. While growing up, initially neutral stimuli in the environment that consistently are associated with the reinforcement of a primary drive can acquire the same tendency to evoke drive states. Thus, by way of conditioning, the few primary drives are supplemented with many *acquired* or **secondary drives**. Although these drives are learned, they have the same motivating power as primary drives.

The empirical demonstrations of the behaviourists –

that important behaviours and emotions, and even many drives (though not all) are learned rather than inborn – was very damaging to the early instinct notions. The drive concept indeed did more justice to the complexity and flexibility of human behaviour, but it was still a very *mechanistic* conception. According to **drive theories** people are passive organisms, trapped between physiological drives and situational stimuli. They are like machines that could be completely predictable if the connections between drive reduction and stimuli were known. One of the first psychologists who criticised the mechanistic character of drive theories is the behaviourist **Edward Tolman**. Around 1930 his experiments convinced him that the energy people invest in accomplishing a goal depends on their expectations about their prospects of reaching that goal. For the first time a behaviourist stated that what people think, desire, or aspire to, makes a difference. In the same period the social psychologist **Kurt Lewin** developed a theory in which the interaction between person and situation played a crucial role. Individual behaviour is not determined by the situation as such, but rather by the interpretation of that situation by the person. Lewin and Tolman were the first to attend to the central role of cognitive factors in motivation. Motivation cannot be understood by only looking at the interplay between biological forces and situational factors. In between these two, there are thinking, choosing and deciding persons.

Alongside criticism about the mechanistic character of drive theory, the principle of **drive reduction** came under attack. According to drive theory, a passive organism is impelled to action only

---

[1] The English edition of Freud's work *The Standard Edition* translates the German *Trieb* to instinct. Strictly speaking this is not correct, because Freud distinguished in German between *Instinkt* and *Trieb*. Therefore, we prefer *drive* as a translation of *Trieb* (Brandt, 1961; Eagle, 1984).

FIGURE 10.1	THE YERKES-DODSON LAW

Performance varies with motivation level and task difficulty. For easy or simple tasks, a higher level of motivation increases performance effectiveness. However, for difficult or complex tasks, a lower level of motivation is optimal. A moderate level of motivation is generally best for tasks of moderate difficulty. These inverted u-shaped functions show that performance is worst at both low and high extremes of motivation.

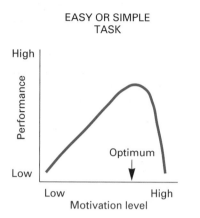

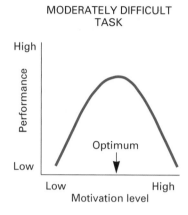

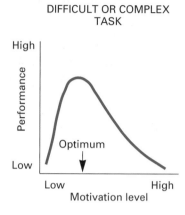

when there is a state of tension. As long as the tension exists, the organism will search for a way to satisfy or reduce it. When this happens, the balance is restored and the organism will cease acting. This conception implies that when all drives are fulfilled, there is no need to do anything at all. In the early 1950s, a number of experiments with healthy animals challenged this view. Animals often do things in the absence of any apparent deprivation in order to increase stimulation: they play and exhibit exploratory and manipulatory behaviours. In experiments, rats deprived of food or water that were placed in a novel environment with plenty of opportunities everywhere to eat or drink, chose to explore instead. Only after they had first satisfied their curiosity, did they begin to satisfy their hunger and thirst (Zimbardo & Montgomery, 1957; Berlyne, 1960; Fowler, 1965). A similar type of motivation was reported in a series of studies in which young monkeys spent much time and energy manipulating gadgets and new objects in their environment, apparently for the sheer pleasure of 'monkeying around', without any extrinsic rewards (Harlow et al, 1950).

Another kind of evidence against the principle of drive reduction came from dramatic experiments on sensory deprivation in humans. The first experiment of this kind was reported by Bexton, Heron and Scott (1954). They paid college student subjects 20 dollars a day to do literally nothing. The students were asked to lie on mattresses for 24 hours a day in a partially sound-deadened room wearing translucent goggles and gloves with cardboard cuffs. Sleep is the best way to deal with this drastic reduction of sensory stimulation, but when sleep was over, very few were

able to tolerate this condition. Most students terminated the experiment despite what at that time was a generous wage. Before that, they showed boredom, irritability and a craving for stimulation. Later experiments also showed that prolonged sensory deprivation leads to aberrations of EEG, autonomic and behavioural indices of arousal (Zubek, 1969). Apparently there is more than drive reduction that makes organisms tick. Under certain circumstances humans and animals need and will work to increase stimulation (Buck, 1988).

Arousal theories

One way to deal with the apparent need for exploration is to drop the assumption that only drive *reduction* is rewarding. Take, for example, body temperature: when you are healthy, your body temperature remains almost constant, despite big alterations in the temperature of the environment. This is made possible by a kind of internal thermostat which first signals deviation from the ideal value and that next undertakes corrective action. When your temperature goes up, the body rectifies this by decreasing it in some way; when it goes down, action also is undertaken, this time to increase it. Many bodily processes operate in accordance with this principle of **homeostasis** principle: organisms attempt to maintain a constant internal environment when confronted by a changing external environment.

The same homeostatic principle can be applied to human action in general. Indeed, arousal-based theories of motivation employ such a principle. Arousal is a measure of the general responsiveness of an organism to activation of the brainstem's reticular system. The concept can be considered synonymous with the one of general drive (Hebb, 1955). Arousal theories state that people have an optimal level of arousal that they try to maintain: when arousal is too high, they feel anxious and will strive for drive reduction; when their arousal is too low, people feel bored and will try to increase their drive.

The concept of **optimal arousal** has been used to identify the way motivational intensity and performance vary with tasks of different difficulty. Some tasks are best approached with high levels of arousal and others with more moderate levels. The key to the level of arousal is task difficulty. With difficult or complex tasks, the optimal level of arousal for success is on the low end of the arousal continuum. Your performance in a game of chess will not profit from the yells of an enthusiastic audience. As the difficulty decreases and the task becomes simpler, the optimal level of arousal – the level required to perform most effectively – becomes greater. A noisy audience would be very stimulating, for example, if you were running a marathon. This relationship has been formalised in the **Yerkes–Dodson law**, which holds that performance of difficult tasks decreases as arousal increases, while performance of easy tasks increases as arousal increases (Yerkes & Dodson, 1908). See *Figure 10.1* (previous page) for an illustration of this principle.

There are individual differences in optimal arousal level, variations in how much arousal different people feel or need in order to function most effectively. Some people seem to need high levels of stimulation and work best in tension-filled settings that would make most people ineffective. They may even put pressure on themselves to increase the arousal level, knowing that greater arousal will help them succeed. Attempts have been made to relate these individual differences to activity within the central nervous system. This line of work goes back to the Russian physiologist Pavlov, who noticed at the beginning of this century that the dogs he used in his classical conditioning experiments displayed individual differences in the 'strength' (meaning sensitivity) of their central nervous systems. A given stimulus produces a greater excitation in the sensitive or 'weak' type of nervous system than it does in the less sensitive, so-called 'strong' one. It may well be that the 'sensation seeker' has a less susceptible, 'strong' type of nervous system; much stimulation is needed to reach his or her optimal level of arousal. The person with an easily affected type of nervous system is satisfied with less perceptible stimuli, but cannot deal with intense stimulation.

The concept of the 'strength' of the nervous system shows some correspondence with the personality dimension introversion-extraversion postulated by Eysenck (see Chapter 12). He suggested that introverts may have an overly responsive nervous system. Extraverts, who prefer a higher level of stimulation, relish risky activities such as skydiving or motorcycle racing and may use drugs to intensify sensations (Zuckerman, 1984, 1991). These individuals, however, are likely to be vulnerable to substance abuse and to destructive behaviours that provide high intensity reactions. In his examination of this subject however, **Ross Buck** states that 'this area is plagued by unusually difficult problems of measurement, and thus far, the theories have been more exciting than the data have been convincing' (Buck, 1988).

 Cognitive Motivation

As we have already explained, drive theory was criticised on two main points: it was too mechanistic and too focused on drive reduction. Arousal theory resolved the last problem by assuming homeostatic principles. The conspicuous desire to seek stimulation could be explained that way. But arousal theory is still a mechanistic theory. It concerns the interaction between a general drive rooted in the central nervous sytem and situational factors. In the 1930s Tolman and Lewin were the first to indicate that motivation comes not from objective realities but from our subjective interpretation of them. For example, the reinforcing effect of a reward is lost if we do not perceive that our actions obtained it. What we do now can be influenced by what we think was responsible for our past successes and failures, by what we believe it is possible for us to do, and by what we anticipate the outcome of an action will be. Cognitive approaches to motivation put higher mental processes such as these in charge of the acting self, rather than physiological arousal, biological mechanisms, or physical stimulus features. These approaches explain why human beings are often more motivated by imagined future events than by stimulus factors in the immediate environment (Nuttin, 1984).

Under the heading **cognitive motivation** we will discuss several theories that give cognition a central place in motivating processes. Our preference for using the broad concept of cognitive motivation, however, does not imply that psychologists agree about the use of this term. In the literature you will find lots of different concepts, like mastery motivation, effectance motivation, competence motivation, curiosity motivation and intrinsic motivation. Nevertheless, we maintain that all of these can be subsumed under the generic heading of cognitive theories of motivation.

Consistency theories

Kurt Lewin (1936) introduced the notion that perceiving a discrepancy between one's current position and another condition – such as a task to be completed, a desired goal, or a group standard – can have motivating effects. Lewin believed that such perceived discrepancies create intrapersonal tension states that motivate behaviour to reduce the discrepancy by completing the task, attaining the goal, or conforming with the group norm.

One of Lewin's students, **Leon Festinger**, carried the motivating effect of discrepancy or incongruity into his theory of cognitive dissonance (1957). According to this theory, discrepancies between beliefs, attitudes and behaviour give rise to a motivational state of dissonance which we then attempt to reduce by changing one or more of the discrepant elements. Suppose you assent to a friend's request to put up a poster on your wall that incites people to moderation in their production of waste. Suppose further that you originally believed that all the fuss about the pollution of our planet is much ado about nothing, because you think in time resourceful scientists will come up with a solution. Your behaviour then, is dissonant with your belief. You will experience this incongruity as unpleasant, and will search for a way to restore cognitive consonance. A way to do so is by changing your belief: you may decide that your faith in science is not warranted after all and therefore we should do something here and now to prevent an ecological disaster. Note still that consistency theories are homeostatic in nature. In this case, the standard as set does not have a physiological origin, but rather a psychological, or to be precise, a cognitive one.

Expectancy-value theories

Cognitive motivation has to do with understanding and getting a grip on the world around us. It feels good when we know how to behave and how to reach goals we have set ourselves. However, it is neither possible nor necessary to comprehend and control everything all of the time. Moreover, a frightening world, as well as our compelling drives, can obstruct our striving toward successful outcomes. Life can even be so demanding and burdensome that a person's motivation to control his or her world becomes severely frustrated. Individuals differ in their personal history of reinforcements, and thus in their willingness to take matters into their own hands. But individual differences do not only arise because of differences in experience. They already exist in newborn babies. Some babies are very curious, while others do not seem very interested in the world around them. Some two-year-old children drive their parents to distraction with their insistence on doing everything themselves, while others act as if they find the world eerie and baffling.

Julian Rotter (1966, 1975, 1990) made the individual differences in the extent to which people perceive they are in control of events the basis of his **locus of control** theory. For Rotter, the probability that we will engage in a given behaviour (studying for an exam instead of meeting friends) is determined by our expectation of attaining a goal (getting a good grade) following the performance of relevant activity, and by the personal value we place on that goal.

Expectation of a future happening is based on our past reinforcement history which, in turn, has helped us develop a broad set of beliefs about who or what is determining the occurrence of positive and negative events in our lives. Some people develop an internal orientation, believing that skill and hard work will lead to positive outcomes. Others develop an external orientation, believing that events are determined by the workings of chance factors, 'fate', powerful other people, and uncontrollable forces. Thus, people with an *internal locus of control* believe that attaining positive outcomes is mostly a matter of their own efforts. They perceive that there is a relationship between their actions and the outcomes that occur in their lives. So, they believe themselves to be master of their own fate. People with an *external locus of control* believe that their behaviour is controlled mainly by internal or external forces beyond their control. They do not perceive that there is a contingent relationship between their behaviour and outcomes that may occur in their daily lives. Consequently, they do not feel accountable for what happens to them, because they feel themselves to be pawns in the hands of others or at the mercy of their own powerlessness.

Because it often feels better to be in control of your own life than to let things happen, 'internals' are frequently better off than 'externals'. In clinical psychology, a feeling of control is considered an important issue in mental health. Job satisfaction, for example, is higher among internals than among externals (Cummins, 1989), and a cross-cultural study found that among residents of the United States of America, India and Hong Kong, externals engaged more often in such self-destructive behaviours as smoking, excessive drinking and unsafe driving (Kelley *et al*, 1986).

Rotter's locus of control theory developed out of a *social learning perspective*, within which behaviours are understood to be controlled by expectancies about reinforcements. The term 'locus of control' refers to whether people believe that outcomes are related to their actions and thereby are controllable. If you join a local action group, in order to prevent the construction of a railway through a bird sanctuary, you probably will do so because you believe your participation will be worthwhile in terms of reaching this goal. In other words, as an internal, you believe your outcomes to be contingent on your behaviour. You will also join this group not only because you expect that doing so will bring about the desired result but because you place *value* on that outcome – in our example here, safeguarding the bird sanctuary. Thus, your action, according to Rotter, emerges from your expectations and values in combination. However, your locus of control may be internal, but you engage in this activity for some external consequence. When behaviour is instrumental to obtaining something else, the motivating principle is called **extrinsic motivation**. Locus of control theory does not explain why people engage in an activity for its own sake, in the absence of external reward. It does not deal with **intrinsic motivation**, where behaviour is carried out without a purpose beyond the immediate rewards of doing it[2]. Things that we do because we simply enjoy doing them, such as walking through the park, singing in the shower, doing crossword puzzles, or keeping a secret diary, are intrinsically motivated. Work, too, can be intrinsically motivated when an individual is deeply interested in the job to be done. In fact, as we will see, all of our cognitive motivation can, in principle, be intrinsic motivation.

Effectance motivation

Why do people seek stimulation, while there is no drive to satisfy, no balance to restore and no reward to gain? Why do people like to explore, control and manipulate their world, without this being a function of 'external' influences? One way to explain this, is to drop the notion of homeostasis, as well as the necessity of external rewards. Hunger, thirst and temperature regulation need not be considered prototypes for all motivational principles. Tendencies to explore, manipulate and seek stimulation have properties very different from those of classical homeostatic drives and they do not need extrinsic rewards to operate. The activity of exploration is rewarding in itself: it is *intrinsically* motivating. Thus, in addition to homeostatic drives, a fundamentally different motivational source is proposed. It concerns a built-in need of the organism to adapt, to learn about and to control the environment. This need does not originate from tissue deficits, but is inherent in the working of the central nervous system. It is not a need that has to be fulfilled, but an emergent property of biological functioning that stimulates the organism to explore and understand.

The existence of this kind of motivation has been formulated most convincingly by **Robert White** (1959). He uses the concept **effectance motivation** to refer to the notion that people are dispositionally motivated to be effective in dealing with their environment. White's notion of effectance motivation is also similar to the kind of motivation thought to underlie cognitive development in the theory of Piaget (Buck, 1988). Children indeed enjoy, and get excited about, mastering their physical environment. However, they want to comprehend not only objects, like balls, trees, or bicycles, but also their social world and their own internal world, the world of desires and feelings. In fact, like adults they spend a great deal of time in understanding the social and internal world. Thus with effectance motivation as a general energising principle, children develop into persons who can deal effectively with the physical, the social and the internal world. In White's words, children develop into competent persons.

Effectance motivation as an energising principle is conceived as a biologically-based need, which makes the striving for **competence** universal. However, biological make-up is merely a condition and not a direct cause of action. We want to put a lot of energy into understanding the world and ourselves as comprehensible and coherent, but this competence is culturally defined. Being a competent person means understanding what is going on in our social worlds and behaving accordingly.

A hierarchy of needs

In the 1950s the humanist psychologist **Abraham Maslow** (1970) formulated a theory of human

Abraham Maslow

---

[2] It could be argued that locus of control theory does account for intrinsic motivation, if 'outcome' is defined as nothing more than an ongoing 'pleasureable state' which in itself is valued – that is to say, if the subjective state which is a consequence of certain activities is valorised.

motivation that does justice to people's desire to look for new goals as well as their need for tension-reduction. Maslow contrasted **deficiency motivation**, in which individuals seek to restore physical or psychological equilibrium, and **growth motivation**, in which individuals do more than reduce deficits as they seek to realise their fullest potential. Growth-motivated people may welcome uncertainty, an increase in tension, and even pain, if they see it as a route toward greater fulfilment of their potential and as a way to achieve their goals. Thus, for example, a person who voluntarily suffers for a religious or political cause may accept pain or humiliation as a necessary part of changing prevailing attitudes and institutions. He or she suffers in order to achieve meaningful goals that are consistent with personal values.

Maslow's theory holds that our basic needs form a **needs hierarchy**, as illustrated in *Figure 10.2*. Our inborn needs are arranged in a sequence of stages from primitive to advanced. At the bottom of this hierarchy are the basic biological needs, such as hunger and thirst. They must be satisfied before any other needs can begin to operate. When biological needs are

FIGURE 10.2	MASLOW'S HIERARCHY OF NEEDS

According to Maslow, needs at the lower level of the hierarchy dominate an individual's motivation as long as they are unsatisfied. Once these are adequately satisfied, the higher needs occupy the individual's attention.

Transcendence
spiritual needs for
cosmic identification

Self-Actualization
needs to fulfill potential,
have meaningful goals

Aesthetic
needs for order, beauty

Cognitive
needs for knowledge,
understanding, novelty

Esteem
needs for confidence, sense
of worth and competence,
self-esteem and respect of others

Attachment
needs to belong, to affiliate,
to love and be loved

Safety
needs for security, comfort,
tranquility, freedom from fear

Biological
needs for water, oxygen, rest,
sexual expression, release from tension

pressing, other needs are put on hold and are unlikely to influence our actions; but when they are reasonably well satisfied, the needs at the next level – safety needs – motivate us. When we are no longer concerned about danger, we become motivated by attachment needs; needs to belong, to affiliate with others, to love and to be loved. If we are well fed and safe and if we feel a sense of social belonging, we move up to esteem needs. These include the needs to like oneself, to see oneself as competent and effective and to do what is necessary to earn the esteem of others.

Next in the hierarchy come cognitive needs. Humans are motivated by strong needs to know our past, to comprehend the puzzles of current existence, and to predict the future. At the next level of Maslow's hierarchy, comes the human desire for beauty and order, in the form of aesthetic needs that give rise to the creative side of humanity. At the top of the hierarchy, are people who are nourished, safe, loved and loving, secure, thinking and creating. These people have moved beyond basic human needs in the quest for the fullest development of their potential for self-actualisation. A self-actualising person is self-aware, self-accepting, socially responsive, creative, spontaneous and open to novelty and challenge, among other positive attributes. Maslow's hierarchy includes a step beyond the total fulfilment of individual potential. Needs for transcendence may lead to higher states of consciousness and a cosmic vision of one's part in the universe. Very few people develop the desire to move beyond the self to achieve union with spiritual forces.

Maslow's theory has had more influence on therapy and education than on psychological research. For Maslow, as for his fellow humanistic psychologist Carl Rogers (1959), the central motivational force for humans is the innate need to grow and actualise one's highest potentials. Other psychologists have suggested that self-actualisation motivation is essentially the motivation to be open to new experiences, ideas and feelings and to explore one's external and mental environments. In other words, Maslow's hierarchy reflects the modern division between biological and cognitive motivation. We return now to our discussion of the latter, namely cognitive motivation.

From competence to self-determination

With effectance motivation as a general energiser, people, in interaction with others, give meaning to their external and internal world. In this way they become competent persons. A competent member of Western society knows how to behave at a party, in a shop, at a railway station, or in a restaurant. Competent persons can, for example, ride a bicycle, cross the road without causing an accident, and know how to prepare food to eat. But as we said before, it is neither possible, necessary or satisfying to be competent at everything all of the time. Some people might dance somewhat clumsily, but they do not necessarily feel uncomfortable about this. People do not act competently automatically; they do so after deliberately making choices. These choices are supposed to be consistent with a coherent set of beliefs, values and principles. In other words, people are supposed to act competently in a way that is in accordance with their self-concept. It is not competence that counts: it is self-determined competence that matters. Children, for example, at first may be stimulated to attain competence in as many activities as possible, but soon they will be urged to make their acts 'their own', by way of a deliberate choice. In other words, people are encouraged thereby to become **autonomous persons**.

The above line of reasoning is advocated by **Edward Deci** and **Richard Ryan** (1985, 1987, 1991). They argue that Rotter's locus of control concept concerns only competence. It is about controlling outcomes, about knowing how to operate in order to reach a goal. However, it is not the activity itself that is pleasant, but the acting person that has to consider it pleasant. People do not enjoy being in control of all activities in general, but rather of specific activities they choose to perform. They are motivated to be the cause of their own behaviour, to be autonomous agents.

Deci and Ryan stress the fact that people not only strive toward competence, but also toward self-determination or autonomy. Autonomous people are intrinsically motivated, because their behaviour is self-determined; they do not need extrinsic rewards to act. Extrinsic rewards can even be detrimental to their motivation. Children who are given extrinsic rewards for behaviour that they were already intrinsically motivated to produce, lose interest. Play becomes work when the performance of fun activities is made contingent upon superfluous rewards, as shown in a series of classroom experiments (Lepper *et al*, 1973). When an extrinsic reward is given, the task itself is enjoyed less (Deci, 1975; Lepper, 1981; Lepper & Greene, 1978). The message is clear: a reward a day makes work out of play.

Extrinsic constraints on people, such as evaluation pressure or close surveillance during an activity, seem to have effects on motivation similar to those of rewards. Typically, students in courses where grades are heavily emphasised might find that their motivation, even for their favourite subjects, dwindles after the final exam; they were working only for the grade. Gold stars, grades, and penalties for failure or misbehaviour are testament to the (false) belief that schoolchildren are extrinsically motivated and must be given external consequences to learn.

According to Deci and Ryan, people's need to be their own cause is as fundamental as their need to control. Thus next to competence motivation they postulate autonomy motivation. Their emphasis on becoming an independent, autonomous and competent self-actualiser may, however, be an **individualistic** culture-bound conception. The mastery that is the goal of competence motivation may develop into self-mastery only in an individualistic culture in which self-determination is a value. In countries with a **collectivistic** ideology, the outgrowth of competence is not directed toward a fully integrated self and toward autonomy. That does not mean that people are less motivated to become competent members of their society. For them, competence and being a respected member of society may mean (instead of self-actualisation) interacting in a coherent and meaningful way with others and caring for their groupmembers (Markus & Kitayama, 1991). We shall examine further the subject of cultural differences later in this chapter in the section on achievement motivation

In the theories about cognitive motivation we have discussed so far, motivation is primarily located within the individual. Motivation is exclusively an individual act, clearly distinguishable from external social pressures. The integrity and independence of Deci and Ryan's autonomous person, for example, is constantly threatened by environmental influences. In his *cognitive behavioural theory*, **Joseph Nuttin** (1984) has designated the interaction between the environment and the individual person as the focal point of attention. The origin of motivated action lies neither in external conditions nor within the individual person, but rather emerges from the existence of the individual within and in relation to a particular situation. The person-environment interaction is crucial for Nuttin, because the person has to cope with his or her environment as soon as plans are translated into action. If someone, for example, wants to become a successful singer, she has to engage in all sorts of activities: she has to spend time on rehearsing, she may have to take lessons and, in all likelihood, she will need to obtain electronic equipment to support her vocal performances. The extent to which she succeeds in making these social and material preparations, is crucial for her reaching the original goal. Failure to accomplish these necessary arrangements will have repercussions for her perception of her chances of reaching the goal. A bad live show, for instance as a consequence of poor equipment, may lead to negative reviews of her performances in the press. This in turn may result in a readjustment of the original objective. She may start wondering if she really wants to be a singer and perhaps decide on a new goal like becoming a studio technician.

The two hypothetical curves represented by a continuous and a dashed line depict the two modes postulated by reversal theory. For comparison, the dotted line making an inverted U-curve represents the single mode of optimal arousal theory.

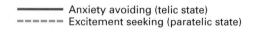

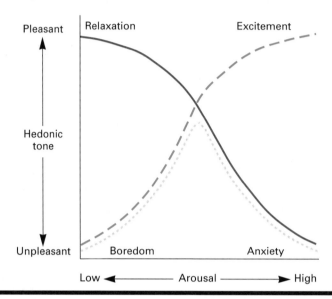

Reversal theory

A theory that also takes the subjective experience of people as its starting point is reversal theory. **Reversal theory** has its origin in Great Britain in the work of **Michael Apter** (Apter 1982, 1989; Kerr *et al*, 1993). One of the central concepts is *arousal*. In this respect reversal theory can be considered a modification of **arousal theories**, because arousal and the pleasure or the displeasure it provokes also plays a central role. The fundamental difference between arousal theories and Apter's work concerns the meaning of the concept of arousal. In arousal theories, arousal is a general drive rooted in the central nervous system. Reversal theory on the other hand takes the subjective experiences of humans as its central concern. Arousal means 'the degree to which one feels oneself to be worked up or emotionally intense about what one is doing' (Apter, 1989). There is another important difference. According to arousal theories organisms fluctuate slightly about a single preferred point, whereas reversal theory claims that people have two preferred points and that they frequently switch or reverse between them. The theory therefore posits *bistability* rather than homeostasis.

With regard to the experience of arousal, people can be in one of two states. In the first state, which is called *telic*, low arousal is preferred: it is felt as pleasant whereas high arousal is experienced as unpleasant. In the telic state, calmness (low arousal, pleasant) is contrasted with anxiety (high arousal, unpleasant). The opposite is true when the person is in the alternative state, which is called *paratelic*. In the paratelic state low arousal is experienced as boredom (unpleasant) and high arousal as excitement (pleasant). It is therefore now high arousal which is preferred. The point being made here is that a given level of arousal may be experienced as either positive or negative. You may experience a quiet Sunday afternoon as serene or dull. You may experience a crowdy and noisy party as exciting or anxiety–provoking. The perceived level of pleasantness, called *hedonic tone*, is different for the two states. The relationship between felt arousal and hedonic tone is shown in *Figure 10.3*.

The paratelic state may be characterised as an arousal-seeking state, the telic state as arousal-avoiding. Each of these states is also characterised by certain important additional features. When in the telic state, people are goal-oriented; they are serious-minded and try to finish their current activity in order to attain their goal. Because of that, they are oriented to the future and are planning ahead. If you want to prepare for an exam, you are better off in the telic state. On the other hand, if you want to have a good time at a party, the paratelic state is more appropriate. People in the paratelic state are oriented toward the here and now. Goals and achievement-related objectives are not primary. Rather they want to play, have fun, be spontaneous.

Reversal theory holds that people frequently reverse between the two states. Being in a state can last several seconds or as much as several hours. Although reversals are considered involuntary, people can place themselves in circumstances that will increase the possibility of reversals occurring. After a hard day's work in the telic state, you may go to a bar where the noise, the witty conversation and the alcohol increase the likelihood of a reversal to the paratelic state. When you are in the paratelic state, but a reversal to the telic state is crucial because you have to study, it is advisable to avoid the company of other people, clear your desk and arrange the things you need, try to relax your muscles and so on.

Its concern with the *experience of arousal*, with subjective rather than behavioural processes, makes reversal theory a phenomenological theory. The theory is concerned with the experience of one's own motivation. However, the way motivation is experienced is clearly structured. Underlying subjective experiences are certain structures and patterns. The telic and paratelic states together constitute but one of these underlying constructions. Others are postulated in the theory. Hence Apter calls his theory a *structural phenomenological theory* of human action.

 ## Social Motivation

Cognitive motivation is the driving force behind our striving toward being a competent member of society. Competence is shaped in interaction with others. For this reason people are by definition social. However, people are not social only because their personal construction of competence has a social origin. They do not only want to give meaning to their social world; they also want *to belong* to their social world, and this need for belongingness is considered a separate motivational system. We can see the working of this **social motivation** in the behaviour of all neonate primates. They all scan the faces of their parents in order to get essential information for survival. This way, an affective bond is formed with the parent. This bond will extend to others so that animals and people accommodate their behaviour to others, not only because it is an efficient way to deal with the social world, but especially because they want to belong to their social world. This wanting to belong is considered a basic need (Buck, 1988). Thus, alongside cognitive motivation, which develops into competence, there exists another basic need, which develops into belongingness. This need is often called

affiliation motivation: one's concern over establishing, maintaining, or restoring a positive affective relationship with another person or a group of persons (Koestner & McClelland, 1992).

Like the further development of competence, the outgrowth of belongingness is also dependent on cultural standards. Every human being starts his or her life with a built-in social need that develops into a kind of attachment or belongingness, but it is culture that gives it its final shape. In collectivistic cultures much value is attached to intimate friendships. The relations between people are supposed to be deep, life-long and full of commitment – it is the quality that counts. In individualistic cultures there exists a strong theme of relatedness, but according to Triandis and his colleagues (1988) this longing for relatedness is shaped into many friendships with lots of non-intimate acquaintances. Thus, friendships can be rather superficial.

It is acknowledged that for humans social motives are among the strongest and most important ones. It is perhaps a characteristic of Western psychology, however, that such recognition has not resulted in a vast body of empirical research, unlike in the case of cognitive motivation. It may be even more characteristic that much research on social motivation directs itself at the negative side of striving toward belongingness. Instead of concentrating on the preference or readiness for experiences of warm, close and intimate interaction with others, Western psychological research focuses on the downside of affiliation examining, for example, topics like evaluation apprehension, social anxiety and fear of failure. It may well be that in some individualistic cultures a cultural shaping of cognitive motivation is predominant, whereas in some collectivistic ones, the cultural shaping of social motivation prevails.

Thus far, we have sampled general theories of motivation. In the next section, we will take a closer look at three very different motives that influence our lives: hunger, sexual motivation and achievement motivation.

INTERIM SUMMARY

The psychological theories of motivation can be categorised in terms of three motivational systems: biological, cognitive and social. Biological motivation includes instinct theories, drive theories and arousal theories. Despite the differences between these theories, they all relate motivation directly to the interaction of physiological processes and external stimuli. Cognitive motivation stresses the subjective interpretation of reality. People want to be competent members of society and, hence, they are eager to understand and master the phenomena that are valued. Cognitive motivation includes consistency theories, expectancy-value theories, theories centred around the intrinsic motivation to be competent and eventually autonomous, and reversal theory. Social motivation concerns the urge to belong to the social world.

✖ HUNGER AND EATING

The primary drives, such as hunger and thirst, represent the body's way of keeping its long-running show on the road. Of the body's many homeostatic mechanisms for maintaining optimal internal conditions, those involved in hunger motivation are among the more complex. Biological regulation by certain brain areas, neurotransmitters, hormones and bodily organs works in tandem with mental, behavioural and social processes to control the organism's motivation to start and to stop eating.

✖ What Regulates Human Feeding Patterns?

To regulate food intake effectively, organisms must be equipped with mechanisms that accomplish four tasks: (a) the detection of internal food need; (b) initiating and organising eating behaviour; (c) monitoring the quantity and quality of the food eaten; and (d) detecting when enough food has been consumed so as to stop eating. Researchers have tried to understand these processes by relating them either to *peripheral* mechanisms in different parts of the body, such as stomach contractions, or to *central* brain mechanisms, such as the functioning of the hypothalamus. Although hunger is probably the most studied motive, our understanding of it – especially in humans – is still incomplete. What do we know about the motivational dynamics of hunger?

Peripheral cues: hunger pangs

Where do sensations of hunger come from? Does your stomach rumble and send out distress signals – pangs and cramps? A pioneering physiologist, **Walter Cannon** (1934), believed that localised sensations of hunger from gastric activity in an empty stomach were the sole basis for hunger. Cannon tested his *peripheral cues hypothesis* in an interesting

demonstration on his student, A. L. Washburn. Washburn trained himself to swallow an uninflated balloon attached to a rubber tube. The other end of the tube was attached to a device that recorded changes in air pressure. Cannon then inflated the balloon in Washburn's stomach; as the student's stomach contracted, air was expelled from the balloon and deflected the recording pen. Reports of Washburn's hunger pangs were correlated with periods when his stomach was severely contracted but not when it was distended. Cannon thought he had proved that stomach cramps were responsible for hunger (Cannon & Washburn, 1912). He went further, arguing that local stimulation was the basis of all biological drives. Cannon advocated looking to the body's peripheral mechanisms to understand the nature of hunger, thirst, sex and other basic drives.

Cannon had only established a *correlation*, not a causal connection. Although hunger pangs accompanied stomach contractions, maybe something else was causing both of those responses. Sure enough, later research showed that stomach contractions are not even a necessary condition for hunger. Injections of sugar into the bloodstream will stop the stomach contractions but not the hunger of an animal with an empty stomach. Human patients who have had their stomachs entirely removed still experience hunger pangs (Janowitz & Grossman, 1950). So, although sensations originating in the stomach may play a role in the way we usually experience hunger, they do not explain how the body detects its need for food.

A multiple-system approach

For many years researchers used models of central regulation, trying to identify 'brain hunger centres' that were responsible for the arousal and cessation of hunger and eating mechanisms. However, that view also proved too limited. The current view of hunger and eating uses a complex biological and psychological model. This multiple-system approach begins by specifying that the brain works in association with many other systems, both biological and psychological, to gather information about an organism's energy requirements, nutritional state, acquired hungers and food preferences, as well as information about social-cultural demands on the person. The brain sends signals to neural, hormonal, organ and muscle systems to start or stop food seeking and eating.

The brain region primarily involved in the control of eating is the *lateral hypothalamus* (the 'hunger centre'), while a separate brain area nearby, the *ventromedial hypothalamus* (the 'satiety centre'), controls

TABLE 10.1 MULTIPLE-SYSTEM MODEL SUMMARISING FACTORS CONTROLLING HUNGER AND FEEDING

Mechanisms Controlling Eating (integrated by lateral hypothalamus)	Mechanisms Controlling Not Eating (integrated by ventromedial hypothalamus)★
FACTORS OF BIOLOGICAL ORIGIN Nutritional deficiencies Low levels of blood glucose (sugar) High levels of fatty acids in the blood — both stimulate lateral hypothalamus Set point (level) of stored fats — when below critical set point, food seeking initiated **FACTORS OF PSYCHOLOGICAL ORIGIN** Specific hunger — learned preference for diets containing substances (salt, calcium, etc.) they lack Stress-induced eating Socially stimulated eating — family and cultural eating rituals; symbolically significant food **FACTORS OF MIXED ORIGIN** Sensory clues — sensory input to central nervous system elicits reflexes activating autonomic nervous system, preparing for digestion, metabolism, storage — palatability of food maintains eating by eliciting reflexes in brain that stimulate the lateral hypothalamus Anticipatory activities — eating that prevents depletion	**FACTORS OF BIOLOGICAL ORIGIN** Metabolic signals High levels of blood glucose Low levels of fatty acids Peripheral signals Full stomach, monitored by pressure detectors, stimulates ventromedial hypothalamus Taste cues from unpalatable foods induce rejection reflex Set point signals Level of stored body fat reaches critical set point of satiety, stimulating ventromedial hypothalamus **FACTORS OF PSYCHOLOGICAL ORIGIN** Fear Conditioned food aversions Conditioned satiety Cultural pressures toward slimness, dieting Eating disorders, such as anorexia ★Includes short-term (stop eating) controls and long-term (suppression between meals) controls

cessation or inhibition of eating. This *dual-hypothalamic mechanism*, together with many inputs and related processes, starts and stops our eating.

Table 10.1 summarises many of the factors believed to be involved in the complex regulation of hunger detection, feeding and satiation. In general, the biological systems are responsive to an organism's energy needs and nutritional state. The psychological systems account for acquired food preferences and are responsive to social, emotional and environmental stimuli that make eating in general and specific foods, in particular, either desirable or aversive. We can only touch briefly on the features of each factor.

Sugar (in the form of glucose in the blood) and fat are the energy sources for metabolism. Evidently, the two basic signals that initiate eating come from receptors that monitor the levels of sugar and fat in the blood. When blood glucose is low or unavailable for metabolism, signals from liver cell receptors are sent to the lateral hypothalamus where certain neurons acting as glucose detectors change their activity in response to this information. When blood

glucose levels fall there is an immediate effect on reported hunger in healthy adults. Other hypothalamic neurons may detect changes in free fatty acids and insulin levels in the blood. Together, these neurons appear to activate appetitive systems in the lateral zone of the hypothalamus and initiate eating behaviour (Thompson & Campbell, 1977).

With free access to food, adult animals and humans will maintain a stable body weight over their lifetime at a level consistent for them. Most organisms have a tightly and efficiently controlled process of balancing nutritive intake with energy expenditures. An internal biological scale weighs the fat in the body and keeps the central nervous system informed. Whenever fats stored in specialised fat cells fall below a certain level, termed the **critical set point**, eat signals are sent out (Keesey & Powley, 1975). This internal set point exerts a major influence on the amount people eat and on their weight.

Besides eating to satisfy hunger, we eat to *prevent* it. Observations of free-ranging animals in their native habitat suggest that they eat before hunger sets in.

Predators invest enormous energy in hunting for prey before hunger weakens them. Similarly, many species gather, store and hoard food. These strategies prevent depletion instead of making up for a deficiency already present (Collier *et al*, 1972). Many of the mechanisms that stop eating are similar to those that start it, but they work through the ventromedial hypothalamus and rely on an opposite set of cues. *Short-term inhibitors* terminate ongoing feeding and *long-term inhibitors* suppress eating activities between meals.

High glucose levels and low levels of free fatty acids in the blood are signals that the set point has been reached; but even before this nutritional information is processed by the brain, several peripheral cues are signalling stop. Pressure detectors in the stomach signal distension, while unpleasant taste cues can induce a *rejection reflex* (including vomiting).

Similar to eating, inhibition of eating is influenced by a host of emotional and learned psychological processes, some occurring during a meal and some between meals. For example, humans and animals do not eat when they are fearful. In addition, animals do not eat much of a new food; they'll sample a bit, then wait for several hours before eating more if no illness has developed. This protective reaction is known as *bait-shyness*. Human children of about two years show a somewhat similar *neophobia*. They tend to shy away from edibles they do not know. However, the instinctive reaction of human children to unknown food is not as strong as in many other animals and is far easier to overcome.

In the case of humans, social and cultural factors determine when, how much, how fast and what people eat. Italian mothers are said to respond to protests of 'No more food, please! I'm not hungry!' with, 'Anyone can eat when they're *hungry*, but eating my food when you're not, shows that you love me'. Human feeding patterns are also determined by religious prescriptions. Eating pork, for example, is a taboo for Muslims and Jews and periods of fasting are common to many religions.

✖ Over-eating and Dieting

The dominant attitude in Western culture toward food and eating is paradoxical. On the one hand, we are continually urged to buy foodstuffs; on the other hand, we are constantly reminded that being slim is a prerequisite for sexual attractiveness. The affluence of modern society partly contributes to the eating disorder *obesity*. A person is obese if his or her body weight exceeds the average for a given height by 20 per cent. Obese people generally have more *fat cells* (adipose tissue) than people of normal weight as a result of either genetic factors or over-feeding at critical periods in infancy (Brownell, 1982; Sjørstrøm, 1980). Beyond infancy, dieting or over-eating changes the *size* of the fat cells, but not their *number*. The number of fat cells people have remains constant throughout life. Consequently, people with a large number of fat cells who diet will lose weight and may become thinner. However, they will still have the same critical set point and so nevertheless will remain hungry, potentially overweight people (Nisbett, 1972). Their bodies are programmed to be fat and rebel against extreme interventions that try to make them slim.

When obese people diet and reach their new reduced weight, their body chemistry is severely affected; it becomes disorganised. Fat cells shrink, menstruation may stop, and thyroid hormone levels and white blood cell counts drop, as do blood pressure and pulse rate. These formerly obese individuals complain of intolerance to the cold, and they are obsessed with thoughts about food.

Sadly, it tends to be the rule that weight loss from dieting programmes is short-term; gradually the body's own weight regulators take over and restore its weight equilibrium (Kolata, 1985; Ogden, 1992). To be effective, any dieting programme must include regular exercise, daily monitoring of food intake, systematic record keeping of calorie intake and weight change, techniques for avoiding severe stress and social (especially family) support. For the obese, dieting is not a question of 'mind over matter'; instead, it is a question of biology asserting itself over psychology.

In some cases, dieting in order to reach the ideal of slenderness may turn into an obsession. The eating disorder *anorexia nervosa* is a relentless pursuit of thinness through self-starvation (Bruch, 1973). Anorexia occurs predominantly among young women of the middle and upper classes in Western societies. The fear of becoming fat leads to a regimen of eating low-calorie food, fasting and long hours of exercise. It generally results in extreme weight loss, sometimes reaching levels that are less than 50 per cent of the average. In some cases, self-starvation leads to death. Anorexia is probably caused by multiple factors, like the cultural obsession with slimness, the fear of being unattractive, rebellion against the parents, or a wish of the sufferer to exert control over some aspects of their lives. There are some indications that hormonal factors also play a role. In all likelihood, however, psychological factors are major contributors to anorexia (Logue, 1986; Noordenbos, 1988). *Bulimia* is another eating disorder that is not uncommon among college and university students. It is characterised by disruptions in self-control (Ruderman, 1986) and by associated eating binges followed by self-induced purging of the food through vomiting or laxatives. Like anorexics, bulimics are preoccupied with their appearance, but unlike anorexics, they are generally of normal weight.

✖ SEXUAL MOTIVATION

While eating is essential to individual survival, sex is not. Some animals and humans remain celibate for a lifetime without apparent detriment to their daily functioning. But to evolution, reproduction is even more important than survival: many animals have evolved to breed fast and die young. In human sexual motivation, nature and culture are linked inextricably, but with respect to the biological processes in sexual motivation, humans have a lot in common with other primates. The influence of cultural factors is, however, confined to humankind. Sexual desire and sexual behaviour are cultural constructs that are relative to the social and historical context (Foucault, 1976). The individual's sexual motivation therefore is always a product of the interaction between physiological processes on the one hand and cultural allowances and constraints on the other.

Academic research on sexual motivation has been dominated in the past hundred years by a focus on biological determinants. Much of what is known about the physiology of sexuality comes from research on nonhuman animals. Though Freud called attention to the importance of human sexual motivation, psychologists in his day did not follow up on his ideas, partly because of the taboos against dealing with human sexuality openly.

In this section, we will first sketch some of the biological factors involved in sexual motivation. Then we will turn our attention to the social and cultural shaping of this powerful motive.

✖ Sexual Arousal in Animals and Humans

If we ask ourselves why animals and humans are motivated by and toward sexual behaviour, we may come up with the necessity of reproduction. Indeed, in many species sexuality is determined totally by its reproductive function. Humans, by contrast, may engage in sex for different reasons, like pleasure or 'love'. Sexual reproduction requires at least two sexual types: males and females. The female produces a few relatively large gametes (eggs) – the energy store for the embryo to begin its growth – and the male produces many relatively small gametes (sperm) that are specialised for mobility (to move into the eggs). This basic sex-cell differentiation is amplified as males and females diverge in physical structure, physiological functions and behaviour.

Sexual arousal plays an obvious role in sexual motivation across many species. Sexual arousal is partly determined by the flow of hormones controlled by the pituitary gland and secreted from the **gonads**, the sex organs. In males, these hormones are known as **androgens** and they are continuously present in sufficient supply so that males are hormonally ready for mating at almost any time; but in the females of many species, the sex hormone, **oestrogen**, is released according to regular time cycles of days or months or according to seasonal changes. Thus, the female is only hormonally receptive to mating at specific times. In both sexes across the animal kingdom hormones may act on both the brain and genital tissue to promote sexual motivation. In most animals at least, it is clear they do so and often lead to a pattern of predictable, stereotyped sexual behaviour for all members of a species. If you've seen one pair of rats in their mating sequence, you've seen them all.

In the human species the relation between hormones and sexual motivation is more complex. Hormonal activity, has no known effect on sexual receptiveness in women. In men, the sex hormone **testosterone** (one of the androgens) is a prerequisite for sexual arousal and performance. Testosterone levels become high enough only after puberty when hypothalamic neurons secrete a special hormone (gonadotropin-releasing hormone) that plays a critical role in establishing and maintaining reproductive activities. When the production of testosterone is inhibited, men tend to lose sexual motivation. Testosterone levels in their turn are subject to external influences: sexual activity increases peak testosterone levels, but this is also influenced by social factors like behaving dominantly (Van de Poll & Van Goozen, 1992). In women, oestrogen is not necessary for sexual behaviour to occur: female sexual arousal does not decline significantly postmenopause when oestrogen levels drop but testosterone remains constant.

Sexual arousal is not only determined by inner states like hormonal flow. Peripheral stimuli can sensitise or activate innate response patterns. In many species, the sight and sound of ritualised display patterns by potential partners is a necessary condition for sexual motivation to occur. Touch, taste and smell can also serve as stimulants for sexual arousal. Some species, for example, secrete chemical signals, called **pheromones**, that attract suitors, sometimes from great distances. In many species, pheromones are emitted by the female when her fertility is optimal. In humans, though, reactions to sex-related odours are quite variable, determined more by who is giving off the smell than by any unlearned, irresistible, olfactory properties of the chemical communication (Hopson, 1979).

✖ Psychological and Social Factors

In humans, sexuality is far more dependent on psychological factors than it is in animals. As a result, it is also more variable in humans than in other species. Human sexuality can be described as including an evolved motivational core focused on mating for reproduction and pleasure from sexual behaviour, along with the societal constraints on and inducements toward sexual activities. Erotic stimuli, which may be physical or psychological, give rise to sexual arousal or feelings of passion. Sexual arousal induced by erotic stimuli is reduced by sexual activities that are perceived by the individual as satisfying, for example by achieving orgasm.

Scientific investigation of human sexual behaviour was given the first important impetus by the work of **Alfred Kinsey** and his colleagues beginning in the 1940s (1948, 1953). They interviewed some 17,000 Americans about their sexual behaviour and revealed – to a generally shocked public – that certain behaviours, previously considered rare and even abnormal, were actually quite widespread, or at least reported to be. However, it was **William Masters** and **Virginia Johnson** (1966, 1970, 1979) who really broke down traditional sexual taboos. They legitimised the study of human sexuality by directly observing ongoing human sexual performance. By doing so, they studied not what people said about sex, but how they actually reacted, during intercourse and masturbation.

Sexual response cycle

To study directly the human response to sexual stimulation, Masters and Johnson conducted controlled laboratory observations of thousands of volunteer males and females during tens of thousands of **sexual response cycles** of intercourse and masturbation. Their pioneering research on sexual arousal dispelled a number of myths and provided a model of the phases of the human sexual response. However, it is important to note that Masters and Johnson studied arousal and response only. They did *not* study the psychologically significant initial phase of sexual responding – that of *sexual desire*, the motivation to seek out a sexual partner or to make oneself available for sexual experience. Further, they focused on genital sexuality. The feminist sexologist Leonore Tiefer (1991) has argued that this focus on penetration and foreplay seriously neglects other sexual priorities and experiences, particularly those of women.

Three of the most significant conclusions drawn by Masters and Johnson are that (a) men and women have similar patterns of sexual responding, regardless of the source of arousal; (b) although the sequence of phases of the sexual response cycle is similar in the two sexes, women are more variable, tending to respond more slowly but often remaining aroused

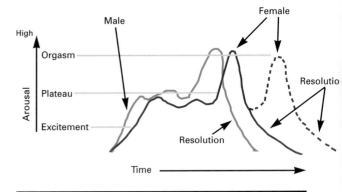

FIGURE 10.4 PHASES OF HUMAN SEXUAL RESPONSE

The phases of sexual response in males and females have similar patterns. The primary differences are in the time it takes for males and females to reach each phase and in the greater likelihood that females will achieve multiple orgasms.

longer; and (c) penis size is generally unrelated to any aspect of sexual performance (except in the man's attitude toward having a large penis). Four phases were found in the human sexual response cycle: excitement, plateau, orgasm and resolution (see *Figure 10.4*).

- In the *excitement phase* (lasting from a few minutes to more than an hour), there are *vascular* (blood vessel) changes in the pelvic region. The penis becomes erect and the clitoris swells; blood and other fluids become congested in the testicles and vagina; a reddening of the body, or sex flush, occurs.

- During the *plateau phase*, a maximum (though varying) level of arousal is reached. There is rapidly increased heartbeat, respiration and blood pressure, increased glandular secretions, and both voluntary and involuntary muscle tension throughout the body. Vaginal lubrication increases and the breasts swell.

- During the *orgasm phase*, males and females experience a very intense, pleasurable sense of release from the sexual tension that has been building. Orgasm is characterised by rhythmic contractions in the genital areas. Respiration and blood pressure reach very high levels in both sexes, and heart rate may double. In men, throbbing contractions lead to ejaculation of seminal fluid. In women, orgasm may be of two different types, achieved from effective stimulation of either the clitoris or the vagina.

- During the *resolution phase*, the body gradually returns to its normal pre-excitement state, with both blood pressure and heartbeat slowing down.

After one orgasm, most men enter a refractory period, lasting anywhere from a few minutes to several hours, during which no further orgasm is possible. With sustained arousal, women are capable of multiple orgasms in fairly rapid succession.

✖ The Mating Game: Sexual Investment Strategies

When sexuality aims at reproduction, animals and humans need a partner to put their sexual motivation into practice. In evolutionary terms, the mating game amounts to the following for most primates and humans: for females, the reproductive environment consists of the behavioural tendencies and abilities of males and of competing females; for males, the reverse holds. The difference comes down to gametes. Males could reproduce hundreds of times a year if they could find enough fertile and willing mates. To produce a child, all they need to invest is a teaspoon of sperm and a few minutes of intercourse. Women can reproduce at most about once a year, and each child reproduced then requires, at minimum, a huge investment of time and energy by the primary care-giver. (Incidentally, the world record for the number of times a woman has given birth falls short of 50, but men can produce many more children. A Moroccan despot, King Ismail the Bloodthirsty, had over 700 children, and the first Emperor of China is said to have begotten over 3,000; both had large harems.)

Thus, the basic problem facing female animals is to find a high-quality male to ensure the best, healthiest offspring from her limited store of eggs. For some animals, such as primates and humans, offspring take so long to mature and are so helpless while growing that substantial parental investment is required (Trivers, 1972). Mothers and fathers must spend time and energy raising the children – unlike fish or spiders which simply lay eggs and depart. Prospective parents have the problem of selecting not just the most healthy, clever, high-status, most thrilling partner, but the most loyal, committed companion who will help raise the children.

Stimuli and social contexts

Although Masters's and Johnson's research focused on the human physiology of sexual responding, perhaps their most important discovery was the central significance of *psychological* processes in both arousal and satisfaction. They demonstrated conclusively that problems in sexual response often have psychological, rather than physiological, origins and can be changed, for example through therapy. Of particular concern, is the inability to complete the response cycle and achieve gratification. This inability is called *impotence* in men and *frigidity* in women. Often the source of the inability is a preoccupation with personal problems, fear of the consequences of sexual activity, or anxiety about a partner's evaluation of one's sexual performance (Bancroft, 1989). However, poor nutrition, fatigue, stress and excessive use of alcohol or drugs can also diminish sexual drive and performance.

Sexual activities can be incited by many stimuli. Behaviourists have focused on associations between stimuli and arousal. Touch is a good example of an unconditioned stimulus. Touch, in the form of genital caresses, is a universal component of sexual foreplay (Ford & Beach, 1951). However, virtually any stimuli that become associated with genital touch and orgasm can become conditioned motivators, whether the stimuli are in the external environment or in one's fantasy. Even a picture of a shoe can lead to sexual arousal in this way (Rachman, 1966). A non-sexual object that becomes capable of producing sexual arousal through conditioning is called a *fetish*. A fetish becomes a psychological problem only when it is necessary for arousal and/or it is objectionable to one's sexual partner.

Psychologists who study sexuality from a cognitive perspective focus on the satisfaction of cognitive desires. They argue that sexual activities are also concerned with 'the attainment of a cognitive state: the conscious perception of sexual satisfaction. This state depends on a combination of experiences originating in the experiencer's body and in that of the sexual partner' (Davidson, 1980). Interpretations of experiences, the meaning of specific sexual events, sexual beliefs and values, imagination and expectation all play a part in human sexual behaviour and satisfaction (Byrne, 1981).

Sexual scripts

Generalised sexual arousal can be channelled into different specific behaviours, depending on how the individual has learned to respond and think about sexual matters. **Sexual scripts** are socially learned programmes of sexual responsiveness that include prescriptions, usually unspoken, of what to do, when, where, and how to do it, with whom, or with what to do it and why it should be done (Gagnon, 1977). Such scripts are crucial for sexual interaction, because they embody what is seen as appropriate behaviour for oneself, as well as expectations of a sexual partner. Different aspects of sexual scripts are constructed in social interaction over one's lifetime. The attitudes and values embodied in one's sexual script define a person's general orientation to sexuality.

Sexual scripts include similar 'stage directions' for most sexual actors within a given culture, socioeconomic group, gender and educational level. However, there are unique features in each individual's personal script, learned through his or her own history of sexual experience. A socially constructed script interacts with personal history and learning, thus creating the enormous variations that are evident in human sexual motivation and behaviour.

Sexual harassment

Differing scripts can create problems of adjustment between partners when they are not discussed or when there is no possibility of negotiation about the script's elements. For example, there is evidence that touch has different meanings for men and women. For women the more a touch was associated with sexual desire, the less it was considered to imply warmth, pleasantness or friendliness. For men, touching is interpreted as having a cluster of meanings: pleasantness, warmth, love and sexual desire. Misunderstandings can arise when one person's 'friendly touch' is perceived by the other as a 'sexual advance' (Nguyen et al, 1975). This study suggested that, from the female perspective, male touch without the rituals of courtship and the preliminaries of respect and commitment is interpreted as a sexual advance – for 'easy,' short-term mating. For males, female touch is interpreted as pleasant in most situations since it is assumed to suggest a willingness to mate.

Two other instances of diverging masculine and feminine scripts have attracted a lot of attention recently: date rape and sexual harassment in the workplace. Date rape is most extensively studied among college and university students in the United States. At European universities, the issue of date rape is not quite such a focal point of public scrutiny. When researchers asked North American college women about their experiences of unwanted sex, they found that over half reported that they had experienced this (Murnen et al, 1989). The researchers also asked the same women how they had been coerced and how they had coped with the incident at the time. The most common responses were ignoring or giving in to the coercion. Many of the women continued to see the men on subsequent occasions, though they often did not continue sexual relations. The authors of this study suggest that women may perceive that their role is to give in eventually to male insistence and coercion. They may feel that male sexual desire is uncontrollable and that, after the rape,

the required female role is to mend the relationship by forgiving the man. Women in the study tended to blame themselves for getting into dangerous situations (even though most attacks came from men who were their friends or whom they knew moderately well) and even to feel guilty about denying sex to their dates.

Surveys of male students show that men who were likely to use physical aggression against their dates endorsed a 'battle of the sexes' attitude. They tend to put the traditional script into practice in which a woman's role is to be passive and coy, offer token resistance and eventually give in, while the man's role is to initiate, persevere and prevail until she has been 'conquered' (Muelenhard & Linton, 1987). Men, however, also reported unwanted sex, although they almost always had the physical power to refuse. The reasons that men had unwanted sex related to their fears about their own sexuality; they were unable to refuse any sexual advance for fear of being labelled as inadequate (Muehlenhard & Cook, 1988).

Sexual harassment is another example of sexual scripts going awry. Harassment is the kind of abuse that includes obscene remarks, offensive jokes, or suggestive comments about one's physical appearance. In more extreme cases it may include threats of being fired, being grabbed at and rape. Because of the unequal distribution of power in relations at work, women are generally the victims of unwanted attention from men. From the perspective of the traditional masculine script, their remarks and touches are seen as innocent hints that are a legitimate part of

Women are often the victims of unwanted attention from men at work.

the 'battle' between the sexes. Many women experience the dropping of sexual hints as annoying, if not threatening. A large scale American survey reported that more than half of the women interviewed said that they had experienced sexual harassment at their place of work (Gutek, 1985). The consequences of being harassed spread beyond office hours. Many victims reported impairment of social relations and an overall lowered satisfaction with their lives (Maypole, 1986).

Homosexuality

Thus far, our discussion of sexual motivation has been undertaken largely with the assumption of heterosexuality in mind. Since Alfred Kinsey's early reports, however, we have known that human sexual orientation is a complex business. Kinsey found that a large percentage of men in his sample had had at least some homosexual experience, and that about four per cent were exclusively homosexual (percentages for women were somewhat smaller). He concluded that the distinction between homosexuality and heterosexuality is not as strict as is often assumed. Recent surveys about sexual orientation in Western countries confirm Kinsey's picture. Most people consider themselves to be heterosexual. About five per cent of the men describe themselves as homosexual. Homosexuality among women is less prevalent, about one per cent see themselves as lesbians. Experiments with one's sexual orientation are not uncommon. From ten to 20 per cent of the men reported that they had had at least one homosexual experience (where one partner reached orgasm). For women these percentages were smaller (Fay et al, 1989; Van Zessen & Sandfort, 1991). Cross-cultural and historical studies have revealed enormous variation in customs and in attitudes about homosexuality (Werner, 1979). In some cultures, homosexuality is strongly suppressed, in some it is acceptable before heterosexual marriage but discouraged after, and, in a very few, it is even favoured over heterosexuality.

Psychology has long neglected homosexuality, or has considered it as a psychological disorder. It was not until 1973 that the American Psychiatric Association removed homosexuality from its list of disorders (Bayer, 1981). Psychological theories have tried to explain homosexuality from a variety of perspectives. Some theories seek to explain the physiological variations that might produce homosexuality, but attempts to identify physiological causes have been inconclusive. Psychoanalysts focus on the individual's family life in early childhood. However, the indications that parents cause

homosexuality in this way are not very compelling (Bell et al, 1981). Behaviourists suggest that early learning experiences about sexual pleasure with same-sex peers play a crucial role (Storms, 1981).

Recently, researchers have begun to explore homosexual motivation from the perspective of self-definition. The common pattern in self-definition of many gays and lesbians is that they report that, around the age of 12, they went through a period of defining themselves as different, but not necessarily in terms of sexual feelings. During adolescence, the difference reveals itself as a difference in sexual preference. Some homosexual boys and girls are at great pains in this period to deny their feelings, for example, by forcing themselves to engage in heterosexual activities. For most homosexuals, the acceptance of their sexual orientation comes in later adolescence and early adulthood when homosexuality is experienced as natural and normal for the self. Social context is crucial to self-definition: its form is partly dependent on the amount of disapproval or support homosexuals receive from family, friends and society (Troiden, 1989).

Celia Kitzinger (1987) studied the accounts British lesbians gave of their subjective experiences of lesbianism. She found that though society constructs lesbianism as a distinct category, the women themselves had many ways of defining their sexual orientation. Some saw their lesbianism as inevitable: they felt they were born that way; others said they became lesbian through radical feminism and saw it as a deliberate political choice. In some accounts the lesbian orientation was described as a burden, or a sin. In most descriptions lesbian women spoke of several narratives, thus showing the multiplicity of meanings they attributed to their sexuality.

Psychological theories about homosexuality are still developing. In all probability, human sexual orientation does not have any one cause. Some people may be born gay or lesbian, but that does not preclude others from choosing to have homosexual experiences. Cultural variation also reminds us how difficult it is to generalise about homosexuality.

ACHIEVEMENT MOTIVATION

The desire to achieve one's goals, whether they involve getting high marks in a psychology examination or climbing to the top of a steep mountain, is a pervasive psychological motive that empowers a wide variety of human actions. **Achievement motivation** is a good example of cognitive motivation. It should not be confused, however, with performing under external pressure. Achievement motivation is concerned with self-motivation to excel on any activity that is significant for the individual: it is intrinsic. It links specific goals, the planning and effort needed to attain them, and feelings of self-worth. However, in some cases achievement motives can become so extreme that they lead to the limitless aspiration of being the best at everything. An important feature of achievement motives is their future orientation. The motivated achiever uses cognitive strategies that rely on long-term instrumental steps toward subgoals and distant goals rather than focusing on the hedonistic value of more readily available, ultimately less valuable, present stimuli (DeCharms & Muir, 1978; Nuttin, 1985).

✖ Need for Achievement

As early as 1938, **Henry Murray** had reasoned on a 'need to achieve' which varied in strength for different people and influenced their tendency to approach success and evaluate personal performances. **David McClelland** and his colleagues (1953) devised a way to measure the strength of this need and then looked for relationships between strength of achievement motivation in different societies, conditions that had fostered it and its results in the world of work. To measure the strength of the need for achievement, McClelland used projections of his subjects' imaginings.

A special projective technique (see Chapter 1) called the **thematic apperception test** (TAT) was used to elicit and classify the subjects' stories. The TAT was originally developed by Murray to identify a limited number of human motives that may be central in people's lives. Murray argued that projective techniques are necessary, because people have limited access to what motivates them. The analysis of (projected) fantasies, however, enables researchers to access the motives of their subjects. In this respect it is interesting to note that recent studies have shown that indirect, fantasy-based measures of achievement show more long-term predictive power than self-reports of achievement (McClelland, Koestner & Weinberger, 1992). In the TAT, subjects are shown a series of ambiguous pictures and are then asked to tell a story about what they thought was happening in each picture and what probable outcomes might be (see *Figure 10.5*, next page). It is assumed that viewers project into a scene reflections of their own values, interests and motives. Murray's inferences drawn from the fantasy stories uncovered a variety of motives: positive ones, but also motives relating to needs for power, dominance and aggression.

McClelland derived measures of several human needs from the TAT stories. The need for achievement was designated as 'n Ach'. It reflected individual differences in the perceived importance of working toward attaining personal goals. A great many studies in both laboratory and real-life settings have validated the usefulness of this construct and measure. For example, persistence in working on an impossible task was found to be greater for those who scored high on the 'n Ach' measure when the task was presented as difficult rather than easy. Low 'n Ach' subjects gave up sooner when they were led to believe the task was difficult, but they persisted longer when faced with the supposedly easy (actually impossible) task. In other research, high-scoring 'n Ach' people were found to be more upwardly mobile than those with low scores. Sons who had high 'n Ach' scores were more likely than sons with low 'n Ach' measures to advance above their fathers' level of occupational attainment (McClelland *et al*, 1976). *Figure 10.5* shows an example of how a high 'n Ach' individual and low 'n Ach' individual might interpret a TAT picture.

The need to achieve clearly energises and directs behaviour, but its dynamism may be inhibited seriously by a **fear of failure**. McClelland's close collaborator **John Atkinson** demonstrated in his experiments that success in a task is determined both by the motive to achieve and the fear of failing. Participants who scored high on fear of failure measures tended to select tasks that were either easy to accomplish or extremely difficult. In the first case they had a high chance of success; in the second case they would probably fail, but without having to blame themselves. After all, as they might rationalise to themselves, the task was too difficult (Atkinson & Feather, 1966).

Emotions (or 'affects' as they are sometimes called in psychology; see below) are central in the theories of achievement motivation. People are assumed to seek or avoid the emotions that are bound up with success and failure. What the high 'n Ach' person really seeks is not success but *pride* of accomplishment. The person scoring high on fear of failure does not really fear failure but rather the *shame* of failure (Mook, 1987). Thus far, achievement motivation was conceptualised as a unidirectional force that pushes the individual – if the motive is not inhibited – toward the completion of significant tasks. However, achievement motivation is also related to the ways in which people perceive what they did or did not accomplish.

✖ Attributions for Success and Failure

Motivation for achievement is complicated by personal attributions: interpretations and beliefs about the

| FIGURE 10.5 | ALTERNATIVE INTERPRETATIONS OF A TAT PICTURE |

Story showing high 'n Ach'

The boy has just finished his violin lesson. He's happy at the progress he is making and is beginning to believe that all his progress is making the sacrifices worthwhile. To become a concert violinist he will have to give up much of his social life and practice for many hours each day. Although he knows he could make more money by going into his father's business, he is more interested in being a great violinist and giving people joy with his music. He renews his personal commitment to do all it takes to make it.

Story showing low 'n Ach'

The boy is holding his brother's violin and wishes he could play it. But he knows it isn't worth the time, energy and money for lessons. He feels sorry for his brother who has given up all the fun things in life to practice, practice, practice. It would be great to wake up one day and be a top-notch musician but it doesn't happen that way. The reality is boring pratice, no fun, and a big possibility of becoming nothing better than just another guy playing a musical instrument in a small-town band.

reasons events turn out the way they do. In his *attributional analysis* of achievement motivation, **Bernard Weiner** (1985) has focused on the person's personal perception of success and failure. According to him, *explanations* of accomplishment are central, rather than the actual successful or unsuccessful performance. People tend to explain their achievement by attributing it to causes. For example, they can explain their accomplishment by pointing to the luck they had or by emphasising the effort they invested. In other words, accomplishment is attributed to luck or effort. Attributions of success and failure are influenced by a variety of factors. First, they are guided by perceived *locus of control*, as discussed earlier, where we can attribute achievement outcomes to internal or external factors. Second, attributions are influenced by the perception of the *stability* or *instability* of the cause to which success or failure is attributed: thus, we can perceive the causes of achievement outcomes as either fixed (stable) or variable (unstable). When the dimension of stability is crossed with the independent dimension of locus of control, four possible interpretations about the causes of outcomes follow, as shown in *Figure 10.6* (next page).

For example, your exam mark in this course may be interpreted as the result of internal factors, such as ability (a stable characteristic) or effort (a varying personal quality). Or it may be viewed as caused primarily by external factors such as the difficulty of the task, the actions of others (a stable, situational problem), or luck (an unstable, external feature). Depending on the nature of the attribution you make for this success or failure, you are likely to experience one of the affective responses depicted in *Table 10.2* (next page). What is important here is that the basis for your personal interpretation may influence your achievement motivation, regardless of the true reason for the success or failure.

The interpretation of success and failure can further be complicated by a third attributional dimension. It is concerned with the question of whether success or failure is *specific,* limited to a particular task or situation, or *global,* applying widely across a variety of settings. We would like to believe our failures are specific and restricted in terms of their effects and that our successes are more general both in terms of their frequency and in terms of their repercussions. People may run into psychological trouble when they come to believe the reverse, that failure is 'general' and success is highly 'specific'.

The attributional dimensions that are involved in explaining successful and unsuccessful performances

FIGURE 10.6	ATTRIBUTIONS REGARDING CAUSES FOR BEHAVIOURAL OUTCOMES

Four possible outcomes are generated with just two sources of attributions about behaviour, the locus of control and the situation in which the behaviour occurs. Ability attributions are made for the internal-stable combination; effort for the internal but unstable combination; luck for the unstable-external combination; and a difficult task (test) when external-stable forces are assumed to be operating.

Locus of Control

	internal	external
stable	ability	task difficulty
unstable	effort	luck

Stability

TABLE 10.2	ATTRIBUTION-DEPENDENT AFFECTS

Our affective reaction to success and failure depends on the kinds of attributions made regarding the cause of those outcomes. For example, we take pride in success when it is attributed to our ability, but are depressed when lack of ability is perceived to cause our failure. Or, gratitude follows success attributed to the actions of others, but anger when they are seen as contributing to our failure.

Attribution	Affects	
	Success	**Failure**
Ability	Competence Confidence Pride	Incompetence Resignation Depression
Effort	Relief Contentment Relaxation	Guilt Shame Fear
Action of others	Gratitude Thankfulness	Anger Fury
Luck	Surprise Guilt	Surprise Astonishment

may turn into *attributional styles* – i.e. the sorts of explanations people tend to give for their successes and failures (Trotter, 1987). **Martin Seligman** has studied the differences between an *optimistic* and *pessimistic* attributional style (Seligman, 1987, 1991). The dichotomy between optimism and pessimism emerged in his research on learned helplessness (see Chapter 7). Recall that about two thirds of the participants became helpless when faced with inescapable noise or insoluble problems. However, there is another side to the story which was ignored initially because it was not as dramatic as the learned-helplessness effects. One third of the subjects turned out to be *invulnerables*, resisting any attempts to make them helpless. They did not give up, kept trying and did not let the negative experience produce the symptoms that plagued the others who were vulnerable to failure. Seligman's research team wondered what could account for this difference in participants? The answer has turned out to be familiar and seemingly simple: optimism versus pessimism. Remarkably, these two divergent ways of looking at the world influence motivation because they represent opposite ways of explaining the causes for one's success and failure. Once formed, these attributional styles operate swiftly, pervasively, and without much thought. The pessimistic attributional style focuses on the causes of failure as being internally generated. Furthermore, the bad situation and one's role in causing it are seen as stable and global – 'It won't ever change and it will affect everything'. The optimistic attributional style attributes failure to external causes – 'The exam was unfair' – and to events that are unstable or modifiable and specific – 'If I put in more effort next time, I'll do better, and this won't affect how I perform any other task that is important to me'. These attributions are reversed when it comes to the question of success. Optimists take full, personal internal-stable-global credit for success. However, pessimists attribute their success to external-unstable-global or specific factors.

Attributions, that is to say beliefs about why we have succeeded or failed, then, are important because they lead to different interpretations of past performance, which, in turn, may lead to different

Martin Seligman

motivation in the future. When we attribute a failure to low ability and difficult tasks, we are likely to give up sooner, select simpler tasks, and lower our goals. When we attribute failure to bad luck or lack of effort, we are likely to have higher motivation to try again for success (Fontaine, 1974; Rosenbaum, 1972; Valle & Frieze, 1976). It is interesting to note that children from individualistic and achievement oriented cultures seem to start out with a sense that intelligence and effort are equivalent. Young children see clever kids as those who work hardest, and young children believe they can make themselves clever by trying hard. Unfortunately, around the age of six, children start to shift over to the prevailing view in such cultural settings, that some people are more gifted than others (Nichols, 1984). People with a high sense of *self-efficacy*, then, seem to retain an enduring faith in their ability to improve themselves (Schunk & Cox, 1986).

✖ Achievement, Culture and Gender

The achievement motive has often been thought of as a fundamental human need (McClelland, 1961). However, the important differences in achievement orientation that have been found across cultures seriously question the universality of 'n Ach'. The debate about the fundamental and universal nature of the achievement motive is also fed by gender differences that have been found in research on achievement.

McClelland himself had an open mind on cultural differences. Although he thought 'n Ach' to be universal, he assumed it to be distributed differentially. In one of his studies McClelland (1955) noted that, in general, Protestant countries (in which achievement and independence tend to be encouraged) were more economically advanced than Catholic countries. In particular he found that men in these 'achieving societies' were more often trained to be self-supporting earlier in life, and thus to value an autonomous success-seeking mode of behaviour.

As we have noted elsewhere, recent cross-cultural research has focused on the difference between individualistic and collectivistic cultures. It is argued that personal achievement is a cardinal feature in most **individualistic** Western cultures. This emphasis on individual success is at odds with the interdependent values upheld in the majority of cultures in Africa, Asia, South America, the Middle East, and Central America (Hofstede, 1980; Triandis, 1990). These deep-rooted cultural differences clearly play vital roles in the motivational psychology of the people. The incongruity of achievement motivation within a

collectivistic culture is all the more compelling because many of the most collective societies in the world (e.g. Japan and China) currently appear focused on accomplishing material achievement. **Hazel Markus** and **Shinobu Kitayama** (1991) report, for example, that the motto 'pass with four, fail with five' is now common among high school students in Japan. It refers to the fact that if a student is sleeping five hours a night, he or she is probably not studying hard enough to pass exams. It appears that the emphasis on achievement in Asian and other collectivistic countries is largely *other* motivated. One achieves because of a desire to fit into the group and to meet the expectations of the group. In a study of academic achievement, North American and Filipino college students were asked to rate their motivations for doing well in academic work (Church & Kagitbak, 1992). The American students ranked achievement and getting good grades higher than did the Filipinos. The Filipino students often described their motives in an interdependent way, stressing the approval of others, and preparing for a proper job. Yang (1986) has proposed distinguishing between two types of achievement motivation: individually oriented and socially oriented. The major difference between the two types is that the latter is concerned with fulfilling the expectations of significant others, typically the family.

The second systematic difference in achievement motivation to be discussed here is the difference between the sexes. In the early laboratory-studies it was found that women obtain lower scores on 'n Ach' than do men (Hoffman, 1972). At the same time, however, it was found that women scored higher on need for affiliation. It was concluded that women were motivated not by internalised standards of excellence ('n Ach'), but rather by a desire for approval from other people (Hoffman, 1972).

Matina Horner (1972) gave an alternative interpretation of the low female scores on achievement motivation. In her research she showed that many women, especially the bright and ambitious ones, had to cope with a motive to avoid success. This **fear of success** originates in the perceived conflict between achievement and femininity, and the perceived connection between achievement and aggressiveness, which is also designated within most societies as gender-inappropiate for females. Thus, for women, the rewards of achievement are contaminated by an accompanying anxiety about being less likeable as a result (Hyde, 1991). Horner's study attracted a lot of attention: the *New York Times* and other newspapers featured stories about the research. The interest in the fear of success explanation was probably due to the fact that Horner seemed to offer a sensible explanation for why more women had not succeeded in high-status occupations.

Recent studies are quite critical of Horner's approach (Mednick, 1989). The methodology of her research was criticised, and follow-up studies showed that fear of success is not exclusively a problem for women: the motive to avoid success was also frequently found in men (Zuckerman & Wheeler, 1975). Although fear of success may be appealing intuitively, the empirical evidence for it is being steadily eroded.

Research on gender differences in achievement motivation has seriously questioned the results that were obtained in the 1960s. In 1974, a review of the available research documented that the evidence for lower achievement motivation in females was weak (Maccoby & Jacklin, 1974). For example, it was shown that many women have a high level of 'n Ach', but that the competitive situation in which it was tested did not arouse their achievement motivation as it did for males. The importance of the context in which achievement takes place is also found in recent studies: women tend to perform better in an all-female group than in a mixed one. The performance of men does not show this patterning of results. Women also take the attitude of their partner toward their accomplishment more seriously than men tend to (Eccles, Adler & Meece, 1984).

The discussion on motivation, gender and culture has shown that individual motives are partly determined contextually. There seems to be a general need among people to become competent and thereby respected members of the society in which they are brought up. If personal achievement is strongly valued in a society, people largely strive for competence in that way. If other values are more prominent, the urge to be a competent member of society will develop in other directions. As always, what men and women in collectivistic or individualistic cultures actually aim to accomplish is the outcome of the interplay between cultural and personal factors.

INTERIM SUMMARY

Three examples of motives were discussed. Hunger is the most studied of all human drives. In early research, the focus was either on peripheral cues or central processing. Both could not entirely explain hunger. Therfore, more recently, an interactive model was postulated. Food intake is regulated by a 'set point', but the regulatory processes do not always function adaptively, which may result in overweightness or eating disorders. Sexual motivation in humans exemplifies the complex interplay between biological and cultural forces. Sexual scripts exert a powerful influence on the actual shaping of sexual behaviour. In some cases, scripts go awry, which may result, for example, in harassment or rape. Achievement motivation provides the impetus for a diverse range of activities. There are gender and cultural differences with respect to the need to achieve. Achievement is also related to the ways in which people attribute their successes and failures.

 ## THE PSYCHOLOGY OF EMOTION

In our discussion of motivation, emotional issues were touched upon on a few occasions, for example, when we discussed the emotional consequences of success and failure, and also in our discussion of sexual motivation. The last section of this chapter is devoted to theories and research about emotion. Among the manifold links between motivational and emotional processes, two general relations stand out. Firstly, motivation may bring about emotions. When we feel motivated, we experience an urge to do something. If we are able to realise our goal, positive feelings like joy generally arise. However, if we are frustrated in what we want, negative feelings, like sadness, come into existence. Secondly, emotions (or 'feelings') can themselves be motivating forces. Being in love, for example, motivates us to minimise the distance between ourselves and the person to whom we are drawn, whilst hatred may urge us to distance ourselves from the individual in question. In general, emotions that occurred in a particular situation tend to become associated with that context in memory. This affective labelling of the situation may motivate us to either approach or avoid it again in the future (Gaskell, 1985).

In the following discussion of the psychology of emotion we will first describe the concept of emotion and some functions emotions serve. Then we will discuss theories of emotion from a biological, cognitive and social constructionist perspective. The section closes by considering the debate about the universal nature of human emotions.

 ## What is an Emotion?

Emotions are elicited by experiences that are important for our general well-being. Reacting emotionally focuses attention on these experiences by marking them as special in some way, by recording them more indelibly in memory and by rousing us to take action. Because emotions involve so many aspects of human functioning, the study of emotions has emerged recently as a central issue in research and theory for a host of psychologists of different theoretical backgrounds.

The history of modern psychology shows that emotions have long been neglected. This was probably due to the tradition in Western philosophy and culture wherein emotions were seen as the enemies of reason: emotions, or rather *passions,* were seen as remnants of our animalistic past. With the rise of cognitive psychology in the 1960s a radically different perspective on emotions was developed. Cognitive theorists argued that the opposition between emotion and reason was artificial because of the fact that emotions generally serve rational functions in human interaction. Rather than 'diseases of the soul', human emotions serve our most personal interests that are crucial for our well-being.

The general consensus among contemporary psychologists employs the term *emotion* to denote various enjoyable or distressing mental states and processes. Emotions include feelings (or **affects**), but the concept of emotion is more encompassing. Emotion is thought of as a complex pattern of bodily and mental changes including physiological arousal, feeling tone, cognitive processes and behavioural reactions made in response to a situation perceived as personally significant (Kleinginna & Kleinginna, 1981). Emotions, in other words, occur when something is at stake for the person concerned. They are generally, but not always, accompanied by bodily excitement (arousal). The cognitive processes are principally concerned with attention and interpretation. The overt behavioural reactions can be expressive (crying, smiling) and action-oriented (running away from the threat). The elements of emotion need further clarification. With respect to the *feeling tone* of emotion this can be done immediately: emotions differ in feeling tone (sometimes also referred to as 'hedonic tone'); sadness feels different from happiness. However, the neurophysiological, cognitive and behavioural aspects of emotion are less evident. Therefore, they are discussed in the following sections.

 Neurophysiological Aspects

Most, though not all, emotions are accompanied by bodily disturbance: a kind of agitation is experienced. The physiological reactions begin with the arousal of the brain as a whole by the *reticular activating system* through which incoming sensory messages pass on their way to the brain (Lindsley, 1951; Zanchetti, 1967). As we saw in Chapter 2, this system functions as a nonspecific, general alarm system for the rest of the brain. Your heart races, respiration goes up, your mouth dries and your muscles tense. In addition to these changes the *autonomic nervous system* (ANS) prepares the body for emotional responses through the action of both its divisions. With mild, unpleasant stimulation, the sympathetic division is more active; with mild, pleasant stimulation, the parasympathetic division is more active. With more intense stimulation of either kind, both divisions are increasingly involved. Physiologically, strong emotions such as fear or anger activate the body's *emergency reaction system* which swiftly and silently prepares the body for potential danger. The sympathetic nervous system takes charge by directing the release of hormones from the adrenal glands which in turn lead the internal organs to release blood sugar, raise blood pressure and increase sweating and salivation. To calm us after the emergency has passed, the parasympathetic nervous system takes over by inhibiting the release of activating hormones. We may remain aroused for a while after an experience of strong emotional activation because some of the hormones continue to circulate in the bloodstream.

The influence of *hormones* on emotion has been shown in several kinds of studies. Changes in emotional response occur in diseases affecting the endocrine glands and when hormones are administered. Steroid hormones, for example, act on many different kinds of body tissue, including nerve cells, by causing them to change their excitability rapidly and directly. They can produce euphoria in short-term low doses but depression in long-term high doses (Majewska *et al*, 1986). Research has also shown that perception of emotional stimuli is accompanied by release of hormones such as adrenalin and noradrenalin. Integration of both the hormonal and the neural aspects of arousal is controlled by the *hypothalamus* and the *limbic system* – old-brain control systems for emotions and for patterns of attack, defence and flight. Either lesioning or stimulation in various parts of the limbic system produces dramatic changes in emotional responding. Tame animals may become killers; prey and predators may become peaceful companions (Delgado, 1969).

Recent neuroanatomy research has focused on the **amygdala** as the part of the limbic system that acts as a gateway for emotion, and as a filter for memory, by attaching significance to the information it receives from the senses. When the amygdala is damaged in accidents or by surgery, a human patient shows no reaction in situations that normally evoke strong emotional responses. Neuroscientist **Joseph LeDoux** (1993) has discovered an anatomical pathway in rats that allows sensory information to go directly to the amygdala before the same information reaches the cortex. The amygdala acts on this raw data to trigger an emotional response *before* the cortex can provide an interpretation of the stimulus event. LeDoux speculates that some people may be overly emotional because their amygdala's response is stronger than the cortex's ability to control it with rational interpretations. The frequent, uncontrollable emotional outbursts of infants may be due to the fact that the parts of the cortex that control emotional responding are not fully developed until some time between 18 and 36 months, long after the amygdala and other emotional centres in the brain are active. In addition, the amygdala seems to record emotional messages in a permanent way; its responsivity is inhibited only by cortical control. When the cortex is surgically prevented from influencing the amygdala, in rats, their strong conditioned fear responses are maintained permanently despite experimental extinction training.

In all complex emotions, the *cortex* is involved through its internal neural networks and its connections with other parts of the body. Research on *lateralisation of emotion* in the human brain is pointing to different emotional centres in the cortex for processing positive and negative emotions. The left hemisphere seems to involve positive emotions, such as happiness, while right-hemisphere activity influences negative emotions, such as sadness and anger (Ahern & Schwartz, 1985; Borod *et al*, 1988; Davidson 1984).

The biochemical responses involved in emotional reactions may differ according to the *meaning* we attach to the situations in which they are experienced. Although tears are associated with sorrow, we cry in response to many types of emotional arousal – for example, when we are angry or extremely happy. Tears also flow from eye-irritating stimuli. When researchers compared the biochemistry of emotional tears and irritant tears, they found that emotional tears (generated when subjects watched a sad film) differ significantly from irritant tears (generated when subjects inhaled the vapour of freshly grated onions). Under emotional conditions, the lacrimal glands secrete a greater volume of tears and also tears with a higher concentration of protein. There are no differences between the sexes on either of these indices (Frey & Langseth, 1986).

Cognitive Aspects

Emotions have attentional properties that are quite powerful. In most instances, they are preoccupying: we may find it difficult to stop thinking about an issue when in an emotional state. Sometimes emotions result in compulsive thinking; then, our whole world revolves around the emotional experience.

The cognitive process of interpretation is crucial in emotion because arousal patterns for many different emotions are similar. The particular emotion that is felt when aroused depends on the way a social situation is interpreted and the meaning attributed to it by the individual. This interpretative process is called **appraisal**, and refers to the contention that sensory experiences lead to emotion only when the stimuli are cognitively interpreted as having personal significance (Arnold, 1960: Lazarus, 1966). The importance of appraisal in emotion comes to the fore if we consider the differences between emotions. Jealousy and anger, for example, are elicited as a result of an unpleasant event for which another person is blamed. Guilt and shame are the result of an event the cause of which is attributed to oneself; this is also the case with pride. One cannot feel guilty about the faults of a Prime Minister (unless perhaps you are a relative); neither can we feel proud about the luck we may have had with the beautiful weather on holiday. As these simple examples show, patterns of appraisal differentiate between emotions.

Behavioural Aspects

Emotions are often outwardly expressed by recognisable facial gestures, bodily postures and tones of voice that are not entirely voluntary. For instance, happiness typically involves smiling, particular patterns of muscle movements around the eyes and a lightness and spontaneity of speech (Oatley, 1992). We will say more about the facial expression of emotion in the section on the alleged universality of emotions at the end of the chapter.

Emotions are generally coupled with a readiness for action. These **action tendencies** differ from emotion to emotion (Frijda *et al*, 1989). When angry, for example, we are motivated to attack and when we are happy we jump with joy. When sad, we may not feel inclined to do anything very much. In other words, emotions tend to go hand in hand with typical actions, or with a typical absence of action, that transform our relation with the world.

FUNCTIONS OF EMOTION

Why do we have emotions? They are functional, because they do many things for us at the motivational, cognitive and communicative levels of experience. Emotions serve a *motivational function* by arousing us to move and to take action with regard to some experienced or imagined event. Action tendencies that are part of emotions may direct and sustain our actions toward specific goals that benefit us, ensuring accomplishment of what is important.

This mandrill monkey is displaying aggression. Notice the bared teeth and clenched jaws that signal others to flee, submit or fight.

The *cognitive function* is mainly concerned with consequences for information processing systems and procedures. **Gordon Bower** (1981), for example, has shown that emotions function in such a way as to affect the processing of information. Most research of this kind is done on **moods**, that is, emotions that last for longer than a few minutes, where the subject is not particularly concerned with how the feeling started. Previously, in Chapter 8, we discussed the effects of moods on memory. Recently, it was found that moods influence people's attraction and interest in activities, other people, stories, films and music (Bower, 1991). It was also shown that happy people offer more creative solutions on standard tests of creativity than do those who are affectively neutral or have been made to experience a negative mood (Isen *et al*, 1987).

Keith Oatley and **Phil Johnson-Laird** (1987) have underscored the twofold *communicative function* which emotions serve: within the cognitive system and between persons. Emotions may amplify or intensify bits of information, or they may signal that something is especially significant, for example because it has self-relevance. In other words, an emotion is like a burglar alarm that signals a disruption, or communicates that something should be attended to: for example, when a successful businessman experiences symptoms of anxiety every time he boasts about his latest successes to his wife; anxiety may communicate an inner conflict of which he was not aware; this new information may motivate the businessman to change his priorities. The communicative function of emotions, however, extends beyond the cognitive apparatus.

Emotions also convey information at the social level (Oatley, 1992). We back off when someone is bristling with anger and approach when another person signals receptivity by a smile, dilated pupils and a 'come hither' glance. They regulate social interaction: as a positive social glue, they bind us to some people; as a negative social repellant, they distance us from others. A substantive amount of research points to the impact of emotion on stimulating prosocial behaviour (Isen, 1984; Hoffman, 1986). When individuals are made to feel good, they are more likely to engage in a variety of helping behaviours. Similarly, when participants in research were made to feel guilty about a misdeed in a current situation, they were more likely to volunteer aid in a future situation, presumably to reduce their guilt (Carlsmith & Gross, 1969).

It is not uncommon that emotions communicate messages that were meant to be concealed from others. For example, when a friend tries to convince you of the fact that he is not angry because you did not show up, but you hear his voice quivering and you see the slight tremble in his hands, these cues lead you to believe that he is not speaking honestly. Emotions may reveal what people are feeling or intending, because they are part of our non-verbal communication system. This silent language of non-verbal bodily messages is difficult to control consciously (Argyle, 1988; Buck, 1984; Mehrabian, 1971).

INTERIM SUMMARY

The concept of emotion refers to mental states and processes that can either be enjoyable or distressing. Emotions include feelings (or affects), but the concept of emotion is more encompassing. It is thought of as a complex pattern of bodily and mental changes including psychological arousal, feeling tone, cognitive processes and behavioural reactions. Emotions occur in response to a situation perceived as personally significant. Emotions serve three functions. The motivational one arouses us to take action. The cognitive function concerns the effects of emotion and moods on the processing of information. The communicative function is twofold: emotions signal within the cognitive system that something important is happening; and between persons, emotions communicate social information. We back away when people look angry and we approach when people smile sympathetically.

✖ THEORIES OF EMOTION

Theories of emotion attempt to explain what causes emotions, what are the necessary conditions for emotion to be engendered and what sequence best captures the way emotions intensify. We will again acknowledge psychology's pluriformity by discussing several perspectives. The biological perspective, which was founded by Darwin, is discussed first. It has dominated thinking about emotion for a long time and it is still influential today. Cognitive theories of emotion, which are discussed thereafter, have been in circulation from the 1960s. Recently, social constructionism has taken part in the debate about the causes and nature of emotion. These theories are discussed in the last part of this section.

✖ The Biological Perspective

Darwin's evolutionary theory laid the groundwork for a biological approach to the study of emotion. In *The Expression of the Emotions in Man and Animals* (1872) he noted similarities of emotional expression between humans and other animals and between adults and children. He took these similarities to be indications of steps in the history of human evolution. Darwin was quite cautious, however, in invoking evolution to explain emotional expression (McGuire, 1993). On the one hand, he argued for the adaptiveness of human emotions. With rage, for example, the heart accelerates, respiration increases and the teeth are clenched. These are all activities necessary to prepare the organism to attack. On the other hand, human emotions were also seen as remnants of previous adaptive behaviour that had persisted in a mild form. For example, when we are angry we still bare our teeth, but few of us do this in order to be ready to bite into our opponent. Thus, even useless aspects of our emotional expressions do not belie their history: they derive from their original adaptive function.

Darwin's followers have generally drawn the adaptiveness of emotions to central stage. Emotions are viewed as inherited, specialised mental states designed to deal with a certain class of recurring situations in the world. They serve an adaptive role in helping organisms to deal with survival issues (Plutchik, 1980). Throughout the history of our species, routinely humans have been attacked by predators, given birth to children, fought each other and confronted their mates' sexual infidelity.

The insight that emotions arise because of their adaptive role in survival, was also shared by **William James** (1890). According to his theory, perceiving a stimulus causes autonomic arousal and other bodily actions that lead to the experience of a specific emotion. As James put it, 'We feel sorry because we cry, angry because we strike, afraid because we tremble' (James, 1890/1950). In short: we feel *after* our body reacts. This view is clearly contrary to common sense. We generally assume that an emotion is induced by the perception of a stimulus, which, in turn, creates a chain of bodily reactions – physiological, expressive and behavioural. The sight of a beautiful person induces feelings of desire. This physically arouses us, which in turn motivates approach reactions and appropriate displays of desire.

James' view that emotion stems from bodily feedback was taken seriously by many psychologists and became known as the *James-Lange theory of emotion*. Carl Lange was a Danish scientist who presented similar ideas in the same year as James. The James-Lange theory is considered a **peripheralist** organic theory because it assigns the most prominent role in the emotion chain to visceral reactions, in particular to the actions of the autonomic nervous system that are peripheral to the central nervous system. Different emotional experiences – of anger, or fear, or joy and so on – from this perspective are envisaged as nothing but an awareness of different physiological response patterns.

Physiologist **Walter Cannon** (1927, 1929) rejected the peripheralist view of emotion in favour of a **centralist** focus on the action of the central nervous system. Cannon stressed the similarity of visceral reactions across different arousal situations – the same heart palpitations accompany aerobic exercise, lovemaking and fleeing danger. He further pointed out that many emotions cannot be distinguished from each other simply by their physiological components. Cannon used rage and fear as an example. They are accompanied by just about the same autonomic discharge, but subjectively are experienced quite differently. According to Cannon, emotion requires that the brain intercedes between the input and output of stimulation and response; it especially requires the involvement of the thalamus and the cortex. Signals from the thalamus get routed to one area of the cortex to produce emotional feeling and to another for emotional expressiveness. The cortical route was expounded by Philip Bard. He argued that an emotion-arousing stimulus has two simultaneous effects, causing both bodily arousal via the sympathetic nervous system and the subjective experience of emotion via the cortex. The views of these physiologists were combined in the *Cannon-Bard theory of emotion*. An emotion stimulus produces two concurrent reactions, arousal and the experience of emotion, which were said not to cause each other.

The debate about the James-Lange theory continues to the present day. The so-called *facial feedback hypothesis* extends the James-Lange line of reasoning by arguing that **facial expression** can be

Facial expression can be helpful in creating emotional experience.

helpful in creating emotional experience. It suggests, for example, that you become angry because you scowl, at least in principle (Ekman, Levinson & Friesen, 1983). Zajonc, Murphy and Inglehart (1989) have added a new element to this hypothesis. They hold that emotions can derive from changes in brain temperature that result from the contraction of facial muscles. Other researchers, however, have recently supported Cannon's critique on the James-Lange theory. Bermond and his colleagues (1991) studied anger and fear with people who suffer from spinal injuries. The paralyses disconnect patients' major sources of bodily excitation. Nevertheless, in such cases there was no evidence of lowered subjective intensity of fear or anger after the injury. Indeed, the experienced intensity of fear and anger was greater following the injury, although, a lowered intensity of physiological disturbance was reported. The debate will no doubt continue. At the moment the cumulative evidence for emotion specific psychophysiological correlates remains inconclusive (Cacioppo *et al*, 1993).

 ## The Cognitive Perspective

Cognitive psychologists take issue with the idea that emotions are automatic reactions to an external event. They also argue that arousal as such is not sufficient to experience an emotion. Cognitivism holds that the event as well as the arousal must be interpreted, that is to say, *appraised*, before an emotion can occur. **Stanley Schachter** was one of the pioneers of this proposition. In their now classic experiment,

participants were autonomically aroused without knowing what caused the arousal. To this end, they were injected with adrenalin (epinephrine). A first group of participants was informed about the effects of the injection. A second group did not receive any information. After the injection had been administered, participants were asked to wait for the experiment to begin. In fact, the experiment took place in the waiting room. Each participant was sitting there alone. Soon he was joined by an alleged fellow participant, who in fact was a confederate of the experimenter. In one condition, the confederate expressed a happy, agreeable mood in the presence of the participant. In the other condition, the confederate acted irritably. Following their stay in the waiting room, the participants were asked to rate how they felt. The results showed that the participants who were correctly informed about the bodily effects of the injection, attributed their arousal to the injection. If the participants in the study had no other explanation for the artificially induced arousal, they labelled it in terms of the characteristics of the immediate situation. So arousal in a context of light-hearted social interaction was experienced as happiness, but where frustration and irritability were expressed, it was experienced as anger (Schachter & Singer, 1962).

An emotion, according to this demonstration, has two components: *arousal* and a *label*. All arousal therein is assumed to be undifferentiated – not very different from the kind of input postulated by James and Cannon. Arousal is assumed as coming first in the emotion sequence. Thus, cognition serves to determine how this ambiguous inner state is labelled. This position has become known as the **two-factor theory of emotion**, which stresses that both physiological arousal and cognitive appraisal are necessary for an emotion to occur. Thus, when there is sympathetic arousal without a known, specified source, a person will search the immediate context for relevant cues to cognitions that can be used to label the arousal and give it meaning as an emotion.

Schachter and Singer showed that independent components of emotion – arousal states and situational cues – could be manipulated experimentally and studied in a laboratory setting. However, some of the specific aspects of the two-factor theory have been challenged. For instance, awareness of one's physiological arousal is not a necessary condition for emotional experience. When experimental subjects are exposed to emotion-inducing stimuli after receiving beta-blockers that reduce heart rate, they still experience anxiety or anger even though minimal signs of physical activation are recordable (Reizenstein, 1983). In addition, experiencing strong arousal without any obvious cause does not lead to a neutral, undifferentiated state, as the two-factor theory assumes. Unexplained arousal is generally interpreted as negative, and taken to mean that something is wrong (Marshall & Zimbardo, 1979; Maslach, 1979). Finally, the two factor theory falls short in explaining the causes of emotion outside the laboratory. The crucial question here is what causes an emotion if it cannot be artificially induced by injecting adrenalin (epinephrine)? Many cognitive theorists now defend the view that emotions are engendered by appraisals. Arousal may accompany the emotion, but this is not a necessary or sufficient condition for emotion to occur (Frijda, 1986; Lazarus, 1991).

Nico Frijda (1986) has developed a comprehensive cognitive theory of emotion. According to him, emotions are sequential processes that follow an orderly pattern (Frijda, 1988). The process typically starts with the perception and appraisal of an event in the social or natural environment. Emotions differ in the kinds of appraisal to which they correspond: fear, for example, is elicited when a situation is appraised as threatening. Events elicit an emotion only if they have *significance* for the individual: emotions occur when something is at stake. The emotion may be accompanied by physiological changes such as increasing heart rate, but it is not a prerequisite. Appraisal results in a tendency to act toward the cause of the emotion. Action tendencies differ from emotion to emotion. Joy, for example, is a happy feeling that comes with a tendency to jump, dance and embrace. Shame is a sad feeling that incites us to disappear from sight. Frijda argues that the tendency to act is the core of an emotion. It may result in actual behaviours, including emotional expressions.

The cognitive theories of emotion of Frijda (1986) and others (e.g., Lazarus, 1991; Mandler, 1975; Oatley & Johnson-Laird, 1987; Scherer, 1984) argue that appraisal is in itself a sufficient cause for an emotion to occur, which does not necessarily mean that bodily excitation is absent. This basic assumption is criticised by psychologists who argue that feelings and preferences are not necessarily derived from appraising a situation, but may be immediate reactions to stimuli, independent of cognitive analysis. We enjoy chocolate and dislike raw liver and we are attracted to smiling faces and repelled by frowns; such immediate 'gut reactions' can occur independently of our reasoning about the stimuli.

Sylvan Tomkins (1962, 1981) was one of the first psychologists to emphasise the pervasive role of immediate, unlearned affective reactions. He points out that infants respond to loud sounds with fear or with difficulties in breathing without cognitive appraisal or prior learning. They seem 'prewired' to respond to certain stimuli with an emotional response general enough to fit a wide range of circumstances. Tomkins sees emotions as the primary motivating

force for human actions that endow any activity with a sense of importance and transform indifference into desire. In this view, without emotion, nothing matters; with emotion, anything can assume significance. Another critique of the cognitive theory of emotion comes from **Robert Zajonc**. He has forcefully argued against the assumed necessity of cognitive elements for affect to occur. Zajonc has shown experimentally how affective judgments (liking and not liking particular words) can be the mere result of greater familiarity with those words. This is called the *mere exposure effect* (Zajonc, 1980). He generalises this observation to the claim that not all affective reactions require cognitive appraisal. Commonly, it is argued to be the other way around: that affect precedes cognition. Zajonc argues we like or dislike something or someone without knowing why. **Richard Lazarus** (1982) has taken issue with Zajonc's claim. A lively debate about cognition and affect has resulted (Lazarus, 1984; Zajonc, 1984). Unfortunately, the debate suffers from definitional problems. Zajonc is not writing about emotion, but about **affect**, which he defines as the positive or negative evaluation of some thing, event or person. As we have seen earlier in this chapter, the concept of emotion is more encompassing. Thus, Zajonc may have a point with general affects, but it is questionable whether emotions can do without appraisal.

✖ The Social Constructionist Perspective

Although cognitivists traditionally focus on the appraisal made by the individual, many among them have recently pointed to the importance of the social context in the production and definition of emotional experience. Oatley (1992), for example, holds that emotions invite others to react, which may result in social interaction. Lazarus (1991) has recently argued that to understand emotions we must spell out the particular person-environment relationship that underlies each emotion. Social constructionists, however, take the issue one step further. They argue that social contexts, which may be large (for example, a culture) or small (for example, a couple), *shape* the emotional life of the individual. Consequently, individual emotional patterns reflect the influence and functions of the social context.

Social constructionists generally emphasise the practical embeddedness of emotions. They prefer to talk about 'doing emotion' instead of 'having an emotion'. According to **James Averill** (1988), emotions are complex syndromes that prescribe behaviour in a certain way. Competent members of a culture know how to behave when they are in love, ashamed, fearful or angry. During an emotion they enter a temporary social role that is derived from the social domain. In his own research on anger, Averill (1982) was able to document the social consequences of anger episodes. Most participants in the study reported that being angry resulted afterwards in a beneficial readjustment of their relationship with the 'object' of their anger. Kenneth and Mary Gergen (1988) have shown how particular social situations result in specific *emotional scenarios*. They found for example, that the sequence in the scenario depends on the way people construct the situation in which they are embedded. If someone, for example, reacts to anger with remorse, the interaction is reconstructed so that the anger scenario ends. When someone, by contrast, reacts with anger *to* anger, an escalation of that emotion is the result.

Many studies in a social constructionist vein focus on the study of emotion vocabularies and the ways in which emotion words are employed in discourse. According to **Rom Harré** (1986) emotion words have a determining influence on emotions, that is, emotions do not have a meaning if they cannot be tagged. In research on emotion 'we would do well to begin by asking: how is the word "anger" and other expressions that cluster around it, actually used in this or that cultural milieu and type of episode?'. Cross-cultural studies of emotional vocabularies clearly show enormous differences in the availability of emotion words. For example, among the Chewong, a small group of aboriginal Malaysians, there are just eight words for emotions; the English language provides its speaker with about 590 emotion words (Oatley, 1993). Nevertheless, it is a moot point as to whether the English have a richer emotional life than the Chewong.

Recently, social constructionists have merged the study of vocabularies with that of emotional practices. It results in a focus on emotion displays as discursive acts (Harré & Gillett, 1994). Emotions are conceived as products of the communicative interaction between people. In other words, both the words they speak and the actions they undertake construct what they experience. In a detailed analysis of the ways in which, for example, a couple talked about jealousy, it was found that their emotional discourse shaped their emotional experience, and thereby also recreated their relationship (Stenner, 1993). This contrasts with the common conception of jealousy and other emotions, where emotion talk is generally seen as a *reflection* of the underlying emotion and of the personalities involved.

By arguing that emotions are put together from parts that derive mainly from culture, social constructionists have put the alleged universality of emotions high on the agenda of psychology. The next section is devoted to this universality issue.

INTERIM SUMMARY

The psychology of emotion has long been dominated by research utilising a biological perspective. These theories hold that emotions are grounded within the workings of biological systems. More recently, cognitive theorists have argued for the centrality of the appraisal process in emotional experiences. According to the cognitivists, the appearance of emotions depends upon the interpretation of physical arousal and social cues in the stimulus situation. Social constructionist theories maintain that the individual emotional experience is shaped largely by processes of communication in socio-cultural contexts.

 ## ARE EMOTIONS UNIVERSAL?

Psychological theories of emotion have generally assumed that people experience emotions similarly, because emotions and their expression are determined by nature. This thesis of **universalism**, however, has been criticised. In Western culture, philosophers, psychologists and others have stressed systematic differences in emotionality between men and women. Other investigators have pointed to cultural differences in emotional experience and expression. Here, we will first briefly discuss the issue of gender.

 ## Gender and Emotion

One of the most persistent ideas about the differences between men and women is that women are more emotional than men. Women are said, for example, to be more expressive, excitable and easily hurt than men. They are also supposed to be more sensitive to the emotions of others. Men are assumed to be rational beings who cannot cope very well with their feelings. Recent research on gender differences in emotion, however, shows that the differences are less clear than is often assumed (Shields, 1991; Fischer, 1993). Men and women differ with respect to fear, sadness, shame and guilt. Women experience these emotions more frequently, more intensely and they express them less reluctantly than men.

This may have to do with the notion that these emotions imply a powerless, or vulnerable self, which is more inconsistent with a traditional masculine identity than with a feminine one. Women, then, more readily admit that they are afraid, sad, ashamed or guilty. For example, a male student may deny that he is scared in anticipation of some important exam and label his feelings as nervousness. A female student, by contrast, may label similar feelings as fear. In general, the empirical studies on gender differences in emotion show that women are not more emotional *per se*, but rather that they show their emotions more often. This greater emotional expressiveness, particularly the most conspicuous difference being that women cry much more than men, may be one of the factors which perpetuates the stereotype of the 'emotional woman' (Fischer, 1993).

✖ Culture and Emotion

Cultural variation in emotion has been studied in detail by cultural anthropologists. They have, for example, described cultural variations in emotion vocabularies, implicit theories of emotion and the local practices with respect to emotional expression. Catherine Lutz (1988) meticulously studied emotional life on Ifaluk, a tiny Micronesian atoll. She described, for instance, how she smiled as she watched a five-year-old girl dance and make silly faces. A woman in the company of Lutz said: 'Don't smile at her – she'll think you are not *song* [justifiably angry]'. The girl was acting out of the emotion *ker* (happiness/excitement), but according to Ifaluk standards her showing off indicated that she was too pleased with herself and not attending to the concerns of others. Mutual concern is the central value on Ifaluk, whereas individual happiness is not valued as it is in most Western countries. Rather, happiness is disapproved by displays of *song* precisely because personal enjoyment may lead one to disregard the interests of others.

The cultural differences between Ifaluk and the West are extensive and so too then are differences in the conditions wherein emotions are expressed and the associated frequencies with which certain ones are displayed. Cultural relativists, however, also have documented differences within the confines of Western culture. It has been argued, for example, that *embarrassment* is a typically British emotion and that the particular mood of sociability and cosiness which the Dutch call 'gezelligheid' is not found in other cultures (Harré, 1990).

Many emotion researchers take issue with relativism. They believe that, despite the variability in emotional experience and behaviour, there is a set of basic emotions that are biologically and experientially distinct. The **emotion wheel** of **Robert Plutchik** (1980, 1984) proposes a set of innate emotions. As *Figure 10.7* shows, the model depicts eight basic emotions, made up of four pairs of opposites:

| **FIGURE 10.7** | THE EMOTION WHEEL |

Plutchik's model arranges eight basic emotions within a circle of opposites. Pairs of these adjacent primary emotions combine to form more complex emotions noted on the outside of the circle. Secondary emotions emerge from basic emotions more remotely associated on the wheel.

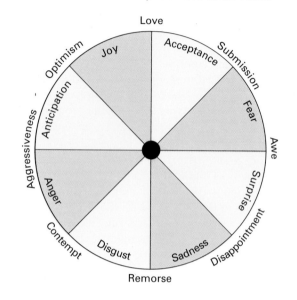

joy-sadness, fear-anger, surprise-anticipation and acceptance-disgust.

All other emotions are assumed to be variations, or blends, of these basic eight. Complex emotions, shown on the outside of the emotional wheel, result from combinations of two adjacent primary emotions. For example, love is conceived as a combination of joy and acceptance; remorse combines sadness and disgust. Plutchik proposes that emotions are most clearly differentiated when they are at high intensities, such as loathing and grief and least different when they are low in intensity, such as disgust and sadness. He also believes that each primary emotion is associated with an adaptive evolutionary response. Disgust is considered an evolutionary outgrowth of rejecting distasteful foods from the mouth, while joy is associated with reproductive capacities.

The universalist conception of emotion as a largely fixed entity which is determined by human nature clearly contrasts with the social constructionist conception. Both views can boast of evidence to support their particular perspective. Theories that view emotion as culturally determined tend to emphasise aspects that are closely connected with the environment, such as the antecedents that may incite an emotion into being. The universalists generally have focused their research on individual emotion elements such as facial expressions. Due to these differences in approach, it is difficult to compare studies. In a recent review, however, Batja Mesquita and Nico Frijda (1992) undertook this task and conclude that global statements about the cross-cultural universality of emotions, or about their cultural determination, are inappropriate. Rather, they advocated that the comparison should focus upon specific aspects of emotion. Mesquita and Frijda observed that cross-cultural similarities as well as differences have been identified in each phase of the emotion process. For example, a particular event, like the loss of a loved one, universally arouses emotions, but the generated tendency to act in particular ways differs from culture to culture. Cultural differences also appear in seeking or avoiding specific kinds of events that could arouse emotions, because of the values attached to these events within the local culture. Support for universality exists, however, for certain specific responses like facial expressions, voice intonations and physiological response modes. Indeed, the facial expressions of emotions have always been central to a universalist account of emotion. The next section discusses this research and the debate in which it has resulted.

Facial Expression of Emotion

If one function of emotion is to prepare and motivate people to respond to the demands of living, then two abilities are essential to coordinate social behaviour. We must be able to communicate effectively our emotional feelings to others and we need to decode the way others are feeling. If, for instance, we can communicate to others that we feel sad and helpless, we increase our chances of soliciting their aid. Similarly, by reading the emotional displays of others, we can predict more accurately when to approach or when to avoid them and when to respond with sensitivity or with firmness.

Emotional facial expression is one of the most effective modes of emotional communication. Ethologists have provided evidence that non-human primates use facial expressions to establish and maintain dominance hierarchies and psychologists have shown that facial expression is an important channel of communication for humans in a variety of social situations. It was found, for example, that children who are good at recognising facial

| FIGURE 10.8 | FACIAL EMOTION EXPRESSIONS |

What emotion is being expressed by each of these faces? Clockwise, starting at the top left, they show happiness, surprise, anger, disgust, contempt, sadness and fear.

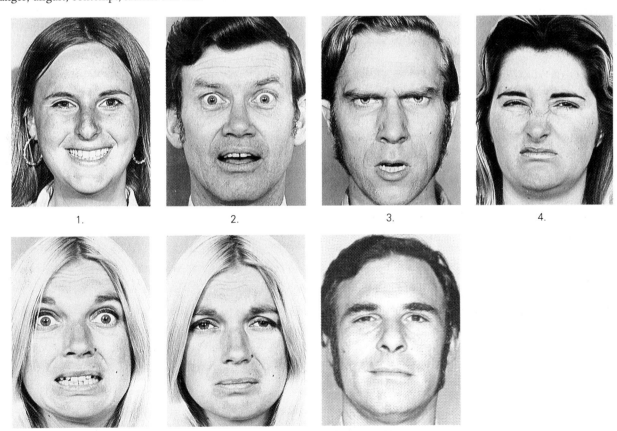

1.   2.   3.   4.

5.   6.   7.

Facial expressions convey a universal message. Although their culture is very different, it is probably not hard for you to tell how these people from New Guinea are feeling.

expressions of emotions in others are more popular among their peers than children who have only developed this capacity to a lesser extent (Manstead, 1992). According to **Paul Ekman**, the leading researcher on the nature of facial expressions, all people speak and understand the same 'facial language', presumably because they are innate components of our evolutionary heritage (Ekman, 1984; Ekman, 1983; Ekman & Friesen, 1975).

This universalist assumption, however, does not exclude cultural influences. According to Ekman, culture plays a role with respect to emotion. The so-called *display rules* prescribe the nature of emotional displays in particular settings. Despite these differences in display, people all over the world, regardless of cultural differences, race, sex, or education, express basic emotions in the same way and, depending on the context, are able to identify the emotions others are experiencing by reading their facial expressions. Take the facial emotion identification test in *Figure 10.8* (previous page) to see how well you can identify these seven universally recognised facial expressions of emotion (Ekman & Friesen, 1986). There is considerable evidence that these seven expressions are recognised and produced worldwide in response to the emotions of happiness, surprise, anger, disgust, fear, sadness and contempt.

Cross-cultural researchers ask people from a variety of cultures to identify the emotions associated with a variety of expressions in standardised photographs. The participants are generally able to identify the expressions associated with the seven listed emotions. Children over age five can detect the emotion depicted in stimulus displays about as accurately as college students.

In one of Ekman's studies, members of a preliterate culture in New Guinea (the Fore culture),

who had almost no exposure to Westerners or to Western culture prior to this experiment, accurately identified the emotions expressed in the Caucasian faces shown in *Figure 10.8*. They did so by referring to situations in which they experienced the same emotion. For example, photograph five (fear) suggested being chased by a wild boar when you did not have your spear and photograph six (sadness) suggested your child had died. Their only confusion came in distinguishing surprise from fear, perhaps because these people are most fearful when taken by surprise. Next, researchers asked other members of the culture (who had not participated in the first study) to model the expressions that they used to communicate six of the emotions (excluding contempt). When North American college students viewed videotapes of the facial expressions of the Fore people, they were able to identify their emotions accurately – with two exceptions. Not surprisingly, the Americans had difficulty distinguishing between the Fore poses of fear and surprise, the same emotions that the Fore had confused in the Western poses.

Emotion researchers generally agree about which specific facial muscle movements are associated with each of the basic emotions (Smith, 1986). Studies that record facial muscle movements while subjects imagine various mood settings show specific patterns of muscle groups that are different for happy, sad and angry thoughts (Schwartz, 1975). For example, the expression of happiness consists of raised mouth corners (a smile) and tightened lower eyelids; the expression of surprise consists of raised eyebrows, raised upper eyelids that widen the eyes and an open mouth; and the expression of fear is very similar to the expression of surprise, except that, in addition to being raised, the eyebrows are pulled together and lowered back down slightly into an eyebrow frown. (The similarity between the two expressions might explain why subjects had such trouble discriminating between them.)

The results from the studies about facial expression are widely accepted among psychologists who study emotion. Some, however, have criticised the approach. Fridlund (1990), for example, asserts that facial expressions are communicative gestures rather than expressions of internal emotional states. In his research he found that people smile more when they watch a film together with others than when alone. James Russell (1994) reviewed the cross-cultural studies on facial expression and elaborates upon a serious critique of the methodology of this empirical tradition. Russell documents that almost all of the studies used preselected photographs of posed facial expressions. So, the participants had to recognise posed expressions rather than facial expressions as they occur in ordinary interaction. The participants further had to express their judgement by ticking the emotion they recognised on a list provided by the experimenter. This list consisted of either emotion names or descriptions of emotional situations. This forced-choice response format seriously constrained the judgement of the participants. If, by contrast, participants were allowed to express their judgement spontaneously, the universal recognition of facial expressions was reduced drastically. The judges then had serious difficulty in distinguishing between expressions of anger, frustration and disgust. The participants also tended to confuse fear and surprise.

In his conclusion, Russell argues that the plausibility of *universalism* has led researchers and theorists on emotion to pursue a one-sided emphasis on supportive evidence. Nevertheless, Russell does not advocate *relativism*. Rather, he strives to raise questions about influential studies on facial expression in order to take the dialogue one step further. Ekman (1994) responded to the challenge by grimly defending the robustness of his own findings, arguing that Russell had neglected important evidence in his review. According to Ekman, Russell erected a 'straw man', a universalist who refuses to admit to cultural variations in facial expression, and who therefore would be easily knocked down if agreement across cultures were demonstarted to be less than perfect. Ekman feels that Russell misrepresents his views, which emphasised both universalities and cultural differences. The Russell-Ekman debate reveals important details in the study of facial expression and key problems associated with its ecological validity. The argument's impact on the universality issue will be considerable, because it is concerned with both the universalist *assumption* and its empirical underpinnings.

recapping main points

⊃ The Psychology of Motivation

Motivation is a dynamic concept used to describe the processes involved in starting, directing and maintaining physical and psychological activities. Psychologists have sought to explain the origins of animal and human behaviour via a host of different theories. These theories can be categorised in terms of three main motivational systems: biological, cognitive and social.

⊃ Theories of Motivation

Theories under the heading of biological motivation concentrate on homeostatic and mechanistic physiological mechanisms. Instinct theories developed out of Darwin's ground-breaking ideas about evolution, but could not accommodate the complexity and flexibility of human behaviour. Drive theories were less rigid, but could not adequately explain why people continue to exert themselves when their drives are satisfied. Arousal theories attempted to explain the conspicuous desire to seek out stimulation, but are still concerned with the interplay between drives and situational stimuli, without paying much attention to the individuals in between. Theories under the heading of cognitive motivation assign the thinking, deciding and choosing person a central place in motivating processes. Consistency theories can be considered as homeostatic with regard to psychological processes. Expectancy-value theory states that the persistence of our behaviour is determined by a combination of our expectation about attaining a goal and the value we attach to that goal. The concept effectance motivation refers to the notion that people are dispositionally motivated to be effective in dealing with their environment. We all want to be competent persons. It is conceived of as a biologically mediated need, but the way it takes form and shape is dependent on the culture we live in. Maslow postulated a hierarchy of needs in which deficiency as well as growth motivation have a place. Deci and Ryan believe that people not only strive toward competence, but also toward self-determination (also referred to as autonomy). Social motivation concerns the need to belong to the social world. Like the further development of competence, the outgrowth of belongingness is also dependent on cultural standards.

⊃ Hunger and Eating

Hunger is the most studied of all human drives. Early researchers mistakenly sought to explain hunger as the result of peripheral stimulation of stomach contractions. Hunger cannot be entirely explained by central processes in the brain. Complex interactions of the brain, hormonal system, local stimulation and psychological factors motivate hunger. Food intake and body weight are regulated according to a 'set point' which is measured by fat stored in specialised fat cells. In some cases, regulation of body weight goes awry and results in obesity, anorexia nervosa or bulimia.

⊃ Sexual Motivation

Sexual motivation in animals is largely controlled by hormones. In human sexual motivation, biological and cultural factors are linked inextricably. The empirical studies of Kinsey and Masters & Johnson provided insight into sexual attitudes and behaviour, especially with regard to the sexual response cycle of men and women. Discrepancies in sexual scripts can lead to serious misunderstandings between the sexes. During the past century, psychologists have attempted to account for homosexuality, but none of the theories has as yet provided a satisfactory explanation of this form of human sexuality.

⊃ Achievement Motivation

Achievement motivation is future oriented and provides the impetus for a diverse range of human activities. People have varying needs for achievement. Women and men tend to differ in their orientation toward achievement, but not in the sense that women accomplish less than men. Societies that emphasise individualism generally value personal achievement strongly, in contrast with collectivistic cultures. Motivation for achievement is influenced by how people interpret success and failure: attributional styles, for example, an optimistic or a pessimistic one, engender different attitudes toward achievement and thus influence motivation.

The Psychology of Emotion

An emotion involves a patterning and complexity of processes, including those at the level of physiological arousal, brain mechanisms, experienced feelings and cognitive appraisal, as well as behavioural and expressive reactions. These changes occur in response to situations perceived as personally significant. The amygdala in the limbic system processes emotional signals in a direct, immediate fashion, while the cortex is involved in interpreting the meaning of the emotional stimulus and providing the big picture. Emotions serve many vital functions at the motivational, cognitive and behavioural levels of experience, such as arousing, directing and sustaining actions.

Theories of Emotion

Three psychological theories of emotion are discussed. The biological perspective holds that emotions are grounded within psychophysiological processes. Some theorists have defended a peripheralist model which makes visceral arousal feedback the important component in emotion. Others have worked from a centralist model in which brain processing causes both arousal and emotional feelings. As an important determinant of emotional experience, cognitive theories highlight the role of the interpretation of arousal and of social cues in the stimulus situation. Social constructionists focus on the communicative nature of emotion by maintaining that the socio-cultural context actually shapes the emotional process.

Are Emotions Universal?

Psychologists generally assume that emotions and emotional expressions are universal. Research on the facial expression of emotion has shown that although cultures vary in the display rules that specify the social appropriateness of showing certain emotions, seven emotional expressions are universally recognised across cultures – happiness, surprise, anger, disgust, fear, sadness and contempt. Recently, however, researchers have taken issue with the alleged universality of emotions and of their expression by documenting cultural and gender differences.

key Terms

achievement motivation
action tendencies
affect
affiliation motivation
amygdala
androgens
appraisal
arousal theories
attributions
autonomous person
biological motivation
centralist theory of emotion
collectivistic
cognitive motivation
competence
consistency theories
critical set point
deficiency motivation
drive theories
drive reduction
effectance motivation
emotion wheel
expectancy value theories
extrinsic motivation
facial expression
fear of failure

fear of success
growth motivation
homeostasis
individualistic
instinct theories
intrinsic motivation
locus of control
monocausality
moods
needs hierarchy
oestrogen
optimal arousal
peripheralist
pheromones
primary drive
reversal theory
secondary drive
sexual scripts
sexual response cycle
social motivation
testosterone
thematic apperception test (TAT)
two factor theory of emotion
universalism
Yerkes-Dodson law

major Contributors

Apter, Michael
Atkinson, John
Averill, James
Bower, Gordon
Buck, Ross
Cannon, Walter (1871–1945)
Darwin, Charles (1809–1892)
Deci, Edward
Ekman, Paul
Festinger, Leon
Freud, Sigmund (1856–1939)
Frijda, Nico
Harré, Rom
Horner, Matina
Hull, Clark (1884–1952)
James, William (1842–1910)
Johnson, Virginia
Johnson-Laird, Phil
Kinsey, Alfred (1894–1956)
Kitayama, Shinobu
Kitzinger, Celia

Lazarus, Richard
LeDoux, Joseph
Lewin, Kurt (1890–1947)
Markus, Hazel
Maslow, Abraham (1908–70)
Masters, William
McClelland, David
McDougall, William (1871–1938)
Murray, Henry (1893–1988)
Nuttin, Joseph (1909–88)
Oatley, Keith
Plutchik, Robert
Rotter, Julian
Ryan, Richard
Schachter, Stanley
Seligman, Martin
Tolman, Edward (1886–1959)
Tomkins, Sylvan
Weiner, Bernard
White, Robert
Zajonc, Robert

Chapter 11

Health Psychology

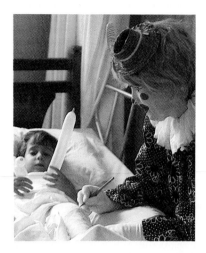

Melanie went to the hospital to visit Emma, a neighbour who had broken her hip. The first thing Melanie saw when the lift door opened at the third floor was a clown with an enormous orange nose dancing down the hall, pushing a colourfully decorated trolley. The clown stopped in front of Melanie, bowed, and then tumbled head over heels to the nurses' station. A cluster of patients cheered. Most of them were in wheelchairs or on crutches. Upon asking for directions, Melanie learned that Emma was in the 'humour room', where a *Tom 'n' Jerry* cartoon was about to start.

In Great Britain, as elsewhere, the idea that laughter may be one of the best medicines has been catching on: since 1991 stress therapist Richard Holden has run over 70 workshops in a Birmingham-based National Health Service laughter clinic. He believes it is important to teach nurses and doctors, as well as patients, how to use humour to enhance their professional practice and to cope with the stresses of health care (Holden, 1993). This is not an isolated case: in Geneva, Switzerland, Dr Tal Schaller at his Foundation Soleil holds frequent 'Hilatherapie' sessions where patients learn to laugh to order in 'waves or cascades'.

Since writer **Norman Cousins**' recovery from a debilitating and usually incurable disease of the connective tissue (*ankylosing spondylitis*), humour has gained new respectability in hospital wards around the world. Cousins, with the co-operation of his physician, supplemented his orthodox medical therapy with a steady diet of Marx Brothers movies and *Candid Camera* film clips. Although he never claimed that laughter alone

produced his cure, Cousins is best remembered for his passionate support of the notion that, if negative emotions can cause distress, then humour and positive emotions can enhance the healing process (Cousins, 1979, 1989).

The idea was popular of course even before it had much empirical support. Today, some progressive hospitals provide patients with videotapes of funny films. For example, Lars Ljungdahl, a general practitioner in Motala, Sweden, regularly takes a 'Comedy Cart' full of humourous books and tapes through the halls of local community health centres. In the United States, Allen Funt, creator of *Candid Camera*, has set up a foundation to distribute his funny videos free of charge to researchers, hospitals and individual patients in the hope of applying humour therapy for distress and illness and investigating the effects of such therapy.

What are the medical benefits of humour? Cousins' doctor found that his sedimentation rate (a measure of inflammation) decreased after only a few moments of robust laughter. This decrease in inflammation was also reflected in Cousins' ability to enjoy two hours of pain-free sleep after ten minutes of hearty laughing (Cousins, 1989). Psychiatric researcher William Fry compares laughter to 'stationary jogging'. Increases in respiration, heart rate and blood circulation created by laughing bring oxygen to the blood at a rate as much as six times greater than during ordinary speech (Fry, 1986). Some biochemical changes, including reductions in the stress hormone cortisol, have also been detected (Berk *et al,* 1989). Salivary immunoglobulin A, which is thought to protect the body against certain viruses, has been found to increase significantly in people who viewed funny tapes for 30 minutes. In addition, people who said they used humour to deal with difficult situations in everyday life had the highest baseline levels of this protective substance (Dillon & Totten, 1989).

The therapeutic use of positive emotions to overcome illness has enhanced public awareness of the relatively new and exciting field of psychoneuroimmunology, the study of potentially healing interactions between brain, body, emotions and the immune system. Researchers hope that advances in this area will help explain the physiological underpinnings of laughter's health promoting effects.

EMOTIONS, SUCH AS the happiness that results from humour, are fundamental to human experience; they give richness to our interactions with people and our contacts with nature, joy to our existence, significance to our memories and hope to our expectations. Emotions, stress, illness and health are all entwined in this humour approach to treating physical ailments.

In this chapter, we will put together these concerns as we look at an emerging and important new area: **health psychology**. Health psychologists investigate the ways in which environmental, social, psychological and biological processes combine and contribute to the development of illness and health. Of concern, in particular, are the ways in which such knowledge can be used to both prevent illness and promote and maintain health – a strategy known as **primary prevention**. **Stress** is a central focus here. If the *demands* on our biological and psychological *resources* and functioning are excessive, we may become overwhelmed and unable to deal with the stressors in our daily lives. In considering the work of health psychologists then, this chapter will later examine how stress affects us and is implicated in the progression of our well-being. But first, let us look at the origins and scope of health psychology in more detail.

◆ HEALTH PSYCHOLOGY – DEVELOPMENT AND DEFINITION

The acknowledgment of the importance of psychological and social factors in health has spurred the growth of this new field. Health psychology is devoted to understanding the way people stay healthy, the reasons they become ill, and the way they respond when illness does occur (Taylor, 1986, 1990). It was only during the latter half of the 1970s in North America and the 1980s in Europe that this new and distinctive sub-discipline formally came into being. The *American Psychological Association* (APA) had set up a task force to examine the role of psychology in relation to physical health. In its report in 1976 it was concluded that insufficient work had been conducted by psychologists on how best to maintain health, how to prevent illness and how best to deliver health care. Shortly afterwards, the APA set up a *Division of Health Psychology* within its formal organisational structure. It was only in 1987, however, that European psychologists followed suit by setting up their equivalent Health Psychology Society, with a similar section within the *British Psychological Society* being established also in that year. In his foundational article, **Joseph Matarazzo** (1980) defined this new arena as follows:

> *Health psychology is the aggregate of the specific educational, scientific and professional contributions of the discipline of psychology to the promotion and maintenance of health, prevention and treatment of illness, the identification of aetiologic and diagnostic correlates of health, illness and related dysfunction and the improvement of the health care system and health policy formation.*

Health can be conceived as a state of *complete* physical, mental and social well-being and not merely the absence of disease or infirmity. This is a key distinguishing feature of health psychology, that interest is focused upon exploring the psychosocial conditions which maintain and accentuate well-being. It is not just concerned with identifying those conditions which pave the way to physical illness or back again to health. Thus, Matarazzo's definition places firm emphasis upon the important role of psychological processes in preventative health care.

The definition highlights a problem for health psychology, however, in that included within it, is mention of the 'treatment of illness', that is to say of **secondary prevention**. The proposition that this is a focal and organising constituent of health psychology has in part led to confusion with clinical psychology and behavioural medicine, both of which exist to take a much more remediative approach to pre-existing mental and physical health difficulties. The latter took its impetus from learning theory, employing behaviour modification techniques to evaluate and manage the treatment of physical disease and physiological dysfunction. As it has developed, however, behavioural medicine has gone beyond its behaviourist roots. Now it is a much broader, more interdisciplinary field, drawing on knowledge from a wide variety of disciplines and focusing on **secondary care**, rather than upon aetiology (Kaptein & van Rooijen, 1990). Importantly, health psychology's distinctiveness lies in its insistence upon identifying psychosocial phenomena which prevent degeneration into ill-health and those which promote and maintain health, effectively decreasing the need for later secondary interventions. Health psychology as defined here, then, is much more closely aligned with that which Matarazzo (1980) has referred to as '**behavioural health**': a *'new interdisciplinary subspecialty . . . concerned with the maintenance of health and the prevention of illness and dysfunction in currently healthy persons'.*

By way of clarification, mention must be made of a third form of intervention, namely **tertiary care**: when a disease or injury progresses to the point of lasting or irreversible damage, then action may be taken to limit its further development or to rehabilitate the person as much as is possible. Physiotherapy after a compound fracture of a limb or giving medication to a patient with terminal cancer for pain relief are examples of tertiary interventions. These are the province, in the main, of behavioural medicine wherein practices are brought in to assist when the proverbial horse of health has long since bolted. Health psychology's focal role here would be to have promoted preventative behaviours that would have made the fracture an unlikely occurence in the first instance, or to have avoided the carcinogenic substances as implicated in the pathogenesis of the life-threatening illness. Nevertheless, the *experience* of illness, plus the diversity of ways in which illnesses are represented, and our reactions to those constructed images of illness necessarily all involve social and psychological processes (Fallowfield, 1991; Radley, 1993). Thereby, they have become of interest to many health psychologists, despite the implications of such work for primary preventative strategy not always being immediately obvious. Although primary care, in terms of theory, research and application, is a central focus, we will be considering health psychology here also with respect to both secondary and tertiary forms of intervention.

◆ The Biopsychosocial Model of Health

During the first half of this century, Western scientific thinking relied exclusively on a biomedical model that entertains a dualistic conception of body and mind. According to this model, the physical body is conceived as *separate* from the psyche; the mind is important only for emotions and beliefs and it has little to do with the reality of the soma (body). However, more recent research has looked at links between the nervous system, the immune system, behavioural styles, cognitive processing and environmental factors which, in combination, can put us at risk of illness or increase our resistance to stress, trauma and disease. Health psychology, then, considers that biological, psychological and social factors are implicated in all stages of health and illness (Taylor, 1990).

This view is termed the **biopsychosocial model** of health and illness (Engle, 1976) and without doubt it has become the guiding framework for health psychology research and practice. By contrast, within conventional medicine much specialisation has developed around particular diseases. Health psychology though, insists upon cutting across these boundaries to focus upon psychosocial processes which may more generally apply and are not disease specific. Such concerns include, for example: the operation of social support; individual differences in coping behaviour; and the role in health of major and minor life events. Thus, the inseparability of the biological, psychological and social aspects of health has necessitated the generation of this new descriptor – biopsychosocial – to aptly reflect the existent synthesis of these interrelated levels of human functioning and experience. Such a framework constitutes a significant challenge to conventional medical models in which health may be reduced to a purely biological level of analysis.

Nevertheless, psychological principles have been applied in the treatment of illness and the pursuit of health for all of recorded time. Many ancient cultures understood the importance of communal health and relaxation rituals in the enhancement of the quality of life. Among the Navajo, for example, disease, illness and well-being have been attributed to social harmony and mind-body interactions. The Navajo concept of *hozho* (pronounced whoa-zo) means harmony, peace of mind, goodness, ideal family relationships, beauty in arts and crafts and health of body and spirit. Illness is seen as the outcome of any disharmony, being caused by evil introduced through violation of taboos, witchcraft, overindulgence, or bad dreams. Tribal healing ceremonies seek to banish illness and restore health, not only through the medicine of the shaman, but also through the combined efforts of all family members who work together with the ill person to re-achieve a state of hozho. The illness of any member of a tribe is seen not as his or her individual responsibility (and fault) but rather as a sign of broader disharmony that must be repaired by communal healing ceremonies. This cultural orientation guarantees a powerful social support network that automatically comes to the aid of the sufferer.

Similarly, among the Nyakusa of Tanzania, Africa, any sign of disharmony or deviation from the expected 'norm' generates a swift communal intervention to set the situation right. Thus, strong anger, the birth of twins, the sudden death of a young person and illness are all signs of an anomaly because they are unusual events for this tribe. Special tribal rituals are quickly enacted around the person or family in which the discord occurs. One feature of these rituals is evidence of the social acceptance of the person(s) afflicted (Wilson, 1959).

◆ Mind and Body in Health and Illness

Health refers to the general condition of the body and mind in terms of their soundness and vigour. As we have stated, it is not simply the absence of illness or injury but is more a matter of outlook and of how well we feel the body is working. 'To be healthy is to have the ability, despite an occasional bout of illness, to live with full use of your faculties and to be vigourous, alert and happy to be alive, even in old age' (Insel & Roth, 1985).

Whilst acknowledging the dangers of inappropriate psychologisation of illness (Goudsmit & Gadd, 1991), your physical health, nevertheless, is inextricably linked to your state of mind, to your behaviour and to the world around you. Health psychologists view health as a dynamic, multidimensional experience. Optimal health, incorporates in the physical, intellectual, emotional, spiritual, social and environmental domains of health the ability to function fully. When you undertake any activity for the purpose of preventing disease or detecting it early on, in the asymptomatic stage, you are exhibiting health behaviour (Kasl & Cobb, 1966). A healthy habit, or behavioural pattern, is one that operates without the necessity of extrinsic reinforcement or incentives and that contributes directly to your overall health (Hunt et al, 1979).

Health psychology, though, has not emerged simply in response to a medical model which dissociates mind from body. Its historical roots prior to this time were already in evidence through links with clinical psychology and behavioural medicine. In addition, the field of psychosomatic medicine has also

long recognised that health cannot be reduced merely to simple biological causes. Indeed, Freud, the founder of psychoanalysis, appreciated how psychological phenomena such as intrapsychic conflict may become converted into physical symptomatology, for example as a temporary state of insensitivity to pain in the absence of any identifiable organic pathology. Health psychologists do not believe though, that all illness is psychological in origin. Such a claim would not be tenable, for example, with respect to infectious disease, though psychological antecedents are likely to be implicated even here.

Is there a difference between illness and illness behaviour? Illness involves documented pathology, such as biological or physiological damage, cell pathology, and blood chemistry. However, if you have missed a lecture you did not really want to go to because of a stomach ache, you were exhibiting illness behaviour. Regardless of whether you were really ill, illness behaviour (saying 'ouch', seeing a doctor, or taking medicine, for example) does not necessarily implicate underlying physical pathology (Taylor, 1990). A growing number of biopsychosocial researchers are calling for the application of behavioural indicators of illness or behavioural outcomes as dependent measures in empirical studies.

◆ Health Psychology and National Resolve

The promotion of health requires not only focusing on the psychology of individuals but also on national and international efforts that go beyond single members of society to systemwide involvement. At the 30th World Health Assembly (1977), a resolution was adopted which specified that the main social goal of governments and of the World Health Organization in the coming decades should be to make possible for all citizens of the world a level of health that would permit each one of us to lead a socially and economically productive life by the year 2000. In the following year at a further international meeting, it was agreed that this goal would best be attained through the provision of extended primary health care services. It was recommended that all governments should formulate national policies to launch and sustain such care as part of comprehensive health service provision.

It is within the context of this wider global initiative that national ones more latterly have been developed. In Great Britain in 1992, the Department of Health issued its 'white paper', The Health of The Nation. This document set out an ambitious plan of targets for the year 2000, for example: to reduce death

TABLE 11.1 HEALTH OBJECTIVES FOR THE YEAR 2000

Priority Area

Health Promotion

1. Exercise and Physical Fitness
2. Nutrition
3. Tobacco/Smoking
4. Alcohol and Other Drugs
5. Family Planning
6. Mental Health and Disorder
7. Violent and Abusive Behaviour
8. Educational and Community-Based Programmes

Health Protection

9. Accidents
10. Occupational Safety and Health
11. Environmental Health
12. Food and Pharmacological Safety
13. Oral Health

Preventive Services

14. Maternal and Infant Health
15. Heart Disease and Stroke
16. Hypertension
17. Cancer
18. Diabetes and Chronic Disabling Conditions
19. HIV Infection
20. Sexually Transmitted Diseases
21. Immunisation and Infectious Diseases
22. Clinical Preventive Services

Surveillance

23. Screening, Monitoring and Data Systems

rates for diseases of the circulatory system, both coronary heart (*cardiovascular*) disease and stroke (*cerebrovascular disease*) by 40 per cent; to reduce the death rate for breast cancer in the population invited for screening by at least 25 per cent; and to reduce the incidence of invasive cervical cancer by at least 20 per cent. By the year 2005 the death rate for accidents among children under 15 should be reduced, its says, by at least 33 per cent. Likewise, in the United States of America, the Department of Health and Human Services, in a report titled *Healthy People 2000*, outlined three national public health goals and objectives for the 1990s: (a) to increase the span of healthy life; (b) to reduce the disparities in health status among different populations, such as the poor, minorities and children; and (c) to provide access to preventive health care services for all people.

In formulating these targets, recognition is being made that cardiovascular disease, cancers of all kinds, strokes and accidents are the four leading causes of premature death in the European and North American regions of the world. On these continents infectious diseases caused by harmful bacteria and viruses, such as tuberculosis and polio, are no longer the main sources of terminal illness. With the exception of those regions

in eastern Europe currently undergoing considerable social and political upheaval, these causes have gone into decline during the twentieth century as a result of advances in preventative measures and secondary medical care. Beyond such geographical areas, however, infectious disease is still a very significant factor in the health profile of many nations, especially so on the African continent.

Implicit in ambitious plans for the development of the new primary care frontier is a recognition that the major health problems and life-threatening illnesses in socially and technologically advanced countries are chronic diseases, ones which are degenerative and progress over a lengthy period of time, specifically heart disease, cancer and stroke. Within the nations of the European Union, for example, circulatory diseases (heart and stroke) account for 44 per cent of all deaths, cancers for 25 per cent (World Health Organization, 1993). Similarly, in the United States these diseases account for approximately two thirds of all deaths (USBC, 1991). We may expect to see further organising efforts to prevent the development of these diseases since the Maastricht Treaty (CECECC, 1993) provides a legal framework (Article 129) within the realm of work and public health in which future plans for coordinated action and provision may be devised.

◆ HEALTH PROMOTION AND MAINTENANCE

Arising from these national and international resolves has been an increasing move amongst health professionals towards primary care: promoting behaviour which facilitates the avoidance of disease, ill-health or injury, towards prevention in the first instance and away from having to 'cure' an already established condition. Treating an illness once it has developed is of course, the traditional medical model of 'secondary care'. Health psychologists and other professionals are increasingly recognising that such a reactive stance is inadequate if we are one day to achieve a 'health-for-all' objective. The more proactive primary care approach is needed, one which necessarily gives ready access to preventative health care services situated within local communities.

Over the past 40 years in particular, the maintenance of health has come to be understood by psychologists and other health professionals as in part to be the long-term consequence of a variety of psychosocial processes. Such processes, for example, may include behaviours we either avoid, for example, smoking tobacco and over-eating; or enact, such as taking exercise regularly. It is recognised, however, that for many people there are often few realistic opportunities to engage in health promoting non-sedentary lifestyles, given the contextual constraints of available personal and local resources. Other examples of such psychosocial processes, nevertheless, might include social cognitions we may make about future challenges, seeing them negatively as threats to security rather than positively as possible achievements; attributing self-critical meaning to

Being often in a hurry, humourless and prone to hostility is detrimental to health and well-being.

interpersonal events that involve loss; comparing ourselves unfavourably with others; or, responding frequently with hostility in social scenarios we find problematic or difficult. Repeated over time, such apparently benign psychological processes have tangible and cumulative implications in terms of the stress and strain placed on our biological and somatic well-being. A careful unpacking and understanding of these processes by health psychologists, then, has very real implications for the form and content of services which are increasingly being required to focus on the primary prevention of illness and on the promotion of well-being. Let us consider health psychology's contributions to knowledge about how to stay healthy – to primary prevention – and thereafter examine in brief its more limited input to secondary and tertiary care.

◆ Staying Healthy – Primary Prevention

The role of behavioural factors in the prevention of disease and the maintenance of health are becoming clearer as the findings of research accumulate (Maes et al, 1994). Health psychologists advocate that we evaluate our beliefs about health, change dysfunctional lifestyles and begin to take those extra behavioural steps toward good health. Modelling beliefs about the maintenance of health and empirically examining hypotheses derived from these theoretical frameworks has been a major task for health psychologists. Integrating the outcomes of research upon Becker's (1974) **Health Belief Model** and Bandura's (1977b) **Self-efficacy Theory**, Rogers (1984), in his emergent **Protection-Motivation Theory**, observes that four elements influence the likelihood of someone engaging in a healthy habit or changing a detrimental one. The person must believe that: (a) the threat to health is of a severe magnitude; (b) the perceived personal vulnerability and/or the likelihood of developing the disorder is high; (c) he or she is able to perform the response that will reduce the threat (i.e. believes in the efficacy of the self in this respect); and that (d) the response will be effective in overcoming the threat (i.e. believes in the efficacy of the response) (Bandura, 1986; Janz & Becker, 1984).

Modifying health behaviours and beliefs, though, is not a simple matter. For example, in adolescence, poor health habits have been associated with 'peer group influence and issues of personal identity' (Botvin & Eng, 1982). Even when health habits change for the better, there is always the threat of relapse. New health habits need to be practised regularly to become automatic. However, it is difficult to make new resolve and new actions routine when you remain in the behavioural setting that reinforced the unhealthy behaviour patterns. Without changing their environment, ex-convicts, recovered drug addicts and weight clinic clients often relapse into former ways of behaving even when they have learned new, more appropriate, healthy behaviours.

Cognitive orientation and health

A series of studies by Israeli psychologists shows that health-oriented individuals have a cognitive orientation related to physical health and absence of symptoms (Kreitler & Kreitler, 1990). This cognitive-motivational factor, which seems to be characteristic of the person, reflects an emphasis on a positive internal atmosphere (feelings of love, joy, contentment), positive daydreams and inhibition of negative emotions; an active sense of personal control and efficacy; repression of daily threats to keep anxiety low; de-emphasis on bodily concerns; and a matter-of-fact problem-solving focus (Kreitler & Kreitler, 1991c).

A surprising result emerging from a considerable body of research is the mental health advantage of maintaining a distorted perception of the self, the world, and the future in the form of *positive illusions* (Taylor & Brown, 1988; Taylor, 1989). When an individual is receiving negative feedback or being threatened in other ways, apparently adaptive behaviour is to filter such incoming information through self-perceptions that are overly positive, unrealistically optimistic, and exaggerate feelings of personal control over events. These characteristics of human thought promote other aspects of mental health such as the abilities to care about others, be happy and content, and engage in productive and creative work. Indeed, a long-term research programme by **Martin Seligman** (1991) and his associates corroborates these findings by pointing the healthy finger at one aspect of personal outlook, namely optimism. Optimistic people have been found to have fewer physical symptoms of illness, to be faster at recovering from certain illnesses, are generally healthier and live longer (Peterson *et al*, 1988).

Talking to sympathetic others about personal problems can also promote good health in tangible ways. A large body of research by health psychologist **James Pennebaker** (1990) has shown that suppressing thoughts and feelings associated with personal traumas, failures and guilty or shameful experiences takes a devastating toll on mental and physical health. Such inhibition of self-disclosure is psychologically hard work and, over time, it undermines the body's defences against illness. Confiding in others neutralises the negative effects of inhibition; there are immediate changes in brainwave patterns and skin conductance levels, drops in blood pressure and improvements in immune functions. This experience of letting go often is followed by improved physical and psychological health weeks and months later.

Health, behaviour and disease

What other preventive strategies are there to be deployed in the struggle against the life-cycle and the onward march of time? One approach is to change or eliminate poor health habits. Examples of this strategy are programmes to help people become or stay healthy, stop smoking, exercise, lose excess weight and be aware of sexually transmitted diseases and how to prevent them.

Illness prevention means developing general strategies and specific tactics to eliminate or reduce the risk that people will get sick. The prevention of illness in the 1990s poses a very different challenge from that at the turn of the century when the primary cause of death was infectious disease. Health practitioners at that time launched the first revolution in public health. Through the use of research, public education, the development of vaccines, and changes in public health standards (such as waste control and sewage disposal systems), they were able to reduce substantially the deaths associated with such diseases as influenza, tuberculosis, polio, measles and smallpox. Life-theatening aspects of these illnesses, then, have been largely surmounted. Nevertheless, psychologists – along with other professionals – must continue to turn their preventative skills to the spectre of re-emerging and new infectious diseases, notably of course, the **Human Immunodeficiency Virus (HIV)**. Only by doing so can it be ensured that we do not return to the position earlier this century of widespread mortality through infectious disease.

If we are to continue to pursue advances in the quality of life, we must address those lifestyle factors which precipitate premature disease and terminal illness. *Table 11.2* (next page) shows that the leading cause of death in Great Britain is coronary heart disease (CHD): of the total number of deaths each year in the UK, one in three men and one in four women die from this disease. CHD is also the main cause of premature death for men, (i.e. before the age of 65). Cancer, though (most frequently of the breast), is the main cause of premature death for women, with a lifetime risk of 1 in 12. Smoking, being overweight, eating foods high in fat and cholesterol, drinking too much alcohol, driving without seat belts and leading stressful lives all play a role in heart disease, cancer, strokes, cirrhosis, accidents and suicide. Changing the

TABLE 11.2   LEADING CAUSES OF DEATH IN GREAT BRITAIN, 1992

Rank	Leading Causes of Death		Number (all ages)	Per Cent of Total Deaths
1	Coronary artery (heart) disease	women	76,364	12
		men	90,389	14
		total	166,753	26
2	Cancer	women	78,894	12
		men	86,002	14
		total	164,896	26
3	Cerebrovascular disease (stroke)	women	47,372	8
		men	28,471	4
		total	75,843	12
4	Respiratory disease	women	35,871	6
		men	33,940	5
		total	69,811	11
	Other causes:	women	87,202	14
		men	69,734	11
		total	156,936	25
		grand total	634,239	

[GREAT BRITAIN 1992 POPULATION: 57,911,647]

Examples of 'other causes' (rank ordered):

Motor traffic accidents	<1
Suicides	<1
Falls	<1
Alcoholic liver disease & cirrhosis	<1
Metabolic & immunity disorders (AIDS)	<1
Fire & flames	<1
Accidental drowning	<1
Murder	<1
Appendicitis	<1
Electrical accidents	<1
Labour & delivery complications	<1
Lightning	<1

Sources: (1) Office of Population Censuses & Surveys (1993) *OPCS Monitor DH2 93/2 Deaths by cause: December quarter 1992 registrations,* OPCS, London (2) Registrar General Scotland (1993) *Annual Report* 1992, General Register Office, Edinburgh.

behaviours associated with these diseases of civilisation could prevent much illness and unnecessary hardship.

The need, then, for a shift toward the values and priorities of a health ethic and the enactment of healthy behaviours is most pronounced in the struggle against preventable diseases. However, we do not all place the same value on health, nor do we all share similar notions of what it is to be optimally healthy at any one time. To prescriptively impose those values on others runs the risk of becoming intrusively moralistic. Notwithstanding such reservations,

though, it is undeniable that you are more likely to stay physically well (and mentally and emotionally you may feel better too) if you practice habits such as those listed in *Table 11.3*.

Primary prevention also involves developing a global consciousness in which avoidance of disease and health promotion are seen within a worldwide framework and not just from a Eurocentric or United States perspective. Because much of the world's expertise in behavioural science, preventive medicine and public health exists in the developed world,

TABLE 11.3 POINTERS TO PHYSICAL HEALTH

1 Developing an optimistic outlook and supportive friendships

2 Taking some exercise every other day for 20 minutes

3 Eating nutritious, balanced meals (high in vegetables, fruits and grains, low in fat and cholesterol)

4 Maintaining a weight appropriate to your build and height

5 Getting 7-8 hours of sleep nightly; taking time to rest/relax daily

6 Drinking alcohol in moderation (but not drinking at all when driving)

7 Wearing: a seatbelt in a car; a crash-helmet on a bike

8 Getting regular medical/dental checkups; complying with medical regimens

9 Engaging in only protected, safe sex

10 Avoiding smoking tobacco or taking other drugs

---

reaching developing world settings requires support for scholars, researchers and practitioners in those regions, and culturally-relevant models of health and behaviour change. A model prevention programme for the Asia-Pacific region, for example, is being developed at the University of Hawaii (Raymond *et al*, 1991).

Changing behaviour and changing health

Lifestyle factors can indeed change, often as the result of supplying information about the consequences of various health behaviours. Unfortunately, though, this is difficult and expensive and mass-media campaigns are not as effective in changing some health behaviours, such as obesity, as had been hoped. Such campaigns may, however, contribute to long-term changes in social attitudes that support lifestyle changes.

A major evaluation of such a campaign aimed at preventing heart disease was conducted in three towns in California. The goals of the study were to persuade people to reduce their cardiovascular risk via changes in smoking, diet and exercise and to determine which method of persuasion was more effective. In one town, a two-year campaign was conducted through the mass media, including television, radio, newspapers, billboards, and mailed leaflets. A second town received the same two-year media campaign plus a personal instruction programme on modifying health habits for high-risk individuals. The third town served as a control group and received no persuasive campaign. How successful were the campaigns in modifying lifestyle? The results showed that the townspeople who had received only the mass-media

campaign were more knowledgeable about the links between lifestyle and heart disease, but they showed only modest changes in their own behaviours and health status, as seen in *Figure 11.1* (next page). In the town where the media campaign was supplemented with personal instruction, people showed more substantial and long-lasting changes in their health habits, particularly in reduced smoking (Farquhar *et al*, 1984; Maccoby *et al*, 1977). Follow-ups reveal that the overall risk of mortality decreased by 15 per cent, and coronary heart disease decreased by 16 per cent, which translates into nearly 560 needless deaths that could be prevented in the next decade if the behaviour changes continue (Perlman, 1990).

Smoking tobacco – a major risk-factor for coronary artery disease – is directly responsible in England every year for about 26,000 deaths from lung cancer and over three times this number from other diseases, notably of the circulatory system (*Department of Health*, 1992). As such it is a major preventable cause of premature death and illness. Annual USA deaths related to smoking climbed to over 400,000 in 1988 from the estimated 188,000 in 1965 (*National Centre for Disease Control Report*, 1991). We are now carrying the burden for past smoking habits. Despite the steady trend toward reduced smoking, especially among the middle aged, around 30 per cent of Europeans and North Americans continue to smoke. There is, of course, considerable variation: in a recent survey of the health behaviours of over seven thousand 17-30-year-old students in eight European countries (Steptoe & Wardle, 1992), 45 per cent of Portugese male subjects reported being smokers, whilst only 12 per cent of female subjects from Belgium reported smoking every day; 30 per cent of male and female participants in England reported regularly smoking more than eight cigarettes a day.

FIGURE 11.1 RESPONSE TO MEDIA HEALTH MESSAGES AND HANDS-ON WORKSHOPS

Knowledge of cardiovascular disease risk factors was greater among residents of Town B, who were exposed to a two-year mass media health campaign, than among residents of Town A, who were not exposed to a campaign. Knowledge gain was greater still when residents of Town C participated in intense wokshops and instruction sessions for several months during the media blitz. As knowledge increased, bad health habits (risk behaviours) and signs (indicators) decreased, with Town C leading the way, followed by Town B.

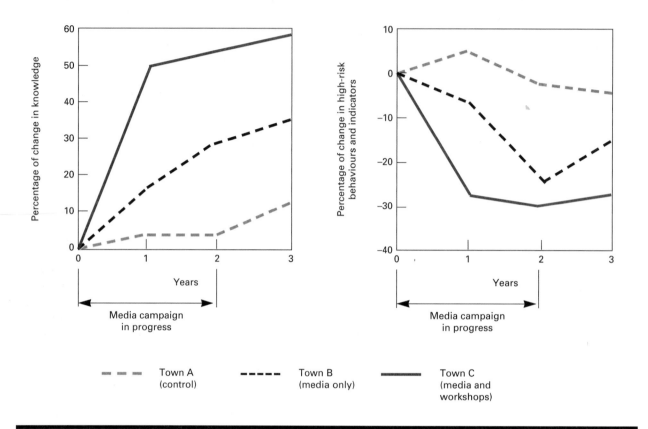

Town A (control)   Town B (media only)   Town C (media and workshops)

Notwithstanding these variations, among those who consume 20-a-day or more, male smokers are 22 times more likely than non-smokers to die of lung cancer, while for women it is 12 times higher for smokers than for non-smokers. Significantly, only ten per cent of smokers initiate this harmful habit after the age of 21. Doubtless, the health and longevity of countless members of society could be protected if the thousands of children who start smoking every day of the year could be discouraged from lighting that first cigarette.

The health benefits of becoming a non-smoker are immediate and substantial for men and women of all ages. Even heavy smokers who kick the habit can improve their chances of avoiding disease and premature death due to smoking. The best health policy appears to be never to start smoking or, failing that, to join the ranks of those who have quit. 90 per cent of those who quit do so on their own, without professional treatment programmes. Because smoking often starts in adolescence, some psychologists have

tried to tackle the problem by studying ways to keep teenagers from smoking. The programmes that seem to be most successful provide anti-smoking information in formats that appeal to adolescents, portray a positive image of the non-smoker as independent and self-reliant, and use peer group techniques – popular peers serve as non-smoking role models – and instruction in ways to help teenagers resist peer pressure (Evans *et al*, 1978).

Regular exercise has been established as an important factor in promoting and maintaining health. In particular, major improvements in health can be gained over a two to three month period from taking part in an exercise such as swimming, bicycling or jogging for just 20 minutes, three times a week. Daily ten-minute brisk walks can also produce beneficial effects on psychological well-being and somatic health (Thayer, 1988). These aerobic exercises are characterised by moderate intensity, moderate duration and moderate endurance. They lead to increased fitness of the heart and respiratory systems, improvement of muscle tone and strength, and many other health benefits. However, most people do not engage in such exercise consistently. Researchers are now exploring the questions of who exercises regularly and why, trying to determine what programmes or strategies are most effective in getting people to start and continue exercising (Dishman, 1982). Findings clearly indicate that people are more likely to exercise regularly if it is easy and convenient to do so and if it involves some socially rewarding interaction with others. For these reasons, some commercial companies are now providing exercise equipment, aerobics classes, or jogging tracks for their employees to use during their lunch breaks and after work.

Health behaviour and beliefs: HIV and AIDS

A deadly virus is the cause of one of today's most daunting preventable diseases – **AIDS**, an acronym for **Acquired Immune Deficiency Syndrome**. Unheard of until 1981, it is now a worldwide epidemic growing in alarming proportions in many countries (see *Table 11.4*, next page). Incidence rates show few signs of decline: Iceland is the exception rather than the rule. In the five years between 1988 and 1993, rates per million in Portugal, for example, have trebled, whilst almost doubling in neighbouring Spain. Notwithstanding differences between countries in identification and notification practices, the figures in *Table 11.4* strongly suggest that there is considerable variation between European nations, both in terms of incidence and rate of change in numbers of people with AIDS.

While thousands of people are dying from this virulent disease, many more are living with its precursor, HIV infection. The World Health Organization (1994) has estimated that the total number of HIV-infected adults currently alive worldwide is 13 to 14 million, with approximately eight million of these cases discernible in sub-Saharan regions of the African continent. HIV (Human Immunodeficiency Virus) attacks human white blood cells (T-Lymphocytes), thus damaging the immune system and weakening the ability to fight other diseases. Being vulnerable to infection by a host of other viruses and bacteria, life-threatening illnesses such as cancer (for example, Karposi's sarcoma), meningitis and pneumonia can ensue. The HIV virus requires direct access to the bloodstream to produce an infection. This can occur via the transmission of the virus from the HIV-positive to the non-infected person in semen, vaginal fluid or blood, usually during either unprotected sexual contact or the sharing of intravenous needles and syringes. In the past, the virus has also been passed through blood transfusions and medical procedures in which infected blood or organs are unwittingly given to healthy people. Some haemophiliac children have contracted HIV in this way whilst others may become infected perinatally during the birth or postnatally through mothers' breast milk (Rogers, 1985). The period of time from initial infection with the virus until symptoms occur (incubation period) can be as long as eight years. Frequently, the symptoms are opportunistic infections such as yeast infections, rashes and warts. At the moment, the diagnosis of AIDS or ARC (AIDS-Related Complex) requires a severe deterioration of the immune system and an episode of a life-threatening infection.

Potentially, everyone is at risk. Although the initial discovery of HIV and AIDS in the United States of America was in the male homosexual community, the disease has spread widely, occurring now in heterosexuals and homosexuals of both sexes, and notably amongst intravenous non-prescription drug users. The understandable fear is that HIV will increase and spread throughout national populations, in just the same way as other sexually transmitted infections such as syphilis and gonorrhea, also on the rise in recent years. According to a *National Centre for Disease Control Report* in the United States (1990), as many as one in 500 North American college students are estimated to be HIV-positive. Given the increasing number of AIDS cases, the anticipated additional burden on health care systems and community health budgets could be unprecedented.

As yet, the natural sciences have not produced a cure for AIDS, nor a vaccine to prevent its spread. Nevertheless, there are medical treatments that will improve the quality and length of life of those who are afflicted with the disease. For example, there is evidence to suggest that the drug AZT slows the progression of the HIV virus, and there are new treatments that can more effectively manage the opportunistic infections, especially pneumonia. Importantly also, changes in public health policy have slowed the proliferation of HIV infection: in France, for example, the liberalisation of the sale of syringes from high-street pharmacists significantly reduced the spread of the virus amongst intravenous drug users, as recorded by Ingold & Toussirt (1993) in Paris, Marseille and Metz. Whilst we wait for a cure, a vaccine or further governmental initiatives, the social and behavioural sciences – of which health psychology is one – can offer their support in the fight against the spread of HIV. Variation in its incidence is as much to do with human behaviour as it is with the virus's ability to replicate itself. The threat of HIV and AIDS, then, offers a considerable challenge to health

TABLE 11.4 AIDS INCIDENCE RATES IN 16 EUROPEAN COUNTRIES, 1988 AND 1993

	1988		Country	1993	
Total Number	Rate per million			Rate per million	Total Number
2138	55		Spain	102	3989
3037	53		France	78	4605
1759	31		Italy	75	4350
4	10		Luxembourg	50	20
126	25		Denmark	44	230
128	12		Portugal	39	378
324	22		Netherlands	27	425
887	16		Great Britain	24	1364
141	14		Belgium	20	205
89	11		Sweden	19	164
5	25		Iceland	17	5
41	12		Ireland	16	58
71	7		Greece	16	167
1326	17		Germany FR	16	1269
25	6		Norway	14	58
17	4		Finland	5	23

AIDS cases and incidence rates per million population, by country and year of diagnosis reported by 31 March 1994, unadjusted for reporting delays.

(note: one decimal place rounded up/down if >/= .5)

Source: European Centre for the Epidemiological Monitoring of Aids, (1994) *Aids Surveillance in Europe: Quarterly Report No.41*, 31st March.

psychology in terms of developing effective strategies for primary prevention and secondary care.

After nearly 15 years of a world inflicted by AIDS, there is now widespread awareness that making permanent changes in patterns of sexual behaviour and in the use of drug-taking equipment are necessary. Yet, amongst intravenous drug users (IDUs), the sharing of needles, 'works' (the syringe itself) and of rinsing water, coupled with the non-use of bleach as a disinfecting cleaning agent, still continues. Likewise, it is widely understood that a monogamous relationship with a non-infected partner or abstinence from unprotected, penetrative sexual activity are advisable options. Many people recognise that it is sensible to know your own HIV status and that of your partner. Despite such awareness,

however, behaviours persist which involve risk of HIV infection. 'Safer sex' is not always practised when risk is evident. Failure to use condoms during sexual contact with a new partner is still commonplace, anticipated loss of pleasurability being a major reason for such non-use (Chapman & Hodgson, 1988).

Often, unreasonable estimates of risk have been made, inappropriate social comparisons with friends and associates drawn, and fictions constructed about their behaviours. Turner *et al* (1988), for example, in a study of Oxford University undergraduates, found that students who were engaging in unprotected sex with a bisexual partner, an intravenous drug user or a prostitute, nevertheless estimated their own risk of infection to be less than for others of their own age and sex. Similarly, a study in the Netherlands (Van der

Plight, 1991) showed that many people continue to entertain an unrealistic sense of optimism with respect to their risk of HIV infection and of AIDS, such an illusion in this instance being of questionable adaptational value. Successful primary prevention, though, cannot be achieved by conceiving risk as a problem located within particular individuals. Despite one person intending to engage in safer sex, whether or not this is achieved depends upon an interpersonal transaction between two people. The ability of a prospective partner to influence decision making may disrupt laudable intentions, as too may the often present disinhibiting effects of alcohol (Stall et al, 1986). As well as supplying information, then, health psychologists can help by providing structured opportunities in which people who feel vulnerable to undesirable forms of social influence can practise the assertiveness and social skills needed to negotiate the interpersonal dynamics of difficult relationships. Moreover, we must continue to emphasise that there are no 'risk groups', only **risk behaviours**. The persistence of this damaging myth, however, allows people who are not members of a minority group to deny that they are in any way at risk and to stigmatise those who are HIV-positive (Phillips, 1991). Health psychologists in primary care must continually dismantle such social misrepresentations of AIDS wherever they may be encountered. Only in so doing will it be possible to promote realistic, behaviourally-based notions of risk and to dispel (or at least limit) misleading group-based ones.

Health psychologist **Thomas Coates** is part of a multidisciplinary research team that is using an array of psychological principles in a concerted effort to prevent the further spread of AIDS (Coates, 1990; Ekstrand & Coates, 1990; Catania et al, 1990). The team is involved in many aspects of applied psychology, such as assessing psychosocial risk factors, developing behavioural interventions, training community leaders to be most effective in educating their members toward healthier patterns of sexual and drug behaviour, assisting with the design of media advertisements, community information campaigns, and systematically evaluating changes in relevant attitudes, values and behaviours.

There is great potential for the media to show people how to practise HIV-prevention behaviours, while developing new healthful social norms and correcting inaccurate perceptions of social norms (Flora, 1991). Special programmes are being developed to reach minorities who are at risk from HIV and AIDS but are not easily accessed by educational and standard media efforts. For example, a recent advertisement designed with the assistance of African-American women addressed in a more sensitive way than previously, the problem of selling sex in return for the drug 'crack'.

◆ Treating Illness – Secondary Prevention

The empirical evidence supporting the biopsychosocial model of health demonstrates that numerous benefits can be derived from psychological treatments of diagnosed pathology or illness. Many investigators now believe that psychological strategies can improve the emotional well-being of individuals. Health psychologists can contribute to the well-being and longevity of people with HIV and AIDS, for example, by promoting psychosocial interventions which boost the immune response. It has been found that aerobic exercise and other behavioural interventions at an early stage can arrest HIV disease by improving immune functioning. In this vein, Antoni et al (1990; 1991) asked gay men to participate in a study where he randomly allocated them to intervention and control groups. All of the men at the beginning of the trial did not know their HIV status. A therapeutic programme occurred some weeks before HIV testing. The intervention included group meetings in which self-defeating beliefs were cognitively restructured. Relaxation training was also given. Both in the weeks before and after being told the results of their HIV test, measures of immunological functioning and of psychological well-being were taken. Antoni and colleagues found that amongst the subjects who discovered they were HIV-positive, those who had participated in the therapeutic programme were significantly less anxious and depressed and, furthermore, displayed better immunological functioning than those allocated to the no-therapy comparison group. Although most of those infected with HIV do not have AIDS (a medical diagnosis), they must live with the continual stress of knowing that this life-threatening disease might suddenly emerge. The results of Antoni's work, then, give hope and respite since psychosocial interventions may extend longevity and quality of remaining life through boosting the immune response. Psychoneuroimmunologists have found that psychosocial variables which have a substantive adverse impact upon immune functioning include bereavment, relationship difficulties, having to provide for others, depression and – as often involved in all of the former – 'stress' (Kiecolt-Glaser & Glaser, 1990). Thus, health psychologists, to be most effective, must initiate remediative strategies and interventions with HIV-positive patients which in particular target these potential psychosocial pitfalls and Achilles heels.

Moving on to other domains in which health psychology can contribute to secondary prevention, it has been found that receiving *information* about one's treatment is a critical factor in recovery from illness. It is better to know what to expect than to be

During 1990 and 1991, Wellings, Field, Johnson and Wadsworth (1994) carried out an extensive and comprehensive interview survey of self-reported sexual behaviour in Great Britain. Of the 26,393 people aged between 16 and 59 years who were randomly selected to take part, 18,876 were interviewed (over 8,200 men and 10,600 women), representing a 71.5 per cent response rate. Though their findings are too numerous to summarise in their entirety here, selected ones are relevant and illustrative. For example, Wellings *et al* found that of the 1,016 men (15.7 per cent of all males in the sample) who reported five or more heterosexual partners in the last five years, only one in five of these men (i.e. 21 per cent, N=203) reported having had an HIV test and so could know of their HIV status. Further, they found that for women and men whose only partner in the last four weeks prior to interview had been a new one (N=128 and 70 respectively), nearly 60 per cent of these women (N=42) and 68 per cent of these men (N=87) had not used a condom on each occasion of sexual intercourse during that time. In addition, they found that one in every six men who designated themselves as widowed, separated or divorced (66 of 421), reported having had two or more heterosexual partners in the last year but had never used a condom during that time. Finally, in answer to the question 'Have you changed your own sexual lifestyle in any way or made any decisions about sex because of a concern about catching AIDS or HIV virus?', from the seven available response options given, fewer than three per cent of all respondents (i.e. fewer than 566 of the 18,876 total

sample) indicated 'not having sex' and 'avoiding some sexual practices' as behaviour changes they had instigated.

Viewed from the perspective of 'risk eradication' these findings leave health psychology with still much to do. Viewed with the more realistic goal in mind of 'risk and harm reduction' however, the self-report results from this study give cause for cautious optimism. Wellings *et al* also found, for example, that since the mid 1980s the prevalence of condom use at first intercourse has increased markedly: self-reports indicated that in 1985 approximately 36 per cent of women and 46 per cent of men used this method of risk-reduction on their first occasion of sexual congress; in 1991 the percentage using a condom at first consummation had risen for women to approximately 80 per cent and to 70 per cent for men. Likewise, findings from a large-scale Dutch survey of sexual behaviour (Van Zessen & Sandfort, 1991) indicated that 40 per cent of those people interviewed said they had changed their sexual practices recently: in particular, this self-reported change predominantly was amongst the younger respondents and those with more

than one sexual partner; they reported using condoms more often than in the past and that they were more cautious about with whom they made love. This increase in the uptake of 'safer sex' practices such as condom use, supports the contention that HIV and AIDS public education campaigns initiated during the latter half of the 1980s were effective in raising awareness and in changing risk-behaviour. Indeed, a conclusion that Wellings *et al* (1994) reach is that those people at apparently greater risk of infection are more likely to have adopted preventive strategies in the context of HIV and AIDS. Thus, continuing to inform people of the relative risks of various forms of behaviour, breaking down the illusion of personal invulnerability, is one way in which health psychologists can productively channel their preventative energies.

Knowledge, then, can help to promote harm reduction. A European multicentre study of 2,330 intravenous drug users (IDUs) interviewed about 'safe' drug injection and condom use (Desenclos, Papaevangelou & Ancelle-Park, 1993) further illustrates the point. Three sub-groups of participants within this sample were identified on the basis of their knowledge about their HIV status: firstly, there were those who had never been tested for HIV and who therefore did not know their status; secondly, there were those who had been tested, found to be 'negative' and had been aware of this for the last six months or more before the time of the survey; and thirdly, were identified a sub-group of intravenous drug users who had been tested, had been found to be 'positive' and had been aware of their HIV status over the last half year or more before the time of

study. Desenclos *et al* asked all members of these groups if they made regular use of condoms in their sexual practices and whether they never shared syringes with others user. They found that the percentages of intravenous drug users who reported making routine use of condoms and who never shared needles, were remarkably similar for the 'untested' and 'HIV-negative' groups (12 per cent and 8.5 per cent; 47 per cent and 46 per cent respectively). In contrast with these comparison groups, however, percentages of

respondents reporting regular condom usage and non-sharing of syringes in the 'HIV-tested-&-positive' group were found to be significantly greater at 37 per cent and 62 per cent respectively. This latter group's more favourable self-reports could well have been motivated in part by a wish to convey a more socially responsible self-image, given their HIV status. But, despite this methodological problem, the results do provide evidence that suggests risk-reduction is associated with knowledge of HIV status.

---

uninformed about an impending medical procedure. Researchers have found that patients who show the best recovery from surgery are those who received complete information before their operations (Janis, 1958; Johnson, 1983).

A recent study conducted by **David Spiegel** further demonstrates the impact of psychosocial treatment on the course of disease. Routine medical care was provided to 86 women with metastatic breast cancer (wherein lumps have appeared that are secondary to the original cite), while an experimental subgroup of 50 also participated in weekly supportive group therapy for one year. These patients met to discuss their personal experiences in coping with the various aspects of having cancer. They had the opportunity to reveal openly in an accepting environment their fears and other strong emotions. Although at the ten-year follow-up all but three of the total sample had died, there was a significant difference in the survival times between those given the psychological treatment and those given only medical treatment. Those patients who participated in group therapy survived for an average of 36.6 months, compared with 18.9 months for the control group. This finding in a well-controlled study indicates that psychological treatments can affect the course of disease, the length of one's life and the quality of life (Spiegel *et al*, 1989).

A negative reaction to this encouraging exploratory research on psychological factors in the treatment of disease was given by a physician apprehensive that medicine was incorporating a biopsychosocial model: 'What I am fearful of is that the "alternative" field will go crazy with this and say, "Aha, we told you all along, psychotherapy cures cancer, so stop your radiation therapy"' (Dr Jimmie Holland, quoted in *Barinaga*, 1989). On the contrary, many health

psychologists want medical treatments to be more flexible and expand to include practices *in addition* to traditional radiation and chemotherapy for the treatment of metastatic cancer (McDaniel *et al*, 1993).

◆ Rehabilitation and Damage Limitation – Tertiary Care

Unlike treatment which aims to 'cure', tertiary care focuses on limiting the further progression of damage or disease and on helping people adjust to an illness if its course is irreversible. For example, a health concern which psychologists are frequently called upon to manage is chronic pain. It is an enduring aspect of many illnesses and injuries, and there are many psychological techniques of pain control, such as biofeedback, hypnosis, relaxation, and visual imagery for distraction (Melzack & Wall, 1988). Likewise, cardiac rehabilitation is an area in which psychologists can make a positive contribution (Bennett, 1993). The restoration of everyday behaviour is an important facet of recovery after a myocardial infarction – a heart attack. However, despite the applicability of a biopsychosocial approach to limiting the progression of further coronary artery disease, psychologists are largely under-represented in cardiac rehabilitation teams, though this involvement varies somewhat across Europe (Maes, 1992).

Many people react to the strain and distress caused by chronic illness with *tension*, resulting in tight muscles, high blood pressure, constricted blood vessels in the brain, and chronic oversecretion of hormones. Fortunately, many of these tension responses can be controlled by a variety of techniques. Relaxation through meditation has ancient roots in many parts of the world. In Eastern cultures, ways to calm the mind and still the body's tensions have been practised for centuries. Today, Zen discipline and Yoga exercises from Japan and India are part of daily life for many people both there and, increasingly, in the West. In our own culture, a growing number of people have been attracted to therapy in, and workshops on, relaxation, and to various forms of meditation.

Stress associated with disability and ongoing disease is the *nonspecific response* of the body to the continued demands made on it both psychologically and physiologically. There is growing evidence that complete relaxation in these circumstances is a potent anti-stress response. The relaxation response is a condition in which muscle tension, cortical activity, heart rate and blood pressure all decrease and breathing slows. There is reduced electrical activity in the brain, and input to the central nervous system from the outside environment is lowered. In this low level of arousal, recuperation from chronic stress can take place. Four conditions are regarded as necessary to produce the relaxation response: (a) a quiet environment, (b) closed eyes, (c) a comfortable position, and (d) a repetitive mental device. The first three lower input to the nervous system while the fourth lowers its internal stimulation (Benson, 1975).

Biofeedback (described in Chapter 7) is a self-regulatory technique used for a variety of special applications, such as control of blood pressure, relaxation of forehead muscles (involved in tension headaches), and even overcoming extreme blushing. Paradoxically, although individuals do not know how they do it, concentrating on the desired result in the presence of this signal produces change in the desired direction. However, while biofeedback can achieve relaxation and reduction in muscle tension, it does not reduce general levels of felt stress (Birbaumer & Kimmel, 1979; Swets & Bjork, 1990).

Chronically ill patients are often given a rehabilitative regimen. This regimen might include medications, dietary changes, prescribed periods of bed-rest and exercise, and follow-up procedures such as check-ups, physiotherapy training and chemotherapy. Failing to adhere to rehabilitative treatment regimens is one of the most serious problems in long-term health care (Rodin & Janis, 1982). The rate of patient non-adherence is estimated to be as high as 50 per cent. The culprit seems to be the nature of the *communication process* between doctor and patient.

Research has shown that healthcare professionals can take steps to improve patient adherence. Patients are more satisfied with their health care when they trust that the efficacy of the treatment outweighs its costs and when practitioners communicate clearly,

make sure that their patients understand what has been said, act courteously, and convey a sense of caring and supportiveness. In addition, health professionals must recognise the role of cultural and social norms in the treatment process and involve family and friends where necessary. Some physicians critical of their profession argue that doctors must be taught to care in order to cure (Siegel, 1988). Compliance-gaining strategies developed by social psychologists are also being used to help overcome the lack of cooperation between patients and practitioners (Zimbardo & Leippe, 1991).

INTERIM SUMMARY

Health psychology is concerned with the psychosocial conditions that maintain and promote well-being and prevent illness. Health is a multidimensional experience. It is not just the avoidance of illness but is also a state of physical, mental and social well-being. It enables us to approach activities of daily living with vigour and to lead a socially and economically productive life. Health psychology considers that biological, psychological and social factors are interrelated phenomena and that they are implicated in all stages of health and illness. This guiding framework for understanding the origins of health is termed the biopsychosocial model.

In terms of application, health psychology's focus is health promotion and primary prevention rather than with secondary or tertiary intervention. Thus, health beliefs and behaviours, within the context of available opportunities provided by the local environment and socio-cultural milieu, are central to health psychology studies and concerns. The primary prevention of chronic degenerative diseases – in particular, heart disease, cancer, stroke and of AIDS – represents major challenges for health psychology.

◆ CAUSES AND CORRELATES OF HEALTH, ILLNESS AND DYSFUNCTION

Health psychologists are very interested in the causes of illness and injury for if we can understand the aetiology (origins) of ill-health from a biopsychosocial perspective, then we may travel a long way down the road to understanding how best to prevent the initial onset of such processes. While poor health habits are important contributors, personality or individual behavioural styles may also play a causal role (H. S. Friedman, 1990).

Personality and Health

Two models relating personality traits to disease are (a) the general personality model (individual differences related to a host of diseases), and (b) the specific trait model (particular personality traits related to specific diseases). Research has asked if there is a general negative affective style or a disease-prone personality characterised by depression, anxiety and, to a lesser extent, hostility. These negative emotional states affect coronary disease, asthma, headache, ulcers and arthritis (H.S. Friedman & Booth-Kewley, 1987). Longitudinal studies have also supported the validity of the link between negative emotional states and illness. Chronic negative emotional states tend to produce pathogenic physiological changes, lead people to practise faulty health behaviours, produce illness behaviour and result in poor interpersonal relationships (Matthews, 1988).

A great deal of research has focused on a particular behavioural style called the **Type-A behaviour syndrome** (Strube, 1990). The Type-A syndrome is a complex pattern of behaviour and emotions that includes being excessively competitive, aggressive, impatient, time-urgent and hostile. Type-A people are often dissatisfied with some central aspect of their lives, are highly competitive and ambitious, and often are loners. Some of these Type-A characteristics are valued in our society, but, in general, the behavioural style is very dysfunctional. Type-A businessmen, for example, are stricken with coronary heart disease more than twice as often as men in the general population (Friedman & Rosenman, 1974; Jenkins, 1976). In fact, many studies have shown that people manifesting the Type-A behaviour syndrome are at significantly greater risk for all forms of cardiovascular disease (Dembroski et al, 1978; Haynes & Feinleib, 1980). New research is relating Type-A behaviour to many subsequent illnesses in addition to heart disease

(Suls & Marco, 1990). Unfortunately, Type-A behaviour patterns are now being seen among college and high-school students and even among children in primary school (Thoresen & Eagelston, 1983). A current focus in Type-A behaviour research is on identifying the specific dimensions of the syndrome which most influence coronary heart disease. In this respect, habitual and frequently expressed anger and hostility have been found to be the coronary toxic components of the Type-A behaviour pattern, whilst an occasional strategic outburst of pique may in fact be socially adaptive (Dembroski & Costa, 1987; Keinan et al, 1992).

Interventions to reduce Type-A behaviour have been successful in most cases (M. Friedman et al, 1986). While the effect is small, both negative affect, as associated with being Type A, and pessimistic explanatory style have demonstrated the possibility for successful intervention (H. S. Friedman & Booth-Kewley, 1988; Peterson et al, 1988). A large-scale intervention programme with more than 1,000 volunteer survivors of a first-time heart attack has found that a behavioural treatment that alters typical Type-A reaction patterns deters a second heart attack and reduces the incidence of death from other causes as well (Thoresen, 1990). Those who had substantially lowered their Type-A behaviour had almost a 50 per cent lower mortality rate over an eight year follow-up period than those who did not change substantially.

The Role of Stress and Stressors

Stress is a unique type of emotional experience that has gained much attention by psychologists and other scientists. Within the broad area of basic and applied

Modern society creates a stressful environment whether we are working or playing.

research on stress, three general questions are of major concern to psychologists: How does stress affect us physically and psychologically? How do common stressors in our society affect our health? How can we cope with stress more effectively?

Our modern industrialised society sets a rapid, hectic pace for our lives. Many of us live in overcrowded conditions, have too many demands placed on our time, are worried about our uncertain future, are holding a frustrating job, or are unemployed, and have little time for family and fun. Would we be better off without stress? A stress-free life would offer no challenge – no difficulties to surmount, no new fields to conquer and no reason to sharpen our wits or improve our abilities. Stress is an unavoidable part of living. Every organism faces challenges from its external environment and from its personal needs. These challenges are life's problems that the organism must solve to survive and thrive.

Stress is the pattern of specific and nonspecific responses an organism makes to stimulus events that disturb its equilibrium and tax or exceed its ability to cope. The stimulus events include a large variety of external and internal conditions that collectively are called **stressors**. A stressor is a stimulus event that places a demand on an organism for some kind of adaptive response. The organism's reaction to external stressors is known as **strain**. An individual's response to the need for change is made up of a diverse combination of reactions taking place on several levels, including physiological, behavioural, emotional and cognitive levels. How can such a complex stress response be studied? In an attempt to better understand the concept of stress, researchers have tried to identify its specific components and their interactions.

Have you ever wondered why some people experience stressful events and seem to suffer little or no negative effects, while others are seriously upset by even minor difficulties This difference exists because the effect of most stressors is not controlled only by the objective features of the stressor. Stress is a personal matter. How much stress we experience is determined by the quality and intensity of a combination of variables: the dimensions of the stressor, the way we interpret the meaning of the stressor, the resources we have available to deal with the stressor, and the amount and nature of the total strain placed on the individual. *Figure 11.2* indicates the elements of the stress process: stressors, stress, cognitive appraisal, resources and stress responses.

Stress, similar to taxes, is a recurring problem most people face. Naturally occurring stressful changes are an unavoidable part of our lives. People close to us get sick, move away or die. We get new jobs, get sacked or laid off, leave home, start college, succeed, fail, begin romances, get married and maybe break up.

In addition to the major life changes, there are also routine frustrations: traffic jams, snoring partners and missed appointments. Unpredictable, catastrophic events, such as major floods or accidents, will affect some of us, and chronic societal problems, such as pollution and crime, will represent important sources of stress for others.

Major life stressors

Unpredictable, uncontrollable and unwanted changes in our life situations are at the root of stress for many of us. Although change puts spice in our lives, too much change at one time can ruin our health. Even events that we welcome, such as winning the lottery or getting promoted, may require major changes in our routines and adaptation to new requirements. Recent studies reveal that one of the most sought changes in a married couple's life, the birth of their first child, is also a major source of stress, contributing to reduced marital satisfaction (Cowan & Cowan, 1988). On the other hand, a review of research on the psychological responses to abortion reveals that distress is generally greatest before the abortion. Distress is less severe for women following the abortion, especially if they have been supported in their decision by others (Adler *et al*, 1990).

Some researchers have viewed stress as resulting from exposure to major life changes or life events (Dohrenwend & Dohrenwend, 1974; Dohrenwend & Shrout, 1985; Holmes & Rahe, 1967). Ask social workers about the stresses of their clients, any one of whom may be unemployed, recently divorced, or living on the streets, or who may have a child selling drugs, or an abusive spouse. Sometimes a person can withstand an enormous amount of felt stress and keep functioning. The reaction depends on the extent and availability of individual resources and on the social and interpersonal contexts in which the stressful events took place. For example, one of the authors of this book, after once being robbed of a small amount of cash, felt relatively happy because, fortunately, he had just spent most of his money on buying a new suit. So the timing of the event made all the difference to the meaning he later attached to it, and consequently to the significance of the theft as a stressor.

The influence of major life changes on subsequent mental and physical health has been a focus of considerable research. It started with the development of the *Social Readjustment Rating Scale* (SRRS), a simple scale for rating the degree of adjustment required by various life events, both pleasant and unpleasant, that many people experience. The scale was developed from the responses of adults who were

FIGURE 11.2   A MODEL OF STRESS

Cognitive appraisal of the stress situation interacts with the stressor and the physical social and personal resources available for dealing with the stressor. Individuals respond to threats on various levels – physiological, behavioural, emotional and cognitive. Some responses are adaptive and others maladaptive or even lethal.

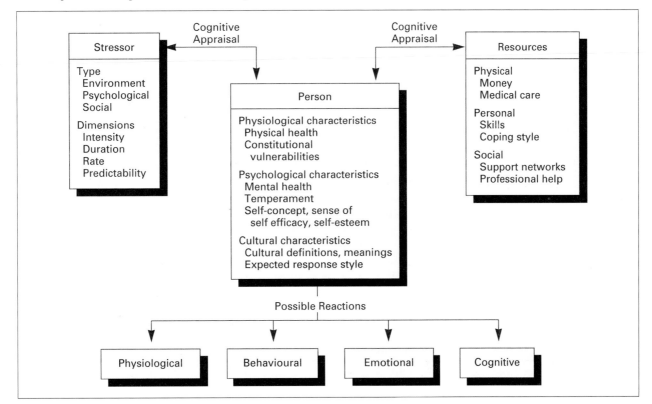

asked to identify from a list those life changes that applied to them. These adults rated the amount of readjustment required to accommodate the events by comparing each to marriage, which was arbitrarily assigned a value of 50 life change units. Researchers then calculated the total number of **life-change units** (LCU) an individual had undergone during that period, using the units as a measure of the amount of stress the individual had experienced (Holmes & Rahe, 1967). A modification of this scale for college students is shown in *Table 11.5* (next page). What is your LCU rating?

Also, compare the relative severity of challenges in your life with those of the four groups outlined in *Table 11.6* (students, mothers, general community members and the elderly) on page 417).

Early studies examined the hypothesis that the greater the life-change intensity, as measured by the SRRS, the greater the risk for subsequent illness. Preliminary studies found support for a relationship between medical problems and the amount of readjustment in life. Patients with heart disease, for example, had higher LCU scores than healthy subjects. Other studies reported that life stress increases a person's overall susceptibility to illness (Holmes &

Masuda, 1974), and LCU values are also elevated for some time after an illness (Rahe & Arthur, 1978).

A modification in measuring the effects of life events is provided in the *Life Experiences Survey* (LES), which has two special features. First, it provides scores for both increases and decreases in change rather than increases only, as in the original scale. Second, its scores reflect individual assessments of the events and their desirability. For example, getting a divorce from a physically abusive and violent spouse might be rated as highly desirable. Thus, this scale goes beyond a mere frequency count of the number of remembered life changes to measure the personal significance of each change (Sarason *et al*, 1978).

One interpretive problem with studies relating stressful life events to illness is that they tend to be retrospective. That is, both the stress measures and the illness measures are obtained by having subjects recall earlier events. This characteristic presents an opportunity for memory distortion to bias the results. For example, subjects who are sick are more likely to remember past negative stressors than subjects who are well. More recently, prospective studies have followed healthy individuals over a period of years; they find significant correlations between the development of medical problems and earlier accumulation of life-stress units (Brown & Harris, 1989; Johnson & Sarason, 1979). Despite such support, the bulk of the current research evidence does not suggest a particularly strong association between major life events and disease (Brett *et al*, 1990).

TABLE 11.5 STUDENT STRESS SCALE

The Student Stress Scale represents an adaptation of Holmes and Rahe's Social Readjustment Rating Scale. Each event is given a score that represents the amount of readjustment a person has to make in life as a result of the change. People with scores of 300 and higher have a high health risk. People scoring between 150 and 300 points have about a 50-50 chance of serious health change within two years. People scoring below 150 have a 1 in 3 chance of serious health change. Calculate your total Life Change Score (LCU) each month of this year and then correlate those scores with any changes in your health status.

Event	Life Change Unit
Death of a Close Family Member	100
Death of a Close Friend	73
Divorce Between Parents	65
Prison Term	63
Major Personal Injury or Illness	63
Marriage	58
Being Fired from Job	50
Failing an Important Course	47
Change in Health of Family Member	45
Pregnancy	45
Sex Problems	44
Serious Argument with Close Friend	40
Change in Financial Status	39
Change of Academic Subject	39
Trouble with Parents	39
New Girlfriend or Boyfriend	38
Increased Workload at School	37
Outstanding Personal Achievement	36
First Term/Year in College/University	35
Change in Living Conditions	31
Serious Argument with Teacher/Lecturer	30
Lower Grades than Expected	29
Change in Sleeping Habits	29
Change in Social Activities	29
Change in Eating Habits	28
Recurrent Car Trouble	26
Change in Number of Family Get-togethers	26
Too Many Missed Lectures/Seminars/Tutorials	25
Change of College	24
Minor Traffic Offence	20
1st Total ☐ (date:)	
2nd Total ☐ (date:)	
3rd Total ☐ (date:)	

TABLE 11.6 SEVERITY OF HASSLES AS PERCEIVED IN FOUR GROUPS

In these New Zealand samples, each hassle type differed significantly in severity among the four groups. The ranked perceived severity was almost reversed for student and elderly groups with time pressures most important and neighbourhood and health pressures least important for students, while the latter were the most important sources of hassles and time pressures were the least for the elderly. Note the hassle priorities for these mothers who had one or more young children at home and no household help.

Frustration type	Students (N = 161)	Mothers (N = 194)	Community (N = 120)	Elderly (N = 150)
Time pressure	1	2	3	4
Future security	2	4	1	3
Finances	3	1	2	4
Household	3	1	2	4
Neighbourhood	4	3	2	1
Health	4	3	2	1

Life's daily hassles

One current view of stress holds that an accumulation of small frustrations places cumulatively greater demands on personal resources over time than do infrequent big jolts of change (Weinberger *et al*, 1987). Life can often be bubbling with low-level frustrations. To what extent do the effects of these minor irritations mount up and alter your health? If you interpret these frustrations as personally salient and harmful or threatening to your well-being, they may affect you more than you might imagine (Lazarus, 1984).

A psychiatrist distributed 100 questionnaires to people waiting for the 7.12 am train from Long Island to Manhattan, New York. From the 40 completed questionnaires returned, it was determined that these average commuters had just gulped down their breakfast in less than 11 minutes, were prepared to spend three hours each day in transit, and, in ten years, had logged about 7,500 hours of rail travel time. Two thirds of the commuters believed their family relations were impaired by their commuting. 59 per cent experienced fatigue, 47 per cent were filled with conscious anger, 28 per cent were anxious, and others reported headaches, muscle pains, indigestion, and other symptoms of the long-term consequences of beating the rat race in the city by living in the country (F. Charaton, personal communication, 1973). In a diary study, a group of white, middle-class, middle-aged men and women kept track of their daily hassles over a one-year period (along with a record of major life changes and physical symptoms). A clear relationship emerged between hassles and health problems: the more

frequent and intense the frustrations people reported, the poorer was their health, both physical and mental (Lazarus, 1981; 1984). As daily challenges decrease, well-being increases proportionately (Chamberlain & Zika, 1990). Although daily stressors have been shown to affect one's mood immediately, people habituate to them so that the negative effects do not carry over to the next day. The exception is cases of interpersonal conflicts (Bolger *et al*, 1989).

An interesting extension of this picture is provided by Evans and Edgerton (1991), who, in a similar diary study of shorter duration, observed in their 100 volunteers that minor desirable events – **daily uplifts** – decreased significantly in frequency during a period commencing four days prior to the onset of a cold. They concluded that immunological suppression associated with such a downswing in pleasurable occurrences, left subjects vulnerable to the development of an infection in the presence of a virus. It may not be just the frustrations of daily life, then, that adversely affect our health and well-being, but also a comparative absence of life's daily pleasures, simple activities such as being with friends, sitting in the sun or doing a job well – all of which have been found to positively affect mood for a whole day (Lewinsohn & Graf, 1973).

Catastrophic events

When an event is negative, uncontrollable, unpredictable, or ambiguous, it is usually experienced as more stressful than if it were not so (Glass, 1977). These conditions hold especially true in the case of catastrophic events.

One afternoon in 1989 a big baseball game was about to begin in San Francisco's Candlestick Park. As the spectators settled into their seats, the brass band started playing. Suddenly, the entire stadium started shaking violently, the lights went out and the scoreboard turned black. 60,000 fans became completely silent. They had just experienced a major earthquake. In the crowd, people watched events on portable television sets as fires broke out in the city; a bridge collapsed; motorways were fractured and numerous deaths occurred.

Shortly after the quake, a team of research psychologists began to study how people coped with the catastrophe. For the study, nearly 800 people were chosen randomly from the San Francisco area and from several comparison cities some distance away. They were interviewed at either 1, 2, 3, 6, 8, 16, 28 or 50 weeks after the quake. The subjects completed a ten-minute telephone survey about their thoughts, social behaviour and health. Three distinct phases of stress reactions were found among the subjects who were city residents. In the *emergency* phase (first three to four weeks), social contact, anxiety and obsessive thoughts about the earthquake increased. The *inhibition* phase (three to eight weeks) was characterised by a sudden decline in talking and thinking about the event, but indirect, stress-related reactions increased, such as arguments and dreams about the earthquake. In the *adaptation* phase (from two months on), the psychological effects of the catastrophe were over for most people. However, as many as 20 per cent of the bay area residents remained distressed about the earthquake one year later (Pennebaker & Harber, 1991).

A great deal of research on the physical and psychological effects of catastrophic events has been

conducted (Baum, 1990). However, these opportunistic studies necessarily have followed a research tradition that differs from studies of personal stressors.

Researchers have found that response to disasters tends to occur in five stages. Typically, there is a period of shock, confusion, even psychic numbness, during which people cannot fully comprehend what has happened. In the next phase, called automatic action, people try to respond to the disaster and may behave adaptively but with little awareness of their actions and poor memory of the experience. In the third stage, people often feel great accomplishment and even a positive sense of communal effort toward a *shared purpose*. Also in this phase, people feel weary and are aware that they are using up their reserves of energy. During the next phase they experience a *letdown*; their energy is depleted and the impact of the tragedy is finally comprehended and felt emotionally. An extended final period of *recovery* follows, as people adapt to the changes brought about by the disaster (Cohen & Ahearn, 1980).

Knowledge of these typical reaction stages provides a model that is helpful in predicting people's reactions when disaster strikes, enabling rescue workers to anticipate and help victims deal with the problems that arise. Responses to events such as floods, tornadoes, aeroplane crashes and factory explosions have all been shown to fit this model of disaster reactions (see the opening case to Chapter 14 as a further example).

Chronic societal stressors

What cumulative effect do overpopulation, crime, economic recession, pollution, AIDS and an awareness of the proliferation of nuclear weapons have on us? How do these and other environmental stressors affect our mental and physical well-being?

Past surveys of the attitudes of students uncovered a general disquiet and uneasiness about the future (Beardslee & Mack, 1983). Studies since 1983 showed a significant increase in teenage school students' expressions of fear, helplessness and anger toward the adult generation. Many young people questioned whether it was worthwhile to work hard to prepare for a future they could not necessarily expect to have if a full-scale nuclear war were ever to become a reality (Hanna, 1984; Yudkin, 1984). Though the Cold War has ended, such fears may yet persist since the possibility of nuclear arms proliferation elsewhere in the world still exists.

Adults, too, have been worried about potential nuclear disasters, but they are also affected by the more immediate concerns of employment and economic security. Many stress-related problems

When an event is unpredictable, such as the 1992 air disaster in Amsterdam, it tends to be more stressful.

increase when the economy is in a downswing; admission to mental hospitals, infant mortality, suicide and deaths from alcohol-related diseases and cardiovascular problems all increase (Brenner, 1976).

Psychologists have found that unemployed men report more symptoms, such as depression, anxiety and worries about health, than do those who are employed. Because these symptoms disappear when the men are subsequently re-employed, researchers have argued that the symptoms are the results of being unemployed rather than indicators of more disturbed workers who are particularly likely to lose their jobs (Liem & Rayman, 1982). According to a recent investigation, high blood pressure among African-Americans (long thought to be primarily genetic) appears to be a consequence of chronic stress caused by low-status jobs, limited education, fruitless job seeking and low socioeconomic status (Klag *et al*, 1991). Hypertension results from frustrations in efforts to achieve basic life goals. It is not linked to genetic factors.

Even pollution creates psychological stress in addition to the severe physical health problems it generates. For example, the release of radioactive steam at the Three Mile Island nuclear power plant in 1979 and the 1986 explosion of the nuclear power factory in Chernobyl, Russia, were dramatic examples of environmental stressors. People living in the area experienced considerable stressful fear about immediate and long-term health consequences. In addition, people all over the world experienced stress as they wondered how these accidents might affect them as well as worrying about other possible nuclear accidents. After Three Mile Island, a legal stipulation required that psychological stress had to be included in the environmental impact survey before the plant could be reopened. One form of chronic societal stress comes from passive exposure to cigarette smoke (as described in the Close-up on the next page).

◆ Stress Moderator Variables

Variables that change the impact of a stressor on a given type of stress reaction are known as stress moderator variables. Moderator variables *filter* the effects of stressors, thereby making likely an alteration in the form which an individual's reaction may take. Before a response to stress begins, a demand on the organism (stressor) must be recognised at some level and evaluated. For example, your level of fatigue and general health status are moderator variables influencing your reaction to a given psychological or physical stressor. When you are in good condition, you can cope with a stressor more successfully than

when you are not.

The cognitive interpretation and evaluation of a stressor is a major moderator variable. **Cognitive appraisal** plays a central role in psychologically constructing and defining the situation: what the demand seems to be, how big a threat it represents, what resources one thinks are available for meeting it, and what coping strategies are appropriate. Some stressors, such as bodily injury or finding one's house on fire, are experienced as threats by almost everyone. However, many other stressors can be defined in a variety of ways, depending on personal biography and life situation, the relation of a particular demand to the individual's most important goals, perceived competence for dealing with the demand and self-assessment of that competence. A predicament that causes acute distress for one person may be all in a day's work for another.

Your appraisal of a stressor and of your resources for meeting it can be as important as the actual stressor. For example, if you believe a stressor is too much for you to deal with, you might create a *negative self-fulfilling prophecy*. In that case, you are likely to fail even when you are ostensibly capable of dealing adequately with the stressor. Cognitive appraisal, on the other hand, may define a stressor not as a threat but as an interesting new challenge against which you can test and positively evaluate yourself. The emotional experience may be one of exhilaration. The most successful athletes get a positive high when thinking about forthcoming competition, while others get nervous planning for the same event, creating a possible handicap even before the race begins. Appraisal of a stressor helps to orchestrate your conscious experience of it and so how successful you are in meeting its demands.

Richard Lazarus, a pioneer in stress research and emotion research, has distinguished two stages in our cognitive appraisal of demands. He uses the term **primary appraisal** for the initial evaluation of the seriousness of a demand. This evaluation starts with the questions 'What's happening?' and 'Is this event good for me, stressful, or irrelevant?' If the answer to the second question is 'stressful', an individual appraises the potential impact of the stressor by estimating whether harm has occurred or is likely to and whether action is required (see *Table 11.7* on page 421). Once a person decides something must be done, **secondary appraisal** begins. The person evaluates the personal and social resources that are available to deal with the stressful circumstance and considers what actions are needed (Lazarus, 1976). Appraisal continues as coping activities are tried; if the first ones do not work and the stress persists, new responses are initiated and their effectiveness evaluated (Lazarus, 1991).

While cognitive appraisals and good health can

Before cigarette advertising on television was banned in many countries, the ruggedly handsome Marlboro Man enjoyed his favourite brand before a campfire. Attractively portrayed men and women pursued high adventure whilst exuding seductive smiles and inhaling smoke as a voice-over counselled viewers: 'You only go around once – grab all the good life you can get'.

However, since the ban on those commercials went into effect, cigarette companies have still managed to get their message across. A study by the National Coalition on Television Violence showed that in 1990, 85 per cent of all cinematic films as surveyed showed characters lighting up. Although cigarette consumption has declined in recent years, the association of smoking with sex, adventure and sophistication (as communicated through advertisements and film) has helped create an environment in which smoking 20 or so cigarettes a day remains the norm for many adults, consumption being greater in countries that do not have anti-smoking campaigns.

Even non-smokers do not completely avoid exposure to cigarette smoke. Passive smoking is inhaling smoke from the cigarettes that other people are smoking. It is especially harmful to children – exposure to tobacco smoke in childhood, and especially, in infancy is associated with increased incidence of respiratory infections, middle-ear disease, and growth deficiencies (Chilmonczyk *et al*, 1990; *Occupational Hazards*, 1990; Rubin, 1990).

A recent study examined the long-term effects of childhood exposure to secondhand smoke (Janerich *et al*, 1990). The

researchers compared the histories of 191 lung cancer patients and a control group of 191 people who did not have lung cancer; none of the subjects had ever smoked. Lifetime exposure to smoke in the home was calculated by multiplying the number of smokers in the household by the number of years the subject had lived there. Exposure to 25 or more 'smoker-years' in childhood and adolescence doubled these non-smokers' risk of developing lung cancer. The researchers estimated that 17 per cent of non-smoker lung cancers were caused by 'passive' smoking in childhood.

Another recent study found that non-smoking spouses of cigarette smokers are 30 per cent more likely to die of heart disease than non-smokers who do not live with smokers (Glantz & Parmely, 1991). Passive smoking kills in the region of one in every 5,000 non-smokers annually; for the population of Great Britain allowing for the proportion of the public who already smoke, this means that, conservatively estimated, eight to nine thousand people a year. This makes it a very significant cause of preventable death (alongside active smoking, alcohol abuse and road traffic accidents).

Even pre-natal exposure to cigarette smoke is dangerous. A mother who smokes during pregnancy increases the probability of miscarriage, birth complications, low birth weight and cot death (Schelkun, 1990). Attention deficits reflecting impulsivity and high activity levels have been found in four to seven-year-olds whose mothers smoked while pregnant. These results held up even when the effects of post-natal exposure to secondhand smoke were taken into account (Kristjansson *et al*, 1989).

The prohibition of smoking in many public places may curb passive smoke health problems. However, it would be problematic to legislate so as determine what smokers do in the privacy of their own homes. Modifying private behaviour requires renewed psychological efforts to change the consciousness, attitudes and behaviour of smokers and non-smokers. Although still a highly contentious issue in numerous countries, many health advocates seek to persuade smokers to respect the rights of others to breath smoke-free air in shared environments and thereby limit the damage to health that might otherwise occur through the passive inhalation of tobacco smoke.

TABLE 11.7 STAGES IN STABLE DECISION-MAKING/COGNITIVE APPRAISAL

Stage	Key Questions
1. Appraising the challenge	Are the risks serious if I don't change?
2. Surveying alternatives	Is this alternative an acceptable means for dealing with the challenge?
3. Weighing alternatives	Have I sufficiently surveyed the available alternatives?
	Which alternative is best?
	Could the best alternative meet the essential requirements?
4. Deliberating about commitment	Shall I implement the best alternative and allow others to know?
5. Adhering despite negative feedback	Are the risks serious if I don't change? Are the risks serious if I do change?

moderate the effects of stressors, psychologist **Suzanne Kobasa** believes a particular personality type and associated outlook on life is even more important in diffusing stress. She identified two groups of subjects from a pool of managers working for a public service company in a large city; the members of one group experienced high levels of stress but rarely were ill, while the members of the second group felt similarly stressed but often experienced illness (Kobasa *et al*, 1979). The stress survivors displayed the attributes of what Kobasa called **hardiness**. Hardiness involves maintaining an outlook that is typified by: firstly, welcoming change as a challenge and not as a threat; secondly, having focused commitment to purposeful activities; and thirdly, having a sense of internal control over one's actions. These three Cs of hardiness – *challenge, commitment* and *control* – are adaptive interpretations of potentially stressful events. Collectively they create resilience, thereby protecting and enhancing well-being during demanding episodes in our lives (Kobasa, 1984).

When students who differed in terms of hardiness (as measured by a questionnaire) were presented with a threat, they also differed in terms of their reactions to the threat. The 60 men and 60 women who had the top third and bottom third scores were selected from over 800 students who completed the hardiness scale. The stressor was an experimental task in which subjects were expected to be videotaped whilst repeating a lecture they had heard previously and were then to be evaluated and questioned by psychology teaching staff. The researcher manipulated the perceived threat and the challenge of the task along with several other hardiness-related variables. She found that the high-hardiness subjects differed from the low-hardiness ones in showing better tolerance of frustration and in appraising the task as less threatening. Additionally, hardiness influenced heart-rate responses among the men (but not the women): high-hardiness men were less physiologically aroused by the event than their low-hardiness counterparts (Wiebe, 1991).

While hardiness has received much attention as a moderator variable which diminishes the undesirable effects of distress, other personality attributes have also been associated with the concept of stress. Are you a daredevil, mountain climber, or off-piste skier? Does your temperament drive you to a life of risk-taking, stimulation and excitement seeking? If this description fits you, you could fit **Type-T personality** mould where the T stands for 'thrills'. Psychologist **Frank Farley** (1990) issues the challenge:

'You may not have heard of this personality, but I will wager that you know some people who show the pattern of characteristics I have listed above.' He adds, 'I believe Type T is at the basis of both the most positive and constructive forces in our nation' . . . (for example, creativity of all kinds) . . . 'and the most negative and destructive forces' . . . (such as vandalism, theft, joy-riding, taking hard drugs, excessive use of alcohol).

Most people fall between the high risk, thrill and stimulation-seeking positions and those who actively avoid any risk or thrill. The Type-T personality and its related Type-T behaviours are further examples of moderator variables that play a role in the psychology of stress.

Physiological Stress Reactions

As people we are often on the move; most of us will move a number of times; often considerable distances from our families, friends and hometowns. Moving involves a host of stressors that function at all levels: loss of the familiar, fear of the unknown, the physical work of packing and moving, and the mental distraction of coping with unpacking and putting your belongings in new places. Getting used to a new environment or new neighbours also creates stress.

These transient states of arousal, with typically clear onset and offset patterns, are examples of acute stress. **Chronic stress** is a state of enduring arousal, continuing over time, in which demands are perceived as greater than the inner and outer resources available for dealing with them (Powell & Eagleston, 1983). An example of chronic stress might be a continuous frustration with the lack of control you have to change the annoying habit of others who seem to constantly monopolise the only nearby telephone kiosk. These acute or chronic states of arousal are expressed on several levels as physiological aspects of the stress response and also as psychological stress reactions.

In Chapter 2, we learned that the brain developed originally as a centre for more efficient coordination of action. Efficiency is flexible responding to changing environmental requirements and also quick, often automatic responding. One set of brain-controlled physiological stress responses occurs when an external threat is perceived (a predator or a menacing loud noise in the night, for example). Instant action and extra strength may be needed if the organism is to survive. A whole constellation of automatic mechanisms has evolved to meet this need. Another set of physiological stress reactions occurs when the danger is internal, and the stability and integrity of the organism are threatened by invading microbes or other disease agents that upset the normal physiological processes.

Emergency reactions to external threats

In the 1920s, **Walter Cannon** outlined the first physiological description of the way animals and humans respond to external danger. He found that a sequence of activity is triggered in the nerves and glands to prepare the body for combat and struggle – or for running away to safety. Cannon called this dual-stress response the **fight-or-flight syndrome**.

At the centre of this primitive stress response is the hypothalamus, which is involved in a variety of emotional responses. The hypothalamus has sometimes been referred to as the stress centre because of its twin functions in emergencies: (a) it controls the autonomic nervous system (ANS); and (b) it activates the pituitary gland.

The ANS regulates the activities of the body's organs. In stressful conditions, breathing becomes faster and deeper, heart rate increases, blood vessels constrict, and blood pressure rises. In addition to these internal changes, muscles open the passages of the throat and nose to allow more air into the lungs while also arising in conjunction with facial expressions of strong emotion. Messages go to smooth muscles to stop certain bodily functions, such as digestion, which are irrelevant to preparing for the emergency at hand.

Another function of the autonomic nervous system during stress is to get adrenaline (epinephrine) flowing. It signals the inner part of the adrenal glands, the adrenal medulla, to release two hormones, adrenalin and noradrenalin (norepinephrine), which, in turn, signal a number of other organs to perform their specialised functions. The spleen releases more red blood corpuscles (to aid in clotting if there is an injury), while the bone marrow is stimulated to make more white corpuscles (to combat possible infection). The liver is stimulated to produce more sugar, building up body energy.

The pituitary gland responds to signals from the hypothalamus by secreting two hormones vital to the stress reaction. The thyrotrophic hormone (TTH) stimulates the thyroid gland, which makes more energy available to the body. The **adrenocorticotrophic hormone (ACTH)**, known as the 'stress hormone', stimulates the outer part of the adrenal glands, the adrenal cortex, resulting in the release of a group of hormones called **steroids**, which are important in metabolic processes and in the release of sugar from the liver into the blood. ACTH also signals various organs of the body to release about 30 other hormones, each of which plays a role in the body's adjustment to this call to arms. However, ACTH also plays a negative role. Its action reduces the ability of natural killer cells to destroy cancer cells and other life-threatening infections. When the body is stressed chronically, the increased production of 'stress hormones' compromises the immune system. A summary of this physiological stress response is shown in *Figure 11.3*.

It is obvious, then, that many bodily processes are activated during the physiological stress response to danger signals. Let us consider their adaptive significance in two different stressful situations.

When a call comes into a firestation, the fire-fighters respond in part with the physiological components of the stress response. Muscles tense, breathing speeds up, heart rate increases, adrenaline flows, extra energy becomes available, and the fire fighters become less sensitive to pain. They will need these responses in order to endure the physical strain of battling a fire. The built-in capacity to deal with physical stressors by mobilising the body's active response systems has been valuable to our species for thousands of years. In studies of African baboon colonies, stress hormone levels are highest when there

FIGURE 11.3 THE BODY'S REACTIONS TO STRESS

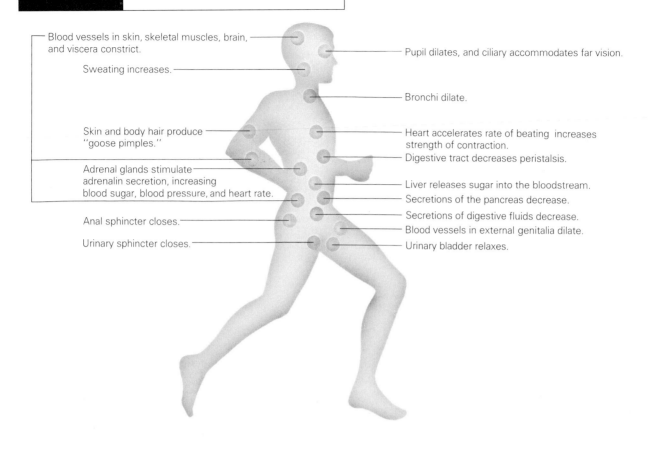

Blood vessels in skin, skeletal muscles, brain, and viscera constrict.

Sweating increases.

Skin and body hair produce "goose pimples."

Adrenal glands stimulate adrenalin secretion, increasing blood sugar, blood pressure, and heart rate.

Anal sphincter closes.

Urinary sphincter closes.

Pupil dilates, and ciliary accommodates far vision.

Bronchi dilate.

Heart accelerates rate of beating increases strength of contraction.

Digestive tract decreases peristalsis.

Liver releases sugar into the bloodstream.

Secretions of the pancreas decrease.

Secretions of digestive fluids decrease.

Blood vessels in external genitalia dilate.

Urinary bladder relaxes.

is least social control and predictability but lowest among dominant males whose behavioural traits reflect high degrees of social skillfulness, outlets for frustration, social affiliation (with infants and females), predictability and control (Sapolsky, 1990).

Now consider people working on a crisis hotline, taking calls from potentially suicidal strangers. These workers undergo the same physiological stress responses as the fire fighters as a result of the psychological stressors they face. However, in contrast to the fire fighters, their physiological responses, except for the heightened attentiveness, are not adaptive. The hotline volunteer cannot run away from the stressor or fight with the caller; the unconditioned fight-or-flight syndrome is out of place and as a response is a biological anachronism and a hindrance. They must, instead, try to stay calm, concentrate on listening, and make thoughtful decisions. These interpersonal skills, though, are not enhanced by the physiology of the stress response. So what has developed in the species as an adaptive preparation for dealing with external danger is now counterproductive for dealing with many contemporary sources of stress. Rather than relying on avoidance ('flight') or hostility ('fight'), we must learn new adaptive stress responses.

The general adaptation syndrome (GAS)

One of the first researchers to systematically investigate the effects of continued severe stress on the body was **Hans Selye**, a Canadian endocrinologist. Beginning in the late 1930s, Selye reported on the complex response of laboratory animals to damaging agents such as bacterial infections, toxins, trauma or forced restraint, heat and cold. According to Selye's theory of stress, there are many kinds of stress-producing agents (stressors) that can trigger the same systematic reaction or general bodily response. All stressors call for adaptation: an organism must maintain or regain its integrity and well-being by restoring equilibrium, or homeostasis. The theory conceptualises stress as a state *within* the organism, rather than being contained within the transactions *between* people. Psychosomatic disorders are problems in organic functioning of the body, such as asthma and peptic ulcers, caused in part by mental and emotional conditions. They are called *diseases of adaptation* because they are conceived as being rooted in the organism's attempts to adapt physiologically to events that are experienced as stressful.

The general adaptive response to such nonspecific

| **FIGURE 11.4** | THE GENERAL ADAPTATION SYNDROME |

Following exposure to a stressor, the body's resistance is diminished until the physiological changes of the corresponding alarm reaction bring it back up to the normal level. If the stressor continues, the bodily signs characteristic of the alarm reaction virtually disappear; resistance to the particular stressor rises above normal but drops for other stressors. This adaptive resistance returns the body to its normal level of functioning. Following prolonged exposure to the stressor, adaptation breaks down; signs of alarm reaction reappear, the stressor effects are irreversible, and the individual becomes ill and may die.

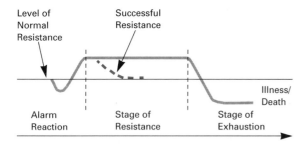

agents was described by Selye as the **general adaptation syndrome (GAS)**. It purports to include three stages: an alarm reaction, a stage of resistance and a stage of exhaustion (Selye, 1956). The GAS is adaptive because, during the stage of resistance, the organism can endure and resist further debilitating effects. This stimulated defence against the stressor develops and maintains an intermediate stage of restoration. The three stages are shown in *Figure 11.4* and *Table 11.8*.

The concept of the general adaptation syndrome has proven valuable to explain disorders that had baffled physicians who had never considered *felt stress* as a cause of illness and disease. Within this framework, many health outcomes can be viewed as the result of the physiological processes involved in the body's long-continued attempts to adapt to a perceived threatening stressor.

On the other hand, because Selye was a physician and because his research focused on reactions to physical stressors among experimental animals, his theory has had little to say about the importance of psychological aspects of stress in the case of human beings. In particular, Selye's critics believe he overstated the role of nonspecific, *systemic* factors in the production of stress-induced illness. The word 'systemic' refers to the workings of the whole body as an integrated system. In research on animals, of course, there was little possibility of accessing and measuring cognitive appraisal, important though it nevertheless may be in other species (Mason, 1975).

Psychoneuroimmunology

A relatively new research area that investigates the effects of stress on the physiological and biological functions of the body is **psychoneuroimmunology (PNI)**. This is the field of endeavour that investigates the inseparable fusion and relation between 'mind' and 'body', particularly the interaction between felt stress and the immune system (Ader, 1990). Our opening case featured the role of humour in enhancing health by altering immunological functioning. Researchers consistently have found a link between stress and declines in indicators of immune activity. For example, a causal link was shown between being exposed to uncontrollable stress and the increase in cancer among susceptible animals (Laudenslager *et al*, 1983). Recall the research in Chapter 7 on conditioning of rats' immune systems to respond to a sweet-tasting solution, subsequently suppressing immune reactions and leading to their untimely demise (Ader & Cohen, 1981; 1993). Also recall the new research on laughter therapy for immune system dysfunction described in the opening case.

Unique white blood cells, **T-lymphocytes**, have a number of subgroups with important functions. Two of these groups are helper and suppressor T-lymphocytes which act by stimulating or shutting off the immunological response to an invading organism. Along with natural killer cells, they provide an important defence against virus-infected cells and cancer cells. The brain can influence the immune system in two ways: through the nerve connections between brain regions and organs in the immune system and through connections of the endocrine system and immune system. The brain triggers the endocrine system to release hormones; receptors for various hormones are located on lymphocyte cells in the immune system, making the immune system responsive to the action of the endocrine system (see Chapter 2).

A number of studies with humans have shown that the quality of interpersonal relationships and their disruption or absence have strong effects on the immune system (Cohen & Syme, 1985; Kiecolt-Glaser & Glaser, 1990). Bereavement and depression also produce immunosuppression: men with wives dying of breast cancer (Schleifer *et al*, 1983) and recently widowed women (Irwin *et al*, 1987) are less able to fight disease and face an increased risk of illness and premature death. As expected, the immune functioning of a group of chronically-stressed individuals living near the damaged Three Mile Island nuclear power plant decreased more than that of a demographically comparable control group (McKinnon *et al*, 1989).

Health psychologist **Judith Rodin** has been studying the mechanisms by which psychological

TABLE 11.8	GENERAL ADAPTATION SYNDROME

Stage I: Alarm Reaction (continuously repeated throughout life)

- Enlargement of adrenal cortex
- Enlargement of lymphatic system
- Increase in hormone levels
- Response to specific stressor
- Adrenaline release associated with high levels of physiological arousal and negative affect
- Greater susceptibility to increased intensity of stressor
- Heightened susceptibility to illness

(If prolonged, the slower components of the GAS are set into motion, beginning with Stage II.)

Stage II: Resistance (continuously repeated throughout life)

- Shrinkage of adrenal cortex
- Return of lymph nodes to normal size
- Sustaining of hormone levels
- High physiological arousal
- Counteraction of parasympathetic branch of ANS
- Enduring of stressor; resistance to further debilitating effects
- Heightened sensitivity to stress

(If stress continues at intense levels, hormonal reserves are depleted, fatigue sets in, and individual enters Stage III.)

Stage III: Exhaustion

- Enlargement/dysfunction of lymphatic structures
- Increase in hormone levels
- Depletion of adaptive hormones
- Decreased ability to resist either original or extraneous stressors
- Affective experience – often depression

variables affect the immune system. She is investigating how giving people, especially the elderly, an increased sense of personal control improves their health through intermediary changes generated in the immune system. In addition, Rodin is exploring how stress factors may explain why 80 per cent of the women undergoing a precise medical procedure to implant a fertilised egg reject it. In part, the rejection may be due to the stress associated with the procedure itself (Rodin, 1990).

 Psychological Stress Reactions

Our physiological stress reactions are automatic, predictable, built-in responses over which we normally have no conscious control. However, our psychological reactions are learned. They depend on our perceptions and interpretations of the world and on our capacity to deal with stress. Psychological stress reactions are behavioural, emotional and cognitive.

Behavioural patterns

The behaviour observed as a reaction to a stressor is a key dependent measure in most psychological studies of stress. Certain stress-related behaviours, such as muscle tension or spasms, can be observed. Similarly, nonconscious reactions, such as grinding one's teeth during sleep (known as *bruxism*) can be used as indexes of stress. However, almost any behaviour can be part of a stress response. To create a base rate of responding, against which to compare stress-related reactions, it is important to have an understanding of the frequency of the behaviour *prior* to the advent of a stressor. For example, consuming sugar-coated pastries can be construed as a behavioural stress response if the person hardly ever ate sweet snacks before being diagnosed as a diabetic.

The behaviour of a person who has been confronted with a stressor depends in part on the level of stress experienced. Very different reaction patterns have been associated with mild, moderate and severe levels of stress.

Mild stress activates and intensifies biologically

significant behaviours, such as eating, aggression and sexual behaviour. Mild stress makes an organism more alert – energies are focused and performance may improve. It may lead to positive behavioural adjustments, such as becoming better informed, becoming vigilant to sources of threat, seeking protection and support from others, and learning better attitudes and coping skills. Continued unresolved mild stressors can cause maladaptive behavioural reactions such as increased irritability, poor concentration, lessened productivity and chronic impatience. However, they pose no problem when they occur only occasionally or are perceived as within one's capacity to control.

Moderate stress typically disrupts behaviour, especially behaviour that requires skilled coordination. Giving a speech or playing in a recital are familiar examples of moderate stress situations. For some people, over-eating is a typical behavioural response to moderate levels of stress. Overt aggressive behaviour can also occur, especially in response to frustration. Moderate stress may also produce repetitive, stereotyped actions, such as pacing in circles or rocking back and forth. These repetitive responses have mixed effects. They are adaptive by reducing a high level of stressor stimulation and lessening an individual's sensitivity to the environment. At the same time, they are nonadaptive by being rigid and inflexible, and in persisting even when the environmental situation makes other responses more appropriate.

Severe stress inhibits and suppresses behaviour and may lead to total immobility. We noted such effects in the case of the dogs and humans that experienced learned helplessness (Chapter 7) when they were shocked electrically, regardless of their actions (Seligman, 1975). It has been argued that immobility under severe stress may be a defensive reaction, representing 'an attempt by the organism to reduce or eliminate the deleterious effects of stress . . . a form of self-therapy' (Antelman & Caggiula, 1980).

Emotional aspects

Most stress is acutely uncomfortable, producing only negative emotions and efforts to lessen the discomfort in direct or indirect ways. Stressful life changes involving loss or separation from friends and loved ones are frequent forerunners of depression. Being left behind is more likely to result in depression than a separation caused by one's own action (Paykel, 1973). Experiencing a cluster of stressful events is another predictor of emotional depression.

Rape and incest victims, survivors of plane and serious automobile crashes, combat veterans, and others who have experienced traumatic events that lie well outside one's usual day-to-day frame of reference, may respond emotionally with a **post-traumatic stress disorder (PTSD)**. PTSD is a psychologically invasive stress response that recurs repeatedly, even long after the traumatic experience. In addition, victims experience an emotional numbing in relation to everyday events and feelings of alienation from other people. The emotional pain of this reaction can result in an increase of various symptoms, such as sleep problems, guilt about surviving, difficulty in concentrating and an exaggerated startle response. The clinical symptoms of PTSD are described as conditioned responses learned in the context of a powerful life-threatening stimulus situation (Keane et al, 1985).

The following excerpt of a discussion about the aftershock of being raped reveals the powerful and enduring emotional dimension of the post-traumatic stress reaction.

Alice: *I was in shock for a pretty long time. I could talk about the fact that I was a rape victim, but the emotions didn't start surfacing until a month later.*

Elizabeth: *During the first two weeks there were people I had chosen to tell who were very, very supportive; but after two weeks, it was like, 'Okay, she's over it, we can go on now'. But the farther along you get, the more support you need, because, as time passes, you become aware of your emotions and the need to deal with them.*

Alice: *There is a point where you deny it happened. You just completely bury it.*

Elizabeth: *It's so unreal that you don't want to believe that it actually happened or that it can happen. Then you go through a long period of fear and anger.*

Alice: *I'm terrified of going jogging. (Alice had been jogging when she was raped.) I completely stopped any kind of physical activity after I was raped. I've started it again . . ., but every time I go jogging I have a perpetual fear. My pulse doubles. Of course I don't go jogging alone any more, but still the fear is there constantly. There's also a feeling of having all your friends betray you. I had a dream in which I was being assaulted outside my student hall. In the dream, everyone was looking out their windows – the faces were so clear – every one of my friends lined up against the windows watching, and there were even people two feet away from me. They all saw what was happening and none of them did anything. I woke up and had a feeling of extreme loneliness.*

(For a systematic analysis of psychological and social issues involved in rape, see Cann et al, 1981; Baron & Straus, 1989.)

British war veterans visiting the World War II Normandy graves of their comrades. The vestiges of prolonged post-traumatic stress reaction have been identified in some war veterans 50 years on. Ambivalence at home toward national involvement in conflict (for example, the Vietnam, Falklands and Persian Gulf wars), heightens the difficulty returning soldiers have in adjusting to civilian life.

The emotional responses of post-traumatic stress can occur in an acute form immediately following a disaster and can subside over a period of several months. These responses can also persist, becoming a chronic syndrome called the **residual stress pattern** (Silver & Wortman, 1980). They can also be delayed for months or even years. Clinicians are still discovering veterans of World War II and the Korean War who are displaying residual or delayed post-traumatic stress reactions (Dickman & Zeiss, 1982).

Cognitive effects

Once a stressor has been interpreted as threatening to one's well-being or self-esteem, a variety of intellectual functions may be adversely affected. These may be when admittedly irrational thoughts create generalisations from any element of the stress situation to remotely similar current stimulus events. In general, the greater the stress, the greater the reduction in cognitive efficiency and the more interference with flexible thinking. Because attention is a limited resource, when we focus on the threatening aspects of a situation and on our arousal, we reduce the amount of attention available for effectively coping with other tasks at hand. Memory is affected too, because short-term memory is limited by the amount of attention given to new input. Also, retrieval of past relevant memories depends on the smooth operation and use of appropriate retrieval cues. Similarly, felt stress may interfere with problem solving, judging and decision making by narrowing perceptions of alternatives and by substituting stereotyped, rigid thinking for more creative responses (Janis, 1982a). Finally, there is evidence that a high level of stress impairs children's intellectual development.

To test the hypothesis that stress affects competence and intelligence, researchers developed a stress index based on such variables as family problems and physical disorders. Stress indexes were calculated for over 4,000 seven-year-old children, and each child's intelligence was tested. The higher the stress index, the lower was the child's IQ. This was particularly true for children with eye problems and for African-American children from poor families. Greater intellectual deficits showed up also in those who had been held back a year or assigned to special education classes. The stress variables combined to

INTERIM SUMMARY

Stress is the pattern of reactions an organism makes in response to stressors, stimulus events that tax its ability to cope. Stress can be negative (distress) or positive (eustress). Change and the need to adapt to biological, social, physical and environmental demands are basic causes of stress. An accumulation of life changes and especially of chronic hassles in everyday existence can become sufficiently stressful to seriously affect functioning and health. Survey studies of natural disasters and catastrophes find evidence for a sequence of stages or phases that marks changing patterns of coping over time. Chronic stressors of society, such as pollution of the environment, passive smoking and our fears of anticipated nuclear disasters, crime, and economic failure strain us biologically and mentally.

We do not react directly to the objective qualities of stressors but, instead, in the form of cognitive appraisal, to our perceptions and interpretations of them. Appraisal is a primary stress moderator, filtering and changing the effect of stressors on our experience of stress. Other moderator variables are our internal and external resources for dealing with a stressor, certain personality attributes such as hardiness, and coping patterns. Cognitive appraisal defines the perceived demand; primary appraisal determines whether the demand is felt as stressful; secondary appraisal evaluates the available personal and social resources and the appropriate action.

Physiological stress reactions are automatic mechanisms facilitating swift emergency action. They are regulated by the hypothalamus and include many emergency body changes, carried out through the action of the autonomic nervous system and the pituitary gland. They lessen sensitivity to pain and provide extra energy for fight or flight. They are useful for combatting physical stressors, but they can be maladaptive in response to psychological stressors, especially when stress is severe or chronic. The general adaptation syndrome is a three-stage pattern of physiological defences against continuing stressors that threaten internal well-being. A resistance stage follows the alarm reaction; psychological defences are activated until adaptive resources fail in the stage of exhaustion. The interaction between body, mind and environmental stimulation is central to the study of psychoneuroimmunology which focuses on the impact of psychosocial variables on the immune system.

Psychological stress reactions include behavioural, emotional and cognitive elements. Mild stress can enhance performance and even be experienced as pleasant and challenging. Moderate stress disrupts behaviour and may lead to repetitive, stereotyped actions. Severe stress suppresses behaviour and typically causes dysfunctional reactions. Emotional stress reactions include irritation, anger and depression. Post-traumatic stress reactions are delayed emotional stress responses that prolong the negative consequences of acutely stressful and unusual experiences. Cognitive stress reactions include a narrowing of attention, rigidity of thought, and interference with judgement, problem solving and memory.

---

influence the performance measured by the IQ test both in the immediate testing situation and also more generally, through interacting with other personal and social factors (Brown & Rosenbaum, 1983).

◆ COPING WITH STRESS

If living is inevitably stressful, and if chronic distress can disrupt our health and even kill us, we need to learn how to manage the causes of stress in order to improve the quality of our lives. Coping refers to the process of dealing with internal or external demands that are perceived as straining or exceeding an individual's resources (Lazarus & Folkman, 1984). Coping may consist of behavioural, emotional, or motivational responses and thoughts. It can also precede a potentially stressful event in the form of **anticipatory coping** (Folkman, 1984). For example,

how do you tell your parents that you are dropping out of the education system, or your lover that you are no longer in love? The anticipation of stressful situations leads to many thoughts and feelings which themselves may be stress-inducing, as in the cases of tests, interviews, speeches or blind dates.

Psychologists have made great advances in conceptualising and measuring coping (Carver et al, 1989; Folkman et al, 1986; Holahan & Moos, 1987). Measures of coping that are targeted for particular groups, such as adolescents experiencing similar stressors, may be more useful than more general coping measures designed for the so-called average person (Wills, 1986).

Human beings have a tremendous potential for adapting, not only biologically over generations but psychologically, within a lifetime – even within a short period of time if they decide they want to change. In this section, we will look at a variety of strategies that people use to alter or reduce the harmful effects of stress.

◆ Coping Strategies

The two main types into which we can categorise coping strategies are determined by whether the goal is to confront the problem directly – *problem-solving focus* – or lessen the discomfort associated with the *stress-emotion-regulation focus* (Billings & Moos, 1982; Lazarus & Folkman, 1984). Several subcategories of these two basic approaches are shown in *Table 11.9*.

'Taking the bull by the horns' is how we can characterise the strategy of facing up to a problem situation. This approach includes all strategies designed to deal directly with the stressor, whether through overt action or realistic problem-solving activities. In school, we may have faced up to a bully or run away; we may have tried to win him or her over with bribes or other incentives. Taking martial arts training or notifying the 'proper authorities' are other approaches that might prevent a bully from continuing to be a threat. In all these strategies, our focus is on the problem to be dealt with and on the agent that has induced the stress. We acknowledge the call to action; we appraise the situation and our resources for dealing with it; and we undertake a response that is appropriate for removing or lessening the threat. Such problem-solving efforts are useful for managing controllable stressors.

The second approach is useful for managing the impact of more uncontrollable stressors. We do not look for ways of changing the external stressful situation; instead, we try to change our feelings and thoughts about it. This strategy that regulates emotions is a remedial coping strategy.

Ego defence mechanisms, such as repression, denial of reality, and rationalisation, are emotion-regulating approaches to personal stress that we often use without conscious awareness. The goal of these defence mechanisms is to protect us from anxieties by enabling us to appraise situations in less self-threatening ways. They lead to coping strategies that are essentially aimed at self-protection rather than at solving problems. At times, however, they cause us to distort reality and, when overused, can lead to maladaptive coping.

What is your typical coping style? 'More' is definitely 'better', as far as coping is concerned (Taylor & Clark, 1986). For coping to be successful, our resources need to match the perceived demand. So, successful coping depends on a match of coping strategies to the features of the stressful event. The availability of multiple coping strategies would, then, be most adaptive because we are more likely to achieve a match and manage the stressful event. When we know that we possess a large repertoire of coping strategies, that metacognition increases our confidence in meeting environmental demands. That self-confidence, that belief in our own self-efficacy (Bandura, 1986), in turn can insulate us from experiencing the full impact of many stressors because believing we have the coping resources readily available immediately bypasses the stressful chaotic response of 'What am I going to do?'

◆ Modifying Cognitive Strategies

A powerful way to handle stress more adaptively is to change our evaluations of stressors and our self-defeating cognitions about the way we are dealing with them. We need to find a different way to think

TABLE 11.9	TAXONOMY OF COPING STRATEGIES

Problem-focused Coping Change stressor or one's relationship to it through direct actions and/or problem-solving activities	**Fight (destroy, remove, or weaken the threat)** **Flight (distance oneself from the threat)** **Seek options to fight or flight (negotiating, bargaining, compromising)** **Prevent future stress (act to increase one's resistance or decrease strength of anticipated stress)**
Emotion-focused Coping Change self through activities that make one feel better but do not change the stressor	**Somatically focused activities (use of drugs, relaxation, biofeedback)** **Cognitively focused activities (planned distractions, fantasies, thoughts about oneself)** **Unconscious processes that distort reality and may result in intrapsychic stress**

about a given situation, our role in it, and the causal attributions we make to explain the undesirable outcome. Two ways of mentally coping with stress are reappraising the nature of the stressors themselves and restructuring our cognitions about our stress reactions.

Reappraising stressors

Learning to think differently about certain stressors, to relabel them, or to imagine them in a less-threatening (perhaps even funny) context are forms of cognitive reappraisal that can reduce stress. Are you worried about giving a speech to a large, forbidding audience? One stressor reappraisal technique is to imagine your potential critics sitting there in the nude – this surely takes away a great deal of their fearsome power. Anxious about being shy at a party you must attend? Think about finding someone who is more shy than you and reducing his or her social anxiety by initiating a conversation.

Restructuring cognitions

A summary of the literature on stress and performance points to an individual's uncertainty about impending events and sense of control over them as the main factors in perceived stress (Swets & Bjork, 1990). Effective coping strategies must counter by providing the person in a stressful setting with some or all of four types of control: information control (knowing what to expect); cognitive control (thinking about the event differently and more constructively); decision control (being able to decide on alternative actions); and behavioural control (taking actions to reduce the aversiveness of the event).

We can manage stress better by changing what we tell ourselves about it and by changing our handling of it. These strategies can lead to cognitive restructuring and more effective coping. For example, depressed or insecure people often tell themselves that they are no good, that they'll do poorly, and – if something goes well – that it was a fluke or just random luck.

Cognitive-behaviour therapist **Donald Meichenbaum** (1977) has proposed a three-phase process to intentionally change this self-fulfilling cycle. In Phase I, people work to develop a greater awareness of their actual behaviour, what instigates it, and what its results are. One of the best ways of doing this is to keep daily diaries. By helping people redefine their problems in terms of their causes and results, diaries can increase their feelings of control. In Phase 2, they begin to identify new behaviours that negate the maladaptive, self-defeating behaviours – perhaps smiling at someone, offering a compliment, or acting assertively. In Phase 3, after adaptive

TABLE 11.10	EXAMPLES OF COPING SELF-STATEMENTS

Preparation	I can develop a plan to deal with it.
	Just think about what I can do about it. That's better than getting anxious.
	No negative self-statements, just think rationally.
Confrontation	One step at a time; I can handle this situation.
	This anxiety is what the doctor said I would feel; it's a reminder to use my coping exercises.
	Relax; I'm in control. Take a slow deep breath.
Coping	When fear comes, just pause.
	Keep focus on the present; what is it I have to do?
	Don't try to eliminate fear totally; just keep it manageable.
	It's not the worst thing that can happen.
	Just think about something else.
Self-reinforcement	It worked, I was able to do it.
	It wasn't as bad as I expected.
	I'm really pleased with the progress I'm making.

behaviours are being emitted, individuals appraise their consequences, avoiding the former internal dialogue of put-downs. Instead of telling themselves, 'I was lucky the tutor put that question to me as I just happened to have read the text last night', they say, 'I'm glad I was prepared for the lecturer's question. It felt good to be able to respond in an informed and thoughtful way'.

This three-phase approach means initiating responses and self-statements that are incompatible with previous defeatist cognitions. Once started on this path, people realise that they are changing and taking full credit for positive developments which promote further successes. *Table 11.10* gives examples of the kinds of self-statements that help in dealing with stressful situations.

One of the major variables that promotes positive adjustments is **perceived control** over the stressor, a belief that you have the ability to make a difference in the course or the consequences of some event or experience. If you believe that you can affect the course of the illness or the daily symptoms of the disease, you are probably adjusting well to the disorder (Affleck *et al*, 1987). However, if you believe the source of the stress is another person whose behaviour you cannot influence or a situation that you cannot change, your chances of a poor psychological adjustment to the chronic condition increase (Bulman & Wortman, 1977).

In a classic study by **Ellen Langer** and **Judith Rodin** (1976), two simple elements of perceived control were introduced into a nursing home environment. Each resident was given a plant to take care of (behavioural control) and asked to choose when to see films (decision control). Comparison subjects on another floor of the institution had neither sense of control; they were given plants that nurses took care of and they saw films at pre-arranged times. On delayed measures several weeks later and a full year later, those elderly patients who had been given some control over the events in this bleak institutional setting were more active, had more positive moods, and were psychologically and physically healthier than the no-control patients. Most amazing is the finding that, one year later, fewer of those in the perceived control situation had died than those on the comparison floor (Langer & Rodin, 1976; Rodin, 1983). Such research findings have important implications for policies and programmes in institutional settings (Rodin, 1986).

Other social and psychological dimensions of the environment can also be critically important in increasing or decreasing stress. For example, the perceived freedom of choice to either enter or not enter a particular environment may determine whether a person will adapt successfully to it. One study determined that elderly women who chose to enter a retirement home lived longer, as a group, than those with an initially comparable health status who entered feeling they had no choice (Ferrare, 1962).

◆ **Supportiveness of the Environment**

We all cope with stress as individuals, but, for a lifetime of effective coping and for the continued success of our species, it is necessary for us to form alliances with others. Isolation can lead to inadequate coping and can itself be the cause of stress. Contemporary research shows that being part of a social support network and living and working in a healthy environment leads to an improvement in coping.

Social support networks

Social support refers to the resources others provide, giving the message that one is loved, cared for, esteemed, and connected to other people in a network of communication and mutual obligation (Cobb, 1976; Cohen & Syme, 1985). In addition to these forms of socioemotional support, other people may provide tangible support (money, transportation, housing) and informational support (advice, personal feedback, information). Anyone with whom you have a significant social relationship – such as family members, friends, co-workers, and neighbours – can be part of your social support network in time of need.

Much research points to the power of social support and its *perceived availability* in moderating personal vulnerability to stress (Cohen & McKay, 1983). When people have other people they can turn to, they are better able to handle job stressors, unemployment, marital disruption, serious illness and other catastrophes, as well as their everyday problems (Gottlieb, 1981; Pilisuk & Parks, 1986). The positive effects of social support go beyond aiding psychological adjustment to stressful events; they can improve recovery from diagnosed illness and reduce the risk of death from specific diseases (House *et al*, 1988; Kulik & Mahler, 1989). Research shows that lack of a social support system clearly increases one's vulnerability to disease and death (Berkman & Syme, 1979). Decreases in social support in family and work environments are related to increases in psychological maladjustment. This negative correlation was found even when the researchers looked at groups who had the same initial levels of support, maladjustment, and life change (Holahan & Moos, 1981). Prospective studies, which control for initial health status,

Where do health psychologists work? Despite the biopsychosocial model having obvious implications for health care, the present role of the health psychologist in an applied setting is still being developed and negotiated. Unlike clinical psychologists whose career routes and courses have been validated and well established for many years, the *practice* of health psychology is still in its infancy, relatively speaking. In Great Britain, for example, somewhat ironically health psychology is most often applied and delivered by clinical psychologists: a new hybrid known as *clinical health psychologists* have begun to emerge, who despite being trained initially in the ways of secondary prevention are being drawn post-qualification as practitioners to developing a primary preventative role. Arguably, there is room for the development of one further hybrid, the occupational health psychologist, who would specialise in promoting practices and relations which enhance well-being, specifically at work. A recent multi-method, multi-measure health study by Marmot *et al* (1991) of over 10,300 British, London-based government workers concluded that attention needs to be paid to social psychological aspects of work (in particular, to perceived autonomy), to job design (notably, to variety) and to the health consequences, psychological and otherwise, of income inequality. Notwithstanding calls for even greater

specialisation, distinctive post-graduate courses in generic health psychology have emerged in recent years and moves are afoot to establish a qualificatory route to a professionally unique role and identity within the health care services. For the moment though, many health psychologists who describe themselves as such, work in a research, academic or educational capacity, mapping out the bedrock of this fast growing discipline.

So, what do practising health psychologists do, apart from those involved in teaching and research? Providing information about health enhancing behaviours to would-be users is one function a health psychologist can fulfill. It is, however, the most rudimentary since it rests on the supposition that knowledge is in itself an amulet which will protect its wearer against harm and disease. In some instances, knowledge of the beneficial consequences of an activity is enough to produce a change in health behaviour, particularly if the

recipient has a pre-existing perceived need for such a personal transformation. Knowledge, though, is frequently not always sufficient for the adoption, initiation and maintenance of health behaviours. A regular intravenous drug user, for instance, is likely to be acutely aware of the health consequences of sharing a hypodermic needle; however, such knowledge may be inadequate as a deterrent to desist from this dangerous practice. A health psychologist's role, then, is much more than that of educator. Centrally, the health psychologist must work to enable people to *influence* and *enhance* their health status (as far as local constraints allow) by creating and being part of a psychological and social environment that supports and sustains primary health cognitions, behaviours and interpersonal transactions, helping individuals and communities where necessary to develop the skills needed to engage beneficially in such processes.

Perceived control over the stressor promotes positive adjustments. Nursing-home residents given plants to care for and the choice of when to see films are more active and have more positive moods.

consistently show an increased risk of death among people whose social relationships are low in quantity and quality (House et al, 1988).

Researchers are trying to identify which types of support are most helpful for specific events (Cohen, 1988; Dakof & Taylor, 1990; Dunkell-Schelter et al, 1987). Different sources of support seem to work best for particular stressors – for example, active and equal participation in childcare by each spouse plus the availability of affordable créche facilities would be ideal for working parents with a newborn child (Lieberman, 1982).

Researchers are also trying to determine when sources of support actually increase anxiety. For example, if your mother insisted on accompanying you to a doctor's appointment or to an interview when you preferred to go alone, you might experience additional anxiety about the situation (Coyne et al, 1988). Too much or too intensive social support may become intrusive and not helpful in the long run; having one close friend may be as beneficial as having many. Research shows that symptoms of depression are more likely to increase for a married person who is unable to communicate well with his or her spouse than for a control subject without a spouse (Weissman, 1987).

Leading health psychologist **Shelley Taylor** studied the effectiveness of the different types of social support given to cancer patients (Taylor, 1986; Dakof & Taylor, 1990). Patients varied in their assessments of the helpfulness of kinds of support. They thought it was helpful to them for spouses but not for physicians or nurses to 'just be there'. On the other hand, it was important to the patients to receive information or advice from other cancer patients or from physicians but not from family and friends. Regardless of the source – whether doctors or family or friends – patients did not find forced cheerfulness or attempts to minimise the impact of their disease helpful.

Other research focuses on the problems caregivers experience as they attempt to provide social support, these problems including giving support that is intense, long-term, unappreciated, or rejected (Coyne, et al, 1988; Kiecolt-Glaser et al, 1987; Schulz et al, 1987).

Payload specialist and scientist-astronaut Millie Hughes-Fulford is one of NASA's psychological researchers who has studied ways to help astronauts cope with the stress of long-duration space travel.

Structuring the physical environment

Psychological researchers involved in space exploration programmes have found that they can help astronauts cope with the stress of long-duration space travel by designing the space capsule in ways that make it more relaxing. The capsule is painted in colours found to be most psychologically pleasing – the walls are darker at the bottom to create an illusion of more height and space. Pictures of Earth's rivers, waterfalls and mountains are found to be the most effective types of posters for combating the sense of separation and isolation space travellers experience.

Psychologists now realise that, in addition to changing behaviour patterns and cognitive styles, stress management should involve restructuring our physical environments to reduce their unhealthy or stress-inducing features.

INTERIM SUMMARY

Coping strategies are means of dealing with the perceived threat of various types of stressors. Two primary coping categories proposed by Lazarus are problem-focused coping, or taking direct actions, and emotion-regulation coping, which is often indirect or avoidant. We can learn to manage stress better through reappraising the nature of the stressors and by restructuring our relevant cognitions. A significant stress moderator is social support. Health is promoted by developing and being an active member of a social support network. However, the quality and nature of the source of social support are important components that affect people's evaluations of the sources. While social isolation is a reliable predictor of psychological, social and medical pathologies, appropriate kinds of social networks are health-promoting. At times, the best coping strategy entails taking action to restructure the physical and/or social environments in which we live, study and work.

◆ HEALTH CARE SYSTEM AND HEALTH POLICY FORMATION

A final focus of health psychology is the delivery of health care that includes health institutions, the health professionals who staff them, and health policies. Within this domain, we will consider two issues in particular: firstly, occupational exhaustion or 'burn-out' amongst care workers; and secondly, methods of delivering care to long-term hospital patients.

◆ Job Burn-out

Providing health care can be an enormously challenging and rewarding career. However, the daily routine of nurses, social workers, casualty and emergency room personnel, hospice workers, and other trained specialists includes dealing with pain, illness, poverty and death. Even the most enthusiastic health care workers run up against the emotional stresses of working intensely with many people suffering from a variety of personal, physical and social problems. The particular emotional stress experienced by these professional health and welfare practitioners has been called 'burn-out', a term that owes its origins to the Graham Greene novel *A Burnt-Out Case* (1961) but which was appropriated and first explored within a social science framework by Freudenberger (1974). **Job burn-out** is a syndrome of emotional exhaustion, depersonalisation and reduced personal accomplishment that is often experienced by workers in professions that demand high intensity interpersonal contact with patients, clients, or the public. **Christina Maslach** is a leading research psychologist on this widespread problem and has found that 'burnt out' health practitioners begin to lose their caring and concern for patients and may come to treat them in detached and even dehumanised ways. They begin to feel bad about themselves and worry that they are failures. Burn-out is correlated with greater absenteeism and turnover, impaired job performance, poor relations with co-workers, family problems, and poor personal health (Leiter & Maslach, 1988; Maslach, 1982; Maslach & Florian, 1988).

Several social and situational factors affect the occurrence and level of burn-out and, by implication, suggest ways of preventing or minimising it. For example, the quality of patient-practitioner interaction is greatly affected by the number of patients for whom a practitioner is providing care – the greater the number, the greater the cognitive, sensory and emotional overload. Another factor in the quality of that interaction is the amount of direct contact with patients. Longer work hours in continuous direct contact with patients or clients are correlated with greater burn-out, especially when the nature of the contact is very difficult and upsetting, such as contact with patients who are dying or who are verbally abusive. The emotional strain of such prolonged contact can be eased by a work schedule that provides chances for a practitioner to withdraw temporarily from such high-stress situations by restructuring the type of contact to using a team rather than only individual contact and by arranging for opportunities for positive feedback for one's efforts (Schau Feli *et al*, 1993).

Individualised care has been shown to be of greater benefit to the patient than task-oriented care.

◆ Personalising Care Delivery

The needs of the care workers, though, must be finely balanced against those of the patients in their charge. The relationship between job burn-out and individual contact with patients in hospital settings presents a dilemma for health care professionals: in particular, it has been shown that *individualised* care (where one nurse carries out all care tasks for a particular patient) is of greater benefit to the health of elderly long-stay patients than is *task-oriented* care, wherein each nurse performs one designated care task for all of the patients on a ward (Miller, 1985). In her study, Miller compared two such wards, one run on the individualised system where each nurse was responsible for between six and eight patients, the other using the task-oriented method where nurses were expected to fulfill a designated function for all 30 patients. She found striking differences between the two in terms of the health behaviour and well-being of the elderly, long-term patients on these two wards. For example, she observed on the individualised ward during the day that nine per cent of such patients were in bed as compared with 45 per cent of elderly patients on the task-oriented ward; 16 per cent required spoon-feeding on the latter ward whilst only four per cent needed this on the individualised unit; and further, she found that 63 per cent of patients on the task-oriented ward were suffering with faecal incontinence whilst only 30 per cent were likewise incapacitated on the individualised ward. Thus, there was less evidence of self-care amongst the patients and more signs of dependency on nursing staff on the ostensibly efficient, task-oriented unit, than on the ward where individual attention was the norm. Of greater concern still was that Miller (1985) also discovered these differences to be mirrored in discharge and mortality rates: there were fewer discharges of patients and more deaths on the task-oriented care ward than on the unit using the personal-care approach.

Individualised care, then, benefits the patient directly. It allows the nurse to get to know the patient and better understand their particular health concerns and needs. A task-oriented approach may advance speed of execution of essential care-related duties, but its largely impersonal style tends to promote an objectification of the patient which is antithetical to building up an understanding of each one as a unique person. There is little time or opportunity in such a system to develop a detailed knowledge of a patient's biography, or to come to know of their capacity for resourcefulness or of their desire to engage in a modicum of self-care. Such a depersonalising method of working can foster feelings of helplessness in the patient and create dependency, ironically increasing the work-load of the already hard-pressed hospital staff, and the risk of patient mortality (Brauer, Mackeprang & Bentzon, 1978). Thus, task-oriented care is ultimately both counter-productive for health care systems and for long-stay patients. Such findings have readily apparent implications for health policies which emphasise maximising the short-term efficiency of staff and the turnover of those in need of care at the expense of regular, one-to-one, extended contact with skilled health professionals – nurses, doctors and psychologists alike. For people undergoing prolonged periods of hospitalisation, then, 'personalised care' means 'quality care'.

◆ POINTERS TO HEALTH

Choices we make about our own health behaviours are governed to an extent by the particular range of opportunities that are available to us. Within such a range, however, and without trying to induce an excessive amount of guilt, no doubt you are aware of making some choices from those possible that contribute to your distress and lack of optimal health:

for example, choosing not to exercise regularly, to commute long distances, not to eat a balanced diet, to be overly competitive, to work too much, to relax too little and not to take time to cultivate friendships. As we have seen, such choices may produce stress that is damaging to your health and well-being.

Instead of waiting for stress or illness to come and then reacting to it, we can set goals and structure our lives and lifestyles in ways that are most likely to forge healthy foundations. Obviously, the exact nature of these will depend on the particular present circumstances and past biography of each individual. However, the following steps are presented as general principles for promoting greater happiness and better mental health. They may encourage you to take more of an active role in your own life and to maintain a positive psychological environment for yourself and others. Having read this health psychology chapter, you might like to consider what other points you would wish to add to these suggestions:

(a) Use situational, not just dispositional, explanations when looking for the causes of your behaviour in current circumstances or in its relation to past ones. Understand the behaviour of others, the *social context*, as setting conditions for your behaviour.

(b) Try not to be self-derogatory. Look for sources of your unhappiness in contextual elements that can be modified by future actions. Give yourself and others *constructive criticism* – what can be done differently next time to produce a more positive outcome?

(c) Compare your reactions, thoughts and feelings to those of comparable individuals in your life currently. In this way, you can gauge the *appropriateness* and relevance of your responses against a suitable social norm.

(d) Maintain close relations with friends with whom you can share feelings, joys and worries. Work at developing, maintaining and expanding these social support networks.

(e) Seek to develop a sense of a balanced time perspective in which you can flexibly focus on the demands of the task, the situation, and your needs; be future oriented when there is work to be done, present oriented when the goal is achieved and pleasure is at hand, and past oriented to keep you in touch with your roots and with a sense of your own personal identity.

(f) Always take credit for your successes and happiness. Share your positive feelings with other people. Keep a note of all the qualities that make you special and unique, and which you can offer others. For example, a shy person can offer a talkative person the gift of attentive listening. Know your sources of personal strength and available coping resources.

(g) When you feel you are losing control over your emotions: distance yourself from the situation by physically leaving it; role-play the position of another person in the situation or conflict; project your imagination into the future to gain perspective on what seems an overwhelming problem now; and talk to a sympathetic listener. Feel and express your emotions.

(h) Remember that failure and disappointment are sometimes blessings in disguise. They may tell you that your goals are not right for you or save you from bigger letdowns later on. Learn from every failure. Acknowledge it by saying, 'I made a mistake' and move on. Every accident, misfortune, or violation of your expectations is potentially a learning opportunity in disguise.

(i) If you discover you cannot help yourself or another person in distress, seek the counsel of a

Cultivating healthy activities with others can promote greater happiness and better mental health.

trained specialist in your health centre or community. In some cases, a problem that appears to be psychological may really be physical, and vice versa. Check out your student counselling services before you need them, and use them without any concern about being stigmatised.

(j) Cultivate healthy pleasures. Take time out to relax, to meditate, to have a massage, to fly a kite, to enjoy hobbies and activities that you can do both alone and with others. By means of these, you can be uplifted to better appreciate yourself and others.

As a postscript, to end where we began this chapter, remember to take time out to laugh with others, perhaps gently at yourself occasionally and at the passing absurdities of the human condition. Use your imagination to discover the unfamiliar, create the unusual, and to get the most out of what appear mundane activities. Learn to play with life, its possibilities and activities (as well as to be goal-oriented and serious-minded), indeed as if it were part of a *Candid Camera* scenario that requires that we smile as often as we can because, after all, 'living well is the best revenge'.

And if all else fails: have a nice cup of tea! Researchers Stensvold, Tverdal, Solvoll and Foss (1992) have found, in a study of over 20,000 Norwegian men and women without history of diabetes or cardiovascular disease, that serum cholesterol, systolic blood pressure and mortality rates are inversely related to tea consumption. Could there be a direct effect, or does greater consumption represent increased social support from those with whom tea drinkers share their brew? We leave the question to be answered by further research.

recapping main points

Health Psychology

Health psychology is a new field that is devoted to the prevention of illness, the maintenance of health and, to a lesser extent, to treatment and rehabilitation. The biopsychosocial model of health and illness looks at the connections among physical, emotional, and environmental factors in illness. Health promotion and maintenance are not just individual matters – they represent an important area where community and government policy can help improve everyone's quality of living. Psychosocial treatment of illness adds another dimension to patient treatment. Studies show that the functioning of the immune system improves with this approach to treatment. Illness prevention in the 1990s will focus on lifestyle factors such as weight, nutrition and risky behaviour. AIDS is one of the most threatening illnesses we face today and can be combatted by reducing risky behaviour and continuing community education.

The Stress of Living

Stress can be negative or positive. Stress is studied using a variety of models. At the root of most stress is change and the need to adapt to environmental, biological, physical and social demands. Cognitive appraisal is a primary moderator variable of stress. Physiological stress reactions are regulated by the hypothalamus and a complex interaction of the hormonal and nervous systems. Psychoneuroimmunology is the study of how psychosocial variables affect the immune system. Depending on its severity, stress can be a mild disruption or lead to dysfunctional reactions.

Coping with Stress

Coping strategies either focus on problems (taking direct actions) or attempt to regulate emotions (indirect or avoidant). Social support is a significant stress moderator. At times, the best coping strategy is to restructure one's work or home environment.

key Terms

acute stress
adrenocorticotrophic hormone (ACTH)
AIDS (acquired immune deficiency syndrome)
amygdala
anticipatory coping
behavioural health
biofeedback
biopsychosocial model
chronic stress
cognitive appraisal
coping
daily hassles
daily uplifts
demands
emotion
emotion-focused coping
fight-or-flight syndrome
general adaptation syndrome (GAS)
hardiness
health
health belief model
health psychology
HIV (human immunodeficiency virus)
illness
illness prevention
job burn-out
life-change units (LCU)
life events
passive smoking
patient non-adherence

perceived control
positive illusions
post-traumatic stress disorder/reaction (PTSD)
primary appraisal
primary care
primary prevention
problem-focused coping
protection-motivation theory
psychoneuroimmunology (PNI)
psychosomatic disorders
relapse
relaxation response
residual stress pattern
resources
risk behaviours
secondary appraisal
secondary care
secondary prevention
social support
social support network
self-efficacy theory
steroids
strain
stress
stress moderator variables
stressor
tertiary care
T-lymphocytes
Type-A behaviour syndrome
Type-T personality

major Contributors

Cannon, Walter (1871–1945)
Coates, Thomas
Cousins, Norman
Farley, Frank
Izard, Carroll
James, William (1842–1910)
Kobasa, Suzanne
Langer, Ellen
Lazarus, Richard
Maslach, Christina

Matarazzo, Joseph
Meichenbaum, Donald
Pennebaker, James
Rodin, Judith
Seligman, Martin
Selye, Hans (1907–82)
Spiegel, David
Steptoe, Andrew
Taylor, Shelley
Tompkins, Sylvan

Chapter 12

Personality and Individual Differences

On the afternoon of 11 February 1990, Nelson Rolihlahla Mandela, aged 71, was released from the gilded cage of Victor Verster prison, where he had lived for the last two years of his prolonged confinement. Just before 4.00pm he walked through the gates of the jail, with his wife Winnie accompanying him, to a long-awaited freedom. Since 5 August 1962, he had endured over 27 years in captivity as a political prisoner and opponent of the apartheid regime in South Africa. Now after 10,000 days of confinement, he was finally free, his release symbolising the imminent emancipation of black South Africans and an end to many years of racial inequality. As he raised his right arm and clenched hand in the Afrika salute, the welcoming crowd of several thousand people roared their approval. The cheers and celebration were echoed by well-wishers throughout the watching world. Four years later, during the last week of April 1994, all that Nelson Mandela had toiled and battled for over the preceding decades of his epic life was realised when the country's first non-racial, one-person-one-vote, national election took place. It was the first time in South Africa's history that the nation's black majority had been given the opportunity to elect its country's leaders. These were joyful, buoyant days for the newly enfranchised electorate as they represented the fulfilment of a hard-fought and protracted struggle against oppression and for the recognition of their fundamental human and democratic rights. The African National Congress (ANC) party of which Nelson Mandela was leader, polled just short of two-thirds of the total vote, securing 252 of the 400 seats in the national assembly. Accordingly, soon afterwards on 10 May 1994, Nelson Mandela was inaugurated in Pretoria as President of South Africa's first democratically elected, multi-racial government. His nation and its people were free at last.

During the transitional period between Mandela's release in 1990 and election as President in 1994, he emerged as an elder statesman of

exceptional political and moral integrity. At a time when he could have become embittered and resentful about his long years spent in captivity and dwelt upon all the pleasures of his family life that he had missed, he neither displayed signs of anger nor of wanting to seek retribution against those who had detained him. Instead, he rose still further as an inspirational and humanitarian figure, binding and healing his fractured nation and, in the process, showing himself to be an open-minded man of tolerance and considered reason, a charismatic leader who would continue to put the needs of his nation's people before those of himself.

During the 1950s he had led a 'Programme of Action' characterised by non-violent resistance to racial apartheid which nevertheless led to the banning in 1960 of the ANC and the outlawing of its members, effectively forcing them underground. After the shooting in the same year at Sharpeville, however, of 69 fleeing African civilians by local police and the ensuing imposition of martial law across the country, his position changed. Following much deliberation (as it was a departure from a 50-year ANC policy), in 1961 Nelson Mandela formed a military organisation which was separate from the ANC called

Umkhonto we Sizwe (MK) – *The Spear of the Nation*. Its objective was to disrupt the apparatus of the state by acts of sabotage, such as the cutting of government telephone lines, and thereby to bring the regime to the negotiating table. Members were instructed that causing loss of life through such acts would not be tolerated. It was not long, though, before Mandela was arrested in August 1962 and put on trial two years later, along with many others, on charges of 'sabotage', 'treason' and 'violent conspiracy' against the South African state. Henceforth, he was assigned the label of 'terrorist' by his opponents and jailed indefinitely as a result of his political and humanitarian convictions.

Despite these adverse experiences, Nelson Mandela emerged as a magnanimous, competent and composed leader. We do not need to look far, however, before we discover the origins of these notable attributes. Born on 18 July 1918, he spent the first nine years of his life as a rural African boy in the village of Mvezo, in the district of Umtata, the capital of the Transkei. Mvezo is home of the Thembu people who are a part of the Xhosa nation – of which Nelson Rolihlahla Mandela is a member. It was here that he enjoyed a childhood of unrestrained freedom, exploring with his young playmates the open fields of rural Africa. It was here that he learned the value of forming bonds of friendship with others and of freedom of movement and expression, the memory of which spurred him on to re-realise such a state throughout his adult life. It is from this context that Mandela derived his strong sense of a cultural identity, of a sense of connectedness with others in a community wherein reciprocal altruism and obligations to members of an extended family were of paramount importance. It was here that Mandela experienced the value of the collective – of the group over and above that of the individual.

Sadly, at the age of nine, Mandela's father died and he became fostered by the wealthy regent of the Thembu people. Mandela's guardian was to be his benefactor for the next ten years, enabling him to take advantage of continued schooling and, thereafter, higher education at both Fort Hare and Witwatersrand universities. The Thembu regent also became his role model in so far as Mandela's later ideas about leadership were significantly informed by his recollections of his guardian as he and the Thembu court dispatched the duties of the chieftaincy. Thus, despite the early loss of his father, these positive learning experiences equipped Mandela with the confidence and capacity to take on a similar role as leader in his subsequent adult life. His cultural identity and self-esteem were strongly reinforced by the supportive presence and positive regard of his generous guardian. From these beginnings, in later years Mandela grew to appreciate and emulate the reasonableness and calmness in a crisis of his great friend and ally Walter Sisulu, who, with Mandela and Oliver Tambo, was to become a founder member of the ANC Youth League and a long-serving comrade and inmate on Robben Island.

IF AS PSYCHOLOGISTS of personality we were to be asked in conversation, '*What kind of man do you think is President Nelson Mandela?*', in all likelihood we might draw on commonplace descriptors to outline his distinctive characteristics – for example: 'resilient' and 'dignified', for successfully enduring hardship as a political prisoner on Robben Island (from 1964 to 1982) and at Pollsmoor maximum security prison (from 1982 to 1988), despite being unable to help his frequently harrassed wife or to attend the funeral of his eldest son, Thembi, killed in a car accident in 1969 ; 'conscientious', 'committed' and 'competent' for, amongst many other things, helping in 1944 to form and actively participate in the ANC Youth League and in 1952 for setting up and running with Oliver Tambo the first black law practice in Johannesburg; and 'genial', 'caring' and 'emotionally stable', for the way in which he has valued and enjoys the companionship of others but also appreciates solitude and opportunities for quiet reflection in which to reaffirm his plans and sense of inner equilibrium – themes which are evident recurrently in the accounts given of interactions with either family and friends or captors and colleagues in his autobiography, *Long Walk to*

Freedom (1994). Certainly, many have recognised these qualities and the significance of his restorative work as arbiter and reconciliator. Indeed, he and former President F.W. de Klerk were jointly awarded the Nobel Peace Prize in 1993.

During the process of selecting these trait descriptors from our individual vocabularies of ordinary language, we might first think over what we have seen and known of Nelson Mandela; then, search for consistencies and continuities in the way in which he has conducted himself across this range of situations and circumstances; and on the basis of such observable evidence, attribute the cause of any cross-situational consistency to either an ongoing internal disposition (to a 'personality trait') or to some recurrent feature of the contexts and environments in which his actions were 'scripted' and took place. Depending also in part upon our own motives, various descriptions then may ensue. Indeed, Nelson Mandela has been characterised and portrayed variously throughout his years of struggle and self-sacrifice. 'Freedom fighter' and 'radical revolutionary' were more complimentary representations of his activities than the derogatory epithets that frequently were used by his adversaries and detractors.

From this brief profile of President Nelson Mandela, you may have formed your own impressions of his personality. Central to our sketched outline has been a search for continuities in observable reaction patterns across the life span, from childhood, through young and middle adulthood and on into old age. However, if psychologists were to focus upon you, what portrait of your personality would they draw? What early experiences might they identify as contributing to how you now act and think? What current conditions in your life exert strong influences on your moods and choices? To what extent does culture or biological disposition influence your personality, intelligence and identity? What makes you different from other individuals who are functioning in many of the same situations and circumstances as you? In this chapter we will consider ways in which such questions can be answered by reviewing available theoretical approaches to personality and by examining measurement techniques used to assess similarities and differences between people.

◻ THE PSYCHOLOGY OF THE PERSON

Psychology is primarily concerned with the individual *person* who is conceived as an embodied social agent capable of self-reflection and moral judgement (Jansz, 1991). Thus, a person is at once both a bodily and psychological unity, having the capacity to behave in accordance with reflections about his or her own preferences. As persons we experience others as having similar capacities. As we have noted elsewhere in this text, cultures differ, however, in the extent to which they place emphasis upon the individual or social origins of personhood. In most Western societies, for example, as well as in mainstream psychology, people are said to *have* a 'self' and 'personality', being conceived as embodied properties of the person over which he or she is assumed to have ownership, responsibility and control. Through such ownership is implicit the notions that people *are* persons and *are* themselves, behaviour being interpreted largely as a reflection of an authentic and distinctive inner-self. Indeed, persons are primarily viewed in this individualistic tradition as autonomous agents, capable of constructing and reconstructing themselves in an image of their own choosing. This notion of the person, however, is in sharp contrast to that which can be found in collectivist cultures wherein the social and relational embeddedness of the self, its identity and of personality is of central explanatory importance (Markus & Kitayama, 1991; Gergen, 1987). Throughout reading this chapter on personality, the cultural and historical relativity of assumptions underlying the ways in which we talk about ourselves as persons need to be continually borne in mind.

Psychologists define *personality* in many different ways, but common to all of the ways are two basic concepts: uniqueness and characteristic patterns of behaviour. We will define personality as the complex set of unique psychological qualities that are said to influence an individual's characteristic patterns of behaviour across different situations and over time. Investigators in the field of personality psychology seek to discover how individuals differ, acknowledging that while there are many similarities between people, there are also numerous differences. They study the extent to which personality traits and behaviour patterns are consistent and thus predictable, from one situational context to another. Personality psychologists, like many developmental ones, are interested in continuities in behavioural functioning over time, as we indicated in our opening account of Nelson Mandela.

Up to this point in the text, we have seen how empirical investigations focus on specific processes that are similar in all of us. In this chapter we will examine the individual as the sum of those separate processes of feelings, thoughts and actions. It is not just that people look different or respond differently to the same stimulus in a common situation. There also seems to be a subjective, private aspect to personality that gives coherence and order to behaviour – a consistent aspect of each of us that we call our 'self'. We will begin by examining the major issues and strategies in the study of personality and then survey the major theories, each of which focuses on slightly different aspects of human individuality. Thereafter, in the second half of this chapter we will examine how psychologists have sought to measure these individual differences by critically reviewing concepts and methods of psychological assessment, including an analysis of intelligence within this context.

The field of personality psychology attempts to integrate all aspects of an individual's functioning. This integration requires the psychologist to build on the accumulated knowledge of all the areas of psychology we have already studied and social psychology, which studies interpersonal and group processes. Personality psychology also goes beyond an interest in the normally functioning individual; it provides the research and theoretical foundation for understanding personal problems and pathologies of body, mind and behaviour (Chapters 11 and 14) as well as a basis for therapeutic approaches to change personality (Chapter 15).

Strategies for Studying Personality

Let us begin by examining your own personality theory. Think of someone you really trust. Now think of someone you know personally who is a role model for you. Imagine the qualities of a person with whom you would like to spend the rest of your life and then of someone you never feel comfortable being around at all. In each case, some of that which springs to mind immediately are personal attributes, such as honesty, reliability, sense of humour, generosity, outgoing attitude, aggressiveness, moodiness and pessimism. You probably have spent a great deal of time trying to get a handle on who you are, on the distinguishing features of your personality, on the personal traits you would like to change, and on those you would like to develop. In all these cases, your judgements were, in fact, naive personality assessments – your **implicit personality theory**. They were based largely on intuition and limited, uncontrolled, non-systematic observations. Such naive judgements can often be accurate, but they are also open to many sources of error. We tend to have one-dimensional impressions of many people because we see them in only one or a few kinds of situations and, often, their behaviour is strongly influenced by features of those situations which in themselves constitute an unrepresentative sample. In addition, you may elicit certain types of reactions from them that they do not typically make around other people.

You should be aware that your impressions of others may be biased by these and other factors, leading you to an interpretation of their personality that may not agree with the way they perceive themselves or the way others see them.

Personality researchers try to assess personality in more systematic ways. Their data come from five different sources:

- *Self-report* data are what people say about their own behaviour, attitudes and traits, often in a personality test or inventory.
- *Observer-report* data reveal what friends, parents, colleagues and other raters or evaluators say about an individual.
- Specific *behavioural* data is systematically recorded information about what a person says or does in a particular situation.
- Life-events data are *biographical* facts (level of education, marriage status or having parents who divorced).
- *Physiological* data include information about heart rate, skin conductance, biochemistry of hormones and neurotransmitter functioning.

These types of data can be interpreted using either of two basic approaches to the study of personality: the idiographic approach and the nomothetic approach. The **idiographic approach** is person-centred, focusing on the way unique aspects of an individual's personality form an integrated whole. It assumes that traits and events take on different meanings in different people's lives. The primary research methodologies of the idiographic approach are the case study and the aggregate case study. A **case study** uses many data sources to form a psychological biography of a single individual; this chapter's opening account is an example of a short case study. The **aggregated case study** is a comparison of idiographic information about many individuals. For example, a summary of the reports on many women with multiple personality disorders, each of whom was studied individually by a given researcher-therapist, is an aggregate case study.

The **nomothetic approach** is variable-centred, assuming that the same traits or dimensions of personality apply to everyone in the same way – people simply differ in the degree to which they possess each characteristic. Nomothetic research looks for relationships between different personality traits in the general population. The correlational method is used to determine the extent to which two traits or types of data tend to show up together in people. The focus of this method is on discovering lawful patterns of relationships among traits and among the traits and behaviour of most people. In nomothetic research, the richness and uniqueness of the individual case is sacrificed for broader knowledge about dimensions of personality that are valid for people in general. When many traits and types of information are studied at one time or answers to numerous questionnaire items from many people are obtained, a multivariate form of correlational analysis, known as **factor analysis**, can be used to examine such a multiplicity of data. This statistical technique enables researchers to search for and explore the underlying dimensions (factors) that the different data points may have in common (Child, 1991).

When psychologists wish to study how personality changes over time, they use either **cross-sectional** or **longitudinal research designs**. In a cross-sectional design, several groups of subjects would be selected, each representing a different age level, and studied at the same time. However, personality development can be better understood through a longitudinal design in which the same group of individuals is studied many times but at different ages over a number of successive years. Some longitudinal studies cover large sections of the life-span – for example, Farrington's (1991) 24-year follow-up study of 'anti-social personality' amongst 400 males from the age of eight to 32. Though such studies are time-consuming and expensive, they provide invaluable information about personality development and its consequences for behaviour at a later date. Often in cross-sectional research it is difficult to establish the direction of the relationship between personality and behaviour. Longitudinal designs hold out the hope of disentangling this 'chicken or egg' problem, of which came first – cause or effect?

Theories About Personality

Theories about personality are hypothetical statements about the structure and functioning of individual personalities (Wiggins & Pincus, 1992). They help us achieve two important goals: (a) understanding the origins, structure and correlates of personality; and (b) predicting behaviour and life events based on what we know about personality. Different theories make different predictions about the way people will respond and adapt to certain conditions.

Before we examine some of the major theoretical approaches, we should ask why there are so many different (often competing) theories. Theorists differ in their approaches to personality by varying their starting points and sources of data and by trying to explain different types of phenomena. Some are interested in the structure of individual personality and others in how that personality developed and will continue to evolve. Some are interested in what

people do, either in terms of specific behaviours or important life events, while others study how people feel about their lives. Some theories try to explain the personalities of people with psychological problems, while others focus on healthy individuals. Finally, some psychologists are interested in personality as a basis for understanding their own and others' predilections for various types of world view and forms of psychological explanation which thereby ensue (Johnson *et al* 1988). Thus, each approach can teach us something about personality and taken together can inform us incrementally about the psychology of personhood.

Theoretical approaches to understanding personality can be grouped into three categories: type and trait, psychodynamic and humanistic, and learning and cognitive theories. We shall now discuss each of these.

INTERIM SUMMARY

The implicit theories we use to understand and predict people's behaviour may be biased because they are based on unsystematic observations; often we make judgements about people after seeing them in only one type of situation. Personality psychologists draw their theories from systematic observations of individuals in many situations. They combine data from self reports, observer reports, specific behaviour observations, life events and physiological measures to obtain a well-rounded picture of human personality. The personality theories we will examine in this chapter are based on different types of data and aim to explain different types of phenomena, such as relations between traits in the general population or case studies of individuals.

TYPE AND TRAIT PERSONALITY THEORIES

Labelling and classifying the many personality characteristics we observe can help us organise human behaviour. However, this is no simple task. In fact, a dictionary search by psychologists **Gordon Allport** and H. S. Odbert (1936) found over 18,000 adjectives in the English language to describe individual differences!

Two of the oldest approaches to describing personality involve classifying people into a limited number of distinct *types* and scaling the degree to which they can be described by different *traits*. What does each concept contribute to our understanding of personality?

▣ Categorising by Types

The most simple way to classify people is according to some distinguishing feature or via a small number of categories. These may include class in school, academic subject, sex, race, honesty and shyness. Some personality theorists also group people according to their **personality types**, distinct patterns of personality characteristics used to assign people to categories. These categories do not overlap: if a person is assigned to one category, he or she is not in any other category within that system. Personality types are all-or-none phenomena and not matters of degree.

Early personality typologies were designed to specify a concordance between a simple, highly visible or easily determined characteristic and some behaviours that can be expected from people of that type. If fat, then jolly; if an accountant, then conservative; if female, then sympathetic. You can appreciate why such systems have traditionally had much popular appeal and still do in the mass media – they simplify a very complicated process of understanding the nature of personality.

One of the earliest type theories was proposed in the fifth century BC by **Hippocrates**, the Greek physician who gave medicine the 'Hippocratic oath'. He theorised that the body contained four basic fluids or humours, each associated with a particular temperament. An individual's personality depended on which humour was predominant in his or her body. Hippocrates paired body humours with personality temperaments according to the following scheme:

- Blood – sanguine temperament: cheerful and active
- Phlegm – phlegmatic temperament: apathetic and sluggish
- Black bile – melancholy temperament: sad and brooding
- Yellow bile – choleric temperament: irritable and excitable

Mention here must also be made of Heymans' personality typology. Inspired by Hippocrates and a founding figure of contemporary personality research, Heymans carried out one of the first large-scale surveys in the history of psychology and produced an empirically derived model of personality types (Heymans & Wiersma, 1918). His typology was represented three-dimensionally in what has become known as *Heymans' Cube*.

Another interesting type theory of personality was advanced by **William Sheldon** (1942), an American physician who related physique to temperament. Sheldon assigned people to three categories based on their **somatotypes** (or body builds):

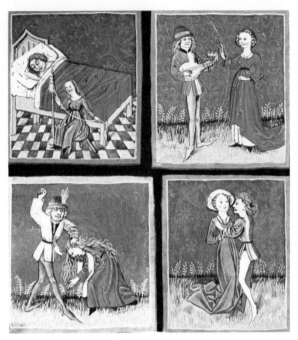

Clockwise: melancholy patient suffers from an excess of black bile; blood impassions sanguine lutist to play; a maiden, dominated by phlegm, is slow to respond to her lover; choler, too much yellow bile, makes an angry master.

- **Endomorphic** (fat, soft, round): these people are relaxed, fond of eating and sociable.
- **Mesomorphic** (muscular, rectangular, strong): these are physical people, filled with energy, courage and assertive tendencies.
- **Ectomorphic** (thin, long, fragile): these are brainy, artistic and introverted people who would think about life, rather than act upon it or engage in consumption.

The typology specified relationships between each physique and particular personality traits, activities and preferences. Sheldon's theory of personality and body types is intriguing, but not substantiated. People come in many different shapes and sizes and cannot be assigned readily to one of Sheldon's three somatotypes. Moreover, it has proven to be of little value in predicting an individual's behaviour (Tyler, 1965).

A popular typology is derived from Carl Jung's theory of personality types (1953). Using the Myers-Briggs Type Indicator (MBTI), people's self-reported preferences are used to measure four dimensions: extraversion-introversion (E-I), sensing-intuition (S-N), thinking-feeling (T-F) and judgement-perception (J-P). If you took this test, you would be assigned to only one side of each dimension and the combination of dimensions would determine which of the 16 possible types best describes you. For example, people of type ENFP (Extraverted-Intuitive-Feeling-Perceiving) are said to be 'enthusiastic innovators' who are 'skilful in handling people' but 'hate

William Sheldon related physique to temperament by assigning people to categories based on their somatotypes. Endomorphic people are fat, soft and round. Mesomorphic people are muscular, rectangular and strong. Ectomorphic people are thin, long and fragile.

uninspired routine'. This is a type system because the categories are distinct or discontinuous and people of one type are supposed to be very much like each other in ways that distinguish them from other types (Myers, 1987). The MBTI typology is widely used, particularly in occupational settings, because people who take the test find the types easy to understand. However, opponents of the system believe that the four dimensions are informative, but that people should be described according to their actual scores on each dimension instead of being collapsed into types.

Describing with Traits

Type theories presume that there are separate, discontinuous categories into which people fit. By contrast, trait theories propose hypothetical, continuous dimensions, such as intelligence or warmth, that vary in quality and degree. **Traits** are generalised action tendencies that people possess in varying degrees; they lend coherence to a person's behaviour in different situations and over time. For example, you may demonstrate honesty on one day by returning a lost wallet and on another day by not cheating on a test. Some trait theorists think of traits as predispositions that cause behaviour, but more conservative theorists use traits only as descriptive dimensions that simply summarise patterns of observed behaviour. Of late, the descriptive endeavour has busied and extended itself by studying the trait terminology of naturally occurring language (Semin & Krahe, 1987; Hofstee, 1990).

Gordon Allport (1937; 1961; 1966) was an influential personality theorist who viewed traits as the building blocks of personality and the source of individuality. Though he was largely responsible for giving the word 'trait' its status as an empirical concept, his contemporary Murray (1938) was implicitly identifying an analogous notion by virtue of postulating a 'need for achievement' which vary in degree from person to person. According to Allport, traits produce coherence in behaviour because they are enduring attributes and are general in scope. Traits connect and unify a person's reactions to a variety of stimuli, as shown in *Figure 12.1*.

Traits may act as intervening variables, relating sets of stimuli and responses that might seem, at first glance, to have little to do with each other. Allport identified three kinds of traits according to how encompassing they are:

- *A cardinal trait* is a trait around which a person organises his or her life. A cardinal trait might be

FIGURE 12.1	SHYNESS AS A TRAIT

Traits may act as intervening variables, relating sets of stimuli and responses that might seem, at first glance, to have little to do with each other.

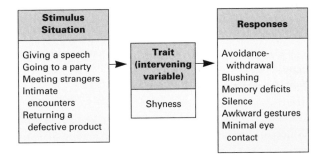

self-sacrifice for the good of others, as we saw in the example of Nelson Mandela in the opening case. Most people do not develop a cardinal trait, however.

- **Central traits** are those said to represent the major characteristics of a person.
- **Secondary traits** are specific, personal features that are less useful for understanding an individual's personality.

According to Allport, traits form the structure of personality, which in turn determines an individual's behaviour. He alleged that an individual's personality can be described if you know the six to ten traits that are central to his or her behaviour. Whether a trait is central or secondary depends on the extent of the influence that trait exerts in the life of the person. Allport saw personality structures, rather than environmental conditions, as the critical determiners of individual behaviour. '*The same fire that melts the butter hardens the egg*', was a phrase he used to show that the same stimuli can have different effects on different individuals. Although he recognised common traits that individuals share in a given culture, Allport is well known as an idiographic trait theorist: he believed that each person has some unique characteristics which allows him or her to be a singular entity, as well as having some common ones, which together form a unique combination of traits. He championed the use of case studies to examine these unique traits, for 'by learning to handle the individuality of motives and the uniqueness of personality, we shall become better scientists, not worse' (Allport, 1960).

In one famous case, Allport studied in depth 301 letters written by a woman named Jenny over an 11-year period. He used factor analysis to examine the way she typically combined key words into units of meaning and found evidence for seven cardinal traits that described the way she expressed herself in the letters. In a separate phase of the study, eight cardinal traits – such as aggressive and sentimental – were derived from the impressions of 36 judges who read the letters. The two independently derived sets of traits were very similar, demonstrating that personality could be reconstructed from other sources when traditional personality tests were unavailable (Allport, 1965; 1966).

Are Traits Heritable?

Where do family resemblances in personality come from? Are they inherited (such as the colour of your eyes) or learned (such as speech mannerisms)? Such questions are of direct relevance to the *nature–nurture controversy*, a debate which is of recurrent and central interest to us as psychologists or as laypersons.

In order to determine the degree to which personality traits and behaviour patterns are inherited genetically, behavioural geneticists study the personality traits of family members who share different proportions of genes and who have grown up in the same or different households. For example, if a personality characteristic such as extraversion is passed on genetically, then extraversion should correlate more highly between monozygotic twins (who have in common 100 per cent of their genes) than among dizygotic twins (who share in common only 50 per cent of their genes) or among other siblings (who share, on the average, only 25 per cent of their genes). However, twins and other siblings are usually raised together: thus, sharing the same family environment might likewise cause their personalities to be correlated. One way of differentiating between the effects of genetic and environmental influences on personality is to find many pairs of twins, some of whom have been raised together in the same family and some of whom have been raised apart (for example, adopted children). On each personality trait researchers (Tellegen *et al*, 1988) then compare the size of correlations between: identical twins reared together; identical twins reared apart; fraternal twins reared together; and fraternal twins reared apart. Thereafter, the size of the correlations are compared to ascertain the percentage of the trait that is inherited and the percentage that can be attributed to environmental influences.

Several large studies of this type have been carried out such as that of 14,000 Finnish co-twins (Rose *et al*, 1988) and the Swedish Adoption/Twin Study (Pedersen *et al*, 1988), as well as many non-twin studies. Heritability studies show that most personality traits are influenced in varying degrees by genetic factors. The findings are similar with many different measurement techniques, whether they evaluate specific traits (such as self-control or sociability) or broad traits (such as extraversion and neuroticism) (Pedersen *et al*, 1988). Nevertheless, there is still disagreement as to the exact degree to which a personality trait is heritable, with estimates ranging from a low of 20 per cent to a high of 60 per cent. There is a consensus amongst researchers, however, that the characteristics which parents pass on to their children genetically have a significant impact on the person they become (Plomin *et al*, 1990).

But what of learning and the environment? Are people stuck with the personality traits they inherit? Current research indicates the environment also has a powerful impact on personality. Behaviour geneticists divide environmental influence into two groups: the *common familial environment*, experienced by all children in a family; and the *unshared environment*, experienced uniquely by each child. For most personality traits, identical twins reared together are no more similar than identical twins reared apart. Traditionally, psychologists have believed that features of the common familial environment, such as the income and education of the parents and their general style of childrearing, cause the children in one family to be more similar to each other than they would have been if raised by different parents. However, twin and adoption studies show that the influence of common familial factors on personality is small (in the region of 10 per cent). Instead, the portion of personality that is not related to genetic factors (in the region of 50 per cent) must be attributed to the unshared environment, the idiosyncratic experiences of each child, (such as the parent–child relationship), the particular relationships with siblings and experiences outside of the home (Bouchard & McGue, 1990).

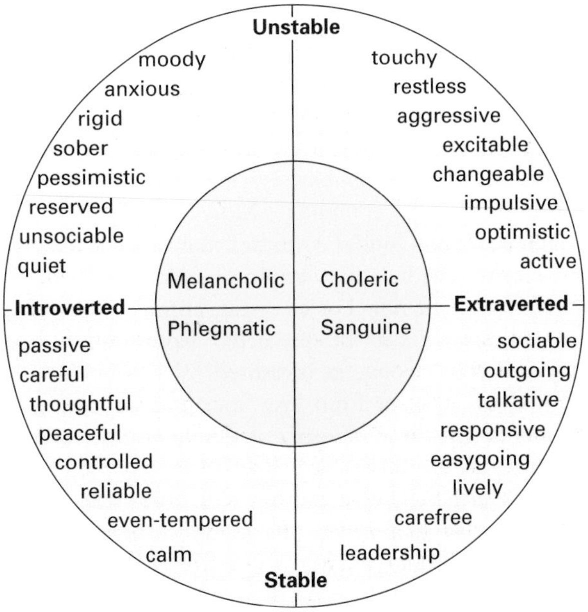

Combining Types and Traits

One of the most important trait theorists is **Hans Eysenck** (1947; 1990) who has proposed a model that links types, traits and behaviour into a hierarchical system. At the lowest level of the hierarchy are single responses, such as acts or cognitions. When they occur regularly, they combine to form sets of habitual responses at the next level. Correlated habitual responses, in turn, form traits at the third level. Correlations among traits form types at the top level.

Eysenck derived three broad dimensions from personality test data, *extraversion*, *neuroticism* and *psychoticism*. He used these dimensions to define the types at the top level of his hierarchy. However, Eysenck does not use these three dimensions to define discrete categories such as those in classical type theories. Instead he discusses general differences – for example, between introverts and extraverts – without claiming that the categories are really discontinuous.

He believes that personality differences on his three basic dimensions are caused by genetic and biological differences between people. He also believes that his hierarchy can be used in combination with other trait models to provide new insights into personality. For example, he has related extraversion-introversion and neuroticism (stability-instability) to the physiological-personality types defined by Hippocrates, as shown in *Figure 12.2*. Because Eysenck's theory is not a strict typology, people can fall anywhere around the circle, ranging from very introverted to very extraverted and from very unstable (neurotic) to very stable. The traits listed around the circle describe people with each

FIGURE 12.2 THE FOUR QUADRANTS OF EYSENCK'S PERSONALITY CIRCLE

combination of scores. For example, a person who is very extraverted and somewhat unstable is likely to be impulsive.

As already discussed in Chapter 10, the extraversion and neuroticism dimensions have been linked to physiological differences between people – for example, in terms of arousal as mediated in particular by the activity of the brainstem structure implicated in the sleep–wake cycle known as the *reticular activating system* (Bullock & Gilliland, 1993). In addition, introverts react more strongly to sensory stimulation and have lower levels of the brain chemical dopamine than do extraverts. Introverts in terms of body type also tend to be more ectomorphic than extraverts, particularly if they are both introverted and neurotic. Neuroticism appears to be somewhat more frequent among people with blood type B than blood type A. The physiological evidence for psychoticism, however, is complex and not well understood (Eysenck, 1990).

Eysenck has also used standard behavioural tests to study how extraverts, as a group, differ from introverts. One finding shows that introverts have lower thresholds for pain than extraverts. Introverts also learn faster than extraverts when unconditioned stimuli are weak or reinforcement is partial rather than continuous. Generally, memory for associations learned under conditions of low arousal is better than for those learned with high arousal. In contrast, extraverts perform better when more aroused, and need more external arousal to maintain their performance, than do the self-stimulating introverts (Howarth & Eysenck, 1968; Revelle *et al*, 1980).

The 'Big Five' Personality Factors

One problem for trait psychology is that different researchers study many different traits and use numerous ways of measuring them, sometimes creating their own idiosyncratic names for the dimensions they seek to assess. Comparing the constructs and measures derived from two competing theories often resembles trying to compare a toothbrush to a computer. More importantly, the resultant terminological confusion can make it difficult to know whether the empirical results of various studies agree or not. For example, criminal behaviour in adolescence can be predicted from either high 'psychoticism' scores, as measured by Eysenck's scale (Jamison, 1984), or from low 'socialisation' scores, as measured by the California Psychological Inventory (Gough, 1968). Should we infer from this pattern of findings that each is measuring a different side of the same coin or that in fact the questionnaires measure quite separate and unique constructs? The answer is unclear.

This problem of confusion led to a search for common dimensions of meaning that would link together the wealth of information accumulating – under different names – in personality psychology. The goal of the search was to develop a common language or descriptive system that all personality psychologists could use to compare and contrast their measures and results. Ideally, such a system should be: comprehensive; easy to understand; independent of any particular theory; and sufficiently flexible to allow for different levels of analysis.

The search for fundamental dimensions of personality began with trait terms found in natural language, in the hope that, over time, people would have developed words to describe the important dimensions they perceived in themselves and others. Several research efforts began with a list of all the traits in the English language that Allport and Odbert (1936) had extracted from the dictionary. The traits were boiled down into about 200 synonym clusters which were used to form bipolar trait dimensions, such as 'responsible–irresponsible'. Next, people were asked to rate themselves and others on the bipolar dimensions and the ratings were factor analysed to determine how the synonym clusters were interrelated. Using this method, several research teams have come to the conclusion that there are five basic dimensions underlying the traits people use to describe themselves and others (Fiske, 1949; Tupes & Cristal, 1961; Norman, 1963; Goldberg, 1981; McCrae & Costa, 1987; de Raad et al, 1988). However, there has not always been agreement as to what each one of these five should be called. For example, the Extraversion dimension is sometimes called Surgency, and the Neuroticism dimension is sometimes called Emotional Stability and scored with reference to its opposite pole. Nevertheless, the five-part structure has been replicated in studies of German and Dutch traits and there is preliminary evidence for some or all of the factors in non-Western languages as well (John, 1990).

The five dimensions are very broad, because each brings into one large category many traits that have unique connotations but a common theme. These five dimensions of personality are known as **The Big Five** and are described in summary form below, the descriptors being those as used by leading researchers **Paul Costa** and **Robert McCrae** (McCrae, 1992). Each dimension is bipolar – terms that are similar in meaning to the name of the dimension describe the high pole and terms that are opposite in meaning describe the low pole.

- *Extraversion:* gregarious, warm and positive vs quiet, reserved and shy.
- *Agreeableness:* straightforward, compliant and sympathetic vs quarrelsome, oppositional and unfeeling.
- *Conscientiousness:* achievement-oriented, dutiful and self-disciplined vs frivolous, irresponsible and chaotic.
- *Neuroticism:* anxious, depressed and self-conscious vs calm, contented and self-assured.
- *Openness to experience:* creative, open-minded and intellectual vs unimaginative, disinterested and narrow-minded.

The Big Five are not meant to replace the many specific trait terms that carry their own nuances and shades of meaning. Rather, they outline a taxonomy that demonstrates the relationships between trait words and between sophisticated theoretical concepts and the personality scales psychologists use. For example, the low Socialisation and high Psychoticism scores that predict criminality have both been shown in factor analyses to be related to the low poles of Agreeableness and Conscientiousness. On the other hand, risk factors for violent crimes all seem to be related to the high pole of Neuroticism ('emotional instability') (af Klinteberg et al, 1992). Thus, we can understand that, in plain English, boys who are likely to become criminals are typically cold, quarrelsome and irresponsible, while those who go on to commit violent crimes are likely to be anxious, temperamental and unstable as well.

As a descriptive system, The Big Five is comprehensive: almost any trait imaginable can be related to one or a few of the dimensions. The dimensions are theory-free and easy to understand because they were derived from natural language. They are very flexible and can accommodate many empirical approaches because they outline a taxonomy for numerous concepts, both broad and specific. Most importantly, the five dimensions have been replicated with many different subject samples, many different types of data and several languages (McCrae, 1992; Hofstee et al, 1992). The Big Five are not universally accepted by all personality psychologists and research continues to determine how each of the dimensions should be precisely interpreted and named. Nonetheless, many researchers accept The Big Five as the broad dimensions of a common descriptive system, and agree in general, if not precisely, upon their meanings.

◻ The Consistency Paradox and Other Critical Issues

Both trait theory and type theory presume that personality characteristics influence behaviour across different types of situations. However, in the 1920s several researchers set out to observe trait-related behaviours in different situations and were surprised to find little evidence that behaviour was cross-situationally consistent at all. For example, two behaviours presumably related to the trait of honesty, lying and cheating on a test, were only weakly correlated among schoolchildren (Hartshorne & May, 1928). More recently theorists who were influenced by behaviourism's environmentalism argued that a person's behaviour is primarily dependent on the situation (Mischel, 1968). They explained the fact that people consider their own behaviour and that of others as consistent across time and situations by referring to the dominant implicit personality theory of Western culture: people are socialised such that they attribute theirs and others' behaviour to relatively stable traits or dispositions (see also Chapter 13 on the fundamental attribution error).

This criticism of type and trait theories has led to the *person-situation debate* in personality theory, in which the relative importance of personal and situational determinants of behaviour is at stake. The observation that personality ratings across time and among different observers are consistent, while behaviour ratings across situations are not consistent, was named by **Walter Mischel** the **consistency paradox** (Mischel, 1968).

One proposed explanation for the consistency paradox is that personality is socially constructed (Hampson, 1982) on the basis of: (a) stereotypes about how physical appearance is related to certain traits; (b) implicit personality theories about what additional traits we can infer from knowledge about a few traits: and (c) cognitive bias to perceive behaviour as consistent even when it is not. For example, people who have been only briefly introduced to an individual make similar guesses about that individual's personality. Ratings made under these circumstances might be attributed to first impressions and stereotypes the raters share. However, the finding that agreement between observers improves as the raters observe more and more of the person's behaviour cannot be explained away so easily (Norman & Goldberg, 1966). Implicit theories of personality and cognitive biases may contribute to, but cannot entirely explain, our stable and consensual perceptions of personality.

Another approach to the paradox that observers typically agree on ratings of most traits for most people but that behaviour is often inconsistent across situations is to measure behaviour more carefully. Many factors may influence behaviour at any one time and in any one situation. Thus, cross-situational consistency should be examined, not by correlating one behaviour in one situation with one behaviour in another situation but by correlating aggregated behaviours, observed many times in each situation (Epstein, 1979). This technique did lead to evidence for the temporal stability of the same behaviour in the same situation over time, showing high correlations of 0.65. Nevertheless, on average, aggregated behaviour in one situation correlated with trait-related aggregated behaviour in another situation only very weakly – the coefficient was a low 0.13 (Mischel & Peake, 1982).

So what is the basis of the consistency paradox? How is it that trait psychology had a long and successful history before anyone ever discovered that behaviour is not cross-situationally consistent? According to Epstein and O'Brien (1985) the answer lies in the realisation that behavioural inconsistency is a problem only for very specific behaviours. They argue that the paradox is not about consistency *per se*, but about levels of analysis – the use of *specific* versus *summary* types of data.

The consistency debate was led primarily by social learning theorists who wanted to isolate very specific behaviours and to identify the situational cues that elicit them. With that information they hoped to encourage adaptive behaviours and modify problem behaviours. They found that specific behavioural measures are fine-tuned to predict the same behaviour in a very similar situation with a high degree of accuracy, but they do not generalise well to different situations.

On the other hand, trait theorists find meaningful relationships between self-reported traits, observer-reported traits, life events and general patterns of behaviour because all of these types of measurement operate at a broad level of analysis in which many different types of behaviours, experiences or events occurring over a period of time are summarised into a single score. Broad summary 'trait' measures are multi-purpose instruments that can predict a range of phenomena, but they do so somewhat less accurately than more specific measures.

Suppose, for example, we would like to learn about aggressive behaviour in children so an effective intervention can be planned to reduce its frequency: such a study of boys with behaviour problems was conducted by Jack Wright and Walter Mischel (1987); they found that aggregated measures of specific aggressive behaviours, such as threatening other children, correlated only 0.35 across different types of situations but correlated more highly, 0.60, across similar situations. A general trait measure of aggressiveness, based on teachers ratings of the boys, correlated well, about 0.50, with specific aggressive behaviours, regardless of the situation. Which measure would you find most useful? If you wanted to predict which children would threaten other children in a particular type of situation, your best bet is a previous observation of the same behaviour in the same type of situation (correlation of 0.60). However, if you did not know what type of situation the children would encounter and you wanted to predict threats in many situations, the trait measure would be a better predictor than previous threats in any particular situation (0.50 vs 0.35). In addition, the trait measure might have a few additional predictions in store: for example, medium-sized correlations with future life events, such as becoming involved in criminal activities (Farrington & West, 1990).

Thus, the cross-situational consistency of activity is only apparent and predictable if the measure used consists of behavioural items that have been aggregated together to form a unity (or 'trait') – which by virtue of being a collection of averaged behaviours appears to be observable and stable across situations. The situational specificity (or 'cross-situational inconsistency') of behaviour only becomes apparent on the other hand, if a single item of behaviour is observed. Epstein and O'Brien (1985) summarise, therefore, that behaviour both can be general and consistent at the aggregate level and specific and inconsistent at the item level. Thereby, it is inappropriate to conceive of behaviour as having its origins in either the person or situation since the observation of consistency or inconsistency and the subsequent attribution of cause to either an internal disposition (a 'trait') or to an external feature of the environment (the 'situation') depends upon the level of behavioural description and analysis being used. Arguably, then, it is not fruitful to frame personality issues in terms of a 'consistency-versus-variability' controversy or in terms of a 'person-situation debate' since these positions are equally tenable. Indeed, it is evident that behaviour cannot be conceived as anything less than the outcome of the interaction between the individual and the environment. False dichotomising between person and situation merely

deflects attention away from answering the important question of "'What in the person, interacts how, with what in the environment". . . to produce behaviour?' (Pervin, 1985).

Undoubtedly, situations are important influences upon the expression of personality. In one sense, details of the situation affect what you will do at any given time. However, research shows that situations differ in the extent to which they enable personality to be expressed in behaviour. Personality traits are likely to influence behaviour when situations are: (a) novel; (b) ill-defined (offering many behavioural alternatives, but no clear guidelines regarding what is proper); and (c) stressful or challenging (Caspi & Bem, 1990).

On the other hand, your personality influences the situations you are likely to get into in the first place. Sometimes you select certain types of situations: for example, going to lots of parties or never raising your hand to answer a question in order to avoid speaking in front of a large group of people. On other occasions, your personality influences the nature of a situation because you evoke particular responses from others. For example, if you typically talk a great deal and in a very loud voice, then other people might contribute less to a conversation with you than they usually do with someone else.

Although trait theorists had not been interested in specific behaviours, the consistency debate forced them to reconceptualise traits in a more precise way, to outline precisely what classes of behaviour should be related to personality traits and under what environmental conditions they would be expressed. As we have noted, however, personality is not reducible to matters of behavioural consistency; instead, patterns of behaviour are produced which appear coherent. A trait may be expressed through different behaviours in different situations and at different ages, but as long as the rationale of a trait predicts the range of behavioural expressions, the pattern seems coherent. For example, Caspi et al (1988) found that boys who were very shy as children, later seemed reluctant to take on new social roles, lagging three to four years behind their non-shy peers in getting married, having children and entering stable careers. Even in the aftermath of the consistency paradox and despite the broad definition and imperfect measurement of personality traits, they still have important implications through their commonplace usage for the ways in which we conceive of ourselves and explain our everyday lives.

Type and trait theories have been criticised, however, for not being real theories because they do not explain how behaviour is caused or how personality, develops; they merely identify and describe characteristics that are simply correlated with behaviour. Longitudinal studies can bring trait theories one step closer to understanding the development of personality but the findings are often interpreted 'post hoc' (instead of being predicted in advance) and are difficult to replicate because frequently different measures from one study to another have been used. Trait theories typically portray a static, or at least stabilised, view of personality structure as it currently exists. By contrast, dynamic theories of personality emphasise conflicting

INTERIM SUMMARY

Type theories, such as those of Sheldon and Myers, use personal characteristics to sort people into discrete groups or types (for example, extraverts or introverts) and attempt to predict behaviour on the basis of a person's type. Trait theories describe people according to continuous dimensions of personality (individuals can be very low on the dimension, very high on the dimension or anywhere in between) and predict behaviour from the degree to which a person is said to possess certain traits. Eysenck combines types, traits, habits and behaviours into a hierarchy in which specific behaviours are correlated into groups; correlated groups of behaviours form habits; correlated habits form traits; and correlated traits form types.

Hundreds of traits have been shown to predict behaviours, physiological responses and life events. In addition, twin and adoption studies suggest that many personality traits are, in part, genetically inherited. Fortunately, we can simplify our knowledge about all these traits by what they have in common. The Big Five dimensions of personality – Extraversion, Agreeableness, Conscientiousness, Neuroticism and Openness to Experience – are the common themes or dimensions that underlay the various traits researchers have studied. Most traits can be accommodated within this taxonomy by specifying their relation to one (or two) of The Big Five personality dimensions.

The observation that personality ratings are consistent across time and across observers while specific behaviours are usually not consistent across situations, came to be called the consistency paradox. Subsequently, researchers realised that specific behaviours are influenced by features of both the situation and of the person. Personality traits, because they are summary measures, are better for predicting general patterns of behaviour in unknown situations. They are especially good predictors of life events because personality traits influence the types of situations people are likely select, the choices they are confronted with and the decisions they make that shape their lives.

forces within the individual and the fast-paced challenges of the environment which together lead to continuous change and development within the individual. We will consider these theories in the next section.

PSYCHODYNAMIC AND HUMANISTIC PERSONALITY THEORIES

By the end of the nineteenth century, Charles Darwin had made the world aware of the common bonds between human beings and animals. Psychologists were quick to borrow Darwin's concept of instinct and transform it from its original use – accounting for patterns of animal behaviour – to account for virtually all human actions. However, identifying something is not the same as explaining it. Psychologists had developed a new term – *instinct* – not a better understanding of the psychological processes it was meant to describe (see Chapter 10). Clearly, they needed a more fruitful approach to understanding behaviour. **Sigmund Freud** provided the new approach. He gave new meaning to the concept of human instinct and, in doing so, revolutionised the very idea of human personality. To Ernest Jones, Freud's biographer, Freud was 'the Darwin of the mind' (1953). Common to all **psychodynamic personality theories**, which are based on Freud's work, is the assumption that personality is shaped and behaviour is motivated by powerful inner forces.

Freudian Psychoanalysis

Freud's theory of personality boldly attempts to explain the origins and course of personality development, the nature of mind, the abnormal aspects of personality and the way personality can be changed by therapy. Here we will focus only on normal personality; Freud's other views will be treated at length in Chapters 14 and 15.

According to psychoanalytic theory, at the core of personality are events within a person's mind (intrapsychic events) that motivate behaviour. Often we are not aware of these motives because they operate at an unconscious level. The psychodynamic nature of this approach comes from its emphasis on these inner well-springs of behaviour. For Freud, no chance or accidental happenings caused behaviour; all acts were determined by motives. Every human action has a cause and a purpose that can be discovered through psychoanalysis of thought associations, dreams, errors and other behavioural clues to inner passions. The wish is parent to the deed. Prominent among our desires, according to Freud, are sexual and aggressive wishes. Through both conscious and unconscious processes, these wishes affect our thoughts and behaviours.

The structure of personality

The primary data for Freud's hypotheses about personality came from clinical observations and in-depth case studies of individual patients in therapy. In this theory, personality differences arise from the different ways in which people deal with their fundamental drives. To explain these differences, Freud pictured a continuing battle between two antagonistic parts of the personality – the id and the superego – moderated by a third aspect of the self, the ego.

The *id*, governed by the pleasure principle, is conceived of as the primitive, unconscious part of the personality – the storehouse of the fundamental drives, especially sexual, physical and emotional pleasures. It operates irrationally, acting on impulse and pushing for expression and immediate gratification without considering whether what is desired is realistically possible, socially desirable or morally acceptable.

The *superego* is the storehouse of an individual's values, including moral attitudes learned from society, corresponding roughly to our common notion of conscience. It develops as a child comes to accept as his or her own values the prohibitions of parents and other adults against socially undesirable actions, helping to form the individual's ideas of the type of person he or she should strive to become.

The *ego* is the reality-based aspect of the self that arbitrates the conflict between id impulses and superego demands. The ego represents an individual's personal view of physical and social reality, his or her conscious beliefs about the causes and consequences of behaviour. Thus, the ego would block an impulse to cheat on an examination because of concerns for the consequences of getting caught and it would substitute the resolution to study harder the next time or solicit the teacher's sympathy. However, as id and superego pressures intensify, it becomes more difficult for the ego to work out optimal compromises.

Four fundamental concepts

The core of the psychodynamic approach is based upon four concepts: psychic determinism, early experience, drives and unconscious processes. Together they provide a conceptually rich perspective on the development and functioning of personality.

Psychic determinism is the assumption that all mental and behavioural reactions (symptoms) are determined by earlier experiences. Freud believed that symptoms, rather than being arbitrary, were related in a meaningful way to significant life events, as illustrated in the cases of in the late 1800s of hysteria (recorded in Europe) for which no adequate physical explanation could be found. Along with his colleague, Joseph Breuer, Freud observed that the particular physical symptom often seemed related to an earlier forgotten event in a patient's life. For instance, under hypnosis, a 'blind' patient might recall witnessing her parents having intercourse when she was a small child. As an adult, her anticipation of her first sexual encounter might then have aroused powerful feelings associated with this earlier, disturbing episode. Her blindness might represent an attempt on her part to undo seeing the original event and perhaps also to deny sexual feelings in herself.

Freud assumed a continuity of personality development from 'the womb to the tomb'. He believed that experiences in infancy and early childhood – especially during the early stages of psychosexual development – had the most profound impact on personality formation and adult behaviour patterns. However, Freud never studied children – only the adult recollections of their childhood experiences. Nonetheless, his emphasis on *early experience* helped to make the scientific study of infant and child behaviour respectable.

Freud's medical training as a neurologist led him to postulate a common biological basis for the mental abnormalities he observed in his patients. He ascribed the source of motivation for human actions to psychic energy found within each individual. How this energy was exchanged, transformed and expressed was a central concern of psychoanalysis. Each person was assumed to have inborn *drives* that were tension systems created by the organs of the body. These energy sources, when activated, could be expressed in many different ways. Freud originally postulated two basic drives. One he saw as involved with the ego, or *self-preservation* (meeting the needs of hunger and thirst). The other he called *eros*, the driving force related to sexual urges and preservation of the species. Of the two drives, Freud was more interested in eros, especially in the energy that came with it, which he called *libido*. However, some of his followers have given the ego drive an important place in personality, as we will see later. Freud greatly expanded the notion of human sexual desires to include, not only the urge for sexual union, but also all other attempts to seek pleasure or to make physical contact with others. Sexual urges demand immediate satisfaction, whether through direct actions or through indirect means such as fantasies and dreams. Clinical observation of patients who had suffered traumatic experiences during World War I and who continued to relive their wartime traumas in nightmares and hallucinations led Freud to add the concept of *thanatos*, or death drive, to his collection of drives and instincts. Thanatos was a negative force that drove people toward aggressive and destructive behaviours. Freud could not work it into his self-preservation or sexual drive theory. He suggested that this primitive urge was part of the tendency for all living things to follow the law of entropy and return to an inorganic state.

According to Freud's belief in the unconscious determinants of behaviour, behaviour can be motivated by drives of which we are not aware. We may act without knowing why or without direct access to the true cause of our actions. There is a manifest content to our behaviour – what we say, do and perceive – of which we are fully aware, but there is also a latent content that is concealed from us by **unconscious processes**. The meaning of neurotic (anxiety-based) symptoms, dreams and slips of the pen and tongue are found at the unconscious level of thinking and information-processing. A 'Freudian slip' occurs when an unconscious desire is betrayed by our speech or behaviour. For example, a host says to an unwanted guest, 'I'm so sorry to see you – I mean so happy to see you'. According to Freud, impulses within us that we find unacceptable still strive for expression: being consistently late for a date with a particular person is supposed to be no accident – allegedly, it is an expression of the way you really feel. Many psychologists today consider this concept of the unconscious to be Freud's most important contribution to the subject of psychology. The notion of an unconscious mind threatens those who want to believe they are in full command of their mental state's ship as it travels along life's tributaries.

Repression and ego defence

Often, the necessary compromise between id and superego involves 'putting a lid on the id'. Extreme desires are pushed out of conscious awareness into the privacy of the unconscious. **Repression** is the psychological process that functions to protect an individual from experiencing extreme anxiety or guilt about having impulses, ideas or memories that are unacceptable and/or dangerous to express. The ego remains unaware of both the mental content that is censored and the process by which repression keeps information out of consciousness. Repression is considered to be the most basic of the various ways in

which the ego defends against being overwhelmed by threatening impulses and ideas.

In psychoanalytic theory **ego defence mechanisms** (mental strategies the ego uses to defend itself in the daily conflict between id and the superego) are considered vital to an individual's psychological coping with powerful inner conflicts. By the use of repression, for example, a person is able to maintain a favourable self-image and to sustain an acceptable social image, though such submerged feelings may continue to play a role in personality functioning. Given strong sexual desires that are frustrated, the ego defence of **sublimation** may allow someone to engage in activities that are indirectly sexual but socially approved – such as producing films containing occasionally mild erotic content. Ego defence mechanisms moderate levels of emotion produced by stress, help keep awareness of certain drives at a minimal level, provide time to help an individual deal with life traumas and they help deal with unresolvable loss (Plutchik *et al*, 1979). For a summary of some of the major ego defences, see *Table 12.1* (next page).

In Freudian theory, anxiety is an intense emotional response triggered when a repressed conflict is about to emerge into consciousness. Anxiety is a danger signal: repression is not working! More defences needed! This is the time for a second line of defence, one or more additional ego-defence mechanisms that will relieve the anxiety and send the distressing impulses back down into the unconscious. For example, a mother who does not like her son and does not want to care for him might use reaction formation which transforms her unacceptable impulse into its opposite: 'I don't hate my child' becomes 'I love my child. See how I smother the dear little thing with love?' Such defences serve important coping functions.

Useful as they are, ego mechanisms of defence are ultimately self-deceptive. When overused, they create more problems than they solve. It is psychologically unhealthy to spend a great deal of time and psychic energy deflecting, disguising and rechannelling unacceptable urges in order to reduce anxiety. Doing so leaves little energy for productive living or satisfying human relationships. Some forms of mental illness result from excessive reliance on defence mechanisms to cope with anxiety, as we shall see in a later chapter on mental disorders.

Criticisms of Freudian theory

Freud's ideas have had an enormous impact on the way many psychologists think about normal and abnormal aspects of personality. However, there probably are more psychologists who criticise

TABLE 12.1   MAJOR EGO DEFENCE MECHANISMS

Denial of Reality	Protecting self from unpleasant reality by refusing to perceive it
Displacement	Discharging pent-up feelings, usually of hostility, on objects less dangerous than those that initially aroused the emotion
Fantasy	Gratifying frustrated desires in imaginary achievements ('day-dreaming' is a common form)
Identification	Increasing feelings of worth by identifying self with another person or institution, often of illustrious standing
Isolation	Cutting off emotional charge from hurtful situations or separating incompatible attitudes into logic-tight compartments (holding conflicting attitudes that are never thought of simultaneously or in relation to each other); also called compartmentalisation
Projection	Placing blame for one's difficulties upon others or attributing one's own 'forbidden' desires to others
Rationalisation	Attempting to prove that one's behaviour is 'rational' and justifiable and thus worthy of the approval of self and others
Reaction Formation	Preventing dangerous desires from being expressed by endorsing opposing attitudes and types of behaviour and using them as 'barriers'
Regression	Retreating to earlier developmental levels involving more childish responses and usually a lower level of aspiration
Repression	Pushing painful or dangerous thoughts out of consciousness, keeping them unconscious; this is considered to be the most basic of the defence mechanisms
Sublimation	Gratifying or working off frustrated sexual desires in substitutive nonsexual activities socially accepted by one's culture

Freudian concepts than support them. What is the basis of some of their criticisms?

Many have criticised Freud because he developed a theory of *normal* personality from his study of those with mental *disorders*. Freud himself was convinced that studying the extremes of human existence helped us understand the ordinary.

Others have criticised Freud's methodology. Although this idiographic approach yields a rich harvest of ideas from which to formulate a complex theory, Freud's theoretical ground is too soft for the heavy methodological equipment necessary to test a hypothesis empirically. For example, how can the concepts of libido and repression of sexual impulses be studied in any direct fashion? A related criticism is that Freudian theory is methodologically flawed as it does not reliably predict what will occur: it is applied only retrospectively – after events have occurred. Using psychoanalytic theory to understand personality typically involves historical reconstruction, not prediction of probable actions and future outcomes. In addition, by over-emphasising the historical origins of current behaviour, the theory misdirects attention away from current stimuli that may be inducing and maintaining the behaviour.

Research that has attempted to isolate predictor variables derived from the theory is beset by problems related to the validity of the dependent measures of psychoanalytic constructs (Silverman, 1976). For example, one researcher predicted that women would hoard more pencils than men, because pencils are phallic symbols and women allegedly have penis envy. He did, in fact, find more hoarding among female subjects (Johnson, 1966), but is there a viable alternative explanation for this finding? Perhaps women simply hoard more pencils because they are more likely than men to be asked if they have one that can be borrowed or because they tend to carry handbags that can hold them.

Freud's theory was developed from speculation based on clinical experience with patients in therapy, almost all of them women with similar symptoms. Thus, another criticism is that the theory has little to say about healthy lifestyles, which are not primarily defensive or defective. Instead, it offers the pessimistic view that human nature develops out of conflicts, traumas and anxieties. As such, it does not fully acknowledge the positive side of our existence nor offer any information about healthy personalities striving for happiness and realisation of their full potential.

Three other criticisms of Freudian theory are that: it is a developmental theory that did not include systematic observations or studies of children; that it minimises traumatic experiences (such as child abuse) by reinterpreting memories of them as fantasies (based on a child's desire for sexual contact with a parent); and that it has an androcentric bias because it uses a male model as the norm, thus positioning women as abnormal if they are different in any way. Whether or not you accept many of Freud's theories, you must agree that Freud changed forever the way we think about the human mind and its complex possibilities and variations.

Post-Freudian Theories

Some of those who came after Freud retained his basic representation of personality as a battleground on which unconscious primal urges fight with social values; but many of Freud's intellectual descendants were also dissidents who made major adjustments in the psychoanalytic view of personality. In general, these post-Freudians have made the following changes:

- They put greater emphasis on ego functions, including ego defences, development of the self, conscious thought processes and personal mastery.
- They view social variables (culture, family and peers) as playing a greater role in shaping personality.
- They put less emphasis on the importance of general sexual urges, or libidinal energy.
- They have extended personality development beyond childhood to include the entire life span.

Among Freud's many celebrated followers, two of the most important were also severe critics, Alfred Adler and Carl Jung.

Alfred Adler (1929) accepted the notion that personality was directed by unrecognised wishes: 'Man knows more than he understands'. However, he rejected the significance of Eros and the pleasure principle. Adler believed that as helpless, dependent, small children we all experience feelings of inferiority. He argued that our lives become dominated by the search for ways to overcome those feelings. We compensate to achieve feelings of adequacy or, more often, over-compensate for inferiority feelings in an attempt to become superior. Personality is structured around this underlying striving; people develop lifestyles based on particular ways of overcoming their

basic, pervasive feelings of inferiority. Personality conflict arises from incompatibility between external environmental pressures and internal strivings for adequacy, rather than from competing urges within the person.

Carl Jung (1959) greatly expanded the conception of the unconscious. For him, the unconscious was not limited to an individual's unique life experiences but was filled with fundamental psychological truths shared by the whole human race. The concept of **collective unconscious** predisposes us all to react to certain stimuli in the same way. It is responsible for our intuitive understanding of primitive myths, art forms and symbols – which are the universal archetypes of existence. An archetype is a primitive symbolic representation of a particular experience or object. Each archetype is associated with an instinctive tendency to feel and think about it or experience it in a special way. Jung postulated many archetypes from history and mythology: the sun god, the hero, the earth mother. Animus was the male archetype, while anima was the female archetype and all men and women experienced both archetypes in varying degrees. In reacting to someone of the opposite sex, then, we react to their particular characteristics as well as to our own male or female archetype. The archetype of the self is the mandala or magic circle; it symbolises striving for unity and wholeness, the integrated personality as balancing opposing forces, such as masculine aggressiveness and feminine sensitivity (Jung, 1973). This view of personality as a constellation of compensating internal forces in dynamic balance was called **analytic psychology**. Jung, although chosen by Freud as the crown-prince of the psychoanalytic movement, led a palace revolt by rejecting the primary importance of libido, so central to Freudian sexual theory. To the

Mandala of Akshobhya

basic urges of sex and aggression Jung added two equally powerful unconscious instincts: the need to create and the need to self-actualise. Jung's views became central to the emergence of humanistic psychology in America (Jung, 1965).

Humanistic Theories

Humanistic approaches to understanding personality are characterised by a concern for the integrity of an individual's personal and conscious experience and growth potential. Humanistic personality theorists, such as **Carl Rogers** and **Abraham Maslow**, believe that a basic drive toward **self-actualisation** is the organiser of all the diverse forces whose interplay continually creates what a person is.

In the humanistic view, the motivation for behaviour comes from a person's unique biological and learned tendencies to develop and change in positive directions toward the goal of self-actualisation. Self-actualisation is described as a constant striving to realise one's inherent potential, to fully develop one's capacities and talents. This innate striving toward self-fulfilment and the realisation of one's unique potential is a constructive, guiding force that moves each person toward generally positive behaviours and enhancement of the self.

Humanistic theories have been described in a variety of ways. To begin with, they are often depicted as being *holistic* because they explain people's separate acts always in terms of their entire personalities. They have also been portrayed as 'dispositional' because they focus on the innate qualities within a person that exert a major influence over the direction that their behaviour will take, such dispositions being said to be oriented specifically toward creativity and growth. Situational conditions are more often seen as constraints, from which once freed, the actualising disposition should actively guide people to choose life-enhancing situations and toward self-actualisation. Humanistic theories are also said to be *phenomenological* because they emphasise an individual's frame of reference and subjective view of reality. This should be characterised by a present-orientation, with the future representing goals to be achieved. Finally, these theories have been described by Rollo May (1975) as having an '*existential* perspective' as they focus on higher mental processes that interpret current experiences and enable us to meet or be overwhelmed by the everyday challenges of existence. A unique aspect of these theories is their focus on free will, separating them from the more deterministic behaviourists and psychoanalysts.

Rogers' Person-centred Approach

Carl Rogers (1947; 1951; 1977) developed the practice of *client-centred* therapy, in which it was up to the client to determine the therapeutic goals and the direction the therapy should take to achieve those goals. Later, Rogers called his therapy *person-centred* because it was an approach for dealing with people in general and with clients as people. Rogers' advice was to listen to what people said about themselves, to their concepts and to the significance they attach to their experiences. As we have noted, at the core of this theoretical approach is the concept of self-actualisation.

The drive for self-actualisation at times comes into conflict with the need for approval from the self and others, especially when the person feels that certain obligations or conditions must be met in order to gain approval. Thus, Rogers stressed the importance of *unconditional positive regard* in raising children. By this he meant that children should feel they will always be loved and approved of, in spite of any of their mistakes and misbehaviour – that they do not have to earn their parents' love. He recommended that, when a child misbehaves, parents should emphasise that it is the behaviour they disapprove of, not the child. Unconditional positive regard is important in adulthood, too, because worrying about seeking approval interferes with self-actualisation. As adults, we need to give and receive unconditional positive regard from those to whom we are close. Most importantly, we need to feel unconditional positive self-regard, or acceptance of ourselves, in spite of the weaknesses we might be trying to change. In recent years, Rogers expanded upon these concepts to create healthy psychological climates that facilitate personal growth in education and inter-racial and inter-cultural harmony.

Such an upbeat view of personality was a welcome treat for many therapists who had been brought up on a hard-to-swallow Freudian diet. Humanistic approaches focus directly on improvement – on making life more palatable – rather than dredging up painful memories that are sometimes better left repressed. Client-centred therapies encourage the clients to write their own recipes for improvement, deciding what aspects of their lives they would like to change.

Criticisms of humanistic theories

It is difficult to criticise theories that encourage us and appreciate us, even for our faults. Who could possibly object to an emphasis on growth, self-concept and fulfilling one's human potential? Behaviourists could and they do. Behaviourists criticise humanistic concepts for being poorly defined both in conceptual and operational terms. They ask, 'what exactly is self-actualisation and when do we know it is to be observed?' Is it an inborn tendency or is it created by the cultural context? Behaviourists also have difficulty understanding how humanistic theories account for the particular characteristics of individuals, judging them to be theories about human nature and about qualities we all share more than about any individual personality or the basis of differences among people. Experimental psychologists contend that too many of the concepts in humanistic psychology are so unclear that they defy testing in controlled research. Although this contention is true for some of the more general humanistic concepts, considerable research has evaluated many of the more specific concepts in humanistic theories of personality (Roberts, 1973). Other psychologists note that, by emphasising the role of the self as a source of experience and action, humanistic psychologists neglect the important environmental variables that also influence behaviour.

Psychoanalytic theorists criticise the humanistic emphasis on present conscious experience. They argue that this approach does not recognise the power of the unconscious. Subjects who have unconscious conflicts and use defensive strategies for dealing with their conflicts cannot accurately describe themselves with simple introspection. Other criticisms of this general theory of personality include the following: (a) it neglects and underestimates the importance of individual history and influences from the past as well as the developmental aspects of personality; (b) it oversimplifies the complexity of personality by reducing it to the 'given' of a self-actualising tendency; (c) it fails to predict how a specific individual will respond in a given situation; and (d) it makes the self unaccountable to sceptical researchers, as some hostile critics conclude – 'In the last analysis, explaining personality on the basis of hypothesised self-tendencies is reassuring double-talk, not explanation' (Liebert & Spiegler, 1982).

INTERIM SUMMARY

Freud's psychodynamic theory of personality identifies unconscious motives and conflicts as important determinants of behaviour. He believed that conflicts occur between three parts of the personality: the id (ruled by the pleasure principle), the superego (ruled by the morality principle) and the ego (ruled by the reality principle). To solve these conflicts and maintain a favourable self-image, the ego often resorts to defence mechanisms such as repression and sublimation. Freud's most

controversial contribution was his theory of psychosexual stages in which sexual desires and conflicts in infancy and early childhood were said to form the cornerstone of adult personality.

Psychodynamic theories that came after Freud generally put greater emphasis on ego functions and social variables and less emphasis on sexual urges; these later theories reconceptualised personality development as a process that continues throughout adult life. Adler argued that the ego's attempt to compensate for feelings of inferiority played a central role in personality development. Jung de-emphasised the sexual drive and incorporated ones drives to create and to self-actualise. He also expanded the unconscious to include the collective unconscious, a storehouse of archetypes of common human experiences.

Humanistic theories emphasise self-actualisation, a basic tendency for humans to develop their potential for creativity and growth. These theories are holistic, dispositional, phenomenological and existential in that they try to understand the whole personality, including the innate qualities, subjective experiences and coping with the challenges of existence that together direct behaviour. Carl Rogers' person-centred therapy permits the client to decide what needs to be changed and in what direction the therapy should proceed. One ingredient that is necessary for self-actualisation, Rogers says, is unconditional positive regard from the self and significant others such as parents, friends or a therapist. Humanistic theories have been criticised because they deal with conscious experiences while ignoring the role of unconscious motives and environmental stimuli. In addition, fundamental concepts such as self-actualisation are loosely defined and difficult to observe.

▣ SOCIAL-LEARNING AND COGNITIVE THEORIES

Common to all the theories we have reviewed is an emphasis on hypothesised inner mechanisms – traits, instincts, impulses, tendencies toward self-actualisation – that propel behaviour and form the basis of a functioning personality. Psychologists with a learning theory orientation, however, have quite a different focus. They look for environmental contingencies – reinforcing circumstances – that control behaviour. From this perspective, behaviour and personality are shaped primarily by the outside environment. Personality, then, is seen as the sum of overt and covert responses that are reliably elicited by an individual's reinforcement history; people are different because they have had different histories of reinforcement. In this view, personality has no active role: it does not cause behaviour as it is defined by behaviour.

This behaviourist conception of personality was first developed by a team of psychologists headed by **John Dollard** and **Neal Miller** (1950). However, as antecedents must be acknowledged the seminal ideas of Kurt Lewin (1935) who was among the first to stress the importance of the social environment to personality: his notion of 'life-space', referring to the environment as it is perceived by the person and determines the actions the individual will take, strongly foreshadows the forthcoming ideas of the social-learning theorists. Nevertheless, this legacy was considerably expanded by **Albert Bandura** and **Walter Mischel** into a meaningful integration of core ideas from the learning – behavioural tradition and the newly emerging ideas from social and cognitive psychology.

Dollard and Miller liberalised the strict behaviourist view of personality by introducing concepts such as learned drives, inhibition of responses and learned habit patterns. Similar to Freud, they emphasised the roles of the motivating force of tension and the reinforcing (pleasurable) consequences of tension reduction. Organisms act to reduce tension produced by unsatisfied drives. Behaviour that successfully reduces such tensions is repeated, eventually becoming a learned habit that is reinforced by repeated tension reduction. Dollard and Miller also showed that one could learn by social imitation – by observing the behaviour of others without having to actually perform the response first. This idea broadened the ways psychologists perceived that effective and destructive habits are learned. Personality emerges as the sum of these learned habits.

Bandura and Mischel agreed that it was vital for personality approaches to recognise the powerful influences that current, specific environmental stimuli exert and to down-play the role of vague, poorly operationalised mechanisms and processes, such as traits and instincts. They also emphasised the importance of learned behavioural patterns based on social learning – observation of others and social reinforcement from others. They went one critical step further to emphasise the importance of cognitive processes as well as behavioural ones, returning a thinking mind to the acting body.

Those who have proposed cognitive theories of personality point out that there are important individual differences in the way people think about and define any external situation. Cognitive theories stress the mental processes through which people turn their sensations and perceptions into organised impressions of reality. Similar to humanistic theories, they emphasise that individuals participate in creating their own personalities. People actively choose their own environments to a great extent; so, even if the environment has an important impact on us, we are not just passive reactors. We weigh alternatives and select the settings in which we act and are acted upon; we choose to enter those situations which are expected to be reinforcing and to avoid those that are unsatisfying and uncertain.

The relationship between situational variables (social and environmental stimuli) and cognitive variables in regulating behaviour is found in a number of personality theories. In this section of our presentation of conceptual approaches to the study of human personality, we will review the personal construct theory of George Kelly and then examine in greater depth the cognitive social-learning theories of Walter Mischel and Albert Bandura.

Kelly's Personal Construct Theory

George Kelly (1955) developed a theory of personality that places primary emphasis on each person's active, cognitive construction of his or her world. He argued strongly that no one is ever a victim of either past history or the present environment. Although events cannot be changed, all events are open to alternative interpretations; people can always reconstruct their past or define their present difficulties in different ways.

Kelly used science as a metaphor for this process of cognitive construction. Scientists develop theories to understand the natural world and to make predictions about what will occur in the future under particular conditions. The test of a scientific theory is its utility – how well it explains and predicts. If a theory is not working well or if it is extended outside the set of events where it does work well, then a new, more useful theory can and should be developed. Kelly argued that all people function as scientists. We want to be able to predict and explain the world around us, especially our interpersonal world. We build theories about the world from units called **personal constructs**. Kelly defined a personal construct as a person's belief about what two objects or events have in common and what sets them apart from a third object or event. An example of such a *triadic comparison* would be as follows: you might say that your uncle and your brother are alike because they are highly competitive; your sister on the other hand is different from them because she likes to 'give in to others'. In such an example, you would seem to be using a construct of 'competitiveness' versus its opposite pole of 'giving in to others' to organise your perceptions of people around you. By applying that construct to many people you know, you might arrange them into categories, or along a scale that ranges from the 'most competitive' people you know to those who are 'most likely to give in to others'. The systematic elicitation of such personal constructs via the method of triadic comparison forms the basis of what Kelly called a *Repertory Grid* (Fransella & Bannister, 1977), a chart containing both qualitative and quantitative information pertaining to an individual's unique world view.

You have many different, sometimes idiosyncratic personal constructs that you can apply to understanding any person or situation. Although many people share some of the constructs you use, some of your constructs are uniquely yours. All of your constructs are put together into an integrated belief system that influences the way you interpret, respond to and feel about each situation you encounter. Chronically accessible constructs are those that you use frequently and automatically. They influence the way you evaluate information and form impressions of others. They are likely to be relatively stable over long periods of time (Lau, 1989; Higgins, 1989). We can think of them as schema, types of knowledge clusters that guide the way one processes information (as we discussed in Chapter 9). Kelly believed that people differ in their readiness to change constructs and that they can run into trouble either by rigidly refusing to change their old ineffective constructs – for example, when adapting to new situations – or by nervously changing their constructs every time the wind turns. There have been many valuable applications of personal construct psychology in clinical practice (Winter, 1992): for example, asking stutterers to explore their personal constructions of verbal fluency has been found to be of significant help to those wishing to overcome their readily apparent disfluency in this respect (Evesham, 1987).

Notably, Kelly emphasised the idiographic nature of each person's system of personal constructs, discussing systems, structures and processes only in general terms and saying little about the content of personal constructs. Recently, Higgins (1990) has elaborated Kelly's theory by outlining different types of constructs, such as facts, guides and possibilities, that deal with aspects of the self, others and social contexts; each type of construct is expected to influence behaviour in particular ways.

Cognitive Social-learning Theory: Mischel

Walter Mischel questioned the utility of describing personality according to traits. As an alternative, he has proposed a cognitive theory of personality that also draws heavily on principles from *social-learning theory*. Similar to other social-learning theorists, Mischel places a great deal of emphasis on the influence of environmental variables on behaviour. In his view, much of what we do and many of our beliefs and values are not best thought of as emerging properties of the self. He sees them instead as responses developed, maintained or changed by our observation of influential models and by specific stimulus-response pairings in our own experience.

Dimensions of individual difference

Mischel also emphasises that people actively participate in the cognitive organisation of their interactions with the environment (Mischel & Peake, 1982). (It is interesting to note that Mischel was a student of Kelly.) People respond differently to the same environmental input because of differences in these person-based variables based in part on previous environmental input. How you respond to a specific environmental input depends on any or all of the following variables or processes (Mischel, 1973):

- *Competencies*: what you know, what you can do and your ability to generate certain cognitive and behavioural outcomes.
- *Encoding strategies*: the way you process incoming information, selectively attending, categorising and making associations to it.
- *Expectancies*: your anticipation of likely outcomes for given actions in particular situations.
- *Personal values*: the importance you attach to stimuli, events, people and activities.
- *Self-regulatory systems and plans*: the rules you have developed for guiding your performance, setting goals and evaluating your effectiveness.

Person versus situational variables

Mischel's approach highlights the adaptive flexibility of human behaviour. Although the person variables previously listed are a continuing influence on our behaviour, we are also able to adapt and change in response to the new demands of our environment. Mischel tried to sort out the tension between consistency and variability by arguing that, because people are so sensitive to situational cues, features of situations are as important as features of people in our attempts to understand behaviours. He hypothesised that person variables will have their greatest impact on behaviour when cues in the situation are weak or ambiguous. When situations are strong and clear, there will be less individual variation in response. For example, in a lift, most of us tend to behave pretty much the same in response to the strong, silent situational demands. At a party, however, where many behaviours are appropriate, person variables will lead to large differences in behaviour. There is extensive evidence in support of this view (Mischel, 1979; Wright & Mischel, 1987; Caspi & Bem, 1990).

Cognitive Social-learning Theory: Bandura

Through his theoretical writing and extensive research with children and adults, **Albert Bandura** (1986) has been an eloquent champion of a social-learning approach to understanding personality. This approach combines principles of learning with an emphasis on human interactions in social settings. From a social-learning perspective, human beings are neither driven by inner forces nor are they helpless pawns of environmental influence. There are uniquely human cognitive processes that are involved in acquiring and maintaining patterns of behaviour and, thus, personality; however, we often gauge our own behaviour according to imposed standards. Because we can manipulate symbols and think about external events, we can forsee the possible consequences of our actions without having to actually experience them and we learn vicariously through observation of other people. Therefore, we do not passively absorb this knowledge; we are capable of self-regulation and we make fine distinctions in the stimulus conditions that lead to a given behaviour and the consequences that follow it. Consequently, when observed behaviour is punished, we still learn the behaviour but do not perform it as we might if we saw it being positively rewarded.

Bandura's theory points to a complex interaction of individual factors, behaviour and environmental stimuli. Each can influence or change the others and the direction of change is rarely one-way – it is reciprocal. Your behaviour can be influenced by your attitudes, beliefs or prior history of reinforcement as well as by stimuli available in the environment. What you do can have an effect on the environment and important aspects of your personality can be affected by the environment or by feedback from your behaviour. In this important concept of social-learning theory called **reciprocal determinism** (Bandura, 1981a), it is necessary to examine all components if you want to understand completely human behaviour, personality and social ecology. So, if you are largely sedentary, do not choose to be active walking or jogging, but if there is a pool

nearby, time spent swimming may become a regular activity. Further, if you are outgoing and like to talk to other people sitting around the pool thereby creating a more sociable atmosphere, this in turn will make it a more enjoyable environment. This is one instance of reciprocal determinism between person, place and behaviour.

Observational learning

Perhaps the most important contribution of Bandura's theory is its focus on **observational learning** as the process by which a person changes his behaviour based on observations of another person's behaviour. In Chapter 7 we saw that this approach challenged traditional behaviouristic theory because it states that a person can learn without overt behaviour. Through observational learning, children and adults acquire an enormous range of information about their social environment – what is appropriate and gets rewarded and what gets punished or ignored. Skills, attitudes and beliefs may be acquired simply by watching what others do and the consequences that follow. This means, for example, that a child can develop a greater identity by observing how men and women behave in their culture and how the culture responds differently to each (S. Bem, 1984). Children may also learn personality traits such as altruism (Straub, 1974) or the ability to delay gratification by observing models that are with them personally or seen indirectly in books, films and on TV.

Self-efficacy

Bandura has recently elaborated the concept of **self-efficacy** as a central part of social-learning theory (1986) and refers to the belief that one can perform adequately in a particular situation. A person's sense of self-efficacy influences his or her perceptions, motivation and performance in many ways. We do not even try to do things or take chances when we expect to be ineffectual. We avoid situations when we do not feel adequate. Self-efficacy is not the same as an overall sense of self-confidence: we should be careful to avoid oversimplifying people's complex self-knowledge and self-evaluation into a simplistic, single label such as self-esteem. However, a sense of self-efficacy can affect behaviour in situations that differ from those in which it was generated, because, once established, positive expectations about one's efficacy can generalise to new situations (Bandura, 1977b).

Beyond our actual accomplishments – often

Albert Bandura

referred to as *enactive attainment* – there are three other sources of efficacy expectations: (a) vicarious experience or our observations of the performance of others; (b) social and self-persuasion (others may convince us that we can do something, or we may convince ourselves); and (c) self-monitoring of our emotional arousal as we think about or approach a task. For example, anxiety suggests low expectations of efficacy; excitement suggests expectations of success.

Besides influencing our choices of activities, tasks, situations and companions, our self-efficacy judgements also influence how much effort we expend and how long we persist when faced with difficulty. How vigorously and persistently a student pursues academic tasks depends more on his or her sense of self-efficacy than on actual ability. Expectations of success or failure can be influenced by feedback from performance, but they are more likely to create the predicted feedback and, thus, to become self-fulfilling prophecies. (In Chapter 15, we will review ways of inducing each of these four types of efficacy expectations through therapy.) Expectations of failure – and a corresponding decision to stop trying – may, of course, be based on the perception that a situation is unresponsive, punishing or unsupportive instead of on a perception of one's own inadequacy (the environment, and not the person, may need to be changed so that reinforcements will follow competent responding). Such expectations are called *outcome-based expectancies*. Perception of one's own inadequacy are called *efficacy-based expectancies* (the person must develop competencies that will boost self-perception of efficacy).

Can a teacher's self-efficacy affect student achievement? The results of a classroom field study strongly support the association between personality and performance variables.

Forty-eight teachers in four American high schools with large numbers of 'culturally deprived' students participated in this study. The researchers measured the teachers' sense of teaching efficacy on self-report scales, made classroom observations of 'climate and atmosphere' and assessed student achievement on standardised tests. Correlations between these and a number of other measures reveal that teachers with a greater sense of self-efficacy tend to maintain a positive emotional climate in their classes, avoiding the harsh modes of behaviour control that tend to characterise low-efficacy teachers. In addition, student achievement on the mathematics test was significantly correlated with the teachers' self-efficacy; students scored higher as teacher self-efficacy was higher. However, this effect was specific to the teaching of mathematics. It did not hold for reading achievement test performance – perhaps because the basic skills language classes the teachers taught did not specifically teach reading (Ashton & Webb, 1986).

▣ Critical Evaluation of Social-learning and Cognitive Theories

Critics hold that behaviouristic approaches to personality have thrown out the baby's vibrant personality and kept the cold bath water. If personality is built upon the learned repetition of previously reinforced responses, where is the origin of new behaviour – creative achievements, innovative ideas, inventions and works of art? Critics also argue that much of the learning that behaviourists observe is highly specific responding that is reinforced because an organism is in a state of deficiency motivation and because other kinds of action and reinforcements are not available. Also, because the focus is on the learning process, what gets obscured is the content of the unique characteristics that form each distinct human personality.

A more specific criticism of cognitive-learning theory schemes is that person and environment are conceived somewhat as separate entities, situations goading persons into action. Rather, as in the case of Bandura's theory, it is through evaluations and appraisals of situations with others, that persons-as-agents actively create an *inter-subjective* environment as mediated by their communicative interactions with others (Rommetveit, 1979). Through such inter-subjectivity, the limits and boundaries of contextual influence are negotiated and 'situations' themselves defined. Thus, through the emergence of the structural properties of these contexts, personalities are scripted, ordered episodes and structured sequences of action become identifiable: Harré *et al* (1985) has called this the *ethogenic approach* to personality.

Cognitive theories are also criticised because they generally overlook *emotion* as an important component of personality. They emphasise rational, information-processing variables, such as constructs and encoding strategies. Emotions are perceived merely as by-products of thoughts and behaviour or just included with other types of thoughts, rather than being assigned independent importance. A great deal of research has demonstrated that emotions have an important effect on cognitive processes such as memory, reaction time and decision-making (Bower, 1981; Zajonc, 1980). Feelings may themselves be important determinants of cognitive content and structure, rather than just 'cognitive coatings'.

A second set of criticisms focuses on the vagueness of explanations about the way personal constructs and competencies are created. Cognitive theorists have little to say about the developmental origins of adult personality; their focus on the individual's perception of the current behaviour setting obscures the individual's history. This criticism is levelled particularly at Kelly's theory, which has been described as more of a conceptual system than a theory because it focuses on structure and processes but says little about the content of personal constructs.

Despite these criticisms, cognitive personality theories have made major contributions to current thinking. Kelly's theory has influenced a large number of cognitive therapists. Bandura's ideas have contributed to the improvement of the way we educate our children and help them to achieve. Mischel's awareness of *situation* has brought about a better understanding of the complexity and significance of the interaction between what the person brings to a behaviour setting and what that setting brings out of the person.

INTERIM SUMMARY

Learning theorists view behaviour as caused, not by internal mechanisms such as traits, but by a combination of environmental stimuli and prior reinforcements. Personality is the sum of the responses that can be reliably elicited from an individual as a function of past learning history. Learning theorists Dollard and Miller added learned drives, inhibition of responses and learned habits to Freudian concepts, such as tension reduction, in an effort to form hypotheses about personality that could be tested in the laboratory. Bandura additionally emphasised that social and cognitive factors – especially observational learning, reciprocal determinism and perceptions of self-efficacy – influence behaviour in important ways.

Kelly suggested that personal constructs influence

the way individuals process information about people, the environment and the behavioural alternatives that are open to them. Chronically accessible constructs are those that people rely on frequently and in a wide range of situations. Mischel has combined social-learning theory with a cognitive approach similar to Kelly's. He emphasises that people adapt flexibly to very subtle changes in environmental conditions or reinforcements. People respond differently to the same situation because they have different competencies, encoding strategies, expectancies, personal values and self-regulatory systems and plans. Social-learning and cognitive theories have been criticised because they consider person and environment as separate entities, tend to overlook emotions and do not pay attention to the developmental aspects of personality.

SELF THEORIES

When cognitive social-learning theories reopened the black box of internal experiences that behaviourists had refused to examine, they found a store of treasures and tribulations. Although the cognitive approach to the self was new, a foundation of self theory had already been laid by philosophers, sociologists, psychodynamic and humanistic psychologists.

The concern for analysis of the self found its strongest advocate in **William James** (1890). James identified three components of self-experience: the *material me* (the bodily self, along with surrounding physical objects); the *social me* (one's awareness of his or her reputation in the eyes of others); and the *spiritual me* (the self that monitors private thoughts and feelings). James believed everything that one associated with one's identity became, in some sense, a part of self. People react defensively when their friends or family members are insulted because a part of the self has been attacked. Some theorists assert that the pride we take in our cars and our attachment to old record albums and memorabilia are evidence of an extended self that also includes possessions (Belk, 1988).

Knowledge is a central concept in theories of the self. Self-insight was an important part of the psycho-analytic cure in Freud's theory and Jung stressed that to fully develop the self, one must integrate and accept all aspects of one's conscious and unconscious life.

Self as Knower Versus Known

Some self theorists make a distinction between the knower and the known. The knower refers to the part of you that experiences thoughts, feelings and perceptions – the part that guides behaviour. The known refers to what Carl Rogers and others have called the **self-concept**; that is, all the conscious or potentially conscious thoughts, ideas and evaluations you have of yourself.

Many psychologists criticised the concept of self as knower because it suggests that there is a little person in the head who integrates experience and directs behaviour. On the other hand, the concept of self as known involves material that is consciously accessible to an individual (Berkowitz, 1988). Thus, we can measure various aspects of the self-concept through self-report – by asking people about their self-beliefs. The self-concept includes many components. Among them are your self-referent memories; beliefs about your traits, motives, values and abilities; the ideal self that you would most like to become, the possible selves that you contemplate enacting; positive or negative evaluations of yourself (self-esteem); and beliefs about what others think of you (McGuire & McGuire, 1988). Importantly, the self as known allows for the possibility that the person act can as his (or her) own audience to himself (or herself): in the process of reflecting upon one's own action, it becomes possible to tacitly discuss self-related themes; thereby, through the telling of such stories about oneself as a person, a **dialogical self** becomes constructed with whom others may converse (Hermans, Kempen & van Loon, 1992).

Dynamic Aspects of Self-concepts

The self-concept is a dynamic mental structure that motivates, interprets, organises, mediates and regulates *intrapersonal* and *interpersonal* behaviours and processes. The content and structure of your self-concept influence the way you process information about yourself and research indicates that the self-schemas, or concepts you frequently use to interpret your own behaviour, influence the way you process information about other people as well (Markus & Smith, 1981; Cantor & Kihlstrom, 1987). The salient aspects of self-concept show developmental changes: very young children think of themselves in terms of physical characteristics, gradually incorporate moods and preferences and finally focus on their interpersonal traits, morals and life philosophies (Damon & Hart, 1986; Livesley & Bromley, 1973). Many aspects of the self-concept are reflected in behaviour. We have already seen from Bandura's work how perceived self-efficacy influences whether and how hard people try to achieve particular goals (Markus & Nurius, 1986; Markus *et al*, 1990).

A person's self-esteem is a generalised evaluative attitude toward the self, which can strongly influence our thoughts, moods and behaviour. Evidence suggests that most people go out of their way to maintain self-esteem and to sustain the integrity of their self concept (Steele, 1988). For example, when experiencing self-doubt people sometimes deliberately sabotage their performance. The purpose of this strategy is to have a ready-made excuse for failure that does not implicate lack of ability (Jones & Berglas, 1978). Thus, if you are afraid to find out whether you have what it takes to be successful, you might enjoy yourself with friends instead of studying for an important exam. That way, if you fail, you can blame it on low effort without finding out whether you really had the ability to make it. Research shows that, most of the time, people do engage in self-verification, trying to know themselves better. However, it seems that sometimes, when confronted by self-doubt, people prefer to remain in the dark about personal problems and engage in self-enhancement processes, trying to be adored rather than known. In self-enhancement, people deny or distort information to sustain a desired self-image (Swann, 1990).

When you deliberately manipulate your public self, trying to create a particular impression on another person, you are engaging in **impression management**. Sometimes you may try to manage your public self without even realising it, in order to maintain an impression that agrees with the way you see yourself. In this process, known as behavioural confirmation, your beliefs about the self control your behaviour (source) in the presence of particular others (target) (Snyder, 1984). Target people are then more likely to react according to the behavioural context established and confirm the original belief about what kind of person you really are. In this way, beliefs create reality. People who are extraverted solicit extraverted behaviours in others (Fong & Markus, 1982); those who are anxious cause anxiety in others (Riggs & Cantor, 1981); and those who are feeling depressed provoke depressed, hostile feelings in others (Strack & Coyne, 1983).

Although separating the self-concept from the self as knower has generated a great deal of research and advanced our understanding of certain types of behaviour, some theorists believe we must ultimately return to an integrated, or unified, conception of self. These theorists promote a conception of the interpersonal self, in which behaviour is directed not by an invisible homunculus (little man) from within the person but by the social context within which the person lives (Rosenberg, 1988). **Hazel Markus** believes that the self is a dynamic construct, deriving its meaning only in interpersonal contexts; without others there can be no self (Markus & Cross, 1990).

There are no clean dichotomies between public and private aspects of the self or between what we think of ourselves and what we think others think of us. All of our interpersonal behaviour becomes incorporated into the self. In addition, much of our behaviour is scripted by the social roles we play and the behaviours we characteristically display in different roles become worked into the self as well.

Much of research into self-concept employs scaled questionnaires to investigate the self, with the majority of these studies tending to focus on the evaluative dimensions of the self-concept. Recently, however, a number of psychologists have readdressed their research endeavours toward *self narratives*, these being stories people tell about themselves in natural language (Freeman, 1993; Gergen & Gergen, 1988). This focus upon the hermeneutics of self ascriptions represents an intriguing signpost to the direction in which self theorising is currently developing.

Critics of self theory approaches, however, argue against its limitless boundaries. Some argue that self is not useful as a theoretical construct, because it simply passes the buck, explaining behaviour by attributing it to an invisible persona that is not accountable to evaluation or research. Paradoxically, other critics argue that the more easily measured self-concept is an empty set of schemata that cannot direct behaviour in the absence of a self as knower.

INTERIM SUMMARY

William James was one of the first psychologists to theorise about the self-concept and its different material, social and spiritual aspects. A distinction is made between the knowing self that is the experiencing agent and the self that is known by the process of self-reflection. New views make the self-concept a dynamic mental structure that not only is involved in interpreting experience and regulating personal and social behaviour but that motivates action as well. Modern researchers are investigating many facets of the self-concept and self-processes, among them self-esteem, self-handicapping, self-verification and self-enhancement.

◻ COMPARING PERSONALITY THEORIES

There is no unified theory of personality that a majority of psychologists can endorse. Several differences in basic assumptions have come up repeatedly in our survey of the various theories. It may be helpful to recap five of the most important differences in assumptions about personality and the approaches that advance each assumption.

1. *Heredity versus environment.* This difference is also referred to as nature vs nurture. What is more important: genetic and biological factors or influences from the environment? Trait theories have been split on this issue: Freudian theory depends heavily on heredity; humanistic, learning, cognitive and self theories all emphasise either environment as a determinant of behaviour or interaction with the environment as a source of personality development and differences.

2. *Learning processes versus innate laws of behaviour.* Should emphasis be placed on modifiability or on the view that personality development follows an internal timetable? Again, trait theories have been divided. Freudian theory has favoured the inner determinant view – a pessimistic one – while humanists postulate an optimistic view that people change as a result of their experiences. Learning, cognitive and self theories clearly support the idea that behaviour and personality change as a result of learned experiences.

3. *Emphasis on past, present or future.* Trait theories emphasise past causes, whether innate or learned; Freudian theory stresses past events in early childhood; learning theories focus on past reinforcements and present contingencies; humanistic theories emphasise present phenomenal reality or future goals; and cognitive and self theories emphasise past and present (and the future if goal-setting is involved).

4. *Consciousness versus unconsciousness.* Freudian theory emphasises unconscious processes; humanistic, learning and cognitive theories emphasise conscious processes. Trait theories pay little attention to either consciousness or unconsciousness; self theories are unclear on this score.

5. *Internal disposition versus external situation.* Learning theories emphasise situational factors; traits play up dispositional factors; and the others allow for an interaction between person-based and situation-based variables.

Each type of theory makes different contributions to our understanding of human personality. Trait theories provide a catalogue that describes parts and structures. Psychodynamic theories add a powerful engine and the fuel to get the vehicle moving. Learning theories supply the steering wheel, directional signals and other regulation equipment. Humanistic theories put a person in the driver's seat. Cognitive theories add reminders that the way the trip is planned, organised and remembered will be affected by the mental map the driver chooses for the journey. Self theories remind the driver to consider the image his or her driving ability is projecting to back-seat drivers and pedestrians.

WHAT IS ASSESSMENT?

Psychological assessment is the use of specified testing procedures to evaluate the abilities, behaviour and personal qualities of people. Educational and occupational psychologists can spend much of their time carrying out such assessment. Gathering information about a person is also especially valuable in helping clinical psychologists detect problems that may require special counselling or treatment. Psychological assessment is often referred to as the measurement of *individual differences*, since assessment scores in essence specify in what sense an individual is different or similar to other people on a given characteristic.

The most well-known assessment procedure is the psychological test and the most famous test is the intelligence test. Such testing is considered by some to be 'one of psychology's unquestioned success stories' (Tyler, 1988). That 'success' is determined in several ways. Psychological tests allow people to be compared on various dimensions of intelligence, specific aptitudes and personality according to objective standards that are not open to the biases of subjective interpreters. They are supposed to be fair comparisons of the mental capacities of all individuals taking the same test under the same conditions. These tests have been perceived as 'tools of democracy', enabling selection of individuals for education and employment to be based on what the individuals know and can show, rather than on who they know and what their family can show (Sokol, 1987).

Despite the widespread use of standardised psychological tests, some psychologists believe that such testing is psychology's worst embarrassment. They argue that many of the tests are not objective measures of ability or characteristics of personality. The tests may overcome the biases of teacher and employer evaluations, but they are themselves biased in more fundamental ways because they are based, in part, on specific learning experiences even though such experiences vary with social class, cultural background and personal experiences. Some people use test scores as evidence of innate mental abilities, evidence that they then use to justify discrimination against the disadvantaged poor, women, minorities and immigrants in educational and career opportunities and in formulating public policy (Gould, 1981; Hirsch *et al*, 1990; Kamin, 1974). It has

also been shown that people can improve on the tasks they practice and worsen at the tasks they neglect. Similarly, practising test-taking actually can improve performance.

The most damning criticism of psychological tests comes from those who believe that testing mental ability contributes to *elitism* - these tests play up the importance of differences between people whilst the remainder of psychology focuses on similarities.

History of Assessment

The key figure in the era of modern intelligence testing was a member of the English aristocracy, **Francis Galton**. His book *Hereditary Genius*, published in 1869, greatly influenced subsequent thinking on the methods, theories and practices of testing. Galton, a half-cousin to Charles Darwin, attempted to apply Darwinian evolutionary theory to the study of human abilities. He was interested in how and why people differ in their abilities. He wondered why some people were gifted and successful while many others were not.

Galton was the first to postulate that: (a) differences in intelligence were quantifiable in terms of degrees of intelligence; (b) these differences formed a bell-shaped curve or normal distribution (where most people clustered in the middle and fewer were found toward the genius extreme or the mental deficiency extreme); (c) intelligence, or mental ability, could be measured by objective tests; and (d) the precise extent to which two sets of test scores were related could be determined by a statistical procedure he called *co-relations*, now known as *correlations*. These ideas proved to be of lasting value.

Galton also believed that: genius was inherited; talent, or eminence, ran in families; nurture had only a minimal effect on intelligence; and intelligence was related to Darwinian species fitness and, somehow, to

Francis Galton (1822–1911)

Who or what we think we are is intimately tied up with our gender identity: our sense of our own masculinity and/or femininity. We are socialised into adopting sets of behaviours, attitudes and values that have been defined by society as being broadly associated with being either a biological male or female. Such gender roles are central to our implicit constructions and representations of our own and other's personalities. Gender, then, is strongly implicated not only in how we behave but also in how we define ourselves – in 'who' we think we are.

Various claims have been made about gendered differences in self-conception. Tronto (1987), for example, has argued that women's value systems are more relationship-centred than those of men as a result of women's often subordinated or 'minority' status. Arguably, such a narrative has become woven over time into the fabric of collective self-conceptions, resulting in further claims being made about the gendered basic of other forms of prosocial behaviour. Indeed, some ecofeminist writers have suggested that women are potentially more environmentalist than men (Diamond & Orenstein, 1990) because as altruistic, other-centred carers, women feel more rooted to the natural environment, more caring about the biosphere and, as potential mothers, have a greater vested interest in maintaining the integrity of the local environment for future generations (Blocker & Eckberg, 1989). Men, on the other hand, frequently cast in the traditional gender role of instrumental supporter and provider, have been portrayed as more concerned about economic

than environmental consequences (George & Southwell, 1986).

Such representations and self-conceptions have been bolstered by women's successful protests and attempts to avert the possibility of ecological and social catastrophy. In the 1970s and 80s, for example, the all-woman encampment next to the Royal Air Force base on Greenham Common in Great Britain successfully brought attention to the folly of nuclear arms proliferation.

More recently, however, environmentally responsible behaviour has become a stronger and more pervasive norm in large segments of the population. Demonstrations against extensive infra-structural projects which destroy natural habitats have become commonplace, whether it be against road building at Twyford Down in the English countryside or against the TGV (high speed railways) in Belgium and the Netherlands. Such concern is evident amongst both women and men. So, is there any longer a basis to former claims about the gendered origins of environmental concern?

In an attempt to resolve this

issue Paul Stern and his colleagues conducted a questionnaire survey of undergraduate students, asking them about their beliefs concerning the consequences of environmental quality and protection for themselves, the welfare of others and of the biosphere. Stern *et al* (1993) also asked how willing students would be to take action to assure protection of the environment: for example, whether or not they would be willing in the future to pay extra taxes in order to fund initiatives to protect the environment. The researchers took such willingness to indicate the degree to which men and women place value upon environmental concerns. 349 students responded to the survey (a 63 per cent response rate). The data produced two interesting findings with respect to gender: firstly, it was observed that the women in the sample had stronger beliefs than men about the consequences of environmental quality for self, others and the biosphere; secondly, however, it was found that there was no difference in the degree to which women and men placed value upon protection of the environment.

Thus, it would appear nevertheless that this cohort of women is more accepting than men of messages that link environmental conditions to potential harm to themselves, others and the biosphere. Women appreciate these connections more readily, seeing the consequences more clearly. Stern *et al* (1993) argue that this awareness may be because regular consumer choices which have direct environmental consequences are more often made by women than men by virtue of their stereotypic sex-role positions. Stern and his colleagues go on to suggest that women are socialised into seeing the interconnectedness of things whereas men's world view is one in which there are separate subjects and objects, the parts being perceived as disconnected rather than inseparable within a unifying whole.

So, even though men are justified in retaining a positive image of themselves in as much as they place equal value as women upon environmental issues, men still have some way to go in terms of reconstructing their relatively fragmented view of the planetary eco-system.

moral worth. Galton attempted to base public policy on the concept of genetically superior and inferior people. He started the *eugenics movement*, which advocated improving the human species by applying evolutionary theory to encouraging biologically 'superior' people to interbreed while discouraging biologically 'inferior' people from having offspring. Galton wrote, 'There exists a sentiment, for the most part quite unreasonable, against the gradual extinction of an inferior race' (Galton, 1884). Among the proponents of these ideas were the psychologists Goddard, Terman and Burt.

Purposes of Assessment

Assessment techniques are used for many different purposes and take place in a multitude of settings. An important distinction is between tests that measure *ability* – which are subdivided into those measuring aptitude (for example, intelligence) and those assessing achievement (for example, how well people do at school) – and tests of *typical performance* which measure people's interests, attitudes or personality characteristics.

Whether psychologists measure ability or a person's typical way of functioning, the goal is to predict behaviour. Error in such predictions, of course, can go in either of two directions. It is possible for a test to predict failure when a student would have been effective. This incorrect prediction is known as a *Type-One Error* (a false negative). Predicting success for a student who eventually drops out is known as a *Type-Two Error* (a false positive). (See also the signal detection matrix in Chapter 6.) Similarly, of course, there are two kinds of accurate predictions: those that predict success that is eventually achieved and those that predict failure that is eventually observed. Good tests reduce both kinds of error and increase both kinds of accurate prediction. Assessment psychology attempts to formalise the procedures by which predictions about individual behaviour can be made accurately. Assessment begins with the measurement of a limited number of individual attributes and samples of behaviour. From this narrow body of information about a person in a testing situation – which can be collected conveniently and inexpensively – predictions are made about his likely reactions at some future time in some other real-life situation that is not identical to the test situation.

When the psychologist's judgement may have a profound impact on a person's life, a complete assessment must involve more than just psychological testing. Tests may be very helpful but results should be interpreted in light of all available information about a person, including medical history, family life, previous difficulties and noteworthy achievements (Matarazzo, 1990).

Basic Features of Formal Assessment

Clearly, there are similarities between our own informal assessments of self and others and the formal assessments of professionals; but there are important differences, too. The methods of assessment psychologists use are developed more systematically, applied in a more organised way, and used for carefully specified purposes. **Psychometrics** is the measurement of psychological functioning, achieving its objectives with statistical analysis and test construction as well as an understanding of mental processes.

We will first consider some of the characteristics that make professional assessments formal. We will then examine some of the techniques and sources of information psychologists use to make assessments.

While some techniques are derived from particular theoretical perspectives, others are based on purely empirical grounds. Empirically constructed techniques are guided only by the data; they are built to make specific predictions and, therefore, utilise the items or questions that do the job regardless of whether or not they make theoretical sense. For example, students might be asked to indicate their views on a series of psychological issues. If males consistently differ from females in their scores on this measure, then it could be used as one test of gender differences, even without offering any theory about why the two groups differ.

To be useful for classifying individuals or for selecting those with particular qualities, an assessment procedure should meet three requirements. The assessment instrument should be: (a) reliable (b) valid and (c) standardised. If it fails to meet these requirements, we cannot be sure whether the conclusions of the assessment can be trusted.

Reliability

Reliability is the extent to which an assessment instrument can be trusted to give consistent scores. If your bathroom scales give you a different reading each morning you step on them, you would call them unreliable because you could not count on them to give consistent results.

One straightforward way to find out if a test is reliable is to calculate its **test–retest reliability**. This is a measure of the correlation between the scores of the same people on the same test given on two different occasions. A perfectly reliable test will yield a correlation coefficient of 1.00. This means that the same exact pattern of scores emerges both times; the same people who got the highest and lowest scores the first time do so again. A totally unreliable test results in a 0.00 correlation coefficient. That means there is no relationship between the first set of scores and the second set; someone who got the top score initially gets a completely different score the second time. As the correlation coefficient moves higher (toward the ideal of 1.00), the test is increasingly reliable.

There are two other ways to assess reliability. One is to administer alternate, parallel forms of a test instead of giving exactly the same test twice. Doing so reduces the effects of direct practice of the test questions, memory of the test questions and the desire of an individual to appear consistent from one test to the next. Reliable tests yield comparable scores on parallel forms of the test. The other measure of reliability is the **internal consistency** of responses on a single test. For example, we can compare a person's score on the odd-numbered items of a test to the score on the even-numbered items. A reliable test yields the same score for each of its halves. It is then said to have high internal consistency on this measure of *split-half reliability*. The best psychological tests have coefficients of reliability above 0.70 (Cronbach, 1951).

Although a reliable test tends to give the same test scores when it is repeated, obtaining different test scores does not necessarily mean that a test is unreliable. Sometimes the variable being measured actually changes from one testing to the next. For example, if you took a test on theories of personality before and after reading this chapter, you would hopefully do better the second time - because you would then actually know more. In addition, many variables other than the one of primary interest may affect test scores; you may have different scores on different occasions because of changes in your mood, fatigue and level of effort. Unless a test is designed to measure mood, fatigue, or motivation, these *extraneous variables* will alter the desired test performance, giving a false picture of your ability.

Validity

The **validity** of a test is the degree to which it measures what an assessor intends it to measure. A valid test of intelligence measures a person's intelligence and predicts performance in situations where intelligence is important. In general, then, validity is not a property of the test itself, but a feature of its use in making accurate predictions about outcomes.

To assess the **criterion validity** of a test, we compare a person's score on the test to his or her score on some other standard, or criterion, theoretically associated with what was measured by the test. Ideally, scores on the criterion directly reflect a personal characteristic or behaviour that is related to, but not the same as, that assessed by the test. For example, if an aptitude test is designed to predict success in college, then college grades would be an appropriate criterion. If the test scores correlate highly with college grades, then the test has criterion validity – also called *predictive validity*. A major task of test developers is finding appropriate, measurable criteria.

For many personal qualities of interest to psychologists, no ideal criterion exists. No single behaviour or objective measure of performance can tell us, for example, how anxious, depressed, or aggressive a person is overall. Psychologists have theories or constructs about these abstract qualities. Constructs are ideas about what affects personal qualities, the way they show up in behaviour and the way they relate to other variables. Although there may be no perfect, direct measure of a construct, there might be several tests or criteria that tap into a part of the construct. For example, we want to know if test items actually tap into constructs of intelligence.

Construct validation is the process of combining what we know about a large set of related measures, such as different tests, judges' ratings and observed behaviours, to determine whether a theoretical construct is useful for understanding the data. Once we have determined that a construct is a good working model that explains a large body of data, we can examine separately each of the measures of the construct. The **construct validity** of a particular test is the degree to which it correlates positively with all the other data that represent valid measures of the construct (Loevinger, 1957). The initial stages of test construction are concerned with construct validity – with discovering the set of evidence about the traits and qualities that underlie the broader construct of interest, such as intelligence or creativity. Construct validity is not a quantitative or static measure of validity but a subjective evaluation of the appropriateness of the available evidence for measuring a given construct. Tests with high construct validity correlate with many, but not all, of the other measures to which they are theoretically related. Sometimes the pattern of which criteria a test does and does not correlate with reveals something new about the measures, the construct, or the complexity of human behaviour. The conditions under which a test is valid may be very specific, so it is always important to ask about a test, 'For what purpose is it valid?'

For example, suppose you design a test to measure the ability of medical students to cope with stress and you find that scores on it correlate well with students' ability to cope with classroom stress. You presume your test will also correlate with students' ability to deal with stressful hospital emergencies, but you discover it does not. Since you have demonstrated some validity, the important question is not whether the test is valid, but when it is valid and for what purpose.

Validity has something in common with reliability. While reliability is measured by the degree to which a test correlates with itself (administered at different times or using different items), validity is measured by the degree to which the test correlates with something external to it (another test, a behavioural criterion, or judges' ratings). Usually, a test that is not reliable is also not valid, because a test that cannot predict itself will be unable to predict anything else. For example, if your year group took a test of aggressiveness today and scores were uncorrelated with scores from a parallel form of the test tomorrow (demonstrating unreliability), it is unlikely that the scores from either day would predict which students had argued most frequently in a week's time – the two sets of test scores would not even make the same prediction!

A third type of validity is based on the content, rather than the correlates, of a test. When test items appear to be directly related to the construct or attribute of interest, the test has **face validity**. Face valid tests simply ask what the test administrator needs to know, without containing any trick questions which a psychologist might interpret differently from the person taking the test. The testee simply answers accurately and honestly. When people taking the test are not motivated to lie about themselves, face valid tests can have excellent criterion and construct validity. Often they can uncover information that no one else would know.

Standardisation and procedural uniformity

Suppose you get a score of 18 on a test designed to reveal how depressed you are. What does that mean? Are you a little depressed, not at all depressed, or about averagely depressed? In itself, your test score provides little information. The score is informative only when it can be compared with scores from other people that provide the **norms** against which your score can be evaluated. These other people form the group on which the test is **standardised**. However, if the standardisation group for the particular test in question consists of psychiatric patients with a mood disorder (i.e. of people dissimilar to you), that your score is below the mean for the group likewise then is not very informative about you. *Group norms* are most useful for interpreting individual scores when the standardisation group shares important qualities with the individuals tested (such as age, social class and experience). As a last prerequisite of a good test, mention must be made of the way it is administered and the responses scored. All persons who take the test should be instructed in the same way and situated in similar conditions. Also, the procedure involved in scoring the responses to a test should be applied uniformly.

Sources of Information

Psychological assessment methods can be organised according to four techniques used to gather information about a person: interviews, life history or archival data, tests and situational observations. They can also be classified according to the person who is supplying the information: the person being assessed or other people reporting on the person being assessed. When the person being assessed is providing the information, the methods are called self reports;

when others are supplying the data, the methods are called observer reports. The technique you choose to use and who you ask to supply information depends on the nature of data you need and the purpose of the assessment. A complete assessment should use as many different techniques and sources of information as are available.

Four assessment techniques

An *interview* is a very direct approach to learning about someone. The interview content and style may be casual and unstructured, tailored to fit the person being interviewed. On the other hand, interviews may be highly *structured*, asking very specific questions in a very specific way. Counsellors find unstructured interviews useful in planning individualised treatment programmes. Structured interviews are preferred for job interviews and psychological research, when it is important that many people be assessed accurately, completely, consistently and without bias.

A well-trained interviewer must have important skills. These abilities are putting the respondent at ease, knowing how to elicit the desired information, maintaining control of the direction and pace of the interview, establishing and maintaining feelings of rapport between interviewer and respondent and finally, bringing the interview to a satisfactory climax.

Interview data may be supplemented with *life history* or *archival data*, information about a person's life taken from different types of available records, especially those of different time periods and in relation to other people. These records may include school or military performances, written work (stories and drawings), personal journals, medical data, photographs and videotapes.

A *psychological test* can measure virtually all aspects of human functioning, including intelligence, personality and creativity. A major advantage of tests over interviews is that they provide *quantitative* characterisations of an individual by using normative comparisons with others.

Tests are economical, easy to use and provide important normative data in quantitative form, but they are not always useful for finding out what a person actually does, especially when a person cannot objectively judge or report his or her own behaviour. Psychologists use *situational behaviour observations* to assess behaviour objectively in laboratory or real-life settings. An observer watches an individual's behavioural patterns in one or more situations, such as at home, at work, or in school. The goal of these observations is to discover the determinants and consequences of various responses and habits of the individual. This approach came out of the traditions

of experimental psychology and social-learning theory. Direct situational observations are especially useful for: (a) finding out the conditions in which problem behaviours occur in order to plan and evaluate behaviour-modification therapy; (b) observing job applicants' behaviour in a joblike situation; and (c) determining whether what people say corresponds to what they do in order to validate test and interview data.

Self-report methods

Self-report methods require respondents to answer questions or give information about themselves. This information may be gathered from an interview, a test, or a personal journal. One very easily administered self-report is the *inventory*, a standardised, written test with a multiple choice, true – false, or rating format. An inventory might inquire about your personality, your health, or your life experiences. For example, you might be asked how frequently you have headaches, how assertive you think you are, or how stressful you find your job to be. Such measures are valuable because they tap into an individual's personal experiences and feelings. They are convenient because they do not require trained interviewers and they are generally easy to score. The greatest shortcoming of self-report measures is that sometimes people are not really 'in touch' with their feelings or cannot objectively report their own behaviour. However, depending on the purpose of the assessment, sometimes a person's subjective experience is actually of more interest to the tester than the objective reality. For example, your perceived competence may be more important than your actual skills in determining whether you enter a challenging and exciting career.

Observer-report methods

In psychological assessment, **observer-report methods** involve a systematic evaluation of some aspect of a person's behaviour by another person, a rater, or judge. Observer reports may consist of very specific situational behaviour observations or more generalised ratings. For example, research assistants may observe a nursery class and record the number of times each child performs particular behaviours, such as pushing, hitting, or sharing a toy, during a particular observation period.

While situational behaviour observations are typically made on-line – at the time the behaviour is performed – *ratings* are typically made after an observation period. Sometimes judges are asked to record specific behaviours and then make overall ratings based on them. Often, ratings are made according to detailed guidelines provided by the developers of an assessment technique. At other times, the guidelines are less precise, allowing spontaneous reactions and informal impressions to play a greater role.

What drawbacks could result from such ratings? One is that ratings may tell more about the judge, or about the judge's relationship with the person, than about the true characteristics of the person being rated. For example, if you like someone, you may tend to judge him or her favourably on nearly every dimension. This type of *rating bias* – in which an overall positive or negative feeling about the person is extended to the specific dimensions being evaluated – is referred to as a **halo effect**. A different type of bias occurs when a rater thinks most people in a certain category (for example, politicians, antiwar protesters, the unemployed) have certain qualities. The rater may 'see' those qualities in any individual who happens to be in that category. This type of bias is called a **stereotype effect**.

Rating biases can be reduced by: (a) phrasing rating items in ways that do not reflect connotations, such as 'keeps to him/herself' in place of 'withdrawn'; (b) making specific rules for each rating level, such as 'if the person does X, give a rating of ten'; and (c) using several raters so that the bias introduced by each judge's unique point of view is cancelled out by the other judges.

Whenever you have more than one observer, you can calculate the **interjudge reliability**, which is the degree to which the different observers make similar ratings or agree about what each subject did during an observation period. Typically, interjudge reliability will be highest when judges record the specific behaviours observed in a specific situation rather than general impressions of behaviour. Therefore, people who see you in different situations will agree more about what you are like (general ratings) than about the precise behaviours that you exhibit.

INTERIM SUMMARY

Assessment is the controlled measurement of individual differences which is used to understand and predict the behaviour of individuals. Galton proposed important early ideas about the measurement of intelligence but extended his theory to make social-political recommendations. Modern-day assessments are used for a variety of research and applied purposes measuring attributes such as general knowledge, cognitive capabilities, attitudes and interests, particular skills and personality traits. The basic applied goal of assessment is to use samples of behaviour to predict future behaviour. The scientific goal of assessment is to use information gathered from systematic assessment of a large number of people to improve understanding of the reasons why people differ on certain attributes and traits that are of theoretical interest to researchers.

We have seen that the information used in assessments can come from many sources. Self-report or observer-report information may be gathered through interviews, compilation of life history data and psychological tests. Observer reports can also be gathered through situational behaviour observations. A comprehensive assessment should include data from as many different sources as possible.

The most important features for any method of assessment is that it should be reliable, valid and standardised. Reliability means that a technique gives consistent scores on different occasions (test–retest reliability), on different test items (parallel forms and split-half reliability) and with different observers (interjudge reliability). Validity means that a technique measures what it is supposed to measure, as shown by its correlation with a related technique (criterion validity) or with a large body of relevant data (construct validity). Finally, a test must always be standardised in order to compare the scores of an individual with the norms set by a certain reference group.

ASSESSING INDIVIDUAL DIFFERENCES

Think of all the ways in which you differ from your best friend or sibling. You differ in terms of various abilities, such as intelligence, but also with respect to preferred and typical ways of functioning. The traditional approach to the study of such non-intellectual differences is personality assessment.

Two assumptions are basic to these attempts to understand and describe human personality: first, there are personal characteristics of individuals that give coherence to behaviour and, second, those characteristics can be assessed or measured. In order to describe and study personality, psychologists use tests designed to reveal important personal traits and the way those traits fit together in particular individuals. This information may be used in psychological research, individual therapy, career counselling, or personnel selection and training. The many different types of personality tests can be classified as being either objective or projective.

▣ Personality Tests

Objective tests of personality are those in which the scoring and the administration is relatively simple and follows explicitly stated rules. Some tests may be scored and interpreted by computer programs. The final score is usually a number scaled along a single dimension (such as 'adjustment' to 'maladjustment') or a set of scores on different traits (such as masculinity, dependency, or extraversion) reported relative to some normative sample. A self-report inventory is an objective test in which individuals answer a series of questions about their thoughts, feelings and actions. Assumptions underlying personality tests fit only the trait approach however and thus are contestable along similar lines: such measures are predicated upon the assumption that they access relatively cross-situationally consistent and enduring internal dispositions – a problematic supposition for reasons as already stated.

Nevertheless, without the benefit of hindsight, one of the first self-report inventories focused on adjustment problems: the *Woodworth Personal Data Sheet* (written in 1917) asked questions such as 'Are you often frightened in the middle of the night?' (see DuBois, 1970). Today, a person taking a personality inventory reads a series of statements and indicates whether each one is true for himself or herself. On some inventories the person is asked to assess how frequently each statement is true or how well each describes his or her typically experienced behaviour, thoughts, or feelings.

The most famous test of this type is the *Minnesota Multiphasic Personality Inventory*, or MMPI (Dahlstrom *et al*, 1975). It is used in many clinical settings to aid in the diagnosis of patients and to act as a guide in their treatment. After reviewing its features and applications, we will briefly discuss two other personality inventories that are used widely with nonpatient populations: the NEO Personality Inventory (NEO-PI) and the Myers–Briggs Type Inventory.

The MMPI

The MMPI was developed at the University of Minnesota during the 1930s. It was first published in the 1940s (Hathaway & McKinley, 1940; 1943). Its basic purpose is to diagnose individuals according to a set of psychiatric labels. The first test consisted of 550 items which subjects determined to be either true or false for themselves or to which they responded, 'Cannot say'. From that item pool, scales were developed that were relevant to the kinds of problems patients showed in psychiatric settings. Norms were established for both psychiatric patients and normal subjects (visitors to the University of Minnesota hospital).

The MMPI scales were unlike other existing personality tests of the time because they were developed using an empirical strategy known as *criterion keying*, rather than the usual intuitive approach. Items were included on a scale only if they clearly distinguished between two groups, for example, schizophrenic patients and a normal comparison group. Each item had to demonstrate its validity by being answered similarly by members within each group, but differently between the two groups. Thus, the items were not selected on a theoretical or rational basis (what the content seemed to mean) but on an empirical basis.

The MMPI has ten clinical scales, each constructed to differentiate a special clinical group (such as schizophrenics or paranoids) from a normal control group. The test is scored by adding up the number of items on a particular scale that a person answered in the same way as the clinical group; the higher the score, the more the person is like the clinical group and less like the normal group.

The test includes validity scales that detect suspicious response patterns, such as blatant dishonesty, carelessness, defensiveness and evasiveness. When an MMPI is interpreted, the tester first checks the validity scales to be sure the test is valid and then looks at the rest of the scores. The pattern of the scores – which are highest, how they differ – forms the 'MMPI profile'. Individual profiles are compared to those common for particular groups, such as paranoids, felons and gamblers.

Recently, the MMPI has undergone a major revision and it is now called the MMPI-2 (Butcher *et al*, 1989). Some items have been dropped, others added and others rewritten to remove sexist language and themes that are no longer culturally relevant. Much of the item pool is unchanged, so the original clinical scales are still scored in the MMPI-2 but the revision uses an improved scoring procedure. The validity scales have changed slightly, and the MMPI-2 has seven validity scales, rather than four. The most dramatic change is the addition of 15 new content scales that were derived using a *rational method* instead of criterion keying. For each of 15 clinically relevant topics (such as anxiety or family problems), items were selected on two bases: if they seemed theoretically related to the topic area and if they statistically formed a homogeneous scale, meaning that each scale measures a single, unified concept. The MMPI-2's clinical and content scales are given in *Table 12.2*. You will notice that most of the clinical scales measure several related concepts and that the names of the content scales are simple and self-explanatory. All of the MMPI-2 scales have good test–retest reliability and have been normed on very large clinical and nonclinical samples.

TABLE 12.2 MMPI-2 CLINICAL AND CONTENT SCALES (1989)

Clinical Scales and Descriptions	Content Scales
Hypochondriasis (Hs): Abnormal concern with bodily functions	Anxiety
Depression (D): Pessimism; hopelessness, slowing of action and thought	Fears
	Obsessiveness
Conversion Hysteria (Hy): Unconscious use of mental problems to avoid conflicts or responsibility	Depression
	Health Concerns
Psychopathic Deviate (Pd): Disregard for social custom; shallow emotions; inability to profit from experience	Bizarre Mentation
	Anger
Masculinity-Femininity (Mf): Differences between men and women	Cynicism
Paranoia (Pa): Suspiciousness; delusions of grandeur or persecution	Antisocial Practices
	Type A (workaholic)
Psychasthenia (Pt): Obsessions; compulsions; fears; guilt indecisiveness	Low Self-Esteem
	Social Discomfort
Schizophrenia (Sc): Bizarre, unusual thoughts or behaviour; withdrawal; hallucinations; delusions	Family Problems
	Work Interference
Hypomania (Ma): Emotional excitement; flight of ideas; overactivity	Negative Treatment Indicators (negative attitudes about doctors and treatment)
Social introversion (Si): Shyness, disinterest in others; insecurity	

The benefits of the MMPI include its established reliability and validity, its ease and economy of administration and its usefulness for research in psychopathology and making decisions about patients. In fact, it is used in over 65 countries and has been the subject of well over 8,000 books and articles (Butcher, 1989). Another benefit is that the item pool can be used for many purposes. For example, you could use criterion keying to build a creativity scale by finding a creative and a noncreative group and selecting the MMPI items that they answered differently. Over the years, psychologists have developed and validated hundreds of special purpose scales in this way and each of these scales can be scored from any MMPI response sheet.

For researchers, one of the most attractive characteristics of the MMPI are the enormous archives, or data banks, of MMPIs collected from different types of people all over the world. Because all of these people have been tested on the same items in a standardised way, they can be compared either on the traditional clinical scales or on special purpose scales. In fact, these MMPI archives allow researchers to apply newly developed special purpose scales to MMPIs taken by people many years earlier, perhaps long before

the construct being measured was even conceived.

However, the MMPI is not without its faults. Its clinical scales have been criticised because they are heterogeneous (measure several things at once) and because the scale names are confusing and do not correspond to what they measure. Complicated clinical lore is required to interpret a profile correctly – schizophrenia, for example, must be diagnosed from a combination of scales and not directly from the Schizophrenia scale. This problem still exists for the clinical scales of the MMPI-2, but its new content scales are less confusing and easier to interpret. Another shortcoming of the MMPI is that as it was formulated originally, it has little to do with personality: the items, including those for the new content scales, were selected to measure clinical problems, so the inventory is not well-suited to measure personality in non-patient populations.

The NEO-PI

The *NEO Personality Inventory* (NEO-PI) was primarily designed to assess personality characteristics in nonclinical adult populations. It measures the five factor model of personality, sometimes called the **Big Five**, which we discussed previously. If you took the NEO-PI, you would receive a profile sheet that showed your standardised scores relative to a large normative sample on each of the five major dimensions: Neuroticism (N), Extraversion (E), Openness (O), Agreeableness (A) and Conscientiousness (C). Also included on your profile would be your standardised scores on facet scales, or specific subscales that measure different aspects of each dimension. For example, the N (Neuroticism) dimension is broken down into six facet scales: Anxiety, Hostility, Depression, Self-Consciousness, Impulsiveness and Vulnerability. There are likewise six facets each for E and O, and new facet scales have been planned for the A and C dimensions in subsequent revisions (Costa & McCrae, 1985). Much research has demonstrated that the NEO dimensions are homogeneous, highly reliable and show good criterion and construct validity (McCrae & Costa, 1987; 1989).

The NEO is being used to study personality stability and change across the life-span as well as the relationship of personality characteristics to physical health and various life events, such as career success or early retirement. In applied settings, a therapist might want to administer both the MMPI-2 and the NEO-PI in order to plan a treatment programme that is well-suited to a patient's personality as well as to his or her psychiatric needs. The NEO may also be useful in career counselling – to help people select jobs that are right for them. However, it has never been validated (or recommended) for making decisions about hiring or promoting employees.

The Myers-Briggs Type Indicator (MBTI)

This popular personality test, based on **Carl Jung's** typology theory (1923; 1971), assigns people to one of 16 categories or types. Developed by Peter Myers and Isabel Briggs, the test attempts to find 'an orderly reason for personality differences' in the ways people perceive their world and make judgements about it (Myers, 1962; 1976; 1980).

Basic differences in perception and judgement are assumed to result in corresponding differences in behaviour. Both perception and judgement are subdivided into dual ways of perceiving – by direct sensing (S) and unconscious intuition (I) – and judging – by thinking (T) and feeling (F). The third factor added to the Myers-Briggs test – preferences for extraversion (E) or introversion (I) – is based on Jung's idea that people focus on either their inner or outer worlds. Sixteen types emerge from the combination of these preferences, such as extraverts who show thinking with intuition or introverts who show sensing with feeling. 'A person's type is the product of conscious orientation to life: habitual, purposeful ways of using one's mind – habitual because they seem good and interesting and trustworthy' (Myers, 1980; Bayne, 1995). A major use of the Myers-Briggs test is relating type to occupation – showing that certain preferences for perceiving, thinking, and extraversion or introversion influence occupational choice and job satisfaction (McCaulley, 1978). Its appeal lies in its ability to categorise people into a small number of types that simplify the enormous complexity of personality differences between individuals. Recent work with the MBTI has indicated that its validity as a measure of four major personality factors has been considerably strengthened by its relationship with indices of The Big Five (Bayne, 1994).

Projective Tests

In a **projective test**, a person is given a series of stimuli that are purposely ambiguous, such as abstract patterns, incomplete pictures and drawings that can be interpreted in many ways. The person may be asked to describe the patterns, finish the pictures, or tell stories about the drawings. In Chapter 6 we saw that people tend to perceive meaningful wholes even when the stimuli do not have a clear, unitary configuration. Projective tests utilise this principle and are based on the further assumption that the way such ambiguous stimuli are perceptually structured, tells us something about the person. The individual is said to '*project*' his or her inner feelings, personal motives and conflicts as derived from prior life experiences onto the stimuli.

Proponents of the use of projective tests share with psychoanalysts the assumption that many of these processes are unconscious. Thus, they argue that in order to access such processes it is not sufficient simply to ask subjects about them. Rather, these phenomena have to be measured *indirectly*. The two most commonly used projective tests are the Rorschach test and the Thematic Apperception Test (TAT).

The Rorschach test

In the *Rorschach test*, developed by Swiss psychiatrist **Hermann Rorschach** in 1921, the ambiguous stimuli are symmetrical inkblots (Rorschach, 1942).

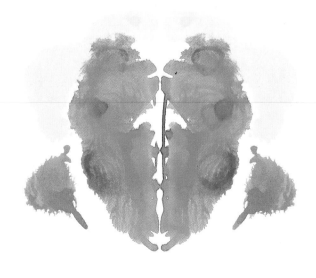

FIGURE 12.3 A SAMPLE RORSCHACH INK BLOT

Some are black and white and some are coloured (see *Figure 12.3*). During the test, a respondent is shown an inkblot and asked, 'Tell me what you see, what it might be to you. There are no right or wrong answers'.

The tester records verbatim what the subject says, how much time she takes to respond, the total time she takes per inkblot, and the way she handles the inkblot card. Then, in a second phase called an inquiry, the respondent is reminded of the previous responses and asked to elaborate on them.

The responses are scored on three major features: (a) the location or part of the card mentioned in the response – whether the respondent refers to the whole stimulus or to part of it and the size of the details mentioned; (b) the content of the response – the nature of the object and activities seen; and (c) the determinants – which aspects of the card (such as its colour or shading) prompted the response. Some scorers also note whether responses are original and unique or popular and conforming.

Interpreting a person's scores into a coherent portrait of personality dynamics is a complex, highly subjective process that relies on clinical expertise and skilled intuition. Ideally, a tester uses these data as a source of hypotheses about a person that are then evaluated through other assessment procedures. Although the Rorschach has questionable reliability and validity, it is recommended as an indirect way to identify sources of information, such as sexual interests or aggressive fantasies, that people may resent being questioned about or lie about on objective tests. It is gaining renewed popularity among clinicians interested in using it along with other forms of personality assessment.

The TAT

In the *Thematic Apperception Test* (developed by American psychologist **Henry Murray** in 1938), respondents are shown pictures of ambiguous scenes and asked to generate stories about them, describing what the people in the scenes are doing and thinking, what led up to each event and how each situation will end (see *Figure 12.4*). The person administering the TAT evaluates the structure and content of the stories as well as the behaviour of the individual telling them, in an attempt to discover some of the respondent's major concerns, motivations and personality characteristics. For example, an examiner might evaluate a person as conscientious if his stories concerned people who lived up to their obligations and if he told them in a serious, orderly way. The test can be used with clinical patients to reveal emotional problems or with normal individuals to reveal dominant needs, such as needs for power, affiliation and achievement (McClelland, 1961).

Statistical versus clinical prediction

Which is better: prediction based on subjective expert judgements of clinical psychologists or cold-blooded objective prediction generated by computer analysis of test scores? Psychologist **Paul Meehl** (1954)

FIGURE 12.4 A SAMPLE CARD FROM THE TAT

answered this irreverent question by comparing computerised predictions about various aspects of the lives of people tested with predictions made by clinical judges. The results surprised many psychologists. The statistical approach was equal or superior to the clinical approach in many instances. Based on probability formulas and actuarial tables of reactions of large numbers of people, the statistical approach was good at predicting specific outcomes (Meehl, 1965; Sawyer, 1966). The judgement of a sensitive, skilled clinician has proven best, however, when no good tests are available, for individual cases studied over time, and to predict the behaviour of rare, atypical cases (Phares, 1984). In practice, then, the best predictions are made when the strengths of each approach are utilised (Holt, 1970).

Personology

Some critics argue that these many different ways of assessing personality use the wrong approach to understanding the richness and uniqueness of personality. Their focus on individual differences and normative comparisons serve us well in ability testing but do us a disservice when extended to personality testing (Rorer & Widiger, 1983). These critics call for an emphasis on understanding what is characteristic and special about individual persons. **Personology** is the study of personality structure, dynamics and development in the individual. The data for this formidable task come from diaries, biographies, literature, case studies, letters, general observations and with life-story questionnaires (McAdams, 1988).

◱ Intelligence Testing

How should we define intelligence? Social scientists have yet to agree on a single definition, but most would include in their measure of intelligence at least three types of skills: (a) adapting to new situations and changing task demands; (b) learning or profiting optimally from experience or training; and (c) thinking abstractly using symbols and concepts (Phares, 1984).

More specific ways of defining intelligence are linked to various theories of human adaptation and intellectual functioning. These theories have emerged from all walks of psychology, including neurological-biology, learning theory and human development.

We will define intelligence as the capacity to profit from experience, to go beyond what is perceived to imagine symbolic possibilities. It is a hypothetical construct, usually equated with higher-level abstract thought processes. Not directly observable, intelligence is verified only by the operations (tests) used to measure it and by how it functions in criterion situations that are developed to validate it.

The way we think about mental functioning and intelligence influences the way we try to assess it. Some psychologists believe that human intelligence can be quantified and reduced to a single score. Others argue that assessment should depend on a schema of the way the different components of a person's intelligence work together (Hunt, 1984; Sternberg, 1985).

Is intelligence a unitary attribute (such as height) meaning that people can be assessed in terms of how smart they are? Is intelligence instead a collection of mental competencies (analogous to athletic abilities) meaning that people's intelligence for different kinds of tasks can be assessed? In this section, we will consider some alternative views about the best way to define and understand intelligence. We will also tackle the question of why intelligence should be measured. We mentioned earlier that, while some people believe that assessment of intellectual abilities is one of psychology's most significant contributions to society, others maintain that it is a systematic attempt by elitists to weed out undesirables (Gould, 1981). We will examine some of the evidence for such conflicting claims, but, first, we need more history to set the stage for these claims.

Historical context

A brief look at the history of intelligence testing will reveal how practical social and political concerns, measurement issues and theory were entwined in the development of intelligence tests for children and adults. The movement to measure intelligence began in France as an attempt to identify children who were unable to learn in school. Soon, however, intelligence testing became big business in America and in some European countries.

The year 1905 marked the first published account of a workable intelligence test. **Alfred Binet** had responded to the call of the French Minister of Public Instruction for the development of a way to more effectively teach developmentally disabled children in the public schools. Binet and his colleague, Theophile Simon, believed that measuring a child's intellectual ability was necessary for planning an instructional programme. Their radical proposal was that education should be fit to the child's level of competence and not that the child be fit to a fixed curriculum.

There are four important features of Binet's approach. First, he interpreted scores on his test as an

A psychologist administers an intelligence test to a four-year-old child. The performance part of this test includes a block design task, an object completion task and a shape identification task.

estimate of current performance and not as a measure of innate intelligence. Second, he wanted the test scores to be used to identify children who needed special help and not to stigmatise them. Third, he emphasised that training and opportunity could affect intelligence and he wanted to identify areas of performance in which special education could help these children. Finally, he constructed his test empirically, rather than tying it to a particular theory of intelligence.

Children of various ages were tested and the average score for normal children at each age was computed. Then, each individual child's performance was compared to the average for other children of his or her age. Test results were expressed in terms of the average age at which normal children achieved a particular score. This measure was called the **mental age** (MA). When a child's scores on various items of the test added up to the average score of a group of five-year-olds, the child was said to have a mental age (MA) of five, regardless of his or her actual **chronological age** (CA) (Binet, 1911). Retardation was then defined operationally by Binet as being two mental-age years behind chronological age. As more children were tested longitudinally, Binet found that those assessed as developmentally disabled at one age

fell further behind the mental age of their birth cohorts as they grew older. A child of five who performed at the level of three-year-olds might, at the age of ten, perform at the level of six-year-olds. Although the ratio of mental age to chronological age would be constant (3/5 and 6/10), the total number of mental-age years of retardation would have increased from two to four.

Binet's successful development of an intelligence test had great impact, first in the United States and then in European countries. A unique combination of historical events and socio-political forces had prepared industrialised countries for an explosion of interest in assessing mental ability. Since the early decades of this century, the interest of psychologists in intellectual assessment has flourished into a mental-measurement industry.

In 1917, when the United States declared war on Germany, it was necessary to establish quickly a military force led by competent leaders. Recruiters needed to determine who of the many people who had been drafted had the ability to learn quickly and benefit from special leadership training. New group administered tests of mental ability were used to evaluate over 1.7 million recruits. Incidentally, a group of famous psychologists, including Lewis Terman, Edward Thorndike and Robert Yerkes, designed these new tests in only a month (Lennon, 1985).

One consequence of this large-scale testing programme was that the American public came to accept the idea that intelligence tests could differentiate people in terms of leadership ability and other socially important characteristics. This acceptance led to the widespread use of tests in schools and industry. Another, more unfortunate, consequence was that the tests reinforced prevailing prejudices, because the army reports indicated that differences in test scores were linked to race and country of origin (Yerkes, 1921). Of course, the same statistics could have been used to demonstrate that environmental disadvantages limit the full development of people's intellectual abilities. Instead, they simply fuelled racist ideology.

Although Binet began the standardised assessment of intellectual ability, statistically-minded American psychologists improved upon his initial work by modifying his scoring procedure, increasing the reliability of the tests and studying the scores of enormous normative samples of people who took the new tests. They also developed the IQ, or **intelligence quotient**. The IQ was a numerical, standardised measure of intelligence, obtained from an individual's score on an intelligence test. Two families of individually administered IQ tests are used widely today: the Stanford-Binet scales and the Wechsler scales.

The Stanford–Binet intelligence scale

Stanford University's **Lewis Terman**, a former public school administrator, realised that Binet's method for assessing intelligence was important. He adapted Binet's test questions for American schoolchildren, standardised administration of the test, and developed age-level norms by giving the test to thousands of children. In 1916 he published the Stanford Revision of the Binet Tests, commonly referred to as the Stanford–Binet Intelligence Scale (Terman, 1916).

With his new test, Terman provided a base for the concept of the intelligence quotient, or IQ (coined by Stern, 1914). The IQ was the ratio of mental age to chronological age (multiplied by 100 to eliminate decimals):

$$IQ = MA \div CA \times 100$$

A child with a CA of eight whose test scores revealed an MA of ten had an IQ of 125 ($10 \div 8 \times 100 = 125$), while a child of that same chronological age who performed at the level of six-year-olds had an IQ of 75 ($6 \div 8 \times 100 = 75$). Individuals who performed at the mental age equivalent to their chronological age had IQs of 100, which was considered to be the average or normal IQ.

The new Stanford–Binet test soon became a standard instrument in clinical psychology, psychiatry and educational counselling. At the same time, Terman's adoption of the IQ concept contributed to the development of a new conceptualisation of the purpose and meaning of intelligence testing. Unlike Binet, Terman believed that intelligence was an inner quality, that it was largely hereditary, and that IQ tests could measure this inner quality throughout the range of abilities that make up intelligence. His implicit message was that IQ reflected something essential and unchanging about human intelligence. 'One's intellectual level was a characteristic one must accept rather than try to change'.

Terman was influenced in his beliefs by the leading assessment theorist of the 1920s, **Charles Spearman**: he had concluded that all mental tests were a combination of an innate general intellectual ability, the **g-factor** and some specific abilities as well (Spearman, 1927). 'It was almost universally assumed by psychologists and by the general public in these early years that individual differences in intelligence were innately determined' (Tyler, 1988).

The Stanford–Binet contains a series of subtests, each tailored for a particular mental age. A series of minor revisions were made on these subtests in 1937, 1960 and 1972 to achieve three goals: (a) to extend the range of the test to measure the IQ of very young children and very intelligent adults; (b) to update vocabulary items that had changed in difficulty with changes in society and (c) to update the norms, or age-appropriate average scores (Terman & Merrill, 1937; 1960; 1972).

IQ scores are no longer derived by dividing mental age by chronological age. If you took the test today, your score would be added up and directly compared to the scores of other people your age. An IQ of 100 would indicate that 50 per cent of those your age earned lower scores. Scores between 90 and 110 are now labelled normal, above 120 are superior, and below 70 are evidence of developmental disability (see *Figure 12.5*).

The Stanford–Binet scales were criticised because the subtests used to measure IQ at different ages focused on different types of skills. For example, two to four-year-olds were tested on their ability to manipulate objects, whereas adults were tested almost exclusively on verbal items. As the scientific understanding of intelligence increased, psychologists found it increasingly important to measure several intellectual abilities at all age levels. A recent revision of the Stanford–Binet now provides different scores for

FIGURE 12.5 DISTRIBUTION OF IQ SCORES AMONG A LARGE SAMPLE

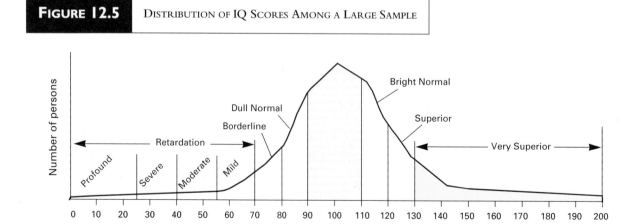

several mental skills, but it has not been widely accepted (Vernon, 1987).

The Wechsler intelligence scales

David Wechsler of Bellevue Hospital in New York set out to correct the dependence on verbal items in the assessment of adult intelligence. In 1939, he published the Wechsler–Bellevue Intelligence Scale, which combined verbal subtests with nonverbal or performance subtests. Thus, in addition to an overall IQ score, subjects were given separate estimates of verbal IQ and nonverbal IQ. After a few changes, the test was retitled the *Wechsler Adult Intelligence Scale* – the WAIS in 1955, and the revised WAIS-R today (Wechsler, 1981).

There are six verbal subtests of the WAIS-R: Information, Vocabulary, Comprehension, Arithmetic, Similarities (stating how two things are alike) and Digit Span (repeating a series of digits after the examiner). These tests are both written and oral. The five performance subtests involve manipulation of materials and have little or no verbal content. In the Block Design test, for example, a subject tries to reproduce designs shown on cards by fitting together blocks with coloured sides. The Digit Symbol test provides a key that matches nine symbols to nine numeric digits and the task is to write the appropriate digits under the symbols on another page. Other performance tests involve Picture Arrangement, Picture Completion and Object Assembly. If you were to take the WAIS-R, you would perform all 11 subtests, and receive three scores: a Verbal IQ, a Performance IQ and an overall or Full-scale IQ.

The WAIS-R is designed for people 18 years or older, but similar tests have been developed for children. The *Wechsler Intelligence Scale for Children– Revised* (WISC-R, 1974) is suited for children ages six to 17, and the *Wechsler Preschool and Primary Scale of Intelligence* (WPPSI) for children ages four to six-and-a-half years. Some subtests were specially created for use with children, but most have a direct counterpart in the WAIS-R. For example, the WAIS-R Digit Symbol test is very similar to the WISC-R Coding test and the WPPSI Animal House test. Digit Symbol and Coding involve matching symbols to numeric digits, while Animal House requires pre-school-age children to match pictures of animals with houses of different colours.

The WAIS-R, the WISC-R, and the WPPSI form a family of intelligence tests that yield a Verbal IQ, a Performance IQ and a Full-Scale IQ at all age levels. In addition, they provide comparable subtest scores that allow researchers to track the development of even more specific intellectual abilities. For this reason, the Wechsler scales are particularly valuable when the same individual is to be tested at different ages, for example, when a child's progress in response to different educational programmes is monitored.

Group tests of intelligence

In addition to the individually given Stanford–Binet and Wechsler scales, there are many other tests that are given to groups of individuals, particularly in schools in the United States and Europe where pupils are sometimes given a group intelligence test in order to predict academic achievement.

Nevertheless, there are many reasons that people's scores on an intelligence test can be lower than their

In these examples from the WISC-R, children are asked to put the frames in order so they make a story.

actual ability. One person may be distracted by unusual surroundings or by extreme test anxiety. Another may misunderstand the instructions because of visual or hearing impairments or difficulty with the English language. These effects contaminate test performance and can invalidate an individual's score on any test. However, the problem is more likely to be noticed (and corrected) when an intelligence test is administered individually than in an anonymous mass testing.

It is important to remember that IQ scores, by themselves, do not tell how much children know or what they can do. A high-school student with an IQ of 100 has knowledge and skills that a fourth-grader with a higher IQ of 120 does not have. In addition, people labelled developmentally disabled on the basis of their IQ scores vary considerably in what they are able to do and in how much they can learn through instruction. Similarly, elderly subjects whose response speed has slowed down perform more poorly than the young on test items where speed is important, but they still have greater wisdom in many measurable domains (Baltes, 1990). Thus, an operational definition such as 'intelligence is what intelligence tests measure', does not cover all that we mean by the concept of human intelligence.

Psychometric theories of intelligence

Psychometrics is the field of psychology that specialises in mental testing in any of its facets, including personality assessment, intelligence evaluation and aptitude measurement. Psychometric approaches to intelligence study the statistical relationships between different measures, such as the 11 subtests of the WAIS-R and then make inferences about the nature of human intelligence on the basis of those relationships. One common approach uses a technique mentioned at the beginning of this chapter called **factor analysis**, a statistical procedure that locates a smaller number of dimensions, clusters, or factors from a larger set of independent variables or items on a test. The goal of factor analysis is to identify a small number of factors that represent the basic psychological dimensions being investigated. Factors are not traits, they are statistical regularities in the data base. However, traits are inferred from the factor; researchers can analyse the nature of the items or information that makes up each factor.

Raymond Cattell (1963), using more advanced factor analytic techniques, determined that general intelligence can be broken down into two relatively independent components he called crystallised and fluid intelligence. **Crystallised intelligence** involves the knowledge a person has already acquired and the ability to access that knowledge; it is measured by tests

of vocabulary, arithmetic and general information. **Fluid intelligence** is the ability to see complex relationships and solve problems; it is measured by tests of block designs and spatial visualisation in which the background information needed to solve a problem is included or readily apparent.

Recent investigations indicate that both crystallised and fluid intelligence are partly inherited and partly learned. In addition, some psychometricians believe there may be no such thing as general intelligence. Instead, there may be four or five relatively independent characteristics of people which influence their performance on different intellectual tasks. Likely candidates for these characteristics are fluid, crystallised, verbal and auditory intelligence as well as speediness (Horn, 1985).

Guilford's structure of intellect

J. P. Guilford, another psychometrician, used factor analysis to examine the demands of many intelligence-related tasks. His *Structure of Intellect* model specifies three features of intellectual tasks: the content, or type of information; the product, or form in which information is represented; and the operation, or type of mental activity performed.

As shown in *Figure 12.6*, in the Structure of Intellect model, there are five kinds of content – visual, auditory, symbolic, semantic and behavioural; six kinds of products – units, classes, relations, systems, transformations and implications; and five kinds of operations – evaluation, convergent production, divergent production, memory and cognition. Each task performed by the intellect can be identified according to the particular types of content, products and operations involved. Further, Guilford believes that each content–product–operation combination (each small cube in the model) represents a distinct mental ability.

There are 150 possible combinations of contents, products and operations; that is, any of the five types of content may take the form of any of the six products ($5 \times 6 = 30$) and on these 30 resulting kinds of information, any of the five types of operation may be performed ($30 \times 5 = 150$). For example, a test of vocabulary would assess your ability for cognition of units with semantic content, while learning a dance routine requires memory for behavioural systems.

This theoretical model is analogous to a chemist's periodic table of elements. By means of such a systematic framework, intellectual factors, similar to chemical elements, may be postulated before they are discovered. In 1961, when Guilford proposed his model, nearly 40 intellectual abilities had been

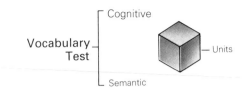

FIGURE 12.6 — THE STRUCTURE OF INTELLECT

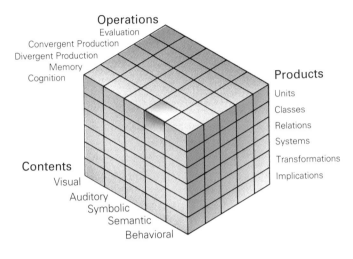

identified. Researchers have since accounted for over 100 (Guilford, 1985).

Since Guilford, many psychologists have broadened their conceptions of intelligence to include much more than performance on traditional IQ tests. However, while Guilford denied mental abilities in terms of the features of the tasks we confront, cognitive scientists such as Hunt, Sternberg and Gardner focus on the different cognitive processes, or mental activities, we use when we learn new things or find a novel solution to a problem. This approach to intelligence as encapsulated in the work of these three psychologists is not considered here as their ideas and research were examined in detail in Chapter 9.

The Use and Misuse of IQ

What purposes do IQ test scores serve? How should an IQ score be interpreted? What damage might be done if an IQ score is used inappropriately? These questions have been the source of many emotionally charged debates because the use of tests has an extensive impact on industry, society and individual lives. We will first outline the issues in this debate and then examine the evidence for each side.

Gender and IQ

Over the last century, psychologists have debated alleged *gender differences* in IQ. For a long time the stereotype prevailed that women are supposedly not as intellectually competent as men, test scores of the time purportedly supporting such a contentious view. We know now however, that the tests used were *sex-biased*, favouring tasks on which men would outperform women. In a review of these studies, Maccoby & Jacklin (1974) concluded they show that on average women score more highly on verbal intelligence subtests than men while the latter, however, score more highly than women on visual spatial intelligence and on mathematical reasoning. Nevertheless, more recent reviews of the literature testify to decreasing evidence of such sex differences, with male test scores over the last two decades on verbal subtests increasingly converging towards those of women. Similarly, female scores on mathematical reasoning have increased to match those of men (Hyde, 1991; Hyde & Linn, 1988). It could be argued that the disappearance of gender differences in IQ subtest scores is attributable to the possibility that boys and girls are treated more liberally as equals following the adoption of increasingly enlightened attitudes. One gender difference has remained: namely on visuo-spatial tests, a higher level of performance for males still being evident (Hyde, 1991). Thus, it continues to be an open question as to whether this test result will undergo change in the future like others before it, as and when the socio-cultural milieu changes once more. The alleged difference remains controversial since it is claimed to be related to sex differences in hemispheric organisation (Benbow, 1988). No doubt further research will seek to address this remaining dissimilarity.

Race and IQ

In most Western countries, the IQ scores of minority group members differ from those of the majority. Although in most cases minorities score lower than the majority on standardised intelligence tests, this is not always the case. In the United States, for example, Asian Americans obtain about the same IQ scores as their white compatriots. However, African Americans and Latinos score, on average, lower than Asian Americans and whites. Of course, there are individuals in all groups who score at the highest (and the lowest) extremes of the IQ scale. How should we interpret IQ scores and what is the source of these group differences? There are three common explanations – genetics, environment and test bias – and each leads to important social consequences.

The *genetic position* claims that IQ tests measure inherent intellectual ability and that some racial or cultural groups score lower because they are genetically inferior. Group differences are used to justify racist views which, in the extreme, support eugenics programmes to limit 'breeding' by undesirable groups, laws restricting the immigration of certain groups and legal inequality that favours the group in power. The 'moderate' consequences of this position are that it feeds intergroup conflict, encourages school segregation and discriminatory hiring practices and argues against funding for intervention programmes that help minorities. However, in our pluralistic culture, it is difficult to determine how much of the variation in intellectual performance on any standard test can be assigned to hereditary factors and what proportion is attributable to environmental influences, or, indeed, why there is so much variation.

The *environmental position* interprets IQ scores as a measure of current functioning and alleges that low scores often reflect social factors. Group differences in IQ scores are believed to be a symptom of larger social problems. The minority groups with the lowest average IQ scores are those for whom poverty, illiteracy and hopelessness are most widespread. People who support the environmental position believe that it was racism and discrimination that landed many minorities in the decaying urban backwaters of our larger metropolitan areas in the first place and still work to keep them there even today. The consequences of this view include

equal opportunity legislation, better schools and intervention programmes which help disadvantaged children build self-confidence and learn the skills necessary to succeed in school.

Proponents of the latter view are also interested in protecting the civil rights of minority group members. They believe that group differences in IQ scores are caused by systematic *bias* in the tests questions, making them invalid and unfair for minorities. Dialect differences between whites and blacks, for example, that could affect an African-European person's verbal scores on a standardised test with a bias toward standard English.

There have been several suggestions made in response to the test bias position. One is that test makers try to improve their tests to make them *culture fair*. Another consequence of this view is that when test bias is seen as the sole cause for group differences, it may become a convenient excuse for legislators to pretend that racial injustice in the larger society is not a serious problem, thereby reducing incentives for supporting remedial action programmes.

Heredity versus environment

There is no question that heredity influences those elusive mental qualities that we call intelligence. Many different lines of research have shown there is a strong genetic basis to a variety of human attributes. Research used to assess the genetic contribution of a given type of functioning compares identical twins (monozygotic, MZ) with same-sex fraternal twins (dizygotic, DZ) and sometimes with siblings. Significant genetic effects have been found on attributes as diverse as heart functioning (Brown, 1990); personality traits (Tellegen *et al*, 1988); and hypnotisability (Morgan *et al*, 1970). So it is reasonable to believe that there is also a genetic basis to intellectual functioning.

The pioneer of research into the relative contribution of heredity and environment to IQ was British psychologist Cyril Burt. In his studies, he compared IQ scores of MZ twins and DZ twins, focusing upon the comparison of MZ twins reared together and MZ twins reared apart. On the basis of this data, he claimed that IQ scores of MZ twins who were reared apart correlated at 0.77, which was interpreted as indicating the genetic determination of IQ (Burt, 1966). After Burt's death, other researchers who wanted to study his pioneering efforts in detail discovered that much of his data could not be traced. Suspicion arose that he had fabricated part of his results. Advocates and adversaries of Burt attacked each other publicly. The debate seemed to come to an end in 1979 when the conclusions of Burt's offical biography by Hearnshaw were accepted by most psychologists. Hearnshaw thought that the evidence suggested Burt had in fact faked part of his data (Hearnshaw, 1979). Recently, however, some proponents of the genetic basis of IQ have argued for the rehabilitation of Burt's work. The resulting debate has given rise to a new episode in the perennial nature–nurture controversy with respect to IQ (Samelson, 1992).

The 'heredity versus environment' issue is focal in the field of *human behavioural genetics*, which has been developed over the past few decades. On the whole, behavioural geneticists claim that both the environment and heredity determine IQ (Plomin & Rende, 1991).

Table 12.3 compares IQ scores of individuals on the basis of their degree of genetic relationship. The greater the genetic similarity the greater the IQ similarity. The correlation between IQ scores increases as we move up in degree of heredity from cousins to siblings to fraternal twins to identical twins. It is also greater between parent and child than between foster parent and adopted child. Environment also reveals its contribution in the greater IQ similarities among those who have been reared together.

A recent large-scale study comparing twins has

TABLE 12.3 IQ AND GENETIC RELATIONSHIP

	Correlationship
Identical twins	
Reared together	0.86
Reared apart	0.72
Fraternal twins	
Reared together	0.60
Siblings	
Reared together	0.47
Reared apart	0.24
Parent/child	0.40
Foster parent/child	0.31
Cousins	0.15

stirred up controversy by claiming that heredity makes a much more important contribution to intelligence than environmental factors. It reports that even when identical twins are raised in different families, as much as 70 per cent of the variance in their IQ scores is due to genetic makeup (Bouchard *et al*, 1990). This figure is being debated, but many psychologists agree that heredity plays an important part in variance of IQ scores. It is difficult to determine the relative roles of genetics and environment in the development of intelligence or other aspects of mental functioning (Plomin, 1989; Scarr, 1988a; Stevenson *et al*, 1987). Children who live in the same family setting do not necessarily share the same critical, psychological environment. You probably are aware of this if you have siblings with interests and lifestyles that differ from your own.

Another problem arises when we use comparisons of IQ scores to make inferences about group differences, using measures of the genetic basis of IQ. A heritability estimate of a particular trait, such as intelligence, is based on the proportion of the variability in test scores on that trait that can be traced to inherited factors. The estimate is found by computing the variation in all the test scores for a given population (college students or manic depressive patients, for example) and then identifying what portion of the total variance is due to genetic or inherited factors (by comparing twins and others whose genetic similarity differ). As more of the total variance is due to heredity, knowing the degree of genetic similarity allows a better prediction of the similarity in test scores within this population. There are two key points regarding heritability estimates. First, the estimates have no implications for individual cases; they pertain only to the average in a given

population of individuals. Thus, we cannot determine how much of your height, which has a high heritability estimate, is due to genetic influences. Second, heritability is based on an estimate within a given group and cannot be used to interpret differences between groups, no matter how large those differences are on an objective test. The fact that on an IQ test one racial or ethnic group scores lower than another group does not mean that the difference between these groups is genetic in origin, even if the heritability estimate for IQ scores is high as assessed within a group. Despite a high heritability estimate in intelligence, education and other advantages can improve performance on IQ tests, while malnutrition, lead poisoning and poor schooling can lower performance (environmental influences). If one group is more environmentally advantaged, it will do better on tests that are responsive to such influences. Those who focus on genetic explanations typically ignore the environmental, situational determinants of mental and behavioural functioning. Those who are stigmatised by genetic inferiority theories suffer by believing they cannot improve their fated genetic destiny.

Another reason that genetic makeup does not appear to be responsible for group differences in IQ has to do with the relative sizes of the differences. For example, even though some studies show that the group average for African Americans is as much as ten to 15 IQ points below the group average for American whites, there is much overlapping of scores and the difference between groups is small compared to the differences among the scores of individuals within each group (Loehlin *et al*, 1975). In fact, geneticist **Stephen Jay Gould** (1981) argues that for human characteristics in general, the differences between the gene pools of different racial groups are minute compared to the genetic differences among individual members of the same group (see also Zuckerman, 1990).

A third argument against the genetic interpretation of group differences is that many other variables are confounded with race, each of which can influence IQ scores (see *Figure 12.7*, next page). For example, in a large-scale, longitudinal study of more than 26,000 children, the best predictors of a child's IQ at age four, for both black and white children, were the family's socio-economic status and the level of the mother's education (Broman *et al*, 1975).

There is ample evidence that environments influence intellectual development. Poverty can affect intellectual functioning in many ways. Poor health during pregnancy and low birth weight are solid predictors of a child's lowered mental ability. So too, poor nutrition, a lack of books and other materials for verbal stimulation, and a survival orientation that leaves parents little time or energy to play with and

FIGURE 12.7	THE RELATIONSHIP BETWEEN HEREDITY, ENVIRONMENT AND IQ

This chart shows evidence for the contribution of heredity and environment to IQ scores. We see similar IQs for fathers and sons (influence of heredity), but the IQs of both fathers and sons are related to social class (influence of environment).

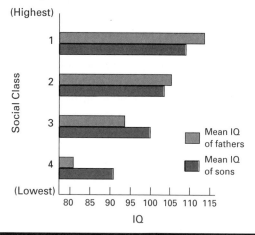

intellectually stimulate their children can be detrimental to performance on tasks such as those on standard IQ tests. We know that a significant proportion of children with low IQs were adversely affected by 'environmental insults', such as lead-based paint chips peeling from walls (Needleman et al, 1990).

When underprivileged black children were adopted by middle-class white families in the United States, they developed IQs significantly above the average of 100. Those who were adopted into these transracial families within the first year of life had higher IQ scores than those adopted later. Thus, when given access to the same cultural and intellectual milieu, black children performed on tests at the same level as their white peers (Scarr & Weinberg, 1976).

More evidence for the importance of the environment comes from the success of intervention programmes. For example, *Head Start* programmes in the United States, in which disadvantaged children are given extra skills and encouragement to succeed in school, have impressive results; they do not change IQ scores directly, but they enhance school performance which then may have a positive impact on many other areas of the child's life (Jordan et al, 1985). Pre-school-age children in Head Start programmes achieve more in school than their peers and are more likely to graduate from high school (Schweinhart & Weikart, 1990). In fact, environmental factors, such as the cognitive complexity and intellectual demands of one's job, can influence IQ throughout adulthood (Dixon et al, 1985). Most adult IQs are stable over many years simply because they remain in environments that provide a stable amount of intellectual stimulation.

Perhaps the best way to summarise these and other relevant findings is to say that both heredity and environment affect intelligence. Heredity plays a big role in differences between individuals but not in differences among groups. Environmental factors play important roles in creating differences between individuals and between groups. Although heredity may make learning easier for some people than for others, genetic makeup alone does not determine level of intellectual achievement. Intervention programmes and enriched learning environments can help overcome the disadvantages of poverty and discrimination.

Validity and test bias in IQ tests

Because group differences do exist in IQ scores, many people are concerned about the appropriateness of using these scores in education and industry. Are they valid predictors of success? Are they equally valid for different racial, sex and cultural groups?

Extensive research shows that IQ scores are valid predictors of examination results from primary school through college, of job status and of performance in certain jobs (Brody & Brody, 1976; Gottfredson, 1986; Lennon, 1985). However, because some groups score lower on IQ and achievement tests than the white middle-class majority on whom these tests are normed, many people are concerned that test scores should not be used to make decisions about the lives of minority school children and job applicants.

How could the tests themselves be biased? One culprit is language differences. Because minority group children may have learned a different language at home, or a non-standard dialect of the language spoken by the majority, the instructions and item content of IQ tests may use words and phrases that are unfamiliar to them. Nonverbal items may be suspect as well. Some critics believe that the abstract nature of these items may be totally foreign to the practical, survival-oriented experience of economically disadvantaged children. As a result of criticisms such as these, many test companies removed biased items from their tests and tried to make tests more culture fair, or equally challenging for people of different cultures.

Unfortunately, decades of attempts have demonstrated that it is impossible to make a test that is both valid and free of any cultural bias, at least, it is impossible to prove that a test is completely culture fair. Even the best IQ and achievement tests show group differences in terms of average scores. How do we know whether those differences are due to test bias or to real group differences in intellectual functioning (Haney, 1982)?

There have been many court battles (mostly in

North America) involving the use of intelligence and ability tests in business and education. In conjunction with affirmative action legislation, the movement to ensure fair testing practices seeks to remove discriminatory practices in our society. Unfortunately, sometimes when standardised tests are forbidden, educators and employers must revert to more expensive, less valid and perhaps more discriminatory assessment procedures, such as interviews or the subjective impressions of teachers or supervisors. The rights and interests of many people must be considered and sometimes poor decisions are made that can have negative consequences for school or business as well as for the student or job applicant involved. The decision to use a test should always be based on the validity and fairness of the test as compared to other selection methods.

approaches encourage us to measure many different components of intellectual functioning by assessing the skills people use to solve all types of problems (see Chapter 9). Because some racial and cultural groups score lower on IQ tests on average than other groups, some critics believe that IQ does not – or should not – tell any story at all. The evidence suggests that group differences reflect both environmental disadvantages and cultural bias in the tests themselves. IQ tests have proven to be equally valid predictors of achievement in school and in certain jobs for members of both groups, suggesting test bias may be less of a problem than environmental disadvantages for intellectual functioning. Group differences in IQ can be reduced through early intervention programmes aimed at giving disadvantaged children an enriched intellectual foundation.

INTERIM SUMMARY

Objective tests such as the MMPI-2, and the NEO-PI are very reliable and valid for specific purposes. Each are valuable research tools, in part because of the enormous archives of data available about them. In applied settings, the MMPI-2 can be used to make rough clinical diagnoses and forming hypotheses about clients. The NEO-PI can be used to find out about a person's preferences, values, interpersonal style and level of functioning. Similarly, the Myers-Briggs test, which identifies 16 different types of people, has been useful in vocational and career counselling. Projective techniques such as the Rorschach test and the TAT depend heavily on the clinician's subjective judgement and are best used as therapeutic icebreakers – sources of preliminary clinical hypotheses to be confirmed by more objective techniques. Test data should always be used in combination with other relevant information, such as interviews, situational observations, medical history, or prior job experience. The personology orientation rejects traditional psychometric testing and the individual differences approach, proposing that the study of personality should focus on the personal uniqueness of each individual.

The construct of intelligence has been defined and measured in many ways. Today, the most popular individually administered tests of intelligence are the Stanford-Binet and the Wechsler scales (the WAIS-R, the WISC-R and the WPPSI). Group tests of intelligence offer somewhat more narrow results because they are restricted to written items. Psychometric analyses of IQ, which are based on statistical relationships between mental measurements, suggest that there are several types of abilities that contribute to IQ scores, such as separate fluid and crystallised types of intelligence. Cognitive science

▣ ASSESSMENT AND YOU

Thus far we have presented some of the major features of assessment techniques and have discussed in detail certain approaches used to assess intelligence, personality and creativity. As a student, you may be struggling with decisions about the kind of job you would like to have when you finish your studies. In our final section, we will first discuss the role of assessment in vocational counselling. Then we will address some of the political and ethical issues posed by the widespread use of formal assessment procedures in our society today.

▣ Vocational Interests and Aptitudes

Have you already determined a career path? Are you still undecided or perhaps thinking of leaving a job you already have? Many assessment instruments have been developed to help people learn what vocations best fit their personalities, values, interests and skills – or, in some cases, to show them before it is too late that the career they have chosen may not be the wisest choice.

Assessing interests

The most widely used test for measuring vocational interests is the *Strong–Campbell Interest Inventory*, which was constructed in 1927 by psychologist **Edward Strong**. The test is based on an empirical approach similar to that used later for the MMPI. First, groups of men in different occupations answered items about activities they liked or disliked. Then the answers of those who were successful in particular occupations were compared with the answers of men in general to create a scale. Subsequent versions of the test have added scales relevant to women and to newer occupations. If you took this test, a vocational counsellor could tell you what types of jobs are typically held by people with interests such as yours, since these are the jobs that are likely to appeal to you.

Both the job and the person are assessed by the employer and employee.

Assessing abilities

Even if a job appeals to you and it suits your personality and fits your values and interests, you are unlikely to be satisfied with it unless you can do it well. Your employer is also unlikely to be satisfied with you if you are unable to do the job for which you were hired.

In order to recommend a career path for you, therefore, a vocational counsellor will want to assess your abilities as well as your interests. Ability has two components: *aptitude* and *achievement*. An **aptitude test** measures your potential for acquiring various skills - not necessarily how well you can perform tasks now but how well you will be able to in the future, presumably with adequate training. An **achievement test**, on the other hand, measures your current level of competence. A test of how well you can speak a foreign language or program a computer would be an example of an achievement test.

Tests have been developed to assess aptitude and achievement in many domains. With knowledge of not only what you like to do but also what you can do well, a counsellor is in a good position to predict your suitability for different jobs (Anastasi, 1982; Sundberg & Matarazzo, 1979; Tyler, 1974).

Tests of ability are also used by companies seeking new employees. The goal of such tests is to match people with the jobs for which they are best suited, thereby increasing the satisfaction of both employees and their employers.

Assessing jobs

Organisations often invest substantial time and money in personnel selection. They rely not only on an assessment of an applicant's characteristics but also on a careful identification and analysis of the requirements of the job (Lewis, 1992). In a job analysis, a specific job is carefully examined to determine the nature and degree of skill required, the amount of effort demanded and the extent to which an individual is responsible for decisions that affect company resources or personnel and to identify any other types of stress the job may entail (Tenopyr & Oeltjen, 1982). The results of **job analyses** are used not only in selecting personnel but also in determining the pay scale for different jobs.

Job assessment is performed in many ways. Workers, supervisors and specially trained job analysts are asked to provide information about the abilities required for particular jobs. Subject-matter experts may rate the relevance of various kinds of knowledge, skills and abilities. An inventory of requirements, including the tasks and duties a worker must perform, can then be prepared for each occupation. One such inventory that has been developed – the *Occupational Analysis Inventory* – provides information about a wide spectrum of occupations and can be very helpful to a job seeker (Pass & Cunningham, 1978).

Some companies supplement other assessment methods with realistic job previews. They show applicants what will be expected of them in the job through films, tapes, employee checklists of most and least-liked aspects of the job and simulations of critical incidents likely to arise (Wanous, 1980). These previews give applicants a clearer picture of what will be expected of them if they take a job and help them decide how well it fits their abilities and interests.

In one study, 11 different assessment methods used in hiring were compared according to how well they predicted an applicant's later job success. The top ranked method was an ability composite based on several psychological tests. Surprisingly, the factors that were not significant in predicting on-the-job success were experience, interview ratings and academic achievement (Hunter & Hunter, 1984).

How one person does at a job often depends on more than knowledge and hard work. Among the other variables affecting job performance might be assertiveness, social skills, appearance and general congruence or fit with a company's picture of its ideal supervisor, manager, or executive. When these types of characteristics are important, personality tests can be used in employee selection – but only for those jobs for which a test has been specifically validated.

Successful performance in a career and in life requires something more than the ability recognised by standardised tests. While the best tests perform the valuable function of predicting how well people will do on the average, there is always room for error when desire, ambition, imagination, self-esteem and personal pride get in the way, for better or for worse. Perhaps it is vital to know when you should believe more in yourself than in the results of a test.

Political and Ethical Issues

The primary goal of psychological assessment is to reduce errors of judgement that bias accurate assessments of people. This goal is achieved by replacing subjective judgements of teachers, physicians, employers and other evaluators with more objective measures that have been carefully constructed and are open to critical evaluation. This is the goal that motivated Alfred Binet in his pioneering work. Binet and others hoped that testing would help democratise society and minimise decisions based on arbitrary criteria of sex, race, nationality, or physical appearance. However, despite these lofty goals, there is no area of psychology more controversial than assessment. Three unresolved issues that are central to the controversy are the fairness of test-based decisions, the utility of tests for evaluating education and the implications of using test scores as labels.

Critics concerned with the fairness of testing practices argue that the costs or negative consequences may be higher for some test-takers than for others. The costs are quite high, for example, when tests on which minority groups receive low scores are used to keep them out of certain jobs. In addition, reliance on testing may make personnel selection too often an automatic attempt to fit people into available jobs.

Instead, sometimes we might benefit more by changing job descriptions to fit the needs and abilities of people.

Testing not only helps evaluate students; it also plays an indirect role in education. The quality of school systems and the effectiveness of teachers are frequently judged on the basis of how well their students score on standardised achievement tests.

These test scores may not accurately reflect what students really know, however. The same tests are used for several years between revisions, so that teachers come to know what is on the test and prepare their students for those items. Scores improve, but the norms are not updated, so students in each school appear to be doing better and better each year until a revision comes out that makes them look inept in comparison to the previous year's students with their inflated scores (Leslie & Wingert, 1990).

As test-takers we sometimes forget that our test scores are, at best, statistical measures of our current functioning. Instead, we imbue them with an absolute significance that is not limited to appropriate normative comparisons. People too often think of themselves as being an IQ of 110 or a B student as if the scores were labels stamped on their foreheads. Such labels may become barriers to advancement as people come to believe that their mental and personal qualities are fixed and unchangeable – that they cannot improve their lot in life. For those who are negatively assessed, the scores can become self-imposed motivational limits that lower their sense of self-efficacy and restrict the challenges they are willing to tackle.

This tendency to give test scores a sacred status has societal as well as personal implications. When test scores become labels that identify traits, states, maladjustment, conflict and pathology within an individual, people begin to think about the 'abnormality' of individual children rather than about educational systems that need to modify programmes to accommodate all learners. Labels put the spotlight on deviant personalities rather than on problems in the environment. Human assessors need to recognise that what people are now is a product of where they have been, where they think they are headed and what situation is currently influencing their behaviour. Such a view can help to unite different assessment approaches and theoretical camps as well as lead to more humane treatment of those who do not fit the norm.

recapting main points

The Psychology of the Person

Personality is what characterises an individual, what is unique about a person across different situations and over time. Personality theorists study the whole person as the sum of feelings, thoughts and actions. Sources of data used in personality research are self reports, observer reports, specific behaviours, life events and physiological measures. The focus of the idiographic approach is the organisation of the unique person. The nomothetic approach attempts to understand all people in terms of individual differences along common dimensions.

Type and Trait Personality Theories

Some theorists categorise people by all-or-none types, assumed to be related to particular characteristic behaviours. Others view traits as the building blocks of personality. Allport, an idiographic theorist, differentiated cardinal, central and secondary traits, while Eysenck combined the type and trait approaches, exploring the relationship between personality and physiological characteristics. Twin and adoption studies reveal that personality traits are partially inherited. The environment is important, but the common familial environment is less important than the unshared environment that is experienced differently by each sibling. The Big Five is a comprehensive, theory-free, descriptive personality system that maps out the relationships between common trait words, theoretical concepts and personality scales. Specific behaviours are not consistent across different situations, although they do show temporal stability when the same behaviour is measured in the same situation. However, the consistency paradox is resolvable if we consider that although trait measures do not predict the cross-situational consistency of individual behavioural items, they do so by aggregating across behaviours.

Psychodynamic and Humanistic Theories

Freud's psychodynamic theory accepted Darwin's emphasis on biological drives as sources of all human motivation. Basic concepts of Freudian theory include psychic determinism; early experiences as key determinants of lifelong personality; psychic energy as powering and directing behaviour; and powerful unconscious processes. Personality structure consists of the id (guided by the pleasure principle), the superego (guided by learned social and moral restrictions), and the reconciling ego (guided by the reality principle). Unacceptable impulses are said to be repressed and ego-defence mechanisms are developed to lessen anxiety and bolster self-esteem.

Post-Freudians have put greater emphasis on ego functioning and social variables and less on sexual urges. They see personality development as a lifelong process. Adler thought each person developed a consistent lifestyle aimed at compensating or overcompensating for feelings of inferiority. Jung emphasised the notion of a collective unconscious, including archetypes (symbols of universal significance); he saw the needs to create and self-actualise as powerful unconscious instincts in all people.

Humanistic theories focus on the growth potential of the individual. These theories are holistic, dispositional, phenomenological, existential and optimistic. At the core of Rogers's person-centred personality theory is the concept of self-actualisation, a constant striving to realise one's potential and to develop one's talents.

Social-learning and Cognitive Theories

Social-learning theorists focus on understanding individual differences in behaviour and personality as a consequence of different histories of reinforcement. Cognitive theorists emphasise individual differences in perception and subjective interpretation of the environment. Bandura's cognitive social-learning theory combines principles of learning with an emphasis on social interactions. Reciprocal determinism, observational learning and self-efficacy are concepts that are critical in the analysis of person–behaviour–situation interactions.

Self Theories

Self theories, which developed primarily from the humanistic tradition, focus on the importance of the self-concept for a full understanding of human personality. The self-concept is a dynamic mental structure that motivates, interprets, organises, mediates and regulates intrapersonal and interpersonal behaviours and processes. The different personality theories vary in their assumptions about many fundamental aspects of human nature, including its structure, influences and processes.

What Is Assessment?

The purpose of psychological assessment is to describe or classify individuals in ways that will be useful for prediction or treatment. A wide variety of personal characteristics may be assessed, including intelligence, personality traits, attitudes, interests, skills and behaviours. A useful assessment tool must be reliable, valid and standardised. A reliable measure gives consistent results on different testings; reliability is an index of the degree to which a test correlates with itself across occasions or across different test forms or items. A valid measure assesses the attributes for which the test was designed; validity is the degree to which a test correlates with one or more related criterion measures. A standardised test is always administered and scored in the same way; norms allow a person's score to be compared to the averages of others of the same age and sex.

Formal assessment is carried out through interviews, review of life history data, tests and situational observations. These important sources of assessment information may come from self-report or observer-report methods. Self-report measures require subjects to answer questions or supply information about themselves; for better or worse, they are tied to subjective reports. Observer-report measures require persons who know or have observed a subject person to provide the information. They may be biased due to halo and stereotype effects, so their reliability should be enhanced by the reports of several independent observers.

Assessing Individual Differences

Personality characteristics are assessed by both objective and projective tests. The MMPI-2 can be used to diagnose clinical problems. It contains ten criterion-keyed clinical scales, seven validity scales, and 15 homogeneous content scales. The NEO-PI is a newer personality test that measures five major dimensions of personality: Neuroticism, Extraversion, Openness, Agreeableness and Conscientiousness. The Myers–Briggs Type Indicator identifies 16 personality types based on Jung's type theory, organised around preferences for sensing, feeling, thinking, intuiting, extraversion and introversion.

All three of the inventories have been used in longitudinal studies of personality structure and development. The MMPI is especially popular for research because there are extensive archives of MMPIs taken by many types of people over many years. Hundreds of special-purpose scales have been constructed from the original item pools and validated in archival data banks. In applied settings, the NEO can be used in informal career counselling or planning therapy in conjunction with an MMPI.

Projective tests of personality are less reliable and valid than objective tests. They are used primarily as a source of clinical hypotheses that must be evaluated through other assessment techniques. Two popular projective tests are the Rorschach test and Murray's TAT. A personology orientation rejects psychometric testing, individual differences and normative comparisons in favour of studying a broad range of idiographic information

recapping main points

about the uniqueness of each person. Vocational assessment includes assessment of an individual's interests, aptitudes and current level of achievement. The Strong–Campbell Interest Inventory compares an individual's interests with those of people who are successful in various occupations. The Occupations Analysis Inventory provides information about the requirements of various jobs.

Though often useful for prediction and as an indication of current performance, test results should not be used to limit an individual's opportunities for development and change. When the results of an assessment will touch an individual's life, it is important that the assessment is as thorough as possible, using all available sources of information.

Assessing Intelligence

Binet began the tradition of intelligence testing in France in the early 1900s. Scores were given in terms of mental ages and were meant to represent children's current level of functioning.

Terman created the Stanford–Binet Intelligence Scale and the concept of IQ. He supported the idea that intelligence was an inner, largely inherited capacity. Wechsler designed special intelligence tests for adults, children and pre-school-age children; each test consists of 11 different subtests and gives separate verbal, nonverbal and full-scale IQs at each age level. Efficient group tests of intelligence are used in education and business.

Psychometric analyses of IQ suggest that several basic abilities, such as fluid and crystallised aspects of intelligence, contribute to IQ scores. Cognitive approaches conceive of and measure intelligence broadly by considering the skills and insights people use to solve all the types of problems they encounter (see Chapter 9).

IQ tests are controversial because, on average, some racial and cultural groups score lower on the tests than other groups. Instead of genetic differences, environmental disadvantages and test bias seem to be responsible for the lower scores of certain groups.

key Terms

achievement test
aggregated case study
analytic psychology
aptitude test
archetype
behavioural confirmation
Big Five
cardinal trait
case study
chronological age (CA)
collective unconscious
consistency paradox
construct validity
criterion validity
cross-sectional (or longitudinal) research designs
crystallised intelligence
dialogical self
ego defence mechanisms
face validity
factor analysis
fluid intelligence
g-factor
halo effect
idiographic approach
implicit personality theory
impression management
intelligence quotient (IQ)
interjudge reliability
internal consistency
job analysis

mental age (MA)
nomothetic approach
norms
observational learning
observer-report methods
parallel forms
personal construct
personality inventory
personality types
personology
projective test
psychic determinism
psychodynamic personality theories
psychological assessment
psychometrics
reciprocal determinism
repression
secondary trait
self-actualisation
self-concept
self-efficacy
self-report methods
somatotypes
standardisation
stereotype effect
sublimation
test-retest reliability
trait
unconscious processes
validity

major Contributors

Adler, Alfred (1870–1937)
Allport, Gordon (1877–1967)
Bandura, Albert
Binet, Alfred (1857–1911)
Cattell, Raymond
Costa, Paul
Dollard, John (1900–80)
Eysenck, Hans
Freud, Sigmund (1856–1939)
Galton, Francis (1822–1911)
Goddard, Henry (1866–1957)
Gough, Harrison
Gould, Stephen Jay
Guilford, J. P.
Hippocrates (c.460–c.377 BC)
James, William (1842–1910)

Jung, Carl (1875–1961)
Kelly, George (1905–66)
Markus, Hazel
Maslow, Abraham (1908–70)
McCrae, Robert
Miller, Neal
Mischel, Walter
Meehl, Paul
Murray, Henry (1893–1988)
Rogers, Carl (1902–87)
Rorschach, Hermann (1884–1922)
Sheldon, William (1898–1970)
Spearman, Charles (1863–1945)
Strong, Edward (1884–1963)
Terman, Lewis (1877–1956)
Wechsler, David (1896–1981)

Chapter 13

Social Psychology

$\mathbf{E}$arly on a summer's Sunday morning a siren shattered the serenity of college student Tommy Whitlow's start to the day. A police car screeched to a halt in front of his home. Within minutes, Tommy was charged with a criminal offence, informed of his constitutional rights, frisked and handcuffed. After he was booked and finger-printed, Tommy was blindfolded and transported to the Stanford County Prison, where he was stripped, sprayed with disinfectant and issued a smock-type uniform with an identity number on the front and back. Tommy became Prisoner 647. Nine other university students were also arrested and assigned numbers.

The prison guards were not identified by name and their anonymity was enhanced by khaki uniforms and reflector sunglasses – Prisoner 647 never saw their eyes. He referred to each of his jailers as 'Mr. Correctional Officer, Sir'; to them, he was only number 647.

The guards insisted that prisoners obey all rules without question or hesitation. Failure to do so led to the loss of a privilege. At first, privileges included opportunities to read, write or talk to other inmates. Later on, the slightest protest resulted in the loss of the 'privileges' of eating, sleeping and washing. Failure to obey rules also resulted in menial, mindless work such as cleaning toilets with bare hands, doing press-ups while a guard stepped on the prisoner's back and spending hours in solitary confinement. The guards were always devising new strategies to make the prisoners feel worthless. Every guard Prisoner 647 encountered engaged in abusive, authoritarian

behaviour at some point during his incarceration. The main difference among the guards was in the frequency and regularity of their hostility toward the prisoners.

Less than 36 hours after the mass arrest, Prisoner 8412, one of the ringleaders of an aborted prisoner rebellion that morning, began to cry uncontrollably. He experienced fits of rage, disorganised thinking and severe depression. On successive days, three more prisoners developed similar stress-related symptoms. A fifth prisoner developed a psychosomatic rash all over his body when the Parole Board rejected his appeal.

At night, Prisoner 647 tried to remember what Tommy had been like before he became a prisoner. He also tried to imagine his tormentors before they became guards. He reminded himself that he was a student who had answered a news-paper advertisement and agreed to be a subject in a two-week experiment on prison life. He had thought it would be fun to do something unusual and he could always use some extra money.

Everyone in the prison, guard and prisoner alike, had been selected from a large pool of student volunteers who, on the basis of extensive psychological tests and interviews, had been judged as law-abiding, emotionally stable, physically healthy and 'normal-average'. In this mock prison experiment, assignment of participants to 'guard' or 'prisoner' had been randomly determined by the toss of a coin. The prisoners lived in the jail around the clock, the guards worked standard eight-hour shifts.

In guard roles, college students who had been

pacifists and 'nice guys' behaved aggressively – sometimes even sadistically. As prisoners, psychologically stable students soon behaved pathologically, passively resigning themselves to their unexpected fate of learned helplessness. The power of the simulated prison environment had created a new social reality – to all intents and purposes a real prison – in the minds of the jailers and their captives.

Because of the dramatic and unexpectedly extreme emotional and behavioural effects observed, those prisoners with extreme stress reactions were released early from their detention in this unusual prison and the psychologists were forced to terminate their two-week study after only six days. Although Tommy Whitlow said he would not want to go through it again, he valued the personal experience because he learned so much about himself and about the origins of human behaviour. Fortunately, he and the other students were basically healthy and they readily bounced back from that highly charged situation. Follow-ups over many years revealed no lasting negative effects. The participants had all learned an important lesson: to never underestimate the power of socially negotiated situations and interpersonal influences to overwhelm the personalities and intentions of even the brightest, most emotionally resilient and moral among us (Haney, Banks & **Philip Zimbardo**, 1973; Haney & Zimbardo, 1977; Zimbardo, 1975; replicated in Australia by Lovibond *et al*, 1979).

SUPPOSE *YOU* HAD been a subject in the Stanford Prison Experiment. What kind of guard would you have been? As a prisoner, would you have blindly obeyed the authorities, become depressed from feeling so helpless, or resisted the situational pressures and acted heroically? We would all like to believe we would be benevolent guards and heroic prisoners, but the best predictor for the way you might react in this setting is the way a typical student, someone possibly resembling you, actually behaved. The results of this study indicate that, despite optimistic beliefs to the contrary, most of us would fall on the latter side of good–bad and hero–victim dichotomies. The results do not offer an upbeat, positive message. However, it is a message that experimental social psychologists feel obliged to pass along.

Social psychology investigates the ways in which people affect one another. Social psychology is the study of the way thoughts, feelings, perceptions, motives and behaviour are influenced by interactions and transactions between people. Social psychologists try to understand behaviour within its social context. This social context provides the complex framework within which we enact the movements, strengths and vulnerabilities of the 'social animal', as so-called by Aronson (1988). Defined broadly, the social context includes: (a) the real, imagined or symbolic presence of other people; (b) the activities, behaviours, utterances, linguistic negotiations and discourses that take place interactively amongst and between people; (c) the environmental features of the physical settings in which behaviour occurs; and (d) the perceptions, beliefs, attitudes, expectations values and norms that covary with behaviour and subjective experience within a given setting (C. Sherif, 1981; Handy, 1987).

The prison experiment in the opening case to this chapter underscores an important theme which has emerged from some of the innovative empirical research that social psychologists have carried out over the past 50 years: the potency of social influence processes with respect to the genesis and control of human conduct. In the first part of this chapter, we will explore this theme and its implications. In doing so, we will consider an extensive body of research that demonstrates the surprising extent to which seemingly minor elements of our interpersonal and socially contextualised worlds have significant influence over our everyday thoughts and actions.

The Stanford Prison Experiment, however, is not typical of all of the research and scholarship conducted in social psychology today, especially in Western Europe. Indeed, past commentators such as the social psychologist **Henri Tajfel** in Britain and **Jos Jaspars** from the Netherlands, argued that social psychology in Europe developed in a way that was distinct in form and focus from that of its North American counterpart (Tajfel, 1984; Jaspars, 1986). In particular, they characterise the European school as emphasising the shared, collective and emergent nature of social behaviour and the American one as focusing upon what are largely conceived as singular actions occurring somewhat mechanistically between self-contained, individual social agents. As

Jaspars (1986) wrote: 'An individual action is not just caused by or directed at other human beings; it is in many ways also a reflection of the society he or she lives in'.

Recognising this, European social psychology is contended by these critics as being more authentically 'social' in its orientation than that which has emanated over the last 50 years from the North American continent. Such a difference, they argue, reflects a tradition of a concern with theoretical and philosophical issues, matters concerning the 'substance' of social psychology. In the United States, on the other hand, they allege that social psychology was more strongly influenced by matters of 'method' and procedure as derived from a conceptually restricting experimental approach to the study of social behaviour. Indeed, on occasions these methods have been reconceived as models for social psychological issues (see Kelley's ANOVA model later in this chapter, for example) which in themselves they are supposed to investigate.

In retrospect, Jaspar's evaluation somewhat caricatures and polarises what has happened and is still occurring in social psychology on either side of the transatlantic divide. Nevertheless, it is perhaps apposite to point out here that a primary interest in conceptual issues has developed strongly in Western European social psychology over the last three decades. This has emerged, however, alongside the seminal contributions of American feminist psychologists and social constructionist scholars. Such a primacy of focus upon conceptual issues has led to a burgeoning and broadening of what is referred to as this more 'social' social psychology. A continuing development of new perspectives and post-modern critiques (on both sides of the Atlantic), of concepts leading methods, has facilitated the beginnings of what Harré & Secord (1972) heralded as a paradigm shift within social psychology, and as manifest subsequently within the work of its protagonists (for example, Shotter, 1975; Gergen, 1985; Potter & Wetherall, 1987; Harré & Gillett, 1994). We will consider these contributions to social psychology later in this chapter.

A second central theme of this chapter, and indeed of social psychology in its more 'social' form, is that 'situations' are defined by people not so much with respect to their objective features but rather in relation to their subjectively realised nature – in the way that as social beings we collectively and intersubjectively perceive, interpret, assign meaning to and represent them. This important dimension of the sub-discipline is called **social cognition** (Fiske & Taylor, 1991). Through the study of such cognitions, we will consider how social realities – stable or transient – come to be constructed for ourselves and others.

Finally, we will look at a third issue for social psychology: how we can solve social problems by applying the findings of research into social processes. Social psychologists are making significant contributions to the improvement of the human condition by taking leading roles in applied fields such as *health psychology*, *environmental psychology*, *psychology and law* and *peace psychology*. On this dimension of social relevance, abstract theory attempts to meet the demands of practical considerations and make a tangible difference to the lives of people and of society.

❖ SOCIAL INFLUENCE PROCESSES: THE DYNAMICS OF SOCIAL SUBJECTIVITY

Throughout our study of psychology, we have seen that psychologists strive to understand the multiple causes and accounts of behaviour. However, depending on their orientation, they tend to look in different places for their answers. Social psychologists believe that the primary focus for understanding behaviour is the nature and workings of the social context in which it occurs. As humans we give sense to our physical, social and bodily environment by creating and negotiating meanings within a community and local moral order (Sabini & Silver, 1982; Harré, 1983), and so by definition we are influenced by others by virtue of our mutual interdependence. Such meaning cannot be conceived simplistically as a private, subjective entity located independently 'within' an individual 'psyche', but rather is created through linguistic interaction and negotiation with others. Social psychologists argue that such pervasive social processes exert considerable control over personal being and behaviour, often dominating preferences for particular forms of activity and overriding an individual's sense of their own values, beliefs and past history of learning. Socio-contextual aspects that appear trivial to most observers – words, labels, signs, rules, social roles, the mere presence or number of other people, a group norm – can considerably influence how we behave. Often, subtle forms of **social influence** affect us without our awareness or full recognition. In this section, we will review some classic empirical research and more recent work that explores the complex staging of social influence processes and their effects upon behaviour.

❖ Social Facilitation

The earliest demonstration that the mere presence of other people has a measurable impact on individual behaviour was conducted by **Norman Triplett** in 1897. The researcher, an avid cyclist, had noticed that racing cyclists had faster times when they were racing with other people than when they were racing against the clock. To determine whether this effect held true for other activities, he had children perform the task of winding fishing reels. Sure enough, the children performed faster when another child was present in the room than when they were alone.

This finding was not simply the result of competition. Later studies found that it occurred also when an individual performed in front of an audience. It was also found in a co-acting group – a group of people engaged in the same behaviour but not interacting with each other, such as when several people play separate games side-by-side. This improvement of performance brought about by the presence of other people is called **social facilitation**.

The social facilitation effect turns out to be more complicated, however, than at first it seemed. Subsequent researchers found that sometimes the presence of others interferes with performance. Standing up before an audience, for example, may cause stage fright. One explanation for these apparently contradictory findings is that the presence of other people has the general effect of increasing an individual's level of arousal, or drive (Zajonc, 1976). This high drive will facilitate performance when a person is engaging in behaviour that is well-learned. However, if the responses are relatively new and not well-learned, as in the early stages of a learning process, then the increased drive can be disruptive and errors ensue. The person may become tense and the level of drive will interfere with optimal performance.

Social loafing is the reverse of social facilitation and can be defined as an unwitting tendency to ease off when performing in a group, regardless of whether the task is interesting and meaningful (Latane, 1981). The negative effects of social loafing are that people not only work less, but they take less responsibility for what they are doing. Social loafing by any one person becomes greater as the size of the group increases. This group effect is attributed to the person's reduced self-attention as he or she must process more external inputs from other group members. When self-attention diminishes, so do the usual self-imposed controls of surveillance on behaviour. Then, people tend to go with the slower flow of the group (Carver & Scheier, 1981; Mullen & Baumeister, 1987). It is interesting to note that social loafing occurs more often in male than in female work groups (Hunt, 1985).

The social facilitation, interference and loafing effects demonstrate the power of even the most rudimentary form of social influence – the mere presence of other people. Most groups, however, involve more dynamic and direct interactions among their members.

 ## Social Roles and Rules

The settings in which you live and function determine the roles available to you. Being a student diminishes the likelihood that you will become a mercenary soldier, drug dealer, shaman or prisoner, for example. Because you have college experience, numerous other **roles**, such as manager, teacher and politician, become more available to you.

Through participation in a culture we each discover the public meanings that have been consensually assigned to specific **social roles** and so for the people who have assumed them. A single action though, can be interpreted in many different ways, depending on the private meaning different people assign to it. For example, defying authority can be interpreted as admirable and heroic, foolish and problematic, or dangerous and subversive. A social role is a socially defined pattern of behaviour that is expected of a person when functioning in a given setting or group. People play many different social roles in the various contexts in which they usually operate.

Participation in a culture also instructs participants as to the social **rules** that everybody lives by. In order to promote social interaction and to achieve the desired outcomes of those in the majority or in power, social settings are often identifiable by the operation of particular rules – specific behavioural guidelines. Some rules are explicitly stated as signs (for example, 'No Smoking'; 'Please Don't Walk On The Grass') or in socialisation practices (for example, showing respect for the elderly; and, to never take sweets from a stranger). Other rules are implicit: they are learned through transactions with others in particular settings. Queuing at the bus-stop, how close you can stand to another person in a lift, having to take a seat in the waiting room at the dental surgery, the polite way to react to a compliment or a gift – all of these depend on our understandings of the implicit rules that have been previously agreed and assigned to these settings. For example, the Japanese do not open a gift in the presence of the gift giver for fear of not showing sufficient appreciation; foreign visitors not aware of this unwritten rule may misinterpret the behaviour as rude instead of sensitive.

Generic prisoner–guard roles

At the conclusion of the Stanford Prison Experiment, guards and prisoners differed from one another in virtually every observable way; yet, just a week before, their role identities had been interchangeable. Chance, in the form of random assignment, had decided their roles and these roles were instrumental in creating status and power differences that were socially validated in the mock prison environment. The social context as it was *intersubjectively* perceived and constructed by the participants, induced a host of differences in the way those in each group thought, felt and acted (see *Figure 13.1*).

No one taught the participants to play their roles. We have to assume that each of the students had the capacity to become either a prisoner or a guard by calling upon stored structures of *collective knowledge* about those roles. Moscovici (1981) refers to these pervasive instances of socially shared and reconstituted thought as **social representations**. Without ever visiting a real prison, we have all learned from other personal experiences something about the interaction between the powerful and the powerless (Banuazizi & Movahedi, 1975). The student participants had already experienced such power differences through many of their previous social interactions: parent–child; teacher–student; doctor–patient; boss–worker. In the mock prison, they refined and intensified their improvised scripts,

basing them on implicitly held social representations of roles within this particular setting.

Thus, the actions of the participants in this simulated prison environment to a degree were stereotypic, reflecting an underestimation of the variety of behaviours possible as a guard or prisoner. A 'guard-type' would have been scripted as someone who simply limits the freedom of 'prisoner-types' by managing their behaviour and making it predictable. In our collective imaginings of these roles then, we may consider that this task is aided commmonly by the use of coercive rules, which include explicit punishment for their violation. Many students in the guard role reported being surprised at how easy it was for them to enjoy controlling other people and how putting on the uniform was sufficient to transform them from college student research subjects into prison guards who had to manage inmates.

Those positioned as prisoners, on the other hand, could only react to the social structure of a prison-like setting as created by those they perceived had power over them to enforce that structure. Rebellion or compliance were the primary options of the prisoners: the first option resulted in punishment in the form of withdrawal of privileges; the second resulted in avoidance of such retraction but also in a loss, nevertheless, of a sense of personal autonomy and dignity. However, some prisoners went beyond strategic compliance and resigned themselves to helplessness. By passively waiting though, they actively changed the dynamics of the social context, in a bid for social power and counter-influence.

FIGURE 13.1	GUARD AND PRISONER BEHAVIOUR

This interaction profile shows categories and frequencies of guard and prisoner behaviour across 25 observation periods over six days in the Stanford Prison Experiment. Note the dramatic difference between the dominating, controlling, hostile behaviour of the guards and the passive-resistance behaviour of the prisoners.

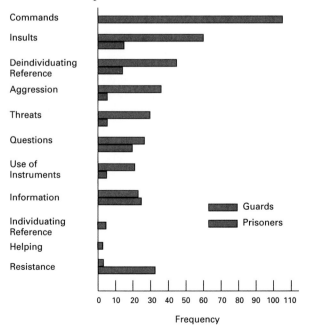

❖ Social Norms

In addition to expectations regarding role behaviours, groups develop many expectations for the ways their members should act. The specific expectations for socially appropriate attitudes and behaviours that are embodied in the stated or implicit rules of a group are called **social norms**. In short, they are shared definitions of desirable behaviour. Social norms can be broad guidelines: if you are member of a Social Democratic Party somewhere in Europe, you may be expected to hold liberal political beliefs. Social norms can also embody specific standards of conduct: if you are a spy, you may be expected to resist any attempt to extract secret information from you, including torture, imprisonment and death. Norms can guide conversation: teaching staff do not talk about their work during meals at 'high table' in Cambridge University, England. Norms can define rigid dress codes for members of groups: businesspeople, gang members and students usually either explicitly or more implicitly expect one another to dress in certain ways.

Social norms can define rigid dress codes for group members.

Adjustment to a group typically involves discovering the set of social norms that regulates desired behaviour in the group setting. This adjustment occurs in two ways: by noticing the uniformities in certain behaviours of all or most members; and by observing the negative consequences when someone behaves in a non-normative way – violating a social norm.

Norms serve several important functions. Awareness of the norms operating in a given group situation helps to orient members and regulate their social interaction. Each participant can anticipate the way others will enter the situation, the way they will dress, what they are likely to say and do, as well as what type of behaviour will be expected of them to gain approval. Some tolerance for deviating from the standard is also part of the norm – wide in some cases, narrow in others. Members are usually able to estimate how far they can go before experiencing the coercive power of the group in the form of ridicule, re-education and rejection. The social control imposed by group norms influences us almost from birth as part of the socialisation process (as discussed in Chapter 4).

Adhering to the norms of a group is the first step in establishing identification with the group and thereby in conferring membership upon novices. Such an alliance allows an individual to have the feeling of sharing in whatever prestige and power the group possesses and to further identify with those of whom they seek to be a part. Group membership and holding to its norms in the first instance will facilitate a positive social identity for its newly accepted initiates (Turner *et al*, 1987). In addition, support for **social identity theory** shows that by virtue of allegiance to a group and the positive sense of self that emerges, participants are likely to favour their new 'ingroup' at the expense of a discriminable 'outgroup'; we evaluate our own group's worth (and by implication, that of ourselves) by comparing it with other groups (Tajfel & Turner, 1979).

Norms emerge in a new group through two

processes: diffusion and crystallisation. When people first enter a group, they bring with them expectations, previously acquired through other group memberships and shared life experiences. These various expectations are diffused and spread throughout the group during the process of members communicating with each other. As people talk and carry out activities together, their expectations begin to converge or crystallise into a common perspective. Informal conversational negotiations and interlocutive transactions lead surreptitiously to a consensus viewpoint.

Sherif's autokinetic effect

The classic experiment that demonstrated **norm crystallisation** was conducted by social psychologist **Muzafer Sherif** (1935). Subjects were asked to judge the amount of movement of a spot of light that was actually stationary but appeared to move when viewed in total darkness with no reference points, a perceptual illusion known as the autokinetic effect. Originally, individual judgements varied widely. However, when the subjects were brought together in a group and stated their judgements aloud, their estimates began to converge. They alleged that they began to see the light move in the same direction and in similar amounts. Even more interesting was the final part of Sherif's study: when alone in the darkened room after the group viewing, these subjects continued to follow the group norm that had emerged when they were together.

Once norms are established in a group, they tend to perpetuate themselves. In later research, these autokinetic group norms persisted even when tested a year later and without peers witnessing the judgements (Rohrer *et al*, 1954). Other research shows that current group members collectively influence incoming members to adhere to the norms, and they in turn directly or indirectly require successive newcomers to conform to the norms. Norms can be transmitted from one generation of group members to the next and can continue to influence people's behaviour long after the original group that created the norm no longer exists (Insko *et al*, 1980). In autokinetic effect studies, researchers replaced one group member with a new one after each set of autokinetic trials until all the members of the group were new to the situation. The group's autokinetic norm remained true to that which had been handed down to them across several successive generations (Jacobs & Campbell, 1961). Indeed, in naturalistic social settings, group rituals often serve the purpose of transmitting from old to new members symbols, history and values which are important to the continuing existence of the group's identity.

Group norms strongly impact on other's conceptual behaviour, as long as the group is sufficiently valued. If the person comes to identify with and value a new group, then he or she will follow and accommodate the norms of the new group. A formal or informal group from which an individual derives attitudes and standards of acceptable and appropriate behaviour and to which the individual refers for information, direction and support for a given lifestyle are known as **reference groups**.

Bennington's liberal norms

Often, the process of being influenced by group norms is so gradual and so subtle that an individual does not perceive what is happening. Some insights into this process are provided by a classic study conducted, not in a laboratory, but in a small New England college for women in 1930s North America. Researcher **Theodore Newcomb** studied the shifts in political and social attitudes experienced by these students during their four years at Bennington College, USA and then followed up the observed effects 20 years later to determine if they were enduring.

Students that came to study at Bennington were from privileged homes and brought along with them conservative values. At the college, however, they met an atmosphere of political and cultural liberalism which was created by the progressive faculty members. In the elections for the US presidency in the 1930s, the majority of first-year students supported the right-wing Republican candidate. The vast majority of the third and fourth-year students voted by contrast for the Democratic and Socialist candidates. Newcomb explained this steady decline in conservatism as students progressed through college

and the shift toward liberal preferences in terms of the close-knit community at Bennington and the reference group norms that were operating.

The strong sense of school spirit included activist concerns and support for the norm of liberalism. Movement toward uniformity of attitudes was reinforced by greater social acceptance. Politically liberal students were most likely to be chosen for positions of leadership and for friendship. These shared values became internalised and accepted by students for whom Bennington pupils became the primary reference group. Those few students who maintained conservative values despite this prevailing ethos had particularly strong ties with their families. Thus, they continued to conform to family standards rather than to those of the school. Interestingly, the legacy of the Bennington experience was still evident 20 years later. At the time of the 1960 presidential election, 60 per cent of the 1935–39 Bennington graduates voted for Democrat candidate John F. Kennedy, whereas only 30 per cent among comparable college graduates did likewise (Newcomb *et al*, 1967). Two decades on, then, ex-Bennington scholars continued to support values which they had come to espouse during their final college year.

These substantial changes in important social and political attitudes were brought about by the gradual construction over four years of shared meanings into a local culture of liberalism, the values of which were expressed and transmitted from one year group to the next through the pervasive influence of group norms. The more people rely on social rewards from a group for their primary sense of self-worth and legitimacy, the greater will be the social influence that the group can bring to bear on them to be the kind of person the group values. Because social contexts include the operation of roles, rules and norms, they can be potent agents of change, affecting people in socially prescribed ways or inhibiting and restraining them from changing in ways that are not deemed socially appropriate or situationally acceptable. In this way, people become not only liberals and conservatives, but pro-life radicals able to attack medical staff working in abortion clinics, religious revolutionaries willing to bomb civilian targets, or members of ethnically prejudiced factions bent on destruction of each other in a central European civil war.

Finally, social norms assume greater force according to the extent that group members are isolated within a social setting, one in which they are detached from contrary points of view and in which sources of information, social rewards and punishments are all highly controlled by group leaders. The thought reform that Chinese communism imposed on its citizens, the 'brainwashing' of prisoners of war, and the alleged coercive persuasion of cult members all have in common this element of intense indoctrination of new beliefs and values within the social isolation of a total situation (Lifton, 1969; Osherow, 1981).

If asked the question, 'How would you act if you were in a situation in which people behaved in a depraved, foolish, or irrational ways?', the lesson of much social psychological research is that, more than likely, we would behave exactly as others have if we were likewise positioned in the same social context. The prudent and wise reply must be, then: 'I do not know; it depends on how powerful I experience social pressures when I'm actually in that setting'. Indeed, your behaviour can best be predicted by knowing the base rate or extent of compliance of those who have already entered into the social scenario in question and by making the conservative assumption that you would probably behave as the majority did. It is only the occasional heroic figure among us who is able to do otherwise, to be the exception to the rule and resist pervasive socio-contextual forces.

◆ Conformity, Rebellion and Influence

It is perhaps unfortunate that conformity is a word that presently has negative connotations for many people. On the one hand, to be able to recognise and act in accordance with the pro-social norms of a group can be read as a sign of tolerance, flexibility or even wisdom. However, when those norms are consensually agreed by reference groups to be morally reprehensible, unthinking conformity to such an aberrant group norm becomes unacceptable. The appalling mass genocide of civilian Jews in concentration camps by Nazi fascism during the Second World War (1940–45) urged psychologists in the last half of the century to examine this latter unacceptable facet of conformist behaviour. What conditions prevailed to allow so many people to collude with one another and take part in the attempted extermination of an entire race? The recent return of 'ethnic cleansing' as a chilling euphemism for genocide makes answering this question as relevant now as it was 50 years ago when psychologists first began to seek viable explanations (McDermott, 1993).

Social psychology's focus upon conformity also takes its impetus from the individualist assumption that for the most part we are self-contained, fully autonomous beings, able to make choices and express free will as if located within an illusory cultural vacuum, uninvolved in the continual flux of social influence. However, as we have seen from a brief review of empirical evidence, this is far from so.

Nevertheless, given the assumption of and value placed upon personal autonomy within individualistic cultures, psychologists working in such settings for the most part have focused upon examining experimental conditions which challenge that autonomy. Reflecting for a moment, social psychology might instead have sought to focus upon identifying conversational ways in which we share and negotiate meanings, together constructing a complex culture in which people in most contexts voluntarily behave according to localised norms and rules. We will look at the possibilities of such a 'common sense' psychology later in this chapter. For now though, let us return to an examination of norms and majority influence in settings and experiments which have imaginatively tried to recreate aspects of our social worlds in microcosm.

In the Bennington Study, conformity to the group norm had clear adaptive significance for the students: they were more likely to be *accepted*, *approved* and *recognised* for various social rewards if they adopted the liberal norm. However, in the autokinetic situation, the subjects were not part of a reference group that controlled such vital social reinforcements and punishments. Their conformity to the crystallised norm of a transient group was not based on normative pressures but rather on other needs, such as the need for cognitive clarity about their world. When uncertain, we typically turn to others to satisfy informational needs that will help us understand what is happening (Deutsch & Gerard, 1955). Two of the reasons that account for why people conform to the perceived requirements of group and comply with those of individuals are **normative influence processes** – wanting to be liked, accepted and approved of by others, the need to *belong* – and **informational influence processes** – wanting to be correct and to understand how best to act in a given social context, the need to *know* (Insko *et al*, 1985).

Majority influence and conformity

Although Sherif demonstrated that perceptions could be socially conditioned, his paradigm was not very relevant to ecologically valid life scenarios because the subjects were judging a very ambiguous stimulus situation where any reaction by others might seem to clarify it. What would happen if individuals were making judgements under conditions where the physical reality was absolutely clear but the rest of the group saw the world differently? That is the circumstance created by **Solomon Asch** (1940; 1956). He believed that physical reality constraints on perception would be stronger than the power of the **social context** to distort individual judgements.

However, Asch was not correct. Rather, his studies produced surprising demonstrations of the influence of a unanimous group majority on the judgements of individuals even under unambiguous stimulus conditions. The **Asch effect**, as the phenomenon has become known, is a classic illustration of **conformity** to a group norm, the tendency for people to adopt the behaviour and opinions presented by other group members.

Groups of seven to nine male college students were led to believe they were in a study of simple visual perception. They were shown cards with three lines of differing lengths and asked to indicate which of the three lines was the same length as the standard line (see *Figure 13.2*, next page). The lines were different enough so that mistakes were rare, and their relative sizes changed on each series of trials.

On the first three trials, everyone agreed on the correct comparison. However, the first person to respond on the fourth trial reported seeing as equal two lines that were obviously different in length. So did the next person and so on, until all members of the group but one unanimously agreed on a judgement that conflicted with the perception of the next to last student. That student had to decide whether to go along with everyone else's view of the two lines and conform or whether to resist the influence of the group and stand by what was clearly visible. That dilemma was repeated in 12 of the 18 trials. Unknown to the 'naive' subject, all of the others in the group were in alliance with the experimenter – confederates – and were following a prearranged script, which also stipulated no communication other than calling out each perceptual judgement. The subject showed signs of disbelief and obvious discomfort when faced with a majority who saw the lines so differently. So, what did this participant and others in the same position do?

Only a quarter of the subjects resisted the group norm and adhered to their judgements; between 50 and 80 per cent of the subjects (in different studies in the research programme) conformed with the false majority estimate at least once; while a third of the subjects yielded to the majority's wrong judgements on half or more of the critical trials. Asch describes some participants who yielded to the majority most of the time as 'disoriented' and 'doubt-ridden', inferring that they 'experienced a powerful impulse not to appear different from the majority' (1952). In other studies, Asch found that strong conformity effects were elicited with a unanimous majority of only three or four people, but that no effects were elicited with just one confederate. Giving the naive subject an ally who dissented from the majority opinion sharply reduced conformity, as can be seen in *Figure 13.2*. With a partner, the subject was usually able to resist the pressures to conform to the majority. Asch also examined the size of the discrepancy between the correct physical stimulus comparison and the majority's position. Maintaining a discrepant judgement increased with the magnitude of the contradiction between one's perception and the group's erroneous judgement. All who yielded to the group underestimated the influence of the social context in which they were embedded and thereby the extent of their conformity; some even claimed they really had seen the lines as the same length (Asch, 1955, 1956).

Numerous studies of conformity have confirmed these results. They hold across a wide range of different types of judgements, with many types of stimuli and even in the absence of an actual face-to-face group (Crutchfield, 1955). The magnitude of the felt influence of the group majority depends on its unanimity. Once it is broken – in any way – the rate of conformity drops dramatically. A person is also more likely to conform when (a) a judgement task is difficult or ambiguous; (b) a group is highly cohesive and the individual feels attracted to it; (c) the group members are perceived as competent and the person feels relatively incompetent on the task; and (d) a person's responses are made public to others in the group. In many cases, people conform and are influenced without awareness that they have been affected, maintaining an illusion of absolute freedom of judgement that is unwarranted by their actions.

Minority influence and non conformity

Given the power of the majority to control resources and reinforcements, the extent of conformity that exists at all levels of our society is not surprising. How can anyone escape group domination and how can anything new (counter-normative) ever come about? How do revolutions and rebellions against the *status quo* emerge? Are there any conditions under which a small minority can turn the majority around and create new norms?

While researchers in North America have focused their studies upon conformity, in part because conforming to, and influencing, the decisions of a democratically elected government is an integral part of maintaining a political and social order, some European social psychologists have instead chosen to examine how the few may influence and change the majority. Leading French psychologist **Serge Moscovici** has pioneered the study of minority influence.

In one study, where six subjects were given colour naming tasks, the majority (four of the participants) correctly identified projected colours as either blue or green. The experimenter's two confederate subjects, however, consistently stated that blue colours were

FIGURE 13.2 · CONFORMITY IN THE ASCH EXPERIMENTS

Faced with a unanimous majority giving an erroneous judgement, the concern of naive subject No. 6 is evident in the photo from Asch's study. A sample of stimulus materials is shown above on the left. The graph illustrates conformity across 12 critical trials when solitary individuals were with a unanimous majority and also their greater independence when paired with a dissenting partner.

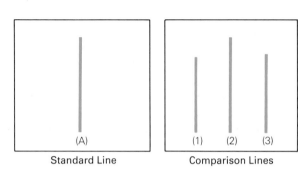

Standard Line

Comparison Lines

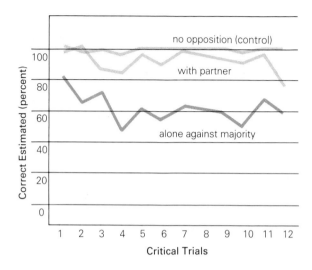

'green'. Gradually, over successive trials, their consistent minority opposition had an effect on the majority: the latter subjects' thresholds of discrimination between blue and green changed. Among the intermediate tones between pure blue and pure green, the majority began to perceive green earlier, a shifting of the boundary between blue and green having been effected toward the green side of the colour continuum (Moscovici, Lage & Naffrechoux, 1969;

Moscovici, 1976; Moscovici & Personnaz, 1991).

How *does* a minority influence the deliberations of the majority? A vocal minority is most influential when it has four qualities: it persists in affirming a consistent position, appears confident, avoids seeming rigid and dogmatic, and is skilled in social persuasion. Eventually, the influence of the many may be undercut by the conviction of the dedicated few (Moscovici, 1980). Majority decisions tend to be made without engaging systematic thought and critical thinking skills of the individuals in the group. They are often taken at face value, given the force of the group's normative influence to shape the opinions of the followers who conform without thinking things through. The persistent minority impels the others to process the relevant information more mindfully (Langer, 1989). Research shows that the decisions of the group as a whole are more thoughtful and creative when there has been minority dissent than in its absence (Nemeth, 1986). The group also better recalls the information after having been exposed to a consistent minority view than to only the majority or inconsistent minority view (Nemeth *et al*, 1990).

Another demonstration of how effective minority social influence can be, comes from research on the way individuals affect jury deliberations. In such simulated contexts, a disagreeing minority within the jury can prevent the unanimous acceptance of the majority point of view. However, a minority group is never well liked and its persuasiveness, when it occurs, must work over time (Nemeth, 1979). To have the most influence on a jury, a minority member must get elected as the chairperson, which can be accomplished quite simply by speaking first in the group, volunteering for the job, or sitting in the 'power seat' at the head of a rectangular table, if there is one. Jurors seated at the ends of a table both initiate and receive the most communication in the group, which allows them to be more influential (Strodtbeck & Hook, 1961).

In society, the majority tends to be the defender of the *status quo*, while the force for innovation and change comes from the minority members or individuals either dissatisfied with the current system or able to visualise new options and create alternative ways of dealing with current problems. In this sense, then, majorities and minorities have distinct forms of influence: the former maintaining social uniformity and compliance; the latter promoting social transformation and conversion. Thus, the conflict between the entrenched majority view and the dissident minority perspective is an essential pre-condition for innovations that can lead to positive social change. As social agents, we are constantly engaged in a two-way exchange with society, a complex mutuality and reciprocity – adapting to its norms, roles and status prescriptions but also acting upon society, being engaged continually in reshaping and renegotiating collectively designated norms (Moscovici, 1985). Important challenges lie ahead for social psychology in further developing our understandings of the dynamics of group processes, of how those processes influence actions and socio-conceptual behaviour and of how group functioning is either maintained or changed.

Authority Influence

We have been considering how groups influence individuals, but there are certain individuals – leaders and authorities – who exert considerable influence over group behaviour and other people. The ultimate demonstration of this effect was seen in the 1930s with the emergence of Adolf Hitler in Germany and Benito Mussolini in Italy. These leaders were able to transform rational individuals into manipulable masses with unquestioning loyalty to a fascist ideology bent on world conquest. Their authoritarian regimes threatened to overrun and destroy the freedom of neighbouring democracies. Much of modern social psychology developed out of this crucible of fear, prejudice and war.

The rise of fascism forced a transfer of scholars and their ideas from Europe to America, where they and their theorising inevitably underwent a transformation as it was adapted to a new national context which espoused the values of rugged, self-contained individualism. Social psychology, though, had existed embryonically in Europe in national traditions of social thought well before this historical period of relocation. The 'Volkerpsychologie' of nineteenth-century Germany ironically emphasised national political, social and cultural development as a shifting setting in which social and individual consciousness develops. A psychology of crowd behaviour was espoused in 1895 by LeBon. The first Institute for Social Psychology in Europe was founded albeit briefly by Hellpach in 1921. With the decanting of this European tradition to America, in the years after 1945, a reconstituted social psychology flowed back from the United States into the void left behind, comprising an unrivalled hegemony which persisted for two decades or so thereafter. As we have suggested, this social psychology was not quite of a form or focus as it had been before. But more of this later.

American experimental social psychology's early concerns were focused on examining the workings of propaganda and persuasive communications (Hovland *et al*, 1949) and the impact of group atmosphere and leadership styles on group members. Of great interest also, was exploring if a pervasive authoritarian personality could have explained the fascist mentality of prejudice and genocide with impunity. Adorno *et al* (1950) put forward the proposition that strict child rearing practices, had been over-anxiously utilised to ensure conformity to social mores. In turn, for fear of likely punitive consequences, the children's legitimate hostility towards their over-controlling parents had been displaced onto alternative weaker or 'inferior' targets, such as members of minority groups. The net effect would have been, they argued, a culturally endemic personality, recognisable by overdeferentiality toward those in positions of power within a given social hierarchy and by aggressiveness toward anyone not identifiable as a member of the prevailing in-group.

Conceptually alluring though such a familial and psychodynamic explanation might be, the balance of evidence and of argument does not support this view. Firstly, given Nazi fascism emerged over the space of one decade, there was insufficient time for German families *en masse* to have adopted such child-rearing practices and to have brought up a new generation which then as mature adults could sustain an oppressive regime. Secondly, if such a personality-based explanation were to be entertained, it cannot explain the occurrence of a frequent uniformity of prejudice amongst individuals in some communities or of sudden swings in such attitudes over brief periods of time. By asking these kinds of personality (or 'dispositional') questions – for example, 'Who are the individuals who could so mistreat others?' – the importance of socio-cultural factors and conditions such as prevailing societal norms are grossly understated. In pursuit of this latter, more viable contextual line of inquiry, subsequent post-war research by **Stanley Milgram** reframed the question into a much more social one: under what conditions or circumstances will people behave in anti-social or inhumane ways, ways which in retrospect they might regard as uncharacterstic of themselves? In so doing, Milgram followed up a concern in an experimental setting for understanding how people can become blindly obedient to the commands of unjust authorities. We will consider this work in detail shortly.

Lewin's group dynamics

The forerunner, however, in North America of Milgram, Asch and Sherif was founding experimental social psychologist **Kurt Lewin**. A German refugee who had escaped Nazi oppression, Lewin, like many others, could not help but wonder how his nation had succumbed so totally to the tyranny of a dictator. As a Professor of Psychology at the University of Berlin from 1927 to 1933, he devoted much time as a practical theorist to political psychology. He witnessed the spectacle of mass rallies of people shouting allegiance to their '*fuhrer*' ('leader'), frightening testimony to the capacity of one person to subvert the minds of so many. Thereby, Lewin came to investigate the ways in which leaders directly influenced their followers and how group processes changed the behaviour of individuals.

He was the founder of **field theory** which considered behaviour to be primarily a function of the person and the present situation. The approach

Kurt Lewin

focused on the interdependence of co-existing events which collectively define the 'field'. As an advocate of Gestalt psychology, Lewin emphasised the primacy of the whole (in this case, the situation or field) over the constituent 'parts'. Lewin effectively started the study of **group dynamics** as we know it today, investigating how group processes change individual functioning, initially conceptualising groups as 'fields of forces'. Perhaps, though, his most important contribution was in demonstrating that it was possible to pose socially significant questions which could be translated into hypotheses and tested in ingenious experimental settings, by reproducing analogues of existent social processes in miniature. In this sense, American social psychology developed as a Lewinian enterprise, his most renowned protégés including leading figures Leon Festinger, Harold Kelley and Stanley Schachter.

In 1939, Lewin and his colleagues Ron Lippitt and Ralph White designed an experiment to investigate the effects of group atmosphere and different leadership styles. The researchers created three experimental groups, allocated to them different types of leaders and observed the groups in action. The subjects were four small groups of ten-year-old boys, meeting after school. The group leaders were men who were trained to play each of the three leadership styles. When they acted as autocratic leaders, the men were to make all decisions about work assignments but not participate in the group activity. As democratic leaders, they were to encourage and assist group decision-making and planning. Finally, when they acted as *laissez-faire* leaders, their job was to allow complete freedom with little leader participation. At the end of each six-week period, the leaders took over a different group and also changed their leadership style according to the researchers' prearranged script. Thus, all groups experienced each of the three leadership styles under a different person, so that the leadership style was largely independent of the leader's personality.

The results of this 'field' experiment produced a

number of informative observations. Firstly, autocratic leaders produced a mixture of effects with respect to their followers, some positive and some quite negative. At times, the boys worked very hard but typically only when the leader – acting as boss – was watching them and they rarely did so when on their own. However, there was little originality in what they produced. What most characterised the boys in the autocratic groups was the frequent enactment of aggressive behaviour. These boys showed up to 30 times the frequency of hostility when led autocratically than they did when with the other types of leaders. They demanded more attention, were more likely to destroy their own property and showed more **scapegoating** behaviour, using weaker individuals as displaced targets for their frustration and anger. Coupled with this greater aggressiveness was more dependence on and submission to the leader's authority: in other words, they behaved not unlike fascists.

As for the *laissez-faire* groups, little benefit was derived from this leadership style. With this form of management, the boys were the most inefficient of all the groups, doing the least amount of work and of the poorest quality. However, when the same groups were democratically run, members worked the most steadily and they were most productive and efficient. The boys showed the highest levels of interest, motivation and originality under democratic leadership. When discontent arose, it was likely to be openly expressed. Almost all the boys preferred the democratic group to the others. Such a leadership style promoted more group loyalty and friendliness. There was more mutual praise, more friendly remarks, more sharing and, overall, more creative playfulness (Lewin *et al*, 1939).

A democratic milieu was demonstrated to be preferable psychologically to the other forms of group atmosphere. Democratic leaders generated the most constructive, prosocial reactions from group members, while autocratic-leader groups generated the most destructive, antisocial ones. Furthermore, general leadership style was shown to be more important than the specific personality of individual leaders. Irrespective of a leader's personality traits as measured by psychometric tests, his impact on the group depended entirely on the leadership style he enacted. Because leadership style was a core feature of the social context in which the boys were embedded, this study was one of the first to show that social influence processes significantly affect what we might otherwise misconstrue as an individual's singular behaviour.

Milgram: obedience to authority

When you think of the long and gloomy history of humankind, you will find more hideous crimes have been committed in the name of obedience than have been committed in the name of rebellion (C. P. Snow, 1961).

What made Adolf Eichmann and other Nazis willing to send millions of Jews to their deaths in gas chambers? Why did military personnel support decisions to drop two atomic bombs on Japan, obliterating in moments the civilian populations of Hiroshima and Nagasaki? More recently, how could Rwandan Hutus have been incited to commit genocide on at least 500,000 of their fellow Tutsi countrymen, women and children? How could Bosnian Serbs incarcerate former neighbouring Bosnian Croats and Muslims in conditions at Omarska that were reminiscent of a World War II concentration camp? How could a Ugandan dictatorship in the mid-1970s have sanctioned and put into effect the 'disappearance' of hundreds of thousands of the country's very own people? Indeed, how was the pervasive collusion necessary for the enactment of these deeds sustained? Did some terrible deficiency of personal disposition or of character lead the people involved in these events to obey blindly the orders of their leaders in unthinking fashion, even

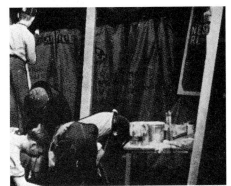

These photos from Lewin's classic study show the three leadership styles in action. The autocratic leader directs work, the democratic leader works with the boys, and the laissez-faire leader remains aloof.

Bosnian Croat and Muslim soldiers incarcerated by Bosnian Serbs.

when those orders violated their own personal values and moralities? Research indicates that such a suggestion – of individualised pathology – is not tenable as a sufficent explanation.

Alas conditions can be created under which most of us would blindly obey an order from an authority figure. But would we have surrendered ourselves to social influence to the extent that, like the American soldiers involved, we would have taken part in the massacre of hundreds of innocent citizens in the Vietnamese village of My Lai (Hersh, 1971; Opton, 1970, 1973)? We would like to think not. Experimental social psychology shows us, though, situational demands can be so persuasive that we would probably do what other human beings have in those circumstances, however atrocious and alien their actions may seem to us outside that setting.

The most convincing demonstration of socio-contextual influence over the behaviour of individuals was created by **Stanley Milgram**, a former student of Solomon Asch. Milgram's research (1965, 1974) showed that the blind obedience of Nazis was less a product of dispositional characteristics (an alleged German national 'personality') than it was the outcome of situational influence that could engulf any one of us. How did he demonstrate this 'banality of evil', that atrocious acts of mass murder could be engaged in by ostensibly good people for what they felt were noble purposes (Arendt, 1963; 1971)? Milgram's obedience research is one of the most controversial in psychology both because of the ethical issues it raises and its significant implications for real world phenomena (Miller, 1986; Ross & Nisbett, 1991).

The obedience paradigm. To disentangle the variables of personality and situation, which are always entwined in natural settings, Milgram used a series of controlled laboratory experiments involving more than 1,000 subjects. Milgram's first experiments were conducted at Yale University with Yale college students and then male residents of New Haven who received payment for their participation. In later variations, Milgram took his obedience laboratory to a high street research unit in Bridgeport, Connecticut. He recruited through newspaper advertisements a cross-section of the population, varying widely in age, occupation and education, and of both sexes.

The basic experimental paradigm involved individual subjects delivering a series of what they thought were increasingly unpleasant electric shocks to another person. They did so not because they were sadistic but because they were participating in a worthwhile cause – or so they believed. They were led to believe that the purpose of the study was to discover how punishment affects memory so that learning and memory could be improved through the proper balance of reward and punishment. In their social roles as teachers, the subjects were to punish each error made by someone playing the role as learner. The main rule they were told to follow was to increase the level of shock by a fixed amount each time the learner made an error until the learning was errorless. The white-coated experimenter acted as the legitimate authority figure: he presented the rules, arranged for the assignment of roles (by a rigged drawing of lots) and ordered the teachers to do their jobs whenever they hesitated or dissented. The dependent variable was the final level of shock (on a shock machine that went up to 450 volts in 15 volt steps) that a 'teacher' gave before refusing to continue to obey the authority. The initial study was simply a demonstration of the phenomenon of obedience. There was no manipulation of an independent

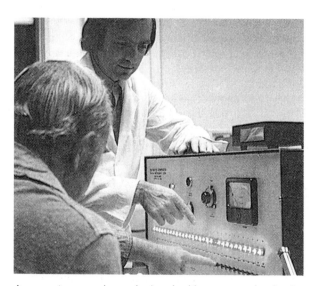

An experimenter shows the 'teacher' how to use the shock generator. How would you behave in this situation?

variable. Later versions, however, did study the effect of varying many situational factors, such as the physical distance between the teacher, the authority and the learner.

The test scenario. The study was staged to make a subject think that, by following orders, he or she was causing pain and suffering and perhaps even killing an innocent person. Each teacher had been given a sample shock of about 75 volts to feel the amount of pain it caused. The learner was a pleasant, mild-mannered man, about 50 years old, who mentioned something about a heart condition but was willing to go along with the procedure. He was strapped into an 'electric chair' in the next room and communicated with the teacher via an intercom. His task was to memorise pairs of words. The learner soon ran into difficulty and began making errors and the teacher began shocking the learner. The protests of the victim rose with the shock level. At 150 volts he demanded to be released from the experiment; at 180 volts he cried out that he could not stand the pain any longer. At 300 volts he insisted that he would no longer take part in the experiment and must be freed. He yelled out about his heart condition and screamed. If a teacher hesitated or protested delivering the next shock, the experimenter said, 'Teacher, you have no other choice; you must go on! Your job is to punish the learner's mistakes'.

As you might imagine, the situation was stressful for the subjects, producing considerable conflict within them. Most subjects complained and protested, repeatedly insisting they could not continue. Their complaints, however, were systematically followed by reassurances from the experimenter that he would accept responsibility for anything that might happen to the learner and by admonitions to 'please continue'. When the learner stopped responding, some subjects called out to him to respond, urging him to get the answer right so they would not have to continue shocking him. Even when there was only silence from the learner's room, the teacher was ordered to keep shocking him more and more strongly, all the way up to the button that was marked 'Danger: Severe Shock XXX (450 volts)'.

Did they obey? How far would the average subject in Milgram's experiment actually go in administering the shocks? Suppose for a moment that you were the subject-teacher. Which of the levels of shock would be the absolute limit beyond which you would refuse to continue?

To shock or not to shock? When 40 psychiatrists were asked this question, they predicted that only a very small percentage of people (0.1 per cent) would continue to 450 volts. The psychiatrists presumed that only those few individuals who were 'abnormal' in some way – for example, harbouring habitually sadistic feelings towards others – would blindly obey

orders to harm another person in an experiment. The psychiatrists based their evaluations on the presumed dispositional qualities of people whom they thought would engage in such acts. In retrospect, this is perhaps unsurprising given the biological and medical focus of their training as mental health practitioners. In so doing, though, they overlooked the influence of the situation to affect the thinking and actions of people caught within such an overpowering social context. Indeed, the majority of subjects obeyed the authority fully: nearly two-thirds delivered the maximum 450 volts to the learner. The average subject did not stop until about 300 volts. It is important to note that most people dissented verbally, but the majority did not disobey behaviourally. From the point of view of the 'victim' of the situation, the confederate learner, that was a critical difference.

Why do we obey authority? From the many variations of situational stimuli that Milgram conducted, we can conclude that the obedience effect is strongest under the following conditions, as shown in *Figure 13.3* (next page): (a) with the social influence of a peer who first models obedience; (b) when there is great remoteness of victim from subject; (c) when there is direct surveillance of the subject by the authority; (d) when a subject acts as an intermediary bystander assisting another person who actually delivers the shock; and (e) when the relative status of the authority figure to the subject is greater. This last finding comes from a replication of the study with school pupils by Rosenhan (1969) in which obedience reached 80 per cent.

Evidence that the obedience effect is due to situational variables and not personality ones is demonstrated by increasing the effect through manipulating the above conditions, and by knocking out the effect through varying other stimulus conditions (experiments 11, 12, 14, 15 and 17 in *Figure 13.3*). For example, subjects do not obey authority when the learner demands to be shocked, when two authorities give contradictory commands or when the authority figure is the victim. The role of personality effects can be ruled out with the finding that personality tests administered to the subjects did not reveal any psychological disturbance or abnormality in the obedient punishers or traits that differentiated those who obeyed from those who refused.

So why did they do it? One possibility is that the subjects did not really believe the 'cover story' of the experiment, knowing that the victim was not really getting hurt. This alternative was ruled out by an independent replication that made the effects of being obedient vivid, immediate and direct for the subjects. Thus, even when the cover story *was* fully believed, subjects still blindly obeyed (Sheridan & King, 1972).

Another alternative explanation for the subjects'

FIGURE 13.3   OBEDIENCE IN 18 EXPERIMENTS

The graph shows a profile of weak to strong obedience effects across Milgram's 19 (one experiment has two variations) experimental variations.

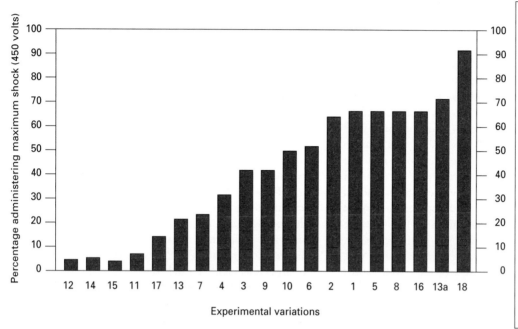

behaviour is that the effect is limited to the **demand characteristics** of the experimental situation. Sometimes cues in the experimental setting influence subjects' perceptions of what is expected of them and systematically influence their behaviour. Is blind obedience to authority in Milgram's study merely a response to the demands of the unusual experimental setting? Can it be shown that the same effect would occur in a real-life situation in which obeying authority could actually harm someone?

A team of psychiatrists and nurses performed the following study to test the potency of obedience in the natural setting of a hospital. A nurse (the subject) received a call from a staff doctor whom she had not met. He told her to administer some medication to a patient so that it could take effect by the time he arrived. He would sign the pharmacy order after he reached the ward. The doctor ordered a dose of 20 milligrams of a drug called Astroten. The label on the container of Astroten stated that five milligrams was the usual dose and warned that the maximum dose was ten milligrams. Would a nurse actually administer an excessive dose of a drug on the basis of a telephone call from an unfamiliar person when doing so was contrary to standard medical practice? When this dilemma was described to 12 nurses, ten said they would disobey. However, what nurses did in actuality was quite different. When another group of them were in the situation for real, almost every nurse

obeyed. 21 of 22 had started to pour the medication (actually a harmless substance) before a physician researcher stopped them (Hofling *et al*, 1966).

A further criticism of Milgram's research, however, was that subjects may have obeyed because they were surprised by the procedure of the experiment, specifically that they did not have time to orient themselves to their problematic role and so were more easily influenced than when outside of the laboratory situation. This aspect of the ecological validity of Milgram's findings was investigated in a Dutch study of obedience. Meeus & Raaijmakers (1987) asked subjects to participate in an occupational selection procedure. Their task was to deliver an important discriminative test to job applicants. They were ordered, however, to put each applicant under pressure, knowing that this would compromise the unemployed interviewee's chances of securing the position. When placed in this experimental condition, 92 per cent of participants obeyed and psychologically coerced the unsuspecting interviewee. In an all-important experimental variation, however, Meeus and Raaijmakers sent each subject a letter one week before the experiment took place. In this communication, participants were informed in advance of the experiment's entire procedure. Thus, participants could decide well before time – and in the context of their everyday lives outside of the laboratory – whether or not they would be a member of this selection committee or behave in a psychologically punitive way. Despite participants having time to orient themselves to the experiment, subjects in the letter-variant condition obeyed with similar frequency to those who had not been informed ahead of time. Thus, the authors concluded that behaviour in this analogous situation could not be explained simply as an experimental artifact but rather represents a compelling instance of ecologically valid, ordinary obedience to authority. The work of Hofling *et al* (1966) and Meeus & Raaijmakers (1987), then, strongly suggests that findings from experimental research have genuine implications for understanding the social psychology of conformity as it occurs beyond the walls of laboratory settings.

Two reasons why people obey authority in these situations can be traced to the effects of normative and informational sources of influence, which we discussed earlier. People want to be liked and they want to be right. They tend to do what others are doing or requesting (normative peer influence and normative authority influence) in order to be socially acceptable and approved. In addition, when in an ambiguous, novel situation, people rely on others for cues as to what is the appropriate and correct way to behave. They are more likely to do so when experts or credible communicators tell them what to do and are less likely to rebel when there is no opportunity with other people to discuss and collectively define the implicit requirements of the situation as unjust and unreasonable (Gamson, Fireman & Rytina, 1982). A third factor in the Milgram paradigm is that subjects were probably confused about how to disobey; nothing they said in dissent satisfied the authority. If they had a simple, direct way out of the situation, for example, by pressing a 'withdraw' button, it is likely more would have disobeyed (Ross, 1988). Finally, obedience to authority in this experimental situation is part of an ingrained habit that is learned by children in many different settings: obey authority without question (Brown, 1986). This heuristic usually serves us and our society well when authorities are legitimate and deserving of our obedience. The problem is that the rule gets overapplied, just as when children first learn the grammatical rules for past tense they add 'ed' to all verbs even when it is wrong to do so.

What is the significance of this obedience research for each one of us? The image of the lone man standing before the tanks of Tiannamen Square during the rebellion of Chinese students in June 1989 behoves us to ask if we could have done the same. We are all likely to face social and moral dilemmas. How we respond, the choices we make, are rendered more under our control once we better understand the influence processes that may otherwise in large part make those choices for us.

Many of the scandals at the highest level of government, military and business involve authorities expecting their subordinates to behave in unethical, illegal or plainly inadvisable ways, with sometimes disastrous consequences (Dixon, 1976). Indeed, national leaders are as subject to the authority influence of their colleagues as much as is any one of us in our daily lives. It was discovered in 1986, for example, that high-level American government officials were involved in a complex, illegal deal that sold arms to Iran in return for the release of American hostages. These officials then diverted the profits from those arms sales to aid the right-wing Contra rebels in Nicaragua. The former director of the National Security Council, Robert McFarlane, testified before a Congressional investigating committee that he was part of the attempt by the White House to deceive Congress about this Iran-Contra affair. He said he 'didn't have the guts' to tell President Reagan that he thought the method for achieving their goal was wrong. Why not? 'To tell you the truth, probably the reason I didn't is because if I'd done that, Bill Casey (former CIA Director), Jeanne Kirkpatrick (former UN ambassador), and Cap Weinberger (Defence Secretary) would have said I was some kind of "Commie", you know' (*Newsweek*, 25 May 1987).

Resisting such socially contextualised influence processes requires being aware of and accepting the fact that they can be sufficiently potent to affect almost anyone, even oneself. Then the social situation needs to be examined critically for the details that do not make sense, for flaws in the 'cover story', or the rationales that are inconsistent upon careful analysis. Most important in resisting all compliance-gaining scenarios is leaving the situation, either physically or psychologically: by taking a 'time out' to think things

Would you have the courage to stand up to authority?

over, never signing on the dotted line the first time; by being willing to appear to make a mistake or appearing to be a poor team player.

As in the case of the Stanford prison study, this obedience research challenges the myth that 'evil' lurks in the minds of 'evil people' – that the 'bad' are different dispositionally from the 'good', who allegedly would never do such things. The purpose in recounting these findings is not to debase human nature but to make clear that even normal, well-meaning people are subject to the human capacity for frailty if positioned in circumstances wherein social situational influences are *potent* and *pervasive*. The 'dark side' of human nature need not continue to be a feature of our human behavioural repertoire if we proactively construct only those social contexts and contingencies that make pro-social forms of activity and belief possible and meaningful.

A victim has a better chance of being helped if the bystanders see the situation as a clear emergency and if they are familiar with the environment.

 Bystander Intervention

Consider a different perspective on the obedience scenario of Milgram's experiments if you were a bystander, would you intervene to help one of the distressed teachers disobey the authority and exit from the situation? Before answering, you might want to consider what social psychologists have discovered about the nature of bystander intervention and the way it reflects another aspect of social influence.

For more than half an hour, 38 law-abiding citizens in the Queens neighbourhood of New York watched a man stalk and fatally stab a woman in three separate attacks. Two times the sound of the bystanders' voices and the sudden glow of their bedroom lights interrupted the assailant and frightened him. Each time, however, he returned and stabbed her again. Not a single person telephoned the police during the assault. Only one witness called the police after the woman was dead (*The New York Times*, 13 March 1964). This newspaper account of the murder of Kitty Genovese shocked a nation that could not accept the idea of such apathy on the part of its responsible citizenry.

Would you have called the police to help Kitty Genovese or intervened in some tangible way? The temptation is to say, 'Yes, of course'. However, we must be careful to resist over-confidence about the way we would react in an unfamiliar situation. Why do bystanders not help in cases such as these? What would make them more likely to do so? A classic series of studies of the bystander-intervention problem was carried out soon after the Kitty Genovese murder by social psychologists **Bibb Latane** and **John Darley** (1968). They created in the laboratory an

ingeneous experimental analogue of the bystander-intervention situation. A college student, placed alone in a room with an intercom, was led to believe that via this, one or more students in an adjacent room could be contacted. During the course of a discussion over the intercom system about personal problems, the lone student heard what sounded like one of the other students having an epileptic seizure and gasping for help.

During the 'seizure' it was impossible for the subject to talk to the other students or to find out what, if anything, they were doing about the emergency. The dependent variable in the experiment was the speed with which the emergency was reported to the experimenter by the lone subject. The major independent variable was the number of people the student thought were in the adjacent discussion group.

It turned out that the likelihood of intervention depended on the number of bystanders thought to be present. The more there were, the slower was the lone participant in reporting the seizure, if this happened at all. As you can see in *Figure 13.4* (next page), everyone in a two-person situation intervened within 160 seconds, but nearly 40 per cent of those who believed they were part of a larger group never bothered to inform the experimenter that another student was seriously ill. Personality tests showed no significant relationship between particular personality characteristics and speed or likelihood of intervening. The best predictor of bystander intervention is the socio-contextual variable of size of the group present. The likelihood of intervention decreases as the group

FIGURE 13.4 BYSTANDER INTERVENTION IN AN EMERGENCY

The likelihood of bystanders intervening in an emergency decreases as the number of other people present increases. Bystanders act most quickly in two-person groups.

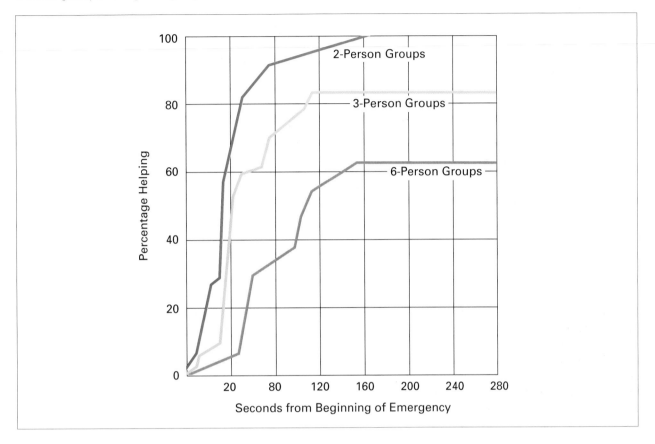

increases in size, probably because each person makes the assumption that others will help, so he or she does not have to make that commitment.

When similar studies of bystander intervention are carried out in field situations rather than in the laboratory, a victim's chances of getting help increase considerably.

A man on a moving New York underground train suddenly collapsed and fell to the floor. A number of bystanders witnessed this event. The experimenters manipulated the situation by varying the characteristics of the 'victim' – an invalid with a cane, a drunk smelling of alcohol or, in a companion study, a disabled person apparently bleeding (or not bleeding) from the mouth. The researchers unobtrusively recorded the bystander responses to these emergency situations. One or more persons responded directly in most cases (81 out of 103) with little hesitation. Help was slower when the apparent cost of intervening was higher (that is, slower for a bloody victim who might require a greater degree of involvement than a victim who simply

collapsed), but it usually still came (Piliavan & Piliavan, 1972; Piliavan et al, 1969).

What accounts for the fact that students do not help as much in a laboratory situation as citizens in a natural setting? Intervention in the laboratory setting is likely to be inhibited for any or all of the following reasons: (a) the college student subjects have already adopted the passive role of 'subject'; (b) they may assume that the experimenter in charge is ultimately responsible for everything that occurs during an experimental session; (c) they often do not actually see the victim-in-distress; and (d) they are severely restricted by obedience to an unstated rule of the laboratory setting – 'stay in your seat; stay put and follow instructions until told you can get up', a heuristic in all likelihood learned at school and further reinforced in college. In unstructured, informal settings, none of these implicit conditions hold and the decision to intervene is based more on an observer's weighing of the personal costs of intervention against the consequences of not doing so.

Despite the higher rate of help in these more ecologically valid field studies, however, it remains that many people do not help and that some settings render help less likely than others. For example, when an experimental accomplice on crutches pretended to collapse in an airport, the percentage of those who helped was much lower than in the subway – 41 per cent as compared with 83 per cent. The important factor seemed to be familiarity with the environment: the subway riders felt more at home on the subway and thus were more likely to deal with the trouble that arose (Latane & Darley, 1970).

Time-urgency and altruism

The presence or absence of other people is one situational factor that apparently affects bystander intervention. In addition, if a bystander is in a hurry to do something else, he or she is less likely to offer help. Could the failure of people to intervene really be due in part to time pressures rather than to personal dispositions? A research team recreated in a study the biblical story of the Good Samaritan, incorporating a special group of research subjects – theological students – who in all probability should be conspicuous in their altruism given their chosen career path.

The students at the Princeton Theological Seminary who were co-opted for the experiment, believed that they were about to have their sermons evaluated, one of which was to focus upon the parable of the Good Samaritan. Before they left the briefing room to have their sermons recorded in a nearby building, they were each told something about the time they had available to get to the studio. Some were randomly assigned to a late condition, in which they had to hurry to make the next session; others to an on-time condition, in which they would just make the next session as scheduled; and a third group to an early condition, in which they had a few spare minutes before they would be recorded.

When each seminarian walked down an alley between the two buildings, he came upon a man slumped in a doorway, in obvious need of help. On their way to deliver a sermon about the Good Samaritan, these seminary students now had the chance to practice what they were about to preach. But did they? Of those who were in a hurry, only ten per cent helped. If they were on time, 45 per cent helped the stranger. Most bystander intervention came from those who were not in a time bind – 63 per cent of these seminarians acted as Good Samaritans (Darley & Batson, 1973).

The manipulation of situational time constraints had a marked effect on the altruism of these young men, increasing it sixfold between the late and early conditions, when all else was held constant. We can hardly attribute the lack of intervention of those in

the late condition to personal callousness or to other individualised dispositions since they were randomly assigned to that condition and had chosen a career based on helping others. It is likely that, while fulfilling their obligation to the researcher to hurry and not be late for their appointment, their single-minded purpose blinded them to distracting, 'task-irrelevant' events that might interfere with that obligation. Some of those who did not help may not have noticed the man in distress, others might have misinterpreted what they saw as a man merely resting.

Eliciting the help of others

To demonstrate the positive effects of situational influence, social psychologist **Tom Moriarity** (1975) arranged two experiments in different 'natural' settings. In the first study, members of the public watched as a thief snatched a women's suitcase in a restaurant when she left her table. In the second, they witnessed a thief snatching a portable radio from a beach blanket when the owner left it for a few minutes. What did these onlookers do? Some did nothing. They let the thieves go on their way. What were the conditions under which some helped and others did not?

In each experiment, the would-be theft victim (the experimenter's accomplice) asked the soon-to-be observer of the crime either 'Do you have the time?' or 'Will you please keep an eye on my bag (radio) while I'm gone?' The first request elicited no personal responsibility and the bystander simply stood by idly as the theft unfolded. However, of those who agreed to watch the victim's property, almost every bystander intervened. They called for help and some even tackled the runaway thief on the beach. The encouraging message is that we can convert apathy to action and transform apparent 'callousness' to demonstrable kindness just by asking for it. The act of requesting a favour can invoke a social obligation that involves other people in ways which materially change the meaning of a situation, thereby altering the likelihood of pro-social behaviour. It makes those others responsible to you and, thereby, responsible for what happens in that shared social context.

INTERIM SUMMARY

Throughout this section, we have explored a theme of great importance within social psychology: the potency and pervasiveness of social influence processes in producing, orchestrating and shaping the behaviour of individual people. We might call this the 'power' of situations, wherein multiple meanings of 'power' refer to three main processes of 'influence' (in the widest sense of that term), namely, the effects of persuasion, authority and of conditions which promote compliance (Turner, 1991). A wide body of controlled experiments and field studies supports the contention that human thought and action are affected by socio-situational influences to a far greater extent than we perhaps realise in our daily lives or would predict. This important social psychological theme was illustrated by a number of studies in which apparently minor or even trivial contextual features altered what was enacted. The mere presence of others can serve to facilitate and intensify reactions in some circumstances. Being assigned to play social roles, even in artificial settings such as a mock prison, can modify behaviour dramatically in ways that may be contrary to strongly held values, beliefs and dispositions. Other potent social influence variables include behavioural rules, signs, symbols and uniforms.

Social norms function within groups to direct and shape their members' behaviour. Informational influence processes lead to conformity and compliance when the situation is ambiguous and the person wants to be 'correct' and act appropriately. Studies of the autokinetic effect revealed how a crystallised norm could influence individual judgements even long after the group was no longer present. The Bennington Study pointed to the potency of social norms in an ecologically valid setting to affect students' core attitudes and values, sometimes for a lifetime. Even in highly structured scenarios, perceptions can be shaped by conformity influences, as demonstrated in Asch's laboratory experiment. Members of a minority can be effective in changing majority opinion if their efforts are consistent, unanimous and non-rigid. One of the most powerful and controversial demonstrations of social influence was Milgram's series of studies on obedience to authority, in which many 'good' people typically behaved in ostensibly 'cruel' ways for the best of motives. Final support for the significance of social influence processes came from studies in which bystander intervention was found to fall away as the number of observing bystanders increased and as bystanders' sense of time urgency was greater. The positive effects of social influence emerges in research that indicates we can induce altruism in others by simply asking for it.

❖ SOCIAL COGNITIONS AND SOCIAL REALITY

In the first part of the chapter we discussed social influence. Now we will shift our attention to a further important consideration and examine the ways in which social agents actively create social reality. As we have seen in the chapters on perception and motivation, people subjectively interpret situations, including social ones. Within social psychology such appraisal is known as **social cognition**. In order to understand how situational influences matter, it is necessary to comprehend the workings of these cognitions. Here, then, we will explore how behavioural settings are perceived by social agents located within them and how meanings are attributed to the various components of a social context.

This second focus of social psychology emphasises how social reality is actively constructed by people's perceptions (shared or otherwise) of their immediate environment, of which other's actions are of course focal constituents. The way 'actors' view a situation can engage psychological processes that in effect change the circumstance so that it comes to be assimilated into their egocentric perception, values and attitudes. It is not so much the physical, objective features of a social setting that control individual and group behaviour; it is a person's mental representation of the particular scenario or situation that matters most. Thereby, social knowledge arises out of a dialectical process between objective and subjective reality (Berger & Luckman, 1966).

For the social psychologist, then, an adequate account of any behaviour includes three basic components: the features of the current situation; the specific content and context of the observed behaviour; and the actor's subjective interpretations of what are considered to be the important elements in the behavioural setting. Taken together, these components broadly constitute the Lewinian notion of 'field'. The complexity of this type of behaviour analysis becomes apparent when it is realised that people often interpret shared events in different ways. Each of us brings a unique phenomenological perspective to his or her personal interpretation and understanding of a given situation. Such subjectivity can minimise focusing upon objective, physical, environmental features as the determinants of social phenomena. When members of a group – whether a small group of friends, a community or a culture – reach a common interpretation of an event, activity or person, their shared phenomenological perspective is known as **social reality**. Social reality is the *consensus* of perceptions and beliefs about a situation generated by the social comparisons made by members of a social group. Thereby, social realities emerge as if 'natural givens' and so become inscribed upon individuals as part of their world view.

In this section, we will see social influence processes from a different perspective, as they are filtered through the viewpoint taken by a person's mental processes. After reviewing a body of field and laboratory studies that illustrates the ways in which our subjective constructions of reality operate, we will outline several theoretical approaches that social psychologists have taken to help them make sense of the ways people think about and perceive their social world. It will become apparent that, throughout much of social psychology, particularly within the North American tradition, there is a marked cognitive orientation (research on person perception, for example, having been informed by work on memory). This cognitive alignment within social psychology, however, focuses specifically upon cognitions about the social world, about ourselves and other people, about settings in which our actions are located; so, more precisely, such perceptions are referred to as 'social cognitions' (Wyer & Carlston, 1979; Eiser, 1980; Fiske, 1993) – the cognitive processes involved in understanding and guiding social behaviour.

 Guiding Beliefs and Expectations

Have you ever disagreed with another spectator about what really took place at an event you both witnessed, at say, for example, a soccer, hockey or rugby match? People's beliefs can lead them to view the same situation from different vantage points and to draw contrary conclusions about what 'really happened'. Think about what often occurs in the sports pages of the local press when, for example, rival soccer teams Manchester City meet Manchester United, or Ajax (Amsterdam) compete against Feyenoord (Rotterdam), or Celtic play Rangers. It is clear that a complex social occurrence, such as a sporting event, cannot be observed in an entirely objective fashion. Social situations become experiential events; they are given significance by observers who selectively encode what is happening in terms of what they expect to see and want to see. In the case of this soccer game, people looked at the same activity, but in effect they saw two different games. In many socially prescribed instances, then, 'reality' is only as we perceive it to be.

Fulfilling prophecies

Can beliefs and expectations go beyond colouring the way we interpret experiences to shape social reality so fundamentally? Much research suggests that the features of some social scenarios can be modified significantly by the beliefs and expectations people have about them. Such social expectancy effects are similar to placebo effects in which belief that a medical treatment will work makes it work for about

a third of all people. For example, ordinary students or underachievers can be transformed into high achievers if their teachers believe they are 'special', or if the students are led to think so.

In George Bernard Shaw's play *Pygmalion* (popularised as the musical *My Fair Lady*), a helpless street waif is transformed into a society lady under the intense training and anticipation of her teacher, Professor Henry Higgins. The effect of such social expectancy, or of what has become known as the 'pygmalion effect', was recreated in a seminal experiment by psychologist **Robert Rosenthal** (in conjunction with school principal Leonore Jacobson).

Some elementary school teachers in Boston were informed by researchers that their psychometric testing had revealed that some of their students were 'academic spurters'. The teachers were led to believe that these particular students were 'intellectual bloomers who will show unusual gains during the academic year'. In fact, there was no objective basis for that prediction; the names of these late bloomers were chosen randomly. By the end of that school year, 30 per cent of the children arbitrarily named as spurters had gained an average of 22 IQ points as measured by a standard intelligence test. Almost all of them had gained at least ten IQ points. Their gain in intellectual performance was significantly greater than that of their control group classmates who had also taken the intelligence test at two time points, thereby controlling for the effects of practice. In absolute terms, their improvement is remarkably significant for any known kind of enriched education programme over such a short time and these were students in ordinary classes (Rosenthal & Jacobson, 1968a; 1968b).

How did the ungrounded expectations of the teachers get translated into such positive student performance? The answer lies in the realisation that the teachers' *expectations* of better academic performances from selected students, led them unwittingly to use *influence strategies* to motivate the targeted students to work harder and more efficiently, thereby fulfilling what they had been led to believe about these pupils. Such strategies were probably communicated in many nonverbal ways, perhaps even nonconsciously, through the teachers' facial expressions and body language.

Rosenthal points to at least four processes that were activated by the teachers' expectations: firstly, they acted more warmly and friendlier, creating a climate of social approval and acceptance; secondly, they put greater demands – involving both quality and level of difficulty of material to be learned – on those for whom there were high hopes; thirdly, they gave

Studying in a group can significantly enhance performance.

more immediate and differentiated feedback (praise and criticism) about the selected students' performance; and fourthly, the teachers created more opportunities for the 'special' students to respond in class, to show their competence and be reinforced, thus giving them incontrovertible evidence that they were good pupils. We could add a fifth factor, the halo effect, in which anything a presumably good student does is interpreted in a positive light or given the benefit of the doubt. This attributional charity is rarely extended to the ordinary students and never to the 'bad' kids (Rosenthal, 1990).

In one sense, this research put some students on the academic fast track. The opposite happens when children are assigned to slow learner or learning disability educational pathways; they often *become* slower when they have been identified in this way. Pessimistic teacher expectations may be responsible for poorer performance of females and some minority students in science and mathematics courses even at college and university level.

A teacher's expectation, then, can act as a **self-fulfilling prophecy** (Merton, 1957). This can be defined as a prediction made about some future behaviour or event that, by the very fact of it having been made, immediately modifies the likelihood of such behaviour being enacted or of a future event occurring. In addition, the probable occurrence or non-occurrence of associated outcomes are likewise changed. Thereby is produced, in this self-fulfilling manner, what was originally expected. Consequently, social reality can be changed in several ways by the operation of such prophecies. For example, a student *expects* he or she will have an enjoyable time at an impending party. By virtue of this prior anticipation,

the student has increased the likelihood of experiencing this satisfying state of affairs.

In Chapter 11, we noted the positive effects on health and well-being of an optimistic outlook on life (Seligman, 1991). Optimism is a general system of beliefs that gets translated into actions that affect health and well-being. Mediating between those general beliefs and specific actions is **social perception**. Research has shown that our wishes and hopes for how life will turn out can actually have some influence on the way it does. The ways we frame future options motivates the ways we reason about paths to attaining them. This motivated reasoning comes to determine the kind of evidence we focus on in making our self-predictions, the methods we use to make those predictions, the confidence we invest in our predictions and our insensitivity to contrary evidence that might disconfirm our predictions (Kunda, 1990). Optimists assume setbacks are temporary and persevere in the face of adversity until they reach their goals.

Confirming expectations

Mark Snyder (1984) uses the term **behavioural confirmation** to refer to the process by which expectations about another person influence others to behave in ways that confirm the original expectation.

In a series of studies, students were led to expect that they would interact with another person who was described in a particular way (not necessarily true), such as, for example, introverted, extraverted, depressed or intelligent. After interacting with the person so identified, the subject rated the person on a variety of dimensions. Typically, the identified person was more likely to act in whatever way the subject expected him or her to behave. The subjects as well as the observers (who did not know about the expectation) agreed that those hypothesised as outgoing were indeed very sociable, that the people identified as introverted behaved less gregariously, and so forth (Kulik, 1983; Snyder & Swann, 1978a). How were these impressions confirmed? Prior expectations become translated into behavioural confirmations by the selective verbal and nonverbal behaviours of the subject with respect the target person. The person identified as 'extraverted' was likely to be asked how she would liven up a party, while the shy target person was asked about what makes it hard to open up to others. These different questions thus elicited different responses that guided and pre-empted the evaluation without the evaluator being aware that their particular line of questioning had played a significant role in constructing the emergent social reality.

Creating and reversing prejudices

Few human frailties are more destructive to the dignity of the people and the social bonds of humanity than **prejudice**. Social psychology has always put the study of prejudice high on its agenda. Understanding its complexity and persistence enables the development of strategies to change prejudicial attitudes and discriminatory behaviour. A decision taken in the United States in 1954 to illegalise segregated public education was based in part upon research presented by social psychologist **Kenneth Clark**, which showed the negative impact on black children of their separate and unequal schooling (Clark & Clark, 1947).

Prejudice is the prime example of social reality gone awry – a situation created in the minds of people that can demean and destroy the lives of others. Prejudice is defined as a learned attitude toward a target object, involving negative affect (dislike or fear), negative beliefs (stereotypes) that justify the attitude and a behavioural intention to avoid, control, dominate or eliminate those in the target group. Because prejudices are often formed on the basis of limited or false information, they are typically unwarranted and irrational. A false belief qualifies as prejudiced when it resists change even in the face of appropriate evidence of its mistakenness. Prejudiced attitudes serve as biasing filters that influence the way people are perceived and treated once they are categorised as members of a target group.

Prejudices are based on biased attitudes toward a specific individual and/or group. The concept of **attitude** is a central one in social psychology. It subsumes evaluative, cognitive and behavioural components. Attitudes are concerned, then, with judging (*cognitive*) something, or someone, to be of

Prejudice is a learned attitude that is usually formed on the basis of limited or false information.

positive or negative valence (*evaluation*). Many, though not all attitudes, are translated into actions (*behaviour*). The specific relation between attitude and action is a subject of controversy in social psychology. Many researchers have tried to predict a variety of actions from expressed attitudes (Fishbein & Ajzen, 1981; Ajzen & Madden, 1986). Few, however, have been successful in this quest for accurate and dependable prediction (Olson, 1993). Prejudiced attitudes have received a considerable amount of attention from psychologists wishing to change these negative evaluations of other people.

Once formed, prejudice exerts a potent influence on the way pertinent information is selectively processed, organised and remembered. Although there are many origins of prejudice and a variety of functions that it serves (Allport, 1954; Pettigrew, 1985; Sarnoff & Katz; 1954), one of its elementary purposes is to satisfy the socio-cognitive goal of simplifying complex interpersonal environments by categorising people in various ways. In so doing, future predictions about others based on such categorisation may be anticipated as still of significant utility but conveniently do not entail the expenditure of the additional cognitive effort needed to make more exact and sensitive behavioural forecasts. In turn, by the operation of these often inadequately, simple socio-cognitive schematas, the expectation is that our interpersonal worlds will miraculously become more manageable and our social behaviour more competent and fulfilling of our needs (Spears & Manstead, 1990). Often, however, the reverse is the result.

The simplest and most pervasive form of categorising consists of an individual determining whether or not people are similar to themself. This categorisation process develops from a 'me versus not-me' orientation to an 'us versus them' orientation. Thus, where membership of a group confers a sense of self-esteem and positive *social identity* upon its adherents, people protect this notion of themselves by maximising perceived differences between their group and that of others – an *outgroup* – (*intergroup* comparisons being made) and by minimising perceived differences between members of the *ingroup* of which one is a part (*intragroup* comparisons being curtailed). These cognitive distinctions between groups result in an *ingroup bias*, an evaluation of one's own group as better than others (Brewer, 1979). Surprisingly, the most minimal of distinctive cues is sufficient to trigger the formation of this bias and, with it, the formation of prejudice, and other social psychological phenomena. The mere fact of belonging to a group has tangible consequences for our attitudes toward other groups.

In a series of experiments by Dutch psychologist **Jaap Rabbie** and his colleagues, subjects were randomly divided into two groups: a blue group and a green group. According to the subjects' group membership, they were given either blue or green pens and asked to write on either blue or green paper. The experimenter addressed subjects in terms of their group colour. Even though these colour categories had no intrinsic psychological significance and assignment to the groups was completely arbitrary, subjects gave a more positive evaluation of their own group than of the other. Furthermore, this ingroup bias, based solely on colour identification, appeared even before the group members began to work together on an experimental task (Rabbie & Horwitz, 1969; Rabbie, 1981).

Social categorisation is the process by which people organise their social environment by categorising themselves and others into groups (Wilder, 1986). This categorisation has been shown to have the following consequences: the perception of similarity of those within one's group and dissimilarity of those in the outgroup; a failure to distinguish among individuals in the outgroup; a reduced influence of outgroup members on the ingroup; and hostile attitudes toward and beliefs in the inferiority of the outgroup (Tajfel, 1982; Tajfel & Billig, 1974). These consequences developed regardless of limited exposure to the outgroups and despite the contrary experience of their individual members with any other outgroup category (Park & Rothbart, 1982; Quattrone, 1986).

Does there need to be an observable, evidential basis to the categorisations which lead to the formation of prejudiced attitudes and discriminatory behaviours? Research suggests not. All that appears to be necessary is any salient cue on which individuals can be sorted into mutually exclusive categories. **Henri Tajfel** (1970) was the first to show that mere categorisation was a sufficient condition to produce intergoup behaviour and prejudice. Like his Dutch colleagues, he allocated schoolboys to one of two groups based on their purported preference for the work of two abstract artists – Paul Klee and Vassilij Kandinsky. Importantly, in this study though, each child knew only to which group he had been assigned – the children did not know which of their classmates had likewise been allocated to their particular group. Thus, they could not identify the other members of their ingroup. The pretext of the experiment was that it was a study of 'decision-making'. Under such an impression, the schoolboys were asked to allot money to recipients using a prepared response booklet. Within these, on each page only the group affiliation of each recipient was made known, not the name or other identifying features. A rule was that the children were not allowed to award money to themselves, thereby eliminating any self-interest.

So, would the mere fact of knowing that one belongs to a particular group have any effect on the patterning of monetary allocation? The results from this **minimal group paradigm** experiment were readily apparent: despite the children's attempts to be fair, there was a consistent bias – a favouritism – toward allocating more money to ingroup recipients as opposed to those they believed were affiliated to the other group. Mere categorisation, then, would appear to be sufficient for discriminatory intergroup behaviour to emerge, a finding which subsequently has been replicated many times (Brewer & Kramer, 1985). On the basis of categorisation, perceived differences between groups become exaggerated, whilst those within them are minimised, this process of **categorical differentiation** being a pervasive one, according to Doise (1976) and Knippenberg & Ellemers (1990). This categorisation process has served as the basis for the formulation of **social identity theory** which proposes that the social part of our identity derives from the groups to which are affiliated (Tajfel, 1981).

It has been suggested, however, that the focus on categorisation as a cognitive process has overlooked an accompanying one, that of **particularisation** (Billig, 1985). Categorisation refers to the process by which a stimulus is placed within a general class. Particularisation, on the other hand, refers to the way in which a particular stimulus is distinguished from that category, or from other stimuli. The two processes, thus, are integral to one another: when people assign an object or person to a category, they are also cognisant at the same time of that which does not belong to such a class. For example, when a person of Welsh origin categorises his Scottish and Irish friends as 'us' (the ingroup), simultaneously he may also be particularising non-Celtic English people and Anglophiles as 'them' (the outgroup).

Despite the clarity of results from minimal group research, a critical question must be asked of it: can the results be generalised to the world beyond the artificially contrived settings of these experiments? The question arises because Tajfel's and other's findings would seem to imply that discrimination and prejudice are inevitable in many walks of life, wherever categorisation is possible. Such an implication has been critiqued by social psychologists who in more recent times have been adopting **rhetorical** or **discourse-analytic** perspectives: **Michael Billig** (1985) and **Jonathan Potter** and **Margaret Wetherell** (1987), for example, suggest that the cognitive emphasis of this work on intergroup relations has missed the *social* psychological point that people can in fact discuss and examine their own assumptions – they can be *reflexive* about human action and thought. Since we can talk about the world and thereby through language continually recreate our implicit categorisations of it, prejudice need not necessarily be an inevitable outcome of what it is to be a social being. However, we are all not equally equipped with or schooled in the linguistic, conceptual and critical competencies needed to engage fully in this rational examination of our socio-cognitive processes. Primary school-age children, the competencies of whom albeit are often underestimated, arguably constitute a case in point.

To examine this concern and that of the generalisability of findings from the minimal group experiments, the work of Jane Elliot, a school teacher, is relevant here. As an educationalist, she wanted her pupils from an all-white, rural Iowa farm community to experience how prejudice and discrimination felt to those in minority groups. She devised an activity to provide her students with that experience. Her demonstration clearly illustrates the arbitrariness of the categorisation involved in prejudice within the ecologically valid setting of the school classroom.

One day Elliot arbitrarily designated brown-eyed children as 'superior' to the 'inferior' blue-eyed children. The superior, allegedly more intelligent, brown-eyes were given special privileges, while the inferior blue-eyes had to obey rules that enforced their second-class status. Within a day, the blue-eyed children began to do more poorly in their schoolwork and became depressed, sullen and angry. They described themselves as 'sad', 'bad', 'stupid' and 'mean'.

Of the brown-eyed superiors, the teacher reported, 'What had been marvellously cooperative, thoughtful, children became nasty, vicious, discriminating little third-graders. . . . It was ghastly'. They mistreated their former friends, called them 'blue-eyes', refused to play with them, got into fights with them and worried that school officials should be notified that the blue-eyes might steal things.

The second day of the activity, Elliott told the class that she had been wrong. It was really the blue-eyed children who were superior and the brown-eyed ones who were inferior. The brown-eyes now switched from their previously 'happy', 'good', 'sweet' and 'nice' self labels to derogatory labels similar to those used the day before by the blue-eyes. Their academic performance deteriorated, while that of the new ruling class improved. Old friendship patterns between children temporarily dissolved and were replaced with hostility until the experiment was ended (Elliott, 1977).

On a more optimistic note, however, the experience of being in a disadvantaged outgroup can have the positive effect of enabling people to develop greater empathy for members of groups that are discriminated against in society. In a replication of Elliott's study, psychologists found that, weeks later, the children who had participated held less prejudicial beliefs than did a comparison group without this experience (Weiner & Wright, 1973). The paradigm of categorising people by arbitrary cues of differentness – eye colour – was equally effective with the adult groups that Elliott instructed. The effects were also long lasting. A ten-year follow-up of her original school students revealed that, as young adults, they were tolerant of group differences and were actively opposed to prejudice (Elliott, 1990).

Thus, the experience of being the victim of prejudice, of categorisation, enabled both children and adults the opportunity to develop an analytical standpoint, to take a reflexive perspective, and examine socio-cognitive processes critically. Albeit that Elliot's demonstration was not an entirely naturalistic one; nevertheless, laudably it approximated to this by incorporating categorisation

Jane Elliot's experiment measured overt changes in prejudicial behaviour among children and changes in their schoolwork. She obtained measures of their feelings toward each other by asking the children to draw pictures of the way they felt. The picture on the left was drawn by a child who felt 'on top', confident, and capable because he had the superior eye colour.

into the workings of school days within the ecologically valid remit of a classroom 'project' – as often are used by energetic, imaginative teachers. Experiences of a more natural still, freely occurring kind, may likewise enlighten us if we take care to discuss these opportunities for empathy after they have arisen. Such critical examination, however, need not inevitably occur since for many, daily living can be pervaded with numerous other competing concerns. In everyday life, then, reflexivity of such a high order is not necessarily a commonplace social reality, desirable though it may be.

Unfortunately, in many classrooms throughout the world, students are made to feel inferior through their negative interactions with other pupils or their teachers. These students often begin to act in ways to confirm this prejudiced belief and come to internalise this sense of academic inadequacy. In turn, this fosters a scenario characterised by envy, suspicion, self-derogation and disidentification with school and academics by those in the outgroup.

Social psychologist **Elliot Aronson** (1978) and his colleagues found a simple way to change the negative dynamics of such classrooms. The research team created conditions in which school pupils had to depend on one another rather than compete against one another to learn required material. In a technique known as *jigsawing*, each pupil was given part of the total material to master and then share with other group members. Performance was evaluated on the basis of the overall group presentation. Thus, every member's contribution was essential and valued. Pupils were made to feel they were team workers rather than competitors, and those in desegregated settings discovered the advantages of sharing knowledge (and friendship) with 'equal and inter-dependent' peers – regardless of race, creed or sex. Indeed, inter-racial conflict has decreased in classes where jigsawing united formerly hostile students in a common-fate team (Aronson & Gonzalez, 1988).

❖ Cognitive Frameworks and Social Contexts

Having seen how social situations are interpreted can influence behavioural outcomes in a variety of ways, we are ready for another important question: how do people go about constructing their views of other people and understanding their transactions with them within a shared social context? They do so by observing the ways that they and others behave over time in various settings. To this observation they add what they have learned about the kinds of events that seem to precede the enactment of certain behaviours.

Such information helps us form a personal theory, or *mental representation*, of what other people apparently are like, what we ourselves are like, and what engenders human actions and reactions. The general process by which we come to identify what we perceive to be the personal attributes of ourselves and others is called **social perception**.

A major task of everyday social perception in guiding our behaviour involves solving problems in *social inference*: fathoming out what behaviour 'means'; forming accurate impressions; and making reliable predictions about what we and others are likely to do under certain circumstances. We are constantly trying to make sense of our world by applying past knowledge and beliefs to present events, assimilating the novel to the familiar and, at times, accommodating the old to the new. To make social inferences and judgements, we rely on a host of cognitive structures such as schemas, scripts, heuristics (described in Chapters 9 and 12) and personal theories.

Social psychology can be said to be cognitively oriented because it has always found in its analysis of human behaviour a prominent place for the role of subjective perceptions, symbolic causal stimuli and imagined results and, above all, for a thinking being that tries rationally (or otherwise) to make sense of the workings of the social world and physical environment. Before examining several of the most important cognitive theories that have guided research in social psychology, we should pause to identify some diverse conceptions of the human being as a social thinker.

Social thinking: a fivefold diversity

The roles that cognition and motivation have played in social psychological theories cast the social thinker into one of five types: consistency seeker, naive scientist, cognitive miser, motivated tactician and peace keeper (Fiske & Taylor, 1991). These views about various types of social thinking reflect different approaches taken in the study of social cognition.

Consistency-seeking thinkers are disturbed by a perceived inconsistency between their thoughts, feelings and actions. This subjective inconsistency motivates them to reduce the cognitive inconsistency. People change their attitudes and their behaviour in response to the need to make their mental worlds cognitively comfortable (Festinger, 1957; Heider, 1958; Abelson *et al*, 1968). How do you bring into line, for example, the cognitions that you are on a diet and that you just consumed a large chocolate bar all on your own?

For the *naive-scientist* thinkers, motivation recedes

into the background as rational analysis takes over. Thoughts and perceptions of inconsistencies do not motivate these thinkers' actions; they are assumed to be able to tolerate cognitive inconsistencies. They should act as mini-scientists, hypothesis testers, in the pursuit of 'truth', their logical conclusions based on reasoned inferences from carefully collected data about the social environment and as compared against available norms. The shortcomings of this *normative model* became apparent when researchers examined the way people actually went about solving problems of social influence (Ross, 1977). They were not very rational or thoughtful much of the time. Instead, researchers found the alleged naive scientist to be cognitively lazy, avoiding mental effort, sustained attention and careful analysis even when it is necessary, and to be cognitively naive, blindly trusting personal theories, overly confident in personal predictions and overly impressed by vivid, exceptional instances at the cost of utilising substantial base-rate data (Nisbett & Ross, 1980). The tendency for human information processing to be susceptible to many types of errors in thinking makes the naive scientist more naive than scientific (Markus & Zajonc, 1985).

When researchers examined what thinking people actually did rather than the way they were supposed to think, the normative model was replaced by a descriptive cognitive model (Kahneman, Slovic & Tversky, 1982). *Cognitive-miser* thinkers are limited in how well they can come up with accurate solutions to problems in social inference because of inherent limitations in cognitive capacity (Taylor, 1981). They seek to simplify complexity by over-using categorical thinking and stereotypes. They search for quick and easy answers rather than slow and carefully arrived at solutions. When the goal of efficiency dominates that of accuracy, errors and cognitive biases slip in because of inherent features of cognitive systems (as we noted in Chapters 8 and 9).

While the cognitive-miser and naive-scientist views had no use for motivation, the currently accepted approach in social cognition once again finds a place for motivation and emotion in directing cognitive processes (Showers & Cantor, 1985; Langer, 1989). *Motivated-tactician* thinkers blend interests in wise, accurate, adaptable solutions with situational demands for efficiency, personal needs for self-esteem and defensive motives. They want to look good, be liked and approved, get what they want and still get it right. A tall order, but that is what the complex social thinker is all about – using the best tactics to achieve personal goals.

The four types of social thinkers so far discussed have been conceived as processing social information in relative isolation. People as social beings, however, attribute meaning to their worlds in interaction *with*

other people. We are constantly engaged in creating and maintaining a social and moral order via our communications with others. Given that meaning–making is a social process, people's ordinary interactions are of central interest. Thus, the socio-cognitive focus shifts from individuals' decontextualised causal attributions to examining shared ways of reasoning as expressed in their accounting practices (Antaki, 1994). As social beings, we account for disruptions of ordinary interaction so that we may repair any disturbance. Through the deployment of these **accounting practices**, we show that we are competent members of our social group and so keep the peace amongst ourselves. Therefore, social thinkers as *peace keepers* are concerned as much with protecting their positive social identities as they are with the exertion of cognitive control.

Dissonance theory: self-justification

The version of consistency theory that has been most influential within the field of social psychology is the theory of **cognitive dissonance**, as developed by **Leon Festinger** (1957). Cognitive dissonance (outlined in brief in Chapter 10) is the state of conflict someone experiences after making a decision, taking an action, or being exposed to information that is contrary to prior beliefs, feelings or values. It is assumed that when cognitions about one's behaviour and relevant attitudes are dissonant – they do not follow psychologically – an aversive state arises that people are motivated to reduce. Dissonance-reducing activities modify this unpleasant state and achieve consonance among one's cognitions. The motivation to reduce dissonance increases with the magnitude of dissonance created by the cognitive inconsistency. When dissonance arises between something we have done and something we believe or value, the magnitude of dissonance becomes greater as the relevant cognitions are more important; the decision to take the dissonant action is perceived as freely chosen and there is minimal justification for having done so (there are barely sufficient incentives).

Two dissonant cognitions, for example, may concern self-knowledge – '*I smoke*' – and a relevant belief – '*smoking causes lung cancer*'. To reduce the dissonance involved, you could take one of several different actions: change your belief – '*the evidence that smoking causes lung cancer is not very convincing*'; change your behaviour by stopping smoking; re-evaluate the behaviour – '*I don't smoke very much*'; or add new cognitions – '*I smoke low-tar cigarettes*' – that make the inconsistency less serious.

Cognitive dissonance produces a motivation to

make discrepant behaviour seem more rational, as if it followed naturally from personal beliefs and attitudes. If you can't deny that you took an action, you might change your attitudes to make them fit your action. The attitude change is then internalised to make acceptable what otherwise appears to be 'irrational behaviour'. You did something you did not believe in when you had the choice to do otherwise and did so in the absence of sufficient external force to justify why you took the discrepant action. Hundreds of experiments and field studies have shown the power of cognitive dissonance to change attitudes and behaviour (Wicklund & Brehm, 1976).

In the classic dissonance experiment, college students told a lie to other students and came to believe in their lie when they got a small, rather than a large, reward for doing so. The non-obvious prediction that behaviour is more affected by a smaller reward contradicted behaviour theory.

Subjects participated in a very dull task and were then asked (as a favour to the experimenter because his assistant had not shown up) to lie to another subject by saying that the task had been fun and interesting. Half the subjects were paid $20 to tell the lie, while the others were paid only $1 (and asked to be on call for future assistance). The $20 payment was sufficient external justification for lying, but the $1 payment was an inadequate justification for lying. The people who were paid $1 were left with two dissonant cognitions: 'The task was dull' and 'I chose to tell another student it was fun and interesting without a good reason for doing so'.

To reduce their dissonance, these $1 subjects changed their evaluations of the task. They later expressed the belief that 'It really was fun and interesting – I might like to do it again'. In comparison, the subjects who lied for $20 did not change their evaluations – the task was still a bore, they had only lied 'for the money' (Festinger & Carlsmith, 1959; Festinger, 1990).

According to dissonance theory, under conditions of high dissonance, an individual acts to justify his or her behaviour after-the-fact, engages in self-persuasion and often becomes a most convincing communicator and convinced target audience. This analysis says that the way to change attitudes is to first change behaviour (eliciting attitude-inconsistent behaviour under a condition of high choice and low justification). Biblical scholars knew this principle: they urged rabbis not to insist that people believe before praying but to get them to pray first and then they would come to believe.

Self-perception theory

People observe how others act and make inferences about the causes of their actions. They also observe themselves in order to figure out the reasons they act as they do. This notion is at the heart of **self-perception theory**, developed by **Daryl Bem** (1972). People infer what their internal states (beliefs, attitudes, motives and feelings) are or should be by perceiving how they are acting and recalling how they have acted in the past in a given situation. They use that self-knowledge to reason backward to the most likely causes or determinants of their behaviour. The self-perceiver responds to the question, 'Do you like psychology?' by saying, 'Certainly; I do all the readings; I pay attention during lectures and I'm getting good marks in the course'. A question of personal preferences is answered by a behavioural description of relevant actions and situational factors. This process should remind you of William James's theory of emotion (Chapter 10) which proposed that we notice our behaviour (running away or laughing) and infer the relevant emotion of fear or happiness.

Self-perception theory is cognitive, with no motivational component posited as energising reactions. By the time we get to be adults, we do have a great deal of self-knowledge without having to infer what it is by perceiving how we just behaved. Self-perception processes occur mainly when we are in ambiguous situations and dealing with unfamiliar events, where we have a 'need for structure regarding some novel attitude object' (Fazio, 1987). One flaw in the process of gaining self-knowledge through self-perception is that people are often insensitive about the extent to which their behaviour is governed by socio-contextual influences. Thus, for example, they may err in inferring their strengths and weaknesses by observing their successes and failures without adequately taking into account the contributions made by the social context. It is remarkable how much we can fail to recognise obvious constraints and supports for our behaviour in 'external' settings, such as social roles that are situationally determined and inter-subjectively defined.

Student research subjects were asked to play a 'University Challenge' type of quiz game in which one contestant was arbitrarily chosen to ask the other difficult questions for which he or she – the questioner – knew the answers. At the end of the session, the questioner, the contestant and observers rated the general knowledge of both questioner and contestant. Although they had only this limited, biased sample of evidence on which to base their inferences, all involved rated the questioner as far more knowledgeable than the contestant or the 'average' university student. The contestant's self-perception was of not being able to answer all the questions that the questioner asked, thus inferring less 'cleverness'. However, the contestant's socio-situational analysis failed to include awareness of the role advantage the questioner had been given in selecting to ask about known esoteric areas of information (Ross et al, 1977).

Attribution theory: causal inferences

One of the most important inferential tasks facing all social perceivers is determining the causes for events. We want to know the 'why's' of life. Why did my boyfriend break off the relationship? Why did she get the job and not me? Why did my parents divorce after so many years of marriage? All such why's lead to an analysis of the possible causal determinants for some action, event or outcome. We are said to be making attributions when we attempt to explain the occurrence of an event by attributing it to a particular cause. **Attribution theory**, then, is a general approach to describing the ways we, as social perceivers, use information to generate 'common-sense' causal explanations for events. This theoretical framework has come to play an important role not only in social psychological thinking but in many other areas of psychology, because it focuses on a fundamental yet ubiquitous aspect of human functioning – the way people make **causal attributions** about events in their lives. Thereby, through the deployment of such explanations, people account to others and to themselves for the origins of, for example, their achievements (Weiner, 1986), their depression (Abramson *et al*, 1978), or, for that matter, the quality of their partnerships (Fincham & Bradbury, 1987).

The intuitive psychologist

The origin of attribution theory came from the writings of **Fritz Heider** (1958), another transplanted European social psychologist working in the United States. Heider argued that people continually make causal analyses as part of their attempts at general comprehension of the social world. Such causal understanding serves the basic functions of predicting future events and trying to control them. If you know what makes your best friend get upset, then you may be able to reduce or induce that reaction by managing those causal conditions. Two general questions that Heider believed are part of most attributional analyses are: firstly, whether the cause of the behaviour is

found within the person (*internal causality*) or within the social context (*external causality*); and secondly, who is responsible for the outcomes? A woman kills her husband; her defence is that he had been battering her for years and she was fearful of her life and her children's when he was drunk, which was becoming ever more frequent. The judicial outcome of the case rests largely on the determination of causality for her admitted crime, given the mitigating circumstances.

Heider suggested that instead of developing theories about how people are *supposed* to think and act, psychologists should discover the personal theories – belief systems – that ordinary people themselves use to make sense of the causes and effects of behaviour. Likewise, Herbert Simon (1955) made a similar and contemporaneous plea in the form of a distinction between 'rational' and 'behavioural' criteria. Heider argued that we are all **intuitive psychologists** who are trying to work out what people are like and what causes their behaviour, akin to professional psychologists who do this for a living. Heider used a simple film to demonstrate the tendency for people to leap from observing actions to making causal inferences and attributing motives to what they see. The film involved three geometric figures that moved around an object without any pre-arranged plan. Research subjects, however, were found always to make up narratives for these shapes, thereby animating the action still further; the figures were transformed by such designations into social actors – personality traits, motives and causes being attributed to their movements so as to explain apparent 'behaviour' (see *Figure 13.5*).

FIGURE 13.5	HEIDER'S DEMONSTRATION OF THE TENDENCY TO MAKE CAUSAL ATTRIBUTIONS

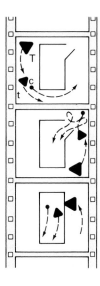

These geometric figures were stimuli in a convincing demonstration of the fact that we infer rather than observe personal characteristics and causes. When subjects were shown a film in which the geometrical forms simply moved in and out of the large rectangle at different speeds and in different patterns, they attributed underlying 'motivations' to the 'characters'. They often 'saw' the triangles as two males fighting over a female (the circle). The large triangle was 'seen' as being aggressive, the small triangle as being heroic, and the circle as being timid. In the sequence shown here, most observers reported seeing T chase t and c into the house and close the door.

The covariation principle

Attribution theory was bolstered by the contributions of **Harold Kelley** (1967) who focused on the issue that often we have to make causal attributions for events under conditions of uncertainty. We may not have sufficient information, the information we have may be poor or vague, our self-confidence may be low, or our capacities may be limited to solving the inferential problem at hand. We then seek out additional information and are susceptible to social influence from peers and experts. In cases where we have access to information about multiple events, Kelley maintains that we tend to employ the **covariation principle** to infer the causes of events – by observing co-occurrences of two events: people will attribute a behaviour to a causal factor if that factor was present whenever the behaviour occurred but was absent whenever it did not occur. For example, in trying to work out why you were unable to sleep one night, you might analyse what events and activities were associated with the experience of insomnia that were in fact absent on those nights when you did sleep well. Caffeine becomes a likely causal candidate if you had late-night coffee and you usually do not drink it. However, many potential causes could be lurking in the explanatory woods: suppose you had just acquired a new bed, that you were upset too about failing a mid-term exam, you were also excited about a big competition the following morning and there was a noisy party next door – in these circumstances, to assess which event or set of events were causally related to your difficulties in sleeping, requires a more complex attributional process in which you must consider multiple events.

Kelley formalised Heider's line of thinking by specifying the variables that people use to make their attributions. His model suggests that causal attribution may proceed as a form of 'analysis of variance' (the anagram for which is ANOVA). This ANOVA model, as it has become known, draws upon the way in which variability in behavioural outcomes may be partitioned by the attributional process to its different sources. In this vein, Kelley proposed that people assess covariation information across three dimensions relevant to the person whose acts they are trying to explain: distinctiveness, consistency and consensus. *Distinctiveness* refers to whether the entity or event is unique such that the effect occurs only when this is present. *Consistency* refers to whether the effect occurs each time and across different situations when the entity is present. *Consensus,* or normativeness, refers to whether other people also experience the same effect with respect to the entity. We use these three sources of information to determine if some experience or effect is due to a cause in ourselves (an 'internal' attribution) or derives from something or someone we perceive to be situated externally to us (an 'external' attribution). Note, though, that we can ascribe casuality to the personal dispositions of ourselves – an internal attribution – or similarly to the personal dispositions of those with whom we are interacting – an external attribution. Thus, in Kelley's terms such dispositional attributions can be both internal or external.

In the insomnia example, you want to know if it is 'you' (your psychological arousal) or an external variable (coffee, mattress, noise) that caused the sleeplessness in order to cope better with the problem in the future. External attributions are likely to be made when there is high distinctiveness, high consistency and high consensus. For example, you get a compliment from an attractive person. You say 'Thanks, I appreciate you mentioning it'. Afterwards, though, you begin to wonder what really caused that effect (the complimenting behaviour). If the behaviour is distinctive (no one else ever compliments you), you might tentatively attribute it to the person with whom you have interacted, believing him or her to be an habitual flatterer or a trickster who is always 'on the make'. If also, however, the person invariably compliments you in many different situations, his or her consistency tells you more – surely – (in conjunction with high distinctiveness) about the person than about the target of the compliment (i.e. you). If in addition, then, the person frequently acts this way with others, the high consensus coupled with the high consistency and high distinctiveness of the behaviour confirms your worst suspicions. You are likely to make an attribution to an external cause (i.e. to the flatterer) and not to features of yourself – to 'internal' such as your appearance which you were hoping had in fact motivated the compliment.

A recent alternative to Kelley's covariation-based model, that has reworked the role of concensus, distinctiveness and consistency information into a new theory of causal attribution, is the *Abnormal Conditions Focus Model* (Hilton & Slugoski, 1986). Within this knowledge-based model, the authors challenge Kelley's (and other's) 'man-as-scientist' notion of causal inference, disputing the assumption that a cause is designated only when the presence or absence of personal and situational factors can be observed to covary with the occurrence of the target event. Rather, they argue that human, 'common-sense' inference processes do not operate through formal logical rules of inference but via *nonlogical, content-based* processes. Denis Hilton and Ben Slugoski demonstrate that common-sense notions of causation are predicated upon an assumption that for a condition to be dignified with causal status, it must be adjudged to be 'abnormal' (i.e. unusual or infrequent) when contrasted against the remaining field of other background conditions that are necessary (but not sufficient) for the target event to occur.

This **contrastive** (rather than covariational) **criterion** of causal ascription, they propose, interacts with knowledge about the perceived normal state of affairs in the world. By such a process, conditions ('abnormal' ones) are selected as causes that would not have been designated, however, by the content-*in*dependent logical rules of inference as laid down in the ANOVA model. Any conditions necessary for the occurrence of the target event that are not designated as 'abnormal' are consigned to the status of plain background conditions. In this way, abnormal conditions become identified as causes of the event or behaviour in question.

The implications of the research on which this model is based are far reaching since causal attributions can be predicted more accurately by this approach than with traditional ANOVA theory. In simplified terms, the model states that when we wish to account for the occurrence of an event, we search over the biography of our recent past, arraying the necessary conditions but for which the event would not have occurred. Then, depending on what contrast we make, we identify a condition that we adjudge to be the 'abnormal' one and ascribe causality to it.

Take the example of a man in his early sixties who has become exhausted and cannot understand the reasons for his symptomatology. In looking for a cause, he searches back over his past, noting that two years previously he was hospitalised for a particularly virulent month-long chest infection. He also recalls that prior to this, he was made redundant from his job. Later, he discloses that since that time, he has not socialised with friends from work or elsewhere. Lastly, he reveals that he has remained at home to look after his chronically arthritic wife. Thus, there are four 'conditions' which may account for his symptomatology. Yet in his attributional search, he ascribes causality to the virus since for him this is the 'abnormal condition': after all, he reasons, many people in his area and of his age are unemployed, have a partner with chronic health problems and have restricted social support networks. Few, though, in his estimation are hospitalised for a month by a flu-like virus. He describes his complaint, then, as 'post-viral fatigue syndrome'.

To his doctor, however, who sees the effects of such viruses on the elderly every day in his surgery, the abnormal condition is his patient's enforced and unwanted redundancy. Therefore, he attributes the presenting symptoms to the

long-term consequences of job-loss and subsequently diagnoses reactive depression. This formulation is supported by the patient confiding further that when he was working he felt like a 'flower in full bloom', but that now he feels 'withered and crumpled'. For the physician, the therapeutic task was to help the patient reconceptualise his somatic state in terms of psychosocial antecedents and thereafter to take action to alleviate his depressed mood. For the elderly man, however, his task was to elicit medication from his doctor that would alleviate what he considered to be his long-standing and organically precipitated illness. Thus, depending on what contrast was made by the doctor or patient, two dissimilar events henceforth were ascribed causal status – and importantly, two different complaints diagnosed.

The emergence of the Abnormal Conditions Focus Model – at the expense of the covariation-based ANOVA theory – also points up the dangers of formulating psychological frameworks around the skeletal outlines provided by statistical techniques, a danger which Jaspars (1986) alludes to in his critique of North American social psychology and as discussed earlier in this chapter. Such analytic methods may be of help to us when we wish to explore empirically derived numeric data. However, it appears unwise to import their underlying principles into the building of models that as a result appear to have neither content nor context, but which seek nevertheless to explain why people do what they do, think what they think or say what they say. Interestingly the authors point out that the abnormal conditions focus model more closely mirrors what occurs when causal ascriptions are made within the ecologically valid context of ordinary conversational exchanges, a theme taken up and elaborated upon by Hilton (1990).

Many studies, however, besides that of Hilton and Slugoski (1986), have been conducted to refine and extend attribution theory (Fiske & Taylor, 1991). These studies reveal the conditions under which the search for causal explanations sometimes proceeds rationally with a systematic search of available information and also when the social thinker is more rationalising than rational. You can probably imagine wanting to believe that something special about you elicited a compliment. If so, you might not want to find out if the attractive person's reaction to you was commonplace. You could end up with the conclusion you desire by distorting the attributional search through selective questioning or by limiting observations. Also, in many ongoing interpersonal situations there is not time for systematic analysis to occur, so heuristic processes take over. When personal goals, motives and strongly held attitudes get in the way of systematic analysis of causes, the attributional process is biased. One class of attributional biases is known as the **self-serving bias**, in which people tend to take credit for their successes while denying responsibility for their failures. This is an instance of the motivated tactician at work, protecting the self-esteem of the social thinker. Within individualistic societies, self-serving biases are quite robust, occurring in many situations for most people. However, researchers disagree about the occurrence of the self-serving bias across cultures. Some have found this bias to be trans-cultural (Fletcher & Ward, 1988); others have demonstrated that in collectivist settings where interdependence is emphasised, there is a bias towards 'modesty' – towards explaining success in terms of contextual factors (Fry & Ghosh 1980; Boski, 1983).

Overemphasising dispositions: the fundamental attribution error

One of the most pervasive attributional biases within individualistic cultures is the tendency for social perceivers to identify dispositional variables as the causes of most behaviours. Many people too readily identify personal traits in the actor – shyness, generosity, honesty, hystericalness – as the causes of his or her observed behaviour. An explanation for the predominance of dispositional accounting practices comes from cultural socialisation theory and stresses the role of the 'cult of the individual' which implicitly advocates notions of personal initiative and responsibility for achievement, immorality, legal liability and madness. Historically, such a 'conversational reality' (Shotter, 1993) has gradually been constructed within our daily explanatory discourses over time, suffusing these practices to the point that such a vocabulary of individualisation has become inscribed upon us and upon our conceptual behaviour. This has led to positioning and containing us within specific linguistically mediated social and relational orders (Rose, 1989).

So, if repeatedly we are focused too much on dispositions, what are we overlooking? Situational attributions and contextual factors tend to get ignored because of the dominating influence of dispositions. Observers take behaviour too much at 'face value', as reflecting something stable about the disposition of the actor, often disregarding prominent situational stimuli that account for the behaviour. **Lee Ross** (1977) has termed this dual tendency to overestimate dispositional causes of behaviour and to underestimate situational ones the **fundamental attribution error** (FAE). Evidence abounds that people infer

TABLE 13.1	REASONS FOR THE FUNDAMENTAL ATTRIBUTION ERROR

Information: Social realities in the situation (norms, power relationships) may be unknown to the observer.

Ideology: People tend to accept the doctrine of personal responsibility for their actions.

Perception: To observers, actors are figures that stand out against the background of the situation.

Language: Western languages have many more terms for describing personality than for describing situations.

dispositions from behaviour even when it is clearly contextually produced, as when they know the person had no choice, or was arbitrarily assigned to engage in the behaviour (for example, the role playing in the University Challenge study), or was in an unusual setting that made most people behave similarly (as in the Milgram study). Not only do we overlook important situational context factors that control behavioural reactions, we also make overly confident predictions when we have only a small amount of trait information (Ross & Nisbett, 1991). *Table 13.1* provides a list of reasons as to why the fundamental attribution error is so deeply ingrained.

Research shows, however, that the fundamental attributional error is absent or at least significantly reduced in societies and settings which emphasise mutual interdependence. Trafimow *et al* (1991), for example, demonstrated how merely being induced temporarily to think of oneself as linked to others led to greater use of context-oriented causal explanations. Conversely, they found also that thinking of oneself as separate and independent from others led to greater use of dispositional attributions. The error of assigning causality to dispositions, then, can only be considered 'fundamental' to those situated within predominantly individualistic cultural settings. Where a collectivist ethos prevails, this error is less likely to be a feature of everyday discourse (Smith & Bond, 1993).

Within individualistic contexts, however, we are perhaps all guilty at times of making the fundamental attribution error. On a societal level, the fundamental attribution error can be seen in the tendency to blame the victim (Ryan, 1976). Many people tend to hold the victims of poverty and racial discrimination personally responsible for their plights. Disregarding socio-contextual influences upon behaviour is in many instances, then, a moral as well as a psychological judgement. Unemployment among minorities can lead, for example, to the attribution 'They're lazy', squalid living conditions to 'They're filthy' and high rates of

When people see evidence of poverty, they infer negative individual dispositions instead of perceiving connections between urban society and urban problems.

crime to 'They're bad'. Somehow, the external societal variables that foster these conditions are largely overlooked and, instead, the consequences of poverty are blamed on the personal deficits of the poor. Similarly, people often blame rape on its victims – as if the unfortunate person invited the assault. This failure of 'attributional charity', ignoring the possible situational causes of negative events, can become part of a more general reactionary political philosophy that has dire social policy implications. This pervasive way of thinking about the causes of behaviour is revealed in a recent article by a conservative lawyer Mona Charen, who was a speech writer for past Republican President Ronald Reagan. In writing about the 'crack' epidemic in major American inner cities, she inadvertently typified the individualistic position of political conservatives. Charen wrote:

> *Conservatives see people destroying their lives by ingesting drugs and conclude that the problem lies not with the society but the lack of self-control on the part of the individuals involved (Charen, 1990).*

Perhaps not far removed from such a sentiment is former British Prime Minister Margaret Thatcher's claim that, contrary to popular belief, there is 'no such thing as society; there are individual men and women, and there are families' (*Womens Own Magazine,* 31 October 1987). Thus, the psychology of the fundamental attribution error has many implications for academic psychology and also, as we can see, for how we think of and construct our political as well as social worlds.

 A *'Social'* Social Psychology?

Let us now return to themes addressed by Jaspars (1986), as mentioned earlier in this chapter. We have considered much of the experimental research within the psychology of social influence and social cognition. We have seen that although this grew out of a largely post-war North American tradition, there have been significant European protagonists (notably Moscovici and Tajfel). In the field of social influence, research has focused both upon intergroup behaviour and upon the influence of the group with respect to 'individual' behaviour. As to social cognition, undoubtedly there has developed a large caucus of experimental work within this arena, both past and present. A growing body of work, however, has been directed at the way in which social realities are represented and negotiated via the shared environment of language rather than upon the personal perceptions and cognitions of individuals. What we perceive as a social reality, then, is very much created in **joint action** (Shotter, 1984). Such a realisation dramatically shifts the focus of psychology and of social science away from the individual as the originator of social realities and behaviour, to focusing upon the constructive aspects of relations *between* individuals. Particularly along these latter lines then, social psychology has been evolving in more ostensibly 'social' directions.

To illustrate this 'social' theme of social psychology, let us briefly return to attribution theory to get a flavour of current directions therein to be found both on the European and North American continents. Dissatisfied with the more cognitive approaches to causal attribution, **Derek Edwards** and **Jonathan Potter** (1993) most recently have proposed what they call a *Discursive Action Model* (DAM) in which the role of language as a form of social action, through conversation, is made more central to developing understandings of causal reasoning. They state that their model is not yet one in the classical sense. Rather, it is formulated at the present time at a meta-theoretical level. A set of principles have been outlined, as too has the phenomena the model covers and the kinds of empirical work needed to test it. Just as Heider, in his original statement, demarcated the general territory of attribution theory at its inception, Edwards and Potter have sought now to do likewise with the Discursive Action Model. At core, this model conceives of attributions as *discursive* actions: that is to say, as things people do through the socio-tactical deployment of language, not as ones they just perceive or think; as such they may constitute a segment of an activity sequence which itself is embedded within interpersonal and intergroup concerns, such as the designation of blame and responsibility. Thus, the discursive model seeks to make conspicuous a more 'social' account of attributions, seeing them as occurring within relational settings and serving social functions. As such, this meta-theoretical model is a significant signpost for the way in which theories of causal reasoning in the future are likely to develop and indeed for the way in which social psychology is currently evolving, particularly within Europe.

In outlining this position, Edwards and Potter (1993) state that empirical support for the model comes from qualitative studies of talk and text. They argue that the use of quantitative experimental methods are inappropriate since such prescriptive forms of investigation by their very nature obscure the subtlety of the relationship between ordinary language and attributional explanation. In particular, they cite an example from Wetherell and Potter (1989) of the way in which excuses for police violence can be constructed through the discursive deployment of 'personality' and 'role' talk as forms of attributional accounting: '*I think the police acted very well; they're only human; . . . they've got to do their job*'. Attributional analyses are situated and performed here within a social context. A universalising trait and an occupational role category are used to actively construct *consensus* – the implication being that anybody and everybody in that circumstance would have behaved in that way. Causality is assigned not just cognitively so as to explain the origins of actions, but rather is employed strategically through social discourse to excuse them.

The emergence of the **discursive turn** in social psychology, as Harré and Gillett (1994) have called it, has gathered momentum particularly over the last two decades since the publication of seminal works by Berger and Luckman (1966) and Harré and Secord (1972). Indeed, its antecedents can be traced back further to philosophers of ordinary language and to Wittgenstein's (1953) assault on the bases of logical positivism. A full consideration here, though, of these underpinning notions lies beyond the scope of this introduction. However, legitimate discontent manifested itself, for example, in terms of **John Shotter's** (1975) important protest against viewing people in psychological investigations as social 'objects', who can simply be scrutinised and understood in the same way that the natural sciences examine phenomena in the 'physical' world.

There has emerged, then, a significant lobby within contemporary social psychology who are in disagreement with the positivist supposition of a hypothetical reality that ultimately is completely knowable through conventional 'scientific' enquiry. Rather, they argue that psychological realities are largely **socially constructed** (as outlined briefly in Chapter 1) through the shared environment of language. They wish to recognise and point out that

how we talk about the world, how we represent it to one another through the rhetoric of language and discourse, significantly shapes what we understand to be 'reality', in all its guises, particularly when we try to fathom the 'whys' and 'wherefores' of human social behaviour. Irrespective of whether reality *is* totally 'constructed', it renders that reality no less 'real' for those engaged within it. Nevertheless, from the constructivist perspective, 'truths' (whether in academic psychology or elsewhere) are viewed as malleable and changeable **narratives** – a position that is sometimes referred to as that of **post-modernism**. Indeed, **Kenneth Gergen** (1985) puts forward the case that all psychological knowledge is socially constructed and *relative* in terms of its historical, linguistic and cultural contexts. In recognition of this ever-changing diversity of 'stories' about reality, a different focus and methodology (largely qualitative and centring on people's verbal accounts of their actions) has been preferred and appropriated, given most detailed exposition of late in the discourse analytic techniques expounded by Potter and Wetherell (1987). Precursors to such analysis, however, have included the participant observation and interview techniques advocated by ethno-methodologists and anthropologists (notably Mead, 1928; 1939).

The implications of this emerging paradigm – of the discursive turn – are manifold for the way in which social psychology is developing both in terms of conceptual debates and methodological issues (Curt, 1994; Stainton-Rogers *et al*, 1995). Utilising here the Discursive Action Model as an example, we have touched upon how these innovations are changing the subject of social psychology. In so doing, we have provided a foretaste of the ways in which this more '*social*' social psychology is evolving.

Social Relevance of Social Psychology

We have seen that two important messages that emerge from social psychology are: firstly, the pervasiveness and persuasiveness of social (situational) influence processes; and secondly, the construction of social reality by the person as a social perceiver in a shared, behavioural setting. When these two fundamental principles are taken together, they lead to a significant conclusion with important implications for how we conduct our lives. Principally people are similar to one another in their key biological and psychological processes. Whenever this assumption of similarity is violated – someone seems or acts differently from us – we should base our subsequent actions on an awareness of two possibilities: firstly, that their situation is likely to be different from ours or may indeed have changed in some way that we have not noticed; and secondly, that their perception of the scenario we are now sharing is very probably different in some important way that we may also not recognise.

The source of much human misunderstanding and social conflict between groups and nations, is the belief that we, as reasonable people, perceive the world or some vital part of it accurately – the only rational way it could be seen – while they, the other side who sees it differently, are wrong. These differences go beyond merely point-of-view variations when we attribute to ourselves personal characteristics that justify this difference – our wisdom, goodness or righteousness – and to them characteristics such as stupidity, foolishness and inadequacies. Each group or nation attributes negative dispositions to other groups and nations and positive ones to itself, all the while ignoring the contextual determinants of the differences that, if changed, can reverse its perceptions and actions.

The error that individuals and societies make by overemphasising such personal or dispositional determinants of behaviour while simultaneously underestimating the situational or contextual factors that are operating can have serious consequences. Such misguided attributions often lead to policy decisions to deal with social problems by changing those who are 'different' through re-education, therapy, conversion, segregation, imprisonment or execution. Social psychological wisdom, however, does not excuse destructive, anti-social deeds by demonstrating their contextual determinants. Rather, it shows that the best way to change problem behaviours is to change or reconstruct problem 'situations'. For example, it does not appear that a governmental so-called 'war on crime' can ever be won by identifying 'criminals' (dispositional finger pointing), by sentencing them to long prison terms and building ever more prisons to hold them without identifying and trying to change the root conditions in society (situational and socio-contextual determinants) that make many disadvantaged people turn to lives of crime in the first instance.

INTERIM SUMMARY

To understand the way situations exert substantial influence over, and are reciprocally related to, many forms of behaviour, social psychologists analyse the way people perceive, interpret and give meaning to features of action within diverse settings and contexts. In so doing, *each* person constructs his or her version of social reality. This is the second

important message, or principle, of social psychology. Research evidence from laboratory and field studies illustrates the way beliefs and expectations can come to guide actions and shape aspects of the behavioural setting. Predictions can become self-fulfilling prophesies that lead to desirable outcomes, such as improved student achievement, by changing the way the relevant behavioural actors view the situation. Our expectancies can be confirmed by our verbal and nonverbal actions which induce in others the actions we expect them to show, without anyone's conscious awareness of the process involved. The cognitive tendency to simplify complex information processing by categorising people can contribute to prejudiced attitudes and discriminatory behaviour against those categorised as different and inferior. Minimal cue differences are sufficient to make extreme categorisations, as in the case of the blue-eyed and brown-eyed schoolchildren. Some effects of prejudice can be reversed by changing aspects of situations that foster new conceptions of the people in them, as demonstrated in the jigsaw classroom research.

Many social psychologists have long endorsed the use of cognitive frameworks in understanding social phenomena. They have been interested in issues of social perception and social cognition, in learning how people go about constructing mental representations of their world. Cognitive theories abound to explain the ways social thinkers make sense of the stimuli and responses they experience and create. Some theoretical approaches emphasise motivation, while others are more purely cognitive. Dissonance theory accounts for the self-justification that people engage in when they have behaved in ways that are discrepant from their internal states. The tension that is created by cognitive dissonance is reduced by changing some aspect of the situation or of oneself. Self-perception theory suggests that we infer our internal states, attitudes, beliefs and emotions from perceptions of our behaviour in its social context. Attribution theory is a general attempt to describe the ways in which people find the causes for the behaviour they observe in others and themselves. Some attributional rules lead to explanations that are based on the perceived traits of the actor and others on the nature of the situation. However, there is a biased tendency to make the fundamental attribution error by over-using dispositional explanations and under-utilising situational ones, even when the evidence is manifestly in favour of the situational dimension. Important social and political implications follow on from the tendency to blame people for failure and negative outcomes versus examining their life situations.

❖ SOLVING SOCIAL PROBLEMS

Numerous social psychologists are strongly motivated by the laudable goal of improving the human condition. European psychologist **Hilde Himmelweit**, for example, has developed what she has called a **societal psychology** as a form of social psychology that is concerned with social issues such as ecology, genocide and medical ethics (Himmelweit & Gaskell, 1990). This concern with improving our societal lot, however, can be thought of as being expressed – broadly speaking – in two major ways. Firstly, studies by social psychologists are often carried out in natural field settings as well as in laboratory analogies of those natural settings – in housing projects, at dances, in nursing homes, in factories or wherever the action is to be found (Rodin, 1985). Efforts are made to include elements of mundane realism in the experimental situation and to capture the conceptual essence of the vital phenomena in simulations of real-world settings. Secondly, the knowledge obtained from basic research and theories is used to explain social phenomena and systematic attempts are made to apply that knowledge to remedy a range of social problems (Deutsch & Hornstein, 1975). A major organisation of social psychologists, the Society for the Psychological Study of Social Issues, is in fact dedicated to just that principle.

Kurt Lewin, a founding figure of social psychology, believed that for psychology to make its greatest contribution, theory and research must be integrated with practical application. 'No action without research, no research without action' was his dictum (1948). He practiced what he preached by conducting research designed to solve social problems, while yielding significant information about the underlying social processes involved. An example is his study of the way to get families during the Second World War to eat food that they did not necessarily like – such as liver and kidneys – but that was plentiful, nutritious and cheap. Lewin arranged for one group of parents to hear a persuasive lecture on the positive effects of serving these meats to their families. Others met in small groups to discuss the issue. The persuasive lecture had little effect on the women's attitudes or behaviour. However, the democratically run discussion groups made many of the women far more likely to take the socially beneficial action of providing the visceral meats for their families (Lewin, 1947).

The key idea in this research was the effectiveness of involving people in the decision-making process – 'participatory management' – and of making public commitments to other members of one's group. Later research showed that workers who are given an active role in decisions about production perform far better on the job, are more efficient and report greater satisfaction than do passive workers who get paid for doing only what they are ordered to do (Coch & French, 1948; Pelz, 1955; 1965). This former commendable approach, however, did not conform to the North American ethic of individualism as it bore a superficial resemblance to what was seen as the unacceptable face of communism. In Japan, however, where societal norms favour group-based behaviour, this approach was enthusiastically enacted. It was a costly missed opportunity for the businesses of other less progressive nations.

The focus on solving social problems moves us a long way from the traditional view of psychology as the study of individual actions and mental processes. We become aware of the person as only one point in a complex system that includes social groups, institutions, cultural values, historical circumstances, political and economic realities and specific situational influences. Modern social psychologists have expanded the domain of their inquiry to include this broader network of interacting elements. Many new areas of application have opened up to both the curious investigator and the psychologist as social change agent.

Social psychological knowledge is applied in many different areas, including law, education, health, politics (international relations, conflict resolution, public policy), consumer behaviour, business, the environment (ecology) and a field of importance to everyone, peace psychology (Oskamp, 1984; Rodin, 1985). We dealt at length with health psychology in Chapter 11. Here we will look at environmental psychology and peace psychology.

 Environmental Psychology

Systematic study of the effects of the larger environment (in contrast to specific stimuli) on behaviour began in the 1950s with studies of behaviour in psychiatric wards, where different physical arrangements of objects and people seemed to produce different patient behaviour. Such studies have led to the new field of **environmental psychology** (Proshansky, 1976; Altman & Christensen, 1990).

Environmental psychologists study the relationships between psychological processes and physical environments, both natural and human-made (Darley & Gilbert, 1985). Environmental psychologists use an ecological approach to study the way people and environments affect each other. The ecological approach emphasises the reciprocity and mutual influence in a person–environment relationship. Person and environment influence each other, and both keep changing as a result. We see a circular pattern – we change the natural environment and create physical and social structures that in turn confine, direct and change us, encouraging certain behaviours and discouraging or preventing others, often in unanticipated ways.

Environmental psychology is oriented not so

Environmental psychologists use an ecological approach to make cities more livable.

Can we make our cities more livable and user-friendly? What features of the environment encourage vandalism and crime? Does crowding cause physical and social pathology? What is the impact of uncontrollable levels of noise in the workplace or the home? Can psychological knowledge contribute to energy conservation programmes? These are among the intriguing questions being studied by environmental psychologists. By reformulating massive social issues into smaller, less overwhelming problems, social psychologists are beginning to obtain small victories that can add up to big ones (Weick, 1984).

Recognition that natural energy is a limited resource throughout the world is leading social psychologists with interests in environmental psychology to develop strategies for aiding people in conserving energy and water in drought-sensitive areas and in reducing reliance on petroleum. The close-up section of this chapter shows one approach to energy conservation involving the use of social psychological principles.

much toward past determinants of behaviour as toward the future being created. This orientation means that environmental psychologists have to be concerned with *values*. Some environments are more nourishing for us than others and some uses of the environment are destructive. This new psychology is concerned with identifying what makes environments supportive and what human behaviours are involved in creating and maintaining those environments, while not trespassing on the health of the ecosystem that makes life possible in the first place (Russell & Ward, 1982).

There is ample evidence of the influence of physical design on psychological activities and processes. Different physical arrangements have been studied in hospital settings, workplaces, homes and entire cities. Different moods, self-images and overt behaviours are consistently found to be related to these physical differences. The way space is partitioned can help bring people together or isolate them. The type of windows in an apartment building can encourage residents to look out at activities on their streets and keep an eye on the neighbourhood or it can discourage such people watching. An architect can design space to appeal to snobbery, to invite informality or to induce confusion (Altman, 1976).

❖ Peace Psychology

Psychologists for Peace is an organisation of psychologists in Great Britain, as elsewhere, who not only study various aspects of the complex issues involved in war and peace but conduct educational programmes on these topics. In addition, they try to have input in relevant political decision-making policies at local and national levels. This organisation is just one example of the dual roles that many psychologists have chosen to play as dedicated social scientists and, at other times, as committed, impassioned advocates of socio-political action based on knowledge and personal values. How to help resolve the dilemmas of superpower competition or, for that matter, many of the domestic and international problems that we now face, poses challenges that psychology is well equipped to study. **Peace psychology** represents an interdisciplinary approach to the prevention of nuclear war and maintenance of peace (Plous, 1985).

Some of these psychologists are conducting research that examines the basis for false beliefs, misperceptions and erroneous attributions on issues relevant to nuclear arms, military strength, risk and national security. They study the fears of children and the anxieties of adults about nuclear war. Exploring some of the individual and cultural forces that create war and promote peace involves studies of propaganda and images of the enemy through content and fantasy analysis of violence and war themes in the

FIGURE 13.6	FACES OF THE ENEMY

Notice how the cartoonists have dehumanised the 'enemy' in each case.

media. Although most cultures oppose individual aggression as a crime, nations train millions of soldiers to kill. Part of this mass social influence involves dehumanising the soldiers of the other side into 'the enemy' – nonhuman objects to be hated and destroyed. This dehumanisation is accomplished through political rhetoric and the media, notably cartoonists, in their vivid depictions of the enemy. Sketches of the enemy can arouse fear and unconscious anxieties and stimulate hostile imaginings and beliefs. A variety of dehumanising faces is superimposed over the enemy to allow him to be killed without guilt. The problem for members of the national militia is how to convert the act of murder into that of patriotism (Keen, 1986). According to army veterans, a soldier's most important weapon in war is not a gun but this internalised view of the hated enemy (see *Figure 13.6*).

We will examine here a few of the directions being taken by some peace psychologists. For quite some time, social scientists have been investigating arms negotiations, international crisis management

Undoubtedly, the unchecked consumption of petroleum products is linked to air pollution, oil-spills and even to war. However, drivers stopped for speeding on a motorway were asked what they thought about slowing down to save oil. Some of their responses included 'I never really thought about it', 'There's a lot of oil around . . .', and 'We have enough . . . to keep us going' (Stipp, 1991).

These views persist despite apparent changes in attitudes toward conservation. A 1989 national poll reported that 80 per cent of people in the USA believed that 'protecting the environment is so important that requirements and standards cannot be too high, and continuing environmental improvements must be made regardless of cost' (Hayes, 1991).

However committed people may feel about the principle of preserving the earth, their actual behaviour is another matter. How do you get people to act differently? An experiment by social psychologist **Elliot Aronson** (1990) suggests that modelling the desired behaviour is much more effective than simply telling people what they should be doing. Administrators at the University of California at Santa Cruz wanted students to conserve energy and water. Because students at UC Santa Cruz claimed to be ardent environmentalists, the bureaucrats believed that displaying a conservation message on signs would lead to significant changes in behaviour.

A sign on the wall of the men's shower room at the sports pavilion encouraged water conservation by urging users to '(1) Wet down. (2) Turn water off. (3) Soap up. (4) Rinse off'. Over a period of five days, only six per cent of the men taking showers followed the

suggested routine. When the sign was placed on a tripod and moved to a more prominent spot at the shower room entrance, compliance went up to 19 per cent. However, the overall effectiveness of the sign was probably negligible, as some users, resenting the sign, knocked it over and took extra long showers.

Finally, all signs were removed and a student modelled the newly required shower-taking behaviour: 'Our stooge entered the shower room when it was momentarily empty, turned on the tap, and waited with his back turned to the entrance. As soon as he heard someone enter, he followed the admonition of the sign: he turned off the water, soaped up, rinsed off and left'. Compliance under this approach jumped to 49 per cent. When two models were used, 67 per cent of those who observed them followed their lead. Aronson concluded that modelling works better than signs because it 'provides a checkpoint from similar people of what is reasonable behaviour in a given situation' (Aronson, 1990).

If governments really want people to conserve energy, perhaps our national leaders should (a) be driven in smaller cars; (b) travel on

public aircraft rather than by special jet; and (c) take showers with a friend. More realistically, recycling of disposable waste products, such as paper, glass and metal, can be vastly expanded by having door-to-door weekly pickups arranged through city contracts with local waste disposal companies and scrap dealers. Any efforts at energy conservation must involve minimal human energy consumption; since most people are not going to go to distant recycling centres, the services have to come to them. Once the service is established, several psychological factors come into play. Seeing neighbours using their different coloured recycling bins once a week creates social pressure for others to conform to this new neighbourhood standard. Periodic feedback from the collecting company or the city about the extent of success of the recycling programme through the media or in flyers sent with bills for standard services (such as electricity or gas supply) will help sustain individual efforts. Another social modelling tactic is to distribute signs to regular recyclers to put in their front windows – 'We recycle to save energy. Will *you* help too?'

and conflict resolution strategies. They have been developing experimental gaming studies to test the utility of different models of the nuclear arms race. These studies use the beliefs and strategies of individual protagonists as the behavioural data that might ultimately motivate the political decisions of national leaders (Guetzkow et al, 1963). Analyses of people in these positions of governmental responsibility suggest that their drive for power may in part be the impetus for the proliferation of nuclear arms.

One approach taken by peace psychology has been to analyse the historical record of actual negotiations and crises. Such a project, which was directed by psychologist **Irving Janis** and political scientist Richard Lebow, has led to some interesting observations. Janis and Lebow categorised the quality of decision making in 19 major international crises since World War II. Characterising these decisions along seven independent dimensions, the researchers found a strong relationship between the way decisions were made and whether or not international conflict intensified. The researchers also found that 'defective decision-making' predominated in more than a third of the crises, and they suggested various safeguards to ensure better decision-making in future crises (Janis, 1985).

Some psychologists believe that to affect policy-making toward nuclear war, it is necessary to study the way those in authority have handled nuclear crises, the most feared events that seem to be least understood by those in charge of nuclear weapons. By learning how decision-makers have made sense of events that could have led to nuclear war, psychologists may be in a position to offer more fully formed decision rules that minimise the cognitive and motivational biases of policy-makers. The goal of their work is to prevent future crises through an understanding of past and current crisis management (Blight, 1987).

Many researchers are focusing their attention on the socio-psychological effects of nuclear war. In such a vein, research psychologists have examined the way we perceive and respond to the threat of nuclear conflict and the reason people who are fearful of destruction by such means do not get involved in activities to promote peace (Allen, 1985; Fiske, 1987). So important was the threat of nuclear war thought to be by the psychological community in the first half of the 1980s, that at a meeting of the Council of the British Psychological Society in October 1984,

clinical psychologist James Thompson's publication, *Psychological Aspects of Nuclear War*, was adopted as the Society's official statement on this frightening threat to humanity (Thompson, 1985). In this volume, he considers reactions to disaster based on past ones such as the Black Death, Hiroshima and Nagasaki, and other topics such as human fallibility and weaponry, implications for civil defence and conflict resolution. Despite the fall of the 'iron curtain' and an end to the 'cold war', possession of nuclear arms and the widespread sale by major nations of conventional military weapons both continue to be features within the ongoing flux of international relations. There is still, then, very much a part to be played by applied social psychology in this arena.

Psychologists, however, have a new role in the revolution that is sweeping away entire political systems and economic orders throughout the world. The transition for hundreds or millions of people from a totalitarian to a democratic mentality and from a central collectivist society to a free-market economy is a change of unprecedented proportions. Generations of communist citizens have never experienced the freedoms and responsibilities of democratic ideas and practices. Democracy is more than a political system; it is a way of thinking about the significance of oneself in shaping shared societal goals. Those who have lived with some sense of security in government-controlled economy and state-run industries must learn to cope with the risks and uncertainties of competitive market economies. Additionally, individuals and whole communities need help to deal with decades of abuses by totalitarian regimes – exiles, imprisonments, forced labour, displacement and ecological catastrophes. This psychological help involves education, research, therapy and social policy planning. The Centre for the Psychology of Democracy is a newly formed organisation of psychologists committed to assisting people and societies in reshaping their lives and country within the framework of democratic principles and practices (Balakrishnan, 1991).

This peace psychology sampler barely touches on the many new directions that researchers and social change agents are taking to reduce the threat of war and increase the prospects for peace. However, it does suggest how the basic research and theories we have been discussing can be applied to solve some of the urgent problems facing us. The goal is to improve the quality of life for people, societies and the global environment.

recapping main points

Social Influence Processes

Human thought and action are affected by social situational influences. Being assigned to play a social role, even in artificial settings, can cause individuals to act contrary to their beliefs, values and dispositions. Social norms shape the behaviour of group members, as demonstrated by the Asch experiments and the Bennington Study. Lewin tested the effect of leadership styles with schoolchildren, demonstrating that socially significant questions could be explored experimentally. Milgram's studies on obedience are a powerful testimony to the influence of situational factors. Bystander intervention studies show that, when among a large group of people or when in a hurry, people are less likely to aid a person in distress. Directly asking for help is an effective way of promoting altruism.

Importantly, 'situations' do not merely exist as a set of physical conditions external to each of us. They as much exist in our perceptions of those external events as they do in terms of any 'objectively' verifiable set of circumstances. Further, those perceptions are in and of themselves shaped and moulded in collective negotiation with others. The meaning we ascribe to a social context or 'situation' is equally a product of our shared social environment, consisting as it does of culturally and historically specific ways of speaking about and representing our world. Thus, 'situations', our perception of them and their influence upon us, are created and recreated intersubjectively, between people, through the sharing and negotiating of our social worlds with one another. Social influence processes, then, by definition are ones with which we are unavoidably suffused. By virtue of being inextricably linked with others, such processes and interdependencies shape our actions, despite our attempts to accommodate and manage the limits of their governance over us. The workings of social influence processes ensure that ultimately we cannot attain a state of absolute self-determination, regardless of our illusions to the contrary, for we live in relation to others.

Social Cognitions and Social Reality

Each person constructs his or her own social reality that is shared by their social group. Beliefs and expectations can guide actions and shape outcomes in any behavioural setting. Prejudice develops as an outcome of the desire to simplify complex information through categorisation. Even minimal cue differences, such as eye colour, are enough basis for extreme categorisations. Some social psychologists often use cognitive frameworks to understand social phenomena. They vary in their use of motivational or purely cognitive factors. Theories using cognitive frameworks include dissonance theory, self-perception theory and attribution theory. A distinctly European brand of social psychology has directed both theory and research toward greater focus on communal transactions and interdependencies, especially through a consideration of conversational realities.

Solving Social Problems

Many social psychologists strive to improve the human condition by applying psychological principles to various social problems. In the field of environmental psychology, researchers look at the way people and environments affect each other. The ecological approach emphasises reciprocity and mutual influence in a person–environment relationship. Environmental psychologists look for ways that human behaviour can make environments supportive without trespassing on the health of ecosystems. Peace psychologists look for ways to help resolve superpower competition and hostilities among nations. They conduct research that examines the basis of false beliefs, misperceptions and erroneous attributions in areas related to national security and nuclear arms. They also study fears about war among children and adults. Social psychology aims to be both practical and theoretical.

key Terms

accounting practices
Asch effect
attitude
attribution theory
autokinetic effect
behavioural confirmation
bystander intervention
categorical differentiation
causal attribution
cognitive dissonance
conformity
contrastive criterion
conversational reality
covariation principle
demand characteristics
discourse analysis
discursive turn
environmental psychology
field theory
fundamental attribution error
group dynamics
informational influence processes
interdependence
intersubjectivity
intuitive psychologists
joint action
minimal group paradigm
modesty bias
narrative

norm crystallisation
normative influence processes
particularisation
peace psychology
phenomenological perspective
post-modernism
prejudice
reference group
roles
rules
scapegoating
self-fulfilling prophecy
self-perception theory
self-serving bias
situation
social categorisation
social cognition
social construction
social context
social facilitation
social identity theory
social influence processes
social loafing
social norms
social perception
social reality
social representations
social role
societal psychology

major Contributors

Aronson, Elliot
Asch, Solomon
Bem, Daryl
Billig, Michael
Clark, Kenneth
Darley, John
Edwards, Derek
Festinger, Leon (1919–89)
Gergen, Kenneth
Harré, Rom
Heider, Fritz (1896–1988)
Hilton, Denis
Himmelweit, Hilde (1919–89)
Janis, Irving (1918–90)
Jaspars, Jos (1934–85)

Kelley, Harold
Latane, Bibb
Lewin, Kurt (1890–1947)
Milgram, Stanley (1933–84)
Moscovici, Serge
Newcomb, Theodore (1903–84)
Potter, Jonathan
Rabbie, Jaap
Rosenthal, Robert
Ross, Lee
Sherif, Muzafer (1906-88)
Shotter, John
Snyder, Mark
Tajfel, Henri (1919-82)
Wetherell, Margaret

Chapter 14

Abnormal Psychology

27 September 1994, 12.50 am: 60-mile-per hour winds whipped up fierce, icy waves in the Baltic Sea. Water had been shipped through the bow doors of the *Estonia* ferry which was on its way to Stockholm with approximately 1,100 people on board. Now unstable, the vessel capsized in the storm. Formerly horizontal decks became vertical drops, down which people could fall or up which they could not clamber to escape. A 'black ferment' of water unforgivingly raged through the ship, submerging the screams of those trapped and drowning. As the ferry lay on her side, 35-year-old Paul Barney, one of two British passengers, stood at the exit of the cafeteria, an Estonian man next to him. Paul had been shouting in despair. He could see no way out. A life-belt, on the other side of a 'ravine', (formerly 'the deck'), represented the faint possibility of survival. Should he jump across the gap to the belt? Before he had chance to decide, the Estonian passenger had made the leap and secured the life-belt. Without warning '. . . a wave came from the back of the boat, over the gunnels and dragged him [the Estonian man] toward me and then down through that vertical ravine'. Paul could not tell if the man had survived. He knew, though, it so easily could have been him that had been washed away. Frantically he looked about. The cafeteria ceiling was now a seemingly insurmountable cliff before him. His eyes fell on some pipework affixed to this flat surface. In an instant he realised these pipes could be climbed like a ladder and so he began his ascent. But would he be able to maintain his grip on the large, rounded pipes? Casting aside this anxiety, he pulled on upwards, elated at having found an escape route. Eventually he reached the hull of the ship.

Though the *Estonia*'s lighting had long since gone out, he could see more clearly now, his view illuminated by the moon. Anticipating he might end up in the water, he had thrown away his heavy boots but taken his fleece jacket with him. In his stockinged feet, he gingerly picked his way along the side of the boat. The surface was wet and slippery. It was also 'pitted with holes', formerly cabin windows, each now a possibly glassless, black abyss into which he could fall. Once at midships, he helped to push a life raft which had self-inflated to the waters edge. As it was launched with all inside, fierce winds and waves flipped the 25-person raft over, throwing everyone out of its confines. Paul scrambled to the top of the raft – now afloat upsidedown – and pulled up others onto the relative safety of the upturned craft's underside. At 1.30 am the *Estonia* sank beneath the waves, entombing and taking to their deaths over 900 people. For the next six and a quarter hours, Paul and initially 13 other people perched precariously on the exposed surface of the life raft, clinging steadfastly to the thin rope around its edge.

Paul knew, though, his ordeal had not ended and that he was far from safe. He recognised that he and the other survivors were in shock. They appeared to him to be unresponsive, 'almost statuesque'. He said to himself: 'You've got to calm down and reduce your heart rate, it's burning up energy; just . . . try and think clearly what's happening here'. Paul and an Estonian girl comforted one another by cuddling together, sharing and conserving precious body heat. At one point, Paul was washed into the sea but managed to scramble back on board. His freezing fingers had great difficulty tying the simplest of knots with which to lash himself onto the raft. At intervals, large waves broke over the raft. Just as some vestige of warmth had been regained, each successive wave '. . . ripped the last of the body heat out of you'. Between these icy blasts, he was becoming dangerously anaethetised to physical sensation: 'It was like . . . I was being numbed by hypothermia'. Paul knew that his body temperature would soon become abnormally low and that in the latter stages of such heat loss he must not allow himself to fall asleep, otherwise he might slip into a fatal unconsciousness. The temptation to slump forward and nod off was overwhelming at times.

Another man on the raft tried to raise their hopes by talking up the likelihood of being saved. But Paul could not subscribe to his unrealistic optimism until more tangible signs were visible. In attempting to raise everybody else's spirits, this vocal individual eventually had little reserves left for himself and died before rescuers reached them. One by one, Paul witnessed his fellow survivors drifting off into an unconsciousness from which they would not return, including the Estonian girl with whom he had felt the glimmer of a short-lived bond. Physically exhausted, it was all he could do to remain on the raft himself. Hours of exposure to the elements had stripped him of his strength. He could no longer keep a young man who was losing consciousness from submerging into the water that had collected in the middle of the raft. For those still conscious, shelter could have been found there from the piercing wind: the raft water '. . . had been warmed up by the sheer volume of people and dead bodies', but Paul could not face lying amongst them. He wanted to keep himself 'separate from the dead . . . always looking out of the raft . . . for something . . . a sign . . . a helicopter . . . some escape route'. By daybreak, his body temperature had fallen to at least $30.8°$ celsius, $6.2°$ below the norm of $37°$. He was perilously close to blacking out and on the verge of death.

Source: interview with Paul Barney, 17 November 1994.

PAUL BARNEY WAS one of the fortunate 140 people, however, who were rescued from the *Estonia* disaster. In the days afterward, having overcome the initial exhaustion and following the jubilation of having survived, Paul became angry at the collosal loss of life. He grieved in particular for the Estonian girl whom he had tried to save and felt survivor's guilt at not being able to have done more for her and others on the raft. A few days after the tragedy, he had time to reflect. Images of the ship's bow being overwhelmed by the sea intruded into his mind, replaying '. . . like a constant video'. He had a sense of almost drifting back into the disaster at times. It was as if he wanted to be there on the raft again with the other survivors: 'It was like a

little club; . . . *that* was life and reality'. The experience was outside the usual frame of reference for those who had not been involved. How could others empathise with him? He wanted to be back with people who had shared this extraordinary event. No one else could really relate to him about the distaster as well as they could. The rest of the world for a while seemed unreal. He felt apart from it, 'a voyeur' – an onlooker – not an active participant. There was another reality, full of un-certainty, of which he had temporarily become a part. For some time afterward, he became 'ultra safety conscious'. The traumatic events of that night had emphasised to him that he was not invulnerable. Fortunately, though, Paul had learned to accept this sense of personal vulnerablity – of 'it *could* happen to me' – during previous travels. Thereby, he was in part protected psychologically from the after-effects of this unexpected and catastrophic event. Also, he knew that he had been highly instrumental in securing his survival. He did not view himself as a passive, helpless victim of the sinking. He felt personally empowered by the way in which he had survived. Thus, despite his initial preoccupations, Paul did not succumb in full to the **post-traumatic stress reaction** which so often afflicts survivors of disasters. Nevertheless, a month and a half later, he realised just how often he was precariously balanced that night on the fine line between life and death. Paul's world view may have been seriously assaulted by the trauma, but his pre-existing psychological hardiness ensured that it was not entirely shattered.

Such an event could have left other less resilient individuals ship-wrecked psychologically for some time to come. A profound uncertainty about their ongoing personal safety in the world could have been engendered. Indeed, for those who were separated from loved ones during the 1987 *Zeebrugge* ferry disaster and were later re-united on dry land, an obsessive fearfulness of losing a relative or spouse to another freak accident became a preoccupation for some survivors, even on returning to the relative safety of their local communities. Traumatic events are themselves 'abnormal' by the very nature of their infrequency and because they threaten our physical integrity and view of the world as a benign place. It is unsurprising, then, that 'abnormal events' can invoke 'abnormal responses' and behaviour. The meaning we attribute to such events though, as in the case of Paul Barney, will in part determine their psychological consequences for us. Traumatic happenings – whether they be 'natural' ones such as a flash-flood or falling tree, 'technological' ones, such as a bridge collapsing, or 'interpersonal' ones, for example, being mugged or sexually assaulted – constitute a subset of rare 'life events' that fortunately happen only to a few of us. Nevertheless, we all experience more commonplace life events at one time or another: breaking up with a partner, getting divorced, losing a job, failing to achieve a much wanted objective or witnessing the ill-health and death of a member of our immediate family. Depending upon the meaning we attribute to such occurrences (in part as a result of our past biography and learning), we will react accordingly. Events which involve for us, for example, a sense of loss, can lead to despair and clinical depression, particularly when the emotional or instrumental support of friends and loved ones is absent or not forthcoming.

We will see in this chapter, then, that for environmental events to influence significantly our psychological well-being, they do not need to be as dramatic, uncontrollable, catastrophic, unpredictable or unusual as the tragic sinking of the *Estonia* car and passenger ferry. Indeed, it will become evident that the ordinary psychological and social environment in which we play out our everyday lives is, more often than not, strongly implicated and embedded within the causation and course of many psychological disorders. In this chapter we will examine how these disorders are conceived, the nature of their correlates and consequences, and explore current explanations of their origins.

◉ THE NATURE OF PSYCHOLOGICAL DISORDERS

Have you ever worried excessively, felt depressed or anxious without really knowing why, been fearful of something you rationally knew could not harm you, believed you were not living up to your potential, had thoughts about suicide, or used alcohol and drugs to escape a problem? Almost everyone will answer 'yes' to at least one of these questions. This chapter looks at the range of psychological functioning that is considered unhealthy or 'abnormal', often referred to as psychological disorder. **Psychopathological functioning** involves disruptions in emotional, behavioural or thought processes that lead to personal distress or that block one's ability to achieve important goals. The field of abnormal psychology, also called *psychopathology*, is the area of psychological investigation most directly concerned with understanding the nature of individual pathologies of mind, mood and behaviour.

As you might expect, the scope of psychological disorder is vast and pervasive, touching the daily lives of millions of us, both directly and indirectly. It can be insidious, working its way into many situations, diminishing our emotional and physical well-being. It can be devastating, destroying the effective functioning of individuals and their families, as well as creating an enormous financial burden through lost productivity and the high costs of prolonged treatment. Whilst rates of psychological disorders vary from one culture to another depending upon what is considered to be 'normal' and 'abnormal' within each, in the United States a study estimated that as many as 32 per cent of all people there have suffered from a form of identified psychological disorder at some point in their lives (Regier *et al*, 1988). Researchers have also found that as many as a quarter of all visits that adults make to professionals for health care are for psychological difficulties (SCP, 1992; Shapiro *et al*, 1984). For example, statistics for schizophrenia also testify to the scale of mental health problems facing our communities. One out of every 100 people are likely to be so diagnosed before the age of 45. This means, for instance, that approximately 580,000 people in the United Kingdom and 150,000 in Holland currently are identifiable as suffering from schizophrenia. About a third of the victims of schizophrenia will never fully recover, even with therapy.

Statistics, however, do not convey the serious impact psychological disorders have on the everyday lives of individuals and families. Throughout this chapter, we will present more statistics, discuss categories of psychological disorders and consider theoretical processes and models that help us understand these problems as well as envision the real people who live with a psychological disorder every day. Their words convey the personal distress and struggles that accompany such conditions.

An instance of psychological disorder is found in the case of Jim Backus, a sociable humourist, comic actor, writer and good golfer. In his later years, however, he became a recluse; when a reporter visited him, he learned that Backus refused to see old friends and feared going into restaurants or working in front of a camera. He even stopped writing and playing golf. The reporter noted: 'The other day Backus sat in a chair in his home, a frightened, insecure man, contrasting tragically with the raucous extraverted Backus of old, needing reassurance that he wasn't, indeed, in the clutches of a life-threatening disease'.

Backus suffered from hypochondriacal fears, believing he was afflicted with Parkinson's disease. Despite reassurances from medical personnel, his panic, depression and fears got steadily worse. He told the interviewer, 'I haven't been out of this house in almost six years. I was terrified when the doorbell rang. I'd run and hide. I'm trying to get over the acute panic right now as we talk . . . Your mind can do this to you. You know it's doing it to you, but you're powerless to stop it'. With the help of his wife, Backus wrote and published the story of this living nightmare in *Backus Strikes Back* (D. M. Scott, 1990).

◎ Deciding What is Abnormal

What is a psychological disorder? Experts in the field of abnormal psychology do not agree completely about what behaviours constitute psychological disorders. As we shall see, there is a great deal of social judgement involved in labelling behaviours as 'normal', 'abnormal' or psychopathological and in classifying mental health problems. The judgement that someone has a mental disorder is typically based on the evaluation of the individual's behavioural functioning by people with some special authority or

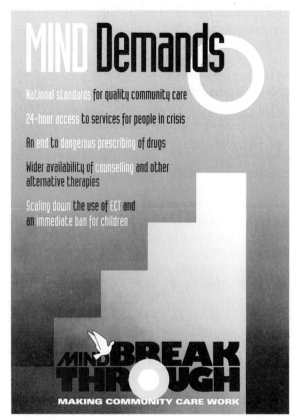

MIND is a UK organisation that helps people in mental distress.

power. The terms used to describe these phenomena – mental disorder, mental illness, or abnormality – depend on the particular perspective, training and cultural background of the speaker, the situation and the status of the person being judged. For example, in some cases, judgements of abnormality are confused with evaluations of morality – it is 'bad' to have hallucinations in our culture because they are taken as signs of mental disturbance, but it is 'good' in cultures where hallucinations are interpreted as mystical visions from spirit force (Helman, 1990).

We have already cited a few statistics about how common psychological problems are, but we have offered only vague definitions of these problems. The first step in classifying someone as having a psychological disorder is making a judgement that some aspect of the person's functioning is abnormal. A **psychological diagnosis** is the identification made by classifying and categorising the observed behaviour pattern into an approved diagnostic system that a disorder, syndrome or condition exists. Such a diagnosis is in many ways more difficult to make than a medical diagnosis and is subject to much greater interpretation. In the medical context, a doctor can rely on physical evidence, such as X-rays, blood tests and biopsies, to inform a diagnostic decision. In the case of psychological disorders, the evidence for diagnosis comes from interpretations of a person's

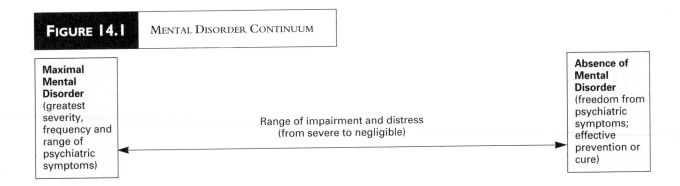

FIGURE 14.1 MENTAL DISORDER CONTINUUM

Maximal Mental Disorder (greatest severity, frequency and range of psychiatric symptoms)

Range of impairment and distress (from severe to negligible)

Absence of Mental Disorder (freedom from psychiatric symptoms; effective prevention or cure)

actions and self-reports. What does it mean to say someone is abnormal or suffering from a psychological disorder? How do psychologists decide what is abnormal? Is it always clear when behaviour moves from the normal to the abnormal category? Judgements about abnormality are far from being clear cut. Mental disorder is best thought of as a continuum, as shown in *Figure 14.1*. Because the definition of abnormality is not very precise, there are no fail-safe rules we can use to identify abnormality.

What follows are six indicators of possible abnormality (Rosenhan & Seligman, 1989):

- *Distress:* experiencing personal distress or intense anxiety.
- *Maladaptiveness:* acting in ways that hinder the accomplishment of personal goals, do not contribute to personal well-being and interfere strongly with the goals and needs of society. Someone who is drinking so heavily that she cannot hold down a job or who is endangering others through her intoxication is displaying maladaptive behaviour.
- *Irrationality:* acting or talking in ways that are irrational or incomprehensible to others. A man who responds to voices that do not exist in objective reality is behaving irrationally.
- *Unpredictability:* behaving unpredictably or erratically from situation to situation, as if experiencing a loss of control. The behaviour may appear to be unresponsive to the effects of social influence and thereby be uncontrollable by usual cultural constraints. A child who smashes his fist through a wall for no apparent reason displays unpredictability.
- *Statistical rarity and undersirability:* behaving in ways that are statistically rare and violate social standards of what is morally acceptable or desirable. Just being statistically unusual, however, does not lead to a psychological judgement of abnormality. For example, possessing genius-level intelligence is extremely rare, but it is also considered desirable. On the other hand, having an extremely low intelligence is also rare but is

considered undesirable; thus, it has often been labelled 'abnormal'.

- *Observer discomfort:* creating discomfort in others by making them feel threatened or distressed in some way (intentionally or otherwise). A man walking down the middle of the street having a vivid conversation with himself creates observer discomfort in the drivers of cars trying to drive around him.

Most of these indicators of abnormality are not immediately apparent to all observers – in other words, they involve a large degree of judgement. At the end of this chapter we will consider the negative consequences and dangers associated with such judgements.

We are more confident in labelling behaviour as 'abnormal' when more than just one of the six indicators are present and valid. The more extreme and prevalent the indicators are, the more confident we can be that they indicate an abnormal condition.

None of these six criteria is a necessary condition shared by all cases of abnormality. For example, during his murder trial, a postgraduate student who had killed his mathematics lecturer with a hammer and then taped to his office door a note that read, 'No office hours today', reported feeling neither guilt nor remorse. Despite the absence of personal suffering, we would not hesitate to label his overall behaviour as abnormal. It is also true that none, by itself, is a sufficient condition that distinguishes all cases of abnormal behaviour from normal variations in behaviour. The distinction between normal and abnormal is not so much a difference between two independent types of behaviours as it is a matter of the degree to which a person's actions resemble a set of agreed-upon criteria of abnormality. When making judgements about normality, it is important to operate from a perspective on mental health as well as from a perspective on mental illness, as shown in *Figure 14.2* (next page).

Before we consider specific examples of abnormality that are classified as psychological disorders, we will explore the approaches and models that psychologists and psychiatrists use to explain how abnormal behaviour develops. Let us begin by looking

FIGURE 14.2   MENTAL HEALTH CONTINUUM

Optimal Mental Health

Individual, group and environmental factors work together effectively, ensuring

- subjective well-being
- optimal development and use of mental abilities
- achievement of goals consistent with justice
- conditions of fundamental equality

Minimal Mental Health

Individual, group and environment factors conflict, producing

- subjective distress
- impairment or underdevelopment of mental abilities
- failure to achieve goals
- destructive behaviours
- entrenchment of inequities

briefly at the way psychological problems have been viewed throughout history and the way these perspectives have contributed to the understanding of psychological disorders.

Historical Perspectives

Throughout history, humans have feared psychological disorders, often associating them with so-called 'evil'. Because of this fear, people have reacted aggressively and decisively to any behaviours they perceived as bizarre or abnormal. Not until very recently have people begun to accept the notion that psychological disorders constitute states that very often are treatable.

Attitudes about the alleged link between mental ill-health and 'evil' may be as old as human history. Archaeologists have found prehistoric skulls in which holes have been drilled. Our ancestors believed such holes would allow the demons that had supposedly possessed a loved one to escape. Similarly, superstitious beliefs abounded with regard to what was once called 'hysteria', an affliction wherein no organic pathology is present but which is characterised nevertheless by a cluster of somatic symptoms that can include paralysis of limbs, insensitivity to pain, tingling skin and impaired vision. **Hysteria** – from the Greek word *hystera* meaning 'womb' – was believed to be caused by a wandering uterus (and so only to affect women) which purportedly was under

the devil's control. Our knowledge of the human body today tells us that this 'wandering womb' hypothesis is anatomical nonsense. Thus, the term hysteria with its misleading connotations has been replaced by 'conversion disorder' to refer more aptly to a condition in which psychological distress has become 'converted' into physical symptomatology.

During the Renaissance (about 1350–1630 AD), intellectual and artistic enlightenment flourished. Oddly enough, amid this intellectual fervour, fear of the devil and evil peaked as the Catholic Church launched a campaign of trials and torture to weed out 'evil' and all non-believers. This Inquisition led to the torture and execution of thousands.

In 1692, in the Massachusetts colony of Salem, numerous young women began experiencing convulsions, nausea and weakness. They reported sensations of being pinched, pricked or bitten. Many became temporarily blind or deaf; others reported visions and sensations of flying through the air. Such strange symptoms sparked a frantic search for an explanation. Many people theorised that the symptoms were the work of the devil who, through the efforts of earthbound witches, had taken over the minds and bodies of the young women. These theories led to a witchcraft panic and to the execution of over 20 women believed to be witches. Detailed analysis strongly suggests that the 'bewitched' Salem women may have been suffering from ergot poisoning – ergot, a fungus that grows on rye, is a source of LSD (Caporeal, 1976; Matossian, 1982).

Until the end of the eighteenth century, the mentally ill in Western societies were perceived as mindless beasts who could be controlled only with chains and physical discipline. They were not cared for in hospitals but were incarcerated with criminals.

In 1905, a group of young artists gathered in Paris to open an exhibition of work that broke entirely from traditional realistic art. These artists had painted their personal impressions of reality. The public reacted to the exhibition with outrage, accused the artists of being wild beasts – fauvists – and suggested that they be committed to institutions for the insane. Among the artists were several whose work is now honoured and highly valued, including Henri Matisse.

Emergence of the medical model

In the latter part of the eighteenth century, a new perspective about the origins of abnormal behaviour emerged – people began to perceive those with psychological problems as sick, suffering from illness, rather than as possessed or immoral. A number of reforms were gradually implemented in the facilities for the insane. **Phillipe Pinel** (1745–1826) was one of the first clinicians to use these ideas to attempt to develop a classification system for psychological difficulties based on the ideas that disorders of thought, mood and behaviour are similar in many ways to the physical, organic symptoms of illness and that each disorder is seen as having a group of characteristic symptoms that distinguishes it from other disorders and from healthy functioning. Disorders are classified according to the patterns of observed symptoms, the circumstances surrounding the onset of the disturbance, the natural course of the disorder and its response to treatment. Such classification systems are modelled after the biological classification systems naturalists use and are intended to help clinicians identify common disorders more easily.

In 1896, **Emil Kraepelin** (1855–1926), a German psychiatrist, was responsible for creating the first truly comprehensive classification system of psychological disorders. Strongly motivated by a belief that there was a physical basis to psychological problems, he gave the process of psychological diagnosis and classification the flavour of medical diagnosis, a flavour that still remains today (Rosenhan & Seligman, 1989). Kraepelin's perspective is most readily seen in the terminology used by psychiatrists. They speak of mental 'illness' and treat mental 'patients' in the hope of 'curing' their 'diseased' brains. The medical model also tends to be based on **organic pathology**, the perspective that mental illness is caused by deficits in structure or neurobiological functioning.

Emergence of psychological models

An alternative perspective to the medical approach focuses on the psychological causes and treatment of abnormal behaviour. This perspective began to emerge most clearly at the end of the eighteenth century. It was helped along by the dramatic work of **Franz Mesmer** (1734–1815) whose legacy remains with us today in the concepts of animal magnetism and mesmerism. Mesmer believed that many disorders, including hysteria, were caused by disruptions in the flow of a mysterious force that he called animal magnetism. He unveiled several new techniques to study animal magnetism, including one that eventually became known as hypnotism but was originally referred to as mesmerism in his honour. While his general theory of animal magnetism was discredited by a scientific advisory commission, his hypnotic techniques were adopted by many researchers, including a prominent French neurologist, **Jean Charcot** (1825–1893). Charcot found that some of the symptoms of hysteria, such as paralysis of a limb, could be eliminated when a patient was under hypnosis. Hypnosis even had the power to induce the symptoms of hysteria in healthy individuals, dramatically illustrating the potential of psychological factors to cause problems that were believed to have an exclusively physical basis.

One of Charcot's students, **Sigmund Freud**, continued to experiment with hypnosis. Freud used his experiments to elaborate his psychodynamic theories of personality and abnormality that continue to exert tremendous influence on current theories of the nature and causes of psychological disorder. Somewhat later in his career, Freud abandoned hypnosis and established what he called 'psychoanalysis' as a treatment for mental health problems (see Chapter 15).

There are many different psychological models used to account for the onset and progress of various mental disorders, some of which we will review. All psychological models share the assumption that the origins of mental disorders and the sources that maintain abnormal behaviour are not primarily biological but rather are psychological. The functionalist perspective does not exclude, however, that in the case of some disorders, organic causes also contribute to the aetiology of the condition.

Psychological models are based on **functional pathology**, the perspective that there is no known organic disorder responsible for the symptoms of mental illness. These models identify learning, reinforcement, motivation, cognitions, cultural factors, family systems and other psychological processes as contributing to mental disorders.

⊙ The Aetiology of Psychological Disorder

Aetiology refers to the factors that cause or contribute to the development of psychological and medical problems. Knowing why the disorder occurs, what its origins are and the way it affects thought and emotional and behavioural processes may lead to new ways of treating and, ideally, preventing it. Approaches to understanding the causal factors in psychological disorders can be grouped into two major categories: biological and psychological.

Biological approaches

Building on the heritage of the medical model, modern biological approaches assume that psychological disturbances are directly attributable to underlying biological factors, most often linked to the brain or nervous system. Biological researchers and clinicians most often investigate structural abnormalities in the brain, biochemical processes and genetic influences (Gottesman, 1991; Meltzer, 1987; Snyder, 1976).

The brain is a complex organ whose interrelated elements are held in delicate balance. Subtle alterations in its chemical messengers – the *neurotransmitters* – or in its tissue can have significant effects. Genetic factors, brain injury and infection are a few of the causes of these alterations. We have seen in earlier chapters that technological advances in scanning techniques, such as PET scans and brain imaging techniques, allow mental health professionals to view the structure of the brain and specific biochemical processes in living individuals without surgery. Using these techniques, biologically oriented researchers are discovering new links between psychological disorders and specific abnormalities in the brain. For example, the brains of some patients with schizophrenic disorders have a larger ventricular area filled with fluid than do normal brains. Also, extreme violence has been linked to brain tumours located in the area of the brain associated with aggressive behaviour – the amygdala (Heath, 1959; Dimond, 1980). Biochemical approaches to psychological disorders have been affirmed by studies showing the ways drugs can alter the normal reality of the mind and by the proven success of drug therapies in alleviating certain symptoms (Bowers, 1980; Papolos & Papolos, 1987). Continuing advances in the field of behavioural genetics have improved researchers' abilities to identify the links between specific genes and the presence of psychological disorders (Joyce, 1989; Tsuang & Vandermey, 1980). However, despite the promise of these approaches, there are still many unknowns about the connections between biology, genes and psychological disorder.

Psychological approaches

Psychological approaches focus on the causal role of psychological or social factors in the development of mental ill-health. These approaches perceive personal experiences, traumas, conflicts and environmental factors as the roots of psychological disorders. We will outline three dominant psychological models of abnormality: the psychodynamic, the behaviourist and the cognitive.

Psychodynamic. Like the biological approach, the psychodynamic model as inspired by classical psychoanalysis holds that the causes of psychological disorder are located inside the person. However, according to Sigmund Freud and followers who developed this model, the internal causal factors are psychological rather than biological and hence are referred to as intrapsychic. As we noted in earlier chapters, Freud developed psychoanalytic theory to explain apparently irrational and senseless behaviour in a rational way. His ideas profoundly changed our basic concept of human nature and our approach to abnormal behaviour. He believed that many psychological disorders were simply an extension of 'normal' processes of psychic conflict and ego defence that we all experience. In the psychodynamic model, early childhood experiences and personal development shape both normal and abnormal behaviour in life.

Behaviour is motivated by drives and wishes of which we are often unaware. Symptoms of psychological disorder have their roots in unconscious conflict and thoughts. If the unconscious is conflicted and tension filled, a person will be plagued by anxiety and other disorders. Much of this psychic conflict is said to arise from struggles between the irrational, pleasure-seeking impulses of the id and the internalised social constraints imposed by the superego. The ego is normally the arbiter of this struggle; however, its ability to perform its function can be weakened by abnormal development in childhood. Individuals attempt to avoid the pain caused by conflicting motives and anxiety with defence mechanisms, such as repression or denial. Defences can become over-used, distorting reality or leading to self-defeating behaviours. When psychic energy is bound up in attempts to defend against the emergence of repression-bound anxiety, little is left for a productive and satisfying life.

Behavioural. Freudian notions gained gradual acceptance among American clinical psychologists and psychiatrists as well as among their European colleagues. However, you will recall that American research psychology from the 1930s to the early 1970s was dominated by a behaviouristic orientation. Those who insisted that observable responses are the only acceptable psychological data had no use for hypothetical unconscious processes.

Behavioural theorists argue that abnormal behaviours are acquired in the same fashion as healthy behaviours – through learning and reinforcement. They do not focus on internal psychological phenomena or early childhood experiences. Instead, they focus on the current behaviour and the current conditions or reinforcements that sustain the behaviour, even if it is not the most adaptive or appropriate response to a situation. The symptoms of psychological disorders arise because an individual has learned self-defeating or ineffective ways of behaving. By discovering the environmental contingencies – the antecedents and consequences – that maintain any undesirable, abnormal behaviour, an investigator or clinician can then recommend treatment to change those contingencies and extinguish the unwanted behaviour (Owens & Ashcroft, 1982; Emmelkamp,

1986). Behaviourists rely on both classical and operant conditioning models to understand the processes that can result in maladaptive behaviour.

Cognitive. The cognitive perspective of human nature that has evolved over the last several decades is often used to supplement behaviouristic views. The cognitive perspective suggests that we should not expect to discover the origins of psychological disorders in the objective reality of stimulus environments, reinforcers and overt responses. Rather, we must look at how we perceive or think about ourselves and about our relations with other people and our environment. Among the cognitive variables that can guide – or misguide – adaptive responses are our perceived degree of control over important reinforcers, beliefs in our own efficacy to cope with threatening events, the ways in which we attribute the causes of our behaviour to internal or external factors and other mental strategies we use to make sense of our problems, successes, failures and unusual experiences (Bandura, 1986).

The cognitive approach assumes that emotional upsets are caused by the mediating processes of perceiving and interpreting events. Psychological problems are the result of distortions in the reality of a situation or of ourselves, faulty reasoning, or poor problem-solving. Sometimes our personal constructions help us and sometimes they harm us; either way, they are our personal way of dealing with the complexities and uncertainties of everyday life (Ellis & Grieger, 1986).

Today, researchers are increasingly taking an **interactionist** perspective within psychopathology, seeing it as the product of a complex interaction between a number of biological and psychological factors (Cowan, 1988). For example, genetic predispositions may make a person vulnerable to a psychological disorder by affecting neurotransmitter levels or hormone levels, but psychological or social stresses or certain learned behaviours may be required for the disorder to develop fully.

INTERIM SUMMARY

We have considered how psychologists conceptualise psychological disorders; they classify behaviour as psychopathological by making a judgement about whether the behaviour is abnormal. Abnormality is judged by the degree to which a person's actions resemble a set of indicators including distress, maladaptiveness, irrationality, unpredictability, statistical rarity, undesirability and observer discomfort. Throughout history, people have tried to explain the origins of psychologocal disorder. Early views regarded psychopathology as the product of so-called 'evil' spirits or 'weak' character. In the latter part of the eighteenth century, emerging modern perspectives considered psychopathological functioning to be a result of psychological factors or underlying bodily disturbances.

Today, biological approaches to the aetiology of disorders of mental health concentrate on structural abnormalities in the brain, biochemical processes and genetic influences. Psychological approaches include the psychodynamic, behavioural and cognitive models. In the psychodynamic model, early childhood experiences, unconscious conflicts and defences play a key role. The behavioural perspective focuses on overt behaviours and the environmental conditions that help produce and maintain them. In the cognitive model, distortions in an individual's beliefs and perceptions of self and the world are at the heart of psychological disorders. Interactionist approaches combine these psychological and biological views.

Alternative Views

In many cultures, folk beliefs about the causes of mental health difficulties are part of a more general view of unexpected personal disasters – sudden illness, infertility, crop failure and premature deaths of loved ones. Such disasters are often attributed to 'evil spirits'. In the traditional explanatory tales of West Africa (Peltzer & Ebigbo, 1989), in beliefs about sorcery among Cree Indians of Canada, in the voodoo practices of Haitians and in the 'evil eye' beliefs still common among many Mediterranean cultures, a person can call upon supernatural, 'evil' power to inflict some disaster or mental affliction on an enemy.

In many cultures, notably those of some African groups and of the southwestern native Americans, psychological disorders are not perceived as intrapsychic, occurring within the mind. Instead they are viewed as intrapopulation, occurring among the people of the community – a more social psychological explanation being preferred. Thus, they suggest disharmony in the relationship of tribal members to their earthly environment and spiritual reality. Treatment in this view consists of communal rituals that renew the vitality of the bonds among afflicted individuals, their society and the natural habitat in which they live (Nobles, 1972).

The importance of socio-cultural explanations of psychological disorders has also been stressed by Western scholars. Many critical theorists have argued that contemporary society is itself disordered, not the people living within it. Thus, psychological disorder can be construed as a 'sane' response to an 'insane' world (Szasz, 1961). In this analysis, societal emphasis upon individual achievement, materialism and consumption are seen as being instrumental in alienating people from themselves and each other. This alternative analytic also proposes that, that which we inter-subjectively decide upon as 'abnormal behaviour' does not recognise the legitimacy of each patient's mode of self-expression; such acts come to be mislabelled, then, as 'symptoms' rather than as justifiable attempts at communication. Indeed, critics of psychiatry and clinical psychology focus upon the widespread use of diagnostic labels to describe mental disturbances, such linguistic practices arguably being culturally and historically bounded. **David Rosenhan** and his colleagues, for example, have shown how professional judgements are influenced by the institutional context in which they take place (as discussed later in this chapter). An escalating use of new psychopathological terminology can in itself lead to a proliferation of socially constructed and reified disorders, something Pincus *et al* (1992) in their revision of the DSM taxonomy wished to guard against. Despite such laudable intentions, however, greater recognition is being made of the socio-negotiative processes that occur when a therapist and client meet, talk and transact about an apparent 'psychological disorder'. Concomitant changes in how therapy is conceived have followed on from such a shift in emphasis (McNamee & Gergen, 1992).

◉ CLASSIFYING PSYCHOLOGICAL DISORDERS

Why is it helpful to have a diagnostic and classification system for psychological disorders? What advantages are gained by moving beyond a global assessment that abnormality is evident to distinguishing among different types of abnormality? Does the conceptual approach to the aetiology of abnormality affect the classification of psychological disorders?

Given the impreciseness of discussions about abnormality and the existence of a number of distinctly different approaches for explaining psychological disorders, it should not surprise you that the diagnosis of mental disturbance often has as much to do with the theoretical orientation of the clinician as it does with the actual symptoms presented (Franklin, 1987). In order to create greater consistency among clinicians and coherence in their diagnostic evaluations, psychologists have helped to develop a system of diagnosis and classification that provides precise descriptions of symptoms and other criteria to help clinicians decide whether a person's behaviour is evidence of a particular disorder.

◉ Goals of Classification

To be most useful, a diagnostic system should provide the following benefits:

- *A common shorthand language:* to facilitate quick and clear understanding among clinicians or researchers working in the field of psycho-pathology, it is helpful to have a common set of terms with agreed-upon meanings. A diagnostic category, such as depression, summarises a large and complex collection of information, including characteristic symptoms and the typical course of a disorder. In clinical settings, a diagnostic system allows mental health professionals to communicate more effectively about the people they are helping. Researchers studying different aspects of mental health and disorder or evaluating treatment programmes must agree on the disorder they are observing. With a good classification scheme (or **taxonomy** as it is also called) individuals can be diagnosed reliably and researchers can design studies to determine the causes of and treatments for different kinds of problems.
- *An understanding of aetiology:* ideally, a diagnosis of a specific disorder should correspond with and suggest the causes of the symptoms. Unfortunately, because there is substantial disagreement or lack of knowledge about the aetiology of many psychological disorders, this goal is difficult to meet.
- *A plan of treatment:* a diagnosis should also suggest what types of treatment to consider for particular disorders. Researchers and clinicians have found that certain treatments or therapies work most effectively for specific kinds of psychological disorders. For example, pharmacological interventions (prescribed drugs) are effective in treating schizophrenia whilst only helpful as adjunctive forms of treatment for depression (wherein psychotherapy is of more use). Further advances in our knowledge of the effectiveness and specificity of treatments will make fast and reliable diagnosis even more important.

◉ DSM-IV and ICD-10

There are two widely used and complementary classification schemes. One has been developed by the American Psychiatric Association and is called the Diagnostic and Statistical Manual of Mental Disorders (DSM). The first version of DSM appeared in 1952 (DSM-I) and listed several dozen mental health disorders. Since that time, significant revisions of this scheme have occurred (1968; 1980; 1987), culminating latterly in 1994 in the fourth edition of the manual. This most recent version is referred to by clinicians and researchers as the **DSM-IV**. It classifies, defines and describes over 200 mental health disorders. Decisions to make changes to diagnostic criteria from previous editions had to be substantiated by explicit statements of rationale and by the systematic review of empirical data (Frances *et al*, 1991; Pincus *et al*, 1992). The DSM-IV has been made compatible with the other guiding taxonomy of mental and behavioural disorders as developed by The World Health Organization and as contained within its International Classification of Diseases (ICD). This is now in its tenth version and is known accordingly as the **ICD-10** (WHO, 1992). Its publication was the result of field-testing of initial proposals as carried out by researchers and clinicians working in some 110 institutes in 40 countries. There is now good agreement between these two major classification systems.

Each of the mental disorders described is seen as a behavioural or psychological syndrome occurring in relation to the locus of the person and associated with present distress, the risk of future distress, impairment in one or more important areas of functioning, or with an important loss of freedom (ICD-10, 1992; DSM-IV, 1994).

Both systems use the term 'disorder' throughout the classifications so as to avoid greater problems inherent in the use of ones such as 'disease' and 'illness', as used by adherents (Goldberg *et al*, 1994) of a more traditional medical model of mental health. However, it must be noted that 'disorder' is not an exact term and may over-state by implication the significance of intrapsychic, person-based processes in the aetiology of certain forms of distress and dysfunction. The pervasive use of the term 'disorder' throughout the DSM-IV and ICD-10 classifications thereby may contribute to an inappropriate 'individualising' of psychological problems and difficulties. Such an implication is to be particularly avoided in those instances where the primary cause of distress is an external provoking agent. Therein, rather than assigning a 'disorder' (as a personal disposition or property), the designation of a 'reaction' (to external events) is a more apposite and less stigmatising form of terminological usage. This argument concerning all-important naming has been put forward, for example, in relation to what is called at present 'post-traumatic stress disorder' (PTSD): in further revisions of the DSM and ICD, it is possible that PTSD may come to be renamed as 'post-traumatic stress reaction' (O'Donohue & Elliot, 1992).

The term 'disorder', then, is used in this chapter under erasure, in the absence of a clearly preferable and more generally applicable signifier. Despite its pervasive occurrence throughout the two major classificatory systems, its use should not be taken as a definitive indication, however, of the originating locus of psychological ill-health. Indeed, distress and dysfunction commonly arise out of a psychosocial **transaction** between the person and environment, rather than exclusively from one or other (Wiener, 1989; Marcus & Wiener, 1989). A still more radical critique proposes that psychiatric diagnostic criteria and 'disorders' are mere social constructions and fascinating examples of social stereotyping. Hallam (1983), for example, argues that they themselves 'should be treated as *objects* of study and not as independent variables determining the *subject* of study'.

To reduce the diagnostic difficulties generated by variability in approaches to psychological disorders, both the ICD-10 and DSM-IV emphasise the description of patterns of symptoms and courses of disorders rather than aetiological theories or treatment strategies, though there is more mention of the latter within the WHO manuals. The diagnostic criteria as outlined within both classificatory frameworks are the products of consensually agreed formulations of currently evolving mental health knowledges and information. The emphasis upon descriptive terms allows clinicians and researchers to use a common language to outline and specify problems, while leaving opportunity for disagreement and continued research about which models best explain them.

To encourage clinicians to consider the social and physical as well as psychological factors that may be associated with a psychological disorder, the DSM-IV (unlike the ICD-10) uses a *multiaxial system* − a number of dimensions or axes that portray information about all of these factors (see *Table 14.1*, next page). Most of the principal psychological disorders are listed on Axis I. Axis II itemises personality disorders and other conditions which may be a focus of clinical attention and accompany Axis I disorders. These include, for example, antisocial behaviour and problems related to abuse and neglect. Axis III incorporates information about physical disorders, such as diabetes, that may be relevant to understanding or treating an Axis I or II disorder. Axes IV (psychosocial and environmental problems) and V (global assessment of functioning) provide important supplemental information about social context and competence that can be extremely useful when planning an individual's treatment or assessing prognosis (the likelihood of favourable future change). For example, when a psychosocial stressor, such as job loss, is associated with the onset of depression, a positive outcome may be predicted since this mental health difficulty is more likely to be a reaction to this external event rather than to some internal cause. A return to a standard level of functioning in these circumstances in all probability will be more swift

TABLE 14.1 THE FIVE AXES OF DSM-IV

Axis	Classes of Information	Description
Axis I	Clinical Disorders	These mental disorders present symptoms or patterns of behavioural or psychological problems that typically are painful or impair an area of functioning (for example, being able to do schoolwork).
Axis II	a) Personality Disorders	These are the dysfunctional strategies of perceiving and responding to the world. Personality characteristics or traits can also be noted on this axis when *no* personality disorder exists.
	b) Mental Retardation	These disorders affect such specific skills as reading, language and articulation.
Axis III	General Medical Conditions	These disorders include physical problems relevant to understanding or managing an individual's mental problems.
Axis IV	Psychosocial & Environmental Problems	On this axis, the clinician rates the amount and degree of psychosocial and environmental difficulties contributing to the current disorder. The coding of these contextual variables varies from none or minimal to extreme. This judgement takes into account the sociocultural values and responsiveness of an average person.
Axis V	Global Assessment of Functioning	This axis considers the highest level of psychological, social and occupational functioning achieved during the past year on a hypothetical continuum of mental health-illness. Usually, the present level can be compared with the previous as an indication of recovery from the presenting problem.

than if the cause of the distress is designated as lying within the individual concerned. Via Axis V, a clinician assesses the highest level of adaptive functioning in the past year. A full diagnosis using the DSM-IV system would consider each of these five axes, thereby involving a more holistic approach to the person and the mental health difficulty. Individuals also may have multiple diagnoses on each of the axes of disorders.

Despite these attempts to evolve a more all-encompassing framework, humanist psychologists – notably **Carl Rogers** and his followers – resist the use of such diagnostic labels, arguing persuasively that clients should be regarded and respected as 'persons', not as subjects to be impersonally categorised by a set of medical diagnostics (Rogers, 1959). Indeed, clinicians need to be continually aware of the potentially deleterious impact that insensitive use of such diagnostic terminology can have upon their clients who understandably may experience such

labelling as a violation of their unique identity and personhood.

Evolution of diagnostic categories

The diagnostic categories and the methods used to organise and present them have shifted with each of the editions of DSM and ICD. These shifts reflect changes in the opinions of a majority of mental health experts about exactly what constitutes a psychological disorder and where the lines between different types of disorders should be drawn. They also reflect changing perspectives among the public about what constitutes abnormality.

The revisions for DSM-IV, for example, were based on the judgements of many mental health experts who worked on advisory panels in specific areas of abnormal behaviour. In the revision process of each DSM, some diagnostic categories were dropped and others were added. The far-reaching consequences of such changes can be illustrated by considering here the elimination in the DSM-III (1980) of the traditional distinction between neurotic and psychotic disorders. **Neurotic disorders**, or neuroses, were originally conceived of as relatively common psychological problems in which a person did not have signs of brain abnormalities, did not display grossly irrational thinking and did not violate basic norms; but he or she did experience subjective distress or a pattern of self-defeating or inadequate coping strategies. **Psychotic disorders**, or psychoses, were thought to differ in both quality and severity from neurotic problems. It was believed that psychotic behaviour deviated significantly from social norms and was accompanied by a profound disturbance in rational thinking and general emotional and thought processes. The DSM-III-R advisory committees felt that the terms 'neurotic disorders' and 'psychotic disorders' had become too general in their meaning to have much usefulness as diagnostic categories. Interestingly, within the latest version of the World Health Organization's taxonomy of mental and behavioural disorders (the ICD-10, 1992), this traditional division between neurotic and psychotic disorders likewise has been dropped for similar reasons, disorders now being arranged into groups according to major common themes or descriptive likenesses. Nevertheless, it must be noted that these two descriptive terms continue to be used by many psychiatrists and psychologists, often in an attempt to characterise the general level of disturbance a person may be exhibiting.

Diagnosing certain behaviour patterns as mental disorders has political and ideological implications. For example, when making revisions for the DSM-III-R, a new diagnostic category was proposed for inclusion on Axis II, namely masochistic personality disorder (Franklin, 1987). **Masochism** was and still is currently diagnosed as one of the psychosexual disorders in which sexual gratification requires being hurt or humiliated. Clinicians on one of the advisory panels recommended it be included as a more pervasive personality disorder in which a person seeks failure on the job, at home and in relationships, rejects opportunities for pleasure and engages in excessive self-sacrifice. Feminist therapists and researchers argued that the diagnosis was biased against women and perpetuated the myth of women's masochism (Caplan, 1985). After a year-long debate, the label was changed to 'self-defeating personality disorder' and put in the appendices of the revised manual under the heading, 'Proposed Diagnostic Categories Needing Further Study'. Notably, it has not been included on Axis II of the DSM-IV.

Are DSM-IV and ICD-10 effective?

In order for a diagnostic system to become a shorthand language for communicating, its users have to be able to agree reliably on what the criteria and symptoms are for each disorder and what the diagnoses would be in specific cases. Reliability has improved substantially with the introduction of the latest, more descriptive and precise taxonomies, although they are still far from complete, especially for certain categories of disorders. Improved reliability has helped facilitate research efforts to improve understanding of psychological disorder and its treatment.

INTERIM SUMMARY

There are several goals that any diagnostic and classification system of psychological disorders should seek to fulfil. They include: (a) providing a common shorthand language for communicating about types of psychological disorder and particular cases in order to facilitate clinical and research work and (b) offering information about aetiology and about preferred modes of treatment. Disagreement over approaches to aetiology and treatment and the lack of knowledge in these areas place limits on how well these goals can be met.

DSM-IV and ICD-10 are the most widely accepted diagnostic and classification systems used by psychologists and psychiatrists. Both emphasise description of symptom patterns rather than identifying aetiology or treatments. The DSM utilises a multi-dimensional system of five axes that encourages mental health professionals to consider psychological, physical and social factors that might be relevant to psychological disorders. The continually evolving diagnostic categories of the DSM system reflect the shifting views of mental health experts and the public about what is or is not abnormal and about how best to describe particular categories of abnormality. The reliability of diagnosis of psychological disorders has improved substantially with the more descriptive and precise DSM-IV. However, some critics have raised concerns about the limited usefulness of the DSM system for making treatment decisions or helping people understand the causes of psychological disorders.

Concerns about the validity of the new DSM-IV and ICD-10 systems no doubt will be raised and tested by future research. Validity in descriptions and diagnoses of mental disorders is a complex concept. It involves, in part, fulfilling the second and third goals of classification systems: identifying aetiology and identifying treatments. One such concern is whether disorders that are regarded as unrelated might be better regarded as similar. This distinction has implications for aetiology and treatment. For example, there are many subtypes of schizophrenia (paranoid, hebephrenic/disorganised, catatonic, undifferentiated, residual) given within both the DSM-IV and ICD-10. Are these best thought of as variants of one basic kind of problem, or are there very different kinds of schizophrenia that have different causes and require different treatments? In answering such questions, we must remain aware of the problem of **nominalism**: that is, by attaching a label to distress and dysfunction of any kind, we may contribute to the construction of a new social role and thereby to a new disorder (Scheff, 1966). In turn, the prevalence of the phenomenon thereby increases – both by virtue of the ensuing increased categorisation and recognition, and by virtue of those who then come to act in accordance with the received meanings of that label.

Some critics argue that, by emphasising theoretically neutral descriptions of disorders, DSM does not include information on important psychological dimensions, such as impulsiveness, perceptual style or prominent defences, that may be helpful for treatment decisions and for understanding the causes of a disorder (Frances & Cooper, 1981; Persons, 1986). Even though ICD-10 and DSM-IV have their critics, they are the most widely used classification systems in clinical practice and are frequently employed in the training of new clinicians.

⊙ MAJOR TYPES OF PSYCHOLOGICAL DISORDERS

Here we turn to the analysis of several categories of psychological disorder. The majority of this section, however, is devoted to a detailed analysis of the most prominent ones: anxiety, mood disorder (for example, depression) and schizophrenic disorders. For each category, we will begin by describing what sufferers experience and how they appear to observers. Then we will consider how each of the major biological and psychological approaches to aetiology helps to explain the development of these disorders. We will selectively highlight widely used explanations and those that have been investigated in research.

There are many other categories of psychological disorder that we will not be able to examine, simply because of space limitations. However, what follows is a summary of some of the most important:

- Sexual disorders (such as that of desire, arousal and orgasm) and dysfunctions (for example, vaginismus – involuntary contraction of the vaginal muscles prior to digital or penile penetration); disorders involving unusual sexual practices – the paraphilias (for example, paedophilia and sexual sadism); and gender identity disorders. (For further reading, see Masters *et al* (1992); Bancroft (1989).)

- Delirium, dementia, amnestic and other cognitive disorders are psychological or behavioural abnormalities associated with temporary or permanent brain damage or malfunction. They may be a product of aging of the brain, neurodegenerative disease (as in the case of Alzheimer's and Parkinson's disease), accidents or excessive ingestion of substances, such as alcohol (leading to, for example, Korsakow's syndrome), lead and many types of pharmacological agents (including barbiturates, amphetamines and opiates). (For further reading, see Kolb & Whishaw (1990); Powell & Wilson (1994).)

- Substance-related disorders include both dependence upon and abuse of alcohol and drugs such as amphetamines, caffeine, cannabis, cocaine, nicotine, opiates, phencyclidine, sedatives, hypnotics and anxiolytics. We discussed many of these issues of substance abuse in the broader context of states of consciousness and in our addiction Close-ups.

- Somatoform disorders involve physical ('soma') symptoms, such as paralysis or pains in a limb, that arise in the absence of any physical or organic cause. This category includes the symptoms of what used to be called 'hysteria' but of what is now known less contentiously as **conversion disorder** – where a psychological difficulty becomes 'converted' into a loss or alteration in physical functioning. (For further reading, see Davison & Neale (1994).)

- Disorders usually first diagnosed in infancy, childhood or adolescence include mental retardation, learning disorders, communication disorders (for example, stuttering), elimination disorders (nocturnal enuresis – bed-wetting; and encopresis – faecal soiling) or behaviour problems (for example, attention-deficit disorder). (For a detailed psychological analysis of these disorders, see Herbert (1991); Rutter & Hersov (1985).)

- Associated with the latter group are the eating disorders: anorexia nervosa (a refusal to maintain body weight at a minimal normal weight for age and height); and bulimia nervos**a** (recurrent binge eating often coupled with self-induced vomiting, use of laxatives and fasting). These typically occur in adolescence or young adulthood. (For further reading on eating disorders, see Chapter 10 in this volume; Wardle (1994).)

As you read about the symptoms and experiences that are typical of the various psychological disturbances, you may begin to feel that some of the characteristics apply to you – at least part of the time – or to someone you know. Some of the disorders that we will consider are not uncommon, so it would be surprising if they sounded completely alien. Many of us have some human frailties that appear on the list of criteria for a particular psychological disorder. Recognition of this familiarity can be a useful way of furthering your understanding of abnormal psychology, but it is important to remember that a diagnosis for any disorder depends on a number of criteria and requires the judgement of a trained mental health professional. Please resist the temptation to use this new knowledge to diagnose friends and family members as pathological. On the other hand, being sensitive to others' needs for counsel and social support in times of personal trouble is always appropriate.

Before exploring anxiety, depression and schizophrenia in depth, we will briefly consider examples of disorders from two additional classification categories: **personality disorders** and **dissociative disorders**. Once again, because of space limitations, our treatment of these disorders will be brief.

◉ Personality Disorders

A personality disorder is a long-standing (chronic), inflexible, maladaptive pattern of perceiving, thinking or behaving. These patterns can seriously impair an individual's ability to function in social or work settings and can cause significant distress. Conceptually, they derive within psychology from a trait approach to personality. They are usually recognisable by the time a person reaches adolescence. As a group, however, personality disorders are among the least reliably judged of all the psychological disorders and are the most controversial. For example, psychologists disagree about whether personality disorders can be said truly to exist since consistency in human behaviour is difficult to observe, moreover, difficult to assign reliably to either internal or external causes (Sampson, 1982). Thus, there is controversy about evaluating lifelong behaviour patterns independently of the contexts in which they have developed. Critical theorists point out that economic, social, family and cultural factors may provide better explanations of the observed behaviour of a given individual than do diagnoses of

TABLE 14.2	SUMMARY OF PERSONALITY DISORDERS

CLUSTER A

Paranoid: pervasive distrust and suspiciousness of others, their motives interpreted as malevolent

Schizoid: pervasive detachment from social relationships and restricted range of emotional expression

Schizotypal: acute discomfort with close relationships, cognitive and perceptual distortions, eccentricities of behaviour

CLUSTER B

Antisocial (*included under 'dissocial' in ICD*): pervasive disregard and violation of the rights of others

Borderline (*subtype of 'emotionally unstable' in ICD*): instability of relationships, self-image of affects and notable impulsivity

Histrionic: pervasive and excessive emotionality and attention seeking

Narcissistic (*included under 'other specific' in ICD*): pervasive grandiosity, need for admiration and lack of empathy

CLUSTER C

Avoidant (*termed 'anxious (avoidant)' in ICD*): pervasive social inhibition, self-perceived inadequacy and marked sensitivity to negative evaluation

Dependent: pervasive and excessive need to be looked after, submissive and clinging behaviour, fears of separation

Obsessive-compulsive (*called 'anankastic' in ICD*): pervasive preoccupation with orderliness, perfectionism, mental and interpersonal control, leading to inflexibility, lack of openness and to inefficiency

personality disorders by themselves (Emler *et al*, 1987).

Despite such serious criticisms, however, the DSM-IV recognises ten types of personality disorders (grouped into three clusters), all of which are recognisable within ICD-10 nomenclature wherein a similar number are specified. A summary of these personality disorders are shown in *Table 14.2*. Here, however, we will discuss two of the better known forms: the narcissistic and antisocial personality disorders.

Narcissistic personality disorder

People with a **narcissistic personality disorder** are observed as having a grandiose sense of self-importance, a preoccupation with fantasies of success or power and a need for constant attention or admiration. These people often respond inappropriately to criticism or minor defeat, either by displaying an apparent indifference to criticism or by markedly over-reacting. Finally, they have problems in interpersonal relationships; they tend to feel entitled to special favours with no reciprocal obligations, exploit others for their own indulgence and have difficulty recognising and experiencing how others feel. For example, an individual with narcissistic personality disorder may express annoyance and no empathy when a friend has to cancel a date because of a death in the family. Many of these features have been validated by empirical studies (Ronningstam & Gunderson, 1990).

Antisocial personality disorder

Antisocial personality disorder which should not be used synonymously with the term 'psychopathy' is marked by a long-standing pattern of irresponsible behaviour that has negative consequences for others and is typically carried out without guilt. Lying, stealing and fighting are indicators commonly observed. People with an antisocial personality often do not experience shame or intense emotion of any kind. Thus, they can retain their composure in situations that would make other people emotionally aroused and upset. Violations of social norms begin early in their lives – disrupting classes, getting into fights and running away from home. Their actions are marked by indifference to the rights of others. Although they can be found among street criminals and con artists, they are well represented among successful politicians and business people who put career, money and power above everything and everyone. In the United States of America, for example, two to three per cent of the population is believed to display antisocial personality disorder.

Men are four times more likely to be so designated than women (Regier *et al*, 1988). Divergent socialisation processes between the sexes may in part explain these differences in recorded antisocial behaviour (Farrington & West, 1993). There are indications, however, that antisocial acts amongst young women are becoming more commonplace given the continuing emergence of instrumentally aggressive female gangs in socially deprived urban areas (Campbell, 1984). Just as for boys, such shows of hostility establish personal reputations and convey status upon individual group members (Emler, 1984). These

These two paintings by Sybil, a multiple personality disorder victim, illustrate differences between the personalities. The painting on the left was done by Peggy, Sybil's angry, fearful personality; the painting on the right was done by Mary, a home-loving personality.

554   CHAPTER 14 ····· ABNORMAL PSYCHOLOGY

trends and processes underline the importance of understanding antisocial personality disorder in relation to the social context in which it may be engendered.

Dissociative Disorders

A **dissociative disorder** is a disturbance in the integration of identity, memory or consciousness. It is important for us to see ourselves as being in control of our behaviour – including our emotions, thoughts and actions. Essential to this perception of self-control is the sense of selfhood – the consistency of different aspects of the self and the continuity of our identity over time and place. Psychologists believe that, in dissociated states, individuals escape from their conflicts by giving up this precious consistency and continuity – becoming dissociated from and, in a sense, disowning part of themselves. Not being able to recall details of a traumatic event – **amnesia** – even though neurological damage is not present, is one example of dissociation (also see Chapter 8). Psychologists have only recently begun to appreciate the degree to which such dissociation of memory from self can be precipitated by instances of sexual and physical childhood abuse. The forgetting of important

personal experiences caused by psychological factors in the absence of any organic dysfunction is termed **psychogenic amnesia** or **functional amnesia**.

Multiple personality disorder (MPD) is a dissociative mental disorder in which two or more distinct personalities exist within the same individual. At any particular time, one of these personalities is dominant in directing the individual's behaviour. Multiple personality disorders have been popularised in books and movies, such as *The Three Faces of Eve* (Thigpen & Cleckley, 1957) and *Sybil* (Schreiber, 1973). Multiple personality disorder is popularly known as 'split personality' and sometimes mistakenly described as schizophrenia, a disorder in which personality often is impaired but is not split into multiple versions. In MPD, although the original personality is unaware of the other personalities, they are conscious of it and often of each other. Each of the emerging personalities contrasts in some significant way with the original self – they might be outgoing if the person is shy, tough if the original personality is weak, and sexually assertive if the other is sexually fearful and naive. Each personality has a unique identity, name, behaviour pattern and even characteristic brain wave activity. In some cases, numerous different characters emerge to help the person deal with a difficult life situation. The emergence of these alternate personalities, each with

TABLE 14.3		RESPONSES TO INQUIRIES REGARDING ABUSE: COMPARING MULTIPLE PERSONALITY DISORDER AND DEPRESSION			

Questionnaire Item	MPD (N = 355) %		Major Depression (N = 235) %		Significance
Abuse Incidence	98		54		p<.0001
TYPE(S)					
Physical	82		24		p<.0001
Sexual	86		25		p<.0001
Psychological	86		42		p<.0001
Neglect	54		21		p<.0001
All of above	47		6		p<.0001
Physical and sexual	74		14		p<.0001
	Mean	S.D.	Mean	S.D.	
Beginning age of abuse	3.3	2.6	7.5	8.7	p<.0001
Ending age of abuse	17.3	7.5	22.6	15.6	p<.001
GENDER					
Female	90.0		73.0		p<.001
Male	10.0		27.0		

its own consciousness, is sudden and typically has been precipitated by a stressful event.

Most often, MPD victims are women who were severely abused physically or sexually by parents, relatives or close friends for extended periods during childhood. One study obtained questionnaire data from 448 clinicians who had treated cases of multiple personality disorders and major depressions (used for comparative purposes). As shown in *Table 14.3* (previous page), the dominant features of the 355 cases of multiple personality disorder (MPD) are an almost universal incidence among mostly female patients of being abused at a very early age, starting around three years old and continuing for more than a decade. Although many of the 255 comparison patients with depression disorder also had a high incidence of abuse, it was significantly less than that experienced by those with MPD (Schultz *et al*, 1989).

MPD victims may have been beaten, locked up or abandoned by those who were supposed to love them – those on whom they were so dependent that they could not fight them, leave them or even hate them. Instead, they have fled their terror symbolically through dissociation. Psychologists believe that multiple personalities develop to serve a vital survival function. Individuals in horrifying situations may protect their egos by creating stronger internal characters to help cope with the ongoing traumatic situation and also to provide relief from their pain by numbing the dominant personality to the abuse. Putnam (1990), a leading researcher in the study of multiple personality disorder, has found that, in the typical case, there are many different alter egos, of different ages and even of both sexes, within the mind of the troubled person. In some circumstances, however, such as during a legal prosecution and courtroom trial, a person may deliberately contrive multiple personalities so as to avoid punishment or to obtain rewards not otherwise attainable (Spanos *et al*, 1985).

Until recently, information on multiple personality disorders has come from single cases treated by one therapist over an extended period of time. Ongoing research, however, is being conducted with the collaboration of many investigators and is enabling clinicians to get a more complete picture of this remarkable disorder that puts on stage too many actors for any one director to manage (Putnam, 1984).

Patients experiencing MPD respond well to treatment that centres on hypnotherapy. The alternate selves emerge under hypnosis and a therapist can assist the patient in eliminating some of them while integrating others into a more effective and coherent single self. The reason hypnotherapy is the treatment of choice with many cases of MPD is because patients apparently use a form of self-hypnosis to develop the characters in the first place, to defend themselves from the hostile environment in which they were forced to live.

During a session in which a therapist was using hypnosis to uncover the source of a female client's chronic problems with dizziness, fainting, nausea, unexplained terrors and suicidal episodes, a strange voice emerged from her. It spoke with a contemptuous intonation, reporting that it 'began with the existence of evil'. The alien voice of the client identified itself as 'a demon'. The therapist's hypothesis was that this aspect of the client's personality probably developed from repeated beatings by her mother and years of sexual abuse by her stepfather during her childhood. Nevertheless, this adult woman had no conscious contact with this other personality nor conscious awareness of her earlier abuse until the hypnotherapy session released her inner 'demon' through guided recall (Kierulff, 1989).

Psychotherapist **Irvin Yalom** (1989) provides an evocatively written account of a similar dual-personality case example wherein he takes an avowedly directive stance. Despite the initial presentation of two personas, Yalom stresses the importance as a clinician of maintaining a 'therapeutically monogamous' and welcoming professional relationship with the prior authentic personality of the MPD client. Gradually over time, the destructive elements of the competing personality are eroded and dissembled as a result of being consistently unreinforced. The constructive components of the inauthentic personality become reintegrated back into the pre-existing persona. The latter is encouraged to re-emerge at the expense of the former by the selective deployment of the therapist's positive regard.

INTERIM SUMMARY

Personality disorders are long-standing, inflexible, maladaptive patterns of perceiving, thinking or behaving that seriously impair an individual's functioning or cause significant distress. Two of the better known personality disorders are narcissistic personality disorder and antisocial personality disorder. Some psychologists reject the diagnosis of a personality disorder, preferring instead to base explanations for such behaviour patterns on external, situational factors. Dissociative disorders involve a basic disruption of the integrated functioning of memory, consciousness or personal identity. In cases of multiple personality, two or more separate identities emerge to cope with the trauma of childhood sexual and physical abuse experienced by those who develop this disorder, most of whom are women.

◉ Anxiety Disorders: Types

Everyone experiences anxiety or fear in certain life situations. The feelings of uneasiness that characterise anxiety and fear are often accompanied by physical reactions, such as a sweaty brow or clammy palms, and may include a sense of impending harm. For some people, anxiety becomes problematic enough to interfere with their ability to function effectively or enjoy everyday life. It has been estimated that 15 per cent of the general population has, at some time, experienced the symptoms that are characteristic of the various anxiety disorders recognised in DSM-IV (Regier et al, 1988). While anxiety plays a key role in each of these disorders, they differ in the extent to which anxiety is experienced, the severity of the anxiety and the situations that trigger the anxiety. We will review four major categories of anxiety: generalised anxiety disorder, panic disorder, phobic disorder and obsessive-compulsive disorder. We have talked already about a fifth kind of anxiety disorder, post-traumatic stress disorder, at the beginning of this chapter and in Chapter 11.

Generalised anxiety disorder

When a person feels anxious or worried most of the time for at least six months, when not threatened by any specific danger or object (i.e. it is 'free-floating'), a **generalised anxiety disorder** is diagnosed. The anxiety might be focused on specific life circumstances, such as unrealistic concerns about finances or the well-being of a loved one, or it just might consist of a general apprehensiveness about impending harm. Often it is related to chronic environmental stress. It occurs in four per cent of the general population (Rapee, 1991) and typically may begin during adolescence. The disorder tends to overlap and to show **comorbidity** with obsessive-compulsive disorder and social phobia (Barlow, 1988), the symptoms and causes of these three not being entirely specific to any one. The way the anxiety is expressed in the generalised form – the specific symptoms – may vary from person to person. The common symptoms can be grouped into three categories:

- *Body tension*: muscular tension, tension headaches, jitteryness, trembling, being easily fatigued, feeling restless, unable to relax, sighing often.
- *Physical arousal*: heart pounding or racing, shortness of breath, sweaty palms, dizziness, epigastric discomfort, lightheadedness, dry mouth, diarrhoea, smothering sensations, flushes.
- *Vigilance*: hyperattentiveness to one's own internal

reactions and to external events, difficulty concentrating, feeling keyed up or on edge, nervousness, sleeping difficulties, irritability.

In spite of these symptoms, a chronically anxious person may continue to function with only mild impairment in his or her social life or job. The constant physical and psychological drain, however, takes a toll (via, for example, immunosuppression) that may manifest as a greater susceptibility to many common ailments, such as colds and other viral infections.

Panic disorder

In contrast to the chronic presence of anxiety in generalised anxiety disorder, sufferers of **panic disorder** experience unexpected (at least initially) and severe attacks of intense anxiety that may last only minutes but which reach a crescendo within no more than ten. This results in a usually hurried exit from wherever the person may be, the situation subsequently being avoided. If associated with specific situational triggers, these distressing episodes are termed *cued panic attacks* and thereby may indicate a phobic reaction. If the attacks are uncued by the external environment, panic disorder is designated. The attacks may occur at least several times a month and typically begin with a feeling of intense apprehension, fear or terror. Invariably, this state becomes focused upon fear of imminent death, losing control of one's actions or of 'going mad'. Feelings of unreality and of depersonalisation are common (Fewtrell & O'Connor, 1995). Also evident are physical symptoms of anxiety, including autonomic hyperactivity (such as rapid heart rate and hyperventilation), dizziness, faintness, nausea or sensations of choking and suffocation.

Because of the apparently unexpected nature of these 'hit and run' attacks, anticipatory anxiety often develops as an added complication in panic disorders. The dread of the next attack and of being helpless and suddenly out of control can lead to avoidance of public places yet fear of being left alone. Thus, in the DSM-IV panic disorder is recognised as occurring with or without agoraphobia, the former being more commonplace.

The following comments made during an attack convey the degree of panic that is experienced by someone with this distressing disorder:

'I'm not going to make it. I can't get help . . . It's like a feeling that sweeps over from the top of my head to the tip of my toes. And I detest the feeling. I'm very frightened. It feels, I just get all, like hot through me and

shaky and my heart just feels like it's pounding and breathing really quick . . . It feels like I'm going to die or something' (Muskin & Fyer, 1981).

Following an initial panic attack, a persistent fear of having another one often arises. This 'fear-of-fear' hypothesis is the principal psychological and cognitive explanation of panic disorder. In this vein, Clark (1986) has suggested during the initial stages of a panic attack, the individual misinterprets the physiological symptoms associated with anxiety (such as palpitations, breathlessness and dizziness). Rather, they are viewed as indications that a catastrophic event (for example, a fatal heart attack or stroke) is about to occur. Clark maintains that this **catastrophising** of somatic symptoms (i.e. focusing selectively on the worst possible outcomes in a situation) is part of a vicious circle. Such fear leads to greater anxiety and thereby to further unpleasant somatic symptoms. These in turn may also be misperceived as heralding an impending catastrophic event, and so on. Readiness to interpret catastrophically bodily sensations means that victims become hypervigilant, continually monitoring their bodily state. The slightest somatic sign becomes noticed and taken as evidence of some serious physical or mental disorder. Thus, the individual gets caught in an escalating fear-of-fear cycle, culminating in an intense attack of panic. Sanderson *et al* (1989) further extend this cognitive explanation, their research indicating that the perceived loss of control accompanying a panic attack is of central importance to understanding an individual's descent into the characteristic spiral of fear.

However, more recently, Hallam (1991) has questioned the distinction between panic as a phobic reaction ('cued') and panic as a product of fearfulness. He argues that a more complex explanation is needed in the form of a psychosocial model which accounts for the probable interaction between **exogenous** (i.e. 'external' to the person) and **endogenous** (i.e. 'internal' to the person) causes.

Phobic disorders

Fear is a rational reaction to an objectively identified external danger (such as a fire in one's home or being attacked in the street) that may induce a person to flee or attack in self-defence. In contrast, a person with a **phobic disorder**, or phobia, suffers from a persistent and irrational fear of a specific object, activity, or situation that creates a compelling desire to avoid it.

Many of us have irrational fears of spiders or snakes (or even multiple-choice tests). Such fears become phobic disorders only when they interfere with our adjustment, cause significant distress or

inhibit necessary action toward goals. Even a very specific, apparently limited phobia can have a great impact on one's whole life.

Myra is a mature student living in the midst of a large, metropolitan area. She has a phobia of dogs (cynophobia). As a girl, her uncle regularly came to visit with his pet Alsatian dog. Her mother would put Myra in the front room to eat her dinner while the adults talked elsewhere in the house. She also put the large dog in there, too. Myra would give all her food to the dog to keep it occupied. When she heard her mother approach, she would quickly take the plate away again. In this way, she avoided contact with the pet and never overcame her fear. Today, she plans her route by foot to college so as to avoid central urban precincts where dogs roam. She avoids streets containing houses in which dogs are kept, adding considerable time and distance to her daily journey. She goes out much less often than she would like. She hyperventilates even in response to the recorded sound of dogs barking. Myra carries a shopping bag wherever she goes so that, if necessary, she may place it between herself and any dog that appears to be coming towards her. She finds it difficult to discriminate mentally between dogs that have healthy-looking coats and wag their tails a lot and those that appear under-fed, have uncared-for coats, no collar, a motionless tail and bark angrily at strangers. Her mental representation of a dog is that they consist in the main of a large salivating mouth, full of big sharp teeth, the sole purpose of which is to bite whatever and whoever is nearby. She could not bring herself to stroke a dog. She does not know how to go about doing so. Hesitancy and awkwardness around them confounds her fear.

Phobias are a relatively common psychological problem. Recent studies suggest between six and 12.5 per cent of the general population suffer some form of phobia at some point in their lives (Regier *et al*, 1988), with approximately twice as many women reporting them than men (Myers *et al*, 1984). Almost any stimulus can come to generate a phobic avoidance reaction (see *Table 14.4*), although some phobias are much more common than others. Seligman (1971) has argued that as a species, we have evolved to be biologically prepared to learn adaptive avoidance reactions to certain kinds of stimuli (such as poisonous snakes and spiders) as opposed to other more benign ones (for example, houses and cuddly toys). The important difference between these sets of stimuli is not so much the ease with which they can elicit the acquisition of a phobic reaction; rather, it is manifest in terms of the rate with which associated

TABLE 14.4 THE COMMON PHOBIAS

Phobia	Approximate Per Cent of All Phobias	Sex Difference	Typical Age of Onset
AGORAPHOBIAS (fear of places of assembly, crowds, open spaces)	10–50	Large majority are women	Early adulthood
SOCIAL PHOBIAS (fear of being observed doing something humiliating)	10	Majority are women	Adolescence

THE SPECIFIC PHOBIAS
Animals
  Cats
  Dogs
  Insects
  Spiders (arachnophobia)
  Birds
  Horses
  Snakes
  Rodents
	5–15	Vast majority are women	Childhood

Inanimate Objects or Situations
  Dirt
  Storms
  Heights
  Darkness
  Enclosed spaces
    (claustrophobia)
	20	None	Any age

Illness–Injury
  Death
  Cancer
  Venereal disease
	15–25	None	Middle age

fear reactions may extinguish thereafter (Öhman *et al*, 1975). The role of prepared learning in the acquisition of phobias, then, may have been somewhat overemphasised. Nevertheless, it is undeniable that stimuli which evoke phobic responses are by no means chance ones and that the different extinction rates of particular fears enhanced our ancestors' chances of survival.

We will now discuss two of the most common phobias: agoraphobia and social phobia.

Agoraphobia

Agoraphobia (from the Greek word 'agora' meaning 'marketplace') is an extreme fear of being in public places or open spaces from which escape may be difficult or embarrassing. Individuals with agoraphobia fear places such as crowded rooms, shopping centres, buses and motorways. They are often afraid that, if they experience some kind of difficulty outside the

home, such as a loss of bladder control or panic attack symptoms, that help might not be available or the situation will be embarrassing for them. These fears deprive individuals of their freedom of movement. In extreme cases, they become prisoners in their own homes. They cannot hold a job or carry on normal daily activities because their fears restrict contact with the outside world. Agoraphobia often begins with reoccurring panic attacks. The afflicted person then seeks to diminish the possibility of a reoccurrence by avoiding places which are appraised as heightening risk. However, both ICD and DSM recognise that agoraphobia may also occur without a prior history of panic disorder.

Agoraphobia is the most commonly cited phobia among people who seek psychiatric or psychological treatment. As many as 60 per cent of all those with phobias who are being treated in clinics suffer from this disorder. Between 2.7 per cent and 5.8 per cent of adults in the general population are estimated to suffer from agoraphobia (NIMH, 1986). Most sufferers of agoraphobia are women for whom the phobia begins either in adolescence or early adulthood, often with an extreme anxiety attack. Besides their fear of going out into public places, agoraphobics may have other psychological problems, such as anxiety, depression and obsessive-compulsive symptoms, more so than do other phobic individuals. However, these do not dominate the clinical picture. Similar to others with extreme anxiety, they may use alcohol and drugs to suppress emotional arousal.

Mitchell (1982) conceives of agoraphobia as a form of separation anxiety. Indeed, according to Rachman (1984), the sufferer is unable to cope with being apart from a person or place of relative safety Supporting such a view, it has been found that the loss of a symbolic place of safety in the form of a loved one often precedes the onset of agoraphobia (Fonagy & Higgitt, 1984). It has also been found that separation anxiety in childhood is more commonplace amongst adults who later become agoraphobic than among those who do not (Gittelman & Klein, 1985).

Consistent with this safety-seeking hypothesis is the sociocultural account of the disproportionate numbers of women amongst agoraphobics. This explanation focuses upon differences between men and women in their traditional sex roles and socialisation (Hallam, 1985). Until the latter half of this century, women largely have been encouraged from a young age to stay at home to fulfil a domestic and nurturant role. Men, on the other hand, have been socialised to make recurrent forays into the outside world for the purposes of economic provision. Thereby, men have opportunity to make excursions which inadvertently may extinguish any fears that might otherwise be engendered about leaving the familiar environment of hearth and home. Women caught in an exclusively domestic role have less occasion to do so and thereby can become phobic of novel, comparatively 'unsafe' situations. If such sociocultural theorising is correct, we should see a diminishing incidence of agoraphobia amongst women as these traditional sex roles are increasingly eroded.

Social phobia

Social phobia is a persistent, irrational fear that arises in anticipation of a public situation involving a comparatively small group of unfamiliar people in which one can be observed and evaluated. Like agoraphobia, a person with a social phobia fears that he or she will act in ways that could be embarrassing. The person recognises that the fear is excessive and unreasonable yet feels compelled by the fear to avoid situations in which public scrutiny and criticism is possible. Panic can be involved in social phobia (Barlow et al, 1985). However, rather than signalling

This crowded scene would cause many agoraphobics to panic.

the possibility of some physically catastrophic event, socially phobic people are fearful that their panic attack may be noticed by others and become the subject of mockery.

Examples of typical social phobias are the fear of choking on food when eating in front of others and the fear of trembling embarrassingly when speaking in public. Sometimes the phobia is more general and may include fears about acting foolishly in social situations and being open to ridicule. In so doing, people who are socially phobic frequently judge their own behaviour with reference to criteria which they would not wish to bring to bear on others (Hope et al, 1989).

Social phobia often involves a self-fulfilling prophecy. A person may be so fearful of the scrutiny and rejection of others that enough anxiety is created to impair performance. Very often such people find it difficult to look at the person to whom they are speaking, thereby creating an awkwardness in their social interactions. Otherwise capable students handicapped by social phobias have been known to drop out of vocational training when they realise that speaking in public is regularly expected of them.

Obsessive-compulsive disorder

Only a year or so ago, 17-year-old Jim seemed to be a normal adolescent with many talents and interests. Then, almost overnight, he was transformed into a

560   CHAPTER 14 ····· ABNORMAL PSYCHOLOGY

'You ask me why I gamble and I tell you, it's the thrill. I know . . . I haven't got a chance, but when I put my money on a horse and hear its name on the speaker, my heart stands still. I know I'm alive' (Newman, 1972).

Approximately two-thirds of the adult population in the UK have gambled at some point in their lives (Cornish, 1978). A review of research by Griffiths (1989) on gambling in teenage children and adolescents shows that self-reports of having gambled over a prior 12-month period range from 65 to 85 per cent. Gambling is a major source of revenue for many companies and charitable organisations. However, when we are playing on fruit and other slot machines, buying a raffle or lottery ticket or playing bingo, few of us think about how our losses will enhance the profits of others. Instead, we fantasise about winning a new car, a house or escaping from the daily grind.

Three to five per cent of the general population feel they cannot control their gambling behaviour (Shaffer, 1989). Such compulsive gambling is a 'chronic and progressive failure to resist impulses to gamble and gambling behaviour that compromises, disrupts, or damages personal, family, or vocational pursuits' (Breo, 1989).

The compulsive gambler is often portrayed as a man in his 40s or 50s. However, this profile is by no means typical of all gamblers. Recent surveys have found that women, young people and ethnic minorities have been under-represented in demographic research on compulsive gamblers. A recent questionnaire study of 9,752 13 to 16-year-old school-children in the UK, found that 14

per cent identified themselves as 'regular' fruit machine players (National Housing & Town Planning Council, 1988). Many school pupils gamble for money and feel they cannot stop, using their lunch funds, stealing or shoplifting to support their activities (Gilman, 1989). The surveys also reveal that people who are unemployed, have a poor record of academic achievement at school, or who are in receipt of low incomes are at an above average risk of becoming compulsive gamblers (Volberg, 1994).

Pathological gambling provides psychologists with the opportunity to study 'addictions' as context-ually contingent behaviours rather than as problems caused by substances that have been ingested, injected or inhaled (Shaffer *et al*, 1989). Nevertheless, as in addic-tions to unprescribed psychotropic drugs, the physiological activity of regular gamblers is discriminable from that of non-regular 'users'. **Mark Griffiths** (1993a) examined the heart rates of 18 to 29-year-olds whilst they gambled on fruit machines. He found that during play the rates of both regular and non-regular slot-machine gamblers increased on average by 22 beats per minute. After cessation of play,

however, whereas the heart rates of non-regular participants did not decrease significantly, those of regular players started to fall immediately. It would appear these seasoned players have developed a physiological 'tolerance' to gambling on fruit machines. Thus, as in other addictions, regular players come to require their 'fix' of either winning or of nearly doing so increasingly more often in order to achieve and maintain the same prior level of pleasurable arousal.

Importantly this research also shows that, as when a win actually occurs, 'nearly winning' likewise involves being physiologically reinforced – but notably in the absence of any financial payout, a phenomenon which Griffiths (1991) has termed 'the psychobiology of the near miss'. Cognitively, regular gamblers are caught up interpreting their misfortunes as evidence of 'constantly nearly winning' rather than of 'consistently losing'.

Help may yet be at hand for pathological gamblers. Studying the cognitive biases of compulsive players, Griffiths (1994) asked participants to verbalise thoughts whilst gambling on a machine. Afterwards, tape-recordings of their stream of consciousness were played back to four subjects who had requested this available feedback. All were shocked at how they had personified the machines and at the irrationality of their thinking. An eventual complete cessation thereafter of gambling activities for one subject was largely attributable to the impact of the audio playback (Griffiths, 1993b). A clinical evaluation of this promising therapeutic technique is currently under way.

lonely outsider, excluded from social life by his psychological disabilities. Specifically, he developed an obsession with washing. Haunted by the notion that he was dirty – in spite of what his senses told him – he began to spend more of his time cleansing himself of imaginary dirt. At first, his ritual ablutions were confined to weekends and evenings, but soon they began to consume all his time, forcing him to drop out of school (Rapoport, 1989).

Jim suffers from a condition known as **obsessive-compulsive disorder** (O-CD) that is estimated to affect up to three per cent of the general population at some point during their lives (Karno et al, 1988).

Obsessions are doubts, fears, images, impulses and thoughts (such as Jim's belief that he is unclean) that recur unbidden or persist despite a person's efforts to suppress them (Akhtar et al, 1975). Obsessions are experienced as an unwanted invasion of consciousness, seem to be senseless or repugnant and are unacceptable to the person experiencing them. Frequently, the individual avoids the situations that relate to the content of the obsessions. For example, a person with an obsessive fear about germs may avoid using bathrooms outside his or her home or refuse to shake hands with strangers.

You probably have had some sort of mild obsessional experience, such as the intrusion of petty worries – 'Did I really lock the door?'; 'Did I turn off the oven?' – or the persistence of a haunting tune you simply could not stop from running through your mind. The obsessive thoughts of people with this obsessive-compulsive disorder are much more compelling, cause much more distress and may interfere with their social or role functioning. Observable in many of us are personality traits such as meticulousness, cleanliness, a strong need for order and indecisiveness. When they occur together and in noticeably marked form, the designation of an obsessional personality disorder (termed 'anankastic' personality in WHO nomenclature) would be appropriate. However, an anankastic personality does not necessarily lead to O-CD, despite the apparent similarities in behaviour between the two (Pollack, 1979). Nor are O-CD sufferers more likely than non-sufferers to have had a personality of this kind prior to onset of the disorder (de Silva, 1994). Thus, obsessive-compulsive personality and obsessive-compulsive disorder are not causally related.

Obsessive thoughts, images or impulses often focus around characteristic themes. A content analysis of the obsessions of 82 people with obsessive-compulsive disorder yielded five broad categories, in the following order of frequency: (1) dirt and contamination, (2) violence and aggression, (3) the orderliness of inanimate objects, (4) sex and (5) religion (Akhtar et al, 1975).

Compulsions are repetitive, covert cognitions or overt purposeful acts (such as Jim's washing)

performed according to certain rules or in a ritualised manner in response to an obsession. Compulsive behaviour is intended to reduce or prevent the discomfort and anxiety associated with some dreaded situation, but it is either unreasonable or clearly excessive. Typical compulsions include irresistible urges to clean, to check that lights or electrical appliances have been turned off and to count objects or possessions. Akhtar et al (1975) distinguish between yielding and controlling compulsions: the former referring to where urges are experienced as being 'forced' upon sufferers; the latter where the repetitive act or thought allows the individual to resist a compulsive urge.

At least, initially, people with obsessive-compulsive disorder resist carrying out their compulsions. When they are calm, they view their compulsion as senseless. When anxiety rises, however, the power of the compulsive behaviour ritual to relieve tension seems irresistible – and must be performed. Part of the distress experienced by people with this mental problem is created by their frustration at recognising the irrationality or excessive nature of their obsessions without being able to eliminate them. People with obsessive-compulsive disorder are also often found to be significantly depressed (Rachman & Hodgson, 1980).

⊙ Anxiety Disorders: Causes

In describing these anxiety disorders, we have given an indication of how psychologists explain the development of each one. However, the four aetiological approaches that we have outlined previously – psychodynamic, behavioural, cognitive and biological – emphasise different casual factors. Let us analyse here how each of these perspectives adds something unique to our understanding of this group of disorders.

Psychodynamic

The psychoanalytic model begins with the assumption that the symptoms of anxiety disorders and obsessions and compulsions come from underlying psychic conflicts or fears. The symptoms are attempts to protect the individual from psychological pain.

In anxiety disorders, intense pain attacks and phobias are the result of unconscious conflicts bursting into consciousness. The unconscious conflicts are seen as having their roots in early childhood experiences. For example, a child's older sibling may be selected for a prestigious sports team. He may see how his older sister receives a great deal of praise for her success but must then move out of the house to attend a college specialising in sport and education in another part of the country. He may then develop a strong desire to be recognised for individual achievement and, at the same time, an intense fear that success will separate him from the comfort and guidance of his parents (Freud, 1926). He may thus develop unconscious conflicting feelings about achievement and recognition. In later life, a phobia may be activated by an object or situation that symbolises the conflict. In our same example, a bridge might come to symbolise the path that the child must traverse from the comforting world of home and family to the world of work, achievement and potential failure and rejection. The sight of a bridge would then force the unconscious conflict into awareness, bringing with it the fear and anxiety common to phobias. So, the individual would develop a fear of bridges – a fear that they might collapse. Avoiding bridges would be his symbolic attempt to stay clear of achievement situations and the anxiety that accompanies them.

In obsessive-compulsive disorders, the obsessive behaviour is an attempt to displace anxiety created by a related but far more feared desire or conflict. By substituting an obsession that symbolically captures the forbidden impulse, a person gains some relief. For example, the obsessive fears of dirt experienced by Jim, the adolescent we described earlier, may have their roots in the conflict between his desire to become sexually active and his fear of 'dirtying' his reputation. Compulsive preoccupation with carrying out a minor ritualistic task also allows the individual to avoid the issue creating unconscious conflict. In some cases, a compulsive act, such as repetitive handwashing, seems intended to undo feelings of guilt over real or imagined sins.

Behavioural

Behavioural explanations of anxiety focus on the way symptoms of anxiety disorders are reinforced or conditioned. They do not search for underlying unconscious conflicts or early childhood experiences because these are phenomena that cannot be measured objectively or observed directly. Behavioural theories are often used to explain the development of phobias, which are seen as classically conditioned fears. A previously neutral object or situation becomes a stimulus for a phobia by being paired with a frightening experience. For example, a man who calls his home from a shopping precinct only to receive the painful information that a loved one has suddenly died may develop a phobia of shopping precincts. After this experience, upon

approaching a shopping precinct he may experience a wave of fear and gloom that cannot be relieved. Phobias continue to be maintained by negative reinforcement: by the reduction in anxiety that occurs when a person withdraws from the feared situation.

Cognitive

Cognitive perspectives on anxiety concentrate on the perceptual processes or attitudes that may distort a person's estimation of the danger that he or she is facing. A person may either overestimate the nature or reality of a threat or underestimate his or her ability to cope with the threat effectively. Faulty thinking processes, such as a tendency to catastrophise – to focus selectively on the worst possible outcomes in a situation – are at the heart of anxiety disorders. As we have seen in the case of panic attacks, a person may attribute undue significance to minor physical sensations. This initiates a vicious cycle wherein they are mistakenly interpreted as signalling impending physical disaster, which in turn increases anxiety, thereby exacerbating the physical sensations and confirming the person's fears (Beck & Emery, 1985).

Before delivering a speech to a large group, a person with a social phobia may feed his or her anxiety by a chain of catastrophising conditions.

'What if I forget what I was going to say? I will look foolish in front of all these people. Then I will get even more nervous and start to perspire and my voice will shake and I'll look even sillier. Whenever people will see me from now on they will remember me as the foolish person who tried to give a speech.'

With each new thought, the anxiety of the speaker escalates. Researchers have indeed found that anxious patients may contribute to the maintenance of their anxiety by employing cognitive biases that highlight threatening stimuli.

Clinically anxious (but not depressed) subjects were compared to normal controls on a task that measured attention to a visual display of 48 threat-related or neutral words (such as injury, agony, failure and lonely). The words were presented in pairs for a brief duration. The pairs consisted of either a neutral word and a threat word or two neutral words. On a random one-third of the 288 trials, a dot of light (a probe) appeared in the area where one of the two words had just been flashed. The subjects pressed a button as quickly as possible when this probe appeared. The dependent variable was the speed with which the probe was detected when it replaced neutral versus threat-related words.

The highly anxious subjects were faster than the controls in detecting the presence of the probe when it appeared in the vicinity of threat words. These subjects had shifted their attention toward threatening stimuli, while normal control subjects had shifted attention away from such material. The study suggested that anxious patients may use an encoding bias mechanism that makes them more susceptible to noticing threatening stimuli (MacLeod et al, 1986).

Biological

The ability of certain drugs to relieve and of others to produce symptoms of anxiety offers evidence of a biological role in anxiety disorders. When a panic-attack sufferer is given an infusion of sodium lactate, the patient usually complains first of palpitations, difficulty catching his or her breath, dizziness, lightheadedness . . . and sweating. Some normal control subjects may complain of these symptoms as well, but only the patient quickly develops overwhelming dread and fear that disastrous physical consequences are imminent (Gorman *et al*, 1989). Studies suggest that abnormalities in sites within the brainstem might be linked to panic attacks. Researchers studying CAT and PET scans of obsessive-compulsive disorder patients have found some evidence that links the disorder and abnormalities in the basal ganglia and frontal lobe of the brain (Rapoport, 1989). Work is under way to investigate how these abnormalities may influence the obsessive-compulsive symptoms.

With regard to the aetiology of phobias, Seligman's (1971) **preparedness** hypothesis suggests we carry around an evolutionary and biologically based tendency to respond quickly and automatically to once-feared stimuli (for example, spiders and snakes). However, this hypothesis has difficulty explaining the hundreds of 'exotic' brands of phobia that have little apparent survival value, among them fear of oneself, fear of responsibility, fear of moving or making changes and fear of the number 13 (triskaidekaphobia)! Nevertheless, it may explain why fear of various kinds of stimuli are lost at different rates.

Each of the major approaches to anxiety disorders may explain part of the aetiological puzzle. Continued research of each approach is needed to further our understanding of the factors that are most important to the aetiology of the disturbances that comprise the anxiety disorders.

INTERIM SUMMARY

Anxiety disorders may affect up to 15 per cent of the population at some time in their lives. The major types of anxiety disorders differ in the extent to which anxiety is experienced, the severity of the anxiety and the situations that elicit anxiety. In generalised anxiety disorder and panic disorder, the predominant symptoms are anxious feelings and physiological symptoms of anxiety. Phobic disorders are characterised by persistent and irrational fears of specific stimuli. A person suffering from obsessive compulsive disorder has recurring thoughts or impulses and ritualised behaviours that persist despite attempts to supress them. Regular gambling can become a compulsive behaviour that can cost the individual his or her family and friends.

Explanations of the origins of anxiety disorders have been made by proponents of each of the biological and psychological approaches that we have considered. Each of these approaches may account for a part of the aetiological puzzle of anxiety.

Mood (Affective) Disorders: Types

A mood disorder is a disturbance of affect, such as excessive *depression* or the latter alternating with **mania**. A person experiencing a period of mania, which is referred to as a *manic episode*, generally acts and feels unusually elated and expansive. However, sometimes the individual's predominant mood is irritability rather than elation, especially if the person feels thwarted in some way. Other symptoms accompany these highly charged mood states which typically last from a few days to months. During a manic episode, a person often experiences an inflated sense of self-esteem or an unrealistic belief that he or she possesses special abilities or powers. The person may feel a dramatically decreased need to sleep and may engage excessively in work or in social or other pleasurable activities. The individual may speak faster, louder or more often than usual, and his or her mind may be racing with thoughts. Caught up in this manic mood, the person shows unwarranted optimism, takes unnecessary risks, promises anything and may give away everything. Samuel was a 20-year-old college student experiencing the symptoms of a manic episode:

Lately Samuel has been feeling fantastic. He has so much energy that he almost never needs to sleep and he is completely confident that he is the top student in his year group. He is bothered that everyone else seems so slow; they do not seem to understand the brilliance of his monologues and no one seems able to keep up with his pace. Samuel has some exciting financial ideas and cannot understand why his friends are not writing out cheques to get in on his schemes.

Samuel has been having problems lately with his bank, which is foolishly insisting that he not overdraw his account. It lacks the visionary wisdom, he is sure, to comprehend his financial wizardry, but its nervous concerns should not be allowed to hold him back. Samuel's other problem is that he is failing several of his courses, but he knows that is only because his lecturers are too dull to appreciate his brilliant contributions and too rigid about certain deadlines. Samuel knows that he is just fine; his euphoria is not dimmed at all by his withdrawing friends, his sinking bank balance and his failure at college.

Bipolar disorder

It is not unusual for people in manic episodes to spend their life savings on extravagant purchases and to engage promiscuously in a number of sexual liaisons or other potentially high-risk actions. When the mania begins to diminish, people such as Samuel are left trying to deal with the damage and predicaments they created during their frenetic period. Those who have manic episodes will almost always also experience periods of severe depression. This condition is called **bipolar disorder**, or **manic-depressive disorder**, to signify the experience of both types of mood disturbances. The duration and frequency of the mood disturbances in bipolar disorder vary from person to person. Some people experience long periods of normal functioning punctuated by occasional, short manic or depressive episodes. A small percentage of unfortunate individuals go right from manic episodes to clinical depression and back again in continuous, unending cycles that are devastating to them, their families, their friends and their co-workers. While manic, they may gamble away life savings or give lavish gifts to strangers, which later adds to guilt feelings when they are in the depressed phase.

Depression

Major depression (sometimes also referred to as **unipolar depression**) has been called the 'common cold of psychopathology' (Seligman, 1973) because it occurs so frequently and almost everyone has experienced elements of the full scale disorder at some

TABLE 14.5	CHARACTERISTICS OF CLINICAL DEPRESSION
Characteristic	**Example**
Dysphoric Mood	Sad, blue, hopeless; loss of interest or pleasure in almost all usual activities
Appetite	Poor appetite; significant weight loss
Sleep	Insomnia or hypersomnia (sleeping too much)
Motor Activity	Markedly slowed down (motor retardation) or agitated
Guilt	Feelings of worthlessness; self-reproach
Concentration	Diminished ability to think or concentrate; forgetfulness
Suicide	Recurrent thoughts of death; suicidal ideas or attempts

time in life. We have all, at one time or another, experienced grief after the loss of a loved one or felt sad or upset when failing to achieve a desired goal. These sad feelings, which most of us experience in our lives, are only one symptom experienced by people suffering from a clinical depression (see *Table 14.5*). As opposed to victims of bipolar depression, those who suffer from 'recurrent major depression' (DSM-IV; ICD-10 'recurrent depressive disorder') do not experience manic highs but rather repeatedly suffer episodes of low mood.

Novelist William Styron wrote a moving story about his experience with severe depression. The pain he endured convinced him that clinical depression is much more than a bad mood; it is best characterised as 'a daily presence, blowing over me in cold gusts' and 'a veritable howling tempest in the brain' that can begin with a 'grey drizzle of horror' and result in 'death' (*Darkness Visible*, Random House, 1990).

People diagnosed with major depression differ in terms of the severity and duration of their symptoms. While many individuals only struggle with clinical depression for several weeks at one point in their lives, others experience depression episodically or chronically for many years. Estimates of the prevalence of affective disorders reveal that about 20 per cent of females and ten per cent of males suffer a major depression at some time in their lives. Bipolar disorder is much rarer, occurring in about one per cent of adults and distributed equally between males and females.

Both major depressive and bipolar disorders take an enormous toll on those afflicted, their families and society. One European study found that those with recurrent depression spend a fifth of their entire adult lives hospitalised, while 20 per cent of sufferers are totally disabled by their symptoms and do not ever work again (Holder, 1986a). In the United States, depression accounts for the majority of all mental hospital admissions, but it is still believed to be underdiagnosed and undertreated (Bielski & Friedel, 1977). According to a 1983 NIMH survey, 80 per cent of those suffering from clinical depression never receive treatment.

Mood (Affective) Disorders: Causes

What factors are involved in the development of affective disorders? Because of its prevalence, major depression has been studied more extensively than bipolar disorder. We will look at it from the cognitive, psychodynamic, behavioural and biological approaches.

Cognitive

At the centre of the cognitive approach to major depression are two theories. One theory suggests that **negative cognitive sets** lead people to take a negative view of events in their lives for which they feel responsible. The **learned helplessness model** proposes that depression arises from the belief that one has little or no personal control over significant life events. **Aaron Beck** (1983; 1985; 1988), a leading researcher on depression, has argued that depressed people have three types of negative cognitions which he calls the *cognitive triad of depression*: negative views of themselves, negative views of ongoing experiences and negative views of the future. Depressed people have a tendency to view themselves as inadequate or defective in some way, to interpret ongoing experiences in a negative way and to believe that the future will continue to bring suffering and difficulties. This pattern of negative thinking clouds all experiences and produces the other characteristic signs of depression: an individual who always anticipates a negative outcome is not likely to be motivated to pursue any goal, leading to the paralysis of will that is prominent in depression.

In the learned helplessness view, developed by **Martin Seligman**, individuals learn, correctly or not, that they cannot control future outcomes that are important to them. This conclusion creates feelings of helplessness, that lead to depression (Abramson *et al*,

1978; Peterson & Seligman, 1984; Seligman, 1975). Suppose that Marie has just received a poor mark for her psychology exam. Marie attributes the negative outcome on the exam to an *internal* factor ('I'm stupid'), which makes her feel sad, rather than an *external* one ('The exam was really hard'), which would have made her angry. Marie could have chosen a less *stable* internal quality than intelligence to explain her performance ('I was tired that day'). Rather than attributing her performance to an internal, stable factor that has *global* or far-reaching influence (stupidity), Marie could even have limited her explanation to the psychology exam or course ('I'm not good at psychology courses'). The learned helplessness theory suggests that individuals such as Marie who attribute failure to internal, stable and global causes are vulnerable to depression.

A study of college students supports the notion that depressed people have a negative type of attribution style. Depressed students attributed failure on an achievement test to an internal, stable factor – their lack of ability – while attributing successes to luck. In comparison, on an achievement test, non-depressed students took more credit for successes and less blame for failures than they were due, blaming failures on an external factor – bad luck (Barthe & Hammen, 1981).

While this and other studies have demonstrated the common presence of negative attributional styles and thoughts in depressed people, there is considerable debate over the key proposition of the cognitive model of depression – that cognitive factors play a causal role in the development of depression. Despite the appeal of the model and its successful application in therapies for depression, it remains plausible that the negative cognitive patterns are, in fact, a consequence rather than a cause of depression.

Research has confirmed what many people already believed about depression – that major changes in one's life, especially those that involve a loss of some sort, such as the death of a loved one, divorce or loss of a job (also referred to as 'exit events'), often precede the onset of depression (Brown & Harris, 1978, 1989; Paykel & Dowlatshahi, 1988). Exit events are seen as important precipitators of depression in both behavioural and psychodynamic approaches, but in very distinct ways.

Psychodynamic

In the psychoanalytic approach, unconscious conflicts and hostile feelings that originate in early childhood are seen to play key roles in the development of depression. Freud was struck by the degree of self-criticism and guilt that depressed people displayed. He believed that the source of this self-reproach was anger, originally directed at someone else, that had been turned inward against the self. The anger was believed to be tied to an especially intense and dependent childhood relationship, such as a parent–child relationship, in which the person's needs or expectations were not met. Losses, real or symbolic, in adulthood trigger hostile feelings that were originally experienced in childhood. A part of the person who was the object of these conflicting feelings of love and anger (the parent) becomes incorporated into the ego of depressed people. The anger that is reactivated by a later loss is now directed toward the person's own ego, creating the self-reproach and guilt that is characteristic of depression. Whilst it is difficult to empirically substantiate such psychodynamic processes, Brown and Harris (1989) in their seminal work on depression, recognise, however, that the psychological effects of loss and trauma in later life can be exacerbated by the way in which such events may resonate with and 'match' adversity experienced previously.

Behavioural

Rather than searching for the roots of depression in past relationships or for the unconscious meaning of a recent loss experience, one behavioural approach focuses on the effects of the amount of positive reinforcement and punishments a person receives (Lewinsohn, 1975; Lewinsohn et al, 1979). In this view, depressed feelings result from a lack of sufficient positive reinforcements and from experiencing many punishments in the environment following a loss or other major change in one's life. These life changes may lead a person to spend less time in activities that had previously provided gratification. Without sufficient positive reinforcement from the environment, a person begins to feel sad and withdraws further. This state of sadness and withdrawal is initially reinforced by increased attention and sympathy from others. Typically, however, friends, who at first respond with support, grow tired of the depressed person's negative moods and attitudes and begin to avoid him or her. This reaction eliminates another source of positive reinforcement, plunging the person further into depression. This cycle of reduced reinforcement can also be initiated when a person is unskilled in obtaining social reinforcements (has difficulty making friendships or gaining support from others) or moving to a new environment. Research shows that depressed people give themselves fewer rewards and more punishment than others and that

FIGURE 14.3	PET SCANS OF BIPOLAR DEPRESSION

PET scans indicate a higher level of cerebral glucose metabolism during manic phases than during depressive phases. The top and bottom rows show the patient during a depressive phase. The middle row shows the manic phase. The colour bar on the right indicates the glucose metabolism rates.

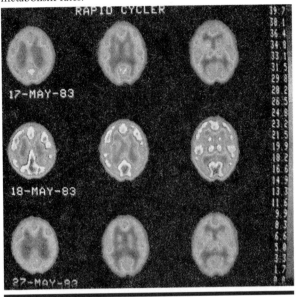

they underestimate their levels of reward while overestimating their levels of punishment (Rehm, 1977; Nelson & Craighead, 1977).

Biological

The ability of certain drugs such as *lithium* (a salt compound) to relieve symptoms of mania and depression has provided support for a biological view of bipolar disorder. Reduced levels of two chemical messengers in the brain, *serotonin* and *noradrenaline* (norepinephrine), have been linked with depression, and drugs that are known to increase the levels of these neurotransmitters are commonly used to treat depression. However, the exact biochemical mechanisms of depression have not yet been delineated. Researchers have used PET scans to show differences in the way the brain metabolises cerebral glucose (a type of sugar utilised to produce energy) during manic and depressive phases (see *Figure 14.3*), but such differences may be the *consequence* rather than the *cause* of the two mood states.

While our overall understanding of the cause of bipolar disorder remains limited, there is some growing evidence that it is influenced by genetic factors. Because family members usually share the same environment, similarities among family members

FIGURE 14.4 SEASONAL AFFECTIVE DISORDER

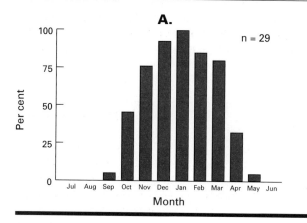

A.

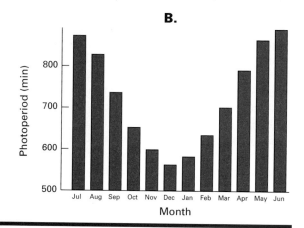

B.

do not prove that the cause of a psychological disorder is hereditary. To separate the influence of heredity from environmental or learned components researchers study twins and adopted children (Plomin & McClearn, 1993).

Studies of identical twins (twins who have the same genetic material) show that, when one twin is afflicted by bipolar disorder, there is an 80 per cent chance that the second twin will have the disorder. The rate at which pairs of individuals share a trait is called the **concordance rate**. Adoption studies demonstrate that the concordance rates of bipolar disorder for an adopted child with his or her biological parents is stronger than with the adoptive parents. While these studies suggest that genetic factors play some part in bipolar disorder, more direct evidence of this role seemed to come from a study that linked bipolar disorder to a specific gene in a unique population of people. In this study, the pattern of transmission of bipolar disorder was traced among the Amish community in Pennsylvania, USA (Egeland *et al*, 1987).

The Amish are ideal subjects for such research because they have large families, keep detailed genealogical records, are genetically isolated and display few behavioural factors, such as alcoholism or violence, that could confound the findings. All 15,000 members of the religious sect are descended from just 30 couples who migrated from Europe in the early eighteenth century. Although their incidence of manic depression is the same as that of the rest of the population, there is a genetic tendency for the associated extreme mood swings to run in some but not other Amish families. Researchers isolated a piece of DNA that was common in all bipolar members of one extended Amish family. The defective gene was passed on to children half of the time and of those who received it, 80 per cent had at least one manic episode in their lives. Not all who had the genetic vulnerability developed the symptoms of bipolar

disorder, suggesting that other biological or psychological variables, which have not yet been identified, may also play an important role in aetiology. The implicated gene was localised at the tip of chromosome 11.

This result was hailed as a real breakthrough – until the predictions made from this genetic analysis to other Amish relatives failed to be supported. When a team of independent researchers checked out the procedures and evaluated the predictions of Egeland's team, they were forced to blow the whistle and declare that the evidence was unconvincing (Kelso *et al*, 1989). At present, two other possibilities are being pursued in this domain: firstly, the gene for manic depression may not be on chromosome 11; or, secondly, the Amish may have two such genes, only one of which is in that chromosome location (Barinaga, 1989). Whatever, as yet the 'jury is still out' and deliberating upon the proposed genetic basis of bipolar disorder.

A dramatic example of a biological approach to understanding one type of psychological disorder comes from an experiment that sheds new light on an unusual form of depression. Some people regularly become depressed during the winter months, especially in the long Scandinavian winters (see *Figure 14.4*). This disturbance in mood has been appropriately named *seasonal affective disorder* or SAD. An internal body rhythm involving the hormone *melatonin*, which is secreted by the pineal gland into the blood, has been linked to SAD. In most species, including humans, the level of melatonin rises after dusk and falls at or before dawn. Melatonin is implicated in sleep processes as well as circadian (24-hour) rhythms that set the body's biological clock.

When depressed patients and normal control subjects were exposed to bright light in the morning, the melatonin cycle was changed. Bright morning light reduced the symptoms of depression in those patients who regularly suffered from recurring winter depression. While it is not clear that disrupted melatonin cycles are responsible for causing the depressive symptoms of SAD, it does appear that a biological intervention that 'resets' their abnormal circadian rhythm is an effective treatment (Lewy et al, 1987).

Sex Differences in Depression

The finding that women are twice as likely to experience unipolar depression as men has challenged psychologists to account for this difference (Boyd & Weissman, 1981). One proposal by **Susan Nolen-Hoeksema** (1987) points to the response styles of men and women once they begin to experience negative moods. According to this view, when women experience sadness, they tend to think about the possible causes and implications of their feelings. In contrast, men attempt actively to distract themselves from depressed feelings, either by focusing on something else or by engaging in a physical activity that will take their minds off their current mood state. This model suggests that it is the more *ruminative* response style of women, the tendency to focus obsessively on problems, that increases women's vulnerability to depression. From a cognitive approach, paying attention to one's negative moods can increase thoughts of negative events which eventually increase the quantity and/or the intensity of negative feelings.

The response styles of both men and women can be seen as a product of socialisation. In Western Europe and many other cultures, a stereotypic female schema may still involve placing relative emphasis on passivity, paying attention to feelings and experiencing emotions fully as well as sharing them with others. In contrast, the stereotypic male schema is focused upon being tough, physical and non-emotional and on not displaying signs of 'weakness' by talking about distressing mood states.

The response styles of men may have certain advantages in terms of reduced vulnerability to depression, but they create other problems. Some researchers have pointed to the maladaptive tendency of men to distract themselves by *acting out* their depressed feelings in excessive drinking and drug use or in violent behaviour. They cite statistics that indicate that twice as many men as women are alcoholic and suggest that alcoholism is often a mask for depression (Williams & Spitzer, 1983).

A recent review of the research on the origins of sex differences in rates of unipolar major depression has been carried out by McGrath et al (1990). Their report suggests that women's higher risk for

depression can only be understood as the product of an interaction between a number of psychological, social, economic and biological factors.

Of relevance here is the landmark study of **George Brown** and **Tirril Harris** (1978). They found that amongst 458 18 to 65-year-old women living in the London borough of Camberwell, 68 per cent of those women who were observed to be clinically depressed had experienced one or more stressful life events during the preceding 12 months; only 20 per cent of women who were not depressed had experienced a similar number of these events. Such events often involved 'loss' of some kind, of a loved-one for example or of a hope, a vision of the future. Further, they found that there was a raised incidence of such events amongst women within lower socio-economic groups and that this difference was mirrored by a greater risk of depression amongst 'working' versus 'middle'-class women. However, they also noted that of those who experienced a stressful life event, only one in five women became depressed. An important further result from Brown and Harris' (1978) research explains why this is so: they observed that a stressful event was potent as a 'provoking agent' for depression only if psychosocial 'vulnerability factors' were also evident. In particular, they observed that an individual was more susceptible to the deleterious effects of a stressful live event and to depression if that person also had either: (a) no confiding relationship to provide support in a crisis; (b) no occupation outside of the home; (c) three or more children under the age of 14 at home to look after; or (d) had lost her mother before the age of 11. The first vulnerability factor – no confiding relationship – has been found to be the most significant psychological Achilles heel of the four. Later work has confirmed the key role of low self-esteem (Brown et al, 1990), and that only when loss of a mother is followed by inadequate substitute parental care or by abuse does it render women vulnerable to depression later (Bifulco et al, 1987; 1994). In summary, women (and men) who are 'vulnerable' in any of the above four ways are more likely to feel disempowered and hopeless in response to a loss event and, therefore, to become clinically depressed than are those who are not psychosocially susceptible as described.

Thus, factors which predispose women to depression relate to the experience of being female as determined and constructed within many cultures. This includes the greater likelihood for women living in relatively impoverished financial circumstances while being entrapped as the primary care-giver for young children and elderly parents, with no possibility of calling on support elsewhere or of deriving self-esteem and feelings of empowerment from occupational roles and relationships outside of the home. Such findings indicate that the causes of depression may be a complex combination of factors

TABLE 14.6 SUICIDE RATES PER 100,000 AGES 25–44 IN 15 COUNTRIES 1986–88

Rank ♂	Country	Rate for Males	Rank ♀	Country	Rate for Females
15	FINLAND	59	15	DENMARK	18
14	DENMARK	41	14	FINLAND	13
13	FRANCE	36	14	SWEDEN	13
12	LUXEMBOURG	33	12	FRANCE	11
11	SWEDEN	31	11	NORWAY	10
10	NORWAY	28	10	NETHERLANDS	9
9	GERMANY FR	25	10	GERMANY	9
8	USA	24	10	LUXEMBOURG	9
7	GREAT BRITAIN	16	7	USA	6
6	IRELAND	16	6	GREAT BRITAIN	5
5	NETHERLANDS	15	6	IRELAND	5
4	PORTUGAL	11	4	PORTUGAL	4
3	ITALY	10	3	ITALY	3
2	SPAIN★	9	2	SPAIN★	2
1	GREECE	6	2	GREECE	2

★ *1986-88 figures for Spain not available; 1984-86 used here*

Source: Charlton, J. *et al* (1993). Suicide deaths in England and Wales: trends in factors associated with suicide deaths. *Population Trends, 71,* 34–42.

involving numerous psychosocial transactions (Wiener, 1989) and that there are multiple paths leading from 'normal' mood states and behaviour to those associated with major depression.

Depression and suicide

'The will to survive and succeed had been crushed and defeated . . . There comes a time when all things cease to shine, when the rays of hope are lost' (Shneidman, 1987). This sad statement by a young suicidal man reflects the most extreme consequence of any psychological disorder – suicide. While most depressed people do not commit suicide, most suicides are attempted by those who are suffering from depression (Shneidman, 1985). Depressed people commit suicide at a rate 25 times higher than non-depressed people in comparison groups (Flood & Seager, 1968).

Rates of reported suicides vary from country to country and in accordance with numerous demographic variables, including age, sex, socio-economic status, employment status, occupation and partnership or marital status. For every completed suicide there may be eight to 20 suicide attempts (US National Centre for Health Statistics, 1984). A suicide usually affects at least six other people intimately. Finland and Denmark have exceptionally high rates of suicide amongst males: 59 and 41 respectively per 100,000 of 25 to 44-year-old males between 1986 and 1988 committed suicide as compared with 21 per 100,000 in the United States of America during the same period. The breakdown of suicides by country and sex for the 25 to 44-year old age-group is shown in *Table 14.6*. The lowest rates of recorded suicide are for men and women living in Greece. Notable is the cluster of Scandinavian countries amongst those with the highest rates. Also remarkable is the on average 3 to 4 times greater suicide rate of men than women. Charlton *et al* (1993) attribute this difference in Great Britain to the increasing trend for men to remain single or to become divorced. They also acknowledge the importance of high unemployment, exposure to armed combat, increasing risk of imprisonment, an increase in the misuse of alcohol and other drugs and the emergence of the HIV virus.

Despite apparently high numbers, suicide is under-reported since single-car fatal accidents and other deaths that may be suicidal are not listed as such without the evidence of a suicide note, and because the potential stigma leads family members to deny suicide when it occurs. Because depression occurs more frequently in women, it is not surprising that women attempt suicide about three times more often than men do. Attempts by men, however, are more successful. This difference is largely because women tend to use less lethal means, such as sleeping pills (Perlin, 1975).

One of the most alarming social problems in recent decades is the spectre of youth suicide (Coleman, 1987; Diekstra, 1990). In 1992 in England and Wales, for example, 412 young men and 73 young women between the ages 15 and 24 were recorded as having died from suicide and self-inflicted injury (Office of Population Censuses & Surveys, 1993). 325 of these were 20 to 24-year-old males. What lifestyle patterns are most commonly found to be associated with youth suicides? Among males, the majority of suicides are found in those who abuse drugs and are seen as aggressive and unruly. The next most common pattern is the hard-driving male perfectionist who is socially inhibited and overly anxious about many social or academic challenges. Among females, depression ranks as the primary predictor of youth suicide. The symptoms of depression reflect serious emotional disorders that often go unrecognised or not treated.

In addition to long-standing psychological problems of maladjustment, there are several precipitating factors that can trigger suicidal actions. The breakup of a close relationship is the leading traumatic incident for both sexes. Other significant incidents that create shame and guilt that can overwhelm and lead to suicide attempts include being assaulted, beaten, raped or arrested for the first time (Egmond et al, 1993). Suicide is an extreme reaction to these acute stressors that occurs especially when adolescents feel unable to cry out to others for help.

Youth suicide is not a spur-of-the-moment impulsive act, but, typically, it occurs as the final stage of a period of inner turmoil and outer distress. The majority of young suicide victims have talked to others about their intentions or have written about them. Thus, talk of suicide should always be taken seriously (Shafii et al, 1985). Because girls are more often part of a social support network than are boys, they are more able to confide in others about their distress (Holden, 1986a; 1986b). Recognising the signs of suicidal thinking and the experiences that can start or intensify such destructive thoughts is a first step toward prevention. Shneidman (1987) has studied and treated people with suicidal tendencies for 40 years and concludes that 'suicide is the desperate act of a perturbed and constricted mind, in seemingly unbearable and unresolvable pain . . . The fact is that we can relieve the pain, redress the thwarted needs

and reduce the constriction of suicidal thinking'. Being sensitive to signs of suicidal intentions and caring enough to intervene are essential for saving lives of youthful and mature people who have come to see no exit for their troubles except total self-destruction.

Although suicide rates are generally lower for non-whites than whites, there is one startling exception in the United States: among 'native American' youth, suicide is five times greater than among youth of the general population. **Teresa La Framboise**, who has been studying the problem, identifies the social causes of youth suicide among this group of people. With poverty and unemployment high in depressed Indian communities, suicide rates are boosted by 'family disruption, pervasive hardship, a severe number of losses (whether through death, desertion, or divorce), substance abuse, the increased mobilities of families and the incarceration of a significant caretaker' (La Framboise, 1988). In addition, the native American belief that the living continuously interact with their ancestors in the spiritual world, means that death holds little fear.

INTERIM SUMMARY

Affective disorders involve disturbances in mood. One main type of affective disorder is major depression (also known as unipolar depression), which is characterised by sad feelings as well as by a collection of thoughts and motivational and physical symptoms. Because it occurs so frequently and elements of it have been widely experienced, this form of depression has been called the 'common cold of psychopathology'. A second type of affective disorder, bipolar disorder, is much rarer and is marked by the alternating occurrence of depression and periods of mania during which a person experiences intense elation or irritability and other cognitive and motivational symptoms. Theories and research on the causes of affective disorders suggest that a number of different biological and psychological factors are responsible for the development of depression. Explanations for the greater incidence of major depression in women support the notion that the causes of affective disturbances may be a complex combination of processes and that it is likely that there is more than one path from 'normal' behaviour to depression.

Most suicides are attempted by people suffering from depression. More women than men attempt suicide, but men are more likely to complete the suicide. In recent years, there has been an alarming increase in youth suicide, notably among socially and economically disadvantaged sections of the general population.

◉ SCHIZOPHRENIC DISORDERS

Everyone knows what it is like to feel depressed or anxious, even though most of us never experience these feelings to the degree of severity that constitutes a disorder. Schizophrenia, however, is a disorder that represents a qualitatively different experience from normal functioning (Bellak, 1979). A **schizophrenic disorder** is a severe form of psychological disorder in which personality seems to disintegrate, perception is distorted, emotions are blunted, thoughts are bizarre and language is strange. The person with a schizophrenic disorder is the one we conjure up when we think about psychosis as so-called 'madness' or 'insanity'.

Those with schizophrenia do not necessarily first develop other types of mental disorders nor do very disturbed 'neurotic' individuals eventually become schizophrenic. For many of the millions of people afflicted with this disorder, it is a life sentence without possibility of parole, endured in the solitary confinement of a mind that must live life apart from others. Approximately, one in every 100 people at one time or another have suffered from this most mysterious and tragic mental disorder (Regier et al, 1988). Many of the beds in mental institutions are currently occupied by schizophrenic patients. For as yet unknown reasons, the first occurrence of schizophrenia typically occurs for men before they are 25 and for women between 25 and 45 years of age (Lewine et al, 1981).

Mark Vonnegut, son of novelist Kurt Vonnegut, was in his early 20s when he began to experience symptoms of schizophrenia. In *Eden Express* (1975), he tells the story of his break with reality and his eventual recovery after being hospitalised twice for acute schizophrenia. Once, while pruning some fruit trees, he hallucinated – reality became distorted, a different one being created:

I began to wonder if I was hurting the trees and found myself apologising. Each tree began to take on personality. I began to wonder if any of them liked me. I became completely absorbed in looking at each tree and began to notice that they were ever so slightly luminescent, shining with a soft inner light that played around the branches. And from out of nowhere came an incredibly wrinkled, iridescent face. Starting as a small point infinitely distant, it rushed forward, becoming infinitely huge. I could see nothing else. My heart had stopped. The moment stretched forever. I tried to make the face go away but it mocked me . . . I was holding my life in my hands and was powerless to stop it from dripping through my fingers. I tried to look the face in the eyes and realised I had left all familiar ground.

During the weeks after this experience, Mark Vonnegut's behaviour went out of apparent control more often and in more extreme form. He would cry without reason. His terror would evaporate into periods of ecstasy, with no corresponding change in his life situation. 'There were times when I was scared, shaking, convulsing in excruciating pain and bottomless despair.' For 12 days he ate nothing and slept not at all. One day, while visiting friends in a small town, he stripped off his clothes and ran naked down the street. Suicidal despair nearly ended his young, once promising life.

In schizophrenia, thinking becomes illogical, associations among ideas being remote or without apparent pattern. Language may become incoherent – a 'word salad' of unrelated or made-up verbalisations – or an individual may become mute. Emotions may be flat, with no visible expression, or they may be inappropriate to the situation. Psychomotor behaviour may be disorganised (grimaces, strange mannerisms) or posture may become rigid. Even when only some of these symptoms are present, deteriorated functioning in work, social relations and self-care is likely. Interpersonal relationships are often difficult as individuals withdraw socially or become emotionally detached.

Hallucinations often occur, involving imagined sensory perceptions – of smell, visiual ones or, most commonly, auditory hallucinations (usually voices) – that are assumed to be real. A person may hear a voice that provides a running commentary on his or her behaviour or may hear several voices in conversation.

Delusion is also common in schizophrenia. These are false or irrational beliefs maintained in spite of clear contrary evidence. Delusions are often patently absurd, such as the belief that one's thoughts are being broadcast, controlled or taken away by aliens. In other cases, delusions may not seem as outlandish, but they are still not realistic or true. For example, a person may experience delusional jealousy, believing that one's sexual partner is not being faithful or believing that he or she is being persecuted.

Psychologists divide these symptoms between a *positive* category and a *negative* category. During acute or active phases of schizophrenia, the positive symptoms – hallucinations, delusions, incoherence and disorganised behaviour – are prominent. At other times, the negative symptoms – social withdrawal and flattened emotions – become more apparent. Some individuals, such as Mark Vonnegut, just experience one or a couple of acute phases of schizophrenia and recover to live normal lives. Others, often described as *chronic* sufferers, experience either repeated acute phases with short periods of negative symptoms or occasional acute phases with extended periods marked by the presence of negative symptoms. The manifestations of schizophrenia are characterised more by variability than by constancy over time (Liberman, 1982). Even the most seriously disturbed are not acutely delusional all the time.

◉ Major Types of Schizophrenia

Because of the wide variety of symptoms that can characterise schizophrenia, many investigators consider it to be not a single disorder but rather a constellation of separate types. However, so varied is the form and direction which symptoms can take that Boyle (1990) contends they are not reducible to one or more types and that schizophrenia *per se* is in essence a socially constructed diagnostic fiction. Nevertheless the florid nature of many symptoms which are often evident in clinical cases suggests schizophrenia does have substance as a mental health construct and cannot totally be dismissed as the product of inventive but misguided diagnostic practice. Notwithstanding such stimulating dissent within the literature, four broad subtypes of schizophrenia are recognised within the DSM-IV and ICD-10 taxonomies. These are outlined in *Table 14.7*.

Disorganised type

In this subtype of schizophrenia (known within the ICD as *hebephrenic*), a person displays incoherent patterns of thinking and grossly bizarre and disorganised behaviour. Emotions are flattened or inappropriate to the situation. Often, a person acts in

TABLE 14.7	TYPES OF SCHIZOPHRENIC DISORDERS (DSM-IV AND ICD-10)
Type of Schizophrenia	**Major Symptoms**
Disorganised ('*Hebephrenic*' in ICD)	**Inappropriate behaviour and emotions; incoherent language**
Catatonic	**Frozen, rigid, or excitable motor behaviour**
Paranoid	**Delusions of persecution or grandeur with hallucinations**
Undifferentiated	**Mixed set of symptoms with thought disorders and features from other types**

a silly or childish manner, such as giggling for no apparent reason. Language can become so incoherent, full of unusual words and incomplete sentences, that communication with others breaks down. Delusions or hallucinations are common, but are not organised around a coherent theme.

Mr. F. B. was a hospitalised patient in his late 20s. His disorganised speech production is notable, evidenced in his answers to interview questions, sentence completions and proverb interpretations, some examples of which follow:

Q: 'What sort of mood have you been in for the past few days?'
A: 'If the world moved, the world moved.'
Q: 'What is the meaning of the proverb "When the cat's away the mice will play"?'
A: 'Takes less place. Cat didn't know what mouse did and mouse didn't know what cat did. Cat represented more on the suspicious side than the mouse. Dumbo was a good guy. He saw what the cat did, put himself with the cat so people wouldn't look at them as comedians.'

Mr. F. B.'s depersonalised, incoherent speech and delusions are the hallmarks of the disorganised type of schizophrenia.

Catatonic type

The **catatonic** person seems frozen in a stupor. For long periods of time, the individual can remain motionless, often in a bizarre position, showing little or no reaction to anything in the environment. When the individual is moved, he or she freezes in a new position, assuming the waxy flexibility of a soft plastic toy. Catatonic negativity sometimes involves motionless resistance to instructions. Sometimes it involves doing the opposite of what is requested – sitting when told to stand, for example. For the catatonic person, stupor sometimes alternates with excitement. During the excited phase, motor activity is agitated, apparently without purpose and not influenced by external stimuli.

Paranoid type

Individuals suffering from the **paranoid** form of schizophrenia experience complex and systematised delusions focused around specific themes. What follows are the four common types of **delusions**:

- Delusions of *persecution*: individuals feel that they are being constantly spied on and plotted against and that they are in mortal danger.
- Delusions of *grandeur*: individuals believe that they are important or exalted beings – millionaires, great inventors or religious figures such as Jesus Christ; delusions of persecution may accompany delusions of grandeur – an individual is a great person but is continually opposed by evil forces.
- Delusional *jealousy*: individuals become convinced – without due cause – that their mates are unfaithful. They contrive data to fit the theory and 'prove' the truth of the delusion.
- Delusions of *reference*: individuals misconstrue chance happenings as being directed at them. A paranoid individual who sees two people in earnest conversation immediately concludes that they are talking about him or her. Even lyrics in popular songs or words spoken by radio or TV actors are perceived as having some special message for the individual, often exposing some personal secret. The individual may even hallucinate voices or images of people organised around themes of persecution or grandiosity.

The onset of symptoms in paranoid schizophrenic individuals tends to occur later in life than it does in other schizophrenic types. Paranoid schizophrenic individuals rarely display obviously disorganised behaviour. Instead, it is more likely that their behaviour will be intense and quite formal.

Undifferentiated type

This is the coverall category describing a person who exhibits prominent delusions, hallucinations, incoherent speech or grossly disorganised behaviour that fit the criteria of more than one type or of no clear type. The miscellany of symptoms experienced by these individuals does not clearly differentiate among various schizophrenic reactions.

Causes of Schizophrenia

Different aetiological models point to very different initial causes of schizophrenia, different pathways along which it develops and different avenues for treatment. Here will be considered the contributions several of these models can make to our understanding of the way a person may develop a schizophrenic disorder.

Genetic approaches

It has long been known that schizophrenia tends to run in families (Bleuler, 1978; Kallmann, 1946). Thus, the possibility of genetic transmission of some predisposition for schizophrenia is a likely causal candidate. Three independent lines of research – family studies, twin studies and adoption studies – point to a common conclusion: persons related

FIGURE 14.5	GENETIC RISK FOR SCHIZOPHRENIC DISORDER

Out of a sample of 100 children of schizophrenic parents, from ten to 50 per cent will inherit a genetic structure that is associated in the previous generation with schizophrenia. Of these, about five per cent will develop schizophrenia early and five per cent later in life. It is important to note that as many as 40 per cent of the high-risk subjects will not become schizophrenic.

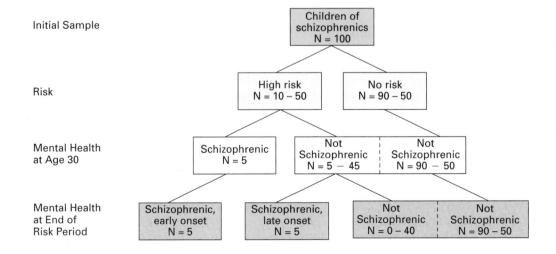

FIGURE 14.6 GENETIC RISK OF DEVELOPING SCHIZOPHRENIA

The graph shows average risks for developing schizophrenia. Data were compiled from family and twin studies conducted in European populations between 1920 and 1987; the degree of risk correlates highly with the degree of genetic relatedness.

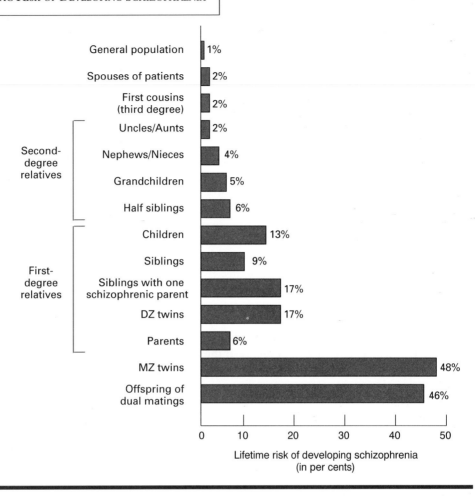

genetically to someone who has been diagnosed as schizophrenic are more likely to show similar symptoms than those who are not (Kessler, 1980).

When both parents are schizophrenic, the schizophrenia risk for their offspring is 46 per cent, as compared to one per cent in the general population. When only one parent is schizophrenic, the risk for the offspring is only 13 per cent. The risk is greater for first-degree relatives (siblings and children), greater in families with many affected relatives and greater where schizophrenic reactions are severe (Hanson *et al*, 1977) (see *Figure 14.5*).

Twin studies show that, when one member of a pair of twins is schizophrenic, the chances that the other will also be affected are four times greater for identical twins than for pairs of fraternal twins, even though, in both cases, the twins usually have shared the same general environments (Gottesman *et al*, 1987). Environmental factors also play a role, as shown by the fact that the concordance rates among identical twins are far from perfect – there are many cases in which one member of the pair develops schizophrenia and the other one never does.

The most compelling evidence for the role of

genetic factors in the aetiology of schizophrenia comes from adoption studies. When the offspring of a schizophrenic parent are reared by a normal parent in a foster home, they are as likely to develop the disorder as if they had been brought up by the biological parent (Heston, 1970; Rosenthal *et al*, 1975). In addition, adoptees who are schizophrenic have significantly more biological relatives with schizophrenic disorders than adoptive relatives with the disorder (Kety *et al*, 1975).

A summary of the risks of being affected with schizophrenia for the various kinds of relatives of a schizophrenic is shown in *Figure 14.6*. Leading schizophrenia researcher **Irving Gottesman** (1991) pooled these data from about 40 reliable studies conducted in Western Europe between 1920 and 1987, dropping the poorest data sets. The data are arranged according to degree of genetic relatedness which correlates highly with the degree of risk. However, limits must be placed on the conclusion that there is a genetic basis for schizophrenia. While there is certainly a strong relationship between genetic similarity and risk of schizophrenia, even in the groups with the greatest genetic similarity, the risk factor is less than 50 per cent. This indicates that, although genes play some role, schizophrenia is a complex disorder with other contributing factors involved.

The genetics of schizophrenia is still undetermined. While one team of researchers claims to have found evidence of a genetic defect on chromosome 5 in seven families with a dominant gene for schizophrenia, another did not replicate this finding with a different family in which one third of 104 relatives was diagnosed as schizophrenic (Barnes, 1988). Critics of the genetic hypothesis of schizophrenia argue that the available evidence is weak for all types of schizophrenia except for chronic forms of the disorder. They point to the fact that 90 per cent of the relatives of schizophrenics do not have schizophrenia (Barnes, 1987). Taken as a whole, the research on genetic influences suggests that genetic factors may contribute to schizophrenia but may not by themselves be sufficient for the development of the disorder (Nicol & Gottesman, 1983). This line of research has not revealed anything about the way in which genes may exert their influence on schizophrenia.

One problem with the current research may be the nature of the diagnosis of schizophrenia. If there is error and variability in that diagnosis, then the relationship with genetic factors may be mixed in different studies. A new line of research uses a biological marker for schizophrenia in place of the traditional diagnosis. A schizophrenia **biological marker** is a biological variable that can be used to index or mark the presence of schizophrenic disorder in the absence of a complex, DSM or ICD diagnosis. For example, persons with schizophrenia are more likely than normal people to have an eye movement dysfunction when they scan the visual field. This biological marker can be quantified in individuals and is shown to be related to the manifestation of schizophrenia in families (Clementz & Sweeney, 1990).

A widely accepted hypothesis for the cause of schizophrenia is the **diathesis-stress hypothesis**. It suggests that genetic factors place the individual at risk, but environmental stress factors must impinge in order for the potential risk to be manifested as a schizophrenic disorder (Fowles, 1992).

Neurochemicals, brain structure and function

Are the brains of individuals who are genetically at risk for schizophrenia unusual in some way? Current research employs brain-scanning techniques to study the way genetic factors might be linked with specific processes in the brain that previously have been associated with schizophrenia (Gershon & Reider, 1992).

Particular neurotransmitters and processes in the brain have been associated with the production and reduction of schizophrenic reactions. The biochemical approach to schizophrenia gained support in the 1950s with the development of a new group of antipsychotic drugs, the *phenothiazines*, that dramatically relieved many schizophrenic symptoms. The success of these neuroleptics led medical researchers to search for the natural biochemical processes that influence the development or remission of schizophrenia. The most promising biochemical research focuses on the influence of a specific neurotransmitter, *dopamine* and its receptor sites in the brain. Dopamine may be responsible for both the abnormalities in movement found in Parkinson's disease and at least some of the symptoms seen in schizophrenia.

The **dopamine hypothesis** holds that schizophrenia is associated with a relative excess of the chemical dopamine at specific receptor sites in the

These four genetically identical women each experience a schizophrenic disorder, suggesting heredity plays a role in the development of schizophrenia. However, for each of the Genain quadruplets, the disorder differed in severity, duration and outcome.

central nervous system (Carlsson, 1978). Schizophrenic symptoms may be the result of an increase in the activity of nerve cells that use dopamine as their neurotransmitter. Support for the dopamine hypothesis has been drawn from research on the effects of the phenothiazines. Commonly prescribed ones include Chlorpromazine Hydrochloride (tradename: Largactil), Haloperidol (tradename: Haloperidol) and Thioridazine (tradename: Melleril). Phenothiazines – some of which are also used in the short-term adjunctive treatment of severe anxiety – seem to be most effective in relieving the positive symptoms of schizophrenia such as hallucinations, delusions and disorganised behaviour. They are also known to block the brain's receptors for dopamine. Recent research has used PET scan technology to look at the density of dopamine receptors in the brains of schizophrenic individuals. These studies, along with examinations of the brain tissue of schizophrenic individuals after death, suggest that in the brains of schizophrenics there may be an increased number of receptors for dopamine rather than increased levels of the neurotransmitter itself (Snyder, 1976). Although impressive evidence has been accumulated for the dopamine hypothesis, we still must be cautious. It is possible that dopamine availability may be one factor in the sequence of development of schizophrenia but not the original cause.

Another area of interest in the biology of schizophrenia is the association of subtle brain abnormalities, such as reduced brain volume in specific areas of the brain or enlarged ventricles (fluid-filled chambers in the brain), with schizophrenic symptoms (Andreasen *et al*, 1990). Further research comparing structure and functions of the brains of twins who are discordant for schizophrenia (one has the disorder, the other does not) and normal control twins is being conducted by interdisciplinary research teams using magnetic resonance imaging and biological and psychological assessment. Through the use of such techniques, progress is being made towards an understanding of hallucinations in terms of the brain functions which may underlie the apparently aberrant cognitive processes typical of schizophrenia. Using scanning technology, McGuire *et al* (1993), for example, have found that there is increased blood flow in Broca's area during auditory hallucinations and that the latter are associated with the production of ordinary 'inner speech', as mapped in other brain imaging research (Paulesu *et al*, 1993). Broca's area has long been recognised as one of the cortical locations involved in the processing of language. It would appear, however, that – in combination with other areas of the cortex – Broca's area may also be implicated in producing one of schizophrenia's most distressing symptoms.

It is unlikely that only one biological trigger will be found to explain the origins of the wide range of schizophrenic symptoms. There is no question, however, that increasingly refined methodology will clarify our understanding of the genetic factors, biochemical processes and neurological factors at work in schizophrenia.

Psychodynamics and family interaction

If it is difficult to prove that a highly specific biological factor is a sufficient cause of schizophrenia, it is equally hard to prove that psychological ones are necessary conditions. Sociologists, family therapists and psychologists have all studied the influence of family role relationships and communication patterns in the development of schizophrenia. Their studies were originally conceptualised as extensions of psychodynamic theory. From a psychodynamic view, schizophrenia allegedly is a regression to an infantile stage of functioning and is marked by a fragile ego that has difficulty distinguishing between the self and the outside world and by immature defences that further distort reality. One psychodynamic model developed by **Margaret Mahler** (1979) traces a schizophrenic individual's difficulty in differentiating between self and the external world to an early, intense symbiotic attachment between mother and child. She believes the two failed to differentiate themselves from each other, were highly dependent on one another, intruded on each other's lives and had difficulty separating.

Research on this type of parent–child relationship and other unusual patterns in role relationships between mothers and fathers and parents and children has not offered consistent evidence in support of the belief that they are linked to schizophrenia. Researchers have provided some evidence for theories that emphasise the influence on the development of schizophrenia of deviations in parental communication (Liem, 1980). These deviations include a family's inability to share a common focus of attention and parents' difficulties in taking the perspective of other family members or in communicating clearly and accurately. Studies suggest that the speech patterns of families with a schizophrenic member show less responsiveness and less interpersonal sensitivity than those of normal families.

Deviant communication in families may contribute to the child's distortion of reality by concealing or denying the true meaning of an event or by injecting a substitute meaning that is confusing (Wynne *et al*, 1979). Anthropologist **Gregory Bateson** used the term **double bind** to describe a situation in which a child receives from a parent multiple messages that are contradictory and cannot all be met. A mother may complain that a son is not affectionate and yet reject his attempts to touch her because he is so dirty. Torn between these different verbal and non-verbal meanings, between demands and feelings, a child's grip on reality may begin to slip. The result may be that the child will see his or her feelings, perceptions and self-knowledge as unreliable indicators of the way things really are (Bateson *et al*, 1956).

Uncertainty still remains over whether the problematic family interaction patterns are a cause of schizophrenia or a reaction to the developing symptoms of schizophrenia. To help answer this question, studies of family interactions before schizophrenia appears in the offspring are needed. One such *prospective* study focused on a pattern of harsh criticism or intrusiveness expressed by a parent toward a teenage child. It revealed that this negative communication pattern is likely to predate the development of disorders similar to, but not quite as severe as, schizophrenia (Goldstein & Strachan, 1987).

This evidence is not sufficient to rally confidence in the hypothesis that family factors play a causal role in the development of schizophrenia. However, there is reliable evidence that family factors do play a role in influencing the functioning of an individual after the first symptoms appear (Brown *et al*, 1962). When parents reduce their 'expressed emotion' – their criticism, hostility and intrusiveness toward a schizophrenic offspring – the recurrence of acute schizophrenic symptoms and the need for rehospitalisation is also reduced (Doane *et al*, 1985).

Cognitive processes

Among the hallmarks of schizophrenia are abnormalities in attention, thought, memory and language. Some cognitive psychologists argue that, instead of being consequences of schizophrenia, these abnormalities may play a role in causing the disorder. One view focuses on the role of attentional difficulties. 'The crucial behaviour, from which other indicators of schizophrenia may be deduced, lies in the extinction of attention to social stimuli to which "normal" people respond' (Ullmann & Krasner, 1975).

Attentional deficits may involve ignoring important environmental or cultural cues that most people use to regulate socially or 'normalise' their behaviour. They may lead a person to notice remote, irrelevant thought or word associations while thinking or talking, thereby confusing these distracting peripheral ideas and stimuli with the main points or central themes of the conversation or thoughts.

The speech of some schizophrenic individuals seems to be under the control of immediate stimuli in the situation. Distracted from complete expression of a simple train of thought by constantly changing sensory input and vivid inner reality, a schizophrenic speaker may make little sense to a listener. The incoherence of schizophrenic speech is due, in part, to bizarre intrusions by thoughts that are not directly relevant to the statement being uttered – intrusions that the person cannot suppress. Normal speaking requires that a speaker remember what has just been said (past), monitor where he or she is (present) and direct the spoken sentence toward some final goal (future). This coherence between past, present and future may be difficult for some schizophrenic individuals, accounting for their inability to maintain long strings of inter-connected words. What comes out is often termed 'word salad', wildly tossed verbal and semantic confusion.

A cognitive approach taken by psychologist **Brendan Maher** (1968) focuses more directly on disturbances in language processes. The bizarre speech of schizophrenic individuals may be a result of deviant processing whenever a person comes to a 'vulnerable' word – one that has multiple meanings to him or her. At that point, a personally relevant, but semantically inappropriate, word is used. For example, a patient may say, 'Doctor, I have pains in my chest and wonder if my box is broken and heart is beaten'. 'Chest' here is a vulnerable word: it can mean either a 'respiratory cage' or a 'container' such as a box. The meaning of the word 'beat' (of the heart) is confounded with that of 'beaten', as in 'to be hit'; and that a heart can be either mechanically or emotionally 'broken' are possible connotations which are also confounded.

Reality testing is also impaired in schizophrenia. While most of us evaluate the reality of our inner worlds against criteria in the external world, individuals with schizophrenic disorders typically reverse this usual reality-testing procedure. Their inner experiences are the criteria against which they test the validity of outer experience (Meyer & Ekstein, 1970). Indeed, research into the cognitive neuropsychology of schizophrenia using non-invasive functional brain imaging techniques, points to a defect in a mechanism that distinguishes between internally and externally generated events (Frith, 1992). For those with schizophrenia, theirs is a world in which thinking it, makes it so – as in the fantasy world of children or the dream world of adults. Thus, it may be that what appears to us as bizarre, inappropriate and irrational behaviour follows from the creation of a closed system that is self-validating and internally consistent. By carefully listening to schizophrenic speech, it is often possible for a clinician to decode the sense in what appears at first to be pure nonsense (Forest, 1976). Thus, the conventional notion that schizophrenia can be characterised as a loss of rationality is challenged. In this vein, Sass (1992) argues that schizophrenia is better understood in terms of *hyperrationality:* there is an evident detachment from action, emotions and the somatic self, plus attendant feelings of entrapment as manifest in acute self-consciousness and heightened self-awareness; these phenomena could be construed thereby as hyperrational responses to alienating aspects of modern life.

The explanations of schizophrenia that we have reviewed, and the questions that remain despite a significant amount of research, suggest how much we have to learn about this powerful psychological disorder. Complicating our understanding is the likelihood that the phenomena we call schizophrenia are probably best thought of as a group of disorders, each with potentially distinct causes (Meltzer, 1982). Genetic predispositions, neurochemical processes and brain structure, family structure and communication and cognitive processes have all been identified as participants in at least some cases of schizophrenia. However, no single one of them explains schizophrenia in every case. We do not yet know the exact ways in which they may combine to cause schizophrenia. Much of the mystery of schizophrenia waits for creative researchers and clinicians to solve.

Is Schizophrenia Universal?

All cultures establish certain rules, or norms, to be followed and roles to be enacted if people are to be considered normal and acceptable members. As we have noted, each culture also maintains more general belief systems about the forces that determine life and death, health and sickness and success and failure. In

What are perceived as symptoms of psychological disorders in some cultures are judged to be perfectly normal behaviours in others. (Photo: John Scofield, © 1962 National Geographic Society.)

other words, there is considerable **cultural relativity** in what is judged as 'mad' or abnormal in different societies. What one culture sees as abnormal, another may see as appropriate (such as wearing your mother's skull around your neck to ward off evil spirits). Also, some styles of psychological disorder are more likely than others to be seen in a particular society (Triandis & Draguns, 1980). For example, a comparison of Filipino and Japanese hospitalised psychiatric patients in Hawaii found that the two cultural groups could be differentiated in terms of aggressive versus ideational symptomatology (Enright & Jaeckle, 1963).

Our view of the origins and manifestations of psychological disorders, then, is broadened by a cross-cultural perspective (Mezzich & Berganza, 1984). What can we learn about schizophrenic disorders from looking at their manifestations in different cultures? From such distinctly contrasting groups as the Inuit of north-west Alaska and the Yoruba of rural Nigeria, we hear descriptions of a disorder in which thoughts, beliefs, feelings and actions are significantly disorganised and part of a socially maladaptive way of relating to and living within the local host community. This pattern resembles what is commonly diagnosed as schizophrenia (Murphy, 1976). From an international pilot study of schizophrenia and later follow-up, the World Health Organization (1973, 1979) concluded that similar rates of the disorder could be identified reliably in disparate cultures. Purportedly the incidence of schizophrenia across diverse cultures is a relatively standard one per cent. Biologically oriented psychologists often point to these findings as further evidence of the biological origins of schizophrenic disorders and of their 'pan-human' universality. It is highly unusual, though, for medical disorders to have the same prevalence across diverse cultures, let alone ones of a mental health kind. This in itself suggests that the data reported in the WHO studies should be treated with caution.

It is notable that the WHO pilot study was carried out in Western and non-Western countries that in large part had already made the transition from rural to urban societies (Sass, 1992). In a pre-existing worldwide survey, Murphy *et al* (1963) found that paranoid schizophrenia is rarely observed in many traditional, rural settings. Had such countries been comprehensively included within the WHO study, differences in the rates of schizophrenic disorders may have been recorded across cultures. In line with such a suggestion, Draguns (1980) observes that cultures notable for their non-antagonistic orientation to nature (viewing it as something to accommodate rather than to master and control), have fewer long-stay psychiatric patients and less of a problem with relapses.

The universality thesis is seriously brought into question, then, if we consider what we do know about schizophrenia. Firstly, it is apparent that there at least four different types of schizophrenic disorder, so it would be unwise to generalise about 'schizophrenia' across cultures as if it were simply one affliction. Secondly, given the multiplicity of types and of symptoms, numerous causal factors appear to be involved and the incidence of some therefore are likely to vary from culture to culture. In addition, as yet, the identity of first causes cannot be specified with absolute certainty: thus, in the absence of known psychogenic or biological markers, a diagnosis of schizophrenia perforce cannot be fully validated. Furthermore, as to the *reliability* of diagnoses, Kleinman (1980) has criticised the WHO pilot study for using a pre-determined definition of schizophrenia which thereby largely pre-empts ensuing findings by '. . . patterning the behaviour observed by investigators . . . systematically filtering out local cultural influences . . . to preserve a homogenous cross-cultural sample'. Such a process gives rise, in Kleinman's (1987) view, to a *category fallacy*: to the '. . . reification of a [*classificatory*] category developed for a particular cultural group that is then applied to members of another culture for whom it lacks coherence and its validity has not been established'. Many cultures, however, consider people abnormal if they exhibit unpredictable behaviour and/or do not communicate with others. We should therefore be wary of regarding these symptoms as universal manifestations of pathology in all known cultural settings. Nevertheless, we should be similarly cautious of dismissing schizophrenic disorders as mere diagnostic artefacts, for the clinical reality of many people's distress behoves us to suspend judgement until replicable, definitive research confirms or disconfirms such a view.

INTERIM SUMMARY

Schizophrenia is a severe form of psychological disorder affecting about one per cent of the population. It is different in kind as well as in degree from the other mental disorders we have considered. Someone with a schizophrenic disorder experiences extreme distortions in perception, thinking, emotion, behaviour and language. Hallucinations and delusions are common and there may be a disintegration of the coherent functioning of personality. Because of the range of behaviour that can characterise schizophrenia, psychologists have identified four subtypes – disorganised, catatonic, paranoid and undifferentiated.

Evidence for the cause of schizophrenia has been found in genetic factors, biochemical and brain abnormalities, family structure and communication, and faulty cognitive processes. Investigators with a medical-model perspective argue that schizophrenia is a disease, not just a matter of faulty mental and behavioural functioning due to stress, trauma or conflict. Despite widely differing views of

psychological disorders across the world, the behaviours of schizophrenia seem to be experienced in many cultures. This cross-cultural commonality leads to the tentative conclusion that schizophrenia appears to be a universal human phenomena.

As with the differing explanations of the aetiology of anxiety and affective disorders, each of the systematic attempts to make sense of the origins of schizophrenic disorders offers only a partial explanation; the development of most cases is likely to be influenced by a number of interacting complex factors.

JUDGING PEOPLE AS ABNORMAL

Although diagnosis and classification yield benefits for research and clinical purposes, these same processes can also have negative consequences. The task of actually assigning a person with the label 'psychologically or mentally disordered' remains a matter of human judgement – thus open to bias and error. The labels of 'mental illness', 'insanity' or 'psychological disorder' can be acquired in a number of ways other than by the diagnosis of a trained clinician. When psychologically untrained people are in the position to judge the mental health of others, their decisions are often vulnerable to biases based on expectations, status, gender, prejudice and context. Too often those identified as psychologically disordered suffer stigma.

The Problem of Objectivity

A mental health difficulty is typically designated on the basis of the following evidence:

- The person is under some form of psychological or psychiatric care.
- Members of the community (doctors, spouses, parents, teachers, judges) agree that the person's behaviour represents a significant degree of maladjustment.
- The person's scores on psychological inventories, school achievement tests or intelligence tests vary by a specified extent from scores of individuals designated as 'normal'.
- The person declares himself or herself to be 'mentally unwell' by applying such terminology directly or by expressing feelings, such as unhappiness, anxiety, depression, hostility or inadequacy, that are excessive and frequent enough to be associated with ongoing emotional disturbance.

- The person behaves publicly in ways dangerous to himself or herself (by making suicidal threats or gestures, by showing problems with self-care) or to others (by demonstrating aggressive or homicidal impulses or gestures).

The criteria psychologists and psychiatrists use to make diagnostic decisions also influence judgements of the legal system and of the insurance and health care businesses. The legal determination of insanity carries with it serious implications regarding a defendant's competence to stand trial and to be held responsible for criminal indictments. It can also deprive a defendant of the right to administer his or her own estate and it can be the basis for an involuntary commitment to a mental hospital for further evaluation or court-ordered care. 'Insanity' is a legal concept that may be informed by psychology but nevertheless is determined by judges and juries. Payments and reimbursements by health insurance for psychological disability and its treatment typically require that the disorder be diagnosed and labelled by a mental health specialist. The ICD-10 and DSM-IV are standard diagnostic guides for this purpose.

The decision to declare someone psychologically 'disordered' or 'insane' is always a judgement about behaviour and thereby the outcome of subjective rather than wholly objective processes. It is a judgement made by one or more people about another individual, often someone of lesser political power or socio-economic status. In some countries, it has been customary to diagnose political dissidents as mentally disordered for their unacceptably deviant ideology and to sentence them to long terms in remote mental hospitals. For example, prior to the demise of communist Russia, artist Mihail Chemiakin was declared insane and exiled for refusing to paint in the government-approved tradition of Soviet socialist realism.

Research has shown that clinicians in many cultures use a double standard to assess the maladjustment of men and women. In one study, both male and female clinicians ascribed more positive characteristics to males and less desirable characteristics to normal, healthy females (Broverman *et al*, 1972). Other research shows that clinicians tend to judge females as maladjusted when they show behaviours that are incongruent with their gender role. When women act 'like men' — use foul language, drink excessively or exhibit uncontrollable temper — they are seen as 'neurotic' or self-destructive. Moreover, clinicians reflect the biases of their society in regarding masculinity as more salient than femininity. Male behaviour that was incongruent with the male gender role was rated as a more serious violation than was female gender role incongruity (Page, 1987).

We have seen throughout the study of psychology that the meaning of behaviour is jointly determined by its *content* and by its *context*. The same act in different settings conveys very different meanings. A man kisses another man: it may signify a gay relationship in the United Kingdom, a ritual greeting in France and a Mafia 'kiss of death' in Sicily. Unfortunately, the diagnosis of a behaviour as 'abnormal' can depend on where the behaviour occurs — even professionals' judgements may be influenced by context. Is it possible to be judged as sane if you are 'a patient' in an insane place? This question was addressed in a classic study by David Rosenhan (1973; 1975).

Rosenhan and seven other sane people gained admission to different psychiatric hospitals by pretending to have a single symptom: hallucinations. All eight of these pseudopatients were diagnosed on admission as either paranoid schizophrenic or manic-depressive. Once admitted, they behaved normally in every way. When a sane person is in an 'insane place', he or she is likely to be judged insane and any behaviour is likely to be reinterpreted to fit the context. If the pseudopatients discussed their situation in a rational way with the staff, they were reported to be using 'intellectualisation' defences, while their notes of their observations were evidence of 'writing behaviour'. The pseudopatients remained on the wards for almost three weeks on average, and not one was identified by the staff as sane. When they were finally released — only with the help of spouses or colleagues — their discharge diagnosis was still 'schizophrenia' but 'in remission'; that is, their symptoms were not active (Fleischman, 1973; Lieberman, 1973).

Rosenhan's research challenged the former system of classifying mental disorders, but it also raised basic issues about the validity of judgements of abnormality in other people, about how dependent such judgements may be on factors other than behaviour itself and about how difficult psychological labels are to remove once they are 'stuck' on a person. In the view of radical psychiatrist **Thomas Szasz**, mental illness does not even exist — it is a 'myth' (1961; 1977). Szasz argues that the symptoms used as evidence of mental illness are merely medical labels that sanction professional intervention into what are social problems — so-called 'deviant people' violating social norms. Once labelled, these people can be treated either benignly or harshly for their problem 'of being different', with no threat of disturbing the existing status quo. British psychiatrist **Ronald Laing** (1967) went further yet, proposing that labelling people as mad often suppresses the creative, unique probing of reality by individuals who are questioning their social context. Laing believed that by regarding the novel and unusual as mad rather than as creative genius, mental diagnosis may hurt both the person and the society (1965; 1970).

Few clinicians would go this far, but there is a movement of psychologists who advocate a contextual or *ecological model* in lieu of the classic medical model (Levine & Perkins, 1987). In an ecological model, abnormality is viewed not as the result of a disease *within* a person but as a product of an interaction *between* individuals and society. Abnormality is seen as a mismatch between a person's abilities and the needs and norms of society. For example, schools typically demand that children sit quietly for hours at desks and work independently in an orderly fashion. Some children are not able to do this and are often labelled 'hyperactive'. The abilities of these children do not conform to the needs of most school settings and they quickly come to the attention of school authorities. However, if these same children were in an alternative school setting where they were free to roam around the classroom and talk to others as part of their work, the mismatch would not exist and these children would not be labelled.

In some cases, prevailing stereotypes can influence the judgements of those with the power to label others. An outrageous example of the medicalisation of deviance is to be found in an 1851 report in a medical journal on 'The Diseases and Physical Peculiarities of the Negro Race'. Its author, Dr Samuel Cartwright, had been appointed by the Louisiana Medical Association to chair a committee to investigate the supposedly 'strange' practices of African–American slaves. 'Incontrovertible scientific evidence' was claimed to have been amassed to justify the accepted practice of slavery. Mysteriously, in the course of doing so, several 'diseases' previously unknown to the white race were discovered. One finding was that black people allegedly suffered from a sensory disease that made them insensitive 'to pain when being punished' – thus, no need to spare the whip.

The committee also invented the disease 'drapetomania', a so-called 'mania to seek freedom' – an alleged mental disorder that caused certain slaves to run away from their keepers. Thus, a pseudo-mental health phenomenon was created to facilitate social control: runaway slaves needed to be caught so that their 'illness' could be properly 'treated' (Chorover, 1981)!

⊙ The Problem of Stigma

From a sociological point of view, people with psychological disorders are labelled as 'deviant'. However, deviance and abnormality are rarely used in a *value-free* statistical sense. The fact that it has been estimated that nearly a third of the general population

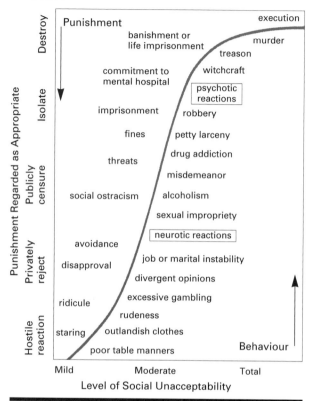

| FIGURE 14.7 | 'LET THE PUNISHMENT FIT THE CRIME' |

This figure illustrates a continuum of behaviours that are deemed increasingly unacceptable and are responded to with increasing severity. Basically, each reaction is a punishment for deviating from a 'norm', so behaviour towards those who act neurotically or psychotically can be seen to resemble reactions to criminality and other forms of 'deviance'.

struggle with some form of psychological disorder at some point in their lives makes mental health problems, at least statistically, relatively normal (Regier *et al*, 1988). In practice, being designated as 'deviant' connotes moral inferiority and so carries with it social rejection. In addition, the term 'deviant' may imply that the whole person 'is different in kind from ordinary people and that there are no areas of his personality that are not afflicted by his "problems" ' (Scott, 1972) – a fundamentally untenable notion.

It has been proposed that each society defines itself negatively by pointing out what is *not* rather than what *is* appropriate, thereby setting boundaries on what is socially acceptable. The construction of 'deviance' and the identification of those who then are 'deviant' serves to clarify these boundaries and to make the rest of the society feel more 'normal', healthy, moral and law abiding (Ericksen, 1966) – despite such psychological comfort being derived from the discomforting of others. There is little doubt that in our society being designated and identified as 'mentally disordered' alas is to be publicly degraded and personally devalued. Society extracts costly penalties from those who vary from its norms (see *Figure 14.7*).

People who are in psychological difficulty are **stigmatised** in ways that most physically unwell people are not. A stigma is a mark or brand of disgrace. In the psychological context it is a set of negative attitudes about a person that sets him or her apart as unacceptable (Clausen, 1981). Negative attitudes toward the psychologically disturbed come from many sources. Prominent among these sources are legal terminology that stresses mental 'incompetence', mass media portrayals of psychiatric patients as prone to violent crime, a family or social group's denial of the mental distress of one of its members and an individual's fear of loss of employment if others discover his or her distress or former mental health care (Rabkin *et al*, 1980). The uncharitable stigmatising process discredits a person as 'flawed' (Jones *et al*, 1984).

A recovered patient wrote, 'For me, the stigma of mental illness was as devastating as the experience of hospitalisation itself'. She went on to describe her personal experience in vivid terms:

'Prior to being hospitalised for mental illness, I lived an enviable existence. Rewards, awards and invitations filled my scrapbook. My diary tells of many occasions worth remembering . . . The crises of mental illness appeared as a nuclear explosion in my life. All that I had known and enjoyed previously was suddenly transformed, like some strange reverse process of nature, from a butterfly's beauty into a pupa's cocoon. There was a binding, confining quality to my life, in part chosen, in part imposed. Repeated rejections, the awkwardness of others around me and my own discomfort and self-consciousness propelled me into solitary confinement.

My recovery from mental illness and its aftermath involved a struggle – against my own body, which seemed without energy and stamina and against a society that seemed reluctant to embrace me. It seemed that my greatest needs – to be wanted, needed, valued – were the very needs which others could not fulfil' (Houghton, 1980).

Negative attitudes toward the psychologically disturbed bias people's perceptions of and actions toward them and also influence their behaviour toward others. A series of experiments conducted in laboratory and naturalistic settings demonstrates the unfavourable influences of the social situation on both the behaviour of a person perceived to be a mental patient (even when not so) and the behaviour of the person making that judgement.

When one member of a pair of male college students was (falsely) led to believe the other had been a mental patient, he perceived the pseudo ex-patient to be inadequate, incompetent and not likable. By making one of a pair of interacting males falsely believe he was perceived by the other as stigmatised, he behaved in ways that actually caused the other naive subject to reject him (Farina, 1980; Farina *et al*, 1971).

Our growing understanding of psychological disorders does more than enable society to reclaim its 'familiar strangers'. In making sense of mental health, we are forced to come to grips with basic conceptions of normality, reality and social values. A mind 'loosed from its stable moorings' does not just go on its solitary way; it bumps into other minds, sometimes challenging their stability. In examining how to understand, treat and, ideally, to prevent psychological disorders, we not only help those who are suffering and losing out on the joys of living, but we also expand available comprehension of what it is to be human.

By whose standards do we judge others to be abnormal?

r ecapping main points

⊃ The Nature of Psychological Disorders

Abnormality is judged by the degree to which a person's actions resemble a set of indicators that include distress, maladaptiveness, irrationality, unpredictability, unconventionality and observer discomfort. In the past, psychological disorders were considered to be the result of so-called 'evil' spirits or weak character. Today, there are a number of approaches to studying aetiology. The biological approach concentrates on abnormalities in the brain, biochemical processes and genetic influences. The psychological approach includes the psychodynamic, behavioural and cognitive models, each involving the social nature of many mental health phenomena. The interactionist approach combines these views.

⊃ Classifying Psychological Disorders

Classification systems for psychological disorders should provide a common shorthand for communicating about general types of disorder and about specific cases. The most widely accepted diagnostic and classification systems are the DSM-IV (American Psychiatric Association) and that within the ICD-10 (World Health Organization). They emphasise descriptions of symptom patterns, though the ICD (WHO) also examines aetiological considerations. The DSM uses a multi-dimensional system of five axes that encourages mental health professionals to consider psychological, physical and social factors that might be relevant to a specific disorder. While the DSM system has been updated over the years to reflect evolving views of psychological disorders, critics contend that it is limited in its ability to add to understanding of aetiology or to make treatment decisions.

⊃ Major Types of Psychological Disorders

Personality disorders are patterns of perception,

thinking or behaviour that are long-standing and inflexible and that impair an individual's functioning. Dissociative disorders involve a disruption of the integrated functioning of memory, consciousness or personal identity. The four major types of anxiety disorders are generalised, panic, phobic and obsessive-compulsive. Biological and psychological explanations of anxiety disorders account for different facets of the aetiology of anxiety. Mood disorders involve disturbances of affect. Major depressive disorder is the most common affective disorder while bipolar disorder is much rarer. Suicides are most frequent among people suffering from depression.

⊃ Schizophrenic Disorders

Schizophrenia is a severe form of psychological disorder. It is characterised by extreme distortions in perception, thinking, emotion, behaviour and language. The four subtypes of schizophrenia are disorganised, catatonic, paranoid and undifferentiated. Evidence for the cause of schizophrenia has been found in a variety of factors including genetics, biochemical and brain abnormalities, family environment and communication, and faulty cognitive processes. The universality of schizophrenic disorders as cross-cultural phenomena is currently a contentious and much-debated issue.

⊃ Judging People as Abnormal

The task of labelling someone psychologically or mentally disordered is ultimately a matter of human judgement. Even professional judgements can be influenced by context and biased by gender, race and other prejudices. Those with psychological disorders are often stigmatised in ways that most physically ill people are not. Understanding psychological disorders enables us to help those who are distressed and suffering with mental health difficulties and to improve our understanding of human nature.

key Terms

aetiology
affective disorder
agoraphobia
amnesia
antisocial personality disorder
catastrophising
catatonic
comorbidity
compulsion
conversion disorder
concordance rate
cultural relativity
biological marker
delusion
diathesis–stress hypothesis
dissociative disorder
dopamine hypothesis
double bind
DSM-IV
endogenous
exogenous
functional pathology
generalised anxiety disorder
hallucination
hebephrenic
hysteria
ICD-10
interactionist perspective

learned helplessness model
major depression (unipolar depression)
mania
manic depression (bipolar disorder)
masochism
multiple personality disorder
narcissistic personality disorder
negative cognitive sets
neurotic disorders
nominalism
obsessive-compulsive disorder
organic pathology
panic disorder
paranoia
personality disorders
phobic disorder
post-traumatic stress
preparedness
psychogenic amnesia
psychopathological functioning
psychotic disorders
reality testing
schizophrenic disorders
social phobia
stigma
taxonomy
transaction

major Contributors

Bateson, Gregory (1904–80)
Beck, Aaron
Brown, George
Charcot, Jean (1825–93)
Freud, Sigmund (1856–1939)
Gottesman, Irving
Griffiths, Mark
Harris, Tirril
Kraepelin, Emil (1855–1926)
La Framboise, Teresa
Laing, Ronald (1927–89)

Maher, Brendan
Mahler, Margaret (1897–1985)
Mesmer, Franz (1733–1815)
Nolen-Hoeksema, Susan
Pinel, Phillipe (1745–1826)
Rogers, Carl (1902–87)
Rosenhan, David
Seligman, Martin
Szasz, Thomas
Yalom, Irving

Chapter 15

Therapies for Personal Change

Rachel is 39-year-old woman who has been referred by her general practitioner (GP) to a community department of clinical psychology based in her local health centre. She complained to her GP of recurrent headaches which she experienced as an uncomfortable constriction of her scalp around her temples, forehead and eyes. She also reported feeling tired and listless most of the time and disinterested in activities about which she used to feel enthusiastic. In the referral letter the GP noted that there was no identifiable physical pathology evident upon examination of Rachel which might account for her headaches and subjective state. Having ruled out any organic cause, Rachel was referred to the clinical psychologist for 'psychogenic pain disorder of unspecified origin'. The GP in the referral letter also mentioned Rachel's lethargy and anhedonia (an inability to take pleasure in everyday activities), commenting in addition that her appearance was uncharacteristically dishevelled. The doctor was aware that in recent months Rachel had discovered through medical tests that she was infertile and would be unable to bear children as she had hoped. Suspecting Rachel might be suffering from a low-mood state (perhaps reactive depression), the general practitioner asked if she would see a clinical psychologist to talk about any difficulties she might be having which could explain her regular tension headaches.

At first interview, the psychologist began by asking Rachel to describe in her own words why she thought she was having frequent headaches. Rachel attributed them to the fact that she was getting insufficient sleep of late, waking early in the morning, and feeling agitated and restless. She also mentioned she found her full-time job as an audio-typist in a small solicitor's office repetitive and unfulfilling. Though these factors *could* be sufficient causes of Rachel's symptoms, as an experienced clinician, the psychologist knew that a

much more thorough exploration of Rachel's present condition and of its antecedents was called for. Only in this way could an appropriate formulation of the aetiology of her tension headaches be arrived at and thereby could a meaningful intervention be planned to help Rachel improve her ongoing quality of life.

The psychologist began by asking Rachel about the history of her headaches, their frequency, duration and intensity. When did they first start? How many times a day or per week do they happen? At what time of day or night do they occur? How long do they last? Do they ever prevent you from engaging in usual activities? Are they accompanied or followed by any other sensations such as anxiety or nausea? How do you cope with a severe one? In this way, the psychologist built up a general picture of the presenting complaint but if necessary would ask Rachel to keep a diary for the following week in which she would note when a headache started and ended, what she was doing before it began and what she did during and after it had ceased. Thereby the psychologist would be able to assess in greater detail how the occurrence of headaches might be related to *antecedent* and to *consequent* events – a form of assessment known as a *functional analysis*. At first interview though, a broader description of this presenting complaint was adequate.

From there the psychologist asked Rachel to describe her present life circumstances, suspending judgement for the moment as to whether or not there were any psychosocial contributors to her condition. Her family history revealed that Rachel lived with her father, who for some years now had been house-bound with coronary artery disease, the symptoms of which were frequent chest pain and breathlessness upon minimal exertion. Her mother had died three years previously. She still missed her greatly, saying she had always been a great source of support to her in times of adversity. Her relationship with her father on the other hand she said had been soured by his bitterness at the loss of his wife and the progression of his debilitating illness. Rachel had one younger sister who now lived in Canada with her husband and family. Rachel had been married during her 20s but the relationship was an unhappy one and had ended in divorce eight years later. There were no childern from the marriage. At present Rachel was single but until recently had been seeing a man a little older than herself of whom she had grown fond. Upon discovering six months ago, however, that Rachel was unable to have children, he had discontinued seeing her, much to her anger and disappointment.

Rachel did not enjoy her job, complaining that her boss was unsympathetic to any of her personal concerns and seemed unappreciative of her efforts to cope with the never ending amounts of work the solicitor's office piled upon her. She said she felt like a mere extension of automata – of her typewriter and audio-playback machine. Since her father had become ill she had stopped even considering going out in the evening to meet a close female friend who lived to the north of the city. He complained bitterly if she left him on his own. She felt trapped both by her father and by her job. She felt let down by her ex-manfriend, strangely deserted by the loss of her mother and that she no longer had anyone to confide in about her dissatisfaction with her existence. Her hopes of a life of her own, of a meaningful relationship, of feeling part of a family or social group again seemed remote possibilities that she thought were now unlikely to happen. She was unable to envisage how her life could possibly change for the better – the past seemed an infinitely better place. She could not remember the last time she had enjoyed herself. She felt worthless and tearful and confessed that unbeknown to her father, of late she had taken to drinking alcohol in her bedroom last thing at night to help her sleep.

Rachel expressed herself slowly and deliberately, seeming emotionally flat and unresponsive. Given her blunted affect and her account of her life circumstances, the psychologist made a more structured assessment of her mental state by asking Rachel to respond to a psychometric measure of depressive mood. This standardised questionnaire showed Rachel to be clinically depressed, the depression being of moderate severity. Thus, the psychologist formulated that Rachel was suffering from a reactive depression which was confounded by regular alcohol consumption (itself being a central nervous system depressant) and that her headaches were a somatic manifestation of stress resulting from her multiple and ongoing psychosocial difficulties.

GIVEN THE MULTI-CAUSAL nature of Rachel's present state, the psychologist is faced with more than one therapeutic possibility: the headaches could become the focus of intervention, with perhaps some form of autogenic relaxation training coupled with biofeedback being desirable; alternatively, the headaches could be conceived as the symptoms of ongoing psychosocial problems and of resultant depressive affect and anxiety. The latter would lead the psychologist into looking for ways of intervening which would empower Rachel and lessen her feelings of entrapment and hopelessness. Necessarily, this would entail examining how she relates assertively or otherwise to her father and to the needs of her over-demanding boss. It may involve engaging Rachel in talking over occupational alternatives or retraining, in construing the importance of re-establishing her social support network, of making time for friends in whom she could confide and from whom she would obtain emotional support.

Given her wish for a meaningful and intimate relationship, a therapist could examine with Rachel ways in which she might meet new people, perhaps through the identification of recreational activities which would bring her into contact with like-minded individuals. Of central concern would also be Rachel's perceptions of her infertility. What meaning does she attribute to this? Here the therapist might wish to examine if Rachel would consider fostering and adoption in the future as possible routeways to the family she had hoped to raise. In addition, the therapist could explore and reappraise with her the way in which the loss of her manfriend had perhaps resonated with the feelings of desertion she felt upon the death of her mother. In the first instance, though, the psychologist might ask Rachel to identify activities which she had enjoyed in the past, but which she has not engaged in since becoming depressed, and to select one or two with a view to enacting them in the coming week. Thereby through such behaviour, Rachel could begin in some small way to re-experience that she is still capable of instigating enjoyable activities. In turn, such a realisation could start to stimulate within her a renewed sense of self-efficacy and a sense of optimism about the future. The depressant effects of alcohol would be discussed with Rachel, the act of solitary, immoderate drinking being of questionable value as a coping strategy.

Through such cognitive and behavioural methods Rachel was helped to emerge over a four-month period from her depression. As her strategies for coping with sources of stress became more active, wide-ranging and successful, her headaches gradually abated. Her world began to hold more desirable possibilities and unfold before her as she took steps to turn into reality her cherished vision of her occupational and interpersonal future. At follow-up one year later, Rachel had changed her job, finding more fulfilment as an office manager for a local children's charity. Though her father remained ill, she had managed to talk with him about their mutual isolation and bereavment; through greater understanding of each other's perspective, her father had come to accept Rachel's need for greater independence and social mobility. She had ceased her solitary drinking and had made new friends through an evening class she had been attending once a week at an adult education centre. Her mood had lifted and she had regained her lost optimism. She felt much more like her old self again and no longer was fixated upon her past.

This opening case highlights the importance of a five-stage therapeutic process consisting of initial *referral*, *assessment*, *formulation* of the problem, *intervention* and *follow-up* evaluation. Such a professional model, focusing as it does largely upon the individual, has emerged in post-industrial, non-collectivist cultural settings. One question which arises then, is how treatment of psychological disorders has been influenced by historical, cultural and social forces? In this chapter we will seek to explore answers to this question amongst others and to examine the nature of the relationship between theory, research and practice. In particular we will consider what can be done to influence a mind bereft of ordinary hope and reason, how behaviour can be modified, how emotions may be altered and abnormalities of the brain can be corrected or accommodated. In so doing, we will examine the major types of treatments currently used by mental health care providers to help people in distress, namely: psychoanalysis, behaviour modification, cognitive therapy, humanistic therapies and drug therapies. We will examine the way these treatments work and also evaluate the validity of claims about their efficacy.

THE THERAPEUTIC CONTEXT

There are different types of therapy for mental disorders and there are many reasons why someone seeks help (and others who could benefit from it do not). Even the purposes or goals of therapy, the settings in which therapy occurs and the kinds of therapeutic helpers are varied. Despite any differences between therapies, however, all are interventions into a person's life, designed to change that person's functioning in some way.

Treatment of mental disorder is in large part determined by its severity. Some disorders such as schizophrenic ones, are so serious that they require long-term, intensive treatment by highly trained professionals, sometimes in institutional settings. On the other hand, relatively minor problems such as a mild phobia of an escalator, do not usually require treatment. In between these two extremes are a range of problems that may be intense but not long lasting; mild but disturbingly repetitive; and varying in the degree of discomfort they cause and in the degree of their interference with daily living.

Overview of Major Therapies

If we think of the brain as akin to a computer, we can say that mental problems may occur either in the brain's hardware or the software that program its actions. The two main kinds of therapy for mental disorders focus on either the hardware or the software.

Biomedical therapies focus on changing the hardware: the mechanisms that run the central nervous system, endocrine system and the metabolism. These therapies try to alter brain functioning with chemical or physical interventions, including surgery, electric shock and drugs, that act directly on the brain–body connection. Only psychiatrists who are medical doctors can administer biomedical therapies.

Psychological therapies, which are collectively called **psychotherapy**, focus on changing the software – the faulty behaviours we have learned and the words, thoughts, interpretations and feedback that direct our daily strategies for living. These therapies are practiced by clinical psychologists as well as by psychiatrists. There are four major types of psychotherapy: psychodynamic, behavioural, cognitive and existential-humanistic.

The *psychodynamic approach*, commonly known as the psychoanalytic approach, views adult suffering as the outer symptom of inner, unresolved childhood traumas and conflicts. Psychoanalysis treats mental disorder with words. It is a 'talking cure' in which a therapist helps a person develop insights about the relation between the overt symptoms and the unresolved hidden conflicts that presumably caused them.

Behaviour therapy treats the behaviours themselves as disturbances that must be modified. Disorders are viewed as learned behaviour patterns rather than as the symptoms of mental disease. Behaviour therapists believe that changing the problem behaviour corrects the disorder. This transformation is accomplished in many ways, including changing reinforcement contingencies for desirable and undesirable responding, extinguishing conditioned fear responses and providing models of effective problem-solving.

Cognitive therapy tries to restructure the way a person thinks by altering the often distorted self-statements a person makes about the causes of a problem. Restructuring cognitions changes the way a person defines and explains difficulties, often enabling the person to cope with them.

Therapies that have emerged from the *existential-humanistic tradition* emphasise the values of patients. Existential-humanistic therapies are directed toward self-actualisation, psychological growth, the development of more meaningful interpersonal relationships and the enhancement of freedom of choice. These therapies have given rise to encounter group and personal growth types of therapy.

Before we examine the conceptual rationale for and methods of each of these types of therapeutic intervention, let us start at the beginning of the process.

Entering Therapy

Most often, people will enter therapy when their everyday functioning violates societal criteria of normality and/or their own sense of adequate adjustment. They may seek therapy on their own initiative after trying ineffectively to cope with their problems, or they may be advised to do so by family, friends, doctors or colleagues. Sudden life changes due to unemployment, death of a loved one or divorce may trigger or worsen one's psychological problems, necessitating outside support. Students often seek therapy in their college mental health facilities because of difficulties in interpersonal relationships and concerns about academic performance. Some people are in treatment because they are legally required by the court to do so in connection with a criminal offence or insanity hearing. Those whose behaviour is judged dangerous to self or others can be involuntarily committed by a court to a mental institution for a limited period of time for treatment, testing and/or observation.

Many people who might benefit from therapy do not seek professional help. Sometimes it is inconvenient for them to do so, but there are many other possible reasons. These reasons include lack of accessible mental health facilities in the community, ignorance of available resources, lack of money, older age, language difficulties, fear of stigmatisation and value systems that devalue seeking help from others.

One's ability to get help can be affected even by the psychological problems themselves. The person with agoraphobia finds it hard, even impossible, to leave home to seek therapy; a paranoid person will not trust mental health professionals. Extremely shy people cannot call for an appointment or go to an initial diagnostic interview precisely because of the problem for which they desire help.

People who do enter therapy are usually referred to as either 'patients' or 'clients'. The term *patient* is preferred by professionals who take a biomedical approach to the treatment of psychological problems. The term *client* is used in preference by professionals who think of psychological disorders as 'problems of living' and not as mental illnesses (Rogers, 1951; Szasz, 1961). We will try to use the preferred term for each approach: *patient* for biomedical and psychoanalytic therapies and *client* for other therapies.

Goals and Settings

The therapeutic process can involve four primary tasks or goals:

- Reaching a diagnosis about what is wrong, possibly determining an appropriate psychiatric (DSM or ICD) descriptor for the presenting problem and for the purposes of classifying the disorder.
- Proposing a probable aetiology, identifying the probable causes of the disorder and the functions being served by the symptoms.
- Making a prognosis, or estimate, of the course the problem will take with and without any treatment.
- Prescribing and carrying out some form of treatment, a therapy designed to minimise or eliminate the troublesome symptoms and, perhaps, also their sources.

There are many settings in which therapy is conducted: hospitals, clinics, schools and private offices. Newer community-based therapies that aim to take the treatment to the client may operate out of local health centres. Finally, therapists who practice **in vivo therapy** work with clients in the life setting that is associated with their problem. For example, they work in airplanes with pilots or flight attendants who suffer from flying phobias or in shopping precincts with people who have social phobias.

Healers and Therapists

A cross-cultural perspective shows that communally oriented societies treat cases of behaviour pathology within a social group context. By contrast, societies with more individualistic values have therapies that generally reflect those dominant values. Most treatment for mental and behavioural problems in Western societies is typically conducted in an environment alien to the patient, in a one-on-one interaction with an expert and stranger who is paid to try to improve a client's well-being or alleviate a patient's suffering.

Although more people seek out therapy now than in the past, people usually turn to trained mental health professionals only when their psychological problems become severe or persist for extended periods of time. When they do, they usually turn to one of five main types of therapists: counselling psychologists, psychiatric social workers, clinical psychologists, psychiatrists and psychoanalysts.

- The term **counselling psychologist** describes a member of the general category of professional psychologists who specialises in providing guidance in areas such as vocation selection, school problems, drug abuse and marital conflict. Typically, these counsellors work in community settings related to the problem areas – within a business, a school, a prison, the military service, or a neighbourhood clinic – and use interviews, tests, guidance and advising to help individuals solve specific problems and make decisions about future options.
- A **psychiatric social worker** is a mental health professional whose specialised training in a school of social work prepares him or her to work in collaboration with psychiatrists and clinical psychologists. Unlike psychiatrists and psychologists, these counsellors are trained to consider first and foremost the social contexts of people's problems – for example, they become acquainted with clients' homes or work settings.
- A **clinical psychologist** is required to have concentrated his or her post-graduate training in the assessment and treatment of psychological problems, completed a period of supervised clinical practice and earned a post-graduate qualification in clinical psychology. These psychologists tend to have a broader background in psychology, assessment and research than do psychiatrists.
- A **psychiatrist** must have completed medical school training to be a medical doctor and also have completed some post-qualificatory specialty training in dealing with mental and emotional disorders. Psychiatrists' training lies more in a biomedical basis of psychological problems. They are the only therapists who can prescribe medications or physically based therapy.
- **Psychoanalysts** must have completed specialised post-graduate training in the Freudian approaches to understanding and treating mental disorders.

Before looking at the various modern approaches in more detail, we will first consider the historical contexts in which treatment of the mentally ill was delivered and then broaden the Western perspective with a look at the healing practices of other cultures.

▚ Historical and Cultural Contexts

What kind of treatment might you have received in past centuries if you were suffering from psychological problems? If you lived in Europe or the United States, the chances are that the treatment would not have helped and could even have been harmful. In other cultures, treatment of psychological disorders has usually been seen within a broader perspective that includes religious and social values which often have been associated with kinder treatment of those with aberrant behaviour.

Western history of treatment

Population increases and migration to big cities in fourteenth-century Western Europe created unemployment, poverty and social alienation. These conditions led to poverty, crime and psychological problems. Special institutions were created to warehouse society's three emerging categories of misfits: the poor, criminals and the mentally disturbed.

In 1403, a London hospital – St Mary of Bethlehem – admitted its first patient with psychological problems. For the next 300 years, mental patients of the hospital were chained, tortured and exhibited to an admission-paying public. Over time, a mispronunciation of Bethlehem – Bedlam – came to mean chaos because of the horrible confusion reigning in the hospital and the dehumanised treatment of patients found there (Foucault, 1975).

In fifteenth-century Germany, the mad were assumed to be possessed by the Devil who had deprived them of reason. As the Inquisition's persecutory mania spread throughout Europe, mental disturbances were 'cured' by painful death. See *The Malleus Malificarum of 1486* (Summers, ed, 1971) to find out about the case made by German clerics against witches.

It was not until the late eighteenth century that the perception of psychological problems as mental illness emerged in Europe. The French physician **Philippe Pinel** wrote in 1801, 'The mentally ill, far from being guilty people deserving of punishment, are sick people whose miserable state deserves all the consideration that is due to suffering humanity. One should try with the most simple methods to restore their reason' (Zilboorg & Henry, 1941).

By the mid-1800s, when psychology as a field of study was gaining some credibility and respectability, 'a cult of curability' emerged throughout the country. Insanity was then thought to be related to the environmental stresses brought on by the turmoil of newly developing cities. Eventually, madness came to be viewed as a social problem to be cured through 'mental hygiene', just as contagious physical diseases were being treated by physical hygiene.

One of the founders of modern psychiatry, German psychiatrist **J. C. Heinroth**, helped provide the conceptual and moral justification for the disease model of mental illness. In 1818, Heinroth wrote that madness is a complete loss of inner freedom or reason depriving those afflicted of any ability to control their lives. Others who 'know best' what is good for the patient must be in charge of care. Heinroth maintained that it was the duty of the state to cure mentally ill patients of diseases that forced them to burden society (Szasz, 1979).

From Heinroth's time to the present, 'In this alliance between psychology and state, the state's protective power to confine the mentally ill has been transformed into a power of the state to treat, through its agent the mental health profession, the mental disorder thought to be the basis of the problem' (White & White, 1981). Heinroth and, later in the 1900s, Clifford Beers spurred on the 'mental hygiene' movement. Eventually, the confinement of the mentally ill assumed a new rehabilitative goal. The asylum then became the central fixture of this socio-political movement. The disturbed were, thus, confined to asylums in rural areas, far from the stress of the city, not only for protection but also to be treated (Rothman, 1971). Unfortunately, many of the asylums that were built became overcrowded. Then the humane goal of rehabilitation was replaced with the pragmatic goal of containing strange people in remote places.

Cultural symbols and rituals of curing

Our review of these historical trends in the treatment of psychological disorders has been limited to Western views and practices which emphasise the uniqueness of the individual, competition, independence, survival of the fittest, a mastery over nature and personal responsibility for success and failure. Both demonology and the disease model are consistent with this emphasis, regarding mental disorder as something that happens inside a person and as an individual's failure.

This view is not shared by many other cultures (Triandis, 1990). For example, in the African world the emphasis is on groupness, commonality, co-operation, interdependence, tribal survival, unity with nature and collective responsibility (Nobles, 1976). It is contrary to the thinking of many non-European cultures to treat mentally ill individuals by removing them from society. Among the Navajo and African cultures, for example, healing is a matter that always takes place in a social context, involving a distressed person's beliefs, family, work and life environment. The African use of group support in therapy has been expanded into a procedure called **network therapy**, where a patient's entire network of relatives, colleagues and friends becomes involved in the treatment (Lambo, 1978).

The research of cultural anthropologists has broadened the conception of 'madness' in all its forms by providing analyses of the explanations and treatments for psychological disorders across different cultures (Bourguignon, 1979; Evans-Pritchard, 1937; Kluckhorn, 1944; Marsella, 1979). In many cultures, the treatment of mental and physical disease is bound up with religion and witchcraft; certain human beings are given special mystical powers to help in the transformation of their distressed fellow beings. Belief systems often personalise the vague forces of fate or chance that intervene in one's life to create problems. This personalisation permits direct action to be taken against presumed 'evil-doers' and direct help to be sought from assumed divine healers (Middleton, 1967).

Common to all folk healing ceremonies are the important roles of symbols, myths and ritual (Levi-Strauss, 1963). Ritual healing ceremonies infuse special emotional intensity and meaning into the healing process. They heighten patients' suggestibility and sense of importance and, combined with the use of symbols, they connect the individual sufferer, the shaman and the society to 'supernatural forces' to be won over in the battle against madness (Devereux, 1981).

One therapeutic practice used in a number of healing ceremonies is dissociation of consciousness, which is induced in either a distressed person or a faith healer. While in Western views dissociation is itself a symptom of mental disorder to be prevented or corrected, in other cultures, as consciousness is altered, good spirits are communicated with and evil spirits are exorcised. The use of ceremonial alteration of consciousness can be seen today among the cult of Puerto Rican Espiritistas in New York City, whose healing ceremonies involve communication with good spirits that are believed to exist outside a person's skin (Garrison, 1977). Some of these non-Western views have begun to work their way into Western practices. The influence of the social-interactive concept and the focus on the family context and supportive community are evident in newer therapeutic approaches that emphasise social support networks and family therapy.

INTERIM SUMMARY

People enter therapy for help with mental or emotional problems that are causing suffering, dysfunctional behaviour or social problems. Biomedical therapies affect physiological processes; psychological therapies try to change thoughts, feelings or behaviours. There are four major types of psychotherapy: the psychodynamic approach focuses on gaining insight into how conflicts from the person's past influences present behaviour; behaviour therapy modifies the behaviours themselves by using conditioning principles; cognitive therapy deals with a person's thoughts; existential-humanist therapies emphasise ways to help a patient fulfil values and achieve personal growth goals.

The therapeutic process involves four tasks: diagnosing what is wrong; establishing the aetiology, or source, of the problem; making a prognosis about probable outcomes with or without treatment; and carrying out a specific kind of treatment. There are various kinds of professionals who work in the therapeutic mould; among them are counselling psychologists, psychiatric social workers, pastoral counsellors, clinical psychologists, psychiatrists and psychoanalysts.

A historical perspective on the treatment of mental disorders shows how conceptions of disease and aberrant behaviour were influenced by religious, social and political agendas of different countries in different eras. Emerging conceptions of the afflicted person as mentally ill led to more humane treatment and hospitalisation in mental institutions. Programmes in mental asylums for rehabilitation of mentally ill patients, however, eventually became custodial warehouses for social misfits.

Cultural anthropologists extend the boundaries of Western psychological views of mental disorder and therapy by revealing a broader socio-religious context. Folk healing typically involves a blend of magic and witchcraft practiced by a healer or shaman. The key ingredients of folk healing are the manipulation of symbols, myths and ritual ceremonies and the patient's total belief in that culturally prescribed system of cure.

■ PSYCHODYNAMIC THERAPIES

Psychodynamic therapies assume that a patient's problems have been caused by the psychological tension between unconscious impulses and the constraints of his or her life situation. These therapies locate the core of the disturbance inside the disturbed person, accepting a general model of a disease core that shows up in overt symptoms.

▣ Freudian Psychoanalysis

Psychoanalytic therapy, as developed by Sigmund Freud, is the premier psychodynamic therapy. It is an intensive and prolonged technique for exploring unconscious motivations and conflicts in neurotic, anxiety-ridden individuals. The major goal of psychoanalysis is 'to reveal the unconscious'. A former president of the American Psychoanalytic Institute explained the premise of psychoanalysis:

We believe an unconscious exists in all humans and that it dictates much of our behaviour. If it is a relatively healthy unconscious, then our behaviour will be healthy, too. Many who are plagued by symptoms from phobias, depression, anxiety or panic may have deposits of unconscious material that are fostering their torment. Only the psychoanalyst is qualified to probe the unconscious . . . (Theodore Rubin, quoted in Rockmore, 1985).

As we saw in earlier chapters, Freudian theory views anxiety (or neurotic) disorders as inabilities to resolve adequately the inner conflicts between the unconscious, irrational impulses of the id and the internalised social constraints imposed by the superego. As an individual progresses through the biologically determined stages from infancy to adulthood, according to Freudian theory his or her particular psychological experiences at each stage determine whether there will be a fixation at an immature stage or progress to a more mature level of development. The goal of psychoanalysis is to establish intrapsychic harmony that expands one's awareness of the forces of the id, reduces over-compliance with the demands of the superego and strengthens the role of the ego.

Of central importance to a therapist is understanding the way a patient uses the process of repression to handle conflicts. Symptoms are considered to be messages from the unconscious that something is wrong. A psychoanalyst's task is to help a patient bring repressed thoughts to consciousness and to gain insight into the relation between the current symptoms and the repressed conflicts from years gone by. In this psychodynamic view, therapy works and patients recover when they are 'released from repression' established in early childhood (Munroe, 1955). Because a central goal of a therapist is to guide a patient toward discovering insights between present symptoms and past origins, psychodynamic therapy is often called **insight therapy**.

The goals of psychoanalysis are ambitious. They involve not just the elimination of the symptoms of psychopathology but a total personality reorganisation. When psychoanalysis overcomes barriers to self-awareness and to freedom of thought and communication, a person can achieve more intimate human associations as well as more intellectual creativity. Because traditional psychoanalysis is an attempt to reconstruct long-standing repressed memories and then work through painful feelings to an effective resolution, it is a therapy that takes a long time (several years at least, with as many as five sessions a week). It also requires introspective patients who are verbally fluent, highly motivated to remain in therapy and willing and able to undergo considerable expense. Some of the newer forms of psychodynamic therapy try to make therapy briefer in total duration. In time-limited psychotherapy, the therapist and patient contract for a specific number of sessions or time period for the treatment. Short-term therapy may be for only a few weeks, perhaps ten sessions, while an intermediate form of therapy gaining popularity with many therapists lasts months or up to a year but is shorter than formal psychoanalysis.

A recent review related improvement in therapy as a function of the number of therapy sessions. This meta-analysis of 2,431 patients in reported studies for over the past 30 years indicates that, by the eigth session, approximately half the patients are measurably improved and that 75 per cent of the patients are measurably improved by six months with weekly sessions (Howard *et al*, 1986).

Psychoanalysts use several techniques to bring repressed conflicts to consciousness and to help a patient resolve them (Langs, 1981; Lewis, 1981). These techniques include free association, analysis of resistance, dream analysis and analysis of transference and counter-transference.

Catharsis and the talking cure

Modern psychotherapy began in 1880 with the case of Fraulein Anna O and her famous physician **Joseph Breuer**. This bright, personable, 21-year-old Viennese woman became incapacitated and developed a severe cough while nursing her ill father. When the physician began to treat her 'nervous cough', he became aware of many more symptoms that seemed to have a psychological origin. Anna squinted, had double vision and experienced paralysis, muscle contractions and anaesthesias (loss of sensitivity to pain stimuli).

Breuer told a young physician named Sigmund Freud about this unusual patient. Together they coined the term *hysterical conversion* for the transformation of Anna O's blocked emotional impulses into physical symptoms (Breuer & Freud, 1895; 1955). The case of Anna O is the first detailed description of physical symptoms resulting from psychogenic causes – a hysterical illness. It was Anna O herself who devised her own treatment, with Breuer acting as therapist. She referred to the procedures as a 'talking cure' and jokingly as 'chimney sweeping'.

In the context of hypnosis, Anna O talked freely, giving full reign to her imagination (free associations). Once she was able to express herself in an open and direct fashion to her therapist, she no longer needed to use the indirect and disguised communication of physical symptoms. According to Breuer, her 'complexes were disposed of by being given verbal expression during hypnosis'.

Breuer and Freud analysed Anna O's disorder in terms of internal psychodynamic forces (instincts and impulses). What they failed to acknowledge fully were the external social obstacles of the time that limited the ambitions and aspirations of all women. In addition, they did not recognise that Anna O's intellectual and emotional involvement with her therapist helped break the monotony of her existence.

Anna O went on to become a pioneer of social work, a leader in the struggle for women's rights, a playwright and a housemother of an orphanage. Her true name was Bertha Pappenheim (Rosenbaum & Muroff, 1984). Although this case played an extremely important role in the development of modern psychotherapy, a provocative new view of Anna O's illness casts doubt on the original diagnosis. A reasonably good alternative diagnosis is that her symptoms were those associated with tuberculous meningitis, which she might have contracted from her father who probably was dying from a form of tuberculosis himself (Thornton, 1984). After Anna O had terminated her treatment with Breuer, she entered a sanatorium from which she was later discharged, relatively recovered from her illness. It is likely that many of her 'hysterical conversion' reactions were of organic not psychological origin, but she may have experienced considerable suppressed rage and guilt from nursing her father for so long and been frustrated by the lack of opportunities for women of her social class.

Free association

The principal procedure used in psychoanalysis to probe the unconscious and release repressed material is called **free association**. A patient sitting comfortably in a chair or lying in a relaxed position on a couch, lets his or her mind wander freely and gives a running account of thoughts, wishes, physical sensations and mental images as they occur. The patient is encouraged to reveal every thought or feeling, no matter how personal, painful or seemingly unimportant.

Freud maintained that free associations are predetermined, not random. The task of an analyst is to track the associations to their source and identify the significant patterns that lie beneath the surface of what are apparently just words. The patient is encouraged to express strong feelings, usually toward authority figures, that have been repressed for fear of punishment or retaliation. Any such emotional release, by this or other processes, is termed **catharsis**.

Among many native American tribes, confession is part of the therapy when a person's disease is believed to be due to the violation of a social rule or taboo. Confession to a ritual healer works as cathartic therapy (La Barre, 1964) and so does the interpretation and acting out of dreams as 'wishes of the soul' (Hallowell, 1976).

Resistance

At some time during the process of free association, a patient will show **resistance** – an inability or unwillingness to discuss certain ideas, desires or experiences. Resistances prevent repressed material from returning to consciousness. This material is often related to an individual's sexual life (which includes all things pleasurable) or to hostile, resentful feelings toward parents. Sometimes a patient shows resistance by coming late to therapy or 'forgetting' a session altogether. When the repressed material is finally brought into the open, a patient generally claims that it is unimportant, absurd, irrelevant or too unpleasant to discuss. The therapist, however, is sensitised to the likelihood of the opposite.

A psychoanalyst, thus, attaches particular importance to subjects that a patient does not wish to discuss. Such resistances are conceived of as barriers between the unconscious and the conscious. The aim of psychoanalysis is to break down resistances and enable the patient to face these painful ideas, desires and experiences. Breaking down resistances is a long and difficult process that is essential if the underlying problem is to be brought to consciousness where it can be resolved.

Dream analysis

Psychoanalysts believe that dreams are an important source of information about a patient's unconscious motivations. When a person is asleep, the superego is presumably less on guard against the unacceptable impulses originating in the id, so a motive that cannot be expressed in waking life may find expression in a dream. Some motives are so unacceptable to the conscious self that they cannot be revealed openly, even in dreams, but must be expressed in disguised or symbolic form. In analysis, dreams are assumed to have two kinds of content: manifest (openly visible) content that we remember upon awakening and latent (hidden) content – the actual motives that are seeking expression but are so painful or unacceptable to us that we do not want to recognise them. Therapists attempt to uncover these hidden motives by using dream analysis, a therapeutic technique that examines the content of a person's dreams to discover the underlying or disguised motivations and symbolic meanings of significant life experiences and desires.

Transference and counter–transference

During the course of the intensive therapy of psychoanalysis, a patient usually develops an emotional reaction toward the therapist. Often the therapist is identified with a person who has been at the centre of an emotional conflict in the past – most often a parent or a lover. This emotional reaction is called **transference**. The transference is called positive transference when the feelings attached to the therapist are those of love or admiration, and negative transference when the feelings consist of hostility or envy. Often a patient's attitude is ambivalent, including a mixture of positive and negative feelings.

An analyst's task in handling transference is a difficult and potentially dangerous one because of the patient's emotional vulnerability; however, it is a crucial part of treatment. A therapist helps a patient to interpret the present transferred feelings by understanding their original source in earlier experiences and attitudes (Langs, 1981).

Personal feelings are also at work in a therapist's reactions to a patient. **Counter-transference** refers to what happens when a therapist comes to like or dislike a patient because the patient is perceived as similar to significant people in the therapist's life. In working through counter-transference, a therapist may discover some unconscious dynamics of his or her own. The therapist becomes a 'living mirror' for the patient and the patient, in turn, for the therapist. If the therapist fails to recognise the operation of counter-transference, the therapy may not be as

effective (Little, 1981). Because of the emotional intensity of this type of therapeutic relationship and the vulnerability of the patient, therapists must be on guard about the ease of crossing the boundary between professional caring and personal involvement with their patients.

▚ Post-Freudian Therapies

Some of Freud's followers have retained many of his basic ideas but modified certain of his principles and practices. In general, these neo-Freudians place more emphasis than Freud did on (a) a patient's current social environment (less focus on the past); (b) the continuing influence of life experiences (not just infantile fixations); (c) the role of social motivation and interpersonal relations of love (rather than of biological instincts and selfish concerns); (d) the significance of ego functioning and development of the self-concept (less on the conflict between id and superego); (g) the extension of psychotherapy to schizophrenic patients; and (f) shorter, time-limited therapy.

In Chapter 14, we noted two other prominent Freudians, Carl Jung and Alfred Adler. To get a flavour of the more contemporary psychodynamic approaches of the neo-Freudians, here we will look at the work of Harry Stack Sullivan, Margaret Mahler, Karen Horney and Heinz Kohut (see Ruitenbeek, 1973, for a look at other members of the Freudian circle).

Harry Stack Sullivan (1953) emphasised the social dimension of a patient's life and its role in creating mental problems. He felt that Freudian theory and therapy did not recognise the importance of social relationships or a patient's needs for acceptance, respect and love. Mental disorders, he insisted, involve not only traumatic intrapsychic processes but troubled interpersonal relationships and even strong societal pressures. A young child needs to feel secure and to be treated by others with caring and tenderness. Anxiety and other mental problems arise out of insecurities in relations with parents and significant others. In Sullivan's view, a self-system is built up to hold anxiety down to a tolerable level. This self-system is derived from a child's interpersonal experiences and is organised around conceptions of the self as the 'good-me' (associated with the mother's tenderness), the 'bad-me' (associated with the mother's tensions) and the 'not-me' (a dissociated self that is unacceptable to the rest of the self).

Therapy based on this interpersonal view involves observing a patient's feelings about the therapist's attitudes. The therapeutic interview is seen as a social setting in which each party's feelings and attitudes are influenced by the other's. The patient is gently provoked to state his or her assumptions about the therapist's attitudes and other assumptions as well. Above all, the therapeutic situation, for Sullivan, was one where the therapist learned and taught lovingly (Wallach & Wallach, 1983).

Margaret Mahler (1979) was one of the first psychoanalysts to recognise and treat childhood schizophrenia. She traced a child's fragmentation of ego and retreat from reality to sources of disharmony in the mother–child relationship. The normal development of an independent ego requires a process of gradual separation of the mother and child, along with an emerging sense of individuation – a unique, stable identity. A child's development can be skewed toward mental disorder by the pathology of the mother, a need on her part not to separate from her child, or re-engulfing of the separated child into an infantile dependency. Mahler also saw a mother's lack of 'emotional availability' as a contributor to abnormal development. A therapist must treat the disturbed parent–child relationship as well as the disturbed child, being sensitive to the conflict over separation-individuation and to the process by which the 'dual unity' of mother and child needs to be differentiated into distinct selves. The therapy works through the phases of this process toward the goal of forming a stable sense of personal identity in the patient (Karon & Vandenbos, 1981).

Karen Horney (1937; 1945; 1950) expanded the boundaries of Freudian theory in many ways. She stressed the importance of environmental and cultural contexts in which neurotic behaviour is expressed. She also took a more flexible view of personality as involving rational coping and continual development that deals with current fears and impulses rather than being determined solely by early childhood experiences and instincts. Horney was one of the first neo-Freudians to question the extent to which Freud's theory was applicable to women. She rejected Freud's phallocentric emphasis on the importance of the penis (male concern for castration by the father and penis envy by females), hypothesising that male envy of pregnancy, motherhood, breasts and suckling is a dynamic force in the unconscious of boys and men (1926). This alternative emphasis is gynocentric, centred on the female womb. Males' intense desires for material achievement and creative products were thus seen as unconscious means of over-compensating for feelings of inferiority in the creative area of reproduction.

Psychodynamic therapies continue to evolve with a varying emphasis on Freud's constructs. One of the most important new directions for these is the modern concern for the self in all its senses, notably the ways one's self-concept emerges, is experienced

by the person and, at times, becomes embattled and requires defending. According to **Heinz Kohut** (1977), a leading proponent of this emphasis on the self and founder of the object relations school of psychoanalysis, the various aspects of self require self-objects, supportive people and significant things that each of us needs in order to maintain optimal personality functioning.

Although psychoanalytic therapy and Freud's theories have been widely criticised (Fisher & Greenberg, 1985), there are still many enthusiastic supporters, especially in many Western European countries and in large urban centres in the United States.

INTERIM SUMMARY

Sigmund Freud's psychoanalytic therapy is the main form of psychodynamic therapy. One of Freud's important contributions was postulating the dynamic role of unconscious processes in normal and pathological reactions. He argued that behaviour is affected by hidden conflicts and drives between the hedonistic impulses of the id and the controlling forces of the superego. The goal of this kind of therapy is to reconcile these conflicts into a stronger ego that mediates these drives. Important concepts in psychodynamic therapy include repression of unacceptable impulses, free association that allows repressed material to surface in undirected speech, resistance of a patient to discuss significant feelings and experiences, and dream analysis to reveal latent meaning in manifest content. Freud's other major contribution involved the notion of transference – the patient's identification of the therapist with significant others – and counter-transference – the therapist's strong emotional reaction to the patient.

Neo-Freudians Harry Stack Sullivan, Margaret Mahler, Karen Horney and Heinz Kohut differ from classic Freudian psychoanalysts in their emphasis on the patient's current social situation, interpersonal relationships, self-concept, differing motivations and sources of mental disorder between women and men, and the use of psychoanalysis to treat severe disorders.

■ BEHAVIOUR THERAPIES

While psychodynamic therapies focus on presumed inner causes, behaviour therapies focus on observable outer behaviours. Behaviour therapies apply the principles of conditioning and reinforcement to modify undesirable behaviour patterns associated with mental disorders. This orientation rejects the medical model along with all assumptions about patients suffering from mental illness that is cured by therapy.

Behaviour therapists argue that abnormal behaviours are acquired in the same way as normal behaviours – through a learning process that follows the basic principles of conditioning and learning. They assert that all pathological behaviour, except where there is established organic causation, can be best understood and modified by focusing on the behaviour itself rather than by attempting to alter any underlying 'disease core'. The term behaviour is used to describe all reactions that are influenced by learning variables – thoughts and feelings as well as overt actions.

The therapies that have emerged from the theories of conditioning and learning are grounded in a pragmatic, empirical research tradition. The central task of all living organisms is to learn how to adapt to the demands of the current social and physical environment. When organisms do not learn how to cope effectively, their maladaptive reactions can be overcome by therapy based on principles of learning (or relearning). The target behaviour is not assumed to be a symptom of any underlying process. The symptom is the problem itself. Behaviourists believe that if the problem behaviour is changed, the problem is solved.

Behaviour modification is defined as 'the attempt to apply learning and other experimentally derived psychological principles to problem behaviour' (Bootzin, 1975). The terms behaviour therapy and **behaviour modification** are often used inter-changeably. Both refer to the systematic use of principles of learning to increase the frequency of desired behaviours and/or decrease that of problem behaviours. The range of deviant behaviours and personal problems that typically are treated by behaviour therapy is extensive and includes fears, compulsions, depression, addictions, aggression and delinquent behaviours. In general, behaviour therapy works best with specific rather than general types of personal problems; with a phobia better than with an inadequate personality. Psychodynamic therapists predicted that treating only the outer behaviour without confronting the true, inner problem would result in **symptom substitution**, the appearance of a new physical or psychological problem. However, research has shown that when pathological behaviours are eliminated by behaviour therapy, new symptoms are not substituted (Kazdin, 1982). 'On the contrary, patients whose target symptoms improved often reported improvement in other, less important symptoms as well' (Sloane et al, 1975).

The earliest recorded use of behaviour therapy was carried out by **Mary Cover Jones** in 1924. She showed how fears learned through conditioning could be unlearned. You may remember the case of Little Albert – in a sense, Cover Jones followed up on Watson's demonstration.

Her subject was Peter, a three-year-old boy who, for some unknown reason, was afraid of rabbits. The therapy involved feeding Peter at one end of a room while the rabbit was brought in at the other end. Over a series of sessions, the rabbit was gradually brought closer until, finally, all fear disappeared and Peter played freely with the rabbit.

Behaviour therapies today are more sophisticated, but they are still based on classical conditioning, operant conditioning or a combination of the two. The development of irrational fears and other undesirable emotional reactions is assumed to follow the paradigm of classical conditioning. Therapy to change these negative responses uses principles of counter-conditioning, substituting a new response for the inadequate one. Operant conditioning principles are applied when the therapeutic task is to increase the frequency of desired actions or decrease undesired habits. Contingency management refers to the general treatment strategy of changing behaviour by modifying its consequences. Special adaptations also have been developed for social learning; generalisation techniques have been developed to make connections between new responses learned in the therapy setting and the client's life situations. Our presentation of behaviour therapy will be organised around these four basic aspects of conditioning and learning approaches to changing behaviour patterns.

▪ Counter-conditioning

Why does someone become anxious when faced with a harmless stimulus, such as a fly, a non-poisonous snake, an open space or a social contact? Is the anxiety due to simple conditioning principles we reviewed earlier? We know that any neutral stimulus may acquire the power to elicit strong conditioned reactions on the basis of prior association with an unconditioned stimulus. However, not everyone who is exposed to situations that are alarming, dangerous or traumatic develop long-lasting conditioned fears that become phobias that lead to avoidance of those situations. In fact, it is surprising that relatively few people do develop such fears. In one survey of 8,000 British schoolchildren exposed to bombing attacks, only four per cent developed anxiety symptoms attributable to the air raids, whilst 96 per cent were unaffected (Agras, 1985).

Although conditioning can be rapidly developed, it is another matter for it to persist. A variety of experimental and observational studies of humans and animals reveals a new understanding of the conditions under which phobias develop and, thus, provide clues as to how to counteract their negative effects with behaviour therapy. According to **Stewart Agras** (1985), a prominent theorist and behaviour therapist for phobias and panic attacks, there are five factors that must be considered in phobic conditioning. First, phobias develop primarily to certain classes of objects that appear to have evolutionary significance because they are dangerous (such as animals) and also of primal threat situations (such as heights and social separation from care-givers). Second, only certain types of fear-evoking conditioned stimuli can be coupled with these objects to produce phobias. They seem to be stimuli that have a relevant sensory association with the feared object (such as tactile stimuli), but not loud sounds for animal phobias (possibly because animals bite the skin). Third, phobias can be learned through social transmission of fear from other individuals. Fourth, emotionally intense fears persist partly because of other people. Significant people may repeatedly show fear of the phobic situation and prevent children and others from exploring it, depriving them of the chance to extinguish fears through experience. Fifth, it appears that certain individuals are born with a predisposition to learn avoidance behaviour more quickly and more persistently than others.

Strong emotional reactions that disrupt a person's life 'for no good reason' are often conditioned responses that the person does not recognise as having been learned previously. To weaken the strength of negative learned associations, behaviour therapists use the techniques of systematic desensitisation, implosion, exposure and aversive learning.

Systematic desensitisation

The nervous system cannot be relaxed and agitated or anxious at the same time because different incompatible processes can not be activated simultaneously. This simple notion was central to a new theory of reciprocal inhibition developed by South African psychiatrist **Joseph Wolpe** (1958; 1973) who used it to treat fears and phobias. First, he showed that strong fears of experimental cats could be overcome. He would relax the cats by feeding them in rooms that were initially different from the one in which they had developed their fear and then in rooms increasingly similar to the original learned fear setting. Finally, the cats were able to eat in the feared room and, as they did, their fear diminished.

On the basis of this simple animal analogue, Wolpe applied this method to cases of human phobias. He taught his patients to relax their muscles

and then to imagine visually their feared situation. They did so in gradual steps that moved from initially remote associations to direct images of it. Psychologically confronting the feared stimulus while being relaxed and doing so in a graduated sequence is the therapeutic technique known as **systematic desensitisation**.

Desensitisation therapy involves three major steps. The client identifies the stimuli that provoke anxiety and arranges them in a hierarchy ranked from weakest to strongest. For example, a student suffering from severe test anxiety constructed the hierarchy in *Table 15.1*. Note that she rated immediate anticipation of an examination as more stressful than taking the examination itself. Then, the client is trained in a system of progressive deep-muscle relaxation. Relaxation training requires several sessions in which the client learns to distinguish between sensations of tension and relaxation and to let go of tension in order to achieve a state of physical and mental relaxation. Finally, the actual process of desensitisation begins: the relaxed client vividly imagines the weakest anxiety stimulus on the list. If it can be visualised without discomfort, the client goes on to the next stronger one. After a number of sessions, the most distressing situations on the list can be imagined without anxiety – even situations that could not be faced originally (Lang & Lazovik, 1963). A number of

TABLE 15.1	HIERARCHY OF ANXIETY-PRODUCING STIMULI FOR A TEST-ANXIOUS COLLEGE STUDENT

1. **On the way to the university on the day of an examination.**
2. **In the process of answering an examination paper.**
3. **Before the unopened doors of the examination room.**
4. **Awaiting the distribution of examination papers.**
5. **The examination paper face down.**
6. **The night before an examination.**
7. **One day before an examination.**
8. **Two days before an examination.**
9. **Three days before an examination.**
10. **Four days before an examination.**
11. **Five days before an examination.**
12. **A week before an examination.**
13. **Two weeks before an examination.**
14. **A month before an examination.**

evaluation studies have shown that this behaviour therapy works remarkably well with most phobic patients and better than any other form of therapy (Smith & Glass, 1977). Desensitisation has also been successfully applied to a diversity of human problems, including such generalised fears as test anxiety, stage fright, impotence and frigidity (Kazdin & Wilcoxin, 1976).

Implosion and flooding

Implosion therapy uses an approach that is opposite to systematic desensitisation. If the latter is a kind of back-door approach, implosion is a fear-in-the-face form of therapy. Instead of experiencing a gradual, step-by-step progression, a client is exposed at the start to the most frightening stimuli at the top of the anxiety hierarchy but in a safe setting. The idea behind this procedure is that the client is not allowed to deny, avoid or otherwise escape from experiencing the anxiety-arousing stimulus situations. He or she must discover that contact with the stimulus does not actually have the anticipated negative effects (Stampfl & Levis, 1967).

One way to extinguish an irrational fear is to force a client to experience a full-blown anxiety reaction. The therapeutic situation is arranged so that the client cannot run away from the frightening stimulus. The therapist describes an extremely frightening situation relating to the client's fear, such as snakes crawling all over his or her body, and urges the client to imagine it fully, experiencing it through all the senses as intensely as possible. Such imagining is assumed to cause an explosion of panic. Because this explosion is an inner one, the process is called implosion; hence the term implosion therapy. As the situation happens again and again, the stimulus loses its power to elicit anxiety. When anxiety no longer occurs, the maladaptive behaviour previously used to avoid it disappears.

Flooding is similar to implosion except that it involves clients, with their permission, actually being put into the phobic situation. A claustrophobic is made to sit in a dark closet and a child with a fear of water is put into a pool. Flooding through stimulating the imagination may involve listening to a tape that describes the most terrifying version of the phobic fear in great detail for an hour or two. Once the terror subsides, the client is then taken to the feared situation, which, of course, is not nearly as frightening as just imagined. Flooding is more effective than systematic desensitisation in the treatment of some behaviour problems (such as agoraphobia) and treatment gains are shown to be enduring for most clients (Emmelkamp & Kuipers, 1979).

Exposure

The question arises as to what is the ingredient common to systematic desensitisation, implosion and flooding therapies? The critical causal ingredient in modifying phobic behaviour patterns is exposure. Therapy that employs a strategy for approaching the feared situation, forcing the client to confront the fear and that reinforces a successful approach is known as **exposure therapy**. This approach works most quickly for specific phobias, such as fear of spiders, but can take longer for fear of flying (Serling, 1986), for example, and as many as 50 hours for complex phobias, such as agoraphobia, that involve many elements. Curiously, research comparing these different treatments for phobia showed that clients least preferred exposure therapy, but found it to be the most effective treatment.

A reversed form of exposure therapy is used to counteract obsessive-compulsive disorders (OCD). Some adults and children are unable to think clearly or to work because they suffer from recurring thoughts that steal into their minds and because of repetitive behaviours which they cannot control. One woman obsessed with dirt compulsively washed her hands over and over until they cracked and bled. She even thought of killing herself because this disorder totally prevented her from leading a normal life. Under the supervision of a behaviour therapist, she confronted the things she feared most – dirt and rubbish – and eventually even touched them, giving up her compulsive avoidance behaviours through supervised response prevention exercises. Eventually she gave up washing and bathing her hands and face for five days. 'The first time I washed my hands normally it was like a miracle to me,' she reported (Londer, 1988). While the majority of those treated by exposure and response prevention therapy for their obsessions improve, for those who do not, the anti-depressant drug clomipramine is an extremely effective adjunct to such approaches. Indeed, pre-treatment with clomipramine often enhances the efficacy of exposure and response-prevention based therapy for OCD.

Aversion therapy

These forms of exposure therapy help clients deal directly with stimuli that are not really harmful, but what can be done to help those who are attracted to stimuli that are harmful or illegal? Drug addiction, sexual perversions and uncontrollable violence are human problems in which deviant behaviour is elicited by tempting stimuli. **Aversion therapy** uses counter-conditioning procedures of aversive learning to pair these stimuli with strong noxious stimuli (such as electric shocks or nausea-producing drugs). In time, through conditioning, the same negative reactions are elicited by the conditional tempting stimuli and the person develops an aversion for them that replaces his or her former desire.

Aversion therapy for a client who is a paedophile (sexually attracted to children) might begin by having him watch slides of children and adults. When he gets aroused to the children's images, he gets an electric shock; when he sees adult slides or is told to imagine socially acceptable fantasies, the shock is extinguished. However, it is difficult for any form of therapy to modify long-standing sexual perversions that have vivid fantasy components that have been repeatedly reinforced with masturbation to orgasm (McConaghy, 1969).

In the extreme, aversion therapy resembles torture, so why would anyone submit voluntarily to it? Usually people do so only because they realise that the long-term consequences of continuing their behaviour pattern will destroy their health or ruin their careers or family lives. They may also be coerced to do so by institutional pressures, as has happened in some prison treatment programmes. Many critics are concerned that the painful procedures in aversion therapy give too much power to a therapist, can be more punitive than therapeutic, and are most likely to be used in situations where people have the least freedom of choice about what is done to them. The film *A Clockwork Orange*, based on Anthony Burgess' novel, depicted aversion therapy as an extreme form of mind control in a police state. In recent years, use of aversion therapy in institutional rehabilitation programmes has become more regulated by laws and ethical guidelines for clinical treatment. The hope is that, under these restrictions, it will be a therapy of choice rather than of coercion.

■ Contingency Management

The operant conditioning approach of **Burrhus Frederic Skinner** to developing desirable behaviour is simple: find the reinforcer that will maintain a desired response, apply that reinforcer (contingent upon the appropriate response) and evaluate its effectiveness. This positive approach has been used to modify behaviour in the classroom, in general and mental hospitals and in homes for the aged (Blackman, 1974). The two major techniques of contingency management in behaviour therapy are positive reinforcement strategies and specific extinction strategies.

Positive reinforcement strategies

When a response is followed immediately by a reward, the response will tend to be repeated and will increase in frequency over time. This central principle of operant learning becomes a therapeutic strategy when it is used to modify the frequency of emission of a desirable response in place of an undesirable one. Dramatic success has been obtained from the application of positive reinforcement procedures to the behaviour problems of children with psychiatric disorders. Two examples were cited in Chapter 7: the case of shaping the behaviour of the little boy who would not wear his glasses and the Premack principle of using running and screaming in a nursery school as reinforcement for sitting still.

Positive reinforcement procedures have been extended to many other settings and problems. We described exposure therapy under counter-conditioning procedures because it emerged out of systematic desensitisation which clearly involves conditioning incompatible responses. However, what is the learning process that makes exposure therapy work? It is the positive reinforcement that comes from the praise of the therapist or the self-praise of the client upon making the desired response. Exposure therapy is clearly a form of contingency management.

Critics of contingency management therapies that use material rewards argue that they work best with those who are under-privileged in some way. Behaviour therapists have generally agreed with this criticism, but they have wanted to maintain the obvious benefits of positive reinforcement systems. One resolution to the problem has been to involve individuals directly in their own contingency management. A behavioural contract is an explicit agreement (often in writing) that states the consequences of specific behaviours. Such contracts are often required by behaviour therapists working with clients on obesity or smoking problems. The contract may specify what the client is expected to do (client's obligations) and what, in turn, the client can expect from the therapist (therapist's obligations).

Behavioural contracting facilitates therapy by making both parties responsible for achieving the agreed-upon changes in behaviour. Treatment goals are spelled out, as are the specific rewards corresponding to meeting planned responsibilities and reaching desired subgoals. The therapeutic situation becomes more structured in terms of what each party can reasonably expect as appropriate content and acceptable interpersonal behaviour. The person with less status and power (patient or child, for example) benefits if a condition for third-party arbitration of alleged contract violation is included (Nelson & Mowrey, 1976). Some parents have found that contracts with their teenagers have generated acceptable behaviour while greatly improving the emotional climate of the home. Reinforcements often include more reasonable parental behaviours (Stuart, 1971).

Extinction strategies

Why do people continue to do something that causes pain and distress when they are capable of doing otherwise? The answer is that many forms of behaviour have multiple consequences – some are negative and some are positive. Often, subtle positive reinforcements keep a behaviour going despite its obvious negative consequences. For example, children who are punished for misbehaving may continue to misbehave if punishment is the only form of attention they seem to be able to earn.

Extinction is useful in therapy when dysfunctional behaviours have been maintained by unrecognised reinforcing circumstances. Those reinforcers can be identified through a careful situational analysis and then a programme can be arranged to withhold them in the presence of the undesirable response. When this approach is possible and everyone in the situation who might inadvertently reinforce the person's behaviour co-operates, extinction procedures work to diminish the frequency of the behaviour and eventually to eliminate the behaviour completely.

Even psychotic behaviour can be maintained and encouraged by unintentional reinforcement. It is standard procedure in many mental hospitals for the staff to ask patients frequently, as a form of social communication, how they are feeling. Patients often misinterpret this question as a request for diagnostic information and they respond by thinking and talking about their feelings, unusual symptoms and hallucinations. Such responding is likely to be counter-productive since it leads staff to conclude that the patients are self-absorbed and not behaving normally. In fact, the more bizarre the symptoms and verbalisations, the more attention the staff members may show to the patient, which reinforces continued expression of bizarre symptoms.

Just as positive reinforcement can increase the incidence of a behaviour, lack of desirable consequences can decrease its incidence. Dramatic decreases in psychotic behaviour sometimes have been observed when hospital staff members were simply instructed to ignore the psychotic behaviour and to give attention to the patients only when they were behaving normally (Ayllon & Michael, 1959). With a break from reinforcement, the target behaviour stops being followed by its usual consequence and should begin to extinguish.

Social-learning Therapy

The focus of behaviour therapies has been expanded by social learning theorists who point out that humans learn – for better or worse – by observing the behaviour of other people. Often we learn and apply rules to new experiences, not just through direct participation, but also through symbolic means, such as watching other people's experiences in life, in a film or on television.

Social-learning therapy is designed to modify problematic behaviour patterns by arranging conditions in which the client will observe models being reinforced for the desirable form of responding. This vicarious learning process has been of special value in overcoming phobias and building social skills. We have noted in earlier chapters that this social-learning approach was largely developed by the pioneering theorising and empirical research of **Albert Bandura** (1977a; 1986). We will only mention two aspects of his approach: imitation of models and social skills training.

Imitation of models

When discussing phobias, we noted that one way such fears could be learned was through vicarious conditioning – through the transmission of fear displayed by others, such as from mother to child. An interesting series of studies with monkeys illustrates this imitation of modelled behaviour.

Young monkeys reared in the laboratory, where they never saw a snake, observed their parents, who had been raised in the wild, react fearfully to real snakes and toy snakes. In less than ten minutes, the young monkeys showed a strong fear of snakes and, by the sixth modelling session, their fear was as intense as that of their parents. The more disturbed the parents were at the sight of the snakes, the greater the fear in their offspring (Mineka et al, 1984).

In a follow-up study, young, laboratory-raised rhesus monkeys observed the fearful reactions of adult monkeys who were strangers to them. As can be seen in Figure 15.1, *the young monkeys showed little fear initially in the pretest, but, after observing models reacting fearfully, they did also, both to the real and toy snakes. This fear persisted in intensity when measured three months later. However, the fear was less strong and showed more variation than that of the other young monkeys who had observed their own parents' fearful reactions (Cook et al, 1985).*

FIGURE 15.1	FEAR REACTIONS IN MONKEYS

After young laboratory-raised monkeys observe adult stranger monkeys showing a strong fear of snakes, they are vicariously conditioned to fear snakes with an intensity that persists over time.

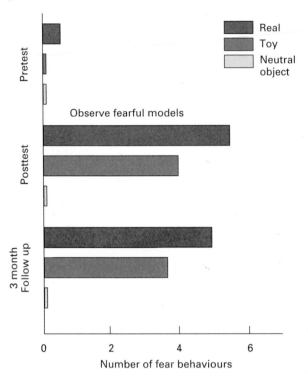

Before desired responses can be reinforced, they must occur. Many new responses, especially complex ones, can be acquired more readily if a person can observe and imitate another person performing the desired behaviour and be reinforced for doing so. If snake fears can be learned by observing such reactions, then it should be possible for people with snake phobias to unlearn them through imitation of models.

In treating a phobia of snakes, a therapist will first demonstrate fearless approach behaviour at a relatively minor level, perhaps approaching a snake's cage or touching a snake. The client is aided, through demonstration and supportive encouragement, to imitate the modelled behaviour. Gradually the approach behaviours are shaped so that the client can pick the snake up and let it crawl freely over him or her. At no time is the client forced to perform any behaviour. Resistance at any level is overcome by having the client return to a previously successful, less threatening approach behaviour.

The power of this form of participant modelling can be seen in research comparing the participant modelling technique just described with symbolic modelling, desensitisation and a control condition (see *Figure 15.2*, next page). In symbolic modelling therapy, subjects who had been trained in relaxation techniques watched a film in which several m fearlessly handled snakes; the subjects could sto film and relax themselves whenever a scene maue them feel anxious. In the control condition, no therapeutic intervention was used. Participant modelling was clearly the most successful of these techniques. Snake phobia was eliminated in 11 of the 12 subjects in the participant modelling group (Bandura, 1970).

Social-skills training

A major therapeutic innovation encouraged by social-learning therapists involves training people with inadequate social skills to be more effective (Hersen & Bellack, 1976). Many difficulties arise for someone with a mental disorder, or even just an everyday problem, if he or she is socially inhibited, inept or unassertive. Social skills are sets of responses that enable people to achieve effectively their social goals when approaching or interacting with others. These skills include knowing what (content) to say and do in given situations in order to elicit a desired response (consequences), how (style) to say and do it and when (timing) to say and do it. One of the most common social-skill problems is lack of assertiveness – inability to state one's own thoughts or wishes in a clear, direct, non-aggressive manner (Bower & Bower, 1991). To help people overcome such a problem, many social-learning therapists recommend behavioural rehearsal – visualising how one should behave in a given situation and the desired positive consequences. Rehearsal can be used to establish and strengthen any basic skill, from personal hygiene to work habits to social interactions. Behavioural rehearsal procedures are being widely used in social skills training programmes with many different populations (Yates, 1985).

Adult pathology has often been preceded by deficits in social skills in childhood (Oden & Asher, 1977). A considerable amount of research and therapy is currently directed at building competence in shy and withdrawn disturbed children (Conger & Keane, 1981; Zimbardo & Radl, 1981). One study demonstrated that pre-school-age children diagnosed as social isolates could be helped to become sociable in a short training period.

Twenty-four subjects were randomly assigned to one of three play conditions: with a same-age peer, with a peer one to one-and-a-half years younger, or with no partner (control condition). The pairs were brought together for ten play sessions, each only 20 minutes long, over a period of about a month. Their classroom behaviour before and after this treatment was recorded and it revealed that the intervention

FIGURE 15.2 PARTICIPANT MODELLING THERAPY

The subject shown in the photo first watched a model make a graduated series of snake-approach responses and then repeated them herself. She eventually was able to pick up the snake and let it crawl about on her. The graph compares the number of approach responses subjects made before and after receiving participant modelling therapy with the behaviour of those exposed to two other therapeautic techniques and a control group.

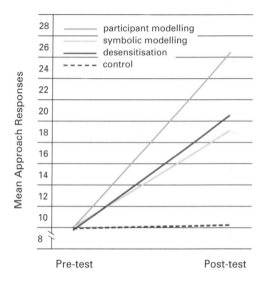

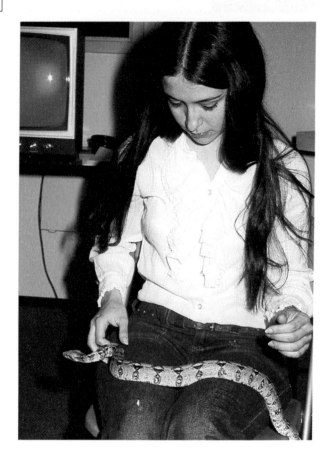

had a strong effect. The opportunity to play with a younger playmate doubled the frequency with which the former social isolates interacted later on with other classmates − bringing them up to the average level of the other children. Playing with a same-age peer also increased children's sociability, but not nearly so much. The researchers concluded that the one-on-one play situation had offered the shy children safe opportunities to be socially assertive. They were allowed to practice leadership skills that were likely to be approved by the non-threatening, younger playmates (Furman et al, 1979).

In another study, social-skills training with a group of hospitalised, emotionally disturbed children changed both verbal and nonverbal components of their behaviour in social settings. The children were taught to give appropriate verbal responses in various social situations (giving help or compliments, making requests). They were also taught to display appropriate affect (for example, to smile while giving a compliment) and to make eye contact and use proper body posture (face the person being talked to). These improved social skills were generalised to 'untreated' situations outside of training. The children also put

them into practice on their own when on the ward. These positive effects continued even months later (Matson *et al*, 1980).

◼ Generalisation Techniques

An ongoing issue of concern for behaviour therapists is whether new behaviour patterns generated in a therapeutic setting will actually be used in the everyday situations faced by their clients. This question is important for all therapies because any measure of treatment effectiveness must include maintenance of long-term changes that go beyond a therapist's couch, clinic or laboratory.

When essential aspects of a client's real-life setting are absent from the therapy programme, behaviours that have been modified by therapy can be expected to deteriorate over time after therapy terminates. To prevent this gradual loss, it is becoming common practice to build **generalisation techniques** into the therapeutic procedure itself. These techniques attempt

604 CHAPTER 15 ····· THERAPIES FOR PERSONAL CHANGE

TABLE 15.2   COMPARISON OF PSYCHOANALYTIC AND BEHAVIOURAL APPROACHES TO PSYCHOTHERAPY

Issue	Psychoanalysis	Behaviour Therapy
Basic human nature	Biological instincts, primarily sexual and aggressive, press for immediate release, bringing people into conflict with social reality.	Similar to other animals, people are born only with the capacity for learning, which follows similar principles in all species.
Normal human development	Growth occurs through resolution of conflicts during successive stages. Through identification and internalisation, mature ego controls and character structures emerge.	Adaptive behaviours are learned through reinforcement and imitation.
Nature of psychopathology	Pathology reflects inadequate conflict resolutions and fixations in earlier development, which leave overly strong impulses and/or weak controls. Symptoms are defensive responses to anxiety.	Problematic behaviour derives from faulty learning of maladaptive behaviours. The symptom is the problem; there is no underlying disease.
Goal of therapy	Psychosexual maturity, strengthened ego functions and reduced control by unconscious and repressed impulses are attained.	Symptomatic behaviour is eliminated and replaced with adaptive behaviours.
Psychological realm emphasised	Motives, feelings, fantasies and cognitions are experienced.	Therapy involves behaviour and observable feelings and actions.
Time orientation	The orientation is discovering and interpreting past conflicts and repressed feelings in light of the present.	There is little or no concern with early history or aetiology. Present behaviour is examined and treated.
Role of unconscious material	This is primary in classical psychoanalysis and somewhat less emphasised by neo-Freudians.	There is no concern with unconscious processes or with subjective experience even in the conscious realm.
Role of insight	Insight is central; it emerges in 'corrective emotional experiences'.	Insight is irrelevant and/or unnecessary.
Role of therapist	The therapist functions as a detective, searching basic root conflicts and resistances; detached and neutral, to facilitate transference reactions.	The therapist functions as a trainer, helping patients unlearn old behaviours and/or learn new ones. Control of reinforcement is important; interpersonal relationship is minor.

to increase the similarity of target behaviours, reinforcers, models and stimulus demands between therapy and real-life settings. For example, behaviours are taught that are likely to be reinforced naturally in a person's environment, such as showing courtesy or consideration. Rewards are given on a partial reinforcement schedule to ensure that their effect will be maintained when rewards are not always forthcoming in the real world. Expectation of tangible extrinsic rewards is gradually faded out while social approval and more naturally occurring consequences, including reinforcing self-statements, are incorporated. Opportunities are provided for patients to practice new behaviours under the supportive guidance of staff members during field trips. Halfway houses also help to transfer new behaviours from the institution to the community setting (Fairweather et al, 1969; Orlando, 1981). Careful attention to ways of increasing the generalisability of treatment effects clearly enhances the long-term success of behaviour therapy (Marks, 1981).

Before turning to cognitive therapies, take a few minutes to review the major differences between the two dominant psychotherapies outlined thus far – the psychoanalytic and the behavioural – as summarised in Table 15.2 (previous page).

INTERIM SUMMARY

Behaviour therapy rejects the medical model and views abnormal behaviour as a set of learned responses that can be modified with principles of reinforcement and conditioning. Behaviour modification attempts to apply these learning principles to problem behaviours in a systematic way. Counter-conditioning includes systematic desensitisation, implosion, flooding, exposure and aversive learning. Systematic desensitisation, developed by Wolpe, uses relaxation and graduated exposure to a feared stimuli to reduce phobic responses. Implosion and flooding are the opposite of systematic desensitisation; they require the client to confront voluntarily the fearful stimulus as it is imagined or in the actual phobic setting. All these phobia modification therapies have in common the key element of exposure therapy, encouraging the client to seek exposure to the feared stimulus. Aversion therapy pairs tempting but destructive stimuli with negative unconditioned stimuli to weaken their attraction.

Contingency management uses operant conditioning to modify behaviour. This conditioning primarily involves the introduction of positive reinforcement strategies and extinction strategies. Positive reinforcement increases the frequency of specific desirable responses, often with an explicit behavioural contract that outlines the goals, commitments and responsibilities of client and therapist. Extinction strategies identify and eliminate rewards that perpetuate undesirable behaviour.

Social-learning therapy, developed by Bandura, uses imitation of models and social-skills training to make individuals feel more confident about their abilities.

In all these therapies, generalisation techniques are used to increase the carry-over of therapeutic gains to clients' real-life settings. These techniques build into the therapy setting elements that will have similarity to the natural features of daily life.

COGNITIVE THERAPIES

Cognitive therapy attempts to change problem feelings and behaviours by changing the way a client thinks about significant life experiences. The underlying assumption of such therapy is that abnormal behaviour patterns and emotional distress start with problems in what we think (cognitive content) and how we think (cognitive process). As cognitive psychology has become more prominent in all areas of psychology, therapies based on cognitive principles have proliferated. These therapies focus on different types of cognitive processes and different methods of cognitive restructuring. We discussed some of these approaches in Chapter 11 as ways to cope with stress and improve health. The two major forms of cognitive therapy involve cognitive behaviour modification (including self-efficacy) and alteration of false belief systems (including rational-emotive therapy and cognitive therapy for depression).

Cognitive Behaviour Modification

We are what we tell ourselves we can be and we are guided by what we believe we ought to do. This is a starting assumption of cognitive behaviour modification. This therapeutic approach combines the cognitive emphasis on the role of thoughts and attitudes in influencing motivation and response with the behaviorism focus on reinforcement contingencies in the modification of performance. Unacceptable behaviour patterns are modified by changing a person's negative self-statements into constructive coping statements.

A critical part of this therapeutic approach is the discovery by therapist and client of the way the client thinks about and expresses the problem for which therapy is sought. Once both therapist and client understand the kind of thinking that is leading to unproductive or dysfunctional behaviours, they develop new self-statements that are constructive and minimise the use of self-defeating ones that elicit anxiety or reduce self-esteem (Meichenbaum, 1977). For example, they might substitute the negative self-statement 'I was really boring at that party; they'll never ask me back' with constructive criticism: 'Next time, if I want to appear interesting, I will plan some provocative opening lines, practice telling a good joke and be responsive to the host's stories'. Instead of dwelling on negatives in past situations that are unchangeable and part of past history, the client is taught to focus on positives in the future that can be realised.

FIGURE 15.3 EFFICACY EXPECTATIONS

According to Bandura (1986), each of the four major sources of efficacy information that an individual can utilise has a specific mode of treatment that operates to induce it.

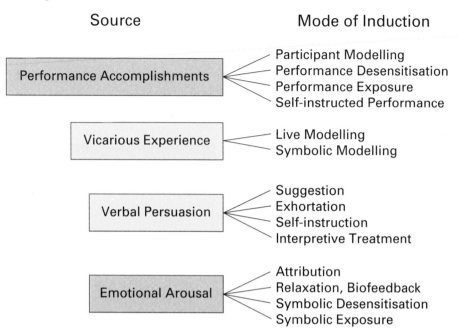

Building expectations of being effective increases the likelihood of behaving effectively. It is through setting attainable goals, developing realistic strategies for attaining them and evaluating feedback realistically that people develop a sense of mastery and self-efficacy (Bandura, 1986). *Figure 15.3* outlines the four major sources of efficacy expectations and the specific modes by which each of them is induced. For example, different types of modelling influence different efficacy sources, just as different types of desensitisation do.

Changing False Beliefs

Some cognitive behaviour therapists emphasise the important role of thoughts but still maintain many behavioural assumptions – such as the rewarding or punishing function of thoughts. Other cognitive therapists put less emphasis on behavioural processes. Their primary targets for change are beliefs, attitudes and habitual thought patterns (or schemas). These cognitive therapists argue that many psychological problems arise because of the way we think about ourselves in relation to other people and the events we face. Faulty thinking can be based on: (a) unreasonable attitudes ('Being perfect is the most important trait for a student to have'); (b) false

premises ('If I do everything they want me to, then I'll be popular'); and (c) rigid rules that put behaviour on automatic pilot so that prior patterns are repeated even when they have not worked ('I must obey authorities'). Emotional distress is believed to be caused by misunderstandings and by failure to distinguish between current reality and one's imagination (or expectations).

Cognitive therapy for depression

A cognitive therapist induces a patient to correct faulty patterns of thinking by applying more effective problem-solving techniques. **Aaron Beck** has successfully pioneered cognitive therapy for the problem of depression. He states the formula for treatment in simple form: 'The therapist helps the patient to identify his warped thinking and to learn more realistic ways to formulate his experiences' (1976). For example, depressed individuals may be instructed to write down negative thoughts about themselves, figure out why these self-criticisms are unjustified and come up with more realistic (and less destructive) self-cognitions.

Beck believes that depression is maintained because depressed patients are unaware of the negative automatic thoughts that they habitually say to themselves, such as 'I will never be as good as my brother'; 'Nobody would like me if they really knew me'; and 'I'm not smart enough to make it in this competitive school'. A therapist then uses four tactics to change the cognitive foundation that supports the depression: (a) evaluating the evidence the patient has for and against these automatic thoughts; (b) reattributing blame to situational factors rather than to the patient's incompetence; (c) openly discussing alternative solutions to the problem; and (d) challenging basic assumptions (Beck *et al*, 1979). This therapy is similar to behaviour therapies in that it centres on the present state of the client.

One of the worst side-effects of being depressed is having to live with all the negative feelings and lethargy associated with depression. One aspect of new therapeutic approaches deals with depression's downward spiral by directing the client in ways not to become further depressed about depression itself (Teasdale, 1985). Becoming obsessed with thoughts about one's negative mood cues memories of all the bad times in life, which further worsens the depressive feelings. By filtering all input through a darkly coloured lens of depression, depressed people see criticism where there is none and hear sarcasm when they listen to praise – further 'reasons' for being depressed (Diamond, 1989).

Rational-emotive therapy

One of the earliest forms of cognitive therapy was the rational-emotive therapy (RET) developed by **Albert Ellis** (1962; 1977). RET is a comprehensive system of personality change based on transforming irrational beliefs that are causing undesirable, highly charged emotional reactions, such as severe anxiety. Clients may have core values demanding that they succeed and be approved, insisting that they be treated fairly and dictating that the universe be more pleasant. A therapist teaches clients how to recognise the 'shoulds', 'oughts' and 'musts' that are controlling their actions and preventing them from choosing the lives they want.

A therapist attempts to break through a client's closed-mindedness by showing that an emotional reaction that follows some event is really the effect of unrecognised beliefs about the event. For example, failure to achieve orgasm during intercourse (event) is followed by an emotional reaction of depression and self-derogation. The belief that is causing the emotional reaction is likely to be 'I am sexually inadequate and may be impotent or frigid because I failed to perform as expected'. This belief (and others) is openly disputed through rational confrontation and examination of alternative reasons for the event, such as fatigue, too much alcohol, false notions of sexual

performance or not wanting to engage in intercourse at that time, or with that particular partner. This technique is followed by a variety of others – those used in behaviour modification, humour and role-playing to replace dogmatic, irrational thinking with rational, situationally appropriate ideas.

Rational-emotive therapy aims to increase an individual's sense of self-worth and the potential to be self-actualised by getting rid of the system of faulty beliefs that block personal growth. As such, it shares much with humanistic therapies, which we consider next.

INTERIM SUMMARY

Cognitive therapy seeks to change a person's behaviour by affecting non-productive, negative or irrational thought patterns about oneself and social relationships. The principles of cognitive behaviour modification involve discovering how the client thinks about a problem, learning more constructive thought patterns and applying these new techniques to other situations. In many cases, the goal is to change false beliefs that a client has internalised about him or herself or about how the world operates.

Two popular types of cognitive therapy have been devised by Aaron Beck and Albert Ellis. Beck uses his therapy to treat depression by getting the client to reality test, reattribute blame appropriately, discuss alternative solutions and challenge false assumptions. Ellis uses rational-emotive therapy to help clients recognise their irrational beliefs that prevent them from living the lives they want.

EXISTENTIAL-HUMANIST THERAPIES

Among the primary symptoms for which many college students seek therapy are general dissatisfaction, feelings of alienation and failure to achieve all they feel they should. Problems in everyday living, the lack of meaningful human relationships and the absence of significant goals to strive for are common existential crises according to proponents of humanist and existentialist perspectives on human nature. These orientations have been combined to form a general type of therapy addressing the basic problems of existence common to all human beings.

The humanistic movement has been called a 'third force in psychology' because it grew out of a reaction

Psychosurgery is the general term for surgical procedures performed on brain tissue to alleviate psychological disorders. In medieval times, psychosurgery involved 'cutting the stone of folly' from the brains of those suffering from 'madness', as shown vividly in many engravings and paintings from that era.

Modern psychosurgical procedures include: severing the fibres of the corpus callosum to reduce violent seizures of epilepsy; severing pathways that mediate limbic system activity (amygdalotomy); and prefrontal lobotomy. The best-known and most frequently used form of psychosurgery in the past has been the prefrontal lobotomy, an operation that severs the white-matter nerve fibres connecting the frontal lobes of the brain with the diencephalon, especially those fibres of the thalamic and hypothalamic areas. The procedure was developed by neurologist **Egas Moniz** who, in 1949, won a Nobel Prize for this treatment which seemed to transform the functioning of mental patients.

The ideal candidates for lobotomy were agitated schizophrenic patients and patients who were compulsive and anxiety ridden. The effects of this psychosurgery were dramatic: a new personality without intense emotional arousal and, thus, without overwhelming anxiety, guilt or anger emerging. In part, this positive effect occurred because the operation disconnected present functioning from memory for past traumas and conflicts and also from future concerns. However, the operation permanently destroyed basic aspects of human nature. Lobotomised patients lost something special: their unique personality. Specifically, the lobotomy resulted in an inability to plan ahead, indifference to the opinions of others, child-like actions and the intellectual and emotional flatness of a person without a coherent sense of self. (One of Moniz's own patients was so distressed by these unexpected consequences that she shot him, partially paralysing him.) Because the effects of psychosurgery are permanent, its negative effects severe and common and its positive results less certain, its continued use is limited to special cases (Valenstein, 1980).

Electroconvulsive therapy (ECT) is the use of electroconvulsive shock for certain psychiatric disorders. It is designed to produce a temporary upheaval in the central nervous system, scrambling the brain's own electrical circuits. The technique consists of applying weak electric current (20–30 milliamps) to a patient's temples for a fraction of a second until a grand mal seizure occurs (loss of consciousness and strong bodily convulsions, followed by a brief coma-like sleep). Patients are prepared for this traumatic intervention by sedation with a short-acting barbiturate and muscle relaxant which minimise the violent physical reactions (Malitz & Sackheim, 1984).

ECT produces temporary disorientation and a variety of memory deficits, most of which are permanent. After a typical series of ECT treatments (every other day), some patients are calmer and more susceptible to psychotherapy when it is available. Today, ECT is often administered to only one side of the brain – the non-dominant hemisphere – so as to reduce the possibility of speech impairment. Such unilateral ECT is reported to be an effective antidepressant (Scovern & Kilmann, 1980).

The effects of ECT were initially hailed as unparalleled in the history of psychiatry. ECT has been especially effective in cases of severe depression; but no one knows exactly why it works. It may increase available noradrenaline (norepinephrine) and other neurotransmitters, or induce a strong psychological reaction, such as determination to avoid another treatment or feeling sufficiently punished to get rid of guilt over an imagined wrong (Fink, 1979). Because the technique involves so many physical reactions, it is unlikely that a single key ingredient can be isolated (Squire, 1986).

In 1985, a US National Institutes of Health panel concluded that ECT 'is demonstrably effective for a narrow range of severe psychiatric disorders' that include depression, mania and some schizophrenias. ECT is often used as emergency treatment for suicidal or severely malnourished, depressed patients and for depressed patients who do not respond to antidepressant drugs or cannot tolerate their side effects. It is effective with patients who have had a recent onset of symptoms; but, while it reduces some of the bizarre symptoms of schizophrenia (such as catatonic posturing), it does not change the problems of cognitive processing that seem central to schizophrenic pathology (Salzman, 1980).

There are many critics of this extreme form of biomedical therapy, especially of its uncontrolled and unwarranted use in many large, under-staffed mental institutions where it may be used simply to make patients docile and manageable or as a punishment (Breggin, 1979). The side effects may include impaired language and memory functioning in some patients as well as loss of self-esteem from not being able to recall important personal information or perform routine tasks. With extensive ECT treatments, signs of personality deterioration may appear. Even today, the debate continues between those who argue it is dramatically effective and opponents who claim its many faults outweigh its limited utility (Diamond, 1989).

Chemotherapy

In the history of the treatment of mental disorder, nothing has ever rivalled the revolution created by the discovery of drugs that could calm anxious patients, restore contact with reality in withdrawn patients and suppress hallucinations in psychotic patients. This new therapeutic era began in 1953 with the introduction of tranquillising drugs, notably chlorpromazine hydrochloride (American and European brand names being *Thorazine* and *Largactil* respectively), into mental hospital treatment programmes.

Chemotherapy is any form of therapy that treats mental and behavioural disorders with drugs and chemicals. The scientific field of psychopharmacology gained almost instant recognition and status as an effective therapy for transforming patient behaviour. With chemotherapy, unruly, assaultive patients became co-operative, calm and sociable. People absorbed in their delusions and hallucinations began to be responsive to the physical and social environment around them. No longer did mental hospital staff have to act as guards, putting patients in seclusion or straitjackets; staff morale improved as rehabilitation replaced mere custodial care of the mentally ill (Swazey, 1974).

Another profound effect of the chemotherapy revolution was its impact on mental hospital populations. The introduction of chlorpromazine and other drugs reversed the steadily increasing numbers of patients and the length of time spent hospitalised. By the early 1970s, it was estimated, for example, that less than half of the United States' mental patients actually resided in mental hospitals; those who did were institutionalised for an average of only a few months as compared with two or so years, as was the case during the 1950s.

Those who benefited most from psycho-pharmacology were younger patients suffering from acute, rather than chronic, psychoses and who had recent, few and short periods of institutionalisation. Older, chronic patients who had been hospitalised for more than five years were not affected as much by chemotherapy, but it still reduced their hallucinations and delusions.

Three major categories of drugs are used today in chemotherapy programmes: *antipsychotic, antidepressant* and *antianxiety* compounds. As their names suggest, these drugs chemically alter specific brain functions that are responsible for psychotic symptoms, depression and extreme anxiety respectively.

Antipsychotic drugs

Antipsychotic drugs alter the psychotic symptoms of delusions, hallucinations, social withdrawal and occasional agitation. Chlorpromazine, derived from the compound phenothiazine, is an antipsychotic drug. Patients treated with such drugs become calm and tranquil but remain alert. Many of these patients are then able for the first time to be treated with psychotherapy.

There are several negative side effects of long-term administration of antipsychotic drugs. *Tardive dyskinesia* is an unusual disturbance of motor control, especially of the facial muscles, caused by antipsychotic drugs. *Agranulocytosis,* a rare blood disease, develops in two per cent of patients treated with Clozapine (brand name: Clozaril), an antipsychotic drug that, in some cases, controls the negative symptoms of schizophrenia.

Antidepressant drugs

The two basic antidepressants are the tricyclics, such as Imipramine hydrochloride (brand name: Tofranil) and Amitriptyline Hydrochloride (brand name: Tryptizol) and the monoamine oxidase inhibitors (MAOIs). A third generation, which consists mostly of tetracyclics but appears to have fewer side effects than earlier variations, is now being used.

One of these third-generation antidepressants is Fluoxetine (a *selective* serotonin re-uptake inhibitor), its brand name being Prozac, which was touted as the new miracle drug whose therapeutic effects were more potent than its competitors. With many millions of people suffering from clinical depression and physicians writing or renewing thousands of Prozac prescriptions every month, sales of this drug alone exceed $500 million in the United States and were expected to top $1 billion by 1995 (Cowley, 1990).

Another remarkable chemical is Lithium salt, the extract of a rock, which can influence the uniquely subtle property of the mind that regulates mood. It has proven effective in the treatment of manic disorders. People who experience uncontrollable periods of hyper-excitement, when their energy seems limitless and their behaviour extravagant and flamboyant, are brought down from their state of manic excess by doses of lithium. Up to eight of every ten manic patients treated with lithium have a good chance of recovery even when other treatments have previously failed (NIMH, 1977). Furthermore, regular maintenance doses of lithium can help break the cycle of recurring episodes of mania and/or depression. Lithium also allows a person to be alert and creative (Ehrlich & Diamond, 1980).

Antianxiety drugs

To cope with everyday hassles, untold millions of people across the world take pills to reduce tension and suppress anxiety. In general, these antianxiety drugs work by sedating the user.

There are three classes of such antianxiety compounds: *barbiturates*, *propanediols* and *benzodiazepines*. Barbiturates have a general relaxing effect, but they can be dangerous if taken in excess or in combination with alcohol. Propanediol drugs, such as Meprobamate (brand name: Equanil), reduce the tension that accompanies agitated anxiety. Benzodiazepine drugs, such as Diazepam (brand name: Valium) and Chlordiazepoxide (brand name: Librium) are effective in reducing generalised fears and anxiety without affecting a person's ability to pay attention or process information. A new class of antianxiety drugs, such as Buspiron Hydrochloride (brand name: Buspar), appears to have fewer negative side effects than other antianxiety drugs.

Caution: your brain on 'good' drugs

Because these tranquillisers work so well, it is easy to become psychologically dependent on them or physically addicted to them. Many people are coping chemically with conflicts or sources of emotional distress rather than confronting their problems, trying to solve them, or accepting pain and grief as part of the human experience.

During the 1970s and 80s Valium was one of the most frequently prescribed drugs in Western Europe and the United States. Now its sales have fallen somewhat, but it is still a highly popular tranquilliser. Valium, though, has a high abuse potential and is being overly relied upon to handle the emotional chores of modern life. Critics point to it as the symbol of the 'pill-for-anything-that-ails-you' mentality that is actively promoted by pharmaceutical companies who make billions in profit from sales. These critics argue that it is self-defeating for people to believe that pills control their stress rather than their own actions. Unfortunately, drug therapy is often given in place of, and not as an adjunct to, the psychotherapy a person may need to learn how to cope effectively with life's recurring hassles.

Here are some cautions about tranquillisers, the drugs that students are most likely to take:

Benzodiazepines should not be taken to relieve anxieties that are part of the ordinary stresses of everyday life. When used for extreme anxiety, they should not be taken for more than four months at a time, and their dosage should be gradually reduced by a physician. Abrupt cessation can lead to withdrawal symptoms, such as convulsions, tremors and abdominal and muscle cramps. Because these drugs depress

the central nervous system, they can impair driving, operating machinery and tasks that require alertness (such as studying or taking examinations). In combination with alcohol (also a central nervous system depressant) or with sleeping pills, benzodiazepines can lead to unconsciousness and even death (Hecht, 1986).

INTERIM SUMMARY

Biomedical therapies try to change directly the physiological aspects of mental illness. These therapies now rely primarily on a range of psychoactive drugs to alleviate the pathological symptoms of behavioural and mental disorders. However, they do not cure the disorder. Psychosurgery, such as the prefrontal lobotomy, once a popular medical treatment, is used infrequently because of the irreversible nature of its negative side effects. Electroconvulsive therapy is undergoing a resurgence of use for severely depressed patients; current techniques are neither as aversive nor have the same kinds of negative consequences as earlier forms. However, both psychosurgery and electroconvulsive therapy are still controversial, extreme treatments for a select class of disorders.

Chemotherapy includes antipsychotic medication for schizophrenic disorders. Antidepressants, such as tricyclics and MAO inhibitors, are used to control depression chemically. Lithium is used to treat bipolar mental disorders. Antianxiety medication is used to reduce tension and sometimes to promote sleep. Antianxiety drugs include barbiturates, propanediols and benzodiazepines. Such medication is particularly susceptible to abuse because it is readily prescribed, is self-administered and has calming, reinforcing effects for millions of normal people suffering from the ordinary stress of living.

DOES THERAPY WORK?

Do these therapies work? The answer is not easily discerned, the methodological issues involved in evaluating therapeutic success being complex and not fully agreed upon by researchers and clinicians.

Time out for a critical thinking exercise: imagine you were hired to collect data to answer the question, 'Does college education work'? Where would you begin, how many different ways are there to reframe your task, and how might you be criticised for collecting the wrong data? Now consider your exercise in light of the question, 'Do these therapies work?'

TABLE 15.3 FACTORS AFFECTING THE SUCCESS OF PSYCHOTHERAPY

Factors*	Conditions leading to success	Conditions making success less likely
Disorder	Neuroticism, especially anxiety	Schizophrenic; paranoid
Pathology	Short duration; not severe	Serious chronic disturbance
Ego strength	Strong; good	Weak; poor
Anxiety	Not high	High
Defences	Adequate	Lacking
Patient's attitudes	Motivated to change	Indifferent
	Realistic expectations for therapeutic change	Unrealistic or no expectations for change
Patient's role in therapy	Active; collaborative; involved; responsible for problem solving	Passive; detached; makes therapist responsible
Therapeutic relationship	Mutual liking and attraction	Unreciprocated attraction
Therapeutic characteristics	Personally well adjusted; experienced	Poorly adjusted

*No differences in outcome and no inconsistencies were found for these factors: age, sex, social class and race.
Source: Adapted with permission from the *Annual Review of Psychology*, vol. 29, copyright ;1978 by Annual Reviews, Inc.

Many conceptual and practical issues and problems plague attempts to assess whether any given therapy is effective or is more effective than other forms of treatment. For example, if we restrict the evaluation of therapy to just one of the hundreds of types of mental disorders, say depression, it still is complex. One expert notes that 'there may be a dozen kinds of depression . . . it's not one disorder, like measles . . . The treatment for depression for one person may look quite different from the effective treatment of depression with another' (Coyne, 1990). Certain general factors seem related to the success of therapy, however; some of these are listed in *Table 15.3*.

Evaluating Therapeutic Effectiveness

British psychologist **Hans Eysenck** (1952) created a furore some years ago by declaring that psychotherapy does not work at all. He reviewed available publications that reported the effects of various therapies and found that patients who received no therapy had just as high a recovery rate as those receiving psychoanalysis or other forms of insight therapy. His claim was that roughly two-thirds of all people with neurotic problems will recover spontaneously within two years of the onset of the problem.

For a variety of reasons, some percentage of mental patients and clients in psychotherapy do improve without any professional intervention. This **spontaneous-remission effect** is one baseline criterion against which the effectiveness of therapies must be assessed. Simply put, doing something must be shown to lead to a significantly greater percentage of improved cases than doing nothing.

Placebo therapy must also be distinguished from substantive therapeutic effects if we are to determine whether client improvement results from specific clinical procedures or just from being in any therapy situation. Many psychologists and psychiatrists believe that the key placebo ingredients in the success of any therapy are a patient's belief that therapy will help and a therapist's social influence in conveying this suggestion (Fish, 1973). Psychiatrist **Jerome Frank** (1963) has compared the processes that take place in modern psychotherapy, religious revivalism, native healing ceremonies and Communist thought-reform programmes. He argues that 'belief is really crucial to all the healing processes of any sort because without the belief the person does not participate in any real way . . . Nothing happens unless they really believe that this could help them' (Frank, 1990).

While most psychotherapy researchers agree with Eysenck that it is important to show that

FIGURE 15.4 DRUG THERAPY AND PSYCHOTHERAPY

Flowchart of stages in the development of treatments for mental/physical disorders.

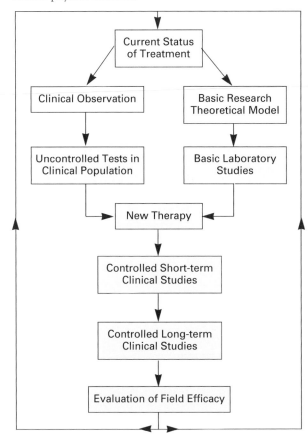

psychotherapy is more effective than spontaneous recovery or client expectations, they criticise his findings because of many methodological problems in the studies he reviewed. A later evaluation of nearly 100 therapy-outcome studies found that psychotherapy did lead to greater improvement than spontaneous recovery in 80 per cent of the cases (Meltzoff & Kornreich, 1970). Thus, we begin to feel a little more confident that the therapeutic experience itself is a useful one for many people much of the time.

A general model of the way theory, clinical observation and research all play a role in the development and evaluation of any form of treatment (for mental and physical disorders) is diagrammed in the flowchart in Figure 15.4. It shows that systematic research is needed to help clinicians discover if their therapies are making the differences that their theories predict.

One well-controlled study compared patients who had undergone psychoanalytic or behaviour therapy with patients who had simply been on a waiting list for therapy. Both types of therapy turned out to be beneficial, with behaviour therapy leading to the greatest overall improvement. The researchers also concluded that the improvement of patients in therapy was 'not entirely due either to spontaneous recovery or to the placebo effect of the non-specific aspects of therapy, such as arousal of hope, expectation of help and an initial cathartic interview' (Sloane et al, 1975). Because of such findings, current researchers are less concerned about asking whether psychotherapy works and more concerned about asking why it works and whether any one treatment is most effective for any particular problem and for certain types of patients (Goldfried et al, 1990).

Some of the confounding variables encountered by using data from various studies to compare the effectiveness of different types of therapy (in a meta-analysis across hundreds of studies) are differences in therapist experience, duration of therapy, accuracy of the initial diagnosis, type of disorder, differences in the severity and types of patient difficulties, the kinds of outcome measures used, the fit between a patient's expectations and the type of therapy offered, and

FIGURE 15.5 DEPRESSION SYMPTOM RELAPSE

For treating severely depressed patients, drugs used in combination with psychotherapy and cognitive therapy are very effective.

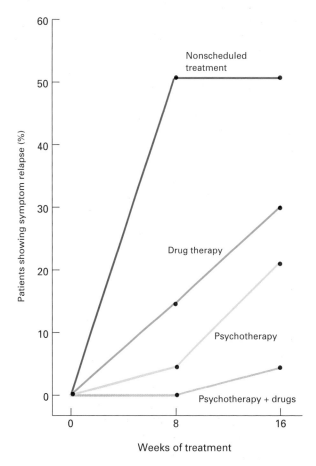

length of follow-up times, to name but a handful (Kazdin, 1986; Kazdin & Wilson, 1980; Smith *et al*, 1980; Smith & Glass, 1977).

We might also wonder whether a combination of therapies is better than a single one for some kinds of disorders. According to research with acutely depressed patients, the answer is yes (see *Figure 15.5*, previous page).

NIMH depression treatment evaluation

A major collaborative research programme to assess the long-term outcome of psychotherapy in treating a specific mental disorder – depression – was co-ordinated and funded during the 1980s by the US National Institutes for Mental Health (NIMH). Its special features included: (a) comparisons of the effectiveness of two different forms of brief psychotherapy – a tricyclic drug treatment and placebo control; (b) careful definition and standardisation of the treatments accomplished by training 28 therapists in each of the four treatment conditions, with each treatment delivered at three different institutions in different cities; (c) random assignment of 240 outpatients who met standard diagnostic criteria for definite major depressive disorder; (d) standardised assessment procedures to monitor both the process of the therapy (by analysis of therapy-session videotapes, for example) as well as a battery of outcome measures administered before treatment began, during the 16-week treatment period, at termination and 18 months later; and (e) independent assessment of the results at an institution separate from any involved in the training or treatment phases of the study (Elkin *et al*, 1989).

The psychotherapies evaluated were two that had been developed, or modified, especially for the treatment of depression in people outside a hospital setting. The methods were also sufficiently standardised to be transmitted to other clinicians in training manuals. Cognitive behaviour therapy and interpersonal psychotherapy, which is a psychodynamically oriented therapy that focuses on a patient's current life and interpersonal relationships, were compared (Klerman *et al*, 1984). Imipramine, a tricyclic antidepressant and a placebo control were administered in a double-blind procedure. For ethical reasons, the placebo patients received more than just an inert pill. They were seen weekly by a psychiatrist who provided minimal supportive therapy along with the placebo.

One set of results from this model programme of therapy outcome is presented in *Figure 15.6*. The graph shows that each of the treatments for severely depressed patients had an effect beyond that of the placebo control, with the antidepressant drug being

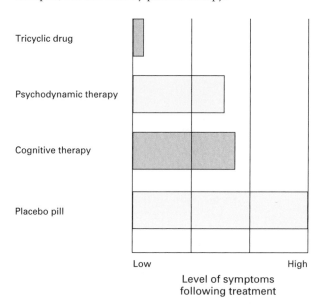

| FIGURE 15.6 | DEPRESSION THERAPIES |

Symptoms of depression are most reduced by drug therapy, and also substantially reduced by dynamic and cognitive therapies, and not at all by placebo therapy.

most effective and the psychodynamic and cognitive therapies having an intermediate level of effectiveness. Other results of note were that: (a) the placebo treatment did help reduce depressive symptoms in patients who were only moderately depressed, but many of them dropped out of the study before it was completed; (b) the positive effects of the drug therapy appeared sooner in treatment than did the psychotherapies and were more consistent across the different institutions; (c) improvement was found across many areas of patient functioning; and (d) patient characteristics, such as marital status, expectation of improvement and daily functioning, also contributed to the success of the two psychotherapy treatments.

The complex analysis of treatments is one of the important contributions of this innovative evaluative research. It serves as a model for the way well-conceived empirical research can be conducted to evaluate the claims of other therapeutic approaches. While various therapists disagree with certain aspects of this clinical comparison study, the programme of rigorous, systematic evaluations of the specific treatments is definitely welcome. Not only can such collaborative research compare the effectiveness of different therapies, it can do a much more valuable service by giving us a new understanding of the complex interaction between therapist, treatment, symptoms, patient and the process of change.

However, some critics argue persuasively that this standardised comparative approach that separates treatment from assessment does not recognise the power of individualised treatments. Instead, it is proposed that assessment be formulated in terms of the therapist's own theory-driven procedure for evaluating therapy outcomes against the goals set for each individual patient (Persons, 1991).

Prevention Strategies

Two friends were walking on a riverbank. Suddenly, a child swept downstream in the current. One of the friends jumped in the river and rescued the child. Then the two friends resumed their stroll. Suddenly, another child appeared in the water. The rescuer jumped in and again pulled the victim to safety. Soon, a third drowning child swept by. The still-dry friend began to trot up the riverbank. The rescuer yelled, 'Hey, where are you going?' The dry one replied, 'I'm going to get the bastard that's throwing them in' (Wolman, 1975).

The moral of this story is clear: preventing a problem is the best solution. All traditional therapies we have examined here share the focus of changing a person who is already distressed or disabled. They begin to do their work after the problem behaviours show up and after the suffering starts. By the time someone elects to go into therapy or is required to, it is often too long after the time when the psychological disorder has 'settled in' and had its disruptive effects on the person's daily functioning, social life, job or career.

The goal of preventing psychological problems (a theme also elaborated upon in Chapter 11 on health psychology) is being put into practice by numerous community mental health centres. The first step toward this goal is the recognition that systematic efforts toward combating psychological problems can take place at any of three levels by reducing the *severity* of existing disorders (using traditional therapies); the *duration* of disorders by means of new programmes for early identification and prompt treatment; and the *incidence* of new cases among the unaffected, normal population that is potentially at risk for a particular disorder (Klein & Goldston, 1977).

The development of this three-stage model has signalled major shifts in the focus and in the basic paradigms of mental health care. The most important of these paradigm shifts are: (a) supplementing treatment with prevention; (b) going beyond a medical disease model to a public health model; (c) focusing on situations and ecologies that put people at risk and away from 'at-risk people'; (d) looking for current precipitating factors in life settings rather than long-standing predisposing factors in people; and (e) not just preventing problems but promoting positive mental health (Albee & Joffe, 1977; Price *et al*, 1980). Indeed, such principles have been emphasised within the emerging field of health psychology, as discussed earlier in this book.

Although the medical model is concerned with treating people who are afflicted, a public health model includes identifying and eliminating the sources of disease and illness that exist in the environment. In this approach, an affected individual is seen as the host or carrier – the end-product of an existing process of disease. Change the conditions that breed illness and there will be no need to change people later with expensive, extensive treatments. The dramatic reduction of many contagious and infectious diseases, such as tuberculosis, smallpox and malaria, has come about through this approach. With psychopathology, too, many sources of environmental or organisational stress can be identified; plans can then be made to alleviate them, thus reducing the number of people who will be exposed to them. The new field of clinical ecology expands the boundaries of biomedical therapies by relating disorders, such as anxiety and depression, to environmental irritants, such as chemical solvents, noise pollution, seasonal changes and radiation (Bell, 1982).

These newer mental health approaches are directing attention toward precipitating factors in a person's current environment and focusing on practical ways to change what is, rather than reinterpreting what was. In recognising that certain situations are likely to foster psychopathology – when people are made to feel anonymous, rejected, isolated or abused – new approaches instruct people in ways to avoid or modify these noxious life situations individually or through community action.

Preventing mental disorders is a complex and difficult task. It involves not only understanding the relevant causal factors but overcoming individual, institutional and governmental resistance to change. A major re-education effort is necessary to demonstrate the long-range utility of prevention and the community mental health approach to psychopathology in order to justify the necessary expense in the face of the many other pressing problems demanding immediate solutions.

Our final Close-up reports on a unique treatment programme developed by a psychologist who gained the support of concerned individuals at many levels – students, teachers, school administrators and government officials – to combat a widespread socio-psychological problem caused by school bullies. The goal was both to reduce and prevent the incidence of abusive confrontation among school children. The methodology used was not the traditional one of

Most of us remember either being bullied or watching someone else being bullied by one of the tough kids in our primary or secondary schools. Sometimes the bullies did it for spare change or lunch money, but often it seemed that they were abusive just to show that they had power. They could make life miserable especially for those kids who, for some unknown reason, were targeted as their favourite victims.

School becomes an aversive environment for children who get picked on, robbed, beaten up or verbally humiliated with clock-like regularity by bullies. Afraid to report the offender to teachers and embarrassed to tell their parents, these children may create excuses to stay away from school and even develop psychosomatic illnesses that justify staying home whenever possible. In any event, for these oppressed youngsters, what should be a joy-filled time of youth becomes a nightmare.

Psychologist **Dan Olweus** (1991) of the University of Bergen, Norway, has found that bullying is a serious and persistent problem in the schools of Sweden and Norway. His research has shown that nine per cent of school-aged children are the victims of bullying classmates and nearly one in seven school children engage in some sort of bullying behaviour. Surprisingly, this is true for girls as well as boys. His research has also shown that most parents and teachers are unaware of the extent of the problem or the involvement of their children in the problem. It does not seem to matter if the school is rural or urban, large or small; bullying seems to be prevalent in all schools.

Contrary to expectation, Olweus found that bullying is

not the result of the bullies' frustration with their poor school performance. The major distinction between the bullies and their victims is simply physical strength. Bullies are stronger and pick on others that are obviously weaker physically. Bullies typically are aggressive not only toward their victims but also toward their teachers, siblings and parents. They have a need to dominate and they tend to be impulsive, acting out whatever they feel. They have little empathy for their victims but are not generally anxious or insecure.

Surveys and interviews reveal a sad portrait of the victims of bullying. They tend to be anxious, insecure, cautious, sensitive and quiet. They react to bullying most typically with tears and social withdrawal. These children view themselves as stupid, ashamed and unattractive. They are usually lonely and physically weak and they feel abandoned. While they do nothing in the way of directly provoking the bullying, the combination of their physical and psychological characteristics marks them as 'victim bait' for the school bully.

Do bullies have any negative

effect beyond the grief they cause their weaker classmates? Olweus believes they do. He has found that bullying is part of a behavioural pattern that is linked to later delinquency and adult criminality. He has shown that more than 35 per cent of young bullies have three or more court convictions by the time they are 24 years old. They create serious problems for themselves and their families, neighbourhoods and society.

How can this serious problem be remedied? Traditional approaches might involve treating the individual bullies with psychotherapy designed to give them insight into their problem or to restructure their cognitions about physical dominance. Olweus decided on a different option: to modify the social and physical ecology in which bullying occurs. To combat the bully problem, Olweus developed and tested an intervention programme based on three principles. The first principle is to create a warm, positive and involved school ethos that also applies firm limits on what is and what is not acceptable behaviour. The second principle is that rule violators should be met with non-hostile and non-physical but consistent reactions from all concerned persons. The third principle is that adults must be willing to be authoritative in interacting with the children; to be caring but within the context of structured guidelines that they enforce. Olweus and his colleagues applied these principles as part of a nationwide programme at the school, class and individual levels. The two goals of the intervention were to reduce as much as possible existing bully/victim problems and to prevent the development of new problems. The programme emphasised education of both school personnel and parents by means of information booklets, folders and videos about the nature and extent of the problem and by means of activities to counteract bullying. Schools were encouraged to provide better supervision of recess time, so that recess was no longer an opportunity for bullies to abuse their targets. The school administration also helped to create parent/teacher discussion groups. Clear rules and sanctions against bullying were put in place. Role-plays of bullying incidents and a series of positive group activities were encouraged. Bullies or victims had serious talks with school authorities and parents.

Did the programme work? Evaluation of the outcome of the intervention was made at several time periods up to two years after it was begun. Outcome data were collected from about 2,500 students in 112 secondary schools and 42 primary and middle schools, with different age-grade cohorts assessed separately. Evaluation showed that the intervention was very successful and resulted in a marked reduction of bullying of both boys and girls across all class levels over the 20-month period of the study. Bullies said that they bullied less and schools reported a general reduction in a variety of anti-social behaviours (such as truancy, vandalism and theft). Not only was bullying reduced in school, it declined as well on the way to and from school. Importantly, most students reported more fun and pleasure during recess.

This unique intervention into a problem of aggression merits our attention because it was conducted nationwide with governmental support, was based on sound psychological principles and adopted an ecological systems approach to analysing and combating a complex problem. We should note also that the programme did not operate as a vague 'war on bullies' campaign as we have seen in some national programmes against drugs, poverty and other pervasive problems. This ecologically sound intervention shows the effectiveness of a sensitive analysis of the components of a socio-psychological problem, education of all those involved and system-wide changes.

giving individual therapy to the bullies but of changing many features of the system and the environment in which bullying occurs.

▨ EPILOGUE

As you come now to the end of *Psychology: A European Text*, upon reflection and when you take your examinations, hopefully you will realise just how much you have learned through your study of this book. Yet in many ways you have just begun to scratch the surface of the possibilities and challenges that await the continuing student of psychology, those dedicated people-watchers who choose to carry on into the more advanced realms of the subject. We hope that you will remain among them and that in time you will contribute to this dynamic enterprise as a researcher or practitioner, or by applying what is known in psychology to the solution of social and personal problems.

The playwright Tom Stoppard appositely reminds us that 'every exit is an entry somewhere else'. As you reach the end of this book, we hope that your entry into further years of academic study will have been facilitated by what you have learned here. Your reading and understanding of this text will perhaps start to enable you to infuse new life into psychology as a subject, to broaden the psychology of others and to strengthen connections between all of the people whom you meet along the way.

recapping main points

⊃ The Therapeutic Context

The four major types of psychotherapy are psychodynamic, behaviour, cognitive and existential humanist; a fifth type of therapy is biomedical. The therapeutic tasks involves diagnosing the problem, finding the source of the problem, making a prognosis about probable outcomes with and without treatment and carrying out treatment. A variety of professionals work under this model. In earlier times, treatment for those with mental problems were usually harsh and dehumanising. It has only been fairly recently in history that people with emotional problems have been treated as individuals with illnesses to be cured. This way of viewing mental illness has led to more humane treatment of patients. Cultural anthropology shows us that many cultures have their own way of understanding and treating mental disorders.

⊃ Psychodynamic Therapies

Psychodynamic therapies grew out of Sigmund Freud's psychoanalytic theory. One of Freud's main contributions to psychodynamic therapy was his postulating of the role of the unconscious in mental processes. Psychodynamic therapy seeks to reconcile conflicts of the id (desires that often remain unconscious) and the superego. Free association, repression, resistance and dream analysis are all important components of this therapy. Neo-Freudians place more emphasis on the patient's current social situation, interpersonal relationships and self-concept and on differences in the psychology of men and women.

⊃ Behaviour Therapies

Behaviour therapy attempts to apply the principles of learning and reinforcement to problem behaviours. Counter-conditioning and systematic desensitisation are two categories of techniques commonly employed. Exposure therapy is the common element in phobia-modification therapies. Contingency management uses operant conditioning to modify behaviour, primarily through positive reinforcement and extinction strategies. Social-learning therapy involves the use of models and social skills training to help individuals gain confidence about their abilities.

⊃ Cognitive Therapies

Cognitive therapy concentrates on changing negative or irrational thought patterns about oneself and social relationships. Cognitive behaviour modification calls for the client to learn more constructive thought patterns in reference to a problem and to apply the new technique to other situations. Cognitive therapy has been used to treat depression. Rational-emotive therapy helps clients recognise that their irrational beliefs about themselves interfere with life and learn how to change those thought patterns.

⊃ Existential-Humanist Therapies

Existential-humanist therapies focus on individuals becoming more fully self-actualised. Therapists strive to be non-directive in helping their clients establish a positive self-image that can deal with external criticisms. Group therapy has grown out of the human potential movement. It has many applications, including community self-help groups and support groups for the terminally ill. Gestalt therapy focuses on the whole person – body, mind and life setting. Family and marital therapy concentrate on situational difficulties and interpersonal dynamics of the couple or family group as a system in need of improvement.

Biomedical Therapies

Biomedical therapies concentrate on changing the physiological aspects of mental illness. These therapies rely on a range of drugs that alleviate the pathological symptoms but do not cure the disorder. Psychosurgery has lost popularity in recent years because of its radical, irreversible side-effects. Electroconvulsive therapy, still sometimes used with depressed patients, remains a controversial technique. Chemotherapy includes antipsychotic medicine for schizophrenic disorders as well as antidepression and antianxiety drugs. Antianxiety medication is particularly susceptible to abuse and should not be used by people suffering from the ordinary stress of living.

Does Therapy Really Work?

Some researchers have argued that therapy for mental illness does not work any better than the passage of time or than non-specific treatment (*placebo*) effects. Research shows that behaviour therapy and psychotherapy are effective for specific types of disorders, but the reasons for this are not clear. Innovative evaluation projects, such as the NIMH study of depression therapies, are helping to answer the question of what makes therapy effective. Prevention strategies have become especially important in the emerging public health model.

key Terms

aversion therapy
behaviour modification
behavioural contract
behavioural rehearsal
biomedical therapy
catharsis
chemotherapy
client
clinical ecology
clinical psychologist
cognitive behaviour modification
cognitive therapy
contingency management
counselling psychologist
counter-conditioning
counter-transference
dream analysis
electroconvulsive therapy (ECT)
existentialism
exposure therapy
flooding
free association
Gestalt therapy
generalisation techniques

human-potential movement
implosion therapy
insight therapy
in vivo therapy
network therapy
participant modelling
pastoral counsellor
person-centred therapy
placebo therapy
prefrontal lobotomy
psychiatric social worker
psychiatrist
psychoanalyst
psychoanalytic therapy
psychosurgery
psychotherapy
rational-emotive therapy (RET)
resistance
ritual healing
social-learning therapy
spontaneous-remission effect
symptom substitution
systematic desensitisation
transference

major Contributors

Agras, Stewart
Bandura, Albert
Beck, Aaron
Breuer, Joseph (1842–1925)
Cover Jones, Mary (1896–1987)
Ellis, Albert
Eysenck, Hans
Frank, Jerome
Freud, Sigmund (1856–1939)
Horney, Karen (1885–1952)
Kohut, Heinz (1913–81)

Mahler, Margaret (1897–1985)
May, Rollo
Moniz, Egas (1874–1955)
Olweus, Dan
Perls, Fritz (1893–1970)
Pinel, Phillipe (1745–1826)
Rogers, Carl (1902–87)
Satir, Virginia
Skinner, Burrhus Frederic (1904–90)
Sullivan, Harry Stack (1892–1949)
Wolpe, Joseph

■ GLOSSARY

Key terms are defined here; additional terms of psychological significance are also defined for your reference.

A

A-B-A design. Experimental design in which subjects first experience the baseline condition (A), then experience the experimental treatment (B), and then go back to the baseline again (A).

Absolute threshold. Minimum amount of physical energy needed to reliably produce a sensory experience.

Accommodation. Process of restructuring or modifying cognitive structures so that the new information can fit more easily into them; also, the process by which the ciliary muscles change the thickness of the lens to permit variable focusing for near and distant objects; concept by Piaget used with assimilation.

Accounting practices. An actor's own statements about why he or she performed the acts in question.

Achievement tests. Standardised tests designed to measure an individual's current level of competence in a given area.

Achievement motivation. An *intrinsic motivation* to excel on any activity that is significant for the individual. Achievement motivation is a form of *cognitive motivation*.

Acquired drives. Learned motivational states.

Acquisition. Classical conditioning experiment stage during which the conditional response is first elicited by the conditional stimulus.

Action potential. A nerve impulse activated in an axon when the graded potential that reaches the axon is above a certain threshold.

Action tendency. A readiness for action that is a part of our emotions.

Acute stress. Transient states of arousal with typically clear onset and offset patterns.

Addiction. Physical state in which the body requires the presence of a certain drug and withdrawal symptoms occur if the drug is not present.

Adolescence. Stage of life commonly defined as beginning at the onset of puberty when sexual maturity or the ability to reproduce is attained.

Adoption studies. Heritability-assessment studies that examine the degree to which children's traits and behavioural patterns (such as IQ and personality) correlate with their biological parents as compared to their adoptive parents.

Adrenocorticotrophic hormone (ACTH). A pituitary hormone which stimulates the adrenal cortex to release hormones important in metabolic processes and in physiological reactions to prolonged stress.

Aetiology. Causes or factors related to the development of a disorder.

Affect. Emotion or mood state.

Affective disorders. Disorders in which the primary symptoms are associated with mood disturbances such as excessive depression, excessive elation, or both.

Afferent pathways. Sensory systems that *detect* and process incoming information to the brain.

Affiliation motivation. A concern about or need for establishing, maintaining, or restoring a positive affective relationship with another person or a group of persons.

Afterimage. Visual sensation occurring after a stimulus has ended.

Age regression. Technique used during hypnosis in which a hypnotised individual receives suggestions that he or she is 'returning' to an earlier period in life.

Ageism. Prejudice against older people, similar to racism and sexism in its negative stereotypes.

Aggregated case study. Research technique used to compare and contrast information about many individuals by combining and summarising the results of a number of individual case studies.

Agoraphobia. Phobia in which there is a fear of being in public places or away from familiar surroundings.

AIDS. Acronym for Acquired Immune Deficiency Syndrome; lethal syndrome caused by a virus that damages the immune system and weakens the body's ability to fight bacteria.

Algorithm. Rote procedure for solving problems in which every possible solution is tried; guaranteed to lead to a correct solution eventually if there is one.

All-or-none law. Property of axon firing in which a uniform action potential is generated when a threshold has been reached, and no nerve impulse is generated when it has not been reached.

Altruism. Putting the welfare, interests, and survival of others above one's own.

Alzheimer's disease. Chronic organic brain syndrome, characterised by gradual loss of memory, decline in intellectual ability, and deterioration of personality; the most common form of dementia in the elderly.

Ambiguity. A property of perceptual situations when stimulus patterns can be perceived in multiple ways.

Amnesia. Loss of memory which is either caused by brain damage, or by psychogenic factors. Anterograde amnesia is a loss of the ability to form memories for newly presented information. Retrograde amnesia is a loss of memory for events that precipitated the amnesia.

Amoral. Lacking in understanding of people's responsibilities to each other; neither moral nor immoral.

Amplitude. Physical property of strength of a sound wave, as measured by its peak-to-valley height.

Amygdala. Portion of the limbic system; brain centre for aggression and some forms of memory.

Analytic psychology. View of psychology as a constellation of compensatory internal forces in a dynamic balance, as proposed by Carl Jung.

Anchoring bias. Insufficient adjustment up or down from an original starting value when judging the probable value of some event or outcome.

Androgens. Male hormones that are secreted from the gonads – the sex organs – and that partly determine male sexual arousal.

Anterograde amnesia. Amnesia in which there is a loss of the ability to form memories for newly presented facts.

Anticipatory coping. Efforts made, in advance of a potentially stressful event to overcome, reduce, or tolerate the imbalance between perceived demands and available resources.

Antisocial personality disorder. Personality disorder in which the symptoms include an absence of conscience and a sense of responsibility to others.

Anxiety. Intense emotional response caused by the preconscious recognition that a repressed conflict is about to emerge into consciousness.

Anxiety disorders. Mental disorders marked by physiological arousal and feelings of tension, tremor, shaking, and intense apprehension without reason.

Apparent motion. Movement illusion in which one or more stationary lights going on and off in succession are perceived as a single moving light; also called the *phi phenomenon*.

Appetitive conditioning. Classical conditioning procedures in which the unconditioned stimulus is of positive value to the organism.

Applied research. Research undertaken with the explicit goal of finding solutions to practical problems.

Appraisal. An interpretative process that refers to the contention that sensory experiences lead to emotion only when the stimuli are cognitively interpreted as having personal significance.

Aptitude tests. Tests designed to measure an individual's potential for acquiring various skills.

Archetype. In Jungian personality theory, a universal, inherited, primitive, symbolic representation of a particular experience or object; part of the collective unconscious.

Archival data. Previously published findings or data already existing in documents, books, or cultural artifacts.

Arousal theory. A class of motivation theories that states that people have an optimal level of physiological arousal that they try to maintain.

Artificial intelligence (AI). 'Computer thought'; computer programs that can make the kinds of judgments and problem solving decisions that humans make.

Asch effect. Phenomenon illustrating influence of a unanimous group majority on the judgments of individuals even under unambiguous conditions; a classic illustration of conformity developed by Solomon Asch.

Assimilation. Process whereby new cognitive elements are fitted; the new elements may be modified to fit more easily; concept developed by Jean Piaget used with accommodation.

Association psychology. View associated with John Locke and other seventeenth-century British philosophers which emphasises the role of experience of mental growth by holding that most knowledge and abilities are determined by experience.

Association cortex. Area of the brain where processes such as planning and decision-making are believed to occur.

Associationism. The view, developed by the British empirical philosophers, that ideals arose from sensory experiences and that thought and memory were composed of chains of these ideas.

Attachment. Close emotional relationship between a child and the regular caregiver; inferred from behaviours that elicit and maintain nearness between the two.

Attitude. Learned, relatively stable tendency to respond to people, concepts, and events in an evaluative way.

Attributions. Individual interpretations and beliefs about the causal determinants of events.

Attribution theory. Cognitive approach that is influential in understanding individual and social behaviour which emphasises inferences about the causes of behaviour.

Audition. The sensation of hearing.

Auditory cortex. Area of the temporal lobes of the cerebral hemisphere which receives and processes auditory signals.

Auditory nerve. Nerve that carries impulses from the cochlea to the cochlear nucleus of the brain.

Autistic thinking. Personal, idiosyncratic process involving fantasy, day-dreaming, unconscious reactions, and ideas that are not testable by external reality criteria.

Autobiographical memory. The capacity of people to recollect their earlier lives.

Autohypnosis. Practice of inducing a hypnotic state in oneself.

Autokinetic effect. Visual illusion in which a stationary point of light in a dark room appears to move slowly from its initial position.

Automaticity. In information processing, an apparently effortless, involuntary process triggered without a person's supporting intention to engage in it.

Autonomic nervous system. Part of the peripheral nervous system that governs activities not normally under voluntary control, such as processes of bodily maintenance.

Autonomous person. A person who has reached self-control and independence by way of critical reflection, and who

thereby turned his or her *competence* into self-determined competence.

Availability heuristic. Heuristic for estimating probabilities, based on dependence on one's personal experience.

Aversion therapy. Behavioural therapy used for individuals attracted to harmful stimuli in which procedures of aversive learning are used to pair a presently attractive substance with other noxious stimuli in order to elicit a negative reaction in the presence of the target substance.

Aversive conditioning. Classical conditioning procedures in which an unconditioned stimulus is of negative value to an organism.

Axon. Extended fibre of a neuron in which nerve impulses occur; transmits signals from the soma to the terminal buttons.

B

Backward conditioning. Temporal pattern in classical conditioning in which a conditioned stimulus comes on after an unconditioned stimulus.

Backward masking. Phenomenon in which a sensory stimulus presented within a certain time interval after another similar stimulus has already been presented, erases or masks the perception or processing of the first stimulus.

Barbiturates. Group of drugs classified as depressants and used in low doses to reduce anxiety and in higher doses for sleep induction.

Base rate. Statistic that identifies the normally occurring frequency of a given event.

Basilar membrane. Membrane in the cochlea which, when set into motion, stimulates hair cells which produce the neural effects of auditory stimulation.

Behaviour. Actions by which organisms adjust to their environment.

Behaviour modification. Behavioural psychotherapeutic approach that involves the use of operant and classical-conditioning procedures to eliminate unwanted responses and reinforce desired ones.

Behaviour analysis. Using systematic variation of stimulus conditions to determine all the ways that various kinds of environmental conditions affect the probability that a given response will occur.

Behavioural confirmation. Process in which people behave in ways that elicit from others specific reactions that they expect and then use those reactions to confirm their beliefs about themselves.

Behavioural contingency. Conditioning approach using systematic variation of stimulus conditions to determine all the ways that various kinds of experience affect the probability of responses; developed by B. F. Skinner.

Behavioural contract. Explicit agreement (often in writing) that states the consequences of specific behaviours; often developed prior to the start of therapy to specify terms of agreement between the parties.

Behavioural data. Factual information about the behaviour of organisms and the conditions under which the behaviour occurs or changes.

Behavioural ecology. Study of the interaction between the environment and the behaviour of the organisms in it; analysis of the ecological settings characteristic for certain behaviours.

Behaviour genetics. Field of research that attempts to identify genetic components in behavioural traits.

Behavioural gerontology. Study of all the psychological issues of ageing and of the elderly.

Behavioural rehearsal. All the procedures used to establish and strengthen any basic skills; often used in social skills training programs.

Behaviourism. Psychological approach that limits the study of psychology to observable behaviour.

Belief-bias effect. Situation that occurs when a person's prior knowledge, attitudes, or values distort the reasoning process by influencing the person to accept invalid arguments.

Bias. Unwanted, systematic source of error in empirical results and conclusions as a result of factors not related to the variables being studied or measured; confounds interpretations.

Biased assimilation. Process in which data consistent with one's beliefs, because they are expected, are given little attention before they are filed away mentally as evidence supporting already held views; any ambiguity in the data is resolved in terms of existing beliefs.

Binocular disparity. Displacement between the horizontal positions of corresponding images in the two eyes.

Biofeedback. Moment-to-moment information about the status of present bodily function as provided to the organism; enabling self-regulation of internal biological processes.

Biofeedback training. Procedure by which an individual acquires voluntary control over nonconscious biological processes by receiving information about successful changes.

Biological constraint on learning. Any limitation on an organism's capacity to learn that is caused by the inherited sensory, response, or cognitive capabilities of members of a given species.

Biological marker. Reliable, biological index of some process or phenomenon of interest (such as depression or schizophrenia).

Biological motivation. A heading encompassing all motivational theories that give physiological arousal, biological mechanisms, or physical stimulus features a central place in motivational processes.

Biological senescing. Process of becoming biologically older over time.

Biological psychology. Psychological approach that explains human functioning in terms of the functioning of *genes*, the brain, the nervous system, and the endocrine system.

Biomedical therapies. Group of therapies used to treat psychological disorders that focus on changing biological or physical mechanisms that may be associated with specific disorders.

Biopsychosocial model. Model of health and illness that suggests that links between the nervous system, the immune system, behavioural styles, cognitive processing, and environmental factors can put people at risk for illness.

Bipedalism. Ability to walk upright; an important development in human evolution.

Bipolar disorder. Substantive disturbance of mood characterised by alternating periods of mania and depression; also known as 'manic depression'.

Bipolar cells. Nerve cells that combine impulses from many receptors and send the results to ganglion cells.

Blind spot. Region of the retina which contains no photoreceptor cells because it is the place where the optic nerve leaves the eye.

Blindsight. Accurate visually guided behaviour that occurs non-consciously in individuals whose visual cortex has been removed.

Blocking. Phenomenon in which the ability of a new stimulus to signal an unconditioned stimulus is not learned when it is presented simultaneously with a stimulus that is already effective as a signal.

Blood-brain barrier. Semi-permeable membrane that keeps foreign substances in the bloodstream from flowing into the brain.

Body image. One's subjective experience of the way one's body looks, may include ideal body.

Bottom-up processing. The bringing in and organising of information from the environment, that starts at the level of sensory information and works its way 'upward' to the brain.

Brain stem. Hindbrain structure in front of the cerebellum which contains the reticular activating system (RAS) and structures involved in the control of basic life processes.

Brightness. Dimension of colour space that captures the intensity of light.

Burnout. Syndrome of emotional exhaustion in which an individual loses concern and emotional feeling as a result of continuing emotional arousal and stress.

Bystander intervention. Act of assisting a person in need of help; research shows that the more people present when help is needed, the less likely it is any one of them will provide.

C

Cardinal trait. Trait around which a person organises his or her life; concept of Gordon Allport.

Case study. Extensive biography of a selected individual; many kinds of data may be collected from a variety of sources; used in idiographic personality study.

Catch trial. Trial on which no stimulus is presented; a technique used to determine whether response biases are operating in sensory detection tasks.

Catharsis. The process and beneficial effect of expressing strongly felt, but usually inhibited, emotions.

Causal theory. Beliefs people have about which factors can bring about a particular outcome and which factors cannot.

Cell assemblies. Term for groups of neurons acting together as a consequence of particular, repeated stimulation; theory proposed by Donald Hebb.

Central core. Area of the brain containing structures involved primarily in autonomic processes such as heart rate, breathing, swallowing and digestion.

Central tendency. Statistical measure that gives a single, representative summary score that can be used as an index of the most typical score obtained by a group. The measures of central tendency are the mode, the median, and the mean.

Central sulcus. Vertical groove that serves to divide the cerebral hemispheres into lobes.

Central nervous system (CNS). Part of the nervous system consisting of the brain and spinal cord.

Central trait. Major characteristic of a person that is assumed to be basic to an understanding of the individual.

Centralist theory of emotion. A view on emotion that, in contrast to the *peripheralist theory of emotion*, stresses the role of the thalamus and the cortex in the production and expression of emotions.

Centration. Thought pattern common during the beginning of the preoperational stage of cognitive development; characterised by the inability of a child to take more than one perceptual factor into account at the same time.

Cerebellum. Structure under the back of the cerebrum which controls balance and motor coordination.

Cerebral cortex. See *cerebrum*.

Cerebral dominance. Tendency for one cerebral hemisphere to play a more dominant role than the other in controlling particular functions.

Cerebral hemispheres. Two halves of the cerebrum, connected by the corpus callosum.

Cerebrum. Upper part of the brain; covered by the cerebral cortex, the outer surface of folds and deep grooves.

Chaining. Operant procedure in which many different responses in a sequence are reinforced until an effective chain of behaviours has been learned.

Chemoreceptors. A class of receptors, situated inside the nose and on the tongue, that *transduces* chemical energy into electrochemical or neural energy.

Chemotherapy. Use of drugs to treat mental and behavioural disorders.

Chromosomes. Large molecules consisting of double strands of DNA and proteins, which contain the genes responsible for hereditary traits. Every human cell contains 46 chromosomes except the germ cells which contain only 23.

Chronic stress. State of arousal, continuing over time, in which an individual perceives demands as greater than the inner and outer resources available for dealing with them.

Chronological age (CA). Number of months or years since birth.

Chunk. Meaningful unit of information.

Chunking. Process of taking single items of information and recoding them by grouping on the basis of similarity or some other organising principle.

Ciliary muscles. Structures attached to the edge of the lens which control its shape.

Circadian rhythm. Consistent pattern of cyclical body activities that lasts approximately 24 hours and is determined by an internal 'biological clock'.

Classical conditioning. Form of learning in which behaviour (conditioned response) comes to be elicited by a stimulus (conditioned stimulus) that has acquired its power through an association with a biologically significant stimulus (unconditioned stimulus); also called *Pavlovian* or *respondent conditioning*.

Classification. Processes which identify and label perceptual objects as members of meaningful categories (for example, *cars, trees,* or *people*).

Client. People who enter therapy conducted by professionals who think of psychological disorders as 'problems of living' and not as mental illnesses.

Clinical psychologist. Individual whose post-graduate training is in the assessment and treatment of psychological problems; unlike a psychiatrist, a psychologist cannot prescribe medications or physical treatments but can administer psychometric tests.

Clinical ecology. Field that relates disorders, such as anxiety and depression, to environmental irritants and sources of trauma.

Closure. Perceptual organising process as a result of which one tends to see incomplete figures as complete.

Coarticulation. The aspect of speech production that holds that the shape of the vocal system for any sound often accommodates to the shape needed for surrounding sounds.

Cochlea. Fluid-filled organ in the inner ear that is the primary organ of hearing.

Cocktail party phenomenon. The phenomenon that one has to direct attention to one out of many possible sources of stimulation occurring at one time, in order to make sense out of the proceedings.

Cognition. Processes of knowing, including attending, remembering, and reasoning; also the content of these processes, such as concepts and memories.

Cognitive appraisal. Recognition and evaluation of a stressor by which one assesses what the demand is, the size of the threat, the resources available for dealing with it, and the strategies which are appropriate.

Cognitive bias. Systematic way of thinking that generally works but may result in errors in drawing inferences or making decisions or judgments when an individual fails to discriminate between appropriate and inappropriate conditions for its use.

Cognitive behaviour modification. Therapeutic approach combining the cognitive emphasis on the importance of thoughts and attitudes to influence motivation and response with the behavioural focus on changing performance through modification of reinforcement contingencies.

Cognitive development. Development of processes of knowing including imagining, perceiving, reasoning, and problem solving.

Cognitive dissonance. Tension-reduction theory about the motivating effects of discrepant or incongruous cognitions and about the ways individuals attempt to reduce this tension.

Cognitive economy. Minimisation of the amount of time and effort required to process information.

Cognitive map. Mental representation of physical space.

Cognitive motivation. A heading encompassing all motivational theories that give the need to be cognitively *competent* a central place in motivational processes.

Cognitive neuroscience. Field of study combining the analysis of the brain's use of neuronal signals to represent and process information with analysis of the mind's cognitive symbol processing.

Cognitive psychology. Study of the higher mental processes and structures.

Cognitive therapies. Psychotherapeutic treatments that attempt to change problem feelings and behaviours by changing the way a client thinks about or perceives significant life experiences.

Cognitivism. Psychological approach that focuses on the rational and information processing aspects of human functioning. Cognitivism is primarily concerned with human thought and all the processes of knowing, attending, thinking, remembering, expecting, solving problems, fantasizing, and consciousness.

Cohort. Group of individuals defined as similar in some way (for example, a birth cohort, individuals born the same year).

Cohort model. A model that describes speech perception in a step-wise fashion and stresses the interaction between the recognition of sounds and the context within the sentence of those particular sounds.

Collective unconscious. In Jungian personality theory, that part of an individual's unconscious which is inherited, evolutionarily developed, and common to all members of the species.

Collectivistic. Countries or cultures that operate from a collectivistic ideology, consider the group as the basic element of human reality. As contrasted with an *individualistic* ideology, this is often connected with an emphasis on commitments toward one's fellow-beings.

Colour space. Three-dimensional model for describing colour experience in terms of hue, saturation, and brightness.

Comorbity. The co-occurrence of two disorders.

Competence. A competent person not only knows how to handle things and events, but also understands what is going on in the world and knows how to behave accordingly.

Complementary colours. Colours opposite each other on the colour circle.

Compliance. Conforming one's outward behaviour to that of others in order to avoid punishment or rejection by members of a valued group.

Compulsion. Undesired repetitive act carried out in stereotypic, ritualistic fashion and one which the individual feels compelled to act out.

Compulsive personality disorder. Personality disorder marked by an excessive concern with rules, roles, trivia, and work, and an inability to express warm and tender emotions.

Concepts. Mental representations of kinds or categories of things; formed through experience with the world.

Concept formation. Identification of the properties of stimuli that are common to a class of objects or ideas.

Concordance rate. Extent to which both members of a set of twins share a particular characteristic or trait used in assessing heritability.

Concrete operational stage. Third of Piaget's cognitive developmental stages (from 7–11 years); characterised by understanding of conservation and readiness for other mental operations involving concrete objects.

Conditional stimulus (CS). In classical conditioning, a previously neutral stimulus that comes to elicit a conditioned response.

Conditional response (CR). In classical conditioning, a response elicited by some previously neutral stimulus; occurs as a result of pairing the neutral stimulus with an unconditioned stimulus.

Conditioned reinforcer. In instrumental conditioning, a formerly neutral stimulus that has become a reinforcer.

Conditioning trial. In classical conditioning, the pairing of a neutral, to-be-conditioned stimulus with an unconditioned stimulus.

Cones. Photoreceptors concentrated in the centre of the retina which are responsible for visual experience under normal viewing conditions and for all experiences of colour.

Configural theory. Theory of learning in which the pairing and presentation of two stimuli is said to result internally in a configural representation of the pattern of this stimulation as a whole.

Conformity. Tendency for people to adopt the behaviour, attitudes, and values of other members of a reference group.

Confounding variable. Something that changes a subject's behaviour, other than the variable an experimenter explicitly introduces, into a research setting.

Connectionism. Originally, a model of learning in which the hypothetical unit that is learned is an association, habit, or stimulus response bond; in contemporary psychology, a model of mental processes that is based on an analogy to the neuron with connections being developed between a series of nodes; see *parallel distributed processing models*.

Consciousness. State of awareness of internal events and of the external environment.

Consensual validation. Mutual affirmation of views of reality.

Consensus criterion. Criterion used when deciding whether an action should be attributed to situational or dispositional factors; it involves deciding whether most people would have behaved in a similar or dissimilar fashion in the same situation.

Conservation. Understanding that physical properties do not change when nothing is added or taken away, even though appearances may change.

Consistency criterion. Criterion used when deciding whether an action should be attributed to situational or dispositional factors; involves deciding whether an action is a reliable one for a particular person.

Consistency paradox. Observation that personality ratings across time and among different observers are consistent, while behaviour ratings across situations are not consistent.

Consistency theory. A class of theories that states that perceiving a discrepancy between one's current position and another condition creates intrapersonal tension. This condition motivates behaviour to reduce the discrepancy.

Consolidation. Process by which learned information is gradually transformed from a fragile short-term memory code to a more durable, long-term memory code.

Constitutional factors. Basic physical and psychological characteristics; shaped by genetic and early environmental influences, they remain fairly consistent throughout a person's life.

Construct validity. Degree to which scores on a test based on the defined variable correlate with scores of other tests, judges' ratings, or experimental results already considered valid indicators of the characteristic being measured.

Context dependence. Principle that material learned when in a particular context will be recalled best when one is exposed to that same context.

Contingency management. General treatment strategy involving changing behaviour by modifying its consequences.

Contrastive criterion. Criterion of causal attribution wherein the ascription of causal status to an event involves contrasting it against the remaining field of other background conditions that are necessary (but not sufficient) for it to occur.

Control condition. Group of subjects in a controlled experiment that share all of the characteristics and procedures of the experimental group except exposure to the independent variable being studied.

Controlled procedures. Consistent procedures for giving instructions, scoring responses, and for holding all other variables constant except for those being systematically varied.

Controlled experiment. Research method in which observations are made of specific behaviours under systematically varied conditions with subjects randomly assigned to treatment conditions.

Controlled-drinking controversy. Dispute triggered by the 1962 report of British physician D. L. Davies which challenged the notion that recovery from alcoholism could only come about with total abstinence by showing that the vast majority of alcoholics participating in controlled drinking maintained moderate, non-problematic drinking over many years.

Convergence. Binocular depth cue in which the two eyes turn inward toward the nose as they fixate on a object that is relatively close.

Convergent thinking. Aspect of creativity in which one uses knowledge and logic to eliminate possibilities and reach the best solution to a problem.

Conversational reality. Social realities and explanatory discourses as implicit within and constructed through everday conversation, negotiations and speech.

Conversion disorder. Psychological disorder in which there is a loss of a specific sensory or motor function in the absence of any physiological or organic cause.

Coping. Means of dealing with a situation perceived to be threatening or challenging.

Corpus callosum. Bundle of myelinated axons that connects the two cerebral hemispheres.

Correlation. Measure of the degree to which two variables are related or covary systematically.

Cortex. See *neocortex*.

Counselling psychologist. Term for the general category of professional psychologists who specialise in providing guidance in a non-medicalising environment in areas such as vocational selection, school problems, drug abuse or marital conflict.

Counterconditioning. Technique used to substitute an unwanted response with a new one by means of conditioning procedures.

Countertransference. Process in which a psychoanalyst develops personal feelings about a client because of perceived similarity of the client to significant people in the therapist's life.

Covariation principle. Postulated social judgment rule regarding the way inferences about the cause of an event are often made in relation to the conditions that vary with the event.

Coverant. Covert operant response that is influenced by the consequences it produces.

Covert behaviours. Unseen psychological processes such as thoughts, images, or feelings, or physiological reactions that cannot be directly observed.

Criterion validity. Degree to which test scores on a specific measure are consistent with some other independent criterion of the characteristic being assessed.

Critical features. Attributes that are necessary and sufficient conditions for a concept to be included in a category.

Critical period. Sensitive time during development when an organism is optimally ready to acquire a particular behaviour if the proper stimuli and experiences occur; also, the period of most rapid biochemical change for a given structure of the brain and nervous system.

Critical set point. Level on an internal biological 'scale' that alerts the central nervous system about the fat in the body; whenever fats stored in specialised fat cells fall below this certain level, signals to eat are sent out; exerts a major influence on the amount eaten and on weight.

Cross-cultural research. Research designed to discover whether some behaviour found in one culture also occurs in other cultures.

Cross-sectional design. Research method in which groups of subjects of different chronological ages are observed and compared at a given time.

Crystallised intelligence. Facet of intelligence involving the knowledge a person has already acquired and the ability to access that knowledge; measured by vocabulary, arithmetic and general information tests; developed by Raymond Cattell.

CT (computer tomography) scanner. Device that scans for abnormalities in brain tissue; allows researchers to link brain structure to the psychological symptoms exhibited by an individual; also known as *CAT Scan*.

D

Data. Reports of observations, factual evidence.

Day-dreaming. Mild form of consciousness alteration in which attention is temporarily shifted away from a response to external stimulation toward responding to an internal stimulus.

Debriefing. Procedure, conducted at the end of an experiment, in which the researcher provides the subject with as much information about the study as possible and makes sure that no one leaves feeling confused, upset, or embarrassed.

Decibel (db). Unit to describe physical intensities of sound.

Declarative memory. Memory of explicit information; also known as *fact memory*.

Declarative learning. Factual knowledge as represented within consciousness – 'knowing that' – but not necessarily apparent from observable actions; contrast with *procedural learning*.

Deductive reasoning. Form of thinking in which one draws a conclusion that is intended to follow logically from two or more statements, or premises.

Deficiency motivation. Motivation in which individuals seek to restore physical or psychological equilibrium.

Dehumanisation. Defense mechanism in which the human qualities and values of other people are psychologically erased or cancelled.

Delayed forward conditioning. Temporal pattern in classical conditioning in which the conditioned stimulus stays on (is delayed) until the unconditioned stimulus comes on.

Delta sleep. Stage during the sleep cycle in which electrical brain activity is characterised by large, slow waves.

Delusions. False beliefs maintained despite contrary external evidence; they may arise from unconscious sources and appear to serve personal needs, such as relieving guilt or bolstering self-esteem.

Demand characteristic. Cue in an experimental setting that influences a subject's perception of what is expected of him/her and systematically influences his/her behaviour within that setting; provides alternative explanations of hypothesized causal effects of given independent variables.

Dementia. Disorder in which memory, reasoning, judgment and other higher mental processes are lost or can no longer be carried out.

Dendrite. Branched fibre of a neuron which receive incoming signals.

Dependent variable. Response, the form or amount of which is expected to vary with changes in the independent variable.

Depressants. Group of drugs including alcohol, barbiturates, and opiates which slows down mental and physical activities by reducing or inhibiting the transmission of nerve impulses in the central nervous system.

Descriptive statistics. Collections of data that are used to describe sets of scores collected from different groups of subjects and to describe relationships among variables.

Detection. The first step in the process of sensation, consisting of making contact with different kinds of physical energy in the external world, by way of the sense organs.

Determinism. Doctrine that all events – physical, behavioural and mental – are determined by specific causal factors that are potentially knowable.

Developmental age. Chronological age at which most children show a particular level of physical or mental development.

Developmental disability. Significant learning difficulty appearing in childhood or early adolescence that continues during the life of the individual unless remediated.

Developmental stage. Period during which physical, mental, or behavioural functioning is different from times before and after it.

Diathesis-stress hypothesis. Predisposition to develop a particular disorder as a consequence of pressure to adjust; interactional effect between stressful demands and personal predispositions.

Dichotic listening. Experimental technique in which a different auditory stimulus is simultaneously sent to each ear.

Diencephalon. Lower part of the forebrain.

Difference threshold. Smallest physical difference between two stimuli that will be recognised as a difference; also known as the *just noticeable difference*.

Discourse analysis. Qualitative examination of natural language ('talk') to discern its multiple functions, focusing upon vocabularies and rhetorical devices used, thereby holding the subject's perspective as of central importance.

Discriminative stimuli. Stimuli which act as predictors of reinforcement signalling when a particular behaviour will result in positive reinforcement.

Discursive remembering. The approach to memory research that is concerned with the ways in which people talk about their past so as to construct a shared present. It does not study the mental processes involved in remembering.

Discursive turn. Contemporary conceptual and methodological movement within critical social psychology towards focusing upon the role of language in the construction of social and psychological realities; term attributable to Rom Harré (& Gillett).

Dishabituation. Recovery from habituation; occurs when novel stimuli are presented.

Dispositional variable. Factor that operates within the individual, such as genetic makeup, motivation, intelligence level and self-esteem.

Dissociative disorder. Psychological reaction in which an individual experiences a sudden, temporary alteration of consciousness in the form of a severe memory loss or loss of personal identity.

Distal stimulus. Objects in the environment that are detected by the sense organs and give rise to *proximal stimuli*.

Distinctiveness criterion. Criterion used when deciding if an action should be attributed to situational or dispositional factors that involves determining if an action is unusual and atypical for a particular person.

Divergent thinking. Aspect of creativity characterised by an ability to produce unusual, but appropriate, responses to standard questions.

Dominant genes. Genes that are expressed in an individual's development.

Dopamine hypothesis. Theory proposing a relationship between psychological disorder (in particular 'schizophrenia') and a relative excess of the neurotransmitter dopamine at specific receptor sites in the central nervous system.

Double bind. Situation hypothesized to contribute to the development of psychotic states (in particular with 'schizophrenia') in which a person receives, from a significant other (for example, a parent or spouse), multiple messages that are contradictory and thereby cannot be met.

Double-blind control. Experimental technique in which bias based on the expectations of experimenters can be eliminated by keeping both subjects and experimental assistants unaware of which subjects get which treatment.

Dream analysis. Psychoanalytic technique involving the interpretation of dreams in order to gain insight into a person's unconscious motives or conflicts.

Dream work. Process in which the censor transforms the latent content of a dream into manifest content that appears to the dreamer; proposed by Sigmund Freud.

Drive. An internal state of tension that guides us towards activities or objects that will reduce the tension; provides the impetus for action.

Drive reduction. A motivational principle that drives the organism to action because of a state of tension. The organism will search for a way to satisfy or reduce the tension. When this happens, the balance is restored, and the organism will cease acting.

DSM-IV. Current *Diagnostic & Statistical Manual* of the American Psychiatric Association that classifies, defines and describes over 200 mental disorders; see also *ICD-10*.

Dual-code model of memory. Theoretical view about the nature of the coding system in memory which proposes that both visual and verbal codes are used to store information in memory, not only verbal codes.

Dualism. Belief that the mechanistic body and brain act separately from the spiritual soul and ephemeral mind.

Dynamic factors. Factors that concern the energetic side of human nature, and the emotional relations between individuals.

E

Early selection. An attentional selection that occurs immediately following sensory registration, that is to say before the meaning of a stimulus can be determined.

Echo. Auditory memory lasting several seconds.

Ecological validity. Extent to which results from a laboratory study can be generalized to 'real life' outside the laboratory.

Ecology. Study of the relationship between organisms and their environments.

Ectomorph. Somatotype characterised by a body build that is thin, long, and fragile in appearance.

EEG. See *electroencephalogram*.

Effectance motivation. A concept introduced by White, referring to the notion that people are dispositionally motivated to be effective in dealing with their environment; the goal of effectance motivation is *competence*.

Efferent pathways. Motor systems that process outgoing information from the brain to the muscles and glands.

Ego defense mechanism. Freudian concept referring to a mental strategy (conscious or unconscious) used by the ego to defend itself from the conflicts experienced in the normal course of life (between the 'id' and 'superego').

Ego. In Freudian theory, that aspect of the personality involved in self-preservation activities and in directing instinctual drives and urges into appropriate channels.

Egocentrism. Aspect of centrism that refers to a preoperational child's difficulty in imagining a scene from someone else's perspective.

Eidetic imagery. Uncommon memory phenomenon in which a few individuals seem to be able to store detailed, whole images of scenes or complex patterns for a relatively long period of time.

Einstellung effect. Mental set, or readiness to respond to new problems using the same procedure, rules, or formula that have worked in the past.

Elaborative rehearsal. Repetition of incoming information in which new information is analysed and related to already stored knowledge.

Electroconvulsive therapy (ECT). 'Shock' treatment in which electric current is applied to a patient's temples for a fraction of a second in order to produce upheaval in the central nervous system.

Electrode. Thin wire through which small amounts of electric current can pass; used in recording electrical activity in the brain.

Electroencephalogram (EEG). Recording of electrical activity of the brain at the scalp.

Electromagnetic spectrum. Energy spectrum which includes X-rays, microwaves, radio waves, TV waves, and visible light waves.

Eliminative materialism. Perspective that wants to eliminate mentalistic terminology – such as 'mind' and 'consciousness' – from the scientific account of human functioning; maintains human functioning is to be explained entirely in neurochemical terms.

Emergent-interaction theory. Perspective on the mind-body problem based on five main hypotheses: (a) brain activities give rise to mental states, but these mental states are different from and not wholly reducible to brain states; (b) the mind and conscious experience are interpreted as emergent properties of brain activity; (c) the phenomenon of 'inner experience' is a high-order emergent property of the way the brain is organised into a hierarchy of increasing degrees of control and regulation of higher levels over lower levels; (d) brain and mind interact; and (e) the conscious mind exerts top-level causal influence over the brain in directing and controlling behaviour.

Emotion wheel. Model of emotion consisting of a set of innate emotions depicting eight basic emotions, made up of four pairs of opposites: joy-sadness; fear-anger; surprise-anticipation; and acceptance-disgust; developed by Robert Plutchik.

Empathy. Feeling someone else's emotion; may represent part of the foundation for a child's future system of moral behaviour.

Empirical investigation. Careful observation of perceivable events or phenomena; a bottom-up type of research based on data collection.

Empirical-analytical methodology. A method of psychological research that relies on objective, empirical evidence, which is gathered in an impartial way and quantified for analysis; this method aims to discover psychological laws that can predict behaviour across time and places.

Empiricism. The philosophical doctrine that considers human knowledge to be the result of learning experiences.

Encephalisation. Increase in brain size; an important development in human evolution.

Encoding. Conversion of information into a code capable of being conveyed in a communication channel.

Encoding specificity principle. Assumption about the close relationship between encoding, storage, and retrieval of information in which subsequent retrieval of information is enhanced if cues received at the time of recall are consistent with those present at the time of encoding.

Endocrine system. Glandular system transferring information between cells in different parts of the body by way of hormonal messengers.

Endogenous. Pertaining to internal conditions and causes; see also *exogenous*.

Endomorph. Somatotype characterised by a body build that is full, round, or soft in appearance.

Endorphins. Class of neurotransmitters involved in many reactions to pleasure and pain; literally, 'endogenous morphines'.

Engram. General term for the coding of acquired information in the brain; also called *memory trace*.

Environmental psychology. Study of the relationships between psychological processes and physical environments, both natural and human-made, emphasising the reciprocity and mutual influence in an organism-environment relationship.

Episodic memory. Component of long-term memory which stores autobiographical information in conjunction with some type of coding designating a time-frame for past occurrences.

ERG theory. Need theory of work motivation which proposes that workers are motivated by three sets of needs: existence needs, relatedness needs, and growth needs; also assumes that higher-level needs can become activated before lower-level needs are met.

Erogenous zones. Areas of the skin surface that are especially sensitive to stimulation and which give rise to erotic or sexual sensations.

Ethology. Observational study of animal behaviour patterns in an animal's natural environment.

Eugenics. Movement that advocated improving the human species by encouraging allegedly biologically 'superior' people to interbreed while discouraging biologically 'inferior' types from having offspring.

Eustress. Positive reaction to a stressor defined as a challenge rather than a threat.

Event-related potential. A brain wave evoked by stimulus events. An ERP, also called an evoked potential, should be distinguished from spontaneous electrical activity of the brain.

Evoked potentials. Patterns of brain activity caused by specific stimuli.

Evolution. Theory that over time, organisms originate and become adapted to their unique environments through the interaction of biological and environmental variables.

Excitation. Stimulation that increases the activity or 'firing rate' of a nerve cell.

Existentialism. Philosophy that emphasises an individual's responsibility and potentiality for existence fully through choice; in psychology, it is the view that the essential problem of existence is to find oneself, be oneself and actualise one's potential.

Exogenous. Pertaining to external conditions and causes; see also *endogenous*.

Expectancy bias. Bias that occurs when a researcher or observer subtly communicates to subjects just what kind of behaviour he or she expects to find, thereby creating that very reaction in them.

Expectancy-value theories. Theories which state that the performance of a specified behaviour is determined by a combination of: (1) our expectation (or, 'belief') as to whether or not there is a contingent relationship between the behaviour and a specified outcome; and (2) upon the value we attach to that outcome.

Experience-sampling method. Experimental method in which subjects wear electronic pagers and are asked to record what they are feeling and thinking whenever the pager signals.

Experimental condition. In a controlled experiment, the subject for whom the independent variable or treatment variables are systematically altered.

Experimental analysis of behaviour. Skinnerian approach to operant conditioning which systematically varies stimulus conditions to discover the ways that various kinds of experience affect the probability of responses; makes no inferences about inner states or non-observable bases for behavioural relationships demonstrated in the laboratory.

Exposure therapy. Therapy that employs strategies for approaching a feared situation, forcing the client to confront the fear and to be reinforced for successfully approaching it.

Extinction. In conditioning, the weakening of a conditioned association in the absence of a reinforcer or unconditioned stimulus.

Extraversion. see *introversion-extraversion*.

Extrinsic motivation. Motivation to engage in an activity for some outside consequence.

F

Face validity. Degree to which the content of a test item appears on first impression (at 'face-value') to be about and therefore measure that psychological property which it purports to.

Facial expression. A term associated with the facial feedback hypothesis that states that facial expression is sufficient to create emotional experience.

Factor analysis. Statistical technique used to analyze multiple data sources; enables the researcher to explore how data are interrelated by examining the meaningful dimensions (factors) that they have in common.

Fear. Rational emotional reaction to an objectively identified external danger that may induce a person to flee an attack in self-defense.

Fear of failure. The fear to fail on a task and to loose face. For some people fear of failure can be a powerful motivator.

Fear of success. A motive to avoid success, rooted in the perceived conflict between achievement and femininity. For women, the rewards of achievement can be contaminated by an accompanying anxiety about being less likeable as a result.

Feature-detection model. Theory that feature-detection cells, cells that respond only when specific patterns are present in their receptive fields, are arranged hierarchically – the simple input from lower centres is combined and expanded at each successive stage along the visual pathway.

Fechner's law. Assertion that the strength of a sensation is proportional to the logarithm of physical stimulus intensity.

Felicity conditions. The situational conditions that must be met in order to enable the accomplishment of a *speech act*.

Feminist psychology. The psychological approach that originated in criticising the male bias in psychology. It developed into gender studies which investigates the impact of societal differences between women and men on the psychological functioning of the female and male individual.

Fetishism. Paraphilia in which sexual excitement is achieved with the aid of non-living objects.

Field dependence. Proposed personality dimension that reflects a person's preference for depending on external versus internal sources of information in perceptual and social situations.

Field theory. Considers behaviour to be primarily a function of the person and the present situation; emphasises the interdependence of these co-existing events which collectively define the 'field'; concept developed by Kurt Lewin.

Fight-or-flight syndrome. Sequence of internal activities triggered when an organism is faced with a threat; prepares the body for combat and struggle or for running away to safety.

Figural goodness. Perceptual organisational process in which a figure is seen according to perceived simplicity, symmetry, and regularity.

Figure. Object-like regions of the visual field.

Figure-ground. A perceptual organisation principle that directs the perceiver to see a figure – an integrated visual experience – standing out against a background.

Fixed action pattern. Unlearned response released by a specific environmental event or object.

Fixed ratio schedule (FR). In operant conditioning, a procedure in which reinforcement is delivered only after a fixed number of responses.

Fixed interval schedule (FI). In operant conditioning, a procedure in which reinforcement is delivered for the first response made after a fixed amount of time has elapsed.

Flooding. Therapy for phobias in which clients are exposed, with their permission, to the stimuli most frightening to them to force them to reality test.

Flow. State of near ecstasy that develops when one is totally focused on an activity in the present moment, increasing the likelihood of creative outputs.

Fluid intelligence. Ability to see complex relationships and solve problems; measured by tests such as block designs and spatial visualisation; developed by Raymond Cattell.

Foetus. Label given to the developing embryo eight weeks after conception until birth.

Formal operational stage. Fourth of Piaget's cognitive developmental stages; characterised by abstract thinking and conceptualisation.

Forward conditioning. Temporal pattern in classical conditioning in which the conditioned stimulus comes on before the unconditioned stimulus.

Fovea. Area of the retina which contains densely packed cones and forms the point of sharpest vision.

Free-floating anxiety. Anxiety not focused on any particular agent or not associated with any known cause.

Frequency. Number of cycles a wave completes in a given amount of time.

Frequency distribution. Array of individual scores arranged in order from highest to lowest.

Free association. Procedure used in psychoanalysis to probe the unconscious in which a patient gives a running account of thoughts, wishes, physical sensations, and mental images as they occur.

Frequency theory. Theory that neural firing rate is determined by a tone's frequency.

Functional fixedness. Inhibition in perceiving a new use for an object previously associated with some other purpose; adversely affects problem solving and creativity.

Functional pathology. Psychotic disorders, not attributable to brain damage or organic factors, that include affective disorders, paranoid states and the schizophrenias.

Functionalism. Perspective on studying mind and behaviour that focused on examination of the intact organism interacting with its environment; study of the contents of consciousness.

Fundamental attribution error. Dual tendency of observers to underestimate the impact of external factors on an actor's behaviour and to overestimate the influence of internal factors.

G

G-factor. General intelligence factor, assumed to be inherited basic intelligence to which is added specific kinds of additional intelligences, or S-factors.

Ganglion cells. Cells which integrate impulses from many bipolar cells into a single firing rate.

Ganzfeld procedure. A procedure, used in parapsychological experiments, in which 'receiver' and 'sender' are placed in different rooms under mild perceptual isolation from the outside world. The sender must concentrate on a 'target', while at the same time, the receiver is invited to verbalise everything that comes to his or her mind. After the session, the receiver is shown four pictures, one of which is the target. The receiver is asked to rate the degree to which each of the pictures matches what was experienced during the ganzfeld procedure.

Garden path sentence. A sentence in which the comprehender assumes a particular meaning but later discovers that this assumption was incorrect, forcing the comprehender to reinterpret the sentence.

Gate-control theory. Theory about pain modulation which proposes that certain cells in the spinal cord act as gates to interrupt and block some pain signals while sending others on to the brain.

Gender. The social and psychological aspects of masculinity and femininity, which do not necessarily match the differences between the male and female *sex*.

Gender role. Set of behaviours and attitudes defined by society that are associated with being male or female and are expressed publicly by the individual.

Gender identity. One's sense of 'maleness' or 'femaleness'; usually includes an awareness and acceptance of one's biological sex.

General adaptation syndrome (GAS). Pattern of nonspecific adaptational physiological mechanisms that occurs in response to continuing threat by almost any serious stressor.

Generalisation techniques. Techniques that attempt to increase the similarity between therapy and real-life settings of target behaviours, reinforcers, models and stimulus demands.

Generalised anxiety disorder. Disorder in which an individual experiences anxiety that persists for at least one month and is not focused on a specific object or situation.

Genetics. Study of the inheritance of physical and psychological traits from ancestors.

Genotype. Genetic constitution of an organism; many genes are not expressed in an individual's development.

Germ cells. In humans, the spermatozoa in the male and the ova in the female; the cells which carry and transmit the genetic information of the parents to the offspring.

Gestalt. German word meaning 'whole configuration', from which is derived *Gestaltism*, the theoretical approach to perception that emphasises whole configurations and emergent properties.

Gestalt psychology. School of psychology founded in Germany that maintains psychological phenomena can be understood only when viewed as organised, structured wholes and not when broken down into primitive perceptual elements.

Gestalt therapy. Therapy that focuses on taking into account all the elements of a person's life, so as to facilitate the emergence of a whole self-characterised by a sense of coherence and cohesion.

Glial cells (glia). Cells which hold neurons close together and facilitate neural transmission by forming a sheath that insulates the axons of some neurons, thereby speeding conduction of electrochemical impulses; they also function in removal of damaged and dead neurons and prevent poisonous substances in the blood from reaching the brain by forming the blood-brain barrier.

Graded potential. Spreading activity along a dendrite or cell body membrane produced by stimulation from another neuron.

Ground. Background areas of the visual field, against which figures stand out.

Group dynamics. Study of how group processes change individual functioning.

Group think. Tendency of a decision-making group to filter out undesirable input so that a consensus may be reached, especially if it is in line with the leader's viewpoint; developed by Irving Janis.

Growth motivation. Motivation in which individuals seek to develop themselves beyond what they have been and done in the past.

Gustation. Sensation of taste.

H

Habituation. Decrease in strength of responding when a stimulus is presented repeatedly.

Hallucination. Vivid perceptions that occur in the absence of objective stimulation; produced by a variety of conditions, such as mental disorders, brain diseases, and intoxication from various drugs.

Hallucinogens. Group of psychoactive drugs that are capable of producing altered states of awareness in which visual, auditory, or other sensory hallucinations occur.

Halo effect. Bias in which an observer judges a liked person favourably on most or all dimensions.

Hardiness. Quality associated with wellness; resulting from employing the three C's of subjective well-being: challenge (welcoming change as a tonic, not a threat), commitment (focused involvement in purposeful activities), and control (sense of internal control to guide actions).

Hawthorne effect. Bias in which the psychological effect of participating in an experiment affects physical variables being manipulated.

Health. General condition of the body and mind in terms of their soundness and vigour; not simply the absence of illness or injury.

Health beliefs. Beliefs about the relationship between health practices and health outcomes.

Health psychology. Field of psychology devoted to

understanding the biopsychosocial origins of health and illness and the way people respond when they become ill.

Heredity. Biological transmission of traits from parent to offspring.

Heritability estimate. Statistical estimate of the degree of inheritance given trait or behaviour; assessed by the degree of similarity between individuals who vary in their extent of genetic similarity.

Hermeneutics. The philosophical reflection on the practice of interpretation and assigning meaning which asserts that conclusions from psychological research are context-bound.

Hertz (Hz). Unit of sound frequency expressed in cycles per second.

Heuristics. Cognitive strategies, or 'rules of thumb', often used as short-cuts in solving complex inferential tasks.

Hippocampus. Part of the limbic system involved in memory.

HIV. Human immunodeficiency virus that attacks white blood cells (T-Lymphocytes) in human blood, thereby weakening the functioning of the immune system; in most cases HIV develops in time into AIDS.

Holistic approach. Theoretical approach in which separate actions are explained in terms of a person's entire personality.

Homeostasis. Constancy or equilibrium of the internal conditions of the body; the tendency of organisms to maintain equilibrium and resist change.

Hormones. Substances secreted into the bloodstream from specialised cells located in various glands; are carried in the blood until they attach themselves to the surface of a target tissues.

Hozho. Navajo north-American Indian concept, referring to harmony, peace of mind, goodness, ideal family relationships, beauty in arts and crafts, and health of body and spirit.

Hue. The dimension of visual sensation that is most closely related to the colour of the perceived object. It derives primarily from the wavelength of the stimulus.

Human potential movement. Therapy movement that encompasses all those practices and methods that release the potential of the average human being for greater levels of performance and greater richness of experience.

Humanistic psychology. The psychological approach that views people as active creatures who rationally strive for the development of their potential.

Hypnosis. Altered state of awareness induced by a variety of techniques and characterised by deep relaxation, susceptibility to suggestions, and changes in perception, memory, motivation, and self-control.

Hypnotic induction. Preliminary set of activities that precedes and prepares a participant for the altered awareness state of hypnosis.

Hypnotisability. Degree to which an individual is responsive to standardised hypnotic suggestions.

Hypochondriasis. Pathological condition characterised by a preoccupation with bodily sensations as possible signs of a serious disease despite medical reassurance.

Hypothalamus. Structure below the thalamus that regulates processes such as eating, drinking, body temperature, and hormonal activity.

Hypothesis. Tentative and testable explanation of the relationship between two (or more) events or variables; often stated as a prediction that a certain outcome will result from specific conditions.

Hysteria. Mental disorder, characterised by a cluster of symptoms that includes paralysis or pains in different parts of the body, dizziness, lameness and blindness, all without clear physical cause; no longer used diagnostically.

I

ICD-10. International classification of diseases, version ten; produced by the World Health Organization; contains a taxonomy of mental health disorders; *see also* DSM-IV.

Icon. Visual memory lasting about half a second.

Id. In Freudian theory, the primitive, unconscious part of the personality which operates irrationally and acts on impulse.

Identification. In perceptual psychology, assigning meaning to percepts by comparing the percept to a memory representation, and attaching a label to it.

Identity crisis. A failure to develop a sense of a coherent *self* which results in a self-image that lacks a central stable core.

Idiographic approach. Methodological approach to the study of personality processes in which emphasis is placed on understanding the unique aspects of each individual's personality rather than on common dimensions on which all individuals can be measured.

Illness. Documented pathology, such as biological or physiological damage, cell pathology and blood chemistry.

Illness prevention. General strategies and specific tactics to eliminate or reduce the risk that people will get sick.

Illusion. Experience of a stimulus pattern in a manner that is demonstrably incorrect, but shared by others in the same perceptual environment.

Illusory conjunctions. Perceptual errors that occur when the primitive features of objects, such as their colours and shapes, are not combined correctly by the visual system.

Immediate memory span. Refers to the limited, brief storage capacity of short-term memory that seems to be between five and nine chunks of information.

Implicit memory. Nonconscious form of memory, marked by the facilitation or improvement in performance of a task when a learner has recently had some experience relevant to the task but is not conscious of that experience.

Implosion therapy. Behavioural, therapeutic technique that exposes a client to stimuli, previously rated by the client as most anxiety-provoking, in an attempt to extinguish the anxiety associated with the stimuli.

Impression formation. Process of knowing other people and of determining their traits, abilities and attitudes.

Imprinting. Primitive form of learning in which an infant animal physically follows and forms an attachment to the first moving object it sees and/or hears.

In-group. Term used by members for their own group, when one group of people is differentiated from another.

***In vivo* therapy.** Therapy approach in which therapists work with their clients in the life settings associated with the clients' problems, such as in airplanes for those who suffer from flying phobias and must fly for their jobs.

Incentive. External stimulus that arouses motives in the laboratory or in everyday settings.

Incremental processing. The notion that in speech production speakers seem to plan one portion of their utterances as they articulate another portion ('increment' means increase, or added amount).

Independent variable. In a controlled experiment, the stimulus that, when varied, is expected to have an affect upon and change some behaviour (the dependent variable).

Index variable. Variable that is itself not causal but is a manifest sign of an underlying causal variable.

Individualism. The ideology that dominates the Western world. It assumes that the individual human being is the basic unit of society. Each individual is seen as a discrete entity, possessing an inner core and free to be uninfluenced by the will of others and to refrain from any involuntary relationships.

Individualistic. Countries or cultures that operate from an individualistic ideology, consider the individual as the basic element of human reality. As contrasted with a *collectivistic* ideology, this is often connected with an emphasis on the self.

Induced motion. Illusion in which a stationary point of light within a moving reference frame is seen as moving and the reference frame is perceived as stationary.

Inductive reasoning. Form of reasoning in which a conclusion is made about the probability of some state of affairs, given the evidence available.

Inference. Logical assumption made on the basis of some evidence other than direct observation about something that is happening inside an organism; the reasoning process of drawing a conclusion on the basis of a sample of evidence or on the basis of prior beliefs and theories.

Inferential statistics. Measures that allow researchers to know what conclusions can legitimately be drawn from data.

Information-processing model. Common approach to studying cognitive processes that proposes that all forms of cognition (such as memory, perception and the structure of knowledge) can be understood by analysing them into component parts; operations are performed on incoming information that goes through a series of stage arranged in a processing hierarchy that moves from simpler to more complex.

Informational influence. Why people conform to group pressures; desire to be correct and right, to understand how best to act in a given situation.

Inhibition. Stimulation that decreases activity or the 'firing rate' of a nerve cell.

Initiation rite. Ritual in many nonindustrial societies which takes place around puberty and serves as public acknowledgment of the passage from childhood to adulthood; also called *rites of passage*.

Insanity. Legal designation for the state of an individual judged to be legally irresponsible or incompetent.

Insight. Phenomenon in problem-solving tasks in which learning results from an understanding of relationships (often sudden) rather than from blind trial and error.

Instinct. A fixed, inborn mechanism that causes every member of a species to act in a specific way.

Instinctual drift. Tendency for learned behaviour to drift toward instinctual behaviour over time.

Instrumental conditioning. Learning in which the relationship that is learned is between a response and its consequences; see also *operant conditioning*.

Intelligence. Global capacity to profit from experience and to go beyond given information about the environment.

Intelligence quotient (IQ). Index of intelligence derived from sources on standardised intelligence tests; obtained by dividing an individual's mental age by chronological age and then multiplying by 100.

Intentionality. The goal-directedness of a phenomenon. Language, for example, is goal-directed.

Interactionist perspective. Behaviour is viewed as the product of a complex interaction between a number of (biological and psychological) factors.

Interdependence. The notion that individuals are dependent upon each other in numreous ways; particulraly in that as humans we give sense to our physical, social and bodily environment by creating and negotiating meanings within a community of others and local moral order.

Interjudge reliability. Degree to which the different observers make similar ratings or agree about what a subject did during an observation period.

Internal consistency. Measure of reliability; the degree to which a test yields similar scores across its different parts, on odd vs. even items, and split halves.

Internal lexicon. The representation of meaningful linguistic units, like words, in long term memory. Also known as *mental lexicon*.

Internalisation. The developmental process in which the child gains voluntary control over communicative forms, including language, that were originally external to him or her.

Interneurons. Neurons providing communication between other neurons; make up the bulk of nerve cells in the brain.

Interposition. Depth cue present when one object blocks off the view of part of another object; also known as *occlusion*.

Intersubjectivity. The standard that is concerned with the consensus among empiricists in the research community.

Intervening variable. Condition or event whose existence is inferred in order to explain a link between some observable input and a measurable response output.

Interview. Face-to-face conversation between a researcher and a respondent for the purpose of gathering detailed information about the respondent.

Intimacy. Capacity to make a full commitment – sexual, emotional and moral – to another person.

Intrinsic motivation. Motivation to engage in an activity for its own sake.

Introspection. Method of gathering data in which trained subjects report their current conscious experience as accurately as possible.

Introversion-extraversion. Personality dimension that describes people by the degree to which they need other people as sources of rewards and cues to appropriate behaviours.

Ion channels. Excitable membrane molecules that produce and transduce signals in living cells.

Ions. Electrically charged particles that flow through the membrane of a cell, changing its polarity and thereby its capacity to conduct electrochemical signals.

J

Job analysis. Study of a specific job focusing on the nature and degree of skill required, the amount of effort demanded, the extent to which an individual is responsible for decisions that affect company resources or personnel, and any other types of stress the job may entail.

Joint action. Acting together through the shared environment of language; thereby constituting different versions of social reality; focuses upon the constructive aspects of relations between individuals.

Judgement. Process by which we form opinions, reach conclusions, and make critical evaluations of events and people based on available material; also the product of that mental activity.

Just noticeable differences. See *difference threshold*.

K

Kinaesthetic sense. Sense concerned with bodily position and movement of the body parts relative to each other.

L

Language acquisition device (LAD). A biologically based mental structure, postulated by Noam Chomsky, that is assumed to facilitate the child's comprehension and production of language.

Late selection. An attentional selection that occurs late in the process of information processing, that is to say after the meaning of a stimulus is determined.

Latent content. In Freudian dream analysis, the actual, but socially or personally unacceptable version of a dream. It is the hidden content of the dream story.

Latent learning. Associations learned from experience and observation in which there is no change in behaviour at the time.

Lateral geniculate nucleus. Relay point in the thalamus through which impulses pass when going from the eye to the occipital cortex.

Lateral inhibition. Tendency for a receptor excited by an intense amount of light to suppress neighbouring receptors receiving less intense light.

Lateral sulcus. Deep horizontal groove that serves to divide the cerebral hemispheres into lobes.

Lateralisation of emotion. Different influence of the two brain hemispheres on various emotions; the left hemisphere seems to influence positive emotions, such as happiness, while negative emotions, such as anger, are more influenced by the right hemisphere.

Law of association. Doctrine which holds that we acquire knowledge through associating ideas – mental events that originate in sensory information from the environment.

Law of common fate. Law of perceptual grouping which states that elements moving in the same direction at the same rate are grouped together.

Law of forward conduction. Principle stating that neurons transmit information in only one direction – from the axon of one neuron to the dendrites or soma of the next.

Law of effect. Basic law of learning which states that the power of a stimulus to evoke a response is strengthened when the response is followed by a reward and weakened when it is not followed by a reward.

Law of Prägnanz. In Gestalt psychology, the general principle that the simplest organisation requiring the least cognitive effort will emerge in our perceptions.

Law of proximity. Law of perceptual grouping which states that the nearest, or 'most proximal', elements are grouped together.

Law of similarity. Law of perceptual grouping which states that the most similar elements are grouped together.

Law of specific nerve energy. Principle that all nerve impulses are virtually identical and that the quality of sensory experience is determined by the type of receptor stimulated.

Learning. Process that results in a relatively permanent change in behaviour or behavioural potential based on experience.

Learned helplessness. General pattern of nonresponding in the presence of noxious stimuli which often follows after an organism has previously experienced noncontingent, inescapable aversive stimuli; concept developed by Martin Seligman.

Learning-performance distinction. Difference between what has been learned and what is expressed in overt behaviour that the organism performs.

Levels of processing theory. Theory regarding the structure and characteristics of the memory system; it postulates a single system of memory in which the only differentiation is in the levels of processing applied to incoming information.

Libido. In Freudian theory, the psychic energy that drives individuals toward sensual pleasures of all types, including sexual.

Life history. Information about a person's life taken from different types of available records such as school or military records, written productions, personal journals and medical data.

Life-change units (LCU). In stress research, the measure of the stress levels of different types of change experienced during a given period; used to predict subsequent illness – as LCU increase above a certain level, the likelihood of illness also increases.

Limbic system. Area at the upper end of the old brain which contains centres for emotional behaviour and basic motivational urges.

Limited capacity. The assumption that we need a selective attention mechanism because the brain cannot deal with the enormous amount of visual stimulation the outside world bombards us with.

Linear perspective. Depth cue based on the illusion that parallel lines converge to a point on the horizon as they recede into distance.

Linguistic relativity. The hypothesis developed by Whorf which holds that language shapes thought; when languages are different, thinking is likewise different.

Locus of control. The extent to which people perceive they are in control of events. People with an internal locus of control believe that attaining positive outcomes is mostly a matter of their own efforts. People with an external locus of control believe that their behaviour mainly is controlled by internal or external forces beyond their control.

Locus of control orientation. Generalised belief about the relationship between actions and outcomes – whether they are caused by what we do or by events outside our control.

Logical positivism. The philosophy which holds that science should concern itself only with 'positive' knowledge, that is based on empirical evidence: reports of observations that are gathered through and by the senses of the observer.

Long-term memory (LTM). Those memory processes associated with the preservation of information for retrieval at any later time, and, theoretically, having the characteristics of unlimited capacity.

Long-term potentiation. High-frequency stimulation of inputs to the hippocampus, which has been found to increase memory strength for new learning by causing changes in the shape of synapses, leading to the formation of new synaptic contacts on nerve cells.

Longitudinal design. Research design in which the same subjects are observed repeatedly, sometimes over many years.

Loudness. Perceptual dimension influenced by the amplitude of a sound wave; sound waves with large amplitudes are experienced as loud, those with small amplitudes as soft.

Lucid dreaming. Being consciously aware that one is dreaming. It is considered a learnable skill that enables dreamers to control the direction of their dreams.

M

Magnetic resonance imaging (MRI). Technique for exploring the living brain; uses magnetic fields and radio waves to generate pulses of energy within the brain.

Magnitude estimation. Method of constructing psychophysical scales by having observers scale their sensations directly into numbers.

Magno cells. A type of *ganglion cell* with relatively long branches and a high conduction rate. Magnolike cells are also found higher up in the visual pathway.

Magno cellular pathway. A visual pathway that leads from the *secondary visual cortex* to the parietal lobes. This pathway probably is concerned with the spatial relationships among stimuli, analysing the 'where' of objects.

Main effect. In a 2×2 research design, the effect that one independent variable has on the dependent variable, regardless of the other independent variable.

Maintenance rehearsal. Active repetition of information in order to enhance subsequent access to it.

Major depression. DSM-IV & ICD-10 category for those who suffer from intense feelings of depression over an extended time, without the manic high phase of bipolar depression; also called '*clinical*' or '*unipolar*' depression.

Mania. Reaction characterised by a recurring period of extreme elation, unbounded euphoria without sufficient reason, and grandiose thoughts or feelings about personal abilities.

Manic depression. see *bipolar disorder*.

Manifest content. In Freudian dream analysis, the dream as it appears to the dreamer after a distortion process that Freud referred to as dream work. It is the acceptable, 'surface' version of the dream story.

Masochism. Psychosexual disorder involving sexual excitement derived from the experience of personal suffering.

Materialism. See *monism*.

Maturation. Continuing influence of heredity during development and later life; important in age-related physical and behavioural changes characteristic of the species.

Mean. Most commonly used measure of central tendency of a distribution; the average value for a group of scores.

Mechanoreceptors. A class of receptors that *transduces* mechanical energy in the outside world into electrochemical or neural energy. They are situated in the inner ear, in the muscles, tendons and joints, and in the skin.

Median. Measure of central tendency of a distribution; the score within a group of observations for which half of the remaining scores have values less than and half have values greater than this number.

Medical model. Paradigm which defines and studies psychological abnormality in a way analogous to that used to study and treat physical illness.

Meditation. Form of consciousness alteration designed to enhance self-knowledge and well-being by losing self-awareness through special rituals and exercises.

Medulla. Area of the brain stem responsible for controlling repetitive processes such as breathing and heartbeat.

Memory code. Representation of information in some encoded form in storage.

Memory trace. See *engram*.

Menarche. Onset of menstruation.

Mental age (MA). In Binet's measure of intelligence, the age at which a child is performing intellectually, expressed in terms of the average age at which normal children achieve a particular score.

Mental map. Cognitive representation of physical space.

Mental processes. The workings of the human mind.

Mental set. Tendency to respond to a new problem in the manner used on a previous problem.

Mere exposure effect. Ability of repeated exposures to the same stimulus to produce greater attraction toward that stimulus, a preference that develops without necessarily being aware of the cognitions involved.

Mesomorph. Somatotype characterised by a body build that is muscular, rectangular and strong.

Metacognition. Thinking about thinking.

Minimal group paradigm. An experimental situation in which participants are made individually aware only of the group or category to which they have been assigned but are not informed of the identity or names of other subjects who have been likewise assigned; thus, each subject is unable to identify other members of his or her in-group.

Mnemonics. Special strategies or devices used during the encoding of new information that use already familiar items to enhance subsequent access to the information in memory.

Mode. Measure of central tendency of a distribution; the score occurring most frequently among the observations.

Model. Conceptual framework which provides a simplified way of thinking about the basic components in a field of knowledge.

Moderator variables. Conditions in a situation and in an individual's functioning that can change the effect of a stressor.

Modesty bias. The tendency notable in collectivist cultures to explain success in terms of contextual factors and not with reference to personal attributes.

Modules. Areas in the brain consisting of relatively isolated networks of neurons, that appear to be specialised in the analysis of limited aspects of the visual field. Within the brain, the various attributes of the visual world are probably analysed separately in different modules.

Monism. View that mind and brain are aspects of a single reality; also called *materialism*.

Monocausality. The principle that a specific behaviour is almost directly caused by an instinct, without for example intervening psychological factors.

Moods. Emotions that last for more than several minutes up to a few hours, where the subject is generally not concerned with how the feeling started.

Mood-congruent processing. Processing of material that is congruent with one's prevailing mood; it is more likely to be attended to, noticed, and processed more deeply with greater elaborative associations; concept developed by Gordon Bower.

Mood-dependent retrieval. Better recall of events experienced earlier that had an emotional component when the person doing the recall is in that same mood; concept developed by Gordon Bower.

Morality. System of beliefs and values which ensures that individuals will act to keep their obligations to others in the society and will behave in ways that do not interfere with the rights and interests of others.

Morpheme. The smallest unit of language that contributes either to the meaning, or to the structure of a sentence, or both.

Motherese. Special form of speech with an exaggerated and high-pitched intonation that adults use to speak to infants and young children; also known as the Baby Talk Register.

Motor cortex. Area of the cerebral cortex located along the front of the central sulcus, devoted to sending messages to the muscles; also known as the *motor projection area*.

Motor neurons. Neurons that carry messages from the central nervous system to the muscles or glands.

MRI. see *magnetic resonance imaging*

Multi-Store Model. The most influential model for human memory as proposed by Atkinson and Shiffrin. The MSM postulates three memory systems: *sensory memory, short-term memory and long-term memory*.

Multiple personality disorder (MPD). Dissociative disorder in which different aspects of a personality function independently of one another, creating the appearance of two or more distinct personalities within the same individual.

Myelin sheath. Covering, made up of glial cells, that insulates some axons, speeding the conduction of nerve impulses.

N

Narcissistic personality disorder. Personality disorder marked by a grandiose sense of self-importance, preoccupation with fantasies of success and power, and a need for constant attention or admiration.

Narcolepsy. Sleep disorder characterised by an irresistible urge to sleep during the daytime.

Narrative. An account of purportedly connected events in order of their occurrence, implicit within which is an explanation of their causal interrelationship.

Nativism. The philosophical doctrine that considers human knowledge to be the result of innate mechanisms.

Natural selection. Darwin's idea that favourable adaptations to features of the environment allow some members of a species to produce more offspring than others.

Naturalistic observation. Observation of naturally occurring behaviours with no attempt to change or interfere with them; data collection without laboratory controls or the manipulation of variables.

Nature. In psychology, nature refers to the inherited, biologically based aspects of human mental and behavioural functioning.

Nature–nurture controversy. Debate in psychology concerning the relative importance of heredity (nature) and learning or experience (nurture) in determining development and behaviour.

Needs hierarchy. Sequence from most primitive level of basic needs to higher levels of needs that are attended to only after lower ones are satisfied; model developed by Abraham Maslow.

Negative reinforcer. Stimulus, not received (terminated or avoided) after a response, that increases the probability of that response occurring.

Negative reinforcement. Condition following a response of not receiving or escaping an aversive stimulus that increases the probability of the response.

Negative cognitive sets. Idea that people take a negative view of events in their lives for which they feel responsible.

Neocortex. Outer layer of the cerebrum, necessary for precise perception and conscious thought; also known as the *cortex*.

Neural network. Circuits or systems of neurons functioning together to perform tasks that individual cells cannot carry out alone.

Neuromodulator. Substance that modifies or modulates the activities of a post-synaptic neuron.

Neuron. Nerve cell specialised to provide rapid communication within and between adjacent cells.

Neuropathic pain. Pain caused by the abnormal functioning or over-activity of nerves.

Neuropsychology. Branch of physiological psychology which studies the foundations of behaviour and mental processes as functions of the activity of the brain and nervous system.

Neuroscience. Branch of the life sciences that deals with the anatomy, physiology, and biochemistry of the brain and nervous system mechanisms involved in the production of normal and abnormal behaviour.

Neurosis. Mental disorder in which there are one or more symptoms related to ineffective attempts to deal with anxiety.

Neurotic disorder. Mental disorder in which a person does not have signs of brain abnormalities and does not display grossly irrational thinking or violate basic norms but does experience subjective distress, especially anxiety.

Neurotransmitter. Chemical messenger released from neurons which cross the synapse and interact with receptors on the post-synaptic cell membrane.

Nociceptive pain. Pain resulting from signals sent from specialised nerve endings in the skin, through the spinal cord, and into the brain.

Nomothetic approach. Methodological approach to the study of personality processes in which emphasis is placed on identifying universal trait dimensions or lawful relationships between different aspects of personality functioning.

Non-REM sleep (NREM). A stage of sleep characterised by the absence of REM (rapid eye movements). It accounts for 75 to 80 percent of total sleep time, and encompasses the phases of deep sleep.

Nonconscious processes. Processes involving information that is not represented in either consciousness or memory, such as the organisation of incoming stimuli into figure and ground.

Norm crystallisation. Convergence of the expectations of a group of individuals into a common perspective as they talk and carry out activities together.

Normal curve. Symmetrical distribution where, in the ideal case, the mean, median, and mode have the same value.

Normative influence. Effect of a group on an individual striving to be liked, accepted and approved of by others.

Normative investigations. Research efforts designed to describe what is characteristic of a specific age or developmental stage.

Norms. Standards based on measurements of a large group of people; used for comparing the score of an individual with those of others within a well-defined group.

Nurture. The environmental influences on human mental and behavioural functioning.

O

Object permanence. Recognition that objects exist independently of an individual's action or awareness.

Observational method. A research procedure in which the behaviour of subjects is registered systematically.

Observational learning. Process of learning new responses by watching the behaviour of another.

Observer bias. Distortion of perceptual evidence due to the personal motives and expectations of the viewer.

Observer-report methods. In psychological assessment, the evaluation of some aspect of a person's behaviour by another person.

Obsessive-compulsive disorder. Mental disorder characterised by obsessions and compulsions.

Oedipus complex. In psychoanalytic theory, the simultaneous appearance of unconscious sexual desire for the parent of the opposite sex and unconscious hatred for the same-sex parent.

Oestrogen. Female hormones that are secreted from the gonads – the sex organs – and that partly determine female sexual arousal.

Olfaction. Sensation of smell.

Olfactory bulb. Centre where odour-sensitive receptors send their signals, located just below the frontal lobes of the cortex.

Operant. Any behaviour emitted by an organism that can be characterised in terms of the observable effects it has on the environment.

Operant conditioning. Learning in which the probability or ratio of a response is changed by a change in its consequences; see also instrumental conditioning.

Operant extinction. Withholding delivery of a positive reinforcer in order to extinguish an operant behaviour.

Operationalization. Defining a variable or condition in terms of the specific procedures an investigator uses to determine its presence.

Opiates. Group of drugs derived from the opium poppy and classified as depressants.

Opponent-process theory. Theory that all colour experiences arise from three systems, each of which include two 'opponent' elements: red vs. green, blue vs. yellow, and black vs. white.

Optic nerve. Axons of the *ganglion cell* that carry information from the eye to the optic chiasma.

Optic chiasma. Region of the brain at which messages from the inner half of each retina cross over to the opposite hemisphere.

Optic tract. Nerve fibres that carry information from the optic chiasma to the visual cortex.

Optimal arousal. Level of arousal at which people best perform tasks of different levels of difficulty.

Organic pathology. Pathology that is caused by a known organic condition.

Organisational psychologist. Psychologist who studies various aspects of human relations, such as communication among employees, socialisation or enculturation of workers, leadership, job satisfaction, stress and burnout, and overall quality of life in work environments.

Orientation constancy. Ability to perceive the actual orientation of objects in the world despite their orientation in the retinal image.

Orienting response. General response of attention to the source of novel stimulation.

Out-group. Term used by members of one group for another group, when one group of persons is differentiated from another.

Over-regularisation. Grammatical error usually appearing during early language development in which rules of the language are applied too widely, resulting in incorrect linguistic forms.

P

Pain. Body's response to noxious stimuli that are intense enough to cause, or threaten to cause, tissue damage.

Panic disorder. Anxiety disorder in which an individual experiences recurrent episodes of intense anxiety and feelings of unpredictability that usually last for a few minutes and include symptoms of autonomic hyperactivity.

Paradigm. Symbolic model in research that represents the essential features of a process being investigated.

Parallel distributed processing model (PDP). Model of the mind in which information is processed in a massively distributed, interactive, parallel system that can carry out various activities simultaneously through exciting or inhibiting the connections between processing units; also known as *connectionism*.

Parallel forms. Different forms of a test used to assess test reliability; the variance of forms reduces effects of direct practice, memory, or the desire of an individual to appear consistent on the same items.

Paranoid disorders. Group of psychotic disorders characterised by well-developed, systematised, intricate delusions.

Paraphilia. Psychosexual disorder in which sexual excitement necessarily and involuntarily demands the presence of nonconventional sexual objects, practices, or circumstances.

Parapsychology. The branch of psychology that studies psi phenomena.

Parasympathetic division. Division of the autonomic nervous system that deals with internal monitoring and regulation of various bodily functions.

Partial reinforcement effect. Behavioural principle that responses acquired under intermittent reinforcement are more difficult to extinguish than those acquired with continuous reinforcement.

Partial-report procedure. Experimental technique used in memory studies in which subjects presented with a pattern containing several individual stimuli are subsequently asked to recall just a portion of the pattern instead of all the information presented.

Participant modelling. Therapeutic technique in which a therapist demonstrates the desired behaviour and a client is aided, through demonstration and supportive encouragement, to imitate the modelled behaviour.

Particularisation. The way in which a particular stimulus is distinguished from a general class of stimuli to which it does not belong or from other stimuli.

Parvo cells. A type of *ganglion cell* with relatively short branches and a low conduction rate. Parvolike cells are also found higher up in the visual pathway.

Parvo cellular pathway. A visual pathway that leads from the *secondary visual cortex* to the temporal lobes. This pathway probably is concerned with the identification of stimuli, analysing the 'what' of objects.

Passive smoking. Inhaling the cigarette smoke of others which is in the atmosphere of one's living or working environment.

Pastoral counsellor. Member of a religious order who specialise in the treatment of psychological disorders, often by combining spiritual direction with practical problem-solving direction.

Patient. Those hospitalised with mental or physical health problems; term used by professionals who take a biomedical approach to the treatment of psychological problems to describe those being treated.

Patient nonadherence. Failure of patients to adhere to medical regimens or to follow physician's recommendations.

Payoff matrix. Detection matrix for estimating gains and losses in a detection trial.

Peace psychology. Interdisciplinary approach to the prevention of nuclear war and the maintenance of peace.

Perceived control. Belief that one has the ability to make a difference in the course or the consequences of some event or experience; often helpful in dealing with stressors.

Percept. What a perceiver experiences.

Perception. Processes that organise information in the sensory image and interpret it as having been produced by properties of objects in the external, three-dimensional world.

Perceptual set. Readiness to detect a particular stimulus in a given context.

Perceptual constancy. Ability to retain an unchanging percept of an object despite variations in the retinal image.

Perceptual defense. Hypothesised perceptual process which protects a person from identifying stimuli that are unpleasant or anxiety provoking.

Performance. External behaviour that indicates learning has taken place; however, performance does not reveal everything that has been learned.

Periphalist theory of emotion. A view on emotion that, in contrast to the *centralist theory of emotion*, stresses the role of visceral reactions, in particular the actions of the autonomic nervous system, in the production and expression of emotions.

Peripheral nervous system (PNS). Part of the nervous system outside of the central nervous system.

Person-centred therapy. Humanistic approach to treating people with problems that emphasises the healthy psychological growth of the individual; based on the assumption that all people share the basic tendency of human nature toward self-actualization; developed by Carl Rogers.

Personal construct. In George Kelly's theory, a person's interpretation of reality; his or her beliefs about the way two things are similar to each other and different from a third.

Personality. Psychological qualities of an individual that influence a variety of characteristic behaviour patterns (both overt and covert) across different situations and over time.

Personality disorder. Chronic, inflexible, maladaptive pattern of perceiving, thinking, and behaving that seriously impairs an individual's ability to function in social or other settings.

Personality inventory. Self-report questionnaire used for personality assessment that includes a series of items about personal thoughts, feelings and behaviours.

Personality type. Distinct pattern of personality characteristics used to assign people to categories; qualitative difference, rather than degree in difference, used to discriminate between people.

Personology. Study of personality structure, dynamics and development in the individual involving data from diaries, biographies, literature, case studies, letters, and general observations.

PET scanner. *See* Positron emission tomography

Phantom limb phenomenon. Experienced by amputees, extreme or chronic pain experienced by amputees in the limb that is no longer there.

Phenomenological perspective. Person's subjective view and interpretation of a situation or environment.

Phenotype. Observable set of characteristics of an organism resulting from the interaction of genotype and the environment.

Pheromones. Chemical signals released by organisms to communicate with other members of the species.

Phi Phenomenon. See *apparent motion*.

Phobic disorder. Pattern of behaviour in which anxiety is associated with some specific external environmental object or situation.

Phoneme. The smallest unit of speech that distinguishes one utterance from another. For example, the /p/ of English 'pin' and the /f/ of English 'fin' are different phonemes.

Photon. Single, indivisible unit of electromagnetic energy.

Photoreceptors. A class of receptors that *transduces* the part of electromagnetic energy we call light into electrochemical or neural energy. They consist of the rods and cones and are situated in the retina.

Physiological zero. Intermediate temperature point at which one feels neither warmth nor cold.

Physiological dependence. Process in which the body becomes adjusted to and dependent on a drug, in part because of depletion of neurotransmitters by the frequent presence of the drug.

Pitch. Sound quality of 'highness' or 'lowness', primarily dependent upon the frequency of the sound wave.

Pituitary gland. Gland located in the brain that secretes a variety of hormones which influence growth and the secretion of other hormones by other glands.

Place theory. Theory that different frequencies produce maximum activation at different locations along the basilar membrane, with the result that pitch can be coded by the place where activation occurs.

Placebo effect. Clinically significant response to a stimulus or treatment that occurs independent of its physiological effect.

Placebo therapy. Therapy independent of specific clinical procedures that results in client improvement.

Pluriformity. The many forms and guises a phenomenon can take. Contemporary psychology is theoretically as well as practically pluriform.

Polygenic. Human characteristic dependent on a combination of several genes.

Pons. Areas of the brain stem involved in dreaming and waking from sleep.

Positive reinforcement. Condition of receiving a stimulus, following a response, that increases the rate or probability of the response.

Positive reinforcer. Stimulus, received after a response, that increases the probability of that response occurring.

Positron emission tomography (PET). Technique for obtaining detailed pictures of activity in the living brain; involves injecting a radioactive substance which is taken up by the active neurons.

Postmodernism. An intellectual movement which questions the validity of scientific method and the notion of objective knowledge, thereby resisting all truth claims; within psychology, this stance focuses attention upon the notion that all forms of knowledge can be regarded as culturally and historically relative and linguistically constructed; thereby from this perspective knowledge in psychology can viewed as composed of malleable and changeable narratives.

Postsynaptic membrane. Membrane of the dendrite on the receiving side of the synapse.

Posttraumatic stress disorder/reaction (PTSD). Reaction in which an individual involuntarily re-experiences the emotional, cognitive, and behavioural aspects of past trauma.

Power function. In psychophysics, a mathematical equation ($S = kIb$) that expresses the relationship between the magnitude of a physical stimulus and the intensity of the sensory experience it evokes.

Prefrontal lobotomy. Operation that severs the nerve fibres connecting the frontal lobes of the brain with the diencephalon, especially those of the thalamic and hypothalamic areas.

Prejudice. Learned attitude toward a target object, with negative affect (dislike or fear), negative beliefs (stereotypes) that justify the attitude, and a behavioural intention to avoid, control, dominate, or eliminate those in the target group.

Premack principle. Principle, formulated by David Premack, that a more preferred activity can be used to reinforce a less preferred one.

Preoperational stage. Second of Piaget's stages of cognitive development (from 2 -7 years); characterised by centrism, discovery of qualitative identity, and increasing use of symbols but continued dependence on appearances.

Preparedness. People and animals are biologically disposed (as a result of evolutionary pressures) and prepared to learn behaviours that are allied to their survival needs; concept developed by Martin Seligman.

Presynaptic membrane. Membrane of the axon on the sending side of a synapse.

Primary appraisal. Term used in stress research referring to the first stage in the cognitive appraisal of a potentially stressful situation; an individual evaluates the seriousness of a demand or potentially stressful situation.

Primary care. Measures that promote the avoidance of disease, ill-health or injury, preventing their development in the first instance and which promote the maintenance and development of health and wellness.

Primary drives. Motivational states induced by biological needs and not dependent on learning.

Primacy effect. Phenomenon that the first information we learn about others has greater impact than does later information.

Primary visual cortex. A part of the occipital cortex where signals from the rods and cones enter the brain. In the primary visual cortex, also called the striate cortex, a first analysis of the complete range of stimulus properties, such as colour, movement and orientation, takes place.

Primary sensations. The result of the process of sensation. Primary or elementary sensations of vision, for example, consist of 'seeing' particular forms, colours and movements.

Priming effect. Triggering of specific memories by a particular cue; typical example of implicit memory.

Proactive interference. Memory phenomenon in which previously stored information interferes with the learning of new, but similar information.

Procedural memory. That component of long-term memory which stores the way in which we remember how things get done and how perceptual, cognitive, and motor skills are acquired, retained and utilised.

Procedural learning. A change in the ability to perform skilled actions – 'knowing how' – as can be inferred from changes in observable behaviour and from improvements in performance; contrast with *declarative learning*.

Progressive relaxation. Technique that teaches people alternately to tense and relax their muscles, in order to learn the experience of relaxation and discover how to extend it to each specific muscle.

Projective test. Method of personality assessment in which an individual is presented with a standardised set of ambiguous, abstract stimuli and asked to interpret the meaning of the stimuli; responses are assumed to reveal inner feelings, motives and conflicts.

Protection motivation theory. Motivation to protect one's health is conceived as depending upon: the magnitude of the threat; the probability of its occurrence; belief that a response will be effective in overcoming the threat; and upon a self-perceived ability to perform the response.

Prototype. Most representative example of a category.

Proximal stimulus. Image on the retina, as contrasted with the *distal stimulus*.

Psi phenomena. Processes of information and energy transfer that cannot be explained in terms of the physical mechanisms thus far discovered and acknowledged by the natural sciences.

Psychiatric social worker. Mental health professional who has received specialised training in a school of social work and whose training emphasises the importance of the social context of people's problems.

Psychiatrist. Individual who has completed all medical school training needed to become a medical doctor and also has completed some postgraduate specialty training in dealing with mental and emotional disorders; a psychiatrist may prescribe medications for the treatment of psychological disorders but is not trained to administer psychometric tests.

Psychic determinism. Assumption that all mental and behavioural reactions are determined by earlier experiences.

Psychoactive drugs. Chemicals which affect mental processes and behaviour by changing conscious awareness of reality.

Psychoanalysis. The psychological approach that explains human functioning in terms of the unconscious determinants of behaviour. Inherited drives and repressed past experiences are assumed to conflict with actual personal needs and thus exert a powerful influence on what the individual does, thinks or feels.

Psychoanalyst. Individual who has completed postgraduate training in an institute that offers specialised training in the Freudian approach to understanding and treatment of mental disorders.

Psychodynamic personality theories. Theories of personality that share the assumption that personality is shaped by, and behaviour is motivated by, powerful inner forces.

Psychogenic amnesia. Amnesia not caused by any physical damage or neurological disorder in which there occurs a sudden inability to recall important personal information and which is precipitated by psychological distress.

Psychogenic fugue. Amnesic state during which an individual travels to a new place and assumes a new identity and lifestyle.

Psychological assessment. Use of specified procedures to evaluate the abilities, behaviours, and personal qualities of people.

Psychological experiment. A controlled laboratory situation in which specific behaviour is measured under systematically varied conditions.

Psychological test. Measuring instrument used to assess an individual's standing relative to others on some mental or behavioural characteristic.

Psychology. Empirical study of the behaviour and mental processes of organisms.

Psychometrics. Field of psychology that is concerned with mental testing and measurement.

Psychometric function. Graph that plots the percentage of detections of a stimulus (on the vertical axis) for each stimulus intensity (on the horizontal axis).

Psychoneuroimmunology (PNI). Research area that investigates the effects of stress on the physiological and biological functions of the body, particularly the effects on the immune system.

Psychopathological functioning. Psychological abnormalities.

Psychophysics. Study of the correspondence between psychological experience and physical stimulation.

Psychosexual disorders. Group of psychological disorders centring on problems of sexual inhibitions and dysfunctions and sexual deviations.

Psychosexual stages. Freud's stages of sexual development in a child which involve successive ways of satisfying instinctual biological urges through stimulation of different areas of the body: the mouth, anus and the genitals.

Psychosocial stages. Successive developmental stages proposed by Erik Erikson that focus on an individual's orientation toward the self and others; these stages incorporate both sexual and social aspects of a person's development and social conflicts that arise from the interaction between an individual and the social environment.

Psychosomatic disorder. Physical disorder aggravated by, or primarily attributable to, prolonged emotional stress or other psychological causes.

Psychosurgery. Surgical procedures performed on brain tissue to alleviate psychological disorders.

Psychotherapy. Group of therapies used to treat psychological disorders that focus on changing maladaptive behaviours, thoughts, perceptions and emotions that may be associated with specific disorders.

Psychotic disorder. Severe mental disorder in which a person experiences impairments in reality-testing manifested through thought, emotional, or perceptual difficulties.

Puberty. Attainment of sexual maturity, indicated for girls by menarche, the onset of menstruation, and for boys by the production of live sperm accompanied by the ability to ejaculate.

Punisher. Aversive stimulus that decreases the probability of the preceding response.

Q

Qualitative methods. The methods of research that are primarily concerned with understanding the people under study rather than predicting their behaviour. Qualitative methods favour the interpretation of naturally occurring sources of data, like what people say verbally or in letters or diaries.

Quantitative methods. The methods of research that translate empirical evidence into numbers, allowing researchers to determine the relationships between the data with mathematical precision.

Questionnaire. Written set of questions.

R

Randomisation. Assignment of subjects to either the experimental or control groups by a chance procedure so that each subject has an equal change of being placed in either group.

Range. Difference between the highest and the lowest scores in a frequency distribution; the simplest measure of variability.

Rapid eye movements (REM). Reliable behavioural signs that indicate a sleeper's mental activity is centred around dreaming.

Rational–emotive therapy (RET). Comprehensive system of personality change based on changing irrational beliefs causing undesirable, highly charged emotional reactions, such as severe anxiety; developed by Albert Ellis.

Rationalism. View, associated with Plato and Descartes, that the human mind came prepared with certain basic ideas that ordered all sensory experience.

Reaction time. Elapsed time between a stimulus presentation and a designated response; used as a measure of the time required for mental processes.

Reaction potential. The likelihood of a particular response occurring.

Realistic thinking. Thinking based on fitting one's ideas to the reality of situational demands, time constraints and operational rules, and based on accurate evaluation of one's personal resources.

Reasoning. Process of logical thinking in which conclusions are drawn from a set of available information; thinking directed toward a given goal or objective.

Recall. Method of retrieval in which an individual is required to reproduce the information previously presented.

Receptive field. The region of retinal stimulation to which a specific *ganglion cell* responds.

Recessive genes. Genes that are expressed in an individual's development only when paired with similar genes.

Reciprocal determinism. Concept of Albert Bandura's social learning theory referring to the notion that a complex reciprocal interaction exists between factors of an individual, behaviour, and environmental stimuli, with each of these components affecting the others.

Recognition. In perceptual psychology, our noticing a *percept* as something we have seen before.

Reductionism. Belief that observable phenomena at one level of analysis can be accounted for by the workings of phenomena at a more basic or fundamental level.

Reference frame. Spatial or temporal context.

Reference groups. Formal or informal groups from which a person derives attitudes and standards of acceptability and appropriateness and to which a person refers for information, direction and support for life-style.

Referentiality. The function of language which holds that meaningful expressions refer to objects, persons and events in the world. It allows us to talk about objects, persons and ideas that are not present in order to put them on the agenda of communication.

Reflection. The function of language which holds that language enables us to think about our own pronouncements.

Reflex. Reaction in which an external stimulus leads to a physical response; an unlearned response elicited by specific stimuli which have biological relevance for an organism.

Reflex arc. Neural circuit including nerve pathways carrying incoming sensory information and pathways carrying outgoing motor signals.

Refractory period. Period of rest during which a nerve impulse cannot be activated.

Reinforcer. An event which changes the strength of a learned response.

Reinforcement contingency. Consistent relationship between a response and the changes in the environment that it produces.

Relapse. Reverting to former behaviour patterns that have been changed; for instance, smoking again after quitting for some period; usually occurs when person returns to original environment where addictive behaviour was maintained.

Relative motion parallax. Source of information about depth in which the relative distances of objects from a viewer determine the amount and direction of their relative motion in the retinal image.

Relaxation response. Condition in which muscle tension, cortical activity, heart rate, and blood pressure all decrease and breathing slows.

Releaser. Environmental cue that evokes a specific response pattern in every member of a species.

Reliability. Degree to which individuals earn the same relative scores each time they are measured.

REM sleep. A stage of sleep characterised by REM (rapid eye movements). It accounts for 20 to 25 percent of total sleep time and is associated with sometimes bizarre and often vivid dreams involving physical activity and emotion.

Replication. Repetition of an experiment under similar conditions in order to see if the same results will be obtained; usually conducted by an independent investigator.

Representativeness heuristic. Cognitive strategy that assigns something to a category on the basis of a few characteristics regarded as representative of the category.

Repression. In Freudian theory, a defense mechanism by which painful or guilt-producing thoughts, feelings, or memories are excluded from conscious awareness.

Research design. Conditions under which an investigator measures behaviour

Residual stress pattern. Chronic syndrome in which the emotional responses of posttraumatic stress persist over time.

Resiliency. Special quality to deal effectively with stressful, traumatic situations and bounce back from their usual debilitating effects; also used to describe children who are termed *invulnerables* because they cope effectively with harsh, abusive environments.

Resistance. Inability or unwillingness of a patient in psychoanalysis to discuss certain ideas, desires, or experiences.

Resistance to extinction. Persistence of the conditional response in the absence of the unconditional stimulus.

Response bias. Systematic tendency, as a result of nonsensory factors, for an observer to favour responding in a particular way.

Reticular formation. Long structure in the middle of the brain stem through which sensory messages pass on their way to higher centres of the brain.

Retina. Layer at the back of the eye which contains photoreceptors.

Retrieval. Recovery of stored information from memory at a later time.

Retrieval cues. Internally or externally generated stimuli available to help with the retrieval of a memory.

Retroactive interference. Memory phenomenon in which the learning of new information interferes with the memory of a previously stored similar item.

Retrograde amnesia. Amnesia in which there is loss of memory for events experienced prior to the event that precipitated the amnesia.

Reversal theory. A theory of motivation, emotion and personality in which the subjective appraisal of arousal and the pleasure or displeasure, with which it is associated, plays a central role; inconsistency in the form of switching (or, reversing) between opposite states is said to characterise human experience.

Ritual healing. Ceremonies which infuse special emotional intensity and meaning into the healing process; they heighten patients' suggestibility and sense of importance; often directed by a shaman and including family members of the afflicted person.

Rods. Photoreceptors that are concentrated in the periphery of the retina, are most active for seeing in dim illumination and do not produce sensations of colour.

Role. Socially defined pattern of behaviour that is expected of a person who has a certain function within a group or setting.

Rorschach test. Projective test used for clinical diagnosis in which the ambiguous symmetrical stimuli are ink-blots.

Rule. Behavioural guideline to act in a certain way in certain situations

Rule learning. Recognition of the behavioural implications of rules, the contexts in which they are relevant, and the perception of reinforcing contingencies for obeying or violating rules.

S

Sample. A carefully selected group of the population, which is assumed to have attributes that are representative of the entire population.

Saturation. The apparent purity of a colour. The more saturated a colour, the more it appears as a hue that is free of white or grey.

Satyriasis. Exaggerated sexual desire in males.

Savings. Term for phenomenon by which a conditioned response which has been extinguished, with further acquisition training, gains strength more rapidly than it did initially.

Savings method. Method of measuring memory originally used by Hermann Ebbinghaus; involves measuring memory by the savings in the amount of time it takes to relearn the original material.

Scapegoating. Process of displacing aggression on a target other than the original source of frustration.

Schedules of reinforcement. In operant conditioning, the pattern of delivering and withholding reinforcement.

Schedules of punishment. In operant conditioning, the pattern of delivering punishment.

Schema. Integrated cluster of knowledge organised around a topic; includes expectations.

Schizophrenic disorders. Group of psychotic disorders characterised by the breakdown of integrated personality functioning, withdrawal from reality, emotional distortions and disturbed thought processes.

Scientific method. A set of principles to govern empirical research in psychology, which stresses intersubjective standards and verifiability of the procedures and the results.

Script. Cluster of knowledge about a sequence of interrelated specific events and actions that are expected to occur in a certain way in particular settings.

Second-order conditioning. Classical conditioning procedure in which a neutral stimulus is paired with a conditioned stimulus rather than an unconditioned stimulus; also called *higher-order conditioning*.

Secondary appraisal. Term used in stress research to refer to the second stage in the cognitive appraisal of a potentially stressful situation in which an individual evaluates the personal and social resources available to deal with the stressful circumstance and determine the needed action.

Secondary care. Measures taken to treat an illness after it has developed.

Secondary drive. Learned drives that supplement the *primary drives*. Although these drives are learned, they have the same motivating power as primary drives.

Secondary trait. Characteristic that is not crucial to an understanding of an individual but nevertheless provides some information about enduring qualities of the person.

Secondary visual cortex. A part of the visual cortex that receives information from the *primary visual cortex*. It consists of relatively isolated networks of neurons, called *modules*.

Selective attention. Refers to the ability to be aware of only part of the available sensory input.

Selective optimisation. Strategy for successful ageing in which one makes the most of gains while minimising the impact of losses that accompany normal ageing; doing fewer things that one does well and doing them better.

Self. In humanistic psychology, the irreducible unit out of which the coherence and stability of a personality emerge.

Self-actualisation. Concept in personality psychology referring to a person's constant striving to realise his or her potential and to develop inherent talents and capabilities; many humanistic psychologists see the need for self-actualisation as the most basic human need; concept developed by Carl Rogers and Abraham Maslow, and earlier by Carl Jung.

Self-concept. Individual's awareness of his or her continuing identity as a person.

Self-construct. Set of beliefs and values that a person holds about his or her personal functioning; also the psychological notion of a self with distinctive characteristics that affect thought, feeling and action.

Self-efficacy. Belief that a person can perform adequately in a particular situation.

Self-esteem. Generalised evaluative attitude toward the self that influences both moods and behaviour and exerts a powerful effect on a range of personal and social behaviours.

Self-fulfilling prophecy. Notion that a hypothesis or expectation about the way someone will act exerts a subtle influence on the person to act in the expected way or for the perceiver to 'see' what is expected.

Self-handicapping. Process of developing, in anticipation of failure, behavioural reactions and explanations that minimise ability deficits as possible causes for the failure.

Self-perception theory. Idea that people observe themselves in order to work out the reasons that they act as they do; people infer what their internal states are by perceiving how they are acting in a given situation; concept developed by Daryl Bem.

Self-report method. Often used research technique in which a personality assessment is achieved through respondents' answers to a series of questions.

Self-serving bias. Class of attributional biases in which people tend to take credit for their successes and yet deny responsibility for their failures.

Semantic. The meaning of words and sentences.

Semantic memory. Aspect of long-term memory which stores the basic meaning of words and concepts.

Sensation. Processes that analyse physical energy in the world (for example, light and sound waves) and convert it into neural activity that codes simple information about the way the receptor organs are being stimulated.

Sensorimotor stage. First of Piaget's stages of cognitive development (from about 0–2 years); characterised by improvement and coordination of sensorimotor sequences, object permanence, and the beginning of internal symbolic representation.

Sensory adaptation. Phenomenon in which visual receptors cells lose their power to respond after a period of unchanged stimulation.

Sensory coding. Way in which intensity of a sensory stimulus is coded in terms of the rate of firing of neural impulses in a sensory system.

Sensory deprivation. A drastic reduction of sensory stimulation, used in experiments that challenged the assumptions of *drive reduction*.

Sensory gating. Brain-directed process in which information in one sensory channel may be enhanced, while information in another is suppressed or disregarded.

Sensory memory. Initial memory processes involved in the momentary preservation of fleeting impressions of sensory stimuli; also called *sensory register*.

Sensory modalities. General term covering all the separate sensory systems that take in information.

Sensory neurons. Neurons that carry messages from the cells in the periphery toward the central nervous system.

Sensory preconditioning. Learning of an association between two paired stimuli prior to any pairing of either one with an unconditioned stimulus.

Sequential design. Research approach in which a group of subjects spanning a small age range are grouped according to year of birth and are observed repeatedly over several years; design combines some features of both the cross-sectional and longitudinal approaches.

Serial position effect. Characteristic of retrieval in which the recall of beginning and end items on a list is better than memory for items appearing in the middle.

Set. Temporary readiness to perceive or react to a stimulus in a particular way.

Sex. Biologically based characteristics that distinguish males from females.

Sex chromosome. Chromosome that contains genes that code for the development of male or female physical characteristics.

Sexual response cycle. Four phases can be distinguished in the human response to sexual stimulation: excitement, plateau, orgasm and resolution.

Sexual scripts. Socially learned programmes of sexual responsiveness that include prescriptions, usually unspoken, of what to do, when, where and how to do it, with whom, or with what to do it, and why it should be done.

Shamanism. Spiritual tradition that has been practised by Native American cultures for nearly 30,000 years; involves both healing and means of allegedly gaining contact with the 'spirit world'.

Shape constancy. The process by which the apparent shape of an object remains constant despite changes in the shape of the retinal image.

Shaping by successive approximations. Operant learning technique in which a new behaviour is produced by reinforcing successive approximations of the final behaviour desired.

Short–term memory (STM). Memory processes associated with the preservation of events or experiences recently perceived; short-term memory is of limited capacity and stores information for only a short length of time without rehearsal.

Significance. A statistical inference measure that shows that the difference between groups or conditions is probably not caused by chance.

Situational variable. External influence on behaviour; also known as *environmental variable*.

Situationism. View that, much more than we realise, our actions are determined by forces and constraints in behaviour settings rather than by personal qualities.

Size constancy. The stability of perceived size despite changes in objective distance and retinal image size.

Sleep apnoea. Upper respiratory sleep disorder in which the person stops breathing while asleep.

Social categorisation. Process by which people organise their social environment by categorising themselves and others into groups.

Social cognition. The cognitive processes employed by people as social beings to individually, collectively and intersubjectively perceive, interpret, assign meaning to and represent aspects of the social environment and that thereby are involved in guiding social behaviour.

Social context. Part of the total environment that includes other people, both real and imagined, interactions, the setting in which the interactions take place, and unwritten rules and expectations that govern the way people relate to each other.

Social constructionism. The psychological approach that criticises mainstream psychology for its almost exclusive focus on the abstract, self-sufficient individual. Social constructionism stresses that persons and psychological notions like 'mind', 'emotion', 'self' and 'memory' are not natural givens, but products of cultural and personal histories and of the immediate social context.

Social facilitation. Facilitating effect that the presence of other people sometimes has on individual performance.

Social identity. Conception of the self which takes its impetus from an individual identifying with the norms, values and members of a perceived social group.

Social influence. Process involved in producing any alteration to a person's intellectual, emotional or behavioural activities which ensues as a result of other people's relations with that individual.

Social learning theory. Learning theory that stresses the role of observation and the imitating of behaviours observed in others; developed by Albert Bandura and Walter Mischel.

Social learning therapy. Therapy utilising imitation of models amd social skills training to enhance self-confidence and self-esteem.

Social loafing. Unconscious tendency to slack off when performing in a group.

Social norms. Expectations that a group has for its members regarding acceptable and appropriate attitudes and behaviour.

Social perception. Process by which a person comes to know or perceive the personal attributes of him or herself and other people.

Social phobia. Phobia in which an individual experiences an irrational fear of speaking, writing, performing artistically or eating in public.

Social reality. Consensus of perceptions and beliefs about a situation that is derived by making social comparisons among members of a social group.

Social referencing. Process of searching for emotional information as a behavioural regulator.

Social representations. Socially shared thought through which collective knowledge comes to be reconstituted; specifically, vocabularies which classify, delineate and thereby in part construct properties of the world and of social reality.

Social role. Socially defined pattern of behaviour that is expected of a person when functioning in a given setting or group.

Social stereotype. Beliefs people have about the personality traits and abilities commonly found among individual members of a particular social group.

Social support. Resources, including material aid, instrumental help, socioemotional support and informational aid, provided by others to help a person cope with environmental and interpersonal demands.

Socialisation. Lifelong process whereby an individual's behavioural patterns, values, standards, skills, attitudes and motives are shaped to conform to those regarded as desirable in a particular society.

Societal psychology. Form of social psychology concerned with those psychological matters as implicated within social issues (for example, in ecology, genocide and medical ethics).

Sodium and potassium pump. Transport mechanism which pushes sodium out of a cell and potassium back into it, thus returning it to resting potential.

Soma. Cell body of a neuron; contains the nucleus and cytoplasm of the cell.

Somatic nervous system. Part of the peripheral nervous system that controls the skeletal muscles of the body.

Somatoform disorders. Group of disorders characterised by bodily (somatic) complaints in the absence of any known organic problems that is assumed to reflect psychological conflicts.

Somatosensory cortex. Area of the parietal lobes that receives sensory input from various body areas.

Somatotype. Descriptive category that classifies a person on the basis of a few salient physical characteristics with the hope of relating these to personality characteristics.

Spatial frequency. Number of dark-light cycles in a pattern over a given distance of visual space.

Speech act. The linguistic utterances that primarily express a form of action. Apologies, orders and requests are examples of speech acts.

Spontaneous recovery. Reappearance of an extinguished conditioned response after a rest period.

Spontaneous remission effect. Improvement of some mental patients and clients in psychotherapy without any professional intervention; a baseline criterion against which the effectiveness of therapies must be assessed.

Spoonerism. A speech error that consists of exchanging the initial sounds of words.

Spreading activation theory. Cognitive model that describes a person's mental dictionary as organised into a network of interconnected words and concepts in which activation of any part vibrates and spreads to related ones.

Standard deviation. Measure of the variability of scores in a distribution indicating the average difference between scores and their mean.

Standardisation. Uniform procedures for treating each participant or for recording data; in test construction, includes giving the test to a large number of representative individuals to establish norms.

State dependence. Characteristic of memory in which retrieval is better if the psychological or physical state present at the time of encoding is similar to that present at the time of retrieval.

Statistics. Mathematical tool used by researchers to help them describe their findings in an objective, uniform way; provides a sound standard for inferring whether the results are real or chance occurrences.

Stereochemical theory. Theory of smell which suggests that receptor sites in odour-sensitive cells have distinctive sizes and shapes corresponding to those of the chemical molecules which stimulate them.

Stereotype effect. Bias sometimes occurring in ratings or observations in which judges' beliefs about the qualities of most people who belong to a certain category influence the perception of an observed individual who belongs to that particular category.

Steroids. Group of hormones which are important in metabolic processes and in release of sugar from the liver into the blood.

Stigma. Negative reaction of people to an individual or group because of some assumed inferiority or source of difference that is degraded; also, what is experienced by the target of stigmatisation.

Stimulus. Environmental condition that elicits a response from an organism.

Stimulus control. Control of the occurrence of a response by means of a dependable signal (a discriminative stimulus) indicating a reinforcer is available.

Stimulus discrimination. Conditioning process in which an organism learns to respond differently to stimuli that are different from the conditioned stimulus on some dimension.

Stimulus generalisation. Automatic extension of conditioned responding to similar stimuli that have never been paired with the unconditioned stimulus.

Storage. Retention of encoded material over time involving neurophysiological changes in certain synapses.

Strain. Organism's reaction to external stressors.

Stress. Pattern of specific and non-specific responses an organism makes to stimulus events that disturb its equilibrium and tax or exceed its ability to cope.

Stress moderator variables. Variables that change the impact of a stressor on a given type of stress reaction.

Stressors. Internal or external events or stimuli that induce stress.

Structuralism. View, associated with Wilhelm Wundt and Edward Titchener, based on the presumption that all human mental experience can be understood as the combination of simple events or elements, that the underlying structure of the human mind can be revealed by analysing all the basic elements of sensation and other experience which forms an individual's mental life; the study of the how and why of experience.

Subject. Participant in an experiment whose behaviour is being observed.

Subjective contours. Perceived contours which do not exist in the distal stimulus, but only in subjective experience.

Subliminal perception. The phenomenon of perceiving something without conscious awareness.

Superego. In Freudian theory, that aspect of personality representing the internalisation of society's values, standards and morals; the inner conscious.

Superior colliculus. Cluster of nerve cell bodies in the mid-brain region of the brain stem involved in the integration of sensory input of different type; assumed to mediate primitive form of sensory perception.

Survey. Method of gathering information from a large number of people; self-report information is gathered in response to a list of questions that follow a fixed format.

Syllogism. Form of deductive reasoning which has a major premise, a minor premise and a conclusion which follows from the premises.

Sympathetic division. Division of the autonomic nervous system that deals with emergency responding.

Symptom substitution. Appearance of a new physical or psychological problem after a problem behaviour has been changed.

Synapse. Gap between one neuron and the next; it is filled with a fluid that does not permit electrical activity to pass across.

Synaptic vesicles. Tiny sacs in the terminal button of the axon which release precisely measured amounts of transmitter chemicals into the synaptic gap.

Synaptic transmission. Relaying of information from one neuron to another.

Syntax. The aspect of language that is concerned with the rules that specify which sequence of words is well formed and acceptable.

Systematic desensitisation. Behavioural therapy technique in which a client is taught to prevent the arousal of anxiety by relaxing.

T

T-lymphocytes. White blood cell that stimulates or shuts off the immunological response to an invading organism.

Tabula rasa. Term associated with the philosophical view of John Locke that, at birth, individuals are born with a 'blank slate' and that all knowledge comes from experience.

Taste buds. Receptors for taste, located primarily on the upper side of the tongue.

Taste aversion learning. Biological constraint on learning in which an organism learns to avoid a food whose ingestion is followed by illness; first studied by Garcia.

Taxonomy. Principles used for the purposes of classification and arrangement of phenomena (see *DSM-IV & ICD-10* as examples)

Teleology. View that an immaterial, purposeful mind gives behaviour its direction by acting on a passive, mechanistic brain.

Temporal contiguity. Principle stating that sensations, movements or ideas occurring closely in time become associated with one another.

Terminal buttons. Swollen, bulblike structures at the branched endings of axons that transmit impulses to the next neuron in the chain.

Tertiary care. Measures taken to limit or slow the further development of a disease, injury or health problem that has progressed to the point of there being lasting or irreversible damage to the person, rehabilitation as far as is possible being implicated.

Test. A standardised instrument to measure psychological attributes like personality or intelligence.

Test-retest reliability. Measure of the correlation between the scores of the same people on the same test given on two different occasions.

Testosterone. Male hormone secreted by the testes; responsible for sex-linked characteristics such as facial hair and deep voice.

Thalamus. Structure below the corpus callosum that serves as a relay station for all incoming sensory information.

Thanatos. In Freudian theory, the death instinct, assumed to drive people toward aggressive and destructive behaviour.

The Big Five. Comprehensive, theory-free, descriptive personality system that maps out the relationships between common trait words, theoretical concepts and personality scales.

Thematic apperception test (TAT). Projective test in which pictures of ambiguous scenes are presented to an individual who is encouraged to generate stories about the stimuli.

Theory. In psychology, a body of interrelated concepts and principles used to explain or predict some psychological phenomenon or to explain how some aspect of brain, mind, behaviour or environment functions.

Theory of signal detection (TSD). Theory that all perceptual judgements combine sensory and decision-making processes.

Thermoreceptors. A class of receptors that *transduces* thermal energy or temperature into electrochemical or neural energy. Thermal energy is sensed in the skin by nerve endings.

Think-aloud protocols. Reports of mental processes and strategies made by experimental subjects while working on a task.

Thinking. Complex mental process of forming a new mental representation by transforming available information.

Three-term contingency. Means by which organisms learn that in the presence of some stimuli, but not others, their behaviour is likely to have a particular effect on the environment; antecedent-behaviour-consequence.

Threshold. Minimum stimulus energy sufficient to excite a neuron and nerve impulse.

Thyrotrophic hormone (TTH). Hormone released from the pituitary gland which stimulates the thyroid gland to make more energy available to the body during a stress reaction.

Timbre. Dimension of auditory sensation which reflects the complexity of a sound wave.

Time perspective. Way we partition the flow of perceived events and experiences into the frames of past, present and future.

Token economy. Technique of positive reinforcement in which individuals are rewarded for socially constructive behaviours by tokens which may later be exchanged for privileges.

Tolerance. Lessened effect of a drug following continued use.

Top-down processing. Perceptual processes in which information from an individual's past experience, knowledge, expectations, motivations and background influence the way a perceived object is interpreted and classified.

Trait. Enduring and continuous quality or attribute which influences behaviour because it acts as a generalised action tendency.

Transactional perception. Theory of 'perception as hypotheses' which stresses the importance of transactions with the environment as the basis for developing hypotheses.

Transduction. The transformation of physical energy into electrochemical or neural energy.

Transference. Process by which a person in psychoanalysis attaches to a therapist feelings formerly held toward some significant person who figured in a past emotional conflict.

Trichromatic theory. Theory that there are three types of colour receptors producing the psychologically 'primary' colour sensations: red, green and blue.

Two-factor theory of emotion. Theory that emotion is the joint effect of two central processes: physiological arousal and cognitive appraisal.

Type-A behaviour syndrome. Competitive, compulsive and hostile behaviour characteristic of a particular style of coping with stress; assumed to increase the risk of coronary heart disease.

Type-T personality. Personality characterised by the desire to take risks and seek out thrills, stimulation and excitement.

U

Unconditional response (UCR). In classical conditioning, the response elicited by an unconditioned stimulus without prior training or learning.

Unconditional stimulus (UCS). In classical conditioning, the stimulus that elicits and reinforces an unconditional response.

Unconscious. In psychoanalytic theory, the domain of the psyche that stores repressed urges and primitive impulses.

Unconscious inference. Helmholtz's term to indicate that perception is a process by which information from a number of sources is unconsciously put together to create a perception.

Unconscious processes. In Freudian theory, mental processes that are not directly observable or subject to verification by self-report, but whose existence is inferred from effects on observable behaviours.

Unipolar depression. Former DSM category for those who suffer from intense feelings of depression over an extended time, without the manic high phase of bipolar depression; also called '*clinical*' or '*major*' depression.

Universalism. The conception that psychological processes, such as emotions, are largely fixed entities that are inherent to human nature, thereby minimalising cultural differences.

Unlimited capacity. The assumption that we have a potentially unlimited capacity for the processing of visual information.

Unrealistic optimism. A bias in judgement toward overconfidence in one's own capacities and underestimation of the risk involved in some behaviours.

V

Validity. Extent to which a test measures what it was intended to measure.

Variable. Factor that varies in amount or kind.

Variable interval schedule (VI). In operant conditioning, a schedule in which reinforcement is delivered after differing lengths of time, regardless of the number of correct responses that have occurred.

Variable ratio schedule (VR). In operant conditioning, a schedule in which reinforcement is given after a changing number of responses.

Verifiability. A criterion to guide scientific research which holds that statements are meaningful only if their truth can be checked in empirical research.

Vestibular sense. Sense that tells us how our bodies are oriented in the world with respect to gravity.

Visual cortex. See *primary visual cortex* and *secondary visual cortex*.

Volley principle. Extension of frequency theory which proposes that when peaks in a sound wave come too frequently for a single neuron to fire at each peak, several neurons as a group could fire at the frequency of the stimulus tone.

W

Weber's law. Assertion that the size of a difference threshold is proportional to the intensity of the standard stimulus.

Wellness. Optimal health, incorporating the ability to function fully and actively over the physical, intellectual, emotional, spiritual, social and environmental domains of health.

Whole-report procedure. Experimental technique used in memory studies in which subjects presented with a pattern containing several stimuli are subsequently asked to recall as many of the individual stimuli as possible.

Wisdom. Expertise in the fundamental pragmatics of life; often reached in late adulthood.

Word association. Technique of personality assessment using an individual's responses to a list of common words to identify unconscious personality dynamics.

Working memory. Short-term memory; material transferred to it from either sensory or long-term memory can be worked over and organised.

Y

Yerkes-Dodson law. Correlation between task difficulty and optimal level of motivation; performance of difficult tasks decreases as arousal increases, while performance of easy tasks increases as arousal increases to form an inverted-U function.

Z

Zeigarnik effect. Motivational effect induced by uncompleted tasks that create 'task tensions' sometimes leading to better recall of uncompleted than completed tasks; Lewinian concept first demonstrated by Bluma Zeigarnik.

REFERENCES

A

Abelson, R.P., Aronson, E., McGuire, W.J., Newcomb, T.J., Rosenberg, M.J. & Tannenbaum, P.H. (Eds.). (1968). Theories of cognitive consistency: A sourcebook. Chicago: Rand McNally.

Abelson, R.P. (1981). Psychological status of the script concept. American Psychologist, 36, 715-729.

Abramson, L.Y., Garber, J., Edwards, N. & Seligman, M.E.P. (1978). Expectancy changes in depression and schizophrenia. Journal of Abormal Psychology, 87, 102-109

Abramson, L.Y., Seligman, M.E.P. & Teasdale, J.D. (1978). Learned helplessness in humans: Critique and reformulation. Journal of Abnormal Psychology, 87, 32-48, 49-74.

Ackerman, D. (1990). A natural history of the senses New York: Random House.

Adams, J. (1979). Mutual-help groups: Enhancing the coping ability of oncology clients. Cancer Nursing, 2, 95-98.

Adams, J.A. (1987). Historical review and appraisal of research on the learning, retention, and transfer of human motor skills. Psychological Bulletin, 101, 41-74.

Adams, J.I, (1986). Conceptual blockbusting (3rd ed.). New York: Norton.

Adams, J.S. (1965). Inequity in social exchange. In L. Berkowitz (Ed.) Advances in experimental social psychology (Vol. 2, pp. 267-299). New York: Academic Press.

Ader, R. (1981). A historical account of conditioned immunobiologic responses. In R. Ader (Ed.), Psychoneuroimmunology. New York: Academic Press.

Ader, R. & Cohen, N. (1981). Conditioned immunopharmacological responses. In R. Ader (Ed.), Psychoneuroimmunology (pp. 281-319). New York: Academic Press.

Ader, R. & Cohen, N. (1993). Psychoneuroimmunology: Conditioning and stress. Annual Review of Psychology, 44, 53-85.

Ader, R. (ed.) (1990). Psychoneuroimmunology 2nd edition, New York, Academic Press.

Adler, A. (1929). The practice and theory of individual psychology New York: Harcourt, Brace & World.

Adler, J., Huck, J., McKillop, P. & Calonius, E. (1987, July 20). Taking life one night at a time. Newsweek, pp. 48-49.

Adler, N.E., David, H.P., Major, B.N., Roth, S.H., Russo, N.F. & Wyatt, G.E. (1990). Psychological responses after abortion. Science, 248, 41-44.

Adorno, T.W., Frenkel-Brunswick, E., Levinson, D.J. & Sanford, R. N. (1950). The authoritarian personality. New York: Harper.

Affleck, G., Tennen, H., Pfeiffer, C. & Fifield, J. (1987). Appraisals of control and predictability in adapting to a chronic disease. Journal of Personality and Social Psychology, 53, 273-279.

af Klinteberg, B., Humble, K., & Schalling, S. (1992). Personality and psychopathy of males with a history of criminal behaviour. European Journal of Personality, 6, 245-266.

Agras, S. (1985). Panic: Facing Fears, phobias and anxiety. New York: Freeman.

Agras, W.S., Taylor, C.B., Kraemer, H.C., Allen, R.A. & Schneider, J.A. (1980). Relaxation training: Twenty-four-hour blood pressure changes. Archives of General Psychiatry, 37, 859-863.

Ahern, G.L. & Schwartz, G.E. (1985). Differential lateralization for positive and negative emotion in the human brain: EEG spectral analysis. Neuropsychologia, 23, 744-755.

Ainsworth, M.D.S. (1973). The development of infant-mother attachment. In B.M. Caldwell & H.N. Ricciuti (Eds.), Review of child development research (Vol. 3). Chicago: University of Chicago Press.

Ainsworth, M.D.S. (1989). Attachments beyond infancy. American Psychologist, 44, 709-716.

Ainsworth, M.D.S., Blehar, M., Waters, E. & Wall, S. (1978). Patterns of attachment. Hillsdale, NJ: Erlbaum.

Ajzen, I. & Fishbein, M. (1977). Attitude-behavior relations: A theoretical analysis and review of empirical research. Psychological Bulletin, 84, 888-918.

Ajzen, I. & Madden, T.J. (1986). Prediction of goal-directed behavior: Attitudes, intentions and perceived behavioral control. Journal of Experimental Social Psychology, 22, 453-74.

Akhtar, S., Wig, N.H., Verma, V.K., Pershod, D. & Verma, S.K. (1975). A phenomenological analysis of symptoms in obsessive-compulsive neurosis. British Journal of Psychiatry. 127, 342-348.

Akil, H. (1978). Endorphins, beta-LPH and ACTH: Biochemical pharmacological and anatomical studies. Advances in Biochemical Psychopharmacology, 18. 125 139.

Alba, J.W. & Hasher, L. (1983). Is memory schematic? Psychological Bulletin, 93, 203-23.

Albee, G.W. & Joffe, J.M. (Eds.). (1977). Primary prevention of psychopathology: Vol.1. Issues. Hanover, NH: University Press of New England.

Albuquerque, E.X., Aguavo, L.G., Warnick, R.K., Ickowicz, R.K. & Blaustein, M.P. (1983, June). Interactions of phencyclidine with ion channels of nerve and muscle: Behavioral implications. Federation Proceedings, 42(9). 2584-2589.

Alden, L.E. (1988). Behavioral self-management controlled-drinking strategies in a context of secondary prevention. Journal of Consulting and Clinical Psychology, 56, 280-286.

Alker, H. & Poppen, P.J. (1973). Ideology in university students. Journal of Personality, 41, 653-671.

Allen, B.P. (1985). After the missiles: Sociopsychological effects of nuclear war. American Psychologist, 40, 927-937.

Allen, V.L. & Wilder, D.A. (1975). Categorization, belief, similarity and intergroup competition. Journal of Personality and Social Psychology. 32, 971-977.

Allison, T. & Cicchetti, D. (1976). Sleep in animals: Ecological and constitutional correlates. Science. 194, 732-734.

Alloy, L.B. & Abramson, L.Y. (1980). The cognitive component of human helplessness and depression. In J. Garber & M.E.P. Seligman (Eds.), Human helplessness: Theory and applications. New York: Academic Press.

Alloy, L.B. & Abramson, L.Y. (1979). Judgment of contingency in depressed and nondepressed students: Sadder but wiser? Journal of Experimental Psychology: General, 108, 441-485.

Allport, G.W. (1937). Personality: A psychological interpretation. New York: Holt, Rinehart & Winston.

Allport, D.A. (1987). Selection for action: some behavioural and neurophysiological considerations of attention and action. In H. Heuer & A.F. Sanders (Eds.). Perspectives on perception and action (pp 395-419). Hillsdale, N.J: Erlbaum.

Allport, D.A. (1989). Visual attention. In M.T. Posner (Ed.). Foundations of cognitive science (pp 631-682). Cambridge, MA: MIT Press.

Allport, G.W. (1954). The nature of prejudice. Cambridge, MA: Addison-Wesley.

Allport, G.W. (1960). Personality and social encounter. Berkeley, CA: Beacon Press.

Allport, G.W. (1961). Pattern and growth in personality. NewYork: Holt, Rinehart & Winston.

Allport, G.W. (1965). Letters from Jenny. New York: Harcourt, Brace' & World.

Allport, G.W. (1966). Traits revisited. American Psychologist, 21, 1-10.

Allport, G.W. (1968). The historical background of modern social psychology. In G. Lindzey & E. Aronson (Eds.), The handbook of social psychology (2nd ed.). Reading, MA: Addison-Wesley.

Allport, G.W. & Odbert, H.S. (1936). Trait-names, a psycholexical study. Psychological Monographs, 47 (1, Whole No. 211).

Allport, G.W. & Postman, L.J. (1947). The psychology of rumor. New York: Holt, Rinehart & Winston.

Almli, C.R. (1978). The ontogeny of feeding and drinking behavior: Effects of early brain damage. Neuroscience and Behavioral Reviews, 2, 281-300.

Altman, I.A. (1976). Environmental psychology and social psychology. Personality and Social Psychology Bulletin, 2, 96-113.

Altman, I. & Christensen, K. (Eds.). (1990). Environment and behavior studies: Emergence of intellectual traditions. New York: Plenum.

Amabile, T.M. (1987). The motivation to be creative. In S.Isaksen (Fd.), Frontiers in creativity: Beyond the basics (pp. 223-254). Buffalo, NY: Bearly.

American Psychological Association. (1982). *Guidelines and ethical standards for researchers*.

American Psychological Association. (1989) *1989 APA directory*. Office of demographic, employment, and educational research.

American Psychiatric Association. *Diagnostic and statistical manual of mental disorders*. First edition, 1952; second edition, 1968; third edition, 1980; revised, 1987; fourth, 1994. Washington, DC: Author.

Amnesty International. (1983). *Chile: Evidence of torture. London:* Amnesty Intemational Publications.

Amoore, J.E. (1965). Psychophysics of odor. *Cold Spring Harbor symposia in quantitative biology, 30,* 623-637.

Anastasi, A. (1982). *Psychological testing* (5th ed.). New York: Macmillan.

Anch, A.M., Browman, C.P., Mitler, M.M. & Walsh, J.K. (1988). *Sleep: a scientific perspective*. Englewood Cliffs, NJ: Prentice-Hall.

Andersen, A. (1985). *Practical and comprehensive treatment of anorexia nervoso and bulimia*. Baltimore: Johns Hopkins University Press.

Anderson, J.R. (1982). Acquisition of cognitive skill. *Psychological Review, 89,* 369-406.

Anderson, J.R. (Ed.). (1981). *Cognitive skills and their acquisition*. Hillsdale, NJ: Erlbaum.

Anderson, J.R. (1976). *Language, memory and thought*. Hillsdale, NJ: Erlbaum.

Anderson, J.R. (1978). Arguments concerning representations for mental imagery. *Psychological Review, 85,* 249-277.

Anderson, J.R. (1990). *Cognitive psychology and its implications,* San Francisco: Freeman.

Anderson, J.R. & Bower, G.H. (1973). *Human associative memory* Washington, DC: Winston & Sons.

Anderson, W.F. (1984). Prospects for human gene therapy. *Science,* 226,401-409.

Andersen, S.M. & Zimbardo, P.G. (1980, November). Resisting mind control. *U.S.A. Today,* pp. 44-47.

Andersson, T. & Magnusson, D. (1990). Biological maturation in adolescence and the development of drinking habits and alcohol abuse among young males: A prospective longitudinal study. *Journal of Youth and Adolescence,* 19, 33-41.

Andreason, N.C. (1988). Brain imaging: Applications in psychiatry. *Science, 239,* 1381-1388.

Andreasen, N.C., Swayze, V.W. & Flaum, M. (1990). Ventricular enlargement in schizophrenia evaluated with computed tomographic scanning: Effects of gender, age and stage of illness. *Archives of General Psychiatry, 47,* 1008-1015.

Andrews, E.L. (1990, April 29). A nicotine drug patch to end smoking. *The New York Times Index* (Vol. 139, Section 1, Col. 1, p. 27, June 3, 1990).

Angier, R.P. (1927). The conflict theory of emotion. *American Journal of Psychology,* 39, 390-401.

Antaki, C. (1994). *Explaining and arguing: social explanations of accounts*. London: Sage.

Antelman, S.M. & Caggiula, A.R. (1980). Stress-induced behavior: Chemotherapy without drugs. In J.M. Davidson & R.J. Davidson (Eds.), *The psychobiology of consciousness* (pp 65-104). New York: Plenum.

Antoni, M.H., Schniederman, N., Fletcher, M.A., Goldstein, D.A., Ironson, G. & Laperriere, A. (1990). Psychoneuroimmunolgy and HIV-1. *Journal of consulting and Clinical Psychology, 58,* 38-49.

Antoni, M.H., Baggett, L., Ironson, G., LaPerriere, A., August, S., Klimas, N., Schneiderman, N. & Fletcher, M.A. (1991). Cognitive-behavioral stress management intervention buffers distress responses and immunologic changes following notification of HIV-1 seropositivity. *Journal of Consulting and Clinical Psychology,* 59, 906-915.

Antrobus, J. (1991). Dreaming: Cognitive processes during cortical activation and high afferent thresholds. *Psychological Review,* 98, 96-121.

Apter, M.J. (1982). *The experience of motivation: the theory of psychological reversals*. London: Academic Press.

Apter, M.J. (1989). *Reversal theory: motivation, emotion and personality.* London: Routledge.

Ardrey, R. (1966). *The territorial imperative*. New York: Atheneum.

Arendt, H. (1971). Organized guilt and universal responsibility. In R.W. Smith (Ed.). *Guilt: Man and society*. Garden City, NY: Doubleday Anchor Books.

Arendt, H. (1963). *Eichmann in Jerusalem: A report on the banality of evil*. New York: Viking Press.

Argyle, M. (1988). *Bodily communication*. London: Methuen.

Ariès, P. (1962). *Centuries of childhood. A social history of family life.* New York: Vintage books.

Ariès, P. & Duby, G. (Eds.) (1985). *Histoire de la vie privée*. Paris: Seuil.

Arkin, R.M. & Baumgardner, A.H. (1985). Self-handicapping. In J.H. Harvey & G. Weary (Eds.), *Attribution: Basic issues and applications*. (pp. 169-202) New York: Academic Press.

Armstrong, D.M. (1968). *A materialist theory of the mind*. London: Routledge & K. Paul.

Arnold, M.B. (1960). *Emotion and personality*. (Vols. I and II). New York: Columbia University Press.

Arnold, M.B. (1970). Perennial problems in the field of emotion. In M.B. Arnold (Ed.), *Feelings and emotions: the Loyola Symposium* (pp.169-185). New York: Academic Press.

Aronson, E. (1988) *The social animal*, 5th ed., New York: Freeman

Aronson, E. (1990). Applying social psychology to desegregation and energy conservation. *Personality, and Social Psychology, Bulletin, 16,* 118-132.

Aronson, E., Blaney, N., Stephan, C., Sikes, J. & Snapp, M. (1978). *The jigsaw classroom*. Beverly Hills, CA: Sage.

Aronson, E., & Gonzalez, A. (1988). Desegregation, jigsaw, and the Mexican-American experience. In P.A. Katz & D. Taylor (Eds.), *Towards the elimination of racism: Profiles in controversy*. New York: Plenum.

Aronson, E., Turner, J.A. & Carlsmith, J.M. (1963). Communicator credibility and communication discrepancy as determinants of opinion change. *Journal of abnormal and Social Psychology, 67,* 31-36.

Asarnow, R.F., Cromwell, R.L. & Rennick, P.M. (1978). Cognitive and evoked response measures of information processing in schizophrenics with and without a family history of schizophrenia. *The Journal of Nervous and Mental Disease. 166,* 719-730.

Asch, S.E. (1940). Studies in the principles of judgments and attitudes: I1. Determination of judgments by group and by ego standards. *Journal of Social Psychology,* 12, 433-465.

Asch, S.E. (1952). *Social psychology*. Englewood Cliffs, N.J.: Prentice-Hall.

Asch, S.E. (1955). Opinions and social pressure. *Scientific American, 193(5),* 31-35.

Asch, S.E. (1956). Studies of independence and conformity: A minority of one against a unanimous majority. *Psychological Monographs,* 70 (9, Whole No. 416).

Asch, S. (1990). In *Discovering Psychology*, Program 19 [PBS video series]. Washington, DC: Annenberg/CPB Program.

Aserinsky, E., & Kleitman, N. (1953). Regularly occurring periods of eye mobility and concomitant phenomena during sleep. *Science,* 118, 273-274.

Ashley, W.R., Harper, R.S. & Runyon, D.L. (1951). The perceived size of coins in normal and hypnotically induced economic states. *American Journal of Psychology,* 64, 564-572.

Ashton, P.T. & Webb, R.B. (1986). *Making a difference: A teacher's sense of efficacy and student achievement*. New York: Longman.

Aspinwall, L.G., Kemeny, M.E., Taylor, S.E., Schneider, S.G. & Dudley, J.P. (in press). Psychosocial predictors of gay men's AIDS risk-reduction behavior. *Health Psychology*.

Associated Press. (1991, April 8). New study on suicide by older people.

Atkinson, R.L., Atkinson, R.C., Smith, E.E. & Bem, D.J. (1990). *Introduction to psychology (10th ed.)*. San Diego, CA: Harcourt Brace Jovanovich.

Atkinson, J.W. & Birch, D. (1970). *The dynamics of action*. NewYork: Wiley.

Atkinson, J.W. & Feather, N.T. (1966). *A theory of achievement motivation*. New York: Wiley.

Atkinson, R.C. & Shiffrin, R.M. (1968). Human memory: A proposed system and its control processes. In K.W. Spence & J.T. Spence (Eds.), *The psychology of learning and motivation: Advances in research and theory* (Vol.2). New York: Academic Press.

Austin, J.L. (1962). *How to do things with words*. Oxford: Oxford University Press.

Averbach, I. & Coriell, A.S. (1961). Short-term memory in vision. *Bell System Technical Journal, 40,* 309-328.

Averill, J.R. (1976). Emotion and anxiety: Sociocultural, biological and psychological determinants. In M. Zuckerman & C.O. Spielberger (Eds.), *Emotion and anxiety: New concepts, methods and*

applications (pp.87-130). Hillsdale, NJ: Erlbaum.

Averill, J.R. (1982). *Anger and aggression: an essay on emotion.* New York: Springer.

Averill, J.R. (1988). Disorders of emotion. *Journal of Social and Clinical Psychology, 6,* 247-268.

Averill, R. (1969). Autonomic response patterns during sadness and mirth. *Psychophysiology, 5,* 399-414.

Ayllon, T. & Azrin, N.H. (1968). *The token economy: A motivational system for theory, and rehabilitation.* New York: Appleton-Century-Crofts.

Ayllon, T. & Azrin, N.H. (1965). The measurement and reinforcement of behavior of psychotics. *Journal of Experimental Analysis of Behavior, 8,* 357-383.

Ayllon, T. & Michael, J. (1959). The psychiatric nurse as a behavioral engineer. *Journal of the Experimental Analysis of Behavior, 2,* 323-334.

Azrin, N.H. & Fox, R.M. (1976). *Toilet training in less than a day* New York: Pocket Books.

Azrin, N.H. & Holz, W.C. (1966). Punishment. In N.K. Honig *(Ed.), Operant behavior* (pp.380-447). New York: Appleton Century-Crofts.

B

Bachman, J.G., O'Malley, P.M. & Johnston, J. (1979). *Adolescence to adulthood: Change and stability in the lives of young men.* Ann Arbor, MI: Institute for Social Research.

Backus, J. & Backus, H. (1984). *Backus strikes back.* Briarcliff Manor: Stein and Day.

Baddeley, A.D. (1982). *Your memory, a user's guide.* New York: Macmillan.

Baddeley, A.D. (1986). *Working memory.* New York: Oxford University Press.

Baddeley, A.D. (1992). What is autobiographical memory? In M.A. Conway, D.C. Rubin, H. Spinnler & W.A. Wagenaar (Eds.), *Theoretical perspectives on autobiographical memory* (pp.13-29). Dordrecht: Kluwer Academic Publishers.

Baddeley, A.D. & Hitch, G. (1974). Working memory. In G.H. Bower (Ed.), *The psychology of learning and motivation* (Vol.8). New York: Academic Press.

Baddeley, A. & Salame, P. (1986). The unattended speech effect: Perception or memory? *Journal of Experimental Psychology: Learning, Memory & Cognition,* 12, 525-529.

Baer, J.S., Kiviahan, D.R., Fromme, K. & Mariatt, G.A. (1991). Secondary prevention of alcohol abuse with college student populations: A skills-training approach. In N. Heather, W.R. Miller & J. Greeley (Eds.), *Self control and the addictive behaviors* (pp.339-356). Sydney: Maxwell MacMillan.

Bahrick, H.P. (1984). Semantic memory content in permastore: Fifty years of memory for Spanish learned in school. *Journal of Experimental Psychology: General, 13,* 1-29.

Bahrick, H.P., Bahrick, P.O. & Wittlinger, R.P. (1975). Fifty years of memory for names and faces: A cross-sectional approach. *Journal of Experimental Psychology: General,* 104, 54-75.

Baillargeon, R. (1986). Representing the existence and the location of hidden objects: Object permanence in 6- and 8-month-old infants. *Cognition, 23,* 21-42.

Baillargeon, R. (1990). In *Discovering Psychology,* Program 5 [PB video series]. Washington, DC: Annenberg/CPB Project.

Baillargeon, R., Spelke, E.S. & Wasseman, S. (1985). Object permanence in five-month-old infants. *Cognition, 20,* 191-208.

Baker, A.A. & Thorpe, J.G. (1957). Placebo response. AMA *Archives of Neurology and Psilchiatrv, 78,* 57-60.

Balakrishnan, S. (1991). Psychology of democracy. *The California Psychologist, 24,* pp. 16, 21.

Baldwin, A.L. & Baldwin, C.P. (1973). Study of mother-child interaction. *American Scientist, 61,* 714-721.

Bales, R.F. (1958). Task roles and social roles in problem-solving groups. In E.E. Maccoby, T.M. Newcomb & E.L. Hartley *(Eds.), Readings in social psychology* (3rd ed.). New York: Holt, Rinehart & Winston.

Bales, R.F. (1970). *Personality and interpersonal behaviour.* New York: Holt, Rinehart & Winston.

Balsam, P.D. & Tomie, A. (Eds.). (1985). *Context and learning.* Hillsdale, NJ: Eribaum.

Baltes, M.M. (1986, November). *Selective optimization with compensation: The dynamics between independence and dependence.* Paper presented at the meeting of the Gerontological Society of America, Chicago.

Baltes, P.B. (1987). Theoretical propositions on life-span developmental psychology: On the dynamics between growth and decline. *Developmental Psychology,* 23, 611-626.

Baltes, P.B. (1990, November). *Toward a psychology of wisdom.* Invited address presented at the annual convention of the Gerontological Society of America, Boston, MA.

Baltes, P.B., Reese, H.W. & Lipsitt, L.P. (1980). Life-span developmental psychology. In M. Rosenzweig & L. Porter (Eds.), *Annual review of psychology.* Palo Alto, CA: Annual Reviews Press.

Banaji, M.R. & Crowder, R.G. (1989). The bankruptcy of everyday memory. *American Psychologist, 44,* 1185-1193.

Bancroft, J. (1989). *Human sexuality and its problems.* Edinburgh: Churchill Livingstone.

Bandura, A. (1965). Influence of models' reinforcement contingencies on the acquisition of imitative responses. *Journal of Personality and Social Psychology, 1,* 589-595.

Bandura, A. (1970). Modeling therapy. In W.S. Sahakian (Ed.), *Psychopathology today: Experimentation, theory and research.* Itasca, IL: Peacock.

Bandura, A. (1973). Aggression: A social learning analysis. Englewood Cliffs, NJ: Prentice-Hall.

Bandura, A. (1977a). *Social learning theory.* Englewood Cliffs, NJ: Prentice-Hall.

Bandura, A. (1977b). Self-efficacy. *Psychological Review, 84,* 191-215.

Bandura, A. (1981b). Self-referent thought: A developmental analysis of self-efficacy. In J.H. Flavell & L. Ross (Eds.), *Social cognitive development: Frontiers and possible futures.* Cambridge: Cambridge University Press.

Bandura, A. (1981a). In search of pure unidirectional determinants. *Behavior Therapy, 12,* 30-40.

Bandura, A. (1982a). The psychology of chance encounters and life paths. *American Psychologist, 37,* 747-755.

Bandura, A. (1982b). Self-efficacy mechanism in human agency. *American Psychologist, 37,* 122-147.

Bandura, A. (1986). *Social foundations of thought and action: A social cognitive theory.* Englewood Cliffs, NJ: Prentice-Hall.

Bandura, A. (1988) Self-regulation of motivation and action through goal systems. In V. Hamilton, G.H. Bower & N.H. Frijda (Eds.), *Cognition perspectives on emotion and motivaton* (pp.37-61). Dordrecht: Kluwer Academic Publishers.

Bandura, A. (1990). Mechanisms of moral disengagement. In W. Reich (Ed.), *Origins of terrorism: Psychologies, ideologies, theologies, states of mind* (pp.161-191). New York: Cambridge University Press.

Bandura, A., Adams, N.E., Hardy, A.B. & Howells, G.N. (1980). Tests of the generality of self-efficacy theory. *Cognitive Therapy and Research, 4,* 39-66.

Bandura, A. & Mischel, W. (1965). Modification of self-imposed delay of reward through exposure to live and symbolic models. *Journal of Personality, and Social Psychology, 2,* 698-705.

Bandura, A., Ross, D. & Ross, S.A. (1963). Imitation of film mediated aggressive models. *Journal of Abnormal and Social Psychology, 66,* 3-11.

Bandura, A., Underwood, B. & Fromson, M.E. (1975). Disinhibition of aggression through diffusion of responsibility and dehumanization of victims. *Journal of Research in Personality, 9,* 253-269.

Bane, M.J. & Ellwood, D.T. (1989). One fifth of the nation's children: Why are they poor? *Science, 245.* 1047-1053.

Banks, W.P. & Krajicek, D. (1991). Perception. *Annual Review of Psychology,* 42, 305-331.

Banks, M.S. & Rennet, P.J. (1988). Optical and photoreceptor immaturities limit the spatial and chromatic vision of human neonates. *Journal of the Optical Society of America, 5,* 2059-2079.

Banuazizi, A. & Movahedi, S. (1975), Interpersonal dynamics in a simulated prison: A methodological analysis. *American Psychologist, 30,* 152-160.

Banyai, E.I. & Hilgard, E.R. (1976).Comparison of active-alert hypnotic induction with traditional relaxation induction. *Journal of Abnormal Psychology, 85,* 218-224

Bar-Tal, D. & Saxe, L. (Eds.). (1978). *Social psychology of education: Theory and research.* Washington, DC: Hemisphere.

Barash, D.P. (1982). *Sociobiology and behaviour, 2nd Ed.* New York: Elsevier.

Barber, T.X. (1969). *Hypnosis: A scientific approach.* New York: Psychological Dimensions.

Barber, T.X. (1976). *Hypnosis: A scientific approach*. New York: Psychological Dimensions.

Barchas, J.D., Ciaranello, R.D., Kessler, S. & Hamburg, D.A. (1975). Genetic aspects of catecholamine synthesis. In R.R.F. Eve, D. Rosenthal, & H. Brill (Eds.), *Genetic research in psychiatry* (pp. 27-62). Baltimore: Johns Hopkins University Press.

Baribeau-Braun, J., Dicton, T.W. & Gosselin, J.Y. (1983). Schizophrenia: A neurophysiological evaluation of abnormal information processing. *Science, 219,* 874-876.

Barinaga, M. (1989). Can psychotherapy delay cancer deaths? Science, 46, 246, 249.

Barinaga, M. (1989). Manic depression gene put in limbo. *Science,* 246, 886-887.

Barinaga, M. (1990). Technical advances power neuroscience. *Science, 250,* 908-909.

Barker, L.M., Best, M.R. & Domjan, M. (Eds.). (1978). *Learning mechanisms in food selection*. Houston: Baylor University Press.

Barland, G. & Raskin, D.C. (1976). *Validity, and reliability of polygraph examinations of criminal suspects* (Report No. 76-11 Contract 75-NI-99-000 1). Washington, DC: U.S. Department of Justice.

Barlow, H.B., Hill, R.M. & Levick, W.R. (1964). Retinal ganglion cells responding selectively to direction and speed of image motion in the rabbit. *Journal of Physiology* (London), 173, 377-407.

Barlow, D.H. (1988). *Anxiety and its disorders: The nature and treatment of anxiety and panic*. New York: Guilford.

Barlow, D.H., Vermilyea, J., Blanchard, E.B., Vermilyea, B.B., DiNardo, P.A. & Cerny, J.A. (1985). The phenomenon of panic. *Journal of Abnormal Psychology, 94,* 320-328.

Barnes, D.M. (1988). Schizophrenia genetics a mixed bag. *Science, 242,* 1009.

Barnes, D. (1987). Defect in Alzheimer's is on Chromosome 21. *Science, 235,* 846-847.

Barnes, D.M. (1987). Biological issues in schizophrenia. *Science, 235,* 430-433.

Barnett, S.A. (1967). Attack and defense in animal societies. In C.D. Clemente & D.B. Lindsley (Eds.), *Aggression* and *defense*. Los Angeles: University of California Press.

Baron, A., Perone, M. & Galizio, M. (1991, in press). Analyzing the reinforcement process at the human level: Can application and behavioristic interpretation replace laboratory research? The *Behavior Analyst, 14.*

Baron, L. & Straus, M.A. (1989). *Four theories of rape in American society: A state-level analysis*. New Haven, CT: Yale University Press.

Barrios, B. A. & Shigetomi, C.C. (1980). Coping skills training: Potential for prevention of fears and anxieties. *Behavior Therapy, 11,* 431-439.

Barron, F. & Harrington, D.M. (1981). Creativity, intelligence and personality. *Annual Review of Psychology, 32,* 439-476.

Barron, F.X. (1963). *Creativity and psychological growth: Origins of personal vitality and creative freedom*. Princeton, NJ: Van Nostrand.

Barrow, H.G. & Tenenbaum, J.M. (1986). Computational Approaches to Vision. In K. Boff, L. Kaufman & J. Thomas *(Eds.), Handbook of perception and human performance* (Vol.21 pp.38-70). New York: Wiley.

Barthe, D.G. & Hammen, C.L. (1981). The attributional model of depression: A naturalistic extension. *Personality & Social Psychology, Bulletin, 7*(1), 53-59.

Bartlett, F.C. (1932). *Remembering: A study in experimental and social psychology*. Cambridge: Cambridge University Press.

Barton, S.B. & Sanford, A.J. (1993). A case study of pragonatic anomaly detection: Relevance driven cohesion patterns. *Memory and Cognition, 21,* 477-487.

Bartoshuk, L. (1990, August/September). Psychophysiological insights on taste. *Science Agenda, 12-13.*

Basseches, M. (1984). *Dialectical thinking and adult development*. Norwood, NJ: Ablex.

Bateson, G., Jackson, D.D., Haley, J. & Weakland, J.H. (1956). Toward a theory of schizophrenia. *Behavioral Science, 1,* 251-264.

Baum, A. (1990). Stress, intrusive imagery and chronic distress. *Health Psychology, 9,* 653-675.

Baum, A., Calesnick, L.E., Davis, G.E. & Gatchel, R.J. (1982). Individual differences in coping with crowding: Stimulus screening and social overload. *Journal of Personality and Social Psychology, 43,* 821-830.

Baum, A. & Valins, S. (1979). Architectural mediation of residential density and control: Crowding and the regulation of social contact. In L. Berkowitz (Ed.), *Advances in experimental social psychology* (Vol. 12). New York: Academic Press.

Baumann, L.J. & Leventhal, H. (1985). I can tell when my blood pressure is up, can't I? *Health Psychology,* 4, 203-218.

Baumrind, D. (1967). Child care practices anteceding three pattems of preschool behavior. *Genetic Psychology Monographs, 75,* 43-88.

Baumrind, D. (1973). The development of instrumental competence through socialization. In A. Pick (Ed.), *Minnesota Symposium in Child Development* (Vol.7). Minneapolis: University of Minnesota Press, 1973.

Baumrind, D. (1985). Research using intentional deception: Ethical issues revisited. *American Psychologist, 40,* 165-174.

Baumrind, D. (1986). Sex differences in moral reasoning: Response to Walker's 1984 conclusion that there are none. *Child Development, 57,* 511-521.

Bavelas, A., Hastorf, A.H., Gross, A.E. & Kite, W.R. (1965). Experiments on the alteration of group structure. *Journal of Experimental and Social Psychology, 1,* 55-70.

Bayer, R. (1981). *Homosexuality and American psychiatry*. New York: Basic Books.

Bayés, R. (1990). The contribution of behavioural medicine to the research and prevention of AIDS. In D.E. Blackman & H. Lejeune (Eds.), *Behaviour analysis in theory and practice: Contributions and controversies*. Hove & London: Lawrence Erlbaum Associates.

Bayley, N. (1969). *Bayley Scales of Infant Development*. New York: The Psychological Corporation.

Baylor, D. (1987). Photoreceptor signals and vision. *Investigative Opthalmology and Visual Science, 28,* 34-49.

Bayne, R. (1994). The 'Big Five' versus the Myers-Briggs. *The Psychologist incorporating the Bulletin of the British Psychological Society,* 7, 1, 14-16.

Bayne, R. (1995). *The Myers-Briggs type indicator: A critical review and practical guide*. London: Chapman & Hall.

Beardslee, W.R. & Mack, J.E. (1983). Adolescents and the threat of nuclear war: The evolution of a perspective. *Yale Journal of Biological Medicine,* 56(2), 79-91.

Beauvoir, S. de (1949). *Le deuxième sexe*. Paris: Gallimard.

Bechtel, W. & Abrahamsen, A. (1991). *Connectionism and the mind: An introduction to parallel processing in networks*. Oxford: Blackwell.

Beck, A.T. (1967). *Depression: Clinical, experimental and theoretical aspects*. New York: Harper & Row.

Beck, A.T. (1976). *Cognitive therapy and emotional disorder*. New York: International Universities Press.

Beck, A.T. (1983). Cognitive theory of depression: New perspectives. In P.J. Clayton & J.E. Barrett (Eds.), *Treatment of depression: Old controversies and new approaches* (pp.265-290). New York: Raven Press.

Beck, A.T. (1985). Cognitive therapy. In R.I. Kaplan & J. Sandock (Eds.), *Comprehensive textbook of psychiatry* (4th ed.). Baltimore: Williams & Wilkins.

Beck, A.T. (1988). Cognitive approaches to panic disorders: Theory and therapy. In S. Rachman & J.D. Maser (Eds.), *Panic: Psychological perspectives*. New York: Guilford Press.

Beck, A.T. & Emery, G. (1985). *Anxiety disorderss and phobias: A cognitive perspective*. New York: Basic Books.

Beck, A.T., Rush, A.J., Shaw, B.F. & Emery, G. (1979). Cognitive therapy of depression. New York: Guilford Press.

Beck, J. (1966). Effects of orientation and of shape similarity on perceptual grouping. *Perception and Psychophysics, 1,* 300-302.

Beck, J. (1972). Similarity groupings and peripheral discriminability under uncertainty. *American Journal of Psychology, 85,* 1-20.

Beck, J. (1982). *Organization and representation in perception*. Hillsdale, NJ: Erlbaum

Beck, M. & Crowley, G. (1990, March 26). Beyond lobotomies: Psychosurgery is safer – but still a rarity. *Newsweek*. p.44.

Becker, G. (1978). *The mad genius controversy: A study in the sociology of deviance*. Beverly Hills, CA: Sage.

Becker, M.H. (1974). The health belief model and sick role behavior. *Health Education Monographs, 2,* 409-419

Beech, R. (1985). *Staying together: A practical way to make your relationship succeed and grow*. Chichester: Wiley.

Beecher, H.K. (1956). Relationship of significance of wound to the pain experienced. *Journal of the American Medical Association,* 161, 1609-1613.

Beecher, H.K. (1959). *Measurement of subjective responses*. New York: Oxford University Press.

Beecher, E. (1972). *Licit and illicit drugs*. Boston: Little, Brown.

Begg, I. & Paivio, A.V. (1969). Concreteness and imagery in sentence meaning. *Journal of Verbal Learning and Behavior, 8,* 821-827.

Bekerian, D.A. & Bowers, J.M. (1983). Eyewitness testimony: Were we misled? *Journal of experimental Psychology: Learning, Memory and Cognition, 9,* 139-145.

Bell, A.P., Weinberg, M.S. & Hammersmith, S.K. (1981). *Sexual preference.* Bloomington: Indiana University Press.

Bell, R.R. (1974). Female sexual satisfaction as related to levels of education. In L. Gross (Ed.), *Sexual behavior* (pp. 3-11). Flushing, NY: Spectrum.

Belk, R.W. (1988). Possessions and the extended self. *Journal of Consumer Research, 15,* 139-168.

Bell, L.R. (1982). Clinical ecology. Bolinas, CA: Common Knowledge Press.

Bell, L.V. (1980). *Treating the mentally ill: From colonial times to the present.* New York: Praeger.

Bellak, L. (Ed.). (1979). *Disorders of the schizophrenic syndrome.* New York: Basic Books.

Belloc, N.B. (1973). Relationship of health practices and mortality. *Preventive Medicine, 2,* 67-8 1.

Belloc, N.B. & Breslow, L. (1972). Relationship of physical health status and family practices. *Preventive Medicine, 1,* 409-42 1.

Bellugi, U., Klima, E.S. & Siple, P.A. (1975). Remembering in signs. *Cognition, 3,* 93-125.

Bem, D.J. (1970). Beliefs, attitudes and human affairs. Belmont, CA: Brooks/Cole.

Bem, D.J. (1972). Self-perception theory. In L. Berkowitz (Ed.), *Advances in experimental social psychology* (Vol.6, pp.1-62). New York: Academic Press.

Bem, D.J. & Allen, A. (1974). On predicting some of the people some of the time: The search for cross-situational consistencies in behavior. *Psychological Review, 81(6),* 506-520.

Bem, D.J. & Honorton, C. (1994). Does psi exist? Replicable evidence for an anomalous process of information transfer. *Psychological Bulletin, 115,* 4-18.

Bem, S.L. (1981a). *The Bem sex role inventory: Professional manual.* Palo Alto, CA: Consulting Psychology Press.

Bem, S.L. (1981b). Gender schema theory: A cognitive account of sex-typing. *Psychological Review, 88,* 354-364.

Bem, S.L. (1984). Androgyny and gender schema theory: A conceptual and empirical integration. In T.B. Sonderegger (Ed.), Nebraska Symposium on Motivation, 1984: *The psychology of gender.* Lincoln, NE: University of Nebraska Press.

Bem, S.L. (1993). *The lenses of gender.* New Haven, CT: Yale University Press.

Benbow, C.P. (1988). Sex differences in mathematical reasoning ability in intellectually talented preadolescents. *Behavioral and Brain Sciences, 11,* 169-232.

Benbow, C.P. & Stanley, J.C. (1987). Sex differences in mathematical reasoning ability. *Science, 222,* 1029-1031.

Benedict, R. (1959). *Patterns of culture.* Boston: Houghton Mifflin.

Beninger, J.R. (1986). *The control revolution: Technological and economic origins of the information society.* Cambridge, MA: Harvard University Press.

Bennett, H.L. (1983). Remembering drink orders: The memory skills of cocktail waitresses. *Human Learning, 2.* 157-169.

Bennett, P. (1993). *Counselling for Heart Disease.* Leicester, BPS Books. **Benson, H.** (1975). *The relaxation response.* New York: Morrow,

Berger, P. & Luckmann, T. (1966). *The social construction of reality: A treatise in the sociology of knowledge.* London: Penguin.

Berglas, S. & Jones, E.E. (1978). Drug choice as a self-handicapping strategy in response to noncontingent success. *Journal of Personality and Social Psychology, 36,* 405-417.

Berk, L.S., Ian, S.A., Fry, W.F., Napier, B.J., Lee, J.W., Hubbard, R.W., Lewis, J.E., & Eby, W.C. (1989). Neuroendocrine and stress hormone changes during mirthful laughter. *American Journal of Medical Science, 298,* 390-396.

Berkman, L.F. & Syme, S.L. (1979). Social networks, host resistance, and mortality: A nine-year follow-up study of Alameda County residents. *American Journal of Epidemiology,* 109,186-204.

Berkowitz, L. (1982). Aversive conditions as stimuli to aggression. *Advances in Experimental Social Psychology,* 15, 249-288.

Berkowitz, L. (1988). Introduction to social psychological studies of the self: Perspectives and programs. in L. Berkowitz (Ed.), *Advances in experimental social psychology,* (Vol.21, pp.57-95). New York: Academic Press.

Berlyne, D.E. (1960). *Conflict, arousal and curiosity.* New York: McGraw-Hill.

Berlyne, D.E. (1967). Reinforcement and arousal. In O. Levine (Ed.), *Nebraska Symposium on Motivation,* 1966. Lincoln: University of Nebraska Press.

Bermond, B., Nieuwenhuyse, B., Fasotti, L. & Schuerman, J. (1991). Spinal cord lesions, peripheral feedback, and intensities of emotional feelings. *Cognition and Emotion, 5,* 201-220.

Bernard, C. (1878). *La science experimentale.* Paris: J. B. Baille'ere & Fils.

Bernard, L.L. (1924). *Instinct.* New York: Holt, Rinehart & Winston.

Berndt, T.J. (1979). Developmental changes in conformity to peers and parents. *Developmental Psychology, 15,* 608-616.

Bernstein, I.L. (1988). What does learning have to do with weight loss and cancer? *Proceedings of the Science and Public Policy Seminar of the Federation of Behavioral, Psychological and Cognitive Sciences.* Washington, DC.

Bernstein, I.L. (1990). Salt preference and development. *Developmental Psychology, 26,* 552-554.

Bernstein, P.A. & Quinna, K. (Eds.). (1988). *Teaching a psychology of people: Resources for gender and sociocultural awareness.* Washington, DC: American Psychological Association.

Berry, J.W. (1967). Independence and conformity in subsistence level societies. *Journal of Personality and Social Psychology, 7,* 415-418.

Berscheid, E., & Walster, E. H. (1978). Interpersonal attraction (2nd ed.). Reading, MA: Addison-Wesley.

Berwick, R.C. & Weinberg, A.S. (1983). The role of grammars in models of language use. *Cognition, 13,* 1-61.

Bexton, W.H., Heron, W. & Scott, T.H. (1954). Effects of decreased variation in the sensory environment. *Canadian Journal of Psychology, 8,* 70-76.

Biaggio, M.K. & Bittner, E. (1990). Psychology and optometry: Interaction and collaboration. *American Psychologist, 45,* 1313-1315.

Biederman, I. (1985). Recognition by components: A theory of object recognition. *Computer Vision Graphics and Image Processing, 32,* 29-73.

Biederman, I. (1987). Recognition by components. *Psychological Review, 94,* 173-211.

Biederman, I. (1989). Higher-level vision. In D.N. Osherson, H.Sasnik, S. Kosslyn, K. Hollerbach, E. Smith & N. Block (Eds.), *An invitation to cognitive science.* Cambridge, MA: MIT Press.

Bielski, R.J. & Friedel, R.O. (1977). Subtypes of depression, diagnosis and medical management. *Western Journal of Medicine, 126,* 347-352.

Bifulco, A., Brown, G.W. & Harris, T.O. (1987). Childhood loss of parent lack of adequate parental care and adult depression: a replication, *Journal of Affective Disorders, 12,* 115-128.

Bifulco, A., Brown, G.W. & Harris, T.O. (1994). Childhood experience of care and abuse (CECA): A retrospective interview measure. *Child Psychology & Psychiatry, 35,* 1419-1435.

Bigelow, H.J. (1850). Dr. Harlow's case of recovery from the passage of an iron bar through the head. *American Journal of Medical* Science, 20, 13-22.

Billig, M. (1985). Prejudice, categorisation and particularisation: from a perceptual to a rhetorical approach. *European Journal of Social Psychology, 15,* 79-103.

Billings, A.G. & Moos, R.H. (1982). Family environments andadaptation: A clinically applicable typology. *American Journal of Family Therapy,* 10, 26-38.

Binet, A. (1894). *Psychologie des grandes calculateurs et joueurs d'echecs.* Paris: Hachette.

Binet, A. (1911). *Les idées modernes sur les enfants.* Paris: Flammarion.

Binkley, S. (1979). A timekeeping enzyme in the pineal gland. *Scientific American, 204(4),* 66-7 1.

Birbaumer, N. & Kimmel, H. (Eds.) (1979). *Biofeedback and selfregulation.* Hillsdale, NJ: Erlbaum.

Bird, O.A. (1974). *Humanities.* Encyclopaedia Brittanica (Macropaedia), Vol. 8, 1179-1183.

Bitterinan, M.E. (1975). The comparative analysis of Teaming. *Science, 188,* 699-709.

Blacher, R.S. (1987). General surgery and anesthesia: the emotional experience. In R.S. Blacher (Ed.), *The psychological experience of surgery* (pp.9-14). New York: Wiley.

Black, I.B., Adler, J.E., Dreyfus, C.F., Friedman, W.F.,LaGamma, E.F. & Blackman, D. (1974). *Operant conditioning: An experimental analysis of behaviour.* London: Methuen.

Black, I.B., Adler, J.E., Dreyfus, C.F., Friedman, W.F.,

LaGamma, E.F., & Roach, A.H. (1987). Biochemistry of information storage in the nervous system. *Science, 236,* 1263-1268.

Blackman, D. (1974). *Operant conditioning: An experimental analysis of behaviour.* London: Methuen.

Blackman, D. (1980). Images of man in contemporary behaviourism. In A.J. Chapman & D.M. Jones (Eds.), *Models of man.* Leicester: British Psychological Society.

Blackman, D. (1991). B.F. Skinner and G.H. Mead: On biological science and social science. *Journal of the Experimental Analysis of Behavior, 55,* 251-265.

Blake, R. & Hirsch, H.V.B. (1975). Deficits in binocular depth perception in cats after altering monocular deprivation. Science, 190, 1114-1116.

Blaney, P.H. (1986). Affect and memory: A review. *Psychological Bulletin, 99,* 299-246.

Blank, A.A., Jr. (1982). Stresses of war: The example of Vietnam. In L. Goldberger & S. Breznitz (Eds.), *Handbook of stress* (pp. 631-643). New York: Free Press/Macmillan.

Blasi, A. (1980). Bridging moral cognition and moral action: a critical review of the literature. *Psychological Bulletin, 88,* 1-45.

Blass, E.M. (1990). Suckling: Determinants, changes, mechanisms, and lasting impressions. *Developmental Psychology, 26,* 520-533.

Blass, E.M. & Teicher, M. H. (1980). Suckling. *Science, 210,* 15-22.

Bleuler, M. (1978). The long-term course of schizophrenic psychoses. In L.C. Wynne, R.L. Cromwell & S. Mattysse (Eds.), *The nature of schizophrenia: New approaches to research and treatment* (pp. 631-636). New York: Wiley.

Blight, J.G. (1987). Toward a policy-relevant psychology of avoiding nuclear war: Lessons for psychologists from the Cuban missile crisis. *American Psychologist, 42,* 12-19.

Bloch, S. & Reddaway, P. (1977). *Psychiatric terror.- How Soviet psychiatry is used to suppress dissent.* New York: Basic Books.

Block, A. (1980). An investigation of the response of the spouse to chronic pain behavior. *Pain, 9,* 243-252.

Block, J. (1990). In *Discovering Psychology,* Program 17 (PBS video series). Washington, DC: AnnenbergicPB Program.

Blocker, T.J. & Eckberg, D.L. Environmental issues as women's issues: General concerns and local hazards. *Social Science Quarterly, 70,* 586-593.

Blodgett, R. (1986, May). Lost in the stars: Psychics strike out (again). *People Expression, 32-35.*

Blos, P. (1967). The second individuation process of adolescence. *Psychoanalytic Study of the Child, 22,* 162-188.

Bly, R. (1990). *Iron John.* New York: Addison-Wesley.

Bohannon, J.N. (1988). Flashbulb memories of the space shuttle disaster: A tale of two theories. *Cognition, 29(2),* 179-196.

Bohman, M., Cloninger, R., Sigvardson, S. & von-Knorring, A.L. (1987). The genetics of alcoholisms and related disorders. *Journal of Psychiatric Research, 21,* 447-452.

Bolger, N., DeLongis, A., Kessler, R.C. & Schilling, E.A. (1989). Effects of daily stress on negative mood. *Journal of Personality and Social Psychology, 57,* 808-818.

Bolinger, D.L. & Gerstman, L.J. (1957). Disjuncture as a cue to constructs. *Word, 13,* 246-255.

Bolles, R.C. & Faneslow, M.S. (1982). Endorphins and behavior. *Annual Review of Psychology, 33,* 87-101.

Bond, C.F. & Brockett, D.R. (1987). A social context-personality index theory of memory for acquaintances. *Journal of personality and social psychology, 52,* 1110-1121.

Bongiovanni, A. (1977). *A review of research on the effects of punishment in the schools.* Paper presented at the Conference on Child Abuse, Children's Hospital National Medical Center, Washington, DC.

Bootzin, R.R. (1975). *Behavior modification and therapy: An introduction.* Cambridge, MA: Winthrop.

Bootzin, R.R. & Nicasio, P.M. (1978). Behavioral treatments for insomnia. In M. Hersen, R. Eisler & P. Miller (Eds.), *Progress in behavior modification.* New York: Academic Press.

Boring, E.G. (1950). *A history of experimental psychology (2nd ed.).* New York: Appleton-Century-Crofts.

Boring, E.G., Langfeld, H.S. & Weld, H.P. (1948). *Foundations of Psychology.* New York: Wiley.

Borke, H. (1975). Piaget's mountains revisited: Changes in the egocentric landscape. *Developmental Psychology, 11,* 240-243.

Borkovec, T.D. (1982). Insomnia. *Journal of Consulting and Clinical Psychology, 50,* 880-985.

Bornstein, P.A. & Quinna, K. (Eds.). *Teaching a psychology of people: Resources for gender and sociocultural awareness.* Washington, DC: American Psychological Association.

Borod, C., Koff, E., Lorch, M.P., Nicholas, M. & Welkowitz, J. (1988). Emotional and non-emotional facial behavior in patients with unilateral brain damage. *Journal of Neurological and Neurosurgical Psychiatry, 5,* 826-832.

Boski, P. (1983). A study of person perception in Nigeria: ethnicity and self versus other attributions for achievement-related outcomes. *Journal of Cross-Cultural Psychology,* 14, 85-108.

Botvin, G.J. & Eng, A. (1982). The efficacy of a multicomponent approach to the prevention of cigarette smoking. *Preventive Medicine, 11,* 199-211.

Botwinick, J. (1977). Intellectual abilities. In J.E. Birren & K.W. Schaie (Eds.), *Handbook of the psychology of aging* (pp 580-605). New York: Van Nostrand Reingold.

Bouchard, T.J., Jr., Lykken, D.T., McGue, M., Segal, N.L., & Tellegen, A. (1990). Sources of human psychological differences: The Minnesota study of twins reared apart. Science, 250, 223-228.

Bouchard, T.J., Jr. & McGue, M. (1981). Familial studies of intelligence: A review. *Science, 2 12,* 1055-1059.

Bouchard, T.J., Jr. & McGue, M. (1990). Genetic and environmental influences on adult personality: An analysis of adopted twins reared apart. *Journal of Personality, 58,* 263-295.

Bourguignon, E. (1973). Introduction: A framework for the comparative study of altered states of consciousness. In E. Bourguignon (Ed.), *Religion, altered states of consciousness and social change.* Columbus: Ohio State University Press.

Bourguignon, E. (1979). Psychological anthropology: *An introduction to human nature and cultural differences.* New York: Holt, Rinehart and Winston.

Bower, G.H. (1972). A selective review of organizational factors in memory. In E.Tulving & W.Donaldson (Eds.), *Organization of memory.* New York: Academic Press.

Bower, G.H. (1981). Mood and memory. *American Psychologist, 36,* 129-148.

Bower, G.H. (1990). In *Discovering Psychology,* Program 9 [PBSvideo series]. Washington, DC: Annenberg/CPB Project.

Bower, G.H. (1991). Mood congruity of social judgements. In J.P. Forgas (Ed.), *Emotion and social judgement* (pp 31-53). Oxford: Pergammon Press.

Bower, G.H. & Hilgard, E.R. (1981). *Theories of learning* (5th ed.). Englewood Cliffs, NJ: Prentice-Hall.

Bower, S.A. & Bower, G.H. (1991). *Asserting yourself: A practical guide for positive change.* Reading, MA: Addison Wesley. (Original work published 1976)

Bowers, K.S. (1976). *Hypnosis for the seriously curious.* New York: Norton.

Bowers, M.B., Jr. (1980). Biochemical processes in schizophrenia: An update. In S.J. Keith & L.R. Mosher (Eds.), *Special Report: Schizophrenia,* 1980. Washington, DC: U.S. Government Printing Office.

Bowlby, J. (1969). *Attachment and loss, Vol.1. Attachment.* New York: Basic Books.

Bowlby, J. (1973). *Attachment and loss: Vol.2. Separation, anxiety and anger.* London: Hogarth.

Boyd, J.H. & Weissman, M.M. (1981). Epidemiology of affective disorders: A reexamination and future directions. *Archives of General Ps.Vchiatry, 38,* 1039-1046.

Boyle, M. (1990). *Schizophrenia: A scientific delusion?* London: Routledge.

Braginsky, B., Braginsky, D. & Ring, K. (1969). *Methods of madness: The mental hospital as a last resort.* New York: Holt, Rinehart & Winston.

Braine, M.D.S. (1976). Children's first word combinations. *Monographs of the Society for Research in Child Development,* 41 (Serial No. 164).

Brandt, L.W. (1961). Some notes on English freudian terminology. *The Journal of the American Psychoanalytic Association, 9,* 337-338.

Bransford, J.D. & Franks, J.J. (1971). The abstraction of linguistic ideas. *Cognitive Psychology, 2,* 331-350.

Bransford, J.D. & Johnson, M.K. (1972). Contextual prerequisites for understanding: Some investigations of comprehension and recall. *Journal of Verbal Learning and Verbal Behavior,* 11, 17-21.

Bransford, J.D. & Johnson, M.K. (1973). Considerations of some problems of comprehension. In W.G. Chase (Ed.), *Visual information processing.* New York: Academic Press.

Bransford, J., Sherwood, R., Vye, N. & Reiser, J. (1986). Teaching, thinking and problem solving. *American Psychologist,* 41, 1078-1089.

Brauer, E. Mackeprang, B. & Bentzon, M. (1978). Prognosis of survival in a geriatric population. *Scandinavian Journal of Social Medicine, 6,* 17-24.

Breakey, W.R. & Fischer, P.J. (1990). Homelessness: The extent of the problem. *Journal of Social Issues, 46,* 31-47.

Breggin, P.R. (1979). Electroshock: Its brain disabling effects. New York: Springer.

Bregman, A.S. (1981). Asking the 'what for' question in auditory perception. In M. Kobovy & J. Pomerantz (Eds.), *Perceptual organization* (pp. 99-118). Hillsdale, NJ: Erlbaum.

Breland, K. & Breland, M. (1951). A field of applied animal psychology. *American Psychologist, 6,* 202-204.

Breland, K. & Breland, M. (1961). A misbehavior of organisms. *American Psychologist, 16,* 681-684.

Brenner, M.H. (1976). *Estimating the social costs of national economic policy: Implications for mental and physical health and criminal violence.* Report prepared for the Joint Economic Committee of Congress, Washington, DC: U.S. Government Printing Office.

Breo, D.L (1989). In treating the pathological gambler, MDs must overcome the attitude, 'why bother'? *Journal of the American Medical Association, 262,* 2599-2603.

Brett, J.F., Brief, A.P., Burke, M.J., George, J.M. & Webster, J. (1990). Negative affectivity and the reporting of stressful life events. *Health Psychology, 9,* 57-68.

Breuer, J. & Freud, S. (1955). Studies on hysteria. In J. Strachey (Ed. and Trans.), *The standard edition of the complete psychological works of Sigmund Freud* (Vol.2). London: Hogarth Press. (Original work published 1895)

Brewer, M.B. (1979). In-group bias in the minimal intergroup situation: A cognitive-motivational analysis. *Psychological Bulletin, 86,* 307-324.

Brewer, M.B. & Kramer, R.M. (1985). The psychology of intergroup attitudes and behaviour. *Annual Review of Psychology, 36,* 219-43.

Bridges, K.M.B. (1932). Emotional development in early infancy. *Child Development, 3,* 324-334.

Brim, O.G. & Kagan, J. (1980). *Constancy and change in human development.* Cambridge: Harvard University Press.

Brislin, R.W. (1981). *Cross-cultural encounters: Face-to-face encounters.* New York: Pergamon.

Broadbent, D.E. (1958). *Perception and communication.* London: Pergamon Press.

Broadbent, D.E. (1971) *Decision and stress.* New York: Academic Press.

Broadbent, D.E. & Gregory, M. (1967). Perception of emotionally toned words. *Nature, 215,* 581-584.

Brody, E.B. & Brody, N. (1976). *Intelligence: Nature, determinants, and consequences.* New York: Academic Press.

Brody, R.V. (1986). Pain management in terminal discase. *Focus: A Review of AIDS Research, 1,* 1-2.

Broman, S.H., Nichols, P.I. & Kennedy, W.A. (1975). *Preschool IQ: Prenatal and early developmental correlates.* Hillsdale, NJ: Erlbaum.

Bronfenbrenner, U. (1977). Toward an experimental ecology of human development. *American Psychologist, 32,* 513-531.

Broughton, R.S. (1991). *Parapsychology: the controversial science.* New York: Ballantine books.

Broverman, I.K., Vogel, S.R., Broverman, D.M., Clarkson, F.E. & Rosenkrantz, P.S. (1972). Sex-role stereotypes: A current appraisal. *Journal of Social Issues, 28*(2), 59-78.

Brown, A.L. & De Loache, J.L. (1978). Skills, plans and self regulation. In R.S. Siegler (Ed.), *Children's thinking: What develops?* (pp. 3-35). Hillsdale, NJ: Eribaum.

Brown, A.M. (1990). *Human universals.* Unpublished manuscript, University of California, Santa Barbara.

Brown, B. & Rosenbaum, L. (1983, May). *Stress effects on IQ.* Paper presented at the meeting of the American Association for the Advancement of Science, Detroit, Mi.

Brown, C.C. (Ed.). (1984). *The many facets of touch.* Skillman, NJ: Johnson & Johnson.

Brown, G.W., Andrews, B., Bifulco, A. & Veiel, H. (1990). Self-esteem and depression:1. Measurement issues and prediction of onset. *Social Psychiatry & Psychiatric Epidemiology, 25,* 200-209.

Brown, G.W. & Harris, T.O. (1978). *Social origins of depression: A study of psychiatric disorder in women.* London: Tavistock Publications.

Brown, G.W. & Harris, T.0. (Eds.). (1989). *Life events and illness.* New York: Guilford.

Brown, G.W. & Harris, T.O. (1989). Depression, In G.W. Brown & T.O. Harris (Eds.), *Life events and illness.* New York: Guilford.

Brown, G.W., Monck, E.M., Carstairs, G.M. & Wing, J.K. (1962). Influence of family life on the course of schizophrenic illness. *British Journal of Preventative Social Medicine, 16,* 55-68.

Brown, J.D. (1991). Staying fit and staying well: Physical fitness as a moderator of life stress. *Journal of Pervonality and Social Psychology, 60,* 555-56 1.

Brown, L. (Ed.). (1989). *State of the world 1989.* New York: Norton.

Brown, R. (1986). *Social psychology: The second edition.* New York: The Free Press.

Brown, R.W. & McNeil, D. (1966). The 'tip-of-the tongue' phenomenon. *Journal of Verbal Learning and Verbal Behavior, 5,* 325-337.

Brownell, K.D. (1982). Obesity: Understanding and treating a serious, prevalent, and refractory disorder. *Journal of Clinical and Consulting Psychology, 50,* 820-840.

Brownell, K.D., Marilatt, G.A., Lichtenstein, E. & Wilson, G.T. (1986). Understanding and preventing relapse. *American Psychologist, 41,* 765-782-

Bruce, C., Desimone, R. & Gross, C.G. (1981). Visual properties of neurons in a polysensory area in superior temporal sulcus of the macaque. *Journal of Neurophysiology, 64,* 216-227.

Bruch, H. (1973). *Eating disorders.* New York: Basic Books.

Bruner, J. (1986). *Actual minds, possible worlds.* Cambridge, MA: Harvard University Press.

Bruner, J. (1990). *Acts of meaning.* Cambridge, MA: Harvard University Press.

Bruner, J.S. (1973). *Beyond the information given.* New York: Norton.

Bruner, J.S. & Goodman, C.C. (1947). Value and need as organizing factors in perception. *Journal of Abnormal and Social Psychology, 42,* 33-44.

Bruner, J.S., Olver, R.R. & Greenfield, P.M. (1966). *Studies in cognitive growth.* New York: Wiley.

Brunswick, A.F. (1980). *Smoking and health: A report of the Surgeon General.* Washington, DC: US Department of Health, Education & Welfare.

Bryant, D.J. (1990). Implicit associative responses influence encoding in memory. *Memory & Cognition, 18,* 348-358.

Buchsbaum, M.S. (1980). The two brains. In 1981 – *yearbook of sciences and the future* (pp. 138-153). Chicago: Encyclopaedia Britannica.

Buck, R. (1984). *The communication of emotion.* New York: Guilford.

Buck, R. (1988). *Human motivation and emotion.* New York: Wiley.

Buhler, C.(1968). Fulfillment and failure in life. In C. Buhler & F. Massarik (Eds.), *The course of human life.* New York: Springer.

Bullock, M. & Gelman, R. (1979). Preschool children's assumptions about cause and effect: Temporal coding. *Child Development, 50,* 89-96.

Bullock, T.H., Orkand, R., & Grinnell, A. (1977). *Introduction to the nervous system.* San Francisco: Freeman.

Bullock, W.A. & Gilliland, K. (1993). Eysenck's arousal theory of introversion-extraversion: A converging measures investigation. *Journal of Personality and Social Psychology, 64,* 1, 113-123.

Bulman, J.R. & Wortman, C.B. (1977). Attribution of blame and coping in the 'real world': Severe accident victims react to their lot. *Journal of Personality and Social Psychology, 35,* 351-363.

Bundesen, C. (1990). A theory of visual attention. *Psychological Review, 97,* 523-547

Burman, E. (Ed.) (1990). *Feminists and psychological practice.* London: Sage.

Burman, E. (1994). Deconstructing developmental psychology. London: Routledge.

Burman, E. & Parker, I. (1993) (Eds.) *Discourse analytic research: repertoires and readings of texts in action.* London: Routledge.

Buros, O.K. (Ed.). (1974). *Tests in print: II.* Highland Park, NJ: Gryphon Press.

Burrows, G.D. & Dennerstein, L. (Eds.). (1980). *Handbook of hypnosis and psychosomatic medicine.* New York: Elsevier/North Holland Biomedical Press.

Burt, C. (1966). The genetic determination of differences in intelligence. *British Journal of Psychology, 57,* 137-153.

Buss, A.R. (1980), *Self-consciousness and social anxiety.* San Francisco: Freeman.

Buss, D.M. (1991). Evolutionary personality psychology. *Annual Review of Psychology, 42.* 459-492.

Butcher, J.N. (1989). Why use the MMPI-2? In J. N. Butcher & J. R. Graham (Eds.), *Topics in MMPI-2 Interpretation.* Minneapolis: MMPI-2 Workshops and Symposia, Department of Psychology, University of Minnesota.

Butcher, J.N., Dahlstrom, W.G., Graham, J.R., Tellegen, A. & Kaemmer, B. (1989). *Manual for the restandarized Minnesota Multiphasic Personality Inventory: MMPI-2. An administrative and interpretive guide.* Minneapolis: University of Minnesota Press.

Butcher, J.N. & Finn, S. (1983). Objective personality assessment in clinical settings. In M.H. Jersen, A.E. Kazdin & A.S. Bellock (Fds.), *The clinical psychology handbook* (pp.329-344). New York: Pergamon.

Butler, M.J. & Rice, L.N. (1963). Audience, self-actualization and drive theory. In J.M. Wepman & R.W. Heine (Eds.), *Concepts of personality* (pp. 79-110). Chicago: Aidine.

Butler, R.A. & Harlow, H.F. (1954). Persistence of visual exploration in monkeys. *Journal of Comparative and Physiological Psychology, 47,* 258-263.

Butler, R.N. & Lewis, M.I. (1982). *Aging and mental health: Positive psychosocial and biomedical approaches* (3rd ed.). St. Louis: Mosby.

Buzan, T. (1976). *Use both sides of your brain.* New York: Dutton.

Bykov, K.M. (1957). *The cerebral cortex and the internal organs.* New York: Academic Press.

Byrne, D. (1971). *The attraction paradigm.* New York: Academic Press.

Byrne, D. (1981, August). *Predicting human sexual behavior.* G. Stanley Hall Lecture presented at the meeting,of the American Psychological Association, Los Angeles, CA.

C

Cacioppo, J.T., Klein, D.J., Berntson, G.G., & Hatfield, E. (1993). The psychophysiology of emotion. In M. Lewis & J.M. Haviland (Eds.) *Handbook of emotions* (pp. 119-143). New York: The Guilford Press.

Cairns, R.B. & Valsinger, J. (1984). Child psychology. *Annual Review of Psychology, 35,* 553-577.

Calambokidis, J. (1986, October 20). [Letter to Greenpeace]

Calkins, M.P. (1988). *Design for dementia: Planning environments for the elderly and the confused.* Owings Mills, MD: National Health Publishing.

Calkins, M.W. (1893). Statistics of dreams. *American Journal of Psychology, 5,* 311-343.

Cameron, P., Frank, R., Lifter, M. & Morrissey, P. (1968, September). *Cognitive functionings of college students in a general psychology class.* Paper presented at the Meeting of the American Psychological Association, San Francisco, CA.

Campbell, A. (1984). *The girls in the gang.* Oxford: Basil Blackwell.

Campos, J.J., Barrett, K.C., Lamb, M.E., Goldsmith, H.H., & Stenberg, C. (1983). *Socioemotional development* (Vol. 2). New York: Wiley.

Cann, A., Calhoun, L.G., Selby, J.W. & Kin, H.E. (Eds.). (1981). *Rape. Journal of Social Issues, 37* (whole no. 4).

Cannon, W.B. (1927). The James-Lange theory of emotion: A critical examination and an alternative theory. *American Journal of Psychology, 39,* 106-124.

Cannon, W.B. (1929). *Bodily changes in pain, hunger, fear and rage* (2nd ed.). New York: Appleton-Century-Crofts.

Cannon, W.B. (1942). 'Voodoo' death. *American Anthropologist, 44,* 169-181.

Cannon, W.B. (1957). 'Voodoo' death. *Psychosomatic Medicine, 19.* 182-19O.

Cannon, W.B. (1934). Hunger and thirst. In C. Murchison (Ed.), *A handbook of general experimental psychology.* Worcester, MA: Clark University Press.

Cannon, W.B. & Washburn, A.L. (1912). An explanation of hunger. *American Journal of Physiology, 29,* 441-454.

Cantor, N. & Kihlstrom, J.F. (1987). Social intelligence: The cognitive basis of personality. In P. Shaver (Ed.), *Review of personality and social psychology, Vol.6* (pp.15-34). Beverly Hills, CA: Sage.

Caplan, G. (1969, November). A psychiatrist's casebook. *McCall's,* p.65.

Caplan, P.J. (1985). The myth of women's masochism. *American Psychologist, 39,* 130-139.

Caplow, T. (1982). *Middletownfamilies: Fifty years of change and continuity.* Minneapolis: University of Minnesota Press.

Caporeal, L.R. (1976). Ergotism: The Satan loosed in Salem? *Science, 192,* 21-26.

Carey, S. (1978). The child as word teamer. In M. Halle, J. Bresnan, & G.A. Miller (Eds.), *Linguistic theory and psychological reality* (pp.

265-293). Cambridge, MA: MIT Press.

Carlsmith, J.M., Lepper, M.R. & Landauer, T.K. (1974). Children's obedience to adult requests: Interactive effects of anxiety arousal and apparent punitiveness of adults. *Journal of Personality and Social Psychology, 30,* 822-828.

Carlsmith, J.M. & Gross, A. (1969). Some effects of guilt on compliance. *Journal of Personality and Social Psychology, 11,* 232-240.

Carlson, J.G. & Wood, R.D. (1974). *Need the final solution be justified?* Unpublished manuscript, University of Hawaii.

Carlsson, A. (1978). Antipsychotic drugs, neurotransmitters and schizophrenia. *American Journal of Psychiatry, 135,* 164-173.

Carlton, J. (1990, December 4). When Californians use leaf blowers, life is less mellow. *The Wall Street Journal,* pp. A1, A7.

Carmichael, L. (1926). The development of behavior in vertebrates experimentally removed from the influence of external stimulation. *Psychological Review, 33,* 51-58.

Carmichael, L. (1970). The onset and early development of behavior. In P.H. Mussen (Ed.), *Carmichael's manual of child psychology* (3rd ed., Vol.1). New York: Wiley.

Carnes, P. (1983). *Out of the shadows: Understanding sexual addiction.* Minneapolis, MN: CompCare Publications.

Carr, T.H. (1979). Orthography and familiarity effects in word processing. *Journal of Experimental Psychology: General, 108,* 389-414.

Carrell, M.R. & Dittrich, J.E. (1978). Equity theory: The recent literature, methodological considerations and new directions. *Academy of Management Review, 3,* 202-210.

Carroll, D.W. (1994). *Psychology of language.* Pacific Grove, CA: Brooks/Cole.

Carskadon, M.A. & Dement, W.C. (1989). Normal human sleep: An overview. In M. Krugger, T. Roth & W.C. Dement (Eds.), *Principles and practice of sleep medicine* (pp.3-13). Philadelphia: Saunders.

Carstensen, L.L. (1987). Age-related changes in social activity. In L. L. Carstensen & B.A. Edelstein (Eds.), *Handbook of clinical gerontology* (pp.222-237). New York: Pergamon Press.

Carstensen, L.L. (1991). Selectivity theory: Social activity in life-span context. In K.W. Schaie (Ed.), *Annual Review of Geriatrics and Gerontology (Vol.II).* New York: Springer.

Cartwright, R.D. (1978). *A primer on sleep and dreaming.* Reading, MA: Addison-Wesley.

Cartwright, R.D. (1982). The shape of dreams. In *1983 Yearbook of science and the future.* Chicago: Encyclopaedia Britannica.

Cartwright, R.D. (1984). Broken dreams: A study of the effects of divorce and depression on dream content. *Psychiatry. 47,* 251-259.

Cartwright, S. (1851, May). The diseases and physical peculiarities of the Negro race. *New Orleans Medical and Surgical Journal.*

Carver, C.S., & Scheier, M.P. (1981). *Attention and self-regulation: A control theory approach to human behaviour.* New York: Springer-Verlag.

Carver, C.S., Scheier, M.F. & Weintraub, J.K. (1989). Assessing coping strategies: A theoretically based approach. *Journal of Personality and Social Psychology 56,* 267-283.

Case, R.S. (1985). *Intellectual development: A systematic reinterpretation.* New York: Academic Press.

Caspi, A. & Bem, D.J. (1990). Personality continuity and change across the life course. In L.A. Pervin (Ed.), *Handbook of personality theory and research* (pp. 549-575). New York: Guilford Press.

Caspi, A., Elder, G.H., Jr. & Bem, D.J. (1988). Moving away from the world: Life-course patterns of shy children. *Developmental Psychology, 24,* 824-833.

Catania, J.A., Kegeles, S.M. & Coates, T.J. (1990). Towards an understanding of risk behavior: An AIDS risk reduction model (ARRM). *Health Education Quarterly, 17,* 53-72.

Cattell, R.B. (1963). Theory of fluid and crystallized intelligence: A critical experiment. *Journal of Educational Psychology, 54,* 1-22.

Cattell, R.B. (1971). *Abilities: Their structure and growth.* Boston: Houghton Mifflin.

Cattell, R.B. (1972). The 16 PF and basic personality structure: A reply to Eysenck. *Journal of Behavioral Science, 1,* 169-187.

Cattell, R.B. (1982). *The inheritance of personality and ability: Research methods and findings.* New York: Academic Press.

Catterall, W.A. (1984). The molecular basis of neuronal excitability. *Science, 223,* 653-661.

Ceci, S.J. & Bronfenbrenner, U. (1991). On the demise of everyday memory. *American Psychologist, 46,* 27-31.

Centers for Disease Control. (1985). *Suicide surveillance report, United States, 1970-1980.* Atlanta: Department of Health and Human Services.

Cermak, L.S. & Craik, F.I.M. (1979). *Levels of processing in human memory*. Hillsdale, NJ: Eribaum.

Chamberlain, K. & Zika, S. (1990). The minor events approach to stress: Support for the use of daily hassles. *British Journal of Psychology, 81*, 469-481.

Chapin, S.F. (1913). *Introduction to the study of social evolution*. New York: Century.

Chapman, R.M., McCrary, J.W. & Chapman, J.A. (1978). Short-term memory: The 'storage' component of human brain responses predicts recall. *Science, 202,* 121 1-1213.

Chapman, S. & Hodgson, J. (1988). Showers in raincoats: attitudinal barriers to condom use in high risk heterosexuals. *Community Health Studies, 12*, 97-105.

Charen, M. (1990, March 11). Say no way: Time for good old selfcontrol. *San Francisco Examiner-Chronicle,* This World Section, p. 3.

Charlton, J., Kelly, S., Dunnell, K., Evans, B. & Jenkins, R. (1993). Suicide deaths in England and Wales: Trends in factors associated with suicide deaths. *Population Trends, 71,* 34-42.

Chase, W.G. & Ericsson, K.A. (1981). Skilled memory. In J.R. Anderson (Ed.), *Cognitive skills and their acquisition*. Hilisdale, NJ: Erlbaum.

Chase, W.G. & Simon, H.A. (1973). Perception in chess. In W.G. Chase (Ed.), *Visual information processing* (pp. 215-281). New York: Academic Press.

Chase, W.G. & Simon, H.A. (1973). Perception in chess. *Cognitive Psychology, 4,* 55-81.

Chasnoff, I.J., Burns, W.J., Schnoll, S.H. & Burns, K.A. (1985). Cocaine use in pregnancy. *New England Journal of Medicine, 313,* 666-669.

Cheek, J.M. & Busch, C.M. (1981). The influence of shyness on loneliness in a new situation. *Personality and Social Psychology Bulletin, 7,* 572-577.

Chen, I. (1990, July 13). Quake may have caused baby boom in Bay Area. *The San Francisco Chronicle,* p. A3.

Cheney, D.L. & Seyfarth, R. (1985). Vervet monkey alarm calls: Manipulation through shared information. *Behavior, 4,* 150-166.

Cherfas, J. (1990, August 31). Science responds to terror. Science, p. 981.

Cherry, E.C. (1953). Some experiments on the recognition of speech, with one and with two ears. *Journal of the Acoustical Society of America, 25,* 975-979.

Chi, M.T.H., Feltovich, P.J. & Glaser, R. (1981). Categorization and representation of physics problems by experts and novices. *Cognitive Science, 5,* 121-152.

Child, D. (1991). *The essentials of factor analysis (second edition)*. London: Holt, Rinehart & Winston.

Chilman, C.S. (Ed.). (1979). *Adolescent sexuality in a changing American society: Social and psychological perspectives (Drew* Publications No. 79-1426). Washington, DC: National Institute of Health.

Chilman, C.S. (1983). *Adolescent sexuality in a changing American society (2nd ed.)*. New York: Wiley.

Chilmonezyk, B.A., Knight, G.J., Palomaki, G.E., Pulkkinen, A.J., Williams, J. & Haddow, J.E. (1990). Environmental tobacco smoke exposure during infancy. *The American Journal of Public Health, 80,* 1205-1208.

Chodorow, N. (1978). *The reproduction of mothering: psychoanalysis and the sociology of gender*. Berkeley: University of California Press.

Chodorow, N. (1989). *Psychoanalysis and feminist theory*. New Haven: Yale University Press.

Chomsky, N. (1965). *Aspects of a theory of syntax*. Cambridge, MA: MIT Press.

Chomsky, N. (1975). *Reflections on language*. New York: Pantheon Books.

Chomsky, N. (1980). *Rules and representations*. New York: Columbia University Press.

Chomsky, N. (1984). *Modular approaches to the study of the mind*.San Diego, CA: San Diego University Press.

Chomsky, N. (1986). *Knowledge of language: Its nature, origin and use*. New York: Praeger.

Chorover, S. (1981, June). *Organizational recruitment in 'open' and 'closed' social systems: A neuropsychological perspective*. Conference paper presented at the Center for the Study of New Religious Movements, Berkeley, CA.

Christy, P.R., Gelfand, D.M. & Hartman, D.P. (1971). Effects of competition-induced frustration on two classes of modeled behavior. *Developmental Psychology, 5, 104-111*.

Church, A.T. & Kagitbak, M.S. (1992). The cultural context of academic motives: a comparison of Filipino and American college students. *Journal of Cross-cultural Psychology, 23,* 40-58.

Churchland, P.S. (1986). *Toward a unified science of the mindbrain*. Cambridge, MA: MIT Press.

Cialdini, R.B. (1985). *Influence: Science and practice*. Glenview, IL: Scott, Foresman.

Ciminero, A.R., Calhoun, K.S. & Adams, H.E. (Eds.). (1977). *Handbook of behavioral assessment*. New York: Wiley.

Claparede, E. (1928). Feelings and emotions. In M.L. Reymert (Ed.), *Feelings and emotions: The Wittenberg Symposium (pp,* 124-139). Worcester, MA: Clark University Press.

Clark, D.M. (1986). A cognitive approach to panic. *Behaviour Research and Therapy, 24,* 461-470.

Clark, E.V. (1973). What's in a word? On the child's acquisition of semantics in his first language. In T.E. Moore (Ed.), *Cognitive development and the acquisition of language*. New York: Academic Press.

Clark, E.V. (1928). Feelings and emotions. In M.L. Reymert (Ed.), *Feelings and emotions: The Wittenberg Symposium (pp.* 124-139). Worcester, MA: Clark University Press.

Clark, H.H. & Clark, E.V. (1977). *Psychology and language: An introduction to psycholinguistics*. New York: Harcourt Brace Jovanovich.

Clark, K. & Clark, M. (1947). Racial identification and preference in Negro children. In T.M. Newcomb & E.L. Hartley (Eds.), *Readings in social psychology*. New York: Holt.

Clarke-Stewart, K.A. (1978). Recasting the lone stranger. In J. Glick & K.A. Clarke-Stewart (Eds.), *The development of social understanding*. New York: Gardner Press.

Clausen, J.A. (1981). Stigma and mental disorder: Phenomena and mental terminology. *Psychiatry, 44,* 287-296.

Clausen, T. (1968). Perspectives on childhood socialization. In J. A.Clausen (Ed.), Socialization and society. Boston: Little, Brown.

Clayman, C.B. (1989). *The American Medical Association Encyclopedia of Medicine*. New York: Random House.

Clearwater, Y. (1990). In *Discovering Psychology,* Program 24 [PBS video series]. Washington, DC: Annent)erg/CPB Program.

Cleek, M.B. & Pearson, T.A. (1985). Perceived causes of divorce: An analysis of interrelationships. *Journal of Marriage and the Family, 47,* 179-191.

Clementz, B.A. & Sweeney, J.A. (1990). Is eye movement dysfunction a biological marker for schizophrenia? A methodological review. *Psychological Bulletin, 108,* 77-92.

Cloninger, C.R. (1987). Neurogenetic adaptive mechanisms in alcoholism. *Science, 236,* 410-416.

Coates, T. (1990). Strategies for modifying sexual behavior for primary and secondary prevention of HIV infection. *Journal of Consulting and Clinical Psychology, 58,* 57-69.

Cobb, S. (1976). Social support as a moderator of stress. *Psychosomatic Medicine, 35,* 375-389.

Coch, L. & French, J.R.P., Jr. (1948). Overcoming resistance to change. *Human Relations, 1,* 512-532.

Cohen, L.B. & Gelber, E.R. 1975). Infant visual memory. In L. Cohen & P. Salapatek (Eds.), *Infant perception: From sensation to cognition, Vol.1 : Basic visual processes* (pp. 347-403). New York: Academic Press.

Cohen, N.J. (1984). Preserved learning capacity in amnesia: Evidence for multiple memory systems. In L.R. Squire & N. Butters (Eds.), *Neuropsychology of memory*. New York: Guilford Press.

Cohen, R.E. & Ahearn, F.L., Jr. (1980). *Handbook for mental health care of disaster victims*. Baltimore: Johns Hopkins University Press.

Cohen, R.Y., Brownell, K.D. & Felix, M.R.J. (1990). Age and sex differences in health habits and beliefs of schoolchildren. *Health Psychology, 9,* 208-224.

Cohen, S. (1988). Psychosocial models of the role of social support in the etiology of physical disease. *Health Psychology, 7,* 269-297.

Cohen, S. & McKay, G. (1983). Social suppose, stress and the buffering hypotheses: A theoretical analysis. In A. Baum, S. E. Taylor, & J. Singer (Eds.), *Handbook of psychology and health* (Vol. 4). Hilisdale, NJ: Erlbaum.

Cohen, S. & Syme, S.L. (Eds.). (1985). *Social support and health*. Orlando, FL: Academic Press.

Coleman, J.C. (1980). Friendship and the peer group in adolescence. In J. Adelson (Ed.), *Handbook of adolescent psychology*. New York: Wiley.

Coleman, L. (1987). *Suicide clusters*. Winchester, MA: Faber & Faber.

Coleman, R.M. (1986). *Wide awake at 3:00 A.M.: By choice or by* *chance?* New York: Freeman.

Collier, G., Hirsch, E. & Hamlin, P. (1972). The ecological determinants of reinforcement. *Physiology and Behavior, 9,* 705-716

Collins, A.M. & Loftus, E.F. (1975). A spreading-activation theory of semantic processing. *Psychological Review, 82,* 407-428.

Conant, J.B. (1958). *On understanding science: An historical approach.* New York: New Amsterdam Library.

Condry, J. & Condry, S. (1976). Sex differences: A study in the eye of the beholder. *Child Development, 47.* 812-819.

Conger, J.J. (1991) *Adolescence and youth* (4th ed.) New York: Harper Collins.

Conger, J.J. (1977) Adolescence and youth: *Psychological development* (2nd ed.) New York: Harper & Row.

Conger, J.C. & Keane, S.P. (1981) Social skills intervention in the treatment of isolated or withdrawn children. *Psychological Bulletin,* 90, 478-495.

Connors, M.M., Harrison, A.A. & Akins, F.R. (1986) Psychology and the resurgent space program. *American Psychologist,* 41, 906-913.

Conrad, R. (1964) Acoustic confusions in immediate memory. *British Journal of Psychology,* 55, 75084.

Conrad, R. (1972) Short-term memory in the deaf: A test for speech coding. *British Journal of Psychology,* 63, 173-180.

Conway, M.A. (1991). In defense of everyday memory. *American Psychologist, 46,* 19-26.

Conway, M.A. (1992). Making sense of the past. In M.A. Conway, D.C. Rubin, H. Spinnler & W.A. Wagenaar (Eds.), *Theoretical perspectives on autobiographical memory* (pp. 3-10). Dordrecht: Kluwer Academic Publishers.

Cook, M., Mineka, S., Woklenstein, B. & Laitsch, K. (1985) Observational conditioning of snake fear in unrelated rhesus monkeys. *Journal of Abnormal Psychology,* 94, 591-610.

Cookerly, J.R. (1980) Does marital therapy do any lasting good? *Journal of Marital and Family Therapy,* 6, 393-397.

Cooper, A.F. (1976) Deafness and psychiatric illness. *British Journal of Psychiatry,* 129, 216-266.

Cooper, L. (1989) Mental models of the structure of visual objects. In B.Shepp & S.Ballisteros (Eds.) *Object perception* (pp.91-119) Hillsdale, NJ: Erlbaum.

Cooper, L.A. & Shepard, R.N. (1973) The time required to prepare for a rotated stimulus. *Memory and Cognition,* 1, 246-250.

Coren, S. & Girgus, J.S. (1978) *Seeing is deceiving: The psychology of visual illusions.* Hillsdale, NJ: Erlbaum.

Coren, S., Porac, C. & Ward, L.M. (1978) *Sensation and perception.* New York: Academic Press.

Coren, S., Ward, L.M. & Enns, J.T. (1994). *Sensation and perception.* New York: Harcourt Brace.

Cornish, D.B. (1978). *Gambling: A review of the literature nad its implications for policy and research.* London: Her Majesty's Stationary Office.

Cornsweet, T.N. (1970) *Visual perception.* New York: Academic Press.

Corsini, R.J. (1977) *Current theories of personality.* Itasca, IL: Peacock.

Cosmides, L. (1989) The logic of social exchange: Has natural selection shaped how humans reason? Studies with the Wason Selection Task. *Cognition,* 31, 187-276.

Costa, P.T., Jr. & McCrae, R.R. (1985). *The NEO personality inventory manual.* Odessa, FL: Psychological Assessment Resources.

Council of the European Communities & the European Communities Commission, (1992). *Treaty on European Union: Maastricht Treaty.* Luxembourg: Office for Official Publications of the European Communities.

Cousins, N. (1979). *The anatomy of an illness as perceived by a patient: Reflections on healing and rejuvenation.* New York: Norton.

Cousins, N. (1983). *The healing heart.* New York: Norton.

Cousins, N. (1989). *Head first: The biology of hope.* New York: Dutton.

Cousins, N. (1990). In *Discovering Psychology,* Program 2 [PBS video series]. Washington, DC: Annenberg/CPB Project.

Cowan, P. & Cowan, P.A. (1988). Changes in marriage during the transition to parenthood. In G.Y. Michaels & W.A. Goldberg (Eds.), *The transition to parenthood: Current theory and research.* Cambridge: Cambridge University Press.

Cowan, P.A. (1988). Developmental psychopathology: A nine-cell map of the territory. In E. Nannis & P.A. Cowan (Eds.), *Developmental psychopathology and its treatment: New directionsfor child development* (No. 39, pp. 5-29). San Francisco: Jossey Bass.

Cowan, W.M. (1979). The development of the brain. In *The Brain*

pp. 56-69). San Francisco: Freeman.

Cowings, P. (1990). In *Discovering Psychology,* Program 24 [PBS video series]. Washington, DC: Annenberg/CPB Program.

Cowles, J.T. (1937). Food tokens as incentives for learning by chimpanzees. *Comparative Psychology Monographs,* 74, 1-96.

Cowley, G. (1990, March 26). The promise of Prozac. *Newsweek, 115,* p. 38.

Cox, T. & McKay, C. (1978). Stress at work. In T. Cox (Ed.), *Stress.* Baltimore, MD: University Park Press.

Coyne, J.C. (1976). Toward an interactional description of depression. *Psychiatry, 39,* 28-40.

Coyne, J. (1990). In *Discovering Psychology,* Program 22 [PBS video series]. Washington, DC: Annenberg/CPB Project.

Coyne, J.C., Aldwin, C. & Lazarus, R.S. (1981). Depression and coping in stressful episodes. *Journal of Abnormal Psychology,* 90, 439-447.

Coyne, J.C. & Downey, G. (1991). Social factors and psychopathology: Stress, social support, and coping processes. *Annual Review of Psychology, 42,* 401-425.

Coyne, J.C., Wortman, C. B. & Lehman, D.R. (1988). The other side of support: Emotional overinvolvement and miscarried helping. In B. Gottlieb (Ed.), *Marshalling social support* (pp.305-330). Newbury Park, CA: Sage.

Craik, F.I.M., & Lockhart, R.S. (1972). Levels of processing; A framework for memory research. *Journal of Verbal teaming and Verbal Behavior,* 11, 671-684.

Craik, K. (1943). *The nature of explanation.* Cambridge: Cambridge University Press.

Cranston, M. (1991). *The noble savage: Jean-Jacques Rousseau,* 1754-1762. Chicago: University of Chicago Press.

Crapo, L. (1985). Hormones: The messengers of life. Stanford, CA: Stanford Alumni Association Press.

Crick, F. & Mitchison, G. (1983). The function of dream sleep. *Nature, 304,* 111-114.

Crick, F. & Mitchison, G. (1986). REM sleep and neural nets. *Journal of Mind and Behavior,* 7, 229-250.

Crick, F.H.C. (1979, September). Thinking about the brain. *Scientific American, 247,* 219-232.

Critelli, J.W. (1984). The placebo: Conceptual analysis of a construct in transition. *American Psychologist, 39,* 57-61.

Cronbach, L.J. (1951). Coefficient alpha and the internal structure of tests, *Psychometrika, 16,* 297-334.

Cronbach, L.J. & Meehl, P.E. (1955). Construct validity in psychological tests. *Psychological Bulletin, 52,* 281-302.

Crook, J.H. (1973). The nature and function of territorial aggression. In M.F.A. Montague (Ed.), *Man and aggression* (2nd ed.). New York: Oxford University Press.

Crosby, F.J. (1982). *Relative deprivation and working women.* New York: Oxford University Press.

Cross, P.G., Cariell, R.B. & Butcher, H.J. (1967). The personality patterns of creative artists. *British Journal of Educational Psychology, 37,* 292-299.

Crowder, R.G. & Morton, J. (1969). Precategorical acoustic storage (PAS). *Perception and Psychophysics,* 8, 815-820.

Crutchfield, R.A. (1955). Conformity and character. *American Psychologist, 10,* 191-198.

Csikszentmihalyi, M., Larson, R. & Prescott, S. (1977). The ecology of adolescent activity and experience. *Journal of Youth and Adolescence,* 6, 281-294.

Csikszentmihalyi, M. (1990). *Flow: The psychology of optimal experience.* New York: Harper & Row.

Culliton, B.J. (1990). Gene therapy: Into the home stretch. *Science,* 249,974-976.

Cumming, E. & Henry, W.E. (1961). *Growing old: The process of disengagement.* New York: Basic Books.

Cummins, R. (1989). Locus of control and social support. Clarifiers of the relationship between job stress and job satisfaction. *Journal of Applied Social Psychology, 19,* 772-788.

Curt, B.C. (1994). *Textuality and tectonics: Troubling social and psychological science.* Buckingham: Open University Press.

Curtiss, S. (1977). *Genie: A psycholinguistic study of a modern-day 'wild child'.* New York: Academic Press.

Cushing, F.H. (1974). *Zuni fetishes.* Las Vegas, NV: KC Publications (Box 14883).

Cutting, J. (1981). Six tenets of event perception. *Cognition, 10,* 71-78.

Cutting, J.E. (1987). Perception and information. *Annual Review of Psychology, 38,* 61-90.

Cutting, J. & Profritt, D. (1982). The minimum principle and the perception of absolute, common and relative motions. *Cognitive Psychology, 14, 211-246.*

Cynader, M.N. & Chernenko, G. (1976). Abolition of directional sensitivity in the visual cortex of the cat, *Science, 193,* 504-505.

Czeisler, C.A., Allan, J.S., Strogatz, S.H., Ronda, J.M., Sanchez, R., Dios, C.D., Freitag, W.O., Richardson, G.S. & Kronauer, R.E. (1986). Bright light resets the human circadian pacemaker independent of the timing of the sleep-wake cycle. *Science, 233,* 667-670.

D

Dackman, L. (1986). Everyday illusions. *Exploratorium Quarterly, 10,* 5-7.

Dahlstrom, W.G., Welsh, H.G. & Dahlstrom, L.E. (1975). An *MMPI handbook, Vol. 1: Clinical interpretation.* Minnesota: University of Minnesota Press.

Dakof, G.A. & Taylor, S.E. (1990). Victims' perceptions of social support: What is helpful from whom? *Journal of Personality and Social Psychology, 58,* 80-89.

Damon, W. & Hart, D. (1986). Stability and change in children's self-understanding. *Social Cognition, 4,* 102-118.

Danziger, K. (1990). *Constructing the subject. Historical origins of psychological research.* Cambridge: Cambridge University Press.

Darley, J.M. & Batson, C.D. (1973). From Jerusalem to Jericho: A study of situational and dispositional variables in helping behavior. *Journal of Personality and Social Psychology, 27,* 100-108.

Darley, J. & Gilbert, D.T. (1985). Social psychological aspects of environmental psychology. In G. Lindzey & E. Aronson (Eds.), *Handbook of social psychology* (2nd ed., Vol. 2, pp. 949-992). New York: Random House.

Darley, J.M. & Goethals, G.R. (1980). People's analysis of the causes of ability-linked performances. In L. Berkowitz (Ed.), *Advances in experimental social psychology* (Vol. 13, pp. 1-37). New York: Academic Press.

Darley, J.M. & Gross, P.H. (1983). A hypothesis-confirming bias in labeling effects. *Journal of Personality and Social Psychology, 44,* 20-33.

Darley, J. & Latané, B. (1968). Bystander intervention in emergencies: Diffusion of responsibility. *Journal of Personality and Social Psychology, 8,* 377-383.

Darwin, C. (1859). *On the origin of species.* London: John Murray.

Darwin, C. (1965). *The expression of emotions in man and animals.* Chicago: University of Chicago Press. (Originally published 1872)

Darwin, F. (Ed.). (1950). *Charles Darwin's autobiography.* New York: Schuman.

Darwin, C.J., Turvey, M.T. & Crowder, R.G. (1972). The auditory analogue of the Sparling partial report procedure: Evidence for brief auditory stage. *Cognitive Psychology, 3,* 255-267.

Davey, G. (1981) (Ed.). *Applications of conditioning* theory. London: Methuen.

Davidson, J.M. (1980). The psychobiology of sexual experience. In J.M. Davidson & R.J. Davidson (Eds.), *The psychobiology of consciousness* (pp. 271-33 1). New York: Plenum.

Davidson, R. (1984). Hemispheric asymmetry and emotion. In K. Schemer & P. Ekman (Eds.), *Approaches to emotion.* Hillsdale, NJ: Erlbaum.

Davies, D.L. (1962). Normal drinking in recovered alcoholics. *Quarterly Journal of Studies on Alcohol, 23,* 94-104.

Davis, G.C. (1985). Oral history: Accounts of lives and times. In G. Lesnoff-Caravalglia (Ed.), *Values, ethics and aging* (pp. 172-184). New York: Human Sciences Press.

Davis, I.P. (1985). *Adolescents: Theoretical and helping perspectives.* Boston: Kluwer-Nijhoff Publishing.

Davis, K. (1988). *Power under the microscope.* Dordrecht/Providence RI: Foris Publications.

Davison, G.C. & Neale, N.M. (1994). *Abnormal psychology, sixth edition.* New York: Wiley

Davison, G.C. & Valins, S. (1969). Maintenance of self-attributed and drug-attributed behavior change. *Journal of Personality and Social Behavior, 11,* 25-33.

Daw, N.W. & Wyatt, H.J. (1976). Kittens reared in a unidirectional environment: Evidence for a critical period. *Journal of Physiology, 257,* 155-170.

Dawes, R.M. (1979). The robust beauty of improper linear models in decision making. *American Psychologist, 34,* 571-582.

Dawes, R., Faust, D. & Meehl, P.E. (1989). Clinical versus actuarial judgment. *Science, 243,* 1668-1674.

Dawkins, R. (1976). *The selfish gene.* Oxford, UK: Oxford University Press.

Day, R.S. (1986, November). *Ways to show it: Cognitive consequences of alternative representations.* Paper presented at the meeting of the Psychonomic Society, New Orleans.

de Bono, F. (1970). *Lateral thinking.* New York: Harper.

De Charms, R. & Moeller, G. (1962). Values expressed in American children's readers: 1800-1950. *Journal of Abnormal and Social Psychology, 64,* 136-142.

De Charms, R.C. & Muir, M.S. (1978). Motivation: Social approaches. *Annual Review of Psychology, 29,* 91-113.

De Raad, B., Mulder, E., Kloosterman, K. & Hofstee, W.K.B. (1988). Personality – descriptive verbs. *European Journal of Personality, 2,* 81-96.

de Silva, P. (1994). *Obsessions and compulsions: Investigation.* In S.J.E. Lindsay & G.E. Powell (Eds.), *Handbook of clinical adult psychology, 2nd edition* (pp.51-70). London: Routledge.

De Valois, R.L. & Jacobs, G.H. (1968). Primate color vision. *Science, 162,* 533-540.

De Valois, R.L. & De Valois, K.K. (1980). Spatial vision. *Annual Review of psychology, 80.*

De Vos, G.A. & Rippler, A.A. (1969). Cultural psychology: Comparative studies of human behavior. In G. Lindzey & E. Aronson (Eds.), *The handbook of social psychology* (2nd ed. pp 323-417). New York: Random House.

Dealing with date rape. (1991, January/February) – *Stanford Observer,* p. 15.

Deaux, K. (1985). Sex and gender. *Annual Review of Psychology 36,* 49-81.

DeCasper, A.J. & Fifer, W.P. (1980). Of human bonding: newborns prefer their mother's voices. *Science, 208,* 1174-1176.

DeCasper, A.J. & Spence, M.J. (1986). Prenatal maternal speech influences newborns' perception of speech sounds. *Infant Behavior and Development, 9,* 133-150.

Deci, E.L. (1975). *Intrinsic motivation.* New York: Plenum.

Deci, E.L. & Ryan, R.M. (1985). *Intrinsic motivation and self-determination in human behavior.* New York & London: Plenum Press.

Deci, E.L. & Ryan, R.M. (1987). The support of autonomy and the control of behavior. *Journal of Personality and Social Psychology, 53,* 1024-1037.

Deci, E.L. & Ryan, R.M. (1991). A motivational approach to self: Integration in personality. In R.A. Dienstbier (Ed.). *Perspectives on motivation.* Nebraska symposium on motivation, 1990, vol. 38 (p. 237-288). Lincoln & London: University of Nebraska Press.

Delgado, J.M.R. (1969). *Physical control of the mind: Toward a psychocivilized society.* New York: Harper & Row.

Delishi, C. (1988). The human genome project. *American Scientist, 76,* 488-493.

Dellas, M. & Gaier, E.L. (1970). Identification of creativity: individual. *Psychological Bulletin, 73,* 55-73.

Dembrowski, T.M. & Costa, P.T., Jr. (1987). Coronary prone behavior: Components of the Type A pattern and hostility. *Journal of Personality 55,* 211-235.

Dembroski, T.M., Weiss, S.M., Shields, J.L. et al (1978). *Coronary-prone behavior.* New York: Springer-Verlag.

Dement, W. C. & Kleitman, N. (1957). Cyclic variations in during sleep and their relations to eye movement, body mobility and dreaming. *Electroencephalography and Clinical Neurophysiology, 9,* 673-690.

Dement, W.C. (1972). *Some must watch, while some must sleep.* San Francisco: Freeman.

Dement, W.C. (1976), *Some watch while some must sleep.* San Francisco: San Francisco Book Co.

Dennett, D.C. (1978). *Brainstorms.* Cambridge, MA: Bradford Books.

Dennett, D.C. (1991). *Consciousness explained.* New York: Little, Brown and Company.

Department of Health, Great Britain, (1992). *The Health of The Nation: A Strategy for Health in England.* London HMSO.

Depue, R.A. & Monroe, S.M. (1983). Psychopathology research. In M. Hersen, A.E. Kazdin & A.S. Bellack (Eds.), *The psychology handbook* (pp. 239-264). New York: Pergamon

Deregowski, J.B. (1980). *Illusions, patterns and pictures: A cultural perspective* (pp. 966-977). London: Academic Press

Descartes, R. (1911). Traitées de L'homme. In E.S. Haldane Ross (Trans.), *The philosophical works of Descartes.* New York: Dover. (Originai work published 1642)

Descartes, R. (1951). The passions of the soul. In E.S. Haldane &

G.T. Ross (Trans.), *The philosophichal works of Descartes*. New York: Dover. (Original work published 1646)

Desenclos, J.C., Papaevangelou, G. & Ancelle-Park, R. (1993). Knowledge of HIV serostatus and preventative behaviour among European injecting drug users. *AIDS*, 7, 1371-1377

Deutsch, J.A. & Deutsch, D. (1963). Attention: Some theoretical considerations. *Psychological Review*, 70, 80-90.

Deutsch, M. & Gerard, H.B. (1955). A study of normative and informational social influence. *Journal of Abnormal and Social Psychology*, 51, 629-636.

Deutsch, M. & Hornstein, H.A. (1975). *Applying social psychology*, Hillsdale, NJ: Eribaum.

Devereux, G. (1961). Mohave ethnopsychiatry psychiatric knowledge and psychic disturbances of an Indian tribe. *Bureau of American Ethology* (Bulletin 175). Washington DC: Smithsonian Institution.

Devereux, G. (1981). *Mohave ethnopsychiatry and suicide: The psychiatric knowledge and psychic disturbances of an Indian tribe*. Bureau of American Ethology (Bulletin 175). Washington, DC: Smithsonian Institution.

DeVries, R. (1969). Constancy of generic identity in the years three to six. *Society for Research in Child Development Monographs. 34* (Serial No. 127).

Diamond, D. (1989, Fall). The unbearable darkness of being. *Stanford Medicine*, pp. 13-16.

Diamond, I. & Orenstein, G.F. (1990). *Reweaving the world: The emergence of ecofeminism*. San Francisco: Sierra Club Books.

Diamond, J. (1990). The great leap forward. *Discover* (Special Issue), pp. 66-77.

Diamond, M.J. (1974). Modification of hypnotizability: A review *Psychological Bulletin*, 81, 180-198.

Dickinson, A. (1980). *Contemporary animal learning theory* Cambridge: Cambridge University Press.

Dickman, H. & Zeiss, R.A. (1982). *Incidents and correlates of post-traumatic stress disorder among ex-Prisoners of War of World War II*. Manuscript in progress. Palo Alto, CA.: Vete Administration.

Diekstra, R.F.W. (1990). Suicidal behaviour and depressive disorders in adolescents and young adults. *Neuropsychology*, 4, 194-207.

Diener, E. (1980). Deindividuation: The absence of self-awaren and self-regulation in group members. In P. Paulus (Ed.), *The psychology of group influence* (pp. 209-242). Hillsdale, NJ: Erlbaum.

Diener, E. & Crandall, R. (1978). *Ethics in social and behavioral research*. Chicago: University of Chicago Press.

Dijk, T. van & Kintsch, W. (1983). *Strategies of discourse comprehension*. New York: Academic Press.

Dijkstra, A. & Kempen, G. (1993). *Taalpsychologie [The psychology of language]*. Groningen: Wolters-Noordhoff.

Dillon, K.M., & Totten, M.C. (1989). Psychological factors affecting immunocompetence and health of breastfeeding mothers and their infants. *Journal of Genetic Psychology*, 150, 155-162.

DiLollo, V. (1980). Temporal integration in visual memory. *Journal of Experimental Psychology: General*, 109, 75-97.

DiMatteo, M.R. & DiNicola, D.D. (1982). *Achieving patient compliance: The psychology of the medical practitioner's role*. New York: Pergamon.

Dimond, S.J. (1980). *Neuropsychology: A textbook of systems and psychological functions of the human brain*. London: Butterworth.

Dion, K.L., Berscheid, E. & Walster, E. (1972). What is beautiful is good. *Journal of Personality and Social Psychology*, 24, 285-290.

Dishman, R.K. (1982). Compliance/adherence in health-related exercise. *Health Psychology*, 1, 237-267.

Dixon, N.F. (1976). *On the psychology of military incompetence*. London: Pimlico.

Dixon, N.F. (1994). Disastrous decisions, *The Psychologist: The Bulletin of The British Psychological Society*, 7, 7, 303-307.

Dixon, R.A., Kramer, D.A. & Baltes, P.B. (1985). Intelligence: a life-span developmental perspective. In B.B. Wolman (Ed.) *Handbook of intelligence* (pp. 301-352). New York: Wiley.

Doane, J.A., Falloon, I.R.H., Goldstein, M.J. & Mintz, J (1985). Parental affective style and the treatment of schizophrenia. *Archives of general psychiatry* 42, 34-42.

Dohrenwend, B.P. & Dohrenwend, B.S. (1974). Social and cultural influences on psychopathology. *Annual Review of Psychology*, 25, 417-452.

Dohrenwend, B.P. & Shrout, P.E. (1985). 'Hassles' in the conceptualization and measurement of life stress variables. *American Psychologist*, 40, 780-785.

Dohrenwend, B.S. & Dohrenwend, B.P. (1974). *Stressful life events: Their nature and effects*. New York: Wiley.

Doise, W. (1976). *L'articulation psychosociologique et les relations entre groupes*. Brussels, de Boeck. Translated as *Groups and individuals: explanations in social psychology*. Cambridge: Cambridge University Press, 1978.

Doll, R. & Peto, R. (1976). Mortality in reaction to smoking: 20 years' observations on male British doctors, *British Medical Journal*, 2, 1525-1536.

Dollard, J., Doob, L.W., Miller, N., Mower, O.H. & Sears, R.R. (1939). *Frustration and aggression*. New Haven, C T: Yale University Press.

Dollard, J. & Miller, N.E. (1950). *Personality and psychotherapy*. New York: McGraw-Hill.

Donchin, E. (1975). On evoked potentials, cognition and memory. *Science*, 790, 1004-1005.

Donchin, E. (1985). *Can the mind be read in brain waves?* Presentation at a Science and Public Policy Seminar. Washington, DC: Federation of Behavioral, Psychological and Cognitive Sciences.

Donnerstein, E. (1980). Aggressive-erotica and violence against women. *Journal of Personality and Social Psychology*, 39, 269-277.

Donnerstein, E. (1983). Erotica and human aggression. In R.G. Green & E. Donnerstein (Eds.), *Aggression: Theoretical and empirical reviews, Vol. 2: Issues in research*. New York: Academic Press.

Donnerstein, E.I. & Linz, D.G. (1986, December). The question of pornography. *Psychology Today*, 56-59.

Dooling, D.J. & Lachman, R. (1971). Effects of comprehension on retention of prose. *Journal of Experimental Psychology*, 88, 216-222.

Dorfman, D.D. (1965). Esthetic preference as a function of pattern information. *Psychonomic Science*, 3, 85-86.

Dorner, G. (1976). *Hormones and brain differentiation*. Amsterdam: Elsevier.

Dorris, M. (1989). *The broken cord*. New York: Harper & Row.

Dowis, R.T. (1984). The importance of vision in the prevention of Teaming disabilities and juvenile delinquency. *Journal of Optometric-Vision Development*, 15, 20-22.

Drabman, R.S. & Thomas, M.H. (1974). Does media violence increase children's tolerance of real-life aggression? *Developmental Psychology*, 10, 418-421.

Draguns, J.G. (1980). Psychological disorders of clinical severity. In H.C. Triandis & J.G. Draguns (Eds.), *Handbook of Cross-Cultural Psychology, Volume 6: Psychopathology*. Boston: Allyn & Bacon.

Driver, P.M. & Humphries, D.A. (1988). *Protean behavior: The biology of unpredictability*. Oxford: Clarendon Press.

Driver, J. & Tipper, S. (1989). On the nonselectivity of selective seeing: Contrasts between interference and priming in selective attention. *Journal of Experimental Psychology: Human Perception and Performance*, 15, 304-314.

Drug Policy Foundation. (1989, September/October). The Drug Policy Letter, Vol. 1 (4).

Dryfoss, J.G. (1990). *Adolescents at risk: Prevalence and prevention*. New York: Oxford University Press.

Duba, R.O. & Shortliffe, E.H. (1983). Expert systems research. *Science*, 220, 261-268.

DuBois, P.H. (1970). *A history of psychological testing*. Boston: Allyn and Bacon.

Dugan, T.F. & Coles, R. (Eds.). (1989). *The child in our times: Studies in the development of resiliency*. New York: Mazel.

Dugdale, R.L. (1912). *The Jukes* (4th ed.). New York: Putnam's Sons.

Dumont, J.P.C. & Robertson, R.M. (1986). Neuronal circuits: An evolutionary perspective. *Science*, 233, 849-853.

Dumont, J.P.C. & Wine, J.J. (1986). The telson flexor neuromuscular system of the crayfish, Ill. The role of feedforward inhibition in shaping a stereotyped behaviour pattern. *Journal of Experimental Biology*, 127, 295-31 1.

Duncan, S. Jr. (1972). Some signals and rules for taking speaking turns in conversations. *Journal of Personality and Social Psychology*, 23, 283-292.

Duncker, K. (1945). On problem solving. *Psychological Monographs*, 58 (No. 270).

Dunkel-Schetter, C., Folkman, S. & Lazarus, R.S. (1987). Correlates of social support receipt. *Journal of Personality and Social Psychology*, 53, 71-80.

Dunning, D., Griffin, D.W., Milojkovic, J.D. & Ross, L. (1990). The overconfidence effect in social prediction. *Journal of Personality and Social Psychology*, 58, 568-581.

E

Eagle, M.N. (1984). *Recent developments in psychoanalysis.* New York: McGraw-Hill.

Eastwell, H.D. (1984). Death watch in East Arnhem, Australia. *American Anthropologists, 86,* 119-12 1.

Ebbinghaus, H. (1913). *Memory.* New York: Columbia University. (Original work published 1885, Leipzig: Altenberg)

Ebbinghaus, H. (1973). *Psychology: An elementary textbook.* New York: Amo Press. (Original work published 1908)

Eccles, J. (1964). Quoted in R.L. Gregory (Ed.), *The Oxford companion to the mind* (p. 164). New York: Oxford University Press.

Eccles, P., Adler, T. & Meece, J.L. (1984). Sex differences in achievement: A test of alternate theories. *Journal of Personality and Social Psychology, 46,* 26-43.

Edge, H.L., Morris, R.L., Palmer, J. & Rush, J.H. (1986). Foundations of parapsychology: Exploring the boundaries of human capability. London: Routledge.

Edmonds, B., Klein, M., Dale, N. & Kandel, E.R. (1990). Contributions of two types of calcium channels to synaptic transmission and plasticity. *Science, 250,* 1 142-1 147.

Educational Testing Service *(1990). Manual and technical report for the School and College Ability Tests, Series III.* Menlo Park, CA: Addison-Wesley.

Edwards, A.E. & Acker, L.E. (1962). A demonstration of the long-term retention of a conditioned galvanic skin response. *Psychosomatic Medicine, 24,* 459-463.

Edwards, B. (1979). *Drawing on the right side of the brain.* Los Angeles: J.P.Tarcher.

Edwards, D.A. (1971). Neonatal administration of androstenedione, testosterone, or testosterone propionate: Effects on ovulation, sexual receptivity and aggressive behavior in female mice. *Physiological Behavior, 6,* 223-228.

Edwards, D. & Middleton, D. (1986). Joint remembering: Constructing an account of shared experience through conversation. *Discourse Processes, 9,* 423-459.

Edwards, D. & Middleton, D. (1988). Conversational remembering and family relationships: How children learn to remember. *Journal of Social and Personal Relationships, 5,* 3-25.

Edwards, D. & Potter, J. (1992). *Discursive psychology.* London: Sage.

Edwards, D. & Potter, J. (1993). Language and causation: a discursive action model of description and attribution. *Psychological Review,* 100, 1, 23-41.

Edwards, D., Potter, J. & Middleton, D. (1992). Toward a discursive psychology of remembering. *The Psychologist: Bulletin of the British Psychological Society, 5 (10)* , 441-446.

Edwards, G. (1980). Alcoholism treatment: Between guesswork and certainty. In G. Edwards & M. Grant (Eds.), *Alcoholism treatment in transition.* London: Croon Helm.

Efron, R. (1990). *The decline and fall of hemispheric specialization.* Hillsdale, NJ: Erlbaum.

Egeland, J.A., Gerhard, D.S., Pauls, D.L., Sussex, J.N., Kidd, K.K., Allen, C.R., Hostetter, A.M. & Housman, D.E. (1987). Bipolar affective disorder linked to DNA markers on chromosome II *Nature, 325,* 783-787.

Eger, E.E. (1990). Auschwitz at 16, Auschwitz at 61. *California State Psychologist,* pp. 6-9.

Egmond, M. van, Garnefski, N., Jonker, D. & Kerhof, A.J.F.M. (1993). The relationship between sexual abuse and female suicide behaviour. *Crisis: the Journal of Crisis Intervention and Suicide Prevention, 3,* 129-139.

Ehrhardt, A.A. & Baker, S.W. (1974). Fetal androgens, human central nervous system differentiation, and behavior sex differences. In R.C. Friedman, R.M. Richart & R.L. Vande Wiele (Eds.), *Sex differences in behavior.* New York: Wiley.

Ehrlich, B.E. & Diamond, J.M. (1980). Lithium, membranes and manic-depressive illness. *Journal of Membrane Biology,* 52, 187-200.

Eich, E., Reeves, J.L. & Katz, R.L. (1985). Anesthesia, amnesia, and the meory/awareness distinction. *Anaesthesiology and Analgesia, 64,* 1143-1148.

Eisenberg, N. & Mussen, P.H. (1989). *The roots of prosocial behavior in children.* New York: Cambridge University Press.

Eiser, J.R. (1980). *Cognitive social psychology.* London & New York: McGraw Hill.

Ekman, P. (1972). Universal and cultural differences in facial expressions of emotion. In J.Cole (Ed.) *Nebraska Symposium on Motivation.* Lincoln, NE: University of Nebraska Press.

Ekman, P. (Ed.). (1973). *Darwin and facial expression: A century of research in review.* New York: Academic Press.

Ekman, P. (1983). Cross cultural studies of emotion. In P. Ekman (Ed.), *Darwin and facial expression: A century of research in review* (pp. 169-222). New York: Academic Press.

Ekman, P. (1984). Expression and the nature of emotion. In K.R. Schemer & P. Ekman (Eds.), *Approaches to emotion.* Hilisdale, NJ: Erlbaum.

Ekman, P. (1985). *Telling lies: Clues to deceit in market place, politics and marriage.* New York: Norton.

Ekman, P. (1994). Strong evidence for universals in facial expressions: a reply to Russell's mistaken critique. *Psychological Bulletin, 115,* 268-287.

Ekman, P. & Friesen, W.V. (1971). Constants across cultures in the face and emotion. *Journal of Personality and Social Psychology, 17,* 124-129.

Ekman, P. & Friesen, W.V. (1975). *Unmasking the face: A guide to recognizing emotions from facial clues.* Englewood Cliffs, NJ: Prentice-Hall.

Ekman, P. & Friesen, W.V. (1986). A new pan-cultural facial expression of emotion. *Motivation and Emotion, 10,* 159-168.

Ekman, P., Levinson, R.W. & Friesen, W.V. (1983). Autonomic nervous system activity distinguishes betweeb emotions. *Science, 221,* 1208-1210.

Ekman, P., Sorenson, E. R. & Friesen, W.V. (1969). Pan-cultural elements in facial displays in emotion. *Science, 764,* 86-88.

Ekstrand, M.L. & Coates, T.J. (1990). Maintenance of safer sexual behaviors and predictors of risky sex: The San Francisco men's health survey. *American Journal of Public Health, 80,* 973-977.

Elkin,I., Shea, M.T., Watkins, J.T., Imber, S.D., Sotsky, S.M., Collins, J.F., Glass, D.R., Pilkonis, P.A., Leber, W.R., Kocherly, J.P., Fiester, S.J. & Parloff, M.B. (1989). National Institutes of Mental Health treatment of depression collaborative research program: General effectiveness of treatments. *Archives of General Psychiatry, 46,* 971-982.

Elliott, J. (1977). The power and pathology of prejudice. In P.G. Zimbardo & F.L. Ruch, *Psychology and life* (9th ed., Diamond Printing). Glenview, IL: Scott, Foresman.

Elliott, J. (1990). In *Discovering Psychology,* Program 20 [PBS video series]. Washington, DC: Annenberg/CPB Program.

Ellis, A. (1962). *Reason and emotion in psychotherapy.* New York: Lyle Stuart.

Ellis, A. (1977). The treatment of a psychopath with rational therapy. In S.J. Morse & R.I. Watson (Eds,), *Psychotherapies: A comparative casebook.* New York: Holt, Rinehart & Winston.

Ellis, A. & Grieger, R. (1986). *Handbook of rational emotive therapy* (Vol. 2). New York: Springer.

Elman, J.L. (1990). Representation and structure in connectionist models. In G.T.M. Altmann (Ed.), *Cognitive models of speech processing: Psycholinguistic and computational perspectives* (pp 345-382). Cambridge, MA: MIT Press.

Eme, R., Maisiak, R. & Goodale, W. (1979). Seriousness of adolescent problems. *Adolescence, 14,* 93-99.

Emler, N. (1984). Differential involvement in delinquency: Toward an interpretation in terms of reputation management. *Progress in Experimental Psychology, 13,* 173-239.

Emler, N., Reicher, S. & Ross, A. (1987). The social context of delinquent conduct. *Journal of Child Psychology and Psychiatry, 28,* 99-109.

Emmelkamp, P.M. (1982). *Phobic and obsessive-compulsive disorders: Theory, research and practice.* New York: Plenum.

Emmelkamp, P.M. (1986). Behavior therapy with adults. In S.L. Garfield & A.E. Bergin (Eds.), *Handbook of psychotherapy and behavior change* (pp. 385-442). New York: Wiley.

Emmelkamp, P.M.G. & Kuipers, A. (1979). Agoraphobia: A follow-up study four years after treatment. *British Journal of Psychology, 134,* 352-355.

Emmons, R.A. (1986). Personal strivings: An approach to personality and its subjective well being. *Journal of Personality, and Social Psychology, 51,* 1058-1068.

Endler, N.S. (1983). Interactionism: A personality model, but not yet a theory. In M.M. Page (Ed.), *Nebraska Symposium on Motivation, 1982: Personality-current theory and research* pp. 155-200). Lincoln, NE: University of Nebraska Press.

Engen, T. (1987). Remembering odors and their names. *American Scientist, 75,* 497-503.

Engle, G.L. (1976). The need for a new medical model: A challenge for biomedicine. *Science, 196,* 129-136.

Enright, J.B. & Jaeckle, W.R. (1963). Psychiatric symptoms and diagnosis in two subcultures. *International Journal of Psychiatry, 9,* 12-17.

Epstein, S. (1979). The stability of behavior: 1. On predicting most of the people much of the time. *Journal of Personality and Social Psychology,* 37, 1097-1126.

Epstein, S. & O'Brien, E.J. (1985). The person-situation debate in historical and current perspective. *Psychological Bulletin,* 98, 3, 513-537.

Epstein, W. (1961). The influence of syntactical structure on learning. *American Journal of Psychology,* 74, 80-85.

Erdelyi, M.H. (1974). A new look at the New Look: Perceptual defense and vigilance. *Psychological Review,* 87, 1-25.

Ericksen, C.W. (1966). Cognitive responses to internally wed anxiety. In C.D. Spielberger (Ed.), *Anxiety and behaviour.* New York: Academic Press.

Ericsson, K.A. & Chase, W.G. (1982). Exceptional memory. *American Scientist,* 70, 607-615.

Ericsson, K.A., Chase, W.G. & Falcoon, S. (1980). Acquisition of a memory skill. *Science,* 208, 1181-1183.

Ericsson, K.A., & Simon, H.A. (1984). *Protocol analysis: Verbal reports as data.* Cambridge, MA: MIT Press.

Erikson, E.H. (1963). *Childhood and society* (2nd. ed.). New York: Norton.

Erikson, E.H. (1968). *Identity: Youth and crisis.* New York: Norton.

Erikson, E. (1990). In *Discovering Psychology,* Program 18 [PBS video series]. Washington, DC: Annenberg/CPB Program.

Eron, L.D., Huesmann, L.R., Lefkowitz, M.M. & Walder, L.O. (1972). Does television violence cause aggression? *American Psychologist,* 27, 253-263.

Estes, W.K. (1944). An experimental study of punishment. Psychological Monographs, 57 (Whole No. 263), Reprinted in Boe, E.E. & Church, R.M. (1968) *Punishment: Issues & Experiments, 108-165,* New York: Appleton-Century-Crofts.

Estes, W.K. (1991). Cognitive architectures from the standpoint of an experimental psychologist. *Annual Review of Psychology,* 42, 1-28.

Evans, F.J. (1989). The independence of suggestibility, placebo response, and hypnotizability. In V.A. Gheorghiu, P. Netter, H.I. Eysenck, & R. Rosenthal (Eds.), *Suggestion and suggestibility* (pp. 145-154). New York: Springer-Verlag.

Evans, G.W., Palsane, M.N., Lepore, S.J. & Martin, J. (1989). Residential density and psychological health: The mediating effects of social support. *Journal of Personality and Social Psychology,* 57, 994-999.

Evans, J.S.B., Barston, J.L. & Pollard, P. (1983). On the conflict between logic and belief in syllogistic reasoning. *Memory and Cognition,* 11, 295-306.

Evans, P.D. & Edgerton, N. (1991). Life-events and mood as predictors of the common cold. *British Journal of Medical Psychology,* 64, 35-44.

Evans, R.I., Rozelle, R.M., Mittelmark, M.B., Hansen, W.B., Bane, A. L. & Havis, J. (1978). Deterring the onset of smoking in children: Knowledge of immediate physiological effects and coping with peer pressure, media pressure, and parent modeling. *Journal of Applied Social Psychology,* 8, 126-135.

Evans-Pritchard, E.E. (1937). *Witchcraft, oracles and magic among the Azande.* Oxford: Oxford University Press.

Evesham, M. (1987). Residential courses for stutterers: combining technique and personal construct psychology. In C. Levy, (Ed.), *Stuttering therapies: Practical Approaches.* London: Croom Helm.

Eysenck, H.J. (1947). *Dimensions of personality.* London: Routledge and Kegan Paul.

Eysenck, H.J. (1952). The effects of psychotherapy: An evaluation. *Journal of Consulting Psychology,* 16, 319-324.

Eysenck, H.J. (1970). *The structure of human personality* (3rd ed.). London: Methuen.

Eysenck, H.J. (1973). *The inequality of man.* London: Temple Smith.

Eysenck, H.J. (1975). *The inequality of man.* San Diego, CA: Educational and Industrial Testing Service.

Eysenck, H.J. & Kamin, L. (1981). *The intelligence controversy: H.J. Eysenck vs. Leon Kamin.* New York: Wiley-Interscience.

Eysenck, H.J. (1990). Biological dimensions of personality. In L.A. Pervin (Ed.), *Handbook of personality, theory and research* (pp. 244-276). New York: Guilford Press.

Eysenck, M.W. (1994). Connectionist models of memory. In M.W. Eysenck (Ed.), *The Blackwell Dictionary of Cognitive Psychology* (pp. 83-84). Oxford: Blackwell.

F

Fagel, A. (1993). *Developing through relationships.* New York: Harvester Wheatsheaf

Fagot, B.L. (1978). The influence of sex of child on parental reactions to toddler children. *Child Development,* 49, 459-465.

Fairweather, G.W., Sanders, D.H., Maynard, R.F. & Crester, D.L. (1969). *Community life for the mentally ill: Alternative to institutional care.* Chicago: Aldine.

Fallowfield, L. (1991). *Breast Cancer.* London: Routledge .

Fanslow, C.A. (1984). Touch and the elderly. In C. Caldwell Brown (Ed.), The many facets of touch (pp. 183-189). Skillman, NJ: Johnson & Johnson.

Fantz, R.L. (1963). Pattern vision in newborn infants. *Science, 140,* 296-297.

Farina, A. (1980). Social attitudes and beliefs and their role in mental disorders. In J.G. Rabkin, L. Gelb & J.B. Lazar (Eds.), *Attitudes toward the mentally ill: Research perspectives* (pp 35-37). Rockville, Md.: National Institute of Mental Health.

Farina, A., Gliha, D., Boudreau, L.A., Allen, J.G. & Sherman, M.I. (1971). Mental illness and the impact of believing others know about it. Journal of Abnormal Psychology, 77, 1-5.

Farina, A. & Hagalauer, H.D. (1975). Sex and mental illness: The generosity of females. *Journal of Consulting and Clinical Psychology, 43,* 122.

Farley, F. (1986, May). The Big T in personality. *Psychology Today,* pp. 44-52.

Farley, F. (1990, May). The Type T personality, with some implications for practice. *The California Psychologist, 23,* 29.

Farquhar, J.W., Maccoby, N. & Solomon, D.S. (1984). Community applications of behavioral medicine. In W.D. Gentry (Ed.), *Handbook of behavioral medicine* (pp. 437-478). New York: Guilford Press.

Farr, M.J. (1984). Cognitive psychology. *Naval Research Reviews, 36,* 33-36.

Farrington, D.P. (1991). Antisocial personality from childhood to adulthood. *The Psychologist incorporating the Bulletin of the British Psychological Society,* 4, 9, 389-394.

Farrington, D.P. & West, D.J. (1990). The Cambridge study of delinquent development: A long-term follow-up of 411 males. In H.J. Kerner & G. Kaiser (Eds.) *Criminality: Personality, behaviour and life history* (pp.115-138). Berlin: Springer-Verlag.

Farrington, D. & West, D.J. (1993). Criminal, penal and life histories of chronic offenders: Risk and protective factors and early identification. *Criminal Behaviour and Mental Health, 3,* 492-523.

Farthing, G.W. (1992). *The psychology of consciousness.* Englewood Cliffs, NJ: Prentice Hall.

Fass, P.S. (1980). The IQ: A cultural and historical framework. *American Journal of Education, 88,* 431-458.

Fausto-Sterling, A. (1993). *Myths of gender: biological theories about women and men,* (2nd ed.). New York: Basic Books.

Fay, R.E., Turner, C.F., Klassen, A.D. & Gagnon, J.H. (1989). Prevalence and patterns of same-gender sexual contact among men. *Science,* 243, 338-348.

Fazio, R.H. (1987). Self-perception theory: A current perspective. In M.P. Zanna, J.M. Olson & C.P. Herman (Eds.), *Social influence: The Ontario Symposium* (Vol. 5, pp. 129-150). Hilisdale, NJ: Eribaum.

Fechner, G.T. (1860). *Elemente der psychophysik.* Germany: Breitkopf und Hartel.

Fechner, G.T. (1966). Elements of psychophysics (Vol. 1, E.G. Boring & D.H. Howes, Eds. and H.E. Adler, Trans.) New York: Holt, Rinehart & Winston. (Original work published 1860)

Feester, C.B., Culbertson, S. & Perron Bore, M.C. (1975). *Behavior principles* (2nd ed.). Englewood Cliffs, NJ: Prentice Hall.

Feester, C.B. & Skinner, B.F. (1957). Schedules of reinforcement. New York: Appleton-Century-Crofts.

Feigenbaum, E.A. & McCorduck, P. (1983). *The fifth generation.* Reading, MA: Addison-Wesley.

Fernald, R. (1984). Vision and behavior in an African cichlid fish. *American Scientist,* 72, 58-65.

Fernald, A. (1990). In *Discovering Psychology,* Program 6 [PBS video series]. Washington, DC: Annenberg/CPB Project.

Fernald, A., Taeschner, T., Dunn, J., Papousek, M., De Boysson-Barthes, B. & Fukui, I. (1989). A cross-cultural study of prosodic modification in mothers' and fathers' speech to preverbal infants. *Journal of Child Language, 16,* 477-501.

Ferrald, D. (1984). *The Hans legacy.* Hillsdale, NJ: Erlbaum.

Ferrare, N.A. (1962). *Institutionalization and attitude change in an aged population*. Unpublished doctoral dissertation, Western Reserve University.

Ferster, C.B., Culbertson, S. & Perron Boren, M.C. (1975). *Behavior principles* (2nd ed.). Englewood Cliffs, NJ: Prentice-Hall.

Ferster, C.B., & Skinner, B.F. (1957). *Schedules of reinforcement*. New York: Appleton-Century-Crofts.

Feshbach, S. & White, M.J. (1986). Individual differences in attitudes toward nuclear arms policies: Some psychological and social policy considerations. *Journal of Peace Research, 23*, 129-138.

Festinger, L. (1954). A theory of social comparison processes. *Human Relations, 7*, 117-140.

Festinger, L. (1957). *A theory of cognitive dissonance*. Stanford, CA: Stanford University Press.

Festinger, L. (1990). In *Discovering Psychology*, Program II [PBS video series]. Washington, DC: Annenberg/CPB Project.

Festinger, L. & Carlsmith, J.M. (1959). Cognitive consequences of forced compliance. *Journal of Abnormal and Social Psychology, 58*, 203-211.

Feuerstein, M., Labbe, E.E. & Kuczmierczyk, A.R. (1986). *Health psychology: A psychobiological perspective*. New York: Plenum.

Fewtrell, D. & O'Connor, F. (1995). *Clinical phenomenology and cognitive psychology*. London: Routledge.

Fields, H.L. & Levine, J.D. (1984). Placebo analgesia: A role for endorphins. *Trends in Neuroscience, 7*, 271-273.

Field, T. (1990). In *Discovering Psychology*, Program 4 (PBS video series). Washington, DC: Annenberg/CPB Project.

Field, T.F. & Schanberg, S.M. (1990). Massage alters growth and catecholamine production in preterm newborns. In N. Gunzenhauser (Ed.), *Advances in touch* (pp. 96-104). Skillman, NJ: Johnson & Johnson Co.

Fincham, F.D. & Bradbury, T.N. (1987). The impact of attributions in marriage: a longitudinal analysis. *Journal of Personality and Social Psychology, 53*, 510-17.

Fink, M. (1979). *Convulsive therapy: Theory and practice*. New York: Raven Press.

Fischer, A.H. (1993). Sex differences in emotionality: Fact or stereotype? *Feminism & Psychology, 3*, 303-318.

Fischer, S. & Greenberg, R.P. (1985). *The scientific credibility of Freud's theories and therapy*. New York: Columbia University Press.

Fish, J.M. (1973). *Placebo therapy*. San Francisco: Jossey-Bass.

Fishbein, M. & Ajzen, I. (1975). *Belief, attitude, intention and behavior: An introduction to theory and research*. Reading, MA: Addison-Wesley.

Fishbein, M. & Ajzen, I. (1981). Attitudes and voting behaviour: An application of the theory of reasoned action. In G.M. Stephenson and J.M. Davis (Eds.), *Progress in applied social psychology, Vol.I*, pp.253-313, London: Wiley.

Fiske, D.W. (1949). Consistency of the factorial structures of personality ratings from different sources. *Journal of Abnormal and Social Psychology, 44*, 329-344.

Fiske, S. (1987). People's reactions to nuclear war: Implications for psychologists. *American Psychologist, 42*. 207-217.

Fiske, S.T., & Taylor, S.E. (1991). *Social cognition*. New York: McGraw-Hill.

Fiske, S.T. (1993). Social cognition and social perception. *Annual Review of Psychology, 44*, 155-194

Fitts, P.M. & Posner, M. (1967). *Human performance*. Belmont, CA: Brooks/Cole.

Fitzgerald, R. & Ellsworth, P.C. (1984). Due process vs. crime control: Death qualification and jury attitudes. *Law and Human Behavior, 8*, 31-51.

Flanagan, O.J. Jr. (1991). *The science of the mind*. Cambridge, MA: The MIT Press.

Flavell, J.H. (1977). *Cognitive development*. Englewood Cliffs, NJ: Prentice-Hall.

Flavell, J.H. (1979). Metacognition and cognitive monitoring: A new area of cognitive-developmental inquiry. *American Psychologist, 34*, 906-911.

Flavell, J.H. (1981). Cognitive monitoring. In W.P. Dickson (Ed.), *Children's oral communication skills* (pp. 35-60). New York: Academic Press.

Flavell, J.H. (1985). *Cognitive development* (2nd ed.). Englewood Cliffs, NJ: Prentice-Hall.

Flavell, J.H., Flavell, E.R. & Green, F.L. (1983). Development of the appearance – reality distinction. *Cognitive Psychology, January, 15(1)*, 95-120.

Fleischman, P.R. (1973). [Letter to the editor concerning "On

being sane in insane places"]. *Science, 180*, 356.

Fletcher, G.J.O. & Ward, C. (1988). Attribution theory and processes: A cross-cultural perspective. In M.H. Bond (Ed.), *The cross-cultural challenge to social psychology* (pp. 230-244). Newbury Park, CA: Sage.

Fletcher, H. (1929). Speech and hearing. New York: Van Nostrand.

Floderus-Myrhed, B., Pedersen, N. & Rasmussen, I. (1980). Assessment of heritability for personality, based on a short form of the Eysenck Personality Inventory: A study of 12,898 twin pairs. *Behavior Genetics, 10*, 507-520.

Flood, R.A. & Seager, C.P. (1968). A retrospective examination of psychiatric case records of patients who subsequently committed suicide. *British Journal of Psychiatry, 114*, 433-450.

Flor, H., Kerns, R.D. & Turk, D.C. (1987). The role of spouse reinforcement, perceived pain and activity levels of chronic pain patients. *Journal of Psychosomatic Research, 31*, 2, 251-259.

Flora, J.A. (1991, May). AIDS prevention among young people. *California Psychologist*, pp. 14, 18.

Fodor, J.A. (1975). *The language of thought*. New York: Thomas Y. Crowell.

Fodor, J.A. (1983). *The modularity of mind: An essay in faculty psychology*. Cambridge, MA: MIT Press.

Fogel, A. (1992). Movement and communication in human infancy: The social dynamics of development. *Journal of Human Movement Studies*.

Foley, V.D. (1979). Family therapy. In R.J. Corsini (Ed.), *Current psychotherapies* (2nd ed., pp. 460-469). Itasca, IL: Peacock.

Folkins, D.H., Lawson, K.D., Opton, E.M., Jr. & Lazarus, R.S. (1968). Desensitization and the experimental reduction of threat. *Journal of Abnormal Psychology, 73*, 100-113.

Folkman, S. (1984). Personal control and stress and coping processes: A theoretical analysis. *Journal of Personality and Social Psychology, 46*, 839-852.

Folkman, S., Lazarus, R.S., Dunkel-Schetter, C., DeLongis, A. & Gruen, R.J. (1986). Dynamics of a stressful encounter: Cognitive appraisal, coping, and encounter outcomes. *Journal of Personality and Social Psychology, 50*, 992-1003.

Fonagy, P. & Higgitt, A. (1984). *Personality, theory and clinical practice*. London: Methuen.

Fong, G.T. & Markus, H. (1982). Self-schemas and judgments about others. *Social Cognition, 1*, 191-204.

Fontaine, G. (1974). Social comparison and some determinants of expected personal control and expected performance in a novel situation. *Journal of Personality and Social Psychology, 29*, 487-496.

Ford, C.S. & Beach, F.A. (1951). *Patterns of sexual behavior*. New York: Harper & Row.

Fordyce, W.E. (1973). An operant conditioning method for managing chronic pain. *Postgraduate Medicine, 53*, 123-128.

Fordyce, W.E. (1976). *Behavioral methods for chronic pain and illness*. St.Louis: C.V.Mosby.

Forest, D.V. (1976). Nonsense and sense in schizophrenic language. *Schizophrenia Bulletin, 2*, 286-38 1.

Forgas, J.P. (1982). Episodic cognition: Internal representation of interaction routines. In L. Berkowitz (Ed.), *Advances in experimental social psychology* (Vol. 5). New York: Academic Press.

Foster, G.M. & Anderson, B.G. (1978). *Medical anthropology*. New York: Wiley.

Foster, K., Wilmot, A. & Dobbs, J. (1990). *General Household Survey 1988, Series GHS, No. 19*. London: Her Majesty's Stationary Office (HMSO).

Foucault, M. (1975). *The birth of the clinic*. New York: Vintage Books.

Foucault, M. (1976). *Histoire de la sexualité: la volonté de savoir*. Paris: Gallimard.

Foulkes, A. (1990). Dreaming and consciousness. *European Journal of Cognitive Psychology, 2(1)*, 39-55.

Fouts, R.S., Bouts, D. & Schoenfeld, D. (1984). Sign language conversational interactions between chimpanzees. *Sign Language Studies, 41*, 1-12.

Fouts, R.S. & Rigby, R. L. (1977). Man-chimpanzee communication. In T. A. Sebeok (Ed.), *How animals communicate*. Bloomington: University of Indiana Press.

Fowler, H. (1965). *Curiosity and exploratory behavior*. New York: Macmillan.

Fowles, D.C. (1992). Schizophrenia: Diathesis-stress revisited. *Annual Review of Psychology, 43*, 303-336.

Fox, M.W. (1974). *Concepts in ethology: Animal and human behavior*. Minneapolis: University of Minnesota Press.

Foy, D.W., Eisler, R.M. & Pinkston, S. (1975). Modeled assertion in a case of explosive rages. *Journal of Behavioral Therapy and Experimental Psychiatry, 6,* 135-137.

Fraisse, P. (1968). Les Emotions. In P. Fraisse & J. Piaget (Eds.), *Traité de psychologie experimentale* (Vol. 5). Paris: Presses Universitaires.

Frances, A. & Cooper, A.M. (1981). Descriptive and dynamic psychiatry: A perspective on DSM-III. *American Journal of Psychiatry, 138,* 1198-1202.

Frances, A.J., Widiger, T.A., First, M.B., Pincus, H.A. et al (1991) DSM-IV: Toward a more empirical diagnostic system. *Canadian Psychology, 32,* 2, 171-173.

Frank, J. (1990). In *Discovering Psychology,* Program 2 [PBS video series]. Washington, DC: Annenberg/CPB Project.

Frank, J.D. (1963). *Persuasion and healing.* New York: Schochen Books.

Frank, J.D. (1979). The present status of outcome studies. *Journal of Consulting and Clinical Psychology, 47,* 310-316.

Frank, J. (1987). The drive for power and the nuclear arms race. *American Psychologist, 42,* 337-344.

Frank, L.R. (Ed.). (1978). *The history of shock treatment.* (Available from L.R. Frank, San Fransisco, CA).

Franklin, D. (1987, January). The politics of masochism. *Psychology Today,* pp. 52-57.

Franks, C.M. & Barbrack, C.R. (1983). Behavior therapy with adults: An integrative perspective. In M. Hersen, A.E. Kazdin & A.S. Bellack (Eds.), *The clinical psychology handbook* (pp. 507-523). New York: Pergamon Press.

Fransella, F. & Bannister, D. (1977). *A manual for repertory grid technique.* London: Academic Press.

Franz, C.E., McClelland, D.C. & Weinberger, J. (1991). Childhood antecedents of conventional social accomplishment in midlife adults: A 36-year prospective study. *Journal of Personality and Social Psychology, 60,* 586-595.

Fraser, S.C. (1974) *Deindividuation: Effects of anonymity on aggression in children.* Unpublished mimeograph report, University of Southern California.

Frederiksen, L.W., Jenkins, J.O., Foy, D.W. & Eisler, R.M. (1976). Social-skills training to modify abusive verbal outbursts in adults. *Journal of Applied Behavior Analysis, 9,* 117-125.

Fredrickson, B.L. (1991). Anticipated endings: An explanation for selective social interaction (doctoral dissertation, Stanford University, 1990). *Dissertation Abstracts International, 3* AAD9l-00818.

Fredrickson, B.L. & Carstensen, L.L. (1990). Choosing social partners: How old age and anticipated endings make people more selective. *Psychology and Aging, 5,* 335-347.

Freedman, D.G. & DeBoer, M.M. (1979). Biological and cultural differences in early child development. *Annual Review of Anthropology, 8,* 579-600.

Freedman, J.L. (1984). Effect of television violence on aggressiveness. *Psychological Bulletin, 96,* 227-246.

Freedman, J.L. & Fraser, S.C. (1966). Compliance without pressure: The foot-in-the-door technique. *Journal of Personality and Social Psychology, 4,* 195-202.

Freedman, J.L. & Doob, A.N. (1968). *Deviancy: The psychology of being different.* New York: Academic Press.

Freeman, F.R. (1972). *Sleep research: A critical review.* Springfield, IL: Charles C Thomas.

Freeman, M. (1993). *Rewriting the self: history, memory, narrative.* London: Routledge.

Freud, A. (1946). *The ego and the mechanisms of defense.* New York: International Universities Press.

Freud, A. (1958). Adolescence. *Psychoanalytic Study of the Child, 13,* 255-278.

Freud, S. (1900). *The interpretation of dreams.* In J. Strachey (Ed. and Trans.), *The standard edition of the complete psychological works of Sigmund Freud* (Vol. 5). London: Hogarth Press.

Freud, S. (1914). *The psychopathology of everyday life.* New York: Macmillan. (Original work published 1904)

Freud, S. (1915). Instincts and their vicissitudes. In S. Freud, *The collected papers.* New York: Collier.

Freud, S. (1923) *Introductory lectures on psychoanalysis* (J. Riviera, Trans.) London: Allen & Unwin.

Freud, S. (1925). The unconscious. In S. Freud, *The collected papers* (Vol. 4). London: Hogarth.

Freud, S. (1926). *Inhibitions, symptoms and anxiety. Standard Edition, Vol. 20.* London: Hogarth.

Freud, S. (1949). *An outline of psycho-analysis.* New York: Norton.

Freud, S. (1949). *A general introduction to psychoanalysis.* New York: Penguin Books.

Freud, S. (1960). *Jokes and their relation to the unconscious.* New York: Norton. (Original work published 1905)

Freud, S. (1961). *Civilization and its discontents* (J. Strachey, Trans.). New York: Norton. (Original work published 1930)

Freud, S. (1976). Three essays on the theory of sexuality. In J. Strachey (Ed. and Trans.), *The standard edition of the complete psychological works of Sigmund Freud* (Vol. 7). London: Hogarth Press. (Original work published 1905)

Freud, S. (1976). Totem and taboo. In J. Strachey (Ed. and Trans.), *The standard edition of the complete psychological works of Sigmund Freud.* (Vol. 13). London: Hogarth Press. (Original work published 1913)

Freudenberger, H.J. (1974). *Staff burnout.* Journal of Social Issues, 30, 159-165.

Frey, W.H. & Langseth, M. (1986). *Crying: The mystery of tears.* New York: Winston Press,

Fridlund, A.J. (1990). Evolution and facial action in reflex, social motive, and paralanguage. In P.K. Ackles, J.R. Jennings, & M.G.H. Coles (Fds.), *Advances in psychophysiology.* Greenwich, CT: JAI Press.

Friedman, H.S. (Ed.). (1990). *Personality and Disease.* New York: Wiley.

Friedman, H.S. & Booth-Kewley, S. (1987). The 'disease-prone personality': A meta-analytic view of the construct. *American Psychologist, 42,* 539-555, 11

Friedman, H.S. & Booth-Kewley, S. (1988). Validity of the Type A construct: A reprise. *Psychological Bulletin, 104,* 381-384.

Friedman, M., Thoresen, C.E., Gill, J.J., Ulmer, D., Powell, L.H., Price, V.A., Brown, B., Thompson, L., Rabin, D.D., Breall, W.S., Bourg, E., Levy, R. & Dixon, T. (1986). Alteration of Type A behavior and its effect on cardiac recurrences in post-myocardial infarction patients: Summary results of the Recurrent Coronary Prevention Project. *American Heart Journal, 11,* 653-665.

Friedman, M., Thoresen, C.E., Gill, J.J., Powell, L.H., Ulmer, D., Thompson, L., Price, V.A., Rabin, D.D., Breall, W.S., Dixon, T., Levy, R., & Bourg, E. (1984). Alteration of Type A behavior and reduction in cardiac recurrences in postmyocardial infarction patients. *American Heart Journal, 11* 108, 237-248.

Friedman, M. & Rosenman, R.F. (1974). *Type A behavior and your heart.* New York: Knopf.

Frijda, N.H. (1986). *The emotions.* Cambridge: Cambridge University Press.

Frijda, N.H. (1988). The laws of emotion. *American Psychologist, 43,* 349-358.

Frijda, N., Kuipers, P. & Peter Schure, E. (1989). Relations among emotion, appraisal, and emotional action readiness. *Journal of Personality and Social Psychology, 57,* 212-228.

Frisby, J.P. (1979). *Seeing: Illusion, brain and mind.* Oxford: Oxford University Press.

Frisby, J.P. (1980). Seeing. Oxford: Oxford University Press.

Frith, C. (1992). *The cognitive neuropsychology of schizophrenia.* Hove: Lawrence Erlbaum Associates.

Fromkin, V.A. (1971). The non-anomalous nature of anomalous utterances. *Language, 47,* 27-52.

Fromkin, V.A. (Ed.). (1980). *Errors in linguistic performance: Slips of the tongue, pen and hand.* New York: Academic Press.

Fromm, E. (1947). *Man for himself.* New York: Holt, Rinehart & Winston.

Fromm, E. & Shor, R.E. (Eds.). (1979). *Hypnosis: Developments in research and new perspectives* (2nd ed.). Hawthome, NY: Aldine.

Frumkin, B. & Anisfeld, M. (1977). Semantic and surface codes in the memory of deaf children. *Cognitive Psychology, 9,* 475-493.

Fry, P.S. & Ghosh, R. (1980). Attributions of success and failure: comparison of cultural differences between Asian and Caucasian children. *Journal of Cross-Cultural Psychology,* 11, 343-63.

Fry, W.F., Jr. (1986). Humor, physiology, and the aging process. In L. Nahemow, K.A. McCluskey-Fawcett, & P.E. McGhee (Eds.), *Humor and aging* (pp.81-98). Orlando: Academic Press.

Fry, W.F. & Allen, M. (1975). Make 'em laugh. Palo Alto, CA: *Science and Behavior Books.*

Fuller, J.L. (1982). Psychology and genetics: A happy marriage? *Canadian Psychology, 23,* 11-21.

Funder, D. (1991). Global traits: A neo-Allportian approach to personality. *Psychological Science, 2,* 31-44.

662　REFERENCES

Furman, W., Rahe, D. & Hartup, W.W. (1979). Rehabilitation of socially withdrawn preschool children through mixed-aged and same-sex socialization. *Child Development, 50,* 915-922.

Furstenberg, F., Jr. (1985). Sociological ventures in child development. *Child Development, 56,* 281-288.

G

Gabriel, C. (1990) The validity of qualitative market research, *Journal of the Market Research Society,* Vol. 32, No.4, p.507-519.

Gagnon, J.H. (1977). *Human sexualities.* Glenview, IL: Scott, Foresman.

Galaburda, A.M., LeMay, M., Kemper, T.L. & Geschwind, N. (1978). Right-left asymmetries in the brain. *Science, 199,* 852-856.

Gallagher, J.M. & Reid, D.K. (1981). *The learning theory of Piaget and Inheider.* Monterey, CA: Brooks/Cole.

Gallup, G., Jr. & Newport, F. (1990, August 6). One in 4 Americans believes in ghosts: Poll shows strong belief in paranormal. *The San Francisco Chronicle,* pp. B1, B5.

Galluscio, E.H. (1990). Biological psychology. New York: Macmillan.

Galton, F. (1869). *Hereditary genius.* London: Macmillan.

Galton, F. (1884). Measurement of character. *Fortnightly Review, 42,* 179-185.

Galton, F. (1907). *Inquiries into human faculty and its development.* London: Dent Publishers. (Original work published 1883)

Gamson, W.A., Fireman, B. & Rytina, S. (1982). *Encounters with unjust authority.* Homewood, Ill.: Dorsey Press.

Garcia, J. (1990). Learning without memory. *Journal of Cognitive Neuroscience, 2,* 287-305.

Garcia, J. & Garcia y Robertson, R. (1985). Evolution of learning mechanisms. In B.L. Hammonds (Ed.), *Psychology and learning: 1984 Master Lecturers* (pp. 187-243). Washington, DC: American Psychological Association.

Garcia, J. & Koelling, R.A. (1966). The relation of cue to consequence in avoidance teaming. *Psychonomic Science, 4,* 123-124.

Gardner, H. (1983). *Frames of mind.* New York: Basic Books.

Gardner, H. (1985). *The mind's new science: A history of the cognitive revolution.* New York: Basic Books.

Gardner, H. (1990). In *Discovering Psychology,* programs 10 and 16 [PBS video series]. Washington, DC: Annenberg/CPB Project.

Gardner, L.I. (1972). Deprivation dwarfism. *Scientific American,* 227(7), 76-82.

Gardner, R.A. & Gardner, B.T. (1969). Teaching sign language to a chimpanzee. *Science, 165,* 664-672.

Gardner, R.A., Van Cantfort, T.E. & Gardner, B.T. (1992). Categorical replies to categorical questions by cross-fostered chimpanzees. *American Journal of Psychology, 105,* 27-57.

Garfield, P. (1975). Psychological concomitants of the lucid dream state. *Sleep Research, 4,* 184.

Garmezy, N. (1976). Vulnerable and invulnerable children: Theory, research and intervention. *Journal Abstract Supplement Service. Catalog of selected Documents in Psychology, 6,* 96.

Garmezy, N. (1977). The psychology and psychopathology of Allen Head. *Schizophrenia Bulletin, 3,* 360-369.

Garmezy, N. & Mattysse, S. (Eds.). (1977). Special issue on the psychology and psychopathology of attention. *Schizophrenic Bulletin, 3(3).*

Garner, W.R. (1974). *The processing of information and structure.* Potomac, MD: Lawrence Erlbaum Associates.

Garrett, M.F. (1984). The organization of processing structures for language production. In D. Caplan, A.R. Lecours, & A. Smith (Eds.), *Biological perspectives on language* (pp. 108-124). Cambridge, MA: MIT Press.

Garrett, M.F. (1988). Processes in language production. In F.J. Newmeyer (Ed.), *Linguistics: The Cambridge Survey, Vol. III. Language: Psychological and biological aspects* (pp. 69-96). Cambridge: Cambridge University Press.

Garrison, V. (1977). The 'Puerto Rican syndrome' in psychiatry and Espiritismo. In V. Crapanzano & V. Garrison (Eds.), *Case studies in spirit possession.* New York: Wiley Interscience.

Gaskell, J. (1985). Positive and negative emotional gradients during first use of the dissecting room. *Motivation and Emotion, 9,* 11-19.

Gawin, F.H. (1991). Cocaine addiction: Psychology and neurophysiology. *Science, 251,* 1580-1586.

Gay, P. (1988). *Freud: A life for our time.* New York: Norton.

Gayle, H.D., Keeling, R.P., Garcia-Tunon, M., Kilbourne, B.W., Narkunas, J.P., Ingram, F.R., Rogers, M.F. &

Curran, J.W. (1990). Prevalence of Human Immunodeficiency Virus among university students. *New England Journal of medicine, 323, 1538-1541.*

Gazzaniga, M. (1970). *The bisected brain.* New York: Appleton Century Crofts.

Gazzaniga, M. (1985). *The social brain.* New York: Basic Books.

Gazzaniga, M. (1990). In *Discovering Psychology,* Program 14 [PBS video series]. Washington, DC: Annenberg/CPB Program.

Gazzaniga, M. (1980). *Psychology.* New York: Harper & Row.

Geen, R.G. (1991). Social motivation. *Annual Review of Psychology, 42,* 377-400.

Geer, J.H., Davidson, G.C. & Gatchel, R.I. (1970). Reduction of stress in humans through nonveridical perceived control of aversive stimulation. *Journal of personality and Social Psychology, 16,* 731-738.

Geldard, F.A. (1972). *The human senses* (2nd ed.). New York: Wiley.

Gelman, R. (1979). Preschool thought. *American Psychologists, 34,* 900-905.

Gelman, R. & Baillargeon, R. (1983). A review of Piagetian concepts. In J. Flavell & E. Markman (Eds.), *Handbook of child psychology* (Vol. 3, pp. 167-230). New York: Wiley.

George, D. & Southwell, P. (1986). Opinion on the Diablo Canyon Nuclear power plant. *Social Science Quarterly, 67,* 722-735.

Gerbner, G., Gross, L., Signorielli, N. & Morgan, M. (1986, September). *Television's mean world: Violence profile no. 14- 15.* Philadelphia: University of Pennsylvania, The Annenberg School of Communication.

Gergen, K.J. (1985). The social constructionist movement in modern psychology. *American Psychologist, 40,* 266-275.

Gergen, K.J. (1987). Toward self as a relationship. In K. Yardley & T. Honess (Eds.), Self & identity: Psychosocial Perspectives, Chichester: Wiley.

Gergen, K.J. & Gergen, M.M. (1988). Narrative and the self as relationship. In L. Berkovitz (Ed.), *Advances in experimental social psychology, Volume 21,* (pp. 17-56). New York: Academic Press.

Gergen, K.J., Gergen, M.M. & Barton, W. (1973, October). Deviance in the dark. *Psychology Today,* pp. 129-130.

Gershon, E.S. & Rieder, R.O. (1992). Major disorders of mind and brain. *Scientific American, 267,* 3, 127-133.

Geschwind, N. (1979). Specializations of the human brain. *Scientific American, 241(3),* 180-199.

Gevins, A.S., Morgan, N.H., Bressler, S.L., Cutillo, B.A., White, R. M., Illes, J., Greer, D.S., Doyle, J.C. & Zeitlin, G.M. (1987). Human neuroelectfic pattems predict performance accuracy. *Science, 235,* 580-585.

Gevins, A.S., Shaffer, R.E., Doyle, J.C., Cutillo, B.A., Tannehill, R.S. & Bressler, S.L. (1983). Shadows of thought: Shifting lateralization of human brain electrical potential patterns during brief visuo-motor task. *Science, 220,* 97-99.

Ghoneim, M.M. & Block, R.I. (1992). Learning and consciousness during general anesthesia. *Anesthesiology, 76,* 279-305.

Gibbs, J.C. (1977). Kohlberg's stages of moral judgment: A constructive critique. *Harvard Educational Review, 47,* 43-61.

Gibbs, J.C., Arnold, K.D. & Burkhart, J.E. (1984). Sex differences in the expression of moral judgment. *Child Development, 55,* 1040-1043.

Gibson, E.J. & Walker, A.S. (1984). Development of knowledge of visual-tactual affordances of substance. *Child Development, 55(2),* 453-460.

Gibson, F. (1990, Autumn). When drinking kills: The tragic story of Ted McGuire. *The Student Body,* pp.1-8.

Gibson, J.J. (1950). *The perception of the visual world.* New York: Houghton-Mifflin.

Gibson, J.J. (1966). *The senses considered as perceptual systems.* New York: Houghton-Mifflin.

Gibson, J.J. (1979). *An ecological approach to visual perception.* New York: Houghton-Mifflin.

Gibson, J.T. & Haritos-Fatouros, M. (1986, November). The education of a torturer. *Psychology Today,* pp. 50-58.

Gieringer, D.H. (1988). Marijuana, driving, and accident safety. *Journal of Psychoactive Drugs, 20(1),* 93-101.

Gieringer, D. (1990). How many crack babies? *The Drug Policy Letter, 2:2,* pp. 4-6.

Gilliam, H. (1986, July 6). Fencing out world prosperity. *San Francisco Chronicle,* p. 18.

Gillig, P.M. & Greenwald, A.G. (1974). Is it time to lay the sleeper effect to rest? *Journal of personality and Social Psychology, 29,* 132-139.

Gilligan, C. (1982). *In a different voice: Psychological Theory and women's development.* Cambridge, MA: Harvard University Press.

Gilligan, S., & Bower, G.H. (1984). Cognitive consequences of emotional arousal. In C. Izard, J. Kagan & R. Zajonc (Eds.), *Emotions, cognitions, and behaviour* (pp.547-588). Cambridge: Cambridge University Press.

Gilman, L. (1989, July/August). Teens take to gambling: lifelong addiction can start with a lottery ticket. *American Health: Fitness of Body and Mind*, p. 113.

Gist, R. & Stolz, S.B. (1982). Mental health promotion and the media: Community response to the Kansas City hotel disaster. *American Psychologist, 37,* 1136-1139.

Gittelman, R. & Klein, D.F. (1985). Childhood separation anxiety and adult agoraphobia. In A.H. Tuma & J.D. Maser (Eds.), *Anxiety and the Anxiety Disorders*. Hillsdale, NJ: Erlbaum.

Givens, A. (1989a). Dynamic functional topography of cognitive tasks. *Brain Topography, 2,* 37-56.

Givens, A. (1989b). Signs of model making by the human brain. In E. Basar & T.H. Bullock (Eds.), *Brain dynamics 2* (pp. 408-419). Berlin: Springer-Verlag.

Glantz, S. & Parmley, W.W. (1991, January). Passive smoking and heart disease: Epidemiology, physiology and biochemistry. *Circulation, 83, 1-12.*

Glanzer, M. & Cunitz, A.R. (1966). Two storage mechanisms in free recall. *Journal of Verbal Learning and Verbal Behavior, 5,* 351-360.

Glaser, R. (1984). Education and thinking: The role of knowledge. *American Ps,vchologist, 39,* 93-104.

Glass, D.C. (1977). *Behavior patterns, stress and coronary disease*. Hillsdale, NJ: Erlbaum.

Glass, A.L., Holyoak, K.J. & Santa, J.L. (1979). *Cognition*. Reading, MA: Addison-Wesley.

Glassman, A.H., Jackson, W.K., Walsh, B.T. & Roose, S.P. (1984). Cigarette craving, smoking withdrawal and clondine. *Science, 226,* 864-866.

Glassman, R.B. (1983). Free will has a neural substrate: Critique of Joseph F. Rychlak's *Discovering free will and personal responsibility, Zygon, 18,* 67-82.

Glucksberg, S. & Danks, J.H. (1975). *Experimental psycholinguistics*. Hilsdale, NJ: Erlbaum.

Goffman, E. (1959). *The presentation of self in everyday life*. New York: Doubleday.

Goffman, E. (1963). *Stigma*. Englewood Cliffs, NJ: Prentice-Hall.

Gold, P.E. (1984). Memory modulation: Neurobiological contexts. In G. Lynch, J.L. McGaugh & N.M. Weinberger (Eds.), *Neurobiology of learning and memory* (pp. 374-382). New York: Guilford Press.

Gold, P.E. (1987). Sweet memories. *American Scientist, 75,* 151-155.

Goldberg, D. (1994). *Psychiatry in medical practice* (2nd Ed.). London: Routledge.

Goldberg, L.R. (1981). Language and individual differences: The Search for universals in personality lexicons. In L. Wheeler (Ed.), *Review of personality and social psychology* (Vol.2, pp.141-165). Beverly Hills, CA: Sage.

Goldfried, M.R., Greenberg, L. & Marmar, C. (1990). Individual psychotherapy: Process and outcome. *Annual Review of Psychology, 41,* 659-688.

Golding, S.L. (1977). The problem of construal styles in the analysis of person-situation interactions. In D. Magnusson & N.E. Endler (Eds.), *Personality at the crossroads* (pp. 401-408). Hillsdale, NJ: Erlbaum.

Goldstein, E.B. (1980). *Sensation and perception*. Belmont, CA: Wadsworth.

Goldstein, M. & Rodnick, E.H. (1975). The family's contribution to the etiology of schizophrenia: Current status. *Schizophrenia Bulletin, 14,* 48-63.

Goldstein, M.J. & Strachan, A.M. (1987). The family and schizophrenia. In T. Jacob (Ed.), *Family interaction and psychopathology: Theories, methods and findings* (pp. 481-507). New York: Plenum.

Gomes-Schwartz, B., Hadley, S.W. & Strupp, H.H. (1978). Individual psychotherapy and behavior therapy. *Annual Review of Psychology, 29,* 435-471.

Gonzalez, A. (1990). In *Discovering Psychology*, Program 20 [PBS video series]. Washington, DC: Annenberg/CPB Program.

Gonzalez, A. & Zimbardo, P.G. (1985, March). Time in perspective. *Psychology Today*, pp. 20-26.

Goodman, D.A. (1978). Learning from lobotomy. *Human Behavior, 7*(1),44-49.

Goodman, L.S. & Gilman, A. (1970). *The pharmacological basis of therapeutics* (4th ed.). New York: Macmillan.

Goodstadt, M.S. (1986). Alcohol education research and practice: A logical analysis of the two realities. *Journal of Drug Education, 16,* 349-365.

Goossens, F.A. & Van Ijzendoorn, M.H. (1990). Quality of infant's attachment to professional caregivers: Relation to infant-parent attachment and day-care characteristics. *Child Development, 61,* 832-837.

Gordon, C. & Gergen, K.J. (1968). *The self in social interaction* (Vol. 1). New York: Wiley.

Gorman, B.S. & Wessman, A.E. (1977). *The personal experience of time*. New York: Plenum.

Gorman, J.M., Liebowitz, M.R., Fyer, A.J. & Stein, J.M. (1989). A neuroanatomical hypothesis for panic disorder. *American Journal of Psychiatry, 146,* 148-16 1.

Gorney, R. (1976, September). Paper presented at annual meeting of the American Psychiatric Association.

Gottesman, I.I. (1963). Genetic aspects of intelligent behavior. In N. Ellis (Ed.), *Handbook of mental deficiency: Psychological theory and research*. New York: McGraw-Hill.

Gottesman, I.I. (1990). In *Discovering Psychology*, Program 21 [PBS video series]. Washington, DC: Annenberg/CPB Program.

Gottesman, I.I. (1991). *Schizophrenia genesis: The origins of madness*. New York: Freeman.

Gottesman, I.I., McGuffin, P. & Farmer, A.E. (1987). Clinical genetics as clues to the 'real' genetics of schizophrenia. *Schizophrenia Bulletin, 13,* 23-47.

Gottesman, I.I. & Shields, J. (1972). *Schizophrenia and genetics: A twin study vantage point*. New York: Academic Press.

Gottesman, I.I. & Shields, J. (1976). A critical review of recent adoption, twin, and family studies of schizophrenia: Behavioral genetics perspective. *Schizophrenia Bulletin, 2,* 360-401.

Gottfredson, L.S. (1986). The g-factor in employment. *Journal of Vocational Behavior, 29,* 293-296.

Gottlieb, B.H. (Ed.). (1981). *Social networks and social support*. Beverly Hills, CA: Sage.

Gottleib, G. (1983). The psychobiological approach to developmental issues. In M.M. Haith & J.J. Campos (Eds.), *Handbook of child psychology: lnfant and developmental psychobiology* (pp. 1-26). New York: Wiley.

Goudsmit, E.M. & Gadd, R. (1991). All in the mind? The psychologisation of illness. *The Psychologist: Bulletin of the British Psychological Society* 4, 449-453

Gough, H.G. (1961). Techniques for identifying the creative research scientist. In *Conference on the creative person*. Berkeley: University of Califomia, Institute of Personality Assessment & Research.

Gough, H.G. (1968). An interpreter's syllabus for the California Psychological Inventory. In P.McReynolds (Ed), *Advances in psychological assessment*, vol. one (pp.55-79). Palo Alto, CA: Science and Behaviour Books.

Gould, J.L. & Marler, P. (1984). Ethology on the natural history of Teaming. In P. Marler & H. Terrace (Eds.), *The biology of learning* (pp. 47-74). Berlin: Springer-Verlag.

Gould, S.J. (1981). *The mismeasure of man*. New York: Norton.

Graesser, A.C. Hoffman, N.L. & Clark, L.F. (1980). Structural components of reading time. *Journal of Verbal Learning and Verbal Behavior, 19,* 135-151.

Graf, P., Squire, L.R. & Mandler, G. (1984). The information that amnesic patients do not forget. *Journal of Experimental Psychology: Learning, Memory and Cognition, 10,* 164-178.

Graf, R. & Torrey, J.W. (1966). Perception of phrase structure in written language. *American Psychological Association Convention Proceedings*, 83-88.

Grant, P.R. (1986). *Ecology and evolution of Darwin's finches*. Princeton, NJ: Princeton University Press.

Gray, C.R. & Gummerman, K. (1975). The enigmatic eidetic image: A critical examination of methods, data and theories. *Psychological Bulletin, 82,* 383-407.

Green, W.H., Campbell, M. & David, R. (1984). Psychosocial dwarfism: A critical review of the evidence. *Journal of the American Academy of Child Psychiatry, 23,* 39-48.

Green, D.M. & Swets, J.A. (1966). *Signal detection theory and psychophysics*. New York: Wiley.

Greene, G. (1961). *A Burnt-Out Case*. London: Penguin.

Greenfield, P.M. & Smith, J.H. (1976). *The structure of communication in early language development*. New York: Academic Press.

Greening, T. (Ed.). (1984). Special peace issue. *Journal of Humanistic Psychology, 23 (3).*

Greeno, C.G. & Maccoby, E.E. (1986). How different is the 'different voice'? *Signs, 11*, 310-316.

Greenwald, A.G. (1992). New Look 3: unconscious cognition reclaimed. *American Psychologist, 47*, 766-779.

Greenwald, A.G., Spangenber, E.R., Pratkanis, A.R. & Eskenazi, J. (1991). Double-blind tests of subliminal self-help audiotapes. *Psychological Science, 2*, 119-122.

Grice, H.P. (1975). Logic and conversation. In P. Cole & J.L. Morgan (Eds.), *Syntax and semantics: Vol. 3. Speech acts* (pp. 41-58). New York: Seminar Press.

Griffin, D.R. (1984). Animal thinking. *American Scientist, 72*, 456-464.

Griffin, D.W. & Ross, L. (1991). Subjective construal, social inference, and human misunderstanding. In M.P. Zanna (Ed.), *Advances in Experimental Social Psk,chology* (pp. 319-359). New York: Academic Press.

Griffiths, M. (1989). Gambling in Childern and Adolescents. *Journal of Gambling Behaviour, 5, 1*, 66-83.

Griffiths, M. (1991). Psychobiology of the near miss in fruit machine gambling. *Journal of Psychology, 125*, 347-357.

Griffiths, M. (1993a). Tolerance in gambling: An objective measure using the psychophysiological analysis of male fruit machine gamblers. *Addictive Behaviours, 18*, 365-372.

Griffiths, M. (1993b). Pathological gambling: Possible treatment using an audio playback technique. *Journal of Gambling Studies, 9, 3*, 295-297.

Griffiths, M. (1994). The role of cognitive bias and skill in fruit machine gambling. *British Journal of Psychology, 85*, 351-369.

Groot, A.D. de (1965). *Thought and choice in chess.* The Hague: Mouton.

Groot, A.D. de (1969). *Methodology. Foundations of inference and research in the behavioural sciences.* The Hague: Mouton.

Grossman, S.P. (1979). The biology of motivation. *Annual Review of Psychology, 30*, 209-242.

Group for the Advancement of Psychiatry. (1950). *Revised electro-shock therapy report, special volume: Report No. 15*, 1-3.

Guetzkow, H., Alger, C.F., Brody, R.A., Noel, R.C. & Snyder, R.C. (1963). *Simulation in international relations.* Englewood Cliffs, NJ: Prentice-Hall.

Guilford, J.P. (1961). *Psychological Review, 68*, 1-20.

Guilford, J.P. (1967). *Crystalized intelligences: The nature of human intelligence.* New York: McGraw-Hill.

Guilford, J.P. (1973). Theories of intelligence. In B.B. Wolman (Ed.), *Handbook of general psychology.* Englewood Cliffs, NJ: Prentice-Hall.

Guilford, J.P. (1985). The Structure-of-Intellect model. In B.B. Wolman (Ed.), *Handbook of intelligence.* New York: Wiley.

Guilleminault, C. (1989). Clinical features and evaluation of obstructive sleep apnea. In M. Kryser, T. Roth & W.C. Dement (Eds.), *Principles and practice of sleep medicine* (pp. 552-558). New York: Saunders Press.

Guilleminault, C., Dement, W.C. & Passonant, P. (Eds.). (1976). *Narcolepsy.* New York: Spectrum.

Gummerman, K., Gray, C.R. & Wilson, J.M. (1972). An attempt to assess eidetic imagery objectively. *Psychonomic Science, 28*, 115-118.

Gunzenhauser, N. (Ed.). (1990). *Advances in touch: New implications in human development.* Skillman, NJ: Johnson & Johnson Co.

Gur, R.C. & Gur, R.E. (1974). Handedness, sex and eyedness as moderating variables in the relation between hypnotic susceptibility and functional brain asymmetry. *Journal of Abnormal Psychology, 83*, 635-643.

Gurman, A.S. & Kniskern, D.P. (1978). Research on marital and family therapy: Progress, perspective, and prospect. In S.L. Garfield & A.E. Bergin (Eds.), *Handbook of psychotherapy and behaviour change: An empirical analysis* (2nd ed.). New York: Wiley.

Gutek, B.A. (1985). *Sex and the workplace.* San Fransisco: Jossey-Bass.

Gynther, M.D. (1981). Is the *MMPI* an appropriate assessment device for blacks? *Journal of Black Psychology, 7*, 67-75.

H

Haas, K. (1965). Understanding ourselves and others. Englewood Cliffs, NJ: Prentice-Hall.

Habot, T.B. & Libow, L.S. (1980). The interrelationship of mental and physical status and its assessment in the older adult: Mindbody interaction. In J.E. Birren & R.B. Sloane (Eds.), *Handbook of mental health and aging* (pp. 701-716). Englewood Cliffs, NJ: Prentice-Hall.

Hachberg, J. (1988). Perception of objects in space. In E.R. Hilgard

(Ed.), *Fifty years of psychology* (pp. 57-74). Glenview: Scott Foresman.

Hackett, C.F. (1960). The origin of speech. *Scientific American, 203*, 89-96.

Haier, R.J. (1980). The diagnosis of schizophrenia: A review of recent developments. In S.J. Keith & L.R. Mosher (Eds.), *Special report: Schizophrenia, 1980* (pp. 2-13). Washington, DC: U.S. Government Printing Office.

Hall, G.S. (1904). *Adolescence: Its psychology and its relations to physiology, anthropology, sociology, sex, crime, religion and education* (Vols. 1 & 2). New York: Appleton.

Hall, G. & Pearce, J.M. (1979). Latent inhibition of a CS during CS-US pairings. *Journal of Experimental Psychology: Animal Behavior Processes, 5*, 31-42.

Hallam, R. (1983). Agoraphobia: Deconstructing a clinical syndrome. *Bulletin of the British Psychological Society, 36*, 337-340.

Hallam, R. (1985). *Anxiety: Psychological perspectives on panic and agoraphobia.* New York: Academic Press.

Hallam, R. (1991). A look forward: Psychosocial perspectives. In J.R. Walker, G.R. Norton & C.A. Ross (Eds.), *Panic Disorder & Agoraphobia*, (pp.470-503). New York: Brooks Cole.

Hallowell, A.I. (1976). Ojibwa world view and disease. In *Contributions to anthropology: Selected papers of A.I. Hallowell* [Introductions by R.D. Fogelson et al. Chicago: University of Chicago Press. (Original work published 1963)

Hamilton, V. (1980). An information processing analysis of environmental stress and life crisis. In I.G. Sarason & C.D. Spielberger (Eds.), *Stress and anxiety* (Vol. 7). New York: Hemisphere Publishing.

Hammer, D.L. & Padesky, C.A. (1977). Sex differences in the expression of depressive responses on the Beck Depression Inventory. *Journal of Abnormal Psychology, 86*, 609-614.

Hampson, S.E. (1982). *The construction of personality: An introduction.* London: Routledge.

Handy, J.A., (1987). Psychology and social context. *Bulletin of the British Psychological Society, 40*, 161-167.

Haney, C. (1984). On the selection of capital juries: The biasing effects of the death-qualification process. *Law and Human Behavior, 8*, 121-132.

Haney, C., Banks, C. & Zimbardo, P.G. (1973). Interpersonal dynamics in a simulated prison. *International Journal of Criminology and Penology, 1*, 69-97.

Haney, C. & Zimbardo, P.G. (1977). The socialization into criminality: On becoming a prisoner and a guard. In J.L. Tapp & F.L. Levine (Eds.), *Law, justice and the individual in society: Psychological and legal issues* (pp. 198-223). New York: Holt, Rinehart & Winston.

Hanna, S.D. (1984). *The psychosocial impact of the nuclear threat on children.* Unpublished manuscript. (Available from Physicians for Social Responsibility, 639 Massachusetts Ave., Cambridge, MA 02139, USA).

Hanson, D., Gottesman, I. & Meehl, P. (1977). Genetic theories and the validation of psychiatric diagnosis: Implications for the study of children of schizophrenics. *Journal of Abnormal Psychology, 86*, 575-588.

Hare-Mustin, R.T. & Maracek, J. (1988). The meaning of difference: Gender theory, postmodernism and psychology. *American Psychologist, 43*, 455-464.

Hare-Mustin, R.T. & Maracek, J. (Eds.) (1990). *Making a difference: Psychology and the construction of gender.* New Haven: Yale University Press.

Hareven, T. (1985). Historical changes in the family and the life course: Implications for child development. *Monographs of the Society for Research in Child Development, 50* (Serial No. 21 1), 8-23.

Harlow, H.F. (1965). Sexual behavior in the rhesus monkey. In F. Beach (Ed.), *Sex and behavior.* New York: Wiley.

Harlow, H.F., Harlow, M.K. & Meyer, D.R. (1950). Learning motivated by a manipulation drive. *Journal of Experimental Psychology, 40*, 228-234.

Harlow, H.F. & Zimmerman, R.R. (1958). The development of affectional responses in infant monkeys. Proceedings of the *American Philosophical Society, 102*, 501-509.

Harner, M.J. (1973). The sound of rushing water. In M.J. Hamer (Ed.), Hallucinogens and shamanism (pp. 15-27). Oxford: Oxford University Press.

Harper Atlas of World History. (1986). New York: Harper & Row.

Harré, R. (1983). *Personal being.* Oxford: Blackwell.

Harré, R. (1986). An outline of the social constructionist viewpoint. In R. Harré (Ed.), *The social construction of emotions* (pp. 2-15). Oxford: Basil Blackwell.

Harré, R. (1990). Embarrassment: a conceptual analysis. In R.A. Crozier (Ed.), *Shyness and embarrassment* (pp. 181-204). Cambridge: Cambridge University Press.

Harré, D., Clarke, D.D. & de Carlo, N. (1985). *Motives and mechanisms.* London: Methuen.

Harré, R. & Gillett, G. (1994). *The discursive mind.* London: Sage.

Harré, R. & Secord, P.F. (1972). *The explanation of social Behaviour.* Oxford: Basil Blackwell.

Harris, B. (1979). Whatever happened to Little Albert? *American Psychologist, 34, 151-160.*

Harris, G., Thomas, A. & Booth, D.A. (1990). Development of salt taste in infancy. *Developmental Psychology, 26,* 534-538.

Harris, P. (1989). The prevalence of visual conditions in a population of juvenile delinquents. *Journal of the American Optometric Association, 37,* 461-468.

Harris, P.L. (1989). *Children and emotion: The development of psychological understanding.* Oxford: Blackwell.

Harris, P.L. (1993). Understanding emotion. In M. Lewis & J.M. Haviland (Eds.), *Handbook of emotions* (pp. 237-247). New York: The Guilford Press.

Harris, P.L., Olthof, T., Meerum Terwogt, M. & Hardman, C.E. (1987). Children's knowledge of situations that provoke emotions. *International Journal of Behavioural Development, 10,* 319-343.

Harris, P.R. (1980). *Promoting health-preventing disease: Objectives for the nation.* Washington, DC: U.S. Government Printing Office.

Harrison, J. (1978). Male sex role and health. *Journal of Social Issues, 34, 1,* 65-86.

Harshman, R.A., Crawford, H.J. & Hecht, E. (1976). Marijuana, cognitive style, and lateralized hemispheric functions. In S. Cohen & R.C. Stillman (Eds.), *The therapeutic potential of marijuana* (pp. 205-254). New York: Plenum.

Hart, R.A. & Moore, G.I. (1973). The development of spatial cognition: A review. In R.M. Downs & D. Stea (Eds.), *Image and environment.* Chicago: Aldine.

Hartmann, E.L. (1973). *The functions of sleep.* New Haven, CT: Yale University Press.

Hartmann, E. (1989). Boundaries of dreams, boundaries of dreamers: Thin and thick boundaries as a new personality measure. *Psychiatric Journal of the University of Ottawa, 14,* 557-560.

Hartmann, E. (1990). In *Discovering Psychology,* Program 13 [PBS video series). Washington, DC: Annenberg/CPB Program.

Hartmann, D.P., Roper, B.L. & Bradford, D. (1979). Some relationships between behavioral and traditional assessment. *Journal of Behavioral Assessment, 1,* 3-21.

Hartshorne, H. & May, M.A. (1928). *Studies in the nature of character,* Vol.1: Studies in deceit. New York: Macmillan.

Hartshorne, H. & May, M.A. (1929). *Studies in the nature of character, Vol. 2: Studies in science and self-control.* New York: Macmillan.

Hartup, W.W. (1989). Social relationships and their developmental significance. *American Psychologist, 44,* 120-126.

Harvey, O.J. & Consalvi, C. (1960). Status and conformity in informal groups. *Journal of Abnormal and Social Psychology, 60,* 182-187.

Harvey, P.H. & Krebs, J.R. (1990). Comparing brains. *Science, 249,* 140-146.

Hasenfus, N. & Magaro, P. (1976). Creativity and schizophrenia: An equality of empirical constructs. *British Journal of Psychiatry* 129,346-349.

Hass, A. (1979). *Teenage sexuality: A survey of teenage sexual behavior.* New York: Macmillan.

Hastorf, A.H. & Cantril, H. (1954). They saw a game: A case study. *Journal of Abnormal and Social Psychology, 49,* 129-134.

Hatfield, E. & Speecher, S. (1986). *Mirror, mirror. The importance of looks in everyday life.* New York: State University of New York Press.

Hathaway, S.R. & Mckinley, J.C. (1943). *The Minnesota Multiphasic Personality Inventory.* Minneapolis: University of Minnesota Press.

Hauri, P. (1977). *The sleep disorder.* T. Kalamazoo, MI: Upjohn.

Hayes, D. (1991). Harnessing market forces to protect the earth. *Issues in Science and Technology, 7,* 46-51.

Hayes-Roth, B. & Hayes-Roth, F. (1979). A cognitive model of planning. *Cognitive Science, 3,* 275-310.

Haynes, S.G. & Feinleib, M. (1980). Women, work and coronary heart disease: Prospective findings from the Framingham Heart Study. *American Journal of Public Health, 70,* 133-141.

Haynes, S.N. (1983). Behavioral assessment. In M. Hersen, A.E. Kazdin, & A.S. Bellack. (Fds.), *The clinical psychology handbook* (pp. 397-425). New York: Pergamon.

Haynes, S.N. & Wilson, C.C. (1979). *Behavioral assessment: Recent advances in methods and concepts.* San Francisco: JosseyBass.

Hazan, C. & Shaver, P. (1987). Romantic love conceptualized as an attachment process. *Journal of Personality and Social Psychology, 52,* 511-524.

Hearnshaw, L.S. (1979). *Cyril Burt psychologist.* London: Hodder & Stoughton.

Heath, A.C., Jardine, R. & Martin, N.G. (1989). Interactive effects of genotype and social environment on alcohol consumption in female twins. *Journal of Studies of Alcohol, 50,* 38-48.

Heath, R.G. (1959). Physiological and biochemical studies in schizophrenia with particular emphasis on mid-brain relationships. *International Review of Biology, 1,* 299-331.

Heather, N. & Robertson, I. (1983). *Controlled drinking (2nd ed.).* New York: Methuen.

Hebb, D.O. (1949). *The organization of behavior: A neuropsychological theory.* New York: Wiley.

Hebb, D.O. (1955). Drives and the CNS (conceptual nervous system). *Psychological Review, 62,* 243-254.

Hebb, D.O. (1966). *A textbook of psychology* (2nd ed.). Philadelphia: Saunders.

Hebb, D.O. (1974). What is psychology about? *American Psychologist, 29,* 71-79.

Heber, R. (1976, June). *Sociocultural mental retardation: A longitudinal study.* Paper presented at the Vermont Conference on the Primary Prevention of Psychopathology.

Hecht, A. (1986, April). A guide to the proper use of tranquilizers. *Healthline Newsletter,* pp. 5-6.

Heckman, J.R. & Oldham, G.R. (1980). *Work redesign.* Reading, MA: Addison-Wesley.

Hedlund, J.L. (1977). MMPI clinical scale correlated. *Journal of Consulting and Clinical Psychology, 45,* 739-750.

Heider, E.R. (1972). Universals in colour naming and memory. *Journal of Experimental Psychology, 93,* 10-20.

Heider, F. (1958). *The psychology of interpersonal relationships.* New York: Wiley.

Heider, F. & Simmel, M. (1944). An experimental study of apparent behavior. *American Journal of Psychology, 57,* 243-259.

Heider, R. (1944). Social perception and phenomenal causality. *Psychological Review, 51,* 358-374.

Helman, C.G. (1990). Cross-cultural psychiatry, in C.G. Helman, *Culture, health and illness.* London: Butterworth-Heinmann.

Helmholtz, H. von. (1962). Treatise on physiological optics (Vol.3). J.P. Southall, (Ed.) and (Trans.). New York: Dover Press (Original work published 1866).

Helson, R. (1971). Women mathematicians and the creative personality. *Journal of Consulting and Clinical Psychology, 36,* 210-220.

Henderson, N.D. (1980). Effects of early experience upon the behavior of animals: The second twenty-five years of research. In E.C. Simmel (Ed.), *Early experiences and early behavior: Implications for social social development* (pp. 39-77). New York: Academic Press.

Hensel, H. (1968). Electrophysiology of cutaneous thermoreceptors. In D.R. Kenshalo (Ed.), *The skin senses* (pp. 384-399). Springfield, IL: Charles C Thomas.

Herbert, M. (1989). *Discipline: A positive guide for parents.* Basil Blackwell: Oxford.

Herbert, M. (1991). *Clinical child psychology: Social learning, development and behaviour.* London: Wiley.

Hering, E. (1861-1864). *Beitrage zur physiologie.* Leipzig: W. Engelmann.

Heritage, J.C. (1985). Recent developments in conversation analysis. *Sociolinguistics, 15,* 1-18.

Herman, M. (1972). The poor: Their medical needs and the health services available to them. *Annals of the American Academy of Political and Social Science, 399,* 12-21

Hermans, H., Kempen, H. & Vann Loon, R. (1992). The dialogical self: Beyond individualism and rationalism. *American Psychologist, 47,* 23-33.

Herrnstein, R.J., Nickerson, R.S., de Sanchez, M. & Swets, J.A. (1986). Teaching thinking skills. *American Psychologist, 41,* 1279-1289.

Herrnstein, R.J. & Wilson, J.Q. (1985). *Crime and human nature.* New York: Simon & Schuster.

Hersen, M. & Bellack, A.J. (1976). Assessment of social skills. In A.R. Cimincro, K.R. Calhoun & H.E. Adams (Eds.), *Handbook of behavioral assessment* (pp. 509-554). New York: Wiley.

Hersh, S.M. (1971). *My Lai 4: A report on the massacre and its aftermath.* New York: Random House.

Hess, E.H. (1972). Pupillometrics: A method of studying mental, emotional and sensory processes. In N.E. Greenfield & R.A. Steinbach (Fds.), *Handbook of psychophysiology.* New York: Holt, Rinehart & Winston.

Hess, W. & Akert, K. (1955). Experimental data on the role of hypothalamus in the mechanism of emotional behavior. *Archives of Neurological Psychiatry, 73,* 127-129.

Hester, R.K. & Miller, W.R. (Eds.). (1989). *Handbook of alcoholism treatment approaches: Effective alternatives. New* York: Pergamon.

Heston, L.L. (1970). The genetics of schizophrenia and schizoid disease. *Science, 112,* 249-256.

Heymans, G. & Wiersma, E.D. (1918). Beiträge zur speziellen Psychologie auf Grund einer Massenuntersuchung. *Zeitschrift für Psychologie.*

Higgins, E.T. (1989). Continuities and discontinuities in self-regulatory and self-evaluative processes: A developmental theory relating selfand affect. *Journal of personality, 57,* 407-444.

Hilgard, E. (1965). *Hypnotic susceptibility.* New York: Harcourt Brace Jovanovich.

Hilgard, E.R. (1968). *The experience of hypnosis.* New York: Harcourt Brace Jovanovich.

Hilgard, E.R. (1973). The domain of hypnosis with some comments on alternative paradigms. *American Psychologist, 28,* 972-982.

Hilgard E.R. (1980). Consciousness in contemporary psychology. *Annual Review of Psychology, 31,* 1-26.

Hilgard, E.R. & Hilgard, J.R. (1974, Spring-Summer). Hypnosis in the control of pain. *The Stanford Magazine,* 58-62.

Hilgard, E.R. & Hilgard, J.R. (1983). *Hypnosis in the relief of pain.* Los Altos, CA: William Kaufmann.

Hilgard, J.R. (1974). Imaginative involvement: Some characteristics of the highly hypnotizable and the nonhypnotizable. *International Journal of Clinical and Experimental Hypnosis, 22,* 281-298.

Hilgard, J.R. (1979). *Personality and hypnosis: A study of imaginative involvement* (2nd ed.). Chicago: University of Chicago Press.

Hill, W.F. (1990). *Learning: A survey of psychological interpretations.* New York: Harper & Row.

Hille, B. (1984). *Ionic channels of excitable membranes.* Sunderland, MA: Sinauer Associates.

Hilton, D.J. (1990). Conversational processes and causal explanation. *Psychological Bulletin, 107,* 1, 65-81.

Hilton, D.J. & Slugoski, B.R. (1986). Knowledge-based causal attribution: the abnormal conditions focus model. *Psychological Review, 93,* 1, 75-88.

Himmelweit, H. & Gaskell, G. (Eds.) (1990). *Societal psychology.* London: Sage.

Hinton, G.F. & Anderson, J.A. (1981). *Parallel models of associative memory.* Hilisdale, NJ: Eribaum.

Hirsch, H.V.B. & Spinelli, D.N. (1970). Visual experience modifies distribution of horizontally and vertically oriented receptive fields in cats. *Science, 168,* 869-871.

Hirsch, J., Harrington, G. & Mehler, B. (1990). An irresponsible farewell gloss. *Educational Theory, 40,* 501-508.

Hirschfield, R.M.A. & Cross, C.K. (1982). Epidemiology of affective disorder: Psychosocial risk factors. *Archives of General Psychiatry, 39,* 35-46.

Hite, S. (1987). *Hite report: Women and love: A cultural revolution in progress.* New York: Knopf.

Hitler, A. (1933). *Mein Kampf.* Cambridge, MA: Riverside.

Hobson, J.A. (1988). *The dreaming brain.* New York: Basic Books.

Hobson, J.A. (1989). *Sleep.* New York: Scientific American Library.

Hobson, J.A., & McCarley, R. W. (1977). The brain as a dream state generator: An activation-synthesis hypothesis of the dream process. *American Journal of Psychiatry, 134,* 1335-1348.

Hochberg, J. (1968). In the mind's eye. In R.N. Haber (Ed.), *Contemporary theory and research in visual perception.* New York: Holt, Rinehart & Winston.

Hochberg, J. (1988). Perception of objects in space. In E.R. Hilgard (Ed.), *Fifty years of psychology* (pp.57-74). Glenview, IL: Scott Foresman.

Hockett, C.F. (1966). The problem of universal in language. In H.J. Greenberg (Ed.), *Universal in language* (pp. 1-29). Cambridge, MA: MIT Press.

Hofer, M. (1981). *The roots of human behavior: An introduction to the psychobiology of early development.* San Francisco: Freeman.

Hoffman, L.W. (1972). Early childhood experience and women's achievement motives. *Journal of Social Issues, 28,* 129-155.

Hoffman, M. (1986). Affect, cognition and motivation. In R. Sorrentino & E. Higgins (Eds.), *Handbook of motivation and cognition: Foundations of social behavior* (pp. 244-280). New York: Guilford.

Hoffman, M.L. (1987). The contribution of empathy to justice and moral judgment. In N. Eisenberg & J. Strayer (Eds.), *Empathy and its development* (pp. 47-80). New York: Cambridge University Press.

Hofling, C.K., Brotzman, E., Dalrymple, S.,Graves, N. & Pierce, C.M. (1966). An experimental study in nurse-physician relationships. *Journal of Nervous and Mental Disease, 143(2),* 171-180.

Hofstede, G. (1980). *Culture's consequences: International differences in work-related values.* Beverly Hills, CA: Sage.

Hofstee, W.K.B. (1990). The use of everyday personality language for scientific purposes. *European Journal of Personality, 4,* 77-88.

Hofstee, W.K.B., De Raad, B. & Goldberg, L.R. (1992). Integration of the big five and circumplex approaches to trait structure. *Journal of Personality and Social Psychology, 63,* 146-163.

Holahan, C.J. & Moos, R. (1981). Social support and psychological distress: A longitudinal analysis. *Journal of Abnormal Psychology, 90,* 365-370.

Holahan, C.J. & Moos, R.H. (1987). Personal and contextual determinants of coping strategies. *Journal of Personality and Social Psychology, 52,* 946-955.

Holden, C. (1978). Patuxent: Controversial prison clings to belief in rehabilitation. *Science, 199,* 665-668.

Holden, C. (1986a). Depression research advances, treatment lags. *Science, 233,* 723-725.

Holden, C. (1986b). Youth suicide: New research focuses on a growing social problem. *Science, 233,* 839-841.

Holden, R. (1993). *Laughter: The Best Medicine.* London, Thorsens.

Holding, D.H. (1985). *The psychology of chess skills.* Hillsdale, NJ: Erlbaum.

Holen, M.C. & Oaster, T.R. (1976). Serial position and isolation effects in a classroom lecture simutation. *Journal of Educational Psychology, 68,* 293-296.

Holender, D. (1986). Semantic activation without conscious identification in dichotic listening, parafoveal vision, and visual masking: a survey and appraisal. *Behavioral and Brain Sciences, 9,* 1-23.

Holland, P.C. & Rescorla, R.A. (1975). Second-order conditioning with food unconditioned stimulus. *Journal of Comparative and Physiological Psychology, 88,* 459-467.

Hollender, M.H. (1980). The case of Anna O.: A reformulation. *American Journal of Psychiatry, 137,*797-800.

Holloway, M. (1990, October). Profile: Vive la différence. *Scientific American,* pp. 40-42.

Holmes, D. (1990). The evidence for repression: an examination of sixty years of research. In J.L. Singer (Ed.), *Repression and dissociation. Implications for personality theory, psychopathology, and health* (pp. 85-102). Chicago: University of Chicago Press.

Holmes, D.S. (1984). Meditation and somatic arousal: A review of the experimental evidence. *American Psychologist, 39,* 1-10.

Holmes, J.A. & Stevenson, C.A.Z. (1990). Differential effects of avoidant and attentional coping strategies on adaptation to chronic and recent-onset pain. *Health Psychology, 9,* 577-584.

Holmes, T.H. & Rahe, R.H. (1967). The social readjustment rating scale. *Journal of Psychosomatic Research, 11(2),* 213-218.

Holmes, T.H. & Masuda, M. (1974). Life change and stress susceptibility. In B.S. Dohrenwend & B.P. Dohrenwend, (Eds.), *Stressful life events: Their nature and effects* (pp. 45-72). New York: Wiley.

Holt, P. (1990, September 4). Coming to terms with depression [Review of *Darkness visible: A memoir of madness*]. San Francisco Chronicle.

Holt, R.R. (1970). Yet another look at clinical and statistical prediction: Or is clinical psychology worthwhile? *American Psychologist, 25,* 337-349.

Homme, L.E., de Baca, P.C., Devine, J.V., Steinhorst, R. & Rickert, E. J. (1963). Use of the Premack principle in controlling the behavior of nursery school children. *Journal of the Experimental Analysis of Behavior, 6,* 544.

Honorton, C. (1985). Meta-analysis of psi ganzfeld research: a response to Hyman. *Journal of Parapsychology, 49,* 51-91.

Honzik, M.P. (1984). Life-span development. *Annual Review of Psychology, 35,* 309-33 1.

Hooper, J. & Teresi, D. (1986). *The three-pound universe,* New York: Macmillan.

Hoorens, V. (1993). Self-enhancement and superiority biases in social comparison. In W. Stroebe & M. Hewstone (Eds.) *European Review of Social Psychology, Volume 4* (pp. 113-141). Chichester: John Wiley & Sons.

Hope, D.A., Gansler, D.A. & Heimberg, R.G. (1989). Attentional focus and causal attributions in social phobia: implications from social psychology. *Clinical Psychology Review, 9,* 49-60.

Hopson, J.L. (1979). *Scent signals: The silent language of sex.* New York: Morrow.

Hopson, J.L. (1988, July/August). A pleasurable chemistry. *Psychology Today,* pp. 29-33.

Horn, J.L. (1985). Remodeling old models of intelligence. In B.B. Wolman (Ed.), *Handbook of intelligence* (pp. 267-300). New York: Wiley.

Horne, J.A. (1988). *Why we sleep: The functions of sleep in humans and other mammals.* Oxford: Oxford University Press.

Horner, M.S. (1972). Toward an understanding of achievement related conflicts in women. *Journal of Social Issues, 28,* 157-175.

Horney, K. (1937). *The neurotic personality of our time.* New York: Norton.

Horney, K. (1939). *New ways in psychoanalyses.* New York: Norton.

Horney, K. (1945). *Our inner conflicts: A constructive theory of neurosis.* New York: Norton.

Horney, K. (1950). *Neurosis and human growth.* New York: Norton.

Horowitz, R.M. (1984). Children's rights: A look backward and a glance ahead. In R.M. Horowitz & H.A. Davidson (Eds.), *Legal rights of children* (pp. 1-9). New York: McGraw-Hill.

Horton, L.E. (1970). Generalization of aggressive behavior in adolescent delinquent boys. *Journal of Applied Behavior Analysis, 3,* 205-21 1.

Horvath, A.T. (1991). Beyond AA. *The California Psychologist, 24,* 13, 26.

Horvath, F.S. (1977). The effects of selected variables on the interpretation of polygraph records. *Journal of Applied Psychology, 62,* 127-136.

Hosobuchi, Y., Rossier, J., Bloom, F. E. & Guillemin, R. (1979). Stimulation of human periaqueductal gray for pain relief increases immunoreactive B-endorphin in ventricular fluid. *Science, 203,* 279-281.

Houghton, J. (1980). One personal experience: Before and after mental illness. In I.G. Rabkin, L. Gelb & J.B. Lazar (Eds.), *Attitudes toward the mentally ill: Research perspectives* (pp. 7-14). Rockville, MD: National Institute of Mental Health.

House, J.S., Landis, K.R. & Umberson, D. (1988). Social relationships and health. *Science, 241,* 540-545.

Hovland, C.I., Janis, I.L. & Kelley, H.H. (1953). *Communication and persuasion.* New Haven, CT: Yale University Press.

Hovland, C.I., Lumsdaine, A.A. & Sheffield, F.D. (1949). *Experiments on mass communication.* Princeton, NJ: Princeton University Press.

Hovland, C.I., Lumsdaine, A.A. & Sheffield, F.D. (1949). *Studies in social psychology in World War II – Vol. 31 Experiments in mass communication.* Princeton, NJ: Princeton University Press.

Howard, D.T. (1928). A functional theory of emotions. In M.L. Reymert (Ed.), *Feelings and emotions: The Wittenberg Symposium* (pp. 140-149). Worcester, MA: Clark University Press.

Howard, K.I., Kopta, S.M., Krause, M.S. & Korlinsky, P.E. (1986). The dose-effect relationship in psychotherapy. *American Psychologist, 41,* 159-164.

Howarth, E. & Eysenck, H.J. (1968). Extroversion, arousal and paired associate recall. *Journal of Experimental Research in Personality, 3,* 114-116.

Hrubec, Z. & Omenn, G.S. (1981). Evidence of genetic predisposition to alcoholic cirrhosis and psychosis: Twin concordance for alcoholism and its end points by zygosity among male veterans. *Alcoholism (NY), 5,* 207-215.

Hubel, D.H. (1979). The brain. *Scientific American, 24/(9),* 45-53.

Hubel, D.H. (1990). In *Discovering Psychology,* Program 7 [PBS video series]. Washington, DC: Annenberg/CPB Project.

Hubel, D.H. & Wiesel, T.N. (1959). Receptive fields of single neurons in the cat's striate cortex. *Journal of Physiology (London), 148,* 574-591.

Hubel, D.H. & Wiesel, T.N. (1962). Receptive fields, binocular interaction, and functional architecture in the cat's visual cortex. *Journal of Physiology* (London), 160, 106-154.

Hubel, D.H. & Wiesel, T.N. (1979). Brain mechanisms of vision. *Scientific American, 241(9),* 150-168.

Huesmann, L.R. & Malamuth, N.M. (Eds.). (1986). Media violence and antisocial behavior. *Journal of Social Issues, 42* (Whole issue).

Hughes, D., Johnson, K., Rosenbaum, S., Butler, E. & Simons, J. (1988). *The health of America's children: Maternal and child health data book.* Washington, DC: Children's Defense Fund.

Hughes, J., Smith, T.W., Kosterlitz, H.W., Fotergill, L.A., Morgan, B.A., & Morris, H.R. (1975). Identification of two related pentapeptides from the brain with potent opiate antagonist activity. *Nature,* 258, 577-579.

Hull, C.L. (1943). *Principles of behavior. An introduction to behavior theory.* New York: Appleton-Century-Crofts.

Hull, C.L. (1952) *A behavior system: An introduction to behavior theory concerning the individual organism.* New Haven, CT: Yale University Press.

Hultsch, D.F. & Dixon, R.A. (1984). Memory for text materials in adulthood. In P. Battes & 0. Brim (Eds.), *Life-span development and behavior* (Vol. 6, pp. 77-108). New York: Academic Press.

Hultsch, D.F., Hertzog, C., & Dixon, R.A. (1990). Ability correlates of memory performance in adulthood and aging. *Psychology and Aging, 5(3),* 356-368.

Hume, D. (1951). In L.A, Selby-Bigge (Ed.), *Inquiries concerning the human understanding and concerning the principles of morals.* London: Oxford University Press. (Original work published 1748)

Humphrey, N.K. (1976). The social function of intellect. In P.P.G. Bateson & R.A. Hinde (Eds.), *Growing points in ethology* (pp. 303-317). Cambridge, MA: Cambridge University Press.

Humphrey, T. (1970). The development of human fetal activity and its relation to postnatal behaviour. In H.W. Reese & L.P. Lipsitt *(Fds.), Advance in child development and behavior* (Vol. 5). New York: Academic Press.

Hunt, E. (1984). Intelligence and mental competence. *Naval Research Reviews, 36,* 37-42.

Hunt, M. (1985). *Profiles of social research: The scientific study of human interactions.* New York: Russell Sage Foundation.

Hunt, W.A., Matarazzo, J.D., Weiss, S.M. & Gentry, W.D. (1979). Associative Teaming, habit, and health behavior. *Journal of Behavioral Medicine, 2,* 111-123.

Hunter, J.E. & Hunter, R.F. (1984). Validity and utility of alternative predictors of job performance. *Psychological Bulletin, 96,* 72-98.

Hunter, F. & Youniss, J. (1982). Changes in functions of three relations during adolescence. *Developmental Psychology, 18,* 806-811.

Hurlburt, R.T. (1979). Random sampling of cognitions and behavior. *Journal of Research in Personality, 113,* 103-111.

Hurvich, L.M. & Jameson, D (1957). An opponent process theory of color vision. *Psychological Review, 64,* 384-404.

Hurvich, L.M. & Jameson, D. (1974). Opponent processes as a model of neural organization. *American Psychologist, 29(2),* 88-102.

Huston, A. (1985). *Television and human behaviour.* Transcript of a Science and Public Policy Seminar. Washington, DC: Federation of Behavioural, Psychological, and Cognitive Sciences.

Hyde, J.S. (1991). *Half the human experience: The psychology of women.* Lexington, MA: Heath & Company.

Hyde, J.S. & Linn, M.C. (1988). Gender differences in verbal ability: A meta-analysis. *Psychological Bulletin, 104,* 53-69.

Hyland, M. (1981). *Introduction to theoretical psychology.* London: MacMillan.

Hyman, I.A., McDowell, E. & Raines, B. (1977). Corporal punishment and alternatives in the schools: An overview of theoretical and practical issues. In J.H. Wise (Ed.), *Proceedings: Conference on corporal punishment in the schools* (pp. 1-18). Washington, DC: National Institute of Education.

Hyman, R. (1985). The ganzfeld psi experiment: a critical appraisal. *Journal of Parapsychology, 49,* 3-49.

Hyman, R. (1994). Anomaly or artifact? Comments on Bem and Honorton. *Psychological Bulletin, 115(1),* 19-24.

Hyman, R. & Honorton, C. (1986). A joint communiqué: the psi ganzfeld controversy. *Journal of Parapsychology, 50,* 351-364.

I

I.S.D.D. (1992). *National audit of drug misuse in Britain*, London: Institute for the Study of Drug Dependence.

Ickes, W., Layden, M.A. & Barnes, R.D. (1978). Objective self awareness and individuation: An empirical link. *Journal of Personality, 46,* 146-16 1.

Inglis, J. & Lawson, J.S. (1981). Sex differences in the effects of unilateral brain damage on intelligence. *Science, 212,* 693-695.

Ingold, F.R. & Toussirt, M. (1993). Transmission of HIV among drug addicts in three French cities: implications for prevention. *U.N. Bulletin of Narcotics,* 45, 1, 117-134.

Insel, P.L. & Roth, W.T. (1985). *Core concepts in health.* Palo Alto, CA: Mayfield.

Insko, C.A., Smith, R.A., Alicke, M.D., Wade, J. & Taylor, S. (1985). Conformity and group size: The concern with being right and the concern with being liked. *Personality and Social Psychology Bulletin,* 41-50.

Insko, C.A., Thibaut, J.W., Moehle, D., Wilson, M.,Diamond, W.D., Gilmore, R., Solomon, M.R. & Lipsitz, A. (1980). Social evolution and the emergence of leadership. *Journal of Personality and Social Psychology, 39,* 43l-448.

Institute of Medicine, Division of Mental Health and Behavioral Medicine. (1989). *Prevention and treatment of alcohol problems: Research opportunities.* Washington, DC: National Academy Press.

Irwin, M., Daniels, M., Smith, T.L., Bloom, E. & Weiner, H. (1987). Impaired natural killer cell activity during bereavement. *Brain Behavior Immunology, 1,* 98-104.

Isen, A. (1984). Toward understanding the role of affect in cognition. In R. Wyer & T. Srull (Fds.), *Handbook of social cognition (pp.* 174-236). Hillsdale, NJ: Eribaum.

Isen, A.M., Daubman, K.A. & Nowicki, G.P. (1987). Positive affect facilitates creative problem solving. *Journal of Personality and Social Psychology, 52,* 1122-1131.

Isen, A.M., Horn, N. & Rosenhan, D.L. (1973). Effects of success and failure on children's generosity. *Journal of Personality and Social Psychology, 27,* 239-247.

Itani, J. (1961). The society of Japanese monkeys. *Japan Quarterly,* 8(4), 421-430.

Itard, J.M.G. (1962). *The wild boy of Aveyron* (G.& M. Humphrey, Trans.). New York: Appleton-Century-Crofts.

Iversen, L.L. (1979). The chemistry of the brain. *Scientific American, 241(9),* 134-149.

Izard, C. (1971). *The face of emotion.* New York: Appleton-Century-Crofts.

Izard, C.E. (1990). The substrates and functions of emotion feelings: William James and current emotion theory. *Personality and Social Psychology Bulletin, 16,* 626-635.

J

Jacob, F. (1977). Evolution and tinkering. *Science, 196,* 161-166.

Jacobs, B.L. (1987). How hallucinogenic drugs work. *American Scientist, 75,* 386-392.

Jacobs, B.L. & Trulson, M.E. (1979). Mechanisms of action of L.S.D. *American Scientist, 6* 7, 396-404.

Jacobs, R.C. & Campbell, D.T. (1961). The perpetuation of an arbitrary tradition through several generations of a laboratory microculture. *Journal of Abnormal and Social Psychology, 62,* 649-658.

Jacobson, E. (1970). Modern treatment of tense patients. Springfield, IL: Charles C Thomas.

Jacoby, L.L., Kelley, C.M. & Dywan, J. (1989). Memory attributions. In H.L. Roediger III & F.I.M. Craik (Eds.), *Varieties of memory and consciousness: Essays in honour of Endel Tulving* (pp. 391-422). Hilsdale, NJ: Erlbaum.

Jahn, R.G. (1992). On the Bayesian analysis of random event generator data. *Journal of Scientific Exploration,* 6, 1, 23-45.

Jahn, R.G. (1994). Series position effects in random event generator experiments. *Journal of Scientific Exploration,* 8, 2, 197-215.

Jahoda, G. (1992). *Crossroads between culture and mind.* London: Harvester Wheatsheaf.

James, J. (1953). The origin of guardian spirits of sweat lodge. As told to V.F. Ray in E.E. Clark, *Indian legends of the Pacific Northwest* (p. 183). Berkeley, CA: University of California Press.

James, W. (1884). What is an emotion? *Mind, 9,* 188-205.

James, W. (1890). *The principles of psychology* (2 vols.). New York:

Holt, Rinehart & Winston.

Jamison, R.N. (1984). Differences in personality between American and English children. *Personality and Individual Differences, 5(2),* 241-244.

Janerich, D.T., Thompson, W.D., Varela, L.R., Greenwaid, P., Chorest, S., Tucci, C., Zaman, M.B., Metamed, M.R., Kiely, M. & McKneally, M.F. (1990). Lung cancer and exposure to tobacco smoke in the household. *The New England Journal of Medicine, 323,* 632-636.

Janis, I.L. (1958). *Psychological stress.* New York: Wiley.

Janis, I.L. (1982a). Decision making under stress. In L. Goldberger & S. Breznitz (Eds.), *Handbook of stress* (pp. 69-87). New York: Free Press.

Janis, I.L. (1982b). *Groupthink: Psychological studies of policy decisions and fiascoes* (2nd ed.). Boston: Houghton Mifflin.

Janis, I.L. (1985). International crisis management in the nuclear age. *Applied Social Psychology Annual, 6,* 63-86.

Janis, I.L. (1990). In *Discovering Psychology,* Program II [PBS video series]. Washington, DC: Annenberg/CPB Project.

Janis, I.L. & Frick, F. (1943). The relationship between attitudes toward conclusions and errors in judging logical validity of syllogisms. *Journal of Experimental Psychology, 33,* 73-77.

Janowitz, H.D. & Grossman, M.I. (1950). Hunger and appetite: Some definitions and concepts. *Journal of the Mount Sinai Hospital, 16,* 231-240.

Jansz, J. (1991). *Person, self and moral demands: Individualism contested by collectivism.* Leiden: DWSO Press.

Janz, N.K. & Becker, M.H. (1984). The health belief model: A decade later. *Health Education Quarterly, 11,* 1-47.

Jaspars, J. (1986). Forum & focus: a personal view of European Social Psychology. *European Journal of Social Psychology,* 16, 3-15.

Jelicic, M., Bonke, B., Wolters, G. & Phaf, R.H. (1992). Implicit memory for words presented during anaesthesia. *European Journal of Cognitive Psychology, 4,* 71-80.

Jemmott, J.B., III, Croyle, R.T., & Ditto, P.H. (1988). Common sense epidemiology: Self-based judgments from lay persons and physicians. *Health Psychology, 7,* 55-73.

Jenkins, C.D. (1976). Recent evidence supporting psychologic and social risk factors for coronary disease. *New England Journal of Medicine, 294,* 987-994, 1033-1038.

Jenkins, J.G. & Dallenbach, K.M. (1924). Oblivescence during sleep and waking. *The American Journal of Psychology, 35,* 605-612.

Jenkins, J.J. (1979). Four points to remember: A tetrahedral model of memory experiments. In L.S. Cermak & F.I.M. Craik (Eds.), *Levels of processing in human memory* (pp. 429-446). Hillsdale, NJ: Erlbaum.

Jenni, D.A. & Jenni, M.A. (1976). Carrying behavior in humans: Analysis of sex differences: *Science, 194,* 859-860.

Jensen, A.R. (1962). Spelling errors and the serial position effect. *Journal of Educational Psychology, 53,* 105-109.

Jensen, A.R. (1973). *Educability and group differences.* New York: Harper & Row.

Jervis, R., Lebow, R.N. & Stein, J.G. (1985). *Psychology and deterrence.* Baltimore: Johns Hopkins University Press.

Johanson, C. & Fischman, M. (1989). The pharmacology of cocaine related to its abuse. *Pharmacological Reviews, 41,* 3-52.

John, E.R., Prichep, L.S., Fridman, J. & Easton, P. (1988). Neurometrics: Computer-assisted differential diagnosis of brain dysfunction. *Science, 239,* 162-169.

John, E.R. (1990). In *Discovering Psychology,* Program 3 [PBS video series]. Washington, DC: Annenberg/CPB Project.

John, O.P. (1990). The 'Big Five' factor taxonomy: Dimensions of personality in the natural language and in questionnaires. In L.A. Pervin (Ed.), *Handbook of personality theory and research* (pp.67-100). New York: Guilford Press.

Johnson, G.B. (1966). Penis envy or pencil hoarding? *Psychological Reports,* 19, 758.

Johnson, J.A., Germer, C.K., Efran, J.S. & Overton, W.F. (1988). Personality as the basis for theoretical predilections. *Journal of Personality and Social Psychology,* 55, 5, 824-835.

Johnson, J.E. (1983). Psychological interventions and coping with surgery. In A. Baum, S.E. Taylor, & J.E. Singer (Eds.), *Handbook of psychology and health* (Vol. 4). Hillsdale, NJ: Erlbaum.

Johnson, J.H., & Sarason, I.B. (1979). Recent developments in research on life stress. In V. Hamilton & D.M. Warburton (Eds.), *Human stress and cognition: An information processing approach* (pp. 205-233). Chichester, England: Wiley.

Johnson, M.K., Hashtroudi, S. & Lindsay, D.S. (1993). Source monitoring. *Psychological Bulletin, 114,* 3-28.

Johnson, T.D. & Gottlieb, G. (1981). Visual preferences of imprinted ducklings are altered by the maternal call. *Journal of Comparative and Physiological Psychology, 95(5),* 665-675.

Johnson-Laird, P. (1983). Mental models. Cambridge, England: Cambridge University Press.

Johnson-Laird, P.N. & Byrne, R.M.J. (1989). Only reasoning. *Journal of Memory and Language, 28,* 313-330.

Johnston, J. & Dark, V. (1986). Selective Attention. *Annual Review of Psychology, 37,* 43-75.

Johnston, L.D., Bachman, J.G. & O'Malley, P.M. (1982). *Student drug use, attitudes and beliefs: Notional trends 1975-1982.* Rockville, MD: National Institute on Drug Abuse.

Johnston, L.D., O'Malley, P.M. & Bachman, J.G. (1989). *Drug use, drinking, and smoking: National survey results from high school, college, and young adult populations, 1975-1988.* Rockville, MD: U.S. Department of Health and Human Services.

Jones, E. (1953). *The life and works of Sigmund Freud.* New York: Basic Books.

Jones, E. (1990). In *Discovering Psychology,* Program 22 [PBS video series]. Washington, DC: Annenberg/CPB Program.

Jones, E.E. (1985). Major developments in social psychology during the last five decades. In G. Lindzey & E. Aronson (Eds.), *The handbook of social psychology* Vol. 1, pp.47-107. New York: Random House.

Jones, E.E. & Berglas, S. (1978). Control of attributions about the self through self-handicapping strategies: The appeal of alcohol and the role of underachievement. *Personality and Social Psychology Bulletin, 4,* 200-206.

Jones, E.E. & Davis, K.E. (1965). From acts to dispositions: The attribution process in person perception. In L. Berkowitz (Ed.), *Advances in experimental social psychology* (Vol. 2). New York: Academic Press.

Jones, E.E., Farina, A., Hastod, A.H., Markus, H., Miller, D.T. & Jones, E.E. & Nisbett, R.E. (1972). The actor and the observer: Divergent perceptions on the causes of behavior. In E.E. Jones et al. (Eds.), *Attribution: Perceiving the causes of behavior.* Morristown, NJ: General Learning Press.

Jones, E.E., Farina, A., Hastod, A.H., Markus, H., Miller, D.T. & Scott, R.A. (1984). *Social stigma: The psychology of marked relationships.* New York: Freeman.

Jones, E.E. & Pittman, T. (1982). Toward a general theory of strategic self-presentation. In J. Suls (Ed.), *Psychological perspectives on the self* (pp.231-262). Hillsdale, NJ: Erlbaum,

Jones, M.C. (1924). A laboratory study of fear: The case of Peter, *Pedagogical Seminary and Journal of Genetic Psychology, 31.* 308-315.

Jones, R. (1978). The third wave. In A. Pines & C. Maslach (Eds.), *Experiencing social psychology.* New York: Knopf.

Jones, W., Cheek, J.M. & Briggs, S.R. (1986). *Shyness: Perspectives on research and treatment.* New York: Plenum.

Jordan, T.G., Grallo, R., Deutsch, M. & Deutsch, C P. (1985). Long-term effects of enrichment: A 20-year perspective on persistence and change. *American Journal of Community Psychology, 13,* 393-414.

Joyce, L. (1989, Fall). Good genes, bad genes. *Stanford Medicine,* pp. 18-23.

Joyce, L. (1990, Fall). Losing the connection. *Stanford Medicine,* pp.19-21.

Joyce, L. (1990, Winter). Fast Asleep. *Stanford Medicine,* pp. 28-31.

Julesz, B. (1981). Textons, the elements of texture perception and their interaction. *Nature, 290,* 91-97.

Julesz, B. (1981). Figure and ground perception in briefly presented isodipole textures. In M. Kubovy & J.R. Pomerantz (Eds.), *Perceptual organization* (pp. 27-54). Hillsdale, NJ: Erlbaum.

Jung, C.G. (1923/1971). *Psychological types* (Bollingen Series XX). The collected works of C.G. Jung (Vol.6.). Princeton: Princeton.

Jung, C.G. (1953). *Collected works.* New York: Bollingen Series/ Pantheon.

Jung, C.G. (1959). The concept of the collective unconscious. In *The archetypes and the collective unconscious, collected works* (Vol. 9, Part 1, pp. 54-74). Princeton, NJ: Princeton University Press. (Original work published 1936)

Jung, C.G. (1965). *Memories, dreams, reflections.* New York: Random House.

Jung, C.G. (1973). *Memories, dreams, reflections* (Rev. ed., A. Jaffe, Ed.). New York: Pantheon Books.

Just, M.A. & Carpenter, P.A. (1980). A theory of reading: From eye fixations to comprehension. *Psychological Review, 87,* 329-354.

K

Kagan, J. (1990). In *Discovering Psychology,* Program 5 [PBS video series]. Washington, DC: Annenberg/CPB Project.

Kagan, J. & Klein, R.E. (1973). Cross-cultural perspectives on early development. *American Psychologist, 28,* 947-961.

Kagan, J., Reznick, J.S. & Snidman, N. (1986). Temperamental inhibition in early childhood. In R. Plomin & J. Dunn (Eds.), *The study of temperament: Changes, continuites and challenges.* Hillsdale, NJ: Erlbaum.

Kagan, J. & Snidman, N. (1991). Infant predictors of inhibited and uninhibited profiles. *Psychological Science, 2,* 40-44.

Kahn, M. (1966). The physiology of catharsis. *Journal of Personality and Social Psychology, 3,* 278-286.

Kahneman, D. (1973). Attention and effort. Englewood Cliffs, NJ: Prentice-Hall.

Kahneman, D. (1990). In *Discovering Psychology,* Program II [PBS video series]. Washington, DC: Annenberg/CPB Project.

Kahneman, D., Slovic, P. & Tversky, A. (Eds.). (1982). *Judgment under uncertainty: Heuristics and biases.* Cambridge, MA: Cambridge University Press.

Kahneman, D. & Snell, J. (1990). Predicting utility. In R. Hogarth *(Ed.), Insights in decision making.* Chicago: University of Chicago Press.

Kahneman, D. & Treisman, A. (1984). Changing views of attention and automaticity. In R. Parasuraman, D.R. Davies, & J.Beatty (Eds.), *Varieties of attention* (pp. 29-6 1). New York: Academic Press.

Kahnemann, D. & Tversky, A. (1973). On the psychology of prediction. *Psychological Review, 80,* 237-251.

Kaij, L. (1960). *Alcoholism in twins. Studies on the etiology and sequelae of abuse of alcohol.* Stockholm, Sweden: Alonquist & Winkell Publishers.

Kalat, J.W. (1974). Taste salience depends on novelty, not concentration in taste-aversion teaming in the rat. *Journal of Comparative and Physiological Psychology, 86,* 47-50.

Kalat, J.W. (1984). *Biological psychology.* (2nd ed.). Belmont, CA: Wadsworth.

Kalish, R. A. (1985). The social context of death and dying. In R.H. Binstock & E. Shanas (Eds.), *Handbook of aging and the social sciences* (pp. 149-172). New York: Van Nostrand Reingold.

Kallmann, F.J. (1946). The genetic theory of schizophrenia: An analysis of 691 schizophrenic index families. *American Journal of Psychiatry, 103,* 309-322.

Kamin, L.J. (1969). Predictability, surprise, attention, and conditioning. In B.A. Campbell & R.M. Church (Fds.), *Classical conditioning: A symposium.* New York: AppletonCentury-Crofts.

Kamin, L.J. (1974). *The science and politics of IQ.* Potomac, MD: Erlbaum.

Kandel, D. (1973). Adolescent marijuana use: Role of parents and peers. *Science, 181,* 1067-1070.

Kandel, E.R. (1976). *The cellular basis of behavior.* San Francisco: Freeman.

Kandel, E.R. (1979). Cellular insights into behavior and teaming. *The Harvey Lectures,* Series 73, 29-92.

Kanigel, R. (1981). Storing yesterday. *Johns Hopkins Magazine, 32,* 27-34.

Kanizsa, G. (1979). *Organization in vision.* New York: Praeger.

Kaplan, J. (1983). *The hardest drug: Heroin and public policy.* Chicago: University of Chicago Press.

Kaplan, R.M. (1985). The controversy related to the use of psychological tests. In B.B. Wolman (Ed.), *Handbook of intelligence* (pp. 465-504). New York: Wiley.

Kaplan, R.M. (1990). *Behavior as the central outcome in health care.* American Psychologist, 45, 1211-1220.

Kaptein, A.A. & van Rooijen, E. (1990). Behavioural Medicine – Some Introductory Remarks. In A.A. Kaptein, H.M. van der Ploeg, B. Garssen, P.J.G. Schreurs, & R. Beunderman, R. (Eds.), *Behavioural Medicine,* (pp.3-13). London: Wiley

Karl, L. (1960). *Alcoholism in twins. Studies on the etiology and sequelae of abuse of alcohol* Stockholm, Sweden: Alonquist & Winkell Publishers.

Karlsson, J.L. (1978). *Inheritance of creative intelligence.* Chicago: Nelson-Hall.

Karno, M., Golding, J.M., Sorenson, S.B. & Burnham, A. (1988). The epidemiology of obsessive-compulsive disorder in five US communities. *Archives of General Psychiatry, 45,* 1094-99.

Karon, B.P. & Vandenbos, G.R. (1981). *Psychotherapy of*

schizophrenia: The treatment of choice. New York: Jason Aronson.

Kasl, S.V. & Cobb, S. (1966). Health behavior and illness behavior: 1. Health and illness behavior. *Archives of Environmental Health, 12,* 246-266.

Kastenbaum, R. (1986). *Death, society and the human experience.* Columbus, OH: Merrill.

Kaufman, L. & Rock, I. (1962). The moon illusion. *Scientific American, 207(7),* 120-130.

Kaufmann, Y. (1984). Analytical psychotherapy. In R. J. Corsini & Contributors (Eds.), *Current psychotherapies* (3rd ed., pp. 108-126). ltasca, IL: Peacock.

Kaushall, P.I., Zetin, M. & Squire, L.R. (1981). A psychological study of chronic, circumscribed amnesia: Detailed report of a noted case. *Journal of nervous and Mental Disorders, 169,* 383-389.

Kay, D.W.K. & Bergman, K. (1982). Epidemiology of mental disorders among the aged in the community. In J.E. Birren & R.B. Sloane (Eds.), *Handbook of mental health and aging* (pp.34-56). Englewood Cliffs, NJ: Prentice-Hall.

Kay, P. & Kempton, W. (1984). What is the Sapir-Whorf hypothesis? *American-Anthropologist, 86(1),* 65-79.

Kazdin, A.E. (1980). *Behavior modification in applied settings* (2nd ed.). Homewood, IL: Dorsey.

Kazdin, A.E. (1982). The token economy: A decade later. *Journal of Applied Behavior Analysis, 15,* 431-445.

Kazdin, A.E. (1986). Comparative outcome studies of psychotherapy: Methodological issues and strategies. *Journal of Consulting and Clinical Psychology, 54,* 95 105.

Kazdin, A.E. & Wilcoxin, L.A. (1976). Systematic desensitization and nonspecific treatment effects: A methodological evaluation. *Psychological Bulletin, 83,* 729-758.

Kazdin, A.E. & Wilson, G.T. (1980). *Evaluation of behavior therapy: Issues, evidence, and research strategies. Lincoln:* University of Nebraska Press.

Keane, T.M., Zimering, R.T. & Caddell, J.M. (1985). A behavioral approach to assessing and treating post-traumatic stress disorder in Vietnam veterans. In C.R. Figley (Ed.), *Trauma and its wake.* New York: Bruner/Mazel.

Keen, S. (1986). *Faces of the enemy: Reflections of the hostile imagination.* New York: Harper & Row.

Keesey, R.E. & Powley, T.L. (1975). Hypothalamic regulation of body weight. *American Scientist, 63,* 558-565,

Keinan, G., Ben-zur, H., Zilka, M. & Carel, R.S., (1992). Anger in or out, which is healthier? An attempt to reconcile inconsistent findings. *Psychology & Health,* Vol. 7, pp. 83-98.

Keller, H. (1902). *The story of my life.* New York: Doubleday, 1954.

Keller, H. (1990). In D. Ackerman, A *Natural History of the Senses.* New York: Random House.

Kelley, H.H. (1967). Attribution theory in social psychology. In D. Levine (Ed.), *Nebraska Symposium on Motivation* (Vol.15). Lincoln, NE: University of Nebraska Press.

Kelley, H.H. (1971a). *Attribution: Perceiving the causes of behavior.* New York: General Learning Press.

Kelley, H.H. (1971b). Attribution in social interaction. In E.E. Jones, D.E. Kanouse, H.H. Kelley, R.E. Nisbett, S. Valins, & B. Weiner (Eds.), *Attribution: Perceiving the causes of behavior.* New York: General Leaming Press.

Kelley, H.H. & Thibaut, J.W. (1978). *Interpersonal relations: A theory of interdependence.* New York: Wiley-Interscience.

Kelley, K., Cheung, F., Rodriguez-Carillo, P., Wan, C.K. & Becker, M.A. (1986). Chronic self-destructiveness and locus of control in cross-cultural perspective. *Journal of Social Psychology, 126,* 573-577.

Kellman, P.J. & Spelke, E.S. (1983). Perception of partly occluded objects in infancy. *Cognitive Psychology, 15,* 483-524.

Kelly, G.A. (1955). *A theory of personality: The psychology of personal constructs* (2 vols.). New York: Norton.

Kelman, H.C. & Hamilton, L. (1989). *Crimes of obedience: Toward a social psychology of authority and responsibility.* New Haven, CT: Yale University Press.

Kelsoe, J.R., Ginns, E.I., Egeland, J.A., Gerhard, D.S., Goldstein, A. M., Bale, S.J., Pauls, D.L., Long, R.T., Kidd, K.K., Conte, G., Housman, D.E. & Paul, S.M. (1989). Reevaluation of the linkage relationship between chromosome 11p loci and the gene for bipolar affective disorder in the Old Order Amish. *Nature, 342,* 238-243.

Kemp, M. (1990). *The science of art: Optical themes in Westem art from Brunelleschi to Seurat.* New Haven: Yale University Press.

Kempen, G. & Hoenkamp, E. (1987). An incremental procedure grammar for sentence formulation. *Cognitive Science, 11,* 201-258.

Kennedy, G.C. (1953). The role of depot fat in the hypothalamic control of food intake in the rat. *Proceedings of the Royal Society,* 140 (Series B), 578-592.

Kennedy, S., Kiecolt-Glaser, J.K. & Glaser, R. (1988). Immunological consequences of acute and chronic stressers: The mediating role of interpersonal relationships. *British Journal of Medical Psychology, 61,* 77.

Kerkhof, G.A. (1985). Inter-individual differences in th human circadian system: a review. *Biological Psychology, 20,* 83-112.

Kerr, J.H., Murgatroyd, S. & Apter, M.J. (Eds.) (1993). *Advances in reversal theory.* Amsterdam/Lisse: Swets & Zeitlinger.

Kesey, K. (1962). *One flew over the cuckoo's nest.* New York: Viking Press.

Kessen, S. & Cahan, E.D. (1986). A century of psychology: From subject to object to agent. *American Scientist, 74,* 640-649.

Kessler, S. (1980). The genetics of schizophrenia: A review. In S.J. Keith & L.R. Mosher (Eds.), *Special report: Schizophrenia, 1980* (pp. 14-26). Washington, DC: U.S. Government Printing Office.

Kett, J.F. (1977). *Rites of passage: Adolescence in America, 1790 to present.* New York: Basic Books.

Kety, S.S., Rosenthal, D., Wender, P.H., Schulsinger, F. & Jacobsen, B. (1975). Mental illness in the biological and adoptive families of adopted individuals who have become schizophrenic: A preliminary report based on psychiatric interviews. In R.R. Fieve, D. Rosenthal, & H. Brill (Eds.), Genetic research in psychiatry (pp. 147-165). Baltimore: Johns Hopkins University Press.

Kevles, D.J. (1985). *In the name of eugenics: Genetics and the use of human heredity.* New York: Knopf.

Kiecolt-Glaser, J.K. & Glaser, R. (1990). Stress & immune function in humans. In R. Ader, (Ed.), *Psychoneuroimmunology,* (2nd ed.), (pp.849-867). New York Academic Press.

Kiecolt-Glaser, J.K., Glaser, R., Shuttleworth, E.C., Dyer, C.S., Ogrocki, P. & Speecher, C.E. (1987). Chronic stress and immunity in family caregivers of Alizheimer's disease victims. *Psychosonwtic Medicine, 49,* 523-535.

Kierulff, S. (1989, March). *Conversation with a demon.* Symposium conducted at the meeting of the California State Psychological Association, San Francisco, CA.

Kihlstrom, J.F. (1987). The cognitive unconscious. *Science, 237,* 1445-1452.

Kihlstrom, J.F. & Harackiewicz, J.M. (1982). The earliest recollection: A new survey. *Journal of Personality, 50,* 134-148.

Kihlstrom, J.F., Schacter, D.L., Cork, R.C., Hurt, C.A. & Behr, S.E. (1990). Implicit and explicit memory following surgical anesthesia. *Psychological Science, 1,* 303-306.

Kim, U. (1994). Individualism and collectivism: Conceptual clarification and elaboration. In U. Kim, H.C. Triandis, Ç. Kâğitçibaşi, S.-C. Choi & G. Yoon (Eds.), *Individualism & collectivism: Theory, method and applications,* London: Sage.

Kimmel, D.C. & Weiner, I.B. (1985). *Adolescence: A developmental transition.* Hillsdale, NJ: Erlbaum.

Kimura, D. (1985, November). Male brain, female brain: The hidden difference. *Psychology Today,* pp. 50-58.

King, R.J. (1986). Motivational diversity and mesolimbic dopamine: A hypothesis concerning temperaments. In R. Plutchik & H. Kellerman (Eds.), *Emotion: Theory, research, and experience: Biological foundations of emotions* (Vol. 3, pp. 363-380). Orlando, FL: Academic Press.

King, R.J., Mefford, I.N., Wang, C., Murchison, A., Caligari, E.J. & Berger, P.A. (1986). CSF dopamine levels correlate with extraversion in depressed patients. *Psychiatry Research, 19,* 305-310.

Kinsey, A.C., Martin, C.E. & Pomeroy, W.B. (1948). *Sexual behavior in the human male.* Philadelphia: Saunders.

Kinsey, A.C., Pomeroy, W.B., Martin, C.E. & Gebhard, R.H. (1953). *Sexual behavior in the human female.* Philadelphia: Saunders.

Kintsch, W. (1974). *The representation of meaning in memory.* Hillsdale, NJ: Erlbaum.

Kintsch, W. (1981). Semantic memory: A tutorial. In R.S. Nickerson (Ed.), *Attention and performance* (Vol. 8). Hillsdale, NJ: Erlbaum

Kintsch, W. & Keenan, J. (1973). Reading rate and retention as a function of the number of propositions in the base structure of sentences. *Cognitive Psychology, 5,* 257-274.

Kintsch, W. & Van Dijk, T.A. (1978). Toward a model of text comprehension and production. *Psychological Review, 85,* 363-394.

Kipnis, D. (1991). The technological perspective, *Psychological Science, 2,* 62-69.

Kitzinger, C. (1987). *The social construction of lesbianism*. London: Sage.

Klag, M.J., Whelton, P.K., Grim, C.E. & Kuller, L.H. (1991). The association of skin color with blood pressure in U.S. blacks with low socioeconomic status. *Journal of the American Medical Association, 265,* 599-602.

Klatzky, R. (1980). *Human memory: Structures and processes* (2nd ed.). San Francisco: Freeman.

Klatzky, R.B. (1991). Let's be friends. *American Psychologist, 46,* 43-45.

Klaus, M. & Kennel, J. (1976). *Maternal-infant bonding.* St. Louis, MO: Mosby.

Klein, D.C. & Goldston, S.E. (Eds.). (1977). *Primary prevention: An idea whose time has come.* Washington, DC: U.S. Government Printing Office.

Klein, G. (1970). *Perception, motives and personality,* New York: Knopf.

Klein, G.S. & Schlesinger, H.J. (1949). Where is the perceiver in perceptual theory? *Journal of Personality, 18,* 32-47.

Klein, R.H. (1983). Group treatment approaches. In M. Hersen, A.E. Kazdin & A.S. Bellack (Eds.), *The clinical psychology handbook.* New York: Pergamon Press.

Klein, W.M. & Kunda, Z. (1993). Maintaining self-serving social comparisons: biased reconstruction of one's past behaviors. *Personality and Social Psychology Bulletin, 19,* 732-739.

Kleinginna, P.R. & Kleinginna, A.M. (1981). A categorized list of motivation definitions with a suggestion for a consensual definition. *Motivation and Emotion, 5,* 263-29 1.

Kleinke, C.L. (1986). Gaze and eye contact: A research review. *Psychological Bulletin, 100,* 78- 100.

Kleinman, A. (1980). *Patients and healers in the context of culture.* Berkeley: University of California.

Kleinman, A. (1987). Anthropology and psychiatry. *British Journal Psychiatry, 151,* 447-454.

Kleinmuntz, B. & Szucko, J.J. (1984). Lie detection in ancient and modem times: A call for contemporary scientific study. *American Psychologist, 39,* 766-776.

Klerman, G.L. (1986). Historical perspectives on contemporary schools of psychopathology. In T. Millon & G.L. Klerman *(Eds.), Contemporary directions in psychopathology: Toward the DSM-IV* (pp. 3-28). New York: Guilford Press.

Klerman, G.L., Weissman, M.M., Rounsaville, B.J. & Chevron, E.S. (1984). *Interpersonal psychotherapy of depression.* New York: Basic Books.

Klinger, E. (1987, May). The power of daydreams. *Psychology Today,* pp. 37-44.

Klinnert, M.D., Campos, J.J., Sorce, J.F., Emde, R.N. & Svejda, M. (1983). Emotions as behavioral regulators: Social referencing in infancy. In R. Plutchik & H. Kellerman (Eds.), *Emotion: Theory, research and experience* (Vol.2, pp. 57-86). New York: Academic Press.

Kluckhorn, C. (1944). Navaho Witchcraft. *Papers of the Yale University Peabody Museum* (Vol.24, No.2). New Haven, CT: Yale University.

Knippenberg, A. van & Ellemers, N. (1990). Social identity and intergroup differentiation. *European Review of Social Psychology, 1,* 137-169.

Kobasa, S.O. (1984). How much stress can you survive? *American Health, 3,* 64-77.

Kobasa, S.O., Hilker, R.R. & Maddi, S.R. (1979). Who stays healthy under stress? *Journal of Occupational Medicine, 21,* 595-598.

Koch, R., Graliker, B., Fishier, K. & Ragsdale, N. (1963). Clinical aspects of phenylketonuria. In *First Inter-American Conference on Congenital Defects.* Philadelphia: Lippincott.

Koch, S. (1951). Theoretical psychology, 1950: An overview. *Psychological Review, 58,* 295-301.

Koch, S. & Leary, D.E. (1985). A *century of psychology as science.* New York: McGraw-Hill.

Koestler, A. (1964). *The act of creation.* London: Hutchinson.

Koestner, R. & McClelland, D.C. (1992). The affiliation motive. In C.P. Smith (Ed.), *Motivation and personality. Handbook of thematic content analysis* (pp. 205-210). Cambridge: C.U.P.

Koh, S.O. & Peterson, R.A. (1974). A perceptual memory for numerousness in 'nonpsychotic schizophrenics'. *Journal of Abnormal Psychology, 83,* 215-226.

Kohlberg, L. (1964). Development of moral character and moral ideology. In M.L. Hoffman & L.W. Hoffman (Eds.), *Review of child development research (Vol.1).* New York: Russell Sage Foundation.

Kohlberg, L. (1966). A cognitive-developmental analysis of children's sex-role concepts and attitudes. In E.E. Maccoby (Ed.), *The development of sex differences.* Stanford, CA: Stanford University Press.

Kohlberg, L. (1967). Moral and religious education and the public schools: A developmental view. In T. Sizer (Ed.), *Religion and public education.* Boston: Houghton Mifflin.

Kohlberg, L. (1969). Stage and sequence: The cognitive-developmental approach to socialization. In D.A. Goslin (Ed.), *Handbook of socialization theory and research.* Chicago: Rand McNally.

Kohlberg, L. (1973). Stages and aging in moral development: Some speculations. *Gerontologist, 13(4),* 497-502.

Kohlberg, L. (1981). *The philosophy of moral development.* New York: Harper & Row.

Köhler, W. (1925). *The mentality of apes.* New York: Harcourt Brace Jovanovich.

Köhler, W. (1947). *Gestalt psychology.* New York: Liveright.

Kohut, H. (1977). *The restoration of the self.* New York: International Universities Press.

Kolata, G. (1985). Why do people get fat? *Science, 227,* 1327-1328.

Kolata, G. (1986). Maleness pinpointed on Y chromosomes. *Science,* 234,1076-1077.

Kolb, B. (1989). Development, plasticity and behavior. *American Psychologist, 44,* 1203-1212.

Kolb, B. & Whishaw, I.Q. (1990). *Fundamentals of human neuropsychology, 3rd edition.* New York: Freeman & Company.

Kolb, L.C. (1973). *Modern clinical psychiatry.* Philadelphia: Saunders.

Kondo, T., Antrobus, J. & Fein, G. (1989). Later REM activation and sleep mentation. *Sleep Research, 18,* 147.

Konecni, V.J. & Ebbesen, E.B. (1984). The mythology of legal decision making. *International Journal of Law and Psychiatry, 7,* 5-18.

Konecni, V.J. & Ebbesen, E.B. (1986). Courtroom testimony by psychologists on eyewitness identification issues: Critical notes and reflections. Law and Human Behavior, 10, 1, 17-126.

Korchin, S.J. (1976). *Modern clinical psychology.* New York: Basic Books.

Korn, J. (1987). Judgments of acceptability of deception in psychological research. *Journal of General Psychology, 1, 14,* 205-216.

Korn, J. W. (1985). Psychology as a humanity. *Teaching of Psychology, 12,* 188-193.

Kosecoff, J.B. & Fink, A. (1982). *Evaluation basics: A practitioner's manual.* Beverly Hills, CA: Sage Publications.

Koslow, S.H. (1984). Preface. In *The neuroscience of mental health: A report on neuroscience research* (DHHS Publication No. ADM 84-1363). Rockville, MD: National Institute of Mental Health.

Kosslyn, S.M. (1980). *Image and mind.* Cambridge, MA: Harvard University Press.

Kosslyn, S.M. (1983). *Ghosts in the mind's machine: Creating and using images in the brain.* New York: Norton.

Kosslyn, S.M. (1985). Computational neuropsychology: A new perspective on mental imagery. *Naval Research Reviews, 37,* 30-50.

Kosslyn, S.M., Holtzman, J.D., Farah, M.J. & Gazzaniga, M.S. (1985). A computational analysis of mental image generation: Evidence from functional dissociations in split-brain patients. *Journal of Experimental Psychology: General, 114,* 311-341.

Kraft, C.L. (1978). A psychophysical contribution to air safety: Simulator studies of visual illusions in night visual approaches. In H. Pick, H.W. Leibowitz, J.R. Singer, A. Steinschneider & H.W. Stevenson (Eds.), *Psychology from research to practice* (pp.363-385). New York: Plenum.

Kraft, D.P. (1984). A comprehensive prevention program for college students. In P.M. Miller & T.D. Nirenberg (Eds.), *Prevention of Alcohol Abuse.* New York: Plenum.

Krajick, K. (1990, July 30). Sound too good to be true? Behind the boom in subliminal tapes. *Newsweek,* p.61.

Krasner, L. (1985). Applications of teaming theory in the environment. In B.L. Hammonds (Ed.), *Psychology arid learning: 1984 master lecturers* (pp. 51-93). Washington, DC American Psychological Association.

Kreitler, S. & Kreitler, H. (1990a). Cognitive orientation and sexual dysfunctions in women. *Annals of Sex Research, 3,* 75-104.

Kreitler, S. & Kreitler, H. (1990b). Repression and the anxiety defensiveness factor: Psychological correlates and manifestations. Personality and lndividual Differences, 11, 559-570.

Kreitler, S. & Kreitler, H. (1990c). *The cognitive orientation of health and susceptibility to illness in college students.* Unpublished manuscript, Psychology Department, University of Tel Aviv, Tel Aviv.

Kreitler, S. & Kreitler, H. (1991). The psychological profile of the health-oriented individual. *European Journal of Personality 5,* 35-60,

Krieger, L. & Garrison, J. (1991, August 4). Hospitals praised for AIDS care. *San Francisco Examiner,* p. B-2.

Krieger, L.M. (1990, October 12). Huh? I can't hear you. *San Francisco Examiner,* pp.DI6-D17.

Krippendorff, K. (1980). *Content analysis: an introduction to its methodology.* Beverly Hills, CA: Sage.

Kristjansson, E.A., Fried, P.A. & Watkinson, B. (1989). Maternal smoking during pregnancy affects children's vigilance performance. *Drug and Alcohol Dependence,* 24, 11-19.

Krosnick, J.A., Betz, A.L., Jussim, L.J. & Lynn, A.R. (1992). Subliminal conditioning of attitudes. *Personality and Social Psychology Bulletin, 18,* 152-162.

Kruschke, J.K. (1992). ALCOVE: An exemplar-based connectionist model of category learning. *Psychological Review, 99,* 22-44.

Kubler-Ross, E. (1969). *On death and dying.* Toronto: Macmillan.

Kubler-Ross, E. (1975). Death: The final stage of growth. Englewood Cliffs, NJ: Prentice-Hall.

Kubovy, M. & Pomerantz, J.R. (Eds.). (1981). *Perceptual Organization.* Hillsdale, NJ: Erlbaum.

Kuffler, S.W., Nicholls, J.G. & Martin, A.R. (984). *From neuron to brain: A cellular approach to thefunction of the nervous system* (2nd ed.). Sunderland, MA: Sinauer Associates.

Kuklick, H. (1987). The testing movement and its founders. *Science,* 237,1358-1359.

Kulik, J.A. (1983). Confirmatory attribution and the perpetuation of social beliefs. *Journal of Personality and Social Psychology, 44,* 1171-1181.

Kulik, J.A. & Mahler, H.I.M. (1989), Social support and recovery from surgery. *Health Psychology, 8,* 221-238.

Kunda, Z. (1990). The case for motivated reasoning. *Psychological Bulletin, 108,* 480-498,

Kupfermann, I. et al. (1974). Local, reflex, and central commands controlling gill and siphon movements in Aplysia. *Journal of Neurophysiology, 37,* 996-1019.

Kurtines, W. & Greif, E.B. (1974). The development of moral thought: Review and evaluation of Kohlberg's approach. *Psychological Bulletin, 8,* 453-470.

Kutas, M. & Hillyard, S.A. (1980). Reading senseless sentences: Brain potentials reflect semantic incongruity. *Science, 207,* 203-205.

L

La Piere, R. (1934). Attitudes versus actions. *Social Forces, 13,* 230-237.

LaBarre, W. (1964). Confessions as psychotherapy in American Indian tribes. In A. Kiev (Ed.), *Magic, faith and healing.* New York: Free Press.

LaBerge, S. (1986). *Lucid dreaming.* New York: Valentine Books.

LaBerge, S. (1990). *In Discovering Psychology, Program 13* (PBS video series]. Washington, DC: Annenberg/CPB Program.

LaBerge, S., Nagel, L.E., Dement, W.C. & Zarcone, V.P., Jr. (1981). Evidence for lucid dreaming during REM sleep. *Sleep Research, 10,* 148.

LaBerge, S. & Rheingold, H. (1990). *Exploring the world of lucid dreaming.* New York: Ballantine

Labouvie-Vief, G. (1985). Intelligence and cognition. In J.E. Birren & K.W. Schaie (Eds.), *Handbook of the psychology of aging* (2nd ed., pp. 500-530). New York: Van Nostrand Reingold.

Lacan, J. (1974). *Télévision.* Paris: Seuil.

Lacan, J. (1979). *The four fundamental concepts of psychoanalysis.* Harmondsworth: Penguin Books.

Lachman, S. (1983). The concept of Learning: Connecting and selecting. *Academic Psychology Bulletin, 5,* 155-166.

Lachman, S.J. (1983). A physiological interpretation of voodoo illness and voodoo death. *Omega, 13(4),* 345-360.

Lachman, R. & Naus, M. (1984). The episodic/semantic continuum in an evolved machine. *Behavioral and Brain Sciences, 7,* 244-246.

LaFramboise, T. (1988, March 30). Suicide prevention. In *Campus Report* (p.9). Stanford, CA: Stanford University.

LaFramboise, T. (1990). In *Discovering Psychology,* Program 21 [PBS video series]. Washington, DC: Annenberg/CPB Program.

Laing, R.D. (1965). *The divided self.* Baltimore: Penguin.

Laing, R.D. (1967, February 3). Schizophrenic split. *Time,* p. 56.

Laing, R.D. (1967). *The politics of experience.* New York: Pantheon.

Laing, R.D. (1970). *Knots.* New York: Pantheon.

Laird, J.D. & Brester, C. (1990). William James and the mechanisms of emotional experience. *Personality and Social Psychology Bulletin, 16,* 636-65 1.

Lakoff, R. (1975). *Language and woman's place.* New York: Harper & Row.

Lambert. J.-L. (1990). The development of thinking in mentally retarded children: Has behaviourism something to offer? In D.E. Blackman & H. Lejeune (Eds.), *Behaviour analysis in theory and practice: Contributions and controversies.* Hove & London: Lawrence Erlbaum Associates.

Lambert, N.M. (1981). Psychological evidence in Larry P. versus Wilson Riles. *American Psychologist, 36,* 937-952.

Lambo, T.A. (1978). Psychotherapy in Africa. *Human Nature, 1(3),* 32-39.

Lane, H. (1976). *The wild boy of Aveyron.* Cambridge, MA: Harvard University Press.

Lane, H. (1986). The wild boy of Aveyron and Dr. Jean-Marc Itard. *History of Psychology,* 17, 3-16.

Lang, P.J. (1979). A bioinformational theory of emotional imagery. *Psychophysiology, 16,* 495-512.

Lang, P.J. & Lazovik, D.A. (1963). The experimental desensitization of a phobia. *Journal of Abnormal and Social Psychology, 66,* 519-525.

Langer, E. (1975) The illusion of control. *Journal of Personality and Social Psychology, 32,* 311-328.

Langer, E. (1978). Rethinking the role of thought in social interaction. In J.H. Harvey, W.J. Ickes & R.F. Kidd (Eds.), *New directions in attribution research* (Vol. 2, pp. 35-38). Hillsdale, NJ: Erlbaum.

Langer, E. (1989). *Mindfulness.* Reading, MA: Addison-Wesley.

Langer, E. (1990). In *Discovering Psychology,* Program 19 [PBS video series]. Washington, DC: Annenberg/CPB Program.

Langer, E.J. & Rodin, J. (1976). The effects of choice and enhanced personal responsibility for the aged: A field experiment in an institutional setting. *Journal of Personality and Social Psychology, 34,* 191-198.

Langlois, J.H. & Downs, A.C. (1980). Mothers, fathers and peers as socialization agents of sex-typed play behaviors in young children. *Child Development, 51,* 1237-1247.

Langs, R. (Ed.). (1981). *Classics in psychoanalytic technique.* New York: Jason Aronson.

Langs, R. (Ed.). (1991). *Classics in psychoanalytic technique.* New York: Jason Aronson.

Lanzetta, J.T., Sullivan, D.G., Masters, R.G. & McHugo, G.J. (1985). Viewers' emotional and cognitive responses to televised images of political leaders. In S. Kraus & R.M. Perloff (Eds.), *Mass media and political thought: An information processing approach* (pp. 50-67). Beverly Hills, CA: Sage.

Lashley, K.S. (1929). *Brain mechanisms and intelligence.* Chicago: University of Chicago Press.

Lashley, K.S. (1950). In search of the engram. In *Physiological mechanisms in animal behavior: Symposium of the Society for Experimental Biology.* New York: Academic Press.

Lasswell, H.D. (1948). The structure and function of communication in society. In L. Bryson (Ed.), *Communication of ideas.* New York: Harper.

Latané, B. (1981). The psychology of social impact. *American Psychologist, 36,* 343-356.

Latané, B. & Darley, J.M. (1968). Group inhibition of bystander intervention in emergencies. *Journal of Personality and Social Psychology, 10,* 215-221.

Latané, B. & Darley, J.M. (1970). *The unresponsive bystander: Why doesn't he help?* New York: Appleton-Century-Crofts.

Latham, G.P. & Yuki, G.A. (1975). A review of research on the application of goal setting in organizations. *Academic Management Journal, 18,* 824-845.

Lau, R.R. (1989). Construct accessibility and electoral choice. *Political Behavior, 11,* 5-32.

Lau, R.R., Bernard, T.M. & Hartman, K.A. (1989). Further explorations of common sense representations of common illnesses. *Health Psychology, 8,* 195-219.

Laudensiager, M.L., Ryan, S.M., Drugan, R.C., Hyson, R.L. & Maier, S F. (1983). Coping and immunosuppression: Inescapable but not escapable shock suppresses lymphocyte proliferation. *Science, 231,* 568-570.

Lawton, M.P. (1977). An ecological theory of aging applied to elderly housing. *Journal of Architecture and Education, 31,* 8-10.

Lazarus, R.S. (1966). *Psychological stress and the coping process.* New York: McGraw-Hill.

Lazarus, R.S. (1975). A cognitively oriented psychologist looks at biofeedback. *American Psychologist, 30,* 553-561.

Lazarus, R.S. (1976). *Patterns of adjustment* (3rd ed.). New York: McGraw-Hill.

Lazarus, R.S. (1981, July). Little hassles can be hazardous to your health. *Psychology Today,* pp. 58-62.

Lazarus, R.S. (1982). Thoughts on the relations between emotion and cognition. *American Psychologist, 37,* 1019-1024.

Lazarus, R.S. (1984). On the primacy of cognition. *American Psychologist, 39,* 124-129.

Lazarus, R.S. (1984). Puzzles in the study of daily hassles. *Journal of Behavioral Medicine, 7,* 375-389.

Lazarus, R.S. (1991). Progress on a cognitive-motivationalrelational theory of emotion. *American Psychologist, 46,* 819-834.

Lazarus, R.S. & Folkman, S. (1984). *Stress, appraisal and coping.* New York: Springer.

Leask, J., Haber, R.N. & Haber, R.B. (1969). Eidetic imagery in children: II. Longitudinal and experimental results. *Psychonomic Monograph Supplements, 3* (3, Whole No. 35).

Le Ny, J.-F. (1985). European roots of behaviourism and recent developments. In C.F. Lowe, M. Richelle, D.E. Blackman & C.M. Bradshaw (Eds.), *Behaviour analysis & contemporary psychology,* Hove & London: Lawrence Erlbaum Associates.

LeBon, G. (1895). *Psychologie des foules.* Paris:Alcan (English trans. *The Crowd,* London, Unwin. Ross, E.A., 1908, Social Psychology, New York, Macmillan.

LeBon, G. (1960). *The crowd.* New York: Viking Press. (Original work published 1895)

LeDoux, J. (1989). Cognitive-emotional interactions in the brain. *Cognition and Emotion, 3,* 267-289.

LeDoux, J.E. (1993). Emotional memory systems in the brain. *Behavioural Brain Research, 58(1-2),* 69-79.

LeDoux, J.E., Wilson, D.H. & Gazzaniga, M.S. (1977). A divided mind: Observations on the conscious properties of the separated hemispheres. *Annals of Neurology, 2,* 417-421.

Leeper, R.W. (1948). A motivational theory of emotion to replace 'emotions as disorganized response'. *Psychological Review, 55,* 5-21.

Leerhsen, C. (1990, February 5). Unite and conquer: America's crazy for support groups. *Newsweek,* pp. 50-55.

Leger, D. (1992). *Biological foundations of behavior: An integrative approach.* New York: Harper Collins.

Leiberman, M.A. (1982). The effects of social supports on responses to stress. In L. Goldberger & L. Bresnitz (Eds.), *Handbook of Stress* (pp. 764-783). New York: Free Press.

Leibowitz, H.W. (1988). The human senses in flight. In E.L. Wiener & D.C. Nagel (Eds.), *Human factors in aviation* (pp. 83-1 10). New York: Academic Press.

Leiter, M.P. & Maslach, C. (1988). The impact of interpersonal environment on burnout and organizational commitment. *Journal of Organizational Behavior, 9,* 297-308.

Lemert, E.M. (1962). Paranoia and the dynamics of exclusion. *Sociometry, 25,* 2-20.

Lenneberg, E.H. (1962). Understanding language without ability to speak: A case report. *Journal of Abnormal and Social Psychology, 65,* 415-419.

Lenneberg, E.H. (1969). On explaining language. *Science, 164,* 635-643.

Lenneberg, E.H. & Roberts, J.M. (1956). *The language of experience* (memoir 13). Indiana, Ill: University of Illinois Press.

Leowontin, R.C., Rose, S. & Kamin, L.J. (1984). *Not in our genes: Biology, ideology and human nature.* New York: Pantheon.

Lepper, M.R. (1981). Intrinsic and extrinsic motivation in children: Detrimental effects of superfluous social controls. In U.A. Collins (Ed.), *Aspects of the development of competence: The Minnesota Symposium on Child Psychology* (Vol. 14, pp. 155-214). Hillsdale, NJ: Erlbaum.

Lepper, M.R. & Greene, D. (Eds.). (1978). *The hidden costs of reward.* Hillsdale, NJ: Erlbaum.

Lepper, M.R., Greene, D. & Nisbett, R.E. (1973). Undermining children's intrinsic interest with extrinsic reward: A test of the overjustification hypothesis. *Journal of Personality and Social Psychology, 28(1),* 129-137.

Lerner, R.M., Orlos, J.R. & Knapp, J. (1976). Physical attractiveness, physical effectiveness and self-concept in adolescents. *Adolescence, 11,* 313-326.

Leslie, C. & Wingert, P. (1990, January 8). Not as easy as A, B, or C. *Newsweek,* pp. 56-58.

Lettvin, J.Y., Maturana, H.R., McCulloch, W.S. & Bitts, W.H. (1959). What the frog's eye tells the frog's brain. *Proceedings of the Institute of Radio Engineers, 47,* 1940-1951.

Levelt, W.J.M. (1983). Monitoring and self-repair in speech. *Cognition, 14,* 41-104.

Levelt, W.J.M. (1989). *Speaking: From intention to articulation.* Cambridge, MA: MIT Press.

Levenson, R.W., Carstensen, L.L., Friesen, W.V. & Ekman, P. (1991). Emotion, physiology and expression in old age. *Psychology and Aging, 6,* 28-35.

Leventhal, H. (1970). Findings and theory in the study of fear communications. In L. Berkowitz (Ed,), *Advances in experimental social psychology* (Vol. 5, pp. 120-186). New York: Academic Press.

Leventhal, R. (1984). A perceptual motor theory of emotion. In K.R. Schemer & P. Ekman (Eds.), *Approaches to emotion* (pp. 271-291). Hillsdale, NJ: Erlbaum.

Leventhal, H. & Cleary, P.D. (1980). The smoking problem: A review of the research and theory in behavioral risk modification. *Psychological Bulletin, 88,* 370-405.

Levi, P. (1985). *A quiet city: Moments of reprieve.* New York: Simon & Schuster.

Levi-Strauss, C. (1963). The effectiveness of symbols. In C. LeviStrauss (Ed.), *Structural anthropology.* New York: Basic Books.

Levine, J.D. (1978, August). *Paper presented at the World Congress on Pain, Montreal.*

Levine, M. (1987, April). *Effective problem solving.* Englewood Cliffs, NJ: Prentice-Hall.

Levine, M. & Perkins, D.V. (1987). *Principles of community psychology: Perspectives and applications.* New York: Oxford University.

Levine, M.W. & Shefner, J.M. (1981). *Fundamentals of sensation and perception.* Reading, MA: Addison-Wesley.

Levine, R., Lynch, K., Miyake, K. & Lucia, M. (1989). The Type A city: Coronary heart disease and the pace of life. *Journal of Behavioral Medicine, 12,*509-524.

Levinson, B.W. (1967). States of awareness during general anesthesia. In J. Lassner (Ed.), *Hypnosis and psychosomatic medicine* (pp. 200-207). New York: Springer-Verlag.

Levinson, D.L. (1978). *The seasons of a man's life.* New York: Knopf.

Levinson, D.L. (1986). A conception of adult development. *American Psychologist, 41,* 3-13.

Levinson, D.L. (1990). In *Discovering Psychology,* Program 18 [PBS video series]. Washington, DC: Annenberg/CPB Program.

Levy, J. & Trevarthen, C. (1976). Metacontrol of hemispheric function in human split brain patients. *Journal of Experimental Psychology: Human perception and performance, 2,* 299-312.

Lewin, K., Lippitt, R. & White, R.K. (1939). Patterns of aggressive behavior in experimentally created 'social climates'. *Journal of Social Psychology, 10,* 271-299.

Lewin, K. (1935). *A dynamic theory of personality: Selected papers.* New York: McGraw Hill.

Lewin, K. (1936). *Principles of topological psychology,* New York: McGraw-Hill.

Lewin, K. (1947). Group decision and social change. In T.N. Newcomb & E.L. Hartley (Eds.), *Readings in social psychology.* New York: Holt, Rinehart & Winston.

Lewin, K. (1948). *Resolving social conflicts.* New York: Harper.

Lewin, K. (1951). *Field theory in social science.* New York: Harper.

Lewin, K. (1990). In *Discovering Psychology,* Program 19 [PBS video series]. Washington, DC: Annenberg/CPB Program.

Lewin, R. (1985). Gregarious grazers eat better. *Science, 228,* 567-568.

Lewin, R. (1987). The origin of the modern human mind. *Science, 236,* 668-670.

Lewine, R.R., Strauss, J.S. & Gift, T.E. (1981). Sex differences in age at first hospital admission for schizophrenia: Fact or artifact? *American Journal of Psychiatry, 138,* 440-444.

Lewinsohn, P.M. (1975). The behavioral study and treatment of depression. In M. Hersen, R.M. Eisler & P.M. Miller (Eds.), *Progress in behavior modification* (pp. 19-64). New York: Academic Press.

Lewinsohn, P.M. & Graf, M. (1973). Pleasant activities and depression. *Journal of Consulting and Clinical Psychology, 41,* 261-8.

Lewinsohn, P.M., Mischef, W., Chaplins, W. & Barton, R. (1980). Social competence and depression: The role of illusory self-perceptions. *Journal of Abnormal Psychology, 89,* 203-212.

Lewinsohn, P.M., Youngren, M.A. & Grosscup, S.J. (1979). Reinforcement and depression. In R.A. Depue (Ed.), *The* *psychiobiology of depressive disorders: Implications for the effects of stress.* New York: Academic Press.

Lewis, C. (1981). The effects of parental firm control: A reinterpretation of findings. *Psychological Bulletin, 90,* 547-563.

Lewis, C. (1992). *Employee selection.* Cheltenham: Stanley Thorne.

Lewis, D.O. (1990, May 11). [interview]. *San Francisco Chronicle.*

Lewis, H.B. (1981). *Freud and modern psychology-Vol. 1: The emotional basis of mental illness.* New York: Plenum.

Lewis, J.W., Cannon, J.T. & Liebeskind, J.C. (1980). Opiod and nonopiod mechanisms of stress analgesia. *Science, 208,* 623-625.

Lewis, M. (1991). Ways of knowing; Objective self-awareness or consciousness. *Developmental Review, 11,* 231-243.

Lewis, M. (1993). The emergence of human emotions. In M. Lewis & J.M. Haviland (Eds.), *Handbook of emotions* (pp. 223-237). New York: The Guilford Press.

Lewy, A.J., Sack, R.L., Miller, S. & Hoban, T.M. (1987). Antidepressant and circadian phase-shifting effect of light.*Science, 235,* 352-354.

Leyland, C.M. & Mackintosh, N.J. (1978). Blocking of first and second-order autoshaping in pigeons. *Animal Learning and Behaviour, 6,* 391-394.

Liberman, R.P. (1982). What is schizophrenia? *Schizophrenia Bulletin. 8,* 435-437.

Lidz, T., Fleck, S. & Cornelison, A.R. (1965). *Schizophrenia and the family.* New York: International University Press.

Lieberman, L.R. (1973, April 3). [Letter to *Science* concerning "On being sane in insane places"]. *Science, 179.*

Lieberman, M.A. (1977). Problems in integrating traditional group therapies with new forms. *International Journal of Group Psychotherapy, 27,* 19-32.

Lieberman, M.A. (1982). The effects of social support on responses to stress. In L. Goldberger & S. Breznitz (Eds.), *Handbook of stress* (pp. 764-783). New York: Free Press.

Lieberman, P. (1963). Some effects of semantic and grammatical context on the production and perception of speech. *Language and Speech, 6,* 172-187.

Liebert, R.M. & Spiegler, M.D. (1982). *Personality: Strategies and issues.* Homewood, IL: Dorsey Press.

Liem, J.H. (1980). Family studies of schizophrenia: An update and commentary. In S.J. Keith & L.R. Mosher (Eds.), *Special report: Schizophrenia,* 1980 (pp. 82-108). Washington, DC: U.S. Government Printing Office.

Liem, R. & Rayman, P. (1982). Health and social costs of unemployment: Research and policy considerations. *American Psychologist, 37,* 1116-1123.

Lifton, R.K. (1969). *Thought reform and the psychology of totalism.* New York: Norton.

Light, L.L. (1991). Memory and aging: Four hypotheses in search of data. *Annual Review of Psychology, 42,* 333-376.

Lillard, A.S. & Flavell, J.H. (1990). Young children's preference for mental-state over behavioral descriptions of human action. *Child Development, 61,* 731-742.

Lindsay, D.S. & Reed, J.D. (1994). Psychotherapy and memories of childhood sexual abuse: A cognitive perspective. *Applied Cognitive Psychology, 8,* 281-338.

Lindsay, P.H. & Norman, D.A. (1977). *Human information processing* (2nd ed.). New York: Academic Press.

Lindsley, D.B. (1951). Emotion. In S.S. Stevens (Ed.), *Handbook of experimental psychology.* New York: Wiley.

Linn, R.L. (Ed.). (1989). *Intelligence: Measurement, theory and public policy – Proceedings of a symposium in honor of Lloyd G. Humphreys.* Urbana, IL: University of Illinois Press.

Linton, M. (1975). Memory for real-world events. In D.A. Norman & D.E. Rumelhart (Eds.), *Explorations in cognition (Chapter 14).* San Francisco: Freeman.

Linton, M. (1986). Ways of searching and the contents of memory. In D.C. Rubin (Ed.), *Autobiographical memory* (pp. 50-67). Cambridge: Cambridge University Press.

Lipsitt, L.P. & Reese, H.W. (1979). *Child development.* Glenview, IL: Scott, Foresman.

Lipsitt, L.P., Reilly, B., Butcher, M.G. & Greenwood, M.M. (1976). The stability and interrelationships of newborn sucking and heart rate. *Developmental Psychobiology, 9,* 305-310.

Little, M.I. (1981) *Transference neurosis and transference psychosis.* New York: Jason Aronson.

Livesley, W.J. & Bromley, D.B. (1973). *Person perception in childhood and adolescence.* London: Wiley.

Livingstone, M. & Hubel, D. (1988). Segregation of form, color, movement, and depth: Anatomy, physiology and perception. *Science, 240,* 740-749.

Locke, E.A. (1982). *A new look at work motivation: Theory V* (Technical Report GS-12). Arlington, VA: Office of Naval Research.

Locke, E.A., Shaw, K. N., Saari, L.M. & Latham, G.P. (1981). Goal setting and task performance: 1969-1980. *Psychological Bulletin, 90,* 125-152.

Locke, J. (1975). *An essay concerning human understanding.* Oxford: P.H. Nidditch. (Original work published 1690).

Lockhart, R.S. & Craik, F.I.M. (1990). Levels of processing: A retrospective commentary on a framework for memory research. *Canadian Journal of Psychology, 44,* 87-122.

Loehlin, J.C., Lindzey, G. & Spuhler, J.N. (1975). *Race differences in intelligence.* San Francisco: Freeman.

Loevinger, J. (1957). Objective tests as instruments of psychological theory. *Psychological Reports, 3,* 635-694.

Loftus, E.F. & Kaufman, L. (in press). Why do traumatic experiences sometimes produce good memory (flashbulbs) and sometimes no memory (repression)? In E. Winograd & U. Neisser (Eds.), *Affect and accuracy in recall.* New York: Cambridge University Press.

Loftus, E.F. (1979). *Eyewitness testimony.* Cambridge, MA: Harvard University Press.

Loftus, E.F. (1984). The eyewitness on trial. In B.D. Sales & A. Alwork (Eds.), *With liberty, and justice for all.* Englewood Cliffs, NJ: Prentice Hall.

Loftus, E.F. (1993). The reality of repressed memories. *American Psychologist, 48,* 518-537.

Loftus, E.F. & Klinger, M.R. (1992). Is the unconscious smart or dump? *American Psychologist, 47,* 761-765.

Logan, F.A. (1960). *Incentive.* New Haven, CT: Yale University Press.

Logue, A.W. (1986). *The psychology of eating and drinking.* New York: Freeman.

Londer, R. (1988, July 24). When you've just got to do it: Millions of Americans are slaves to their obsessions. *San Francisco Examiner-Chronicle,* This World Section, p. 9.

London, K.A., Mosher, W.D., Pratt, W.F. & Williams, L.B. (1989, March). *Preliminary findings from the National Survey, of Family Growth, Cycle IV.* Paper presented at the annual meeting of the Population Association of America, Baltimore, MD.

Loomis, A.L., Harvey, E.N. & Hobart, G.A. (1937). Cerebral states during sleep as studied by human brain potentials. *Journal of Experimental Psychology, 21,* 127-144.

Lorenz, K. (1937). Imprinting. *The AUK, 54,* 245-273.

Lott, B. & Lott, A.J. (1985). Learning theory in contemporary social psychology. In G. Lindzey & E. Aronson (Eds.), *The handbook of social psychology* (3rd ed., Vol. 1, pp. 109-135). Hillsdale, NJ: Erlbaum.

Lovaas, O.I. (1968). Learning theory approach to the treatment of childhood schizophrenia. In *California Mental Health Research Symposium: No. 2. Behaviour theory and therapy*: Sacramento. CA: Department of Mental Hygiene.

Lovaas, O.I. (1977) *The autistic child: Language development through behaviour modification.* New York: Halsted Press.

Lovibond, S.H., Adams, M. & Adams, W.G. (1979). The effects of three experimental prison environments on the behavior of nonconflict volunteer subjects. *Australian Psychologist, 14,* 273-285.

Lowe, C.F., Harzem, P. & Hughes, S. (1978). Determinants of operant behaviour in humans: Some differences from animals. *Quarterly Journal of Experimental Psychology, 30,* 373-386.

Lowe, C.F. & Horne, P.J. (1985). On the generality of behavioural principles: Human choice and the matching law. In C.F. Lowe, M. Richelle, D.E. Blackman & C.M. Bradshaw (Eds.), *Behaviour analysis & contemporary psychology,* Hove & London: Lawrence Erlbaum Associates.

Lubow, R.E., Rifkin, B. & Alex, M. (1976). The context effect: The relationship between stimulus preexposure and environmental preexposure determines subsequent Teaming. *Journal of Experimental Psychology: Animal Behaviour Processes, 2,* 38-47.

Luchins, A.S. (1942). Mechanization in problem solving. *Psychological Monographs, 54* (No. 248).

Luchins, A.S. (1957). Primacy-recency in impression formation. In C.I. Hovland (Ed.), *The order of presentation in persuasion* (pp. 34-35). New Haven, CT: Yale University Press.

Ludwig, A.M. (1966). Altered states of consciousness. *Archives of General Psychiatry, 15,* 225-234.

Lunde, A.S. (1981). Health in the United States. *Annals of the American Academy of Political and Social Science, 453,* 28-69.

Luria, A.R. (1976). *Cognitive development: Its cultural and social foundations.* Cambridge, MA: Harvard University Press.

Lutz, C. (1988). *Unnatural emotions: everyday sentiments on a Micronesian atoll and their challenge to Western theory.* Chicago: University of Chicago Press.

Lykken, D.T. (1979). The detection of deception. *Psychological Bulletin, 86,* 47-53.

Lykken, D.T. (1981). *A tremor in the blood: Uses and abuses of the lie detector.* New York: McGraw-Hill.

Lykken, D.T. (1984). Polygraphic interrogation. *Nature, 307,* 681-684.

Lynch, G. (1986). *Synapses, circuits and the beginnings of memory.* Cambridge, MA: MIT Press.

Lynch, J.J. (1979). *The broken heart: The medical consequences of loneliness.* New York: Basic Books.

Lynn, S.J., Rhue, J.W. & Weekes, J.R. (1990). Hypnotic involuntariness: a social cognitive analysis. *Psychological Review, 97,* 169-184.

Lyons, N. (1983). Two perspectives: On self, relationships and morality. *Harvard Educational Review, 53,* 125-146.

M

Maccoby, E.E. (1980). *Social development: Psychological growth and the parent-child relationship.* San Diego, CA: Harcourt Brace Jovanovich.

Maccoby, E.E. (1988). Gender as a social category. *Developmental Psychology, 24,* 755-765.

Maccoby, E.E. (1990). In *Discovering Psychology,* Program 17 [PBS video series]. Washington, DC: Annenberg/CPB Program.

Maccoby, E.E. & Jacklin, C.N. (1974). *The psychology of sex differences.* Stanford, CA: Stanford University Press.

Maccoby, E.E. & Jacklin, C.N. (1987). Gender segregation in childhood. In H. Reese (Ed.), *Advances in child behaviour and development* (Vol. 20). New York: Academic Press.

Maccoby, N., Farquhar, J.W., Wood, P.D. & Alexander, J.K. (1977). Reducing the risk of cardiovascular disease: Effects of a community-based campaign on knowledge and behavior. *Journal of Community Health, 3,* 100-114.

Mace, W.M. (1977). James J. Gibson's strategy for perceiving: Ask not what's inside your head, but what your head's inside of. In R. Shaw & J. Bransford (Eds.), *Perceiving, acting and knowing.* Hillsdale, NJ: Erlbaum.

Machlowitz, M. (1980). *Workaholics: Living with them, working with them.* Reading, MA: Addison-Wesley.

Mack, J. (1990). In *Discovering Psychology,* Program 24 [PBS video series]. Washington, DC: Annenberg/CPB Program.

Mackintosh, N.J. (1975). A theory of attention. *Psychological Review, 82,* 276-298.

Mackintosh, N.J. (1994). *Animal learning and cognition.* San Diego: Academic Press.

Maclean, P.D. (1990). *The triune brain in evolution.* New York: Plenum Press.

MacLeod, C., Mathews, A. & Tata, P. (1986). Attentional bias in emotional disorders. *Journal of Abnormal Psychology, 95,* 15-20.

Maes, S. (1992). Psychosocial aspects of cardiac rehabilitation in Europe. *British Journal of Clinical Psychology, 31,* 473-483.

Maes, S., Leventhal, H. & Johnston, M. (Eds.). (1994). *International review of health psychology.* Volume 3, Chichester (Eng.), Wiley

Magnani, F. (1990). In *Discovering Psychology,* Program 9 [PBS video series]. Washington, DC: Annenberg/CPB Project.

Magnusson, D. (1987). Adult delinquency in the light of conduct and physiology at an early age: A longitudinal study. In D. Magnusson & A. Ohman (Eds.), *Psychopathology* (pp. 221-324). Orlando, FL: Academic Press.

Magnusson, D. & Bergman, L.R. (1990). A pattern approach to the study of pathways from childhood to adulthood. In L.N. Robins & M. Rutter (Eds.), *Straight and devious pathways from childhood to adulthood* (pp. 101-115). Cambridge: Cambridge University Press.

Magnusson, D. & Endler, N.S. (1977). Interactional psychology: Present status and future prospects. In D. Magnusson & N.S. Endler (Eds.), *Personality at the crossroads: Current issues in interactional psychology.* Hillsdale, NJ: Erlbaum.

Maher, B.A. (1968, November). The shattered language of schizophrenia. *Psychology Today,* pp. 30ff.

Maher, B.A. (1974). Delusional thinking and cognitive disorder. In M. London & R.E. Nisbett (Eds.), *Thought and feeling: Cognitive alteration of feeling states.* Chicago: Aldine.

Maher, B. & Ross, J.S. (1984). Delusions. In H.E. Adams & P.B. Sulker (Eds.), *Comprehensive handbook of psychopathology* (pp. 383-987). New York: Plenum.

Mahler, M.S. (1979). *The selected papers of Margaret S. Mahler (2 vols.).* New York: Jason Aronson.

Mahoney, M.J. (1974). *Cognition and behaviour modification.* Cambridge, MA: Ballinger.

Maier, N.R.F. (1931). Reasoning in humans: II. The solution of a problem and its appearance in consciousness. *Journal of Comparative Psychology, 12,* 181-194.

Maier, S.F. & Seligman, M.E.P. (1976). Learned helplessness: Theory and evidence. *Journal of Experimental Psychology, 105,* 3-46.

Maier, S. (1984, March). Stress: Depression, disease and the immune system. *Science and public policy seminars.* Washington, DC: Federation of Behavioral, Psychological and Cognitive Sciences.

Main, M., Kaplan, N. & Cassidy, J. (1985). Security in infancy, childhood and adulthood: A move to the level of representation. In I. Bretherton & E. Waters (Eds.), *Growing points of attachment theory and research: Monographs of the Society of Research in Child Development, 4* (Serial No. 209, pp. 66-104).

Majewska, M.D., Harrison, N.L., Schwartz, R.D., Barker, J.L. & Paul, S.M. (1986). Steroid hormone metabolites are barbiturate-like modulators of the GABA receptor. *Science, 232,* 1004-1007.

Main, M. & George, C. (1985). Responses of abused and disadvantaged toddlers to distress in age mates: A study in the day care setting. *Developmental Psychology, 21,* 407-412.

Malamuth, N.E. & Donnerstein, E. (1982). The effects of aggressive-pornographic mass media stimuli. *Advances in Experimental Social Psychology, 15,* 103-136.

Malamuth, N.E. & Donnerstein, E. (1984). Pornography and sexual aggression. New York: Academic Press.

Malatesta, C.Z. & Kalnok, M. (1984). Emotional experience in younger and older adults. *Journal of Gerontology, 39,* 301-308.

Malitz, S. & Sackheim, H.A. (1984). Low dosage ECT: Electrode placement and acute physiological and cognitive effects.*American Journal of Social Psychiatry, 4,* 47-53.

Mandela, N.R. (1994). *Long walk to freedom: The autobiography of Nelson Mandela.* London: Little, Brown and Company.

Mandler, G. (1972). Organisation and recognition. In E. Tulving & W. Donaldson (Eds.), *Organisation and memory.* New York: Academic Press.

Mandler, J.M. (1992). How to build a baby: 11 conceptual primitives. *Psychological Review, 99,* 587-604.

Mandler, G. (1975). *Mind and emotion.* New York: Wiley.

Manfredi, M., Bini, G., Cruccu, G., Accornero, N., Beradelli, A. & Medolago, L. (1980). Congenital absence of pain. *Archives of Neurology, 38,* 507-511.

Mann, L. (1979). *On the trail of progress: A historical perspective on cognitive processes and their training.* New York: Grune & Stratton.

Manning, C.A., Hall, J.L. & Gold, P.E. (1990). Glucose effects on memory and other neuropsychological tests in elderly humans. *Psychological Science, 1,* 307-31 1.

Manschreck, T.C. (1989). Delusional (paranoid) disorders. In H.I. Kaplan & B.J. Sadock (Eds.), *Comprehensive textbook of psychiatry* (pp. 816-829). Baltimore: William & Wilkins.

Manstead, A.S.R. (1992). Communicative aspects of children's emotional competence. In K.T. Strongman (Ed.), *International Review of Studies on Emotion, Vol. 2* (pp. 167-197). Chichester: John Wiley.

Manuck, S.B., Cohen, S., Rabin, R.S., Muldoon, M.F. & Bachen, E.A. (1991). Individual differences in cellular immune response to stress. *Psychological Science, 2,* 111-115.

Marcel, A.J. (1983). Conscious and unconscious perception: An approach to the relation between phenomenal experience and perceptual processes. *Cognitive Psychology, 15,* 238-300.

Marcus, A.D. (1990, December 3). Mists of memory cloud some legal proceedings. *The Wall Street Journal,* p. B1.

Marcus, D. & Wiener, M. (1989). Anorexia nervosa reconceptualized from a psychosocial transactional perspective. American Journal of Orthopsychiatry, 59, 346-354.

Marek, G.R. (1975). *Toscanini* London: Vision Press.

Mariatt, G.A. (1978). Behavioural assessment of social drinking and alcoholism. In G.A. Mariatt & P.E. Nathan (Eds.), *Behavioural approaches to alcoholism.* New Brunswick, NJ: Rutgers Center for Alcohol Studies.

Mariatt, G.A. (1983). The controlled-drinking controversy: A commentary. *American Psychologist, 38,* 1097-1110.

Markman, E.M., Cox, B. & Machida, S. (1981). The standard object-sorting task as a measure of conceptual organization. *Developmental Psychology, 17,* 115-117.

Marks, I. (1981). *Cure and care of neuroses: Theory and practice of behavioral psychotherapy.* New York: Wiley.

Marks, R. (1976-1977). Providing for individual differences: A history of the intelligence testing movement in North America. *Interchange, 1,* 3-16.

Markus, H. & Cross, S. (1990). The interpersonal self. In L.A. Pervin (Ed.), *Handbook of personality theory and research* (pp. 576-608). New York: Guilford Press.

Markus, H., & Cross, S. & Wurf, E. (1990). The role of the self system in competence. In R.J. Sternberg & J. Lollgian, Jr. (Eds.), *Competence considered* (pp. 205-225). New Haven, CT: Yale University Press.

Markus, H. & Kitayama, S. (1991). Culture and the self: Implications for cognition, emotion and motivation. *Psychological Review, 98,* 224-253.

Markus, H. & Nurius, P. (1986). Possible selves. *American Psychologist, 41,* 954-969.

Markus, H. & Smith, J. (1981). The influence of self-schemas on the perception of others. In N. Cantor & J.F. Kihlstrom (Eds.), *Personality, cognition, and social interaction* (pp. 233-262). Hilisdale, NJ: Erlbaum.

Markus, H. & Zajonc, R.B. (1985). The cognitive perspective in social psychology. In G. Lindzey & E. Aronson (Eds.), *The handbook of social psychology: Vol. 1. Theory and methods* (3rd ed., pp. 137-230). New York: Random House.

Marler, P.R. & Hamilton, W.J. (1966). *Mechanisms of animal behaviour.* New York: Wiley.

Marmot, M.G., Davey-Smith, G., Stansfield, S., Patel, C., North, F., Head, J., White, I., Brunner, E. & Feeney, A. (1991). Health inequalities among British civil servants: the Whitehall II study. *The Lancet,* June 8, pp. 1387-1393.

Marquis, J.N. (1970). Orgasmic reconditioning: Changing sexual object choice through controlling masturbation fantasies. *Journal of Behavior Therapy and Experimental Psychiatry, 1,* 263-271.

Marr, D. (1982). *Vision: A computational investigation into the human representation and processing of visual information.* San Francisco: W.H. Freeman.

Marr, D. & Nishihara, H.K. (1978). Representation and recognition of the spatial organization of three-dimensional *shapes. Proceedings of the Royal Society of London (Series B), 200,* 269-294.

Marsella, A.J. (1979). Cross-cultural studies of mental disorders. In A.J. Marsella, R.G. Sharp & T.J. Ciborowski (Eds.), *Perspectives on cross-cultural psychology* (pp. 233-262). New York: Academic Press.

Marshall, G.D. & Zimbardo, P.G. (1979). Affective consequences of inadequately explained physiological arousal. *Journal of Personality and Social Psychology, 37,* 970-988.

Marslen-Wilson, W. & Tyler, L.K. (1980). The temporal structure of spoken language understanding. *Cognition, 8,* 1-71.

Martin, C.L. & Halverson, C.F. (1981). A schematic processing model of sex typing and stereotyping in children. *Child Development, 52,* 1119-1134.

Martin, G. & Pear, J. (1983). *Behavior modification: What it is and how to do it* (2nd ed.). Englewood Cliffs, NJ: Prentice-Hall.

Martin, J.A. (1981). A longitudinal study of the consequences of early mother-infant interaction: A microanalytic approach. *Monographs of the Society for Research in Child Development, 46* (203, Serial No. 190).

Masangkay, Z.S., McCluskey, K.A., McIntyre, C.W., SimsKnight, J., Vaughn, B. & Flavell, J.H. (1974). The early development of inferences about the visual percepts of others. *Child Development, 45,* 357-366.

Maslach, C. (1974). Social and personal bases of individuation. *Journal of Personality and Social Psychology, 29,* 411-425.

Maslach, C. (1979). Negative emotional biasing of unexplained arousal. *Journal of Personality and Social Psychology, 37,* 953-969.

Maslach, C. (1982). *Burnout: The cost of caring.* Englewood Cliffs, NJ: Prentice-Hall.

Maslach, C., & Florian, V. (1988), Burnout, job setting and self-evaluation among rehabilitation counselors. *Rehabilitation Psychology, 33,* 135-157.

Maslach, C., Stapp, J. & Santee, R.T. (1985). Individuation: Conceptual analysis and assessment. *Journal of Personality and Social Psychology, 49,* 729-738.

Maslow, A.H. (1954). *Motivation and personality.* New York: Harper.

Maslow, A. (1968). *Towards a psychology of being* (2nd ed.). New York: Van Nostrand-Reinhold.

Maslow, A.H. (1970). *Motivation and personality* (Rev. ed.). New York: Harper & Row.

Mason, J.W. (1975). An historical view of the stress field: Parts 1 & 2. *Journal of Human Stress, 1,* 6-12, 22-36.

Masters, J.C. (1981). *Developmental psychology. Annual Review of Psychology, 32,* 117-151.

Masters, W.H. & Johnson, V.E. (1966). *Human sexual response.* Boston: Little, Brown.

Masters, W.H. & Johnson, V.E. (1970). *Human sexual inadequacy.* Boston: Little, Brown.

Masters, W.H. & Johnson, V.E. (1979). *Homosexuality in perspective.* Boston: Little, Brown.

Masters, W.H., Johnson, V.E. & Kolodny, R.C. (1992). *Human sexuality, 4th edition.* New York: HarperCollins.

Matarazzo, J.D. (1972). *Wechsler's measurement and appraisal of adult intelligence* (5th ed.). Baltimore: Williams & Wilkins.

Matarazzo, J.D. (1980). Behavioral health and behavioral medicine: Frontiers for a new health psychology. *American Psychologist, 35,* 807-817.

Matarazzo, J.D. (1984). Behavioral immunogens and pathogens in health and illness. In B.L. Hammonds & C.J. Scheirer (Eds.), *Psychology and health: The Master Lecture Series, Vol. 3* (pp. 9-43). Washington, DC: American Psychological Association.

Matarazzo, J.D. (1990). Psychological assessment versus psychological testing: Validation from Binet to the school, clinic, and courtroom. *American Psychologist, 45,* 999-1017.

Matas, L., Arend, R.A. & Sroufe, L.A. (1978). Continuity of adaptation in the second year: The relationship between quality of attachment and later competence. *Child Development, 49,* 547-556.

Matossian, M. (1982). Ergot and the Salem witchcraft affair. *American Scientist, 70,* 355-357.

Matson, J.L., Esveldt-Dawson, K., Andrasik, F., Oliendick, T.H., Petti, T. & Hersen, M. (1980). Direct, observational, and generalization effects of social skills training with emotionally disturbed children. *Behavior Therapy, 11,* 522-53 1.

Matthews, K.A. (1988). Coronary heart disease and Type A behavior: Update on an alternative to the Booth-Kewley and Friedman (1987) quantitative review. *Psychological Bulletin, 104,* 373-380.

Maugh, T.H. (1982). Sleep-promoting factor isolated. *Science, 216,* 1400.

May, R. (1961). *Existential psychology.* New York: Random House.

May, R. (1969). *Love and will.* New York: Norton.

May, R. (1975). *The courage to create.* New York: Norton.

May, R. (1972). *Power and innocence: A search for the sources of violence.* New York: Delta.

May, R. (1977). *The meaning of anxiety* (Rev. ed.). New York: Norton. (Original work published 1950).

Mayer, G.R., Butterworth, T., Nafpaktitis, M. & Sulzer-Azaroff, B. (1983). Preventing school vandalism and improving discipline: A three-year study. *Journal of Applied Behavior Analysis, 16,* 355-369.

Mayer, J. (1955). Regulation of energy intake and body weight: The glucostatic theory and lipostatic hypothesis. *Annals of the New York Academy of Sciences, 63,* 15-43.

Mayer, R.E. (1981). *The promise of cognitive psychology.* San Francisco: Freeman.

Maypole, D.E. (1986). Sexual harassment of social workers at work: injustice within? *Scial Work, 31,* 29-34.

Mayr, E. (1974). Behavior programs and evolutionary strategies. *American Scientist, 38,* 650-659.

Mazur, J. (1990). *Learning and behavior.* Englewood Cliffs, NJ: Prentice-Hall.

McAdams, D.P. (1988). *Power, intimacy and the life story: Personological inquiries into identity.* New York: The Guilford Press.

McAdams, D.P. (1994). *The person.* New York: Harcourt, Brace.

McAdams, D.P. & Vaillant, G.E. (1982). Intimacy motivation and psychosocial adjustment: A longitudinal study. *Journal of Personality Assessment, 46,* 586-593.

McCabe, K. (1990). Beyond cruelty. *The Washingtonian,* pp. 72-77.

McCall, R.B. (1977). Childhood IQs as predictors of adult education and occupational status. *Science, 197,* 483-485.

McCarley, R. (1990). In *Discovering Psychology,* Program 13 [PBS video series]. Washington, DC: Annenberg/CPB Program.

McCarthy, S.J. (1979, September). Why Johnny can't disobey. *The Humanist*, pp. 30-33.

McCaulley, M.H. (1978). *Application of the Myers-Briggs Type Indicator to medicine and health professions* [Monograph I]. Gainesville, FL: Center for Applications of Psychological Type.

McClelland, D.C. (1955). Some social consequences of achievement motivation. In M.R. Jones (Ed.), *Nebraska Symposium on Motivation* (Vol. 3). Lincoln, NE: University of Nebraska Press.

McClelland, D.C. (1961). *The achieving society*. Princeton, NJ: Van Nostrand.

McClelland, D.C., Atkinson, J.W., Clark, R.A. & Lowell, L. (1953). *The achievement motive*. New York: Appleton-Century-Crofts.

McClelland, D.C., Atkinson, J.W., Clark, R.A. & Lowell, E.L. (1976). *The achievement motive* (2nd ed.). New York: Irvington.

McClelland, D.C., Koestner, R. & Weinberger, J. (1992). How do self-attributed and implicit motives differ? In C.P. Smith (Ed.), *Motivation and personality*. Handbook of thematic content analysis (pp. 49-72). Cambridge: C.U.P.

McClelland, J.L. & Elman, J.L. (1986). Interactive models in speech perception: the TRACE model. In J.L. McClelland, D.E. Rumelhart & the PDP Research Group (Eds.), *Parallel distributed processing: Vol. 2. Psychological and biological models* (pp. 58-121). Cambridge, MA: MIT Press.

McClelland, J.L. & Rumelhart, D.E. (1985). Distributed memory and the representation of general and specific information. *Journal of Experimental Psychology: General*, 114, 159-188.

McClelland, J.L. & Rumelhart, D.E. (1988). *Explorations in parallel distributed processing: A handbook of models, programs and exercises*. Cambridge, MA: MIT Press/Bradford Books.

McClelland, J.L., Rumelhart, D.E. & the PDP Research Group (Eds.)(1986). *Parallel distributed processing*. Vol. 2: Psychological and biological models. Cambridge, MA: MIT Press.

McClintock, M.K. (1971). Menstrual synchrony and suppression. *Nature*, 229, 244-245.

McCloskey, M. & Egeth, H.E. (1983). Eyewitness identification: What can a psychologist tell a jury? *American Psychologist*, 38, 550-563.

McCloskey, M., Wible, C.G. & Cohen, N.J. (1988). Is there a special flashbulb memory mechanism? *Journal of Experimental Psychology*, 117(2), 171-181.

McConaghy, N. (1969). Subjective and penile plesthsmograph response following aversion-relief and apomorphine aversion therapy for homosexual impulses. *British Journal of Psychology*, 115, 723-730.

McCormick, D.A. & Thompson, R.F. (1984). Cerebellum: Essential involvement in the classically conditioned eyelid response. *Science*, 223, 296-299.

McCoy, E. (1988). Childhood through the ages. In K. Finsterbusch *(Ed.), Sociology 88/89* (pp. 44-47). Guilford, CT: Duskin.

McCrae, R.R. (1982). Consensual validation of personality traits: Evidence from self-reports and ratings. *Journal of Personality and Social Psychology*, 43, 293-303.

McCrae, R.R. (1987). Creativity, divergent thinking and openness to new experience. *Journal of Personality and Social Psychology*, 52, 1258-1265.

McCrae, R.R. (ed) (1992). The five-factor model: Issues and applications (Special issue). *Journal of Personality*, 60, (2).

McCrae, R.R. & Costa, P.T. (1987). Validation of the five-factor model of personality across instruments and observers. *Journal of Personality and Social Psychology*, 52, 81-90.

McCrae, R.R. & Costa, P.T., Jr. (1989). Rotation to maximize the construct validity of factors in the NEO Personality Inventory. *Multivariate Behavioral Research*, 24, 107-124.

McCrae, R.R., Costa, P.T., Jr. & Busch, C.M. (1986). Evaluating comprehensiveness in personality systems: The California Q-Set and the five factor model. *Journal of Personality*, 54, 430-446.

McDaniel, S.H., Hepworth, J. & Doherty, W.J. (1993). *Medical family therapy: psychosocial treatment of families with health problems*. New York: Basic Books.

McDermott, M.R. (1993). On cruelty, ethics & experimentation: profile of Philip G. Zimbardo. *The Psychologist, incorporating The Bulletin of The British Psychological Society*, 6, 10, 456-459.

McDougall, W. (1908). *An introduction to social psychology*. London: Methuen.

McGaugh, J.L. (1983). Hormonal influences on memory. *Annual Review of Psychology*, 34, 297-323.

McGaugh, J.L. & Herz, M.J. (1972). *Memory consolidation*. San Francisco: Albion.

McGaugh, J.L., Weinberger, N.M., Lyffch, G. & Granger, R.H. (1985). Neural mechanisms of Teaming and memory: Cells, systems and computations. *Naval Research Reviews*, 37, 15-29.

McGhee, P.E. (1979). *Humor: Its origin and development*. San Francisco: Freeman.

McGinnies, E. (1949). Emotionality and perceptual defense. *Psychological Review*, 56, 244-25 1.

McGinnis, J.M. (1991). Health objectives for the nation. *American Psychologist*, 46, 520-524.

McGlashan, T.H., Evans, F.J. & Orne, M.T. (1978). The nature of hypnotic analgesia and placebo response to experimental pain. *Psychosomatic Medicine*, 31, 227-246.

McGrath, E., Keita, G.P., Strickland, B.R. & Russo, N.F. (1990). *Women and depression: Risk factors and treatment issues*. Hyattsville, MD: American Psychological Association.

McGuire, R.J., Carlise, J.M. & Young, B.G. (1965). Sexual deviations as conditioned behavior: A hypothesis. *Behavioral Research and Theory*, 12, 185-190.

McGuire, P.K., Shah, P. & Murray, R.M. (1993). Increased blood flow in Broca's area during auditory hallucinations in schizophrenia. *The Lancet*, 342, 703-706.

McGuire, T.R. (1993). Emotion and behavior genetics in vertebrates and invertebrates. In M. Lewis & J.M. Haviland (Eds.) *Handbook of emotions* (pp. 155-167). New York: The Guilford Press.

McGuire, W.J. & McGuire, C. V. (1988). Content and process in the experience of self. In L. Berkowitz (Ed.), *Advances in experimental social psychology* (Vol. 21, pp. 97-144). New York: Academic Press.

McGuire, W.J., McGuire, C.V., Child, P. & Fujioka, T.A. (1978). Salience of ethnicity in the spontaneous self-concept as a function of one's ethnic distinctiveness in the social environment. *Journal of Personality and Social Psychology*, 36, 511-520.

McKean, K. (1986, October). Pain. *Discover*, pp. 82-92.

McKinnon, W., Weisse, C.S., Reynolds, C.P., Bowles, C.A. & Baum, A. (1989) Chronic stress, leukocyte subpopulations and humoral response to latent viruses. *Health Psychology*, 8, 389-402.

McLearn, G.E. & De Fries, J.C. (1973). *Introduction to behavioral genetics*. San Francisco: Freeman.

McLintock, T.T.C., Aitken, H., Dowie, C.F.A. & Kenny, G.N.C. (1990). Post-operative analgesic requirements in patients exposed to positive intraoperative suggestions. *British Journal of Medicine*, 301, 788-790.

McMillan, J.R., Clifton, A.K., McGrath, D. & Gale, W.S. (1977). Women's language: uncertainty or interpersonal sensitivity and emotionality? *Sex Roles*, 3, 545-559.

McNamee, S. & Gergen, K.J. (1992) (Eds.). *Therapy as social construction*. London: Sage.

McNeil, B.J., Pauker, S.G., Sox, H.C., Jr. & Tversky, A. (1982). On the elicitation of preferences for alternative therapies. *New England Journal of Medicine*, 306, 1259-1262.

Mead, M. (1928). *Coming of age in Samoa*. New York: Morrow.

Mead, M. (1939). *From the South Seas: Studies of adolescence and sex in primitive societies*. New York: Morrow.

Meador, B.D. & Rogers, C.R. (1979). Person-centered therapy. In R.J. Corsini (Ed.), *Current psychotherapies* (2nd ed., pp. 131-184). ltasca, IL: Peacock.

Meaney, M. (1990). In *Discovering Psychology*, Program 17 [PBS video series]. Washington, DC: Annenberg/CPB Program.

Meany, M.J., Aitken, D.H., Van Berkel, C., Bhatnagar, S. & Sapolsky, R.M. (1988). Effect of neonatal handling on age-related impairments associated with the hippocampus. *Science*, 239,766-768.

Meany, M.J., Stewart, J. & Beatty, W.W. (1985). Sex differences in social play: The socialization of sex roles. *Advances in the Study of Behavior*, 15, 1-58.

Mednick, M.T. (1989). On the politics of psychological constructs: stop the bandwagon I want to get off. *American Psychologist*, 44, 1118-1123.

Meehl, P.E. (1954). *Clinical versus statistical prediction*. Minneapolis: University of Minnesota Press.

Meehl, P.E. (1965). Seer over sign; The first good example. *Journal of Experimental Research in Personality*, 1, 27-32.

Meeker, M. (1985). Toward a psychology of giftedness: A concept in search of measurement. In B.B. Wolman (Ed.), *Handbook of intelligence* (pp. 787-800). New York: Wiley.

Meeus, W. & Raaijmakers, Q. (1987). Administrative obedience as a social phenomenon. In W. Doise & S. Moscovici (Eds.), *Current issues in European social psychology, Vol.2*. Cambridge: Cambridge University Press, p.183-230.

Mehrabian, A. (1971). *Silent messages*. Belmont, CA: Wadsworth.

Meichenbaum, D. (1975). A self-instructional approach to stress management: A proposal for stress innoculating training. In D.C. Spielberger & I.G. Sarason (Eds.), *Stress and anxiety* (Vol.1, pp. 237-263). New York: Wiley.

Meichenbaum, D. (1977). *Cognitive-behavior modification: An integrative approach*. New York: Plenum.

Meier, R.P. (1991). Language acquisition by deaf children. *American Scientist, 79*, 60-70.

Meisner, W.W. (1978). *The paranoid process*. New York: Jason Aronson.

Meltzer, H.Y. (1982). What is schizophrenia? *Schizophrenia Bulletin, 8*, 433-435.

Meltzer, H.Y. (1987). Biological studies of schizophrenia. *Schizophrenia Bulletin, 13*, 827-838.

Meltzoff, A.N. (1988). Infant imitation and memory: Nine-month olds in immediate and deferred tests. *Child Development, 59*, 217-225.

Meltzoff, A.N. & Borton, R.W. (1979). Intermodal matching by human neonates. *Nature, 282*, 403-404.

Meltzoff, J. & Kornreich, M. (1970). *Research in psychotherapy*, New York: Atherton.

Melville, J. (1977). *Phobics and obsessions*. New York: Penguin Books.

Melzack, R. (1973). *The puzzle of pain*. New York: Basic Books.

Melzack, R. (1980). Psychological aspects of pain. In J.J. Bonica (Ed.), *Pain*. New York: Raven.

Melzack, R. (1989). Phantom limbs, the self and the brain (the D.O. Hebb Memorial lecture). *Canadian Psychology, 30*, 1-16.

Melzack, R. & Wall, P. (1988). *The Challenge of Pain*. London: Penguin.

Menzel, E. M. (1978). Cognitive mapping in chimpanzees. In S.H. Hulse, H. Fowler & W.K. Honzig (Eds.), *Cognitive processes in animal behavior* (pp. 375-422). Hillsdale, NJ: Erlbaum.

Meredith, M.A. & Stein, B.E. (1985). Descending efferents from the superior colliculus relay integrated multisensory information. *Science, 227*, 657-659.

Merikle, P.M. (1992). Perception without awareness: critical issues. *American Psychologist, 47*, 792-795.

Merton, R.K. (1957). *Social theory and social structures*. New York: Free Press.

Mervis, C.B. & Rosch, E. (1981). Categorization of natural objects. *Annual Review of Psychology, 32*, 89-115.

Mesquita, B. & Frijda, N.H. (1992). Cultural variations in emotion: A review. *Psychological Bulletin, 112*, 179-204.

Meyer, N. (1974). *The seven percent solution*. New York: Dutton.

Meyer, M.M. & Ekstein, R. (1970). The psychotic pursuit of reality. *Journal of Contemporary Psychotherapy, 3*, 3-12.

Mezzich, J.E. & Berganza, C.E. (Eds.). (1984). *Culture and psychopathology*. New York: Columbia University Press.

Middleton, J. (Ed.). (1967). *Magic, witchcraft and curing*. Garden City, NY: The Natural History Press.

Milam, J. & Ketcham, K. (1981). *Under the influence: A guide to the myths and realities of alcoholism*. Seattle: Madrona Publications.

Milavsky, J.R., Kessler, R.C., Stipp, H.H. & Rubens, W.S. (1982). *Television and aggression. Results of a panel study*. New York: Academic Press.

Milgram, S. (1965). Some conditions of obedience and disobedience to authority. *Human Relations, 18*, 56-76.

Milgram, S. (1974). *Obedience to authority*. New York: Harper & Row.

Milgram, S. (1977, October). Subject reaction: The neglected factor in the ethics of experimentation. *Hastings Center Report, pp.* 19-23.

Milgram, S. (1990). In *Discovering Psychology*, Program 19 [PBS video series]. Washington, DC: Annenberg/CPB Program.

Milgram, S. & Jodelet, D. (1976). Psychological maps of Paris. In H.M. Proshansky, W.H. Ittleson & L.G. Rivlin (Eds.), *Environmental psychology*. New York: Holt, Rinehart & Winston.

Miller, A. (1985). Nurse/patient dependency – is it iatrogenic? *Journal of Advanced Nursing, 10*, 63-69.

Miller, A.G. (1986). *The obedience paradigm: A case study in controversy in social science*. New York: Praeger.

Miller, G.A. (1956). The magic number seven plus or minus two: Some limits on our capacity for processing information. *Psychological Review, 63*, 81-97.

Miller, G.A. (1962). Some psychological studies of grammar. *American Psychologist, 17*, 748-762.

Miller, G. & Gildea, P. (1987). How children learn words. *Scientific American, 257*, 94-99.

Mills, K.C. & McCarty, D. (1983). A data based alcohol abuse prevention program in a university setting. *Journal of Alcohol and Drug Education, 28*, 15-27.

Miller, L. (1990). Neuropsychodynamics of alcoholism and addiction: Personality, psychopathology and cognitive style. *Journal of Substance Abuse Treatment, 7*, 31-49.

Miller, N.E. (1941). The frustration-aggression hypothesis. *Psychological Review, 48*, 333-342.

Miller, N.E. (1948). Fear as an acquired drive. *Journal of Experimental Psychology, 38*, 89-101.

Miller, N.E. (1978). Biofeedback and visceral teaming. *Annual Review of Psychology, 29*, 373-404.

Miller, N.E. (1983). Behavioral medicine: Symbiosis between laboratory and clinic. *Annual Review of Psychology, 34*, 1-31.

Miller, N.E. (1985). The value of behavioral research on animals. *American Psychologist, 40*, 423-440.

Miller, P.Y. & Simon, W. (1968). The development of sexuality in adolescence. In J. Adelson (Ed.), *Handbook of adolescent psychology* (pp. 383-407). New York: Wiley.

Miller, P.Y. & Simon, W. (1980). The development of sexuality in adolescence. In J. Adelson (Ed.), *Handbook of adolescent Psychology*. New York: Wiley.

Miller, W.R. (1983). Controlled drinking: A history and critical review. *Journal of Studies on Alcohol, 44*, 68-83.

Miller, W.R. & Hester, R.K. (1980). Treating the problem drinker: Modem approaches. In W.R. Miller (Ed.), *The addictive behaviors*. Oxford, England: Pergamon Press.

Millstein, S.G. & Irwin, C. E., Jr. (1987). Concepts of health and illness: Different constructs of variations on a theme? *Health Psychology, 6*, 515-524.

Milner, B. (1966). Amnesia following operation on the temporal lobes. In C.W. Whitty & O.L. Zangwill (Eds.), *Amnesia (pp.* 109-133). London: Butterworth.

Milojkovic, J.D. (1982). Chess imagery in novice and master. *Journal of Mental Imagery, 6*, 125-144.

Mineka, S., Davidson, M., Cook, M. & Keir, R. (1984). Observational conditioning of snake fear in rhesus monkeys. *Journal of Abnormal Psychology, 93*, 355-372.

Minuchin, S. (1974). *Families and family therapy*. Cambridge, MA: Harvard University Press.

Mischel, W. (1968). *Personality and assessment*. New York: Wiley.

Mischel, W. (1973). Toward a cognitive social Teaming reconceptualization of personality. *Psychological Review, 80*, 252-283.

Mischel, W. (1976). *Introduction to personality* (2nd ed.). New York: Holt, Rinehart & Winston.

Mischel, W. (1979). On the interface of cognition and personality; Beyond the person-situation debate. *American Psychologist, 34*, 740-754.

Mischel, W. (1984). Convergences and challenges in the search for consistency. *American Psychologist, 39*, 351-364.

Mischel, W. & Peake, P. (1982). Beyond déja vu in the search for cross-situational consistency. *Psychological Review, 89(6)*, 730-755.

Misgeld, V., Deisz, R.A., Dodt, H.U. & Lux, H.D. (1986). The role of chloride transport in postsynaptic inhibition of hippocampal neurons. *Science, 232*, 1413-1415.

Mishkin, M. (1982). A memory system in the monkey. *Philosophical Transactions of the Royal Society of London, 298*, 85-95.

Mishkin, M. & Appenszeller, G. (1987). The anatomy of memory. *Scientific American, 256*, 80-89.

Mishkin, M., Malamut, B. & Backevalier, J. (1984). Memories and habits: Two neural systems. In G. Lynch, J.L. McGaugh & N.M. Weinberger (Eds.), *The neurobiology of learning and memory* (pp. 65-77). New York: Guilford Press.

Mishkin, M. & Petri, H.L. (1984). Memories and habits: Some implications for the analysis of Teaming and retention. In L.R. Squire & N. Butters (Eds.), *Neurophysiology of memory* (pp. 287-296). New York: Guilford Press.

Mitchel, R. (1982). *Phobias*. Harmondsworth: Penguin.

Miyake, K., Chen, K. & Campos, J.J. (1985). Infant temperament mother's mode of interaction, and attachment in Japan: An interim report. In I. Bretherton & E. Waters (Eds.), *Growing points of attachment theory and research. Monographs of the Society for Research in Child Development, 50* (1-2, Serial No. 209), 276-297.

Moar, I. (1980). The nature and acquisition of cognitive maps. In D. Cantor & T. Lee (Eds.), *Proceedings of the international conference on environmental psychology*. London: Architectural Press.

Modern couples say they are happy together: Poll differs with Shere Hite report. (1987, October 27). *Washington Post, p.* WH-8.

Moinar, J.M., Rath, W.R. & Klein, T.P. (1990). Constantly compromised: The impact of homelessness on children. *Journal of Social Issues, 46,* 109-123.

Moncrieff, R.W. (1951). *The chemical senses.* London: Leonard Hill.

Money, J. & Ehrhardt, A.A. (1972). *Man and woman, boy and girl.* Baltimore, MD: Johns Hopkins University Press.

Money, J., Hampson, J.G. & Hampson, J.L. (1957). Imprinting and the establishment of gender role. *AMA Archives of Neurology and Psychiatry, 77,* 333-336.

Moniz, E. (1973). Prefrontal leucotomy in the treatment of mental disorders. *American Journal of Psychiatry, 93,* 1379-1385.

Monroe, S.M. (1983). Major and minor life events as predictors of psychological distress: Further issues and findings. *Journal of Behavioral Medicine, 6,* 189-205.

Monson, T.C., Hesley, J.W. & Chemick, L. (1982). Specifying when personality traits can and cannot predict behavior: An alternative to abandoning the attempt to predict single-act criteria. *Journal of Personality and Social Psychology, 43,* 385-399.

Montague, A. (1986). *Touching: The human significance of the skin.* New York: Harper & Row.

Montgomery, G. (1990). The mind in motion. [Special issue]. *Discover,* pp. 12-19.

Mook, D.G. (1987). *Motivation. The organization of action.* New York/London: W.W. Norton and Company.

Moore, B.S., Underwood, B. & Rosenhan, D.L. (1973). Affect and altruism. *Developmental Psychology, 9,* 99-104.

Moore, P. (1990). In *Discovering Psychology,* Program 18 [PBS video series]. Washington, DC: Annenberg/CPB Program.

Moos, R. (1979). *Evaluating educational environments.* San Francisco: Jossey-Bass.

Moos, R.H. & Engel, B.T. (1962). Psychophysiological reactions in hypertensive and arthfitic patients. *Journal of Psychosomatic Research, 6,* 227-241.

Moos, R. & Lemke, S. (1984). Supportive residential settings for older people. In I. Altman, M.P. Lawton & J.F. Wohlwill (Eds.), *Elderly people and the environment* (pp. 159-190). New York: Plenum.

Moran, J. & Desimone, R. (1985). Selective attention gates visual processing in the extrastriate cortex. *Science, 229,* 782-785.

Morehouse, R.E., Farley, F.H. & Youngquist, J.V. (1990). Type T personality and the Jungian classification system. *Journal of Personality Assessment, 54,* 231-235.

Morgan, A.H., Hilgard, E.R. & Davert, E.C. (1970). The heritability of hypnotic susceptibility of twins: A preliminary report. *Behaviour Genetics, 1,* 213-224.

Morgan, A.H., Johnson, D.L. & Hilgard, E.R. (1974). The stability of hypnotic susceptibility: A longitudinal study. *International Journal of Clinical and Experimental Hypnosis, 22,* 249-257.

MORI (Market & Opinion Research International) (1990). *Teenage smoking.* London: Health Education Authority.

Moriarty, T. (1975). Crime, commitment and the responsive bystander: Two field experiments. *Journal of Personality and Social Psychology, 31,* 370-376.

Moriarity, T. (1990). In *Discovering Psychology,* Program 19 [PBS video series]. Washington, DC: Annenberg/CPB Program.

Morris, C., & Heckman, J. (1969). Behavioral correlates of perceived leadership. *Journal of Personality and Social Psychology, 13,* 350-361.

Morris, J.J. & Clarizio, S. (1977). Improvement in IQ of high risk, disadvantaged preschool children enrolled in a developmental program. *Psychchological Reports, 41(1),* 111-114.

Morrison, M.A. (1990, May). Addiction in adolescents. The *Western Journal of Medicine,* p. 543-546.

Moscovici, S. (1976). *Social influence and social change.* New York: Academic Press.

Moscovici, S. (1980). Toward a theory of conversion behavior. In L. Berkowitz (Ed.), *Advances in experimental social psychology* (Vol. 13, pp. 209-239). New York: Academic Press.

Moscovici, S. (1981). On social representations. *In Social cognition,* (Ed) J.P. Forgas. London: Academic Press.

Moscovici, S. (1985). Social influence and conformity. In G. Lindzey & E. Aronson (Eds.), *Handbook of social psychology* (3rd ed.). (pp.347-412). New York: Random House.

Moscovici, S., Lage, E. & Naffrechoux, M. (1969). Influence of a consistent minority on the responses of a majority in a colour perception task. *Sociometry, 32,* 265-79.

Moscovici, S. & Personnaz, B. (1991). Studies in social influence VI: Is Lenin orange or red? Imagery and social influence. *European Journal of Social Psychology, 21,* 101-118.

Motley, M.T. (1987, February). What I meant to say. *Psychology Today, pp.24-28.*

Mowrer, O. (1960). *Learning theory and symbolic processes.* New York: Wiley.

Muehlenhard, C.L. & Cook, S.W. (1988). Men's self-reports of unwanted sexual activity. *The Journal of Sex Research, 24,* 58-72.

Muehlenhard, C.L. & Linton, M.A. (1987). Date rape and sexual aggression in dating situations: incidence and risk factors. *Journal of Counseling Psychology, 34,* 186-196.

Muhlhausler, P. & Harre, R. (1991). *Pronouns and people.* Oxford: Blackwell.

Mullen, B. & Baumeister, R.F. (1987). Group effects on selfattention and performance: Social loafing, social facilitation, and social impairment. In C. Hendrick (Ed.), *Review of personality and social psychology.* Beverly Hills, CA: Sage.

Munroe, R.L. (1955). *Schools of psychoanalytic thought.* New York: Dryden.

Munsterberg, H. (1927). *On the witness stand: Essays on psychology and crime.* New York: Clark Boardman. (Original work published 1908)

Murnen, S.K., Perolt, A. & Byrne, D. (1989). Coping with unwanted sexual activity: Normative responses, situational determinants, and individual differences. *The Journal of Sex Research, 26,* 85-106.

Murphy, J.M. (1976). Psychiatric labeling in cross-cultural perspective. *Science, 191,* 1019-1028.

Murray, J.P. & Kippax, S. (1979). Children's social behavior in three towns with differing television experience. *Journal of Communication, 28,19-29.*

Murray, H.A. (1938). *Explorations in personality.* New York: Oxford University Press.

Murray, L. & Trevarthen, C. (1986). The infant's role in mother-infant communications. *Journal of Child Language, 13(1),* 15-29.

Murphy, H.B.M., Wittkower, E.W., Fried, J. & Ellenberger, H. (1963). A cross-cultural survey of schizophrenic symptomatology. *International Journal of Social Psychiatry, 9,* 237-249.

Muskin, P.R. & Fyer, A.J. (1981). Treatment of panic disorder. *Journal of Clinical Psychopharmacology, I,* 81-90.

Mussen, P.H., Honzik, M.P. & Eichorn, D.H. (1982). Early adult antecedents of life satisfaction at age 70. *Journal of Gerontology, 37,* 316-322.

Myers, D.G. (1987). *Social psychology* (2nd ed). New York: McGraw-Hill.

Myers, I.B. (1962). *The Myers-Briggs type indicator.* Palo Alto, CA: Consulting Psychologists Press.

Myers, I.B. (1976). Introduction to type (2nd ed.). Gainesville, FL: Center for Applications of Psychological Type.

Myers, I.B. (1980). *Gifts differing.* Palo Alto, CA: Consulting Psychologist Press.

Myers, R.E. & Sperry, R.W. (1958). Interhemispheric communication through the corpus callosum: Mnemonic carry-over between the hemispheres. *Archives of Neurology and Psychiatry, 80,* 298-303.

Myers, J.K., Weissman, M.M., Tischler, G.L., Holzer, C.E., Leaf, P.J., Orvaschel, H.A., Anthony, J.C., Boyd, J.H., Burke, J.E., Kramer, M. & Stoltzman, R. (1984) Six-month prevalence of psychiatric disorders in three communities: 1980-1982. *Archives of General Psychiatry, 41,* 959-967.

Nadi, S.N., Nurnberger, J.I. & Gershon, E.S. (1984). Muscafinic cholinergic receptors on skin fibroblasts in familial affective disorder. *New England Journal of Medicine, 311(4),* 225-230.

N

Nancy Nurse spoofs the healing profession. (1987, Spring). *Wellness New Mexico,* pp. 19-2 1.

Nasrallah, H.A. & Weinberger, D.W. (1986). *The neurology, of schizophrenia: Handbook of schizophrenia, Vol.* 1. Amsterdam: Elsevier.

Nathans, J., Thomas, D. & Hogness, D.S. (1986). Molecular genetics of human color vision: The genes encoding blue, green, and red pigments. *Science, 232,* 193-202.

National Assessment of Educational Progress. (1983). *The third national mathematics assessment: Results, trends, and issues* (1 3MA-0I). Denver, CO: Educational Commission of the States.

National Housing & Town Planning Council (1988) *Gambling machines and young people.* London: National Housing and Town Planning Council.

National Institute on Drug Abuse. (1982). *Student drug use, attitudes and beliefs: National trends 1975-1982.* Washington, DC: U.S. Government Printing Office.

National Institutes of Mental Health. (1977). *Lithium and the treatment of mood disorders* (DHEW Publication No. ADM 77-73). Washington, DC: U.S. Government Printing Office.

National Institutes of Mental Health. (1982). *Television and behavior: Ten years of scientific evidence and implications for the eighties:* Vol. 1. Summary report. Washington, DC: U.S. Government Printing Office.

National Institutes of Mental Health. (1986). *Useful information on phobias and panic* (DHHS Publication No. ADM 86-1472). Washington, DC: U.S. Government Printing Office.

Natsoulas, T. (1978). Consciousness. *American Psychologist, 33* (10), 906-914.

Natsoulas, T. (1981). Basic problems of consciousness. *Journal of Personality and Social Psychology, 41,* 132-178.

Nauta, W.J.H. & Feirtag, M. (1979). The organization of the brain. *Scientific American,* 24/(9), 88-111

Navon, D. & Gopher, D. (1980). The difficulty resources and dual-task performance. In R.S. Nickerson (Ed.), *Attention and performance VIII* (pp. 297-318). Hilisdate, NJ: Erlbaum.

Neale, M.A. & Bazerman, M.H. (1991). *Cognition and rationality in negotiation.* New York: Free Press.

Needleman, H., Schell, A., Belinger, D., Leviton, A. & Allred, E. (1990). The long-term effects of exposure to low doses of lead in childhood: An 11 year follow-up report. *New England Journal of Medicine, 322,* 83-88.

Neisser, U. (1967) *Cognitive psychology.* Englewood Cliffs: Prentice-Hall (of New York: Appleton-Century Crofts.

Neisser, U. (1976). *Cognition and reality.* San Francisco, CA: Freeman.

Neisser, U. (1978). Memory: What are the important questions. In M.M. Gruneberg, P.E. Morris & R.N. Sykes (Eds.), *Practical aspects of memory* (pp. 3-24). London: Academic Press.

Nelson, K.E. (1971). Accommodation of visual tracking patterns in human infants to object movement patterns. *Journal of Experimental Child Psychology, 16,* 180-196.

Nelson, R.E. & Craighead, W.E. (1977). Selective recall of positive and negative feedback, self-control behaviors and depression. *Journal of Abnormal Psychology, 86,* 379-388.

Nelson, R.K. (1989, Spring). Hunters and animals in a native land: Ancient ways for the new century. *Orion Nature Quarterly,* pp. 48-53.

Nelson, Z.P. & Mowrey, D.D. (1976). Contracting in crisis intervention. *Community Mental Health Journal, 12,* 37-43.

Nemeth, C. (1979). The role of an active minority in intergroup relations. In W. Austin & S. Worchel (Eds.), *The social psychology of intergroup relations.* Monterey, CA: Brooks/Cole.

Nemeth, C.J. (1986). Differential contributions of majority and minority influence. *Psychological Review, 93,* 23-32.

Nemeth, C.J., Mayseless, O., Sherman, J. & Brown, Y. (1990). Exposure to dissent and recall of information. *Journal of Personality and Social Psychology, 58,* 429-437.

Nesselroade, J.R. & Baltes, P.B. (1974). Adolescent personality development and historical change: 1970-1972. *Monographs of the Society for Research in Child Development, 39.*

Neugarten, B.L. (1976). *The psychology of aging: An overview* [Master lectures on developmental psychology]. Washington, DC: American Psychological Association.

Neumann, O. (1987). Beyond capacity: A functional view of attention. In Hotteuer & A.F. Sanders (Eds.), *Perspectives on perception and action.* Hillsdale, NJ: Erlbaum.

Neumann, O. (1990). Visual attention and action. In: O. Neumann & W. Prinz (Eds.), *Relationships between perception and action.* Berlin, Heidelberg: Springer.

Neumann, O., Van der Heijden, A.H.C. & Allport, D.A. (1986). Visual selective attention: Introductory remarks. *Psychological Research, 48,* 185-188.

Newcomb, T.M. (1963). Persistence and regression of changed attitudes: Long-range studies. *Journal of Social Issues, 19,* 3-4.

Newcomb, T.M., Koenig, D.E., Flacks, R. & Warwick, D.P. (1967). *Persistence and change: Bennington College and its students after twenty-five years.* New York: Wiley.

Newcomb, M.D. & Bentler, P.M. (1988). *Consequences of adolescent drug use: Impact on the lives of young adults.* Newbury Park, CA: Sage.

Newell, A., Shaw, J.C. & Simon, H.A. (1958). Elements of a theory of human problem solving. *Psychological Review, 65,* 152-166.

Newell, A. & Simon, H.A. (1972). *Human problem solving.* Englewood Cliffs, NJ: Prentice-Hall.

Newman, O. (1972). Gambling: Hazard and reward. London: Athlone.

Newsome, W.T. & Pare, E.B. (1988). A selective impairment of motion perception following lesions of the middle temporal visual area. *Journal of Neuroscience, 8,* 2201-2211.

Newton, I. (1671-1672). New theory about light and colors. *Philosophical Transactions of the Royal Society of London, 80,* 3075-3087. In D.L. MacAdam (Ed.), *Sources of color science.* Cambridge, MA: MIT Press.

Nguyen, T., Heslin, R. & Nguyen, M.L. (1975). The meanings of touch: Sex differences. *Journal of Communication, 25,* 92-103.

Nhat Hanh, T. (1991). *Peace is every step: The path of mindfulness in everyday life.* New York: Bantam.

NIAAA. (1984). *Report of the 1983 Prevention Planning Panel.* Rockville, MD: NIAAA.

Nichols, M.P. (1984). *Family therapy: Concepts and methods.* New York: Gardner Press.

Nicol, S.E. & Gottesman, I.I. (1983). Clues to the genetics and neurobiology of schizophrenia. *American Scientist, 71,* 398-404.

Nicoll, C., Russell, S. & Katz, L. (1988, May 26). Research on animals must continue. *The San Francisco Chronicle,* p.A25.

Nideffer, R.M. (1976). Altered states of consciousness. In T.X. Barber, *Advances in altered states of consciousness and human potentialities (Vol.* 1, pp. 3-35). New York: Psychological Dimensions.

Nielsen, T.A., Kuiken, D.L. & McGregor, D.L. (1989). Effects of dream reflection on waking affect: Awareness of feelings, Rorschach movement, and facial EMG. *Sleep, 12,* 277-286.

Nietzel, M.T., Bernstein, D.A. & Milich, R. (1991). *Introduction to clinical psychology.* Englewood Cliffs, NJ: Prentice-Hall.

Nisbett, R.E. (1972). Hunger, obesity and the ventromedial hypothalamus. *Psychological Review, 79,* 433-453.

Nisbett, R.E. & Ross, L. (1980). *Human inference: Strategies and shortcomings of social judgment.* Englewood Cliffs, NJ: Prentice Hall.

Nisbett, R.E. & Wilson, T.D. (1977). Telling more than we can know: Verbal reports on mental processes. *Psychological Review, 84,* 231-259.

Nobles, W.W. (1972). African psychology: Foundations for black psychology. In R.L. Jones (Ed.), *Black psychology.* New York: Harper & Row.

Nobles, W.W. (1976). Black people in white insanity: An issue for black community mental health. *Journal of Afro-American Issues, 4,* 21-27.

Nolen-Hoeksema, S. (1987). Sex differences in unipolar depression: Evidence and theory. *Psychological Bulletin, 101,* 259-282.

Nolen-Hoeksema, S. (1990). *Sex differences in depression.* Stanford, CA: Stanford University Press.

Noordenbos, G. (1988) *Onbegrensd lijnen. Een onderzoek naar culturele en seksespecifieke factoren in de ontwikkeling van anorexia nervosa [Limitless dieting. A study of cultural and genderspecific factors in the development of anorexia nervosa].* Leiden: DSWOPress.

Norman, D.A. & Rumelhart, D.E. (1975). *Explorations in cognition.* San Francisco: Freeman.

Norman, W.T. (1963). Toward an adequate taxonomy of personality attributes: Replicated factor structure in peer nomination personality ratinngs. *Journal of Abnormal and Social Psychology, 66,* 574-583.

Norman, W.T. & Goldberg, L.R. (1966). Raters, ratees and randomness in personality structure. *Journal of Personality and Social Psychology, 4,* 681-691.

Novick, L. (1990). Representational transfer in problem solving. *Psychological Science, 1,* 128-132.

Nungesser, L.G. (1990). *Axioms for survivors. How to live until you say goodbye.* Santa Monica, CA: IBS Press.

Nunner-Winkler, G. (1984). Two moralities? A critical discussion of an ethic of care and responsibility versus an ethic of rights and justice. In W.M. Kurtines & J.L. Gewirtz (Eds.), *Morality, moral behavior, and moral development* (pp. 348-361). New York: Wiley.

Nuttin, J. (1984). *Motivation, planning and action. A relational theory of behavior dynamics.* Leuven: Leuven University Press; Hillsdale, N.J.: Lawrence Erlbaum Associates.

Nuttin, J. (1985). *Future time perspective and motivation: Theory and research method*. Hillsdale, NJ: Erlbaum.

O

O'Connor, S., Hesselbrock, V., Tasman, A. & DePalma, N. (1987). P3 amplitudes in two distinct tasks are decreased in young men with a history of paternal alcoholism. *Alcoholism, 4,* 323-330.

O'Donohue, W. & Elliot, A. (1992). The current status of post-traumatic stress disorder as a diagnostic category: problems and proposals. *Journal of Traumatic Stress, 5,* 3, 421-439.

O'Sullivan, C. (1990, December 15). Quoted in G. Eskenazi, When athletic aggression turns into sexual assault. *The New York Times Index* (Vol. 139, p. 18, March 17, 1990).

Oatley, K. (1992). *Best laid schemes. The psychology of emotions.* Cambridge: Cambridge University Press.

Oatley, K. (1993). Social construction on emotion. In In M. Lewis & J.M. Haviland (Eds.) *Handbook of emotions* (pp. 341-353). New York: The Guilford Press.

Oatley, K. & Bolton, W. (1985). A social-cognitive theory of depression in reaction to life events. *Psychological Review, 92,* 372-388.

Oatley, K. & Johnson-Laird, P.N. (1987). Towards a cognitive theory of emotions. *Cognition & Emotion, 1,* 29-50.

Occupational Hazards. (1990). Survey cites passive smoking hazards. *Occupational Hazards, 52,* 19-20.

Oden, S. & Asher, S.R. (1977). Coaching children in social skills for friendship making. *Child Development, 48,* 495-506.

Offer, D. & Offer, J.B. (1975). *From teenage to young manhood.* New York: Basic Books.

Offer, D., Ostrov, E. & Howard, K.I. (1981a). *The adolescent: A psychological self-portrait.* New York: Basic Books.

Offer, D., Ostrov, E. & Howard, K.I. (1981b). The mental health professional's concept of the normal adolescent. AMA *Archives of General Pvychiatry, 38,* 149-153.

Office of Population Censuses & Surveys (1993). *Mortality statistics cause, England & Wales, Series DH2 No 19.* London: Her Majesty's Stationary Office.

Ogden, J. (1992). *Fat chance! The myth of dieting explained.* London: Routledge.

Öhman, A., Erixon, G. & Loftberg, I. (1975). Phobias and preparedness: Phobic versus neutral pictures as conditional stimuli for human autonomic responses. *Journal of Abnormal Psychology, 34,* 41-45.

Oldham, D.G. (1978a). Adolescent turmoil: A myth revisited. In S. C. Feinstein & P.L. Giovacchini (Eds.), *Adolescent psychiatry* (Vol. 6). Chicago: University of Chicago Press.

Oldham, D.G. (1978b). Adolescent turmoil and a myth revisited. In A.H. Esman (Ed.), *The psychology, of adolescence.* New York: International University Press.

Olds, J. (1973). Commentary on positive reinforcement produced by electrical stimulation of septal area, and other regions of the rat brain. In E.S. Valenstein (Ed.), *Brain stimulation and motivation: Research and commentary.* Glenview, IL: Scott, Foresman.

Olds, J. & Milner, P. (1954). Positive reinforcement produced by electrical stimulation of septal area and other regions of the rat brain. *Journal of Comparative and Physiological Psychology, 47,* 419-427.

Olin, B.R., Hebel, S.K., Connell, S.I., Dombek, C.E. & Kastrup, E.K. (Eds.). (1990). *Drug facts and comparisons.* St. Louis, MO: J.B. Lippincott.

Olson, J. (1993). Attitude and attitude change. *Annual Review of Psychology, 44,* 117-154.

Olton, D.S. (1979). Mazes, mazes, and memory. *American Psychologist, 34,* 583-596.

Olton, D.S., Aaron, A. & Noonberg, R. (1980). *Biofeedback: Clinical applications in behavioral medicine.* Englewood Cliffs, NJ: Prentice-Hall.

Olweus, D. (1991). Bully/victim problems among school children: Basic facts and effects of a school-based intervention program. In K. Rubin & D. Pepler (Eds.), *The development and treatment of childhood aggression.* Toronto. Ontario: Erlbaum.

Olweus, D., Block, J. & Radke-Yarrow, M. Eds.). (1986). *The development of anti-social and pro-social behavior: Research, theories, and issues.* New York: Academic Press.

Oppel, J.J. (1854-55). Ueber geometrisch-optische Tauschungen. *Jahresbericht des physikalischen Vereins zu Frankfurt a. M., 34-47.*

Opton, E.M. (1970). Lessons of My Lai. In N. Sanford & C. Comstock (Eds.), *Sanctions for evil.* San Francisco: Jossey-Bass.

Opton, E.M., Jr. (1973). 'It never happened and besides they deserved it'. In W.E. Henry & N. Sanford (Eds.), *Sanctions for evil* (pp. 49-70). San Francisco: Jossey-Bass.

Orlando, N.J. (1981). Mental patient as therapeutic agent-self change, power and caring. *Psychotherapy: Theory, Research, and Practice, 7,* 58-62.

Orne, M.T. (1972). On the stimulating subject as a quasi-control group in hypnosis research: What, why, and how? In E. Fromm & R.E. Shor (Eds.), Hypnosis: *Research developments and perspectives* (pp. 399-443). Chicago: Aldine.

Orne, M.T. (1980). Hypnotic control of pain: Toward a clarification of the different psychological processes involved. In J.J. Bonica (Ed.), *Pain* (pp. 155-172). New York: Raven Press.

Ornstein, R.E. (1986a). *Multimind: A new way of looking at human behaviour.* Boston: Houghton-Mifflin.

Ornstein, R.E. (1986b). *The psychology of consciousness* (Rev. ed.). New York: Penguin Books.

Ornstein, R., & Sobel, D. (1989). *Healthy pleasures.* Reading, MA: Addison-Wesley.

Osborne, R. (1987, Winter). Whale Museum opposed biopsy research project. *Orca Update,* p. 6.

Osherow, N. (1981). Making sense of the nonsensical: An analysis of Jonestown. In E. Aronson (Ed.), *Readings in the social animal.* San Francisco, CA: Freeman.

Oskamp, S. (1984). *Applied social psychology.* Englewood Cliffs, NJ: Prentice-Hall.

Oskamp, S. (Ed.). (1985). International conflict and national public policy issues. *Applied Social Psychology Annual, 6.*

Owen, D. (1985). *None of the Above: Behind the Myth of Scholastic Aptitude.* Boston, MA: Houghton Mifflin.

Owens, R.G. & Ashcroft, J.B. (1982). Functional analysis in applied psychology, *British Journal of Clinical Psychology, 21,* 181-189.

P

Page, S. (1987). On gender roles and perception of maladjustment. *Canadian Psychology, 28,* 53-59.

Paivio, A. (1983). The empirical case for dual coding. In J.C. Yuille (Ed.), *lmagery, memory and cognition* (pp. 307-332). Hillsdale, NJ: Erlbaum.

Paivio, A. (1986). *Mental representations: A dual coding approach.* New York: Oxford University Press.

Palmer, S.E. (1975). The effects of contextual scenes on the identification of objects. *Memory and Cognition, 3,* 519-526.

Palmer, S.E. (1981). The psychology of perceptual organization. In J.Beck (Ed.), *Organization and representation in perception (pp. 269-339).* Hillsdale, NJ: Erlbaum.

Palmer, S.E. (1984). The psychology of perceptual organization: A transformational approach. In A. Rosenfeld & J. Beck (Eds.), *Human and machine vision.* New York: Academic Press.

Palmer, S.E. (1989). Reference frames in the perception of shape and orientation. In B. Shepp & M. Ballisteros (Eds.), *Object Perception* (pp. 121-163). Hillsdale, NJ: Erlbaum.

Palys, T.S. (1986). Testing the common wisdom: The social content of video pornography. *Canadian Psychology, 27,* 22-35.

Papolos, D.F. & Papolos, J. (1987). *Overcoming depression.* New York: Harper & Row.

Pappas, A.M. (1983). Introduction. In A.M. Pappas (Ed.), *Law and the status of fhe child* (pp. xxvii-lv). New York: United Nations Institute for Training and Research.

Paraplegic reaches summit after 9-day mountain climb. (1989, July 27). *The New York Times,* p. A1O(N).

Park, B. & Rothbart, M. (1982). Perception of out-group homogeneity and levels of social categorization: Memory for the subordinate attributes of in-group and out-group members. *Journal of Personality and Social Psychology, 42,* 1051-1068.

Park, R.D. & Walters, R.H. (1967). Some factors influencing the efficacy of punishment training for inducing response inhibition. *Monographs of the Society for Research in Child Development, 32 ,* Whole No. 109).

Parks, T. (1965). Post-retinal visual storage. *American Journal of Psychology, 78,* 145-147.

Parpal, M. & Maccoby, E.E. (1985). Maternal responsiveness and subsequent child compliance. *Child Development, 56,* 1326-1334.

Parrott, J. & Gleitman, H. (1984, April). *The joy of peekaboo or* *reappearance?* Paper presented at the meeting of the Eastern Psychological Association, Baltimore, MD.

Pass, J.J. & Cunningham, J.W. (1978). Occupational clusters based on systematically derived work dimensions: Final report. *Journal of Supplemental Abstract Service: Catalogue of selected documents: Psychology,* 8, 22-23.

Paul, G.L. (1969). Outcome of systematic desensitization: 11, Controlled investigations of individual treatment technique variations, and current status. In C. M. Franks (Ed.), *Behavior therapy: Appraisal and status.* New York: McGraw-Hill.

Paul, S.M., Crowley, J.N. & Skoinick, P. (1986). The neurobiology of anxiety: The role of the GABA/benzodiazepine complex. In P.A. Berger & H.K.H. Brodie (Eds.), *American Handbook on psychiatry: biological psychology* (2nd ed.). New Program 8 PBS video York: Basic Books.

Paulesu, E., Frith, C.D. & Frackowiak, R.S.J. (1993). The neural correlates of the verbal component of working memory. *Nature,* 362, 342-344.

Pavlov, I.P. (1927). *Conditioned reflexes* (G.V. Anrep, Trans.) London: Oxford University Press.

Pavlov, I.P. (1928). *Lectures on conditioned reflexes: Twenty-five years of objective study of higher nervous activity (behavior of animals)* (Vol. 1, W.H. Gantt, Trans.). New York: International Publishers.

Pavlov, I.P. (1990). In *Discovering Psychology* Program 8 [PBS video series]. Washington, DC: Annenberg/CPB Project.

Paykel, E.S. (1973). Life events and acute depression. In J.P. Scott & E.C. Senay (Eds.), *Separation and depression* (pp. 215-236). Washington, DC: American Association for the Advancement of Science.

Paykel, E.S. & Dowlatshahi, D. (1988). Life events and mental illness. In S. Fisher & J. Reason (Eds.), *Handbook of Life Stress, Cognition and Health.* Chichester: Wiley & Sons.

Pear, T.H. (1927). Skill. *Journal of Personnel Research,* 5, 478-489.

Pearce, M. (1988). A memory artist. *The Exploratorium Quarterly,* 12, 13-17,

Pearce, J.M. (1987). A model of stimulus generalization for Pavlovian conditioning. *Psychological Review,* 94, 61-73.

Pearce, J.M. (1994). Similarity and discrimination: A selective review and connectionist model. *Psychological Review,* 101, 587-607.

Pearce, J.M. & Hall, G. (1980). A model for Pavlovian learning: Variations in the effectiveness of conditioned but not of unconditioned stimuli. *Psychological Review,* 87, 532-552.

Pearce, J.M. & Wilson, P.N. (1991). Failure of excitatory conditioning to extinguish the influence of a conditioned inhibitor. *Journal of Experimental Psychology: Animal Behavior Processes.* 17, 519-529.

Pedersen, N.L., Plomin, R., McClearn, G.E. & Friberg, L. (1988). Neuroticism, extraversion and related traits in adult twins reared apart and reared together. *Journal of Personality and Social Psychology,* 55, 6, 950-957.

Pedersen, P.E., William, C.L. & Blass, E.M. (1982). Activation and odor conditioning of suckling behavior in 3-day-old albino rats. *Journal of Experimental Psychology:* Animal *Processes,* 81 329-341.

Peele, S. (1984). The cultural context of psychological approaches to alcoholism: Can we control the effects of alcohol? *American Psychologist,* 39, 1337-1351.

Peele, S. (1985). The implications and limitations of genetic models of alcoholism and other addictions. *Journal of Studies on Alcohol.* 47, 63-73.

Pelletier, K.R. & Peper, E. (1977). Developing a biofeedback model: Alpha EEG feedback as a means for main control. *The International Journal of Clinical and Exxperimental Hypnosis,* 25, 361-371.

Pelletier, L. & Herold, E. (1983, May). *A study of sexual fantasies among young single females.* Paper presented at the meeting of the World Congress of Sexuality, Washington, DC.

Peltzer, K. & Ebigbo, P. (1989) (Eds.). *Clinical psychology in Africa.* Enugu: Uinversity of Enugu Press.

Pelz, E.B. (1965). Some factors in 'Group decision'. In H.Proshansky & B. Seidenberg (Eds.), *Basic studies in social psychology,* (pp. 437-444). New York: Holt, Rinehart & Winston. (Original work published 1955)

Pendery, M.L., Maltzman, I.M. & West, L.J. (1982). Controlled drinking by alcoholics? New finding and a reevaluation of a major affirmative study. *Science,* 217, 169-174.

Penfield, W. & Baldwin, M. (1952). Temporal lobe seizures and the technique of subtotal lobectomy. *Annals of Surgery,* 136, 625-634.

Penfield, W. & Perot, P. (1963). The brain's record of auditory and visual experience. *Brain,* 86, 596-696.

Pennebaker, J.W. (1990). *Opening up: The healing power of confiding in others.* New York: Morrow.

Pennebaker, J.W. & Harber, K.D. (1991, April). *Coping after the Loma Prieta earthquake: A preliminary report.* Paper presented at the Western Psychological Association Convention, San Francisco, CA.

Pennebaker, J.W., Kiecolt-Glaser, J.K & Glaser, R. (1988). Disclosure of traumas and immune function: The health implications for psychotherapy. *Journal of Consulting and Clinical Psychology,* 56, 239.

Penrose, L.S. & Penrose, R. (1958). Impossible objects: A special type of visual illusion. British Journal of Psychology. 49.

Peplau, L.A. & Conrad, E. (1989). Beyond non-sexist research: The perils of feminist methods in psychology. *Psychology of Women Quarterly,* 13, 379-400.

Perlman, D. (1990, July 18). Heart risk lowered in community experiment. *San Francisco Chronicle,* pp. 1, A6.

Perlmutter, C. (1989, September). The dance of healing: Psychiatrist Carl Hammerschiag offers healing lessons based on Native American traditions. *Prevention, 41,* 69.

Perlmutter, M. & Hall, E. (1985). *Adult development and aging.* New York: Wiley.

Perls, F.S. (1967). Group vs. individual therapy. *ECT. – A Review of General* Semantics, 34, 306-312.

Perls, F.S. (1969). *Gestalt therapy verbatim.* Lafayette, CA: Real People Press.

Perlin, S. (Ed.). (1975), *A handbook for the study of suicide.* New York: Oxford University Press.

Perrett, D.I. & Mistlin, A.M. (1987). Visual neurons responsive to faces. *Trends in Neuroscience,* 10, 358-364.

Persons, J.B. (1986). The advantages of studying psychological phenomena rather than psychiatric diagnoses. *American Psychologist, 41,* 1252-1260.

Persons, J. (1991). Psychotherapy outcome studies do not accurately represent current models of psychotherapy. *American Psychologist, 46,* 99-106.

Pert, C.B. & Snyder, S.H. (1973). Opiate receptor: Demonstration in the nervous tissue. *Science, 179, 1011-1014.*

Pervin, L.A. (1985). Personality: Current controversies, issues and directions, *Annual Review of Psychology,* 36, 83-114.

Peters, T.J. & Waterman, R.H., Jr. (1983). *In search of excellence: Lessons from America's best-run companies.* New York: Warner.

Peterson, C. & Seligman, M.E.P. (1984). Explanatory style and depression: Theory and evidence. *Psychological Review,* 91, 341-374.

Peterson, C., Seligman, M.E.P. & Vaillant, G.E. (1988). Pessimistic explanatory style is a risk factor for physical illness: A thirty-five year longitudinal study. *Journal of Personality and Social Psychology,* 55, 23-27.

Peterson, J.L. & Zill, N. (1981). Television viewing in the United States and children's intellectual, social, and emotional development. *Television and Children,* 2, 21-28.

Peterson, L.R. & Peterson, M.J. (1959). Short-term retention of individual verbal items. *Journal of Experimental Psychology,* 58. 193-198.

Petit, C. (1987, April 9). San Francisco doctors find brain damage in 2 of 10 cocaine users. *San Francisco Chronicle,* p.8.

Pettigrew, T.F. (1985). New pattems of racism: The different worlds of 1984 and 1964. *Rutgers Law Review,* 37, 673-706.

Pfaffman, C. (1959). The sense of taste. In J. Field (Ed.), *Handbook of physiology: Section 1. Neurophysiology (Vol.* 1). Washington, DC: American Physiological Society.

Pfefferbaum, A. (1977). Psychotherapy and psychopharmacology. In J.D. Barchas, P.A. Berger, R.D. Ciacanello & G.R. Elliott (Eds.), *Psychopharmacology: From theory to practice* (pp. 481-492). New York: Oxford University Press.

Pfungst, O. (1911). *Clever Hails (the horse of Mr. Von Ostein)* (R. Rosenthal, Trans.). New York: Holt, Rinehart & Winston.

Phares, E.J. (1984). *Clinical psychology: Concepts, methods and professionals* (Rev. ed.). Homewood, IL: Dorsey.

Phelps, M.E. & Mazziotta, J.C. (1986). Positron emission tomography: Human brain function and biochemistry. *Science,* 228,799-809.

Phillips, D.P. (1983). The impact of mass media violence on U.S. homicides. *American Sociological Review,* 48, 560-568.

Phillips, K. (1991). The primary prevention of AIDS. In K. Phillips & M. Pitts, (Eds.), *The psychology of health: an introduction*, (pp. 139-155). London Routledge.

Piaget, J. (1929). *The child's perception of the world*. New York: Harcourt & Brace.

Piaget, J. (1954). *The construction of reality in the child*. New York: Basic Books.

Piaget, J. (1960). *The moral judgement of the child*. New York: Basic Books.

Piaget, J. (1965). *The moral judgment of the child* (M. Gabain, Trans.). New York: Macmillan.

Piaget, J. & Inhelder, B. (1967). *The child's conception of space*. New York: Norton.

Piaget, J. (1977). *The development of thought: Equilibrium* cognitive structures. New York: Viking Press.

Piecione, C., Hilgard, E.R. & Zimbardo, P.G. (1989). On the degree of stability of measured hypnotizability over a 25-year period. *Journal of Personality and Social Psychology, 56,* 289-295

Pifer, A. & Bronte, L. (Eds). (1986). *Our aging society: Paradox and promise*. New York: Norton.

Piliavin, J.A. & Piliavin, I.M. (1972). Effect of blood on reactions to a victim. *Journal of Personality and Social Psychology, 23,* 353-361.

Piliavin, I.M., Rodin, J. & Piliavin, J.A. (1969). Good Samaritanism: An underground phenomenon? *Journal of Personality and Social Psychology* 13, 289-300.

Pilisuk, M. & Parks, S.H. (1986). *The healing web: Social networks and human survival* Hanover, NH: University Press of New England.

Pincus, H.A., Frances, A.J., Davis, W.W., First, M.B. *et al* (1992). DSM-IV and new diagnostic categories: holding the line on proliferation. *American Journal of Psychiatry, 149,* 1, 112-117.

Pines, M. (1981, October 4). Genie: The 'Wild Child' of California. *San Francisco Examiner-Chronicle,* This World Section, pp. 8-14.

Pines, M. (1983, November). Can a rock walk? *Psychology Today,* pp. 46-54.

Pinkerton, J. (Ed.). (1814). *A general collection of the best and most interesting voyages and travels in all parts of the world, 1808-1814.* London: Longman, Hurst, Rees, & Ome.

Pious, S. & Zimbardo, P. G. (1984, November). The looking glass war. *Psychology Today* pp. 48-59:

Pittenger, J.B. (1988). Direct perception of change. *Perception, 17,* 119-133.

Pitts, F.N. (1969). The biochemistry of anxiety. *Scientific American,* 220(2), 69-75.

Place, E.J.S. & Gilmore, G.C. (1980). Perceptual organization in schizophrenia. *Journal of Abnormal Psychology,89,* 409-418.

Plight, J. van der (1991). Health education: risk perception and unrealistic optimism. In M. Johnston, M. Herbert & T. Marteau (Eds.), *European health psychology,* (pp. 124-125), Leicester: British Psychological Society.

Plomin, R. (1989). Environment and genes: Determinants of behavior. *American Psychologist, 44,* 105-111.

Plomin, R., Chipuer, H.M. & Loehlin, J.C. (1990). Behavioral genetics and personality. In L.A. Pervin (Fd.), *Handbook of personality theory and research* (pp. 225-243). New York: Guilford Press.

Plomin, R., & Danists, D. (1987). Genetics and shyness. In W.W. Jones, J.M. Cheek & S.R. Briggs (Eds.), *Shyness: Perspectives on research and treatment* (pp. 63-80). New York: Plenum.

Plomin, R., DeFries, J.C. & McClearn, G.E. (1980). *Behavioral genetics: A primer.* San Francisco: Freeman.

Plomin, R. & McClearn, G.E. (1993). *Nature, nurture & psychology.* Washington: American Psychological Association.

Plomin, R. & Rende, R. (1991). Human behavioural genetics. *Annual Review of Psychology, 42,* 105-111.

Plous, S. (1985) Perceptual illusions and military realities: A social psychological analysis of the nuclear arms race. *Journal of Conflict Resolution, 29,* 363-389.

Plous, S. (1986, February). *The effects of anchoring on subjective probability estimates of an imminent nuclear war.* Paper presented at the meeting of the California State Psychological Association, San Francisco, CA.

Plutchik, R., Kellerman, H. & Conte, H.Q. (1979). A structural theory of ego defenses and emotions. In C. Izard (Ed.), *Emotions and psychopathology* (pp. 229-257). New York: Plenum.

Plutchik, R. (1980). *Emotion: A psychoevolutionary synthesis.* New York: Harper & Row.

Plutchik, R. (1984). Emotions: A general psychoevolutionary theory.

In K. Schemer & P. Ekman (Eds.), *Approaches to emotion*. Hillsdale, NJ: Erlbaum.

Pollack, J.M. (1979). Obsessive-compulsive personality: a review. *Psychological Review,* 86, 225-241.

Pomerantz, J. & Kubovy, M. (1986). Theoretical approaches to perceptual organization. In K.R. Boff, L. Kaufman & I.P. Thomas (Eds.), *Handbook of perception and human performance* (Vol. 3, pp. 1-46). New York: Wiley.

Poon, L.W. (1985). Differences in human memory with aging: Nature, causes and clinical implications. In J.E. Birren & W.K. Schaie (Eds.), *Handbook of the psychology of aging (pp.427-462).* New York: Van Nostrand Reinhold.

Popper, K. (1934) The logic of scientific discovery. New York: Harper & Row.

Porter, G. (1987). *Socioeconomic transformations [Review of The control revolution]. Science, 236,* 970-972.

Posner, M.I. (1978). Cumulative development of attentional theory. *American Psychologist, 37,* 168-179.

Posner, J.K. (1982). The development of mathematical knowledge in two West African societies. *Child Development 53,* 200-208.

Posner, M.I. (1988). Structures and functions of selective attention. In T. Boil & B. Bryant (Eds.), *Master lectures in clinical neuropsychology* (pp. 173-202). Washington, DC: American Psychological Association.

Posner, M.I. (1990). *In Discovering Psychology,* Program 10 (PBS video series). Washington, DC: Annenberg/CPB Project.

Posner, M.I. & Snyder, C.R. (1974). Attention and cognitive control. In R.L. Solso (Ed.), *Information processing and cognition: The Loyola Symposium* (pp. 55-88). Potomac, MD: Erlbaum.

Posner, M.I. & Snyder, C.R. (1975). Facilitation and inhibition in the processing of signals. *Journal of Experimental Psychology: General, 109,* 160-174.

Posner, M.I. & Petersen, S.E. (1990). The attentional system of the human brain. *Annual Review of Neuroscience, Vol 13,* 25-42.

Post, F. (1980). Paranoid, schizophrenic-like and schizophrenic states in the aged. In J.E. Birren & R.B. Stone (Eds.), *Handbook of mental health and aging* (pp. 591-615). Englewood Cliffs, NJ: Prentice-Hall.

Postman, L. & Phillips, L. (1965). Short-term temporal changes in free recall. *Quarterly Journal of Experimental Psychology, 17,* 132-138.

Potter, J. & Wetherall, M. (1987). *Discourse and social psychology: Beyond Attitudes and Behaviour.* London: Sage.

Pound, E. (1934). *The ABC of reading.* New York: New Directions Publishing Co.

Powell, G.E. & Wilson, B.A. (1994). Neurological problems: Treatment and rehabilitation. In S.J.E. Lindsay & G.E. Powell (Eds.), *Handbook of clinical adult psychology, 2nd edition* (pp.688-704). London: Routledge.

Powell, L.H. & Eagieston, J.R. (1983). The assessment of chronic stress in college students. In E.M. Altmaier (Ed.), *Helping students manage stress-new directions for student services (Vol,* 21, pp. 23-41). San Francisco: Jossey-Bass.

Powley, T.L. (1977). The ventromedial hypothalamic syndrome, satiety and a cephalic phase hypothesis. *Psychological Review,* 84, 89-126.

Pratkanis, A.R. & Greenwald, A.G. (1988). Recent perspective on unconscious processing: Still no marketing applications. *Psychology & Marketing, 5,* 337-353.

Premack, D. (1965). Reinforcement theory. In D. Levine (Ed.), *Nebraska Symposium on Motivation* (pp. 128-180). Lincoln, NE: University of Nebraska Press.

Prentice-Dunn, S. & Rogers, R.W. (1983). Deindividuation in aggression. In R.G. Green & E.I. Donnerstein (Eds.), *Aggression: Theoretical and empirical reviews* (Vol. 2, pp. 155-171). New York: Academic Press.

Prentky, R.A. (1980). *Creativity and psychopathology.* New York: Praeger.

Pribram, K.H. (1979). Behaviorism, phenomenology and holism in psychology: A scientific analysis. *Journal of Social and Biological Sciences, 2,* 65-72.

Pribram, K.H. & Gill, M.M. (1976). *Freud's 'Project' reassessed.* New York: Basic Books.

Price, R. (1953/1980). *Droodies.* Los Angeles, CA: Price/Stem/Sloan.

Price, R.H., Ketterer, R.F., Bader, B.C. & Monohan, J. (Eds.). (1980). *Prevention in mental health: Research, policy and practice (Vol.* 1). Beverly Hills, CA: Sage.

Prince, A. & Pinker, S. (1988). On language and connectionism: Analysis of a parallel distributed processing model of language acquisition. *Cognition, 28,* 73-194.

Proshansky, H.M. (1976). Environmental psychology and the real world. *American Psychologist, 31*, 303-310.

Pullum, G.K. (1991). *The great Eskimo vocabulary hoax and other irreverent essays on the study of language.* Chicago: University of Chicago Press.

Putnam, F.W. (1984, March). The psychophysiologic investigation of multiple personality disorder [Symposium on Multiple Personality]. The Psychiatric Clinics of north America, 7(1), 31-40.

Putnam, F.W. (1990). In *Discovering Psychology*, Program 14 [PBS video series]. Washington, DC: Annenberg/CPB Program.

Pylyshyn, Z.W. (1984). *Computation and cognition. Toward a foundation for cognitive science.* Cambridge, MA: MIT Press.

Pynoos, R.S. & Nader, K. (1989). Children's memory and proximity to violence. *Journal of the American Academy of Child and Adolescent Psychiatry, 28*, 236-241.

Q

Quattrone, G.A. (1982). Overattribution and unit formation: When behavior engulfs the person. *Journal of Personality and Social Psychology, 42*, 593-607.

Quattrone, G.A. (1986). On the perception of a group's variability. In S. Worchell & W. Austin (Eds.), *The psychology of intergroup relations* (Vol. 2, pp. 25-48). New York: Nelson-Hall.

Quattrone, G.A., Lawrence, C.P., Warren, D.L. Souza-Silva, K., Finkel, S.E. & Andrus, D.E. (1984). *Explorations in anchoring: The effects of prior range, anchor extremity, and suggestive hints.* Unpublished manuscript, Stanford University.

R

Rabbie, J.M. (1981). The effects of intergroup competition and cooperation on intra- and intergroup relationships. In J. Grzelak & V. Derlega (Eds.), *Living with other people: Theory and research on cooperation and helping.* New York: Academic Press.

Rabbie, J.M. & Horwitz, M. (1969). Arousal of ingroup-outgroup bias by a chance win or loss. *Journal of Personality and Social Psychology, 13*, 269-77.

Rabbie, J.M. & Wilkens, G. (1971). Intergroup competition and its effect on intragroup and intergroup relations. *European Journal of Psychology, 1*, 215-234.

Rabkin, J.G., Gelb, L. & Lazar, J.B. (Eds.). (1980). *Attitudes toward the mentally ill: Research perspectives* [Report of an NIMH workshop]. Rockville, MD: National Institutes of Mental Health.

Rachman, S. (1966). Sexual fetishism: An expert mental analogue. *Psychological Record, 6*, 293-296.

Rachman, S. (1984). Agoraphobia – a safety-signal perspective. *Behaviour, Research & Therapy, 22*, 59-70.

Rachman, S. & Hodgson, R. (1980). Obsessions and compulsions. Englewood Cliffs, NJ: Prentice-Hall.

Radke-Yarrow, M., Zahn-Waxier, C. & Chapman, M. (1983). Children's presocial dispositions and behavior. In P.H. Mussen *(Ed.), Handbook of child development: Socialization, personality, and social development* (Vol. 4, pp. 469-545). New York: Wiley.

Radley, A. (1993). The role of metaphor in adjustment to chronic illness. In R. Radley (Ed.) *Worlds of illness, biography and cultural perspectives on health & disease,* (pp. 109-123), London: Routledge

Rahe, R.H. (1988). Anxiety and physical illness. *Journal of Clinical Psychiatry, 49*, 26-29.

Rahe, R.H. & Arthur, R.J. (1978, March). Life change and illness studies: Past history and future directions. *Journal of Human Stress,* pp. 3-15.

Rahe, R.H. & Arthur, R.J. (1977). Life-change patterns surrounding illness experience. In A. Monat & R.S. Lazarus *(Eds.), Stress and coping* (pp. 36-44). New York: Columbia University Press.

Raiffa, H. (1982). *The art and science of negotiation.* Cambridge, MA: Harvard University Press.

Rakic, P. (1985). Limits of neurogenesis in primates. *Science, 227*, 1054-1057.

Rapee, R.M. (1991). Generalised anxiety disorder: A review of clinical features and theoretical concepts. *Clinical Psychology Review, 11*, 419-440.

Rapoport, J.L. (1989, March). The biology of obsessions and compulsions. *Scientific American,* pp. 83-89.

Rasmussen, G.L. & Windle, W.F. (1960). *Neural mechanisms of the auditory and vestibular systems.* Springfield, IL : Charles C Thomas.

Ray, O. & Ksir, C. (1987). *Drugs, society, and human behavior.* St. Louis: Times Miffor/Mosby.

Ray, W.J. & Cole, H.W. (1985). EEG alpha activity reflects attentional demands, and beta activity reflects emotional and cognitive processes. *Science, 228*, 750-752.

Raymond, J.S., Chung, C.S. & Wood, D.W. (1991). Asia-Pacific prevention research: Challenges, opportunities, and implementation. *American Psychologist, 46*, 528-53 1.

Rayner, K., Carlson, M. & Frazier, L. (1983). The interaction of syntax and semantics during sentence processing: Eye movements in the analysis of semantically biased sentences. *Journal of Verbal Learning and Verbal Behavior, 22*, 358-374.

Reason, J. (1978). Motion sickness: Some theoretical and practical considerations. *Applied Ergonomics, 9*, 163-167.

Regier, D.A., Boyd, J.H, Burke, J.D., Rae, D.S., Myers, J.K., Kramer, M., Robins, L.N., George, L.K., Karno, M. & Locke, B.Z. (1988). One-month prevalence of mental disorders in the United States. *Archives of General Psychiatry, 45*, 977-986.

Rehm, L.P. (1977). A self-control model of depression. *Behavior Therapy, 8*, 787-804.

Reich, P.A. (1986). *Language development.* Englewood Cliffs, NJ: Prentice Hall.

Reicher, G.M. (1969). Perceptual recognition as a function of meaningfullness of stimulus material. *Journal of Experimental Psychology, 81*, 275-280.

Reid, T. (1785/1850). *Essays on the intellectual powers of man.* Cambridge: J. Bartlett.

Reinisch, J.M. (1981). Prenatal exposure to synthetic progestions increases potential for aggression in humans. *Science, 21* 1171-1173.

Reisenzein, R. (1983). The Schachter theory of emotion: Two decades later. *Psychological Bulletin, 94*, 239-264.

Reiser, B.J., Black, J.B. & Abelson, R.P. (1985). Knowledge structures in the organization and retrieval of autobiographical memories. *Cognitive Psychology, 17*, 89-137.

Reisman, J. (1986, January 16). *A content analysis of Playboy, Penthouse, and Hustler magazines with special attention to the portrayal of children, crime, and violence.* Supplementary testimony given to the United States Attorney General's Commission on Pornography, New York.

Reiterman, T. & Jacobs, J. (1983). *Raven: The untold story of Jim Jones and his people.* New York: Dutton.

Rescorla, R.A. (1966). Predictability and number of pairings in Pavlovian fear conditioning. *Psychonomic Science, 4*, 383-384.

Rescorla, R.A. (1972). Information variables in Pavlovian conditioning. In G. Bower (Ed.), *The psychology of learning and motivation* (Vol. 6). New York: Academic Press.

Rescorla, R.A. (1980). *Pavlovion second-order conditioning: Studies in associative learning.* Hillsdale, NJ: Erlbaum.

Rescorla, R.A. (1988). Paviovian conditioning: It's not what you think it is. *American Psychologist, 43*, 151-160.

Rescorla, R.A. & Wagner, A.R. (1972). A theory of Pavlovian conditioning: Variations in the effectiveness of reinforcement and non reinforcement. In A.H. Black & W.F. Prokasy (Eds.), *Classical conditioning, II: Current research and theory* (pp. 64-94). New York: Appleton-Century-Crofts.

Rest, J.R. & Thoma, S.J. (1985). Relation of moral judgment development to formal education. *Developmental Psychology, 21*, 709-714.

Reston, N.J. (1986, December 24). Questions about the President's memory. *The New York Times.*

Restrepo, D., Miyamoto, T., Bryant, B.P. & Teeter, J.H. (1990). Odor stimuli trigger influx of calcium into olfactory neurons of the channel catfish. *Science, 249*, 1166-1168.

Revelle, W., Humphreys,. M.S., Simon, L. & Gilliland, K. (1980). The interactive effect of personality, time of day and caffiene: a test of the arousal model. *Journal of Experimental Psychology: General, 109*, 1-31.

Reynolds, J.E. (Ed.). (1989). *Martindale: The extra pharmacopoeia.* London: The Pharmaceutical Press.

Richelle, M.N. (1993). *B.F. Skinner: A reappraisal.* Hove: Lawrence Erlbaum Associates.

Richter, C.P. (1957). On the phenomenon of sudden death in animals and man. *Psychosomatic Medicine, 19*, 191-198.

Richter, C.P. (1965). *Biological clocks in medicine and psychiatry* Springfield, IL: Charles C Thomas.

Riggs, J.M. & Cantor, N. (1981). *Information exchange in social interaction: Anchoring effects of self-concepts and expectancies.* Unpublished manuscript, Gettysburg College.

Rips, L.I. (1983). Cognitive processes in propositional reasoning. *Psychological Review, 90(1),* 38-71.

Rips, L. (1988). Deduction. In R.J. Stemberg & E.E, Smith (Eds.), *The psychology of human thought (pp.* 118-152). Cambridge: Cambridge University Press.

Riskind, J.H. (1984). They stoop to conquer: Guiding and self-regulatory functions of physical posture after success and failure. *Journal of Personality and Social Psychology, 47,* 479-493,

Ritz, M.C., Lamb, R.J., Goldberg, S.R. & Kuhar, M.J. (1987) Cocaine receptors on dopamine transporters are related to selfadministration of cocaine. *Science, 237,* 1219-1223.

Roach, A.H. (1987). Biochemistry of information storage in the nervous system. *Science, 236,* 1263-1268.

Robbins, L.C. (1963). The accuracy of parental recall of aspects of child development and of child rearing practices. *Journal of Abnormal and Social Psychology* 66, 261-270.

Roberts, T.B. (1973). Maslow's human motivation needs hierarchy: A bibliography. *Research in Education* (ERIC Document Reproduction Service No.ED069691).

Robins, L.N., Helzer, J.E., Weissman, M.M., Orvaschel, H., Gruenberg, E. Burke, J.D. & Regier, D.A. (1984). Lifetime prevalence of specific psychiatric disorders in three sites. *Archives of General Psychiatry, 41,* 949-958.

Robinson, J.O. (1972). *The psychology of visual illusion.* London: Hutchinson.

Rock, I. (1975). *An introduction to perception.* New York: Macmillan.

Rock, I. (1983). *The logic of perception.* Cambridge, MA: Bradford Books/MIT Press.

Rock, I. (1986). The description and analysis of object and event perception. In K.R. Boff, L. Kaufman & J.P. Thomas (Eds.), *Handbook of perception and human performance* (Vol.2, pp. 33-71). New York: Wiley.

Rock, I. & Gutman, D. (1981). The effect of inattention on form perception. *Journal of Experimental Psychology: Human Perception and Performance,* 7, 275-285.

Rockmore, M. (1985, March 5). Analyzing analysis. *American Way,* pp. 71-75.

Rodin, J. (1983, April). Behavioral medicine: Beneficial effects of self control training in aging. *International Review of Applied Psychology, 32,* 153-181.

Rodin, J. (1985). The application of social psychology. In G. Lindzey & E. Aronson (Eds.), *Handbook of social psychology* (3rd ed., Vol. 2, pp. 805-882). New York: Random House.

Rodin, J. (1986). Aging and health: Effects of the sense of control. *Science, 233,* 1271-1276.

Rodin, J. (1990). In *Discovering Psychology,* Program 23 [PBS video series]. Washington, DC: Annenberg/CPB Program,

Rodin, J., Bohm, L.C. & Wack, J.T. (1982). Control, coping, and aging: models for research and intervention. In L. Bickman (Ed.), *Applied social psychology annual* (pp. 153-180). London: Sage.

Rodin, J. & Janis, I.J. (1982). The social influence of physicians and other health care practitioners as agents of change. In H.S. Freedman & M.R. DiMatteo, *Interpersonal issues in health care* (pp. 33-49). New York: Academic Press.

Rodin, J. & Salovey, P. (1989). Health psychology. *Annual Review of Psychology, 40,* 533-579.

Roediger, H.L. (1980). Memory metaphors in cognitive psychology. *Memory & Cognition,* 8, 231-246.

Roediger, H.L. (1990). Implicit memory. *American Psychologist,* 45, 1043-1056.

Roediger, H.L., & Crowder, R.G. (1976). A serial position effect in recall of United States presidents. *Bulletin of the Psychonomic Society,* 8, 275-278.

Roediger, H.L. & Wheeler, M.A. (1992). Discursive remembering: A brief note. *The Psychologist: Bulletin of the British Psychological Society, 5,* 452-453.

Roffwarg, H.P., Munzio, J.N. & Dement, W.C. (1966). Ontogenetic development of the human sleep-dream cycle. *Science, 152,* 604-619.

Rogers, C.R. (1947). Some observations on the organization of personality. *American Psychologist, 2,* 358-368.

Rogers, C.R. (1951). *Client-centered therapy: Its current practice, implications and theory.* Boston: Houghton-Mifflin.

Rogers, C.R. (1959). A theory of therapy, personality and interpersonal relationships, as developed in the client-centered framework. In S. Koch (Ed.), *Psychology: A study of a science* (Vol. 3). New York: McGraw-Hill.

Rogers, C.R. (1977). *On personal power: Inner strength and its revolutionary impact.* New York: Delacorte.

Rogers, M.F. (1985). AIDS in children: a review of the clinical, epidemiologic and public health aspects. *Pediatric Infectious Diseases,* 4, 230-6.

Rogers, R.W. (1984). Changing health-related attitudes and behavior: The role of preventive health psychology. In J.H. Harver, J.E. Maddux, R.P. McGlynn, & C.D. Stoltenberg (Eds.), *Social perception in clinical and consulting psychology* (Vol. 2, pp. 91-112). Lubbock, TX: Texas Tech University Press.

Rogoff, B. (1990). *Apprenticeship in thinking: Cognitive development in social context.* New York: Oxford University press.

Rohrer, J.H., Baron, S.H., Hoffman, E.L. & Swinder, D.V. (1954). The stability of autokinetic judgment. *Journal of Abnormal and Social Psychology, 49,* 595-597.

Rommetveit, R. (1979). On the architecture of intersubjectivity. In R. Rommetveit & R.M. Blaker (Eds.), *Studies of language, thought and verbal communication.* London: Academic Press.

Ronningstam, E. & Gunderson, J.G. (1990). Identifying criteria for narcissistic personality disorder. *American Journal of Psychiatry, 147,* 918-922.

Rook, K. (1984). Promoting social bonding: Strategies for helping the lonely and socially isolated. *American Psychologist, 37,* 1389-1407.

Rorer, L.G. & Widiger, T.A. (1983). Personality structure and assessment. *Annual Review of Psychology, 34,* 431-463.

Rorschach, H. (1942). *Psychodiagnostics: A diagnostic test based on perception.* New York: Grune & Stratton.

Rosch, E.H. (1973). Natural categories. *Cognitive Psychology, 4,* 328-350.

Rosch, E.H. (1978). Principles of categorization. In E. Rosch & B.B. Lloyd (Eds.), *Cognition and categorization* (pp. 27-48). Hillsdale, NJ: Eribaum.

Rosch, E.H., Mervis, C.B., Gray, W.D., Johnson, D.M. & Boyes-Braem, P. (1976). Basic objects in natural categories. *Cognitive Psychology, 8,* 382-439.

Rose, S. (1973). *The conscious brain.* New York: Knopf.

Rose, N. (1989). Individualizing psychology. In J. Shotter & K.J. Gergen, (Eds.) *Texts of identity.* London: Sage.

Rose, N. (1990) *Governing the soul: the shaping of the private self.* London: Routledge.

Rose, R.J., Koskenvuo, M., Kaprio, J., Sarna, S. & Langinvaino, H. (1988). Shared genes, shared experiences and similarity of personality: Data from 14,288 adult Finnish co-twins. *Journal of Personality and Social Psychology, 54,* 161-171.

Rosenbaum, M. & Muroff, M. (Eds.). (1984). *Fourteen contemporary reinterpretations.* New York: Free Press.

Rosenbaum, M. & Berger, M.M. (Eds.), (1975). *Group psychotherapy and groupfunction* (Rev. ed.). New York: Basic Books.

Rosenbaum, R.M. (1972). *A dimensional analysis of the perceived causes of success and failure.* Unpublished doctoral dissertation, University of California, Los Angeles.

Rosenberg, D. (1990, November 19). Bad times at Hangover U.: College parties lead to ER or drunk tank. *Newsweek, 116,* p.81.

Rosenberg, S. (1988). Self and others: Studies in social personality and autobiography. In L. Berkowitz (Ed.), *Advances in experimental social psychology* (Vol. 21, pp. 57-95). New York: Academic Press.

Rosenhan, D.L. (1969). Some origins of concern for others. In P. Mussen, J. Langer, & M. Covington (Eds.), *Trends and issues in developmental psychology.* New York: Holt, Rinehart & Winston.

Rosenhan, D.L. (1973). On being sane in insane places. *Science,* 179, 250-258.

Rosenhan, D.L. (1975). The contextual nature of psychiatric diagnoses. *Journal of Abnormal Psychology, 84,* 462-474.

Rosenhan, D.L. (1990). In *Discovering Psychology,* Program 21 TPBS video series]. Washington, DC: Annenberg/CPB Program.

Rosenhan, D.L. & Seligman, M.E.P. (1989). *Abnormal Psychology* (2nd ed.). New York: Norton.

Rosenthal, D. (Ed.). (1963). *The Genain quadruplets.* New York: Basic Books.

Rosenthal, D., Wender, P.H., Kety, S.S., Schulsinger, F., Weiner, J. & Rieder, R. (1975). Parent-child relationships and psychopathological disorder in the child. *Archives of General Psychiatry* 32, 466-476.

Rosenthal, N.E., Sack, D.A., Gillin, J.C., Lewy, A.J., Goodwin, F.K., Davenport, Y., Mueller, P.S., Newsome, D.A. & Wehr, T.A. (1984). Seasonal affective disorder: A description of the syndrome and preliminary findings with light therapy. *Archives of General Psychiatry, 41*, 72-80.

Rosenthal, R. & Jacobson, L.F. (1968a). *Pygmalion in the classroom.* New York: Holt.

Rosenthal, R. & Jacobson, L.F. (1968b). Teacher expectations for the disadvantaged. *Scientific American, 218(4)*, 19-23.

Rosenthal, R. (1990). In *Discovering Psychology*, programs I and 20 (PBS video series]. Washington, DC: Annenberg/CPB Project.

Rosenweig, M., & Leiman, A.L. (1982). *Physiological psychology.* Lexington, MA: D. C. Heath.

Rosenzweig, M.R. (1984a). U.S. psychology and world psychology. *American Psychologist, 39*, 877-884.

Rosenzweig, M.R. (1984b). Experience, memory and the brain. *American Psychologist, 39*, 365-376.

Ross, D.F., Read, J.D. & Toglia, M.P. (Eds.). (1994). *Adult eyewitness testimony: Current trends and developments.* New York: Cambridge University Press.

Ross, L. (1977). The intuitive psychologist and his shortcomings. In L. Berkowitz (Ed.), *Advances in experimental social psychology* (Vol. 10). New York: kcademic Press.

Ross, L. (1988). Situational perspectives on the obedience experiments. [Review of The obedience experiments: A case study of controversy in social science]. *Contemporary Psvchology, 33*, 101-104.

Ross, L., Amabile, T. & Steinmetz, J. (1977). Social roles, social control and biases in the social perception process. *Journal of Personality and Social Psychology, 37*, 485-494.

Ross, L. & Lepper, M.R. (1980). The perseverance of beliefs: Empirical and normative considerations. In R.A. Shweder & D. Fiske (Eds.), *New directions for methodology of behavioral science: Follible judgments in behavioral research* (pp. 17-36). San Francisco: Jossey-Bass.

Ross, L. & Nisbett, R.E. (1991). *The person and the situation: Perspectives of social psychology.* New York: McGraw-Hill.

Roth, J.D., Le Roith, D. & Shiloach, J. (1982). The evolutionary origins of hormones, neurotransmitters, and other extracellular chemical messengers. *New England Journal of Medicine, 306*, 523-527.

Roth, T., Roehrs, T., Carskadon, M.A. & Dement, W.C. (1989). Daytime sleepiness and alertness. In M. Kryser, T. Roth & W.C. Dement (Eds.), *Principles and practice of sleep medicine (pp. 14-23).* New York: Saunders.

Rothman, D.J. (1971). *The discovery of the asylum: Social order and disorder in the new republic.* Boston: Little, Brown.

Rotter, J. (1966). Generalized expectancies for internal versus external control of reinforcement. *Psychological Monographs, 80*, (Whole No. 609), 1-28.

Rotter, J.B. (1975). Some problems and misconceptions related to the construct of internal versus external control of reinforcement. *Journal of Consulting & Clinical Psychology, 43*, 56-67.

Rotter, J.B. (1990). Internal versus external control of reinforcement: a case history of a variable. *American Psychologist, 45*, 489-493.

Rotton, J. & Frey, J. (1984). Psychological costs of air pollution: Atmospheric conditions, seasonal trends, and psychiatric emergencies. *Population and Environment: Behavioral and Social Issues, 7*, 3-16.

Rovee-Collier, C.K., Sullivan, M.W., Enright, M., Lucas, D. & Fagen, J.W. (1980). Reactivation of infant memory. *Science, 208*, 1159-1161.

Rozee, P. & Van Boemel, G. (1989). The psychological effects of war trauma and abuse on older Cambodian refugee women. *Women and Therapy, 8*, 23-50.

Rozin, P. (1976). The evolution of intelligence and access to the cognitive unconscious. In J.M. Sprague & A.A. Epstein (Eds.), *Progress in psychobiology and physiological psychology (pp.245-280).* New York: Academic Press.

Rozin, P. & Fallon, A.E. (1987). A perspective on disgust. *Psychological Review, 94*, 23-41.

Rozin, P. & Kalat, J.W. (1971). Specific hungers and poison avoidance as adaptive specializations of teaming. *Psychological Review, 78*, 459-486.

Rubin, B.K. (1990). Exposure of children with cystic fibrosis to environmental tobacco smoke. *The New England Journal of Medicine, 323*, 782-788.

Rubin, D.C. & Baddeley, A.D. (1989). Telescoping is not time compression: A model of the dating of autobiographical events. *Memory & Cognition, 17*, 653-661.

Rubin, D.C, Wetzler, S.E. & Nebes, R.D. (1986). Autobiographical memory across the lifespan. In D.C. Rubin (Ed.), *Autobiographical memory* (pp. 202-221). Cambridge: Cambridge University Press.

Rubin, J.Z., Provenzano, F.J. & Luria, Z. (1974). The eye of the beholder: Parents' views on sex of newborns. *American Journal of Orthopsychiatry, 44*, 512-519.

Rubin, L.B. (1976, October). The marriage bed. *Psychology Today*, pp.44-50,91-92.

Rubin, Z. (1973). *Liking and loving.* New York: Holt, Rinehart & Winston.

Ruble, D.N. & Nakamura, C.Y. (1972). Task orientation versus social orientation in young children and their attention to relevant social cues. *Child Development, 43*, 471-480.

Ruderman, A.J. (1986). Dietary restraint: a theoretical and empirical review. *Psychological Bulletin, 99*, 247-262.

Rudy, J.W. & Wagner, A.R. (1975). Stimulus selection in associative learning. In W.K. Estes (Fd.), *Handbook of learning and cognition* (Vol. 2). Hillsdale, NJ: Erlbaum.

Ruitenbeek, H.M. (1973). *The first Freudians.* New York: Jason Aronson.

Rumelhart, D.E. (1970). A multicomponent theory of the perception of briefly exposed visual displays. *Journal of Mathematical Psychology, 7*, 191-218.

Rumelhart, D.E. & McClelland, J.L. (1986). *Parallel distributed processing: Explorations in the microstructure of cognition (2* vols.). Cambridge, MA: MIT Press.

Runner tells why she tried to kill herself. (1986, December 22). *San Francisco Examiner-Chronicle*, Sports Extra Section, p. 66.

Ruse, M. (1981). Are there gay genes? Sociobiology and homosexuality. *Journal of Homosexuality*, 6, 5-33.

Rushton, J P., Fulker, D.W., Neale, M.E., Nim, D.K.B. & Eysenck, H.J. (1986). Altruism and aggression: The heritability of individual differences. *Journal of Personality and Social Psychology, 50*, 283-305.

Russell, B. (1948). *Human knowledge, its scope and limits.* New York: Simon & Schuster.

Russell, J.A. (1994). Is there universal recognition of emotion from facial expression? A review of the cross-cultural studies. *Psychological Bulletin, 115*, 102-141.

Russell, J.A. & Ward, L.M. (1982). Environmental psychology. *Annual Review of Psychology, 33*, 651-688.

Russell, D. & McAuley, E. (1986). Causal attributions, causal dimensions, and affective reactions to success and failure. *Journal of Personality and Social Psychology, 50*, 1174-1185.

Russell, T.G., Rowe, W. & Smouse, A.D. (1991). Subliminal self-help tapes and academic achievement: an evaluation. *Journal of Counseling and Development, 69*, 359-362.

Russo, N.F. & Denmark, F.L. (1987). contributions of women to psychology. *Annual Review of Psychology, 38*, 279-298.

Rutter, M. (1979). Maternal deprivation, 1972-1978: New findings, new concepts, new approaches. *Child Development, 50*, 283-305.

Rutter, M. & Hersov, L. (1985). Child & adolescent psychiatry, 2nd edition. Oxford: Blackwell.

Ryan, W. (1976). *Blaming the victim.* (Rev. ed.). New York: Vintage Books.

Rychlak, J. (1979). *Discovering free will and personal responsibility.* New York: Oxford University Press.

Ryle, G. (1949). *The concept of mind.* London: Hutchinson.

Rylsky, M. (1986, February). A town born of the atom. *Soviet Life*, p.8.

Rymer, R. (1993). *Genie, an abused child's flight from silence.* New York: Harper Collins.

S

Sabini, J. & Silver, M., (1982). *Moralities of everyday life.* Oxford: Oxford University Press;

Sacks, O. (1973). *Migraine: Evolution of a common disorder.* Berkeley: University of Califomia Press.

Sachs, O. (1985). *The man who mistook his wife for a hat and other clinical tales.* New York: Summit.

Sachs, S. (1990, May 28). Romanian children suffer in asylums. *San Francisco Chronicle*, p. A]2.

Sacks, H., Schlegoff, E.A. & Jefferson, G. (1974). A simplest systematic for the organization of turn-taking in conversations. *Language, 50*, 696-735.

Saegert, S. & Hart, R. (1976). The development of sex differences in the environmental competence of children. In P. Bumett (Ed.), *Women in society.* Chicago: Maarouta.

Saks, M.J. (1977). *Jury verdicts: The role of group size and social decision rule*. Lexington, MA: Lexington Books.

Salmon, D.P., Zola-Morgan, S. & Squire, L.R. (1987). Retrograde amnesia following combined hippocampus-amygdala lesions in monkeys. *Psychobiology, 15*, 37-47.

Salovey, P. & Birnbaum, D. (1989). Influence of mood on healthrelevant cognitions. *Journal of Personality and Social Psychology, 57*, 539-551.

Salovey, P. & Rodin, J. (1985). Cognitions about the self: Connecting feeling states and social behavior. In L. Wheeler (Ed.), *Review of Personality and Social Psychology* (Vol. 6, pp. 143-167). Beverly Hills, CA: Sage.

Salzman, C. (1980). The use of ECT in the treatment of schizophrenia. *American Journal of Psychiatry, 137*, 1032-1041.

Salzman, C.D., Britten, K.H. & Newsome, W.T. (1990). Cortical microstimulation influences perceptual judgements of motion direction. *Nature, 346*, 174-177.

Samelson, F. (1992). Rescuing the reputation of Sir Cyril Burt. *Journal of the History of the Behavioural Sciences, 28*, 221-233.

Sampson, S.E. (1982). *The construction of personality: an introduction*. London: Routledge & Kegan Paul.

Sampson, E. (1993). *Celebrating the other*. London: Harvester Wheatsheaf.

Samuelson, W. & Zeckhauser, R. (1988). Status quo bias in decision making. *Journal of Risk and Uncertainty* 1, 7-59.

Sanchez-Craig, M., Annis, H.M., Bornet, A.R. & MacDonald, K.R. (1984). Random assignment to abstinence and controlled drinking: Evaluation of a cognitive-behavioral program for problem drinkers. *Journal of Consulting & Clinical Psychology,* 52,390-403.

Sanders, R.S. & Reyhen, J. (1969). Sensory deprivation and the enhancement of hypnotic susceptibility. *Journal of Abnormal Psychology, 74*, 375-381.

Sanderson, W.C., Rapee, R.M. & Barlow, D.H. (1989). The influence of an illusion of control on panic attacks induced via inhalation of 5.5% carbon dioxide-enriched air. *Archives of General Psychiatry, 46*, 157-162.

Sapolsky, R.M. (1990). Adrenocortical function, social rank and personality among wild baboons. *Biological Psychiatry 28,* pp.1-17.

Sarason, I.G., Johnson, J.H. & Siegel, J.M. (1978). Assessing the impact of life changes: Development of the Life Experiences Survey. *Journal of Consulting and Clinical Psychology, 46*, 932-946.

Sarbin, T.R. & Coe, W.C. (1972). *Hypnosis: A social psychological analysis of influence communication*. New York: Holt, Rinehart & Winston.

Sarnoff, I. & Corwin, S.M. (1959) Castration anxiety and the fear of death. *Journal of Personality, 27*, 374-385.

Sarnoff, I. & Katz, D. (1954). The motivational basis of attitude change. *Journal of Abnormal and Social Psychology, 49*, 115-124.

Sass, L.A. (1992). *Madness and modernism*. New York: Basic Books.

Satir, V. (1967). *Conjoint family therapy* (Rev. ed.). Palo Alto, CA: Science and Behavior Books.

Sawyer, J. (1966). Measurement and prediction, clinical and statistical. *Psychological Bulletin, 66*, 178-200.

Scammon, R.E. (1930). The measurement of the body in childhood. In J. Hanis, C.M. Jackson, D.G. Patterson, & R.E. Scammon (Eds.), *The measurement of man*. Minneapolis: University of Minnesota Press.

Scardamalia, M. & Bereiter, C. (1985). Fostering the development of self-regulation in children's knowledge processing. In S.F. Chapman, J.W. Segall & R. Glaser (Eds.), *Thinking and learning skills: Research and open questions, Vol 2* (pp. 563-577). Hillsdale, NJ: Erlbaum.

Scarr, S. (1988a). How genotypes and environments combine: Development and individual differences. In N. Bolger, A. Caspil G. Downey, & M. Morehouse (Eds.), *Persons in context: Developmental processes*. New York: Cambridge University Press.

Scarr, S. (1988b). Race and gender as psychological variables: Social and ethical issues. *American Psychologist, 43*, 56-59.

Scarr, S. (1981). *Race, social class, and individual differences in IQ*. Hillsdale, NJ: Eribaum.

Scarr, S. & Eisenberg, M. (1993). Child care research: issues, perspectives, and rules. *Annual Review of Psychology ,44*, 613-644.

Scarr, S. & Weinberg, R.A. (1976). I.Q. test performance of black children adopted by white families. *American Psychologist, 31*, 726-739.

Schacter, D.L. (1987). Implicit memory: History and current status. *Journal of Experimental Psychology: Learning, Memory and Cognition, 13*, 501-518.

Schacter, D.L., Kihlstrom, J.F., Kihlstrom, L.C. & Berren, M.B. (1989). Autobiographical memory in a case of multiple personality disorder. Journal of Abnormal Psychology, 98, 508-514.

Schachter, S. (1959). *The psychology of affiliation*. Stanford, CA: Stanford University Press.

Schachter, S. & Singer, J. (1962). Cognitive, social and physiological determinants of emotional state. *Psychological Review, 69*, 379-399.

Schaffer, H.R. (1984). *The child's entry into a social world*. New York: Academic Press.

Schaie, K.W. (1978). Towards a stage theory of adult cognitive development. *International Journal of Aging and Human Development, 8(2)*, 129-138.

Schaie, K.W. (1980). Intelligence and problem solving. In J.E. Birren & R.B. Sloan (Eds.), *Handbook of mental health and aging* (pp. 262-284). Englewood Cliffs, NJ: Prentice-Hall.

Schaie, K.W. (1989). The hazards of cognitive aging. *The Gerontologist, 29*, 484-493.

Schaie, W. (1990). In *Discovering Psychology*, Program 18 [PBS video series). Washington, DC: Annenberg/CPB Program.

Schaie, K.W. & Willis, S.L. (1986). Can decline in adult intellectual functioning be reversed? *Developmental Psychology, 22*, 223-232.

Schanberg, S.M. (1990). In *Discovering Psychology*, Program 4 [PBS video series]. Washington, DC: Annenberg/CPB Project.

Schanberg, S.M., Kuhn, C.M., Field, T.M. & Barolome, J.V. (1990). Maternal deprivation and growth suppression. In N.Guzenhauser (Fd.), *Advances in touch* (pp.3-10). Skillman, NJ: Johnson & Johnson Co.

Schank, R.C., & Abelson, R. (1977). *Scripts, plans, goals and understanding: An inquiry into human knowledge and structures*. Hillsdale, NJ: Eribaum.

Schaulfeli, W.B., Maslach, C. & Marek, T. (1993). (Eds.). *Professional burnout: Recent developments in theory and research*. London: Taylor & Francis.

Scheff, T.J. (1966). *Being mentally ill: A sociological theory*. Chicago: Aldine.

Scheier, M.F., Magovern, G.J., Sr., Abbott, R.A., Matthews, K.A., Owens, J.F., Ferebvre, R.C. & Carver, C.S. (1989). *Journal of Personality and Social Psychology, 57*, 1024-1040.

Scheikun, P.H. (1990). Secondhand smoke – more than annoying. *Cooking Light, 4*, 14-17.

Scherer, K.R. (1984). On the nature and function of emotion: A component process approach. In K.R. Schemer & P. Ekman *(Eds.), Approaches to emotion* (pp. 293-317). Hillsdale, NJ: Erlbaum.

Schleifer, S.J., Keller, S.E., Camerino, M., Thornton, J.C. & Stein, M. (1983). Suppression of lymphocyte stimulation following bereavement. *Journal of the American Medical Association, 250*, 374-377.

Schmidt, W.E. (1987, June 7). Paddling in school: A tradition is under fire. *The New York Times*, pp. A1, A22.

Schneider, D.J. (1991). Social cognition. *Annual Review of Psychology, 42*, 527-56 1.

Schneider, D.J., Hastorf, A.H. & Ellsworth, P.C. (1979). *Person perception* (2nd ed.). Reading, MA: Addison-Wesley.

Schneider, W. (1984). Developmental trends in the meta-memorymemory behavior relationship. In D.L. Forrest-Pressley, G.E. Mackinnon, & P.G. Waller (Eds.), *Metacognition, cognition, and human performance*. New York: Academic Press.

Schneider, W. & Shiffrin, R.M. (1977). Controlled and automatic information processing: 1, Detection, search, and attention. *Psychological Revieiv, 84*, 1-66.

Schneidman, E.S. (Ed.). (1976). *Deaths of man*. New York: Quadrangle.

Schrag, P. (1978). *Mind control*. New York: Delta.

Schreiber, F. (1973). Sybil. New York: Wamer Books.

Schreiner, L. & Kling, A. (1963). Behavioral changes following rhinencephalic injury in the cat. *Journal of Neurophysiology, 16*, 634-659.

Schultz, R., Braun, R.G. & Kluft, R.P. (1989). Multiple personality disorder: Phenomenology of selected variables in comparison to major depression. *Dissociation, 2*, 45-51.

Schulz, R. (1976). Effects of control and predictability on the physical and psychological well-being of the institutionalized aged. *Journal of Personality and Social Psychology, 33*, 563-573.

Schulz, R. (1978). *The psychology of death, dying and bereavement.* Reading, MA: Addison-Wesley.

Schulz, R., Tompkins, C., Wood, D. & Decker, S. (1987). The social psychology of caregiving: The physical and psychological costs of providing support to the disabled. *Journal of Applied Social Psychology, 17,* 401-428.

Schunk, D.H. & Cox, P.D. (1986). Strategy training and attributional feedback with Teaming disabled students. *Journal of Educational Psychology, 78,* 201-209.

Schwanenflugel, P.J., Blount, B.G. & Lin, P.J. (1991). Cross-cultural aspects of word meanings. In P.J. Schwanenflugel (Ed.), *The psychology of word meanings* (pp. 71-90). Hillsdale, NJ: Erlbaum.

Schwartz, B. (1984). Psychology of teaming and behavior (2nd ed.). New York: Norton.

Schwartz, B. & Lacey, H. (1982). *Behaviorism, science and human nature.* New York: Norton.

Schwartz, G.E. (1975). Biofeedback, self-regulation and the patterning of physiological processes. *The American Scientist, 63,* 314-324.

Schwartz, G.E., Brown, S.L .& Ahern, G.L. (1980). Facial muscle patterning and subjective experience during affective imagery: Sex differences. *Psychophysiology, 17,* 75-82.

Schwartz, P. & Strom, D. (1978). The social psychology of female sexuality. In I. Sherman & F.L. Denmark (Eds.), *Psychology of women: Future directions of research* (pp. 149-177). New York: Psychological Dimensions.

Schweder, R.A. & Bourne, E. (1982). Does the concept of the person vary cross-culturally? In A.J. Marsella & G.M. White *(Eds.), Cultural conceptions of mental health and therapy, (pp. 97-137).* London: Reidel.

Schweinhart, L.J. & Weikart, D.P. (1990). Research support for Head Start. *Science, 248,* 1174-1175.

Scott, J.P., Stewart, J.M. & De Ghett, V.J. (1974). Critical periods in the organization of systems. *Developmental Psychobiology, 7,* 489-513.

Scott, R.A. (1972). A proposed framework for analyzing deviance as a property of social order. In R.A. Scott & J.D. Douglas (Eds.), *Theoretical perspectives on deviance.* New York: Basic Books.

Scott, R.A. (1984). *Social stigma: The psychology of marked relationships.* New York: Freeman.

Scott, V. (1984, June 13). A six-year nightmare for Jim Backus [United Press]. *San Francisco Chronicle,* p.58.

Scovern, A.W. & Kilmann, P.R. (1980). Status of electro-convulsive therapy: Review of outcome literature. *Psychological Bulletin, 87,* 260-303.

Searle, J.R. (1969). *Speech acts: An essay in the philosophy of language.* Cambridge: Cambridge University Press.

Searle, J.R. (1992). *The rediscovery of the mind.* Cambridge, MA: MIT Press.

Sears, R.R.(1961). Relation of early socialization experiences to aggression in middle childhood. *Journal of abnormal and Social Psychology, 63,* 466-492.

Sears, R.R. (1977). Sources of life satisfactions of the Terman gifted men. *American Psychologist, 32,* 119-128.

Sears, P. & Barbee, A.H. (1977). Career and life situations among Terman's gifted women. In J.C. Stanley, W.C. George, & C.H. Solano (Eds.), *The gifted and the creative: A fifty year perspective* (pp. 28-65). Baltimore: Johns Hopkins University Press.

Sebeok, T.A. & Rosenthal, R. (1981). The clever Hans phenomenon. *Annals of the New York Academy of Sciences,* Whole Vol. 364.

Secretary of Health and Human Services. (1990). *Alcohol and health.* Alexandria, VA: Editorial Experts.

Selfridge, O.G. (1955). Pattern recognition and modem computers. *Proceedings of the Western Joint Computer Conference. New* York: Institute of Electrical and Electronics Engineers.

Seligman, M.E.P. (1971). Preparedness and phobias. *Behavior Therapy, 2,* 307-320.

Seligman, M.E.P. (1973). Fall into helplessness. *Psychology Today, 7,* 43-48.

Seligman, M.E.P. (1975). *Helplessness: On depression, development and death.* San Francisco: Freeman.

Seligman, M.E.P. (1987). *Predicting depression, poor health and presidential elections.* Washington, DC: Federation of Behavioral, Psychological and Cognitive Sciences.

Seligman, M.E.P. (1991). *Learned optimism.* New York: Norton.

Seligman, M.E.P. & Maier, S.F. (1967). Failure to escape traumatic shock. *Journal of Experimental Psychology, 74,* 1-9.

Selman, R. (1980). *The growth of interpersonal understanding. New* York: Academic Press.

Selye, H. (1956). *The stress of life.* New York: McGraw-Hill.

Selye, H. (1974). Stress without distress. New York: New American Library.

Selye, H. (1976). *Stress in health and disease.* Reading, MA: Butterworth.

Selye, H. (1978). On the real benefits of eustress. *Psychology Today, 12,* pp. 60-64.

Selye, H. (1980). The stress concept today. In I.L. Kutash & L.B. Schlesinger (Eds.), *Handbook on stress and anxiety (pp. 127-129).* San Francisco: Josey-Bass.

Semin, G.R. & Krahe, B. (1987). Lay conceptions of personality: Eliciting tiers of a scientific conception of personality. European Journal of Social Psychology, 17, 199-209.

Semin, G.R. & Papadopoulou, K. (1990). The acquisition of reflexive social emotions: The transmission and reproduction of social control through joint action. In G. Duveen & B.B. Lloyd (Eds.), *Social representation and the development of knowledge* (pp. 74-86). Cambridge: Cambridge University Press.

Serling, R.J. (1986). Curing a fear of flying. *USAIR,* pp.12-19.

Settler, J.M. (1982). *Assessment of children's intelligence and special abilities.* Boston: Allyn & Bacon.

Sex addicts: Many are professionals who exhibit varied behaviors. (1989, August 5). *Addiction Letter,* p. 9.

Sexton, V.S. & Hogan, J.D. (Eds.) (1992) *International psychology: Views from around the world,* Lincoln, University of Nebraska Press.

Shaffer, H.J. (1989), Conceptual crises in the addictions: The role of models in the field of compulsive gambling. In H.J. Shaffer, S.A. Stein, B. Gambino, & T.N. Cummings (Eds.), *Compulsive gambling: Theory, research and practice.* Lexington, MA: D.C. Heath.

Shaffer, H.J., Stein, S.A., Gambino, B. & Cummings, T.N. (Eds.). (1989). *Compulsive gambling: Theory, research and practice.* Lexington, MA: D.C. Heath.

Shafii, M., Carrigan, S., Whittinghill, J.R. & Derrick, A. (1985). Psychological autopsy of completed suicide in children and adolescents. *American Journal of Psychiatry, 142,* 1061-1064.

Shallice, T. (1978). The dominant action system: An informationprocessing approach to consciousness. In K.S. Pope & J.L. Singer (Eds.), *The stream of consciousness: Scientific investigations into the flow of human experience* (pp.117-157). New York: Plenum.

Shapiro, A.K. (1960). A contribution to a history of the placebo effect. *Behavioral Science, 5,* 109-135.

Shapiro, D.H. (1985). Clinical use of meditation as a self-regulation strategy: Comments on Holmes's conclusions and implications. *American Psychologist, 40,* 719-722.

Shapiro, S., Skinner, E.A., Kessler, L.G., Von Korff, M., German, P.S., Tischler, F.L., Leaf, P.J., Benham, L., Cottler, L. & Regier, D.A. (1984). Utilization of health and menta) healtb services. *Archives of General Psychiatry, 41,* 971-978.

Shatz, M. & Gelman, R. (1973). The development of communication skills: Modifications in the speech of young children as a function of listener. *Monographs of the Society for Research in Child Development, 38* (5, Serial No. 152).

Shatz, M., Wellman, H.M. & Silber, S. (1983). The acquisition of mental verbs: A systematic investigation of the first reference to mental state. *Cognition, 14,* 301-32).

Shaw, R. & Turvey, M.T. (1981). Coalitions as models for ecosystems: A realist perspective on perceptual organization. In M. Kubovy & J.R. Pomerantz (Eds.), *Perceptual organization* (pp. 343-346). Hillsdale, NJ: Erlbaum.

Sheehy, G. (1976). *Passages: Predictable crises of adult life.* New York: Dutton.

Sheffield, F.D. (1966). New evidence on the drive-induction theory of reinforcement. In R.N. Haber (Ed.), *Current research in motivation* (pp.111-122). New York: Holt.

Sheffield, F.D. & Roby, T.B. (1950). Reward value of a nonnutritive sweet taste. *Journal of Comparative and Physiological Psychology, 43,* 471-481.

Sheingold, K. & Tenney, Y.J. (1982). Memory for a salient childhood event. In U. Neisser (Ed.), *Memory observed. San* Francisco: Freeman.

Sheldon, W. (1942). *The varieties of temperament: A psychology of constitutional differences.* New York: Harper.

Shepard, R.N. (1978). Externalization of mental images and the act of creation. In B.S. Randhawa & W.E. Coffman (Eds.), *Visual learning,* thinking and communicating. New York: Academic Press.

Shepard, R.N. (1984). Ecological constraints on intemal

representation: Resonant kinematics of perceiving, imagining, thinking and dreaming. *Psychological Review, 91*, 417-447,

Shepard, R.N. (1990). *Mind sights: Original visual illusions, ambiguities, and other anomalies, with a commentary on the play of mind in perception and art*. New York: Freeman.

Shepard, R.N. & Cooper, L.A. (1982). *Mental images and their transformations*. Cambridge, MA: MIT Press.

Shepard, R.N. & Jordan, D.S. (1984). Auditory illusions demonstrating that tones are assimilated to an internalized musical scale. *Science, 226*, 1333-1334.

Shepp, B. & Ballisteros, M. (Eds.). (1989). Object Perception. Hillsdale, **NJ**: Eribaum.

Sheridan, C.L. & King, R.G. (1972). Obedience to authority with an authentic victim. *Proceedings of the 80th Annual Convention*, American Psychological Association, Part 1, 7, 165-166

Sherif, C.W. (1981, August). *Social antipsychological bases of social psychology*. The G. Stanley Hall Lecture on social psychology, presented at the annual convention of the American Psychological Association, Los Angeles, CA.

Sherif, M. (1935). A study of some social factors in perception. *Archives of Psychology, 27(187).*

Sherif, M. & Sherif, C.W. (1979). Research on intergroup relations. In W.G. Austin & S. Worchel (Eds.), *The social psychology of intergroup relations* (pp. 7-18). Monterey, CA: Brooks/Cole.

Sherif, M., Harvey, 0.J., White, B.J., Hood, W.E. & Sherif, C.W. (1961). *Intergroup conflict and cooperation: The Robber's Cave experiment*. Norman, OK: University of Oklahoma Press.

Sherman, J.A. (1963). Reinstatement of verbal behavior in a psychotic by reinforcement methods. *Journal of Speech and Hearing Disorders, 28*, 398-40 1.

Sherrington, C.S. (1906). *The integrative action of the nervous system*. New York: Scribner.

Sherrod, K., Vietze, P. & Friedman, S. (1978). *Infancy*. Monterey, CA: Brooks/Cole.

Shields, S.A. (1991). Gender in the psychology of emotion: a selective research review. In K.T. Strongman (Ed.), *International Review of Studies on Emotion*. Volume 1 (pp. 227-247). New York: Wiley.

Shiffman, S.S., & Erickson, R.P. (1971). A theoretical review: A psychophysical model for gustatory quality. *Physiology and Behavior, 7*, 617-633.

Shirley, M.M. (1931). *The first two years*. Minneapolis: University of Minnesota Press.

Shneidman, E. (1987, March). At the point of no return. *Psychology Today*, pp. 54-59.

Shortliffe, E.H. (1983). Medical consultation systems: Designing for doctors. In M.S. Sime & M.J. Coombs (Eds.), *Designing for human computer communication* (pp. 209-238). London: Academic Press.

Shotter, J. (1975). *Images of man in psychological research*. London: Methuen.

Shotter, J. (1984). *Social accountability and selfhood*. Oxford: Blackwell.

Shotter, J. (1989). Social accountability and the social construction of 'you'. In J. Shotter & K. Gergen (Eds.), *Texts of identity* (pp. 133-151). London: Sage.

Shotter, J. (1993). *Conversational realities: Constructing life through language*. London: Sage.

Showers, C. & Cantor, N. (1985). Social cognition: A look at motivated strategies. *Annual Review of Psychology, 36*, 275-305.

Shweder, R.A. (1991). *Thinking through cultures: expeditions in cultural psychology*. Cambridge, MA: Harvard University Press.

Siegler, R.S. (1983). Information processing approaches to cognitive development. In W. Kessen (Ed.), *Handbook of Child Psychology: History, theory and methods (Vol.1)*. New York: Wiley

Siegel, B. (1988). *Love, medicine and miracles*. New York: Harper & Row.

Siegel, J.M. (1990). Stressful life events and use of physician services among the elderly: The moderating role of pet ownership, *Journal of Personality and Social Psychology. 58*, 1081-1086.

Siegel, S. (1977). Morphine tolerance acquisition as an associative process. *Journal of Experimental Psychology: Animal Behaviour Processes*, 3, 1-13.

Siegel, S. (1979). The role of conditioning in drug tolerance and addiction. In J.D. Keehn (Ed.). *Psychopathology in animals and clinical applications* (pp.143-167). New York: Academic Press.

Siegel, S. (1984). Pavlovian conditioning and heroin overdose: Reports by overdose victims. *Bulletin of the Psychonomic Society 22*, 428-430.

Siegel, S., Hinson, R.E., Krank, M.D. & McCully, J. (1982).

Heroin 'overdose' death: The contribution of drug-associated environmental cues. *Science, 216*, 436-437.

Siegman, A.W. & Feldstein, S. (1985). *Multichannel integrations of nonverbal behaviour* Hillsdale, NJ: Erlbaum.

Silberfeld, M. (1978). Psychological symptoms and social supports. *Social Psychiatry, 13*, 11-17.

Silver, R. & Wortman, E. (1980). Coping with undesirable life events. In J. Garber & M.E.P. Seligman (Eds.), *Human helplessness: Theory and application*. New York: Academic Press.

Silverman, L.H. (1976). Psychoanalytic theory: 'The reports of my death are greatly exaggerated'. *American Psychologist, 301* 621-637.

Simmel, E.C. (1980). *Early experiences and early behavior: Implications for social development*. New York: Academic Press.

Simon, H. (1955). A behavioral model of rational choice. *Quarterly Journal of Economics, 69*, 99-118.

Simon, H. (1973). The structure of ill-structured problems. *Artificial Intelligence, 4*, 181-202.

Simon, H. (1985). *Using cognitive science to solve human problems*. Presentation at a Science and Public Policy Seminar, Federation of Behavioral, Psychological, and Cognitive Sciences, Washington, DC.

Simon, H. (1990a). A mechanism for social selection and successful altruism. *Science, 250*, 1665-1668.

Simon, H. (1990b). In *Discovering Psychology*, Program 10 [PBS video series]. Washington, DC: Annenberg/CPB Project.

Simon, H.A. & Gilmartin, K. (1973). A simulation of memory for chess positions. *Cognitive Psychology, 5*, 29-46.

Simpson, E.E.L. (1974). Moral development research: A case study of scientific cultural bias. *Human Development, 17*, 81-106.

Sinclair, J.D. (1983, December). The hardware of the brain. *Psychology Today*, pp.8, 11, 12.

Singer, C. (1958). *From magic to science: Essays on the scientific twilight*. New York: Dover.

Singer, J. (1990). *Seeing through the visible world: Jung, Gnosis, and chaos*. New York: Harper & Row.

Singer, J.L. (1966). Daydreaming: An introduction to the experimental study of inner experience. New York: Random House.

Singer, J.L. (1975). Navigating the stream of consciousness: Research in daydreaming and related inner experience. *American Psychologist*, 30, 727-739,

Singer, J.L. (1976). Fantasy: The foundation of serenity. *Psychology Today, 10*, pp.32ff.

Singer, J.L. (1978). Experimental studies of daydreaming and the stream of thought. In K.S. Pope & I.L. Singer (Eds.), *The stream of consciousness: Scientific investigations into the flow of human experience* (pp. 187-223). New York: Plenum.

Singer, J.L. & Antrobus, J.S. (1966). *Imaginal processes inventory*. New York: Authors.

Singer, J.L. & McCraven, V.J. (1961). Some characteristics of adult daydreaming. *Journal of Psvchology, 51*, 151-164.

Sinnott, J.D. (Ed.). (1989). *Everyday problem solving: Theory and applications* New York: Praeger.

Sjoberg, B.M. & Hollister, L.F. (1965). The effects of psychotomimetic drugs on primary suggestibility. *Psychopharmacologia, 8*, 251-262.

Sjorstrom, L. (1980). Fat cells and body weight. In A.J. Stunkard (Ed.), *Obesity*. Philadelphia: Saunders.

Skeels, H.M. (1966). Adult status of children with contrasting early life experiences. Monographs of the Society for Research in Child *Development*, 31(3).

Skinner, B.F. (1938). *The behavior of organisms*. New York: Appleton-Century-Crofts.

Skinner, B.F. (1953). *Science and human behavior*. New York: Macmillan.

Skinner, B.F. (1957). *Verbal behavior*. New York: Appleton-Century-Crofts.

Skinner, B.F. (1966). What is the experimental analysis of behavior? *Journal of the Experimental Analysis of Behavior* 9, 213-218

Skinner, B.F. (1976). *About behaviorism*. New York: Vintage Books.

Skinner, B.F. (1981). Selection by consequences. *Science*, 2 13, 501-504.

Skinner, B.F. (1987). Whatever happened to psychology as the science of behavior? *American Psychologist, 42*, 8, 780-786.

Skinner, B.F. (1990). Can psychology be a science of mind? *American Psychologist, 45*, 11, 1206-1210.

Skinner, B.F. (1990). In *Discovering Psychology*, programs 8 and 18 [PBS video series]. Washington, DC: Annenberg/CPB Project.

Skolnick, A. (1986). Early attachment and personal relationships across the life course. In P.B. Baltes, D.M. Featherman, & R.M. Lemer (Eds.), *Lifespan development and behavior* (Vol.7, pp.173-206). Hillsdale, NJ: Erlbaum.

Slade, P.D. & Bentall, R.P. (1988). *Sensory deception: a scientific analysis of hallucination.* Baltimore: Johns Hopkins University Press.

Sleep disorders can be a nightmare. (1990, September 26). *Associated Press.*

Sloane, R.B., Staples, F.R., Cristol, A.H., Yorkston, N.J. & Whipple, K. (1975). *Psychotherapy versus behavior therapy.* Cambridge, MA: Harvard University Press.

Slobin, D. (1979). *Psycholinguistics* (2nd ed.). Glenview, IL: Scott, Foresman.

Slovic, P. (1984). *Facts vs. fears: Understanding perceived risk.* Presentation at a Science and Public Policy Seminar. Federation Behavioural, Psychological, and Cognitive Sciences, Washington, DC.

Small, G.W. & Nicholi, A.M., Jr. (1982). Mass hysteria among schoolchildren. *Archives of General Psychiatry, 39,* 721-724.

Smart, M.S. & Smart, R.C. (1973). *Adolescents: Development* and relationships. New York: Macmillan.

Smiley, P. & Huttenlocher, J. (1989). Young children's acquisition of emotion concepts. In C. Saarni & P.L. Harris (Eds.) (1989). *Children's understanding of emotion* (pp. 27-50). Cambridge: Cambridge University Press.

Smith, C. & Lloyd, B. (1978). Maternal behavior and perceived sex of infant revisited. *Child Development, 49,* 1263-1265.

Smith, C.A. (1986). *The information structure of the facial expression of emotion.* Dissertation, Stanford University.

Smith, C.A. (1989). Dimensions of appraisal and physiological response in emotion. *Journal of Personality and Social Psychology, 56,* 339-353.

Smith, C.A. & Ellsworth, P.C. (1987). Patterns of appraisal and emotion related to taking an exam. *Journal of Personality and Social Psychology, 52,* 475-488.

Smith, D. (1982). Trends in counselling and psychotherapy. *American Psychologist, 37,* 802-809.

Smith, D. & Kraft, W.A. (1983). DSM-III: Do psychologists really want an alternative? *American Psychologist, 38,* 777-785.

Smith, J. & Baltes, P.B. (1990). Wisdom-related knowledge: Age/cohort differences in response to life-planning problems. *Developmental Psychology, 26,* 494-505.

Smith, E.E. & Medin, D.L. (1981). *Cognitive Science Series: 4. Categories and concepts.* Cambridge, MA: Harvard University Press.

Smith, M.L. & Glass, G.V. (1977). Metaanalysis of psychotherapy outcome studies. *American Psychologist, 32,* 752-760.

Smith, M.L., Glass, G.V. & Miller, T.I. (1980). *The benefits of psychotherapy.* Baltimore: Johns Hopkins University Press.

Smith, P. & Bond, M.H. (1993). *Social psychology across cultures: analysis and perspectives.* London: Harvester Wheatsheaf.

Smith, S.M., Brown, H.O., Toman, J.E.P. & Goodman, L.S. (1947). The lack of cerebral effects of d-tubercurarine. *Anesthesiology, 8,* 1-14.

Smith, T.W. (1991, May/June). Adult sexual behavior in 1989: Number of partners, frequency of intercourse and risk of AIDS. *Family Planning Perspectives, 23,* 102-107.

Smuts, A.B. & Hagen, J.W. (1985). History and research in child development. *Monographs of the Society for Research in Child Development, 50* (Serial No. 211), 4-5.

Snow, C.P. (1961, January 7). In the name of obedience. *Nation, 3.*

Snow, R. (1983). The relationship between vision and juvenile delinquency. *Journal of the American Optometric Association, 54,* 509-511.

Snowden, C.T. (1969). Motivation, regulation and the control of meal parameters with oral and intragastric feeding. *Journal of Comparative and Physiological Psychology, 69,* 91-100.

Snyder, C.R. & Fromkin, H.L. (1980). *Uniqueness: The human pursuit of difference.* New York: Plenum.

Snyder, C.R. & Smith, T. (1982). Symptoms as self-handicapping strategies: The virtue of old wine in new bottles. In G. Weary & H. Mirels (Eds.), *Integrations of clinical and social psychology* New York: Oxford University Press.

Snyder, S.H. (1974). Catecholamines as mediators of drug effects in schizophrenia. In F.0. Schmitt & F.G. Worden (Eds.), *The neurosciences: Third study program* (pp. 721-732). Cambridge, MA: MIT Press.

Snyder, S.H. (1976). The dopamine hypothesis of schizophrenia, *American Journal of Psychiatry*, 133, 197-202.

Snyder, S.H. (1981). Dopamine receptors, neuroleptics and schizophrenia. *American Journal of Psychiatry, 138,* 460-464.

Snyder, S.H. & Childers, S.R. (1979). Opiate receptors and opioid peptides. *Annual Review of Neurosciences, 2,* 35-64.

Snyder, S.H. & Mattysse, S. (1975). *Opiate receptor mechanisms.* Cambridge, MA: MIT Press.

Snyder, M. (1984). When beliefs create reality. In L. Berkowitz (Ed.). *Advances in experimental social psychology, 18,* 247-305. New York: Academic Press.

Snyder, M. & Franker, A. (1976). Observer bias: A stringent test of behavior engulfing the field. *Journal of Personality and Social Psychology, 34,* 857-864.

Snyder, M. & Jones, E.E. (1974). Attitude attribution when behavior is constrained. *Journal of Experimental Social Psychology, 10,* 585-600.

Snyder, M. & Swann, W.B., Jr. (1978a). Behavioral confirmation in social interaction: From social perception to social reality. *Journal of Experimental Social Psychology, 14,* 148-162.

Snyder, M. & Swann, W.B., Jr. (1978b). Hypothesis-testing processes in social interaction. *Journal of Personality and Social Psychology, 36,* 1202-1212.

Sobell, M.B. & Sobell, L.C. (1973). Individualized behavior therapy for alcoholics. *Behavior Therapy, 4,* 49-72.

Sobell, M.B. & Sobell, L.C. (1984). The aftermath of heresy: A response to Pendery et al (1982) critique of 'individualized behavior therapy for alcoholics'. *Behaviour Research and Therapy, 22,* 413-440.

Sociaal Cultureel Planbureau (SCP) (1992). *Sociaal cultureel rapport [Social-cultural report].* The Hague: VUGA.

Sokol, M.M. (Ed.). (1987). *Psychological testing and American society, 1890-1930.* New Brunswick, NJ: Rutgers University Press.

Solvic, P. (1984). *Facts vs. fears: Understanding perceived risk.* Presentation at a Science and Public Policy Seminar. Federation of Behavioral, Psychological, and Cognitive Sciences, Washington, DC.

Sonnenstein, F.S., Pleck, J.H. & Ku, L.C. (1989). Sexual acting, condom use and AIDS awareness among adolescent males. *Family Planning Perspectives, 21,* 152-158.

Sorce, J.F., Emde, R.N., Campos, J. & Klinnert, M.D. (1985). Maternal emotional signaling: Its effect on the visual cliff behavior of 1-year-olds. *Developmental Psychology, 2* 195-200.

Sorenson, R.C. (1973). *Adolescent sexuality in contemporary America.* Cleveland: World.

Spanos, N.P. & Gottlieb, J. (1976). Ergotism and the Salem village witch trials. *Science, 194,* 1390-1394.

Spanos, N.P., Weekes, J.R. & Bertrand, L.D. (1985). Multiple personality: A social psychological perspective. *Journal of Abnormal Psychology, 94,* 362-376.

Spearman, C. (1923). *The nature of 'intelligence' and the principles of cognition.* London: Macmillan.

Spearman, C. (1927). *The abilities of man.* London: Macmillan.

Spears, R. & Manstead, A.S.R. (1990). Consensus estimation in social context. *European Review of Social Psychology, 1,* 81-109.

Speisman, J.C., Lazarus, R.S., Mordkoff, A.M. & Davison, L.A. (1964). The experimental reduction of stress based on ego defense theory. *Journal of Abnormmal and Social Psychology, 68,* 367-380.

Spelke, E., Hirst, W. & Neisser, U. (1976). Skills of divided attention. *Cognition, 4,* 215-230.

Spelke, E.S., von-Hofsten, C. & Kestenbaum, R. (1989). Object perception in infancy: Interaction of spatial and kinetic information for object boundaries. *Developmental Psychology, 25(2),* 185-196.

Spence, D.P. (1967). Subliminal perception and perceptual defense: Two sides of a single problem. *Behavioral Science, 12,* 183-193.

Sperling, G. (1960). The information available in brief visual presentations. *Psychological Monographs, 74,* 1-29.

Sperling, G. (1963). A model for visual memory tasks. *Human Factors, 5,* 19-31.

Sperry, R.W. (1952). Neurology and the mind-brain problem. *American Scientist, 40,* 291-312.

Sperry, R.W. (1968). Mental unity following surgical disconnection of the cerebral hemispheres. *The Harvey Lectures,* Series 62. New York: Academic Press.

Sperry, R.W. (1976). *Changing concepts of consciousness and free will.* Perspectives in Biology and Medicine, 20, 9-19.

Sperry, R.W. (1987). Consciousness and causality. In R.L. Gregory *(Ed.), The Oxford companion to the* mind (pp. 164-166). New York: Oxford University Press.

Spiegel, D., Bloom, J. R., Kraemer, H. C. & Gottheil, E. (1989, October 14). Effect of psychosocial treatment on survival of patients with metastatic breast cancer. *The Lancet,* pp. 888-891.

Spiegel, D., Bloom, J.R. & Yalom, I. (1981). Group support for patients with metastatic cancer. *Archives of General Psychiatry, 38,* 527-533.

Spiro, R.J. (1977). Remembering information from text: The state of schema approach. In R.C. Atkinson, R.J. Spiro, & W.E. Montague (Eds.), *Schooling and the acquisition of knowledge.* Hillsdale, NJ: Erlbaum.

Spitz, R.A. & Wolf, K. (1946). Anaclitic depression. *Psychoanalytic Study of Children, 2,* 313-342.

Spitzer, R. (1981, October). Nonmedical myths and the DSM-III. *APA Monitor.*

Spong, P. (1988, September 17). [Letter to Shari Anderson, President of the Puget Chapter of the American Cetacean Society.

Springer, S.P. & Deutsch, G. (1984). *Left brain, right brain (2nd* ed.). San Francisco: Freeman.

Squire, L.R. (1986). Memory functions as affected by electroconvulsive therapy. *Annals of the New York Academy of Sciences, 462,* 307-314.

Squire, L.R. (1986). Mechanisms of memory. *Science, 232,* 1612-1619.

Squire, L.R., Amaral, D.G., Zola-Morgan, S., Kritchevsky, M. & Press, G. (1989). Description of brain injury in the amnesic patient N.A. based on magnetic resonance imaging. *Experimental Neurology, 105,* 23-35.

Squire, L.R., Knowlton, B. & Musen, G. (1993). The structure and organization of memory. *Annual Review of Psychology, 44,* 453-495.

Squire, L.R. & Slater, P.C. (1975). Forgetting in very long-term memory as assessed by an improved questionnaire technique. *Journal of Experimental Psychology: Human Learning and Memory, 104,* 50-54.

Squires, S. (1985, August 19). It's hard to tell a lie. *San Francisco Chronicle,* This World Section, p.9.

Squire, S. (1988, January 3). Shock therapy. *San Francisco Examiner-Chronicle,* This World Section, p. 16.

Staats, A.W., Gross, M.C., Guay, P.F. & Carlson, C.C. (1973). Personality and social systems and attitude-reinforcer discriminative theory: Interest (attitude) formation, function, and measurement. *Journal of Personality and Social Psychology, 26,* 251-261.

Staats, A.W., Minke, K.A., Martin, C.H. & Higa, W.R. (1972). Deprivation-satiation and strength of attitude conditioning: A test of attitude-reinforcer-discriminative theory. *Journal of Personality and Social Psychology, 24,* 178-185.

Staats, A.W. & Staats, C.K. (1958). Attitudes established by classical conditioning. *Journal of Abnormal and Social Psychology, 57,* 37-40.

Staff. (1989, January). You've come a long way, baby, part II. *University of California, Berkeley, Wellness Letter,* p. 1.

Staff. (1990, Fall). Changing the image: regulating alcohol advertising. The Student Body (p.7). Stanford, CA: Stanford University.

Staff. (1990). *1989 survey results from monitoring the future: A continuing study of the life styles and values of youth.* Ann Arbor, MI: University of Michigan, Institute for Social Research.

Stainton-Rogers, R., Stenner, P., Gleeson, K. & Stainton-Rogers, W. (1995). *Social psychology: a critical agenda.* Cambridge: Polity Press.

Stall, R., McKusick, L., Wiley, J., Coates, T.J. & Ostrow, D.G. (1986). Alcohol and drug use during sexual activity and compliance with safe sex guidelines for AIDS: the AIDS Behavioral Research Project. *Health Education Quarterly,* 13, 359-71.

Stam, H.J. (1991). The re-emergence of theory in psychology. *Theory & Psychology, 1,* 5-11.

Stampfl, T.G. & Levis, D.J. (1967). Essentials of implosive therapy: A Teaming theory-based psychodynamic behavioral therapy. *Journmal of Abnormal Psychology, 72,* 496-503. *Stanford Daily.* (1982, February 2, pp. 1, 3, 5).

Stangler, R.S. & Printz, A.M. (1980). DSM-III: Psychiatric diagnosis in a university population. *American Journal of Psychiatry, 137,* 937-940.

Stanley, J. (1976). The study of the very bright. *Science, 192,* 66-69.

Stanovich, K. (1986). *How to think straight about psychology.* Glenview, IL: Scott, Foresman.

Stapp, J. & Fulcher, R. (1981). The employment of APA members. *American Psychologist, 36,* 1263-1314.

Stayton, D., Hogan, R. & Ainsworth, M.D.S. (1971). Infant obedience and matemal behavior: The origins of socialization reconsidered. *Child Development, 42,* 1057-1069.

Steele, C.M. (1988). The psychology of self-affirmation: Sustaining the integrity of the self. In L. Berkowitz (Ed.), *Advances in experimental social psychology* (Vol. 21, pp.261-302). New York: Academic Press.

Steers, R.M. & Porter, L.W. (1974). The role of task-goal attributes in employee performance. *Psychological Bulletin, 81,* 434-452.

Stein, M., Keller, S.E. & Schleifer, S.J. (1985). Stress and immunomodulation: The role of depression and neuroendocrine function. *Journal of Immunology, 135,* 827-833.

Steiner, J. (1980). The SS yesterday and today: A sociopsychological view. In J.E. Dimsdale (Ed.), *Survivors, victims, and perpetrators: Essays on the Nazi holocaust (pp.* 405-456). Washington, DC: Hemisphere Publishing.

Steininger, M., Newell, J.D. & Garcia, L.T. (1984). *Ethical issues in psychology.* Homewood, IL: Dorsey.

Stellar, E. (1954). The physiology of motivation. *Psychological Review, 61,* 5-22.

Stem, M. & Karraker, K.H. (1989). Sex stereotyping of infants: A review of gender labeling studies. *Sex Roles, 20,* 501-522.

Stenberg, C.R., Campos, J.J. & Emde, R.N. (1983). The facial expression of anger in seven-month-old infants. *Child Development, 54,* 178-184.

Stenner, P. (1993). Discoursing jealousy. In E. Burman & I. Parker (Eds.), *Discourse analytic research* (pp. 114-133). London: Routledge.

Stensvold, I., Tverdal, A., Solvoll, K. & Foss, O.P. (1992). Tea consumption: Relationship to cholesterol, blood pressure, and coronary and total mortality. *Preventative Medicine,* 21, 4, 546-553.

Steptoe, A. & Wardle, J., (1992). Cognitive predictors of health behaviour in contrasting regions of Europe. *British Journal of Clinical Psychology,* 31, 485-502.

Steriade, M. & McCarley, R. W. (1990). *Brainstem control of wakefulness and sleep.* New York: Plenum.

Stern, P. & Aronson, E. (Eds.). (1984). *Energy use: The human dimension.* New York: Freeman.

Stern, P.C., Dietz, T. & Kalof, L. (1993). Value orientations, gender and environmental concern. *Environment & Behaviour, 25(3),* 322-348.

Stern, R.M. & Ray, W.J. *(1977).* Biofeedback. Chicago: Dow Jones-Irwin.

Stern, W. (1914). The psychological methods of testing intelligence. *Educational Psychology Monographs* (No.13).

Stern, W.C. & Morgane, P.S. (1974). Theoretical view of REM sleep function: Maintenance of catecholomine systems in the central nervous system. *Behavioral Biology,* 11, 1-32.

Sternberg, R. (Ed.). (1982). *Handbook of human intelligence.* Cambridge, MA: Cambridge University Press.

Sternberg, R. (1985). *Beyond IQ.* Cambridge, MA: Cambridge University Press.

Sternberg, R. (1986a). Inside intelligence. *American Scientist, 74,* 137-143.

Sternberg, R. (1986b). A triangular theory of love. *Psychological Review, 93,* 119-135.

Sternberg, R. (1990). In *Discovering Psychology,* Program 16 [PBS video series). Washington, DC: Annenberg/CPB Program.

Sternbach, R.A. & Tursky, B. (1965). Ethnic differences among housewives in psychophysical and skin potential responses to electric shock. *Psychophysiology, 1,* 241-246.

Sternberg, R.J., Conway, B.E., Ketron, J.L. & Bernstein, M. (1981). People's conceptions of intelligence. *Journal of Personality and Social Psychology, 41,* 37-55.

Stevens, C.F. (1979). The neuron. *Scientific American, 241(9),* 54-65.

Stevenson, J., Graham, P., Fredman, G. & McLaughlin, V.A. (1987). Twin study of genetic influences on reading and spelling ability and disability. *Journal of Child Psychiatry, 28,* 229-247.

Stipp, D. (1991, January 30). Split personality. Americans are loath to curb energy use despite war concems. *The Wall Street Journal,* pp. A1, A5.

Storms, M.D. (1981). A theory of erotic orientation development. *Psychological Review, 88,* 340-353.

Strack, S. & Coyne, J.C. (1983). Social confirmation of dysphoria: Shared and private reactions to depression. *Journal of Personality and Social Psychology, 50,* 149-167.

Straub, E. (1974). Helping a distressed person: Social, personality and stimulus determinants. In L. Berkowitz (Ed.), *Advances in experimental social psychology* (Vol. 7). New York: Academic Press.

Strien, P.J. van (1987). Model disciplines, research traditions, and the theoretical unification of psychology. In: W.J. Baker et al. (Eds.),

Current issues in theoretical psychology, pp. 333-344. Amsterdam: North-Holland.

Strodtbeck, F.L. & Hook, L.H. (1961). The social dimensions of a twelve-man jury table. *Sociometry, 24,* 397-415.

Stroebe, M.S. & Stroebe, W. (1983). Who suffers more? Sex differences in health risks of the widowed. *Psychological Bulletin, 93,* 279-301.

Stroebe, M.S. & Stroebe, W. (1987). *Bereavement and health. The psychological and physical consequences of partner loss.* Cambridge: Cambridge University Press.

Stroebe, W., Stroebe, M.S., Gergen, K.J. & Gergen, M. (1982). The effects of bereavement on mortality: A social psychological analysis. In J.R. Eiser (Ed.), *Social psychology and behavioral medicine* (pp. 527-560). New York: Wiley.

Strong, E.K. (1927). Differentiation of certified public accountants from other occupational groups. *Journal of Educational Psychology, 18,* 227-238.

Stroop, J.R. (1935). Studies of interference in serial verbal reactions. *Journal of Experimental Psychology, 18,* 643-662.

Strube, M.J. (Ed.). (1990). *Type A behavior.* Corte Madera, CA: Select Press.

Strupp, H. (1990). *In Discovering Psychology,* programs 21 and 22 (PBS video series]. Washington, DC: Annenberg/CPB Program.

Stuart, R.B. (1971). Behavioral contracting with families of delinquents. *Journal of Behavior Therapy and Experimental Psychiatry, 2,* 1-11.

Study finds that deaf babies 'babble' in sign language. (1991, March 22). *The New York Times,* p.1.

Styron, W. (1990). Darkness visible: A memoir of madness. New York: Random House.

Suchman, A.L. & Ader, R. (1989). Placebo response in humans can be shaped by prior pharmalogic experience. *Psychosomatic Medicine, 51,* 251.

Suedfeld, P. (1980). *Restricted environmental stimulation: Research and clinical applications.* New York: Wiley.

Sullivan, A. (1908). Letters to Sophia C. Hopkins. In H. Keller, *The Story of My Life.* New York: Doubleday, 1954.

Sullivan, H.S. (1953). *The interpersonal theory of psychiatry. New* York: Norton.

Suls, J. & Fletcher, B. (1985). The relative efficacy of avoidant and nonavoidant coping strategies: A metaanalysis. *Health Psychology, 4,* 249-288.

Suls, J. & Marco, C.A. (1990). Relationship between JAS- and FTAS-Type A behavior and non-CHD illness: A prospective study controlling for negative affectivity. *Health Psychology, 9,* 479-492.

Summers, M. (Ed.). (1971). *The Malleus maleficarum of Heinrich Kramer and James Spranger.* New York: Dover. (Original work published 1486)

Sundberg, N.D. (1977). *Assessment of persons.* Englewood Cliffs, NJ: Prentice-Hall.

Sundberg, N.D. & Matarazzo, D. (1979). Psychological assessment of individuals. In M.E. Meyer (Ed.), *Foundations of contemporary psychology* (pp.580-617). New York: Oxford University Press.

Svenson, O. (1981). Are we all less risky and more skillful than our fellow drivers? *Acta Psychologica, 47,* 143-148.

Sutker, P.B., Allain, A.N. & Winstead, D.K. (1993). Psychopathology and psychiatric diagnoses of World War II Pacific theatre prisoner of war survivors and combat veterans. *American Journal of Psychiatry, 150,* 2, 240-245.

Swann, W.B., Jr. (1985). The self as architect of social reality. Ill B. Schlenker (Ed.), *The self and social life (pp.* 100-126). New York: McGraw-Hill.

Swann, W.B., Jr. (1990). To be adored or to be known?: The interplay of self-enhancement and self-verification. In R.M. Sorrentino & E.T. Higgins (Eds.), *Handbook of motivation and cognition* (Vol.2). New York: Guilford Press.

Swazey, J.P. (1974). *Chlorpromazine in psychiatry: A study of therapeutic innovation.* Cambridge, MA: MIT Press.

Sweet, W.H., Ervin, F. & Mark, V.H. (1969). The relationship of violent behavior to focal cerebral disease. In S. Garattini & E. Sigg (Eds.), *Aggressive behavior.* New York: Wiley.

Swets, J.A. & Bjork, R.A. (1990). Enhancing human performance: An evaluation of 'new age' techniques considered by the U.S. Army. *Psychological Science,* 1, 85-96.

Swets, J.A. (1992). The science of choosing the right decision threshold in high-stakes diagnostics. *American Psychologist, 47,* 522-532.

Swift, W. J., Andrews, D. & Barklage, N.E. (1986). The relationship between affective disorders and eating disorders: A review of the literature. *American Journal of Psychiatry, 143,* 290-299.

Szasz, T.S. (1961). The myth of mental illness. New York: Harper & Row.

Szasz, T.S. (1977). *The manufacture of models.* New York: Dell

Szasz, T.S. (1979). *The myth of psychotherapy.* Garden City, NY: Doubleday.

T

Tajfel, H. (1970). Experiments in intergroup discrimination. *Scientific American, 223,* 96-102.

Tajfel, H. (1981). *Human groups and social categories.* Cambridge: Cambridge University Press.

Tajfel, H. (Ed.). (1982). *Social identity and intergroup relations.* New York: Cambridge University Press.

Tajfel, H. (Ed.) (1984). *The social dimension.* C.U.P. Maison des Sciences de l'Homme: Cambridge, Paris.

Tajfel, H. & Billig, M. (1974). Familiarity and categorization in intergroup behavior. *Journal of Experimental Social Psychology,* 10,159-170.

Tajfel, H., Flament, C., Billig, M.G. & Bundy, R.P (1971). Social categorisation and intergroup behaviour. *European Journal of Social Psychology,* 1, 149-78.

Tajfel, H. & Turner, J.C. (1979). An integrative theory of intergroup conflict. In W.C. Austin & S. Worchel (eds), *The Social Psychology of Intergroup Relations,* Monterey, Calif.: Brooks/Cole.

Talbot, J.D., Marrett, S., Evans, A.C., Meyer, E., Bushnell, M.C. & Duncan, G.H. (1991). Multiple representations of pain in the human cerebral cortex. *Science, 251,* 1355-1358.

Tannen, D. (1990). *You just don't understand. Women and men in conversation.* New York: William Morrow and Company.

Tanner, J.M. (1962). *Growth at adolescence* (2nd ed.). Oxford: Blackwell Scientific Publications.

Targ, R. & Harary, K. (1984). *The mind race: Understanding and using psychic abilities.* New York: Villaed Books.

Tarpy, R.M. *(1982). Principles of animal learning and motivation.* Glenview, IL: Scott, Foresman.

Tart, C.T. (1969). *Altered states of consciousness.* New York: Wiley.

Tart, C.T. (1971). *On being stoned: A psychological investigation of marijuana intoxication.* Palo Alto, CA: Science and Behavior Books.

Taylor, F.W. (1911). *Principles of scientific management.* New York: Harper & Row.

Taylor, S.E. (1980). The interface of cognitive and social psychology. In J.H. Harvey (Ed.), *Cognition, social behavior, and the environment* (pp. 189-211). Hillsdale, NJ: Erlbaum.

Taylor, S.E. (1981). A categorization approach to stereotyping. In D.L. Hamilton (Ed.), *Cognitive processes in stereotyping and intergroup behavior* (pp.88-114). Hillsdale, NJ: Erlbaum.

Taylor, S.E. (1982). The availability bias in social perception and interaction. In D. Kahneman, P. Slovic & A. Tversky (Eds.), *Judgment under uncertainty: Heuristics and biases* (pp.190-200). Cambridge: Cambridge University Press.

Taylor, S.E. (1986;1991). *Health psychology.* New York: Random House.

Taylor, S.E., (1989). *Positive Illusions, Creative Self-Deception and the Healthy Mind.* New York: Harper Collins.

Taylor, S. E. (1990). Health psychology: The science and the field. *American Psychologist, 45,* 1, 40-50.

Taylor, S.E. & Brown, J.D. (1988). Illusion and well-being: A social psychological perspective on mental health. *Psychological Bulletin, 103,* 193-210.

Taylor, S.E. & Clark, L.F. (1986). Does information improve adjustment to noxious events? In M.J. Saks & L. Saxe (Eds.), *Advances in applied social psychology* (Vol. 3, pp. 1-28). Hillsdale, NJ: Erlbaum.

Taylor, S.E., Crocker, J., Fiske, S.T., Sprinzen, M. & Winkler, J.D. (1979). The generalizability of salience effects. *Journal of Personality and Social Psychology,* 39.

Taylor, S.P., Vardaris, R.M., Rawtich, A.B., Gammon, C.B., Cranston, J.W. & Lubetkin, A.I. (1976). The effects of alcohol and delta-9-tetrahydrocannabinol on human physical aggression. *Aggressive Behavior,* 2, 153-161.

Taylor, W., Pearson, J., Mair, A. & Burns, W. (1965). Study of noise and heating in jute weaving. *Journal of the Acoustical Society of America,* 38, 113-120.

Teasdale, J.D. (1985). Psychological treatments for depression: How do they work? *Behavior Research and Therapy, 23,* 157-165.

Teitelbaum, P. (1966). The use of operant methods in the assessment and control of motivational states. In W.K. Honig (Ed.), *Operant behavior.* New York: Appleton-Century-Crofts.

Tellegen, A. & Atkinson, S. (1974). Openness to absorbing and self-altering experiences ('absorption'), a trait related to hypnosis. *Journal of Abnormal Psychology, 83,* 268-277.

Tellegen, A., Lykken, D.T., Bouchard, T.J., Wilcox, K.J., Segal, N.L. & Rich, S. (1988). Personality similarity in twins reared apart and together. *Journal of Personality and Social Psychology,* 54, 1031-1039.

Templin, M. (1957). Certain language skills in children: Their development and interrelationships. *Institute of Child Welfare Monograph,* Series No.26. Minnesota: University of Minnesota Press.

Tennant, L., Cullen, C. & Hattersley, J. (1981). Applied behaviour analysis: Intervention with retarded people. In G. Davey, (Ed.), *Applications of conditioning* theory. London: Methuen.

Tenopyr, M.L. & Oeltjen, P.D. (1982). Personnel selection and classification. *Annual Review of Psychology, 33,* 581-618.

Terman, L.M. (1916). *The measurement of intelligence.* Boston: Houghton-Mifflin.

Terman, L.M. & Merrill, M.A. (1937). *Measuring intelligence.* Boston: Houghton-Mifflin.

Terman, L.M. & Merrill, M.A. (1960). *The Stanford-Binet intelligence scale.* Boston: Houghton-Mifflin.

Terman, L.M. & Merrill, M. A. (1972). *Stanford-Binet intelligence scate-manualfor the third revision, Form L-M.* Boston: Houghton-Mifflin.

Terwee, S.J.S. (1990). *Hermeneutics in psychology and psychoanalysis.* Heidelberg/New York: Springer Verlag.

Thatcher, R.W., Walker, R.A. & Giudice, S.(1987). Human cerebral hemispheres develop at different rates and ages. *Science, 236,* 1110-1113.

Thayer, R.E. (1988). *The Biopsychology of Mood & Arousal.* Oxford: Oxford University Press.

Thienes-Hontos, P., Watson, C G. & Kucala, T. (1982). Stress-disorder symptoms in Vietnam and Korean War veterans. *Journal of Consulting and Clinical Psychology, 50,* 558-561.

Thigpen, C.H. & Cleckley, H.A. (1957). *Threefaces of Eve.* New York: McGraw-Hill.

Thomas, G. & O'Callaghan, M. (1981). Pavlovian principles and behaviour therapy. In G. Davey, (Ed.), *Applications of conditioning* theory. London: Methuen.

Thompson, D.A. & Campbell, R.G. (1977). Hunger in humans induced by 2-Deoxy-D-Glucose: Glucoprivic control of taste preference and food intake. *Science, 198,* 1065-1068.

Thompson, J.A. (1985). *Psychological aspects of nuclear war.* Chichester: The British Psychological Society & John Wiley & Sons Limited.

Thompson, K. (1988, Oct. 2). Fritz Perls. *San Francisco Examiner Chronicle,* This World Section, pp. 14-16.

Thompson, P. (1980). Margaret Thatcher: A new illusion. *Perception, 9,* 483-484.

Thompson, M.J. & Harsha, D.W. (1984, January). Our rhythms still follow the African sun. *Psychology Today,* pp. 50-54.

Thompson, R. (1990). In *Discovering Psychology,* Program 9 [PBS video series]. Washington, DC: Annenberg/CPB Project.

Thompson, R.F. (1972). Sensory preconditioning. In R.F. Thompson & J.F. Voss (Eds.), *Topics in learning and performance.* New York: Academic Press.

Thompson, R.F. (1975). *Introduction to physiological psychology.* New York: Harper & Row.

Thompson, R.F. (1984, February 4). Searching for memories: Where and how are they stored in your brain? *Stanford Daily.*

Thompson, R.F. (1986). The neurobiology of learning and memory. *Science, 233,* 941-944.

Thompson, R.F. (1987). The cerebellum and memory storage: A response to Bloedel. *Science, 238,* 1729-1730.

Thoresen, C. (1990, June 29). *Recurrent coronary prevention program: Results after eight and a half years.* Address given to First International Congress of Behavioral Medicine, Uppsala, Sweden.

Thoresen, C.E. & Eagleston, J.R. (1983). Chronic stress in children and adolescents [Special edition: Coping with stress]. *Theory into Practice, 22,* 48-56.

Thorndike, E.L. (1898) Animal intelligence. *Psychological Review Monograph Supplement, 2* (4, Whole No. 8).

Thorndike, E.L. (1911). *Animal intelligence.* New York: Macmillan.

Thorndyke, P.W. & Hayes-Roth, B. (1979). *Spatial knowledge acquisition from maps and navigation.* Paper presented at the Psychonomic Society Meeting, San Antonio, TX.

Thorne, B. & Luria, Z. (1986). Sexuality and gender in children's daily worlds. *Social Problems, 33,* 176-190.

Thornton, E.M. (1984). *The Freudian fallacy: An alternative view of Freudian theory.* New York: The Dial Press/Doubleday.

Tiefer, L. (1991). Historical, scientific, clinical, and feminist criticisms of 'The human response cycle' model. *Annual Review of Sex Research, 2,* 1-23.

Tillich, P. (1952). *The courage to be.* New Haven, CT: Yale University Press.

Timberlake, W. (1993). Animal behavior: A continuing synthesis. *Annual Review of Psychology, 44,* 675-708.

Timiras, P.S. (1978). Biological perspectives on aging. *American Scientist, 66,* 605-613.

Tipper, S.P. & Driver, J. (1988). Negative priming between pictures and words in a selective attention task: Evidence for semantic processing of ignored stimuli. *Memory and Cognition, 16,* 64-70.

Tolman, E.C. (1948). Cognitive maps in rats and men. *Psychological Review, 55,* 189-208.

Tolman, E.C. & Honzik, C.H. (1930). 'Insight' in rats. *University of California Publications in Psychology, 4,* 215-232.

Tomkins, S. (1962). *Affect, imagery, consciousness* (Vol. 1). New York: Springer.

Tomkins, S. (1981). The quest for primary motives: Biography and autobiography of an idea. *Journal of Personality and Social Psychology, 41,* 306-329.

Tompkins, R.D. (1981). *Before it's too late... : The prevention manual on drug abuse for people who care.* Englewood Cliffs, NJ: Family Information Center.

Torrey, E.F. (1990). In *Discovering Psychology,* Program 21 [PBS video series]. Washington, DC: Annenberg/CPB Program.

Tourangeau, R. & Ellsworth, P.C. (1979). The role of facial response in the experience of emotion. *Journal of Personality and Social Psychology, 37,* 1519-1531.

Trafimow, D., Triandis, H.C. and Goto, S.G. (1991). Some tests of the distinction between the private self and the collective self. *Journal of Personality and Social Psychology Bulletin,* 60, 649-55.

Tranel, D. & Damasio, A.R. (1985). Knowledge without awareness: An autonomic index of facial recognition by prosopagnosics. *Science, 228,* 1453-1454.

Treisman, A. (1960). Contextual cues in selective listening. *Quarterly Journal of Experimental Psychology,* 12, 242-248.

Treisman, A. (1986). Properties, parts and objects. In K. Boff, L. Kaufman, & J. Thomas (Eds.), *Handbook of perception and human performance, Vol.* 2. New York: Wiley.

Treisman, A. (1988). Features and objects: The fourteenth Bartlett Memorial Lecture. *The Quarterly Journal of Experimental Psychology, 40,* 201-237.

Treisman, A. & Gormican, S. (1988). Feature analysis in early vision: Evidence from search asymmetries. *Psychological Review, 95,* 15-48.

Treisman, A. & Sato, S. (1990). Conjunction search revisited. *Journal of Experimental Psychology: Human Perception and Performance, 16,* 459-478.

Treisman, A. & Souther, J. (1985). Search asymmetry: A diagnostic for preattentive processing of separable features. *Journal of Experimental Psychology: General,* 114, 285-310.

Treisman, U. (1989). *A study of mathematics performance of black students at the University of California, Berkeley.* Unpublished manuscript, Dana Center, University of California, Berkeley.

Triandis, H. (1990). Cross-cultural studies of individualism and collectivism. In J. Berman (Ed.), *Nebraska Symposium on Motivation,* 1989 (pp.42-133). Lincoln, NE: University of Nebraska Press.

Triandis, H.C., Bontempo, R., Villareal, M.J., Asai, M. & Lucca, N. (1988). Individualism and collectivism: Cross-cultural perspectives on self-ingroup relationships. *Journal of Personality and Social Psychology, 54,* 323-338.

Triandis, H.C. & Draguns, J.G. (Eds.). (1980). *Handbook of cross-culture psychology: Vol. 6, Psychopatholgy.* Boston: Allyn & Bacon.

Trinder, J. (1988), Subjective insomnia without objective findings: A pseudodiagnostic classification. *Psychological Bulletin, 103,* 87-94.

Triplett, N. (1897). The dynamagenic factors in pacemaking and competition. *American Journal of Psychology, 9,* 507-533.

Trivers, R.L. (1972). Parental investment and sexual selection, In B.

Campbell (Fd.), *Sexual selection and the descent of man* (pp. 139-179). Chicago: Aldine.

Trivers, R.L. (1983). The evolution of cooperation. In D.L. Bridgeman (Ed.), *The nature of pro-social behavior*. New York: Academic Press.

Troiden, P.R. (1989). The formation of homosexual identities. *Journal of Homosexuality, 17(1-2)*, 43-73.

Tronick, E., Als, H. & Brazelton, T.B. (1980). Moradic phases: A structural description analysis of infant-mother face to face Interaction. *Merrill-Palmer Quarterly 26*, 3-24.

Tronto, J. (1987). Beyond gender difference to a theory of care. SIGNS: *Journal of Women in Culture and Society, 12*, 644-663.

Trotter, R.J. (1987, February). Stop blaming yourself. *Psychology Today*, pp. 30-39.

Tryon, W.W. (1979). The test-trait fallacy. *American Psychologist*, 34,402-406.

Tsuang, M.T. & Vandermey, R. (1980). *Genes and the mind: Inheritance ofmental illness*. New York: Oxford University Press.

Tucker, O.M. (1981). Lateral brain functions, emotion, and conceptualization. *Psychological Bulletin, 89*, 19-46.

Tulving, E. (1972). Episodic and semantic memory. In E. Tulving & W. Donaldson (Eds.), *Organization of memory*. New York: Academic Press.

Tulving, E. (1983). *Elements of episodic memory*. Oxford: Clarendon Press.

Tulving, E. (1985). Memory and consciousness. *Canadian Psychology, 26*, 1-12.

Tulving, E. (1989). Remembering and knowing the past. *American Scientist, 77*, 361-367.

Tulving, E. & Pearlstone, Z. (1966). Availability versus accessibility of information in memory for words. *Journal of Verbal Learning and Verbal Behavior, 5*, 381-39 1.

Tulving, E. & Schacter, D.L. (1990). Priming and human memory systems. *Science, 247*, 301-306.

Tulving, E. & Thomson, D.M. (1973). Encoding specificity and retrieval processes in episodic memory. *Psychological Review*, 80,352-373.

Tupes, E.G. & Christal, R.C. (1961). *Recurrent personality factors based on trait ratings* (Tech. Rep. No. ASD-TR-61-97). Lackland Air Force Base, TX: U.S. Air Force.

Turing, A.M. (1950). Computing machinery and intelligence. *Mind, 59*, 433-460.

Turner, C., Anderson, P., Fitzpatrick, R., Fowler, G. & Mayon-White, R. (1988). Sexual behaviour, contraceptive practice and knowledge of AIDS of Oxford University students. *Journal of Biosocial Science*, 20, 445-51

Turner, J.C. (1991). *Social influence*. Milton Keynes: Open University Press.

Turner, J.C., Hogg, M.A., Oakes, P.J., Reicher, S.D. & Wetherell, M.S. (1987). *Rediscovering the social group: a self-categorization theory*. Oxford: Blackwell.

Turner, R.H. & Killian, L.M. (1972). *Collective behavior* (2nd ed.). Englewood Cliffs, NJ: Prentice-Hall.

Tversky, A. (1990). In *Discovering Psychology*, Program II [PBS video series]. Washington, DC: Annenberg/CPB Project.

Tversky, A. & Kahneman, D. (1973). Availability: A heuristic for judging frequency and probability. *Cognitive Psychology, 5*, 207-232.

Tversky, A. & Kahneman, D. (1980). Causal schemata in judgments under uncertainty. In M. Fishbein (Ed.), *Progress in social psychology*. Hillsdale, NJ: Erlbaum.

Tversky, A. & Kahneman, D. (1983). Extensional versus intuitive reasoning: The conjunction fallacy in probability judgment. *Psychological Review, 90*, 293-315.

Tversky, A. & Kahneman, D. (1986). Rational choice and the framing of decisions. *Journal of business, 59*, S25I-S278.

Tversky, B. (1981). Distortions in memory for maps. *Cognitive Psychology, 12*, 407-433.

Twain, M. [S.L. Clemens]. (1923). *Mark Twain's speeches*. New York: Harper & Row.

Tyler, L.E. (1965). *The psychology of human differences* (3rd ed.). New York: Appleton-Century-Crofts.

Tyler, L.E. (1974). *Individual differences*. Englewood Cliffs, NJ: Prentice-Hall.

Tyler, L. (1988). Mental testing. In E.R. Hilgard (Ed.), *Fifty years of psychology* (pp. 127-138). Glenview, [L: Scott, Foresman.

Tzeng, O.J.L. & Wang, W.S.Y. (1983). The first two R's. *American Scientist*, 71, 238-243.

U

U.S. Bureau of the Census. (1984). *Educational attainment in the United States: March 1981 and 1980* (Current Population Reports, Series P-20, No. 390). Washington, DC: U.S. Government Printing Office.

U.S. Bureau of the Census. (1985a). *Marital status and living arrangements: March 1984* (Current Population Reports, Series P-20, No. 399). Washington, DC: U.S. Government Printing Office.

U.S. Bureau of the Census. (1985b). *Statistical abstract of the United States: 1986* (106th ed.). Washington, DC: U.S. Government Printing Office.

U.S. Bureau of the Census. (1986a). *Demographic and socioeconomic aspects ofaging in the United States* (Current Population Reports, Series P-23, No. 138). Washington, DC: U.S. Government Printing Office.

U.S. Bureau of the Census. (1986b). *Money income and poverty status of families atid persons in the United States: 1985* (Current Population Report, Series P-60, No. 154). Washington, DC: U.S. Government Printing Office.

U.S. Bureau of the Census, (1991). *Statistical Abstracts of the United States*, (111th ed.). Washington D.C.: Government Printing Office.

U.S. Department of Health, Education and Welfare. (1979). *Healthy people: The Surgeon General's report on health promotion and disease prevention* (USPHS Publication No. 79-55071). Washington, DC: U.S. Government Printing Office.

U.S. National Center for Health Statistics. (1984). *Vital statistics of the United Slates*. Quoted in U.S. Department of Commerce, Bureau of the Census, Statistical Abstract of the United States. (104th ed.). Washington, DC: U.S. Government Printing Office.

U.S. Public Health Service. (1986). *Surgeon General's report on Acquired Immune Deficiency Syndrome*. Washington, DC: U.S. Government Printing Office.

U.S. Women Today (1983, Nov. 11-20). *The New York Times poll, reported in the International Herald Tribune*.

Ullmann, L.P. & Krasner, L. (1975). *Psychological approach to abnormal behavior* (2nd ed.). Englewood Cliffs, NJ: Prentice Hall.

Ullman, S. (1979). *The interpretation of visual motion*. Cambridge, MA: MIT Press.

Ultan, R. (1969). Some general characteristics of interrogative systems. *Working Papers in Language Universals, 1*, 41-63.

Underwood, B.J. (1948). Retroactive and preactive inhibition after five and forty-eight hours. *Journal of experimental Psychology, 38*, 28-38.

Underwood, B.J. (1949). Proactive inhibition as a function of time and degree of prior learning. *Journal of experimental Psychology, 39*, 24-34.

Unger, R. & Crawford, M. (1992). *Women and gender. A feminist psychology*. New York: McGraw-Hill.

United Press International. (1984, April 12). *Testimony of child molesting* [Press Release, Senate Judiciary Subcommittee hearings on Child Molesting, Washington, DC].

United Press International. (1990, September 4). In P. Shenon, Crisis of drugs remains top priority, Bush says. *The New York Times*, Section A, col. 4, p. 22, Sept. 6, 1990.

United Press International. (1990, September 5). Lest we forget that drug crisis – small signs of progress, but still lots to do. *Los Angeles Times*, Section B, p. 6.

V

Vaillant, G.E. (1977). *Adaptation to Life*. Boston: Little, Brown.

Valenstein, E.S. (Ed.). (1980). *The psychosurgery debate*. New York: Freeman.

Valle, V.A. & Frieze, I.H. (1976). Stability of causal attributions as a mediator in changing expectations for success. *Journal of Personality and Social Psychology, 33*, 579-587.

Van de Poll, N.E. & Van Goozen, S.H.M. (1992). Hypothalamic involvement in sexuality and hostility: comparative psychological aspects. In D.F. Swaab, M.A. Hofman, M. Mirmiran, R. Ravid & F.W. van Leeuwen (Eds.), *The human hypothalamus in health and disease – Progress in brain research Volume 93* (pp. 343-361). Amsterdam: Elsevier Science Publishers.

Van der Heijden, A.H.C. (1990). Visual information processing and selection. In: O. Neumann & W. Prinz (Eds.), *Relationships between perception and action*. Berlin, Heidelberg: Springer.

Van der Heijden, A.H.C. (1992). *Selective attention in vision.* London/New York: Routledge.

Van der Veer, R. & Valsiner, J. (1991). *Understanding Vygotsky. A quest for synthesis.* Oxford: Blackwell.

Van Eeden, R. (1913). A study of dreams. *Proceedings of the society for psychical research, 26,* 431-461.

Van Geert, P. (1994). *Dynamic systems of development. Change between complexity and chaos.* New York: Harvester Wheatsheaf.

Van Geert, P. & Mos, L. (1990). *Annals of Theoretical Psychology: Developmental Psychology.* New York: Plenum.

Van Wagener, W. & Herren, R. (1940). Surgical division of commissural pathways in the corpus callosum. *Archives of Neurology and Psychiatry, 44,* 740-759.

Vaughan, E. (1977). Misconceptions about psychology among introductory psychology students. *Teaching of Psychology, 41* 138-141.

Venn, A.J. & Guest, C.S. (1991). Chronic morbidity of former prisoners of war and other Australian veterans. *Medical Journal of Australia, 155,* 10, 705-707.

Vernon, P.E. (1987). The demise of the Stanford-Binet Scale. *Canadian Psychology, 28,* 251-258.

Vivano, F. (1989, October 8). When success is a family prize. *San Francisco Examiner-Chronicle,* This World Section, pp. 7-9.

Vogel, F. & Motulsky, A.G. (1982). *Human genetics.* New York: Springer-Verlag.

Volberg, A. (1994). The prevalence and demographics of pathological gamblers: Implications for public health. *American Journal of Public Health, 84(2),* 237-241.

Von Békésy, G. (1960). *Experiments in hearing.* New York: McGraw-Hill.

Von Békésy, G. (1961). Concerning the fundamental component of periodic pulse patterns and modulated vibrations observed in the cochlear model with nerve supply. *Journal of the Acoustical Society of America, 33,* 888-896.

Von Helmholtz, H. (1962), Treatise on physiological optics (Vol. 31 J. P. Southall, Ed. and Trans.). New York: Dover Press. (Original work published 1866).

Von Hofsten, C., & Lindhagen, K. (1979). Observations on the development of reaching for moving objects. *Journal of Child Psychology, 28,* 158-173.

Von Restorff, H. (1933).Über die Wirkung von Bereichsbildungen im Spurenfeld. In W. Köhler & H. von Restorff, Analyse von Vorgänen im Spurenfeld, I. *Psychologische Forschung, 18,* 299-342.

Von Wright, J.M., Anderson, K. & Stenham, U. (1975). Generalization of conditioned GSRs in dichotic listening. In P.M.A. Rabbit & S. Dornic (Eds.), *Attention and performance* (pp. 194-204). New York: Academic Press.

Vonnegut, M. (1975). *The Eden express.* New York: Bantam.

Vygotsky, L.S. (1978). *Mind in society. The development of higher psychological processes.* Cambridge, Mass.: Harvard University Press.

Vygotsky, L.S. (1987). Thinking and speech. In *The collected works of L.S. Vygotsky, Volume 1* (pp. 39-285). New York: Plenum Press.

W

Wagenaar, W.A. (1986). My memory: A study of autobiographical memory over six years. *Cognitive Psychology, 18,* 225-252.

Wagenaar, W.A. (1988). *Identifying Ivan. A case study in legal psychology.* London: Harvester Wheatsheaf.

Wagenaar, W.A. (1992). Remembering my worst sins: How autobiographical memory serves the updating of the conceptual self. In M.A. Conway, D.C. Rubin, H. Spinnler & W.A. Wagenaar (Eds.), *Theoretical perspectives on autobiographical memory* (pp. 263-274). Dordrecht: Kluwer Academic Publishers.

Wahba, M. A. & Bridwell, L.G. (1976). Maslow reconsidered: A review of research in the need hierarchy theory. *Organizational Behavior and Human Performance, 15,* 212-240.

Waldron, I. (1976, March). Why do women live longer than men? *Journal of Human Stress,* 2-13.

Waldron, T.P. (1985). *Principles of language and mind: An evolutionary theory of meaning.* Boston: Routledge and Kegan Paul.

Waldrop, M.M. (1984). Artificial intelligence: I, Into the world (research news). *Science, 223,* 802-805.

Waldvogel, S. (1948). The frequency and affective character of childhood memories. *Psychological Monographs, 62* (Whole No. 291).

Walker, B.B. & Sandman, C.A. (1977). Physiological response patterns in ulcer patients: Phasic and tonic components of the electrogastrogram. *Psychophysiology,* 14, 393-400.

Walker, L. (1984). Sex differences in the development of moral reasoning: A critical review. *Child Development, 55,* 667-691.

Wallach, M.A. & Wallach, L. (1983). *Psychology's sanction for selfishness.* San Francisco: Freeman.

Waller, J.H. (1971) Achievement and social mobility: Relationships among IQ score, education, and occupation in two generations. *Social Biology, 18,* 252-259.

Wallis, C. (1984, June 11). Unlocking pain's secrets. *Time,* pp. 58-66.

Walsh, R.N. & Vaughan, F. (Eds.). (1980). *Beyond ego: Transpersonal dimensions in psychology.* Los Angeles: Torcher.

Walters, C.C. & Grusec, J.E. (1977). *Punishment.* San Francisco: Freeman.

Walters, R.G. (1974). *Primers for prudery: Sexual advice to Victorian America.* Englewood Cliffs, NJ: Prentice-Hall.

Walton, R.E. (1977). Successful strategies for diffusing work innovations. *Journal of Contemporary Business, 6,* 1-22.

Wanous, J.P. (1980). *Organizational entry: Recruitment, selection, and socialization of newcomers.* Reading, MA: Addison-Wesley.

Ward, W.C., Kogan, N. & Pankove, E. (1972). Incentive effects in children's creativity. *Child Development, 43(2),* 669-676.

Warden, C.J. (1931). *Animal motivation: Experimental studies on the albino rat.* New York: Columbia University Press.

Wardle, J. (1994). Disorders of eating & weight: Investigation; Treatment. In S.J.E. Lindsay & G.E. Powell (Eds.), *Handbook of clinical adult psychology, 2nd edition* (pp.514-561). London: Routledge.

Warren, R.M. & Warren, R.P. (1970). Auditory illusions and confusions. *Scientific American, 223,* 30-36.

Warshaw, L. (1979). *Managing stress.* Reading, MA: Addison-Wesley.

Wason, P.C. (1966). Reasoning. In B.M. Foss (Ed.), *New horizons in psychology, Volume 1* (pp. 135-151). Harmondsworth: Penguin Books.

Wason, P.C. & Shapiro, D. (1971). Natural and contrived experience in reasoning problems. *Quarterly Journal of Experimental Psychology, 23,* 63-71.

Wasser, S.K. (1990). Infertility, abortion, and biotechnology: When it's not nice to fool mother nature. *Human Nature, 1,* 3-24.

Wasserman, E.A., Elek, S.M., Chatlosh, D.L. & Baker, A.G. (1993). Rating causal relations: The role of probability in judgements of response-outcome contingency. *Journal of Experimental Psychology: Learning and Motivation, 14,* 406-432.

Watkins, L.R. & Mayer, D.J. (1982). Organization of the endogenous opiate and nonopiate pain control systems. *Science,* 216, 1185-1193.

Watson, J.B. (1913). Psychology as the behaviorist views it. *Psychological Review, 20,* 158-177.

Watson, J.B. (1919). *Psychology from the standpoint of a behaviorist.* Philadelphia: Lippincott.

Watson, J.B. (1926). *Behaviorism.* New York: Norton.

Watson, J.B. (1930). *Behaviorism.* New York: Norton.

Watson, J.B. & Rayner, R. (1920). Conditioned emotional reactions. *Journal of Experimental Psychology, 3,* 1-14.

Weakland, J.H., Fish, R., Watzlawick, P. & Bodin, A.M. (1974). Brief therapy: Focused problem resolution. *Family Process, 13,* 141-168.

Weaver, C.A. III. (1993). Do you need a 'flash' to form a flashbulb memory? *Journal of Experimental Psychology: General, 122,* 39-46.

Weber, E. H. (1834). *De pulsu, resorptione, auditu et tactu: Annotationes anatomical et physiological.* Leipzig: Koehler.

Weber, M. (1958). *The Protestant ethic and the spirit of capitalism* (T. Parsons, Trans.). New York: Scribners. (Original work published 1904-1905).

Webb, W.B. (1974). Sleep as an adaptive response. *Perceptual and Motor Skills, 38,* 1023-1027.

Webb, W.B. (1981). The return of consciousness. In L.T. Benjamin, Jr. (Ed.), *The G. Stanley Hall Lecture Series, 100* (Vol. 1), pp. 133-152. Washington, DC: American Psychological Association.

Wechsler, D. (1974). *Wechsler intelligence scale for children – revised.* New York: Psychological Corp.

Wechsler, D. (1981). *Manual of the Wechsler Adult Intelligence Scale – revised.* New York: Psychological Corp.

Weick, K.E. (1984). Small wins: Redefining the scale of social problems. *American Psychologist, 39,* 40-49.

Weigel, R.H. & Newman, L.S. (1976). Increasing attitude behavior correspondence by broadening the scope of the behavioral measure. *Journal of Personality and Social Psychology, 33,* 793-802.

Weil, A.T. (1977). The marriage of the sun and the moon. In N.E.

Zinberg (Ed.), *Alternate states of consciousness* (pp. 37-52). New York: Free Press.

Weinberger, M., Hiner, S.L. & Tierney, W.M. (1987). In support of hassles as a measure of stress in predicting health outcomes. *Journal of Behavioral Medicine, 10*, 19-31.

Weiner, B. (1980). *Human motivation.* New York: Holt, Rinehart & Winston.

Weiner, B. (1985). An attributional theory of achievement motivation and emotion. *Psychological Review, 92*, 548-573.

Weiner, B. (1986). *An attributional theory of motivation and emotion.* New York: Springer-Verlag.

Weiner, B., Frieze, I., Kukla, A., Reed, L., Rest, S. & Rosenbaum, R.M. (1971). Perceiving the causes of success and failure. In E.E. Jones et al. (Eds,), *Attribution: Perceiving the causes of Behavior.* Morristown, NJ: General Learning Press.

Weiner, B., Russell, D. & Lerman, D. (1978). Affective consequences of causal ascriptions. In J.H. Harvey, W.J. Ickes & R.F. Kidd (Eds.), *New directions in attribution research (Vol. 2).* Hillsdale, NJ: Erlbaum.

Weiner, M.J. & Wright, F.E. (1973). Effects of undergoing arbitrary discrimination upon subsequent attitudes toward a minority group. *Journal of applied Social Psychology, 3*, 94-102.

Weins, A.N. & Matarazzo, J.D. (1983). Diagnostic interviewing. In M. Hersen, A.E. Kazdin & A.S., Bellack (Eds.), *The clinical psychology handbook* (pp. 309-328). New York: Pergamon.

Weinstein, N.D. (1982). Community noise problems: Evidence against adaptation. *Journal of Environmental Psychology, 2*, 87-97.

Weinstein, N.D. (1980). Unrealistic optimism about future life events. *Journal of Personality and Social Psychology, 39*, 806-820.

Weinstein, N.D. (1990a). Optimistic biases and personal risks. *Science, 246*, 1232-1233.

Weinstein, N.D. (1990b). Determinants of self-protective behavior: Home radon testing. *Journal of Applied Social Psychology, 20*, 783-801.

Weisenberg, M. (1977). Cultural and racial reactions to pain. In M. Weisenberg (Ed.), *The control of pain.* New York: Psychological Dimensions.

Weiss, B. & Laties, V.G. (1962). Enhancement of human performance by caffeine and amphetamines. *Pharmacological Review, 14*, 1-27.

Weiss, P. (1991, April). The sexual revolution: Sexual politics on campus: A case study. *Harper's Magazine*, pp. 58-72.

Weiss, R.S. (1973). *Loneliness: The experience of emotional and social isolation.* Cambridge, MA: MIT Press.

Weiss, R.S. (1987). Reflections on the present state of loneliness research. *Journal of Behavior and Personality, 2(2)*, 1-16.

Weiss, R.F., Buchanan, W., Alstatt, L. & Lombards, J.P. (1971). Altruism is rewarding. *Science, 171*, 1262-1263.

Weissman, M.M., Prusoff, B.A., DiMascio, A., Neu, C., Goklaney, M. & Kierinan, G.L. (1979). The efficacy of drugs and psychotherapy in the treatment of acute depressive episodes. *American Journal of Psychiatry, 136*, 555-558.

Weissman, W.W. (1987). Advances in psychiatric epidemiology: Rates and risks for depression. *American Journal of Public Health, 77*, 445-451.

Weisstein, N. (1968). *Kinder, Kirche, Kuche as scientific law: Psychology constructs the female.* Boston: New England Free Press.

Welker, R.L. & Wheatley, K.L. (1977). Differential acquisition of conditioned suppression in rats with increased and decreased luminance levels as CS+S. *Learning and Motivation, 8*, 247-262.

Wellings, K., Field, J., Johnson, A.M. & Wadsworth, J. (1994). Sexual behaviour in Britain: the national survey of sexual attitudes and lifestyles. London: Penguin.

Wellman, H.M. (1990). *The child's theory of mind.* Cambridge MA: MIT Press.

Wellman, H.M. & Estes, D. (1986). Early understanding of mental entities: A reexamination of childhood realism. *Child Development, 57(4)*, 910-923.

Wellman, H.M. & Gelman, S.A. (1992). Cognitive development: foundational theories of care domains. *Annual Review of Psychology, 43*, 337-375.

Welner, A., Reish, T., Robbins, I., Fishman, R. & van Doren, T. (1976). Obsessive-compulsive neurosis. *Comprehensive Psychiatry, 17*, 527-539.

Wender, P.H. (1972). Adopted children and their families in the evaluation of nature-nurture interactions in the schizophrenic disorders. *Annual Review of Medicine, 23*, 255-372.

Werker, J.D. & Lalonde, C.E. (1988). Cross-language speech

perception: Initial capabilities and developmental change. *Developmental Psychology, 24(5)*, 672-683.

Werker, J.F. & Pegg, J.E. (1992). Infant speech perception and phonological acquisition. In C.A. Ferguson, L. Menn & C. Stoel-Gammon (Eds.), *Phonological development. Models research and implications* (pp. 285-311). Timonium, MD: York Press.

Werner, D. (1979). A cross-cultural perspective on theory and research on male homosexuality. *Journal of Homosexuality, 41* 345-361.

Wertheimer, M. (1923). Untersuchungen zur lehre von der gestalt, II. *Psychologische Forschung, 4*, 301-350.

Wertsch, J.V. (1979). From social interaction to higher psychological processes: A clarification and application of Vygotsky's theory. *Human Development, 22*, 1-22.

Wertsch, J.V. (1985). *Vygotsky and the social formation of mind.* Cambridge, MA: Cambridge University Press.

Wertsch, J.V., McNamee, G.D., McLane, J.G. & Budwig, N.A. (1980). The adult-child dyad as a problem solving system. *Child Development, 51*, 1215-1221.

Wertsch, J.V. & Stone, C.A. (1985). The concept of internalization in Vygotsky's account of the genesis of higher mental functions. In J.V. Wertsch (Ed.), *Culture, communication, and cognition: Vygotskian perspectives* (pp. 162-179). New York: Cambridge University Press.

Wertsch, J.V. & Tulviste, P. (1992). L.S. Vygotsky and contemporary developmental psychology. *Developmental Psychology, 28*, 548-557.

Wetherell, M. & Potter, J. (1989). Narrative characters and accounting for violence. In J. Shotter & K. Gergen (Eds.) *Texts of Identity* (pp.206-219). Newbury Park, CA: Sage

Wever, E. G. (1949). *Theory of hearing.* New York: Wiley.

Wever, R.A. (1979). *The circadian system of man: Results of experiments under temporal isolation.* New York: Springer Verlag.

Weyler, J. (1984, September 11). An unforgettable moment: It's one Gabfiele wishes she could forget. *Los Angeles Times*, Part III, PP1, 10.

Whalen, R., & Simon, N. G. (1984). Biological motivation. *Annual Review of Psychology, 35*, 257-276.

Whitbourne, S.K. & Hulicka, I.M. (1990). Ageism in undergraduate psychology texts. *American Psychologist, 45*, 1127-1136.

White, B.W., Saunders, F.A., Scadden, L., Bach-Y-Rita, P. & Collins, C.C. (1970). Seeing with the skin. *Perception & Psychophysics, 7(J)*, 23-27.

White, G.L., Fishbein, S. & Rutstein, J. (1981). Passionate love and the misattribution of arousal. *Journal of Personality and Social Psychology, 41*, 56-62.

White, M.D. & White, C A. (1981). Involuntarily committed patients' constitutional right to refuse treatment. *American Psychologist, 36*, 953-962.

White, R.K. (1952). *Lives in progress.* New York: Dryden Press.

White, R.W. (1959). Motivation reconsidered. The concept of competence. *Psychological Review, 66*, 297-333.

Whorf, B.L. (1956). *Language, thought and reality.* Cambridge, MA: MIT Press.

Whyte, W.F. (1943). *Streetcorner society: the social structure of an Italian slum.* Chicago: University of Chicago Press.

Wicklund, R.A. & Brehm, J.W. (1976). *Perspectives on cognitive dissonance.* Hillsdale, NJ: Erlbaum.

Widrow, B. & Hoff, M.E. (1960). *Adaptive switching circuits.* IRE WESCON Convention Record, Pt. 4, 96-104.

Wiebe, D.J. (1991). Hardiness and stress modification: A test of proposed mechanisms. *Journal of Personality and Social Psychology, 60*, 89-99.

Wiener, M. (1989). Psychopathology reconsidered: depressions interpreted as psychosocial transactions. *Clinical Psychology Review, 9*, 295-321.

Wiggins, J.S. & Pincus, A.L. (1992). Personality: Structure and assessment. *Annual Review of Psychology, 43*, 473-504.

Wilcoxon, H.G., Dragoin, W.B. & Kral, P.A. (1971). Illness induced aversions in rat and quail: Relative salience of visual and gustatory cues. *Science, 171*, 826-828.

Wilder, D.A. (1986). Social categorization: Implications for creation and reduction of intergroup bias. *Advances in Experimental Social Psychology, 19*, 291-355.

Wilkinson, S. (Ed.)(1986). *Feminist social psychology. Developing theory and practice.* Milton Keynes: Open University Press.

Williams, J.H. (1983). *The psychology of women* (2nd ed.). New York: Norton.

Williams, J.B.W. & Spitzer, R.L. (1983). The issue of sex bias in

DSM-III. *American Psychologist, 38,* 793-798.

Williams, T. (1989, Spring). Attitudes toward wildlife in 2049 A.D. *Orion Nature Quarterly,* pp. 28-33.

Wills, T.A. (1986). Stress and coping in early adolescence: relationships to substance use in urban school samples. *Health Psychology, 5,* 503-529.

Wilson, E.D., Reeves, A. & Culver, C. (1977). Cerebral commissurotomy for control of intractable seizures. *Neurology, 27,* 708-715.

Wilson, E.O. (1973). The natural history of lions. *Science, 179,* 466-467.

Wilson, J.P. (1980) Conflict, stress and growth: The effects of war on the psychosocial development of Vietnam veterans. In C.R. Figley & S. Leventman (Eds.), *Strangers at home: Vietnam veterans since the war* (pp. 123-165). New York: Praeger.

Wilson, T.D. & Lassiter, G.D. (1982). Increasing intrinsic interest with superfluous extrinsic constraints. *Journal of Personality and Social Psychology, 42,* 811-819.

Wilson, M. (1959). *Communal rituals among the Nyakusa.* London: Oxford University Press.

Wing, C.W. & Wallach, M.A. (1971). *College admissions and the psychology of talent.* New York: Holt, Rinehart & Winston.

Wingerson, L. (1990). *Mapping our genes.* New York: Dutton.

Winfield, A. & Byrnes, D.L. (1981). *The psychology of human memory.* New York: Academic Press.

Winning through intimidation. (1987, August 31). *U.S. News and World Report.*

Winter, D.A. (1992). *Personal construct psychology in clinical practice: Theory, research and applications.* London: Routledge.

Winton, W.M., Putnam, L.E. & Krauss, R.M. (1984). Facial and autonomic manifestations of the dimensional structure of emotions. *Journal of Experimental Social Psychology, 20,* 196-216.

Wintrob, R.M. (1973). The influence of others; Witchcraft and rootwork as explanations of behavior disturbances. *Journal of Nervous and Mental Diseases, 156,* 318-326.

Wise, S.P. & Desimone, R. (1988). Behavioral neurophysiology: Insights into seeing and grasping. *Science, 242,* 736-740.

Wispé, L.G. & Drambarean, N.C. (1953). Physiological need, word frequency and visual duration threshold. *Journal of Experimental Psychology, 46,* 25-31.

Witkin, H.A., Dyk, R.B., Faterson, H.F., Goodenough, D.R. & Karp, S.A. (1962). *Psychological differentiation.* New York: Wiley.

Witkin, H.A. & Goodenough, D.R. (1977). Field dependence and interpersonal behavior. *Psychological Bulletin, 84,* 661-689.

Witkin, H.A., Moore, C.A., Goodenough, D.R. & Cox, P.W. (1977). Field-dependent and field-independent cognitive styles and their educational implications. *Review of Educational Research, 47,* 1-64.

Witkin-Lanoil, G. (1988). *The male stress syndrome: How to recognize and live with it.* New York: Newmarket Press.

Wittgenstein, L.J.J. (1953). *Philosophical investigations.* Blackwell: Oxford.

Wolf, M., Risley, T. & Mees, H. (1964). Application of operant conditioning procedures to the behavior problems of an autistic child. *Behavior Research and Therapy, 1,* 305-312.

Wolitzky, D.L. & Wachtel, P.L. (1973). Personality and perception. In B.J. Wolman (Ed.), *Handbook of general psychology* (pp. 826-857). Englewood Cliffs, NJ: Prentice-Hall.

Wolman, C. (1975). Therapy and capitalism. *Issues in Radical Therapy, 3(1).*

Wolpe, J. (1958). *Psychotherapy by reciprocal inhibition.* Stanford, CA: Stanford University Press.

Wolpe, J. (1973). *The practice of behavior therapy* (2nd ed.). New York: Pergamon.

Woodruf-Pak, D.S. & Thompson, R.F. (1988). Cerebeller correlates of classical conditioning across the life span. In P.B. Baltes, D.M. Featherman & R.M. Learner (Eds.), *Life span development and behavior* (Vol. 9, pp. 1-37). Hillsdale, NJ: Erlbaum.

Woods, D.L., Hillyard, S.A., Courchesne, E. & Galambos, R. (1980). Electrophysiological signs of split-second decision making. *Science, 207,* 655-657.

Woodworth, R.S. & Schlossberg, H. (1954). *Experimental psychology* (Rev. ed.). New York: Holt.

Woolridge, D.E. (1963). *The machinery of the brain.* New York: McGraw-Hill.

Workman, B. (1990, December 1). Father guilty of killing daughter's tend in '69. *San Francisco Examiner-Chronicle,* pp. 1, 4.

World Health Organization. (1973). The international pilot study of schizophrenia. Geneva: WHO.

World Health Organization. (1979) *Schizophrenia: An international follow-up study.* Chichester: Wiley.

World Health Organization. (1992). *The ICD-10 classification of mental and behavioural disorders: Clinical descriptions and diagnostic guidelines.* Geneva: World Health Organization.

World Health Organisation. (1993). *Health for All Indicators,* Copenhagen: Regional Office for Europe.

World Health Organisation, (1994). AIDS: Global data – the current global situation of the HIV/AIDS pandemic. *WHO Weekly epidemiological record,* Geneva, Vol. 69, No. 26, 189-192.

Wortman, C.B. & Dunkel-Schetter, C. (1979). Interpersonal relationships and cancer: A theoretical analysis. *Journal of Social Issues, 35,* 120-155.

Wright, J.C. & Mischel, W. (1987). A conditional approach to dispositional constructs: The local predictability of social behaviour. *Journal of Personality and Social Psychology, 53(6),* 1159-1177.

Wundt, W. (1907). *Outlines of psychology* (7th ed., C.H. Judd, Trans.). Leipzig: Englemann. (Original work published 1896).

Wyer, R.S. & Carlston, D.E. (1979). *Social cognition, inference and attribution.* Hillsdale, N.J.: Erlbaum.

Wynne, L.C., Roohey, M.L. & Doane, J. (1979). Family studies. In L. Bellak (Ed.), *The schizophrenic syndrome.* New York: Basic Books.

Y

Yalom, I.D. (1989). *Love's executioner and other tales of psychotherapy.* London: Penguin.

Yalom, I.D. & Greaves, C. (1977). Group therapy with the terminally ill. *American Journal of Psychiatry, 134,* 396-400.

Yang, K.S. (1986). Chinese personality and its change. In M.H. Bond (Ed.), *The psychology of the Chinese people* (pp. 106-170). Oxford: Oxford University Press.

Yates, B. (1985). *Self-management.* Belmont, CA: Wadsworth.

Yates, B.T. (1980). *Improving effectiveness and reducing costs in mental health.* Springfield, IL: Charles C Thomas.

Yates, F.A. (1966). *The art of memory.* London: Routledge and Kegan Paul.

Yeltsin says KGB unit refused plotter's orders to seize him. (1991, August 26). *San Francisco Examiner-Chronicle,* p. A 10.

Yerkes, R.M. (1921). Psychological examining in the United States Army. In R.M. Yerkes (Ed.), *Memoirs of the National Academy of Sciences: Vol. 15.* Washington, DC: U.S. Government Printing Office.

Yerkes, R.M. & Dodson, J.D. (1908). The relation of strength of stimulus to rapidity of habit formation. *Journal of Comparative Neurology and Psychology, 18,* 459-482.

Young, P.T. (1961). *Motivation and emotion.* New York: Wiley.

Young, T. (1807). On the theory of light and colours. In *Lectures in natural philosophy* (Vol. 2, pp. 613-632). London: William Savage.

Yudkin, M. (1984, April). When kids think the unthinkable. *Psychology Today,* pp. 18-20, 24-25.

Z

Zadeh, L.A. (1965). Fuzzy sets. *Information Control, 8,* 338-353.

Zahn-Waxler, C. & Radke-Yarrow, M. (1982). The development of altruism: Alternative research strategies. In N. Eisenberg-Berg (Ed.), *The development of presocial behavior* (pp. 109-138). New York: Academic Press.

Zajonc, R.B. (1968). Attitudinal effects of mere exposure. *Journal of Personality and Social Psychology, Monograph Supplement, 9* (2, Part 2), 1-27.

Zajonc, R.B. (1976). Family configuration and intelligence. *Science, 192,* 226-236.

Zajonc, R.B. (1980). Feeling and thinking: Preferences need no inferences. *American Psychologist, 35,* 151-175.

Zajonc, R.B. (1984). On the primacy of affect. *American Psychologist, 39,* 117-129.

Zajonc, R.B., Murphy, S.T. & Inglehart, M. (1989). Feeling and facial efference: implications of the vascular theory of emotion. *Psychological Review, 96,* 395-416.

Zammuner, V.L. (1991). Strategies in discourse production: Computational models. In G. Dehiere & J.P. Rossi (Eds.), *Text and text processing* (pp 387-402). Amsterdam: North-Holland.

Zanchetti, A. (1967). Subcortical and cortical mechanisms in arousal and emotional behavior. In G.C. Quarton, T. Melnechuk & F. O. Schmitt (Fds.), *The neurosciences: A study program*. New York: Rockefeller University Press.

Zborowski, M. (1969). *People in pain*. San Francisco: Jossey-Bass.

Zeigarnik, B. (1927). Uber das leehalten von Eriedigten und unerleighten Handbegen. *Psycholische Forschung*, 9, 1-85 [Classic research on task tensions from uncompleted tasks].

Zelnik, M., Kim, Y.J. & Kantner, J.F. (1979). Probabilities of intercourse and conception among U.S. teenage women, 1971-1976. *Family Planning Perspectives, II,* 177-183.

Zessen, G. van & Sandfort, T. (1991). *Seksualiteit in Nederland [Sexuality in the Netherlands]*. Amsterdam/Lisse: Swets & Zeitlinger.

Zettle, R.D. (1990). Rule-governed behavior: A radical behavioral answer to the cognitive challenge. *The Psychological Record. 40,* 41-49.

Zilboorg, G. & Henry, G.W. (1941). *A history of medical psychology*. New York: Norton.

Zimbardo, P.G. (1970). The human choice: Individuation, reason and order versus deindividuation, impulse, and chaos. In W.J. Arnold & D. Levine (Eds.), *Nebraska Symposium on Motivation,* 1969. Lincoln, NE: University of Nebraska Press.

Zimbardo, P.G. (1975). On transforming experimental research into advocacy for social change. In M. Deutsch & H. Hornstein (Eds.). *Applying social psychology: Implications for research, practice and training*. Hillsdale, NJ: Erlbaum.

Zimbardo, P.G. (1990). *Shyness: What it is, what to do about it* (Rev.ed.). Reading, MA: Addison-Wesley. (Original book published 1977.)

Zimbardo, P.G., Andersen, S.M. & Kabat, L.G. (1981). Induced hearing deficit generates experimental paranoia. *Science, 212,* 1529-1531.

Zimbardo, P.G. & Leippe, M. (1991). *The psychology of attitude change and social influence*. New York: McGraw-Hill.

Zimbardo, P.G. & Montgomery, K.D. (1957). The relative strengths of consummatory responses in bunger, thirst, and exploratory drive. *Journal of Comparative and Physiological Psychology, 50,* 504-508.

Zimbardo, P.G. & Radl, S. (1981). *The shy child*. New York: McGraw-Hill.

Zimmerman, D.H. & West, C. (1975). Sex roles, interruptions and silences in conversation. In B. Thorne & N. Henley (Eds.), *Language and sex: Differences and dominance* (pp. 105-129). Rowley, MA: Newbury House.

Zola, I.K. (1973). Pathways to the doctor-from person to patient. *Social Science and Medicine, 7,* 677-689.

Zubek, J.P. (Ed.) (1969). *Sensory deprivation*. New York: Appleton-Century-Crofts.

Zubeck, J.P., Pushkar, D., Sansom, W. & Gowing, J. (1961). Perceptual changes after prolonged sensory isolation (darkness and silence). *Canadian Journal of Psychology, 15,* 83-100.

Zucker, R.S. & Lando, L. (1986). Mechanism of transmitter release: Voltage hypothesis and calcium hypothesis. *Science, 231,* 574-579.

Zuckerman, M. (1979). Sensation seeking and risk taking. In C.E. Izard (Ed.), *Emotions in personality and psychopathology*. New York: Plenum.

Zuckerman, M. (1984). Sensation seeking: a comparative approach to a human trait. *The Behavioral and Brain Sciences, 7,* 413-471.

Zuckerman, M. (1990). Some dubious premises in research and theory on racial differences: Scientific, social and ethical issues. *American Psychologist, 45,* 1297-1303.

Zuckerman, M. (1991). *Psychobiology of personality*. Cambridge: Cambridge University Press.

Zuckerman, M. & Wheeler, L. (1975). To dispel fantasies about the fantasy-based measure of fear of success. *Psychological Bulletin, 82,* 932-946.

ACKNOWLEDGMENTS

PHOTOGRAPH CREDITS

Unless otherwise acknowledged, all photographs are the property of Scott, Foresman. Page abbreviations are as follows: T—top, C—centre, B—bottom, L—left, R—right.

Chapter One

3	Associated Press
10	Rex Features
27	Rich Friedman/Black Star
31	Christopher Springmann
34	Jeff Albertson/The Picture Cube
35	Tony Stone Images

Chapter Two

41	Tony Stone Images
43	By permission of the Darwin Museum, Down House
47	Omikron/SS/Photo Researchers
49	Giraudon/Art Resource, NY
50	Tony Stone Images
51	Warren Anatomical Museum, Harvard University Medical School
53T	Dan McCoy/Rainbow
53B	Steven E. Petersen, Washington University School of Medicine, St Louis
54	Dan McCoy/Rainbow
74	Jim Pickerell/Tony Stone Worldwide

Chapter Three

87	Tony Stone Images
88	John W. Verano/National Museum of Natural History/Smithsonian Institution
93R	From *Mind Sights* by Roger N. Shepard. Copyright 1990 by Roger N. Shepard. Reprinted with permission of W.H. Freeman and Company.
95	Reprinted (abstracted/excerpted) with permission from Vol.239, Jan.8, 1988, p.163/*Science*. Copyright 1995 American Association for the Advancement of Science.
96	Endel Tulving, American Scientist, July–Aug. 1989, p.365, Photo: Dr David Bryant, Northeastern University, Boston.
98	Copyright 1977 J. Allan Hobson and Hoffman-La Roche Inc./Courtesy DREAMSTAGE.
107	Tony Stone Images
109	P. Chock/Stock Boston
111	R.D.Ullman

Chapter Four

117	D.McKay
119	Bibliothèque Nationale
120	Courtesy Dr. Lew Lipsitt
122	From A Child Is Born, New York: Dell, 1977, p.42. Lennart Nilsson/Bonnier Fakta.
131L	Peter Menzel/Stock Boston
131C	George Goodwin/Monkmeyer Press Photo Service
131R	Robert Mayer/Tony Stone Worldwide
141	Thomas McAvoy. Copyright 1955/Life Magazine Time Warner Inc.
142	Courtesy Stephen LaBerge
145	Rex Features
148T	Miro Vintoniv/The Picture Cube
148L	James Chimbidis/Tony Stone Worldwide
148R	Christopher Langridge/Sygma
159	Tony Stone Images
161	Tony Stone Images

Chapter Five

165	Brown Brothers
166	Tony Stone Images
180	Ken Briggs/Photo Researchers
181	Fritz Goro. Copyright 1944/Life Magazine Time Warner Inc.
186	From Frisby, J., Seeing: Illusion, Brain, and Mind. Oxford University Press, 1980. The Kobal Collection/SuperStock International.
193	Associated Press
198	Courtesy Dr. Daryl Tanelian
199	Fuji Photos/The Image Works

Chapter Six

203	Tony Stone Images
211L	"Gestalt Bleue" by Victor Vasarely. Copyright © ADAGP, Paris and DACS, London 1995.
211R	1995 M.C. Escher Heirs, Collection of C.V.S. Roosevelt, Washington, D.C./Cordon Art-Baarn-Holland.
211B	"Slave Market and the Disappearing Bust of Voltaire". (1940) Oil on canvas, $19^1/_4 \times 25^3/_8$ inches. Collection of The Salvador Dali Museum, St. Petersburg, Florida. Copyright 1995 Salvador Dali Museum, Inc.
216	Courtesy of Mrs Broadbent
217	Courtesy of Anne Triesman
227L	Esao Hashimoto/Earth Scenes
229L	Holt Studios/Earth Scenes
231	Susan Schwartzenberg/The Exploratorium for Scott Foresman
233	Dr Peter Thompson, University of York, England.

Chapter Seven

241	Tony Stone Images
245	Courtesy John Hopkins University
246	The Bettmann Archive
250	Professor Philip G. Zimbardo
253	Tony Stone Images
257	Richard Wood/The Picture Cube
263	Yerkes Primate Research Centre, Emory University
267	Copyright 1985 American Psychological Association. Reprinted with permission from *Psychology Today* magazine.
274	Norman Baxley/Discover Publications/Family Media

Chapter Eight

281	Associated Press
287	Flilp Chalfant/The Image Bank
300	Associated Press
302	Courtesy of Gordon Bower
308	Rex Features

Chapter Nine

317	G. Rancinan/Sygma
327	Courtesy Howard Gardener
328	Joe Feingersh/Tom Stack & Associates
333	Courtesy of WGBH Boston
336	Louise Carter
351	Tony Stone Images

Chapter Ten

355	Rex Features
357	Rich Clarkson/*Sports Illustrated*
359L	Joyce Wilson/*Animals Animals*
359R	Robert Brenner/Photo Edit
363	Courtesy of WGBH Boston
374	Tony Stone Images
378	Courtesy of Martin Seligman
383	George Harrison
385	Tony Stone Images
389	Dr Paul Ekman and the University of California
390	Dr Paul Ekman and the University of California

Chapter Eleven

397	William C.Buzzard/Uniphoto
402	Hulton Deutsch Collection
410	Tony Stone Images
413L	The Image Works
413C	Robert Brenner/Photo Edit
413R	David H. Wells/The Image Works
419	Associated Press
420	Tony Stone Images
427	Rex Features
432	Tony Stone Images
433T	Mike Douglas/The Image Works
433B	Courtesy of WGBH Boston
435	Tony Stone Images
436	Tony Stone Images

Chapter Twelve

441	Rex Features
446	Zentralbibliothek, Zurich
447	Robert Brenner/Photo Edit
457	Mandala Of Akshobhya. Collection of the Newark Museum. Purchase 1920. Shelton Collection.
463	Courtesy Albert Bandura
467	National Portrait Gallery, London
468	Associated Press
477T	Reprinted by permission of the publishers from Thematic Apperception Test, by Henry A. Murray, Cambridge, MA: Harvard University Press, copyright 1943 by the President and Fellows of Harvard College; Copyright 1971 by Henry A. Murray
481	Courtesy The Psychological Corporation
489	Rex Features

Chapter Thirteen

495	Professor Philip G. Zimbardo
500L	Tim Brown/Tony Stone Worldwide
500R	A. Nogues/Sygma
504	William Vandivert
506	Courtesy of WGBH Boston
507	Courtesy Dr. Ronald Lippitt
508T	Associated Press
508B	Professor Philip G. Zimbardo
511	AP/Wide World
512	Charles Gupton/Southern Light
517	Tony Stone Images
518	Ethan Hoffman
520	Courtesy Mrs Jane Elliott and ABC Television. Photos by Charlotte Button
528	Hulton Deutsch Collection
532	Tony Stone Images
533	From Keen, S., Faces of the Enemy: Reflections of the Hostile Imagination. Copyright 1986 by Sam Keen. All rights reserved. Reprinted by permission of HarperCollins Publishers, Inc.
534	Tony Stone Images

Chapter Fourteen

539	Rex Features
540	Rex Features
542	Courtesy of the UK organisation MIND
560	Associated Press
561	Rex Features
576	NIMH
583	Hulton Deutsch Collection

Chapter Fifteen

587	Tony Stone Images
604	Professor Philip G. Zimbardo
620	Rex Features

LITERARY CREDITS

Chapter 1

18	Table 1.1. From Sexton, V.S. & Hogan, J.D. (eds) (1992). *International psychology: Views from around the world.* Lincoln: University of Nebraska Press.

Chapter 2

45	Figure 2.2. From *Human Evolution: An Illustrated Introduction*, by Robert Lewin. Copyright © 1984 by W.H. Freeman and Company. Reprinted by permission.
56	Figure 2.4. By Lynn O'Kelley.
57	Figure 2.5. By Lynn O'Kelley.
79	Figure 2.21. By Lynn O'Kelley.
81	Figure 2.24. From *The Harvey Lectures*, Series 62, by R.W. Sperry. Copyright © 1968 by Academic Press. Reprinted by permission of the author and the publisher.

Chapter 3

101	Figure 3.7. From 'Ontogenetic Development of the Human Sleep-Dream Cycle,' by H.P. Roffwarg *et al.*, in *Science*, April 1966, Vol.152, No.9, p.604-19. Copyright © 1966 by AAAS. Reprinted by permission of the American Association for the Advancement of Science.

Chapter 4

121	Figure 4.2. By Lynn O'Kelley. Redrawn from *The Brain*, by W.M. Cowan. Copyright © 1979 by W.H. Freeman and Company. Reprinted by permission.
123	Figure 4.4. From *The First Two Years*, by Mary M. Shirley. Reprinted by permission of the University of Minnesota Press.
127	Table 4.1. From p.18 of *Child Development*, by L.P. Lipsitt and H.W. Reese. Copyright © 1979 by HarperCollins Publishers. Reprinted by permission of the publisher.
134	Figure 4.6. From 'Representing the Existence and the Location of Hidden Objects: Object permanence in 6- and 8- month-old Infant,' by Renee Baillargeon, in *Cognition, 23* (1986), p.21-41. Reprinted by permission of the author and North-Holland Publishing Company.
150	Table 4.5. Adapted from *The adolescent: A Psychological Self-Portrait*, by Daniel Offer, Eric Ostrov, and Kenneth I. Howard. Copyright © 1981 by Basic Books, Inc. Reprinted by permission of the publisher.

152   Table 4.6. From *Adaptation of Life*, by George Vaillant. Copyright © 1977 by George E. Vaillant. Reprinted by permission.

Chapter 5

170   Table 5.2. From *New Direction in Psychology*, by Roger Brown, Eugene Galanter, and Eckhard H. Hess. Copyright © 1962 by Holt, Rinehart and Winston, Inc. Reprinted by permission of Dr Eugene Galanter.

173   Table 5.3. From *Introduction to Psychology*, 10th ed., by Atkinson *et al.* Copyright © 1990 by Harcourt Brace Jovanovich, Inc. Reproduced by permission of the author.

178   Figure 5.8. Adapted from *Seeing: Illusion, Brain and Mind*, by John P. Frisby. Copyright © 1979 by John P. Frisby. Reprinted by permission of Oxford University Press.

191   Figure 5.20. From *The Science of Musical Sounds*, by D.C. Miller. Macmillan Company, 1926. Reprinted by permission of Case Western Reserve University.

192   Figure 5.21. From *Theory of Hearing*, by Ernest Glen Weaver. Copyright © 1949 by John Wiley & Sons, Inc. Reprinted by permission of the author.

Chapter 6

209   Figure 6.5. From *Fundamentals of Sensation and Perception*, by M.W. Levine and J. Shefner. Reprinted by permission of Michael W.Levine.

215   Figure 6.8. From '*The Effect of Inattention on Form Perception*,' by I. Rock and D. Gutman, Journal of Experimental Psychology: Human Perception and Performance, I. Copyright © 1981 by the American Psychological Association. Reproduced by permission.

216   Figure 6.11. From *Cognitive Psychology and Information Processing: An Introduction*, by Roy Lachman, Janet I. Lachman, and Earl C. Butterfield. Reprinted by permission of the authors and Lawrence Erlbaum Associates, Inc.

226   Figure 6.17. From 'Impossible Objects: A Special Type of Visual Illusion,' by L.S. Penrose and R. Penrose, in *British Journal of Psychology, 1958, Vol.49*, p.31. Reprinted by permission of The British Psychological Society.

228   Figure 6.19. From *Sensation and Perception*, by Stanley Coren, Clare Porac, and Lawrence M. Ward. Copyright © 1979 by Harcourt Brace Jovanovich, Inc. Reprinted by permission of the publisher.

230   Figure 6.21. Adapted from Figure 38 of 'The Perspective of a Pavement,' in *The Perception of the Visual World*, by James W. Gibson. Copyright © 1950 and renewed 1977 by Houghton Mifflin Company. Adapted by permission of the publisher.

234   Figure 6.25a. From *Droodles*, by R. Price. Copyright © 1953, 1980 by Price Stern Sloane, Inc., Los Angeles.
Figure 6.25b. From *The Logic of Perception*, by I. Rock. Copyright © 1983 by the Massachusetts Institute of Technology. Reprinted with permission.
Figure 6.26a. From 'Representative and Recognition of the Spatial Organization of Three-Dimensional Shapes,' by D. Marr and H.K. Nishihara, in *Proceedings of the Royal Society of London*, 1978, p.200B. Reprinted by permission.
Figure 6.26b. From 'Recognition by Components: A Theory of Object Recognition,' by I. Biederman, in *Computer Vision Graphics and Image Processing*, 1985, p.32. Reprinted by permission.

Chapter 7

248   Figure 7.2. From *Psychology*, by William Buskist. Copyright © 1991 by HarperCollins Publishers, Inc. Reprinted by permission.

249   Figure 7.3. Reprinted by permission of HarperCollins Publishers, Inc.

252   Figure 7.4. From *Psychology*, by William Buskist. Copyright © 1991 by HarperCollins Publishers, Inc. Reprinted by permission.

254   Figure 7.5. From ' Predictability and Number Pairings in Pavlovian Fear Conditioning,' by Robert A. Rescorla, in *Psychonomic Science, Vol.4*, No.11. Reprinted by permission of the Psychonomic Society, Inc.
Figure 7.6. From *Psychology*, by William Buskist. Copyright © 1991 by HarperCollins Publishers, Inc. Reprinted by permission.

258   Figure 7.8. From *Introduction to Psychology*, by Christopher Peterson. Copyright © 1991 by HarperCollins Publishers, Inc. Reprinted by permission.

271   Figure 7.10. From 'Learned Association Over Long Delays,' by Sam Revusky and John Garcia, in *The Psychology of Learning and Motivation*, Vol.IV, edited by Gordon H. Bower. Orlando, Fla.: Academic Press, 1970. Reprinted by permission.

273   Figure 7.11. From 'Degrees of Hunger, Reward and Non-reward, and Maze Learning in Rats,' by E.C. Tolman and C.H. Honzik, in *University of California Publication in Psychology*, Vol.4, No.16, December 1930. Reprinted by permission of the University of California Press.

Chapter 8

288   Figure 8.2. From *Human Memory: Structures and Processes*, 2nd ed., by Roberta Klasky. Copyright © 1975, 1980 by W.H. Freeman and Company. Reprinted by permission.

292   Figure 8.4. From 'Short-Term Retention of Individual Verbal Items,' by Lloyd R.Peterson and Margaret Jean Peterson, in *Journal of Experimental Psychology*, September 1959, Vol.58, No.3. Copyright © 1959 by the American Psychological Association, Inc. Reprinted by permission of the authors.

298   Figure 8.6. From 'Two Storage Mechanisms in Free Recall,' by Murray Glanzer and Anita R. Cunitz, in *Journal of Verbal Learning and Verbal Behaviour*. Copyright © 1966 by Academic Press, Inc. Reprinted by permission of the author and the publisher.

300   Figure 8.7. From 'Remembering Odors and Their Names,' by T. Engen, in *American Scientists*, 1987, Vol.75, p.498. Reprinted by permission of Sigma XI, The Scientific Research Society.

311   Figure 8.8. By Lynn O'Kelley.

313   Figure 8.9. By Lynn O'Kelley.

Chapter 9

317   Text reprinted by permission of Edith Eva Eger, Ph.D.

325   Figure 9.4. From *How to Solve Problems: Elements of a Theory of Problems and Problem Solving*, By Wayne A.Wickelgren. Copyright © 1974 by W.H. Freeman and Company. Reprinted by permission.

Chapter 10

360   Figure 10.1. From *Psychology*, 3rd ed., by Rathus. Copyright © 1987 by Holt, Rinehart and Winston, Inc. Reprinted by permission.

366   Figure 10.3. From '*Reversal Theory: Motivation, Emotion and Personality*' by Michael Apter. Copyright © 1989 by Routledge, London.

372   Figure 10.4. From p.207 of *Human Sexualities*, by J.H. Gagnon. Copyright © 1977 by HarperCollins Publishers, Inc. Reprinted by permission.

378 Figure 10.6. Adapted from *Human Motivation*, by Bernard Weiner, Copyright © 1980 by Bernard Weiner. Reprinted by permission of the author.

388 Figure 10.7. From 'A Language for the Emotions,' by Robert Plutchik, in *Psychology Today*, February 1980. Copyright © 1080 by Sussex Publishing. Reprinted by permission.

Chapter 11

404 Table 11.2. Adapted from *OPCS Monitor DH2 93/2 Deaths by cause: December quarter 1992 registrations*, OPCS, London. The office of Population Censuses & Surveys. Also adapted from the Annual Report 1992, by the General Register Office, Edinburgh, Scotland.

406 Figure 11.1. From *Health and Human Services*, Office of Disease Prevention and Health Promotion.

408 Table 11.4. Selection of figures taken from Suicide deaths in England and Wales: Trends in Factors associated with suicide deaths. *Population Trends, 71*, 34-42. Charlton, J. *et al*, 1993.

417 Table 11.6. Adapted from Table 3, p.475, of 'The Minor Events Approach to Stress: Support for the Use of Daily Hassles,' by Kerry Chamberlain and Sheryl Zika, in *British Journal of Psychology*, 1990, Vol.81. Reprinted by permission.

421 Table 11.7. Adapted from p.333 of *Decision Making: A Psychological Analysis of Conflict, Choice, and Commitment*, by I.L. Janis and L. Mann. Copyright © 1977 by The Free Press, a Division of Macmillan, Inc. Adapted with permission of The Free Press.

424 Figure 11.4. From Figure 7.10 of *Psychology*, by Michael S. Gazzaniga. Reprinted by permission of HarperCollins Inc.

425 Table 11.8. From Table 6.1, p.147, of *Health Psychology*, by Feuerstein, New York: Plenum Publishing Corporation, 1986. Reprinted with permission.

Chapter 12

449 Figure 12.2. From *The Inequality of Man*, by H.J. Eysenck. Copyright © 1973 by Hans J. Eysenck. Reprinted by permission of the author.

480 Figure 12.5. From *Wechsler's Measurement and Appraisal of Adult Intelligence*, 5th ed., by J.D. Matarazzo. Copyright © 1972 by Oxford University Press, Inc. Reprinted by permission.

483 Figure 12.6. From P.161 of *Way Beyond the IQ: Guide to Improving Intelligence and Creativity*, by J.P. Guilford. Buffalo, N.Y.: Barely Limited, 1977. Reprinted by permission of the author.

485 Figure 12.3. From 'Familial Studies of Intelligence: A Review,' by T.J. Bouchard, Jr., and M. McGue, in *Science*, 1981, Vol.212, p.1055-59. Copyright © 1981 by the AAAS. Reprinted by permission of the American Association for the Advancement of Science.

486 Figure 12.7. From 'Achievement and Social Mobility: Relationships Among IQ Score, Education and Occupation in Two Generation,' by Jerome H. Waller, in *Social Biology*, September 1971, Vol.18, No.3. Copyright © 1971 The American Eugenics Society.

Chapter 13

510 Figure 13.3. From *The Obedience Experiments: A Case Study of Controversy in the Social Sciences*, by A.G. Miller. Copyright © 1986 by Praeger Publishers. Reprinted by permission of Greenwood Publishing Group, Inc., Westport, Conn.

513 Figure 13.4. Adapted from 'Bystander Intervention in Emergencies: Diffusion of Responsibilities,' by Darley and Latane, in *Journal of Personality and Social Psychology*, 1968, Vol.8, No.4, p.377-84. Copyright © 1968 by the American Psychological Association. Adapted by permission of the author.

524 Figure 13.5. From 'An Experimental Study of Apparent Behaviour,' by F. Heider and M. Simmel, in *American Journal of Psychology*, 1944, Vol.57, p.243-59. Reprinted by permission of the University of Illinois Free Press.

Chapter 14

543 Figure 14.1. From p.9 of *Mental Health for Canadians: Striking a Balance*. Minister of National Health and Welfare, 1988.
Figure 14.2. From p.9 of *Mental Health for Canadians: Striking a Balance*. Minister of National Health and Welfare, 1988.

555 Figure 14.3. From 'Multiple Personality Disorder: Phenomenology of Selected Variables in Comparison to Major Depression,' by R. Schults, B.G. Braun, and R.P. Kluft, in *Dissociation*, 1989, Vol.2, p.45.

559 Table 14.4. From *Abnormal Psychology*, by David L. Rosenhan and Martin E.P. Seligman. Copyright © 1984 by W.W. Norton & Company, Inc.

568 Figure 14.4. From p.72-80 of *Archives of General Psychiatry*, 1984, Vol.41, by Rosenthal *et al*. Reprinted by permission.

573 Table 14.7. From *Diagnostic and Statistical Manual of Mental Disorders*, 3rd ed., Revised. Copyrights © 1987 by the American Psychiatric Association. Reprinted with permission.

574 Figure 14.5. From 'Genetic Theories and the Validation of Psychiatric Diagnosis: Implications for the Study of Children of Schizophrenics,' by Daniel R. Hanson *et al.*, in *Journal of Abnormal Psychology*, 1977, Vol.86, p.575-88. Copyright © 1977 by the American Psychological Association, Inc. Reprinted by permission of the authors.

575 Figure 14.6. From *Schizophrenia Genesis*, by Guttesman. Copyright © 1991 by W.H. Freeman and Company. Reprinted by permission.

Chapter 15

599 Table 15.1. From *The Practice of Behaviour Therapy*, 2nd ed., by J. Wolpe. Copyright © 1973 by Pergamon Books Ltd. Reprinted with permission.

603 Figure 15.1. From p.603 of *Journal of Abnormal Psychology*, Vol.94, by Cook *et al*. Copyright © 1985 by the American Psychological Association. Adapted by permission.

604 Figure 15.2. From 'Modelling Therapy,' by Albert Bandura. Reprinted by permission of the author.

605 Table 15.2. Adapted from *Modern Clinical Psychology: Principles of Intervention in the Clinic and Community*, by Sheldon J. Korchin. Copyright © 1976 by Sheldon J. Korchin. Reprinted by permission of Basic Books, Inc., Publishers.

607 Figure 15.3. From p.69 of *Panic*, 1988, by A. Agras.

617 Figure 15.4. From p.555-58 of *American Journal of Psychiatry*, 1979, Vol.136, by Weissman *et al*. Reprinted with permission.

618 Figure 15.6. From Figure 1, p.976, of 'NIMH Treatment of Depression Collaborative Research Program,' by I.Ilkin *et al.*, in *General Psychiatry*, Vol.46. Reprinted by permission.

Strack, S. 465
Straub, E. 462
Straus, M.A. 426
Strodtbeck, F.L. 505
Stroebe, M. 161
Stroebe, W. 161
Strong, E. 487, 492
Strube, M.J. 413
Stuart, R.B. 602
Suchman, A. 241
Suedfeld, P. 107
Sullivan, A. 165
Sullivan, H.S. 165, 596, 597
Suls, J. 413
Summers, M. 592
Sundberg, N.D. 488
Sutker, P.B. 251
Svenson, O. 332
Swann, W.B., Jr. 465, 517
Swazey, J.P. 614
Sweeney, J.A. 576
Swets, J.A. 171, 172, 412, 430
Syme, S.L. 424, 431
Szasz, T. 547
Szasz, T.S. 592, 590

T

Tajfel, H. 519, 496, 497, 500,
   519, 521, 522, 526
Talbot, J.D. 198
Tannen, D. 349
Targ, R. 112
Taylor, S. 398-400, 403, 429,
   433
Taylor, S.E. 91, 321, 331, 332
Teasdale, J.D. 608
Teicher, M.H. 120
Tellegen, A. 448, 484
Templin, M. 137
Tennant, L. 259
Tenney, Y.I. 303
Tenopyr, M.L. 488
Terman, L.M. 469, 479, 480, 492
Terwee, S.J.S. 22
Thatcher, R.W. 132
Thayer, R.E. 406
Thigpen, C.H. 555
Thoma, S.J. 155
Thomas, G. 246
Thompson, D.A. 369
Thompson, K. 610
Thompson, J.A. 535
Thompson, R. 310, 311, 313
Thompson, R.F. 250, 274
Thomson, D.M. 295
Thoresen, C. 413
Thorndike, E.L. 256, 257, 268,
   273, 274, 277, 278
Thorndyke, P.W. 323
Thornton, E.M. 595
Tiefer, L. 372
Timberlake, W. 243
Tipper, S.P. 218
Tolman, E. 323, 359, 361
Tolman, E.C. 273
Tomie, A. 273
Tomkins, S. 386
Totten, M.C. 398
Toussirt, M. 407

Trafimow, D. 527
Treisman, A. 217
Trevarthen, 124
Trevarthen, C. 81
Triandis, H.C. 7, 327, 379, 579,
   592
Trinder, J. 102
Trivers, R.L. 373
Troiden, P.R. 375
Tronick, E. 124
Tronto, J. 468
Trotter, R.J. 378
Tsuang, M.T. 546
Tulving, E. 91, 96, 285, 286,
   295, 299
Tulviste, P. 140
Tupes, E.G. 450
Turing, A.M. 328
Turner, C. 408
Turner, J.C. 500
Turvey, M.T. 213
Tverdal, A. 437
Tversky, A. 333, 334, 522
Tversky, B. 296
Tyler, L. 340, 343, 467, 480
Tyler, L.E. 446, 488

U

Ullmann, L.P. 578
Underwood, B.J. 304

V

Vaillant, G. 147, 151, 152
Valenstein, E.S. 613
Valle, V.A. 379
Valsiner, J. 125, 139
Van Strien, P.J. 17
Van de Poll, N.E. 371
Van den Bos, G.R. 597
Van der Heijden, A.H.C.
   219-221, 341
Van der Heijden, L. 220
Van der Mey, R. 546
Van der Plight, J. 409
Van der Veer, R. 139
Van Dijk, T. 343
Van Eeden, R. 104
Van Egmond, M. 571
Van Geert, P. 125
Van Goozen, S.H.M. 371
Van Ijzendoorn, M.H. 143
Van Loon, R. 465
Van Rooijen, E. 399
Van Wagener, W. 81
Van Zessen, G. 410
Van Zessen, G. 375
Venn, A.J. 251
Vernon, P.E. 481
Volberg, A. 561
Von Békésy, G. 191
Von Helmholtz, H. 183, 187,
   191, 212, 214, 231
Von Hofsten, C. 124
Von Restorff, H. 299
Vygotsky, L.S. 136, 139, 140,
   146, 162

W

Wadsworth, J. 410
Wagenaar, W.A. 281, 305, 307,
   308
Wagner, A.R. 249, 255, 276
Walker, L. 155
Walker-Andrews, 133
Wall, P. 411
Wallace, 593
Wallach, M.A. 597
Wallis, C. 197
Walters, C.C. 260
Wanous, J.P. 488
Ward, W.C. 527, 532
Wardle, J. 405, 553
Warner Schaie, K. 153
Warren, R.P. 340
Warren, R.M. 340
Washburn, A. 368
Wason, P. 324, 325
Wasserman, E.A. 274
Watkins, L.R. 76
Watson, J. 244, 245, 251
Watson, J.B. 9, 10
Weaver, C.A. III. 302
Webb, W.B. 100, 463
Weber, E. 173
Wechsler, D. 479, 481, 487, 492
Weick, K.E. 532
Weikart, D.P. 486
Weil, A.T. 97
Weinberg, R.A. 486
Weinberger, M. 376, 417
Weiner, B. 378, 524
Weiner, M.J. 520
Weinstein, N.D. 332, 335
Weisenberg, M. 199
Weiss, R.F. 251
Weissman, M.M. 569
Weissman, W.W. 433
Weisstein, N. 15
Wellings, K. 410
Wellman, H.M. 130, 132, 134,
   330
Werker, J.D. 135
Werner, D. 375
Wertheimer, M. 224
Wertsch, J.V. 139, 140
West, D.J. 554
West, 159
West, C. 349
West, D.J. 452
Wetherell, M. 27, 348, 497, 519,
   529
Wever, E.G. 192
Wever, R.A. 98
Wheeler, M.A. 309
Wheeler, L. 380
Whishaw, I.Q. 552
Whitbourne, S.K. 157
White, M.D. & White, C.A. 592
White, R. 363, 506
Whorf, B. 350, 351
Whyte, W.F. 27
Wicklund, R.A. 523
Widiger, T.A. 478
Widrow, B. 276
Wiebe, D.J. 421
Wiener, M. 549, 570
Wiersma, E.D. 446
Wiesel, T. 14, 185

Wiesel, T.N. 223
Wiggins, J.S. 445
Wilcoxin, L.A. 600
Wilder, D.A. 519
Wilkinson, S. 15
Williams, T. 35
Williams, 272
Williams, J.B.W. 569
Williams, J.H. 145
Willis, S.L. 159
Wills, T.A. 428
Wilson, B.A. 552
Wilson, E.D. 81, 618
Wilson, M. 400
Wilson, P.N. 255
Wingerson, L. 48
Wingert, P. 489
Wingfield, A. 297
Winter, D.A. 461
Wise, S.P. 187
Witkin, H.A. 236
Wittgenstein, L.J.J. 529
Wolf, M. 143, 264
Wolman, C. 619
Wolpe, J. 599
Woodruf-Pak, D.S. 250
Woods, D.L. 94
Wortman, C.B. 427, 431
Wright, J.C. 520
Wright, J. 451, 452, 462
Wundt, W. 6, 89, 93
Wyer, R.S. 516
Wynne, L.C. 577

Y

Yalom, I. 556
Yalom, I.D. 611
Yang, K.S. 379
Yates, B. 603
Yates, F.A. 306
Yerkes, R. 479
Yerkes, R.M. 361
Young, T. 183, 187
Yudkin, M. 418

Z

Zadeh, L.A. 319
Zahn-Waxler, C. 156
Zajonc, R.B. 385, 386, 464, 522,
   498
Zammuner, V.L. 345
Zanchetti, A. 381
Zeckhauser, R. 333
Zeiss, R.A. 427
Zettle, R.D. 272
Zika, S. 417
Zilboorg, G. 592
Zimbardo, P.G. 150, 158, 188,
   360, 386, 412, 496, 603
Zimmerman, D.H. 142, 349
Zubeck, J.P. 107
Zubek, J.P. 360
Zucker, R.S. 71
Zuckerman, M. 361, 380, 485

SUBJECT INDEX